The Alabaster Carvers

Raymond Henry State

Published by

MELROSE BOOKS

An Imprint of Melrose Press Limited
St Thomas Place, Ely
Cambridgeshire
CB7 4GG, UK
www.melrosebooks.co.uk

FIRST EDITION

Cover designed by Melrose Books

ISBN 978-1-912026-12-8

Printed and bound in Great Britain by:
TJ International Ltd, Padstow, Cornwall

FSC www.fsc.org MIX Paper from responsible sources FSC® C013056

FRONT COVER:

This is the effigy of Sir Robert Goushill and his wife, the former Duchess of Norfolk, Elizabeth FitzAlan, in Hoveringham church, Nottinghamshire. This effigy was carved between 1403 and 1425 in pure white alabaster and probably shows the early work of the Chellaston kervers. Sir Robert was murdered in 1403 following the battle of Shrewsbury during Henry IV's reign. The effigy shows the attention of latter day graffiti artists made worse by the fact that the tomb was removed from the original church during its demolition in 1865 and not protected. The Victorians then made things worse by squeezing the tomb into an alcove far too small for it so that the effigy of the lady had to be mutilated to make it fit. Sir Robert displays late 14th century armour, camail hood and hauberk and rests his head on a great helm (or tilting helmet) with an orle or garland around the steel headpiece. One glove is removed and he once clasped the hand of his wife. He has a short Esse (SS) collar round his neck from which the pendant has been broken (*see* Appendix E). This is one of three linked effigies associated with Shrewsbury; the others being Bakewell and Tideswell both in Derbyshire. Photos: the author.

This is a picture of Ratcliffe-on-Soar in 1950s. The 11th-century church contains four fine 16th and 17th century alabaster monuments to the Sacheverell family. Photo: the author's collection.

The Author

Ray State is a member of the Ratcliffe-on-Soar, Nottinghamshire History Group and the Southwell Diocese Church History Group. A professional engineer, he worked for the railway for 52 years before retiring in 2012. He moved to the small village of Ratcliffe-on-Soar in 1998 where he was given the research papers of deceased village historian Harry Collins. Harry had produced a booklet on village history but almost 75% of his work was unpublished. The author set about publishing all Harry's work in the form of a diary based loosely on the Saxon Chronicles. This was published in 2008 as *The Ratcliffe Chronicles*[1] in which the history of the church featured prominently.

The 11th-century Ratcliffe church contains many carved alabaster slabs and four fine tombs of the Sacheverell family from the 16th and 17th century, one of which is also a mural. What was clear was that the records on the tombs were fragmentary and in some cases conflicting. Research into these for the Chronicles opened up the possibility of investigating many of the other Nottinghamshire tombs.

The village has a close involvement in the gypsum industry. The parish is on the edge of the Nottingham and Derby gypsum and alabaster mining area, and some mining took place in the 18th century on the northern boundary and at the junction of the Rivers Soar and Trent, known as Redhill. Alabaster from Redhill was used in the Marble Hall in Kedleston Hall, Derbyshire, possibly in the main hall at Holkham, Norfolk and the mausoleum at Brocklesby, Lincolnshire. In the 18th century, the Redhill mine, or quarry, was in the ownership of Assheton Curzon (1st Baron Curzon), the brother of Lord Curzon of Kedleston.

The village's involvement in alabaster (and gypsum mining) has spurred the author to look at the history of alabaster mining and carving, and the findings are contained in the following pages.

Notes:

1. British Library, shelfmark, General Reference Collection YC.2009.b.2260 © Ratcliffe-on-Soar History Group 2008. Other Books: *The Pride and the Lion* (2011), British Library, shelfmark, General Reference Collection YD.2012.b.1257.

The author (on the right) discusses a finer point with photographer John Allen. Photo: Janet State.

Acknowledgements

This book would not have been written without the help and patience of my family. Above all, I wish to thank my wife, Janet, who has endured an unceasing round of church visits but has assisted in commenting, proof reading and taking photographs. Janet's family have been of great assistance too. The Maryon and Miles families have carted me round East Anglia looking for remote churches on a number of occasions. I wish also to thank my neighbours, Paul and Stephanie Grimley, and John and Barbara Allen, for their encouragement and the excellent photographs they have taken. My thanks also go to Anthony Goode, Johnny Garlick and Douglas Kent of the Society for the Protection of Ancient Buildings (SPAB) for the original idea of the book. I also wish to thank the organisers of the Southwell Church History Project, John Beckett and Chris Brooke, for their support in making archive material available. Alan Baker provided the information on the railways of Staffordshire and George Roberts of the Tower of London, who worked with me to investigate the tombs there, especially the Cholmondeley tomb.

The members of the congregation of our church cluster have acted as scouts bringing details of far churches. In particular, I thank Jill and Chris Hinds, Mike Staves and Anne Farnsworth whose late husband identified the Montréal reredos for me.

The many church wardens and incumbents of the churches and cathedrals have been of great help as have the archivists of a number of stately homes, archives and public buildings. There are too many to name them all, but those at Tutbury Museum, Gloucester Cathedral, Holkham Hall and The Breakers, Rhode Island (the Preservation Society of Newport County) have been particularly helpful. I also wish to thank Simon Lake of the New Walk Museum, Leicester for his assistance in identifying Cumberland albabaster.

I thank you all.

Ray State

CONTENTS

Diagrams and Pictures

The Alabaster Beds

Monument Populations

Timelines

Timelines are in a central group

Figures

Figures are in the text or in a central gallery as indicated below

The Guilds and the Mystery Plays

Modern Alabaster

Armour and the Carver

Alabaster Mines and Quarries

Foreword

There have been many learned papers on the subject of alabaster. Many of these are listed in the bibliography. Amongst these, the books by Francis Cheetham and the thorough review of Gothic tombs by Arthur Gardner are excellent references, whilst the papers by the late R Firman of Nottingham University give a competent history of the mining of alabaster. Nigel Llewellyn's book *Funeral Monuments in Post-Reformation England* picks up the story from where Gardner stopped and is highly recommended as are those by Sally Badham and Jon Bayliss.

Gardner paid tribute to earlier writers including Lawrence Weaver, Gough, Blore, Richardson, Hollis and Stothard, but observes that little attention was directed towards the material used. Gardner collaborated with Prof Edward S Prior who correctly observed that the understanding of the materials used was the key in any study of monument styles. Later writers such a William St John Hope and F H Crossley are also commended.

In fact, the study of alabaster seems to fall into several groups. There are those who follow the geology, those who follow the art form and the history of the objects and those who study the identity of the persons to whom the monuments were erected. Some use the monuments to describe the purpose and liturgy surrounding their creation. Some have attempted to match carvings to a group of kervers[1] and/or to their location in a structured way, but with limited success. Some have attempted to locate the source of the alabaster used for carvings, again without firm conclusions. It is noted that when historians veer into geology and vice versa, some assumptions made are very questionable. In fact, anyone looking for an overall picture of the alabaster industry at its peak from 1330 to about 1670 will need to read all the books to get a balanced view.

The reasons for this are not clear, but many of the books fail to identify all the locations at which alabaster was mined and the dates of operation and fail to observe the affect of transportation on the location where carving was undertaken. There is a temptation by some authors to trivialise the effort in moving large objects in medieval times and the cost of transport. The suggestion that a local jobbing freestone carver could obtain a block of alabaster weighing several tons at short notice from afar is unlikely to be true. This is where another group make an appearance. The engineer is interested in mining techniques, equipment, lifting and transport, the study of which can open up new aspects of the study of the alabaster trade not previously perceived. This book has a slight engineering overlay.

Francis Cheetham has carried out an almost complete review of the medieval alabaster tablets of the 14th, 15th and 16th century (*see Alabaster Images of Medieval England*, 2003) and this was outstanding for the time. However, where Cheetham comments on individual tomb effigies, the linking of styles, faces and dress in his books, the detail is fragmented. Cheetham gave the clear impression that the Nottingham school predominated the carving throughout the period. The *Ampleforth Journal* published in January 1918 has an interesting suggestion on page 100. It says there is 'evidence' that panels between 1350 and 1380 were manufactured in London and in York between 1380 and 1420, and only after this did Nottingham rise to importance. It cites the fact that the London panels were oblong and had carefully moulded sides, the York had an integral embattled canopy, but Nottingham had a canopy carved as a separate item as well as showing declining quality in the carving. It is noted that between 1432 and 1449 there were at least six bequests of images to York churches (St John Hope). As this book is not reviewing the carved tablets and panels, I will not evaluate further, but offer the above as possible evidence of the distribution of carvers.

Therefore, the term Nottingham school needs to be defined. It is widely and often inaccurately used to describe all the medieval carving of the 15th and 16th century. Whilst the town was indeed the centre for panel carving, the evidence of effigy carving is thin to non-existent as is the presence of quarries in the Nottingham area. In fact, no alabaster was extracted in Nottinghamshire until the 18th century (*see* Appendix M). Up to the late 16th century all the alabaster came from quarries well to the west of the town and whilst the carriage of stone for panels was quite feasible, the cartage of alabaster by land or water for effigy carving was extremely challenging (*see* Appendix C). In addition, the town of Nottingham was perched on a sandstone ridge bounded by the castle mound on west and the Mapperley Ridge to the east and therefore quite small. The River Leen skirted the castle and the Trent was almost a mile away to the south. Alabaster carving was carried out in the streets around the church of St Mary, namely St Mary's Gate, and the aptly named Stony Street and on the south side of the market square as stated in the borough records. The tightly packed town had little room, narrow steep streets and mainly wooden buildings wholly unsuited to carving large alabaster blocks. In addition, no effigy carver can be identified in the borough records which is hardly surprising as the carriage of blocks weighing several tons into the city was a challenge. Authors cite, inaccurately, the River Trent as a means of transport without any consideration of the problems that river experiences. Although Nottingham could be reached by boats from the Humber, navigation west of the town towards the alabaster sources was risky and Appendix C details the difficulties with navigation in this direction.

One of the most comprehensive books is *Alabaster Tombs* by Arthur Gardner. Written in 1939 it covers the alabaster effigies of the period to the Reformation about

1549 (and some to 1566), but demonstrates the difficulties experienced by authors in establishing the facts in the pre-computer era. There are errors and assumptions which modern research is able to resolve, but this should not detract from the brilliant work of this author.

There is a general consensus that the Renaissance monuments from the second half of the 16th century and the mural monuments of Dutch style have not been fully researched. Nigel Llewellyn comments that a full census of monuments in the era has yet to be produced and observes that from 1549 to 1670, some 4000 monuments were created. In this period, the old traditional sources of alabaster were reducing and new locations were being sought. In addition, the movement away from the East Midlands of some effigy carving fragmented the industry. As a result much attention in this book has been placed on the period from about 1560 to 1670 in an attempt to describe the work of the carvers in these years and produce a catalogue of monuments (Appendix D).

As stated, there is little to be gained from repeating the work of Francis Cheetham covering the reredos and retables of the Middle Ages and a comment on these is therefore muted, being restricted to observations where samples were recovered from hidden locations within buildings. It does, however, take Gardner's work further and attempts to trace the alabaster kervers art across the East Midlands and other centres between the 14th and the end of the 17th century. Some later sculptors in alabaster are mentioned as well.

The research into the mural monuments has included the records of Nicholas Stone ably summarised by Walter Spiers for the Walpole Society in the 7th Volume, dated 1918–1919, but these are now believed to be incomplete and the population of Stone monuments is far greater than previously believed. Nevertheless, the work of Walter Spiers is much commended to researchers. Spiers examined Nicholas Stone's notebook and account book now held by the John Soane Museum, Lincoln's Inn Fields, London and described most of the work as it existed in 1940. Another writer, Adam White, is currently preparing a complete review of Nicholas Stone's work and I have supplied him with the details I know and will leave the precise details of this carver to him.

What is clear is that the Dutch influence was apparent much earlier than 1613 when Stone returned to London from Amsterdam, and that the work of the Jannsen (or Johnson) family in London from 1564 and the Hollemans family in Burton on Trent from 1594 is significant. Nicholas Stone's Dutch brother-in-law, Hendrik de Keyser, traded in Nottingham in the mid-17th century making the period under review heavily influenced by the Dutch/Flemish styles. There are others and an analysis of all the carvers identified during the research is included.

There are times when it is necessary to stray from the East Midlands, especially when kervers from outside the area carried out work, or where effigies can be traced along distribution routes. The London carvers became increasingly important at the end of the 16th century along with provincial workshops such as that of Samuel and Stephen Baldwin of Gloucester and Stroud. For these it has been found beneficial to look at transport and the means by which carvings and raw blocks of alabaster were moved to and from these more remote places.

As stated, there have been several style shifts and these are worth restating. Cheetham defines the periods of tablet and image industry from *circa* 1367 to its destruction in 1549. Gardner noted that the Gothic style of table tombs held sway from early 14th century until the mid-16th century and after a period of mixed Gothic/Renaissance form, the Renaissance and Jacobean style predominated from about 1560. Gardner disliked the Renaissance style and refused to describe them. He did group the tombs, and this is disliked by some researchers, but I have repeated the grouping for continuity purposes to be used or ignored. At the beginning of the 17th century, there was a major shift in style with the introduction of the mural monument. As stated, this form appears to have been introduced from Holland and there is a full discussion later.

I have included a list of monuments (Appendix D) with a commentary on the importance of the person and/or the form of carving and its method of treatment by the kerver. The art was so broad that it covered retable panels, free-standing images, mural tablets, floor slabs, tomb tables and effigies. In the case of the latter, the presence of the Yorkist or Lancastrian decoration on some tombs has been treated in some detail (Appendix E). The list in Appendix D is in ascending date order. This has been done to enable work by individual carvers and the period of quarry and mine working to be identified. Some may not find this useful in identifying monuments in a certain area so a cross index by location/county has been added referenced to the sequential list.

The kervers of the East Midlands, and later London and other centres, were real people with real lives. They had a great skill in fashioning images and effigies and their work was highly prized from kings to minor bureaucrats even if some authors criticise their lack of individuality and the later decline in quality. Their work spread over all Western Europe and it is outside England where most images and tables, rather than effigies, survived the ravages of time. However, despite the destruction of the Reformation, some images and tables survived in Britain and these have been listed. Despite this wide customer base the industry was small. Firman estimates that between 1350 and 1550 the output of quarries averaged 70 tons per year – only sufficient for 18 effigial monuments and that there is a strong case that, up to the Reformation, all alabaster mining and almost all carving was carried out in a geographic area some 20 miles long and about 3 miles wide. This is the area bounded by Marchington/Fauld in Staffordshire and Nottingham City following the rivers Dove and Trent. It is quite possible that carving took place in York and Lincoln, both reachable by boat, and others linked to coastal shipping played their part. Towards to end of the 16th century, roads had improved significantly. From a study of the monuments of the Samuel Baldwin workshop in Gloucestershire, it is probable that he sourced its alabaster from Fauld and Chellaston. However, he may well have used Watchet alabaster as well. It is inconceivable that the alabaster made the river and sea journey involving several hundred miles when Gloucester was only 70 miles from the quarries by land. It is therefore likely that Baldwin used road transport requiring a mere 160 tons to 250 tons over the 60-year life of the workshop, or little more than 3 to 4 tons a year. Therefore, with increasing transport capability, carving became more widespread in the 17th century.

In 1549–1550, the business of the image makers of Nottingham was destroyed when the reforming acts of Edward VI banned the placing of images within the Protestant Church (*see* Appendix H). However, the image trade was in serious decline before this, due to the reforming policies of Thomas Cromwell and Archbishop Cranmer. Not to be daunted, the kervers concentrated on effigies and table slabs. However, with the alabaster now required in larger pieces, which required additional transport costs, there was a human migration westwards towards Burton on Trent (later Coventry) which was closer to the alabaster beds. In consequence, alabaster working in Nottingham City ceased.[2]

In later sections (Appendix M), the alabaster mining areas will be described, but it is important to note that the alabaster seams in general were never very thick. Firman observes that the alabaster was in near-surface deposits becoming gypsum at lower levels, which is why the deep mines of Gotham produced little or no alabaster. In addition, alabaster at the top of a seam could be white, becoming increasingly veined lower down. However, whilst the shallow pits of Chellaston were a prime source of white alabaster, the steeply rising ground at Fauld seems to have provided little or no pure white stone. In the first instance, only the white alabaster was sought and the green, brown- and purple-veined alabaster was discarded.[3] The pure white alabaster beds of Chellaston began to be worked out by the second quarter of the 16th century,[4] but the appearance of the Dutch carvers who stained their effigies increased the demand for alabaster with purple or brown veining. So, at the time when the carvings were gilded or painted, this veining was of little concern. In addition to Chellaston, there were veined alabaster mines at Tutbury (Castle Hay) and Fauld in Staffordshire and a quarry at Ratcliffe. In the 18th century, a further change took place in that the veining was valued as a decorative feature. These were shallow-worked quarries and only at Fauld was mining employed. The rise in the interest in Gothic architecture produced a minor resurgence mid-19th century, which resulted in some reopening of old workings mainly at Chellaston, but at Fauld production never really ceased, with alabaster continuing to be mined in a small way. Alabaster quality was not as good as it was in the medieval period, but sufficiently attractive at Fauld for the mine to continue in production into the late 20th century providing alabaster for the USA[5] and the London carvers. English mining all but ceased in the second decade of the 20th century and most modern church alabaster is Italian. However, some alabaster was extracted from Fauld for Leicester Cathedral in 2015 (*see* later).

Gardner estimated that some 331 Gothic alabaster tombs existed in England in 1940 covering the 14th and to the mid-16th century, with 507 effigies. This estimate is much lower than the number carved as some will have been destroyed in the Dissolution of the Monateries and priories and the sensitivity of alabaster to fire means that many were destroyed in fires over the years.[6] This is particularly true of London churches many of which were destroyed in the Great Fire of 1666 and the later Blitz. The distribution of the extant tombs indicates that the majority (40%) are in the East Midlands and Yorkshire and the bulk of the remainder along the coastal fringe of England. These underline the role of the East Midlands 'school' and its water transport links – but *see* later.

Nigel Llewellyn in his book *Funeral Monuments in Post-Reformation England* has analysed the number of monuments created after 1560 and before 1660 – *see* Tables 1.1 and 1.2 (pages 8 & 9 of his book) – and, although not absolutely clear, indicate that some 4000 monuments in stone exist, which is believed to be about 75% of those originally created.[6] Not all of these used alabaster. One fact emerging from Llewellyn's tables is the high density of tombs in the Home Counties with 37% located there as compared to the East Midlands. This is the reverse of Gardner's Gothic distribution, reinforcing the view that the centre of carving, post-Reformation, had moved to London. Slab manufacture, however, remained the province of the East Midlands at 38% with a further 13% in the immediate adjoining West Midlands counties. This will be discussed in full later.

This book cannot claim to be the final word on alabaster monuments. Its purpose is a compendium to bring together monuments, sources of alabaster, transport, carvers and quarries in a structured way to allow those who follow to dig deeper and refine their knowledge. To this end, it is not a book in which every statement is referenced to its source and my preference is to use notes as a means of amplification rather than a demonstration of how well read I am. This may well attract criticism from those who prefer a rigid academic approach, but that is a risk worth taking to protect the flow of the book. However, where sources contain large blocks of information, such as the CMS publications, I have referenced these in full. In Appendix D, I have kept the tables to basic location, date, carver and material source and placed all other information as structured notes. The index numbers in column 1 allow a researcher to quickly identify the population of extant monuments between dates, a feature not available from any other source. I have no compunction in allocating carvers and quarries to certain monuments. This may cause those who need absolute proof (beyond reasonable doubt) before accepting a suggestion to have some disquiet, but the reader must understand that in the period that the monument was carved there were limited sources and carvers, which makes the allocation a sound bet on the balance of probability. In Appendix G, I have attempted to identify anyone associated with the alabaster trade. The names are taken from a number of sources particularly the law as they often seemed to need to sue each other. Some names may be questionable in respect of alabaster work, but somewhere, someone has made the link and so the reader can make a judgment to use or ignore.

Notes:

1. It was present in the 11th century in Old English as ceorfan (ker-van) which means to carve. Kerver is an Anglo-Saxon word for a wood-carver or sculptor. Chaucer (1343–1400) writing about Theseus in *The Knight's Tale* in *The Canterbury Tales*, says, '*Ne purtreyour, ne Kerver of images*'. In the same passage Chaucer says, '*And north-ward in a touret on the wal of albastre whyt and red coral*'. This indicates he was fully aware of the trade in alabaster and at the time the predominant colour was white. This was not a surprise as he was related through marriage with John of Gaunt who we know arranged for alabaster from Tutbury for a tomb to Blanche for which Chaucer penned the *Book of the Duchess* about her.
2. In 1634, Dutch artisan and brother-in-law to Nicholas Stone, Hendrik de Keyser, set up a workshop in Nottingham remaining until 1647 when he returned to Holland.
3. Although white alabaster was sought, the price of this would be high. As a result, veined alabaster was used especially when locally sourced.
4. At one point, the Chellaston History Group appears to have reopened the old quarries supplying alabaster to a number of users. The group has produced a fine book by the late John Young called simply *Alabaster* dated 1990. This book is written in anecdotal form with the result that understanding the historical development is difficult.

5 Francis Cheetham reports that Epstein's sculpture, *Jacob and the Angel*, carved in 1940 and now in Tate Britain, was formed from a large block of alabaster from Fauld Mine. In addition, the statue of *Adam* by the same carver in the great hall at Harewood House, Yorkshire dating from 1938 is also Fauld alabaster (*see* A50). A few years ago, this showed a uniform mid-brown stain which was attributable to the atmosphere and was cleaned and stripped of this staining in 2011. It is believed by the author that the staining is unlikely to have been atmospheric and was probably applied by the carver in 1940.

6. Appendix D9 attempts to catalogue some of the alabaster monuments which have vanished.

1
Introduction

Those who visit ancient churches will have noticed wall memorials, panels, slabs, effigies and altar pieces made from stone. Many are carved in freestone,[1] but some are exquisitely carved from a translucent mineral sometimes white, pink or cream, but often stained with purple, green or brown streaks. These are often mistaken for marble, but are, in fact, alabaster.[2]

These decorative items can date from the medieval to the Middle Ages and into the Tudor and Stuart period when it was popular to decorate churches with tables, grave slabs, screens and tombs. This practice lost favour towards the end of the 17th century as its position was assumed by pure marble, but it had a minor resurgence in the 18th century grand houses and some churches before petering out in the late 20th century.

In England, one of the main centres for alabaster work was the East Midlands. Here, craftsmen known as alabasterers, alabastermen, kervers, image makers, stainers or marblers plied their art. Records show that the trade was well established in the 14th century, but alabaster for monumental construction was applied much earlier.[3]

This book describes the work of the 'kervers' of Staffordshire, Derbyshire and Nottinghamshire and where samples of their carvings can be observed. However, much alabaster was exported to London, Lincoln, Gloucester, Norwich and York and beyond, so the work of these distant carvers will also be included.

Notes:

1. Although freestone is the term for any locally workable stone in terms of monuments, it usually relates to members of the limestone family.
2. The guides at Southwell, Nottinghamshire refer to the veined alabaster as 'smokey bacon'. The term may well be a derivative of 'streaky bacon' alabaster which is attributed to historian Alec Clifton-Taylor (1907–1985). The name alabaster comes from the Egyptian town of Alabastron.
3. Mr William Henry St John Hope in a paper read at Nottingham in July 1901 (*Royal Archaeological Journal* Vol 61) stated that the earliest alabaster effigy he had found was 1290. However, Francis Cheetham disagrees stating the first effigy was 1340 – *see* notes on Hanbury. St John Hope also wrote the illustrated catalogue on the *Early Working of Alabaster* dated 1913 for the Society of Antiquaries (British Library 001730240) and the *Funeral Effigies of the Kings and Queens of England* 1907 with reference to those in Westminster Abbey (British Library 001730242). In 1891, he wrote on the *Sculptured Alabaster Tablets Called St John's Heads* (British Library 001730246). St John Hope observed that Edward Richardson's paper of 1853 in the *Archaeological Journal* (Vol X 116 to 123) contained all that was practically known at the time. He also observes that Richardson seemed unaware of the importance of Nottingham.

2
ALABASTER

Alabaster is found in two forms. The first is an anhydrous sulphate of calcium known as gypsum and in its fibrous or granular form it appears as a pure white stone known as alabaster. This is soft (Mohs hardness 1.5 to 2) and can be scratched or carved very easily, but after exposure to air the stone hardens. This type is the most common found today in Britain.[1] This is sometimes known as selenite. According to Corsi, selenite is only found in England, in Volterra and Castellina Marittima in Italy and in small deposits in China and Oklahoma. Not all Italian alabaster is selenite.

Selenite is deposited in cold water and is principally coloured white or translucent, but can be veined red, black, purple, brown or pink. The Italian, Chinese and particularly that in Oklahoma can produce a rare black anhydrite alabaster.[2]

The second is a carbonate of calcium known as calcite.[3] This is harder than gypsum alabaster (Mohs hardness 3), but can still be carved with metal implements.

In addition, calcite will effervesce when touched by hydrochloric acid whereas gypsum alabaster will remain unaffected.[4]

Calcite is the material of the ancients.[5] It was mined extensively in Egypt around Hatnub, Mallawi, Asyut, Suez and Tel el Armana, and was carved into statues, used for drinking cups and even sliced thinly to provide screens or for glazing windows.[6] A form of calcite can also be found in Catalonia (Spain), Tivoli (Rome), Algeria and Mexico and in the six US States of California, Arizona, Oklahoma, Utah, Colorado and Virginia.

Egyptian alabaster can be seen at its best in the Alabaster Mosque of Muhammad Ali in Cairo, Egypt. This mosque, built between 1830 and 1848, is in a Turkish style and both the courtyard and the interior walls are veined alabaster.[7]

Calcite (travertine) is deposited under hot spring conditions and is richly patterned by bushy growths tinted red, yellow, purple or brown by iron oxides. It is gypsum alabaster which is the main subject of this book.

Figure 1. A small modern sphinx made from Egyptian golden calcite alabaster. Photo: the author.

Figure 2. The interior of the Alabaster Mosque in Cairo. With permission of *Wikipedia.*

Notes:

1. The chemical formula is $CaSO_4 + 2(H_2O)$ – a sedimentary deposit of the limestone family. Alabaster is a crystalline form of gypsum also called Derby spar, or satin spar.
2. The Alabaster Caverns State Park, near Freedom, Oklahoma has a natural cavern which is wholly made from alabaster.
3. The chemical formula is $CaCO_3 + 2(H_2O)$. Calcite alabaster is a crystalline form of stalagmitic limestone also called onyx-marble, or travertine. Geologists use the latter term, or oriental alabaster, to distinguish it from selenite. Note that onyx can also be used for a kind of agate.
4. The difficulty in identifying alabaster from marble can be overcome by using the 'torch test'. A torch with a strong beam can be placed on the surface. If the light diffuses through the stone into the interior then the material is alabaster. In addition the 'touch test' can be applied in which marble is identified by being cold.
5. In Shakespeare's *Othello*, a lady is described as being '… as smooth as monumental alabaster'.
6. St Peter's Basilica in the Vatican City, Rome, has an amber alabaster window in the chancel dating from 1660. Known as the Dove of the Holy Spirit the pictures of this can be seen on the internet.
7. Elizabeth M Hewitt writing in 1910: Gypsum is a hydrous calcium sulphate, with a composition (from a Nottingham sample) of: calcium sulphate, 77%; water, 21%; impurities, 1.6%. The crystalline form, or selenite, is very rarely found in these marls and only lining accidental cavities. The commonest variety is the saccharoidal, which is massive, brilliantly white and amorphous. The more compact, transparent form of this, known as alabaster, has not been found in any quantity in Nottinghamshire, though worked at Chellaston over the Derbyshire border. The fibrous variety consists of long narrow crystals packed closely side by side obliquely to the edges of the vein or round the boundaries of the saccharoidal masses. The play of light upon these crystals has obtained for the variety the name of satin stone, under which title it has been much worked at East Bridgford for ornaments. The workable variety occurs in thick nodular beds or floors, in large spheroidal or lenticular masses called balls or bowls, or in rows of cakes. In places where any large lump occurs, the stratification of the surrounding marls is disturbed on all sides as though irregularly pushed out by the growth of the lump. This has suggested that the mineral was originally deposited in an anhydrous form as anhydrite, and that subsequent additions of water have caused it to swell by entering into combination to produce gypsum. This explanation is rendered more probable by the occurrence of centres of anhydrite in some of the larger masses at Newark and the discovery of a mass of the same mineral 9 feet thick in the Permian marls at Southcar boring, where no doubt it has been protected from infiltration. The gypsum beds occur principally on two horizons, one not far from the base which has been worked at Clarborough and Little Gringley in the north of the county, and one at about 100 feet from the top of the marls worked at Newark, Hawton, Shelton Orston, East Bridgford, Barton, Thrumpton, Gotham and Kingston. The gypsum industry is an important one, 76,584 tons having been raised in the county during 1901, out of 200,000 tons raised in the whole of the United Kingdom.

3
THE BRITISH ALABASTER BEDS

Geological evidence shows that Keuper marl (now Mercian Mudstone) extends in a long bed from just west of Lyme Regis, Dorset, through West Somerset, South Wales, Gloucestershire, Leicester, East Staffordshire, East Nottinghamshire, Isle of Axholme, the Derwent valley east of York and finally ending on the south bank of the Tees at Middlesbrough. Isolated deposits can be found in West Cumbria, Sussex and into the Fylde, Lancashire.

These mudstones can be subdivided by colour and form, but there appears to be no relationship between these subdivisions and the formation of alabaster.

In addition, Permian marl is found in small narrow deposit from Southwell (Nottinghamshire), Worksop, Ledsham (near Pontefract) and Ripon also ending on the Tees near Darlington. An isolated deposit can be found in the Vale of Eden, Cumbria.

Gypsum can be found in both marl deposits, and mining was undertaken in the Eden Valley (19th and 20th century), Yorkshire, Isle of Axholme (16th century), Somerset and South Wales. However, the largest deposits were in Nottinghamshire, North Leicestershire, Staffordshire and South Derbyshire.

Firman in his 1991 paper says that only carvable alabaster within the Nottinghamshire gypsum beds came from Redhill with those seams extending eastward from there being too coarse and granular to be suitable for carving. This is particularly true of the Newark and nearby quarries where even if fine grain seams were located it was too thin to provide blocks of the required size. In the answer to an 1869 question made of the Orston quarry by a prospective alabaster customer, it was stated that '... the largest block that can be obtained would be 18 inches by 2ft and the same width'. There is however no record of any being supplied by the quarry. There are spasmodic reports of alabaster being obtained from the Gotham mines for ornament carving, and firm evidence for this use comes from the Kingston mine in the 1920s and 1930s – *see* Appendix M.

Alabaster has been found in the mudstones of Watchet, Somerset and at Penarth in Glamorgan. However, the main centres for production were in the Forest of Needwood in a seam stretching in a band from Draycott in the Clay and Fauld in Staffordshire, through Tutbury to Chellaston and Aston-on-Trent in Derbyshire.[1] These seams parallel the rivers Dove and Trent. The extent of these beds can be seen on the geological maps of the British Geological Society and are denoted CBp.[2] The extent of these beds is shown in the following diagrams.

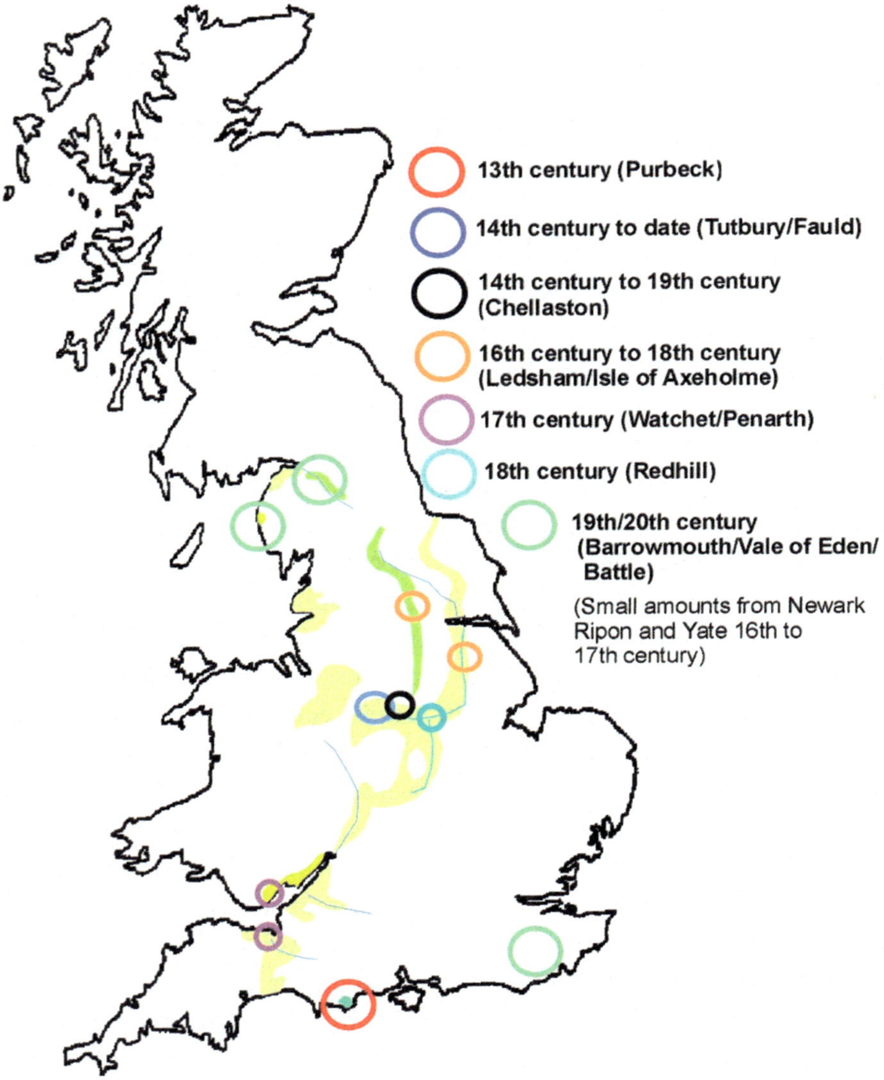

Diagram A. The Keuper Marl (Mercian Mudstone) beds are shown in yellow and the Permian in green. Not all produced workable gypsum and still fewer produced alabaster. The alabaster (and one false marble) sites are shown with their dates of working. *See* Appendix M for description of each area. There is no significance in the size of the circles. Drawn by the author.

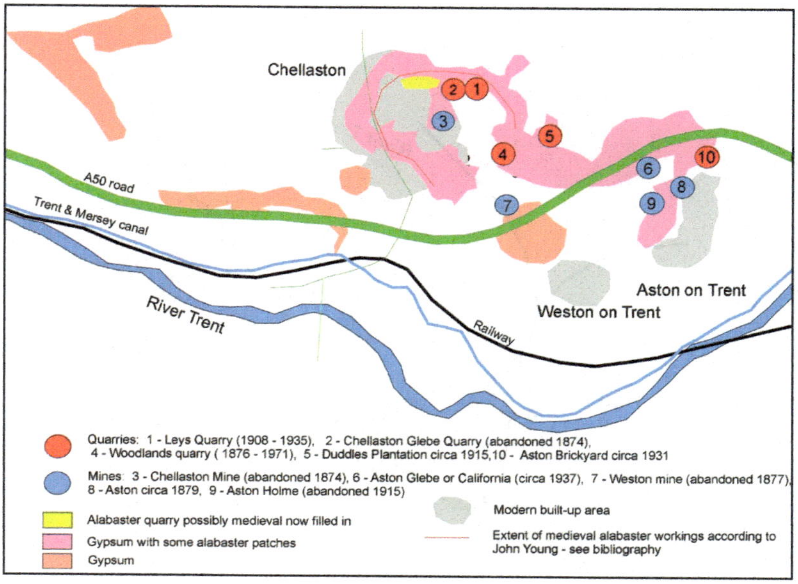

Diagram B. The Chellaston gypsum and alabaster beds in the Trent Valley. The medieval workings are believed to have been a quarry shown above in yellow, but the whole of the ground within the red line was worked at some time in antiquity. The 18th, 19th and 20th century mines and quarries are shown, but only the abandonment dates are known for certain. The most likely source of Gilbert Scott's alabaster is the Woodlands quarry shown as No 4. When surface quarrying was worked out, mining was undertaken, but these were shallow and short unlike the deep and long mines at Fauld. Data from British Geological Survey and redrawn by the author.

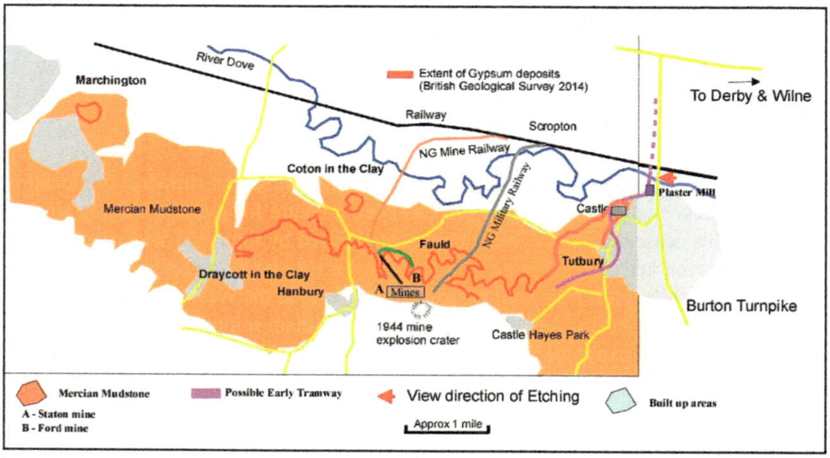

Diagram C. The Forest of Needwood (Fauld, Tutbury and Castle Hay) gypsum and alabaster beds in the Dove Valley. The location of the 12th century quarry which was the source of the alabaster for Tutbury church is not known and may well be the footings for the castle. Appendix M explores this area in greater detail, but the closeness of Castle Hay and the Fauld Mines can be seen. Note the crater of the 1944 munitions explosion. Data from British Geological Survey and drawn by the author.

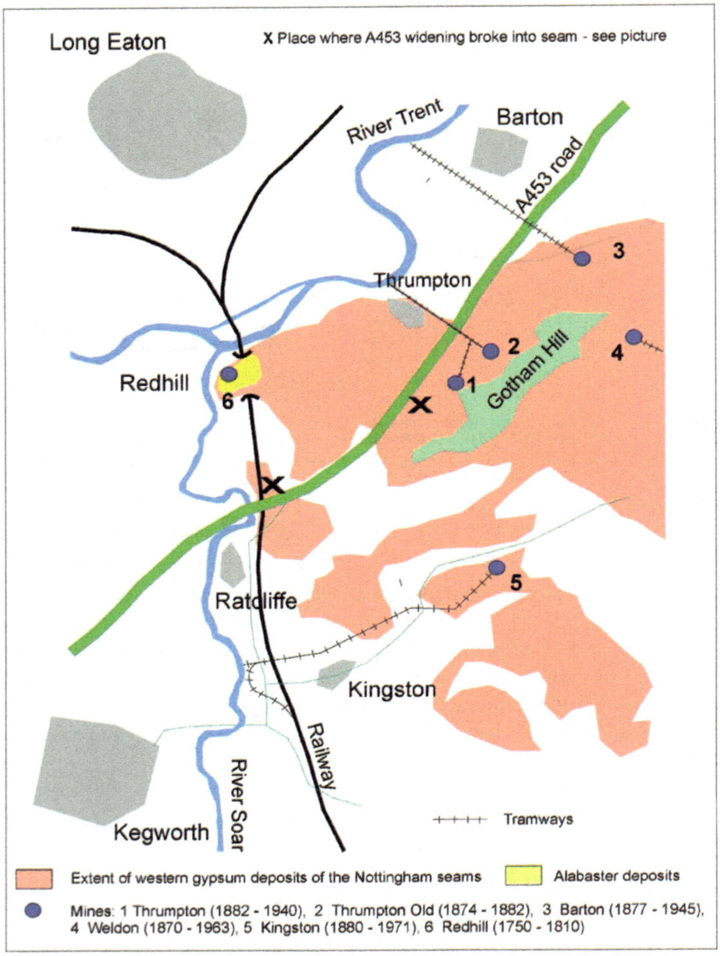

Diagram D. The western edge of the Nottinghamshire gypsum seams showing the location of the quarried alabaster deposits in yellow. This area has been a centre for gypsum mining since the 18th century although this ceased in 1971. The seams were exposed by the A453 widening in the summer of 2013 at the points marked X (*see* Figure 7). The alabaster is to be found only in the cliff face which abuts the River Soar although it may well pass under the Soar to the west where is was disturbed by the Normanton Hills fault. Records of alabaster from the Gotham mines are thin, but alabaster from the Kingston mine (5) was extracted and used in Kingston church, in Kingston Hall and for making ornaments – *see* later. Data from British Geological Survey and drawn by the author.

Diagrams of the alabaster of the Permian marl beds at Ledsham (Fairburn)[3] near Pontefract in Yorkshire, which may be the source for the York carvers and the Somerset and Glamorgan beds, are shown in Appendix M. These and the East Midlands beds and those from Watchet are, currently, the only known British sources of carvable alabaster.

The centre for alabaster today is Florence, Italy where varieties of alabaster are mined from underground galleries in the district of Volterra. Tuscan alabaster occurs in nodular masses embedded in limestone interstratified with marls of the Miocene and Pliocene age.

Figure 3. *The Last Supper* carved from Italian Tuscan alabaster *circa* 1970. The pale honey colour of this sulphate of calcium material can be compared to the golden colour of the calcite alabaster shown above. Photo: the author.

In its purest form alabaster is pure white with a translucent look, but Italian alabaster can be honey coloured. It may be veined with oxides of iron which produce orange, brown or purple staining. Where many alabaster memorials are grouped together from the same quarry over perhaps 100 years, the quality of the material can be seen to deteriorate as the pure white strata are worked out. Around Chellaston in Derbyshire the stone was particularly pure being found in great detached blocks.[4,5] It is suggested that carving continued at Shardlow and Weston on Trent into the 20th century,[6] but evidence is thin.

There have been many attempts at scientifically identifying alabaster from a given quarry and Firman (pages 174 to 175) summarised the situation that existed in 1984. He found that the results were inconclusive, but recent work on the use of isotopes may yet yield results (*see* the work of Wolfram Kloppmann in the Appendix M, Section 13).

The carvers of the 14th, 15th and 16th century were reluctant torecord from where they obtained their raw materials. The location of carvers close to the East Midlands quarries (*see* later) makes a firm link with the alabaster from that source which, whilst not absolute proof, provides convincing evidence these quarries provided the raw materials from which most, if not all, the medieval effigies were carved. In fact, apart from Tutbury/Fauld and Chellaston it has proved impossible to identify any other quarries capable of producing alabaster in the sizes required until the last quarter of the 16th century. This is discussed again in Section 4.

Despite purist protests there is therefore a clear case that all monuments carved in alabaster from 1300 to 1570 had their material sourced in the East Midlands.

This is reinforced by the study of the colour of the alabaster. Firman suggests that the Chellaston quarry mined white or translucent alabaster (occasionally a green tinge) and discarded any that had veining. This is borne out by later reworking of the Chellaston quarries in the late 19th century which produced alabaster in fine white condition as demonstrated at Mackworth church, Derbyshire (Appendix K). I would agree with this suggestion which accounts for the downturn in output towards the end of the 16th century when the lack of machinery and drilling technology meant that fine white seams could not always be followed.

Fauld, on the other hand, seems to have produced only veined alabaster. The *circa* 1340 effigy at Hanbury, generally recognised as being locally sourced and carved, is heavily veined dark brown at a time when white stone was valued.[7] The veining appears to have been patchy and may well have been minimal at Castle Hay and more severe as the seams were mined further west. This still requires more work to confirm, but the probability is high.

Notes:

1. In Chellaston the alabaster was known as 'Patrick' and sold under the name of Derby spar a term more attributable to fluorspar.
2. CBp stands for Cropwell Bishop Plate and denotes the geological plate which extends from the Vale of Belvoir into Staffordshire. The British Geological Society gives the sub-name Newark and Tutbury Gypsum for the entire area.
3. There are records of gypsum and alabaster being mined in West and North Yorkshire in medieval times and certainly problems have been encountered in the current millennium with the collapse of gypsum caves in Ripon, North Yorkshire where the mineral outcrops into the River Ure. A commentator, Thomas Fuller, wrote in the early 1600s 'At Fairbourne (Fairburn), near Ledsham, Leeds are several quarries of alabaster – the finest used for images and funerary monuments – for which are dug up (blocks) of 1 ton weight and sometimes 2 or 3 tons weight'. The quarry was still shown as being worked in 1750, but probably not for carving stone. There is also a reference to Buttercrambe near York, but Cheetham believes these were gypsum quarries as the records show it was used to make plaster-of-Paris for the Minster. A reference in a 1579 book gives St David's, Wales and Beau Maris, near Leicester as minor sources of alabaster.
4. Nottingham enjoyed a considerable reputation for its skilled 'kervers' in alabaster possibly only rivalled by Burton on Trent. The 'Journal of the Royal Archaeological Institute' of

June 1906 records a paper by Monsieur Camille Entart in which he records 'significant quantities of alabaster sculptures, principally from the Nottingham school which are imported for use throughout France during the 15th century'. France was not the only customer, for there is a well-preserved reredos in the Reynistaour Archeological Museum in Reykjavick, Iceland as well as an elaborate altarpiece in Ferrara, Italy, both of which show English execution. Monsieur Entart also found that much alabaster was exported through Hull which was easily reached by river boat down the Trent. The Iceland reredos can be seen at https://digital.library.cornell.edu/catalog/ss:269108.

5. During the A453 widening around Ratcliffe in the summer of 2013 huge blocks of gypsum/alabaster were discovered close to railway and at the junction of New Kingston Lane. Ratcliffe village acquired a 5–7 ton block which is now been placed on the village green.
6. Lady Victoria Manners, *Arts Journal* September, October and November 1903.
7. As will be discussed later John of Gaunt instructed his steward at Tutbury to obtain alabaster for Blanche's tomb in Old St Paul's in 1370 with the directive that if no suitable stone could be found there he was to '... look elsewhere'. This could well be due to no good white stone being available from Staffordshire whereas Chellaston (also in Duchy of Lancaster's domain) was known to have some. Unfortunately, the fire of 1666 removed any possibility of confirming this.

4

Mining and Quarrying (*see also* Appendix M)

Gypsum may have been quarried by the Romans. In some places the gypsum outcrops into cliffs (such as at Redhill, Nottinghamshire and Watchet, Somerset) and here it can be gathered by hand on the surface.

Figure 4. Fine-grained white gypsum outcropping from red Keuper marl (Mercian Mudstone) in the cliff face at Redhill, Ratcliffe-on-Soar, Nottinghamshire in 2012. Gypsum of this quality was collected and used for plaster, but 300m further north a large outcrop of crystalline gypsum which was alabaster quality was found and mined for some 50 years. Photo: Janet State.

Figure 5. During the excavation for the A453 road in September 2013 the alabaster and gypsum seam was exposed to the east of Ratcliffe. In the background a rock breaker is at work as the density was too much for the scrapers. The overburden was little more than 3 metres above the top of the seam, but the thickness could not be gauged. The adit of the Thrumpton mine was some 300m to the right, but the extent and direction of the mine workings is not known. Photo: John Allen, September 2013.

Figure 6. This is the pile of broken gypsum removed from the cut before being taken away. Some of these are nodules removed complete from the earth and weigh some 2 to 3 tons. Photo: John Allen September 2013.

Figure 7. Ratcliffe's monster nodule of 5 to 7 tons donated by Lang-Rourke the contracting firm for the A453 road in 2015. Photo: the author.

As seen in the above photographs the seams are often close to the surface. In these circumstances quarrying was employed, but where the beds sloped downwards, mining was undertaken.[1] This was true of the beds east of the River Soar particularly around Gotham where the mines were all drift adits. At the peak of development the East Midlands area had 17 major mines/quarries (Fauld and Castle Hay, the Chellaston and Aston group, Thrumpton, Kingston, Burton on the Wolds, Redhill, East Leake, Barton, Silver Seal (Bunny), Weldon (Sheppards), Winser, Cuckoo Bush, Glebe, Marblaegis (East Leake) and Sileby – only Marblaegis, Sileby and Fauld remain. In 2025 the current planning conditions for Marblaegis Mines expire and planning consent to extend to 2042 is being sought in 2016. The application reveals some interesting details such that the mine has an annual capacity of 600,000 tons and that the Silver Seal, Marblaegis and Glebe Mines are connected underground with Kingston being used to drain all three with the mining area extending to 3852 hectares (14 sq miles). Planning consent to mine another 1780 hectares under Gotham Hill covering seven other closed mines still exists. In 2016 only five English mines and a quarry were working. However, of the original number, only five, namely the Chellaston group, Burton on the Wolds, Fauld, Kingston and Redhill,[2] provided carvable alabaster. George Fellows also mentions Wheatley near Newark as being a source.[3]

Gypsum is used in the manufacture of plaster. The first traces of this are in ancient buildings some 9000 years old, but it is known that Egyptians burnt gypsum for plaster around 5000 years ago and this was adopted by the Romans. In medieval times some plaster making was carried out locally, but most medieval plasters are lime based containing only traces of gypsum. In the 16th century plaster was imported from France and plaster making as we know it today did not commence until the 19th century. The source of gypsum in Paris was a mine in Montmartre and its use increased after 1666 when the French king took fright at the scale of damage done in the London fire of that year. He ordered all timber building to be coated in plaster from which the term 'plaster of Paris' is derived.

The mining or quarrying of alabaster, however, is much earlier. In Tutbury the Norman church has a doorway, the crown of which is constructed of alabaster. It is not clear if this was contemporary with the church itself, but it must be one of the first uses of this local stone (*see* Appendix M).

In St Werburgh's Church of the village of Hanbury, close to Tutbury, there is an alabaster effigy which it is claimed, dates from about 1303.[4] This is one of the earliest effigies made from this material found by Gardner during his research in the 1930s. The effigy is cross-legged in keeping with the styles of the early medieval freemasons.[5] Gardner points out that the effigy is in veined alabaster unlike that quarried in Chellaston and with the style and method of carving following 13th century practice is probably the work of a local freemason experimenting with some new local material. The stone is probably Fauld or Tutbury (Castle Hay) alabaster; the two alabaster centres being only a few kilometres away to the east.

Figure 8. The '1303' effigy in locally mined alabaster in Hanbury church, Staffordshire (for details *see* Appendix D and note G28). Photo: the author.

It is well known that alabaster mining was established under the patronage of the Duchy of Lancaster and that effigy carving was initially done by royal or provincial carvers. It would seem that some local quarrying was conducted from the 12th to the dawn of the 14th century around Fauld and Tutbury, but by mid-14th century it was more organised and the new quarries had opened at Chellaston where 'alabaster of fine quality was to be had'.[6]

Records in Yorkshire show that quarries in Ledsham (Fairburn), Yorkshire (near Leeds) were in operation in the 17th century, but it is likely that mining began decades earlier, as a monument believed to be Ledsham alabaster was carved in 1590 (*see* A16). The Ledsham alabaster was probably used by York carvers. Positive identification of monuments using Ledsham alabaster is difficult.

Further away, alabaster was found in Somerset and in South Glamorgan. The veins of gypsum were deposited in the Severn estuary and have been seriously eroded over time. The remnants exist in the Alabaster Cliffs between Watchet and Blue Anchor, Somerset. These can be seen today as pink and white with black veins where the sea has eroded the cliffs. The veins at Penarth across the estuary are a violent red but soft and mainly used for rockeries although as Appendix M will indicate, the alabaster has been used for decorative purposes in some churches and public buildings. Monuments carved from Watchet alabaster are hard to find, but the fonts at Williton and Elworthy, Somerset and a monument at Lydiard Tregoze, Wilts may well be in alabaster mined from this source.

There has, from time to time, been speculation as to the size of the alabaster industry. Whilst authors such as Llewellyn make a spirited, and probably near correct, estimate of the number of monuments post-Reformation, the destruction wrought by that event means that the true monument populations to 1560 are speculative (*see* Diagram E below).

Diagram E shows the distribution of effigies and slabs between 1300 and 1700 based on Firman's work carried out in 1991 to which is added additional information from Appendix D.

Firman suggested that taking into account the additional effigies identified by local historians and the Royal Commission on Historic Monuments (RCHM) the population throughout the country would probably be far larger than that indicated (Firman's 1991 paper Figure 5 page 172). He estimated that some 800 alabaster monuments were still to be found and identified giving a population of almost 2000 to the year 1670. This is not a proven fact. Diagram E shows the additional effigies extracted from Appendix D of this book and while there are, for some years, full agreement with Firman's estimates his extrapolation is shown to be flawed. The population of extant effigies and murals, including slabs, but excluding tablets and altar panels, to 1670 is closer to 1600 than 2000. Whilst the inclusion of known lost monuments slightly flattens the graph, no allowance is made for those lost in religious houses during the Reformation, but since this had run its course by 1553 it has no affect on the peak and its decline some 80 years later.

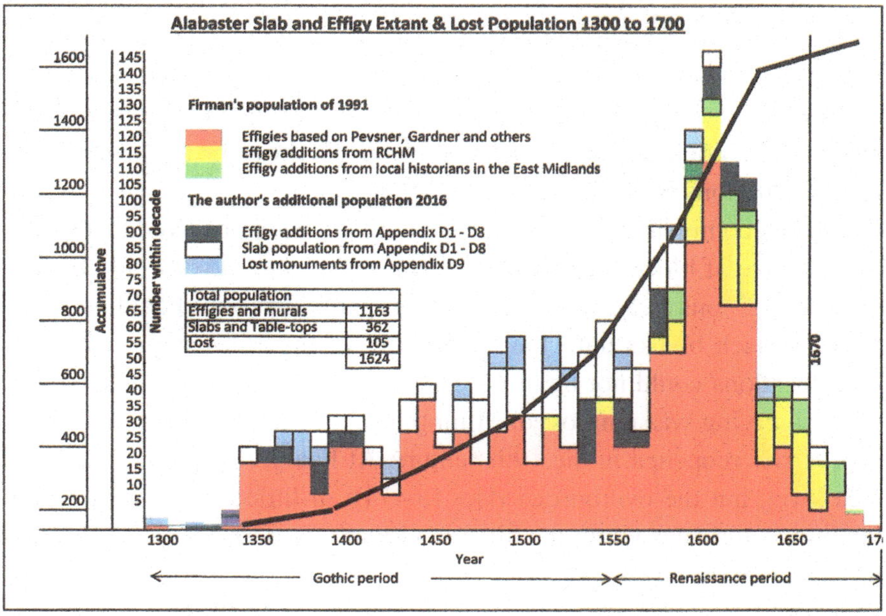

Diagram E: The population of extant effigies and slabs 1330 to 1700 based firstly on Firman analysis of 1991 to which are added further examples from Appendix D of this book. This takes into account known lost monuments from Appendix D9. The peak years of 1560 to 1640 are evident as is the sharp decline from the onset of the Civil War onwards. From 1660 the population of pure marble prevented alabaster from re-establishing its position. Drawing by the author.

What Diagram E shows is the steep rise in alabaster effigy carving in the opening years of the 17th century and the near total collapse at the onset of the Civil War, never to recover. The fall in demand for alabaster probably saw the end of the small quarries such as Watchet and Ledsham, and possibly Chellaston, leaving the Fauld group alone to supply the needs of the market. The alabaster slab market had virtually vanished by 1600.

Later, we will discuss the peak years of outputs from Ledsham, Watchet, Redhill and Penarth, but it is clear that the linking of a monument with these quarries is more difficult. This is made even more suspect by the staining of monuments which often means the colour of the alabaster cannot be determined. Even so some work has been done by matching colours and this is dealt with in some detail later.

Despite all this, the identification of quarries with monuments will remain contentious. At the cost of repeating statements already made the assumption that carvable alabaster was found all over England is flawed. This means that for any effigy carved within a certain timescale only a very limited number of sources are available and in some cases only one quarry/mine was working at the time. On the basis of this I have no hesitation to allocate a source based on strong (almost irrefutable) probability.

Some writers give the impression of a thriving industry and some, more intent on the effigy design, describe the obtaining of alabaster as a trivial matter. Both assumptions have to be treated with caution. Trafford-Wynne, writing in 1907, observes that 18 blocks of 15 ton each had been obtained from Fauld (234cu ft^2) and in 1951 Bray reported that the average size of a block obtained from the same mine was 4 tons going on to say that 900 tons was produced in that year.

Firman when commenting on the alabaster at Ledsham, observed that he estimated the minimum size of block for **two** recumbent medieval effigies would be 6ft x 3ft x 4ft (72cu ft or 4.5 tons to 5 tons). It is most probable that only Fauld and Chellaston could produce such blocks until the last quarter of the 16th century. The operation of the two locations could not be more different. At Chellaston, the overburden was shallow so quarrying was employed. Mining does not seem to have been undertaken until the quarries reopened in the 19th century. At Fauld, the quarry was about 261ft above sea level, but the overburden rises to 474ft in little over ¼ of a mile making the extending of the quarry into the hillside virtually impossible. This difference may explain why Chellaston was famed for its white alabaster as it worked only the top of the seam whilst Fauld was forced to mine the lower veined strata.

The size of slabs varies. A straw poll indicates a range from some 6ft to 7ft 6 inches long and 3ft to 3ft 6 inches wide and about 6 inches thick, but smaller slabs exist. Assuming the average slab was 6ft 6 inches x 3ft 6 inches x 6 inches (11.4cu ft or .75 ton) the total alabaster production for the extant population is little more than 204 tons.

In support of his estimate of output, Firman in his 1984 paper, produced the block diagram for the period 1300 to 1700, revised and shown above as Diagram E. Taking only the period to 1670 the population estimate of existing effigies, murals, and slabs is 1519 with 105 known to be lost. This gives us a start in being able to estimate the size of the industry. Based on Firman's estimates for effigies and counting the number of recumbent effigies other than those on murals and making an estimate for tomb slabs and tomb chests indicates a figure between 4000 and 4500 tons. Murals are harder to estimate for, but if the average consumption is between 6.5 and 7.5 tons then another 3000 and 3500 tons can be added for the period 1550 to 1670. Therefore, the total output for 1300 to 1670 based on known population is some 7200 to 8200 tons over the 370 years of the industry.

Of course we do not know how many tombs were lost in monasteries and priories during the Reformation or for reredos and retable panels most of which are also lost. However, if we even double the estimates for 1300 to 1550 we have another 2500 tons making a likely output of some 9700 to 10,500 tons which is still small as compared with the freestone quarrying. This is highlighted by consideration of a single cathedral such as Salisbury which required some 70,000 tons of freestone over more or less the same period.

The mining was not even and the rate per decade would not have exceeded 100 tons until 1400, 150 tons at the Reformation and peaked at 570 tons in the period to the onset of the Civil War. This is somewhat lower than Firman's estimates which stated that output up to the Reformation from Chellaston was 20 tons per year (200 tons per decade) and 50 tons from Tutbury/Fauld (500 tons per decade). This makes the total 70 tons per year for all applications. His full arguments can be read in his paper (page 174) and only key points are reproduced here.

Comparing the two estimates:

Firman 1984	–	Output by 1550: 70 tons per year
Diagram E	–	Output by 1550: 15 tons per year

This is a serious discrepancy and made even greater if the full 260 years of effigy carving is taken into account. However, it must be noted that Firman estimated in 1984, that some 800 medieval monuments were still to be found and identified. It is believed Firman overstated the output and in support of this contention we note his comment '... an average production of only 12 tons a year would be needed to support the known effigy carving' seems more to the point. With slab and other items included, the Firman estimate rises to 19 tons per year which correlates closely to the estimate in Diagram E.

There is little serious doubt that the sources of the raw material to 1550 can only be Tutbury/Fauld and Chellaston. The conclusion is that the industry was small and that output could be maintained by just two or three men per location working full time which is why few records survive. It is also worth observing that with a relatively low demand for alabaster in the 14th and 15th century, all the needs could be supplied from the East Midlands quarries without any need to prospect elsewhere. This would change in the last quarter of the 16th century.

At first the carving was not local. The early effigy carvers 1300 to 1370 are mainly royal or London based, but they were responsible for only a handful of monuments – nine (1300–1370). From 1370 the carvers of Nottingham, Burton, Chellaston and York became organised and appear to have formed a monopoly of effigy and panel carving for lesser nobility and gentry until the end of the Gothic period. This is a sensible assumption based on the need to minimise the cost of transport (*see* Appendix C), but also because few carver's names have been recorded outside the East Midlands and Yorkshire until the arrival of the Dutch mid-16th century.

After 1550 the output rose sharply as the number of carvers increased. In addition the mural monument required more alabaster than the effigial tombs of the Gothic period. This may have meant that Fauld increased production towards Firman's estimates and it is significant that Ledsham and Watchet produced alabaster in this period.

Appendix D4 shows that the number of identified monuments carved in alabaster after 1670 falls sharply as marble became the fashion. As hinted earlier, this fall in business may well have seen the smaller quarries of Chellaston, Ledsham and Watchet cease production.

Firman in his 1984 paper observed that a number of historians had attempted to match styles and deduce the probable sculptor. In particular he mentioned Jon Bayliss and his work on the Burton upon Trent carvers which had permitted the writer to examine the textures and structures of the alabaster from the supply quarries.[7] He could find no pattern in any aspect of the alabaster which gave a direct link to the quarry and the author directs the reader to Firman's paper for the arguments. One detail worth noting is that Firman found the alabaster which was used for Sandys tomb at Southwell (A17) had an abnormally high sediment content which sets it apart from others analysed. This may yet support the contention that this alabaster is from the Permian beds of Ledsham. Firman goes on to hypothesise that the effigies at Sheriff Hutton, Yorks do have a similar texture to samples from Rippon Park in the Permian field or Hillam (near Ledsham), but this is yet to be examined in detail.

However, Firman's scientific approach seems to ignore colour and more relevant, the names of the quarries actually working at the time the alabaster was obtained. Later the current author will take a much more direct approach to the allocation of alabaster sources.

At this point it is pertinent to mention the work of Dr Wolfram Kloppmann in Orleans, France. In 2013 he published a paper on his work in the use of isotopes in the identification of sources of alabaster to existing monuments. His work on a 1572 tomb in Uppsala in Sweden (R187) has been traced to the Newark and Tutbury gypsum seams in south Nottinghamshire and Staffordshire as part of the CBp (Cropwell Bishop Plate) although the only sample he had was from the Newark area. Samples of alabaster from Redhill and Kingston have been supplied to broaden the sample, but the results from these are currently unknown. This use of isotopes will be discussed in more detail later.

The conclusion is that that the alabaster production was always small involving a limited number of quarries/mines and a small workforce. The limited availability of good stone has had an influence on the location of carving in a way which has received limited attention. This book will explore those influences in the following chapters.

Notes:

1. The Gotham hills have steep sides and quarrying is not feasible due to the depth of the overburden. All the mines here are 19th century or later. Firman records that Leland (1543), Burton (1622) and Plot (1686) mention quarries in the area, but without any mention of mines. Farey in 1811 on the other hand, implies that mining was in hand at Fauld in 1811, and this is supported by Trafford-Wynne in 1907 who said that mining at Fauld had been carried out for at least 100 years and that it started as a quarry whilst describing Redhill from the start as a quarry. Nichols mentions a quarry at Thrumpton, Nottinghamshire in 1795, but since the Redhill quarry is technically in Thrumpton Park it is assumed that this and the Redhill quarry are the same. We may assume that the first and possibly only, purely alabaster mine was at Fauld commencing *circa* 1790.
2. Despite the evidence in note 1 above, there remain doubts about whether Redhill was a mine or a quarry. It may well have commenced as a mine, but in the Board of Agriculture's Report entitled *A General View of the Agriculture of the County of Nottingham* 1794, Robert Lowe of Oxton is recorded as writing 'At Redhill at the junction of the Soar and Trent there is an alabaster quarry from which Lord Yarborough and Lord Scarsdale (Curzon) obtained their columns. The alabaster is not so fine quality as in the past and the modern method of obtaining it is by blasting which so shakes the hillside that it is difficult to secure a large or sound block. It is extensively used for the making of Plaster of Paris'. (British Library system number 002220977). Any mine adits would have been cut by the railway tunnel constructed in 1840, but in the records of the Midland Counties Railway there is no mention of intersecting tunnels although other 'finds' are stated including skeletons[8] and a Celtic Shield Boss, now in the Pump Room Museum, Leamington whilst the records notes that the ground is 'mainly red marl and gypsum'.
3. George Fellows of Beeston Fields, Nottingham, *Arms, Armour and Alabaster Round Nottingham* 1907 – a brief description of some local alabaster altar tombs (with illustrations) – British Library 001214422.
4. Mr William Henry St John Hope in a paper before 1901 stated that the earliest alabaster effigy he had found was 1290. It is possible that St John Hope had the Hanbury effigy in mind knowing that Richardson had dated it to 1240 in 1853. However, in the 1901 paper on Nottingham he states '... it must be at least 70 or 80 years later' and that 'Lord Dillon agrees'. There is therefore uncertainty as to what St John Hope was referring to. Cheetham says that the Hanbury effigy is unlikely to date earlier than 1340. The alabaster is heavily veined making the source most likely to be Fauld quarry rather than Castle Hay.
5. The myth remains that the cross-legged pose means the depicted knight died in battle. As early as 1592 William Wyrley dispelled this assumption, pointing out that many were produced long after the Palestine wars had ended. Some 16th and 17th effigies use the pose, amongst them being Sir G Carew's effigy in Exeter dating from 1589 imitating the medieval style out of choice. Few cross-legged effigies exist in alabaster probably because the carving was too difficult and the cross-legged pose made the effigy liable to damage. On the other hand the mail armour of the 13th and early 14th century suited a cross-legged pose whereas the plate armour did not. Whatever the reason the pose was all, but abandoned by 1360.
6. The Rolls of John of Gaunt *circa* 1371. Young's *Alabaster* page 18 shows the location of the Chellaston quarries named as Leys, Woodlands, Pit Close and Parsons although subsequent investigations by a BGS report has questioned some of these names – diagram in Section 3.

7. Nottingham University has offered the following suggestions as to the first century in which each centre has reported alabaster mining:

13th century	Nore Down (Purbeck marble)
14th century	Tutbury/Fauld, Chellaston, Ripon
15th century	no new quarries
16th century	Isle of Axholme, Newark
17th century	Watchet, Penarth
18th century	Redhill, Ledsham (Fairburn)
19th century	Barrowmouth, Vale of Eden all in Cumbria
20th century	Battle, Kingston

I agree with most of the above, but I have no data on Ripon, and Ledsham was definitely working in the 17th century and may well have been started in the 16th century. Newark is mainly gypsum, but a small amount of surface alabaster may have been recovered, but not enough to make an impact. The History of Mining in Cumbria is very clear in that although some alabaster was mined at Barrowmouth, little was of carvable quality, but *see* Appendix M. Nothing is known about Battle – but again note later comments.

8. The Celtic King Lear (Leire) is reputed to be buried in a tunnel under the river Soar which was known as the Leire in Celtic times. This is assumed to be just north of Leicester, but the geology does not fit well with this assumption except in two places – Sileby and Redhill both places where the gypsum beds protrude under the river. Unlike the gravel and alluvial deposits which populate most of the valley, the gypsum beds can be tunnelled without supports and are largely water-resistant. Of the two locations, Redhill has the better claim in that a Celtic shrine existed on the cliff above the junction of the Soar and the Trent in Lear's time and the shield boss found buried in 1895 is a votive offering indicating that the Soar/Trent junction was an important place for the Celts. This is pure whimsy, but one day it may be proved that Lear's burial was the first known tunnel in alabaster.

5
ALABASTER PRODUCTS

5.1 Introduction

It is clear that from early times the suitability of alabaster for carving objects was understood and appreciated especially by the Egyptians and others at the beginning of civilisation. However, the carvings of the ancient world are outside the scope of this book and the decoration of religious houses with alabaster products does not seem to have been fashionable in the Western world until the dawn of the 14th century. With the introduction of the tomb came the founding of chantry[1] chapels which were often established by building an aisle to the east, alongside the chancel. The tomb would be found within this chapel or between the pillars which separate this chapel and the chancel or placed within the chancel in front of the altar. In modern times incumbents have found these in the way and so it will be found that many have been moved with loss of some detail, pushed into corners or niches too small for their setting. In some cases the tomb has been reordered placing parts above or to one side or in some cases mixing the effigy of a knight with an unrelated lady.

The objects that are known to have been carved from alabaster are covered by the following subject headings:

Notes:

1. The origins of chantry are cantare (to sing) in Latin or adapted to cantaria (license to sing Mass) in medieval times.

5.2 Effigies

Effigies created by freemasons date from Saxon times, but the migration from freestone to alabaster seems to have begun around about the first quarter of the 14th century. The techniques in using freestone and alabaster are wholly different and it is possible the freemasons did not take to the new material with any enthusiasm. As a result a new breed of artisan emerged more in keeping with wood carving than masonry. The alabaster when newly mined was soft enough to be carved with a knife and polished with abrasives (*see* records of Nicholas Stone). It is likely that a contract for a tomb may have a freemason-sculptured tomb chest and canopy and the effigy 'bought in' from a new artisan known as an alabasterer. Later the alabasterer would make the tomb chest as well and sometimes the canopy. Many medieval effigies remain as the 16th century Reformation and the 17th century Commonwealth did not see them as a threat except where destruction on political grounds held sway. The effigies were mainly carved from a single block, but often, particularly when large blocks became difficult to obtain, small parts were carved separately and 'glued' in place. The records of Nicholas Stone contain details of this.

5.3 Slabs

Grave markers in the form of slabs can be found from the 12th century. The majority are cross slabs carved in freestone with various designs of cross. This population is outside the scope of this book, but a small number are made from alabaster, amongst them the one at Teversal, Nottinghamshire (S26) which, with a date of 1538, is very late for this form. The Southwell Church History Project group[1] has co-operated with a census of such slabs indicating carving centres around Mansfield, Tickhill and Southwell all using locally quarried stone. None of these centres appear to have been involved in alabaster carving.

Many cross slabs are without inscriptions and in the Midlands were gradually supplanted by slabs of alabaster with inscribed images and marginal text.

This practice grew in popularity from the 15th century especially amongst some families who could not afford the cost of a tomb and who settled for church burials marked by a slab. Many churches continue to show incised slabs of freestone and slate, but many, especially in the East Midlands, have incised slabs of alabaster. These are often carved with an image of the owner and carry a citation round the border usually in Latin. The slab is more likely to be of white alabaster as these are relatively thin and can be won from the beds more easily than the rectangular blocks required for effigies. The incisions are filled with pitch which highlights the image and text.

Many slabs have received damage due to repeatedly being walked on or suffered from water damage. Nevertheless, the slabs reflect a style of carving which again favours wood carving and previous authors refer to these as 'Arts and Crafts' rather than sculpture. The population of slabs is concentrated in the Midlands and South Yorkshire.

Notes:

1. http://southwellchurches.nottingham.ac.uk/_main/hindex.php

5.4 Panels and Retables

Increasing ornamentation of churches in the 13th century saw the introduction of altar screens known as retables. These often stood on the altar and had wooden frames with hinges so that the sides could be folded in to totally enclose the panels. It was found that alabaster carving suited these ornaments. Not only was alabaster light, but it could be easily carved to depict stories from the Bible and images of saints. Cheetham gives a typical size of the panels as:

Horizontal form	45cm (17.75 inches) high by 65cm (25.5 inches) long
Vertical form	40cm (15.75 inches) high by 26cm (10.25 inches) wide

There are variants to this and the thickness is not stated, but must be about 5 to 6 cm (about 2.5 inches) thick. Many had staples and pins[1] on the back for mounting in the wooden frames and they were highly coloured. It is believed that the panels were supplied individually for mounting elsewhere. Not only did these ease transport, but the wooden frame could be tailored to suit the individual altar. Retables in English churches were systematically destroyed during the Reformation around 1549 so that no complete domestic retables or reredos remain (*see* Appendix D9). However, many English carved reredos and retables exist on the continent and some have been purchased and returned to this country. Amongst these are the 'Swansea' retable in the Victoria and Albert Museum and the reredos in the chapel of Haddon Hall in Derbyshire. Although the details of the panel carving are not included in the book, some individual panels remain and these are listed in Appendix D where they have been found hidden or secreted away only to be discovered much later.

Figure 9: The 'Swansea' retable in the Victoria and Albert Museum. This bears clear similarities to that in Montréal, France. The museum example was obtained from Germany. Photo: © Victoria and Albert Museum, London.

Notes:

1. Francis Cheetham says that the panels were secured by 'latten' wires fitted into holes and set with lead plugs. Latten is a copper alloy.

5.5 Images

Images, unlike retables which told a story, were used for veneration and in some cases pilgrimage. In the 14th century through to the 15th century the East Midland carvers found alabaster suitable for freestanding images and ornaments. Items can vary from mundane domestic objects such as condiment containers to large statues.

In English churches up to the Reformation, images were common, but like retables, they suffered destruction so that almost none survived. Considering the vast population of images that would have existed in 1530 there are few survivors, but some images were collected and exported and some were hidden from the commissioners sent to see that they were removed. Those hidden include the 'Flawford Three'[1] now in the Nottingham Castle Museum – *see* later for description. One notable Nottingham product was an ornament which consisted of a platter containing the head of John the Baptist. These were intended for domestic use in private chapels as shrines and suffered almost total destruction too, although alabaster collectors were able to assemble many samples from Europe (*see* Index of V&A collection). St John Hope detailed a number of instances where alabaster objects were left as bequests of wills. The details can be found on page 228 of his 1901 paper.

Notes:

1. Flawford is a lost village in South Nottinghamshire, but its ancient name is Flawforth a name which is still used locally. *See*: http://flawford.org.uk/saxonchurch.htm and Appendix H.

5.6 Later Reredos

Victorian Gothic Revival in the 19th century established the fashion of reredos. The reredos is usually mounted on the wall behind the altar. Many reredoses are in freestone (*see* Barrow on Soar, Leics), but follow the Gothic style favoured by the medieval carvers. However, the ease of carving and the quality of the carving meant that many reredoses were carved in alabaster. Much is Italian and high quality, but in some cases local alabaster was used (Kingston on Soar and Thrumpton, Nottingham) which displays much veining and inclusions. A resurgence of Gothic taste during the 19th century saw many reredoses reinstated in churches. The work of Nathaniel Hitch between 1871 and 1935 is particularly interesting – *see* Appendix G.

5.7 Mural Wall Hung Tablets and Monuments

From the first quarter of the 17th century it became fashionable to place wall hung memorials inside churches. The appearance of these coincides with the arrival of carvers from the Low Countries in the second quarter of the 16th century. The fashion in Europe was for effigies and tomb chests, but with classical entablature behind and rising above the tomb, comprising an architrave, frieze or cornice supported by columns. Heraldry and symbols such as obelisks were also present. This style grew slowly from the late 1550s, but peaked in the first quarter of the 17th century. Later, the effigy and tomb chest was abandoned and only the entablature remained sometimes with smaller kneeling figures. The mural monument had several important features. Firstly, the cost (without recumbent effigies) was a quarter of the cost of a table tomb and effigy and secondly, being hung on the wall did not take up floor space. This opened up the option of commemoration of the departed one which was more cost effective than a table effigy and able to be introduced into smaller churches. The mural monument now became available to a lower stratum of gentry and so the use proliferated. In some cases it was now possible to commemorate individuals long after their death (*see* Nettlestead, Kent and Woodham Ferrers, Essex). Sometimes mural monuments commemorate people buried in the churchyard or elsewhere and can be huge or little more than rectangular panels. The large wall monuments of Nicholas Stone and others of the Dutch school were highly coloured, but later monuments are in natural stone.

One view on the introduction of lofty mural monuments is the 16th century use of high-backed pews. In the 17th century architects such a Christopher Wren railed against these church furnishings on the grounds they interfered with lines of view of the architecture and monuments. One means of overcoming this was to raise the height of monuments so they towered over the furniture.

By the time of the Reformation the attention of the congregation towards the altar and the sacrament had been replaced by focus on the pulpit and the sermon being presented and so the styles changed. Old low effigial tombs in the chancel could be hidden from view and this new interest in the pulpit meant that high monuments were needed to attract the attention of audiences. The result of this change in focus was that arches and pillars or columns and high heraldic devices, which could be seen from afar, appeared.

5.8 Church Furniture

Most church furniture is wooden or freestone. However, in some parts of Britain alabaster has been used. In Hanbury church, Staffordshire there are floor slabs, a font and a pulpit all made from alabaster. The church is only a few miles from the Tutbury and Fauld Mines and this provides the opportunity to use this material. Another church rich in alabaster is Mackworth near Derby – *see* Appendix K. At Kingston on Soar, Nottingham the Tudor church was rebuilt at the direction of Lord Belper of Kingston Hall in 1900. Being a director of British Gypsum the benefactor arranged for an alabaster reredos and font to be installed.[1] Both are in Fauld alabaster, but the kerb of the font is in a translucent alabaster which has been identified as coming from the Kingston mine about a mile away to the east.[2]

Notes:

1. As Lord Belper was also the patron of Ratcliffe-on-Soar it was to that church that Kingston's displaced Tudor font was directed so that the church there now has two fonts.
2. The mine closed in 1983 and the kilns and building were demolished in 1986. Richard Woodfield, mine manager 1958–1965, died in 1971 and a small tablet to him in the church is made from Kingston alabaster.

The tablet to Richard Woodfield in Kingston on Soar church, Nottinghamshire. He was Kingston mine manager and the stone is Kingston alabaster.

6
Evolution of Church Carving

6.1 Early Forms of Image and Effigy

Modern monuments and statues viewed through 20th and 21st century eyes have a definite purpose. They commemorate the life and achievements of people and the evolution of objects and technology, but also may stray into things which would have seemed strange in times past, such as animals. The danger is to view medieval monuments in the same light.

The pre-Christian world especially the Egyptian, Greek and Roman produced statues and effigies both of gods and people, but with the coming of Christianity in the west the depiction of such 'idols' fell out of favour. In Britain, Christianity came in the mid-4th century only to revert to paganism in the 5th before Christianity was restored in the mid-7th century. Burials were unmarked or denoted by mounds for both Christian and pagan burials and not until very much later were grave markers used. Even then, the grave marker was unlikely to commemorate a person. The burial practice to the 11th century was to bury the body with the minimum of ceremony, but changes were on the way.

6.2 Early Medieval

It is well known that the burial of a person as powerful as William I in 1087 was done in a haphazard manner and with little decorum. His body was stripped and left unattended until approval of the place and time of burial by which time the decomposition was so far advanced that the smell resulted in the monks wrapping up the funeral quickly. Nearly 200 years later the burial of Henry III in 1272 was conducted with much ceremony and with an effigy clothed in robes of state including the crown. Still later the burial of Edward II in 1327 was conducted after 'lying in state'; lasting 3 months. It is worth observing that the three months may well have been sufficient for the carving of the alabaster memorial to the king as it was recorded that 'an effigy fully clothed lay close to the coffined body and which formed the focal point of the obsequies'. However, the effigy was more likely to have been wooden and may have provided the model for the later permanent alabaster tomb. The reason for this change of style of interment and its influence on monument design is worth discussing.

6.3 The Cult of Purgatory[1]

The early Norman liturgy taught that on death the soul went either to heaven or hell depending on the quality of a person's life on earth. All Souls Day was established in the 10th century to focus prayers for the departed, but the concept of purgatory[2] was not mentioned until sometime in the 11th century but was ill defined. Between 1170 and 1200, attempts were made to define the state of purgatory and this action assisted in the schism between the Eastern and Western churches.

As the 12th century progressed, the theory was expounded in that there was an intermediate state called purgatory in which the soul resided before the Last Judgement during which the final resting place was decided. There was, however, no biblical support for this concept. The treatment of the soul and its time in purgatory was thought to be influenced by the deeds of the person when alive and the degree of intersession made on the dead person's behalf by those still living. The popularity of this belief grew so fast that Pope Innocent IV had to give a papal definition in 1254 at the First Council of Lyon which is still authoritative today. His decree said:

> *Since the Greeks themselves believe and profess truly and without hesitation that the souls of those who die after receiving penance but without having had the time to complete it, or who die without mortal sin but guilty of venial sins or minor faults are purged after death and may be helped by suffrages of the church, we, considering that the Greeks assert they cannot find any certain and proper name to designate this place of purgation, this name shall be Purgatory. We wish that in future this expression be also accepted by them. In the temporal fire, sins not of course crimes or capital errors which could not have been forgiven through penance, but slight and minor sins are purged for if they have not been forgiven during existence they weigh down the soul after death.*

Any opposition to this belief had collapsed by 1300 and was probably further accentuated by the repeat visitation of the plague. The establishment of the state of purgatory in which the soul could only be purged through forgiveness after death became all important.

There was a problem in that with the anonymity of burial the continuity of prayer and intercession would soon be lost. There was, therefore, established a need by which the deceased could be identified and prayers offered to ensure the soul was moved speedily to heaven. Thus was established the effigy by which the religious and secular populace could identify the deceased and offer prayers direct for the person's soul. More details can be found in Christopher Daniels' book with the unsettling title of *Death and Burial in Medieval England* which sets out the attitudes in the funerary rites of the period 1300 to the Reformation.

This practice was encouraged by the church. There is a view that the church promoted 'the cult of the dead' and a 'catechism of fear', but this may be unfair. Certainly the church benefited from the money that was poured into chantries, chapelries and intercession contributions, all geared to the praying for souls in purgatory. Later, the pope assumed the ability to release souls from purgatory through indulgencies (or pardons) taking his authority from Matthew 16:19 that Peter (the first pope) could bind or loose souls. This evolved so that many strata of the established church could issue indulgences in which a person could be excused from temporal punishment in purgatory for sins on earth. This was done in exchange for money collected through pardoners (*see Canterbury Tales* by Chaucer). In 1476 it was decreed that indulgences could be purchased for the departed as well as those who were still alive. Few monuments display the details of these pardons and most of them that do, are brasses. However, an incised freestone slab of uncertain date at Hungerford, Berks which, in some quarters, is attributed to Robert de Hungerford, displays the details of his pardon and declares that he purchased some 550 days from 14 bishops. In the church of Edvin Ralph, Hereford a *circa* 1310 slab to Maud d'Eddefin prompts the observer to say a prayer or ave by which she will be rewarded with 30 days pardon by one bishop and 60 by another. These are rare examples.

The fact that purgatory, as such, could not be found in the Bible and that the pope (and others) could arbitrarily decide the fate of a person, often through paid intercession or indulgencies, was much resented by Henry VIII and his ministers. This was one of the reasons for the Reformation during which purgatory was, by 1543, to vanish from the English liturgy. It is also worth observing that the abandonment of purgatory also saw the termination of church building for more than a century. This was not helped by there being four changes in theological direction between 1540 and 1560 which left the populace in some disarray as well as removing the source of funds for such capital projects.

To return to the cult of purgatory, intercession took a number of different forms. The good deeds could be the endowment of a hospital, a chapel in a church, priory or monastery, a college dedicated to the training of priests[3] or, most popular, the willing of a chantry. It could also be a penance or pilgrimage.[4] A chantry was the establishment of a priest or group of priests whose sole task was to pray for, or hold intercessions for, the departed. Priests would hold a Mass for the soul of the person and it was believed that the more Masses which were held could seriously shorten the length of time in purgatory.[5] For those who were rich, a will could specify that thousands of Masses should be said and these could be paid for by endowment of land, or other benefices, which would provide the income to support those who sang them.

The records of Bromsgrove, Worcestershire church contain the details of a complete chantry foundation made by Eleanor the widow of Humphrey Stafford *circa* 1479 (G184). This is too long to repeat here but can be found in *Bromsgrove Church: Its History and Antiquities* by William Alfred Cotton. The chantry was for one chaplain who would say Mass at the altar for the royal family, herself, Sir Humphrey her husband and their five children. The chantry was to be managed by Thomas Lyelton, justice of the common pleas, who was granted 10 marks per year on the basis they would pay the same to the chaplain in two equal parts. The chantry appears to have been maintained at least until 1512, but would not have survived the Reformation.

Pilgrimage was an important method of gaining the help of a saint. Pilgrimages to St Peter in Rome, to St James in Santiago de Compostela in Spain (*see* G106) and above all, to St Thomas Beckett in Canterbury were the most popular.

The church saw this rite of pilgrimage as a revenue stream and cultivated the process. However, whilst these endowments were available to the rich the poor had no such option. Here, the church had another solution. During a routine Mass[6] the priest would pray for all souls of the departed and one day, 2nd November, was set aside for specific prayers for all souls which we know today as All Souls Day. The church considered that those unable to purge themselves by the recounting of deeds, or the personal intercessions, could be cleansed of sin in purgatory by these prayers. In addition, individual souls could be helped by prayers at the anniversary of their death. This was known as obit possibly the source of the later term requiem Mass and could be a big event. Daniel records that an undated obit was held with attendees that included 9 named high clergy, 18 vicars, 18 chantry priests, 10 secondaries and 14 choristers – 69 people in all. The cost came to 6s 7d.

The installation of a tomb in a chantry chapel was to be the manifestation of the focus of prayers and devotions in response to the cult of purgatory.

Notes:

1. The origins and maintenance of purgatory are well documented by Sally Badham in her 2015 book *Seeking Salvation* which is highly recommended.
2. The Latin *purgatorium* was used.
3. This could backfire. Thomas de Wynwyck, treasurer of the Bishop of York misappropriated funds from the 'sale' of the advowson of Ratcliffe-on-Soar, Nottinghamshire for the founding of a college called St Mary's Hall within Oriel College, Oxford. This was discovered by the Pope who ordered a recovery of the funds and when he was ignored organised an attack on the church on the night of the 9th October 1381. The attack failed and earned the leader a period in outlawry for which he was fined 1500 marks. (Richard II, Calendar of Patent Roles, Close Roles 1381 to 1385 – leader pardoned at Windsor 17th Feb 1385.)
4. The pilgrimage to the shrine of St Thomas Beckett in Canterbury is described in Chaucer's Canterbury Tales. There were others. Walsingham, Norfolk was (and still is) popular as was St Wulfstan's tomb at Worcester. A tomb in Ashby de la Zouch (G106), depicts a pilgrim and has trappings of a pilgrimage to Santiago de Compostella in Spain where St James is buried.
5. The will of Joan Lady Cobham *circa* 1361 (*see* G211) specified some 7000 Masses at a cost of £29 3s 4d and Alice Lady West ordered that 4400 Masses should be sung for her husband Sir Thomas West, herself and all Christian souls in 1395. This had to be in haste and completed within 14 nights of her death (Page 12 of Hartshorne).
6. Indroit, Kyrie, Gloria, prayers, epistle, Alleluia, sequence, gospel, offertory, Sanctus, prayers of consecration, Pater Noster, Agnus Dei, post communion and final prayers.

6.4 Role of the Clergy

At the end of the 13th century (1299) there was some approximately 40,000 secular clergy spread across 9500 parishes as stated by J H R Moorman, 1945, in *Church Life in England in the Thirteenth Century*. By the late 14th century the plague had reduced this population but it was followed by a recovery in the 15th century.

At dissolution the clergy population is estimated at 26,500. In 1291 there were 60 livings worth £100 or more but typically the living would be about £10. When the church was attached to a priory or monastery or other religious house, this was the corporate rector appropriating the major Tithes, the lesser going to the vicar appointed by the rector. So valuable were these appropriations in the late 14th century that waves of sub-appropriations were often made to help fund other religious centres.

The role of the clergy in the erection of monuments and their freedom to act is unclear. Diocesan policy seems to have dictated that chapels attached to mother churches should not conduct funerals or have monuments and in such churches which were later raised to full status at the Reformation no monuments in the building or graveyard can be found earlier than *circa* 1550. Although Kingston on Soar had a chapel, the lords of the manor of Kingston were buried at the mother church as indicated by Isobel Babington's slab in Ratcliffe (S54, 1487). All clergy had to take account of diocesan policy, but those who were attached to lower religious houses had also to take note of their policy too. This was especially important where intramural burials were involved.

6.5 Intramural Burials

The position of monuments within a religious building was dictated by status and diocesan policy. Few intramural burials were permitted before the mid-13th century, but the rules were gradually relaxed such that at the beginning of the 14th century the church building became a recognised place of burial for those who could afford it. Even then the location within the structure of the building was reserved for certain groups. The chancel was seen as the suitable resting place for high clergy with the laity confined to the nave or transepts. The sectors of the laity, who could afford to do something special, such as the noble families, could create a side chapel and so from this period we find designated chapels into which family burials could be made. The lesser laity who could not afford the cost of a side chapel could be buried along the length of the nave along the processional route followed by the priest during the Sunday Mass.

Ultimately the church saw this as a revenue stream. For a fee, deserving laity were permitted burial in formerly sacred places and it is recorded that some churches charged almost 7s for burial in the chancel and 3s for the same in the nave – *see* Saul page 117. After the Reformation the rules were much relaxed and burials anywhere in the church were permitted. In particular, the patron or lord of the manor sought precedence over ordinary laity in the burial within the chancel as witnessed by the high population of mid to late 16th century monuments which can be found there. Into the 17th century this concession was granted to lesser laity until in the 19th century ordinary people could stipulate that they were to be buried 'where they formerly worshipped'.

In studying the locations in a church it will be perceived that early monuments paid due regard to the conventions of the Catholic Church, but as the centuries wore on the need for ostentatious display overturned conventions giving rise to the dictation of the location and style by those with the local power. This can be starkly seen by the large number of mural monuments often highly painted in formerly sacred locations.

As stated above, chapels of mother churches were not allowed to bury people. They could hold funeral services but the burial had to be in the main church. This restriction was for two reasons. Firstly, the ground around the chapel may not be consecrated and secondly, the revenue from the burial was guarded as income for the mother church. The Church of England developed its canon law by establishing authority to make changes and install monuments through the award of a faculty. In the 16th and 17th century this control was erratic and many monuments were erected by local agreements without recourse to the ecclesiastical courts. In addition, permission was not required when monuments were placed in 'private' aisles or chapels. This was particularly true when these locations were paid for by local landowners and maintained at their cost. This sometimes caused disputes when incoming landowners found their inherited chapel was full, or had inappropriate monuments. Such a case involved the chapel at Humberstone church which resulted in a long court case – *see* note L6.

6.6 Forms of Intercession

Group intersession was assisted by the bederoll (Old English bede – prayer, roll – list). The bederoll was a list of names of souls for which to pray, which was read out in church. This was a public occasion which not only provided an opportunity to pray for the dead, but also to encourage the living to get onto the bederoll themselves. Bedesmen could be appointed by someone to recite prayers on their behalf, or were the recipients of alms distributed by the deceased's under the terms of his will. The bedesman (or woman) dates to Anglo-Saxon times and is one whose duty is to pray for others, but later came to relate to any poor person who receives alms and is thereby bound to pray for his benefactor (a bedehouse is an ancient name for an almshouse).

It is clear that there were many ways in which intercession could be effected to enable a soul to remain for as short a time as possible in purgatory.

This desire was reflected in the development of monuments. The inscription, 'orate pro anima …' was added to a monument to prompt visitors and others to pray for the soul of the deceased. It was often preceded by 'hic jacet …' (here lies …) or occasionally 'ici gist …' in French and included the name and the date of death which was required so that the correct intercession and obit could be made. A description of the good works of the commemorated were included, all to increase the degree of intercession.

It may be this change in practice was a principal reason for the abandonment of solely relying on heraldic insignia since this could not identify the individual which was a key feature of both sets of prayers. The addition of bedesmen, saints and other family members either on the tomb or adjacent both in the form of images and identified by heraldic symbols, widened the cache of people who would increase the number of prayers being offered. Bedesmen can be found on the tombs at Abergavenny, Mon (G120), Callington, Devon (G54), Clifton Campville, Staffordshire (G161), Elford, Staffordshire (G159), Harewood (G196), Yorks (G206), Llandaff, Wales (GNP118), Lowick, Northamptonshire (G123), Malpas, Cheshire (G53), Newport, Shrops (G151), Norbury, Derbyshire (G62), North Aston, Oxford (G143), Stanton Harcourt, Oxford (GNP77), Shrewsbury, Shrops (GNP82), Strelley, Nottinghamshire (G139), Tong, Shrops (G149), Westminster, Middlesex (G117) and Windsor, Berks (G37), and indicating the wide attraction of such images.

The presence of 'weepers', small figures on the tomb chest which are not angels, bedesmen or saints seems to indicate the involvement of family or associates in the chantry process. Whether these are to show the people who prayed for the soul of the deceased, or to remind the onlooker of who was part of the deceased's 'family' is uncertain. The presence of heraldry and, later, scrolls on which text could be painted would support this view.

6.7 Customer Requirements

There is much to suggest that patrons were not very adventurous in their requirements. They relied on personal recommendation and observed styles in the selection of workshops and families tended to stay with workshops that they trusted.

As the number of fine carved alabaster monuments increased, so customers specified that their monuments should look like one already installed. As a result the similarities in style and design provide a clue to their creator. This will be discussed later.

The Herberts of Abergavenny (G119) and Gascoignes and Redmans of Harewood (G192 & G193) had long tradition of grand alabaster tombs mainly from the same workshop. The conservatism extended to the preference of ensuring status and family links were included at the expense of design which was left to the workshop although when monuments were created close together in time there could be great similarities (*see* Layer Marney, Essex). In a few cases, the contract for the monument states 'to be made' like another seen elsewhere, usually close by, such as those at Strelley and Wollaton, Nottinghamshire. The introduction of alabaster, probably by the House of Lancaster, opened the door for lesser nobility and eventually landed gentry to employ a range of monuments. The presence of provincial workshops meant that these did not need to look to London and so the cost of monuments fell to within the orbit of the less wealthy. (*See* page 105 of Saul's book.)

The Spencer family of Althorpe, Northamptonshire used the Hollemans workshop for their monuments in Great Brington church (R59). The Foljambes of Chesterfield (M115 & M116) specified a wish for their monuments to be like that in Great Cubley (G73) made by Harpur and Moorecock. Favourite workshops could fall from grace and in the case of the Spencer family, the work of Garrett Hollemans II, when he inherited the workshop from his father, was not to the quality expected and he was quietly dropped.

The details of the 1418 contract for Ralph Greene's monument at Lowick (G122) may be the only ones to survive from this period. Written in French, the original no longer survives. However, the contents were copied by Hartshorne who reprinted the contract in *Recumbent Effigies of Northampton*. Extracts have been made by St John Hope and Crossley so there are no shortages of published versions. Commissioned by Ralph's widow Katherine, it refers to Ralph's effigy as '... an esquire armed at all points with a helm under his head and a bear at his feet'. The effigy of Katherine herself was to be shown holding hands with her husband and there was to be '... two tabernacles called gablettes[1] at their heads with angels holding shields on the side of the chest'. The whole was to be stained and gilded and an arch of alabaster to be placed above the tomb. This arch no longer exists, but the monument remains much as Katherine specified. More details are contained in Appendix W.

Contracts also exist for alabaster tombs at Somerton (R75), Breedon on the Hill (R74) and Bisham (A20) and also for the lost monument in London Charterhouse (D9/11). Contracts for bronze effigies also exist and the details of these and the ones in alabaster can be found in Appendix W.

Notes:

1. A gablette is a low canopy over the head of the effigy.

6.8 Costs (for an estimate of current value *see* table in Appendix W)

The cost of the Lowick effigies was £40, Bisham £43 – both from Chellaston – whilst a freestone effigy cost £17 6s 8d for Nicholas Loveine. The annual income of a knight would be between £40 and £300. A large canopied monument would take a year to deliver. The Lowick contract stipulated that delivery was to be within 14 months, that is, by Easter 1420. The setting of delivery dates would be, in some cases, the responsibility of the testator's executor. Wills would be proved in the diocesan court and the executor would be obliged to carry out its conditions. There are cases of executors dragging their heels and in a few cases simply not carrying out the work, but most felt morally obliged to see that the terms of the will were carried out in full. (For more details *see* Saul page 113.)

6.9 Latin Versus English

One of the tools for intercession was script. Many monuments at the start of the period under scrutiny do not carry an inscription and rely on heraldry for identification. It is not clear when inscriptions became common, but by 1400 they can be found on tombs in the larger churches.

The rise in inscriptions can be linked to the developing need to seek prayers of intersession and the rise in literacy. However, this change was diminished somewhat by the use of Latin, the province of the clergy and the landed gentry. To counter this, inscriptions were stylised so that the form of the message could be recognised and only the name need be determined which was often in English.

Hic jacet (Here lies) ... Name ... ***armiger*** (knight or Sir) ... ***et mortuus est*** (who died) ... Date ... ***orate pro anime*** (pray for the soul) ... ***cujus amime propicietur deus*** (that his soul may be given to god).

Words in this form found a place along the rim of the tomb chest on a chamfer which was often castellated.

Gardner quotes the inscription on Herteshull's tomb of 1365 at Ashton, Northamptonshire which is a mixture of Latin and French, but gives no translation:

Monsr Johan d'Herteshull gist ycy dieu de sa aime eyt mercy amen
(Monsieur John d Herteshull teacher of god in his mercy and love, amen)

It begs the question that Herteshull was known as a knight, but may well have been of the clergy.

The Dodford inscription fully in Latin and mentioned in G125 reads:

Hic jacet Johes Cressy miles d'nus isti ville quondam capitani de lycieux orbef at pontleveque in Normandia et Cociliari dni regis in Francia qui obiit apud tove in Loirina IIII° March M^o^CCCCXLIIII cui anie propicietur deus Amen
(Here lies John Cressy soldier and captain of Lycieux Orbef and Ponteveque in Normandy and Cociliari for the king in France who died in Tove Loirina 4th March 1444 pray that his soul may be given to god. Amen)

Here the unusual stating of his appointment in France is inscribed. This may be the only Gothic monument described in this way.

Saul records that one of the earliest monuments to be written in English was that of a woman in Stow (Lincs) dating from 1300 to 1340. Most early inscriptions were on brasses which reflects their popularity with the lower levels of society whose Latin was limited, but English and Latin maintained a parallel existence into the 15th century. The target for the use of one or other of the languages is demonstrated by that of John Statham at

Morley, Derbyshire from 1454, and the ancestor of the Sacheverells of Ratcliffe-on-Soar. His obituary clearly directed heavenward is in Latin whilst the details of his good works directed at the laity, are in English. English text did not outnumber Latin until the 16th century, exemplified by the fact that Ralph Sacheverells tomb at Ratcliffe-on-Soar (G136) of 1539 is in formalised Latin[1] albeit in an odd script, whilst his son Henry Sacheverell of 1558 (T9) displays his epitaph in English albeit in Gothic script. Inscriptions on alabaster tombs in the medieval period into the early 16th century were simple comprising a call for prayers, the name, or names, of the deceased and the date.

From 1520 onward, more biographical details can be found. Inscriptions could be found along the edge of the tomb chest or on scrolls. Where saints are depicted the scrolls are arranged to indicate speech. In a largely illiterate period the use of Latin may seem strange. Whilst the language had been the working medium for clerics from Saxon times it would have been unintelligible to the population as a whole yet it remained dominant as the means of textual inscription into the 16th century. The Reformation with its rejection of Catholic rights firmly established English as the language of funerary art. However, towards the mid-17th century the restoration of the monarchy resulted in restored interest in Latin.

In some cases texts are incomplete. This may indicate that the tomb was created before the demise of the depicted and not added later as intended. In the instance of Henry Sacheverell in Ratcliffe, who died in 1585, the date of death is omitted. However, the style of the tomb is very much later and as his son's will of 1625 provides for its manufacture, the only conclusion is that no-one was alive in 1625 who could remember when Henry died.[2]

Text provides much useful information to researchers but should be treated with care.

Notes:

1. The tomb of Ralph Sacheverell may not be what it seems. *See* discussion on G136.
2. As one of the columns which supports the chancel wall obstructed the desired position of the 1585 Henry it had to be moved forward to allow the two tombs to be directly opposite each other which resulted in the 1625 Henry's tomb covering one of lancet windows.

6.10 In Mine Own Image

Most medieval effigies were not portraits. They were not the work of incompetent masons but were intended to represent types. A man in armour of the finest sort with a wife dressed in accordance with the fashion of the period made a statement. In fact costume was all important. Not that the church approved of some ladies attire and form. In this there was often conflict: the tomb maker wishing to show off his skills with finery, headgear and hairstyles whilst the clergy made disapproving noises. The patron would also specify fashion. In the case of the 1595 monument for the Gage family the patron wrote that he wished his wives to have French hoods (despite these being somewhat old-fashioned by that date), long hair wired and tied in a cornet and with gowns buttoned and girded with a farthingale long enough to cover the feet. He even supplied samples of the costume for the carver to copy.

Gardner suggests that the ideal age for knights was 33 – the age that they hoped to appear as at the resurrection, making portraiture unnecessary.

One of the earliest effigies which can be considered as a portrait is that of Richard II (late 14th century) in Westminster Abbey commissioned during his lifetime and that of his wife Anne of Bohemia (1394). The tomb of Philippa of Hainault (died 1369) also in Westminster can also be considered as a likeness as can the tombs of Edward II in Gloucester (1328–1330) and Henry VII and his wife Elizabeth of York, all of which may also verge on portraiture. What distinguishes these is that they were all of royalty and the products of royal masons and sculptors who had access to the person or to images. Even so, Gardner considers that the effigy of Edward II must be considered as an ideal representation of a king rather than a likeness. In the same manner, early female effigies held sway to the artist's concept of the Madonna.

The origin of the anonymous recumbent effigy can be found in the vertical statuary in major church facades. These were shown as living images and in the transposition from vertical to horizontal form the problem with the depiction of the person from the living to dead had to be overcome. Effigies were shown with cushions and later great helms under the head and with the feet on objects or animals, but the clothes were stiff and representative of a standing figure. The presence of the adornments at the head and feet have been given meaning but is more likely to be because in the translation from vertical to horizontal, support for the vulnerable head and feet of the effigy had to be made by the carver to prevent damage. This was particularly important when images were carved in alabaster. In the case of the three wives of Henry Sacheverell in Ratcliffe-on-Soar (M2) carved in 1625, all three are shown in the costume correct for the date in which they died, but the heads are not portraits, all being very similar. In the case of the third wife, Lucy, the head is identical to another in Gotham (M24) both effigies being carved within a few months of each other.

In the 15th century signs of aging appeared, but they are few and far between. Bishop Beckyngton at Wells (G156) has been given some appearance of age and the knight at Ash, Kent (G99) has a bald forehead as does the judge at Willoughby on the Wolds (G24) although this may be a repair. Gardner considers that the Duke of Suffolk at Wingfield (G163) and the priest at St Mary Redcliffe, Bristol (1474, G89) may be likenesses. However, the latter has striking resemblance to the judge at Yatton (1475, G155) indicating that the features are again a standard likeness. This list just about exhausts the effigies which may have a portrait feature until the onset of the last quarter of the 16th century.

In any case, the effigies of the 14th and early 15th century have a bascinet and gorget or camail which results in little more than the eyes, nose and mouth being visible which makes little scope for portraiture.

One interesting item from the Reformation period is the possible 1547 effigy of Sir William Fielding at Monks Kirby (R113) which may well have been carved during his lifetime and altered as he grew older. The hair line shows that at one time it was down over his forehead and later cut back to show receding hair (*see* Chatwin 1922).

As regards the chin and upper lip, moustaches do feature as do occasionally beards on the chin, but in the period to the end of the 15th century these were considered to be a hindrance under a helmet. So a clean shave predominates. Beards reappeared in Tudor times. The transition tomb of Thomas Essex at Coventry (T12) is one of the first after which beards are almost universal (however, the tomb may have been destroyed in the 1940 blitz).

Kneeling figures in medieval times are rare. Saul records that one of the first was that of Edward Lord Despenser (G10) in his chantry chapel in Tewkesbury. The kneeling figure was not popular as when represented as full size effigy, took up proportionally more room and apart from being shown on a number of incised slabs made no impact until the arrival of the mural monument in which the kneeling effigy is almost universally applied either representing the deceased or his or her family.

With the advent of Puritanism post-1550s many people saw the making of human effigies as conflicting with the second commandment:

> 'Thou shalt not make unto thee any graven image or ant likeness of anything that is heaven above or the earth below or the waters under the earth'.

This was not universally accepted and many Anglicans argued that the sculpture of lay people was an example of the recognition of good behaviour. This demonstrates the first moves from the effigy representing intercession for the soul to that of the recognising the life of the individual. Although religious scenes disappeared and were replaced by secular imagery the effigies were occasionally satirised. The Renaissance form of monument where the effigy is resting on one elbow with his hand under their cheek in contemplation was referred to in the John Webster's Jacobean play *The Duchess of Malfi* in that: 'Prince's images on their tombs do not lie as they are wont, seeming to pray up to heaven: but with their hands under their cheeks as if they died of toothache and they are not carved with their eyes fixed upon the stars but as if their minds were wholly bent upon the world'.

Some portraiture began to appear. The effigy on the tomb of the Archbishop of York Edwin Sandys in Southwell, Nottinghamshire (A17) is clearly a portrait as the pictures below demonstrates.

Figure 10. The head of Bishop Sandys in 1588, as seen on his tomb and from a portrait. Photos: the author and *Wikipedia.*

This was almost certainly carved in York where portraits of the bishop would be known but this is a rare example and nondescript heads continued to be made. The work of the Baldwin workshop in Gloucester (1606–1667) tends to buck this trend and their effigies have a uniqueness which tends to portraiture.

Not so at Burton. As previously stated, the tomb of Henry Sacheverell at Ratcliffe (1625, R5) has wife Lucy with a face identical to that of the wife of St Andrew in Gotham (M23, also 1625, Figures 32 & 33). The two villages are only about 5 miles apart and both wives were living at the time of their husband's death yet they do not seem to have been bothered about being depicted in the same way.

6.11 Status

The Green contract for Lowick Northamptonshire (G122) refers to the carving being 'honestly and competently' carved. Whilst the term 'competently' is well understood today the term 'honest' had a different meaning in medieval England. In 1570 the Archbishop of York set down an edict that stone altars were to be removed and replaced by an 'honest' table. In this context the term 'honest' can be attributable to fit for purpose, properly fashioned or honourable and, in respect of monuments, can be found in wills linked to the desire to have one constructed according to the 'estate' of the deceased. In other words the monument must be constructed with due regards to the recipient's status. In this context what is 'honest' depends on the calling of the deceased. For a priest the representation of a chalice was very important as well as the form of dress especially the Mass vestments. Many inscribed slabs show a tonsured head, a further sign of status. For landed gentry, 'estate' meant being represented by appropriate attire. Knights would be shown in armour even if the real life use of such symbols of military service was thin. All three monuments to the Sacheverell family in Ratcliffe-on-Soar church from 1558 to 1625 show the deceased in fine Elizabethan and Stuart armour whereas their business was certainly not military and they only appeared so attired at the occasional muster. For non-knightly men of status, such as judges and lawyers the symbol of status would be the robes and headgear of their calling.

However, the conveying of status was communicated in other ways. The monument may display awards (*see* Appendix E on collars) or garters or more commonly, heraldry. The inclusion of coats of arms had several purposes. Firstly, it displayed the depth of family connections through marriage both with the deceased or the children and secondly, it permitted observers to identify who the person was who was being commemorated.

In addition, status may be conferred by the inclusion of an inscription setting the ancestral connection with high-status family members. The deceased may be so concerned with this in that the inscription may be set out in the will, but most likely the deceased's executor would have received verbal instructions and would be free to agree the actual words with the mason. In any case the inscription into the 17th century had a style which emphasised the deceased's good pedigree and judgment in making good matches. The inscription on Henry Sacheverell's tomb shown in Figures 11A and 11B is a case in point.

It was not common for testators to specify the material from which their monument is to be made. Occasionally there is mention of 'marble stone' but there is disagreement as to whether this is what it means and Nigel Saul has interpreted this as being brass mounted in a freestone block or slab. What is certain is that the distribution of monuments in certain materials is dependent on geography. The highest population of brass monuments is in the southern part of England with alabaster slabs in the Midlands and freestone slabs in the North reflecting the transport requirements and the access to workshops. However, alabaster is the material which is more often mentioned by name. Alabaster was liked due to its translucent appearance and ease of carving. With the distribution of reredos and retable panels and images in this material over a wide area centred on Nottingham, the laity soon were specifying a monument in this new medium. We find Lord Latimer specifying such a tomb in Guisborough Priory in 1380 (D9/17) and Countess of Cambridge one in Roche Abbey in 1440 (D9/30).

6.12 Inheritance

By the beginning of the 15th century the importance of inheritance through the male line became a dominant feature of medieval life. This had a curious twist in the case of monuments. It became important to commemorate past family lines as a means for preserving the line for the future. Suddenly, parents and grandparents were commemorated with dates which have confused later researchers. The incised freestone slab at Lambley, Nottinghamshire carries a date of 1398 but the slab was laid by Ralph, Lord Cromwell in the mid-15th century as he became aware that his line was about to come to an end with no heir.

The same issues drove the Cobhams in their desire for commemoration at Lingfield, Surrey (G166 and L1). Another twist was the need to emphasis kinship on the monument of the deceased himself. Up to the end of the 14th century solitary effigies are found, but from the 15th, the commissioning of multiple effigies became popular. The inclusion of the wife, and sometimes wives, indicated the good lineage of the deceased and increasingly children and sometimes parents were included. This together with coats of arms, some of which are suspect, showed to the world the good connections of those commemorated and also increased the potential numbers of people who might pray for the soul of the departed.

This was important in the middle ages. As previously stated, the church preached the cult of purgatory which could be mitigated through good works and prayers for the departed which would be magnified by broadening the family connections to as many as possible. In fact, the number of solitary effigies in the period just before the Reformation became few in number and restricted to widows and clergy. It has been suggested that the monuments provide a legal dimension in that they provided a visual confirmation of the right to inheritance which could be called on in disputes, or during inquisition post-mortems. However, the number of monuments cited in disputes is few in number but the option remained.

Tradition played a part in the carving. Where a single female effigy is carved, the man was always placed on the right (dexter) while the woman was placed on the left (sinister).

As for the man, the woman's monument had some symbols. The key and shears appear on early monuments, but these do not appear to have survived into the alabaster period. Another feature is that a woman has her feet on a lapdog, the symbol of fidelity (the man sometimes has a lion, the symbol of strength). The presence of female saints such as Anne, Helen, Zita and Elizabeth as well the Virgin Mary can be attributed to the woman, but apart from this and the costume very little other symbolic representation is present on the woman's effigy.

6.13 Summarising the Period to the Reformation

The positioning of effigies in churches until the Reformation had one purpose and that was to identify the departed and to garner intercessions in the form of prayers in order to seed the soul through purgatory. The addition of wives on tombs only increased the number of people who would provide prayers. The duration of the period in which prayers were said was increased by granting chantries in that people not connected with the deceased would be paid to offer prayers and the person for whom prayers should be directed was identified through painted or carved coats of arms.

Additional features such as angels, saints and bedesmen only emphasised the good works and charity of the deceased by which further prayers could be offered.

Alabaster was very suited to this purpose. It was easier to carve than any of the 'false' marbles and gave finer detail than freestone. Its cost was less than both 'false' and true marble although the transportation cost of this in comparison to locally mined stone could be prohibitive.

At the Reformation all this changed.

6.14 The Disturbance of the Reformation

The style and purpose of monuments changed in the 16th century. Gardner saw this change in simplistic terms in that he offered the opinion that a transition period lasting from about 1550 to 1566 in which the Gothic depiction on tombs was gradually replaced by the Renaissance form as a style change.

Nigel Llewellyn sees this change as much more subtle. The Renaissance concept is thought to have emerged in the 14th century in Italy and found a base in Florence until it spread into most of Europe in the 16th century. Its basis is in the desire to look back at the Classic period mainly Greek and reflect this in the art form. Llewellyn dismisses the view that England embraced the Renaissance style as an import from Italy and points out that English monuments follow a style which may have had its roots in Italy but was heavily influenced by Dutch modifications.

However, he also offers alternative views in that masons had been commandeered by Henry VIII in the 1540s for grand building projects which continued into the 1570s as fortifications became paramount and church building dried up. This suggestion assumes that masons used for large building projects were the same as those who carved monuments, a suggestion which may well be challenged. The coarse statistics for alabaster monuments for 1500 to 1550 show approximately two monuments carved per year (101 in 50 years) but there is no reduction in the transition period at three and a half per year (68 in 20 years) and rising to more than six per year in the period 1571 to 1599.

A similar coarse analysis of the number of carvers working 1500 to 1550 is 24, 1551 to 1570 is 8 and 1571 to 1599 is 25. There is therefore no discernible dip in the ability to build tombs in the period immediately post-Reformation and the cause of the dip in carvers is most likely the departure of Protestant carvers during the Marian period and the wait for stability and an indication of policy towards tomb building in the first years of Elizabeth I. In fact it was not until 1560 (or 1562) that Elizabeth stated clearly her support for monuments, by which time the religious artefacts so beloved by the earlier Gothic carvers were set aside for the new Renaissance form which took time to learn or was brought in by foreign carvers. Llewellyn's claim to the diversion of carvers onto building work is probably incorrect.

Up to the Reformation (*circa* 1538) monument creation was in the hands of domestic carvers who had followed the same Gothic style for some 200 years. Around 1540 Italian sculptors who had been trained in Renaissance style and which included Benedetto do Rovezzano and Nichol da Madonna were invited to England by the ruling class which included Henry VIII.

However, amongst the visitors was a Dutchman, William Cure. It may be that Henry saw in the continental form the confirmation of the departure from the old ways displayed by the Gothic style despite the Renaissance being fundamentally Catholic. In William Cure he may have seen strong Lutheran traits as the storm clouds of Dutch resistance to Spanish rule began to gather.

In fact after Henry VIII's death, the development of the 'English' monument style stalled with the hostility to imagery during Edward VI's reign followed by the re-establishment of the Gothic style during the reign of Mary I. The uncertainty continued after Mary's death in 1559 until the 1562 ruling by Elizabeth I. It is most likely the transition period beloved by Gardner existed because the carvers could not determine what depiction would be acceptable to the customers and so hedged their bets by producing a mixed style. Nigel Llewellyn discusses this (page 27 and 28) but draws no firm conclusions.

By 1566 the Gothic form was all but abandoned. However, it was not replaced by a pure Italian Renaissance form but by one with strong Dutch leanings. Appendix C shows that immigration of Dutch carvers started as early as 1550 but this gathered pace as the century progressed until by 1600 most carving was done by Dutchmen or Dutch-trained carvers.

The 'Dutch' style embraced Ionic and Corinthian columns, massive heraldic displays, marble inlays and bright colours. The recumbent effigy was retained but increasingly kneeling figures at prayer stalls appeared together with inscriptions in English and depiction of one or more offspring. The recumbent effigy slowly disappeared towards the mid-16th century in favour of mural monuments and demi-figure-like busts in a frame.

It is interesting to note that the evolution of style was enabled by political events in the mid-16th century and again in mid-17th century almost 100 years later. The Dutch 'Renaissance' style brought in by the Reformation and Tudor dynasty was rapidly terminated by the Civil War and the Commonwealth. The restoration of the monarchy in 1660 did not see its reintroduction as its place was taken by the Baroque and the last of the alabaster mural type ceased about 1670 never to be seen again in any volume.

6.15 Summarising the Period Post-Reformation

In the immediate period post-Reformation 1545 to 1553 effigies were seen in the same light as religious images and liable for suppression. The Marian period to 1559 saw this abate only for it to be reinstated at the beginning of Elizabeth's reign. Elizabeth's proclamation of 1561–1562 (*see* Appendix H), established the role of effigies within religious houses but the purpose had changed.

Effigies no longer sought intercession but were the celebration of the life of the deceased. The importance of status led to massive heraldic devices and representation of children, inscriptions in English which stated the deceased's deeds, awards and decorations.

6.16 Inscriptions

Inscriptions on grave markers date back to the Saxon times when both Latin and Old English were used. The period immediately after the Conquest saw the addition of French to society and after 1100 the abandonment of Old English. As far as monuments are concerned the period from the Norman Conquest to the beginning of the 13th century was a time when textual inscriptions were largely discontinued especially for secular monuments. The reasons for this are many. The monument-specifying populace often preferred burial in monastic surroundings in which there was continuity of records as compared with the parish church in which the turnover of priests was high. As a result there was little need to identify the monument itself. As fashion for interment in the parish grew so did the need to maintain identification of those commemorated by tombs. This was at first satisfied by the use of heraldry. The use of crests and symbols dates to the early Crusades and this was refined and regulated such that the art of heraldry was established probably about 1140.

Heraldic device appeared on tombs by the end of the 12th century and evolved into a style which saw not only the device of the person commemorated but the devices of the family connections. The first alabaster tombs carried shields in one form or another on which the heraldic device would be painted. One of the first secular, non-royal effigies, is that at Hanbury, Staffordshire (1340, G28) which displays a shield on which the Hanbury coat of arms would most likely have been painted but with no textual inscription although the tomb chest on which it originally stood has been lost. This would be useful whilst the populace were largely illiterate. In fact textual inscription had begun to reappear from 1300 but this was by no means universal.

The reason for this reintroduction was due to increasing literacy and, as previously stated, the growing popularity of parish burials where the use of heraldry alone could not preserve the identity of the departed. It therefore became the norm that both heraldry and inscription would be used one to establish the status and family connections and the other to identify the commemorated so that intercessions for their souls could be correctly focused. Latin was the official liturgy of the church throughout Europe and so it was natural that inscriptions should be written in this language despite its lack of functional suitability. Latin was the language of government and law as well as the church. When Latin inscriptions reappeared literacy was improving and more of the populace could understand certain words but this is not the only reason for its growing popularity. With religious intercessions and liturgy in Latin there was an assumption that the 'recipients' of the intercession and prayers would only understand this language. The inscriptions can therefore be seen to be directed heavenwards.

One curious feature is that French intercession emerged late in England. Despite this language being dominant from 1066 it did not appear on monuments until late in the 13th century some 200 years after the Conquest. Its role was brief and by the end of the 14th century was in serious decline so that few alabaster monuments have French inscriptions and then only those commemorating laity. English and Latin became dominate but occasional relapses into French occurred especially where French wives and/or their attendants were depicted.

6.17 Figures and Furniture

In the beginning of alabaster carving, additional figures were incorporated into the design. In the case of the Hanbury effigy (*circa* 1340) the cushion on which its head rests is supported by angels and this would be repeated. Later knightly effigies were shown with the head resting on a great helm.[1] Ladies heads nearly always rested on a cushion and this was often supported by angels too but could also be legendary animals such as a wyvern or griffon. The feet on the Hanbury effigy were resting on a dog and animal representations were almost universally used until the Reformation. Dogs for ladies and lions for men were the most popular. A few had bedesmen designed to elicit prayers for the departed and even fewer had other images such as clerks – *see* individual monument descriptions. The depiction of relations on monuments did not commence until after 1550.

Traditional subjects such as the resurrection, the crucifixion, the trinity and saints appear on medieval tombs but cease from about 1540 except in protected areas and for a brief resurgence during Mary Tudor's reign.

Heavenly graces Cardinal virtues faith, hope and charity often on Roman dress, cherubs and angels in classical pose appear increasingly post-Reformation.

Prayer stalls or desks with effigies either singly or in pairs were not known in medieval times. These were common in Continental Europe, the first depiction was in brasses created about 1540. Prayer desks increasingly appeared during the second half of the 16th century but from the beginning of the 17th century the numbers proliferated.

Seated effigies are rare and usually restricted to women. One of the earliest is that at Kelstern, Lincolnshire (M87). This 1604 monument to Elizabeth South shows a seated lady facing forward with one hand on a cushion and the other on her lap. The arms may well have held a chrisom at some point. One foot rests on a skull. She wears a late Elizabethan costume with bum roll and high-backed ruff. Two smaller cherubs are at her side. There is no attempt at depicting any form of prayer. The monument at All Saints Church in Fulham to Margaret Legh (M577) dating from 1605, whilst not alabaster, is very similar in that the seated lady is similarly costumed and again faces forward. She is cradling a child with another chrisom shown vertical to her left. This monument to Legh is attributable to Maximilian Colt and although the figures are similar, the surrounds are not the same. The South monument is a simple arch with little adornment whilst the Legh memorial shows all the style and flare of Colt with columns and an extraordinary heraldic device above. Another seated effigy which may also be by Maximilian Colt is the one to Mary Plomer at All Saints Radwell, Herts (M100). She gazed wistfully into the distance holding a chrisom in her arms and with an hour glass by her side. There are similar memorials at East Donyland, Essex (M596, 1613) and at Gawsworth, Cheshire (R47). Although few, these monuments form a small group associated with sadness over the loss of a child in childbirth.

Women who are depicted on tombs with their husband are either on the same level or tiered below the man. The exception to this is where the woman of very high birth as compared to her husband. An example of this is Catherine Grey's tomb in Salisbury (M105) where she was of royal lineage and Edward Seymour, Earl of Hertford of lowly birth.

Notes:

1. Hartshorne suggested that the first effigy to show a great helm was that of the freestone tomb of Sir Oliver de Ingham at Ingham, Norfolk dating from 1343–1344.

6.18 Painting and Staining (*see also* Appendix R)

It is unclear as to the beginning of painting of monuments. No monuments prior to 1400 exist with paint but many shows signs of being waxed or oiled. There is spasmodic evidence in the first half of the 15th century, but staining becomes more prevalent from 1465. The use of paint and stains may emanate from the growing fashion of display of heraldic devices which could be carved, but could also be painted more cheaply. The number of tomb chests displaying blank shields or scrolls on which words or coats of arms can only have been painted means that some painting must have been prevalent. In the golden age of retable and reredos panel making in Nottingham (1390 to 1540) there were probably as many painter/stainers working as carvers (*see* Appendix G), but records are thin until the end of the 16th century. The status of these workers was not high and so few records survive.

At the turn of the 17th century, painters are mentioned in relation to the Mary, Queen of Scots marble memorial in Westminster (1612) and the Bottesford tombs (1592). One, James Mauncey, is recorded as a serjeant painter. Painter records appear more frequently as the 17th century progressed and their charges for work begin to account for a large percentage of the cost of monument. Typically, painters' charges could vary from 17% (Bottesford) to 30% (Westminster) of the total cost. There emerged a new status of gentlemen painters skilled in heraldic matters and the term herald painter is often used.

Painting of 17th century monuments was almost universal with the advent of the Dutch carvers. The polychromy of these monuments has been widely criticised in modern times as being garish and displaying poor taste in the post-Reformation period. Attempts have been made to remove paint to display the alabaster beneath and in some cases repainted to make the memorial look like stone (M23, Gotham, Nottinghamshire but the monument was cleaned in 2015). However, it is now seen that the polychromy appearance of these monuments was how they were intended and restorers have been following the old practices.

Not much is known about the paints used. It appears that the permeable alabaster would be treated with layers of oil and egg-based protein. After this, unpainted areas may well have been waxed which today gives older monuments a golden-brown hue. If being painted there would follow lead-based undercoats and a series of coloured oil glazes and then further applications of wax. There are suggestions that the honey colour is the result of exposure to years of candle fumes mixed with insect droppings but there has been little or no investigation into this.

This is explored further in Section 6.21 and Appendix S.

6.19 Cadavers

Saul in his book identifies 175 surviving monuments that depict a corpse or cadaver. Few of these are alabaster most being brasses. Those that are alabaster include Arundel (G168, 1435), Wells (G156, 1465), Bury St Edmunds (A26, 1467), Ewelme (G142, 1477), Holme (A84, 1491), Wollaton (A3, 1528), Kinlet (M296, 1548 or 1580), Hackington (R193, 1592), Breedon (M95, 1598), Montgomery (M213, 1600), Gawsworth (R46, 1608), Edensor (R277, 1616), Burford (R51, 1628), Bishop Burton (R192, 1649) and D4/54, the lost monument in St Paul's, although some have wooden or freestone cadavers. Christina Welch of Winchester University investigated 37 cadaver non-brass monuments between 1425 and 1558 but many are not alabaster. The full list is referenced under Wordpress Historical Context ECCM37.

Saul attempts to explain the depiction of this macabre form of memorial (pages 311 to 334) but without a clear conclusion. The statement of human mortality included on memorials seems to have been a northern European cult and appears to be a mixture of pessimism, moral concern and a change in clerical teaching post the Black Death era. Compared with the production of conventional memorials' the number depicting a cadaver was very small but worthy of comment. Those that were made appear to be as a result of requests in wills or created within the lifetime of those commemorated indicating that there was no general theme for this style and that each tomb was made to the individual's requirements. Christina Welch, referenced above, makes a more determined attempt at defining the reasons behind cadaver tombs to which the reader is directed for research (*see* Appendix A).

6.20 Clasped Hands

Eight alabaster monuments show effigies with clasped hands, Warwick (1469, G171), Strelley (1391, G25), Elford (1391, G158), Hoveringham (1403, GNP68), Lowick (1419, G122), Aston on Trent (1450, G60), Warrington (1462, GNP40) and Macclesfield (1491, G50). The significance of this pose has been debated. In most cases the gauntlet is taken off and held in the left hand in order to leave the right free to hold that of the lady or else placed on the side (*see* frontispiece). Clasped hands derived popularity after 1360 and only one monument is known prior to this. The peak was after 1400 but died away after 1460, that at Macclesfield being amongst the last.

It is easy to see affection in the reason for the depiction but most medieval marriages were arranged and technically loveless. However, this must be countered by the emergence of clasped hands with the development of printing and the verse-writing of authors such as Chaucer. At the same time churches were beginning to cite biblical teaching which stated that husbands and wives should become one and emphasised the importance of love which unites a man and a woman.

This does not mean that some relationships were not loving ones. The affection that John of Gaunt had for his wife Blanche is known and this was reflected in Blanche's monument in St Paul's (now lost – *see* D9/13). Despite the lack of information about the personal life of those depicted on effigies it is likely that some hand-holding has its basis in affection between the couple.

There is, however, one other aspect – the position of the hands. Styles vary. In some cases the woman's hand is clasped firmly by the man, just pressed together or in a few cases the man's hand is grasped by the woman. In the case of Lowick, Katherine Green simply specified to Sutton and Prentys that '... the hand of one figure was to hold the hand of the other'. The carvers interpreted this by placing Katherine's right hand in the right hand of Ralph in a neutral pose which may reflect the fact that it was Katherine who commissioned the monument. This style is repeated at Elford (G158, 1408), but at Strelley (G25, 1405), Sir Samson clasps the hand of his wife in a clear masculine way. It has been suggested that the person who does the clasping is the dominant one in the relationship and there is some evidence that when the woman is depicted in clasping the hand of her husband she was a significant heiress in her own right bringing wealth to the union. In all the population of effigies the depiction of hand-holding is low and the reasons for this remain unclear.

6.21 Colour

Gardner states that all effigies were gorgeously coloured. This sweeping statement may need some qualification. Time has faded any colour, especially on the Gothic memorials and incompetent restorers and others have removed what little remained. In 1998, when I moved to Ratcliffe-on-Soar, I was told that the churchwarden, who had died only a few years earlier, so disliked the colour on the Sacheverell tombs that she would take sandpaper to the alabaster.

Nottingham had many painters and stainers who mainly worked on the reredos and retable panels, so staining of alabaster was well practiced by the end of the 14th century. A description of their work is included as Appendix S.

The evidence for staining of effigies in the 14th century is thin. In Appendix D the first effigy noted with a YES in the 7th column is that of Bishop Wykeham at Winchester (G90, 1404) but this has been restored *circa* 1894, so the origin of the colour is uncertain. In fact reliable evidence of staining does not emerge until the 16th century.

The exception is that a number of effigies show a light brown or dark honey-coloured patina which is uniform across the whole carving. One of the best examples is the effigy of Henry Pierrepont at Holme Pierrepont (G135, *see* picture below). Appendix S offers some suggestions as to the how this patina might have been applied evenly at all points but at this time the method remains elusive.

Gardner recorded that Edward Richardson described the paint on the Elford monuments (G158 & G159) which he subsequently removed along with the graffiti. These two monuments are recorded as having gold tips on the coronet and the plumes of the helm, green on the leather of the SS collar, crimson belt and sword hilt, blue mantle and many others (*see also* page 32 of *Alabaster Tombs of the Pre-Reformation Period in England*). Even so a large part of the effigies remained unstained and the only colour is on the tomb chest heraldry.

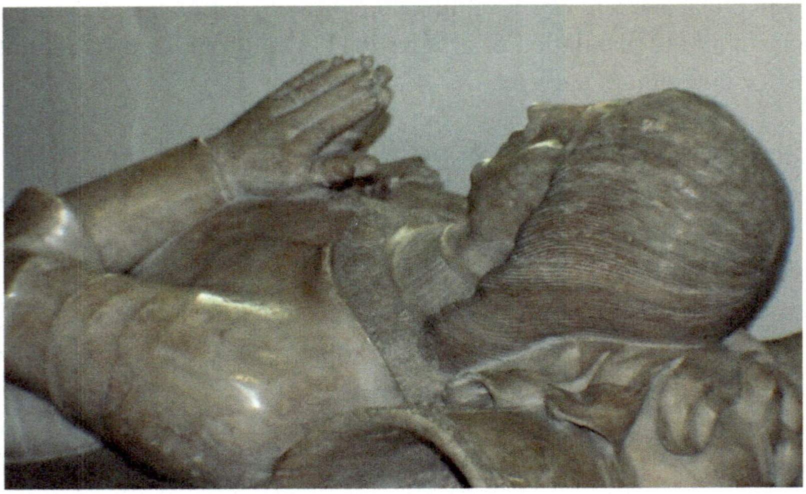

Figure 12. Henry Pierrepont's effigy of 1499 at Holme Pierrepont, Nottinghamshire displays a rich dark honey colour evenly distributed over the surface. This does not seem to be painted and there is no evidence of paint on any part of the monument. The effigy sports a Yorkist collar which raises questions about the date or identity of this tomb. In addition the tomb chest has the lozenges of a period much later than 1499 leading to speculation that this may be a recovered effigy and repositioned post-Reformation. Photo: the author.

Stothard in his 1817 research found paint on the 1393 tomb of Sir Hugh Calverley at Bunbury, Cheshire (G2) but the colour was applied on the figure leaving the armour unpainted. He found a similar scheme at Ashwellthorpe (G121) of 1417. Despite this evidence the general covering of all of the tombs of Gothic design with paint is uncertain and may not have been as universal as claimed by Gardner and many other commentators.[1] The effigy of Bishop Wykeham of 1404 at Winchester (G90) and the freestone effigy of Bishop Chichele at Canterbury has evidence of all-over painting but both have been restored by Victorian restorers and so the matter remains uncertain.

This was to change with the adoption of the Renaissance style. From the third quarter of the 16th century tombs become increasingly coloured until the onset of the mural monuments which are invariably all coloured. The painting of effigies is clearly a continental import but from the end of the 16th century the pure white alabaster was becoming increasingly more difficult to obtain and the veining may well have been seen as an impurity which needed to be covered. A notable exception is the fine monument to Edwin Sandys in Southwell of *circa* 1590 which uses (Ledsham) veined alabaster to good effect and shows no evidence of having been painted.

In the 18th and 19th century the veining was seen as decorative as witnessed by the Marble Halls in Kedleston and Holkham, Norfolk and the dining room at The Breakers, Rhode Island.

For more details *see* Appendix S.

Notes:

1. In 2011 I was present when two students minutely examined the 1539 tomb of Ralph Sacheverell in Ratcliffe. They claimed to have observed traces of paint in the otherwise virgin alabaster which even today I have been unable to see.

6.22 Allegorical Figures

The use of angels, animals, bedesmen and saints on medieval tombs and the existence of cadavers have previously been discussed. These have direct meaning. From the last quarter of the 16th century allegorical figures appeared on Renaissance tombs especially those of the mural form.

The ornamental finial or obelisk is regarded as a symbol of the ending of life. This symbol appears with increasing frequency as the century progressed until almost every tomb had at least one. Some were huge and free-standing, but most were on the entablature over the main tomb. It seems that as a family line neared extinction the monuments and the allegorical figures got larger and more lavish.

Other allegories include putti, wreaths, skulls, strapwork and human figures. Father Time were popular. The meaning to be conveyed by these is not always clear. For example the association with putti (plural of Italian Putto from the Latin *putus* – meaning boy or child) can be love, heaven, peace, prosperity or leisure.

It is not intended to discuss these in detail. The reader can obtain the meaning of any figures from the internet.

7

The Alabaster Trade

Descriptions of the alabaster trade vary widely. In some cases it has been stated, that the numbers involved were huge and geographically widespread. Most only identify the few whose work has been recorded in contracts or within state papers. Appendix G lists nearly 300 alabaster workers, stainers and polishers which have been identified through contracts, research, borough records or accounts of purchases. This list spans some 600 years but is by no means complete. It does provide a starting point for more detailed research. Some have only a remote connection such as a Latoner (brass worker) in the 16th century who installed his brass on an alabaster slab which was almost certainly bought in.

It can be postulated that the numbers involved in alabaster work were never high but their output was prodigious. As previously stated the transport logistics dictated the location of the workers but it is also clear that some moved about the country during installation and it may be the fact that some finishing was done on site.

Apart from royal masons and carvers, the alabaster carving of the 14th to mid-16th century was the prerogative of the East Midlands. The location of the first quarries has been discussed but the rise of Nottingham needs some explanation. The source of alabaster in the 14th century was equidistant from Derby and Burton on Trent yet it was the more remote town of Nottingham which rose to prominence. In Appendix C the transport issues are discussed and it is concluded that with water transport predominating, Nottingham was the highest point on the Trent that reliable transport could be guaranteed. Nottingham was a compromise with a concentration of skilled workers reasonably close to the source of the raw material yet with good links to other parts of the country.

The distribution of monuments in this period radiates outward from the Midlands with pockets of monuments where the delivery could be by river and sea. The mid to late 16th century saw a collapse of the reredos and retable trade and the improvement in transportation and this resulted in other locations rising to prominence, principally London. East Midlands carving ceased in the 17th century but continued as a major source of the raw alabaster.

Nigel Llewellyn observes that the output of the carvers from 1566 to 1670 was prodigious and that '... most monuments are, genuinely, collective productions and tomb makers could produce a range of work and (were) not exponents of a personnel style'. He goes on '... in the present state of knowledge the majority of funeral monuments remain anonymous. Perhaps as few as one in ten can be documented or convincingly attributed to a specific hand'. This is very true and the identification of a particular carver by studying the style and form is problematical. Nevertheless, in the following pages an attempt is made to catalogue those monuments which can be traced to a particular carver. This can be reasonably accomplished by logic. The combination of limited number of carvers when the tomb was commissioned, the location, features of the monument and in some cases continuity of orders makes the probability very high.[1] Nevertheless the reader should be wary.

In respect of the post-Reformation monuments, Saul looked into the distribution and the population. He found that the counties close to London were the most densely populated – that of Kent, Surrey and Sussex, were particularly dense but none had much in the way of carvable stone and were heavily dependent on the London trade. Some Kentish gentry used local 'marble' – *see* Appendix I. Sussex was notoriously conservative and pre-Reformation imagery lasted well into the second half of the 16th century. Saul suggests that the density of tombs in Hampshire, Wiltshire and Dorset was much like that of Sussex reflecting the coastal transport capability and the closeness to the Thames. Purbeck 'marble' continued to be used and workshops in the Stroud Valley and towards Hereford supplied North Wiltshire with a mixture of stone although the source of alabaster was the East Midlands and the new mining activity at Watchet. Berkshire, Oxford, Buckingham and Warwickshire also had access to navigable rivers for the London trade but even here the East Midland workshops are represented.

Of the western counties Somerset is the densest and observers suggest that many were locally made. The mining of alabaster in the cliffs at Watchet was in hand by 1633, but may well have commenced years earlier. Saul observes that the London carvers did not generally export to the western counties but the mason marks on a font at Williton, near Watchet, Somerset would seem to indicate the presence of itinerant carvers belonging to the London workshop of Nicholas Stone. This font is carved from pink Watchet alabaster but it is not clear if the carving of more complex memorials could be accomplished by these travelling workmen. Certainly the notebooks of Nicholas Stone reveal 'expense' payments to his workers which may indicate travel costs and his brother-in-law was employed in Nottinghamshire in 1634 to erect and finish a fireplace for John Byron in Newstead Abbey.

In East Anglia the population of post-Reformation monuments in Essex, Hertfordshire, Cambridgeshire, Suffolk and Norfolk is high. Again the proximity to the coast and to the rivers Lee, Stour and Orwell as well as the Broads indicates that the London carvers could easily reach their markets. This compares favourably with the pre-Reformation distribution when Cambridgeshire and Hertfordshire were also completely absent from the alabaster memorial list. This represents the improved transport capabilities of the

17th century when many rivers were made navigable by the introduction of flash locks. Strangely the coastal ports of East Anglia are absent from the monument list which indicates nothing more than the fact that the memorial contracting gentry lived well away from the dangerous East Coast.

Moving to the Midlands counties, Bedford, Northampton, Leicestershire, Lincolnshire, Nottinghamshire and Derbyshire are well populated which is consistent with their proximity to the Fauld and Chellaston alabaster quarries and mines. In Lincolnshire the presence of the limestone belt exemplified by the Barnack quarries produced much stone for monuments but the rivers Trent, Soar, Welland and Nene, all navigable in part, provided a delivery route for both uncarved stone and finished items.

In the Welsh Marches counties the early pre-Reformation trade in monuments provided by the East Midlands carvers gave way, *circa* 1580, to local carvers as can be found in the index to carvers (Appendix G), but which includes workshops led by Gildon, the Baldwins and Reeves. Any alabaster carving had to use material from the East Midlands (Trent Valley) or from Watchet, there being no other source of this stone. Saul observes that the penetration of these markets by London workshops was thin, owing to coastal and river transport having to navigate both the Lizard and the treacherous Severn.

The northern counties are thinly populated with post-Reformation monuments, for what reason is not immediately clear.

Notes:

1. The 1625 tomb of Henry Sacheverell in Ratcliffe is a case in point. The Sacheverells were rural squires whose parcels of land extended from the borders of Lincolnshire to Cheshire. Although Henry had lodgings in London his business was in the East Midlands and therefore the carving of his tomb has a high probability of being placed with the Hollemans of Burton on Trent.

7.1 Early Uses in the 12th Century and 13th Century

On the banks of the River Dove in Staffordshire is the attractive village of Tutbury. This ancient village is the site of Tutbury Castle, the infamous prison of Mary, Queen of Scots at various times between 1569 and 1585 and owned by the Earl of Shrewsbury and his wife Bess of Hardwick.

Nestling beneath the ramparts is Tutbury Priory church which shows clear Norman origins. It is claimed that the west door was partially constructed from locally mined alabaster in the 11th century but Francis Cheetham and Dr Firman are of the opinion that this cannot be before 1160. However, in 1967 Walker identified slabs of alabaster used to support the buttresses of the south aisle and that he saw gypsum in the footings. In addition, an alabaster sarcophagus was uncovered from the graveyard. Firman himself noted a well-worn roundel of alabaster on the west side of the Rolleston on

Dove's 13th-century church porch (2 miles south-east of Tutbury). These inappropriate uses of this stone indicate that alabaster may well have been used earlier.

Whatever is the true date of the first discovery, Tutbury church demonstrates an early use of alabaster in a religious building in England. The church and castle are on steeply rising ground and the local alabaster deposits lie in the ridges and folds in the hills on the west side of the Dove Valley. Firman believes that the alabaster was found when the foundations for the castle were dug and was also used as supports for the buttresses on the south side of the church and for the construction of the alabaster coffin found in the churchyard. Much of the castle dates from the 13th century but the chapel is reputed to be 12th century contemporary with Tutbury church. It is possible that this alabaster find allowed further exploration and other deposits outcropping into the hill side close to Tutbury village before these were worked out and exploration moved west toward Castle Hay. This location was quarried by local masons but few records remain from this time. Firman observes that the outcrop on which the church and castle stands was an isolated outlier of the main seam geomorphologically similar to Row Hill near Fauld and Hound Hill at Marchington and this seems to be supported by the maps of the Geological Survey of Nottingham.

William Henry St John Hope claimed to have found an effigy dated 1290 but the author has been unable to confirm this. It is likely this reference is related to the Hanbury effigy of 1340 of which more will be said later.

The closeness of Burton on Trent to the Tutbury alabaster may account for records of 'alabaster painters' in 1317. Later Burton was to emerge as a significant centre for carving.

Apart from local use of alabaster in a small way the major development occurred in the next century.

7.2 Developments in the 14th Century

Gardner believed that the first effigy to be carved from alabaster was that now in Hanbury church, Staffordshire. He dated this to 1300 and it is likely that St John Hope had this effigy in mind when he reported that the earliest effigy was dated 1290.

It is without doubt that the effigy at Hanbury, attributed by Gardner to Sir John de Hanbury is both very interesting and of an early date. Francis Cheetham, quoting Blair 1992 pages 3 to 15, disputes the date and believes the effigy is Sir Henry de Hanbury in 1340 and I am inclined to support this view with some reservations.

The effigy is of a 'crusader' knight with long shield and in the process of sheathing his sword believed to denote that his crusading was done. His legs are crossed, being one of the very few alabaster effigies so depicted. Gardner offered the opinion that it was the work of a local mason experimenting with a 'new' material and this could be true, the current Fauld Mine being less than a mile away but there is no proof that the mine was working in the 14th century. However, Firman believes that the Fauld hillside may have had a quarry in the 14th century and also at Castle Hay about 2 miles south-west of Tutbury. An early etching of Fauld shows quarry-working.

Why a member of the de Hanbury family should be shown as a crusader some 140 years after the last of the crusades is curious and may be considered out of fashion in the age of Edward III. Certainly other effigies in the latter half of the 14th century show clear Gothic styles in keeping with the period. Either the Hanbury effigy is much earlier than Francis Cheetham believes or Gardner is correct and the work is the product of a local carver out of touch with the style of the times.

The Hanbury effigy and those in Gloucester dating from 1327 to 1340 are heavily veined and there is very clear circumstantial evidence that the source was the Tutbury/Fauld beds, which were the only English quarries working at that time. This gives us the first reference source for alabaster and this will be explored later in the book.

The earthworks at Tutbury date to 1068 when the land was granted to Hugh d'Avranches but was in the domain of the Ferrers by 1071. Tutbury Manor later belonged to Robert de Ferrers 6th Earl of Derby but was besieged and destroyed in 1264 in a rebellion. The manor came to the Duchy of Lancaster, being granted by Henry III (1216 to 1272) to Richard Crouchback, Earl of Chester and First Earl of Lancaster between 1266 and 1270. Thus began a long association of the area and the use of alabaster within the House of Lancaster.

John of Gaunt (1340–1399), son of Edward III and related to the House of Lancaster by marriage inherited the manor and rebuilt Tutbury castle in the 14th century probably *circa* 1362.

John visited Tutbury many times with both his first wife Blanche and his second wife Constance. His tomb in old St Paul's had an alabaster effigy and it may be during his tenure at Tutbury that the value of alabaster for carving was firmly established. It certainly established the royal connection.

Edward III (1327 to 1377) used alabaster in the early 14th century for a monument at Gloucester (Francis Cheetham says that the Gloucester monuments date from 1330 and in view of the date of accession for Edward III there is some support for this). If so then Gloucester may inherit the claim to have the earliest effigy in alabaster. These early monuments show the use of composite materials, the tomb in Gloucester consisting of an alabaster effigy resting on a Purbeck marble[1] table under an elaborate freestone canopy. Gardner believes this to be the work of the royal masons all the stone being transported in block. There are records of Gloucester masons working in Westminster 'for which stone had to be imported from elsewhere there being no local supplies'. These may have been working on the tomb of John of Eltham (G18). The interesting thing about the Gloucester effigies is that they are reputed to have a likeness to the king which was not a common practice until the end of the 16th century.

Crossley, in his 1921 book, had an interesting view on the early 14th-century tombs. He suggests that the Black Death, which peaked in 1350, heralded a watershed in tomb carving as the period 1300 to 1350 was the era of the mason-sculptors, men who were trained in noble architecture who turned their hand to tomb-making. The analysis of extant alabaster tombs from this period reveal ten effigial and two slab/tomb chest tombs of very individual styles and decoration consistent with a distributed carver base. After 1350 and following a severe reduction in population mason-sculptors were in short supply. Only two tombs are noted in the decade following 1350 but from 1360 the numbers grow and as Crossley states, this coincided with the rise of the alabastermen. However, gone were the soaring architectural monuments of the nobility to be replaced by a more gentle horizontal style, if more formalised, which would be attractive to the lower classes. The growth of population gave rise to the new merchant class who not only could invest in a tomb but could found rural chantries and chapels into which the tomb was to be placed. Such a man was William de la Pole, a Hull merchant, a supporter of Edward III and baron of the exchequer although the identity of his tomb in Hull (G32) of 1367 is being disputed but his descendants are indisputably buried in Wingfield church, Suffolk (A36 and G163).

Nigel Saul in his 2011 book – page 67 – makes reference to a record in the Exchequer Rolls of Scotland 1359–79 that Queen Philippa, wife of Edward III ordered six cartloads of alabaster from Tutbury in 1362 for her own use. *See* A78 for the probable use of this consignment.

In Chatwin's book *Monumental Effigies in Warwickshire* reference is made to John of Gaunt's register for 13th June 1374. In this, instructions were given to John's agent in Tutbury to send six cartloads of alabaster for the construction of a tomb for John's wife Blanche who had just died. Two special blocks were to be selected for the principal figures and if not available 'had to be sought elsewhere'. This suggests that by 1374 the Chellaston quarries were in operation and that Blanche's tomb was fashioned in London. Alan Cameron of Nottingham University points out that Chellaston was, until 1565, land which was part of the Duchy of Lancaster but the duchy operated as an absentee landlord, the locals negotiating rights through the manorial court. Whether the blocks were Tutbury or Chellaston alabaster may never be known because this tomb and that of John of Gaunt, assembled at a cost of £486, did not survive, being destroyed in the Great Fire of 1666.

The carting of large blocks of alabaster some 120 miles to London or 107 miles to Gloucester was some extraordinary feat as the same chronicler relates that Purbeck marble was brought to London by sea from the ancient port of Newton near to Poole, Dorset. It is most likely the carriage of the Purbeck marble to Gloucester was also by sea and transhipped for carriage up the Severn. For an appreciation of the transport issues *see* Appendix C.

The blocks mentioned above are clearly for effigies and tombs but in the same time frame the monarch was contracting for other church monuments. In 42EdwardIII (1367–8 and 1368–9) a sum of £166 13s 4d was paid to Peter the Mason for making an alabaster tabula or reredos for the chapel of the Order of the Garter in Windsor Castle.

From the Issue Roll of 45EdwardIII (1370–1 and 1371–2) we learn that Peter le Maceon (Mason), therein described as of Nottingham, was paid the further sum of 50 marks, or £33 6s 3d, in discharge of 300 marks which the king owed to the same Peter 'for a table of alabaster made by him and placed upon the high altar within the free Chapel of St. George at Windsor'. This great reredos, for this was what it was, cost the huge sum (for that time) of £200, and if the Nottingham carvers could already command the royal patronage, their work must have been of a high standard. Unfortunately, nothing of Peter's reredos now exists at Windsor since this was destroyed during the Reformation (but *see* the retable at Montréal, France below and A144).

In the archives at Nottingham is a debate on the identity of Peter. Authors John Blair and Nigel Ramsey, in 1991, put forward the proposition that the Nottingham trade was in shipping and forwarding alabaster products rather than working the stone. They claim that Peter was a Chellaston carver. In evidence they point out that Nottingham never had a guild of alabasterers unlike Coventry,[2] Lincoln (established *circa* 1525), York (established before 1509[3]) and possibly Norwich.[4] In fact it has been observed by others that the peak years for Nottingham carving were after 1478 and this will be discussed later.

It is possible that Peter received the label 'of Nottingham' simply because it was the point of shipping and the closest major city, neither Chellaston nor Derby being of any significant size.

Even more intriguing is the debate over Peter's true name. It is claimed Peter was Peter Steppyngleye (Steppingley) of the county of Bedford and that the term 'mason' was his trade. Both Peter the Mason and Peter Steppyngleye are recorded as having an establishment in St Mary's Gate from 1365 where Steppyngleye's wife was recorded as being Alice. Neither of these two entries are the same date and it is a coincidence that both reside in the same street unless they are one and the same. Steppyngleye's son was Richard (called son of Peter) and is recorded in the Borough records from 1363 to 1380 as a 'leger' (stonecutter). There was also another son called John of which there is no other trace.[5]

Documents on Chellaston (*see Alabaster* by John Young) shows that in Derbyshire there were workshops as well as the quarrying of alabaster material. This does not prove that all monuments and panels were necessarily sculptured upon the site of the quarries or near them. Like other stone, alabaster was capable of being transported away in the rough and worked to its purposes in many places, as we have seen in respect of John of Gaunt's requirements.

The precise starting of quarrying in Chellaston is uncertain but the discovery of medieval pottery on the site of Ley Quarry with coins of Edward I, II and III would suggest that the quarry was working by 1377.

In Cheetham's books and others who quote the alabaster trade, it is suggested that Nottingham was the centre for all alabaster carving. However, the evidence for this is thin.

In the paragraphs above it is pointed out that Nottingham did not have a guild of alabasterers and a search of the borough records only reveals Peter the Mason (alias Steppyngleye) and one other (*see* Appendix G). Therefore the full degree to which carving was carried out in the borough in the 14th century cannot be firmly established.

In the period to about 1375 it would appear that alabaster in the rough was possibly supplied to remote carvers but large and smaller pieces were probably carved locally. Later carting or 'packing' to Nottingham and Burton for working was undertaken but possibly not until the 15th century. Authors had tended to group these workshops together as the 'Nottingham school' but this is an over-simple generalisation which masks the totality of the trade.

At some point the trade, formerly alabasterers or alabastermen implying workers in alabaster, became known as imagers or image makers implying that the trade developed into the making of images. However, despite this being apparently applied to the 15th century, there is a record of two images residing in Basilica de Santa Croce in Gerusalemme, Rome for which Pope Urban VI had been given an English export licence in 1382.[6]

In drawing the details of the trade in the late 14th century to a conclusion, there is clear evidence that the Derbyshire carvers were active but Nottingham may have been just the retail and dispatching centre. The majority of existing monuments from this time are chest tombs and effigies leading support to the fact that these were worked close to the point of mining.

Whatever the truth the area between Burton on Trent and Nottingham achieved a reputation for the working of alabaster which it was to retain into the 16th century.

Francis Cheetham in his books on medieval carving points out that the 14th century trade in images and panels for retables and reredoses was not restricted to religious houses. He records that individuals purchased items for private devotion, many appearing in wills and other bequests. This trade although present in the 14th century, reached a peak in the following one when a specialisation of the Nottingham carvers was in a plaque depicting the head of St John the Baptist.

A strange entry in 'The Select Cases of Chancery 1364–1471', as recorded in *Archaeological Journal* for 1920, show that in Dartmouth, Devon an application was made in 1390 by Henry and William Mayn, merchants, to export alabaster images to Seville in a ship called *St George*. Why Dartmouth, which is far from the centre of alabaster production, was involved is hard to fathom but in 1390 it was appointed as the sole port for the export of tin. Wendy R Childs in 2003 offered the opinion that this was not the only export to Spain of alabaster and cites the Basque towns as additional entry ports. The entry states '... images of alabaster' amongst a long list of general merchandise showing that it was part of a normal cargo and the images may well have arrived by coastal barque and been transhipped to ocean-going vessels in Dartmouth's fine harbour. The interest in images may stem from the reclaiming of towns and cities from the Muslims and the re-equipping of mosques which seems to have been a continuous process from the 13th to 15th century.

Notes:

1. Purbeck marble is actually 'polishable fossily limestone'. The Church of St Nicholas Studland has a fine effigy in Purbeck marble of Sir Henry d'Estoke, Sheriff of Dorset dated 1240. Thisindicates that this material was used for effigies long before alabaster. The History of Dorset has an interesting comment in that it blames the decline in the use of Purbeck marble to the mining of alabaster which was more easily worked.
2. Folio 121 of the 14th Register of Trades in Coventry lists 'alabasterer' as a guild and that a carver from Tutbury joined the guild. It is undated but may be 1355. Transcribed in 1935.
3. http://www.communigate.co.uk/york/freemenofyork/page6.phtml There is some evidence that stainers and carvers were active from 1456.
4. Francis Cheetham whilst acknowledging that some local monuments are attributable to a 'Norwich school' there is no documentary evidence of such a school in Norfolk or of a guild. The accounts for Swaffham church record repairs to the altar screen by an alabasterman in 1520 but there is no evidence he was from Norwich.
5. Nottingham Borough Records 1100 to 1400 and the File of Correspondence held in the Nottingham City Library.
6. In September 2016 an attempt was made to find these during a visit to Rome. They were located in the Museum of the Holy Cross of Jerusalem attached to the Basilica of the same name. One featured St Paul and the other St Peter, otherwise they were the standard product of the late 14th century.

7.3 Developments in the 15th Century

The status of the Nottingham carvers and stainers is exemplified by the purchase of alabaster for the Abbott of Fécamp in Normandy in 1414.[1]

Thoroton Records, Volume XI 1908, pages 89 to 98[2] have a full description of the purchase of alabaster from Chellaston for the abbott of Fécamp. This description, drawn from the abbey records sheds much light on the fame which East Midlands alabaster trade had achieved and the method of conducting business.

The description is for a 'charter party'. This is the anglicised form of charte partie (divided charter), a medieval form of contract in which the contract is parted with wavy lines drawn across the page such that when the two halves are married together they can be seen to match. This form is believed to be the origin of the term 'indentures'.

Abbott Estaud d'Estouteville had charged one of his monks, Dan Nicholas Ducroq, to supervise the arrangements and his instructions to the agents were dated 9th July 1414. This may seem strange but the abbey frequently did this.

It is clear they were aware of the location of the alabaster centres but unclear as to how to get there. In consequence they contracted with an English captain to act as guide. This was Walter Neasham the captain of the brig *Friday* (or Gaulter Nyersham as written by Ducroq). The *Friday* worked out of Newcastle and was to that town that Neasham brought the four envoys of the abbott: Maitre Alexandre de Berneval, the architect of Rouen; Martin Lausse (or Lause); Raoul le Pappe (or Pape); and Jean Deparis (or de Paris). Berneval first appears in the records of Fécamp as a simple mason in 1409 but in 1413 he entered into a contract with the abbott to construct an unidentified monument for the abbey for which the English alabaster formed a part. He was again recorded carrying out work for the abbey in 1420 but died in 1440, his monument being a tomb slab with his portrait and an epitaph.

The ship set out from Harfleur on the 13th July 1414 arriving in Newcastle after five or seven days at sea. Here they stayed for eight days. There is a claim that they stayed in the house of a merchant who was to act as their 'purse bearer'. In those days a merchant would act as a 'clearing house' for purchases in foreign countries using the loaned money for purchases in the home country, probably for things like wine. Such arrangements existed into the 20th century until rates of exchange were established. The Newcastle merchant is said to have advanced the envoys 200 gold crowns, probably against a 'charte partie' (Charta Parti or Charter Party). This is not borne out by the reports contained in Appendix V as Neasham was reported thereafter as the 'purse bearer'. However, the taking of the envoys all the way to Newcastle instead of Hull is strange. It is possible that Neasham did volunteer as 'purse bearer' but always intended to use one of his contacts in Newcastle, so the report of a loan may not be completely false.

The envoys under the guidance of Neasham purchased horses and began their journey to Nottingham. It took four days, the group lodging in Darlington, York and Doncaster. After one night in Nottingham they arrived in Chellaston to meet Thomas Prentys. Berneval does not record what they saw but they would have observed alabaster being won in large blocks from the beds and carving taking place, but on their return to Nottingham they would have seen alabaster being worked there too.

The contract was signed in Nottingham. There is some uncertainty as to whether Prentys lived in Nottingham or he travelled there to sign the contract. The contract called for the alabaster to be free on board at the port of Hull and the price to Prentys was 40 ecu (understood to be 40 gold crowns). Unfortunately, there does not appear to be any record of the tonnage but the contract stipulates that the alabaster had to be partially worked.

With that, the envoys left Nottingham progressing south with Neasham still acting as guide, departing for Dieppe from Winchelsea, Sussex taking the four purchased horses with them. The port of Winchelsea was granted to Fécamp in pre-Norman times. The grant was annulled during the reign of Harold only to be later restored by William I.

To continue the story, Neasham then made the long journey back to Newcastle and collecting the *Friday*, sailed to Hull to await the arrival of the alabaster by barge from Nottingham. The contract said that Neasham was to be paid for every ton burden the value of 5 to 6 ecu of gold (probably 5 to 6 gold crowns) but again we have no knowledge of the tonnage. When Fauld sent alabaster in 1894 to the USA the blocks were in 15-ton slabs, but it is unlikely that the tonnages would be as big as this.

Berneval died in 1440 and is famous for the rose window in Rouen.[3,4]

The purchase of the alabaster for Fécamp appears to indicate that by 1414 carving had started in Nottingham. This is supported by evidence in the borough records and the records of the *forinsec pleas*. There is increasing reference to the carriage of alabaster (in the rough) to Nottingham and the appearance of alabasterers in disputes and in 'fines' to the town council.

Logistics dictate that the carting of rough blocks some 3ft by 2ft by 3 inches thick for retable panels by mule, in panniers, is not difficult and the Chellaston/Nottingham mule trains could probably make the journey in a day-and-a-half. The movement of a block for an effigy is another matter and such carving, when it commenced, would be done local to the quarry.

We may assume that from the first quarter of the 15th century carvers found that having a workshop in Nottingham close to the retail and transport was more convenient. Therefore in pre-Reformation Britain the main Nottingham trade was in images and panels with those depicting the head of John the Baptist predominating. However, there must have been some trade in tombs and Nottingham Alabasterer Walter Hilton is reported as constructing a tomb for Richard III in the church of Greyfriars in Leicester between 1493 and 1500. It is suggested that Henry VII authorised the construction whilst passing through Leicester.[5]

In the 15th century it would appear that there was gravitation towards Nottingham which concentrated on the smaller items whilst the effigy trade expanded west of Chellaston to Burton on Trent where accommodation was better and transport distances short.

In this time the Chellaston/Castle Hayes Park/Fauld field continued to provide the majority of the carvable alabaster for the country. As well as the locations named there are records that 'the whole of the bank of red marl between the Forest or Chase of Needwood and the River Dove from Marchington to Tutbury has alabaster in it but that at Castle Hayes Park is incomparably the best of which they make gravestones, candlesticks, plates and fruit dishes or whatever the buyer demands'. Firman believes that quarries were worked at Hound Hill (Marchington) and Row Hill (Fauld).

Burton on Trent continued to work alabaster in a small way. Nicholas Michelson and Robert Bounde were named as image makers in 1401 and 1424 respectively and William Howeton in 1439, whilst a painter called Couper provided an image of the Virgin Mary for a church in Coventry *circa* 1462 for 40s. Robert Bocher and Gilbert Twyst are recorded as supplying several monastic houses with objects. These latter two may well have entered into lawsuits for payment from St Albans Abbey, Holy Trinity Priory, Wallingford and St Bartholomew's Hospital, Newbury. In the Wallingford Priory rolls for 1481–1482, there appears a note over the supply of a 'tabula' in alabaster. This account may only have survived as it was used to wrap a parcel of deeds.

The accounts of Tintinhull, Somerset record a payment of 26s 8d for an alabaster altar slab and the sale of another alabaster slab[6] to Robert Shearne for 1s in 1433, as well as 1d to an alabasterman as an advance in 1451–1452. The full payment of 37s 3d for a 'table' was made in 1453.

It has been estimated that by 1530 some 10,000 churches, monasteries and priories had one or more objects or tombs in alabaster.

Notes:

1. A more detailed version is contained as Appendix V.
2. Also see a paper by Mr. John Bilson, FSA, on 'A French purchase of alabaster in 1414', in The *Archaeological Journal* of March, 1907 (vol, LXIV. 32–37). The remit for the charter party and the report of the abbot is attached as Appendix V.
3. The coast is known as the 'Cote d'albastre' or 'Alabaster Coast', more to do with the whiteness of the cliffs than for any other reason.
4. His tomb in Saint-Ouen, Rouen commemorates both Alexander and Colin Berneval and a drawing is contained in Greenhill Vol 2 Figure 117b. This shows a fine incised slab with a Nottingham-style canopy which may well be in alabaster. They hold architect tools and features such as a tracery moulding. The faces are carved with different expressions.
5. The tomb of Richard III is dealt with in more detail later and in Appendix R.
6. One can imagine that the sale to Robert Shearne was an offcut after the altar slab was trimmed.

7.4 Expansion and Collapse in the 16th Century

As to the 16th century, Cheetham offers the opinion that the records of alabasterers in Nottingham after 1529 are thin with Richard Starkey being the last. Although he offers no solution for this it is clear that whilst Chellaston provided tombs there is no record of the carving of images and altar pieces which remained the sole prerogative of Nottingham. After 1530 with the Reformation taking hold this trade collapsed and from 1549 when Edward VI brought in the Books and Images Act there would be no call for this work leaving the imagers with no trade (*see* Appendix H).

John Leland writing in the 16th century records many stainers were working in Burton on Trent between 1535 and 1543 and in 1571 the will of Richard Parker refers to himself as a stainer. Parker is believed to be the kerver of the tomb of the first Earl of Rutland at Bottesford in 1543. It would appear that after the collapse of the image trade in Nottingham the centre of carving moved west to Burton. The navigation of the Trent above the confluence with the Soar was gradually improved in the 16th century allowing transport to be eased. In addition a bridge over the Trent had been built at Burton on Trent improving access to the South.

Richard Parker was the son-in-law of Margery Walker reported as a 'trader in tables' who died in 1546. It was clear she was continuing to trade after the death of her husband, probably also a kerver, and that Burton was not just concentrating on tombs but also trading in figures and panels probably for export. It is unclear as to the law at that time. As stated the installation of images in English churches was banned from 1549 but would be repealed following Mary's enthronement in July 1553. The more relaxed attitude of the Elizabethans may have permitted the carving of religious objects for export but the policy is as yet unclear. What is known is that in 1550 one year after the 1549 law reached the statute books, shiploads of images turned up for sale in French ports which were obviously as a result of Tudor merchants making a quick sale out of looted ornaments.

In the case of York, eight stainers and three marblers are recorded from about 1456 to 1525.[1] The evidence of York-made tombs are scarce, but those at Sheriff Hutton, Methley and Harewood are credited to the York school. The source of alabaster for York is uncertain. The quarries at Fairburn near Ledsham (5 miles north of Pontefract) are believed to have been working in the late 16th century but if York alabasterers were working in the 15th century then the alabaster had to come from the East Midlands fields. This would not be too much of a problem, the Trent, Humber and York Ouse providing a suitable transport medium. As to Buttercrambe (2 miles east of Stamford Bridge) little or no information is forthcoming as to dates between which the quarries were working. However, Francis Cheetham believes that these quarries were only a source of gypsum.

As to London, details of work in the 16th century are fragmented but it is worth mentioning that many nobles who had estates in the Midlands were familiar with the local alabaster work and also most certainly carried their ideas and requirements to London. In fact most of the London tombs were carved in that city but there is no evidence of images and altarpieces being carved which may all have come from Nottingham and in any case there were no sources of alabaster in London other than those emanating from the East Midlands fields.[2]

In Lincoln, unlike Nottingham, there was a guild of painters, gilders, stainers and alabastermen in 1525–1526, but evidence of their work is uncertain with the sole example of the Wollaton tombs. The census of guilds in 1388 failed to identify an alabasterers guild in Lincoln, London or Norwich. Even later in the case of Norwich, the extent of carving in the city is uncertain. With no alabaster in the vicinity any working of the stone had to be sourced from the Midlands and whole tombs could have been imported as the tomb at Ashwellthorpe (G121) shows clear signs of being carved by Prentis or Sutton at Chellaston.

From the above we can deduce that carving in Norwich, Lincoln and maybe Bristol was a minor activity. London concentrated on tombs and mainly for the South-East (the Bottesford tomb may be an exception) and York workshops carved for local nobility.

Particular instances of a trade in block alabaster for use elsewhere are known. Late medieval commerce, as we know it, would favour both the block trade and the worked trade. We know that Caen stone was imported in block and in ashlar form and also that Purbeck marble was supplied in block, in paviors, and in worked pieces. White stone was shipped from the cliff at Beer and conveyed to Exeter, no doubt also to other places, since furniture and monuments of this material appear in many churches along the English Channel. It seems natural that, with improving river navigation, alabaster 'in the rough' should go from Tutbury to Burton on Trent or from Chellaston to Swarkestone and be carried down the River Trent to Nottingham and beyond.

Once in Nottingham the difficult part of the river was past and the onward transport to the Humber at Trent Falls would be easy. There was water-carriage on to York via the Ouse or to Lincoln by the Witham channel, and so by coastal trader to Norwich, a place to which stone was continually coming by sea and river, since no freestone could be quarried locally.

The mining at Chellaston involved the Harpur family. Richard Harpur married Jane Finderne and so acquired Chellaston Manor. A surviving sub-lease refers to Chellaston having a 'plaster pit to get plaster in' and it is believed mining continued after Richard's death in 1577.

Since memorial effigies of Purbeck marble can be found distributed as if coming from London along Watling Street in Northamptonshire, it seems that block alabaster could easily go by the same road to London. Nevertheless, the difficulties of carriage by road of such bulky items in the Middle Ages should not be understated (*see* Appendix C).

In 1549 the trade in images and retable panels was abruptly terminated (*see* Appendix H). Quite what happened to the carvers is unclear, but after this date, nothing is heard about Nottingham kervers, although we have seen that Burton on Trent continued to trade. The records of effigies is such that it is clear carving continued into the Stuart era.

It may be that with the carvers turning to the larger monuments, the transport of large blocks for these to Nottingham was uneconomic and that the carvers abandoned the city for the places closer to the alabaster mining. One thing for certain is that the influence of Flemish and Italian styles came to fore. Gardner complains bitterly about the abandonment of the Gothic style from about 1560 and refused to describe the

Renaissance successors. Gone were the arcades and images on the sides of tomb chests to be replaced by inscriptions and weepers representing the family of the departed. The style of the effigies changed too with the abandonment of medieval armour for Tudor plated armour and a less formal setting. The styles and settings will be discussed later but the change from Gothic seems to be synchronised with the departure from Nottingham.

This is the period of the Royley family and others of the Burton 'school'. However, later, Coventry opened as a centre.

Richard Royley was trading as a slab maker in 1540 and may have acquired the premises of Richard Parker as both are noted as occupying premises in Horninglow St, Burton on Trent. Little can be gleaned about him but in 1580 there are records of a Richard Royley and his son Gabriel working in the same vicinity as tomb makers. The connection between the two is unclear. The detail of their work is included in Appendix G.

About the same time a Dutchman by the name of Garrett Hollemans arrived in Burton from Holland. This was the first of three generations of Hollemans carvers, the details of which are contained in Appendix G.

It is very clear that the flight from Nottingham was sudden and terminal and that between about 1540 to the late 17th century the centre for alabaster carving was Burton on Trent. The records of this town suggest that the alabaster trade in Burton died in 1676 when such tomb effigies became unfashionable but the Civil War and the Puritan ethics had depressed this trade much earlier.

Notes:

1. This does not imply that the trade ceased in 1525. In fact, there is evidence that the tomb to Bishop Sandys in Southwell Minster was carved in Ledsham alabaster by York carvers *circa* 1590.
2. There is a suggestion that with the working out of the Purbeck marble quarries in Dorset the Weymouth shippers began trading in alabaster but there is little evidence for this. It is possible they were trading in alabaster from the Somerset Levels in which case, like Nottingham, they were just middlemen and the shipping was probably from Bridgwater.

7.5 The Entry of the Mural Tablet in the Late 16th Century to the Commonwealth

As stated above, as the 17th century dawned, the centre for slab and tomb effigies was Burton on Trent with the Royley and Hollemans families in the fore. This is well supported with the Tutbury and Fauld Mines 5 and 7 miles away by road to the north. In 1600 Nottingham was still the head of navigation on the Trent. The shallows at Sawley and Wilford deterred navigation except when the river was in flood and goods from the west of Nottingham were carried to a wharf below Trent Bridge. Moves to improve navigation, opposed by vested interests in Nottingham, extended the head of navigation to Wilden (Wilne) Ferry, but the date of this is uncertain.[1] In 1699, an Act of

Parliament approved navigation to Willington which resulted in Nottingham blocking the arches of Trent Bridge with chains. Locks were built at King's Mill and Burton Mills but Burton was not reached until 1712 when the Soho Wharf opened in that town but this was 36 years after the alabaster trade there had ceased. The rights for transport were leased to George Hayne and Leonard Fosbrooke who would not let any load to be carried to and from Nottingham except in their own boats. Their lease expired in 1762. The Trent and Mersey Canal was completed in 1777 and in 1805 the Trent above Wilden Ferry was closed to all navigation.

It can be concluded that much of the Burton trade in the 17th century was wholly or partly delivered by road.

In Europe, the carving trade had developed its own style. In particular, the Flemish workshops had established the mural style in which recumbent effigies still existed but to which were added kneeling effigies of the family in a high entablature rising up the wall. In fact kneeling effigies on tombs before 1570 are rare (*see* tomb M329 in the Tower of London).

In the 1560s, Holland was under the control of Spain but the Protestant revolt of 1566–1568 which was to rumble on for some 80 years saw a number of Flemish or Flemish-trained carvers fleeing to England. They brought with them the mural style which gradually gained acceptance as the century progressed. Amongst these were the Jannsen family, Cure and Hollemans family and Epiphanius Evesham – *see* Appendix G. Appendix D3 reveals a growing number of mural monuments to 1600 although the recumbent effigy alone remained in the majority.

James I came to the throne in 1603, ushering in the Stuart era. There was a surge in the production of murals especially from 1613.

In that year a man returned from Holland having moved there in 1606 to train under Dutch sculptor and architect Hendrik de Keyser. The story of Nicholas Stone is contained in Appendix B but it is necessary to set the scene here.[2]

Nicholas Stone left behind his notebooks which reveal the details of monuments created after 1613. The advantage of the mural tomb was that it took little or no floor space being built into the wall and, in addition, cost much less than the chest tomb with effigy. Nicholas Stone's notebooks and accounts show that a plain mural tablet could be had for as little as £20 (equivalent to £6,000 today) and a mural tomb with effigies for £80 (equivalent to £24,000) or less.

Nicholas Stone was to become master mason to James I and working in Long Acre, London from 1613 to his death in 1647. His workshop continued under the direction of his son John Stone until 1667 before being inherited by a cousin, Stoakes, finally closing sometime after 1670.

In fact, the resurgence of the mural style may have permitted relatives to commemorate their loved ones long after their demise. It may be found that many of those that appear in the 16th century were created later. In particular, records show that at Woodham Ferrers, Cecily Sandys (M4, died 1611) was not commemorated until 1619 and in Nettlestead in Kent (M37), a death in 1598, was not commemorated until 1636.

This does not mean that chest effigies ceased in 1613 but the trauma of the English Civil War seems to have terminated the attraction of the chest tomb in most cases. It has been found that, whereas many chest tombs escaped attention in 1550, any non-human effigy present on a tomb in 1650 appears to have been attacked by those who saw it as idolatry. Some were caged to prevent damage by Puritans. There are some which were installed after the Restoration but they are few in number (*see* Appendix D4 onwards).

The effect of the English Civil War (1642 to 1649) was severe on Nicholas Stone's business and his notebooks record a downturn in business from the time of the Battle of Edge Hill until his death in 1647. It is now known that Nicholas Stone's account books are incomplete and other works may emerge. His brother-in-law Hendrik de Keyser Junior appears to have been domiciled in Stony Street, Nottingham possibly as early as 1634 and until 1647 when he returned to Holland. More details on this man are included in Appendix B.

The rise of Puritanism in mid-17th century changed the fashion for church monuments. The flamboyant Renaissance tombs of the early Stuart period gave way to simple slabs or mural tablets with plain frames and alabaster too became less desirable. After the Restoration in 1660 monuments were made from marble, slate or freestone and alabaster work went into decline.

Notes:

1. Richard Stone in *The River Trent* says that Leonard Fosbrooke the lessee of Wilne Ferry across the Derwent extended the navigation first to Shardlow and then to Wilne. Stone says 'by early 17th century' and certainly Wilne was trading in 1684.
2. Appendix B only gives a brief outline of Stone's work. A more detailed commentary is to be published by Adam White in the future.

7.6 The Rise of the Stately Home

Alabaster working remained in the doldrums until its suitability for structural and other large building work was discovered in the mid-18th century.

It was found that alabaster blocks could be formed into large columns for which the brown or purple staining, when polished, was highly decorative. About 1710 the Curzon family of Kedleston Hall, Derbyshire acquired the manor of Ratcliffe-on-Soar, Nottinghamshire, building a new manor house in 1714 and demolishing the old one in 1719. About 1750 the manor came to Assheton Curzon under the will of his father and he set about exploiting the minerals of his estate. It had long been known that gypsum outcropped into the red marl cliffs of Redhill at the junction of the Rivers Soar and Trent, but at the north face of Red Hill a large deposit of alabaster was found. This was quarried *circa* 1759–1762 and was used to make the columns in the Marble Hall in Kedleston, which featured prominently in the film *The Duchess*. By this time the navigation of the Trent had improved and to a lesser extent that of the Derwent[1] and the blocks could be loaded directly on to barges at the quarry and taken by boat to a wharf below the weir at Derby, from which is was short road journey to Kedleston.

Ratcliffe alabaster was also used in the mausoleum at Brocklesby, Lincolnshire. Again the transport was by boat to Barton on Humber which is only a short distance by road to the estate of Charles Anderson-Pelham, 1st Baron Yarborough who commissioned the mausoleum to his family. It was the work of architect James Wyatt and constructed in 1787. The carver is unknown. The construction was described in the *Proceedings of the Church Monuments Society* 1992 pages 86 to 96. The alabaster is in the form of half-columns inside the mausoleum flanking the three recesses.

The 'marble' hall in Holkham, Norfolk is also worthy of attention. Holkham Hall was commissioned in 1734, but the date of the building of the alabaster entrance hall is unclear but may well date from 1763–1764 as it is credited to Lady Leicester, widowed in 1759. Many sources state the alabaster is 'pink Derbyshire', but records in the archives at Holkham place show some deliveries from Castle Hay in Staffordshire and the rest from an unnamed source which is likely to be Redhill. This is in keeping with the columns at Kedleston which they resemble.

Extraction of alabaster from the Ratcliffe quarries continued to the late 18th century when an agricultural review of the area commented tartly that 'alabaster was being won at Redhill but gunpowder was being used which so broke up the blocks that they were not worth recovering. The explosions have greatly disturbed the people and animals of the surrounding farms'. It is believed that extraction ceased about this time or may have drifted into the first decade of the 19th century. Certainly evidence post-1810 is lacking. For more details *see* Appendix U.

Nothing is known about any mines at Tutbury at this time, but it is believed that they were still in operation. Later the Fauld Mine and the one at Draycott in the Clay moved over to the production of gypsum for the plaster trade.

Exploration of the minerals to the east of Ratcliffe in the 18th century occurred, but this too was for gypsum and no alabaster was recovered.

Notes:

1. The River Derwent below Derby is shallow and winding and never really suitable for navigation until being eventually bypassed by the Derby Canal in the late 18th century. However, Derby Museum has established that wherries did manage to reach Derby in the late 17th century, tying up at a dock just north of the present railway station.

7.7 The Rise of Victorian Gothic in the 19th Century and Beyond

The Victorian era, which commenced in about 1837, saw Gothic architecture again coming to the fore. The Victorian ethos saw the old medieval and Stuart Renaissance styles as outdated and set out 'improving' churches and other buildings.[1]

As a result there was resurgence in reredoses and retables in which alabaster had a minor role. In some cases reredos were created from freestone but in the style of the medieval carvers of the 14th century (Barrow on Soar) or in Italian alabaster or marble sometimes with locally sourced alabaster surrounds (Thrumpton and Kingston on Soar, Nottinghamshire). The Italian alabaster generally shows the colour and fine grain of calcite but the local-mined alabaster is veined and often has severe inclusions and faults. The reason for using this is that in most cases the sponsor of the refurbishment owned gypsum mines or quarries and/or owned the land where alabaster had been mined in history.

Ultimately there was a reaction to the Victorian 'vandalism'. In 1877 William Morris and other notable members of the Pre-Raphaelite Brotherhood formed the Society for the Protection of Ancient Buildings (SPAB) in Queen Square, Bloomsbury. Morris told the assembly that 'Well meaning architects were scraping away the historic fabric of too many buildings in their quest for restoration'. The detail of the development of SPAB can be found on their website: http://www.spab.org.uk/.

However, for many churches such concerns came too late. Some alabaster monuments were moved and damaged in the process (Ordsall and Hoveringham, Nottinghamshire) or removed in their entirety. Churches used for schoolrooms and other gatherings of juveniles resulted in the carving of initials into the soft surface of effigies and in some cases the breaking off of hands, heads and swords for souvenirs.

It was not all bad news. The Victorians liked alabaster where it could be won easily and there is fine alabaster furniture in some churches (Hanbury, Staffordshire, Kingston on Soar, Nottingham and particularly Mackworth, Derbyshire – *see* Appendix K).

In 1894 Cornelius Vanderbilt Junior built a new mansion, called The Breakers, on Rhode Island, USA. How he came to learn about alabaster is uncertain but his relationship with the Curzons was strong and it is most likely that he saw the Marble Hall at Kedleston. By that time mining at Ratcliffe had ceased but the mine at Fauld, Staffordshire was still working and it is to that location that Vanderbilt's architect came. In the end some 18 blocks of alabaster, some weighing 15 tons, were mined and carried by narrow-gauge railway from the mine about 3 miles to the interchange sidings with the North Stafford Railway at Tutbury. From there they were taken to Liverpool for shipment to New York. The alabaster was used in the lounge and dining room of The Breakers and can be seen on their website.[2] *See also* the Fauld Section of Appendix M. The columns and cornices show the deep veining of the Staffordshire alabaster.

In the 20th century the move to retain historical buildings and the difficulty in getting permission for monuments in churches has resulted in the decline in the use of alabaster. However, restoration of existing monuments has gathered pace and as a result a return to the ancient quarries for alabaster has resulted, as witnessed by the mining at Chellaston.

Notes:

1. Douglas Kent of SPAB has written to the author saying that sheer scale of the rise of Victorian Gothic is not always appreciated. Over 6000 churches and cathedrals in Britain were restored between 1840 and 1870 under the Gothic Revival. The purpose, far from a desire to conserve material fabric, was to rebuild them to achieve stylistic purity and stimulate greater piety. William Morris claimed that restoration created 'a feeble and lifeless forgery'. John Ruskin, the art critic and an early member of the SPAB was equally forthright: 'Do not let us talk then of restoration from beginning to end.' Restoration can come from an overtly scholarly approach. This explains why, historically, the Society made little pretence at being academic. February 2017. The author observes that whereas this Victorian restoration activity was detrimental to the building fabric it did spur a revival of Gothic tomb building.
2. http://www.newportmansions.org/explore/the-breakers

8
THE KERVERS

In the following section, I have used the medieval word **kerver** which to some may be questionable for the later artisans, but is useful if research is carried out.

8.1 Overview and Case Study

When alabaster effigy-carving became fashionable the monument carvers of England had been active in this field for some 200 years. The use of local freestone meant that carving could be localised as transport was not an issue. Some stone was better than others. Limestone and sandstone is freely found, but the latter was less durable so few early monuments in this are to be found. In the case of Purbeck marble, the hardness of this limestone meant that it was durable and took a polish and this made it a favourite of the nobility. The closeness of the Dorset quarries to the sea meant that coastal ships could carry the raw material further so that by 1330 London and maybe others became well established as carving centres for this stone.

Carvers followed fashion or styles and changes in religious practices, but the basic demand came from the customer who would see effigies which they liked and wished to be copied for themselves. When alabaster carving commenced *circa* 1327–1330, the popularity spread outwards from the first monuments initially within royal and noble circles and then to the lesser gentry from the centres where the raw materials could be easily obtained.

Any researcher into the alabaster carvings will note that the features of the effigies in many cases are somewhat alike. It is almost impossible to think that no precautions were taken to ensure that they should bear a resemblance to the persons whom they portrayed and in many instances, the features show so much character and individuality that it can scarcely be accidental. However, as many tombs were carved after the person had died and with no portrait available the faces can only represent the general shape and fashion of the times.

A study of the visages of many effigies shows the hairstyles and features consistent with the times. For men the 15th-century faces show the Plantagenet hair and are clean-shaven whereas those of the 16th century show the changes in hair and beard style, a practice which was maintained into the 17th century.

In the case of costume and, in particular, the changes in ceremonial armour, the effigies are interesting to study. Ralph Sacheverell's tomb in Ratcliffe (G136) shows a clean-shaven man with a 15th-century hair style and armour which would be considered out-of-date in 1539 when Ralph died. However, round his neck is an Esse (SS) collar with a Tudor rose pendant[1] which could only have been awarded after 1520. This leads to speculation that the kerver, whilst receiving clear instruction about including the SS honour, was not fully familiar the changes in armour style and represented Ralph in a style with which he was familiar.

Nineteen years later, the tomb of Ralph's son, Henry (T9) shows the full round beard as can be seen being worn by the portraits of Henry VIII. His armour, whilst still Gothic in style, has Tudor features. Ralph's grandson, also Henry (1585, R4), and great grandson, yet another Henry (1625, R5), show increasingly pointed beards beloved by the Elizabethans and early Stuarts. The armour styles are also in keeping with the times. The conclusion is that from the mid-16th century the kervers caught up with the current fashion in armour and produced effigies which would be easily recognised.

The same is not true of the ladies depicted on the tombs. Ralph Sacheverell's lady shows the decorated gable hood which was not fashionable until after 1520, but which was largely superseded by the French hood from about 1530. The conclusion that can be drawn is that the kervers may have been more familiar with ladies' fashions than those of their knights.

The ladies on Henry Sacheverell's tomb of 1625 are of particular interest. Henry had three wives between 1590 and 1616. All three are depicted in dress commensurate with the years that they died. Mary Gittings (died 1600) shows the late Elizabethan hood and the full ruff and a bum-rolled skirt. Elizabeth Copley (died 1616) shows the early Stuart dress but also with hood and full ruff whilst Lucy Boughton (died 1667) shows the late Stuart dress with bib and half-ruff which largely fell out of favour by 1630. The tomb was constructed contemporary with the death of Henry in or about 1625–1626.[2]

In tracing the dates, styles and origins of the effigies it may be that dress and fashion are the key to identification of the kervers and locations.

Notes:

1. *See* Appendix E and G136. This tomb is not what it appears to be.
2. Although the second Henry died in 1585 his tomb was not made until 1625 as provision for it was made in his son's will. There are other features. The recumbent effigies are very alike and the two tombs align on either side of the chancel such that the third Henry's tomb covers the window, an unnecessary decision seeing that a blank wall exists less than two metres away. The decision to cover the window allows the two tombs to be directly opposite each other.

8.2 Early Kervers (1327 to 1359) – Diagram F

Extant Effigy Population: 11 (Gardner, Class I)
Extant Slab and Tabletop: 3

These kervers are mostly anonymous, possibly some attached to the crown. They are chiefly located in the South and experimenting with a new material possibly at the behest of influential patrons such as John of Gaunt. The Lakenhams were active in London in this period and as described as marblers may well have migrated from Purbeck marble to alabaster. However, evidence is scant. The effigy at York (G30) of 1346 is credited to John Orchard but the date makes this suspect as he was London-based and especially as he would need alabaster from Tutbury area. Orchard was mainly a latoner (brass-worker), but at some point in his career inlaid brass on alabaster. However, he may well have travelled to York to fulfil a contract on a tomb carved by someone else, so his involvement cannot be completely dismissed.

The effigies at Hanbury (G28), Longford (GNP18) and Stamford (GNP54) appear to be the first stirrings of the Midlands kervers as it is hard to imagine that the rural sponsors would look to London for their creation. Nevertheless, the kervers responsible remain unknown.

It is clear that these early alabaster effigies provided a spur for others and the sponsors would appreciate the reduced cost over Purbeck and other false marbles and the quality of the finished production over freestone.

Henry Yeaveley became active from about 1350. As his name implies he had family contacts close to the Staffordshire quarries and thus may well have been familiar with the use of alabaster. He was not a kerver, but an architect working with Thomas Wreck (Wrek) and Stephen Lote whose work is described in the next section. Little of any work in alabaster between 1350 and 1360 in which Yeaveley is associated is currently known, but his close association with others justifies a mention.

The effigy at Hanbury is cross-legged as are three others in this period. This style did not last much beyond 1360, but the reasons for its demise are unclear. Freestone and Purbeck cross-legged effigies also appear to have ceased about this time and, although the cross-legged form may not have suited alabaster, the abandonment may hold more for the design falling out of favour than any technical limitations.

The tomb of Edward II at Gloucester set the style. His son, Edward III, having just shed himself of the restrictions placed on him by his mother and her lover, Roger Mortimer, clearly wanted to make statement. The choice of Gloucester for the tomb was by necessity as Edward II died in nearby Berkeley a few years earlier and he was buried in Gloucester with some ceremony. What attracted Edward III to alabaster rather than Purbeck marble is uncertain, but something had drawn the king's attention to the mineral. Contemporary accounts say that Edward, having been buried with much pomp, had a wooden effigy with a copper crown provided for the funeral which was stated as being 'temporary'. With this effigy being finely carved, and the rest of the tomb made from oolite and Purbeck marble, the only permanent material which could match the wooden effigy would be alabaster.

The source of the alabaster can only be the Tutbury area, then in the hands of the Duchy of Lancaster, which is the only place that large blocks of the stone could be obtained in 1329. The transport would be difficult but certainly not impossible for someone with authority such as the crown and details of similar transport events can be found in Appendix C.

The mid-1300s were the time of the Black Death. It may not be significant, but worth noting that most of the rural effigies were carved in the period after 1349 when the disease struck London and it may well be that the kernel of the Trent Valley carving industry was formed from kervers fleeing the plague in the South. The records of Burton on Trent show that the plague visited the town late in 1349 and again in 1361 so the kervers may well not have fled there. Nottingham did not fare much better so if this migration did take place it may have been to a rural location.

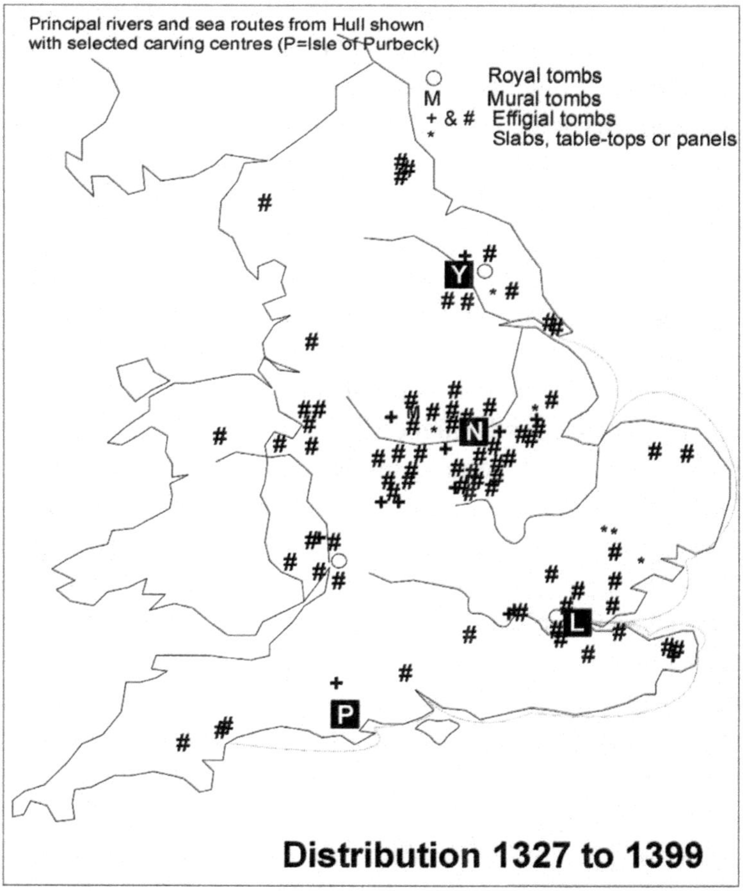

Diagram F. The distribution of tombs 1327 to 1359 (+) and 1360 to 1399 (#) with rivers and coastal routes shown. It is difficult to envisage the post-1360 cluster in the Midlands can be anything, but the work of local workshops. Almost all those in the East, South and North-east are in proximity to rivers and ports and may also be the work of Midland kervers. The cluster round Gloucester may be influenced by the royal tomb of 1328–1329. Drawn by the author.

It is also to be noted that all the tombs in this period were classified as Class I by Gardner. Leaving aside the royal tombs, of the seven remaining the most remote are the one (possibly two) at Dorchester on Thames and one at Stamford and these merit further research.

8.3 London and the First Nottingham Kervers (1360 to 1399) – Diagram F

Extant Effigy Population: 71 (Gardner, Class II)
Extant Mural Population: 1
Extant Panel, Slab and Tabletop Population: 5

With reference to the kerver timeline (central pages), this shows a dominance of named London carvers but the distribution above shows a different picture. Although London kervers are many, their work may have remained centred on English 'marble' with some work in alabaster. It is unbelievable that Trent Valley alabaster was shipped south for carving and then back to be installed in the Northern churches for which they were intended, only a few miles from the quarry. The conclusion is that there is a number of Trent Valley kervers who have yet to be identified working between 1360 and 1399.

Henry Yeaveley continued work in London throughout this period and he almost certainly promoted the use of alabaster although documentary evidence is thin. The South, predominantly London, continued to play a significant role in the next 40 years and this will be dealt with later but the 1360s saw the first reports of Nottingham kervers.

The sandstone ridge on which Nottingham was founded was attractive to the Normans who built a castle on the highest point in 1068. Over the next 300 years the town grew to the east of the castle along this ridge with St Mary's Church predominant on the next highest point. Either side of the church were two streets – St Mary's Gate and Stony Street and it is here that the borough records list the first fines (local taxes) paid by kervers. As stated in Section 1, the records of Windsor show that a retable of alabaster was supplied by Nottingham kerver Peter the Mason who as Peter Steppyngleye had premises in St Mary's Gate in 1365.

For a Nottingham kerver to have received such a commission the activity of alabaster carving must have commenced much earlier, but we cannot be certain when. Also we cannot ascertain if Steppyngleye was a lone kerver or whether there were more workshops.

Cox, in his review of Derbyshire churches observed that Osberton in Nottinghamshire which was the seat of the Foljambes, had an alabaster altar panel of Thomas Beckett in its museum which was removed from Beauchief Abbey (D9/6A). This is recorded as much mutilated but still inscribed with the statement that it was presented as an altarpiece by Sir Godfrey Foljambe in 1350. Part of the museum was disbursed in April 2008 through Christie's and the current whereabouts of the panel is not known. In any case, the date would seem to indicate that panel carving was in hand years earlier than believed.[1]

Why Nottingham rose to prominence when it was some 19 miles from the nearest supply of alabaster requires some explanation. Apart from being a town in 1350 it had better communication than either Derby or Leicester. The situation with transport in the town is discussed in detail in Appendix C, but it is worth restating that Nottingham was the only major East Midlands town which, in the 14th century, had reliable navigation with the sea. It also had the only bridge over the Trent. This would be essential for the kervers to supply their customers by water when they could not rely on royal patronage to secure land transport.

In the history of Nottingham alabaster work, no evidence of the carving of tomb effigies in the town can be established. It is clear that the Windsor retable was carved in sections and again Appendix C has a description of the probable material supply chain which established the fact that Nottingham produced small objects such as retable and reredos panels, statues and images and triptych panels.

What is clear is that the Nottingham kervers looked to Chellaston for their supply and therefore there is much confidence that Chellaston quarries were working in the mid-1350s. Certainly the quarries were well established by the 1370s when first Queen Philippa acquired six cartloads in 1362 for an unspecified reason, but most probably her tomb (A78) and then John of Gaunt obtaining alabaster for his wife's tomb in St Paul's, London (*see* Appendix C and Section 1) a few years later.

As to the East Midlands tomb effigy-carving in this period the evidence is scant.

Diagram F above shows the extant effigy distribution for the years 1327 to 1399. The early tombs from 1327 to 1359 are widely distributed with only two in the alabaster catchment area. However, as can be seen, the period 1360 to 1399 produces a distribution much closer to the Trent Valley. There is an absolute certainty that all alabaster for all these tombs from 1327 came from the Tutbury/Chellaston beds. Although it is difficult to identify East Midlands kervers in this period the proposition that alabaster was carried to London and then carried back as finished effigies, as previously stated, is preposterous.

The London kervers – Wreck, Lote and Orchard may well be the creators of some of the Southern effigies but as can be seen the coastal trade based on Hull would have no trouble supplying customers in Suffolk, Essex, Kent, Sussex and ports as far west as Falmouth with Purbeck marble as a return load. Hull would also trade with the North-east Coast, making Durham accessible via the River Wear where coal would be the reverse cargo. Also connected to Hull via the Humber were the Yorkshire towns via the York Ouse, Calder and Swale. Thus there was a ready-made transport system in place which would mean that raw stone and finished effigies could be moved with ease (*see also* Appendix C).

Francis Cheetham in his book *English Medieval Alabasters* identifies a number of styles for the retable and reredos panels. Those in the period to 1399 all have a chamfered raised edge like a picture frame.[2] No Nottingham panel has been attributed with a frame edge like this. The style changes which can be attributable to the 15th century and beyond will be dealt with later. Francis Cheetham also suggests that the panel carving in Nottingham town was an offshoot of the effigy carving industry, but fails to indicate when this extension took place. Clearly the panel carving and effigial carving went on side by side in the Trent Valley, but it is likely that some kervers had a foot in both camps as the next section will reveal.

As has been stated, the kervers outside of London are unknown. Appendix D1 shows that the effigy at Swine (G189) of 1372 is identified to a York workshop, whilst those at Spilsby (GNP51 and GNP52), Strelley (G25) Nuthall (G131) and Layer Marney, Essex (G8) have been identified as 'Trent Valley'.

Speculation as to location of these 'Trent Valley' kervers has failed to find their workshops. As has been stated Nottingham has been a popular suggestion, but this must be tempered with the knowledge that movement of large blocks of stone to Nottingham was problematical, the steepness and narrowness of the approach roads and the likelihood that none of the workshops there were of sufficient size to support effigial carving makes this unlikely. I favour the emergence of workshops at Chellaston and possibly Burton on Trent. Certainly, as the next section will discuss, the Sutton/Prentys workshop at Chellaston was well established by 1414 and Nicholas Michelson was recorded as working at Burton in 1401.

It may well be that the exporting of alabaster started in this period. Jean de Liege was in London in 1366 when he was commissioned to make the effigy of Philippa of Hainault (A78). His biography claims that he took the style of this tomb back to France and there are records of alabaster tombs and statues made by this carver up to 1381. It is therefore likely that the Liege's tomb in Rouen was seen by admirers which spurred the purchase of alabaster in 1414 described in the next section. The Grove Encyclopaedia makes about 50 references to continental tombs which contain alabaster in this period but none is identified with its source in England and some are positively identified with Spain and Northern Italy. These are widely distributed, but must have acted as a 'shop window' for the new material.

The lone mural monument Bakewell (M1, Figure 13) is an oddity comprising a frame and two forward-facing demi-figures looking out as if the frame was a window.[3] The kerver is unknown. It would be the 17th century before anything else like this was produced.

Much more research is required for this period.

Notes:

1. Francis Cheetham observes that the Osberton panel is *circa* 1375 and links it in style with the Foljambe mural in Bakewell (M1) of the same date so doubt remains.
2. These can be seen in the book on page 67 and Figures 53, 91, 92, 135, 161, 171, 172, 186 and 199 and may well be attributable to the London workshops.
3. *See* Figure 13.

8.4 Fame Spreads (1400 to 1459) – Diagram G

Extant Effigy Population: 109 (Gardner, Class II and III)

Extant Mural Population: 0

Extant Panel, Slab and Tabletop Population: 39

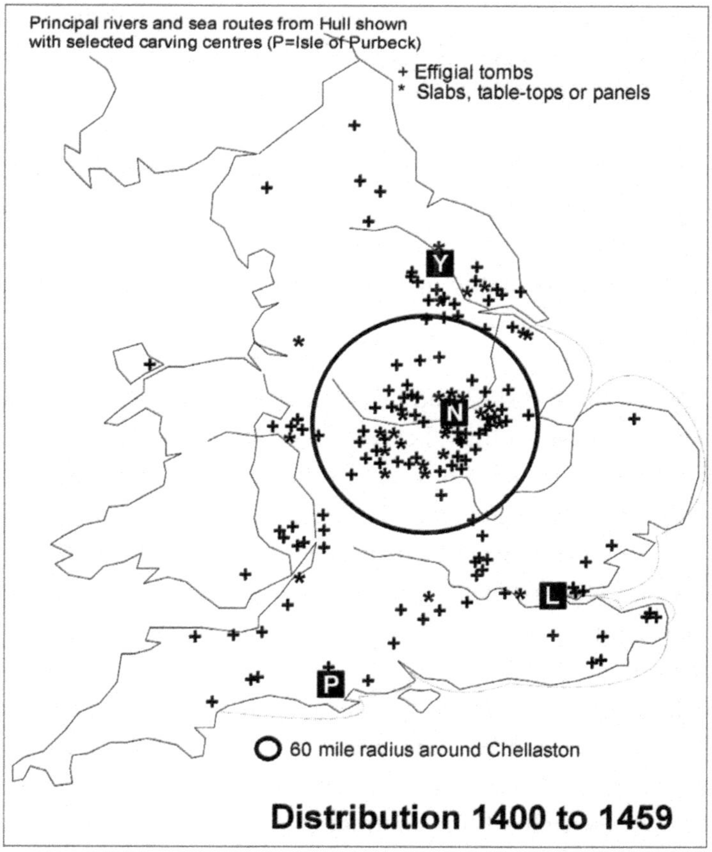

Diagram G. The distribution of effigial tombs (+) and others (*) 1400 to 1459 with rivers and coastal routes shown. Once again a significant cluster exists around the Trent Valley. On the basis that Chellaston was able to deliver to Lowick by road in 1419 a radius of 60 miles encloses almost half the population. The 60 mile radius includes the upper reaches of the Warwick Avon and Severn which makes the distribution on the Severn estuary interesting. Drawn by the author.

It is clear that by 1400 the fame of the unnamed Trent Valley alabaster kervers and their source of raw materials had spread abroad. Appendix V gives details of the 1414 purchase of alabaster by the Abbey of Fécamp in Normandy, but the records of Francis Cheetham indicate that England was supplying retable and reredos panels and images to Europe by 1391. This is assumed to be London. However, he mentions a ship's manifest for that year which included two alabaster images valued at 5s for a crossing from the port of Boston in Lincolnshire which had perforce to be made in Nottingham.

Trade with France had been a staple business for English captains for decades. Until 1554 England owned the port of Calais and trade flourished under the Hanseatic League, despite the disruption of disputes such as the Hundred Years War from 1337 to 1450.

Whereas raw alabaster blocks and small objects found a market in Europe, there appears not to have been any trade in effigies. It may be that the cost of transport which, in most cases, was borne by the customer, was too much to make effigies viable. It may also be the case that in this period permission was needed for the export of alabaster objects. It is not determined if any charge was made by the crown for an export license but it may well be that finished effigies would attract significant export duty. It is also possible that the English style for somewhat austere tomb chests and simple effigies did not attract the continental customers. Whatever the reason, the English kervers saw little or no trade abroad for effigial carving.

Unfortunately, once again, the majority of the extant effigies cannot be associated with a kerver.

We have one window in that the Fécamp purchase (Appendix V) and the contract for Green's Lowick tomb (G122 and L1) clearly identifies Robert Sutton and Thomas Prentys as quarrymen and effigy kervers located at Chellaston. This would be on or before 1414, but we do not know when the two men first set up their workshop. However, we know that the Fécamp charter party came specifically to meet the two kervers and so their work must have been seen in France or that the Chellaston quarry as used by Jean de Liege (probably Rouen – *see* B129) was a satisfactory source. This means that the commissioning of the Chellaston workshop was probably in the early 1400s or even earlier.

We can make other assumptions. The distance between Lowick, Northamptonshire and Chellaston is some 60-miles and with no possibility of any form of river transport, it can be concluded that the delivery by land transport for non-royal customers was well established by the time of this contract in 1419.[1]

The diagram for 1400 to 1459 above shows the distribution of extant effigies which is densely packed in the Midlands. Taking Lowick as the standard delivery distance, a circle drawn with Chellaston as the centre nearly embraces them all. In addition the 60 mile radius cuts the headwater wharfs on the rivers Avon and Severn and possibly the Weaver and the Dee opening new markets for the Trent Valley workshops. The York cluster can be assumed to be distributed by means of the York Ouse, Calder and Swale.

There are tantalising glimpses of other workshops. The 1408 tomb of the Duke of Brittany in Nantes (A15) is clearly identified with three alabastermen, Thomas Colyn, Thomas Holewell and Thomas Poppehowe, about which nothing else is known. Saul offers the opinion that these were Trent Valley Kervers and Gardner suggests that there were similarities with the tomb in Staindrop (G104) based on an old drawing, but these names are absent from the borough records and forinsec pleas of the counties. The tomb did not survive the French Revolution.

An unknown kerver in York is credited with the tombs at Methley (G194) and some at Harewood (possibly G192, GNP104 and G193), and later a named kerver, William Cowebrigge is to be found working in York at the start of what was to be a significant activity in the second half of the 15th century.

There are some locations worth discussing. The tomb in Anglesey could have been delivered by sea from the Cheshire ports, but that at Greystoke is more difficult to explain. However, the effigy has clear Trent Valley characteristics whilst being carved from Chellaston alabaster so its origins are most likely to be the East Midlands. The remaining monuments are close to waterways or sea ports. One such is Chillingham, Northumberland (Figure 14). This tiny church is close to Chillingham Castle, about 15 miles from Seahouses, has a chapel which is dominated by the huge tomb chest in carved limestone which stands about 5ft high and holds two alabaster effigies. The chest side has crocketted niches in which stand images of saints interspersed with smaller angels holding shields (GNP65, Figure 15) and retains some original paint. The survival of these post-Reformation is unusual and is probably due to its remoteness and the protection of the castle. The effigies are also partially stained and show Trent Valley features. The effigy of Sir Ralph Grey carries a short SS collar and has a face which may be a likeness. This is one of only two in Northumbria, the other being at Bothal (GNP66) of 1513 which shows clear Burton on Trent features demonstrating that the Trent Valley carvers were capable of trading to remote parts. Gardner seems not to have travelled to Northumberland to photograph these monuments.

It is therefore assumed that apart from some monuments in the Thames Valley and some in Yorkshire and in the Home Counties, the Trent Valley kervers dominated this period.

In the case of retable and reredos panels, the style change mentioned above meant that the chamfered frame edge gave way to an embattled canopy at the top. Again Francis Cheetham illustrates these in his book (*see* 8.2).[2] The panels with this feature are mainly dated from 1400 to 1430 and it is suggested are the product of York workshops as no embattled canopied panels can be positively identified with Nottingham or London. After 1430 the panels have no edge features, but are plain with a separate panel with a frieze which can be identified with the Trent Valley and specifically Nottingham. This continues into the next period.

Notes:

1. A 1987 thesis in Salford University entitled 'The Transport System of Medieval England and Wales' by Frederick Edwards determined that Wansford was the headwater of the River Nene which is some 15 miles from Lowick. It is therefore possible to have delivered by means of the Trent, Hull, Sutton Bridge and the Nene – a circuitous journey involving at least three transhipments and an additional 60 miles. On the other hand, the Roman road, now known as the A6, passes within 4 miles of Lowick and 2 miles of Chellaston, making this a real possibility.
2. For embattled panels *see* page 68, and Figures 64, 67, 73, 93, 104, 131, 136, 137, 167, 174, 175, 176, 179, 187, 200, 201, 202 and 203.

8.5 Plantagenet Dominance (1460 to 1485) – Diagram H

Extant Effigy Population: 52 (Gardner, Class IV)
Extant Mural Population: 0
Extant Panel, Slab and Tabletop Population: 32

This period is dominated by the Civil War now known colloquially as the War of the Roses. Over these 24 years there were 12 battles as widely separated as Hexham and Barnet, leading one to believe that movement by land was easier than in the first half of the 15th century.

The war does not seem to have affected the rate of commissioning monuments but the locations of monuments in this period are more dispersed, as shown below:

Now only a quarter of the effigial monuments (13) are within the 'catchment' area of the Trent Valley. There are, however, three interesting clusters around York, Dorset and London.

The dominance of the Sutton/Prentys Chellaston workshop appears to have ended around this period. This does not mean that Chellaston alabaster ceased to be quarried only that the carving moved westwards to Burton upon Trent. Here, at least three carvers appear as alabasterers. Richard Couper, Robert Bosher (Bocher) and Gilbert Twist are the three named and from the value the objects accredited to them, they were carving items of some importance being destined for locations which include St Albans Abbey, Wallingford Priory and St Bartholomew's Hospital, Newbury. Burton must have been highly regarded for important religious establishments like these to place commissions. It is highly likely that the 1460s saw the start of Burton's alabaster effigy industry and it is possible that Chellaston effigy carving never recommenced after the demise of Sutton and Prentys workshop *circa* 1466.

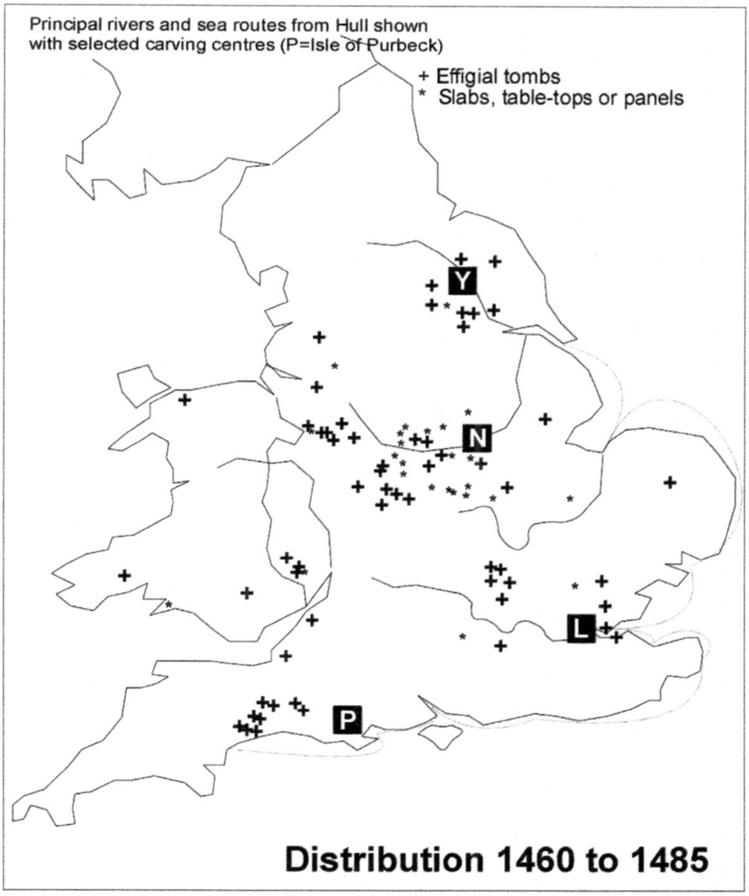

Diagram H. The distribution of effigial tombs (+) and others (*) 1460 to 1485 with rivers and coastal routes shown. The cluster around the Trent is now mainly slabs reflecting the rise in the Nottingham slab trade. The cluster around York is mainly effigies and may well be York carved. The group in Dorset is of particular interest and discussed in the text. Drawn by the author.

As to Nottingham, this period saw the peak in alabaster panel-carving but the number of workers in the town was never large. The rise of the Hylton family is documented in Appendix R but there were others including Sherwood and Godeman. Once more, there are no records of effigy carving in Nottingham and the town still did not lend itself to such work. Hylton may well have carved ledger stones and slabs as indicated by Appendix R, but this was probably the largest product from this centre. The take-up of slabs and tabletops in place of effigial tombs appears significant in Nottinghamshire, Staffordshire, Leicestershire and Derbyshire as a cost-effective alternative to effigies.

As to York, the list of freeman indicates alabasterers present from 1456. Saul claims that an unnamed one was active in the city as early as 1401 although he ceased work in

1430 (*see* Section 8.4). The largest workshop was that of John and Thomas Roper and it may be that this period was pinnacle of the York school. It is a small but significant point that the rise of the York workshops may be linked to the reign of the Yorkist kings whereas the decline in the largely Lancastrian Trent Valley workshops is the counterpoint.

The important issue is the source of alabaster for York there being no useable quarries in Yorkshire at this time and all stone would need to come from the Trent Valley. The state of the River Ouse as a navigable river is unclear prior to 1479 when a charter for improving navigation was granted to the city. However, a 2014 report on the river at Selby states that it has always been tidal to the town and this obstructed navigation and, in addition, it had a dangerous tidal bore known as an aegir. In the case of the Yorkshire Derwent, the mayor of York was instructed to improve the navigation as far as Sutton on Derwent, about 7 miles from York in 1462. Information held at Merchant Adventurer's Hall at York claims that sea-going vessels could reach the city but is vague about the dates and as both the Ouse and the Yorkshire Derwent are torturous such claims are questionable.[1]

In respect of the coal trade from Tyneside it is stated that to reach Sutton the mineral had to be transhipped at Goole into smaller boats. There is circumstantial evidence that the rise in York carving coincides with the improvement in navigation of both Ouse and Derwent but it was with river boats rather than seagoing ships.

Certainly some six alabasterers are named in the period and this sudden population increase was most likely due to transport improvements in the Ouse/Derwent Valleys. A number of writers credit all the period's Yorkshire effigies to the York school and in view of the closure of the Chellaston workshops and the slow ramping-up of Burton this may well be correct. It was not to last.

In London the author can find no named carvers in this period. It is therefore probable that for the London area tombs the carving was carried out at Burton or York and exported through Hull. However, more work on the London effigies is required.

The most intriguing is the Dorset/Somerset cluster of eight. The churchwarden records of the parish of Tintinhull, Somerset haves the following entry for 1451–1452:

> 'And paid a certain man called alabaster man an equipment and agreement for one slab of alabaster – 1d'.

This is clearly not a carved item and the purpose to which the church wardens intended to put the alabaster is not known. In the extensive Tintinhull church records over many decades there is no further mention of 15th-century alabaster, but it is noted that in the same year, the church demolished and rebuilt its rood loft and the slab may be associated with that event. In the forinsec pleas of Nottingham, for 1490 there is an entry for

William Bott who was described as an 'alabaster salesman' for the alabaster workshop of Nicholas Hill. Bott had failed to return to Hill all the proceeds of alabaster sales hence the entry in the pleas. This does tend to indicate that the workshops employed travellers to drum up sales but the value of the Tintinhull sale at 1d makes it uncertain that the 'alabaster man' was from the North.

In the Isle of Purbeck the carvers had experienced a trade downturn when alabaster became popular. Some authors offer the opinion that the grouping of monuments in Dorset and South Somerset represents the Purbeck carvers attempting to regain their business by carving in alabaster. Some go as far as suggesting the sea cliffs of Dorset provided alabaster but geologists point out that large nodules are not present and the small amount of alabaster/gypsum mined went to making plaster. Certainly the customs records of Wareham and Poole (1460 to 1479) list a significant number of exports of carved alabaster goods to France in this period and one record, if taken literally, indicates that alabaster was *imported* through Poole. If so then this may mean that Purbeck took in Trent Valley alabaster for reworking. However, one record does not make a clear case so the Dorset and Somerset cluster remains an interesting if unproven case.

Some authors link the Dorset cluster to the exports to Ireland through Bristol. The Jakes family were active in this town during the 1470s, exporting alabaster objects to Ireland and to the Iberian Peninsula. Irish commentators attribute the few remaining English alabasters in Ireland to the Nottingham school so questions here remain too.

Of the eight 'Dorset' effigies, the two at Melbury Sampford (G81, 1467 and G80, 1470) show the biggest departure from Trent Valley style with portrait-like features and a form of carved salet not seen elsewhere. Those at Puddletown (two effigies, G79 and GNP27), Marnhull (G78) and Stourton Caundle (G82) also show some departure from Trent Valley styles. The Dorset cluster remains an intriguing if undocumented group which may well prove to be locally carved.

One defining feature of this period is the Yorkist collar (Appendix E). The SS collar[2] although established in 1371, long before the dispute between the Houses of Lancaster and York, was devised as a Lancastrian livery emblem. The Yorkists created their own in the form of a collar of suns and roses with a number of different pendants. As would be expected the appearance of the Yorkist collar on effigies is from 1461 to 1485 and the Tudors looked unfavourable on any Yorkist trappings after this. Despite this, a number of Yorkist collars appear on effigies after 1485, the last being the 1499 effigy in Holme Pierrepont church (G135). Some Yorkist collared effigies seem to have attracted disproportionate attention from Tudor vandals. That at Sutton Bonington (GNP73) and Minster in Sheppey (GNP39), both with Yorkist collars, are extensively damaged in a very similar way to that at Puddletown (GNP27).

The dawn of the Tudor dynasty saw it all change again.

Notes:

1. The same 1987 thesis in Salford University entitled 'The Transport System of Medieval England and Wales' by Frederick Edwards states that the Ouse was navigable to the mouth of the Ure north of York and the Derwent to Stamford Bridge. The Ure itself was navigable to Boroughbridge. It is therefore quite possible to have alabaster delivered to York by means of the Trent and one or other of these rivers without transhipment.
2. The term SS has connotations with the 1930s Nazi party and the current preferred term is collar of esses. However, most readers will appreciate there is no political connection and for clarity the term SS has been retained.

8.6 Tudor Gothic (1486 to 1540) – Diagram I

Extant Effigy Population: 140 (Gardner, Class IV and V)
Extant Mural Population: 0
Extant Panel, Slab and Tabletop Population: 111

Following Bosworth in 1485 the new Tudor dynasty made strident moves to reconcile the houses of York and Lancaster. Insurrections by Lambert Simnel in 1487 and later Perkin Warbeck in 1497 temporarily disturbed the peace but Henry VII was able to establish a peaceful country under joint nobility. The Yorkist trappings were the first to be discarded, including the Yorkist collar, but as we have previously described, some diehards succeeded in being buried with the emblem carved on their effigy – *see* Section 8.5 above.

The Tudors needed a new emblem and although the term 'Wars of the Roses' is a 19th-century manifestation, the emblem chosen by the Tudors was the combined white and red rose now known as the Tudor rose. This appears on monuments until the end of the period under review but its application to the SS collar may well not have happened until the reign of Henry VIII – *see* Appendix C.

The distribution of extant effigies is shown in Diagram I:

With the Trent Valley in the doldrums during the Yorkist period (1460 to 1485), it is somewhat surprising that it appears to have risen again to dominate in the 1490s. The diagram above shows a massive cluster around Nottingham and Burton, comprising 60 effigies (43%) with a further 12 (8%) just across the county line in Yorkshire. The popularity of alabaster slabs is also seen with as much of 75% of the population within 60 miles of the River Trent. The westward penetration into Cheshire and Shropshire is noted and a southward push along the line of the Derby to London road (now the A6) and the Derby to Bristol road (now the A38). The cluster in Oxfordshire is less clear regarding access.

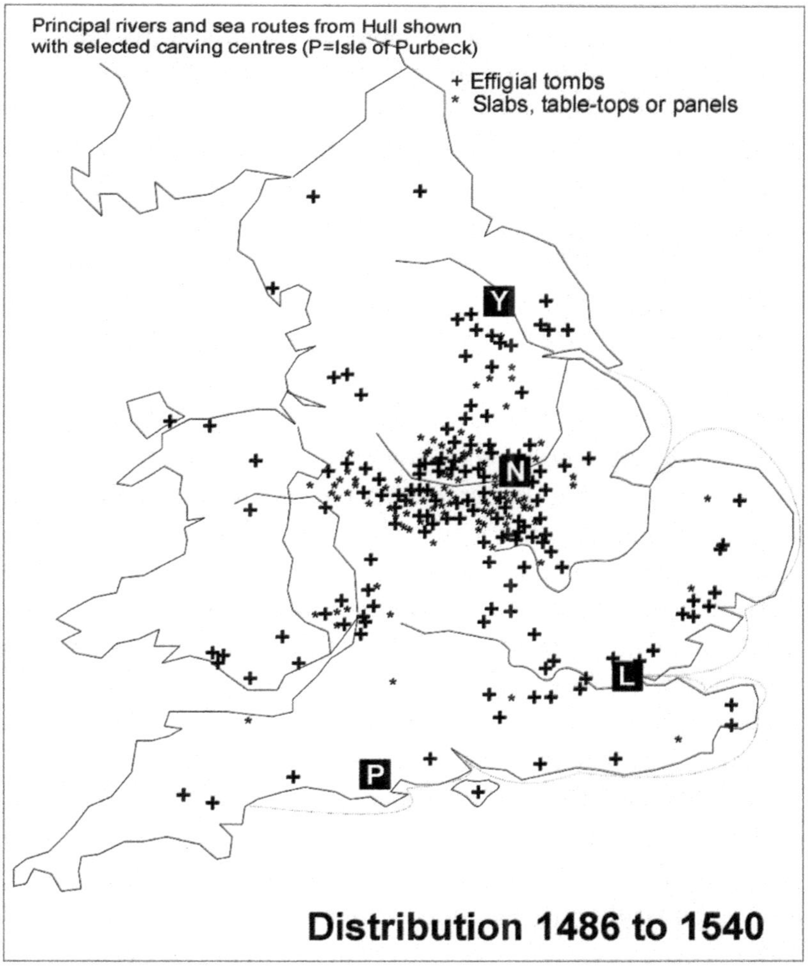

Diagram I. The distribution of effigial tombs (+) and others (*) 1486 to 1540 with rivers and coastal routes shown. The cluster around the Trent and Ouse now represents more than 50% of the effigial tombs carved and 70% of the slabs. The southern distribution hugs the coast. The central counties are sparsely served, as they were in the previous two centuries. However, some remote locations are served including Anglesey, Cumberland and Northumberland. Purbeck alabaster carving, if it ever existed, seems to have ceased. Drawn by the author.

In this period the carvers of Nottingham town, including the Hyltons (*see* Appendix R), were at their most productive. Their status must have been quite widely known for them to have received a commission as important as that of Richard III's tomb in Leicester but their work did not seem to extend to effigy-carving which seems by now to have been firmly established in Burton on Trent.

At Burton, kervers Harpur and Moorecock had established their workshop by 1490. About equidistant from the Fauld/Castle Hay quarries and those at Chellaston, transport to Burton would not be difficult with the former on the ridge above the Trent Valley and the latter a mere 8 miles away along an old straight Roman road (now the A38). These two kervers rose to prominence after being commissioned to carve the Foljambe tomb at Chesterfield (GNP25) which was to be a copy (counterfeit) of one they had carved at Great Cubley (G73). Altogether only the two tombs, above, have been positively identified to these men but they appear to have been active for some 40 years and it has been suggested that North Aston (1490, G143), Strelley (1501, G139), Little Chart (1509, G101), Harewood (1510, G206, Figure 16) Norton (1510, G94), Tamworth (1512, G160), Tong (1517, G149), Ashover (1518, G69, Figure 17), Prestwold (1520, G110, Figure 18), Tower of London (1521, T28, Figure 23), Malpas (1522, G53, Figures 19 and 20), Godshill (1522, G91), Exton (1523, GNP79), Elford (1525, G159), Macclesfield (1528, G52) and Llandaff (1528, GNP118) show features common to this workshop. Further study may reveal more over time. Moorecock may have died before 1520 leaving Harpur to carry on alone until he ceased work in 1528. No record can be found of either man in Burton church archives. One 'signature' feature of the workshop was the way the cording was looped on the chest (Figure 20 – the Brereton lady at Malpas). This is mainly found on the female effigies but in the case of Sir John Cheyne in Salisbury (G182), his garter robes are secured in an identical manner. Cheyne was Henry VII's flag-bearer after William Brandon was killed in the final skirmish at Bosworth in 1485, and died in 1499 but the tomb and effigy, which also carries an SS collar, was not made until 1509.

Around 1522 Richard Parker established his presence in Burton. Whether he acquired the Harpur and Moorecock workshop, then winding down, is unknown, but Burton history suggests that both Parker and Harpur were located on Horninglow Street, Burton. John Bayliss has identified 12 monuments in the period under review which includes slabs as well as effigies. We will discuss Parker again in this and the next section.

The first two decades of the 16th century saw changes which ultimately would see the demise of the Trent Valley kervers. In 1510 a Norfolk kerver Cornelius Harman opened a workshop in Norwich and he is credited with the monuments located in Essex and Cornwall. Details of work in alabaster are lacking, but he merits inclusion as it demonstrates two points. Firstly, he is of Dutch/Flemish extraction, being one of the early migrant carvers fleeing from the Spanish and who later came to dominate the alabaster trade, and: secondly, he sometimes worked in Cornish catacleuse marble, indicating the developing coastal trade in minerals.

Like Nottingham, Lincoln is not credited with a carver's guild but one John Hippis of Lincoln is stated to have carved the tomb to the Willoughbys in Wollaton (A6, 1514). Lincoln had 11 or 12 guilds, one being a masons' guild to which the alabasterers may have belonged. This was a religious rather than occupational guild and was suppressed by Henry VIII *circa* 1540. Only three carvers are recorded for Lincolnshire after 1540 and none in Lincoln.

In York there were three alabasterers recorded but the extent of their work in alabaster is unclear. Thomas Drawswerd is the one who worked longest but even here the identification of monuments is difficult. York would subsequently disappear as a carving centre.

In London, the Tudors looked outwards beyond the shores of England to the continent. Here the Renaissance was in full swing. As will be seen in the next section, Renaissance forms would be introduced to English monument carving after the Reformation, but before that Florentine Pietro Torregiano was invited to England in 1511 and Benedetto da Rovezzano in 1520. Both stayed for several years. There are a number of monuments to these carvers but the extent to which they carved in alabaster is not yet determined. Their work was Renaissance in style and may well have influenced the alabaster-carving industry beyond London. These two are the only named carvers working in London between 1486 and 1540, and the lack of jobbing carvers may well be the reason for the absence of a reasonable population of alabaster monuments in London. In fact of the 140 effigial monuments in this period only two are in London,[1] four in the Home Counties and a smattering on the Berks/Wilts borders. This does not indicate any significant alabaster carving in London to 1540.

The absence of Dorset monuments, so different from the previous 25 years, is noted. It may well be that alabaster carving by the Purbeck workshops did not endure but the Tintinhull records again provide an interesting item. In 1514 the churchwarden records state:

> 'Two payments of 10/1d to painters W Wheler and W Ootts for their labour for painting an alabaster retable'.

The assumption is that retable panels were supplied unpainted. The following year there is another entry for two un-named painters called 'father and son' for £2 1s10d and in 1516, 2d for painting the king's crown assumed to mean an image.

Although a link is tenuous it is worth observing that the Purbeck trade seems to have blossomed with the rise in Yorkist fortunes as did York, and suffered a decline with the advent of the Tudors – the very reverse of that experienced by the Trent Valley during the Plantagenet reign. No obvious link with either faction can be seen, but may well be worth a detailed study.

The Dorset cluster was replaced by a new cluster of 13 in Cheshire and Shropshire. There is no evidence of carvers in the West and as several monuments in nearby Worcestershire and Hereford have been identified with Parker and Royley which means that the likelihood is that all these are all products of the Burton workshops.

If the assumptions are correct the Trent Valley kervers had greatly expanded their influence in the first half of the 16th century but it was not to last.

Nicola Shilliam offers the suggestion that Richard Parker of Burton was influenced by the Renaissance styles of Pietro Torrigiano. Considering the long life of the Parker workshop this may well only be true of his work post-1540 covered in the next section. Certainly Gardner seems to support this suggestion, saying that Renaissance features did not appear until his transition period (Class VI, 1548 to 1560).

However, sampling the monuments attributable to Parker between 1522 and 1540 indicates a creeping introduction of Renaissance features supporting Nicola Shilliam's suggestion. The 1531 monument at Kinlet (T10) has much detail which is not Gothic in style, spiral pilasters appear from 1536 (Fawsley, G127) and pilasters with vases from 1537 (Stowe by Chartley, T26). This sample is small but there are five others (G96, G111, A229, R128 and A230), all 1529 to 1539 which may well demonstrate a growing Renaissance style.

At this point it is necessary to discuss the effect of the Reformation. The destruction of the images and other Catholic trappings is discussed elsewhere but the Reformation appears not to have had any lasting effect on new effigy work. True, some existing urban and rural effigial tombs had angels and other symbols removed but the creation of new effigial tombs continued unabated. The fate of tombs within suppressed priories and monasteries is another matter. The fate of Richard III's tomb in Leicester Cathedral is discussed in Appendix R, but throughout the country, tombs were removed or destroyed or left to the elements. There arose a fine trade in second-hand components of tombs. The CMS has discussed this in some detail in the past, but it is clear that some tomb effigies were removed and the inscriptions including the deceased's name re-carved.

Amongst these is Ralph Sacheverell's 1539 tomb in Ratcliffe-on-Soar (G136, Figures 21 and 22) which shows signs of the inscription being recut as well the fact that his lady beside him may well not be the one he married. He also sports an SS collar to which he was not entitled. The belief is that the effigy is his uncle Richard (died 1534) who was entitled to the SS collar and whose tomb may have been recovered from the Newarke in Leicester when that was suppressed. It was then rebranded by Ralph's son Henry, who may also have 'liberated' tomb effigies for himself and his wife as they too show distinct alterations. As to the tomb chest, it may well be that a new chest was created for the 'new' effigies. In the case of Ratcliffe, the tomb chest is clearly Gothic whilst that of Henry (1558 or earlier) is Renaissance. The lozenge-pattern seen on the former tomb chest, according to Crossley, is stated to be a feature of Trent Valley.

Another example is the tomb of Sir Richard Cholmondeley in St Peter ad Vincula,

Tower of London (T28, Figure 23). There is no proof that he ever had an effigial tomb having possibly been buried in the priory of the Crutched Friars or at Our Lady of Barking in 1521. The records of the Tower state clearly that his son erected a tomb to his father in 1554 but the effigies may be some 35 years apart in their carving dates and both predate the knight's death. On the other hand, the tomb chest while basic Gothic has Renaissance spiral pilasters, a very post-1530 feature. The details of this tomb are currently being researched by the author and the Tower staff, and may well prove this to be correct, in which case it is another example of the reuse of tomb components. There may be many more.[2]

By 1540 the suppression of the monasteries and priories was well in hand. There is more evidence of tomb-moving in the next section.

Despite the suppression of Nottingham carving, the dominance of the Trent Valley workshops continued to evolve as this period drew to a close.

Notes:

1. One is the 1521 tomb to Richard Cholmondeley which has been subject of extensive research by the author and the Tower of London and may well have been removed from a church in Cheshire *circa* 1554. For more details *see* T28 and G53.
2. One tomb which may also be a 'changeling' is that to Sir Henry Pierrepont in Holme Pierrepont, Nottinghamshire (G135). The requirements for the tomb appear in the deceased's will of 1499, which is the year he died. The effigy is in Gothic style with a Yorkist collar despite this being 14 years since that decoration was last awarded. The tomb chest is of a style 40 years later and resembles that at Ratcliffe. As the tombs are known to have been moved about it is possible that a new chest was made mid-16th century or even that the effigy with its pre-1485 collar was liberated from elsewhere.

8.7 Reformation and Transition (1541 to 1566) – Diagram J

Extant Effigy Population: 65 (Gardner, Class VI)
Extant Mural Population: 5
Extant Panel, Slab and Tabletop Population: 65

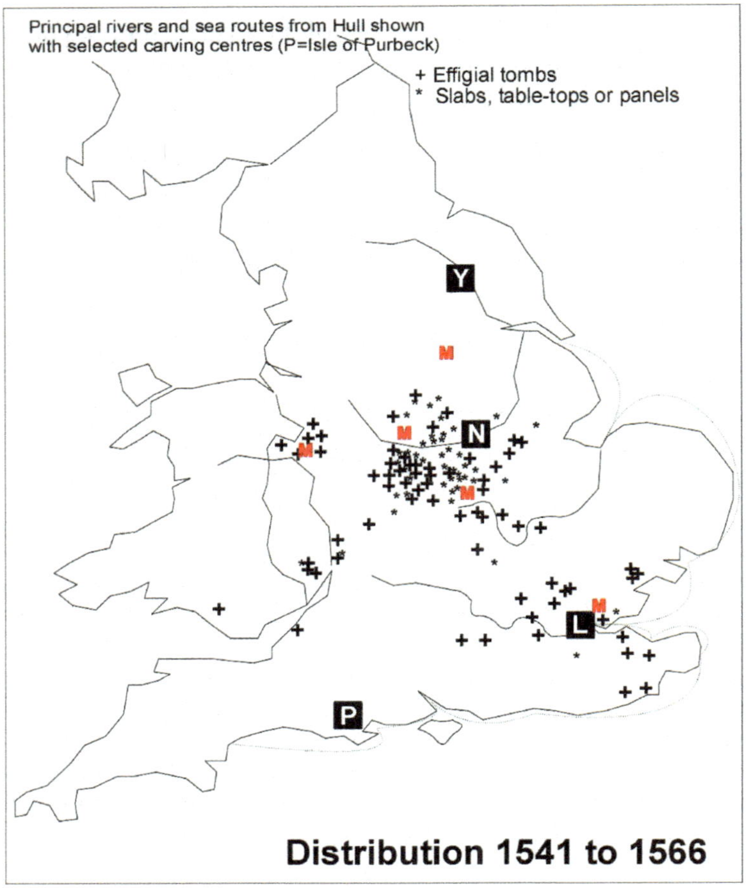

Diagram J. The distribution of effigial tombs (+) and others (*) 1541 to 1566 with rivers and coastal routes shown. This was period of change with the Reformation having a major effect on churches and the transition from Gothic to Renaissance form. Yet again the biggest cluster is based in the Trent Valley but has shrunk in extent. Note the five murals marked M. Drawn by the author.

As stated the Reformation was well in hand by 1540. Henry VIII, with Thomas Cromwell, had dissolved the priories and monasteries and, apart from suppressing chantries and shrines and revising the liturgy, the initial effect on church monuments was minimal. This was to change over the next decade as the policies of Edward VI were far more harmful. Across the nation in Edward's time, images, reredos, retables and symbols of saints were removed and destroyed. This time is covered in more detail in Appendix H.

The period 1547 to 1559 saw no less than four monarchs, one pretender and see-sawing religious direction, so it would be expected that monumental carving would be depressed.

However, the population of effigies seems to have been unaffected by these changes. Very few were destroyed (apart from those in suppressed religious houses) and the rate of new carving increased by 50% with the kervers responding to the religious doctrine of the times. Gone were images of saints, angels, mythical beasts and requests for intersession. Also gone were inscriptions in Latin although these later were reintroduced at the end of the 16th century.

The map above shows that Burton on Trent workshops continued to dominate with the Parker workshop now having new competition from that of Gabriel Royley. The architect Robert Smythson was busy in the East Midlands from 1556 until 1601 and some commissions came from this source.

It will be noted that Dorset, Lincoln and Yorkshire are devoid of monuments although John Tarbotons and Philip Gillo where reported as working in the latter county. The only monument credited to either is a wooden effigy identified with the Tarbotons which is stated to be 'in Gothic style dating from this period'. The demise of the York carvers in the 1540s could be due to the fact that they were attached to one of the religious guilds which was suppressed by Henry VIII. York was to briefly rise again.

In Lincoln one Henry Kinder is recorded as working in 1560 but nothing is known of his monuments. Thomas Goodlord is credited with the tomb at Spilsby in Lincolnshire in 1580, otherwise carving in the county was at low ebb. In Nottingham the alabaster trade was decimated with the banning of their key products and apart from one later mention, was never to recover.

The cluster around London is unassigned apart from one attributed to the Cure workshop at Southwark. In the 1540s the first Dutchman arrived in London in the form of William Cure, apparently at the request of Henry VIII although this cannot be confirmed. In 1549 he set up a workshop at Southwark outside of, but close to, the city. After his retirement in 1559 his eldest son Cornelius inherited the business being credited with the alabaster monument at Bisham (R44) and it may well be that some of the twelve other unknown monuments in the home counties may be from the Southwark workshops. In 1560 they were joined by Richard Stevens, also a Dutch émigré, who also opened a workshop. These two established Southwark as a centre setting the basis for the subsequent dominance of London.

This period saw the first mural monuments with Kinlet (1548, M296), Rolleston on Dove (1555, R211), Greens Norton (1558, M362), Chesterfield (1558, M115, Figures 24 to 26) and St Peter's ad Vincula in the Tower of London (1564, M329, Figure 27). This list must be treated with caution. Only the last one is likely to be the correct date, having been attributed to the Cure workshop in London. Of the others the construction of the tomb may be much later with Kinlet *circa* 1580, Rolleston *circa* 1600, Greens Norton, late 16th century and Chesterfield post-1584 and attributable to the Hollemans workshop of which more details will be provided in the next section. I have retained these four in the period to 1566 as readers may search for the deceased's death date.

In this period 43 (64%) out of the 65 extant effigial monuments are definitely Trent Valley-carved, with the Royley and Parker workshops predominant, and almost all the slabs. There are a further 10 likely to be attributable to the Trent Valley with further research. This total is a large percentage of the remaining monuments but it represents only two and a half monuments per year neither taxing for the raw material supply or the availability of carvers. The workshops were most likely family businesses with one or two resident carvers, an apprentice and a stainer/painter. In fact the records of the Parker workshop include one Margery Walker, the mother-in-law, who traded in images and had a working relationship with a carver in Coventry and a 'warehouse' in Bristol. It may well be that she traded in second-hand goods removed from churches by Edward VI's commissioners and sold on to Europe. It may also be that a travelling salesperson was employed as we have found in the records of Nottingham and Tintinhull in the previous century. Whatever the means, the reputation of the Burton carvers was widespread.

One important point is that no tombs will have been placed in priories and monasteries as these had all been suppressed by 1541.[1]

Nicola Shilliam cites increasing Renaissance features after 1540 such as pilasters with Corinthian capitals, urns, floral scrolls and candelabra at the corners of freestanding tomb-chests, medallions and putti, in place of angels. Relations appeared on tomb-chest sides in place of Gothic features.

Richard Parker is to be found listed on the Lichfield 'census' of 1532, the details of which are set out in B200. Parker continued to work to 1571 but may have retired before this. The most significant contract was that for the Manners at Bottesford (T7, 1543) for which the details still exist. The monument retains some Gothic detail, such as the hands in horizontal position and chamfered edge text, but the tomb chest has corner pilasters with urns, and the 'weepers' facing forward are without additional features, and are depicted on a plain background. The old Gothic richness of the effigy-carving is in contrast to the simplicity of the tomb chest allowing this to be noted as a transition tomb of the classic type.

Parker's work in the last decades of the workshop became increasingly Renaissance in style occasionally adopting features from his neighbour such as the shields in circles.

In 1540 the Royley workshop opened in Burton on Trent and appears to have adopted a Renaissance style from the onset. The tomb chests made by this workshop also depict spiral or twisted pilasters (copied from early Parker tombs) and carved circles within which are shields as well as 'weepers' in the form of relatives singly or in groups.

Notes:

1. The recovery of tombs from suppressed religious houses by relatives does not affect the population of this period.

8.8 Elizabethan Renaissance and the First Dutch Influence (1567 to 1602) – Diagram K

Extant Effigy Population: 125
Extant Mural Population: 69
Extant Panel, Slab and Tabletop Population: 78

This period saw the emergence of more countrywide centres of carving. Output per year doubled but at seven and a half monuments per annum is hardly outstanding. In 1567 the Trent Valley workshops were still going strong and would be throughout the period under review. In London, the Cure workshop at Southwark was emerging as a force, and other urban and provincial workshops were starting up. Also in London, Garrett Jannsen arrived from Holland in 1567. He later anglicised his name to Johnson and with his sons the workshop prospered to about 1611. In 1568 another Dutch migrant arrived in the form of Garrett Hollemans and finding Southwark somewhat overcrowded, settled in Burton on Trent, although the location of the workshops is uncertain. This had advantages and disadvantages in that Burton was remote from the London market but close to the source of alabaster. The Hollemans market embraced much of the East Midlands.

In the diagram (above) the red and black cross cluster representing the Royley and Parker workshops' products is concentrated in Warwickshire, Northamptonshire, Nottinghamshire, Derbyshire, Staffordshire and Leicestershire. A small cluster in Shropshire and Cheshire can also be attributed to them. There are a few remote locations in Bedford, Bucks, Lancashire and Yorkshire but other than these the two carvers appear not to have made any impact in the rest of the country. In light of the fact that the London workshops made no penetration in the North until 1587 with a small number of monuments (Stamford, M64, Quorndon, R85 and Brockelsby, M123), it is reasonable to assume that all 124 (47%) extant monuments in the Midland counties, carved in the period 1566 to 1587, can be attributed to the Trent Valley workshops. Beyond that date there is penetration of the Midlands market by London as described below.

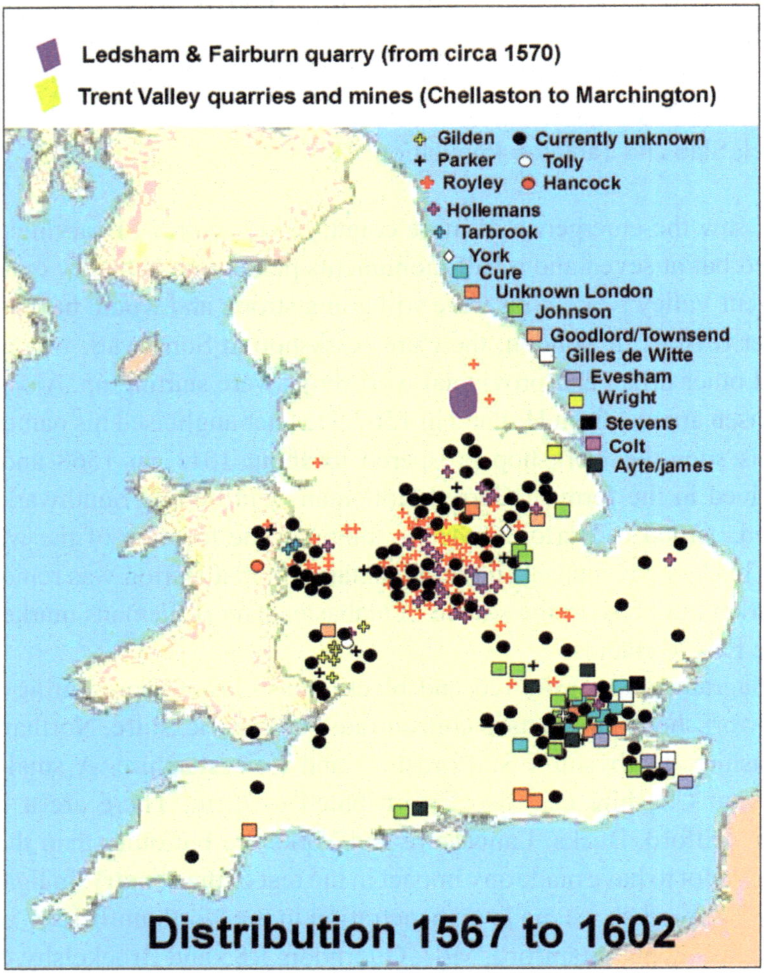

Diagram K. The distribution of monuments by workshop (London by a square box and others by a cross) 1567 to 1602 without rivers and coastal routes shown. This is coloured to represent the known distribution of work by individual workshops. Yet again the cluster around the Trent Valley predominates but note the significant group around London emanating from the Southwark workshops of Cure, Johnson (Jannsen), Evesham and others. The separation between monument types has not been made to avoid confusion. Drawn by the author.

The London workshops beginning with that of the Cure family served London and the Home Counties as indicated by the tight cluster around the capital. Where they used alabaster the material came from the Trent Valley quarries. Although alabaster was obtained from Ledsham *circa* 1570 onwards, the identification of monuments in this stone are fugitive. It is possible London used European imported alabaster, but no trace can be found and the costs of such imports would make the trade uncompetitive. Therefore, the above statement can be made with some surety.

The Cures were joined by other workshops as the square boxes indicate. It was not until the end of the 16th century that the London workshops made any penetration into the Midlands but this was to grow in the next period.

As stated above, in Burton on Trent the Parkers and Royleys were joined by the Hollemans in the 1570s but there is only one possible attribution before 1584 (Quorndon, R198, 1574). The Hollemans' customers in this period were in the Midlands too but there are a number of odd attributions. A slab in Queenhill, Worcs (S8, 1584) is attributed to the Hollemans as is one at Hornsey, north London (S10, 1590) and a mural at Hintlesham, Suffolk (M211, 1594). It may well be that all the customers had Midlands association and indeed Henry Field at Queenhill was from a well-known Kings Norton family and George Rey at Hornsey was a Staffordshire man.

Figure 28. One of the children on the tomb chest of Hugh Armstrong of Wysall, Nottinghamshire dated to 1572 and attributable to the Royley workshop. The shield surface is carved and would probably have been stained. The figure is emancipated and may indicate the loss of quality which some observers claim about the workshop at that time. Photo: the author.

Most of the cluster in the Welsh Marches can be attributed to the Gildon workshop at Hereford and the unknowns here are likely to be attributable to this workshop.

An interesting monument which stands out is that to York Archbishop Edwin Sandys in Southwell, Nottinghamshire (A17).

Figure 28A. The tomb of Edwin Sandys in Southwell Minster, Nottinghamshire. The style is unlike the Trent Valley workshops and the alabaster is not from the East Mildlands CBp seams. Sandys was an arch-Protestant fleeing to France during reign of Mary I. The presence of high-church robes and the medieval angels holding the cushion and the bedesmen at the feet would seem to be out of keeping with his beliefs which has yet to be explained. The small effigies of Cecily, his wife and Samuel, his eldest son are present. She has her tomb in Woodham Ferrers, Essex (M4) and he in Wickhamford, Worcs (R67). Photos: the author.

This effigial monument is dated about 1588–1590 and not only is in a style which cannot be attributed to the Trent Valley, the alabaster cannot be matched with the quarries in the same area either. The carving is superb and in full Renaissance with some reservations. The visage is a close likeness to the portraits of Sandys in York and the robes are very high-church. The alabaster is very hard and the veining is purple-brown. The alabaster may well be from the Permian marl deposits in Ledsham, in which case this is a rare example of alabaster from this source. The possibility of confirming this lies with the work of Wolfgang Kloppmann in Orleans, France who is experimenting with isotopes to match the carved works with quarries (*see* Appendix M Section 13). Although there are no samples from Ledsham the proof that the alabaster is not from the Trent Valley beds is all that is required.

If this is of Ledsham alabaster then there is a possibility that this is a York carving. The problem is the identification of a York workshop in this period. The only one known is Philip Gillo whose works are difficult to find. However, the Southwell tomb was commissioned by Edwin's son, Samuel, who has his own Baldwin-carved alabaster monument at Wickhamford, Worcs (R67) and who, at the time of Edwin's death, was residing in Woodham Ferrers, Essex and therefore well acquitted with the London market. In fact he also commissioned a monument to his mother Cecily between 1611 and 1619 in Woodham Ferrers church (M4, Figure 29), but which has all the trappings of the London carvers.

The Sandys monument in Southwell remains a mystery which is yet to be solved.

For the first time it is possible to identify a tomb which was made in London for a location close to source of alabaster. In 1587 it seems a commission was given to the Cure workshop for a tomb in Stamford, Lincs for a relative of the Cecils (M64). In 1591–1594 the Manners of Belvoir Castle commissioned tombs (R7 & R29) from the Johnson (Jannsen) workshop in Southwark for installation in Bottesford church. The details of this have survived and are included in Appendix C. A year later the same workshop supplied a tomb to Glentworth, Lincs (M84) for the Wray family probably also using Boston as the transit port. More were to follow.

In Burton on Trent, the Royley workshop continued until the first decade of the 17th century. Other authors[1] have observed that the descendants of the founder showed demising skills and adherence to a style increasingly out of fashion with the tomb-purchasing community.

In the midst of the two important centres there were smaller workshops. In Bilborough on the western fringes of Nottingham a carver known as William Hargrave produced tombs for local gentry. Almost nothing can be gathered about this carver but authors credit five effigies,[2] three murals[3] and a tablet to him between 1587 and 1619.[4]

Another was John Gildon (B75). Although his works in alabaster are rare, his tombs for the Harfords at Bosbury (R241 and R242) show a clear understanding of the Renaissance art sufficient for him to be called the Michelangelo of Hereford.

Notes:

1. John Bayliss in the 'CMS Journal' 1991, Vol 2 and others.
2. Quorndon (R85), Langer (R283), Saundby (R284), Old Dalby (M324), Colwick Old Church (now at Newstead, M291), Averham (M595), Brooke, Rutland (R282) and Bunny (M410) as well as the lost tomb at Breadsall (D9/94A).
3. The mural at Newstead (M291) lacks the refinement of the London carvers. When recovered from Colwick in 1937 the tomb was in poor shape having been exposed to the elements for some years. Restoration has been undertaken including repainting.
4. Bilborough in the late 16th century was a coal mining village and it is possibly that Hargrave worked in Nottingham or in Beeston.

8.9 English Forms of Dutch Renaissance (1603 to 1670) – Diagram L

Extant Effigy Population: 164
Extant Mural Population: 357
Extant Panel, Slab, Tablet and Tabletop Population: 57

The Tudor era came to an end in 1603 with the death of Elizabeth I. James I of England (VI of Scotland) came to the throne and the next 67 years saw the biggest surge in alabaster monuments for nearly three centuries.

In 1600 there were 18 alabaster workshops at work, 10 in London, 3 in Burton/Nottingham, 2 in York, 1 in Cheshire, 1 in Sandon, Staffordshire and 1 in Dorset – up from 12 in 1566 of which only 3 were in London (*see* Timelines 3 and 4). This rose to 21 by 1630 but fell to 13 by the period end in 1670. The Trent Valley workshops had declined to the point that only the Hollemans workshop in Burton on Trent was a serious supplier of alabaster products and these were mainly supplied to customers in the East Midlands. Therefore London and the busy Baldwin workshops at Gloucester predominated. Diagram L (black M) shows that London workshops were trading all over England and many of the currently unidentified carvers of rural monuments may well be from this source. Transport had improved to the point that distribution was no longer tied to the rivers and coast although these continued to play their part.[1] As to the source of raw alabaster, this has to be the East Midlands and Yorkshire. At the beginning of the period Ledsham and Fairburn are recorded as working and possibly Chellaston although evidence for this is thin. The prime source, however, was Castle Hay and Fauld in Staffordshire. Thus these quarries may have supplied alabaster for some 400 to 500 monuments over 67 years. This is not an over large commitment being just five to seven monuments per year all of which may have been shipped through Hull.[2] In 1633 Watchet in Somerset joined the list of working Quarries.

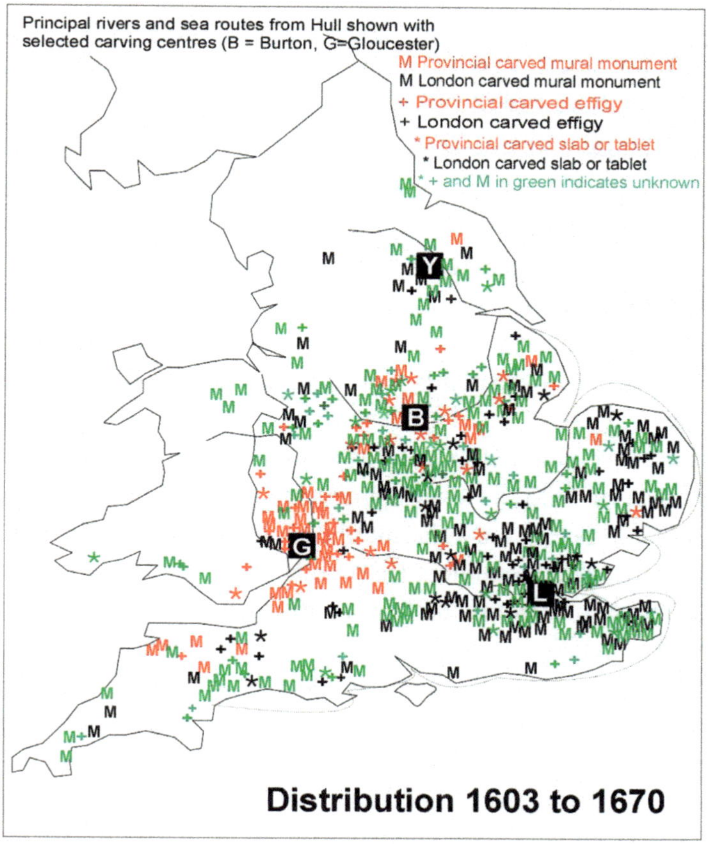

Diagram L. The diagram shows the distribution of effigial tombs (+), murals (M) and others (*) from 1603 to 1670 with rivers and coastal routes shown. This is coloured to show the spread of the mural style probably outwards from London. By this time the transport situation had changed meaning that distribution was now no longer tied to the coasts and rivers. The cluster around Gloucester is mainly the work of the Baldwin workshop. The black symbols show that the London workshops were now trading far from their South-east heartland. The red cluster around the Trent Valley is mainly from the Hollemans workshop in Burton. Kent, Suffolk, Norfolk and Cambridge are now much more populated whilst the Midland counties continue to be a popular location for alabaster products. London carving has reached Devon, Dorset, Cornwall, York and Lancashire. Drawn by the author.

The style that blossomed was the mural. Effigies alone on tomb chests continued to be carved but were now replaced in popularity by the wall-mounted mural comprising kneeling figures usually in front of prayer stalls with prayer books or with hands in prayer (Figures 27 and 40). Supporters in the form of children appeared. The mural had a high entablature supported by columns and large heraldic devices and finials, pinnacles or obelisks. Another feature was that much was painted so as to be very striking to the eye (Figure 30). The ornamental finial which is a common addition at the time is regarded as a symbol of the ending of life.

The preference for painted tombs may have influenced the choice of alabaster. In earlier sections we have discussed the fact that pure white alabaster was sought for its lustre although many of the medieval tombs were also stained. Now the heavily veined Fauld alabaster could be used as it would be covered in paint.

Although the Fauld and Castle Hay mine and quarry may have been the prime source we know that a 'Dutchman' was exploiting the cliffs at Watchet for alabaster from 1633.[3] It is inconceivable that the Baldwin workshop just 50 miles away up the Bristol Channel and the Severn did not exploit these reserves. The Baldwin monuments in Appendix D4 show the alabaster sources, where identified are mainly Fauld, but the monument at Lydiard Tregoze of 1634 (R165) has a distinct pinkish hue and the date of 1634 corresponds with Gerard's observations on the mining of the cliffs at Watchet.

Some monuments combine the features of the mural with a recumbent effigy. That at Ratcliffe-on-Soar of 1625 to Henry Sacheverell (R5, M2 and the corresponding one to his father, R4) and one at the adjacent church at Gotham (M23) are interesting for a number of reasons. The monument (Figure 31) appears to be the standard mural of the period but Henry is shown recumbent on his own tomb chest with his three wives kneeling at prayer stalls each depicted in the dress appropriate to the date of their death. Mary Gittings (died 1600) shows an identical Queen of Scots headdress which is contemporary with that on the effigy of Jane Ireton (R4) and has clear Elizabethan trappings. The second wife is Mary Copley (died 1616) in Stuart dress and hood and the third wife is Lucy Broughton (died 1667) who later married Sir Thomas Grantham (died 1630, *see* R21). Lucy has a late Stuart dress with a half-ruff which is rare on murals. Even more strange are the features of Lucy which are almost identical to those of the wife of William St Andrew at Gotham (M23, Figures 32 and 33).

As stated earlier, the Ratcliffe mural is placed over the lancet window of the chancel which was totally unnecessary since a large blank wall was available a few metres away. However, the mural was positioned to be directly opposite the effigial tomb of Henry's father which entailed covering the window. The scroll work supporting the entablature and on the tomb chest is coarse and heavy and wholly unlike the fine carving of the London workshops. The detail incorporated is good but the execution is poor and the belief is that the two Ratcliffe monuments and at least one at Gotham are from the latter days of the Hollemans' workshop, which like that of Royley some 50 years before had declined in quality with the death of their founder. Nevertheless, the workshop continued in being until the 1650s.

The Gotham and Ratcliffe mural monuments have another feature in common in that they both have inlays of cockleshell marble. This false marble, which is actually a fossilised limestone, is described in Appendix I and seems to be a feature only of the Northern carvers.

In London, the productive workshops of Johnson, Cure, Colt, Marshall, Stone, Wright, Christmas, Evesham and later Stanton dominated the market from 1603 to the start of the Civil War in 1642. In the West the Baldwin workshop carved out a niche in Gloucestershire, Herefordshire, Worcestershire, Wiltshire and Somerset. Like the Hollemans workshop the quality took a downward step after the death of Samuel in 1647 and after his son Stephen carried on with the carving but with declining sales until it closed in 1670. The goodwill may have been assumed by the Reeve workshop (*see* next section).

The finesse of the London carvers can be seen in monuments such as that to Sir William Skipwith of 1631 at Prestwold, Leicestershire (M41, Figure 34). Sir William, despite being in armour, no longer rests his head on a great helm but on a rolled-up mat whilst his lady still has a cushion but devoid of images or animals. However, the quality can be seen in the entablature which has a decorated arch, fine small heraldic devices and strapwork with the inscription picked out in black marble.

The same quality but a very different style can be seen in a monument in St Peter ad Vincula in the Tower of London. The tombs to Sir Richard and Sir Michael Blout (M329) were built in two stages by the Cure workshop (Figure 27). The first stage built between 1564 and 1574 was an early mural and so good that the extended tomb of 1610 followed the same style. The double arch and the two groups of kneeling figures carved in the 16th century would be copied and repeated with variations in hundreds of monuments.

A good example from the Colt workshop can be seen at Framlingham in the form of the tomb to the Earl of Surrey (A32, Figure 35). The Earl was executed in 1547, but the tomb, commissioned by the Howard family, was not constructed until 1614. The two recumbent effigies are matched by two kneeling nobles at the foot and three at the head and although there is a nod to the Gothic style of the mid-Tudor period, the whole has a very Continental Renaissance feel. This tomb is the only Howard tomb in Framlingham carved in alabaster but the rich history of the other tombs shows a link to the tombs in Thetford Priory which may have used this stone. The details of this are contained in note X100.

Whereas the London workshops tended to produce a limited range of styles, the Baldwin workshop in Gloucester offered a range of monuments in different forms according to the requirements of his customers. Appendix Y sets out the work of the workshop between 1603 and 1651. The high-rise mural can be found being carved alongside an effigial tomb either with recumbent effigies or leaning on one elbow as observed by John Webster (Section 6.10).

The Gloucester Cathedral monuments show his early mural works. The monument to Elizabeth Williams (Figure 36, 1622) who died in childbirth shows Elizabeth resting on one elbow contemplating her baby in the form of a chrisom. Note that the chrisom, cuffs, floppy ruff and face are left unstained to emphasise these against the black of the dress and mourning hood. On Thomas Machen's tomb (M60, 1615), his wife Christian has a severe expression on her face on which the features have been painted (Figure 37) and which may be a likeness. It will be noted that almost all dresses on Jacobean mural tombs have ladies in black.

The latter effigies are particularly well carved. Those to the Sandys family at Miserden, Gloucs (R56, 1644) and Wickhamford (R67, 1626) are particularly fine.[4] As found in other workshops the quality diminished after Samuel Baldwin's son Stephen assumed the reigns when Samuel died in 1645.

The English Civil War, which started in 1642 and ended in 1651, may have had a dampener on the customer demand for monuments. Certainly Walter Spiers writing on the work of Nicholas Stones seems to think so. Money was tight especially within the Royalist enclaves of the West Country, North-east, North-west and Wales whilst Royalist towns such as Oxford and Newark are absent from the lists apart from one small tablet. In addition, parliamentary areas although smaller held most of the wealth, control of the navy and the major ports, including London. With London now the major carving centre the monuments are largely found in the Home Counties with occasional deliveries in border or in Royalist areas.

The political affinities of the carvers are unclear. John Stone observed at the Restoration that his father Nicholas had been 'imprisoned for his loyalty' but the duration appears to be short. The reason is unclear but may be due to the monies received from Charles I which was paid in arrears. Certainly, something made his brother-in-law suddenly leave Nottingham and return to Amsterdam around this time. The delivery of alabaster from the East Midlands was probably disrupted so cutting off the route by which the raw material reached London. Although the upper reaches of the Trent and Nottingham were in parliamentary hands, Newark stood astride the navigable arm of the Trent with the castle walls actually on the river bank. It was just possible to use the Muskham arm through Averham but there were shallows and the Kelham Bridge to pass. With this arm in the hands of the vesting Parliamentarians, the rafting of freight round Newark was likely or else road had to be used.

With peace in 1651, trade picked up but it was not to last. In 1660 the monarchy was restored bringing with it a new fashion for marble. Appendix D4 shows 30 monuments carved between 1652 and 1660 and just 19 between 1661 and 1670. The Stone, Baldwin and Hollemans workshops all closed between 1656 and 1667. The Burman and Marshall workshops closed soon after, along with a number of lesser names. As the 1670s dawned we note that only the major workshops of Sweet, Stanton, Besnier, Cibber, Cartwright and Reeve were working.

One unusual monument can be found in Shenfield church in Essex. The tomb to Elizabeth Robinson is dated to 1652 (A224) and carved by Thomas Burman. It is ahead of its time having Baroque features without any entablature.

Figure 38. The alabaster tomb of 1652 to Elizabeth Robinson in Shenfield church, Essex by Thomas Burman. Its simplicity is ahead of its time with the only nod to the old style being in the skull and the charnel house carved at one end of the tomb chest. Photo: Janet State.

Notes:

1. The notebook of Nicholas Stone records that the chimney piece for Newstead Abbey was shipped from the Thames to Hull and thence by river to Nottingham and only then carted to Newstead.
2. The Port of Hull Archives have no specific record of alabaster but at less that 100 tons a year at peak the consignment would be of no matter as compared with coal.
3. A West Country traveller called Gerard recorded this in 1633 (Roger Firman's notes) and it is noted that Nicholas Stone exported two large consignments of alabaster to Amsterdam (Appendix B) which his Dutch brother-in-law William de Keyser had obtained. The Dutch connection is strong.
4. Sir Samuel Sandys was the son of Edwin (A17) and Cecily (M4). These three monuments could not be more different in style, one being York carved, one London and the other Gloucester.

8.10 Marble Period and Decline (1670 to 1750)

Extant Effigy Population: 4
Extant Mural Population: 18
Extant Panel, Statue, Slab, Tablet and Tabletop Population: 37

The decline in alabaster monuments post-1670 is almost terminal with the carving of alabaster effigial tombs diminishing almost to the vanishing point and only 18 murals as shown in Appendices D4 and D5. Most significant is the rise in wall tablets. The wall tablet is less expensive than a mural and uses less space in a church. They usually do not include an effigy but some do. A typical wall tablet without effigy from around this period is that to John Hutchinson in Owthorpe church, Leicestershire (Figure 39, 1663) in which the elements of the murals of the previous decades survive in the coat of arms over the cornice and two symbolic obelisks. However, the ornamentation is restricted to images and figures on the margin.

The main thrust is the inscription. An ardent Republican, John Hutchinson was the constable of Nottingham Castle during the English Civil War and signed Charles I's death warrant in 1649. Arrested as a regicide in 1662 and imprisoned in Sandown Castle, he died of pleurisy in 1663 and the tablet was erected by his wife Lucy, the daughter of Sir Allan Apsley, Lieutenant of the Tower and granddaughter of St John of Lydiard Tregoze (R165). Lucy wrote a hagiography of John Hutchinson and exercised her dismay at his treatment in Sandown in the text of the inscription. Hutchinson's Puritan beliefs saw him arrange to break out the stained glass in both Owthorpe and Ratcliffe church but there is no record of any attack on any of the effigies.[1]

Typical of the tablet with an effigy is the one to Samuel Bevercotes in Ordsall church, Nottinghamshire (Figure 40). This mutilated monument, although dated from 1603–1613, retains the columns, coat of arms and obelisks of the mural period and is typical of the wall tablets that became popular. This monument has been moved at least twice, losing its backing stone, inscription and one obelisk.

Why alabaster fell out of favour so quickly is not clear. The Restoration introduced the Baroque style which favoured unpainted effigies and tomb chests. In this period most quarries had ceased or were at low ebb and possibly the only working quarry/mine was Fauld which, as we know, had veined alabaster. This was of no import when the monument was painted but now this veining may not have suited the carvers of Baroque monuments. As a result true marble was employed for most monuments.

However, it would appear that the veining was seen as decorative for tablets and the appreciation of this feature would be utilised throughout the next two centuries.

What is significant is that the large London workshops are represented in the list of alabaster monuments until the 1690s after which a number of provincial carvers appear. Amongst these are William Byrd of Oxford and John Weston of Exeter but there are many others mostly anonymous (*see* Appendix D4 and D5). William Byrd's monument to Fettiplace in Swinbrook, Oxford (M207) is a triple-tiered mural which is reputed to be in Castle Hay alabaster. The style is not new since Swinbrook had an earlier triple-tiered Fettiplace monument dating from 1613 which may or may not be by Byrd.

The workshop of John Weston may well have produced more monuments than have been identified and he may have used Watchet alabaster. He appears from the identified monuments to have made only wall tablets and his products can be found at

Exeter (M238), Whitchurch (M241), Dartmouth (M240) and Denbury (M242). There also appears to be a workshop in Barnstaple and the monuments at Tawstock are signed by both Thomas Jewell the Elder and Thomas Jewell the Younger. The 2006 thesis on Devon monuments (*see* bibliography) suggests this workshop was active from 1690 to 1758 making tablets for local churches and the one made by them in Tawstock is possibly Watchet alabaster (M237). One in Bittenden (M233) is also a possibility.

In summary, this period seems to have seen the abandonment of alabaster by the big London workshops for marble. This may be customer-driven who embraced the continental shift to Baroque marble. Alabaster continued to be used by provincial workshops that saw a market in tablets rather than the grand murals of the early 17th century. What the effect was on the alabaster quarries is uncertain but it is likely that only those in Staffordshire survived.

Notes:

1. Being related to the Sacheverells through the daughter of Henry (died 1585), he would not have an inclination to deface these. However, in 2013 the author was asked to try to identify an effigy found in a cave beneath Nottingham Castle. The limestone effigy was clearly from the mid-17th century and clothed as a doctor. The only effigy from this period which is known to be missing is that to Dr Huntington Plumtre, a long-term opponent of Hutchinson who was buried in June 1660 in St Mary's, Nottingham. A confirmed atheist, which did not prevent him from a wish to be buried in the church, his presence would no doubt be an irritant to the religious Hutchinson who may well have arranged to have the effigy removed to the castle which he was in the process of dismantling under the orders of Cromwell. Fragmentary evidence of a tomb exists but neither Thoroton nor Throsby found one. Seeing as they were writing later than 1660 it is possible that the effigy had already been removed by then. The effigy remains where it was found, a mystery yet to be solved.

8.11 The Rise of the Marble Halls (1750 to 1770) (*see* Appendix U)

Extant Monuments: None

If the period after 1670 was thin on alabaster monuments, the period under review has no recorded extant monuments in alabaster at all. Marble ruled for those who could afford a splendid tomb and freestone for those that could not.

However, the late 17th century to the mid-18th century saw a boom in the building of stately houses. The list of the 25 top stately houses in *BritainExpress.com* reveals that all were built or rebuilt between 1690 and 1798 with the peak in the 1720 to 1770 period.

The Palladian style emerged with colonnaded fronts behind which were grand entrance halls. There were departures from the norm such as Ickworth House, Suffolk where the central edifice was a rotunda but most country house owners wanting to make a similar statement to impress visitors, settled on the colonnade.

One such owner was Lord Nathaniel Curzon of Kedleston Hall, Derbyshire. The

Curzon family had occupied the estate at Kedleston since 1297 and had lived in a series of manor houses gradually extending the boundaries which at one point meant removing a complete village. The current hall was commissioned in 1759 from Robert Adams. It is not intended to deal with the construction of the entire building, just the entrance hall, and here we must look towards Nathaniel Curzon's brother.

In 1714 Nathaniel Curzon's father acquired the manor of Ratcliffe-on-Soar, building a new house there.[1] In 1719 the old manor was demolished. The estate was bounded on one side by the River Soar and on the north side by the River Trent against which the gypsum-rich cliffs of Redhill faced. In 1758 the old man died leaving Kedleston to his elder son Nathaniel and Ratcliffe to his younger son Assheton. Exploitation of the cliffs had commenced about 1750 and later Thoroton recorded that skeletons and coffins had been uncovered during 'mining operations for gypsum'. This is no surprise as the Redhill site had been occupied by Celts and Romans from about 300BC to 410AD. It is possible that these activities may have exposed a large seam of white and pale-brown-veined alabaster before it was used at Kedleston. This will be discussed again when we look at Holkham Hall.

Assheton Curzon's acquisition of Ratcliffe drew Adam's attention to the alabaster at Redhill and in his design of Kedleston he decided to use this stone for the columns to the entrance hall. The blocks were mined in six to eight foot lengths, roughed out on site and carried by river boat to Derby by way of the Trent and Derwent and thence by wagon to Kedleston where they were finished and fluted.[2]

In all some 20 columns were made and these can now be seen in the Marble Hall in Kedleston (Figure 41).

In addition, the door frames of rooms such as the library are also of alabaster showing the same colouring as the columns and these too are likely to be from Redhill. However, the floor of the Marble Hall is believed to be formed of Italian marble but this is uncertain.

We can now turn our attention to Holkham Hall, Norfolk. This Palladian mansion was the vision of Thomas Coke. Started in 1734 the mansion was unfinished when Thomas died in 1759. It was completed by his successors.

The records at Holkham indicate that alabaster was purchased as early as 1755 (Appendix U) and carried on until 1758. Castle Hay is mentioned by name as a source leading to speculation about the quarry which is contained in Appendix M Section 1. It has columns which are a size and colour very close to those at Kedleston leading to the suggestion that these too were obtained from Redhill and may pre-date those obtained for Kedleston. However, some written histories state that the marble hall at Holkham was not completed until after 1759 so the matter as to which came first is uncertain. The columns are fluted like those at Kedleston.

The account records are very specific. The entry for 1755 states 'Alabaster comes from Castle Hay' followed by 'Benjamin Carter and Joseph Pickford carving chimney pieces'.[3] The 1758 entry just states 'More alabaster delivered – Alabaster columns arrived' followed by 'William Atkinson carving door surrounds'. For more discussion on this *see* Appendix U.

Although the Holkham records are unclear, the belief is that the columns were carried down the Trent to Gainsborough where they were loaded onto a seagoing boat for shipment to Wells-next-the-Sea, Norfolk.

The third use of Redhill alabaster is in the Mausoleum at Brocklesby, Lincolnshire. The Brocklesby estate was owned by the Pelham family from 1565 but in 1770 Charles Anderson Pelham, First Baron Yarborough, commissioned Capability Brown to lay out the grounds. The mausoleum was built between 1786 and 1794 by James Wyatt as a memorial to Yarborough's wife Sophia who died in 1786, aged 33. The mausoleum is built as rotundas within which are niches supported by pairs of alabaster columns. The niches are filled with marble statues made in Italy by unknown carvers.[4]

These three locations are the best-known recipients of large blocks of alabaster in the period under review. However, many others employed this stone in chimney pieces. The records of Nicholas Stone mention many chimney pieces made for stately houses between 1612 and 1647. That at Newstead Abbey for Sir John Byron made in 1635 from 'marble and other pieces' is not currently firmly identified but may be the one in the assembly room which is the only one of three chimney pieces not made of limestone and the only one to contain black marble (Figure 42). Kedleston Hall has at least one chimney piece of alabaster in which is inlaid cockleshell marble. This shelly limestone is described in Appendix I and seems to only appear on items in the East Midlands. Two other chimney pieces which are in alabaster from this period are two at Burton Agnes Hall (X55)[5] and one at Newburgh Priory (X56). The latter may not be in English alabaster. Another location in which cockleshell marble is used to good effect is Bolsover Castle, Derbyshire.[6] In fact Bolsover has no less than six chimney pieces which contain alabaster as described in note X47.

It would appear that veined alabaster which was used in the 17th century, but masked with stain and paint, was seen as decorative in the 18th century in the grand houses of the nobility.

Notes:

1. The building still stands as Manor Farm. The dining room of the old manor was retained as a barn until 1830.
2. The museum at Derby confirms that the Derwent was navigable with some difficulty to just below the Derwent weir in Derby from about 1696 when Wilne became the head of navigation on the Trent. The records of the mining activity of the Curzons in the 18th century in Kedleston are lost owing to a later member of the family ordering their destruction. Therefore for the details of the mining we have to rely on observers such as Thoroton and Throsby. Visible on the ground at Redhill are the remnants of an aggered

ridge which curves to run along the Soar to the south bank of the Trent until obliterated by the 1840 railway bridge. There ares no purpose in this other than to provide a level path above the annual flooding, from the quarry face to the Trent.

3. The records of Joseph Pickford the Derbyshire carver state 'Travelling to Fauld to select alabaster for Holkham'. Later his son states '... alabaster from Chellaston from a quarry owned by my father'. However, there is no proof that the latter observation is related to Holkham or any other stately home.
4. 'Church Monuments Society Journal' Vol VII 1992 has the details.
5. Although the one in the entrance hall was installed *circa* 1765 it may date from the 16th or 17th century having come from the demolished Barmston Manor.
6. http://planning.bolsover.gov.uk/WAM/doc/Drawing-1530959.pdf

8.12 Alabaster in the Doldrums (1770 to 1850)

Extant Effigy Population: 1
Extant Mural Population: 1
Extant Statue and Tablet Population: 12

Alabaster continued to be unpopular in this period. The majority of alabaster products were tablets of no great importance.

The solitary effigy is a rather nice recumbent carving for Bishop James Bowstead in Eccleshall church, Staffordshire (R210) from 1843. This is carved in Fauld alabaster but almost nothing can be established about the carver.

The statue and mural from this period are only partially carved in alabaster. The interesting mural at Gaddesby, Lincs depicts Colonel Edward Hawkins Cheney (died 1848) who fought at Waterloo in 1815 (M541). He is depicted astride a horse which has been injured. At Waterloo he had no less than four horses shot from under him. The statue is probably made from marble but the base and relief are in alabaster. The statue was formerly in Gaddesby Hall but moved in 1917 on log rollers to the church when the hall was sold. The *Melton Times* (4th June 2015) states that the statue was carved in Rome and dragged from the station to the hall by 15 horses but this may be speculation.

At Burley in Rutland a statue in marble dated 1813 to Charlotte Finch (A193) has an alabaster base.

Otherwise this period is very uninteresting but that was due to change.

8.13 Gothic Revival (1850 to 1900)

Extant Effigy Population: 21
Extant Mural Population: 3
Extant Tablet Population: 16
Tomb Chest: 4
Statue: 2

The populist term known as Gothic Revival is a bit of a misnomer. The Gothic style was never quite extinguished by the Renaissance and Baroque and began to re-emerge as a popular style in the last quarter of the 18th century. It was only after 1840 that this gathered pace. The leaders were those who espoused philosophy and social change and who saw the medieval Gothic as something pure – a representation of the spirit in an artistic form. In an even more narrow sense, pressure groups such as the ecclesiological movement saw that only Gothic features should be present in English churches. What began as a preference for architecture soon spilled over into monuments. Along with this came resurgence in the use of alabaster.

In the 50 years to 1900 some 21 effigies in alabaster were carved, some four times the number in almost 200 years from 1670. This led to a renewed interest in the quarries such as Chellaston where new seams and drifts were explored with encouragement from people such as Gilbert Scott. The revival did not rest solely with monuments as pulpits, reredos, altars, fonts and other church furniture were carved. Most extraordinary are the churches at Mackworth, Derbyshire and Hanbury, Staffordshire which contain much fine furniture carved in alabaster. These are dealt with in detail in Appendix J, but some of the carvers we will meet again.

The rediscovery of alabaster was matched by resurgence in the number of carvers. Between 1800 and 1850 the names of only 10 carvers can be determined, but between 1850 and 1900 the list grows to 45, some in business throughout the period under review.

The quality of the revival style can be seen in the two effigies in the church at Welshpool, Montgomeryshire (A62 of 1853 & A77 of 1891). Both effigies reside in niches and display the medieval symbols of angels holding the head cushion and dogs at the feet. The alabaster is highly polished. The two effigies were carved some 38 years apart, one by Edward Richardson with design input by Gilbert Scott who is also credited with the design of the second, although the carver of this is uncertain.

Even those who commissioned tombs saw the need for representation in medieval style. The effigy of Francis Scawen Blunt in Crawley Friary church (A121 of 1875) is carved in the form of a medieval friar; Blunt having converted to Catholicism before his death. Designed by his brother, Wilfred, the carving work was carried out by Neville Northey Burnhard, but others were involved (for more details *see* A121).

Not all carvings were Gothic in form. The three listed murals, Westminster (M466),

Middle Clayton (M545) and Louth, Lincolnshire (M547), are all demi-figures or busts in an alabaster frame.

Different again is the monument to the 8th Earl of Lothian in Blickling church, Norfolk (A122) of 1870. The tomb chest is clearly Gothic but the two huge angels standing at the head and foot have a Baroque feel whilst the effigy in a winding sheet is Renaissance. A mixture of styles which produces an impressive and striking monument.

The 1871 monument to Blanche Foljambe in Tickhill church, Yorkshire (A101) on the other hand is pure Renaissance.

Therefore although the main drive was to celebrate the Gothic form the finished form was sometimes anything but Gothic. This may be because of the wide range of carvers in this period had their own preferences.

The emergence of carvers and designers who may have produced just one monument can be gauged by reference to Appendix G, lines 247 to 285, which shows a number of 'itinerant' carvers and sculptors amongst the well known names such as Rhind, Marshall, Street, Scott and Nathaniel Hitch. Then there are the big workshops such as Boulton and Son, Field and Allan of Edinburgh, Bridgeman, William Vickers and Farmer and Brindley. Edward Richardson (B80) who died in 1869 was largely involved in monument restoration and some repairs have been severely criticised as inappropriate. His workshop was at 17 Melbury Terrace, Marylebone, a place well known to me as 10 years of my working life was spent at 14 Melbury Terrance, the railway offices built in 1960 adjacent to the site of the demolished workshop. Richardson was larger than life and had a high profile; writing and presenting on monuments and their restoration (*see* B80 for observations made by the *Derby Mercury* in 1851).

Although effigial monuments are in the majority the cost-effective wall-tablet continued to be popular not least because floor space within churches became difficult to find. It was not unknown for incumbents to arrange for old monuments to be evicted to make room for new ones. The strange case of the Millbrook effigies is retold in Appendix O and is a variation on this theme but Appendix D9 also lists cases where effigial monuments have been destroyed by overzealous vicars. On a lighter note the 1950s Bernard Miles monologue, Appendix H, Note 6, describes the late Victorian habit of using the monuments to sharpen agricultural implements. The same observation has been made about the Greystoke monuments (G4 and GNP15).

In the mid-1800s fine alabaster was seen as being suitable for making decorative items for the home. This was not the first time as borough records of Nottingham in the 15th century show that such items were made using off-cuts from the panel-making. Appendix M, Section 3 describes the 'bauble' industry in north Leicestershire sourced from the Chellaston quarries, which embraced the townships of Whitwick and Loughborough and villages in between. The local term for alabaster was Derbyshire spar. The items made include candlesticks, plates, dishes, vases and Stanhopes, all of which were sold to seaside outlets for the souvenir trade. Extant samples are hard to find – but *see* after next section.

At the very end of the period there was a large export order for alabaster to the USA. The Vanderbilt family made their money out of railroads and in the 1890s the third-generation descendant, Cornelius Vanderbilt II, commissioned a summer retreat in Rhode Island known as The Breakers. The architect was Richard Morris Hunt who designed an Italian Renaissance mansion. Both the dining room and the billiard room have alabaster decoration. Nothing is known about the source for the latter but the source for the dining room is the Fauld Mine in Staffordshire. The dining room walls are supported by 12 Corinthian columns in veined alabaster in a similar fashion to the Marble Halls at Kedleston and Holkham (*see* Appendix M, Section 1). How Vanderbilt and Hunt found their way to a remote Staffordshire mine is unclear but the Vanderbilts married into English aristocracy and it is likely that Cornelius visited Kedleston on more than one occasion. With the Redhill site overgrown and disturbed by the boring of a second railway tunnel, Hunt must have been directed to Fauld, then the only mine capable of providing long blocks.[1] Appendix M, Section 1 shows a photograph of the blocks destined for The Breakers standing on railway wagons in Scropton Sidings.

We now move into the 20th and 21st century

Notes:

1. The notebook of Nicholas Stone has two interesting entries for alabaster exports. An entry for 21st August 1632 states 'Sent to Peter de Keyser four blocks of alabaster the length of which came to 76ft'. Peter was in Amsterdam. This was repeated for the 24th August 1634. If Stone's note is to be believed the average length of each block would be 19ft which would be more or less the same length as the Vanderbilt blocks. In 1632 and 1634 Fauld would be incapable of handling such bocks and Redhill was not yet exploited, so there is a suggestion that Watchet was the source. The purpose of these exports has not been identified.

8.14 Modern Alabaster (1900 to date)

Extant Effigy Population: 6
Extnt Mural Population: 3
Extant Tablet Population: 27 (incomplete and excluding war memorials)
Statue: 1

It will be seen that alabaster church monuments declined severely after the First World War with the exception of war memorials, many of which were placed in churches. Some of these, known to have alabaster in their design, are listed in Appendix D8, but are not described being of a largely standard format. The handful of effigies and murals are noted for their variety of style and quality of the carving. Three depict bishops.

Dealing with the murals first, two are identical, one in St Paul's Cathedral crypt and the other in St Thomas's Hospital (M155 and M156). In 1910 Florence Nightingale died and was commemorated by these wall murals in which she is shown attending a wounded soldier. The cameo carving is in white marble. Florence Nightingale has also a marble memorial in the Santa Croce church in Florence, Italy and also a statue outside the Derby Royal Infirmary.

The mural in Brocklesby church is unusual in that it has a kneeling soldier in an alabaster frame which is carved in 17th-century style (M551, Figure 43) complete with heraldic device, columns with strapwork and black marble inscription panel. Carved by Charles Jagger, it was commissioned in this style to complement the adjacent Pelham family monuments which were carved in 1587 (M123) and 1629 (M318), both by William Wright. Jagger is well-known for his monuments depicting the First World War.

As regards the effigies post-1900 those at Hoar Cross, Staffordshire (A126) are particularly well executed. This church was built as a mausoleum to Hugo Meynell-Ingram killed in a hunting accident in 1871. His monument was formerly in marble but was replaced by one in alabaster when his wife, Emily Meynell-Ingram, died. Her effigy, also in alabaster, is adjacent to that of Hugo on either side of the chancel. In an unusual manner the heads were carved separately from the rest of the effigy.

The monument to Bishop Ridding in Southwell Minster (1904, A81) could not be more different. The kneeling effigy is bronze but the base and prayer desk is Fauld alabaster and well crafted by William Caröe who also designed the tomb in St David's, Pembroke. A picture of the Southwell monument can be seen on:

http://www.churchmonumentssociety.org/Nottinghamshire.html#Southwell_Minster

The tomb to the Countess of Maidstone in St David's, Pembroke (1932, R71) is one of the last effigial monuments to be made. This is magnificently carved and depicts a recumbent lady with facial features believed to be a likeness. There is a hint of Gothic in that there is a pet Pomeranian dog at her feet and its ashes are reputed to be in an urn nearby. An alabaster angel sits on a corbel close by. This tomb can be seen on:

http://www.churchmonumentssociety.org/Pembrokeshire.html

In Gloucester Cathedral there is a fine tomb to Bishop Charles Elicot (A194 of 1905).

Figure 44. Bishop Charles Elicot in Gloucester Cathedral dating from 1905. The tomb chest has the medieval crocketted canopies within which are images of saints. A larger niche holds a mitre. The effigy is believed to be marble and carved by William Silver Frith. Photo: the author.

Yet another variation can be seen in Bishop Lloyd's tomb in the cathedral church of Newcastle upon Tyne (A135 of 1908). Carved by Frederick Pomeroy, the bishop lies recumbent under a grand medieval canopy with two guardian angels at his feet. This can be viewed on:

http://www.victorianweb.org/sculpture/pomeroy/64.html

The last is the effigy at Corsham, Wiltshire (A199 of 1970) to Lady Eleanor Methuen. Carved by Fred Kormis in rose alabaster, this tomb is pure Renaissance in style. The tomb chest is plain except for an inscribed image of a reclining lady and at the feet of the effigy is a seated girl. Again the carving is exceptional.

What the period lacks in numbers it makes up in quality and variety.

In 1902 an American arrived in England who later became a British citizen. This was Jacob Epstein. A controversial sculptor mixing within artistic and Bohemian circles, he carved two large statues in alabaster between 1938 and 1940. One called *Adam* was huge and the other smaller one was *Jacob and the Angel.* These had an eventful career being shown in a drapers shop in Blackpool before going on the road with a travelling fair and then being lodged in Tussaud's waxworks. They have now found a permanent home, *Adam* in Harewood House and *Jacob and the Angel* in the Tate Gallery. As far as can be established these are his only works in alabaster and with the history of the two statues in freak shows earned Epstein criticism, especially when set alongside the anti-Semitism of the early war years. Epstein made no more large statues.

As to the source of the alabaster, the only alabaster mines working in the 1930s were those at Fauld. In Appendix M, Section 1 there is a photograph taken in the 1930s of a train emerging from the Fauld Mine with wagons containing three large blocks of alabaster. This photograph seems to have been specially posed and may well be the blocks for Jacob Epstein who at the time had his studio in Essex, as no other contemporary carver can be identified as taking such large blocks.

As regards the other mines and quarries, Chellaston appears to have ceased production during the First World War bringing to an end the Leicestershire bauble trade. However, the mines around Gotham continued to trade but only produced gypsum, with the exception of just one. The exception was the Kingston mine which encountered a seam of translucent alabaster that prompted the mine owner, Lord Belper, to open the Kingston Fine Arts Company. This traded from 1929 to 1936 (*see* Appendix M, Section 8). Kingston church, rebuilt in 1905, contains a reredos and font in Fauld alabaster but the curb edge to the font is in Kingston alabaster as is the plaque to one of the mine managers on the nave wall. Another Kingston alabaster plaque can be found in the chancel of nearby Thrumpton church. Kingston mine closed in 1963, all the Gotham area mines following soon after.

At Fauld, the section worked by Ford was taken over by the Ministry of War in the 1940s as a munitions dump. This dump exploded in 1944 (*see* Appendix M) producing a huge crater which today is a prohibited area due to unexploded ordinance. Although this put an end to the mineral extraction there, the nearby Staton mine was unaffected. This continues to trade today, but alabaster extraction ceased in the 1950s. This would seem to have ended English alabaster production. However, the discovery of Richard III's body in a Leicester car park in September 2012 and his subsequent burial in Leicester Cathedral meant that the cathedral's old altar had to be removed leading to the carving of a new one in Fauld alabaster by Northamptonshire carver James Elliott in 2015 (Appendix R, X41 and B195).

Elsewhere, Watchet alabaster continues to be collected in a small way for ornaments and church furniture inlay as does Penarth alabaster. The latter stone is red in hue and has mainly been used as rockery stone but the alabaster has been used in Roath (1870), Baglan (1875, X64), Kemberton, Shrops (1882, A143), Pontardawe church (1885, X71), Treochy church (1895), Cowbridge church (1896, X16), Llanfeiddan church (1896), Pen y Fai church (1900, X79), Caerphilly church (1902), Clydach church (1903) and Hopkinstown (1914). Penarth alabaster was also in Cardiff Empire Theatre but this has been demolished (*see* D9/111). George Eley Halliday and William Clark were instrumental in the use of Penarth alabaster.

Figure 45. James Elliott working on a block of Fauld alabaster in April 2015. Lying around are off-cuts of Wharfedale limestone used for Richard III's tomb. Photo: the author.

This brings to an end our story of some seven centuries of alabaster carving. There remains the need to discuss certain aspects of tomb-carving.

9
Armour and Knights

In 1600 there were 18 alabaster workshops at work, 10 in London, 3 in Burton/Nottingham, 2 in York, 1 in Cheshire, 1 in Sandon, Staffordshire and 1 in Dorset – up from 12 in 1566 of which only 3 were in London (*see* Timelines 3 and 4). This rose to 21 by 1630 but fell to 13 by the period end in 1670. The Trent Valley workshops had declined to the point that only the Hollemans workshop in Burton on Trent was a serious supplier of alabaster products and these were mainly supplied to customers in the East Midlands. Therefore London and the busy Baldwin workshops at Gloucester predominated. Diagram L (black M) shows that London workshops were trading all over England and many of the currently unidentified carvers of rural monuments may well be from this source. Transport had improved to the point that distribution was no longer tied to the rivers and coast although these continued to play their part.[1] As to the source of raw alabaster, this has to be the East Midlands and Yorkshire. At the beginning of the period Ledsham and Fairburn are recorded as working and possibly Chellaston although evidence for this is thin. The prime source, however, was Castle Hay and Fauld in Staffordshire. Thus these quarries may have supplied alabaster for some 400 to 500 monuments over 67 years. This is not an over large commitment being just five to seven monuments per year all of which may have been shipped through Hull.[2] In 1633 Watchet in Somerset joined the list of working Quarries.

The knightly effigy as a monument form survived long after knighthood ceased to have any military meaning. The knight effigy was common in Europe in the 12th century but not in England. The freestone effigy to Aubrey (or Alberie) de Vere now in St Stephen's Church, Bures, Suffolk is believed to date from 1141, but this remained one of the few until about 1270 when armoured effigies became more numerous. The location of these in monastic houses was the norm probably in memory of grants by the testator to the particular house. In the case of Aubrey de Vere's monument, it was found in a garden close to the site of Colne Priory in the 1920s. In the same church is the freestone effigy to Robert de Vere, 5th Earl of Oxford (Figure 46). It was formerly located in Colne Priory, later moved to the Tudor house built on the site and finally relocated to St Stephen's. By 1300 knightly effigies began to appear in cathedrals and churches. The material was Purbeck marble or freestone until about 1330 when alabaster made its first appearance. Temple Church in London has a fine collection of Purbeck marble effigies. Patrons found that the alabaster provided white stone or polychrome finish and fine detail at a reduced cost and therefore Purbeck fell out of favour.

Figure 46. The freestone effigy of Robert de Vere, 5th Earl of Oxford in Bures, St Stephen's Church, Suffolk. Carved *circa* 1296 and formerly in Colne Priory it shows the some of the features of the period. Although the legs are crossed the hands are in prayer and not sheathing the sword. The conventions of feet on an animal and head on a cushion supported by angels can be seen. Photo: Janet State.

The origin of the knight form has been identified with the popularity of men in armour on cathedral facades. Saul states that the early horizontal and vertical effigies have the same model. Gardner draws our attention to the similarity between the statues on Wells Cathedral and some West Country effigies but this is unproven. The transition from vertical to horizontal maintained the straight-legged format but at some point (possibly mid-13th century) the carvers introduced a novel form. The knight would have his legs crossed and his hand on the hilt of his sword, either in the process of drawing it or replacing it in the scabbard. In the case of the limestone effigy in Dorchester on Thames the angle of the hand on the hilt and the representation of movement would tend to indicate that the knight is drawing his sword but some effigies show a much more tranquil setting seeming to indicate the sheathing of the sword signifying 'crusading done'. Ultimately the hands were removed from the sword and placed in the prayer position as seen at Bures. The cross-legged style may have lost favour in the mid-14th century or the carvers may have found the crossed-leg style too problematical when using alabaster as only five in this material have survived, namely Bedale (14th century, A160), Westminster (1337, G18), Hanbury (1340, G28) and Wantage (1361, G1).

As the centuries progressed the detail and quality of the armour improved. That of the Earl of Warwick *circa* 1439 depicts fine Milanese armour in all its detail leading to the assumption that the carver had a set of armour on hand during carving. In some cases the armour depicted is many decades out of date for the period of the monument. Ralph Sacheverell's monument in Ratcliffe-on-Soar of 1539 (G136) depicts armour (and a hairstyle) more in keeping with a period some five decades earlier yet his lady has a decorated gable hood and gown fashionable in the first quarter of the 16th century. It can be speculated that the carver, probably from Burton on Trent, would not have seen a man in armour for years and may have had an old suit from the Wars of the Roses period which was used to provide the model whilst ladies in the latest fashion would be seen in Horninglow Street every day. On the other hand, Ralph's visage on his effigy is youthful with the conclusion that the carver may have wished to depict the testator in his prime with appropriate attire. The pauldron is not well-carved and has no visible articulation such that as it is shown, the knight would be unable to raise his arm.

Almost wholly absent on the alabaster monuments are the artefacts of chivalry, especially the war horse. The horse was vital to medieval knights and continued in importance for war well into the 19th century, yet its depiction on English monuments appears to have ceased about 1350, just as alabaster became popular, unlike the monuments in Europe. At the same time the martial deeds of knights appear also to have been omitted from inscriptions, which is unfortunate as we are left without a clear reason for why certain individuals received decorations that sometimes appear on effigies (*see* SS collars). One item of chivalry which did endure is that of the great helm. In the period to the mid-15th century the placing of a knight's head on a cushion was the norm but increasingly the laying of his head on a helm, often with an ornate crest, became the standard. The great helm is a remnant from the days when tournaments or tourneys were popular, knights often forming teams which were identified with crests of a certain design. Later in the 16th century, crests can be identified with the insignia of the family. In the case of Ratcliffe on Saor's Sacheverell family the goat crest was a play on origins of the name being based on the Norman word cheverall, or goat. In fact, all four monuments display great helms with the goat crest, but in the case of three effigies the only martial activity they took part in was the occasional muster. The depiction of armour seems to have taken a significant change part way through the 15th century. Before that time those depicted in armour were most likely to be aristocrats and knights of the realm whose use of armour was common. After that time the non-martial gentry who were major land owners were allowed to assume the distinction of armour on their memorials in recognition of their status as lords rather than knights. *See also* Appendix N.

10

Styles and Forms

As this book will reveal, it is impossible to examine the various monuments enumerated above without coming to the conclusion that the similarity in all the knightly effigies with orles can only be accounted for by their issue from such a common centre as the workshop of the Chellaston/Nottingham carvers, amongst which were Thomas Prentys and Robert Sutton. They had the alabaster at their doors, as a deposit of considerable thickness covering several square miles, and they, their predecessors and successors must have done a great trade in monumental sculpture. Appendix G lists the names of people in the alabaster trade.

It is evident that some of the most splendid alabaster tombs in England in the period to about 1560 were sent out from the Chellaston and Burton on Trent workshops, for it is tolerably certain that the carvers of the Lowick tomb also wrought the grand memorials of Thomas Earl of Arundel (*circa* 1416) and his countess at Arundel and of Henry IV and Queen Joan at Canterbury, both of whoms tombs are distinguished by similar 'gablettes' over the heads of the effigies. Gablettes can also be seen on the great tomb of Ralph Neville Earl of Westmorland (*circa* 1425) and his two wives at Staindrop, Durham, which is of the same design as King Henry's.

Meanwhile, there are other groups of tombs that clearly emanated from a common centre, which may also have been Chellaston/Burton but which Lawrence Stone suggests is London. One group contains the three Episcopal effigies of William Courtenay (G15, *circa* 1396) at Canterbury, William of Wykeham (G90, *circa* 1404) at Winchester, and Simon Langham (G20, *circa* 1376) at Westminster. The fine detail which includes the draping of the stem of the crosier and the angels who sit bolt upright with their wings trailing are a London feature and can also be seen on Bishop Sheppey's tomb at Rochester (A216, 1361) and on Bishop Ralph's tomb at Wells (G26, 1363). Another group includes the fine effigy of John Earl of Arundel (*circa* 1434), at Arundel, and the tomb at Canterbury with effigies of Margaret Holland (*circa* 1439) and her two husbands, John Earl of Somerset (*circa* 1408–1409), and Thomas Duke of Clarence (*circa* 1421).

Bedesmen

A small number of extant memorials contain bedesmen. The term means man of prayer from Old English 'bede', to pray. A bedesman in real life was pensioner or almsman who was paid to pray for the soul of his lord but in some quarters it became desirable to make provision for a permanent presence.

Bedesmen in some form appear randomly on three monuments from 1372 to 1416 but their form is variable. The 1425 Ralph Neville monument at Staindrop (G104) included two clerks at desks at the foot of the effigy in place of the usual animal. The reason is not altogether clear but may well be associated with the founding of a chapel. This form is not known to have been repeated.

There are 25 further extant monuments which contain bedesmen in two forms. One form is contained in niches on the tomb chest and the other as small figures at the feet of the effigy either on or by the side of the animal or sitting on the tomb chest.

There is consensus that the Staindrop memorial was carved in the Trent Valley and a strong suspicion that all the other 25 were likewise carved in this location making bedesmen a very East Midlands feature.

Those at Norbury (1483, G62), Strelley (1501, G139), Callington (1503, G54), Harewood (1510, G206) and Godshill (1522, G91) have the bedesman astride or sideways sitting on an animal whilst Lowick (1498, G123), Westminster (1506, G117) and Chichester (1536, G169) have them appearing from the sole of the feet. At Stanton Harcourt (1490, G141) and Prestwold (1520, G110) the bedesmen appear sitting in niches on the tomb chest.

Figure 47. The bedesman on the tomb chest at Prestwold, Leicestershire. Although the effigies are *circa* 1520 (G110) the chest is believed to have been formerly a tabletop tomb of 1487. Photo: Janet State.

Bedesmen are not common on continental tombs but that of Bishop Ramon d'Escales (died 1398) in the Basilica de Santa Maria del Mar in Barcelona (*see* Figure 112 and Appendix M, Section 13) has eight fine bedesmen carved on the tomb chest. The bedesmen on this can be compared to that at Prestwold shown above.

11
Retables, Carved Tablets and Images

11.1 Altarpieces

There can be no finer reference source for these than Francis Cheetham's books especially *Alabaster Images of Medieval England* written in 2003 and hence I will not deal with these in detail. What Cheetham describes is the form and style of the tablets, with many illustrations, and this book is commended to the researcher.

However, it is necessary to give an outline of the trade here and say where examples can be found. The altarpiece for Edward III at Windsor in 1367 clearly defines the start of the trade and the creation of this is described in Section 7.2 above. From that time until 1550 the population of tablets probably runs into the thousands. Many of these were exported to places as far flung as Iceland, Spain and Germany. A Danish Commission on Archaeology reports that in 1450 they could count 79 retables and images in 43 Danish churches and it is safe to assume these were from the Nottingham school. There is an altarpiece in Santiago de Compostela, Spain, a gift of an English priest John Goodyear in 1456, one in the Victoria and Albert Museum known as the Swansea Altarpiece and one in Montréal, Languedoc, France.

The latter is described below:

The Carved Retable of Montréal, Languedoc, France

In the Church of Our Lady in Montréal, France there is a retable (wooden screen holding paintings or carved tablets) which is a triptych (central panel with hinged side panels). Formerly over the altar the retable is housed in an alcove at the side of the choir. The history of the church claims that the alabaster carvings came from Nottingham during the Hundred Years War (1337 to 1453). In 1971 the central three carved panels were stolen but two remain both depicting the life of the Virgin Mary. This retable may give some indication as to the detail of the Windsor reredos.

Figure 48. The retable showing the three carvings in the centre replaced by photographs. Photo: the author.

Figure 49 (left). The Virgin Mary as a maiden welcomes Gabriel (kneeling). Photo: the author
Figure 50 (right). Mary being crowned represented as an old woman. Legend has it she lived in Ephesus up to the age of 60 years. Photo: the author.

These carved alabaster panels are contemporary with those carved for Windsor and indicate the type of work carried out by Nottingham kervers in the late 14th and early 15th century. *See* Thoroton Volume XI 1908 flyleaf for photograph of the Montréal altarpiece *before* the centre panels were stolen.

Almost all the population of English tablets were destroyed in the 16th century (*see* Appendix H), but a few remain outside of museums. A list of the ones of which I am aware is included below:

Place	Subject
Abinger, Surrey, St James	Crucifixion. This survived a direct hit from a V1
Barkway, Herts	Group of fragments found in east wall
Barling, Essex	Statue of Virgin walled up in north aisle
Bletchingley, Surrey, St Mary the Virgin	Adoration of the Magi. Has a very nice 1870 reredos by Street
Blyth, Nottinghamshire	Painted slabs
Canterbury, Kent, St Mary's Elham	St Thomas
Carlton in Lindrick, Nottinghamshire	Painted sculpture of Trinity now in private hands
Chessington, Surrey, St Mary the Virgin	Annunciation once part of a retable. The local history dates this to 1376
Coddenham, Suffolk, St Mary	Crucifixion. Found walled up in a Tudor cottage in the village and restored to the rood screen
Drayton, Berks	Parts of reredos
East Rudham, Norfolk, St Mary probably the best collection in a parish church	The Annunciation, St John, Crucifixion, Coronation of the Virgin, St Anthony, St John the Baptist. Fragments. It is believed these were buried in the wall at one time and found in 1871
Haddon Hall, Derbyshire. Imported from Europe	Mocking of Christ
Hawley Hampshire	Betrayal
Horton on Trym, Gloucs	Figures
Lydiate RC church, Lancashire	St Catherine and St Cuthbert formerly in the chapel of Lydiate Hall. These are mounted in the pulpit
Milton, Cambs	Figure of St Leonard found in wall
Naworth Castle, Cumbria	St Oswald formerly in Lancercost Priory
North Leverton, Lincs	A panel found in the rood loft the current location unknown
Norwich, Norfolk, Cathedral,	Angels
Norwich, Norfolk, St Peter Mancroft	Female Saints.
Norwich, Norfolk, St Stephen's Chapel	Prophets formerly part of reredos
Nottingham, St Mary's Church	St Thomas
Sandy, Bedfordshire	Figurines
Shrewsbury, Salop, St Mary's	Trinity
Stewkely, Buckingham, St Michael's and All Angels	Remnant of retable may have been reformed 1867. There is also 15th century pieta of the Virgin and Child which was found in the chancel
Upton, Bucks	14th-century sculpture of the trinity found in north wall
Wells Cathedral, Somerset	Annunciation
Willoughby on the Wolds, Nottinghamshire	Panel in a 15th-century tomb chest
Wimborne Minster, Dorset	Parts of a reredos panel found in chancel
Workington, Cumbria, The Priory	Crucifixion and Ascension
Yarnton, Oxford, St Bartholomew	Adoration of the Magi formerly found at St Edmund Hall, Oxford. These 15th-century tablets have been fitted into a reredos but one was sent to the British Museum and one to the Victoria and Albert Museum in London

John the Baptist tablets are in Leicester City Museum, Worcester Cathedral and National Museum of Iceland. For the best collection of medieval panels the reader is directed to the V&A Museum and the Castle Museum in Nottingham.

11.2 Images

As stated elsewhere the existence of carved alabaster images in England from the 15th and 16th century is almost non-existent. The images recovered from the abandoned Church of St Peter at Flawford,[1] Nottinghamshire are described in Appendix H and these remain three of the few complete examples of medieval image-making unless more images are found hidden in the future.

It is clear that congregations were unhappy about the destruction of their church icons and Flawford is not the only example of the actions of worshippers to hide them from Edward VI's commissioners. In the list above, the tablet at Coddenham was found hidden in a cottage but there are others. In 1930 a number of alabaster figures and panels were found outside St Helen's Church in the village of Thorganby, North Yorkshire, now in the Yorkshire Museum. The fragments comprise three figures which were believed to be freestanding and two altar panels. Similar fragments are also reported from Skipwith, a short distance away from Thorganby, but here they may represent a destroyed retable rather than one dismantled.

There are other finds in or around country churches. The church at East Rudham, Blunham in Bedfordshire, Preston in Lancashire and at Whittlesford, Cambridgeshire have all yielded remains of buried icons. See the paper by William Anderson for further finds of hidden medieval alabasters (Appendix A).

For details of the Flawford images, *see Medieval English Alabaster Carvings in Nottingham Castle* by Francis W Cheetham, 1962 and *Unearthed* by the same author.

Notes:

1. There is dispute as to whether the village is Flawford or Flawforth. Certainly the adjacent road is Flawforth Lane, but at the time of writing this matter has not be settled.

12

Conclusion

The previous chapters of this book give the history of the carving of alabaster. From the 14th century, the mineral was seen as a substitute for Purbeck marble, being easier to carve and probably less expensive and better than freestone. The purpose of the monuments has been described and this took a shock in the mid-16th century at the Reformation. Notwithstanding that, the monument industry soldiered on but with a change of emphasis towards the celebration of the person depicted rather than to encourage prayers for the soul.

The peak years were in the late 16th and early 17th centuries before the trade came to a sudden and abrupt halt around 1670. This can be attributed to the Restoration and the introduction of marble. The early 17th-century tombs vary greatly in quality and have a style which can become tedious. However, the period saw some of the most colourful tombs that have ever been seen in England.

The wilderness years of the 18th century saw yet another change in that alabaster was seen as being suitable for decoration of stately houses before descending yet again into obscurity. The Gothic Revival reawakened interest in alabaster and it can be said that what the period lacks in numbers is matched by the quality of the 19th and 20th-century carvers.

In the latter years alabaster has been seen as suitable for baubles, domestic trinkets and inlays until this, too, became unfashionable. The latest adventure has been the 2015 altar at Leicester which not only shows the Fauld alabaster in its true colours but the design is unique since it enables the alter to be moved on wheels. I will leave this to be described by James Elliott himself in his presentations and future book.

The remaining sections of this book are individual essays on aspects of the alabaster trade and disciplines which affected the prosecution of the trade.

It only leaves me to thank the reader for their patience and attention.

GALLERY

Figure 11: The Inscription on Henry Sacheverell's tomb at Ratcliffe on Soar.

Figure 13. A very early mural from 1376 at Bakewell, Derbyshire.

Figure 14. Chillingham church, Northumberland.

Figure 15. The end of a tomb in Chillingham, Northumberland.

Figure 16. The 1510 tomb of Edward Redman in Harewood.

Figure 17. The 1518 tomb to Thomas Babyngton in Ashover.

Figure 18. The unknown 1520 tomb in Prestwold church, Leicestershire.

Figure 19. The 1521 tomb to Sir Randal Brereton in Malpas church.

Figure 20. Detail of Eleanor Brereton in Malpas church.

Figure 21. Ralph Sacheverell's tomb of 1539 in Ratcliffe on Soar.

Figure 22. Detail of the inscription on Ralph Sacheverell's tomb.

Figure 23. Sir Richard Cholmondeley's tomb in the Tower of London.

The Foljambe mural in Chesterfield church:

Figure 24. Left

Figure 25. Centre

Figure 26. Right

Figure 27. An early mural of 1564 in the Tower of London.

Figure 29. The tomb to Cecily Sandys in Woodham Ferrers church, Essex.

Figure 30. The tomb of 1624 to Henry Bellasis in York Minster.

Figure 31. The tomb of 1625 to Henry Sacheverell in Ratcliffe on Soar.

Figure 32. The head and shoulders of Lucy Sacheverell in Ratcliffe on Soar.

Figure 33. The head and shoulders of the wife of William St Andrew's in Gotham.

Figure 34. The tomb to Sir William Skipwith
in Prestwold church, Leicestershire.

Figure 35. The tomb of the Earl of Surrey in Framlingham church, Suffolk.

Figure 36. The Baldwin tomb of Elizabeth Williams in Gloucester Cathedral.

Figure 37. The head of the wife of Thomas Machen in Gloucester Cathedral.

Figure 39. A typical wall tablet in Owthorpe church.

Figure 40. Ordsall, Nottinghamshire. A wall monument showing a small effigy.

Figure 41. The Marble Hall at Kedleston, Derbyshire.

Figure 42. A chimney piece at Newstead Abbey.

Figure 43. A war memorial in Brockelsby Church, Lincolnshire.

Timelines

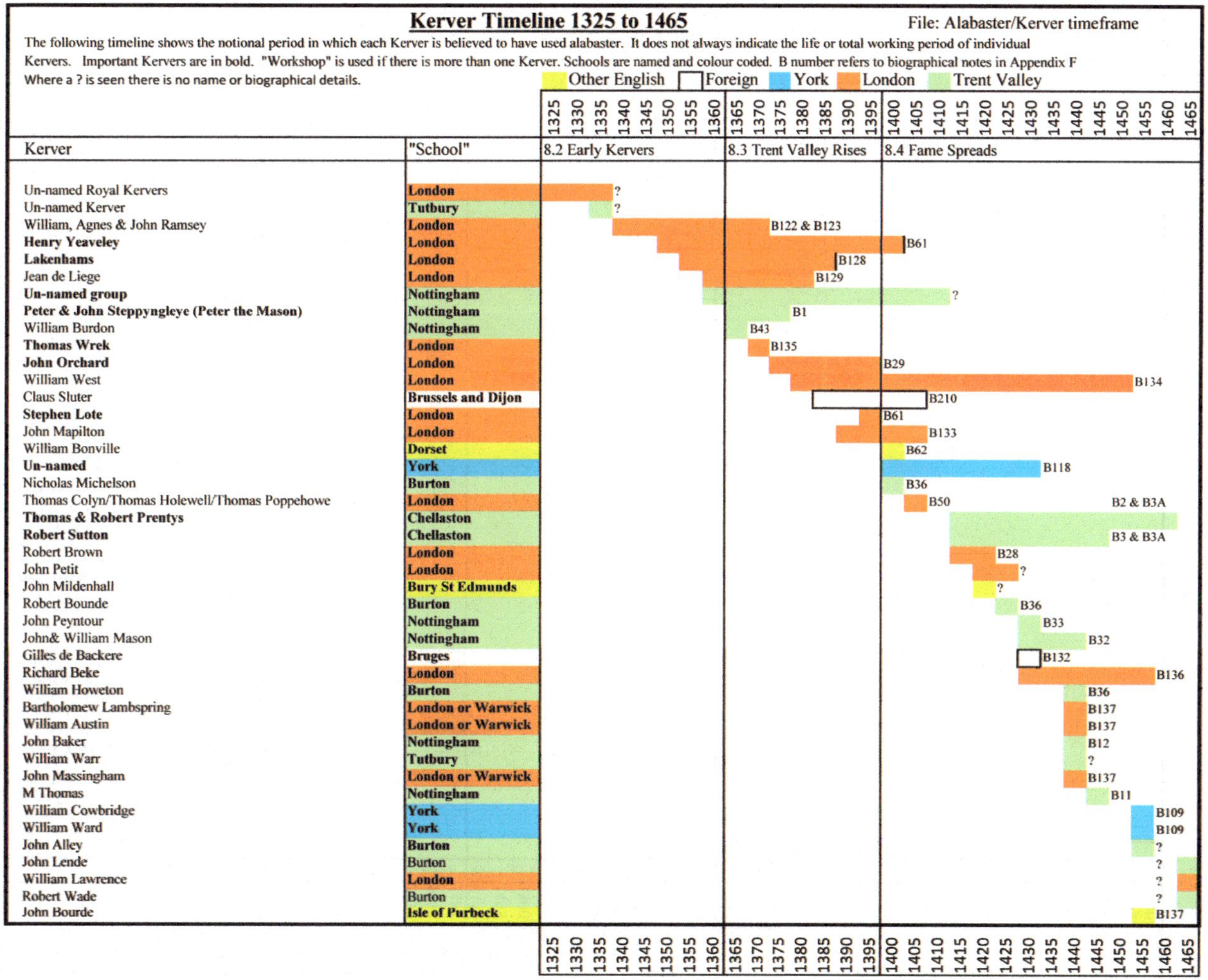
Kerver Timeline 1325 to 1465
File: Alabaster/Kerver timeframe
The following timeline shows the notional period in which each Kerver is believed to have used alabaster. It does not always indicate the life or total working period of individual Kervers. Important Kervers are in bold. "Workshop" is used if there is more than one Kerver. Schools are named and colour coded. B number refers to biographical notes in Appendix F
Where a ? is seen there is no name or biographical details.
Other English
Foreign
York
London
Trent Valley
1325 1330 1335 1340 1345 1350 1355 1360 1365 1370 1375 1380 1385 1390 1395 1400 1405 1410 1415 1420 1425 1430 1435 1440 1445 1450 1455 1460 1465
Kerver
"School"
8.2 Early Kervers
8.3 Trent Valley Rises
8.4 Fame Spreads
Un-named Royal Kervers London ?
Un-named Kerver Tutbury ?
William, Agnes & John Ramsey London B122 & B123
Henry Yeaveley London B61
Lakenhams London B128
Jean de Liege London B129
Un-named group Nottingham ?
Peter & John Steppyngleye (Peter the Mason) Nottingham B1
William Burdon Nottingham B43
Thomas Wrek London B135
John Orchard London B29
William West London B134
Claus Sluter Brussels and Dijon B210
Stephen Lote London B61
John Mapilton London B133
William Bonville Dorset B62
Un-named York B118
Nicholas Michelson Burton B36
Thomas Colyn/Thomas Holewell/Thomas Poppehowe London B50
Thomas & Robert Prentys Chellaston B2 & B3A
Robert Sutton Chellaston B3 & B3A
Robert Brown London B28
John Petit London ?
John Mildenhall Bury St Edmunds ?
Robert Bounde Burton B36
John Peyntour Nottingham B33
John& William Mason Nottingham B32
Gilles de Backere Bruges B132
Richard Beke London B136
William Howeton Burton B36
Bartholomew Lambspring London or Warwick B137
William Austin London or Warwick B137
John Baker Nottingham B12
William Warr Tutbury ?
John Massingham London or Warwick B137
M Thomas Nottingham B11
William Cowbridge York B109
William Ward York B109
John Alley Burton ?
John Lende Burton ?
William Lawrence London ?
Robert Wade Burton ?
John Bourde Isle of Purbeck B137
1325 1330 1335 1340 1345 1350 1355 1360 1365 1370 1375 1380 1385 1390 1395 1400 1405 1410 1415 1420 1425 1430 1435 1440 1445 1450 1455 1460 1465

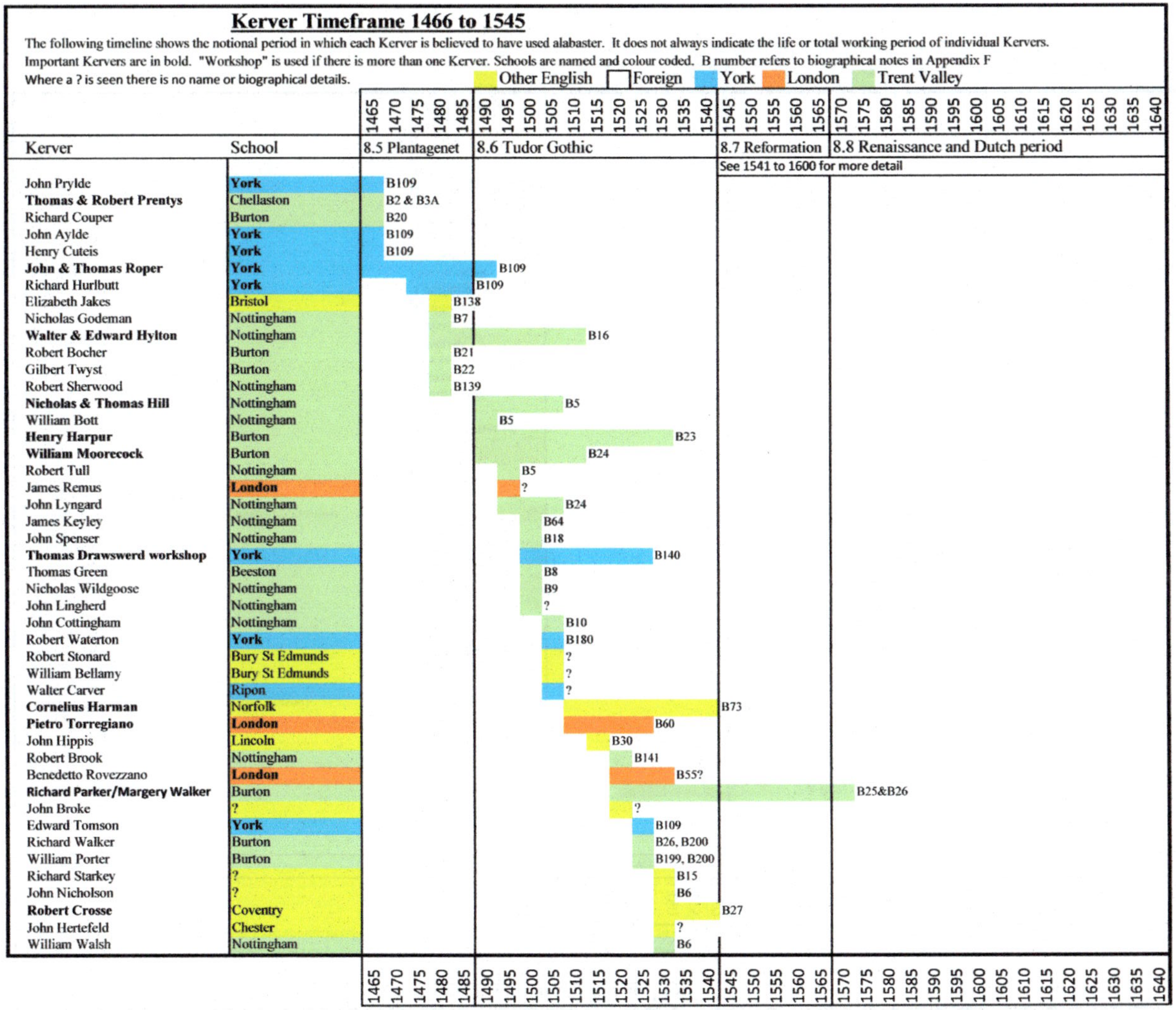
Kerver Timeframe 1466 to 1545
The following timeline shows the notional period in which each Kerver is believed to have used alabaster. It does not always indicate the life or total working period of individual Kervers.
Important Kervers are in bold. "Workshop" is used if there is more than one Kerver. Schools are named and colour coded. B number refers to biographical notes in Appendix F
Where a ? is seen there is no name or biographical details.
Other English
Foreign
York
London
Trent Valley
1465 1470 1475 1480 1485 1490 1495 1500 1505 1510 1515 1520 1525 1530 1535 1540 1545 1550 1555 1560 1565 1570 1575 1580 1585 1590 1595 1600 1605 1610 1615 1620 1625 1630 1635 1640
Kerver
School
8.5 Plantagenet
8.6 Tudor Gothic
8.7 Reformation
8.8 Renaissance and Dutch period
See 1541 to 1600 for more detail
John Prylde York B109
Thomas & Robert Prentys Chellaston B2 & B3A
Richard Couper Burton B20
John Aylde York B109
Henry Cuteis York B109
John & Thomas Roper York B109
Richard Hurlbutt York B109
Elizabeth Jakes Bristol B138
Nicholas Godeman Nottingham B7
Walter & Edward Hylton Nottingham B16
Robert Bocher Burton B21
Gilbert Twyst Burton B22
Robert Sherwood Nottingham B139
Nicholas & Thomas Hill Nottingham B5
William Bott Nottingham B5
Henry Harpur Burton B23
William Moorecock Burton B24
Robert Tull Nottingham B5
James Remus London ?
John Lyngard Nottingham B24
James Keyley Nottingham B64
John Spenser Nottingham B18
Thomas Drawswerd workshop York B140
Thomas Green Beeston B8
Nicholas Wildgoose Nottingham B9
John Lingherd Nottingham ?
John Cottingham Nottingham B10
Robert Waterton York B180
Robert Stonard Bury St Edmunds ?
William Bellamy Bury St Edmunds ?
Walter Carver Ripon ?
Cornelius Harman Norfolk B73
Pietro Torregiano London B60
John Hippis Lincoln B30
Robert Brook Nottingham B141
Benedetto Rovezzano London B55?
Richard Parker/Margery Walker Burton B25&B26
John Broke ? ?
Edward Tomson York B109
Richard Walker Burton B26, B200
William Porter Burton B199, B200
Richard Starkey ? B15
John Nicholson ? B6
Robert Crosse Coventry B27
John Hertefeld Chester ?
William Walsh Nottingham B6

Kerver Timeframe 1546 to 1602

The following timeline shows the notional period in which each Kerver is believed to have used alabaster. It does not always indicate the life or total working period of individual Kervers. Kervers. Important Kervers are in bold. "Workshop" is used if there is more than one Kerver. Schools are named and colour coded. B number refers to biographical notes in Appendix F

Where a ? is seen there is no name or biographical details.

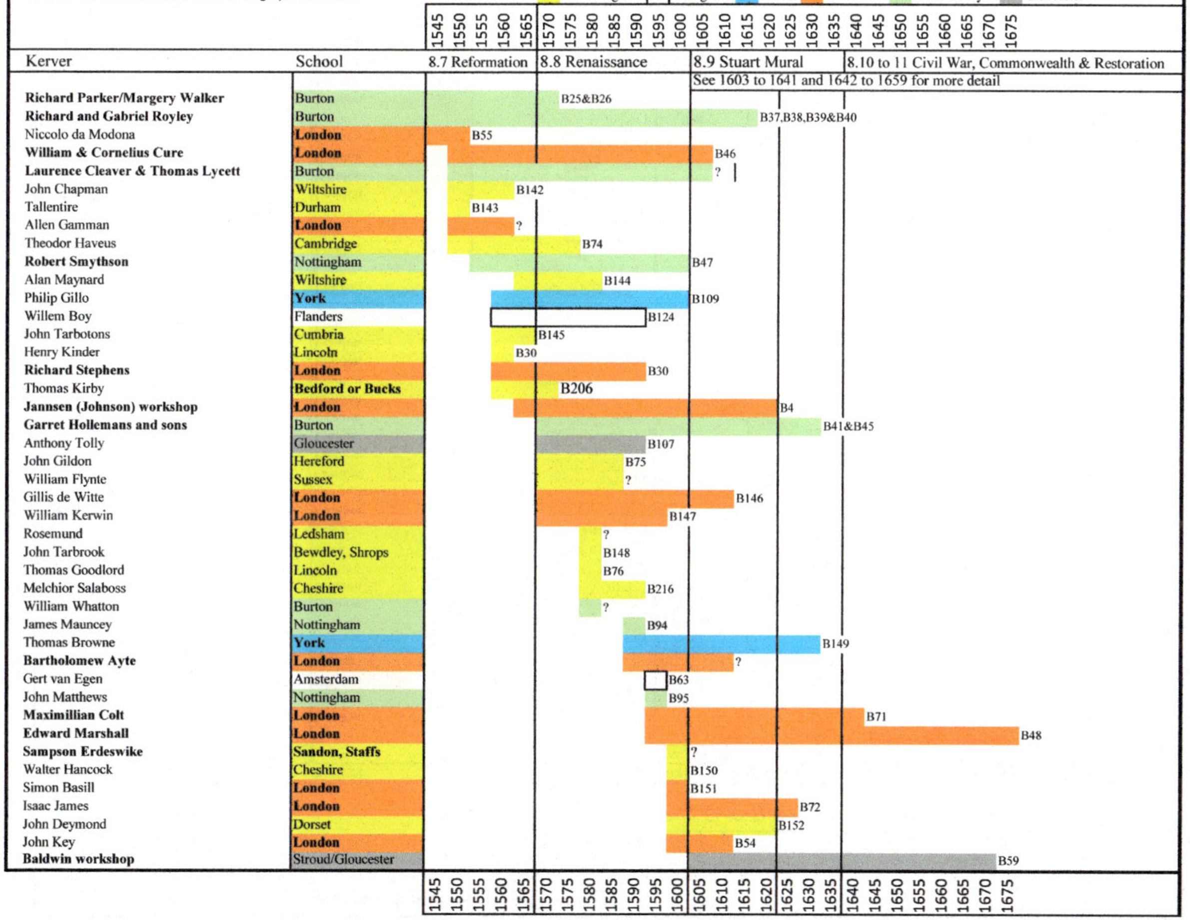

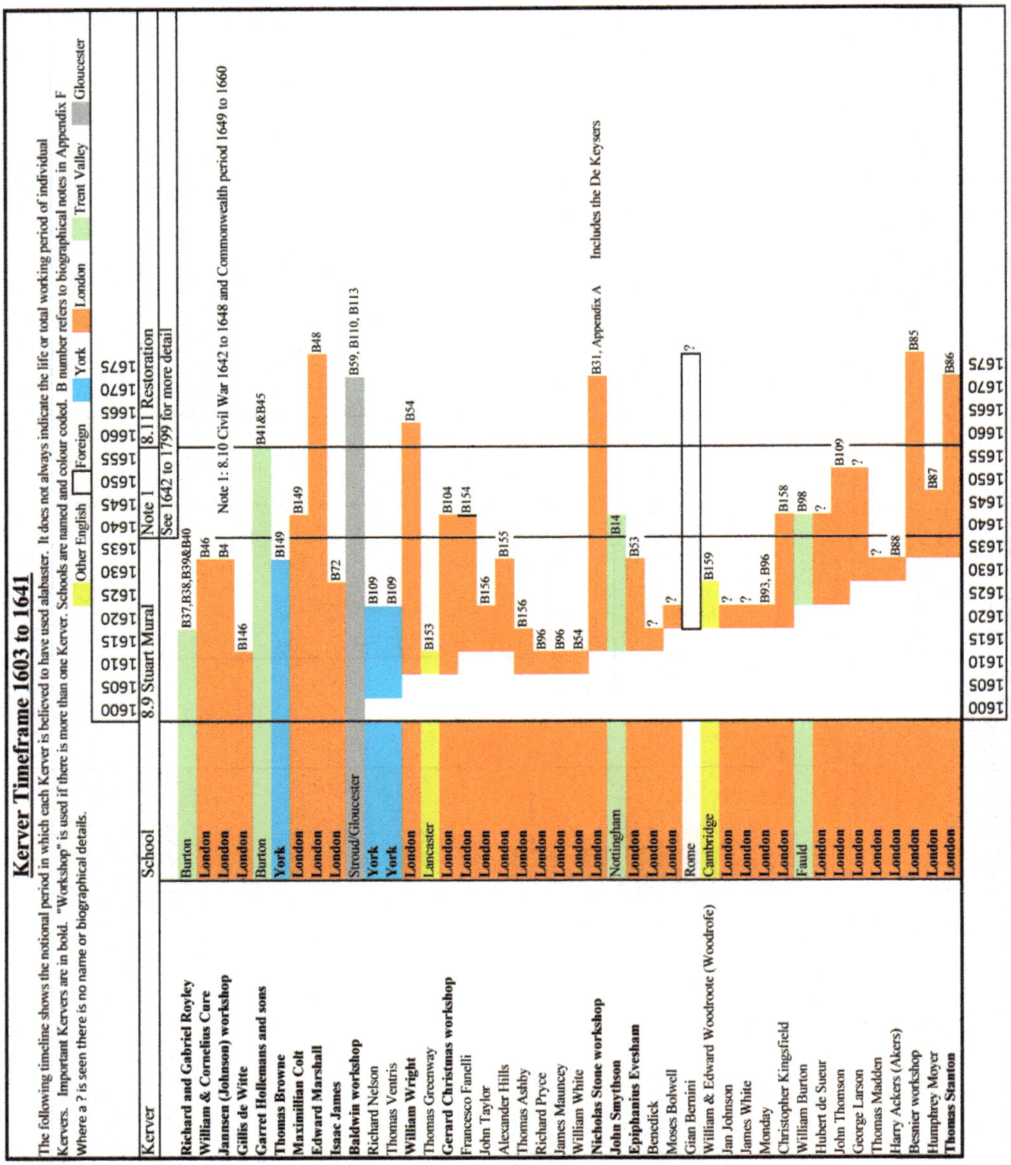
Kerver Timeframe 1603 to 1641
The following timeline shows the notional period in which each Kerver is believed to have used alabaster. It does not always indicate the life or total working period of individual Kervers. Important Kervers are in bold. "Workshop" is used if there is more than one Kerver. Schools are named and colour coded. B number refers to biographical notes in Appendix F
Where a ? is seen there is no name or biographical details.
Other English
Foreign
York
London
Trent Valley
Gloucester
Kerver
School
8.9 Stuart Mural
Note 1
8.11 Restoration
See 1642 to 1799 for more detail
Note 1: 8.10 Civil War 1642 to 1648 and Commonwealth period 1649 to 1660
Includes the De Keysers
Richard and Gabriel Royley
William & Cornelius Cure
Jannsen (Johnson) workshop
Gillis de Witte
Garret Hollemans and sons
Thomas Browne
Maximillian Colt
Edward Marshall
Isaac James
Baldwin workshop
Richard Nelson
Thomas Ventris
William Wright
Thomas Greenway
Gerard Christmas workshop
Francesco Fanelli
John Taylor
Alexander Hills
Thomas Ashby
Richard Pryce
James Mauncey
William White
Nicholas Stone workshop
John Smythson
Epiphanius Evesham
Benedick
Moses Bolwell
Gian Bernini
William & Edward Woodroote (Woodrofe)
Jan Johnson
James White
Monday
Christopher Kingsfield
William Burton
Hubert de Sueur
John Thomson
George Larson
Thomas Madden
Harry Ackers (Akers)
Besnier workshop
Humphrey Moyer
Thomas Stanton
Burton
London
York
Stroud/Gloucester
Lancaster
Nottingham
Rome
Cambridge
Fauld
B37,B38,B39&B40
B46
B4
B146
B41&B45
B149
B48
B72
B59, B110, B113
B109
B54
B153
B104
B154
B156
B155
B96
B31, Appendix A
B14
B53
B159
B93, B96
B158
B98
B88
B85
B87
B86
1600
1605
1610
1615
1620
1625
1630
1635
1640
1645
1650
1655
1660
1665
1670
1675

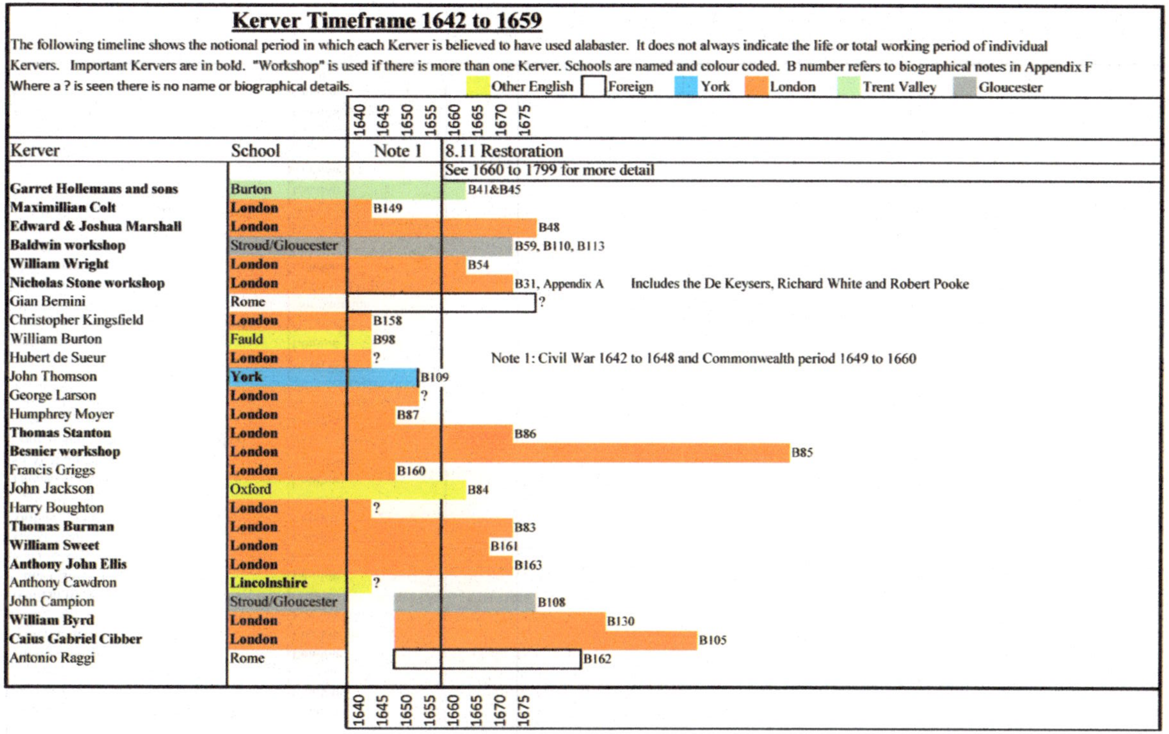
Kerver Timeframe 1642 to 1659
The following timeline shows the notional period in which each Kerver is believed to have used alabaster. It does not always indicate the life or total working period of individual Kervers. Important Kervers are in bold. "Workshop" is used if there is more than one Kerver. Schools are named and colour coded. B number refers to biographical notes in Appendix F
Where a ? is seen there is no name or biographical details.
Other English
Foreign
York
London
Trent Valley
Gloucester
1640 1645 1650 1655 1660 1665 1670 1675
Kerver
School
Note 1
8.11 Restoration
See 1660 to 1799 for more detail
Garret Hollemans and sons
Burton
B41&B45
Maximillian Colt
London
B149
Edward & Joshua Marshall
London
B48
Baldwin workshop
Stroud/Gloucester
B59, B110, B113
William Wright
London
B54
Nicholas Stone workshop
London
B31, Appendix A
Includes the De Keysers, Richard White and Robert Pooke
Gian Bernini
Rome
?
Christopher Kingsfield
London
B158
William Burton
Fauld
B98
Hubert de Sueur
London
?
Note 1: Civil War 1642 to 1648 and Commonwealth period 1649 to 1660
John Thomson
York
B109
George Larson
London
?
Humphrey Moyer
London
B87
Thomas Stanton
London
B86
Besnier workshop
London
B85
Francis Griggs
London
B160
John Jackson
Oxford
B84
Harry Boughton
London
?
Thomas Burman
London
B83
William Sweet
London
B161
Anthony John Ellis
London
B163
Anthony Cawdron
Lincolnshire
?
John Campion
Stroud/Gloucester
B108
William Byrd
London
B130
Caius Gabriel Cibber
London
B105
Antonio Raggi
Rome
B162
1640 1645 1650 1655 1660 1665 1670 1675

Kerver Timeframe 1660 to 1799

The following timeline shows the notional period in which each Kerver is believed to have used alabaster. It does not always indicate the life or total working period of individual Kervers. Important Kervers are in bold. "Workshop" is used if there is more than one Kerver. Schools are named and colour coded. B number refers to biographical notes in Appendix F. Where a ? is seen there is no name or biographical details.

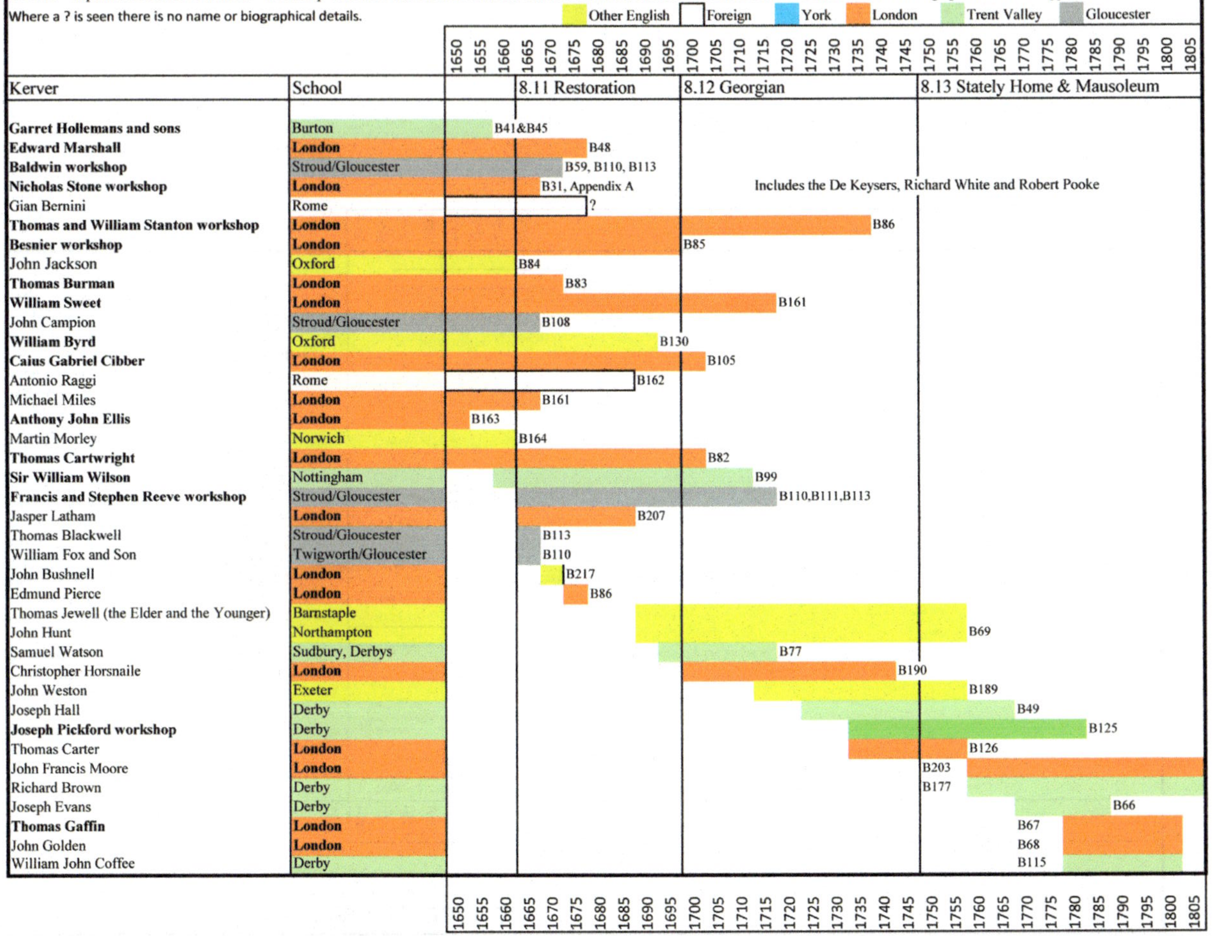

Kerver Timeframe 1800 to 1899

The following timeline shows the notional period in which each Kerver is believed to have used alabaster. It does not always indicate the life or total working period of individual Kervers. Important Kervers are in bold. "Workshop" is used if there is more than one Kerver. Schools are named and colour coded. B number refers to biographical notes in Appendix F

Where a ? is seen there is no name or biographical details.

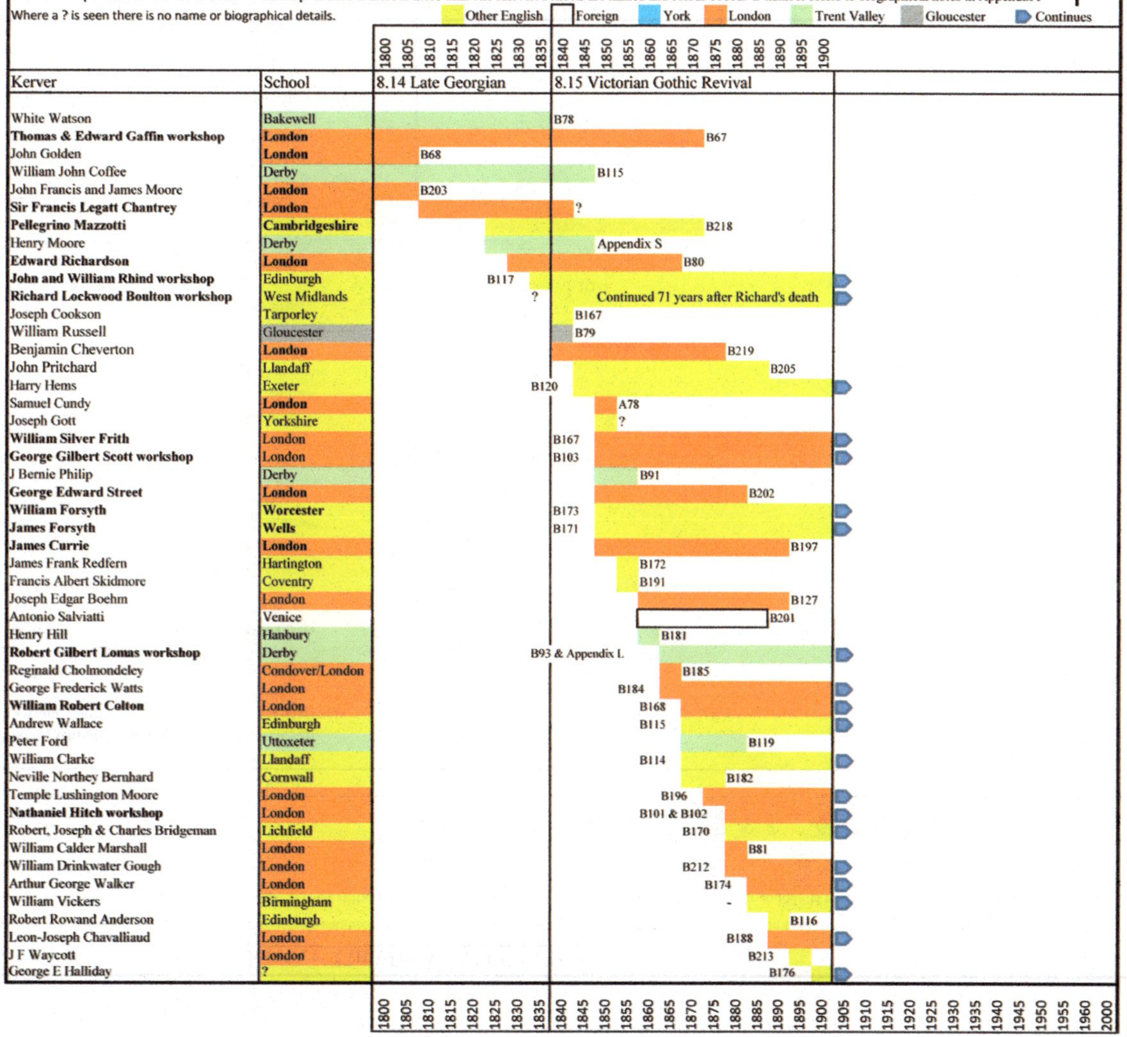

Kerver Timeframe 1900 to Date

The following timeline shows the notional period in which each Kerver is believed to have used alabaster. It does not always indicate the life or total working period of individual Kervers. Important Kervers are in bold. "Workshop" is used if there is more than one Kerver. Schools are named and colour coded. B number refers to biographical notes in Appendix F Where a ? is seen there is no name or biographical details.

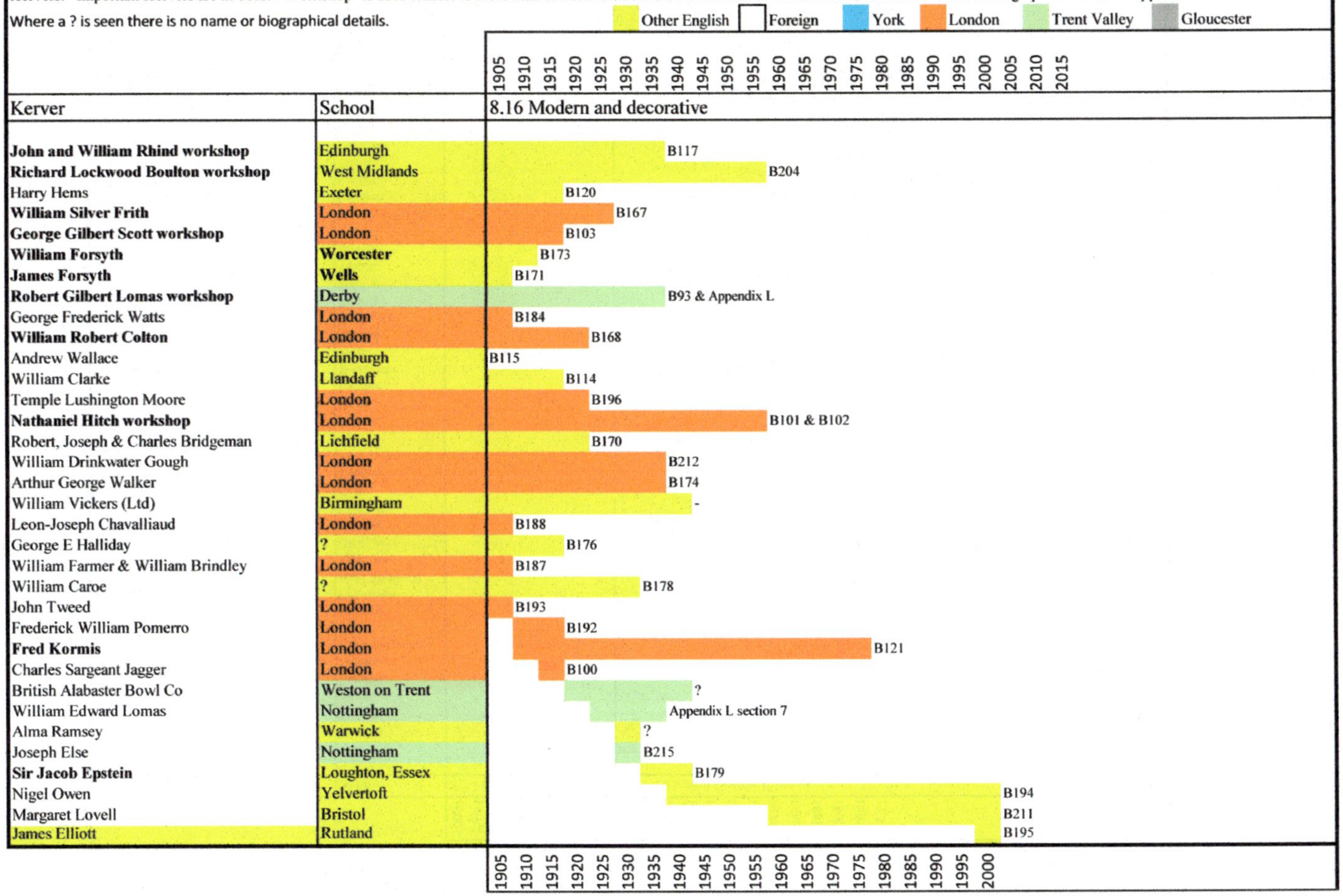

Appendix A
Bibliography

Alabaster Sources

Bray, A (1951). *Gypsum and Alabaster in Staffordshire.* Mine and Quarry Engineer, issue 17, pages 239-333

Cooper, A H (1996). *Technical Report WA/96/30 – Gypsum: Geology, Quarrying, Mining and Geological Hazards in the Chellaston and Aston-on-Trent Areas*

Cranstone, David (2007). *Whitehaven Coast Archaeological Survey.* Consultants for the National Trust, June 2007

Farey, J (1811). *A General View of the Agriculture and Minerals of Derbyshire – Vol 1*

Firman, R J (1984). *Geological Approach to the History of English Alabaster.* Mercian Geologist, Vol 9, March 1984, page 161 to 178

Firman R J (1991). *Gypsum in Nottinghamshire.* Peak District Mines History Society, winter 1991, pages 189 to 203

Firman R J (1964). *Gypsum Working in the Parish of Orston, Nottinghamshire*, Peak District Mines History Society, October 1964, pages 167 to 182, and 189 to 203

Forbes, B G. *Folded Permian Gypsum of Rippon Parks, Yorkshire.* Proceedings Yorkshire Geological Society, Vol 31, pages 351 to 358

Gerard, Thomas (1632). *The Particular Description of the County of Somerset.* Somerset Record Society, Vol 15, 1900, page 12. It appears that Thomas Gerard was aware of the writings of William Burton but it seems unlikely they were friends. Gerard was also a follower of Leland's work. Gerard died in 1634

Hewitt, E M. *Gypsum or Alabaster and Industries Except Coalmining.* Victoria History of the County of Nottingham, Vol 2, pages 319 to 324 and 330 to 370

Jenkins, David (1973). *The History of BPB Industries.* British Plasterboard Company history

King, William (1850). *Guide to Port Hamilton and Fleswick Beach.* Edited by Joseph Hodgson (Putty Joe) of Whitehaven

Kloppmann, Wolfram (2013) with L. Leroux, P. Bromblet, C. Guerrot, E. Proust, A. H. Cooper, N. Worley, S.-A. Smeds, H. Bengtsson. *Tracing Medieval and Renaissance Alabaster Works of Art Back to Quarries: A Multi-Isotope (Sr, S, O) Approach.* Article first published online: Archaeometry Journal, 20 Jan, 2013

Laid, F C (1810). *A Typographical and Historical Description of Nottinghamshire.* London

Lowe, Robert (1794). *Board of Agriculture's Report entitled 'A General View of the Agriculture of the County of Nottingham'*

Plot, Robert (1686). *A Natural History of Staffordshire 1686.* Keeper of the Ashmolean Museum, Oxford

Taylor, S T (1983). *Datable Stable Isotope Study of the Mercian Mudstones.* Sedimentology, Vol 30, pages 11 to 31

Trafford-Wynne, T (1907). *Gypsum and Its Occurrence in the Dove Valley.* Transactions of the Institute of Mining Engineers, Vol 32, pages 171 to 192

Vellacott, C H (1912). *Quarrying Section from The Victorian History of the County of York*, Vol 2 page 380

Woodward, H B (1906). *A History of the County of Somerset.* Section on geology, Vol 1, pages 1 to 33

Young, John (1990). *Alabaster.* Issued by Chellaston History Group, 1990. ISBN 0 906753 18 X

Carvers and sculptors

Badham, Sally and Oosterwijk, Sally (2010). *Monumental Industry: The Production of Tomb Monuments in England and Wales in the Long 14th Century.* ISBN 978-I-907730-00-9 (Seven extant contracts)

Bayliss, Jon (1993). *A Dutch Carver, Garrett Hollemans I in England.* Church Monuments Society, 1993, Vol 8

Bayliss, Jon (1991). *Richard and Gabriel Royley of Burton on Trent, Tomb Makers.* Church Monuments Society, 1991, Vol 6

Bilson, John, F.S.A (1907). *A French Purchase of Alabaster in 1414. A* paper in the Archaeological Journal (vol. IXIV. 32–37)

Broome, John (1995). *Samuel Baldwin – Carver of Gloucester.* Church Monument Society, 1995

Cheetham, Francis (2001). *The Alabaster Men: Sacred Images From Medieval England.* London: Daniel Katz Ltd

Christian, R (1959). *Alabaster Industry in the Trent Valley.* Derbyshire Countryside, Vol 24, pages 14 to 16

Gardner, Arthur (1951). *English Medieval Sculpture.* (730.941)

Gunnis (2009). *Biographical Dictionary of British Sculptors 1660 to 1851.* A revised work of the *Dictionary of British Sculptors* by Gunnis revised by Ingrid Roscoe, Emma Hardy and M G Sullivan, ISBN 9780300149654. Published 2009. Also the Henry Moore database

Kettle, Ann J (2008). *A List of Families in the Archdeaconry of Stafford 1532–33.* Staffordshire Records Society 1976, reprinted 2008

Newham, C B (2013). *Book of Effigies and Book of Effigies II.* ISBN 978-1-906265-20-5 and 2014, ISBN 978-1-906265-21-2

Ramsey, Nigel. *English Medieval Industries: Craftsmen, Techniques and Products – Alabaster*

St John Hope, William Henry (1913). *Early Working of Alabaster.* Possibly published 1904, for the Society of Antiquaries (British Library 001730240)

Walpole Society Publications

Volume 21, 1932–1933, J G Mann – *English Church Monuments 1536 to 1625*

Volume 7, 1918–1919, Walter Lewis Spiers – *The Notebook and Account book of Nicholas Stone* (http://archive.org/details/volumeofwalpoles07walpuoft)

White, Adam (1999). *A Biographical Dictionary of London Tomb Sculptors 1560 to 1660.* Walpole Society, Vol 61 pages 1 to 163

Carving Style

Anderson, William (2004). *Rediscovery, Collecting and Display of English Medieval Alabasters.* A paper to The Journal of the History of Collections

Antiquarian Transactions. Pre-Reformation effigies in Cheshire, Claude Blair, Lancs and Cheshire Society, Vol 60

Medieval effigies in the County of Durham, Claude Blair,

Medieval effigies in the County of Northumberland

Badham, Sally (2011). *Medieval Church and Churchyard Monuments*. ISBN 9780747808107

Beasley, S M (1978). *The Attribution of Alabaster Tomb Carvings to Schools.* A thesis held by the University of Bradford

Blore, Edward. *The Monumental Remains of Noble and Eminent Persons*

Cheetham, Francis W (2003) reprint. *Alabaster Images of Medieval England*

Cheetham, Francis W (1984). *English Medieval Alabasters.* Reprinted 2005

Craven, Maxwell (2012). *Country Images*. March 2012

Crease, Jane Rosemary (2008). *Incomparable Sepulchres. The Alabaster Chest Tomb in Yorkshire c.1350–c.158*. Vol. I. An unpublished University of York PhD thesis (2008), p. 289

Crossley. F. *English Church Monuments AD 1150 to 1500*

English Alabasters from the Hildeburgh Collection. V&A publication (731.263)

Esdaile, Katherine A (1946). *English Church Monuments 1510–1840.* Batsford Ltd (726.8)

Entart, Monsieur Camille (1906*). Journal of the Royal Archaeological Institute June 1906*

Fellows, George (1907). *Arms, Armour and Alabaster Round Nottingham – a brief description of some local alabaster altar tombs (with illustrations).* Beeston Fields, Nottingham. British Library 001214422

Gardner, Arthur (1940). *Alabaster Tombs of the Pre-Reformation Period.* Cambridge University Press

Gough, Richard (1786 and 1796). *Sepulchral Monuments of Great Britain.* He employed Jacob Schnebbelie, Samuel Hieronymous Grimm and others to provide the illustrations for his topographical publications

Hildeburgh, Dr W L (1949). *English Alabaster Carvings as Records of Medieval Religious Drama.* Society of Antiquaries

Hodgkinson, Terence (1976). *English Medieval Alabasters.* (736.5)

James, Clive (2006). *Church Monuments of Devon and Cornwall 1660 to 1750.* A thesis of July 2006

Kelly, Francis M and Schwabe, Randolph (1939). ***A Short History of Costume and Armour.*** Vols 1&2 1066 to 1485, Published 1939

Kemp, Brian (1985). *Church Monuments.* ISBN 9780852637685

Kirby J, Nash Susie and Canon, Joanne. *Trade in Artists' Materials, Markets and Commerce to 1700.* ISBN 978190492258. This contains:

ORO.open.uk/25605. *The Supply of alabaster in Northern and Mediterranean Europe in the Later Middle Ages.* ISBN 1-904982-25-5 and 978-1-904982-25-8

Lipińska, Dr Aleksandra (2009). *Decline, Break or Continuation? Southern Netherlandish alabaster sculpture in the 17th century.* University of Wroclaw, Poland. Paper CODART, March 2009

Mann, J G (1933). *English Church Monuments 1536 to 1625.* Walpole Society, Vol XXI, 1932–1933

Manners, Lady Victoria (1903). *Art Journal September, October and November*

Mercer, E. *English Art 1553 to 1625*

Oliver A. *Incised Effigies of Staffordshire*

Richardson, Edward (1851). *Alabaster in England.* Archaeological Journal 19;116. Probably *circa* 1850–1851

Richardson, Edward (1853). *Notices of Medieval Sculpture and Workings in Alabaster.* The Archaeological Journal, 1853

Sherlock Peter (2008). *Monuments and Memory in Early England*

St John Hope, William Henry (1901). Royal Archaeological Journal Vol 61 July 1901, paper read in Nottingham

Ward, Matthew (2013). *The Livery Collar-Politics and Identity in 16th Century England.* University of Nottingham thesis, August 2013

Weaver, Lawrence (1915). *Memorials and Monuments, Old and New*

Lawrence Weaver, 1915

Weever, John and Harper, Thomas (1631). *Ancient Funerary Monuments.* Mainly Rochester, Canterbury, London and Norwich but not completed. This is the first book on the history of tombs. The book, seen at the Southwell Minster Archives in Feb 2014, is a work of art. Its advantage for the researcher is that Weever faithfully reproduces the inscriptions on monuments some of which have subsequently been lost

Woods, Dr Kim (2007). *Imported Images – Netherlandish late Gothic Sculptures in England 1400–1550.* ISBN 1900289830, Paul Watkins Publishing

Church Furniture

Pridham, Harvey (1863). *Ancient Church Fonts of Somerset.* Later edited by A Webb

Churches, Cathedrals and Other Locations

Alec Clifton-Taylor's (1987). *The Pattern of English Building.* (Authors note: The source of the term 'streaky bacon' in relation to alabaster)

Bond, Shelagh M (1958). *Monographs of Windsor. Volume 12: The Monuments of St. George's Chapel Windsor Castle*

Briggs, Joseph (1872). *Sculptural Monuments of Derbyshire.* Derbyshire Records Office, accession no D4626/1

Britton, John (1826). *Antiquities, Wells, Exeter and Worcester.* Also that by Henry Winkler, 1836 and 1892

Burton, W (1622). *The Description of Leicestershire: containing matters of antiquity, history, armoury and genealogy*

Chatwin, Philip (1921). *The Monumental Effigies of Warwickshire.* Birmingham Archaeological Society Transactions, Vol XLVII, 1921

Cheetham, Francis W (1962). *Medieval English Alabaster Carvings in Nottingham Castle*

Cotton, William Alfred (1881). *Bromsgrove Church: Its History and Antiquities*

Cox, J Charles (1875). *Notes on the Churches of Derbyshire*

Downing, Mark. *Military Effigies of England and Wales in Six Volumes.* Monumental Books, Shrewsbury

Edwards, K C (1966). *Nottingham and Its Region.* The British Association, pages 231 to 235

Guilford, Everard L (1912). *Memorials of Old Nottingham*

Jeavons, S (1955). *Monumental Effigies of Staffordshire*

Hartshorne, Charles Henry (1867). *Recumbent Monument Effigies of Northamptonshire (An Endeavour to Classify the Sepulchral Remains in Northamptonshire)*

Hearne, T (1769). *The Itinerary of John Leland 1535 to 1543 and 1536 to 1539*

Lysons, Daniel and Samuel (1817). *Magna Britannia Vol 5 Derbyshire.* Rector of Rodmarton, Gloucestershire and Keeper of his Majesties Records at the Tower

Morgan, Octavius (1872). *Some Account of the Ancient Monuments of the St Mary's Priory Church of Abergavenny*

Nichols, John (1811). *The History and Antiquities of the County of Leicester.* London (available on download from University of Leicester)

Notes on Narburgh Church 27th August 1844 (available on the internet)

Oliver, Andrew (1881). *Notes on the Incised Effigies of Derbyshire and Staffordshire*

Richard Stone (2005). The River Trent ISBN 1 86077 356 7

Routh, Pauline. *Medieval Effigial Alabaster Tombs in Yorkshire.* (731.76)

Shaw and Stebbings (1801). *The History and Antiquities of Staffordshire.* In two volumes published by J Nichols, London

Sinclair, William (1909). *Memorials of St Paul's Cathedral*

St John Hope, William Henry (1907). *Funeral Effigies of the Kings and Queens of England with Reference to Those in Westminster Abbey.* British Library 001730242

Smith, Brian W (1990). *Kingston on Soar – Further Chapters in the History of an Estate Village.* Contains interviews with the last Kingston mine manager and workers.

Snow John (1598). Survey of London

Somerville, R (1960). *Guide to Tutbury Castle, Duchy of Lancaster.* London

Stone, L (1955). *Sculpture in Britain: The Middle Ages.* Also 1972

Stothard, Charles Alfred (1817). *Monumental Effigies of Great Britain.* This book was started in 1811. Stothard (1786–1821) made many drawings of tombs

Thoroton and Throsby (1696 and 1740). *Thoroton's Antiquities of Nottinghamshire in two Volumes*

Tudor Trails:

Tudor Trail – a booklet on Tudor monuments by Graham Beaumont

Holme Pierrepont Trail – booklet issue by Holme Pierrepont church

Warwick, G T (1967). *The Victorian History of the County of Staffordshire.* Section on Gypsum, Vol 2, pages 197 to 203

Whinney, Margaret (1988). *Sculpture in Britain 1530–1830.* Pelican History of Art, first published 1964

People Other Than Carvers

Camden Series (1911). *John of Gaunt 1374 Register* (pages 212 to 213), also 1379 to 1383 and 1371 to 1375

Religion and Religious Practices

Llewellyn, Nigel. *Art of Death: Visual Culture in the English Death Ritual 1500 to 1800*

Welch, Christina (2013). *English Carved Cadaver Monuments of the Late-Medieval Social and Religious Elite.* Fieldwork in Religion, Vol 8, 2013 – For Prayers and Pedagogy. Winchester University

Slabs

Greenhill, Frank Alan. *Incised Effigial Slabs – A Study of engraved stone memorials in Latin Christendom 1100 to 1700 in two Volumes.*

Vol 1 – ISBN: 0571107419. Publisher: Faber and Faber – 1976-03-08

Vol 2 – ISBN: 0571108806 *Incised Slabs of Lincolnshire*

ISBN: 0951007602, 1986 *Incised Slabs of Leicester and Rutland.* 1958

Tablets, Reredos and Retables

Hildeburgh, W L (1944). *Some Presumably Fragments of an English Alabaster Retable and Assembled Notes on English Alabaster Carving in Spain.* The Society of Antiquaries, London, 1944

St John Hope, William Henry (1891*). Sculptured Alabaster Tablets called St John's Heads.* British Library 001730246

The Carved Retable of Montréal, Languedoc, France. Booklet issued by the church

Tomb Conservancy

Larson, John (1979). *The Conservation of Alabaster Monuments in Churches.* The Conservator, Vol 3, 1979

Appendix B

Nicholas Stone and the de Keysers

To the middle of the 16th century church memorials were either floor slabs or tomb effigies. From the first decade of the reign of Elizabeth I a new memorial style made its appearance.

This was the mural. Unlike a slab or tomb the mural takes up less floor space being attached or built into the wall. There is firm evidence of the existence of mural monuments in Europe, particularly Holland, for some time and that its introduction to Britain was through the work of the Dutch émigrés.

However, the peak period for this style was in the first half of the 17th century before its popularity collapsed after the English Civil War. One carver of renown was Nicholas Stone. Nicholas Stone was a prolific record keeper and his notebooks and account books are preserved in the John Soane Museum in London. In 1919 Soane curator Walter Spiers published the details of the Stone papers for the '7th Volume of the Walpole Society' and these are a factual and accurate reproduction of the Stone records.

Nicholas Stone was born in Devon and, in 1606, whilst in London met and befriended Hendrik de Keyser the Elder, a Dutch sculptor of some status in his home town of Amsterdam. Stone was invited to train under De Keyser which he did, subsequently marrying Maria de Keyser, Hendrik's daughter. In 1613 he returned to England settling in Long Acre, London where he established a workshop.

Nicholas had three sons and a daughter. All three men followed him into the carving trade but only John Stone survived Nicholas who died in 1647.

Between 1613 and 1647 he produced a welter of carvings. Spiers considers that Stone brought back the mural style from Holland, but we now know that the style was seen in London as early as 1564. However, he produced a range of large murals as well as chest effigies and small murals, tablets and floor slabs. Nicholas died in 1647 shortly after his wife. On his death John Stone carried on the business and on his death it came to a cousin who traded for a time before closing the business in the 1670s.

Stone records carving his mural monuments from 1615, but these may not be the earliest. The account book for 1613 to 1631 is missing and the notebook was created from memory in 1642. Therefore, many monuments for 1613 to 1631 may be omitted and a reconciliation of the two books shows significant variation. Many monuments omitted from one or other of the books was found (and photographed) by Spiers in 1919. It is possible that the Soane Museum has records of only a fraction of the monuments created by the Stone workshops and this is currently under investigation by Adam White. Certainly on page 80 of the Walpole Society publication, Spiers admits to the fact that the notebook is unlikely to be a complete list. He refers to several monuments being mentioned in the account book which do not appear in the notebook. In addition, as the reader will see, the sequential pages of the notebook have random dates indicating that although Stone may have started in sequence his later entries are less so. For example Folio 22, possibly 1641, has dates for 1632 embedded. In addition to this, august bodies such as the Victoria and Albert Museum have laid claim to Nicholas Stone monuments which do not appear in either book.

In addition to his sons, Stone employed his brothers-in-law especially William and Hendrik de Keyser. The notebooks contain much personal chatter.

Rozalin Coope said that Hendrik, born 1613, was married in 1642, but the register for St Nicholas Church in Nottingham, confirms that Hendrik married Elizabeth Bellamy on the 6th July 1639. Hendrik was in Nottingham supervising some chimney-piece work at Newstead Abbey.[1] Elizabeth died in child birth in 1642 and a possible daughter Dorothea De Keyser may have married a John Syll several decades later. Hendrik returned to London in 1647 but soon moved to Amsterdam to remarry in 1658 and die in 1665.[2]

William came to England in 1620 and was apprenticed to Nicholas Stone. He may have been sent to find sources of alabaster *circa* 1633. Dismissed from the workshop by John Stone in 1653 he returned to Amsterdam, but came back to London in 1658.

The outbreak of the Civil War in 1642 severely damaged the carving business of the workshop. John Stone later confirmed that Nicholas was arrested in 1647 for an unstated reason but may be due to receiving monies due from Royalists or refusing to sign the covenant. The imprisonment was probably of short duration but probably expedited the speedy departure of Hendrik back to Amsterdam. The historical records of Nicholas Stone (summarised on Spiers, pages 80 to 84) do not betray Stone's sympathies with either parliament or the king. He does not mention the raising of the king's standard at Nottingham in 1642 which might be expected from a Royalist. The mention of the Battle of Edge Hill (page 84) is made without comment and the skirmish at Brentford is followed by a statement regarding the king's withdrawal from London but again without any indication as to his leanings.

The Civil War must have affected Stone's trade. His work for landed gentry many of whom were Royalists must have taken a downturn whilst the emerging proletariat were Puritan and not given to ostentatious monuments. Places like Oxford were soon 'off bounds' and supplies disrupted. In the East Midlands the transport from the alabaster beds at Tutbury, Chellaston and Fauld were soon disturbed by the presence of Parliamentary forces in Nottingham whilst Royalists held Newark sitting astride the Trent for the duration of the war. Royalists from Ashby held Swarkestone Bridge blocking transport south and attacked King's Mill both of which were key points in the provision of materials. It may be that Stone transferred his purchases to Ledsham in Yorkshire or Watchet, Somerset which was less susceptible to disruption by either force.

The notebook contains some other interesting snippets. Stone notes at one point 'For hands and feet a mortar composed of quicklime or gypsum mixed with casein (skimmed milk cheese) is used'. This provided for a strong adhesive for alabaster and marble products throughout the 17th century and may still have been employed into the 19th century. Casein, a phosphoprotein, is well known in the manufacturer of some paints and was used in binding safety matches. It was also used for gluing some wooden-framed aircraft including the WW2 Mosquito.

The notebook also discussing polishing the carvings for which he purchased various-size grains of sand the cost of which also appear in the account book.

The books of Nicholas Stone are an interesting window into the workings of a 17th century workshop comprising a mixture of technical, accounting, family chatter and management notes. The full version of the Walpole Society publication can be viewed online at:

https://archive.org/details/volumeofwalpoles07walpuoft

Notes:

1. Examination of all the chimney pieces in Newstead in July 2016 reveals all but three are plain limestone of no particular interest. The three worthy of inspection are in the library, salon and assembly rooms. From Stone's description the one that fits best is the assembly room (Figure 42) but this cannot be confirmed.
2. The letter from Thomas de Keyser, 19th December 1639:

   The letter opens with some domestic arrangements and an account of purchases made by Stone for the family in Amsterdam.

   The next section is repeated here with comments:

   I have heard with pleasure of the good health of your children in Rome. Our brother Hendrik came here in Amsterdam (on) the 2nd November (1639) three or four days before brother Peter married, but not knowing that his brother was a bridegroom: he came here on business, and told us as you wrote that he had got married in England. He left here again for Hull on the 5th December (1639). We hope the Lord God will grant him a safe journey in all these bad storms.

   Written in Amsterdam this 19th December 1639 by your zealous brother until death Thomas de Keyser.

Comment:
There is some evidence that Hendrik de Keyser came to England *circa* 1634. He appears to have worked for Nicholas Stone in erecting the Byron pieces in 1637–1638 and settled in Nottingham. The Nottingham Borough records show that he was living in Stony Street Nottingham on the 28th July 1643 when he was charged £0.6s.8d by the authorities for rates. There are no other records in the Nottingham Archives. Thomas (above) says that Hendrik came to Amsterdam 'on business'.This indicates that he may have been acting for Stone or in business in his own right. On the strength of the letter it would appear that in the 13 years that Hendrik was in England he traded in his own right and may have made some East Midland monuments.

Appendix C
Transport of Alabaster

Care must be taken to avoid giving 20th century views on the ease of the transport of heavy objects in the 14th to 17th century. Experienced art commentators have a tendency to trivialise the movement of alabaster slabs and blocks around the country which leads to false assumptions. Francis Cheetham in *Unearthed* (*see* bibliography) concludes that road transport was more common than previously believed. This assumption is based on the very thin evidence of the movement of the Windsor retable and the disputes between carvers and carters in 15th century. In fact most of this evidence is in relation to small panels and relatively light images over short distances and is not representative of the general medieval transport scene. Neither can the transport of the Windsor retable in the 14th century be taken as normal. As will be shown, not only was this inordinately expensive but in order to ensure safe passage the towns on the way had to be put on guard – a process which was only available to royalty.

In fact the transport problems were so great that it had a tendency to dictate the location where alabaster was sourced and place where it was carved. Another factor was that transport tended to be in the summer months when the ground would be hard except during early winter when frosts would freeze the mud. Of the 15 extant contracts for work covering 10 tombs, 7 have delivery schedules in the months of August and September.

The transport arrangements of John of Gaunt in 1371 have already been stated but it is worth quickly reviewing the transport scene which existed in those times.[1]

The movement of heavy objects was solved very early in English history. The movement of bluestones for the construction of Stonehenge is a case in point but there are other examples closer to the East Midlands. In 1998 a log boat dating from 3500 BC was found in Shardlow Quarry still with its cargo of sandstone blocks mined from the cliffs at King's Mill (about 5 miles upstream). The cargo may have weighed several tons and it demonstrates that water could be used to transport heavy object with success.

It is fortunate that both the mines at Fauld/Tutbury and Chellaston are close to rivers and so are those at Ledsham/Buttercrambe, Yorkshire, whilst the Somerset and Cumbrian quarries[2] were on the coast. In the case of Purbeck marble the blocks were mined at Downshay or Afflington, carried along the Marbler's Road and loaded onto ships at Owers Point in the old port of Newton Studland, Dorset. Therefore it is probable that, like Purbeck Marble, water featured large in the transport of alabaster.

In the case of Ledsham and Fairburn, the date of the opening of the quarries is uncertain,[3] but it is most likely that, at some time, blocks of alabaster were carried down the River Swale and into the River Ouse for the York carvers. Buttercrambe is on the River Derwent. However, it is also possible for York to have received alabaster from the Derbyshire mines by way of the Rivers Trent, Humber and Ouse. Section 7.3 in the main body of the text and Appendix V detail the arrangements for carriage of the alabaster for the Abbey of Fécamp in 1414 which sheds much light on the arrangements in medieval times. The rights to the navigation of rivers until 1472 are unclear. It is probable that navigation was only obstructed by mill weirs and fisheries and that boatman were free to use the river for transport. In 1472 the rights were affirmed by a statute known as 'An Act for Taking Away Wears and Fishgarths' such that navigation of any river could only be revoked by legislation in parliament or by the river silting up. This is the last time parliament expressed its will on the rights of river navigation.[4] This Act is still on the statute book.

It is necessary to examine the rivers of the East Midlands to see the problems which faced the carriers. Although the Trent is wide and deep at its confluence with the Humber, it was tidal to Gainsborough and only navigable at all times of the year to Nottingham. Richard Stone's *The River Trent* describes the early problems with navigation. Beset by floods and shallows and often frozen in winter, the book describes the difficulty in navigation above Nottingham into the heartland of the alabaster area.

Eight miles above Nottingham three other rivers join the Trent which are the Soar, the Derbyshire Derwent and the Dove. Like the Trent none of these were known for their navigation capacity. The Soar is disturbed by the Normanton Hills Fault which made navigation almost impossible above Ratcliffe. Attempts were made by Thomas Skipwith of Cotes in 1636 to make the river navigable to Loughborough but after about 5 miles of straightening and dredging the work had to be abandoned and within a year floods had undone the work. Skipwith being a Royalist was largely prevented from attending the works as the area around the mouth of the Soar was occupied by the Sacheverell and Hutchinson families both ardent Parliamentarians.

In the case of the Derbyshire Derwent its shallowness and meanders provided a real problem. It never received any attempt to be made navigable before the 17th century. A wharf was then opened in Derby, close to what is now the Eagle Centre which remained in business until abandoned when the Derby Canal opened in 1796.

The Dove is the smallest and narrowest of all the rivers but it passed within half a mile of the mines at Tutbury and Fauld and with the evidence of a number of flash locks being present from early days. It would be reasonable to assume that water was used to transport the alabaster blocks to Burton on Trent and beyond but no such evidence is forthcoming.

As for the Trent itself the meanders around Sawley and its shallowness leading to numerous fords limited its usefulness until the 18th century. Richard Stone records that locks were installed in 1712 at the worst places, namely Winshill and King's Mill, which enabled the Soho Wharf in Burton to be opened. Even then the 'locks' were of the 'flash' design meaning that water levels had to be managed by opening mill sluices which was often disrupted by irate millers and required much manpower to haul the boats through the flash. Richard Stone states that King's Mill was the loading point for Chellaston gypsum and alabaster to avoid the problem with navigating Swarkestone Bridge. This bridge was first mentioned in documents about 1204 as the Pont de Cordy and was almost certainly a wooden structure (the remains of wooden bridges over former courses of the Trent dating from the 11th and 13th century were found at Hemmington along with the log boat in the 1990s). The archaeological evidence points to the bridge being rebuilt in stone *circa* early 14th century which accords to the royal grant of tolls issued for its repair dated 1324 and 1347. Local tradition that the bridge was rebuilt by two sisters (*see* Prestwold, G110) has no foundation in documentary evidence. The current bridge dates from 1795 and now carries the A514. In the period of alabaster production at Burton, Swarkestone Bridge was an impediment to navigation. For more details *see Conservation Area Histories – Swarkestone – District of South Derbyshire*.

However, single-masted ketches were able to reach Burton by the mid to late 18th century, probably after Swarkestone Bridge was rebuilt with wider and taller arches. These could be loaded to 40 tons (12 tons when water was low). The movement of boats along these rivers could be by sail but at the time haulage by men was resorted to, which was very expensive.

A study of the medieval river transport entitled *The Transport system of Medieval England and Wales – a Geographical Synthesis* by James Frederick Edwards – a thesis of Salford University dated 1987 – lists the highest point on each significant river that was navigable. Selected rivers have been ploted on Diagram M below. Unfortunately, the dates for the survey are absent but examination of a few details indicates a period around 1500. This reveals that river cartage was possible almost everywhere except along the spine of England. In the case of Burton, transport eastwards was not difficult and westward was possible by road with a little effort as the following diagram shows.

The 15th century records of the Borough of Nottingham reveal disputes with carriers which can only indicate overland cartage. The stated destinations of the carters indicate the contracts are for small blocks for ornaments or thin blocks for retables probably no more than 2.5ft by 1.5ft and 4 inches thick. These would weigh about 119lbs or 1.1cwt – an analysis of the alabaster panels in the Victoria and Albert Museum indicates a range of sizes but few indicate uncarved weights above 1.7cwt. Stone estimates a medieval horse could be loaded to 2.5cwt or 280lbs and the Early Railways Conference in Newcastle in June 2016 put the estimate higher at 3cwt or 336lbs which would tend to indicate two panels carried in panniers.

Diagram M. Selected rivers of England and Wales showing the highest point that the river was navigable. As can be seen the Towns of Burton and Nottingham were close to the river Trent and to the alabaster sources. It was possible to reach the Fen rivers by means of the Foss Dyke without resorting to coastal shipping. In this way the 1419 effigies (G122) from Chellaston could reach Lowick by means of the Nene which had its head of navigation at Wansford (27 miles from Lowick) but would entail a total journey of over 120 miles. This could be reduced to 60 miles by using the road. The Severn can be accessed by the Warwick Avon whose navigation in medieval times reached Kenilworth (40 miles from Burton). If delivery to Lowick was by road it is therefore likely that the Burton alabastermen could move blocks and part finished works at least up to 60 miles. Drawn by the author.

The Pack-horse Convoy. [By Louis Huard.]

Figure 51. A packhorse convoy showing panniers. From a 17th century print by Lou Huard.

14th and 15th century cartage from the alabaster fields at Fauld or Tutbury (20 miles west of Nottingham) would take about a day and a half by a train of four horses or about a day from Chellaston (about 15 miles from Nottingham). A four-horse train could deliver some 10 to 16 slabs a week to the Nottingham carvers.

Local land cartage was estimated as being some three times more expensive than the river but would ensure a regular supply free of the dangers of the water. However, for longer distances prices rose almost exponentially.

In 1367 the kerver Peter the Mason agreed a contract for cartage to carry finished retable panels from Nottingham the 130 miles to Windsor for £30, employing some 80 horses 20 carts and 20 men. We do not know exactly what the sizes of the panels were but it is clear that Peter did not trust either the water transport or the pack horse and settled for carrying the panels in carts, the inference being that each was hauled by four horses. Such was the importance of this wagon train that the king issued a letter patent to all sheriffs '... to detain or imprison all persons who shall obstruct the passage of the materials'. The transportation took 17 days (20th October 1367 to 6th November 1367) which indicates just 7 miles per day. It is interesting to speculate that the date may have been carefully chosen. The autumn frosts would have hardened the ground yet the thermal lag would have prevented snow disrupting the transport. Any earlier would have meant the wagons having to face a mud bath which again would have stalled the convoy. It is interesting to compare this with the Nazi conquest of Russia where offensives took place after frosts had hardened the Russian mud roads but before the winter snows.

Francis Cheetham investigated the shipping of alabaster in the 15th century. He noted that the Mary of Hull belonging to Cornelius de Grave left her home port with two tables of alabaster on the 20th May 1465. The cargo belonged to Jacob Jonson a non-Hanseatic merchant and was valued at £7. The destination is not recorded. On the same ship a cargo for Adrian Barbour also non-Hanseatic also contained two tables of alabaster but valued at £3.16s.

In 1479 the pinnace *Le Gabriel* of Poole whose master was Robert Gosselyn departed with two tables of alabaster to the value of £3, the property of William Filat. At Wareham another pinnace *Nicholas* 'departed' in August 1479 with six tables and a cask of images valued at £6, the property of Richard Harres. Interestingly, the clerk recording the customs wrote intravit (import) instead of exivit (export) which has always been treated as a clerical error but wonders if this ship arrived from Hull with a load of raw alabaster. Four weeks after the *Nicholas* entry, in September 1479 it was *The Mary* of Poole (Master John Duet) which departed with one table valued at 20s and four days later the *Margaret* of Kyhavy[5] (Master John Wade) left with one more. Could these be the tables which arrived on the *Nicholas* a short time earlier? In 1483 an un-named ship whose master was William Mellit left with 20 tables at a princely sum of £26.13s. 4d.

The use of these Dorset ports far from Nottingham may be surprising but, as we have seen, tables could be carried by pack horses and the short sea crossing to Normandy would be attractive rather than the dangerous passage down the East Coast. In 1442 a licence was granted to Modbury Abbey, Dorset for the shipping of a table from Poole to St Pierre sur Dives in France. Modbury had strong links with Tutbury and this may well provide a connection.

Even into the 17th century water transport was preferred. In the records of Nicholas Stone, a London carver, there are costs for transportation entered in his account book. In March 1637 he had contracted to supply John Lord Byron in Newstead Abbey with an alabaster chimney piece. The account reads:

For 3 parcels, packing and bound with hoops	£1: 0:0
Carriage to the water, 8s wharfage and cranage 3s (8 miles – 12d/mile)	11:0
Freight to Hull (270 miles – 1.33d/mile)	£1:10:0
Total:	£3: 1:0

It will be observed that some 300 years after the carriage of the Windsor retables water transport was one tenth the cost of road transport and therefore must have featured large in the logistic decisions.

In a subsequent note Nicholas Stone suggests that he used Blackwall Wharf as his departure point on the Thames which may account for the high cost of cartage across London. The use of Blackwall avoided the long drag round the Isle of Dogs (and possibly the city wharfage charges).

The apparent rule that animal-drawn land transport was some four to five times more expensive than water is supported by the work done by Douglas Knoop and G P Jones in their 1949 book *The Medieval Mason*. They examined rolls and expenses accounts over a long period with the following result:

- Between 1268 and 1280 stone was carried the 5 miles from the Eddisbury quarry in Cheshire to the Vale Royal Abbey for which they paid £347. In the same period the quarrymen's wages were £104 showing that land carriage raised the cost at the Abbey by 300%.
- On the other hand 2290 tons of stone was carried from Maidstone to Rochester in 1368 for the repair of Rochester Castle. This cost £47 against Quarrying costs of £119 giving an uplift of just 30%. The difference being that rafting the stone 12 miles down the Medway was employed.
- Even when river was used for the majority of the journey the cartage element could raise costs. Thevedale and Huddlestone quarries provided stone for York Minster in 1415. Although the distance by road was little more than 20 miles the cheapest route was cartage to Tadcaster or Cawood was employed so that stone was rafted down the Swale and hauled up the Ouse. At Huddleston quarry surface costs of £9 14s were lifted to £31 7s (or 350%) by virtue of the 11 miles cartage. At Thevedale the cartage distance was only 4 miles so that quarry surface costs of £12 8s were uplifted to £34.15s at York (280%) despite the additional distance down the Swale all of which was rafted.
- Knoop and Jones give other examples which can be found on pages 50 to 52 of their book.

In 1812 whilst the Napoleonic Wars were at their height the cost of land transport was three times that of canal or river. However, peace in 1815 released a lot of horses and men from military service and in 1816 many of these had been pressed into providing cartage services. Road transport fell such that it was only 20% higher, but slowly rose as the economy recovered (6th Early Railway and Canal Conference Newcastle June 2016).

The cost of road carrying recovered to a high level into the start of the railway era. The comparison of costs between water and road down to the 19th century can be gauged by the comparing the cost of moving a new locomotive of 7 tons by road from Newcastle to Carlisle in April 1828 and the carriage of an identical locomotive from

Newcastle to New York, USA by sea in October 1828. The former cost £25 for some 80 miles (6s a mile) whilst the latter cost £32 for some 4000 miles (1.9d per mile) – a factor of nearly 50 (account book of Robert Stephenson & Co, National Railway Museum, York). The cost of transport to Carlisle or New York consumed just 5% of the total cost of manufacture showing that although land carriage was less cost effective than road it mopped up less of the overall cost of the product than some centuries earlier when tombs were being transported. It will be observed that the cost to Carlisle in 1828 would be the same as the cost of alabaster from the East Midlands to London a century before but that the tonnage had doubled.

It is ironic that the movement of these two locomotives established the rail industries in England and on the North American continent which revolutionised the carriage of heavy goods.

Details exist for the transport of the tomb for the Bottesford tombs from 1591. The tombs (R7 and R29) were carved in Southwark, London and unfortunately there are no details of the acquisition of the raw materials. However, we know that the finished or part-finished components were shipped to Boston, Lincs and then by cart for the 27 miles to Bottesford. The Rutland Papers MSS IV (1905) has details of the carriage. Some 15 carts were required and a man was required to stand guard over a cart whose axle had broken and liquid refreshment provided for those who watched with him.

There are no statements as to the transportation from Hull up the Trent but in 1635 there were regular sailings from Hull to Nottingham via the Humber and Trent Falls. Neither are there any costs for this, but it is believed that Stone had an agent in Nottingham from 1637 in the form of his brother-in-law Hendrik de Keyser who was deputised to assemble the chimney piece in Newstead Abbey. Transportation up the Trent and onwards by road would almost certainly be arranged locally.

T P Connor in CMS Vol XXIX 2014 investigated transport costs for graveyard chest tombs from the late 16th century onward. He found that in 1694 the cost of transport of a chest tomb from London to Manston represented 14% of the total manufacturing costs. Assuming this is not Manston, Kent close to North Foreland point which would be suitable for river transport down the Thames, the cartage of some 115 miles to Manston, Dorset would seem to be a bargain. More representative of the costs is the 1570 record of transport of a stone load from Upwey quarry to Dorchester, a distance of some 4 miles which consumed 85% of the total cost. In 1699 transport consumed 48% of the cost of the provision of Ham stone for Mapperton rectory.

Considering the rutted tracks at the time, the large number of horses would be essential. The carts before the 17th century would be two wheeled and the panels wrapped in hide and laying on beds of straw. In *An Economic History of Modern Britain* by J H Clapham 1926, there is a good summary of the roads up to 1829. Turnpike trusts came into existence in the 17th century (*circa* 1662) and reached the peak of about

1000 in the 1820s. As a rule of thumb a rider and horse could make 35 to 50 miles per day on 17th century roads. Stagecoaches some 15 to 20 miles and goods wagons about 10 miles. The turnpike trusts were often incompetent, corrupt or overwhelmed by the task and only covered major routes usually the old Roman roads. Local roads were the responsibility of the parish and often in poor shape. It is estimated that of the 125,000 miles of (so called) roads in England only 21,000 miles (17%) were turnpikes in 1820. Clapham says that 10 dray horses had a life span of only four years in the country but the equivalent capacity of 8 horses in London had a life span of six years or more.

The records of Nottingham state that the city fathers had regularised the road transport by 1781. They set down that the charges for east Nottinghamshire towns from London should be 12d per stone (14lbs) in summer and 13d in winter and that this rate may have been fixed as early as 1691. This gives an approximate cost of £8 per ton in summer and £8 13s in winter. The wagons were to be hauled by 8 or 10 horses and managed by a man on a pony with a whip. The cost of a 3 ton block from the East Midlands to London by road would therefore be in the order of £25 (today this would be £2,790 in accordance with price indices but £35,000 in respect of labour and transport). It can be seen that water transport was used wherever possible.

Figure 52. As turnpike trusts improved roads the pack horse gave way to stage wagons in the 18th century. The wide wheels allowed the load to be distributed on the poor road surface but were disliked by the trusts as they broke up the surface. Normally 10 horses were in harness but this old print shows only 8. The similarity of this wagon and the *Conestoga* wagons of the prairies of America from 1717 will be noted. From an 18th century print.

A statement to a select committee in 1819 complained that the condition of some turnpikes was such that the mails could be delayed several hours by being buried up to their axles in loose gravel. The forced amalgamation of turnpike trusts and the attention of Telford and McAdam greatly improved turnpikes during the next 10 years.

Figure 53. A mail coach prepares for departure from London *circa* 1806. From *The Story of the British People In Pictures* 1936.

The benefits of the canals can be gauged by the toll rates for several navigations. In 1824 the Kensington Canal in London listed the toll for alabaster as 1d per ton between the Thames and Stamford Bridge. Nearer to home, the Cromford Canal quoted 1½d per ton for alabaster originating on the canal but 4½d if it came by way of the Erewash navigation which it would have to do from the Chellaston quarries. This is dated 1790. The Carlisle Canal quoted 2d per ton in 1819.

In the same year (1828) the cost to a passenger travelling inside a mail coach from London to Liverpool was £4 4s 3d taking 36 hrs. In 1841 parliament legislated for the carriage of a passenger in third class at 1d per mile making Liverpool reachable within 8 hrs at a cost of 16s.

In fact the railway revolutionised the transport from the mid-1830s. The North Stafford Railway opened its line through Tutbury in the 1860s and the Fauld Mine was connected to sidings by a narrow-gauge railway still shown on the 1961 maps of the area. A photograph, dated 28th June 1894, exists depicting 15-ton blocks of alabaster standing on North Stafford Railway wagons at Scropton Sidings having been dug by hand from the Fauld Mine (Figure 96). These blocks were destined for the mansion of Cornelius Vanderbilt in the USA and would have travelled to Liverpool to be shipped by sea to New York. Correspondence with the proprietors of The Breakers, Rhode Island, reveals Fauld alabaster in the great hall and in the dining room reminiscent to the Marble Hall in Kedleston. The Vanderbilts were related to the Curzons and there is every reason to assume that Cornelius had seen the Marble Hall at some point in time.

The medieval carvers would be fully aware that transport would be difficult. The logistics of the alabaster trade meant that the lighter the object the cheaper and easier it would be to carry it to its destination. In the 14th century it is for this reason that much roughing out of blocks and carving was done close to the place when alabaster was won from the ground. As a result we see Chellaston and Tutbury as the centres. However, these places were remote and therefore difficult to recruit workers and very soon workshops in Nottingham were opened. These would be carving small objects and panels which could receive their raw materials easily by pack horse but, even here, it is possible that carvers such as Peter the Mason still retained their base in South Derbyshire. Cheetham offers the opinion that large object carving remained in the country whilst the carving of images and panels grew in Nottingham town and I would agree with this. The major expansion of this work occurred in the second half of the 15th century until killed off in the mid-16th century. Effigy carving appears to have gravitated to Burton in the 16th century when that town underwent expansion later adding Coventry to its outposts.

As for other centres only York had any indigenous supplies of alabaster. In the 13th century and into the 14th royal carvers of London (and Gloucester) had to use sea-born Purbeck marble which was not easy to work for effigies. In 1330, the realisation that finer work could be produced by using alabaster meant better carved effigies, but also meant that they could only get their supplies from the East Midlands.

Of the 11 extant effigies dating from 1330 to 1360 4 are royal tombs (all 1330 to 1348), 4 are local nobility associated with the alabaster mining area and only 3 are remote gentry. It can be concluded that royalty started the fashion which was copied by others who were unconcerned about transport difficulties or costs, being able to pay whatever it took and legislate for its safe passage.

This essay allows the transport issues surrounding the alabaster trade to be assessed.

Figure 54. Detail from *Castle Grinding Mill* by Joshua Wood Whymper (1813–1902) dated 1880 but likely to be much earlier as this method of unloading blocks had ceased some decades earlier. Blocks of limestone or sandstone are being delivered to strengthen the banks of the River Don in Sheffield. The carter is levering a block off a wagon. Two timbers are lodged under the lip of the wagon and the intention is to lever the block beyond its tipping point so that it slides down the timbers. A risky and dangerous practice used until shear-legs or tripods became commonplace. Two men watch the process from a safe distance and the boy is strangely behind the wagon instead of attending the horses. He may be steadying the wagon as it would tip as soon as the block touched the slide. Whatever was on that side cannot be seen clearly but may well be the timbers visible beneath the wagon. It is clear Whymper had knowledge of the carriage of stone. The height of the wagon platform makes for an unstable arrangement but is necessary to provide a slope of about 60° on the timbers as any less may mean the block does not slide so breaking the timbers. In the Middle Ages such practices would be used for moving uncarved blocks of alabaster. From an old print.

Notes:

1. Michael Hicks writing in *History Magazine* October 2015 states that the carters at Southampton at the turn of the 15th century took three days to Salisbury (23m) or six days to Gloucester (94m). A carter named Stephen Kyng carried 56 loads between 1447 and 1448 during which he covered some 4000 miles (average 71 miles/journey).
2. The Barrowmouth gypsum and alabaster mine appears not to have opened until the end of the 18th century *circa* 1794 (or 1739). Located south of Whitehaven it was so close to the sea that it was threatened with erosion. It also had an early inclined plain for carriage of mined materials to the top of the cliffs. (A Review of the Archaeology from St Bees to the River Sark *circa* 2009.)
3. Cheetham says that the quarries were open in the 17th century and the Southwell Minster effigy of Bishop Sandys would tend to support the fact that large blocks were being won by 1590. Other writers say that serious mining was not undertaken until the 18th century when it was reported that 'large blocks of alabaster were being obtained from quarries at Ledsham'.
4. Google: 1472 Act for wears and Fishgarthes. The fines for obstructing navigation was punitive but the Act allowed millers and fisheries to provide methods of opening their defences to allow boats to pass which led to the use of flash locks.
5. Could this be Keyhaven in Hampshire?

Appendix D1 to D12

Notes on the Use of the Appendices

These appendices cover the period from 1327 to date and specific subjects as listed below:

D1	–	1330 to 1399
D2	–	1400 to 1499
D3	–	1500 to 1599
D4	–	1600 to 1699
D5	–	1700 to 1799
D6	–	1800 to date
D7	–	Undated
D8	–	Others
D9	–	Vanished
D10	–	Non-Church Alabaster
D11	–	Significant Non-Alabaster Monuments
D12	–	Kings and Queens of England

Unlike other publications the lists are in date order which may difficult for those searching a specific location. To overcome this there is a separate alphanumeric index following these notes for readers to access specific locations. This gives the place, dates, appropriate note and table. To find the details for a location, refer to the location index, choose a date and table and go to that date within the appropriate table.

Appendix tables D1 to D8, D10 to D11

Number	Location	Building	Monument	Date	Armour or other features	Painted/collar or Garter	Source	Kerver	Notes Image

Number – A sequential number to allow a reader to see population. To find a population between dates note the number on the first line of the start date and the number on the last line of the end date. Deduct one from the other gives the population. If the reader requires specific monument types then further analysis is required.

Location – The location name and county. Where the county is obvious this is omitted e.g. Oxford.

Building – Mainly a church. Postcode if known is added.

Monument – Effigy, mural, tablet etc. The letters denote the subject, K (knight), L (lady), C (civilian), J (judge or other legal), P (priest), B (bishop), R (royal) etc. The Roman numerals in brackets ( ) relate to Gardner – *see* below:

According to Gardner effigial monuments can be categorised into groups. Many researchers do not agree but for completeness it is repeated here to use or discard as appropriate. Gardner arranged his classes according to style changes in the design of armour but this has to be tempered with caution. The classes are as follows:

Class I – 1330 to *circa* 1360 Early Experimental Gothic, some horizontal panels, mail armour
Class II – 1360 to *circa* 1420 Middle Gothic, embattled top to vertical panels, camail and jupon armour
Class III – 1420 to *circa* 1450 Late Middle Gothic, early plate armour
Class IV – 1440 to *circa* 1485 Late Gothic, late plate armour
Class V – 1482 to *circa* 1542 Final Gothic, simplification of armour
Class VI – 1539 to *circa* 1566 Transition, mainly Gothic with Renaissance elements such a family, simple Tudor armour

Note that some classes overlap. The change in styles was not sharp. The predominance of the Trent Valley in classes II to V allows the cut-off date to be specified with some surety but even here some older carves perpetuated the early class form for a number of years. Later after 1560 the rise in London whilst the Trent Valley carvers were still active and the importation of Renaissance and Dutch styles meant that the change point became more fluid. Trent Valley carvers maintained a Gothic element for some 16 years after the first Renaissance elements appeared. The overlap between effigial and mural monuments is even more fluid. After the Commonwealth effigial monuments of all types were in decline leading to plain tablets. When effigies again began to be popular the customer preferences moved to marble and it is not until the Victorian Gothic Revival did alabaster again become popular.

The lists below includes slabs. The history and details of the incised slabs of Britain and the Western World is covered by Frank Allan Greenhill in his magnum opus *Incised Effigial Slabs Volumes 1 and 2*. This is thorough but although he details the slab trade in alabaster (Volume 1, pages 19 to 24) his catalogue fails to record which slabs are made from which material. This oversight makes it difficult for researchers only interested in slabs made from certain stones. As a result the following tables list the slabs which are known to be made from alabaster whilst cross referencing to Greenhill's work.

Date – Dates of construction are problematical. In some cases monuments were created in the person's lifetime and sometimes many years after the death. Where this known, the date of creation is shown where not, the date of death is given and variations are given in the note. Dates in brackets are alternative dates which, at this time, could not be reconciled.

Features – A brief and limited list of specific features noted during analysis.

Painted/collar – Whether the tomb carries paint and specific livery and other decorations. Ga = garter (m man, w woman), SS = Lancastrian SS collar (2) indicates both effigies, Y = Yorkist collar of suns and roses, P = plain livery collar, Chain = simple chain collar. Yes = currently painted, No = no paint trace, Was = known to have been painted at some time.

Source – The source of the alabaster and some notes on colour.

Kerve – The kerver or school believed to responsible.

Notes – The Note column refers the reader to the observations and owner of the monuments. I have tried to lead the reader to a variety of source material. Notes beginning AO are details in Andrew Oliver's book on Derbyshire and Staffordshire slabs dated 1881 available on line, G listed with picture by Gardner with numerals in brackets indicating the illustration number, GNP listed by Gardner without picture, for slabs GH1 = Greenhill Vol 1 + page no, GH2 = Greenhill Vol 2 + page no, S = slab, T = transition, TT = tabletop, A = not attributable to other groups, R = Renaissance, M = mural with figures but the notes embrace tablets without, Q = foreign tombs related to the book text, L = notes on linked monuments, LS Pxxx = plate numbers from Lawrence Stone's Book, X = other notes and observations. Notes containing a D relate to Mark Dowling series of books where the first number is the volume and the second number is the page (example 4D77 = volume 4 of Dowling page 77). This may be incomplete as not all volumes have been scrutinised. CMS-CG indicates an image in the County Guides of the Church Monuments Society which can be accessed on line. The Southwell History Project website is very useful for images of Nottinghamshire tombs.

<u>Appendix tables D9 and D12</u>

Appendix D9 lists alabaster monuments known to have existed but have since vanished. For interest D12 lists the burial places and monuments of the monarchs of England.

Index to Monuments Listed in Appendices D1 to D12

Commemorative Items

This index covers tombs, murals and tablets in which an individuals or groups are commemorated. In the main tables the monuments are listed in date order. Refer to the following alphabetical list to find individual locations and notes. For the physical details go to the appropriate D table and search within date and for historical details go to the appropriate note. Notes commencing L refer to linked items.

Totals as at publication:

Table	D1 = 92 (91 effigies 1 slab)
	D2 = 312 (236 effigies and 78 slabs)
	D3 = 535 (382 effigies and 152 slabs)
	D4 = 685 (621 mural and effigies, 48 tablets and 16 slabs)
	D5 = 31
	D6 = 93
	D7 = 2
	D8 = 145
	D9 = 151

Total so far = 2046

Location	Date	Note	Table
Abbess Roding, Essex	1613	M611	D4
Aberavon, Wales	1633	M612	D4
	1890	-	D8
Abergavenny, Monmouth	1450	G118	D2
	1470	G119	D2
	1510	G120	D3
	1631	R180	D4
Acton, Cheshire	1399	GNP1	D1
Acton Burnell, Shrops	1591	R213	D3
	1632	M295	D4
Adbaston, Staffs	1441	S188	D2
Adwick le Street, Yorks	1580	S70,GH2,GH1	D3
Albrighton, Shrops	1555	T17	D3
Albury, Herts	1570	M583	D3
	1891	–	D8
Alcester, Warwicks	1559	D179	D3
Aldbourne, Wilts	1510	TT4	D3
	1617	M76	D4
Aldermaston, Berks	1526	G38	D3
Alfreton, Derbys	1467	X107	D8
	1611	X107	D8
	1682	X107	D8
	1860	X107	D8
Allenton Maultreverer Yorks	1458	GNP10	D2
Altringcham, Cheshire	1921	M641	D8
Alvingham, Lincs	1360	GNP122	D1
Amersham, Bucks	1636	M356	D4
Amport, Hants	1500	X60	D8
Ampton, Suffolk	1628	M452	D4
	1638	M511	D4
Apethorpe, Northants	1440	G130	D2
Appleby, Cumb	1616	M443	D4
Appleby Magna, Leics	1396	GNP45	D1
Arras, France	1585	A102	D10
Arundel, Sussex	1416	G167	D2
	1435	G168	D2
Ash, Kent	1498	G99	D2
	1617	M79	D4
	1618	M80	D4
Ashbourne, Derbys	1372	G212	D1
	1403	G212	D2
	1447	G58	D2
	1483	GNP21	D2
	1505	S169	D3
	1581	R115	D3
	1590	S91,L33	D3
	1591	R183	D3
	1592	M392	D3
	1789	A131	D5
	1805	N540	D6
	1882	X67	D8
	1896	–	D8
Ashby de la Zouch, Leics	1483	G106, X15	D2
	1526	S48	D3
	1561	G112	D3
Ashby Folville	1347	A112	D1
	1485	S49	D2
	1607	R221	D4
	1629	R220	D4
Ashby St Ledger, Northants	1634	M311	D4
	1657	M312	D4
Ashover, Derbys	1518	G69	D2
Ashley, Staffs	1593	R16	D3
Ashprington, Devon	1692	A189	D4
Ashton, Northants	1365	G22	D1
Ashwell, Rutland	1481	S192	D2
	15th cent	GNP80	D2
Ashwellthorpe, Norfolk	1417	G121, L1	D2
Astley, Warwicks	1457	GNP?	D2
	1483	G176	D2
	1530	G177	D3
	?	–	D9/124
Aston, Warwicks	1370	GNP10	D1
	1390	GNP92	D1
	1460	GNP90	D2
	1462	GNP91	D2
	1626	M276	D4
Aston on Trent, Derbys	1450	G60, L1, L12	D2
Aston on Trent Hall, Derbys	?	–	D10
Aston Bottrell, Shrops	1588	S71,L27	D3
Aston Flamville, Leics	1549	S231,L32,L33	D3
	1552	TT12	D3
Atcham, Shrops	1524	S34	D3
Attenborough, Notts	1621	M373	D4
Aubourn, Lincs	1587	R219	D3
Audley, Staffs	1360	GNP85	D1
	1623	R261	D4
	1656	S267	D4
Avening, Gloucs	1615	M166	D4
Averham, Notts	1611	M595	D4
Aylesbury, Bucks	1380	GNP2	D1
	1584	R150	D3
Aymestrey, Hereford	1522	S255	D3
Bacton, Hereford	1578	M133	D3

Location	Date	Note	Table
Baglan, South Wales	1875	X64	D8
Bakewell, Derbys	1376	M1	D1
	1403	GNP17	D2
	15th cent	G72	D2
	1566	T13	D3
	1611	M594	D4
	1880	No add details	D8
Banbury, Oxford	1438	S209	D2
Barcelona, Spain	1364	Appendix M Sec 13	
	1406	Appendix M Sec 13	
Barcheston, Warwick	1555	T18	D3
Bardney, Lincs	1446	S47	D2
	1508	S162	D3
Barlborough, Derbys	1399	A111	D1
Barling Magna, Essex	15th	X77	D8
Barlow, Derbys	1467	S154	D2
Barmston, Yorks	1420	G195	D2
	1634	TT45	D4
	1645	TT46	D4
Barnstaple, Devon	1634	M235	D4
	1653	M234	D4
Barnwell, Northants	1625	M245	D4
Barrow-on-Trent, Derbys	14th cent	G56	D1
Barthomley, Cheshire	1389	G3	D1
	1529	GNP14	D3
Barton in Fabis, Notts	1598	M403	D3
	1606		D11
	1616	R19	D4
	1671	M22	D4
Bath, Somerset	1605	M415	D4
	1606	X49	D11
	1618	R20	D4
	1619	R254	D4
	1633	M291	D4
Bath, Eyre Mortuary, Chapel	1863	No add detail	D8
Batley, Yorks	1396	G207, L17	D1
Battle, Sussex	1548	T16	D3
Beachamwell, Norfolk	15th cent	–	D9/47A
Beaumaris, Wales	15th	G209	D2
Beckbury, Shrops	1505	S32	D3
	1595	–	D9/87
Beckington, Somerset	1619	M442	D4
Bedale, Yorks	14th	A160	D1
Beddington, Surrey	1611	M250	D4
Belton, Lincs	1641	M81	D4
Belton, Rutland	1558	S17	D3
Berkeley, Gloucs	1364	G11	D1
	1490	G87, A85	D2
	1615	R1	D4
Berkhamsted, Herts	1305	–	D9/3
	1920	–	D8
Berry Pomeroy, Devon	1641	–	D9/99
Betley, Staffs	1610	M421	D4
Beverley, Yorks	1665	M28	D4
Bilborough, Notts	1592	–	D9/83A
Bingham, Notts	1458	A237	D2
Birmingham, St Martin	1390	GNP89	D1
	1500	GNP94	D3
	1874	X34	D8
	1908	X70	D8
Bisham Abbey, Berks	1421	A20, L1	D2
	1566	R44	D3
	1605	W3	D4
	1609	M96, X53	D4
Bishop Burton, Yorks	1649	R192	D4
Bishops Cleeve, Gloucs	1636	R162	D4
Bishops Hull, Somerset	1609	M121	D4
Bittadon, Devon	1691	M233	D4
Blackburn, Lancs	1612	M446	D4
Blackmore, Essex	1594	A228	D3
Blakesley, Northants	1614	M315	D4
Bletchingley, Surrey	1559	TT43	D3
	1625	M488	D4
	1450	G40	D2
	1616	S181	D4
	1693	–	D9/104
Blickling, Norfolk	1870	A122	D6
Blithfield, Staffs	1480	S142	D2
	15th cent	–	D9/114
	1508	S144	D3
	1513	S141	D3
	1534	S61	D3
	1541	S145	D3
	1557	S62	D3
	1586	S64	D3
	1593	S63	D3
	1673	S143	D4
Blore Ray, Staffs	1618	M21	D4
Blunham, Beds	14th cent	X45	D8
	1620	R258	D4
Bodiam, Sussex	1423	A211	D2
Bolsover, Derbys	1617	M142	D4
	17th	X47	D10
	18th	B126	D10
Boscastle, Cornwall	1611	M418	D4
Boreham, Essex	1589	R138	D3

Location	Date	Note	Table
Bosbury, Hereford	1573	R241	D3
	1575	R242	D3
Boston, Lincs	1430	A233	D2
	15th cent	–	D9/23A
	16th cent	GNP57	D3
	16th cent	GNP58	D3
Boston, Mass, USA	1420	Q3	D2
Bothal, Northumberland	1513	GNP66	D3
Bottesford, Leics	1414	G103, L15	D2
	1421	G105, L15	D2
	1543	T7	D3
	1563	R6	D3
	1591	R7	D3
	1591	R29	D3
	1612	R8	D4
	1632	M89	D4
Bottisham, Cambs	1599	M228	D3
	1638	M229	D4
Bowdon, Cheshire	1519	S268	D3
	1630	M496	D4
Bovet Tracey, Devon	1626	M239	D4
Boxted, Suffolk	1675	A39	D4
	1725	A39	D5
Bradford, Yorks	1767	M538	D5
	1911	M550	D6
	1919	M556	D6
	1990	A200	D6
	1918	X58	D8
Bradgate, Leics	1614	M205	D4
Bradley, Staffs	1633	M223	D4
Bradwell Juxta Coggeshall, Essex	1592	M165	D3
Bramfield, Suffolk	1629	R164	D4
Bramley, Hants	1532	–	D9/60
	1604	M414	D4
Brasted, Kent	1649	M260	D4
Bray, Berks	1622	M110	D4
Breadsall, Derbys	15th cent	–	D9/115
	1616	–	D9/94A
Breaston, Derbys	1720	X61	D8
Bredon, Worcs	1611	M168	D4
Bredwardine, Hereford	1415	GNP34	D2
Breedon-on-the-Hill, Leics	1494	S79, L25	D2
	1545	S81, L30	D3
	1571	R73	D3
	1585	R74	D3
	1598	M95	D3
Brereton, Cheshire	1618	M476	D4
Brewood, Staffs	1517	S226	D2
	1556	T19	D3
	1560	T20	D3
	1615	R83	D4
	1630	M134	D4
	1632	R84	D4
	1643	M522	D4
Bridgend, Glamorgan	1906	X84	D8
Brightling, Sussex	1954	M558	D6
Brinsop, Hereford	1926	X85	D8
Bristol, Somerset	1474	G89	D2
	1550	R229	D3
	1602	S164	D4
	1603	X10	D11
	1606	X10	D4
	1615	M167	D4
	1617	R35	D4
	1627	M243	D4
	1627	M171	D4
	1630	M495	D4
Bristol, St Mark's Chapel	1602	R34	D4
Broad Hinton, Wilts	1645	R175	D4
Brocklesby, Lincs	1587	M123	D3
	1629	M318	D4
	1770	W2	D10
	1914	M551	D6
Bromham, Beds	1603	R252	D4
Bromham, Wilts	1492	G183	D2
Bromsgrove, Worcs	1450	G184, L13	D2
	1490	G185	D2
	1490	GNP43	D2
	1550	GNP100	D3
	1859	No add details	D8
Broome, Norfolk	1927	No add details	D6
Brooksby, Leics	1481	S124	D2
Broughton, Lincs	1404	GNP53	D2
Broughton, Oxford	1456	GNP74	D2
	1470	GNP75	D2
Broxbourne, Herts	1609	A167	D4
Bulkington, Warwicks	1530	TT30	D3
Bunbury, Cheshire	1393	G2	D1
	1602	S163	D4
Bunny, Notts	1603	M410	D4
	1741	M411	D5
Burbage, Leics	1578	S21	D3
	1643	M521	D4
Bures, St Mary, Suffolk	1300	X1	D10
Bures, St Stephen, Suffolk	1141	A25	D10
	1370	G29	D1
	1420	G113	D2

Location	Date	Note	Table
Burford, Oxford	1628	R51	D4
Burghfield, Berks	1460	A47	D2
Burford, Shrops	1426	G147	D2
Burghill, Hereford	1450	G93	D2
Burley, Rutland	15th cent	GNP78	D2
	1813	A193	D6
Burscough, Lancs	–	GNP42	D2
	1504	–	D9/48B
Burton Agnes, Yorks	1481	G198	D2
	1727	X55	D8
Burton Joyce, Notts	1550	S53	D3
	1617	S235	D4
Burton-by-Lincoln, Lincs	1639	M320	D4
Burton on Trent (Stapenhill)	1496	S6	D2
Burton on Trent, Derbys	15th cent	–	D9/40
Burton Pedwardine, Staffs	1610	M319	D4
Bury St Edmunds, Suffolk	1467	A26	D2
	1501	A27	D3
	1533	–	D9/62
	1536	A28	D3
Burwell, Cambs	1613	M334	D4
Bushbury, Warwick	1593	S98	D3
	1594	S257	D3
Buxton, Derbys	1908	X66	D10
Caerleon, Monmouth	15th cent	X96	D8
	19th cent	–	D8
Caerphilly, South Wales	1902	–	D8
Caldecote, Warwicks	1570	*See* D9/77	D3
	1616	M435	D4
	1648	M436	D4
Caldey Island, Pembroke	1390	–	D9/23
Callington, Devon	1503	G54	D3
Cambridge	1624	R262	D4
Cambridge, Gonville & Caius	1575	M635	D4
Canterbury, Kent	1292	–	D9/1
	1348	G14	D1
	1390	G16	D1
	1396	G15	D1
	1413	G97, L1	D2
	1437	G98	D2
	1589	M486	D3
	1625	M485	D4
	1627	M491	D4
	1632		D4
	?	–	D9/124
Canterbury Old Priory, Kent	1540	–	D9/71
Cardiff, Empire Theatre	1900	–	D9/111
Cardiff, Ely Rise	19th cent	–	D10
Cardiff, St Catherine, Wales	?	–	D8
Cardiff University	1903	–	D10
Cardington, Shrops	1607	M141	D4
Carlton Curlieu, Leics	1622	R195	D4
Carmarthen, Wales	?	–	D9/125
Castle Donington, Leics	15th cent	A145	D9/113
	1529	G111	D3
Chalfont St Giles, Bucks	1671	M532	D4
Charlecote, Warwick	1601	R65, L10	D4
	1605	M120, L10	D4
Charlton, Surrey	1612	A203	D10
Charwelton, Northants	1564	R13	D3
Chatsworth House Chapel, Dby	1688	A130	D4
	1698	–	D9/105
	1711	–	D9/106
	?	–	D10
Cheadle, Cheshire	1461	G46	D2
	1473	G47	D2
Cheam, Surrey	1590	M147	D3
	1603	M108	D4
	1604	A165	D4
Checkendon, Oxford	1629	M494	D4
	1673	M533	D4
Checkley, Staffs	1560	R234	D3
Chellaston, Derbys	1523	S198	D3
	1557	S92	D3
	1880	No add details	D8
	1400	–	D9/26
Chellaston Methodist, Derbys	1880	A74	D8
Chelmsford, Essex	1920	–	D8
Chelsea, Middlesex	1581	M573	D3
Cheltenham, Gloucs	1877	No add details	D8
Chenies, Bucks	1555	T29	D3
	1559	R230	D3
	1601	A161	D4
	1603	A165	D4
	1611	A184	D4
	1623	R259	D4
	1653	R271	D4

Location	Date	Note	Table
	1891	A183	D6
Chester Cathedral	1863	R288	D8
	1902	R289	D8
Chesterfield, Derbys	1411	–	D9/27A
	1433	X22	D9/29
	1451	X22	D9/31
	1469	X22	D9/32
	1510	GNP25, L2, L7	D3
	1558	M115	D3
	1585	R62, L7	D3
	1588	S7, L7	D3
	1592	M116	D3
	1595	R63, L7	D3
	1604	R64, L7	D4
Chesterton, Warwicks	1585	R119	D3
Chetnole, Dorset	1865	A176	D8
Chevening, Kent	1590	R196	D3
	1613	M217	D4
	1615	M216	D4
Chichester, Sussex	15th cent	–	D9/42
	1293	X74	D11
	1503	GNP88	D3
	1536	G169	D3
	1596	M564	D3
	1896	A202	D6
	1907	M278	D6
	1928	M563	D6
Chicksands, Beds	15th	X76	D8
Chiddingly, Sussex	1612	M131	D4
Chigwell, Essex	1595	M258	D3
	1631	M497	D4
Chilham, Kent	1631	R137	D4

Location	Date	Note	Table
Chillingham, Northumberland	1443	GNP65	D2
Chilton, Bucks	1608	R31	D4
	1631	M93	D4
Chilton, Suffolk	1491	G165	D2
	1500	G164	D3
	1626	M138	D4
Chipping Campden, Gloucs	1629	M130	D4
	1633	M54	D4
	1642	M129	D4
Chipping Norton, Oxford	1502	G144	D3
Chipping Sodbury, Gloucs	1501	S195	D2
	1872	M543	D6
Christchurch, Hants	1445	GNP31	D2
	1784	M539	D5
Church Gresley, Derbys	1699	A107	D4
Churchover, Warwick	1641	M111	D4
	1641	M112	D4
Cirencester, Gloucs	1638	M188	D4
	1896	–	D8
Claverley, Shrops	1448	S186	D2
	1559	R90	D3
	1599	M228	D3
	1577	S19	D3
Clevedon, Somerset	1415	S163	D2
Clifton, Bedford	1549	G34	D3
Clifton, Notts	1403	G133&G134	D2
	1457	S127	D2
	15th cent	A235	D2
	1520	S126	D3

Location	Date	Note	Table
	1587	R121	D3
Clifton Campville, Stafford	1545	G161	D3
Clumber, Notts	?	–	D8
Clydach, Wales	1903	–	D8
Coates-by-Stow, Lincs	1470	S212	D2
	1653	M321	D4
Cobham, Kent	1561	R276	D3
Cobham, Surrey	1361	G211	D1
Cockayne Hatley, Beds	1627	M490	D4
Cockersand, Lancs	1540	–	D9/70
Codsall, Staffs	1630	R281	D4
Cofton Hackett, Worcs	1514	S224	D2
	1528	GNP96	D3
Coleshill, Warwick	1519	G178	D2
	1549	TT33, L32	D3
	1558	GNP98	D3
	1587	R136	D3
Colmworth, Beds	1641	M198	D4
Colne Priory, Essex – *see* Bures	–	–	–
Colston Bassett, Notts	1892	X21	D6
Compeigne, France	!6th	A22	D10
Compton Verney House, War	1636	R267	D4
Compton Winyates. Warwick	15th cent	GNP95	D2
Condover, Shrops	1587	R199	D3
	1598	M221	D3
	1868	A123	D6
Corsham, Wilts	1970	A199	D6
Cossington, Leics	1556	TT13	D3
Cothelstone, Somerset	1603	R57	D4

Location	Date	Note	Table
Coughton Court, Warwick	1586	A91	D3
Coventry, Warwicks	1525	T12	D9/56
	1539	T25	D9/67
	1546	T12	D3
Cowbridge, South Wales	16th cent	–	D9/44
	1616	M567	D4
	1896	X16	D8
Coxwold, Yorks	1605	M98	D4
	1631	M454	D4
Crediton, Devon	1605	M177	D4
	1630	M176	D4
Cranborne, Dorset	1641	M224	D4
Cranbrook, Kent	1490	–	D9/36A
	1550	–	D9/73A
Cranford, Middlesex	1612	M157	D4
Cranham, Gloucs (Prinknash)	1913	M566	D6
Crawley, Sussex	1875	A121	D6
Crayford, Kent	1650	M602	D4
Criech, Fife	1421	S205	D2
Crich, Derbys	1490	–	D9/39
	1513	S173, L27	D3
	1583	S172	D3
	1592	S202	D3
Crouch Hill, Herts	1933	M572	D8
Crowcombe, Somerset	1808	M292	D6
Croxall, Staffs	1350	S103	D1
	1480	S116	D2
	1485	S118	D2
	1487	S119	D2
	1490	S194	D2
	1500	S117	D3
	1520	S120	D3
	1521	S227	D3
	1530	S114	D3
	1554	S115	D3
	1605	S121	D4
Cumnor, Berks	1607	M417	D4
Curry Mallet, Somerset	1642	M535	D4
	17th cent	M536	D4
Dalby, Lincs	1621	M82	D4
	1631	M83	D4
Dale Abbey, Derbys	15th cent	–	D9/24
	1855	M542	D6
Dalton le Dale, Durham	1420	GNP29	D2
Darfield, Yorks	1410	GNP103	D2
	1658	M30	D4
	1695	A40	D4
Darley Dale, Derbys	1514	S107	D2
	1550	S174	D3
	?	S175	D3
Dartmouth, Devon	1727	M240	D5
Daventry, Warwick	1471	A24	D2
Dauntsey, Wilts	1455	S148	D2
Daybrook, Notts	1895	–	D8
Deene, Northants	1531	G128	D3
	1865	A196	D6
Denbury, Devon	1736	M242	D5
Dennington, Suffolk	1441	G162, L13	D2
Denton, Lincs	1440	S217	D2
	1602	M407	D4
Derby Cathedral	1480	S75	D2
	1601	M145	D4
	1859	No add details	D8
	1920	–	D8
Derby, King St	19th cent	–	D10
Derby, St Andrew	1887	–	D9/109
Derby, St Werburgh	?	–	D9/121
Didsbury, Lancs	1612	M326	D4
Dijon, Cote d'Or, France	1404	A157	D2
	1423	A83	D10
Dodford, Northants	1444	G125	D2
Dorchester, Dorset	1899	A156	D8
Dorchester on Thames, Oxford	14th cent	A137	D1
	1354	A41	D1
	1390	GNP11	D1
Dorney, Bucks	1607	M377	D4
Dover, Kent	1374	–	D9/12
Doveridge, Staffs	1359	S156	D1
	1495	S104	D2
Down Ampney, Gloucs	1637	M187	D4
Draycott-in-the-Moors, Staffs	1522	S222	D3
	1560	R91	D3
	1662	R272	D4
Droitwich, Worcs	1616	M189	D4
Dronfield, Derbys	15th cent	G65	D2
Dublin, Ireland	1855	X30	D8
Duffield, Derbys	1536	G70	D3
	1600	S203	D4
Dunmow, Essex	1460	G83	D2
	1480	G84	D2
Dunster, Somerset	1428	GNP83, L13	D2
	1493	S214	D2
Durban, South Africa	1910	–	D8
Durham Cathedral	1341	–	D9/5
	1350	A21	D8

Location	Date	Note	Table
	1367	G6	D1
	1372	–	D9/11A
	1380	G7 & L16	D9/15
	1388	G7	D1
Dyrham and Hinton	1581	R246	D3
Easebourne, Sussex	1542	G170	D3
	1592	R80	D3
East Bridgford, Notts	1627	M62	D4
East Donyland, Essex	1613	M596	D4
East Harling, Norfolk	1370	G21	D1
East Horndon, Essex	1440	X38	D2
	15th/16th cent	–	D9/117
East Horsley, Surrey	1626	R207	D4
East Lockinge, Berks	1633	M45	D4
East Shefford, Berks	1440	G33, L11	D2
East Sutton, Kent	1585	M598	D3
	1609	M599	D4
	1805	A133	D6
	1810	A132	D6
Easton Maudit, Northants	1612	M202	D4
	1631	M201	D4
Easton Neston, Northants	1577	M31	D3
	1612	R17	D4
Eastchurch, Kent	1622	A223	D4
Eastling, Kent	1592	M603	D3
Eastrington, Yorks	1427	S164	D2
	1462	GNP107	D2
Eastwell/Boughton Aluph – *see* London V&A			

Location	Date	Note	Table
Eccleshall, Staffs	1554	TT14	D3
	1578	TT38	D3
	1609	M293	D4
	1843	R210	D6
Edensor, Derbys	1616	R277	D4
Edinburgh, St Cuthbert	1880	A118	D8
Edinburgh, St Giles	1874	M544	D6
	1888	A95	D6
	1892	M195	D6
	1904	A93	D6
	1918	M194	D6
Edgcote, Northants	1585	R118	D3
	1608	R112	D4
Edgmond, Shrops	1425	S177	D2
Edinburgh, Museum of Scotland	17th cent	–	D10
Edmondthorpe, Leics	1654	M206	D4
Eggesford, Devon	1630	M230	D4
	1648	R20	D4
Egham, Surrey	1595	M160	D3
	1612	M161	D4
	1638	M162	D4
	1663	M163	D4
Egmanton, Notts	1579	S22	D3
Elford, Staffs	1370	GNP84	D1
	1408	G158	D2
	1525	G159	D3
Ellesborough, Bucks	1638	M175	D4
Ellough, Suffolk	1877	M285	D6
Elmley Castle, Worcs	1632	R54	D4
Elmore, Gloucs	1472	–	D9/33
Elstow, Beds	1594	M90	D3
Elvaston, Derbys	1610	R158	D4

Location	Date	Note	Table
Ely, Cambs	1337	–	D9/4
	1609	M375	D4
	1636	M374	D4
	1853	A158	D6
Emneth, Norfolk	1617	R10	D4
Englefield, Berks	1605	M44	D4
English Bicknor, Gloucs	1918	X14	D8
Enville, Staffs	1559	T24	D3
Eton College, Bucks	1623	M126	D4
Etwall, Derbys	1503	S168	D3
	1541	A231	D3
Eversley, Hants	1862	A195	D6
Everton, Beds	1624	M383	D4
Everton, Notts	1440	S11	D2
Ewelme, Oxford	1477	G142	D2
Exeter, Devon	1376	–	D9/14A
	1419	G75	D2
	1575	M341	D3
	1621	R144	D4
	1626	R143	D4
	1628	A146	D4
	1715	M328	D5
	?	–	D9/118
Exton, Rutland	1524	GNP79	D3
	1600	M32	D4
Eydon, Northants	1919	M555	D6
Eye, Hereford	1510	G94	D3
	1563	T3	D3
Eyeworth, Beds	1616	M91	D4
	1623	A69	D4
	1638	M92	D4
Falmouth, Cornwall	1617	M441	D4

Location	Date	Note	Table
Faringdon, Berks	1553	T2	D3
	1583	S200	D3
	1600	M338	D4
Farthinghoe, Northants	1635	A37	D4
Faversham, Kent	1618	M604	D4
	1651	M605	D4
Fawsley, Northants	1533	G127	D3
Fawsley, Worcs	1616	M437	D4
Fécamp, France	1414	Appendix V	D8
Felbrigg, Norfolk	1669	M215	D4
Felsted, Essex	1620	R160	D4
Fenny Bentley, Derbys	1580	G71	D3
Fenny Drayton, Leics	1543	(GNP50, TT5) L30	D3
	1554	TT42	D3
	1596	R43	D3
	1628	M99	D4
	All	X110	–
Finchingfield, Essex	1889	M640	D8
Flawford (Flawforth), Notts	1380	Appendix H	D8
Flaxley, Gloucs	1856	X62	D8
Flaxton, Northants	1660	M317	D4
Fledborough, Notts	1360	G132	D1
Fletching, Sussex	1596	R251	D3
Flitton, Beds	1614	A70, A71	D4
Forncett St Peter, Norfolk	1520	TT39	D3
Fornham, Suffolk	1500	–	D9/48A
Forton, Staffs	1633	M401	D4
Fountains Abbey, Yorks	15th cent	–	D9/41
Fowey, Cornwall	1610	M143	D4
Framlingham, Suffolk	1554	A29	D3
	1557	A30	D3
	1557	A31	D3
	1560	R11	D3
	1614	A32	D4
	1636	TT44	D4
Freckenham, Suffolk	14th cent	X35	D1
Fryerning, Essex	1572	A227	D3
	1613	M617	D4
Folesworth, Leics	14th cent	–	D9/22
	1631	R224	D4
	1657	R225	D4
Fulham, Middlesex	1593	M393	D3
	1600	M394	D4
	1605	M395	D4
	1609	M396	D4
	1610	M578	D4
	1664	M397	D4
	1918	M398	D8
Fulmer, Bucks	1631	M585	D4
Fyfield, Oxford	1442	X92	D11
Gaddesby, Leics	1498	S216	D2
	1500	–	D11
	1848	M541	D6
Gawsworth, Cheshire	1608	R46	D4
	1619	A182	D4
	1626	R47	D4
	1643	R270	D4
Gayton, Northants	1558	TT15	D3
Gazeley, Suffolk	1604	M14	D4
Geddington, Northants	1533	S229	D3
Gedling, Notts	1487	S277	D2
Gilston, Herts	1636	M517	D4
	1657	M456	D4
Glasgow, St Francis	1910	–	D8
Glastonbury, Somerset	1470	G154	D2
Glenfield, Leics	15th cent	A222	D2
Glentworth, Lincs	1592	M84	D3
Glossop, Derbys	1572	S180	D3
Gloucester Cathedral	1327	G9	D1
	1457	G86	D2
	15th cent	A48	D2
	1535	G88	D3
	1588	M58	D3
	1604	R25	D4
	1615	M60	D4
	1622	M55	D4
	1623	M57	D4
	1626	X11	D11
	1630	M59	D4
	1638	R26	D4
	1713	X57	D11
	1905	A194	D6
Gloucester, St Nicholas	1626	R263	D4
	1626	X11	D11
	1645	M526	D4
Gnosall, Staffs	15th cent	A219	D2
Godshill, IOW	1522	G91	D3
Gotham, Notts	1624	M24	D4
	1625	M23	D4
	1746	M458	D5
	1881	M25	D6
Grafton Regis, Northants	1415	TT22	D2
Grandborough, Bucks	15th cent	X99	D2
Great Addington, Northants	1490	GNP64	D2
Great Brington, Northants	1522	R14	D3

Location	Date	Note	Table
	1586	R59	D3
	1599	R60	D3
	1638	R269	D4
Great Cubley, Derbys	1435	GNP20, L2	D2
	1491	G73, L2	D2
Great Grimsby, Lincs	1408	S185	D2
	1410	S184	D2
Great Hale, Lincs	1652	S183	D4
	1668	M337	D4
Great Hallingbury, Essex	17th cent	X105	D4
Great Malvern, Worcs	1615	R170	D4
Great Milton, Oxford	1616	M174	D4
	1695	A190	D4
Great Mitton, Lancs	1594	R222	D3
	1629	M327	D4
Great Parndon, Essex	1661	M615	D4
Great Warley, Essex	1633	M502	D4
Great Waltham, Essex	1609	R166	D4
Great Wilne, Derbys	1622	M448	D4
Great Wishford, Wilts	1629	M222	D4
Greatham, Hants	1632	R285	D4
Greens Norton, Northants	1457	G126	D2
	1558	M362	D3
	1606	M363	D4
	1607	M316	D4
Greensted, Ongar	1585	M388	D3
Grendon, Warwicks	1460	GNP93	D2
	1539	S23	D3
	1592	R125	D3
	1612	M423	D4
Gresford, Denbigh	1602	M263	D4
	1638	M262	D4
Greystoke, Cumbria	1367	G4	D1
	1436	GNP15	D2
Grove, Notts	1455	S150	D2
Guisborough, Yorks	1380	–	D9/17
Haccombe, Devon	1373	G74	D1
Hackington, Kent	1592	R193	D3
Hackleton & Horton, Northants	1546	T27	D3
	1580	R149	D3
Haddington, Lothian	1638	–	D9/98
Hainton, Lincs	1587	M85	D3
	1595	A57	D3
	1610	M86	D4
Halesowen, Shrops	1417	–	D9/27C
Halsall, Lancs	1470	G102	D2
	1490	GNP43	D2
	1523	GNP43	D3
Halsham, Yorks	15th cent	G202	D2
Hambleden, Bucks	1450	X39	D2
	1633	M504	D4
Hampton Gay, Oxford	1665	M474	D4
Hanbury, Staffs	1340	G28	D1
	1595	TT2	D3
	1624	M481	D4
	?	X83	D8
Hardingstone, Northants	1606	M415	D4
Hardwick, Northants	1604	M413	D4
Harefield, Middlesex	1610	M361	D4
	1617	M438	D4
	1623	M439	D4
	1636	M440	D4
Harewood, Yorks	1419	G193.L3.L12	D2
	1426	GNP104, L3	D2
	1430	G192, L3	D2
	1465	G196	D2
	1487	G197	D2
	1497	S208	D2
	1510	G206	D3
Harewood House. Yorks	1938	A50	D10
Harlaxton, Lincs	1410	GNP56, L12	D2
Harlton, Cambs	1623	M376	D4
	1631	M453	D4
Harpham, Yorks	1349	TT26	D1
Harrington, Northants	1588	M220	D3
Hartington, Derbys	1856	–	D9/108
Hartshorn, Derbys	15th cent	S245	D2
Haugh, Lincs	1606	M548	D4
Haughton, Staffs	1520	S269	D3
Haughmond Abbey, Shrops	1528	S221	D3
Haversham, Bucks	1422	G39	D2
Hawkeden, Suffolk	1471	–	D9/32B
Hawnby, Yorks	1608	M249	D4
Hawstead, Suffolk	1610	M571	D4

Location	Date	Note	Table
	1617	M9	D4
Heacham, Norfolk	1927	No add details	D6
Headingley, Yorks	1895	–	D8
Healaugh, Yorks	1568	R98	D3
Hereford	1375	G13	D1
	14th cent	–	D9/7
	14th cent	–	D9/20
	1474	GNP35	D2
	1500	G95	D3
	1566	T3	D3
	1617	R227	D4
	1636	M384	D4
	?	X88	D8
Highclere, Hants	1601	R39	D4
Hillesdon, Bucks	1558	T14	D3
	1576	R130	D3
Hintlesham, Norfolk	1594	M211	D3
	1624	M212	D4
Hinton on the Green, Gloucs	1490	S160	D2
Hinton Ampnor, Hants	1638	R200	D4
Hinton St George, Somerset	1588	R78	D3
	1728	R49	D5
Hinxhill, Kent	1632	M500	D4
Hirwaun, Wales	1936	–	D8
Hitcham, Bucks	1580	M385	D3
	1624	M386	D4
Hitcham, Suffolk	1636	M507	D4
Hoar Cross, Staffs	1904	A126	D6
Hoby, Leics	1567	R100	D3
Holcombe Regis, Devon	1634	M579	D4
Holdenby, Northants	1490	S215	D2
Holkham, Norfolk	1636	M305	D4
	1639	M306	D4
Holkham Hall, Norfolk	1756	W4	D10
Holme, Notts	1491	A84	D2
Holme Lacy, Hereford	1555	T4	D3
Holme Pierrepont, Notts	13th cent	GNP69	D1
	1499	G135, L14	D2
	1615	R3	D4
Holme next the Sea, Norfolk	1607	M601	D4
Honiton, Devon	1886	–	D9/110
Hope under Dinmore, Herford	1559	S36	D3
Hopkinstown, South Wales	1914	–	D8
Hornby, Yorks	1422	G188	D2
Hornchurch, Essex	1617	M475	D4
	1625	M487	D4
	1638	M510	D4
Horndon on the Hill, Essex	1634	M506	D4
Hornsea, Yorks	1430	TT25	D2
Hornsey, Middlesex	1590	S10	D3
Horseheath, Cambs	1613	M425	D4
Horwood, Devon	1450	G76	D2
Hothfield, Kent	17th cent	A225	D4
Hougham, Kent	1607	M606	D4
Hoveringham, Notts	1403	GNP68	D2
Howden, Yorks	1491	G210	D2
Hulcote, Beds	1615	M34	D4
Hull – *see* Kingston upon Hull	–	–	–
Humberstone, Leics	1451	TTI, L6	D2
	1500	L6	D9/48
Hungerford, Berks	1891	X90	D8
	1918	M582	D6
Hunsworth, Norfolk	1506	–	D9/50
Hurst, Berks	1631	M33	D4
Huyton, Lancs	1360	GNP6	D1
Hythe, Kent	1597	M180	D3
Ickenham, Suffolk	1472	–	D9/33A
Ightham, Kent	1638	M607	D4
	1641	M608	D4
Ilam, Derbys	1626	R208	D4
Illington, Norfolk	?	X89	D8
Ilstom, South Wales	1892	–	D8
Ilston on the Hill, Leics	1639	M323	D4
Ilton, Somerset	1470	G157	D2
Ingatestone, Essex	1573	R140	D3
	1593	M484	D4

Location	Date	Note	Table
	1621	M483	D4
	1624	M482	D4
Ingham, Norfolk	1364	A208	D1
Inkberrow, Worcs	1631	R266	D4
Instow, Devon	1633	M231	D4
Ipsley, Warwick	1558	S18	D3
Ipswich, St Stephen's, Suffolk	1637	M288	D4
Irthingborough, Northants	1490	GNP62 & 63	D2
Isfield, Sussex	1631	R38	D4
Kedleston, Derbys	1406	G63	D2
	1456	G67	D2
	1547	S60	D3
	1664	M26	D4
Kedleston Hall, Derbys	1760	W1	D10
Kedington, Suffolk	1503	A33	D3
	1520	A34	D3
	1609	M16	D4
	1610	M15	D4
	1653	M17	D4
Keele, Staffs	1593	M431	D3
	1613	A170	D4
	1615	M430	D4
Kegworth, Leics	1606	–	D9/92
Keighley, Yorks	1910	–	D8
Kelstern, Lincs	1604	M87	D4
Kemberton, Shrops	1882	A143	D8

Location	Date	Note	Table
Kempsey, Worcs	1620	R157	D4
Kendal, Cumbria	1920	M569	D6
	1920	M570	D6
Kenilworth Castle, Warwick	?	–	D10
Kentchurch, Hereford	1616	R171	D4
Kidderminster, Worcs	1445	G186	D2
	1473	A154	D2
	1568	R55	D3
	1630	M109	D4
Kidwell, Dyffryn House	15th cent	–	D10
Kilkenny, Ireland	15th cent	A56 & A140	D2
King's Pyon, Hereford	1440	X38	D2
Kingsbury, Middlesex	1932	A119	D8
Kingsbury, Warwicks	1360	GNP9	D1
King's Lynn, Norfolk	1623	M310	D4
	1623	M308	D4
	1675	M309	D4
Kings Norton, Warwick	1513	S55	D3
	1588	S90	D3
	1631	M277	D4
Kingston on Soar, Notts	1537	A96	D9/65
	1900	A96	D8
	1933	A114	D8
Kingston upon Hull, Yorks	1366	G32	D1
	1490	A147	D2

Location	Date	Note	Table
	1666	X33	D8
Kington, Hereford	1469	GNP36	D2
Kinlet, Shrops	1410	G146	D2
	1478	G150	D2
	1531	T10	D3
	1548	M296	D3
Kinnersley, Hereford	1633	M503	D4
Kinver, Staffs	15th cent	A221	D2
	16th cent	A220	D3
Kirby Bellars, Leics	1360	GNP4	D1
	1380	GNP5	D1
Kirkby Mallory, Leics	1594	S99	D3
	1595	S260	D3
Kirk Langley, Derbys	1511	S223	D2
	1559	S68, L31	D3
Kirkleatham, Yorks	1659	M531	D4
Kirklees, Thornhill, Yorks	1449	A153	D2
Knipton, Lancs	1523	S238	D3
Knowlton, Kent	1721	M609	D5
Lambourn, Berks	1558	T1	D3
	1649	X54	D4
Lamport with Faxton, Northants	1616	M3	D4
Landogo, Monmouth	1889	–	D8
Landwade, Suffolk	1620	M339	D4
	1689	M340	D4
Langar, Notts	1537	S136	D3

Location	Date	Note	Table
	1558	A1	D3
	1590	R283	D3
Langford, Norfolk	1727	A129	D5
Langham, Rutland	1533	S197	D3
Lanhydrock, Cornwall	1915	M552	D6
Latton, Essex	1583	M389	D3
Layer Marney, Essex	1360	G8	D1
Leaveland, Kent	1606	M365	D4
Ledbury, Hereford	1596	S178	D3
	1630	M186	D4
	1638	M514	D4
Lee, London	1604	M565	D4
Leeds, Yorks	1895	–	D8
Leicester, Cathedral	1520	G107	D2
	1589	S4	D3
	1609	S5	D4
	1638	M588	D4
	1656	M77	D4
	2015	X41	D8
Leicester. Greyfriars	1495	A45, TT3	D9/37
Leicester, St Margaret	1496	A151	D2
Leicester, Trinity Hospital	1394	G17	D1
Leigh, Essex	1641	M519	D4
Leigh, Staffs	1523	GNP87	D3
Leigh, Worcs	1606	X48	D11
	1615	M429	D4

Location	Date	Note	Table
	1640	A136	D4
Leighton, Shrops	1540	TT40	D3
Leighton Bromswold, Hunts	1567	R103	D3
	1572	R104	D3
Lenton, Lincs	1606	M88	D4
Letherington, Suffolk	1628	–	D9/96
Leyton, Essex	1612	A168	D4
	1612	M253	D4
Lichfield, Staffs	1530	–	D9/58
	1880	A117	D8
	1880	A197	D6
Lilford, Northants	1635	–	D9/97
Lillingstone, Dayrell, Bucks	1571	R32	D3
Lincoln Cathedral, Lincs	1705	S264	D5
	1732	S265	D5
	1894	A174	D6
Lincoln, St Mary Wigford	1618	R21	D4
Lingfield, Surrey	1453	G166, L1	D2
Linton, Kent	1615	M450	D4
	1627	M449	D4
Litchborough, Northants	1618	R217	D4
Little Baddow, Essex	1639	M614	D4
Little Chart, Kent	1509	G101	D3
Little Easton, Essex	1610	A60	D4

Location	Date	Note	Table
Little Gaddesden, Herts	1611	M584	D4
Little Waltham, Essex	1663	M613	D4
Little Warley, Essex	1641	M127	D4
	1658	M128	D4
	17th cent	–	D4
Little Wilne, Derbys	1491	S106	D2
Livermore Magna, Suffolk	1539	X35	D9/68
Llandaff, Wales	15th cent	GNP116	D2
	1500	GNP115	D3
	1500	GNP117	D3
	1528	GNP118	D3
Llandaff, Insole Court, Wales	1880	X80	D10
Llandegai, Wales	1480	GNP112	D2
	1650	M528	D4
Llanfarchell (Whitchurch)	1578	R72	D3
Llanfleiddan, Wales	1896	–	D8
Llanrwst, Denbigh	1639	M225	D4
Llansanfraed, Monmouth	1786	X108	D5
Lockeley, Hants	1892	–	D8
Lockington, Leics	1500	G109	D3
	1509	S58, L29	D3
	1540	S74	D3
	1555	S59, L29	D3
Lod, Israel	1870	X52	D8
Lolworth, Cambs	1480	S213	D2

Location	Date	Note	Table
Longford, Derbys	1350	GNP18	D1
	1416	G59	D2
London, Aldgate	1571	M251	D3
London, Bayswater	1874	X31	D8
London, Bishopsgate	1400	G114	D2
	1594	TT24	D3
	1605	M208	D4
	1609	R2	D4
	1643	M523	D4
	1903	M610	D6
London, Chancery Lane	1610	M18	D4
London, Charterhouse	1371	A64	D9/11
	1615	M7	D4
London, Crooked Lane	1562	–	D9/75
London, Crouch Hill	1933	M572	D8
London, Eastcheap	16th cent	–	D9/45
London, Faringdon	16th cent	–	D9/46
	16th cent	–	D9/47
London, Grey Friars	1359	A44	D9/9
	1537	–	D9/66
London, Hackney	1569	M364	D3
	1582	R226	D3
London, Haringey	1610	M433	D4
	1614	A63	D4
	1616	M434	D4
London, Great St Helen's	1474	G116	D2
	1579	TT35	D3
	1599	M402	D3
London, St Dunstan in the East	15th cent	–	D9/87B
London, St Giles in the Fields	1663	R273	D4
London, St Giles, Cripplegate	1602	–	D9/90
	1606	–	D9/91
London, St Martin's in the Fields	1588	R49	D3
London, St Mary Graces	1380	A43	D9/16
London, St Michael, Crooked Ln	1381	–	D9/19
London, St Paul's	1358	–	D9
	1376	A18	D9
	1631	R197	D4
	1910	M156	D6
	1872–98	X63	D8
London, St Paul's (old)	1358	–	D9/8
	1374	A18	D9/13
	1381	–	D9/18
	1519	–	D9/54
	1569	–	D9/76
	1592	–	D9/84
	1595	–	D9/86
	17th cent	–	D9/88
London, St Stephen	1902	–	D8
London, St Thomas Hospital	1917	M155	D10
London, Sherehog	1613	–	D9/94
London, Smithfield	1623	M279	D4
	1641	M280	D4
	1659	M281	D4
	1660	M282	D4
	1704	M283	D5
	1738	M284	D5
London, South Kensington	1877	No add details	D8
London, Southwark	1618	M149	D4
	1625	M146	D4
	1626	X4	D4
	1633	X5	D4
London, Temple Church	1585	A67	D3
	1618	M114	D4
London, Tower of London	1447	G115	D2
	1521	T28, L36, L2	D2
	1554	T28, L36	D3
	1564	M329	D3
	1610	M429	D4
	1651	M330	D4
London, V&A	1510	A141	D10
	1580	–	D10
	1627	M489	D4
	1630	A56	D4

Location	Date	Note	Table
London, Westminster Abbey	1337	G18	D1
	1369	A78	D1
	1376	G19	D1
	1376	G20	D1
	1506	G117	D3
	1532	–	D9/61
	1568	M153	D3
	1578	R50	D3
	1585	R159	D3
	1586	R181	D3
	1587	M445	D3
	1588	M122	D3
	1589	R155	D3
	1596	R40	D3
	1596	M464	D3
	1597	A142	D3
	1597	M404	D3
	1598	R151	D3
	1598	R152	D3
	1599	M463	D3
	1600	M462	D3
	1603	R48	D4
	1605	R153	D4
	1606	R41	D4
	1606	M106	D4
	1607	M152	D4
	1608	A166	D4
	1609	A180	D4
	1616	A181	D4
	1618	A179	D4
	1623	R260	D4
	1631	M467	D4
	1631	M473	D4
	1632	R142	D4
	1652	–	D9/101
	1639	M516	D4
	1662	M469	D4
	1676	M472	D4
	1681	M465	D4
	1708	A192	D5
	1875	M468	D6
	1876	M466	D6
	1880	A75	D8
	1884	A178	D6
	1907	M471	D6
	1947	M470	D6
	1960	S263	D6
	1971	A177	D6
London, Westminster, Minster	1589	R139	D3
London, Westminster,St Margaret	1595	M400/M133	D3
London, Whitefriars	1416	A152	D2
London, Windsor Hotel	1908	X66	D10
Long Buckby, Northants	1726	A134	D5
Long Melford, Suffolk	1350	A21	D8
	1580	R148	D3
Long Whatton, Leics	1577	S113	D3
Longford, Derbys	1404	GNP121	D2
	1610	R36	D4
Los Angeles, California	1750	–	D10
Louth, Lincs	1892	M547	D6
Lowdham, Notts	1520	S1	D3
Lowick, Northants	1419	G122, L1	D2
	1498	G123, L14	D2
Ludlow, Shrops	1581	R247	D3
	1592	M297	D3
	1612	M298	D4
	1635	M505	D4
	1637	R268	D4
Lugwardine, Hereford	1634	M190	D4
	1637	M508	D4
Luton, Beds	1881	A175	D8
Lutterworth, Leics	1440	GNP47	D2
Lydiard Tregoze, Wilts	1634	R165	D4
Lynsted, Kent	1618	M35	D4
	1622	M36	D4
Mabe (Falmouth), Cornwall	15th cent	A150	D8
Macclesfield, Cheshire	1463	G48	D2
	1470	G49	D2

Location	Date	Note	Table
	1495	G50	D2
	1513	G51	D3
	1528	G52	D3
Mackworth, Derbys	1607	M103	D4
	1876	Appendix K	D8
	1902	Appendix K	D8
	1903	Appendix K	D8
Maesteg, South Wales	1895	–	D8
Madeley, Staffs	1522	TT28, L23	D3
Madingley, Cambs	1635	M226	D4
	1692	M227	D4
Madley, Hereford	1585	R244	D3
Maida Vale, London	1895	–	D8
Maldon, Essex	1602	M132	D4
Malmesbury, Wilts	14th cent	X8	D11
Malpas, Cheshire	1495	S166	D2
	1522	G53, L36	D3
	1605	R236	D4
Mamble, Worcs	1561	R145	D3
Manchester, Alexandra Park	1908	X66	D8
Manchester. Lancs	1890	X69	D8
Marchington, Staffs	1593	TT19	D3
Margam Abbey, Glam	1559	R233	D3
	1585	R245	D3
	1623	M477	D4
	1631	R231	D4
	1638	R232	D4
	All	X109	-
Margaretting, Essex	1625	M619	D4
Market Drayton, Shrops	1595	S24	D3
Marlborough, Wilts	1626	M244	D4
Marlesford, Suffolk	1641	M286	D4
Marnhull, Dorset	1478	G78	D2
Marston-on-Dove, Derbys	1560	S93	D3
	1595	S259	D3
	1597	S258	D3
Martley, Worcs	1459	GNP99	D2
Masham, Yorks	1612	M264	D4
Matlock, Derbys	1576	S94	D3
Mavesyn Ridware, Staffs	1403	TT36	D2
	1478	S135	D2
	1557	S132	D3
	1585	S134	D3
	1592	TT32, L8	D3
Melbourne, Derbys	1530	G151	D3
	1613	S108	D4
	1673	S109	D4
	1679	S110	D4
Melbury Sampford, Dorset	1467	G80	D2
	1470	G81	D2
Melton Mowbray, Leics	15th cent	GNP71	D2
	1597	S31	D3
	1628	S236	D4
Merevale, Warwicks	1440	G173, L11	D2
Meriden, Warwicks	1404	G172	D2
Mersham, Kent	1595	M405	D3
	1626	M179	D4
Merton, Surrey	1600	M144	D4
Methley, Yorks	1424	G194, L3	D2
	1461	G199	D2
Middle Claydon, Bucks	1539	G43	D3
	1608	M381	D4
	1653	M382	D4
	1877	M545	D6
Millbrook, Beds	1602	R79	D4
Millom, Cumbria	1494	G55	D2
Minster Lovell, Oxford	15th cent	GNP76	D2
Minster-in-Sheppey	1475	G100	D2
	1558	GNP39	D3
Miserden, Gloucs	1614	X12	D11
	1644	R56	D4
Misterton, Leics	1567	R97	D3
Mitcham, Surrey	1623	–	D9/95
Mitton, Lancs	1594	R126	D3
Mixbury, Oxford	1548	–	D9/72
Modbury, Devon	15th cent	GNP26	D2
Monken Hadley, Hereford	1616	M158	D4

Location	Date	Note	Table
Monks Kirby, Warwicks	1547	GNP97	D3
	1580	R114	D3
Montgomery, Powis, Wales	1360	GNP111	D1
	15th cent	GNP119	D2
	1600	M213	D4
Montréal, France	1420	Q1	D8
Morley, Derbys	1543	A232	D3
	1625	S111	D4
	1628	S276	D4
	1638	S204	D4
	1640	S237	D4
	1660	S112	D4
Mottram, Cheshire	1517	–	D9/53
Montresor, Indre et Loire, France	1523	A82	D10
Much Cowarne, Hereford	1617	R253	D4
Much Dewchurch, Hereford	1575	R172	D3
	1625	M185	D4
Much Marcle, Hereford	1635	R178	D4
Nailstone, Leics	1586	S25	D3
Nancy, Musee de Lorain, France	16th cent	A103	D10
Nantes, France	1399	A15,X18,X23	D9/27
	1408	A15	D2
Nantwich, Cheshire	1390	A5	D1
	1614	A65	D4
Narborough (Narburgh), Norfolk	1607	M119	D4
	1678	M261	D4
	1679	L9	D4
Neen Solas, Wilts	1624	M299	D4
Nether Alderley, Cheshire	1591	–	D9/83
Netherbury, Dorset	15th cent	GNP28	D2
Nettlestead, Kent	1598	M37	D3
Nettlestead, Suffolk	1625	M18	D4
	1636	M38	D4
Newark, Notts	1532	X43	D11
	1639	M359	D4
	1655	M357	D4
	1659	M358	D4
	1727	M360	D5
Newbold on Avon	1401	S57	D2
	1441	S149	D2
	1454	TT17, L12	D2
	1583	R16	D3
Newburgh Priory, Yorks	1766	X56	D8
Newbury, Berks	1481	B21, B22	D9/35
Newcastle on Tyne	1631	M498	D4
	1634	M499	D4
	1908	A135	D6
Newent, Gloucs	1370	GNP3	D1
Newport, Mon	15th cent	GNP60	D2
	19th cent	-	D8
Newport, Shrops	1530	G151	D3
Newstead Abbey, Notts	1567	TT16, L33	D3
	1609	M391	D4
	1623	M136	D4
Newton Solney, Derbys	1375	GNP19	D1
Newton St Cyr, Devon	1637	M509	D4
Nicholaston, Wales	1894	–	D8
Norbury, Derbys	1460	S210	D2
	1473	G61	D2
	1483	G62	D2
	1491	S271	D2
	1500	S153	D3
	1531	S176	D3
North Aston, Oxford	1490	G143	D2
North Bradley, Wilts	1630	M335	D4
North Cockerington, Lincs	1370	GNP7	D1
Northleigh, Oxford	1411	G140	D2
	1596	M301	D3
North Mimms, Herts	1584	TT18	D3
North Ockendon, Essex	1606	M638	D4
	1607	R287	D4
	1643	M639	D4
North Stoneham, Hants	1613	M173	D4
North Walsham, Norfolk	1608	M107	D4
North Witham, Lincs	1658	M529	D4
Norton, Derbys	1510	GNP22, L2	D3

Location	Date	Note	Table
	1535	S230	D3
	1541	S233, L34	D3
	15th cent	S273	D3
Norton, Northants	1602	M408	D4
Norton, Worcs	1614	M191	D4
	1621	M192	D4
Norton in Hales, Shrops	1606	M300	D4
Norwich, Norfolk	1499	GNP61	D2
	15th cent	A149	D8
	1594	–	D9/85
	1609	M140	D4
	1611	M139	D4
	1613	R110	D4
	1613	R111	D4
	1896	M549	D6
Noseley, Leics	1402	S76	D2
	1406	S101	D2
	1467	S77	D2
	1474	S147	D2
	1525	S52	D3
	1600	S69	D4
	1629	M20	D4
	1659	M39	D4
	17th cent	S102	D4
Nottingham, St Mary	1413	GNP70	D2
	1416	G137	D2
	1637	M170	D4

Location	Date	Note	Table
	No Date	S29	D7
Nottingham, St Peter	1469	–	D9/32A
	1637	M600	D4
Nuneaton, Warwicks	1560	R58	D3
Nuthall, Notts	1395	G131	D1
	1562	S272	D3
	1919	M554	D6
Oakham, Rutland	1898	–	D8
Oakley, Hants	1520	A155	D3
Ogbourne St Andrew, Wilts	1695	M246	D4
Old Dalby, Leics	1562	S27	D3
	1580	R133, L35	D3
	1603	M324	D4
Old Leake, Lincs	15th cent	GNP59	D2
Ordsall, Notts	1603	M40	D4
Orlingbury, Northants	1370	GNP12	D1
Orton on the Hill, Leics	1511	S33	D3
Ormskirk, Lancs	1490	GNP41 & 42	D2
Otterden, Kent	1620	M355	D4
Over Peover, Cheshire	1410	G44	D2
	1456	G45, L1, L13	D2
	1515	S89	D3
	1573	S88	D3
	1586	R120	D3
Owthorpe, Notts	1663	M219	D4
	1713	M218	D5
Oxford	1425	A138	D2

Location	Date	Note	Table
	1522	G145	D3
	1559	R129	D3
	1615	M164	D4
	1620	M304	D4
	1645	M525	D4
Oxford, Broadgate	1522	A210	D3
Oxford St John's Chapel	1667	A186	D4
Oxnead, Norfolk	1608	R204	D4
	1636	M586	D4
Packington, Leics	1534	S234	D3
	1539	–	D9/69
	1560	S95	D3
	1587	S9	D3
Panton, Lincs	14th cent	–	D9/112
Paston, Norfolk	1629	M492	D4
	1632	M493	D4
Patshull, Staffs	1514	–	D9/57
	1532	A229	D3
Paulerspury, Northants	1595	–	D9/87A
	1626	R280	D4
Peatling Magna, Leics	1597	TT20	D3
	1614	TT21	D4
	1618	M322	D4
Peatling Parva, Leics	1480	S191	D2
Peckleton, Leics	1544	S65, L30	D3
Pembroke, Wales	1603	M196	D4

Location	Date	Note	Table
Pembroke College, Oxford	1522	–	D9/55
Penkridge, Staffs	1502	S167	D3
	1529	S196	D3
	1558	T23	D3
	1574	R89	D3
	1610	R88	D4
Penmynydd, Anglesey	1410	G208	D2
Pen-y-Fai. Wales	1900	X79	D8
Pentlow, Essex	1542	TT41	D3
Peterborough, Cambs	1643	–	D9/100
	1894	A104	D8
Pickering, Yorks	1380	GNP13	D2
	1407	GNP101	D2
Pinner, Middlesex	1656	M336	D4
Pitchford, Shrops	1530	S39	D3
	1587	S40	D3
	1587	S40	D3
Pitchford Staffs	1534	S14	D3
Pleshey, Essex	1920	–	D8
Plumtree, Notts	1534	–	D9/63
Plymtree, Devon	16th cent	X78	D8
Polesworth, Warwicks	1447	G175	D2
Pontardawe, South Wales	1885	X71	D8
Porchester Castle, Hants	1619	M13	D4
Porlock, Somerset	1440	G153, L13	D2
Presbury, Cheshire	1495	S251	D2
	1572	S87	D3
	1573	S252	D3
	1577	–	D9/80
Preston, East Yorks	15th cent	A144	D8
Preston in Holderness, Yorks	14th cent	–	D9/21
Prestwold, Leics	1487	TT23	D9/36
	1499	GNP48 & TT10	D2
	1520	G110	D2
	1531	–	D9/59
	1631	M41	D4
	1682	M203	D4
	?	X75	D8
Priories and monasteries (gen)	1530/53	X29	D9/57
Puddletown, Dorset	1470	GNP27 & G79	D2
Pusey, Berks	1485	S193	D2
Putley, Hereford	1875	A127	D8
Quarrendon, Bucks	1612	–	D9/93
Quatt Malvern, Shrops	1614	R216	D4
Queenhill, Worcs	1584	S8	D3
Quorndon, Leics (Quorn)	1502	S41	D3
	1551	S42	D3
	1557	S15	D3
	1560	S16	D3
	1574	Q2	D9/75
	1587	R85	D3
Radbourne, Derbys	1432	S105	D2
	1454	TT37	D2
	1500	G109	D3
	1684	M331	D4
Radcliffe, Lancs	1410	S266	D2
Radley, Berks	1633	M378	D4
Radwell, Herts	1595	M102	D3
	1605	M100	D4
	1625	M101	D4
	1625	M629	D4
Raglan, Monmouth	17th cent	X106	D4
Ratcliffe on Soar, Notts	1458	S239	D2
	1480	S190	D2
	1487	S54	D2
	1497	S157	D2
	15th cent	S240	D2
	1500	S242	D2
	1505	S158	D3
	1505	S275	D3
	1519	S122	D2
	1524	S241	D3
	1539	G136, L14, X37	D3
	1558	T9, X37	D3
	?	S123	D3
	1625	R4	D4
	1625	R5, X37	D4

Location	Date	Note	Table
	1663	S128	D4
Redmarshall, Durham	1440	GNP30	D2
Repton, Derbys	1482	GNP22	D2
	1563	S2	D3
	1617	M42	D4
Riddlesworth, Norfolk	1617	M154	D4
Ripley, Derbys	19th cent	–	D8
Risley, Derbys	16th cent	X82	D8
Rivenhall, Essex	1608	R69	D4
Roath, South Wales	1870	No add details	D8
Robertsbridge, Kent	1417	–	D9/27B
Roche Abbey, Yorks	1440	–	D9/30
Rochester, Kent	1361	A216	D1
	1550	–	D9/74
	1598	R250	D3
	1886	M367	D6
	1902	X81	D8
Rock, Worcester	1560	S249	D3
Rockingham	1584	R117	D3
Rodney stoke Somerset	1630	R278	D4
Rolleston on Dove, Staffs	1485	S30	D2
	1536	R128	D3
	1555	R211	D3
	1615	S44	D4
	1638	M294	D4
	1928	M597	D6

Location	Date	Note	Table
Rome, Italy	1382	A16, X18	D8
Romford, Essex	1576	M256	D3
	1605	M255	D4
	1605	M257	D4
Ross on Wye, Hereford	1529	G96	D3
	1609	M182	D4
	1636	R167	D4
	1651	R169	D4
Rothley, Leics	1486	TT7	D2
	1520	TT29	D3
	1544	A4, TT6, L34	D3
	1567	R100	D3
	1648	M527	D4
	15th/16th-cent		D9/116
Rouen, France	1376	B129	D9/14
Rowington, Warwick	1558	S35	D3
Royston, Herts	1360	GNP38	D1
Ruabon, Wales	1526	GNP114	D3
Rufford, Lancs	1463	S165	D2
	1588	–	D9/82
Rufford, Notts	1383	–	D9/19A
Rushton, Northants	1562	R92	D3
Ryther	1475	G200	D2
Saddington, Leics	1628	S179	D4
Salisbury, Wilts	1407	G180	D2
	1459	G181	D2

Location	Date	Note	Table
	1509	G182	D3
	1621	M105	D4
	1624	M200	D4
	1628	M273	D4
	1628	M274	D4
	1628	M199	D4
Saltcoats, Ayrshire	1929	X68	D8
Sandon, Staffs	1545	S80	D3
	1600	S138	D4
Santiago de Compostella, Spain	1456	X15 & X18	D8
Sapcote, Leics	?	–	D9/120
Sapperton, Gloucs	1630	M169	D4
Saundby, Notts	1599	R284	D3
	1885	X102	D6
Sawley, Derbys	1496	G68	D2
Saxelby, Leics	1531	S56	D3
Saxilby, Lincs	1370	A234	D1
Scarning, Norfolk	1623	M222	D4
Scawby, Lincs	1640	M74	D4
Screveton, Notts	1583	A2	D3
Scropton, Derbys	1495	S250	D2
	1515	GNP24	D2
Seckington, Warwicks	14th cent	A125	D1
	1603	M412	D4
Seighford, Staffs	1593	R125	D3
Selby, Yorks	1407	S72	D2

Location	Date	Note	Table
	1411	GNP102	D2
	1504	S73	D3
	1526	S276	D3
Selling, Kent	1550	R203	D3
Selston, Ashfield, Notts	1630	M43	D4
Seville, Spain	1390	X59	D8
Shareshill, Staffs	1562	R93	D3
Sheepstor, Devon	1641	M518	D4
Sheffield, Yorks	1538	A230	D3
	1590	R18	D3
Shelford, Notts	1587	R70	D3
Shenley Church End, Bucks	1607	M416	D4
Sherborne, Dorset	1717	M368	D5
Sherborne, Gloucs	1909	M61	D6
Sheriff Hutton, Yorks	1484	G203	D2
Shifnal, Shrops	1596	R214	D3
Shinfield, Berks	1627	M580	D4
Shipton Moyne, Gloucs	1599	R177	D3
	1640	R174	D4
Shipton under Witchwood, Ox	1614	M427	D4
Shirland, Derbys	1537	TT11	D3
Shrewsbury, Shrops	1471	S45	D2
	1473	S78	D2
	1529	GNP82	D3
Shottesbrooke, Berks	1536	R238	D3

Location	Date	Note	Table
Shouldham Thorpe, Norfolk	1600	S100	D4
Skeffington, Leics	1543	S50	D3
	1600	–	D9/89
	1651	M325	D4
Slebech, Wales	1475	GNP113	D2
Smisby, Derbys	1548	S82	D3
	1627	M451	D4
Snarford, Lincs	1582	R27	D3
	1613	M71	D4
	1619	M72	D4
Solihull, Warwicks	1577	S96	D3
Somercotes, Derbys	1879	No add details	D8
Somerton, Oxford	1583	R75	D3
Sotterley, Suffolk	1638	M290	D4
South Cockingham, Lincs	1623	R28	D4
South Cowton, Yorks	1493	G204	D2
	15th cent	G205	D2
	15th cent	GNP108	D2
South Harting, Sussex	1609	R76	D4
	1616	R77	D4
South Normanton, Derbys	1890	X87	D8
South Ockendon, Essex	1601	M636	D4
South Scarle, Notts	1510	S146, L27	D3
South Walsham, Norfolk	1612	M420	D4
Southwell, Notts	1450	GNP72	D2

Location	Date	Note	Table
	1590	A17	D3
	1904	A81	D6
Spetchley, Worcs	1614	R53	D4
Spilsby, Lincs	1372	GNP51	D1
	1396	GNP52	D1
	1582	M63, L20	D3
	1612	M422, L20	D4
Spixworth, Norfolk	1635	M210	D4
Spratton, Northants	1370	G23	D1
Sprotbrough, Yorks	1458	S159	D2
	1577	TT31	D3
Sprowston, Norfolk	1667	R274	D4
St Albans, Herts	1481	B21, B22	D9/35
	1895	A92	D6
	No date	X6	D7
St Brides super Ely, Wales	1658	M193	D4
St David's, Pembroke	1932	R71	D6
St John's Wood, London	1879	A72	D8
	1900	A73	D8
St Minver, Cornwall	1657	M236	D4
St Osyth, Essex	1620	R68	D4
St Peter Port, Guernsey	1886	X72	D8
	1889	–	D8
Stafford	1568	R94	D3
Staindrop, Durham	1425	G104	D2
	1564	X51	D11

Location	Date	Note	Table
Stallingborough, Lincs	1612	M70	D4
Stamford, Lincs	1350	GNP54	D1
	1587	M64	D3
	1598	M66	D3
Stamford, Burghley House	18th cent	A116	D10
Standish, Lancs	1658	R223	D4
Standon Herts	1587	M150	D3
	1606	M151	D4
Standon, Staffs	1526	R212	D3
	1562	S84	D3
Stanford on Soar, Notts	1498	S219	D2
	1695	M345	D4
	1893	–	D8
Stanford on Avon, Northants	1558	T8	D3
	1606	M314	D4
	1606	R218	D4
	1613	M313	D4
Stanford on Terne, Worcs	1493	G187	D2
Stansted Mountfitchet, Essex	1614	A61	D4
Stanton by Bridge, Derbys	1530	S67	D3
	1558	S66, L31	D3
	1879	X65	D8
Stanton Harcourt, Oxford	1471	G141	D2

Location	Date	Note	Table
	1490	GNP77	D2
	1688	M303	D4
Staunton, Notts	1582	S130	D3
Stanwell, Middlesex	1623	M380	D4
Stapleford, Notts	1571	S140	D3
Staveley, Derbys	1509	–	D9/51
	1510	S171, L27	D3
Stenigot, Lincs	1592	M65	D3
	1607	M67	D4
Stone, Staffs	1537	–	D9/64
Stonton Wyville, Leics	1590	A236	D3
Stoke on Tern, Shrops	1566	R215	D3
Stoke by Nayland, Suffolk	1634	M289	D4
Stoke Dry, Rutland	1496	S274	D2
	1590	R122	D3
Stoke Edith, Hereford	1470	GNP37	D2
Stoke Newington, Middlesex	1580	M461	D3
Stourton, Leics	1562	R131	D3
Stourton Caundle, Dorset	1560	G82	D3
Stowe Bardolf, Norfolk	1623	M307	D4
Stowe by Chartley, Staffs	1537	T26	D3
Stowting, Kent	1916	M553	D6
	1640	M581	D4
Stratford on Avon, Warwick	1592	R124	D3

Location	Date	Note	Table
	1614	M343	D4
	1616	M344	D4
	1629	M342	D4
	1649	M590	D4
	1732	M591	D5
Streatham, London	1610	A88	D4
Streatley, Berks	1893	–	D8
Strelley, Notts	1391	G25	D1
	1421	S151	D2
	1438	S152	D2
	1501	G139, L14	D3
Stretton Sugwas, Hereford	1473	S189	D2
Sturton le Steeple, Notts	1687	A188	D4
Stroud, Gloucs	1613	M426	D4
Strubby, Lincs	1648	M75	D4
Stutton, Suffolk	1662	M632	D4
Sudbury, Derbys	1600	R235	D4
Sudeley, Castle, Gloucs	1548	–	D9/73
Sutton, Beds	1605	R30	D4
Sutton Cheney, Leics	1633	R191	D4
Sutton Coldfield, Warwick	1554	R82	D3
	1715	M457	D5
Sutton Bonington, Notts	1470	GNP73	D2
Sutton on the Hill, Derbys	1634	M460	D4

Location	Date	Note	Table
Sutton-at-Hone, Kent	1625	M587	D4
Swarkestone, Derbys	1482	TT34	D2
	1573	R105	D3
	1577	TT8	D3
	1622	A38	D4
	1627	R106	D4
Swepstone, Leics	1591	GNP49	D3
Swimbridge, Devon	1654	M232	D4
Swine, Yorks	1372	G189, L37	D1
	1403	G191, L37	D2
	1410	G190, L3	D2
Swinbrook, Oxford	1613	M302	D4
	1686	M207	D4
Swineshead, Lincs	1610	M69	D4
Tamworth, Staffs	1512	G160	D3
Tate Gallery, London	1940	A51	D10
Tatenhill, Staffs	1641	M520	D4
Tathwell, Lincs	1626	M73	D4
Tavistock, Derbys	1600	M406	D4
Tawstock, Devon	1623	M209	D4
	1700	M237	D5
Temple Balsall, Warwicks	1663	A185	D4
Temple Guiting, Gloucs	1920	–	D8
Tenbury Wells, Worcs	1564	R206	D3
Tenby, Wales	1482	GNP120	D2
Tenterden, Kent	1622	M459	D4
Tettenhall, Staffs	1417	A13	D2
	1517	S225	D2
	1578	–	D9/81
Teversal, Notts	1538	S26	D3
	1562	S27	D3
	1674	M534	D4
Tewkesbury, Gloucs	1349	G19	D1
	1375	A124	D1
	1900	M561	D6
Thakeham, Sussex	1528	S13, L28	D3
Thame, Oxford	1559	R190	D3
Thetford??	16th cent	X100	D9/43
Theydon Mount, Essex	1577	A226	D3
	1587	M634	D4
	1626	M633	D4
	1631	M616	D4
	1668	R286	D4
Thornhill, Yorks	1481	G201	D2
	1614	X50	D11
	1622	A173	D4
	1627	M379	D4
	1931	X86	D8
Thornton, Bucks	1467	G41, G42 & A85	D2
Thorpe Mandeville, Northants	1597	A217	D3
Thorpe Salvin, Yorks	1461	S206	D2
Throwley, Kent	1592	R37	D3
	1668	M94	D4
Thrumpton, Notts (dates from)	1695	A14	D
Thrumpton Hall, Notts	?	–	D10
Thurlaston, Leics	1440	S129	D2
	1509	G108	D3
	1584	S139, GH2	D3
Thurstaston, Wirral	1885	–	D8
Tichborne, Hants	1619	M247	D4
	1621	M576	D4
Tickhill, Yorks	15th cent	S3	D2
	1513	A46	D3
	16th cent	–	D9/119
	1871	A101	D6
Tideswell, Derbys	1440	G57	D2
	1876	A80	D6
Tilton on the Hill, Leics	1638	M513	D4
Titchfield, Hants	1592	R22	D3
	1594	R81	D3
Tittleshall, Norfolk	1598	M178	D3
Tiveton, Devon	1419	–	D9/28
Tixover, Rutland	1623	M455	D4
Toft monks, Norfolk	1624	M259	D4
Toledo, Spain	1505	A215	D3
Tombland, Norfolk	1617	M6	D4
Tonbridge, Kent	1615	R66	D4
Tong, Shrops	1360	GNP123	D1
	1409	GNP81	D2
	1451	G148, L1, L13	D2

Location	Date	Note	Table
	1515	A87	D2
	1517	G149	D2
	1531	S228	D3
	1576	R86	D3
	1624	M135	D4
	1632	R87	D4
	1735	–	D9/107
	?	–	D9/122
Tortworth, Gloucs	1614	R156	D4
Trent, Dorset	1604	M369	D4
Treochy, Wales	1895	–	D8
Truro, Cornwall	1615	M432	D4
	1620	R256	D4
	1855	X44	D6
	1915	M568	D6
Tunstall, Kent	1613	M124	D4
	1647	M125	D4
	1654	A59	D4
	1740	M537	D5
Turnastone, Hereford	1522	S51, L23	D3
Turvey, Beds	1504	G35	D3
	1562	R240	D3
	1571	R239	D3
	1601	A159	D4
Tutbury, Staffs	1343	–	D9/6
	1919	X111	D86
Twickenham, Surrey	1642	M328	D4

Location	Date	Note	Table
Tydd St Mary	1389	A110	D1
Uffculme, Devon	1663	R202	D4
Uffington, Berks	1599	R237	D3
Uffington, Lincs	1607	M68	D4
Ufford, Cambs	1621	M332	D4
	1911	M333	D6
Uppsala, Sweden	1572	R187	D3
Upton, Northants	1537	G129	D3
Upton Hellions, Devon	1631	M589	D4
Uttoxeter, Staffs	1391	–	D9/25
	1523	R209	D3
	1539	TT27	D3
	1918	–	D8
Uxbridge, Middlesex	1638	M512	D4
Waddesdon Manor, Bucks	18th cent	–	D10
Wadworth, Yorks	1430	GNP105	D2
Waltham Abbey, Essex	1600	R42	D4
	1619	R255	D4
Wallingford, Berks	1481	B21, B22	D9/35
Wallington, Surrey	1612	M252	D4
Walthamstow, Essex	1632	M159	D4
Wanstead, Essex	1610	–	D9/92A
	1638	M622	D4
	1699	M621	D4
Wantage, Berks	1361	G1	D1
	1621	M447	D4
Warrington, Lancs	1462	GNP40	D2

Location	Date	Note	Table
Warter, Yorks	1499	–	D9/38
Warwick	1371	G171	D1
	1456	X17	D11
	1577	–	D9/79
	1584	A79	D3
	1588	A66	D3
Warwick Castle Chapel	1456	X17	D11
Washington DC, USA	1400	X97	D8
Waterperry, Oxford	1610	M183	D4
Watford, Herts	1600	A161	D4
	1619	M12	D4
	1630	M113	D4
Watton at Stone, Herts	1480	S218	D2
Wawne, Yorks	1437	S161	D2
Wednesbury, Staffs	1521	S38	D3
	1602	M409	D4
	1559	G179	D3
	1613	A172	D4
	1880	A113	D8
	1885	M546	D6
	1903	M546	D6
	1910	M546	D6
Weekley, Northants	1557	T21	D3
	1601	A162	D4
	1644	M524	D4
Welford, Berks	1610	M294	D4
Welford, Northants	1454	S187	D2

Location	Date	Note	Table
	1585	M390	D3
	1888	X73	D8
Wellingore, Lincs	1435	GNP55	D2
Wellington, Somerset	1607	R163	D4
Wells, Somerset	1305	A90	D9/2
	1329	X26	D11
	1363	G26	D1
	1440	G152	D2
	1451	G156	D2
	1465	S28	D2
	1472	A89	D2
	1608	R194	D4
	1614	M428	D4
	1679	–	D9/103
	1703	X27	D11
	1897	A115	D8
Welshpool, Montgomery	1853	A62	D6
	1891	A77	D6
Welwyn, Herts	1923	M557	D6
Wentworth, Yorks	1460	GNP106	D2
	1587	R275	D3
	1611	M575	D4
Weobley, Hereford	1430	GNP33	D2
	1437	G92	D2
Westhide, Hereford	1524	S253, L23	D3
Westonbirt, Gloucs	1892	A49	D6
West Dereham, Norfolk	1612	M419	D4
West Hallam, Derbys	1484	S247	D2
	1598	R249	D3
	1624	M478	D4
	1662	M479	D4
West Ham, Essex	1613	M248	D4
	1631	M254	D4
West Leake, Notts	14th/15th cent	X94	D11
West Malling, Kent	1594	M399	D3
West Thurrock, Essex	1607	M387	D4
West Wickham, Kent	1620	R257	D4
Weston under Wetherley	1584	M117	D3
Warwick	1584	A79	D3
Weddington, Warwicks	1639	M515	D4
Wetheral, Cumb	1500	GNP16	D3
Wethersfield, Essex	1490	G85. L18	D2
Whatton, Notts	1380	GNP8	D1
	1501	S12	D3
Wheathamstead, Herts	1543	T6	D3
	1637	M630	D4
Whichford, Warwick	1537	S170	D3
Whitchurch, Shrops	1550	T30	D3
Whitchurch, Denbigh	1568	M137	D3
	1578	R109	D3
Whitchurch, Devon	1722	M241	D5
Whitkirk, Yorks	1531	GNP110	D3
Whitmore, Staffs	1580	S83	D3
Whittlesford, Cambs	15th cent	A148	D8
Whitwick, Leics	1390	GNP44	D1
Wickhambrook, Suffolk	1630	R279	D4
Wickhamford, Worcs	1626	R67	D4
Wield, Hants	1617	A191	D4
Wiggenhall, Norfolk	1624	M628	D4
Wighill, Yorks	1635	R205	D4
Willesley, Derbys	15th cent	S244	D2
	1505	S86, L26	D3
	1571	S85	D3
	1577	S254	D3
Williton, Somerset	1666	Appendix M	D8
Willoughby on the Wolds, Notts	1362	G24	D1
	1395	GNP67	D1
	1448	G138, L11	D2
Willingale, Essex	1641	M618	D4
Wilton, Wilts	1626	M276	D4
Wimborne, Dorset	1444	G77	D2
	1606	M371	D4
	1628	M372	D4
	1650	M370	D4
Winchester, Hants	1366	G12	D1
	1404	G90	D2
	1687	A58	D4
	1873	A100	D8
Windsor, Berks	1367	A10	D9/10
	1513	G36	D3

Location	Date	Note	Table
	1526	G37	D3
	1584	R141	D3
	1612	A169	D4
	1863	No add details	D8
Wing, Bucks	1575	R33	D3
	1616	M46	D4
Wing, Kent	1552	R24	D3
Wingfield, Suffolk	1361	A36	D11
	1415	X95	D11
	1491	G163	D1
Wingham, Kent	1458	–	D9/31A
	1624	M480	D4
Winkburn, Notts	1570	S131	D3
Wirksworth, Derbys	1558	R228	D3
	1564	S199	D3
	1584	R135	D3
	1688	M348	D4
	1719	M347	D5
	1798	M346	D5
	1813	M351	D6
	1814	M350	D6
	1819	M352	D6
	1836	M354	D6
	1866	M353	D6
	1869	M349	D6
Wistow, Leics	1658	M530	D4
Witham, Essex	1585	R147	D3

Location	Date	Note	Table
Withybrook, Warwick	1602	TT9	D4
Withyham, Sussex	1663	–	D9/102
Woking, Sussex	1899	–	D8
Wollaton, Notts	1514	A6	D2
	1528	A3	D3
Wolstanton, Notts	1571	R12	D3
Wolverhampton, Staffs	1575	R107	D3
	1575	R243	D3
	1585	R108	D3
	1585	R248	D3
Wombourne, Staffs	1720	X97	D5
Woodbridge, Suffolk	1587	A35	D3
	1627	M19	D4
Woodchester Priory, Gloucs	1863	A201	D6
Woodcote, Shrops	1527	S220	D3
Woodham Ferrers, Essex	1619	M4	D4
Wootton Wawen, Warwicks	1428	G174	D2
	1605	X46	D11
Worfield, Shrops	1589	R264	D4
	1626	R265	D4
Worcester	1216	X7	D11
	1388	A109	D1
	1400	A23	D8
	1400	X20	D2
	1477	–	D9/34

Location	Date	Note	Table
	1502	X7	D11
	1591	R183	D3
	1596	R184	D3
	1608	R185	D4
	1613	M184	D4
	1616	R186	D4
	1627	R182	D4
	1682	M197	D4
	1867	No add details	D8
	1873	A100	D8
	1877	A99	D6
	1878	A97	D6
	1888	A98	D6
Worksop, Notts	1366	A212	D1
	1406	A213	D2
	15th cent	GNP71	D2
	?	–	D9/126
Wormington, Gloucs	1532	S248	D3
Wrangle, Lincs	1626	R161	D4
Wreay, Cumberland	1840	No add details	D8
Writtle, Essex	1920	–	D8
Wrotham, Kent	1588	S201	D3
Wroxeter, Shrops	1555	T11	D3
	1570	R101	D3
	1618	R102	D4
Wroxton, Oxford	1631	R154	D4
Wysall, Notts	1572	R9	D3

Location	Date	Note	Table	Location	Date	Note	Table	Location	Date	Note	Table
Yalding, Kent	1637	M366	D4		1615	M51	D4		1916	M265	D6
Yarnton, Oxford	1609	R15	D4		1624	M48	D4	Woodford, Essex	1595	M620	D4
Yatton, Somerset	1449	G155	D2		1624	M172	D4	Yougal, Co Cork	1620	M214	D4
Yelvertoft, Northants	1439	G124	D2		1628	M104	D4	Youlgreave, Derbys	1488	G64	D2
York, Minster	1346	G30 D2	D1		1629	M52	D4		1492	M47	D2
	1403	S262	D2		1648	M49	D4		1613	M424	D4
	1505	–	D9/49		1797	M270	D6	Yoxall, Staffs	1565	R95	D3
	1589	S261	D3		1854	M270	D6	Ysbyty Ifan. Wales	15th cent	A106	D2
	1606	M50	D4		1891	M271	D6				
	1615	M5	D4		19th cent	X40	D8				

Index to Non-commemorative Items Contained in Appendices D1 to D12

This index covers church furniture, panels, reredos, items in country houses and palaces other than chapels. In the main tables the items are listed in date order. Refer to the preceding alphabetical list to find individual locations and notes. For the physical details go to the appropriate D table and search within date and for historical details go to the appropriate note. Notes commencing L refer to linked items.

Appendix D1 – 14th Century 1300 to 1399

Number	Location	Building	Monument	Date	Armour or other features	Painted/collar or Garter	Source	Kerver	Notes Image
D1/1	Dorchester on Thames, Oxford	Church, St Peter & St Paul OX10 7HH	Effigy, K	13th cent	Cross-legged, crusader, shield		Material unknown		A137
D1/2	Gloucester	Cathedral GL1 2LX	Effigy (I), R	1327–1330 Poss later	Kingly features, cushion, crown	No. Traces of paint. Lion at feet	Tutbury, Purbeck and limestone	Royal sculptors London	G9,L38 (LS P119) (118,122)
D1/3	London, Westminster	Abbey SW1P 3PA	Effigy (I), R	1337 (1340)	Cross-legged, crusader, cushion, shield, bascinet. In prayer not drawing sword	Lion	Tutbury	Royal sculptors London	G18, L38 (LS P123 & 124) (4D113) (11,12,13) (31,119)
D1/4	Hanbury, Staffs	Church, St Werburgh DE13 8TF	Effigy (I), K	1340 (1300–1303)	Cross-legged, crusader, shield, cushion	Feet on dog. Angels holding cushion	Tutbury/Fauld	Local	G28 (117)
D1/5	York	Minster YO1 7HH	Effigy (I), R	1346 (1376)	Jupon. Cushion		Chellaston	John Orchard	G30 (120)
D1/6	Ashby Folville, Leics	Church, St Mary LE14 2TE	Effigy, K	1347	Cushion. Feet on lion.	No	Possibly not alabaster		A112

Number	Location	Building	Monument	Date	Armour or other features	Painted/collar or Garter	Source	Kerver	Notes Image
D1/7	Canterbury, Kent	Cathedral CT1 2EH	Effigy (I), B	1348				London	G14 (184)
D1/8	Tewkesbury, Gloucs	Abbey GL20 5RZ	Effigy (I), K,L	1349 (1348)	Round top bascinet and camail, great helm, framed headdress	No		London or Royal Sculptors	G10 (121,123)
D1/9	Harpham, Yorks	Church, St John of Beverley YO25 4QT	Tabletop, K,L (chest only)	1349 (1430)			Chellaston	York	TT26 GH1/19
D1/10	Longford, Derbys	Church, St Chad DE6 3DS	Effigy (II), K	1350	Cushions			Trent Valley	GNP18 (–)
D1/11	Stamford, Lincs	Church, St Mary PE9 2DN	Effigy (II), K	1350	Bascinet with attached aventail, hip belt	No		Trent Valley	GNP54 (4D77)
D1/12	Croxall, Staffs	Church, St John the Baptist WS13 8RA	Slab, K,L	1350	Pointed bascinet		Chellaston		S103
D1/13	Dorchester on Thames, Oxford	Church, St Peter & St Paul OX10 7HH	Effigy (I), J	1354			Material uncertain	–	A41 (–)
D1/14	Doveridge, Derbys	Church, St Cuthbert DE6 5NP	Slab, P	1359	Mass vestments				S156 GH2(4)
D1/15	Kirby Bellars, Leics	Church, St Peter LE14 2EE	Effigy (II), L	1360 (1370)	Great helm with missing crest	Hip belt. Feet on lion	Chellaston	Trent Valley	GNP4 (–)
D1/16	Layer Marney, Essex	Chapel of Layer Marney Hall CO5 9US	Effigy (II), K	1360 (1414)	Bascinet and great helm. Lion at feet	*ihc Nazare* Decorated hip belt	Chellaston	Trent Valley	G8 (23,102)
D1/17	Huyton, Lancs	Church, St Michael LE36 7SE	Effigy (II), P	1360	Quire habit	No tomb chest	Chellaston		GNP6 (–)

Number	Location	Building	Monument	Date	Armour or other features	Painted/collar or Garter	Source	Kerver	Notes Image
D1/18	Kingsbury, Warwicks	Church, St Peter & St Paul B78 2LR	Effigy (I), K	1360	May have had a shield. Chain mail gypon and bawdric	Damaged			GNP9 (–)
D1/19	Audley, Stafford	Church, St James the Great ST7 8HL	Effigy (II), K	1360	Bascinet and feet on lion Baldric	Decorated hip belt. Both arms lost	Chellaston		GNP85 (–)
D1/20	Alvingham, Lincs	Church, St Adelwold LN11 0QD	Effigy (II), K	1360 (1350)	Lion with long tail	Just a torso much damaged			GNP122 (–)
D1/21	Royston, Herts	Church, St John the Baptist SG8 7DB	Effigy (II), K	1360	Lion supporting cushion under head				GNP38 (–)
D1/22	Fledborough, Notts	Church, St Gregory NG22 0UU	Effigy (II), K	1360 (1375)	Jupon		Chellaston		G132 (–)
D1/23	Montgomery, Wales	Church, St Nicholas SY15 6PT	Effigy (II), K	1360	Bascinet				GNP111 (–)
D1/24	Tong, Shrops	Church, St Bartholomew TF11 8PW	Remnant, -	1360	Angel holding shield				GNP123 (–)
D1/25	Wantage, Berks	Church, St Peter and St Paul OX12 8BL	Effigy (II), K,L	1361	Cross-legged, crusader, cushion, shield	Ga (m)		Gardner suggests local carvers	G1 (129)
D1/26	Rochester, Kent	Cathedral	Effigy, B	1361 (1360)		Yes			A216
D1/27	Cobham, Surrey	Church, St Andrew KT11 3EJ	Effigy, K	1361		Ga (m). Yes modern			G211 (–)
D1/28	Willoughby in the Wolds, Notts	Church, St Mary & All Saints LE12 6SS	Effigy (II), J	1362 (1410)			Chellaston	Trent Valley	G24 (166)
D1/29	Wells, Somerset	Cathedral BA5 2UE	Effigy (II), B	1363	Bishop's robes with staff, gloved hands, hinged mitre	No	Chellaston	Probably London	G26 (191)

Number	Location	Building	Monument	Date	Armour or other features	Painted/collar or Garter	Source	Kerver	Notes Image
D1/30	Ingham, Norfolk	Church, Holy Trinity	Effigy, K,L	1364			Chellaston		A208
D1/31	Berkeley, Gloucs	Church, St Mary GL13 9BN	Effigy (II), K,L	1364	Framed headdress		Chellaston		G11 (113)
D1/32	Ashton, Northants	Church, St Michael & All Angels NN7 2JJ	Effigy (I), K	1365	Camail			Trent Valley	G22 (130)
D1/33	Winchester, Hants	Cathedral SO23 9LS	Effigy (II), B	1366			Chellaston		G12 (125)
D1/34	Hull, Yorks	Church, Holy Trinity HU1 2JJ	Effigy (II), K,L	1366 (1390)	Bearded with long cloak		Claimed as Ledsham but more likely Chellaston	London	G32 X91 (132)
D1/35	Worksop, Notts	Church, St Anne S80 1NJ	Effigy (II), K	1366	Bascinet with garland	Angels holding cushion	Chellaston		A212
D1/36	Greystoke, Cumbs	Church, St Andrew CA11 0TW	Effigy (II), K	1367	Gablette		Chellaston		G4 (137)
D1/37	Durham	Cathedral DH1 3EH	Effigy (II), K,L	1367			Alabaster effigies on sandstone tomb	London	G6 (–)
D1/38	London, Westminster	Abbey SW1P 3PA	Effigy (II), L	1369	-			Possibly the royal masons but may be Jean de Liege of Brabant	A78 (–)
D1/39	Elford, Stafford	Church, St Peter B79 9DD	Effigy (II), K	1370 (1470)	Eagle and chrisom, bascinet and aventail	Hip belt	Chellaston	Trent Valley	GNP84 (–)
D1/40	Newent, Gloucs	Church, St Mary GL18 1AA	Effigy (II), K,L	1370	Framed headdress				GNP3 (–)

Number	Location	Building	Monument	Date	Armour or other features	Painted/collar or Garter	Source	Kerver	Notes Image
D1/41	North Cockerington, Lincolnshire	Church St Mary LN11 0QD	Effigy (II), K	1370 (1380)	Lion at feet otherwise only a torso				GNP7 (4D61)
D1/42	Orlingbury, Northants	Church, St Mary NN14 1JB	Effigy (II), K	1370		Some colour			GNP12 (–)
D1/43	Aston, Warwicks	Church, St Peter and St Paul WA7 3ED	Effigy (II), K	1370 (1360)	Bascinet with band		Chellaston		GNP10 (–)
D1/44	East Harling, Norfolk	Church, St Peter & St Paul NR16 2NB	Effigy (II), K,L	1370 (1392)	Pointed bascinet and camail, jupon with unicorn, framed headdress				G21 (4D122) (133,134)
D1/45	Bures, Suffolk (ex Colne Priory, Essex)	St Stephen's Chapel CO8 5LD	Effigy (II), K	1370	Jupon with star, cushion, camail and bascinet		Chellaston		G29 (30, 139)
D1/46	Saxilby, Lincs	Church, St Botolph LN1 2PE	Effigy, K	1370 (1390)	Head on helm, bascinet and orle with aventail				A234 (4D68)
D1/47	Spratton, Northants	Church, St Andrew NN6 8HH	Effigy (II), K	1371	Pointed bascinet, jupon laced at side	SS with knot pendant			G23 (143)
D1/48	Warwick	Church, St Mary CV34 4RA	Effigy (II), K,L	1371	Jupon and breastplate, nebule (framed) headdress, holding hands	Ga (m) Yes. Weepers. Decorated jupon	Chellaston?		G171 L41 (LS P139) (29,33,37) (148)
D1/49	Swine, Yorks	Church, St Mary HU11 4JE	Effigy (II), K,L	1372	Pointed bascinet and camail, great helm, barbe, crown	Decorated jupon and belt	Chellaston	York	G189 L3, X91 (LS P139) (96,144)
D1/50	Ashbourne, Derbys	Church, St Oswald DE6 1AN	Effigy (II), K,C	1372		No			G212 (–)

Number	Location	Building	Monument	Date	Armour or other features	Painted/collar or Garter	Source	Kerver	Notes Image
D1/51	Spilsby, Lincs	Church St James PE23 5DU	Effigy (II), K,L	1372	Head on great helm, bascinet with aventail and orle. Bedesmen	*ihc Nazare*	Chellaston	Trent Valley	GNP51 L20 (4D75)
D1/52	Haccombe, Devon	Church, St Peter TQ12 4SJ	Effigy (II), Boy	1373	Feet on dog and angels holding cushion	No. Small effigy. Hip belt	Chellaston	Trent Valley	G74 (75)
D1/53	Hereford	Cathedral HR1 2NG	Effigy (II), K	1375	Feathered great helm	No. Ga (m) on left leg	Chellaston effigy	London	G13 (–)
D1/54	Tewkesbury, Gloucs	Abbey GL20 5RZ	Statue, K.	1375		No	Fauld or Castle Hay		A124
D1/55	Newton Solney, Derbys	Church, St Mary DE15 0SR	Effigy (II), K	1375	Angels and lion		Chellaston		GNP19 (–)
D1/56	London, Westminster	Abbey SW1P 3PA	Effigy (II), C,C	1376				John Orchard	G19 (74)
D1/57	London, Westminster	Abbey SW1P 3PA	Effigy (II), B	1376 (1390)	Mass vestments	Angels at head (damaged)	Chellaston	Henry Yeaveley & Stephen Lote	G20 (100,161)
D1/58	Bakewell, Derbys	Church, All Saints DE45 1FD	Mural and effigies (II), K,L	1376	Bascinet and camail	Small window with demi-figures facing forward	Chellaston		M1 (3)
D1/59	Aylesbury, Bucks	Church, St Mary HP20 2 JJ	Effigy (II), K	1380	Bascinet	In poor condition	Chellaston		GNP2 (–)
D1/60	Whatton, Notts	Church, St John of Beverley NG13 9EL	Effigy (II), K	1380	Heraldry on jupon	SS	Fauld		GNP8 (–)
D1/61	Pickering, Yorks	Church, St Peter & St Paul YO18 7BE	Effigy (II), K	1380	Bascinet	Narrow collar with flower decoration			GNP13 X91 (–)
D1/62	Kirby Bellars, Leics	Church, St Peter LE14 2EE	Effigy (II), K	1380 (1390)	Great helm with coronet, pointed bascinet with aventail				GNP5 (4D12)

Number	Location	Building	Monument	Date	Armour or other features	Painted/collar or Garter	Source	Kerver	Notes Image
D1/63	Durham	Cathedral DH1 3EH	Effigy (II), B	1381	Contains a bishop's throne	Decorated canopy niche		Possibly John Orchard, London	G5 (124)
D1/64	Wells, Somerset	Cathedral BA5 2UE	Effigy (II), B	1386	Feet on hares	No	Chellaston		G27 (103, 126)
D1/65	West Tanfield, Yorks	Church, St Nicholas HG4 5JQ	Effigy (II), K,L	1386	Jewelled band, arms on jupon, plume crest	SS with loop pendant. Iron hearse	Chellaston		G31 X91 (154)
D1/66	Durham	Cathedral DH1 3EH	Effigy (II), K,L	1388		Damaged	Sandstone tomb chest with alabaster effigies	London	G7 (–)
D1/67	Worcester	Cathedral WR1 2LA	Effigy (II), P	1388	Vestments	No	Uncertain		A109
D1/68	Barthomley, Cheshire	Church, St Bertoline CW2 5PE	Effigy (II), K	1389	Crocketted niches with figures	SS and hip belt. Angel holding shield	Chellaston	Trent Valley	G3 L1 (64)
D1/69	Tydd St Mary, Lincs	Church, St Mary PE13 5QY	Slab, K	1390			Chellaston		A110
D1/70	Dorchester on Thames, Oxford	Church, St Peter & St Paul OX10 7HH	Effigy (II), K	1390	Bascinet band	No	Chellaston	Trent Valley	GNP11 (–)
D1/71	Nantwich, Cheshire	Church, St Mary CW5 5RQ	Effigy (II), K	1390		No	Chellaston		A5 (–)
D1/72	Canterbury, Kent	Cathedral CT1 2EH	Effigy (II), L	1390	Nebule hair. Buttoned tunic	No. Damaged	Chellaston		G16 (–)
D1/73	Whitwick, Leics	Church St John the Baptist LE67 5HA	Effigy (II), K	1390 (1365)	Great helm with crest, pointed bascinet and aventail	*ihc Nazare* (but may be lost)			GNP44 (4D21)
D1/74	Birmingham, Warwicks	Church, St Martin B5 5BB	Effigy (II), K	1390 (1360)	Bascinet with band. Empty niches	Honey colour. Hip belt	Chellaston	Trent Valley	GNP89 (–)

Number	Location	Building	Monument	Date	Armour or other features	Painted/collar or Garter	Source	Kerver	Notes Image
D1/75	Kingston upon Hull, Yorks	Church, Holy Trinity HU1 2JJ	Effigy, C,L	1390	Merchant's probe for wool		Chellaston		A147
D1/76	Strelley, Notts	Church, All Saints NG8 6PE	Effigy (II), K,L	1391 (1405 or 1410)	Crespine/horned headdress. Holding hands	Chain		Trent Valley	G25 L41 (150)
D1/77	Bunbury, Cheshire	Church, St Boniface CW6 9PN	Effigy (II), K	1393	Blazoned jupon	Was	Chellaston		G2 (158)
D1/78	Leicester, Leics	Trinity Hospital LE1 6WY	Effigy (II), L	1394		Damaged			G17 (248)
D1/79	Willoughby-on-the Wolds, Notts	Church, St Mary & All Saints LE12 6SS	Effigy (II), K	1395	Aventail without bascinet		Fauld		GNP67 (–)
D1/80	Nuthall, Notts	Church, St Patrick NG16 1DA	Effigy (II), K	1395				Trent Valley	G131 (142)
D1/81	Canterbury, Kent	Cathedral CT1 2EH	Effigy (II), B	1396	Likeness			London	G15 (LS P152) (192)
D1/82	Spilsby, Lincs	Church St James PE23 5DU	Effigy (II), K,L	1396 (1420)	Head on great helm, ducal coronet, bascinet with orle and aventail	*ihc Nazare* Restored. Cording on dress	Chellaston	Trent Valley Possibly Sutton and Prentys	GNP52 L20 (4D76)
D1/83	Appleby Magna, Leics	Church, St Michael DE12 7BB	Effigy (II), K,L	1396 (1400–1410)	Great helm, pointed bascinet with aventail. Nebule				GNP45 (4D5)
D1/84	Acton, Cheshire	Church, St Mary CW5 8LE	Effigy (II), K	1399	Single ogee arch canopy	SS Yes			GNP1 (–)
D1/85	Barlborough, Derbys	Church, St James the Greater S43 4ER	Slab, L	1399					A111

Number	Location	Building	Monument	Date	Armour or other features	Painted/collar or Garter	Source	Kerver	Notes Image
D1/86	Barrow on Trent, Derbys	Church, St Wilfrid DE73 7HB	Effigy (II), P	14th cent					G56 (287)
D1/87	Holme Pierrepont, Notts	Church, St Edmund NG12 2LD	Effigy (II), K	14th cent			Chellaston		GNP69 (–)
D1/88	Seckington, Warwicks	Church, All Saints B79 0LD	Effigy, L	14th cent					A125
D1/89	Freckenham, Suffolk	Church, St Andrew IP28 8JF	Panel	14th cent		Part	Chellaston	London	X35
D1/90	Bedale, Yorks	Church, St Gregory DL8 1AF	Effigy, K	14th cent (poss 1306)	Cross-legged		May be limestone		A160
D1/91	Saffron Walden, Essex	Museum	Panel	14th cent			Chellaston		A204
D1/92	Saffron Walden, Essex	Church, St Mary	Panel	14th cent			Chellaston		A205

Appendix D2 – 15th Century 1400 to 1499

GNP = Gothic Gardner 'no picture' list in file, G = Gothic Gardner with picture

Number	Location	Building	Monument	Date	Armour	Painted/collar	Colour/ Source	Kerver	Notes
D2/1	London, Bishopsgate, Middlesex	Church, St Helen's EC3A 6AT	Effigy (II), C,L	1400	Angels holding cushions. Lion and dogs	Carries a sword	Chellaston	London	G114 (131)
D2/2	Worcester	Cathedral WR1 2LA	Effigy, K,L	1400			May not be alabaster		X20
D2/3	Newbold on Avon, Warwick	Church, St Botolph CV211HR	Slab, C,L	1401	Nine men's morris graffiti		Chellaston		S57
D2/4	Noseley, Leics	St Mary Chapel of Noseley Hall LE19 2JA	Slab, L	1402 (1406)			Chellaston		S76 GH2(7)

Number	Location	Building	Monument	Date	Armour	Painted/collar	Colour/ Source	Kerver	Notes
D2/5	Ashbourne, Derbys	Church, St Oswald DE6 1AN	Effigy (II), K	1403 (1412)	–	–	–	Added to his father's tomb chest	G212 (–)
D2/6	Mavesyn Ridware, Staffs	Church, St Nicholas WS15 3QE	Tabletop, K	1403	Camail and bascinet		White with pale brown veining		TT36 AO Fig 3
D2/7	Bakewell, Derbys	Church, All Saints DE45 1FD	Effigy (II), K	1403	Had angels on cushions. Bascinet	SS	Chelleston	Trent Valley	GNP17 (–)
D2/8	Hoveringham, Notts	Church, St Michael & All Angels NG14 7JH	Effigy (II), K,L	1403 (1423)	Holding hands	Short SS Pendant removed	White, Chellaston	Trent Valley	GNP68 L41 (–)
D2/9	Clifton, Notts	Church, St Mary NG11 8NJ	Effigy (II), K	1403?				Trent Valley	G133 (140)
D2/10	Clifton, Notts	Church, St Mary NG11 8NJ	Effigy (II), L	1403?				Trent Valley	G134 (141,236)
D2/11	Swine, Yorks	Church, St Mary HU11 4JE	Effigy (II), K	1403 (1410)	Orle, chaplets on jupon, well carved. Bascinet with crown (coronet)	*ihc Nazare*	Chellaston	York but may well be Trent Valley	G191 L3, X91 (14,109,159)
D2/12	York	Cathedral YO1 7HH	Slab, B	1403			Chellston		S262
D2/13	Longford, Derbys	Church, St Chad DE6 3DS	Effigy (II), K	1404		SS			GNP121 (–)
D2/14	Winchester, Hants	Cathedral SO23 9LS	Effigy (II), B	1404	Three monks at feet. Bishop's mitre	Yes	Veined, Fauld	London May have been repaired by William Byrd *circa* 1664	G90 (LS P152 7 154) (162,163,193)
D2/15	Broughton, Lincs	Church, St Mary DN20 0HY	Effigy (II), K,L	1404 (1409)	Great helm, bascinet with orle and aventail	SS			GNP53 (4D26)

Number	Location	Building	Monument	Date	Armour	Painted/collar	Colour/ Source	Kerver	Notes
D2/16	Meriden, Warwicks	Church, St Laurence CV7 7HX	Effigy (II), K	1404	Jupon with arms. Hip belt with rosettes		White	Trent Valley	G172 (157,232)
D2/17	Dijon, France	Palace of the Dukes of Burgundy	Effigy, K	1404 (1389) (1825)		Partial	Chellaston and Namur black marble	Claus Sluter	A157
D2/18	Kedleston, Derbys	Church, All Saints DE22 5JH	Effigy (IV), K?	1406	Bowl crop hair. Lion at feet	SS Hip belt	Chellaton		G63 (78)
D2/19	Worksop, Notts	Church, St Anne S80 1NJ	Effigy, K	1406	Bascinet	Decorated hip sword belt	Chellaston		A213
D2/20	Noseley, Leics	St Mary Chapel of Noseley Hall LE19 2JA	Slab, L	1406		Possibly an SS collar		Sutton and Prentys	S101 GH2(23 &Pl 141a)
D2/21	Salisbury, Wilts	Cathedral SP1 2EJ	Effigy (II), B	1407		Some paint remains	Purbeck and Chellaston		G180 (–)
D2/22	Pickering, Yorks	Church, St Peter & St Paul YO18 7BE	Effigy (II), K,L	1407	Orle	SS (2)	Fauld		GNP101 X91 (–)
D2/23	Selby, Yorks	Abbey YO8 4PU	Slab, B	1407					S72
D2/24	Elford, Stafford	Church, St Peter B79 9DD	Effigy (II), K,L	1408	Orle, great helm with angels. Jupon with breastplate. Three cusp ogee arches to niches	*ihc Nazare* SS (2). Cross pendant. Holding hands		Trent Valley. Poss Sutton and Prentys	G158 L1, L41 (38,149)
D2/25	Great Grimsby, Lincs	Church, St James DN31 1EP	Slab, C	1408	Houppelande				S185
D2/26	Tong, Shrops	Church, St Bartholomew TF11 8PW	Effigy (II), K,L	1409	Orle. Turk woman crest				GNP81 (–)

Number	Location	Building	Monument	Date	Armour	Painted/collar	Colour/ Source	Kerver	Notes
D2/27	Great Grimsby, Lincs	Church, St James DN31 1EP	Slab, K,L	1410		SS			S184
D2/28	Over Peover, Cheshire	Church, St Lawrence WA16 9HW	Effigy (II), K,L	1410		SS (2)		Trent Valley	G44 (187)
D2/29	Harlaxton, Lincs	Church, St Mary & St Peter NG32 1HD	Effigy (III), J,L	1410	No armour. Chaperon, gorget and liripipe	Face battered. Crespine headdress	Chellaston	Trent Valley	GNP56 L12 (–)
D2/30	Kinlet, Shrops	Church, St John the Baptist DY12 3BL	Effigy (II), L	1410	Crespine	Baby in fold of cloak	Fauld		G146 (225)
D2/31	Penmynydd, Anglesey	Church, St Gredifael LL61 5BX	Effigy (II), K,L	1410 (1382)	Pointed bascinet with ridge & camail	Hip belt. Nebule headress	Chellaston	Trent Valley	G208 (135)
D2/32	Swine, Yorks	Church, St Mary HU11 4JE	Effigy (II), K,L	1410 (1393)	Orle, chaplets on jupon. Lady has side cauls. Crown	SS and chain with pendant (lady) Dogs at feet of lady and lion at knight		York	G190 L3, X91 (145)
D2/33	Darfield, Yorks	Church, All Saints S73 9JX	Effigy (II), K,L	1410		SS		Trent Valley	GNP103 X91 (–)
D2/34	North Leigh, Oxford	Church, St Mary OX29 6TX	Effigy (II), K,L	1410	Houppelande		Chellaston	Sutton and Prentys	A128
D2/35	Radcliffe, Lancs	Church, St Bartholomew	Slab, K,L	1410					S266
D2/36	North Leigh, Oxford	Church, St Mary OX29 6TX	Effigy (II), K,L	1411	Orle	SS (2) *ihc Nazare*		Trent Valley	G140 (LS P155) (1,153)

Number	Location	Building	Monument	Date	Armour	Painted/collar	Colour/ Source	Kerver	Notes
D2/37	Selby, Yorks	Abbey YO8 4PU	Effigy (II), K	1411	Bascinet, great helm, feather crest	SS. Had lion but now lost			GNP102 X91 (–)
D2/38	Canterbury, Kent	Cathedral CT1 2EH	Effigy (III), R,R	1413 (1420 or 1437)	Gablette, Crowns	SS. Yes. Evidence of painting on gilt		Sutton/Prentys (may be parts from Robert Broun and design by Stephen Lote or Richard Beke)	G97 L1 B61 (LS P155) (190)
D2/39	Nottingham	Church, St Mary NG1 1HW	Tomb chest, C [Effigy (III)]	1413 (1475)			Chellaston		GNP70 (–)
D2/40	Bottesford, Leics	Church, St Mary the Virgin NG13 0DA	Effigy (II), K	1414	Great helm with crest, pointed bascinet, orle and aventail	SS, Ga (m) *ihc Nazare*		Sutton and Prentys	G103 L1, L15 (20,204,4D8)
D2/41	Bredwardine, Hereford	Church, St Andrew HR3 6BT	Effigy (III), K	1415 (1450)		SS	Fauld		GNP34 (–)
D2/42	Grafton Regis, Northants	Church. St Mary the Virgin NN12 7SS	Tabletop, K	1415	Early plate armour		Freestone chest. Chellaston	Sutton and Prentys	TT22 L24
D2/43	Clevedon, Somerset	Church, St Andrew BS21 7BY	Slab, K	1415				Sutton and Prentys Thomas Lovell	S163 L24
D2/44	Longford, Derbys	Church, St Chad DE6 3DS	Effigy (III), K	1416		SS Hip belt	Chellaston	Trent Valley	G59 (86)
D2/45	London	Church of the White Friars	Effigy, B	1416					A152
D2/46	Nottingham	Church, St Mary NG1 1HW	Effigy (III), C	1416	Cassock. Had angels. Dog at feet	Round cap. Pointed beard	Chellaston	Trent Valley	G137 (195)

Number	Location	Building	Monument	Date	Armour	Painted/collar	Colour/ Source	Kerver	Notes
D2/47	Arundel, Sussex	Castle chapel BN18 9AB	Effigy (III), C,L	1416	Crown (coronet) and long robe. Gablette	SS		Sutton/Prentys	G167 L1 (6,101,138,188)
D2/48	Ashwellthorpe, Norfolk	Church, All Saints NR16 1EZ	Effigy (III), K,L	1417	Pointed bascinet with garget and orle. Head on helm. Crespine/horned headdress	SS (2)		Sutton/Prentys	G121 L1 (84,85,4D119)
D2/49	Spare								
D2/50	Tettenhall, Staffs	Church, St Michael and All Angels WV6 9AH	Slab, K,L	1417	Long pediment	16 children	Chellaston	Trent Valley	S246 CMS-CG
D2/51	Exeter, Devon	Cathedral EX1 1HS	Effigy (III), B	1419 (1442)	Bishop's robes		Chellaston	Sutton/Prentys?	G75 (197)
D2/52	Lowick, Northants	Church, St Peter NN14 3BH	Effigy (III), K,L	1419	Gablette. Crespine. Holding hands	ihc Nazare	Chellaston	Sutton/Prentys	G122 L1, L41 (LS P156 & 158) (5,19,180)
D2/53	Harewood, Yorks	Church, All Saints LS17 9LQ	Effigy (III), C,L	1419	Judge's robes and head on cushion. Crespine/horned headdress		Chellaston	York but suspect may well be Chellaston	G193 L3, L12 X91 (15,167)
D2/54	Dalton le Dale, Durham	Church, St Andrew SR7 8QX	Effigy (II), K	1420	Camail to shoulders	Damaged. Hip belt	Chellaston	May well be Trent Valley	GNP29 (–)
D2/55	Bures, Suffolk (ex Colne Priory, Essex)	St Stephen's Chapel CO8 5LD	Effigy (III), K,L	1420 (1452)	Orle	SS (2)	White, Chellaston		G113 (164)
D2/56	Barmston, Yorks	Church, All Saints YO25 8PR	Effigy (III), K	1420	Bascinet	SS *ihc Nazare* Angels holding shields	Chellaston	Possibly Sutton and Prentys	G195 L1 X91 (24)

Number	Location	Building	Monument	Date	Armour	Painted/collar	Colour/ Source	Kerver	Notes
D2/57	Bottesford, Leics	Church, St Mary the Virgin NG13 0DA	Effigy (III), K	1421	Great helm, bascinet, gorget and mail cap and orle	SS, Ga *ihc Nazare*		Possibly Sutton and Prentys	G105 L15 (175,4D9)
D2/58	Bisham Abbey, Berks	Abbey SL7 1RW	Effigy (?), K,L	1421			Chellaston	Sutton and Prentys and Robert Broun, London	A20 L1 (–)
D2/59	Strelley, Notts	Church, All Saints NG8 6PE	Slab, K,L	1421	Star on armour		Chellaston		S151 GH2(7)
D2/60	Creich, Fife	Church, St Devenic IV24 3EG	Slab, L	1421	Crespine		Freestone – *see* S205		S205
D2/61	Haversham, Bucks	Church, St Mary MK17 7DT	Effigy (II), L	1422		Angels holding shields		Sutton and Prentys	G39 L1 (43,152)
D2/62	Hornby, Yorks	Church, St Margaret DL8 1NH	Effigy (II), K,L	1422	Orle, fauld of lames. Widows veil and barbe. Pointed bascinet	Little dogs *ihc Nazare*	Chellaston	Trent Valley	G188 X91 (165)
D2/63	Bodiam, Sussex	Castle	Effigy, K	1423		SS			A211
D2/64	Methley, Yorks	Church, St Oswald LS26 9EF	Effigy (III), K,L	1424	Large orle, turban, curled beard. Crespine	SS made of alternative S and crowns. Lady has plain SS	Chellaston	York	G194 L3, X91 (LS P157) (18,90,186)
D2/65	Staindrop, Durham	Church, St Mary DL2 3NJ	Effigy (II), L,K,L	1425	Pointed bascinet with IHS and camail. Bulls. Head crest	SS (3) with triple ring pendant. Clerk bedesmen	Chellaston	Trent Valley (St John Hope attributes this to Sutton/Prentys)	G104 (93,104,146)
D2/66	Oxford	Christ Church chapel OX1 1DP	Effigy, K	1425			Alabaster repairs		A138

Number	Location	Building	Monument	Date	Armour	Painted/collar	Colour/ Source	Kerver	Notes
D2/67	Edgmond, Shrops	Church, St Nicholas TF10 8JW	Slab, P	1425	Bachelor of law costume				S177
D2/68	Harewood, Yorks	Church, All Saints LS17 9LQ	Effigy (III), K,L	1426 (1440)	Orle similar to G193. Horse crest	SS	White with brown mottles. Chellaston	York	GNP104 (LS P154) L3, X91 (–)
D2/69	Burford, Shrops	Church, St John the Baptist WR15 8HG	Effigy (III), L	1426					G147 (249)
D2/70	Eastrington, Yorks	Church, St Michael DN14 7PW	Slab, K,L	1427	Horned headdress			York.	S164 GH1/19
D2/71	Dunster, Somerset	Church, St George TA24 6RY	Effigy (III), K,L	1428		SS			GNP83 L13 (–)
D2/72	Wootton Wawen, Warwicks	Church, St Peter	Effigy (III), K	1428	Bascinet with band	Chain			G174 (168)
D2/73	Harewood, Yorks	Church, All Saints LS17 9LQ	Effigy (III), K,L	1430–1434 (1426)	Orle, eagle buckle on hip belt	SS and flowers	White with brown mottles. Chellaston	York but well might be Chellaston	G192 L3, L37, X91 (17,92,147)
D2/74	Wadworth, Yorks	Church, St John the Baptist DN11 9BW	Effigy (III), K,L	1430	Orle. Plume of feathers crest. Drooping moustache. Side cauls	SS	Chellaston	Possibly Chellaston	GNP105 (–)
D2/75	Boston, Lincs	Church St Botolph PE21 6NP	Effigy (?), K	1430 (1450)	Great helm, bascinet with beavor and orle	Chain and pendant			A233 (4D25)
D2/76	Hornsea, Yorks	Church, St Nicholas HU18 1 AB	Tabletop, P	1430				Possibly York	TT25
D2/77	Weobley, Hereford	Church, St Peter & St Paul HR4 8SD	Effigy (III), K	1430		SS			GNP33 (–)

Number	Location	Building	Monument	Date	Armour	Painted/collar	Colour/ Source	Kerver	Notes
D2/78	Radbourne, Derbys	Church, St Andrew DE6 4LY	Slab, C,L	1432	Curious cap. Baselard. Horned headdress		Chellaston		S105 GH2(15 & plate 102b) AO Fig 7
D2/79	Arundel, Sussex	Castle chapel BN18 9AB	Effigy (III), K	1435	Tabard, bascinet with holes for visor	SS Cadaver		Possibly London	G168 L42 (271)
D2/80	Great Cubley, Derbys	Church, St Andrew DE6 2FB	Effigy (III), K	1435 (1461)	Angels with shields	SS (*see* note) Poss Y collar	Chellaston	Possibly Sutton and Prentys	GNP20 L2 (–)
D2/81	Wellingore, Lincs	Church, All Saints LN5 0HU	Effigy (III), K,L	1435	Bascinet with gorget and orle	SS *ihc Nazare*			GNP55 (4D84)
D2/82	Greystoke, Cumb	Church, St Andrew CA11 0TW	Effigy (IV), K	1436		SS			GNP15 (–)
D2/83	Weobley, Hereford	Church, St Peter & St Paul HR4 8SD	Effigy (III), K,L	1437		SS(2)	Fauld		G92 (89)
D2/84	Canterbury, Kent	Cathedral CT1 2EH	Effigy (III), K,K,L	1437		SS(2)		It is suggested that Richard Beke may have made this	G98 (190)
D2/85	Canterbury, Kent	Cathedral CT1 2EH	Effigy K,L	1437	-	-	-	-	*See* G97
D2/86	Wawne, Yorks	Church, St Peter HU7 5XH	Slab, Abbott	1437	Mass vestments. No mitre				S161 Gh2(2)
D2/87	Strelley, Notts	Church, All Saints NG8 6PE	Slab, K	1438					S152 GH2(7)
D2/88	Banbury, Oxford	Church, St Peter OX16 0AA	Slab, K,L	1438	Horseshoe headdress				S209
D2/89	Yelvertoft, Northants	Church, All Saints NN6 6LF	Effigy (III), P	1439 (1445)	Mass vestments				G124 (288)

Number	Location	Building	Monument	Date	Armour	Painted/collar	Colour/ Source	Kerver	Notes
D2/90	Apethorpe, Northants	Church, St Leonard PE8 5DQ	Effigy (V), K	1440–1402 (1500)	Tabard				G130 (79)
D2/91	Tideswell, Derbys	Church, St John the Baptist SK17 8NU	Effigy (III), K,L	1440 (1423)	Horned headdress	SS with ring pendant *ihc Nazare*	White, Chellaston for effigies and veined brown Fauld for tomb chest	Sutton/Prentys?	G57 (169)
D2/92	East Shefford, Berks	Church, Old Church RG17 7EF	Effigy (III), K,L	1440	Horned headdress			Trent valley	G33 L11 (173)
D2/93	Everton, Notts	Church, Holy Trinity DN10 5BB	Slab, K,L	1440			Fauld		S11 (–)
D2/94	Redmarshall, Durham	Church, St Cuthbert TS21 1EP	Effigy (III), K,L	1440		SS			GNP30 (–)
D2/95	Wells, Somerset	Cathedral BA5 2UE	Effigy (III), P	1440	Mass vestments. Holding challis	Canopy with scenes			G152 (32,47,160)
D2/96	Denton, Lincs	Church, St Andrew NG32 1LG	Slab, L	1440	Veil				S217
D2/97	Porlock, Somerset	Church, St Dubricius TA24 8QJ	Effigy (III), K,L	1440	Orle	SS			G153 L13 (172)
D2/98	Thurlaston, Leics	Church, St Bartholomew LE3 3PF	Slab, L	1440		Poor condition			S129 GH2(23)
D2/99	King's Pyon, Hereford	Church, St Mary HR4 8PT	Effigy (III), K	*Circa* 1440		Torso only. Hip belt	Chellaston	Possibly Trent Valley	GNP32 (–)
D2/100	East Horndon, Essex	Church, All Saints CM13 3LL	Slab, L	1440			Limestone but *see* X38	French	X38

Number	Location	Building	Monument	Date	Armour	Painted/collar	Colour/ Source	Kerver	Notes
D2/101	Merevale, Warwicks	Church, St Mary CV9 2LA	Effigy (III), K,L	1440	Orle and an early form of salet	Angels holding shields			G173 L11 (21,99,170)
D2/102	Lutterworth, Leics	Church, St Mary LE17 4AN	Effigy (IV), C,L	1440–1485 (1403)	Robes over armour, bare head on cushion	Plain			GNP47 (4D14)
D2/103	Dennington, Suffolk	Church, St Mary IP13 8JF	Effigy (III), K,L	1441	Orle. Plate armour. Crespine/horned headdress	SS (2), Ga (m). Loop pendant. Yes. Hawk or eagle foot rest	Chellaston	Trent Valley	G162 L13 (112,176,178)
D2/104	Newbold on Avon, Warwicks	Church, St Botolph CV211HR	Slab, K,L	1441	Chaperon, horned headdress		Chellaston		S149 GH1-252 & Fig 26)
D2/105	Adbaston, Staffs	Church, St Michael and All Angels ST 20 0NP	Slab, K,L	1441 (1468)	Baselard. Horseshoe headdress				S188 GH1(218)
D2/106	Chillingham, Northumberland	Church, St Peter NE66 5NJ	Effigy (IV), K,L	1443	Tabard. Later mural added. Saints	SS and tiret. Part painted	Chellaston effigies and limestone chest and mural	Trent Valley?	GNP65 (–) CMS-CG
D2/107	Wimborne, Dorset	Minster BH21 1EB	Effigy (III), K,L	1444	Holding hands	SS (2),Ga (m)	Purbeck and albaster		G77 (81)
D2/108	Dodford, Northants	Church, St Mary the Virgin NN7 4SU	Effigy (IV), K	1444		SS. Angels in pairs holding shield		Sutton and Prentys	G125 L1 (27,73,215)
D2/109	Kidderminster, Worcs	Church, St Mary DY10 2JN	Effigy (IV), K,L	1445	Tabard and ridged salet with raised visor	SS	Partial		G186 (230)
D2/110	Christchurch, Hants	Priory BH23 1BU	Effigy (IV), K,L	1446 (1461)		SS	Chellaston	Chellaston	GNP31 L37 (–)

Number	Location	Building	Monument	Date	Armour	Painted/collar	Colour/ Source	Kerver	Notes
D2/111	Bardney, Lincs	Church, St Lawrence LN3 5TZ	Slab, K,L	1446	Tiled pavement		Chellaston		S47
D2/112	Ashbourne, Derbys	Church, St Oswald DE6 1AN	Effigy (III), K,L	1447		SS		Sutton/Prentys	G58 L1 (22,45,174)
D2/113	London, Tower of London	Church, St Peter ad Vincula	Effigy (III), C,L,L	1447 (1461 or 1432)	Long robe and coronet. Great helm. Horned headdresses		Chellaston	Sutton or Prentys?	G115 (171)
D2/114	Polesworth, Warwicks	Abbey of St Edith B78 1DU	Effigy (III), L	1447	Crespine headdress	Angels with cushion	Chellaston		G175 (155)
D2/115	Willoughby in the Wolds, Notts	Church, St Mary & All Saints LE12 6SS	Effigy (III), K,L	1448	Head on great helm. Feet on lion. Salet	Angels holding shields	Chellaston	Sutton and Prentys	G138 L1,L11 (16,88,158)
D2/116	Claverley, Shrops	Church, All Saints WV5 7DS	Slab, C,L	1448	Horned headdress				S186 GH1(212)
D2/117	Yatton, Somerset	Church, St Mary BS49 4EE	Effigy (IV), J	1449 (1475)	Head on great helm. Butterfly	Angels holding shields			G155 L39 (292)
D2/118	Thornhill, Kirklees, Yorks	Church, St Michael WO12 0JZ	Effigy, K	1449					A153 X91
D2/119	Bletchley, Bucks	Church, St Mary MK3 6DZ	Effigy (IV), K	1450		SS			G40 (218)
D2/120	Burghill, Hereford	Church, St Mary the Virgin HR4 7SF	Effigy (IV), K,L	1450 (1430)	Horned headdress				G93 (189)
D2/121	Horwood, Devon	Church, St Michael EX39 4PD	Effigy (III), L	1450 (1430)	Children in skirt. Horned headdress		Chellaston		G76 (226)

Number	Location	Building	Monument	Date	Armour	Painted/collar	Colour/ Source	Kerver	Notes
D2/122	Abergavenny, Mon	Church, Priory of St Mary NP7 5ND	Effigy (III), K,L	1450	Bascinet with gorget	SS and lozenge	Chellaston		G118 (48,80)
D2/123	Southwell, Notts	Minster NG25 0HD	Effigy (III), B	1450		Damaged	Chellaston		GNP72 (–)
D2/124	Bromsgrove, Worcs	Church, St John the Baptist B61 7JW	Effigy (III), K,L	1450 (1440)	Orle	SS			G184 L13 (91)
D2/125	Kedleston, Derbys	Church, All Saints DE22 5JH	Effigy (V), K,L	1450 (1456)	Flapped headdress or truncated cone	SS. Cording on dress	Chellaston	Possible Chellaston	G67 (–)
D2/126	Aston on Trent, Derbys	Church, All Saints DE72 2DH	Effigy (III), J,L	1450	Chaperon hat		Chellaston	Thomas Prentys	G60 L1, L12 (151)
D2/127	Hambleden, Bucks	Church, St Mary the Virgin RG9 6RX	Statue	1450					X39
D2/128	Tong, Shrops	Church, St Bartholomew TF11 8PW	Effigy (III), K,L	1451	Orle	SS		Thomas Prentys	G148 L1, L13 (70,181)
D2/129	Humberstone, Leicester	Church, St Mary LE5 1AE	Inscribed tabletop, K	1451	Helmetless	Cartoon like.	Chellaston	Possibly Nottingham	TT1, L6 (–) Figure 118
D2/130	Wells, Somerset	Cathedral BA5 2UE	Effigy (IV), B	1451 (1465)		Yes. Cadaver in stone			G156 L42 (194)
D2/131	Lingfield, Surrey	Church, St Peter & St Paul RH7 6AH	Effigy (IV), K,L	1453	Simple veil		Chellaston. Fine white except for Saracen's head and sea-wolf at feet	Thomas Prentys	G166 L1 (111,116,205)
D2/132	Newbold on Avon, Warwicks	Church, St Botolph CV211HR	Tabletop, K,L	1454	Salet. Pauldron design. Horseshoe headdress		Chellaston	Nottingham	TT17 & L13 GH2(8) (–)

Number	Location	Building	Monument	Date	Armour	Painted/collar	Colour/ Source	Kerver	Notes
D2/133	Radbourne, Derbys	Church, St Andrew DE6 4LY	Tabletop, J,L	1454	Robes and coif. Heart headdress	Angels holding shields		Trent Valley	TT37 GH2(15)
D2/134	Welford, Northants	Church, St Mary the Virgin NN6 6HB	Slab, C,L	1454	Houppelande				S187
D2/135	Grove, Notts	Church, St Helen DN22 0RJ	Slab, K,L	1455	Steeple headdress at an angle	Armour but merchant's hat	Fauld (repairs in Chellaston)		S150 GH2(8)
D2/136	Dauntsey, Wilts	Church, St James the Great SN15 4HT	Slab, K,L	1455				Nottingham	S148 L13 GH2(8)
D2/137	Over Peover Cheshire	Church, St Lawrence WA16 9HW	Effigy (III), K,L	1456		SS	Chellaston	Thomas Prentys	G45 L1, L13 (199)
D2/138	Broughton, Oxford	Church, St Mary the Virgin OX15 5EF	Effigy (III), L	1456		SS			GNP74 (–)
D2/139	Clifton, Notts	Church, St Mary NG11 8NJ	Slab, L	1457		Nearly worn away	Chellatson		S127
D2/140	Gloucester	Cathedral GL1 2LX 1, Seabroke Chapel	Effigy (IV), P	1457	Mitre with pastoral staff	No	Chellaston	Possibly Trent Valley	G86 (127)
D2/141	Greens Norton, Northants	Church, St Bartholomew NN12 8BN	Effigy (IV), K,L	1457		Short SS (2). Loop pendant	Chellaston		G126, L21 (–)
D2/142	Astley, Warwicks	Church, St Mary the Virgin CV10 7QS	Effigy (IV), K	1457		SS			GNP92 (–)

Number	Location	Building	Monument	Date	Armour	Painted/collar	Colour/ Source	Kerver	Notes
D2/143	Ratcliffe on Soar, Notts	Church, Holy Trinity NG11 0EB	Slab, K	1458		Fragment	Chellaston		S239
D2/144	Allerton Mauleverer, Yorks	Church, St Martin HG5 0SE	Effigy (V), K,L	1458 (1500)	Beavor			Possibly early Harpur and Moorecock	GNP109 X91 (–)
D2/145	Bingham, Notts	Church, St Mary and All Saints NG13 8AL	Effigy, K	1458			Chellaston		A146
D2/146	Sprotbrough, Yorks	Church, St Mary DN1 2NR	Slab, L	1458					S159 GH2(3)
D2/147	Salisbury, Wilts	Cathedral SP1 2EJ	Effigy (IV), K	1459	Milanese armour. Decorated belt	SS	Chellaston and Fauld		G181 L37 (LS P171) (220,239)
D2/148	Martley, Worcs	Church, St Peter WR6 6QA	Effigy (IV), K	1459 (1461)		Y			GNP99 (–)
D2/149	Aston, Warwicks	Church, St Peter and St Paul WA7 3ED	Effigy (IV), K,L	1460 (1433)		SS (2)	Chellaston		GNP90, L21 (–)
D2/150	Burghfield, Berks	Church, St Mary RG30 3GT	Effigy, K,L	1460	Tabard	Much damaged	Chellaston		A47 (–)
D2/151	Wentworth, Yorks	Church, Holy Trinity S62 7TW	Effigy (IV), K,L	1460	Tabard	SS with trefoil from which the pendant is missing			GNP106 X91 (–)
D2/152	Grendon, Warwicks	Church, All Saints CV9 3DP	Effigy (IV), L	1460	Small dog				GNP93 (–)
D2/153	Norbury, Derbys	Church, St Mary and St Barlock DE6 2ED	Slab, L	1460	Forked headdress		Chellaston		S210 Page 104 of Crossley

Number	Location	Building	Monument	Date	Armour	Painted/collar	Colour/ Source	Kerver	Notes
D2/154	Dunmow Priory, Essex	Church, St Mary CO1 2BQ	Effigy (IV), K,L	1460 to 1470	Hornedd headdress	SS	Chellaston		G83 (212)
D2/155	Stourton Caundle, Dorset	Church, St Peter DT10 2JN	Effigy (IV), L	1460 to 1480	Remains of angels on cushion		Chellaston		G82 (227)
D2/156	Cheadle, Cheshire	Church, St Giles ST10 1HU	Effigy (III), K	1461 (1454)	Bascinet and gorget	SS			G46 (200)
D2/157	Methley, Yorks	Church, St Oswald LS26 9EF	Effigy (IV), K,L	1461	Tabard Butterfly	Chain, Ga (m)	Chellaston	York or Chellaston	G199 L37, X91 (223)
D2/158	Thorpe Salvin, Yorks	Church, St Peter S80 3JR	Slab, L	1461	Heart headdress				S206
D2/159	Aston, Warwicks	Church, St Peter and St Paul WA7 3ED	Effigy (IV), K	1462		Y			GNP91 (–)
D2/160	Eastrington, Yorks	Church, St Michael DN14 7PW	Effigy (IV), C,L	1462 (1453)	Judges coif and robes worn over armour		Chellaston	Possibly York	GNP107 X91 (–)
D2/161	Warrington, Lancs	Church, St Elphins WA1 2TL	Effigy (IV), K,L	1462	Strange canopies over niches	Iron grill. Weepers and angels with shields	Chellaston		GNP40 (7)
D2/162	Macclesfield, Cheshire	Church, St Michael SK10 1HW	Effigy (IV), K	1463	Holding hands. Basin cut hair	Angels with cushion	Chellaston (dark gold colour)		G48 (201)
D2/163	Rufford, Lancs	Church, St Mary L40 1TA	Slab, K,L	1463					S165
D2/164	Harewood, Yorks	Church, All Saints LS17 9LQ	Effigy (IV), K,L	1465	Barbe and veil	Y with Lion of March pendant	Chellaston. White with brown mottles	Burton or Chellaston	G196 X91 (94,207)

Number	Location	Building	Monument	Date	Armour	Painted/collar	Colour/ Source	Kerver	Notes
D2/165	Wells, Somerset	Cathedral BA5 2UE	Slab, B	1465 (1451)					S28 (194)
D2/166	Bury St Edmunds, Suffolk	Church, St Mary IP33 1RT	Effigy (?), C	1467		SS. Cadaver			A26 L42 (–)
D2/167	Barlow, Derbys	Church, St Lawrence S18 7TQ	Slab, K,L	1467	Horseshoe headdress	Y. Triple canopy. Holding hands			S154 GH2 (plate 80b)
D2/168	Noseley, Leics	St Mary Chapel of Noseley Hall LE19 2JA	Slab, K,L	1467	Heart headdress but poor				S77 GH2(8)
D2/169	Melbury Sampford, Dorset	Church (private hands)	Effigy (IV), K	1467	Salet with flutes and knobs	Y			G80 (231)
D2/170	Thornton, Bucks	Church, St Michael & All Angels MK17 0HJ	Effigy (IV), K	1468		Twisted rope and Lion of March	White, Chellaston	Chellaston?	G41 A85 (217)
D2/171	Thornton, Bucks	Church, St Michael & All Angels MK17 0HJ	Effigy (IV), L	1468			Chellaston	Chellaston?	G42 A85 (228)
D2/172	Kington, Hereford	Church, St Mary HR5 3AG	Effigy (IV), K,L	1469		Y with cross pendant	Fauld		GNP36 (–)
D2/173	Macclesfield, Cheshire	Church, St Michael SK10 1HW	Effigy (IV), K	1470 to 1480		SS			G49 (202)
D2/174	Puddletown, Dorset	Church, St Mary the Virgin DT2 8SN	Effigy (IV), K,L	1470 to 1480	Angels holding shields	Y, some colour remains	Chellaston	Trent Valley	GNP27 (–)
D2/175	Puddletown, Dorset	Church, St Mary the Virgin DT2 8SN	Effigy (IV), K	1470 (1485)	Salet with raised visor. Shield	No, Y with lion pendant	Purbeck quarries Chellaston	Dorset	G79 (97,214)

Number	Location	Building	Monument	Date	Armour	Painted/collar	Colour/ Source	Kerver	Notes
D2/176	Melbury Sampford, Dorset	Church. (private hands) DT2 0LZ	Effigy (IV), K	1470 (1547)	Salet with flutes and knobs	Y			G81 (–)
D2/177	Halsall, Lancs	Church, St Cuthbert L39 8RG	Effigy (IV), P	1470	Almice and alb	Dog at feet. Doctored to fit alcove			G102 (296)
D2/178	Abergavenny, Mon	Church, Priory of St Mary NP7 5ND	Effigy (V), K,L	1470		Y. Madonna			G119 (51)
D2/179	Sutton Bonington, Notts	Church, St Anne LE12 5NJ	Effigy (IV), K	1470		Short Y. Hog pendant			GNP73 (–)
D2/180	Glastonbury, Somerset	Church, St John BA6 9DR	Effigy (IV), C	1470 (1487)			Fauld		G154 (211)
D2/181	Ilton, Somerset	Church, St Peter TA29 9EX	Effigy (IV), L	1470	Butterfly. Cording on cape	Possible Yorkist short collar	Chellaston	Possible Trent Valley	G157 (229)
D2/182	Broughton, Oxford	Church, St Mary the Virgin OX15 5EF	Effigy (IV), K,L	1470		Y Likeness	Chellaston		GNP75 (–)
D2/183	Stoke Edith, Hereford	Church, St Mary HR1 4HQ	Effigy (V), L	1470 (1482)	Butterfly				GNP37 (–)
D2/184	Coates by Stow, Lincs	Church, St Edith LN1 2DW	Slab, K,L	1470	Butterfly		Chellaston		S212
D2/185	Shrewsbury, Shrops	Church, St Mary SY1 1DX	Slab, K,L	1471	Forked headdress		Poss Chellaston		S45
D2/186	Stanton Harcourt, Oxford	Church, St Michael OX29 5RJ	Effigy (IV), K,L	1471	Garter robes	Y, Ga(m). Ga(w). Bedesmen			G141, L21 (177)
D2/187	Daventry, Warwicks	Church, Holy Cross NN11 4BL	Image	1471					A24 (–)

Number	Location	Building	Monument	Date	Armour	Painted/collar	Colour/ Source	Kerver	Notes
D2/188	Kinver, Staffs	Church, St Peter DY7 6HX	Tomb chest	1471	Great helm with wolf's head crest	SS			A221
D2/189	Wells, Somerset	Cathedral BA5 2UE	Effigy, P	1472	Fully wrapped in cope	Alabaster panels	Chellaston		A89 (–)
D2/190	Cheadle, Cheshire	Church, St Giles ST10 1HU	Effigy (IV), K	1473 (1460)	Bare headed	SS			G47 (200)
D2/191	Kidderminster, Worcs	Church, St Mary DY10 2JN	Effigy, L	1473	Four angels holding shields	Unusual canopy with columns and fan vaulting	Uncertain		A154
D2/192	Norbury, Derbys	Church, St Mary and St Barlock DE6 2ED	Effigy (IV), K	1473	Bare headed	Y. Lion of March pendant	Fauld		G61 (35,39,46) (206)
D2/193	Shrewsbury, Shrops	Church, St Mary SY1 1DX	Slab, K,L	1473		Y	Chellaston	Trent Valley	S78
D2/194	Stretton Sugwas, Hereford	Church, St Mary Magdalene HR4 7PT	Slab, C,L	1473	Gypciere and baselard. Butterfly				S189 GH1(218) GH2(Fig 119b)
D2/195	Bristol, Somerset	Church, St Mary Redcliffe BS1 6RA	Effigy (V), P (2 effigies)	1474 (1437)	Mayoral robes. Mass vestments	Yes			G89 (291)
D2/196	Hereford	Cathedral HR1 2NG	Effigy (IV), B	1474	Lion at feet. Angels holding cushion, now damaged	Niches with angels on tomb chest	Chellaston	Possibly Burton	GNP35 (–)
D2/197	London, Bishopsgate	Church, St Helen EC3A 6AT	Effigy (IV), C,L	1474 (1476)	Bare-headed knight Butterfly	Y with Lion of March pendant			G116, L21 (242, 4D87)
D2/198	Noseley, Leics	St Mary Chapel of Noseley Hall LE19 2JA	Slab, K,L	1474					S147 GH2(8)

Number	Location	Building	Monument	Date	Armour	Painted/collar	Colour/ Source	Kerver	Notes
D2/199	Minster in Sheppey, Kent	Church, St Mary & St Sexburga ME12 3QD	Effigy (IV), K	1475		Y	Purbeck chest		G100 (–)
D2/200	Ryther, Yorks	Church, All Saints LS24 9EF	Effigy (IV), K	1475	Elaborate armour	Y and Lion of March pendant			G200 X91 (58,196,235)
D2/201	Slebech, Wales	Church, St John the Baptist SA62 4PD	Effigy (IV), K,L	1475		Y with lion pendant			GNP113 (–)
D2/202	Ewelme, Oxford	Church, St Mary the Virgin OX10 6HS	Effigy (IV), L	1477	Crown	Ga(w). Cadaver. Angels with shields		London	G142 L39. L42 (LS P 170) (28,82,183)
D2/203	Mavesyn Ridware, Staffs	Church, St Nicholas WS15 3QE	Slab, K,L	1477					S133
D2/204	Kinlet, Shrops	Church, St John the Baptist DY12 3BL	Effigy (V), K,L	1478	Butterfly	Y. Weepers under ogee headed niches	Fauld		G150 (42,252)
D2/205	Marnhull, Dorset	Church, St Gregory DT10 1PZ	Effigy (IV), L,K,L	1478	Butterfly	Y	Chellaston		G78 (233)
D2/206	Mavesyn Ridware, Staffs	Church, St Nicholas WS15 3QE	Slab, K	1478					S135 AO Fig 4
D2/207	Dunmow Priory, Essex	Church, St Mary CO1 2BQ	Effigy (IV), L	1480 (1500)	Cording on cape. Angels at cushion	SS	Chellaston	Harpur and Moorecock	G84 (–)
D2/208	Llandegai, Bangor, Wales	Church, St Tegai	Effigy (IV), C,L	1480	Weepers	Y with rose pendant	Chellaston	Possibly York	GNP112 (–)
D2/209	Derby	Cathedral DE1 3GP	Slab, P	1480	Funeral procession in canopy	Mass vestments and almice	Chellaston	Nottingham	S75 GH2(5)

Number	Location	Building	Monument	Date	Armour	Painted/collar	Colour/ Source	Kerver	Notes
D2/210	Croxall, Staffs	Church, St John the Baptist WS13 8RA	Slab, K,L	1480					S116
D2/211	Blithfield, Staffs	Church, St Leonard WS15 3NL	Slab, K,L,L	1480					S142
D2/212	Ratcliffe on Soar, Notts	Church, Holy Trinity NG11 0EB	Slab, C,L	1480	Baselard trimed with fur. Purse	Bull terrier	Chellaston		S190 GH1(218)
D2/213	Peatling Parva, Leics	Church, St Andrew LE17 5QA	Slab, C	1480	Baselard		Chellaston		S191 GH1(218)
D2/214	Lolworth, Cambs	Church, All Saints CB23 8HH	Slab, L,L	1480	French inscription. Butterfly				S213
D2/215	Watton at Stone, Herts	Church, St Andrew & St Mary DG14 3RD	Slab, C.L,L	1480	Flemish headdress with long pediment				S218
D2/216	Burton Agnes, Yorks	Church, St Martin YO25 4NB	Effigy (IV), K,L	1481	Great helm and orle	SS (2)	Chellaston		G198 X91 (55,221)
D2/217	Thornhill, Yorks	Church, St Michael WF12 0JZ	Effigy (IV), K,L	1481	Maiden crest	Y with Lion of March pendant. Weepers	Chellaston	York	G201 X91 (67,234)
D2/218	Ashwell, Rutland	Church, St Mary LE15 7LP	Slab, C,L	1481	Baselard Heart headdress	Purse and sword	Chellaston		S192 GH1(218)
D2/219	Brooksby, Leics	Church, St Michael LE14 2LH	Slab, K,L,L	1481	Heart headdress				S124
D2/220	Tenby, Wales	Church, St Mary SA70 7AZ	Chest (V), K	1482		Tomb chest has niches with family groups	Fauld		GNP120 (–)

Number	Location	Building	Monument	Date	Armour	Painted/collar	Colour/ Source	Kerver	Notes
D2/221	Repton, Derbys	Church, St Wystan DE65 6FH	Effigy (IV), K	1482	Bowl crop hair	Y. Hip belt	Chellaston	Trent Valley	GNP22 (–)
D2/222	Swarkeston, Derbys	Church, St James DE73 1JB	Tabletop, K,L	1482	Pomander	Round-headed niches and angels holding shields			TT34
D2/223	Norbury, Derbys	Church, St Mary and St Barlock DE6 2ED	Effigy (IV), K,L Now V&A Museum	1483 (1491)	Bare headed knight. Butterfly. Standard of mail	Y (2). Boar pendant. Lion and bedesmen		Burton	G62 (10,44,98) (106,213) (237)
D2/224	Ashby de la Zouch, Leics	Church, St Helen LE65 1AA	Effigy (V), C (pilgrim)	1483 (1530)	Palmer's staff. Cockle-shell	SS Pilgrim's hat			G106, X15 (210)
D2/225	Astley, Warwicks	Church, St Mary the Virgin CV10 7QS	Effigy (V), L	1483		Rose			G176 (–)
D2/226	Ashbourne, Derbys	Church, St Oswald DE6 1AN	Effigy (IV), K,L	1483 (1499)	Angels holding shields	No. Lady has necklace of shells			GNP21 (–)
D2/227	Sheriff Hutton, Yorks	Church, St Helen & the Holy Cross YO60 6SX	Effigy (V), C	1484 (1420)	*See* Jane Crease's paper on Sheriff Hutton		Ripon?	York	G203 L37, L3, X91 (267)
D2/228	West Hallam, Derbys	Church, St Wilfrid DE7 6GR	Slab, K,L	1484					S247
D2/229	Rolleston on Dove, Staffs	Church, St Mary DE13 9BE	Slab, K,L	1485	Steeple		Fauld		S30 (–) GH1 (256)
D2/230	Croxall, Staffs	Church, St John the Baptist WS13 8RA	Slab, K,L	1485	Steeple headdress				S118 GH1 (256)

Number	Location	Building	Monument	Date	Armour	Painted/collar	Colour/ Source	Kerver	Notes
D2/231	Ashby Folville, Leics	Church, St Mary LE14 2TE	Slab, K	1485			Chellaston		S49
D2/232	Pusey, Berks	Church, All Saints SN7 8QB	Slab, C,L	1485	Baselard. Embroidered hems		Chellaston		S193 GH1(218) GH2 (257 & fig 41)
D2/233	Rothley, Leics	Church, St Mary & St John LE7 7PN	Inscribed tabletop, K,L	1486	Butterfly and fur lined frontlet				TT7 L25 (–)
D2/234	Prestwold, Leics	Church, St Andrew LE12 5SH	Incised tabletop on Class V chest	1486 (1476)	Horned headdress	Canopy and inscription tapes	Chellaston		GNP48 TT10 GH2 (plate 103a) (–)
D2/235	Harewood, Yorks	Church, All Saints LS17 9LQ	Effigy (IV), K,L	1487	Tabard. Simple veil. Goat crest	SS and roses and O. Pendant obscured	Chellaston	Chellaston or Burton	G197 X91 (114,222)
D2/236	Croxall, Staffs	Church, St John the Baptist WS13 8RA	Slab, K	1487	Chrisom				S119
D2/237	Ratcliffe on Soar, Notts	Church, Holy Trinity NG11 0EB	Slab, L	1487	Domed cap	Low-necked gown	Chellaston		S54 L25
D2/238	Gedling, Notts	Church	Slab, K	1487			Chellaston		S277
D2/239	Youlgreave, Derbys	Church, All Saints DE45 1WS	Effigy (V), K	1488		Y. Angels holding shields	Chellaston	Burton	G64 (76)
D2/240	Wethersfield, Essex	Church, St Mary Magdelene CM7 4BY	Effigy (V), K,L	1490		Y			G85 L18 (283)
D2/241	Berkeley, Gloucester	Church, St Mary GL13 9BN	Effigy (V), K,K	1490 (1463)		Y(2). St Luke. Lion of March pendant			G87 A85 (50)

Number	Location	Building	Monument	Date	Armour	Painted/collar	Colour/ Source	Kerver	Notes
D2/242	Ormskirk, Lancs	Church, St Peter & St Paul L39 3LJ	Effigy (IV), K,L	1490	Short pediment	Battered	Uncertain		GNP41 (–)
D2/243	Holdenby, Northants	Church, All Saints NN6 9DF	Slab, K,L	1490	Short pediment	Battered	Uncertain		S215 L25
D2/244	Hinton on the Green, Gloucs	Church, St Peter WR11 2QR	Slab, A	1490	Mass vestment				S160 GH2(2)
D2/245	Ormskirk, Lancs	Church, St Peter & St Paul L39 3LJ	Effigy (IV), K,L	1490	Short pediment	Battered	Uncertain		GNP42 (–)
D2/246	Irthingborough, Northants	Church, St Peter NN9 5SD	Effigy (V), C,L	1490		Modern tomb chest			GNP62 (–)
D2/247	Irthingborough, Northants	Church, St Peter NN9 5SD	Effigy (V), L	1490	Long pediment				GNP63 (–)
D2/248	Bromsgrove, Worcs	Church, St John the Baptist B61 7JW	Effigy (III), L	1490	Surcoat and mantle. Reticulated coiffure which once held jewels				G185 (250)
D2/249	Halsall, Lancs	Church, St Cuthbert L39 8RG	Effigy (V), K,L	1490					GNP43 (–)
D2/250	North Aston, Oxford	Church, St Mary the Virgin OX25 6JA	Effigy (V), K,L	1490	Bedesmen on chest but without crocketted niches. Flapped headdress	SS with loop & Lion of March pendant.	Fauld for tomb chest but effigies may be Chellaston	Trent valley possibly Harpur and Moorecock	G143 L2 (34,240)
D2/251	Great Addington, Northants	Church, All Saints NN14 4BH	Effigy (V), K	1490		SS, Pendant unknown			GNP64 (–)
D2/252	Stanton Harcourt, Oxford	Church, St Michael OX29 5RJ	Effigy (V), K	1490	Angels holding shields	Y with Lion of March pendant. Bedesmen		Burton	GNP77 (–)

Number	Location	Building	Monument	Date	Armour	Painted/collar	Colour/ Source	Kerver	Notes
D2/253	Croxall, Staffs	Church, St John the Baptist WS13 8RA	Slab, C,L	1490					S194 GH1(218)
D2/254	Wingfield, Suffolk	Church, St Andrew IP21 5RA	Effigy (V), K,L	1491	Garter robes and crown (coronet)	Ga (m). Heraldic lions. Traces of paint		Burton on Trent	G163 (108,275)
D2/255	Howden, Yorks	Church, St Peter & St Paul DN14 7BS	Effigy (V), K	1491					G210 (–)
D2/256	Chilton, Suffolk	Church, St Mary C010 2ZB	Effigy (V), C	1491	Long robe and script, liripipe		Fauld		G165 (269)
D2/257	Great Cubley, Derbys	Church, St Andrew DE6 2FB	Tomb chest without effigy (V), K,L	1491	Crocketted niches with figures			Harpur/ Moorecock	G73 L2 (8)
D2/258	Norbury, Derbys	Church, St Mary and St Barlock DE6 2ED,	Slab, L	1491	Figure in shroud		Chellaston		S271
D2/259	Holme, Notts	Church, St Giles NG23 7RY	Effigy, K,L	1491	Flapped headdress	Cadaver	Possibly Fauld		A84 L42 (–)
D2/260	Little Wilne, Derbys	Church, St Chad DE72 3QH	Slab, K,L	1491	Crossed hands. Butterfly				S106
D2/161	Youlgreave, Derbys	Church, All Saints DE45 1WS	Mural tablet now reredos	1492			Chellaston		M47 (–)
D2/262	Bromham, Wilts	Church, St Nicholas SN15 2JS	Effigy (IV),K	1492	Beavor and cap. Large neck guard	SS	Chellaston		G183 (284)
D2/263	Stanford on Teme, Worcs	Church, St Mary WR6 6SH	Effigy (V), K,L	1493	Group of weepers. Simple crocketted niches	SS			G187 (65)

Number	Location	Building	Monument	Date	Armour	Painted/collar	Colour/ Source	Kerver	Notes
D2/264	South Cowton, Yorks	Church, St Luke DL7 0JB	Effigy (V), K	1493 (1509)	Band over hair	SS & roses and Tudor rose pendant	Chellaston	Trent Valley	G204 X91 (224)
D2/265	Dunster, Somerset	Church, St George TA24 6RY	Slab, L	1493	Flemish headdress with very long lappets		Watchet?	Somerset?	S214 Picture in S214 GH1 (261)
D2/266	Millom, Cumb	Church, St George AA18 4JE	Effigy (V), K,L	1494	Angels with shields	Y		Burton	G55 L39 (71)
D2/267	Breedon the Hill Leics	Church, St Mary & St Hardulph DE73 8AJ	Slab, K,L	1494					S79 & L25 GH2(9)
D2/268	Macclesfield, Cheshire	Church, St Michael SK10 1HW	Effigy (V), K,L	1495	Butterfly. Holding hands	Y, CH			G50 (66)
D2/269	Prestbury, Cheshire	Church, St Peter SK10 4DG	Slab, K,L	1495	Inscription panel at top	No margin text	Chellaston		S251
D2/270	Malpas, Cheshire	Church, St Oswald SY14 8PP	Slab, P	1495	Eucharistic vestments		Chellaston		S166
D2/271	Doveridge, Derbys	Church, St Cuthbert DE6 5NP	Slab, K,L	1495	Great helm				S104
D2/272	Ratcliffe on Soar, Notts	Church, Holy Trinity NG11 0EB	Slab, C,L	1495	Baselard and purse	Three sons and three daughters	Chellaston		S243
D2/273	Scropton, Derbys	Church, St Paul DE65 5PP	Slab, C	1495	Feet on dog				S250 AO Fig 8
D2/274	Sawley, Derbys	Church, All Saints NG10 3AT	Effigy (V), P	1496	Fully wrapped in quire habit		Chellaston	Trent Valley	G68 (128)
D2/275	Batley, Yorks	Church, All Saints WF17 8PA	Effigy (V), K,L	1496	Beavor. Cord work on cloak	Chain collar		Burton	G207 L17, X91 (261)

Number	Location	Building	Monument	Date	Armour	Painted/collar	Colour/ Source	Kerver	Notes
D2/276	Leicester	Church, St Margaret LE1 3EB	Effigy, B	1496 (1519)	Crosier				A151
D2/277	Stoke Dry, Rutland	Church, St Andrew LE15 9JG	Slab, L	1496	Flapped headdress	Fragment	Chellaston		S274 L25
D2/278	Burton on Trent	Church, St Peter (Stapenhill) DE15 9AF	Slab (once a tabletop), K,L	1497			Fauld	Walter Hylton? But more likely locally carved	S6 (Appendix R)
D2/279	Ratcliffe on Soar, Notts	Church, Holy Trinity NG11 0EB	Slab, P	1497	Mass vestments. Tonsure	Challis and clasped missal one on each side	Chellaston		S157 GH2(4)
D2/280	Hereford	Cathedral HR1 2NG	Slab, K,L	1497	Heart headdress. Cider barrel at feet		Chellaston	Possibly Nottingham	S208
D2/281	Lowick, Northants	Church, St Peter NN14 3BH	Effigy (V), K	1498	Stafford knot encircling shields on tomb chest	Bedesmen			G123 L14 (105,209)
D2/282	Gaddesby, Leics	Church, St Luke LE7 4WG	Slab, K,L	1498	Furred edges to frontlet		Chellaston		S216 L25
D2/283	Ash, Kent	Church, St Nicholas CT3 2EN	Effigy (IV), K,L	1498 (1458)	Great helm with angels	SS, loop pendant			G99 (216)
D2/284	Stanford on Soar, Notts	Church, St John the Baptist LE12 5PY	Slab. K.L	1498	Long pediment				S219 GH1 (261)
D2/285	Norwich, Norfolk	Cathedral NR1 4DH	Effigy (V), B	1499		Musket ball imbedded			GNP61 (–)
D2/286	Holme Pierrepont, Notts	Church, St Edmund NG12 2LD	Effigy (IV), K	1499		Short Y. Cross pendant	Honey patina		G135 L14 (87, 246, 257)
D2/287	Kilkenny, Ireland	Black Abbey	Image	15th cent				Trent Valley	A140

Number	Location	Building	Monument	Date	Armour	Painted/collar	Colour/ Source	Kerver	Notes
D2/288	Tickhill, Yorks	Church, St Mary DN11 9LY	Incised slabs	15th cent		One is a cross slab with crude effigies			S3 (–)
D2/289	Ysbyty Ifan, Conwy, Wales	Church, St John LL24 0NR	Effigies, K,L,K	15th cent (Post-1485)		Damaged	Chellaston		A106
D2/290	Willesley, Derbys	Church, St Thomas LE65 2YS	Slab, P	15th cent					S244
D2/291	Hartshorne, Derbys	Church, St Peter DE11 7ER	Slab, K,L	15th cent					S245
D2/292	Ratcliffe on Soar, Notts	Church, Holy Trinity NG11 0EB	Slab, L	15th cent			Chellaston		S240
D2/293	Burley, Rutland	Church, Holy Cross LE15 7SU	Effigy (III), K,L	15th cent (1413–1456)		SS (2)			GNP78 (–)
D2/294	Melton Mowbray, Leics	Church, St Mary LE13 1AE	Effigy (III), L	15th cent (1413–1456)	Crown headdress and whimple	Angels holding cushion	Chellaston		GNP46 (–)
D2/295	Worksop, Notts	Church, St Anne S80 1NJ	Effigy (III), L	15th cent (1413–1456)	Cauls	Fragment	Chellaston		GNP71 (–)
D2/296	Beaumaris, Wales	Church, St Mary & St Nicholas LL58 8LA	Effigy (IV), K,L	15th cent (1440–1485)	Salet with raised visor	SS. St Christopher			G209 (136)
D2/297	Halsham, Yorks	Church, All Saints HU12 8DD	Effigy (IV), K	15th cent (1440–1485)		SS			G202 X91 (208)
D2/298	Minster Lovell, Oxford	Church, St Kenelm OX29 0RT	Effigy (IV), K	15th cent (1440–1485)		St Margaret			GNP76 (49,219)

Number	Location	Building	Monument	Date	Armour	Painted/collar	Colour/ Source	Kerver	Notes
D2/299	Modbury, Devon	Church, St George PL21 0QN	Effigy (IV), K	15th cent (1440–1485) Poss 1503		Damaged			GNP26 (–)
D2/300	Ashwell, Rutland	Church, St Mary LE15 7LP	Effigy (V), P	15th cent (1482–1542)	Vestments. Had angels at head	Damaged. Feet on lion	Chellaston		GNP80 (–)
D2/301	Compton Winyates, Warwicks	Chapel CV35 0UD	Effigy (V), L	15th cent (1482–1542)		Fragment			GNP95 (–)
D2/302	Dronfield, Derbys	Church, St John the Baptist S18 1QB	Effigy (V), K	15th cent (1482–1542)					G65 (–)
D2/303	Gloucester	Cathedral GL1 2LX	Effigy (V), K,L	15th cent (1482–1542)		SS			A48
D2/304	Old Leake, Lincs	Church, St Mary PE22 9NS	Effigy (V), K	15th cent (1482–1542)		Damaged			GNP59 (–)
D2/305	Llandaff, Wales	Cathedral CF5 2LA	Effigy (V), L	15th cent (1482–1542)					GNP116 (–)
D2/306	Montgomery, Wales	Church, St Nicholas SY15 6PT	Effigy (V), K	15th cent (1482–1542)	Chain on bascinet				GNP119 (–)
D2/307	Netherbury, Dorset	Church, St Mary DT6 5LR	Effigy (V), K	15th cent (1482–1542)		SS			GNP28 (–)
D2/308	Newport, Mon	Church, St Woolos NP20 4DF	Effigy (V), K	15th cent (1482–1542)		Fragments			GNP60 (–)
D2/309	South Cowton, Yorks	Church, St Mary DL7 0JB	Effigy (V), L	15th cent (1482–1542)	Truncated steeple. Cords holding cape	Effigy only	Chellaston	Trent Valley	G205 X91 (115)

Number	Location	Building	Monument	Date	Armour	Painted/collar	Colour/ Source	Kerver	Notes
D2/310	South Cowton, Yorks	Church, St Mary DL7 0JB	Effigy (V), L	15th cent (1482–1542)	Cords holding cape	Effigy only	Chellaston	Trent Valley	GNP108 (–)
D2/311	Bakewell, Derbys	Church, All Saints DE45 1FD	Tomb chest without effigy (V)	15th cent (1482–1542) Poss 1477		Angels and weepers			G72 (241)
D2/312	Gnosall, Staffs	Church, St Lawrence	Effigy, K	15th cent	Great helm Decorated belt	Angels on cushions	Chellaston		A219
D2/313	Glenfield, Leics	Church, St Peter	Effigy	15th cent					A222
D2/314	Clifton, Notts	Church, St Mary NG11 8NJ	Effigy, L	15th cent		Lamb at feet	Chellaston	Trent Valley	A235

Appendix D3 – 16th Century 1500 to 1599

GNP = Gothic Gardner 'no picture' list in file, G = Gothic Gardner with picture, R = Renaissance, T = Transition

Number	Location	Building	Monument	Date	Armour and other features	Painted/collar	Source	Kerver	Notes
D3/1	Birmingham, Warwicks	Church, St Martin B5 5BB	Effigy (V), P	1500	Choir vestments		Chellaston	Trent Valley	GNP94 (–) CMS-CG
D3/2	Chilton, Suffolk	Church, St Mary C010 2ZB	Effigy (V), K,L	1500	Tabard	Lady has a SS with a sun pendant	Chellaston and black marble		G164 L18 (282)
D3/3	Hereford	Cathedral HR1 2NG	Effigy (V), P	1500	Lion	Angels holding cushion	Chellaston & limestone chest		G95 (297)
D3/4	Llandaff, Cardigan, Wales	Cathedral CF5 2LA	Effigy (V), K	1500		Lion which may have been black	Chellaston		GNP115 (–)
D3/5	Lockington, Leics	Church, St Nicholas DE74 2RH	Effigy (V), L	1500		Bedesmen			G109 (268)

Number	Location	Building	Monument	Date	Armour and other features	Painted/collar	Source	Kerver	Notes
D3/6	Radbourne, Derbys	Church, St Andrew DE6 4LY	Effigy (V), K,L	1500 (1491)	Great helm	SS			G66 (258)
D3/7	Ratcliffe on Soar, Notts	Church, Holy Trinity NG11 0EB	Slab, C,L	1500	Canopy	Almost totally worn	Chellaston		S242
D3/8	Wetheral, Cumb	Church, Holy Trinity & St Constantine CA4 8HA	Effigy (V), K,L	1500		SS			GNP16 (–)
D3/9	Croxall, Staffs	Church, St John the Baptist WS13 8RA	Slab, K,L	1500	Baselard				S117
D3/10	Norbury, Derbys	Church, St Mary and St Barlock DE6 2ED	Slab, P	1500	Mass vestments holding challis	Canopy	Chellaston		S153 GH2(4) AO Fig 1
D3/11	Netherseal, Derbys	Church, St Peter DE12 8DF	Slab	1500	Mass vestments				S155 GH2(4)
D3/12	Llandaff, Cardigan, Wales	Cathedral CF5 2LA	Effigy (V), K,L	1500 (1526)		SS			GNP117 (299)
D3/13	Strelley, Notts	Church, All Saints NG8 6PE	Effigy (IV), K,L	1501 (1500)	Lion	Bedesmen. Chain collar	Chellaston	Harpur/ Moorecock	G139 L2, L14 (270)
D3/14	Bury St Edmunds, Suffolk	Church, St Mary IP33 1RT	Effigy, K,L	1501					A27 (–)
D3/15	Whatton, Notts	Church, St John of Beverley NG13 9EL	Slab, C	1501	Long hair, bell-mouthed cuffs on gown		Chellaston		S12 GH1(221) (–) CMS-CG
D3/16	Chipping Sodbury, Gloucs	Church, St John the Baptist BS37 6NB	Slab, C,L	1501	Long cloaks and gowns. Mourning dress			Possibly Bristol made	S195 GH2(Fig 123a)

Number	Location	Building	Monument	Date	Armour and other features	Painted/collar	Source	Kerver	Notes
D3/17	Chipping Norton, Oxford	Church, St Mary OX7 5NT	Effigy (V), K,L	1502		Chain			G144 (253)
D3/18	Quorndon, Leics (Quorn) – *see* Q2	Church, St Bartholomew LE12 8DP	Slab. C,L	1502	Long pediment with cinquefoil	No			S41
D3/19	Penkridge, Staffs	Church, St Michael ST19 5AL	Slab, K,L	1502	Long pediment				S167 L27 GH1 (Fig 42)
D3/20	Kedington, Suffolk	Church, St Peter & St Paul CB9 7NN	Effigy, K,L	1503 (1526)	Long pediment	Lozenges with shields on tomb chest			A33 (–)
D3/21	Callington, Cornwall	Church, St Mary PL17 7RE	Effigy (V), K	1503		Ga (m). Bedesmen			G54 (83)
D3/22	Chichester, Sussex	Cathedral PO19 1PX	Effigy (V), B	1503 (1428)			Chellaston		GNP88 (–)
D3/23	Etwall, Derbys	Church, St Helen DE65 6LW	Slab, C,L	1503	Mourning dress		Chellaston		S168
D3/24	Turvey, Bedford	Church, All Saints MK43 8EP	Effigy (V), K,L	1504 (1562)		SS	Chellaston		G35 (–)
D3/25	Selby, Yorks	Abbey YO8 4PU	Slab, B	1504					S73
D3/26	Ashbourne, Derbys	Church, St Oswald DE6 1AN	Slab, C	1505		Very badly worn	Chellaston		S169
D3/27	Beckbury, Shrops	Church, St Milburga TF11 9DG	Slab, K,L	1505	Long pediment				S32 GH2(plate 87b)
D3/28	Ratcliffe on Soar, Notts	Church, Holy Trinity NG11 0EB	Slab, P	1505	Mass vestments. Challis to dexter	Text from Bible poss Job xix VV25	Chellaston		S158 GH2(4)
D3/29	Ratcliffe on Soar, Notts	Church, Holy Trinity NG11 0EB	Slab, L	1505	Incomplete effigy	Coats of arms on slab	Chellaston		S275

Number	Location	Building	Monument	Date	Armour and other features	Painted/collar	Source	Kerver	Notes
D3/30	Willesley, Derbys	Church, St Thomas LE65 2YS	Slab, C	1505					S86 L26 GH2(9)
D3/31	Toledo, Spain	Now in the V&A Museum	Effigy, K,L	*Circa* 1505	Great helm with weeper		Castille	Castilian sculptor	A215
D3/32	London, Westminster	Abbey SW1P 3PA	Effigy (V), K,L	1506	Great helm with holly tree crest. Lion at feet. Lady has wolf at feet	Ga (m). Bedesmen		May well be Burton	G117 (280)
D3/33	Blithfield, Staffs	Church, St Leonard WS15 3NL	Slab, C	1508					S144
D3/34	Bardney, Lincs	Church, St Lawrence LN3 5TZ	Slab, P	1508	Mass vestment, crosier and book		Chellaston		S162 GH2(2)
D3/35	Little Chart, Kent	Church, St Mary TN27 0QH	Effigy (V), K	1509	Lion with split tail	SS. Bedesman	Chellaston	Harpur and Moorecock	G101 L2 (203)
D3/36	Thurlaston. Leics	Church, All Saints LE9 7TA	Effigy (V), K,L	1509		SS (2)	Chellaston		G108 L17 (260)
D3/37	Salisbury, Wilts	Cathedral SP1 2EJ	Effigy (V), K	1509	Garter robes Cording. Long Hair	SS long, with portcullis and double rose pendant, Ga (m)	Chellaston	Trent Valley possibly Harpur and Moorecock	G182 (266)
D3/38	Lockington, Leics	Church, St Nicholas DE74 2RH	Slab, C,L	1509 (1540)	Gable hood				S58 L29 GH2(17)
D3/39	Harewood, Yorks	Church, All Saints LS17 9LQ	Effigy (IV), K,L	1510 (1529)	Tail of lion over sole of sabaton. Saints. Bedesmen	SS with alternating roses with Tudor rose pendant.	Chellaston, White with brown mottles	Harpur/ Moorecock	G206 L2, X91 (53,54,95,107) (243)
D3/40	Chesterfield, Derbys	Church, St Mary and All Saints S40 1XJ	Tomb chest without effigy (V) but is for a K	1510	Crocketted niches			Harpur/ Moorecock	GNP25 L2 L7 (–)

Number	Location	Building	Monument	Date	Armour and other features	Painted/collar	Source	Kerver	Notes
D3/41	Abergavenny, Mon	Church, Priory of St Mary NP7 5ND	Effigy (V), K	1510		SS. Bedesmen. Angels holding shields		Burton	G120 L17, L39 (9)
D3/42	Staveley, Derbys	Church, St John the Baptist S43 3TL	Slab, K	1510					S171 L27
D3/43	South Scarle, Notts	Church, St Helena NG23 7JH	Slab, K	1510			Chellaston		S146 L27 GH2(9)
D3/44	Aldbourne, Wilts	Church, St Michael SN8 2EL	Tabletop, P	1510	Mass vestments and holding challis		Fauld. Limestone chest	Nottingham	TT4
D3/45	Norton, Derbys	Church, St James S8 8JQ	Effigy (V), C,L	1510 to 1520 (1530)	Long pediment. Crocketted niches. Embattled edges			Harpur/ Moorecock	GNP23 L2 (–)
D3/46	Eye, Hereford	Church, St Peter and St Paul HR6 0	Effigy (V), K	1510 to 1520	Tabard	Long SS. Tudor rose pendant	Chellaston, Fauld for tomb chest	Possibly Richard Parker	G94 (255)
D3/47	Orton on the Hill, Leics	Church, St Edith (of Polesworth) CV9 3NG	Slab, C,L	1511	Long pediment	Very worn. Children as feet	Chellaston	Trent Valley	S33
D3/48	Kirk Langley, Derbys	Church, St Michael DE6 4NG	Slab, L	1511	No widow's weeds. Handkerchief				S223
D3/49	Tamworth, Stafford	Church, St Editha B77 2HH	Effigy (V), K,L	1512	Long pediment	SS with Tudor rose pendant		Harpur & Moorecock	G160 L2 (–)
D3/50	Windsor, Berks	Chapel, Rutland, St Georges SL4 1NJ	Effigy (V), K,L	1513	Short pediment	SS. Bedesmen	Fauld?		G36 (40,59,279,281)

Number	Location	Building	Monument	Date	Armour and other features	Painted/collar	Source	Kerver	Notes
D3/51	Blithfield, Staffs	Church, St Leonard WS15 3NL	Slab, C	1513					S141 GH2(9)
D3/52	King's Norton, Warwicks	Church, St Nicholas B38 8RU	Slab, P	1513 (1515)	Mass vestments. Challis and book in hands				S55 L26
D3/53	Macclesfield, Cheshire	Church, St Michael SK10 1HW	Effigy (V), K	1513					G51 (273)
D3/54	Bothal, Northumberland	Church, St Andrew NE61 6SW	Effigy (V), K,L	1513	Tabard. Flapped headdress	Chain	Chellaston	Burton on Trent	GNP66 (–), CMS-CG
D3/55	Tickhill, Yorks	Church, St Mary DN11 9LY	Effigy, K,L	1513 (1525) Rebuilt *circa* 1540	Gable hood which is decorated. Renaissance tomb chest	SS collar with alternating roses. She has chain collar with a pike pendant	Chellaston		A46 X91 (–)
D3/56	Crich, Derbys	Church, St Mary DE4 5DJ	Slab, C	1513					S173 L27
D3/57	Darley Dale, Derbys	Church, St Helen DE4 2GG	Slab, C,L	1514 (1513)	Long pediment. Canopy	Chain			S107 GH2(221)
D3/58	Cofton Hackett, Worcs	Church, St Michael & All Angels B45 8PT	Slab, L,K,L	1514	Long pediment		Chellaston		S224 L27
D3/59	Wollaton, Notts	Church, St Leonard NG8 2AF	Effigy, K	1514 (1549)				John Hippis of Lincoln	A6 (–)
D3/60	Over Peover, Cheshire	Church, St Lawrence WA16 9HW	Slab, K	1515 (1586)				Trent Valley possibly a Parker id 1515/29 and a Royley if later	S89

Number	Location	Building	Monument	Date	Armour and other features	Painted/collar	Source	Kerver	Notes
D3/61	Tong, Shrops	Church, St Bartholomew TF11 8PW	Effigy, K,L	1515					A87 (–)
D3/62	Scropton, Derbys	Church, St Paul DE65 5PP	Effigy (V), L,K,L	1515	Long pediment				GNP24 (–)
D3/63	Tong, Shrops	Church, St Bartholomew TF11 8PW	Effigy (V), K,L	1517	Long pediment	SS with Tudor rose pendant. Bedesmen		Harpur & Moorecock	G149 L2 (25,36)
D3/64	Brewood, Staffs	Church, St Mary & St Chad ST19 9BT	Slab, K,L	1517	Long pediment	No. Row of children	Chellaston	Trent Valley	S226 L28
D3/65	Tettenhall, Staffs	Church, St Michael and All Angels WV6 9AH	Slab, K,L	1517	Long pediment				S225 L27
D3/66	Ashover, Derbys	Church, All Saints S45 0AB	Effigy (V), C,L	1518 (1511)	Long pediment	Yes/SS (*see* note G69)		Harpur/ Moorecock	G69 L2 (61,69,259)
D3/67	Coleshill, Warwicks	Church, St Peter & Paul B46 3AD	Effigy (V), K,L	1519	Spiral pilasters. Long pediment	SS		Thought to be Royley but too early and may well be a Henry Harpur	G178 L2 (285)
D3/68	Ratcliffe on Soar, Notts	Church, Holy Trinity NG11 0EB	Slab, C	1519			Chellaston		S122
D3/69	Bowdon, Cheshire	Church, St Mary WA14 3BN	Slab, K	1519					S268
D3/70	Leicester	Church, St Margaret LE1 3EB	Effigy (V), B	1520	Episcopal habit	Modern tomb chest			G107 (289)
D3/71	Prestwold, Leics	Church, St Andrew LE12 5SH	Effigy (V), L,L	1520	Long pediments	Bedesmen		Henry Harpur	G110 L2 (263)

Number	Location	Building	Monument	Date	Armour and other features	Painted/collar	Source	Kerver	Notes
D3/72	Kedington, Suffolk	Church, St Peter & St Paul CB9 7NN	Effigy, K,L	1520					A34 (–)
D3/73	Rothley, Leics	Church, St Mary & St John LE7 7PN	Incised tabletop, L,K,L	1520 (1530)	Gable hood with short pediment	No. Canopy.	Chellaston		TT29 L29 (–)
D3/74	Lowdham, Notts	Church, St Mary the Virgin NG14 7BQ	Incised Slab, P	1520		No	White		S1 (–)
D3/75	Clifton, Notts	Church, St Mary NG11 8NJ	Slab, L	1520					S126
D3/76	Croxall, Staffs	Church, St John the Baptist WS13 8RA	Slab, C,L	1520					S120
D3/77	Oakley, Hants	Church, St Leonard RG23 7ED	Effigy, K,L	1520	Gable hood	Chain	Chellaston	Trent Valley?	A155
D3/787	Forncett St Peter, Norfolk	Church, St Peter NR16 1LT	Tabletop, C,L	1520 (possibly later)	Spiral pilasters. Lozenges with shields. Long pediment. Fur cape		Fauld	Trent valley. Probably late Parker.	TT39 GH1 (221) GH2 (fig 123b)
D3/79	Haughton, Staffs	Church,	Slab, P	1520	Mass vestments		Chellaston		S269
D3/80	Wednesbury, Staffs	Church, St Bartholomew WS10 9DJ	Slab, C	1521					S38
D3/81	Croxall, Staffs	Church, St John the Baptist WS13 8RA	Slab, K,L	1521					S227 L27
D3/82	London, Tower of London	Church, St Peter ad Vincula	Effigy, K,L	1521 (1554)	Long pediment . Dogs in skirt. Lion with divided tail	SS collar and Tudor rose pendant. Spiral pilasters.	Chellaston	Harpur & Moorecock	T28, G53, L2 and L36

Number	Location	Building	Monument	Date	Armour and other features	Painted/collar	Source	Kerver	Notes
D3/83	Broadgates Hall, Pembroke College, Oxford	St Aldate's Church chapel	Effigy, P	1522	Niches with bedesmen				A210
D3/84	Malpas, Cheshire	Church, St Oswald SY14 8PP	Effigy (V), K,L	1522	Long pediment. Dogs in skirt. Crocketted niches. Lion with divided tail	SS collar and Tudor rose pendant. Bedesmen	Chellaston & Fauld	Trent Valley, probably Harpur (& Moorecock)	G53 L2, L36 (–)
D3/85	Godshill, IOW	Church, All Saints PO38 3HY	Effigy (V), K,L	1522	Long pediment	SS. Bedesmen	Chellaston	Henry Harpur.	G91 L2 (238)
D3/86	Oxford	Church, St Aldates OX1 1BP	Effigy (V), P	1522	University hood				G145 (294)
D3/87	Great Brington, Northants	Church, St Mary NN7 4JB	Effigy, K	1522 (1550?)				Richard Parker?	R14
D3/88	Madeley, Staffs	Church, All Saints CW3 9ND	Tabletop, K,L	1522	Seventeen worn figures on tomb chest		Chellaston	Henry Harpur.	TT28 L2, L23
D3/89	Turnastone, Hereford	Church, St Mary HR2 0RD	Slab, K,L	1522			Chellaston	Henry Harpur	S51 L23 GH2(Pl 88a)
D3/90	Draycott in the Moors, Staffs	Church, St Margaret ST11 9AG	Slab, K,L	1522	Heraldic mantle				S222 L28
D3/91	Aymestrey, Hereford	Church, St John the Baptist HR6 9ST	Slab, K,L	1522 (1506)	Long pediment	Badly worn	Fauld		S255
D3/92	Halsall, Lancs	*See* GNP43	–	1523	–	–	–	–	*See* GNP43
D3/93	Knipton, Leics	Church, All Saints NG32 1RN	Slab, chrisom, C	1523	Chrisom	Small slab	Chellaston		S238
D3/94	Leigh, Staffs	Church, All Saints ST10 4NB	Effigy (V), K,L	1523		Roses			GNP87 (–)

Number	Location	Building	Monument	Date	Armour and other features	Painted/collar	Source	Kerver	Notes
D3/95	Uttoxeter, Staffs	Church, St Mary ST14 8AW	Effigy, L	1523	Cording on cape. Long pediment		Chellaston	Trent Valley	R209
D3/96	Chellaston, Derbys	Church, St Peter DE73 6UA	Slab, P	1523					S198
D3/97	Exton, Rutland	Church, St Peter & St Paul LE15 8AX	Effigy (V), K,L	1524 (1592)	Spiral pilasters. Lion with split tail on feet of knight	Collar with motto. Bedesman	Fauld	Likely to be Harpur and Moorecock	GNP79 L2 (–)
D3/98	Atcham, Shrops	Church, St Eata SY5 6QE	Slab, K	1524					S34
D3/99	Westhide, Hereford	Church, St Bartholomew HR1 3RQ	Slab, C	1524				Henry Harpur	S253 L23
D3/100	Ratcliffe on Soar, Notts	Church, Holy Trinity NG11 0EB	Slab, K,L	1524	Gable hood	No. Children at feet	Chellaston		S241
D3/101	Elford, Staffs	Church, St Peter B79 9DD	Effigy (V), L,K,L	1525	Long pediment Crocketted niches. Dog playing with hem. Gable hood on one and crown (coronet) on other	Long SS. Cross pendant. Bedesmen		Possibly Harpur and Moorecock	G159 L2 (26,179,256)
D3/102	Noseley, Leics	St Mary Chapel of Noseley Hall LE19 2JA	Slab, C	1525				Henry Harpur	S52 L23
D3/103	Windsor, Berks	Chapel, St George SL4 1NJ	Effigy (V), K,L	1526		Ga (m)	Purbeck marble with Chellaston effigies		G37 (–)
D3/104	Standon, Staffs	Church, All Saints ST21 6RN	Effigy, C	1526				Possibly Richard Parker. *See* R128	R212
D3/105	Ruabon, Denbigh, Wales	Church, St Mary LL14 6HP	Effigy (V), K,L	1526		SS with Tudor rose pendant			GNP114 (–)

Number	Location	Building	Monument	Date	Armour and other features	Painted/collar	Source	Kerver	Notes
D3/106	Ashby de la Zouch, Leics	Church, St Helen LE65 1AA	Slab, L,C,L	1526	Gable hoods	Bottom text	Chellaston	Burton	S48
D3/107	Selby, Yorks	Abbey YO8 4PU	Slab Abbot	1526			Chellaston		S270
D3/108	Aldermaston, Berks	Church, St Mary the Virgin RG7 4HR	Effigy (V), K,L	1526	Spiral pilasters. Bedesmen on tomb sides	SS		Burton	G38 (41,57,276) (277,278)
D3/109	Woodcote, Shrops	Church, St Peter	Slab, K,L	1527 (1500)	Long pediment. Canopies		Chellaston	Henry Harpur	S220 L23
D3/110	Thakeham, Sussex	Church, St Mary RH20 3EP	Slab, C	1527				Burton	S13 L28
D3/111	Macclesfield, Cheshire	Church, St Michael SK10 1HW	Effigy (V), K,L	1528	Dog playing with dress hem. Niches with weepers	SS		May be Harpur and Moorecock	G52 L2 (–)
D3/112	Haughmond Abbey, Shrops	Abbey church SY4 4RW	Slab, L	1528					S221
D3/113	Compton Winyates, Warwicks	Church, St George	Effigy (V), K	1528	Tabard	SS			GNP96 (–)
D3/114	Llandaff, Wales	Cathedral CF5 2LA	Effigy (V), K,L	1528 (1530)		SS. Bedesmen		Possibly late Harpur or early Parker	GNP118 L2 (–)
D3/115	Wollaton, Notts	Church, St Leonard NG8 2AF	Effigy (?), K	1528	Cadaver	SS			A3 L42 (–)
D3/116	Kinver, Staffs	Church, St Peter DY7 6HX	Tabletop, K.L,L	1528	Lozenges on chest side		Brass inlaid on alabaster	Burton on Trent	A220
D3/117	Barthomley, Cheshire	Church, St Bertoline CW2 5PE	Effigy (V), P	1529			Chellaston		GNP14 (–)
D3/118	Penkridge, Staffs	Church, St Michael ST19 5AL	Slab, C	1529 (1518)	Long pediment		Chellaston		S196 GH1(221)

Number	Location	Building	Monument	Date	Armour and other features	Painted/collar	Source	Kerver	Notes
D3/119	Ross on Wye, Hereford	Church, St Mary HR9 6QY	Effigy (V), C,L	1529	Crespine/horned headdress. Weepers in simple niches	St Anne and young virgin	Chellaston	Possibly Parker	G96 (52,63,295)
D3/120	Castle Donington, Leics	Church, St Edward King and Martyr DE74 2LA	Effigy (V), K,L	1529 (1536)		SS. Bedesmen		Richard Parker	G111 (262)
D3/121	Shrewsbury, Shrops	Church, St Mary SY1 1DX	Effigy (V), K,L	1529 (1532)	Long pediment	Yes. Bedesman			GNP82 (-)
D3/122	Astley, Warwicks	Church, St Mary the Virgin CV10 7QS	Effigy (V), L	1530	Long pediment				G177
D3/123	Croxall, Staffs	Church, St John the Baptist WS13 8RA	Slab, K	1530	Chrisom				S114
D3/124	Stanton by Bridge Derbys	Church, St Michael OX29 5RJ	Slab L,	1530					S67
D3/125	Pitchford, Shrops	Church, St Michael SY5 7DP	Slab, K,L	1530	Gable headdress		Chellaston	Attributed to Richard and Gabriel Royley but date a bit early	S39
D3/126	Newport, Shrops	Church, St Nicholas TF10 8BP	Effigy (V), C,L	1530		Bedesmen			G151 (300)
D3/127	Bulkington, Warwick	Church, St James CV12 9JT	Tabletop, K,L,L	1530		Eight sons and two daughters			TT30 L29
D3/128	Melbourne, Derbys	Church, St Michael with St Mary DE73 8JH	Slab, C	1530					S137 GH2(17)

Number	Location	Building	Monument	Date	Armour and other features	Painted/collar	Source	Kerver	Notes
D3/129	Deene, Northants	Church, St Peter NN17 3EJ	Effigy (V), L,C,L	1531	Judges robe in red	Yes			G128 (301)
D3/130	Norbury, Staffs	Church, St Mary and St Barlock DE6 2ED	Slab, L	1531	Shrouded figure		Chellaston		S176
D3/131	Tong, Shrops	Church, St Bartholomew TF11 8PW	Slab, K,L	1531					S228 L28
D3/132	Saxelby, Leics	Church, St Peter LE14 3PA	Slab, K	1531					S56 L29
D3/133	Kinlet, Shrops	Church, St John the Baptist DY12 3BL	Effigy (VI), K,L	1531 (1540)	Gable hood	SS	Chellaston	Richard Parker	T10 (62) CMS-CG
D3/134	Whitkirk, Yorks	Church, St Mary LS15 0AA	Effigy (VI), K,L	1531 (1546)	Spiral pilasters and columns. French hood	Weepers	Fauld	Royley	GNP110 X91 (–)
D3/135	Patshull, Staffs	Church, St Mary WV6 7HY	Effigy, K,L	1532	Round-headed niches with figures	No. Gable hood. SS collar with Tudor rose pendant	Fauld	Richard Parker	A229
D3/136	Wormington, Gloucs	Church, St Katherine WR12 7NL	Slab, K,L,L	1532		Very worn	Chellaston		S248
D3/137	Langham, Rutland	Church, St Peter & St Paul LE15 7JE	Slab, C,L	1533					S197
D3/138	Geddington, Northants	Church, St Mary Magdalene NN14 1AJ	Slab, K,L	1533	Gable hood				S229

Number	Location	Building	Monument	Date	Armour and other features	Painted/collar	Source	Kerver	Notes
D3/139	Fawsley, Northants	Church, St Mary NN11 3BS	Effigy (V), K,L	1534	Spiral pilasters. Gable hood. Figures	Yes, SS	Chellaston	Richard Parker	G127 (LS P191 & 192) (58,60,274)
D3/140	Pitchford, Shrops	Church, St Michael SY5 7DP	Slab, K,L	1534 (1540)	Gable hood. Pen holder			Royley workshop	S14 GH1(fig 43)
D3/141	Blithfield, Staffs	Church, St Leonard WS15 3NL	Slab, K,L,L,L	1534 (poss 1508)	Tabard. Jewelled pediment	Three wives	Chellaston		S61 L27
D3/142	Packington, Leics	Church, Holy Rood LE65 1WL	Slab, C,L	1534					S234
D3/143	Gloucester	Cathedral GL1 2LX	Effigy (V), B	1535 (1539)			Stained		G88 (290)
D3/144	Norton, Derbys	Church, St James S8 8JQ	Slab, K,L	1535	Gable hood				S230
D3/145	Shottesbrooke, Berks	Collegiate church LS6 3SW	Effigy, D	1535		Effigy lying in coffin			R238
D3/146	Rolleston on Dove, Staffs	Church, St Mary DE13 9BE	Effigy, B	1536		No		Richard Parker	R128
D3/147	Duffield, Derbys	Church, St Alkmund DE56 4BA	Effigy (V), K,L	1536		SS. Bedesmen			G70 (265)
D3/148	Chichester, Sussex	Cathedral PO19 1PX	Effigy (V), B	1536	Bishop's robes	Yes. Bedesmen	Fauld	Possibly Trent Valley	G169 (198)
D3/149	Bury St Edmunds, Suffolk	Church, St Mary IP33 1RT	Effigy, K,L	1536	Short pediment	Canopy is lost. Modern tomb chest			A28
D3/150	Framlingham, Suffolk	Church, St Michael IP13 9BJ	Tomb chest, K,L (no effigy)	1536 (1557)		No	Limestone	Tomb chest by a French carver – *see also* note in A29.	A30 X100

Number	Location	Building	Monument	Date	Armour and other features	Painted/collar	Source	Kerver	Notes
D3/151	Upton, Northants	Church, St Michael NN5 4UX	Effigy (V), K,L	1537	Tabard	SS with Tudor rose pendant		Poss Richard Parker	G129 (293)
D3/152	Shirland, Derbys	Church, St Leonard DE55 6AW	Tabletop, K,L	1537 (1546)	Tabard. Long flowing mantle	Children at feet	Chellaston	Royley	TT11
D3/153	Stowe by Chartley, Staffs	Church, St John the Baptist ST18 0LD	Effigy, K,L,L	1537		Ga (m) collar	Chellaston (white)	Richard Parker	T26
D3/154	Langar, Notts	Church, St Andrew NG13 9HG	Slab, C	1537				Not yet identified	S136 GH2(18)
D3/155	Whichford, Warwick	Church, St Michael CV36 5PG	Slab, P	1537	Mass vestments			Nottingham	S170
D3/156	Sheffield, Yorks	Cathedral S1 1HA	Effigy, K,L,L	1538 (1567)				Richard Parker	A230
D3/157	Teversal, Notts	Church, St Katherine NG17 3LH	Slab, L	1538				Richard Parker?	S26
D3/158	Uttoxeter, Staffs	Church, St Mary ST14 8AW	Tabletop, C	1538		Family group on chest side	Fauld		TT27 CMS-CG
D3/159	Ratcliffe on Soar Notts	Church, Holy Trinity NG11 0EB	Effigy (IV), K,L	1539 (1548)		No, long SS with Tudor rose pendant	Chellaston (white)	May be Richard Parker	G136 L14, X37 (77,110,247)
D3/160	Middle Claydon, Bucks	Church, All Saints MK18 2EY	Effigy (VI), L	1539	Gable hood. Baluster pilasters		Fauld	May be Royley	G43 (264)
D3/161	Grendon, Warwicks	Church, All Saints CV9 3DP	Slab, L	1539	Long pediment	Infant called William Chetwynd	Fauld		S23
D3/162	Lockington, Leics	Church, St Nicholas DE74 2RH	Slab, P	1540			Chellaston		S74 GH2(5)

Number	Location	Building	Monument	Date	Armour and other features	Painted/collar	Source	Kerver	Notes
D3/163	Leighton, Shrops	Church, St Mary SY5 6RN	Tabletop, K,L	1540					TT40
D3/164	Etwall, Derbys	Church, St Helen DE65 6LW	Effigy, K,L,L	1541				Richard Parker	A231
D3/165	Norton, Derbys	Church, St Bartholomew S8 8JQ	Slab, K,L	1541	Flat cap. Cape and bell-mouthed sleeves			Possibly Burton	S233 GH1(Fig 45 & page 268) L34
D3/166	Blithfield, Staffs	Church, St Leonard WS15 3NL	Slab, K,L	1541	Tabard. Great helm with goat crest		Chellaston		S145 AO Fig 5
D3/167	Easebourne, Sussex	Church, St Mary GU29 0AJ	Effigy (V), K	1542 (1502)	Tabard	SS and roses and Tudor rose pendant			G170 (272)
D3/168	Pentlow, Essex	Church, St Gregory CO10 7SP	Tabletop, C,L	1542		Overpainted	Uncertain material		TT41
D3/169	Wheathampstead, Herts	Church, St Helen AL4 8AA	Effigy (VI), K,L	1543 (1558)	Children holding shields	Chain	Fauld	Royley	T6 (–)
D3/170	Bottesford, Leics	Church, St Mary the Virgin NG13 0DA	Effigy (VI), K,L	1543	Coronet and tabard	Ga (m) collar	Chellaston	Richard Parker	T7 (–)
D3/171	Leicester	Church, St Mary de Castro LE1 5WN	Slab, C,L	1543 (1583)			Poor and thinly carved	Possibly local to Leicester	S97 L30
D3/172	Fenny Drayton, Leics	Church, St Michael & All Angels CV13 6BA	Tabletop with (VI) chest, K,L	1543 (1545)	Well carved. Holding hands	Figures in round-headed niches	Fauld alabaster	Royley but may also be a Parker	GNP50 & TT5 L30 & X110 GH2 (pl 89b) (–)
D3/173	Morley, Derbys	Church, St Matthew DE7 6DE	Effigy, L	1543	Spiral pilasters	Weepers. Yes	Fauld	Richard Parker	A232

Number	Location	Building	Monument	Date	Armour and other features	Painted/collar	Source	Kerver	Notes
D3/174	Skeffington, Leics	Church, St Thomas a Becket LE7 9YB	Slab, K,L	1543		Thirteen children	Chellaston		S50 CMS-CG
D3/175	Peckleton, Leics	Church, St Mary Magdalene LE9 7RA	Slab, C,L,L	1544				Possible Parker	S65 L30 GH2(10)
D3/176	Rothley, Leics	Church, St Mary & St John LE7 7PN	Inscribed tabletop, K,L	1544 (1549)	Rosary			From same workshop as S41	A4, TT6 L34
D3/177	Clifton Campville, Stafford	Church, St Andrew B79 0AR	Effigy (VI), C,L	1545		Chain Bedesmen		Richard Parker	G161 (68)
D3/178	Sandon, Staffs	Church, St Andrew ST18 0DB	Slab, K,L	1545		No		Royley	S80 GH2(11)
D3/179	Coventry, Warwicks	Church, St Michael CV1 5FB	Effigy (VI), K,L,C	1546 (1525)	Civilian has head on great helm	Chain (2)		Royley	T12 (286)
D3/180	Breedon on the Hill Leics	Church, St Mary & St Hardulph DE73 8AJ	Slab, C.L	1545		No		Royley	S81 L30 GH2(11)
D3/181	Hackleton and Horton, Northants	Church, St Mary Magdalene NN4 6BY	Effigy (VI) K,L	1546		SS with Tudor rose pendant. No		Richard Parker	T27
D3/182	Monk's Kirby, Warwicks	Church, St Edith CV23 0QX	Effigy (VI), K,L	1547 (1539)		Lion at feet			GNP97
D3/183	Kedleston, Derbys	Church, All Saints DE22 5JH	Slab, K	1547			Chellaston		S60 L29

Number	Location	Building	Monument	Date	Armour and other features	Painted/collar	Source	Kerver	Notes
D3/184	Battle, Sussex	Abbey, St Mary TN33 0AN	Effigy, K,L	1548	Shell-headed niches	yes	Pink?		T16
D3/185	Kinlet, Shrops	Church, St John the Baptist DY12 3BL	Mural, K,L	1548 (1580)	Kneeling facing forward	Cadaver	Fauld	Possibly Hollemans as monument is probably much later than 1548	M296 L42 CMS-CG
D3/186	Smisby, Derbys	Church, St James LE65 2TN	Slab, K,L	1548		Feet on dog			S82 GH2(11)
D3/187	Clifton, Bedford	Church, All Saints SG17 5EL	Effigy (V), K,L	1549 (1519)					G34 (244,245)
D3/188	Coleshill, Warwick	Church, St Peter & Paul B46 3AD	Tabletop, K,L	1549	Twisted pilasters and shields in lozenges		Chellaston top and Fauld chest	Royley	TT33 L32 GH2(11)
D3/189	Aston Flamville, Leics	Church, St Peter LE10 3AF	Slab, K,L	1549		Five children		Royley	S231 L32 & L33 GH1(266)
D3/190	Whitchurch, Shrops	Church, St Alkmund SY13 1LB	Effigy, K	1550		Garter robes	Chellaston		T30
D3/191	Burton Joyce, Notts	Church, St Helen NG14 5DQ	Slab, K	1550				Nottingham	S53
D3/192	Bromsgrove, Worcs	Church, St John the Baptist B61 7JW	Effigy (VI), L,K,L	1550 (1501)	Gable hood and French hood			Royley	GNP100 (–)
D3/193	Bristol, Somerset	Church, St John the Baptist BS1 2HZ	Effigy, C,L	1550 or earlier	Gable hood	No	Chellaston	Possibly Trent Valley	R229
D3/194	Selling, Kent	Church, St Mary ME13 9RD	Effigy, K	1550		No	Fauld		R203

Number	Location	Building	Monument	Date	Armour and other features	Painted/collar	Source	Kerver	Notes
D3/195	Darley Dale, Derbys	Church, St Helen DE4 2GG	Slab, C,L	1550 (1534)	Gable hood	Children in group at feet	Chellaston		S174 GH1(265) AO Fig 9
D3/196	Quorndon, Leics (Quorn) – *see* Q2	Church, St Bartholomew LE12 8DP	Slab, K,L	1551 (1548)		No	Chellaston	Royley	S42 GH2(11)
D3/197	Wing, Bucks	Church, All Saints LU7 0NX	Tomb chest, K,L (no effigy)	1552 (1567)	Bull's skulls linked by swags			French influence	R24
D3/198	Aston Flamville, Leics	Church, St Peter LE10 3AF	Tabletop, K,L	1552 (1549)		No	Chellaston	Royley	TT12 GH2(11)
D3/199	Faringdon, Berks	Church, All Saints SN7 7HW	Effigy (VI), K,L	1553 (1540)	Tabard. Great helm with dog crest and orle. Gable hood	SS. Shell-headed niches	Fauld	Burton on Trent	T2 (–)
D3/200	Ipsley, Warwicks	Church, St Peter B98 0AJ	Slab, K,L	1553	Gable hood			Royley.	S232
D3/201	Framlingham, Suffolk	Church, St Michael IP13 9BJ	Effigy, K,L	1554 (1560)	Crown. Possible likeness	No	Limestone	Effigies possibly by Burton with tomb chest by a French carver	A29 X100
D3/202	Eccleshall, Staffs	Church, All Saints S11 7PP	Tabletop, B	1554	Shields with coats of arms	No. Spiral intermediate pilasters		Royley	TT14
D3/203	Fenny Drayton, Leics	Church, St Michael & All Angels CV13 6BA	Slab or tabletop	1554				Royley	TT42 X110
D3/204	London, Tower of London	Church, St Peter ad Vincula EC3N 4AB	Effigy, K,L	1554	–	–	–	Relocated tomb for detail *see* 1521	T28, L2 & L36

Number	Location	Building	Monument	Date	Armour and other features	Painted/collar	Source	Kerver	Notes
D3/205	Croxall, Staffs	Church, St John the Baptist WS13 8RA	Slab, Child	1554	Chrisom				S115
D3/206	Sutton Coldfield, Warwicks	Church, Holy Trinity B72 1TJ	Effigy B,	1554 (1555)		Yes		Royley	R82
D3/207	Wroxeter, Shrops	Church, St Andrew SY5 6PH	Effigy (VI), C,L	1555	Judge's coif. Spiral pilasters		Chellaston	Richard Parker	T11 (303)
D3/208	Holme Lacy, Hereford	Church, St Cuthbert HR2 6LQ	Effigy (VI), K,L	1555 (1571)	White	No	Chellaston	Richard Parker	T4 (-)
D3/209	Lockington, Leics	Church, St Nicholas DE74 2RH	Slab, C,L	1555 (1545)	Feet turned out			Royley	S59 L29 GH2(18)
D3/210	Albrighton, Shrops	Church, St Mary Magdelene WV7 3EQ	Effigy, K,L	1555	Spiral pilasters	No SS	Chellaston	Royley	T17
D3/211	Chenies, Bucks	Chapel, St Michael WD3 6ER	Effigy, K,L	1555 (1559)			Fauld		T29
D3/212	Barcheston, Warwicks	Church, St Martin CV36 5AY	Effigy, K,L	1555		No	Chellaston	Royley	T18
D3/213	Rolleston on Dove, Staffs	Church, St Mary DE13 9BE	Mural, C,L	1555 (1600)					R211
D3/214	Cossington, Leics	Church, All Saints LE7 4UU	Tabletop, C	1556	Academic dress	No	Chellaston	Royley	TT13
D3/215	Brewood, Staffs	Church, St Mary & St Chad ST19 9BT	Effigy, K,L,L	1556 (1536)		Yes		Royley	T19

Number	Location	Building	Monument	Date	Armour and other features	Painted/collar	Source	Kerver	Notes
D3/216	Chellaston, Derbys	Church, St Peter DE73 6UA	Slab, C,L	1557			Chellaston	Royley	S92
D3/217	Mavesyn Ridware, Staffs	Church, St Nicholas WS15 3QE	Slab, C,L	1557					S132
D3/218	Blithfield, Staffs	Church, St Leonard WS15 3NL	Slab, L	1557	Tabard. French hood with outer hood		Chellaston	Royley	S62
D3/219	Framlingham, Suffolk	Church, St Michael IP13 9BJ	Effigy, L,L	1557 (1564)		No	Limestone		A31 X100
D3/220	Quorndon, Leics (Quorn) – *see* Q2	Church, St Bartholomew LE12 8DP	Slab, C,L	1557	MQS bonnet	No	Chellaston	Royley	S15 GH2(18)
D3/221	Weekley, Northants	Church, St Mary NN16 9UW	Effigy, J	1557	Judges coif and robes	Plain tomb chest with shield flanked by spiral pilasters	Fauld	Royley	T21
D3/222	Langar, Leics	Church, St Andrew NG13 9HG	Effigy, K,L,L	1558				Royley	A1
D3/223	Belton, Rutland	Church, St Peter LE15 9JU	Slab, C,L	1558				Royley	S17 GH2(11)
D3/224	Minster in Sheppey, Kent	Church, St John in Minster ME12 3PF	Effigy (VI), K	1558	Early strapwork	Ga (m)			GNP39 (–)
D3/225	Greens Norton, Northants	Church, St Bartholomew NN12 8BN	Mural, C	1558			Colonnades in marble, slate inscription		M362
D3/226	Stanford on Avon, Northants	Church, St Nicholas NN6 6JP	Effigy (VI), K,L	1558	Spiral pilasters	Chain	Chellaston	Royley	T8 (304,305) CMS-CG

Number	Location	Building	Monument	Date	Armour and other features	Painted/collar	Source	Kerver	Notes
D3/227	Lambourn, Berks	Church, St Michael and All Angels RG17 8PA	Effigy (VI), K,L	1558	Dolphin at feet. Mary, Queen of Scots cap. Great helm	No	Fauld	Richard Parker	T1 (-)
D3/228	Ratcliffe on Soar Notts	Church, Holy Trinity NG11 0EB	Effigy (VI), K,L	1558		Was	Chellaston. Some brown veining	Royley or Richard Parker	T9, X37 (-)
D3/229	Penkridge, Staffs	Church, St Michael ST19 5AL	Effigy, K,L,L	1558	Spiral pilasters and figures with no shields	Chain. Part	Chellaston	Royley	T23
D3/230	Coleshill, Warwicks	Church, St Peter & Paul B46 3AD	Effigy (VI), K,L	1558				Royley	GNP98 (-)
D3/231	Hillesdon, Bucks	Church, All Saints MK18 4DB	Effigy, K,L	1558	French hood	Chain. No	Chellaston	Richard Parker	T14
D3/232	Rowington, Warwicks	Church, St Laurence CV35 7AA	Slab, C,L	1558				Royley	S35 GH2(18)
D3/233	Gayton, Northants	Church, St Mary the Virgin NN7 3HP	Tabletop, C,L	1558 (1583)		Children		Royley	TT15 GH2(11)
D3/234	Chesterfield, Derbys	Church, St Mary and All Saints S40 1XJ	Mural, K,L,L	1558 (but likely to be post-1584)			Probably Fauld, Waxed	Garrett Hollemans (I)	M115 L7
D3/235	Stanton by Bridge Derbys	Church, St Michael OX29 5RJ	Slab, K,L	1558					S66 L31 GH1 (266)
D3/236	Wirksworth, Derbys	Church, St Mary DE4 4ET	Effigy, K	1558		Yes	Chellaston		R228
D3/237	Ipsley, Warwicks	Church, St Peter B98 0AJ	Slab, K,L	1558 (1583)	Long pediment		Chellaston?	Royley	S18 GH2(11)

Number	Location	Building	Monument	Date	Armour and other features	Painted/collar	Source	Kerver	Notes
D3/238	Alcester, Warwicks	Church, St Nicholas B49 5AL	Effigy (VI), K,L	1559	Spiral pilasters			Royley	G179 (-)
D3/239	Kirk Langley, Derbys	Church, St Michael DE6 4NG	Slab, C,L	1559					S68 L31 GH2(11)
D3/240	Thame, Oxford	Church, St Mary OX9 3AJ	Effigy, K	1559			Purple veined	Repaired by William Byrd after Civil War damage	R190
D3/241	Hope under Dinmore, Hereford	Church, St Mary HR6 0PP	Slab, C,L	1559				Royley	S36
D3/242	Chenies, Bucks	Chapel, St Michael WD3 6ER	Effigy, K,L	1559 (1562 or 1585)		No	Fauld and touchstone	Possibly by an Italian carver but likely to be Trent Valley	R230
D3/243	Claverley, Shrops	Church, All Saints WV5 7DS	Effigy, J,L,L	1559 (1540)	Lion with head turned	No. SS collar	Chellaston and Fauld	Royley or Parker	R90
D3/244	Wednesbury, Staffs	Church, St Bartholomew WS10 9DJ	Slab, C,L	1559				Royley	S37
D3/245	Enville, Staffs	Church, St Mary DY7 5HX	Effigy, K,L	1559	Spiral pilasters			Royley Pevsner	T24
D3/246	Bletchingley, Surrey	Church, St Mary RH1 4PD	Tabletop, C	1559			Uncertain material		TT43
D3/247	Margam Abbey, Glamorgan	Abbey SA13 2TJ	Effigy, K	1559 (1650s)				London	R233 X109
D3/248	Oxford	Trinity College OX1 3BH	Effigy, K,L	1559 (1567)	In alcove behind glass	Chain collar. Traces of colour	Chellaston	Richard Parker	R129
D3/249	Nuneaton, Warwicks	Church, St Nicholas CV11 4AZ	Effigy, K	1560			Fauld	Richard Parker	R58

Number	Location	Building	Monument	Date	Armour and other features	Painted/collar	Source	Kerver	Notes
D3/250	Marston on Dove, Derbys	Church, St Mary DE65 5GB	Slab, C,L	1560				Royley	S93 GH2(18)
D3/251	Framlingham, Suffolk	Church, St Michael IP13 9BJ	Toms chest without effigy, R	1560		No	Limestone		R11 X100
D3/252	Brewood, Staffs	Church, St Mary & St Chad ST19 9BT	Effigy, K,L,L	1560		Yes	Fauld	Royley	T20
D3/253	Quorndon, Leics (Quorn) – *see* Q2	Church, St Bartholomew LE12 8DP	Slab, C,L	1560 (1561)		No	Chellaston	Royley	S16
D3/254	Draycott in the Moors, Staffs	Church, St Margaret ST11 9AG	Effigy, K.L	1560				Royley	R91
D3/255	Checkley, Staffs	Church, St Mary and All Saints ST10 4NJ	Effigy, K,L	1560		Chain			R234
D3/256	Packington, Leics	Church, Holy Rood LE65 1WL	Slab, K,L	1560	MQS bonnet without veil			Royley	S95 GH2(18)
D3/257	Rock, Worcs	Church, St Peter and Paul DY14 9RX	Slab, P	1560			Chellaston	Richard Parker	S249
D3/258	Ashby de la Zouch, Leics	Church, St Helen LE65 1AA	Effigy (V), K,L	1561	Pilaster. Figures with shields on dividing bar. Great helm with crest. Coronets	Ga (m). Was painted. Collar of alternating roses and gathered ribbons	Fauld	Richard Parker	G112 (302)
D3/259	Cobham, Kent	Church, St Mary Magdelene DA13 9BN	Effigy, K,L	1561	Shell-headed niches	Part painted		Possibly Jan Mone, a Flemish carver	R276

Number	Location	Building	Monument	Date	Armour and other features	Painted/collar	Source	Kerver	Notes
D3/260	Mamble, Worcs	Church, St John the Baptist DY14 9JY	Effigy, K,L	1561					R145
D3/261	Teversal, Notts	Church, St Katherine NG17 3JN	Slab, C	1562				Richard Parker	S27 GH2(18)
D3/262	Old Dalby, Leics	Church, St John the Baptist LE14 3LB	Effigy, L,K,L	1562	Feet of knight on dog		Fauld	Richard Parker	R132 L35
D3/263	Rushton, Northants	Church, All Saints NN14 1RL	Effigy, K	1562			Chellaston. White with minimal brown veining	Royley	R92
D3/264	Shareshill, Staffs	Church, St Mary & St Luke WV10 7LA	Effigy, K,L	1562	No longer on tomb chest. (On window sills)	Lion	Chellaston	Royley workshop	R93
D3/265	Standon, Staffs	Church, All Saints ST21 6RN	Slab, C,L	1562	Well carved	Fourteen children		Royley	S84 GH2(11)
D3/266	Stoughton, Leics	Church, St Mary and All Saints LE2 2FJ	Effigy, C,L	1562		Remnants chain	Fauld	Richard Parker	R131
D3/267	Turvey, Bedford	Church, All Saints MK43 8EP	Effigy (V), K,L	1562	Sarcophagus tomb chest			Thomas Kirby	R240
D3/268	Nuthall, Notts	Church, St Patrick	Slab, C,L	1562		Badly worn	Fauld		S272
D3/269	Eye, Hereford	Church, St Peter and St Paul HR4	Effigy (VI), K	1563 (1540)		Long SS. Tudor rose pendant	Chellaston. Modern Fauld tomb chest	Richard Parker	T3 (254)

Number	Location	Building	Monument	Date	Armour and other features	Painted/collar	Source	Kerver	Notes
D3/270	Bottesford, Leics	Church, St Mary the Virgin NG13 0DA	Effigy, K,L	1563					R6
D3/271	Repton, Derbys	Church, St Wystan DE65 6FH	Slab, C,L	1563			Fauld	Royley	S2
D3/272	Charwelton, Northants	Church, Holy Trinity NN11 3YS	Effigy, K,L,L	1564 (probably 1555)		SS collar with Tudor rose pendant	Fauld	Richard Parker	R13
D3/273	Wirksworth, Derbys	Church, St Mary DE4 4ET	Slab, L,K.L	1564			Fauld	Richard Parker	S199
D3/274	London, Tower of London	Church, St Peter ad Vincula EC3N 4AB	Mural, K	1564 (1574)	Kneeling figures			William Cure I (The extension is also shown under 1610)	M329 Figure 27
D3/275	Tenbury Wells, Worcs	Church, St Mary WR15 8BP	Effigy, K,L	1564 (1546)		No	Fauld		R206
D3/276	Yoxall, Staffs	Church, St Peter DE13 8PT	Effigy, C,L	1565 (1584)			Fauld	Royley Pevsner	R95
D3/277	Stoke on Tern, Shrops	Church, St Peter TF9 2EZ	Effigy, K,L	1566 (1603)	Judges coif	Part	Chellaston		R215
D3/278	Hereford	Cathedral HR1 2NG	Effigy (VI), K,L	1566	Lion crest on great helm	Yes. Chain collar	Chellaston	Richard Parker	T5 (-)
D3/279	Bisham Abbey, Berks	Church, All Saints SL7 1RW	Effigies, K,K	1566 (1558)	Strapwork. Rush mat	Part	Chellaston and Fauld	William Cure or a French carver possibly Pierre Bontemps	R44 X53
D3/280	Bakewell, Derbys	Church, All Saints DE45 1FD	Effigy, L,K,L	1566–1567	Long beard	Part. Niches with shields on tomb chest	Fauld	Richard Parker	T13

Number	Location	Building	Monument	Date	Armour and other features	Painted/collar	Source	Kerver	Notes
D3/281	Rothley, Leics	Church, St Mary & St John LE7 7PN	Effigy. K,L	1567		Five sons and six daughters		Royley	R100
D3/282	Hoby, Leics	Church, St Michael LE14 3DR	Slab, L	1567		One son and three daughters all kneeling			S125 GH2(24)
D3/283	Misterton, Leics	Church, St Leonard LE17 4JP	Effigy, K	1567	Shields on tomb chest	Chain collar. Was painted	Chellason	Royley	R97
D3/284	Newstead Abbey, Notts	Chapel NG15 8NA	Tabletop, L,K,L	1567 (1559)	Bottom inscription now illegible		Fauld	Royley	TT16 L33 GH2(11)
D3/285	Leighton Bromswold, Hunts	Church, St Mary PE28 5AY	Effigy, L	1567	French hood			Royley	R103
D3/286	Kidderminster, Worcs	Church, St Mary DY10 2JN	Effigy, K,L	1568	Great helm and lion	Part. Children on back panel in cameo		Richard Parker	R55
D3/287	London, Westminster	Abbey, St Edmunds Chapel SW1P 3PA	Mural tablet, L	1568	No effigy	Part. Decorative border with motifs	Marble and Fauld	London	M153
D3/288	Stafford	Church, St Mary ST16 2AR	Effigy, K,L	1568	Headless knight effigy. Great helm with large tassles.	Lion at feet.	Chellaston	Pevsner Royley	R94
D3/289	Healaugh, Yorks	Church, St John the Baptist LS24 8DA	Effigy, K,L,L	1568		No. Latin inscriptions	Fauld	Royley	R98
D3/290	Whitchurch, Denbigh (Parish church of Denbigh)	Church, St Marcella LL16 4ER	Effigy, K	1568			Fauld		M137
D3/291	London, Hackney	Church, St John E5 0PD	Mural, K,L	1569 (1570)	Reported as being obscured			London	M364

Number	Location	Building	Monument	Date	Armour and other features	Painted/collar	Source	Kerver	Notes
D3/292	Wroxeter, Shrops	Church, St Andrew SY5 6PH	Effigy, K,L	1570 (1578)	Spiral pilasters	Yes		Royley	R101
D3/293	Caldecote, Warwick	Church, St Theobald and St Chad CV10 0UN	Effigy, C	1570				Parts may be in the church	*See* D9/77
D3/294	Winkburn, Notts	Church, St John of Jerusalem NG22 8PQ	Slab, C,L	1570					S131 GH2(18)
D3/295	Albury, Herts	Church, St John the Baptist	Mural, K,K	1570	No effigies	Corithian columns supporting broken pediment			M583
D3/296	Lillingstone Dayrell, Bucks	Church, St Nicholas MK18 5AT	Effigies, C,L	1571 (1556)			Chellaston	Possibly Richard Parker	R32
D3/297	Breedon on the Hill Leics	Church, St Mary & St Hardulph DE73 8AJ	Effigy, K L	1571 (1585)		No	Fauld	Richard and Gabriel Royley	R73
D3/298	Willesley, Derbys	Church, St Thomas LE65 2YS	Slab, C,L	1571				Royley	S85 GH2(11)
D3/299	Stapleford, Notts	Church, St Helen NG9 8FN	Slab, K,L	1571 (1590)	Farthingale				S140 GH2(11)
D3/300	Wolstanton, Staffs	Church, St Margaret ST5 0HU	Effigy, K,L	1571		11 children		Pevsner	R12
D3/301	London, Aldgate	Church, St Katherine Cree EC3A 3DH	Mural, K	1571	Rolled mat. Scroll work around inscription		Fauld	Cornelius Cure	M251

Number	Location	Building	Monument	Date	Armour and other features	Painted/collar	Source	Kerver	Notes
D3/302	Turvey, Bedford	Church, All Saints MK43 8EP	Effigy (V), LK,L	1571			Fauld		R239
D3/303	London, Westminster	Abbey SW1P 3PA	Mural, L,K,L	1571		Yes	Fauld		M444
D3/304	Wysall, Notts	Church, Holy Trinity NG12 5QS	Effigy, K,L	1572	Lion and dog at feet. Carved coat of arms	Chain collar. Fist crest	Fauld	Royley	R9
D3/305	Glossop, Derbys	Church, All Saints SK13 7RU	Slab, P	1572 (1560)	Hammer and trowel				S180
D3/306	Leighton Bromswold, Hunts	Church, St Mary PE28 5AY	Effigy	1572 (1578 or 1581)	Rolled up mat			Royley	R104
D3/307	Prestbury, Cheshire	Church, St Peter SK10 4DG	Slab, K.L	1572				Royley	S87 GH2(11)
D3/308	Uppsala, Sweden	Cathedral	Effigy, R	1572			Fauld	Willem Boy	R187
D3/309	Fryerning, Essex	Church, St. Mary the Virgin and St. Edmund	Effigy, K,L	1572	Rush mat Head on great helm			Cornelius Cure	A227
D3/310	Bosbury, Hereford	Church, Holy Trinity HR8 1QT	Effigy, C	1573			Freestone (*see* B75)	John Gildon	R241
D3/311	Prestbury, Cheshire	Church, St Peter SK10 4DG	Slab, C,L	1573				Royley	S252
D3/312	Ingatestone, Essex	Church, St Edmund & St Mary CM4 9DU	Effigy, K,L	1573			Alabaster and marble	Cornelius Cure	R140
D3/313	Over Peover, Cheshire	Church, St Lawrence WA16 9HW	Slab, K,L	1573 (1586)				Royley	S88 GH2(11)

Number	Location	Building	Monument	Date	Armour and other features	Painted/collar	Source	Kerver	Notes
D3/314	Swarkestone, Derbys	Church, St James DE73 1JB	Effigy, J	1573	Coif. Serjeant robes			Royley with some work carried out by London	R105
D3/315	Penkridge, Staffs	Church, St Michael ST19 5AL	Effigy, K,L	1574	Pilasters with urns, figures with shields. Great helm	Stag head crest	Fauld	Royley	R89
D3/316	Wing, Bucks	Church, All Saints LU7 0NX	Effigy, K,L	1575					R33
D3/317	Wolverhampton, Staffs	Church, St Peter WV1 1TS	Effigy, K,L	1575				Robert Royley	R107
D3/318	Much Dewchurch, Hereford	Church, St David HR2 8DL	Effigy, K,K	1575	Freestone?		Freestone (*see* B75)	John Gildon	R172
D3/319	Bosbury, Hereford	Church, Holy Trinity HR8 1QT	Effigy, C,L	1575			Freestone (*see* B75)	John Gildon	R242
D3/320	Wolverhampton, Staffs	Church, St Peter WV1 1TS	Effigy, K,L	1575		No	Fauld	Robert Royley	R243
D3/321	Exeter, Devon	Cathedral EX1 1HS	Mural, K	1575	Much heraldry	No	Deep brown stained	London	M341
D3/322	Cambridge	Chapel, Gonville and Caius Col	Mural, no effigy	1575	Sarcophagus			London	M635
D3/323	Hillesden, Bucks	Church, All Saints MK18 4DB	Tomb chest (no effigy), C,L	1576	Sarcophagus			Thomas Kirby	R130
D3/324	Romford, Essex	Church, Edward the Confessor RM1 3AB	Mural, K	1576			Fauld	William Cure	M256
D3/325	Tong, Shrops	Church, St Bartholomew TF11 8PW	Effigy, K,L	1576					R86

Number	Location	Building	Monument	Date	Armour and other features	Painted/collar	Source	Kerver	Notes
D3/326	Matlock, Derbys	Church, St Giles DE4 3BZ	Slab, C,L	1576 (1560?)				Royley	S94 GH2(18)
D3/327	Willesley, Leics	Church, St Thomas LE65 2YS	Slab, C,L	1577 (1580)			Chellaston	Royley	S254
D3/328	Swarkestone, Derbys	Church, St James DE73 1JB	Tabletop, K	1577 (1573)			Chellaston	Royley workshop but may be on a tomb chest made in London	TT8
D3/329	Long Whatton, Leics	Church, All Saints LE12 5DB	Slab, K,L	1577					S113 GH2(27)
D3/329	Easton Neston, Northants	Church, St Mary NN12 7HS	Mural, K,L	1577	Small effigies	No	Uncertain		M31
D3/330	Claverley, Shrops	Church, All Saints WV5 7DS	Slab, K,L	1577	Ruff			Royley	S19 GH1(274)
D3/331	Sprotbrough, Yorks	Church, St Mary DN1 2NR	Slab, K,L	1577				Possibly locally carved	TT31 GH2(12)
D3/332	Solihull, Warwick	Church, St Alphege B91 3RQ	Slab, K.L,L	1577 (1537)				Royley	S96 GH2(18)
D3/333	Theydon Mount, Essex	Church, St Michael, CM16 7QQ	Effigy, K,L	1577	Resting on one elbow	Strapwork	Fauld	London	A226 CMS-CG
D3/334	Bacton, Hereford	Church, St Faith HR2 0AR	Mural, L	1578	Kneeling effigy of Elizabeth I	No	Fauld alabaster and freestone	Commissioned by Blanche Parry (*see* St Margaret's, Westminster) in her lifetime	M133 (*see also* M400)

Number	Location	Building	Monument	Date	Armour and other features	Painted/collar	Source	Kerver	Notes
D3/335	Whitchurch, Denbigh (Parish church of Denbigh)	Church, St Marcella LL16 4ER	Effigy, K,L	1578		Yes		Richard (II) and Gabriel Royley (Donbins?)	R109
D3/336	London, Westminster	Abbey, Henry VII chapel SW1P 3PA	Effigy, R	1578		Yes		Cornelius Cure/ Garrett Johnson	R50
D3/337	Llanfarchell, Whitchurch, Denbigh	Church, St Marcella LL16 4ER	Effigy, K,L	1578 (1588)		Yes	Fauld	The name Donbins has been associated but may well be a Royley – *see* note on R119	R72
D3/338	Burbage, Leics	Church, St Catherine LE10 2DE	Slab, K,L,L	1578	French hood			Royley	S21
D3/339	Eccleshall, Staffs	Church, Holy Trinity ST21 6BY	Tabletop, B	1578	Coif Furred cuffs				TT38
D3/340	Egmanton, Notts	Church, Our Lady of Egmanton NG22 0HN	Slab, L,C,L	1579	Wives at a lower level	Worn	Fauld	Royley	S22 Southwell history website
D3/341	London, Bishopsgate	Church, Great St Helens EC3A 6AT	Tabletop – no effigy, K	1579		No		London	TT35
D3/342	Old Dalby, Leics	Church, St John the Baptist LE14 3LB	Effigy, K,L,K	1580	French hood	Chain collar	Chellaston	Richard Parker	R133 L35
D3/343	Hitcham, Bucks	Church, St Mary SL1 7DP	Mural, K,L	1580	Broken pediment			Garrett Johnson	M385
D3/344	Monk's Kirby, Warwicks	Church, St Edith CV23 0QX	Effigy, C,L	1580				Royley	R114

Number	Location	Building	Monument	Date	Armour and other features	Painted/collar	Source	Kerver	Notes
D3/345	Whitmore, Staffs	Church, All Saints ST5 5HR	Slab, K,L	1580 (1560?)				Royley	S83
D3/346	Fenny Bentley, Derbys	Church, St Edmund DE6 1LD	Effigy (V), C,L	1580		Shrouded figure			G71
D3/347	Long Melford, Suffolk	Church, Holy Trinity CO10 9DL	Effigy, K	1580	Rolled up mat			Cornelius Cure	R148
D3/348	Adwick le Street, Yorks	Church, St Laurence DN6 7AD	Slab, K,L	1580	Ruff. Head turned			Possibly locally carved (Doncaster)	S70 GH2(12) GH1(274)
D3/349	Hackleton and Horton, Northants	Church, St Mary Magdalene NN4 6BY	Mural, K	1580	Kneeling effigies	Strapwork			R149
D3/350	Stoke Newington, Middlesex	Church, St Mary N16 9ES	Mural, K,L	1580	Helmet on stand	Some colour	Chellaston		M461
D3/351	Ashbourne, Derbys	Church, St Oswald DE6 1AN	Effigy, K,L	1581	Figures holding shields to one side	No. Lion at feet	Fauld	Richard and Gabriel Royley	R115
D3/352	Dyrham and Hinton, Avon	Church, St Peter SN14 8HA	Effigy, K	1581				John Gildon	R246
D3/353	Ludlow, Shrops	Church, St Lawrence SY8 1AN	Effigy, K,L	1581	Holding a book between his hands. Round-headed niches with pairs of figures	Yes.	Uncertain		R247 CMS-CG
D3/354	Chelsea, Middlesex	Church, Old Church	Mural, K,L	1581		Two sons	Fauld		M573
D3/355	Spilsby, Lincs	Church, St James PE23 5DU	Effigy (II), K,L	1582	Demi-figure	Statues of a green man	Chellaston	Thomas Goodlord – *see* B76	M63 L20
D3/356	Snarford, Lincs	Church, St Lawrence LN8 3SL	Effigy, K,L	1582		Six-column canopy. Painted	Pink		R27

Number	Location	Building	Monument	Date	Armour and other features	Painted/collar	Source	Kerver	Notes
D3/357	Staunton, Notts	Church, St Mary NG13 9PE	Slab, C	1582	No effigy		Chellaston		S130
D3/358	Screveton, Notts	Church, St Wilfred NG13 8JT	Effigy, K,L,L	1583			Fauld		A2
D3/359	Crich, Derbys	Church, St Mary DE4 5DJ	Slab, K,L	1583 (1603)	French hood Slashed sleeves	Skull at feet			S172
D3/360	Faringdon, Berks	Church, All Saints SN7 7HW	Slab, C,L	1583					S200
D3/361	London, Hackney	Church, St John E5 0PD	Tablet, L	1582				Cornelius Cure (later Farmer and Brindley)	R226
D3/362	Latton, Essex	Church, St Mary CM12 2JP	Mural tablet, K,L	1583		Eleven children. Part	Chellaston		M389
D3/363	Somerton, Oxford	Church, St James OX25 6LN	Effigy, K,L	1583	Dog toying with ribbon	No	Chellaston (but poor quality)	Richard and Gabriel Royley	R75
D3/364	Newbold on Avon, Warwicks	Church, St Botolph CV211HR	Effigy, C,L	1583				Royley	R116
D3/365	Wirksworth, Derbys	Church, St Mary DE4 4ET	Effigy, C	1584		Remnants of paint	Fauld and Chellaston		R135
D3/366	Aylesbury, Bucks	Church, St Mary HP20 2 JJ	Effigy, L,L	1584 (1590)				Poss Gerard Johnson	R150
D3/367	Warwick	Church, St Mary CV34 4RA	Mural with effigy, Child	1584		No	Fauld		A79
D3/368	Windsor, Berks	Chapel, St George SL4 1NJ	Effigy, R,L	1584			Pillars of porphyry		R141

Number	Location	Building	Monument	Date	Armour and other features	Painted/collar	Source	Kerver	Notes
D3/369	Weston under Wetherley, Warwicks	Church, St Michael CV33 9BY	Mural, L,L	1584		No	Fauld	Garrett Hollemans	M117
D3/370	Queenhill, Worcs	Church, St Nicholas WR8 0RE	Slab, C,L,L	1584	Badly kept beard			Garrett Hollemans	S8
D3/371	Welford, Northants	Church, St Mary the Virgin NN6 6HB	Tablet with brass insert, K,L,L,L	1584 (1585)		Part (may be restored)	Fauld	Garrett Hollemans	M390
D3/372	North Mimms, Herts	Church, Our Lady AL9 7TN	Tabletop, L	1584				Royley	TT18
D3/373	Thurlaston, Leics	Church, St Bartholomew LE3 3PF	Slab, K,L	1584				Royley	S139 GH2(12)
D3/374	Rockingham, Northants	Church, St Leonard LE16 8TH	Effigy, K,L	1584				Royley	R117
D3/375	Madley, Hereford	Church, St Mary HR2 9DP	Effigy, K,L	1585				John Gildon	R244
D3/376	Margam Abbey, Glamorgan	Abbey SA13 2TJ	Effigy, K	1585		Four kneeling figures		London	R245 X109
D3/377	Chesterton, Warwicks	Church, St Giles CV33 9LG	Effigy, K,L	1585		Partially	Fauld	Royley	R119
D3/378	London	Temple Church EC1A 2DE	Effigy, C	1585 (1600)		Yes		Garret Johnson but may also be John Key or William Wright. Repaired by the Stantons	A67
D3/379	Wolverhampton, Staffs	Church, St Peter WV1 1TS	Effigy, K,L	1585	Rolled mat over cushion			Robert Royley	R108

Number	Location	Building	Monument	Date	Armour and other features	Painted/collar	Source	Kerver	Notes
D3/380	Chesterfield, Derbys	Church, St Mary and All Saints S40 1XJ	Effigy, K,L	1585		Stained	Probably Fauld	Garrett Hollemans (I)	R62 L7
D3/381	Mavesyn Ridware, Staffs	Church, St Nicholas WS15 3QE	Slab, K	1585					S134
D3/382	Breedon on the Hill Leics	Church, St Mary & St Hardulph DE73 8AJ	Effigy, K	1585		No	Fauld	Richard and Gabriel Royley	R74
D3/383	Wolverhampton, Staffs	Church, St Peter WV1 1TS	Effigy, K,L	1585	Carved shields on tomb chest			Robert Royley	R248
D3/384	Edgcote, Northants	Church, St James OX17 1AG	Effigy, K,L	1585				Royley	R118
D3/385	Witham, Essex	Church, St Nicholas CM8 2GS	Effigy, C,L	1585		Yes			R147
D3/386	London, Westminster	Abbey SW1P 3PA	Effigy, K	1585				Johnson workshop (Southwark)	R159
D3/387	Greensted, Ongar, Essex	Church, St Andrew CM5 9LD	Tablet, L	1585		No	Fauld	Attributable to Gilles de Witte.	M388
D3/388	East Sutton, Kent	Church, St Peter & St Paul ME17 3DE	Tablet, K	*Circa* 1585			Fauld		M598
D3/389	Great Brington, Northants	Church, St Mary NN7 4JB	Effigy, K	1586			Fauld	Jasper Hollemans	R59
D3/390	Blithfield, Staffs	Church, St Leonard WS15 3NL	Slab, Child	1586	Death carrying away the child	No. Bottom inscription	Chellaston	Possibly Royley – *see* comment on S64	S64

Number	Location	Building	Monument	Date	Armour and other features	Painted/collar	Source	Kerver	Notes
D3/391	London, Westminster	Abbey SW1P 3PA	Mural, L	1586		Yes		Johnson workshop (Southwark)	R181
D3/392	Nailstone, Leics	Church, All Saints CV13 0DH	Slab, C	1586				Royley	S25 GH2(19)
D3/393	Over Peover, Cheshire	Church, St Lawrence WA16 9HW	Effigy (may be slab), K,L	1586				Royley	R120
D3/394	Coughton Court, Warwick	Church, St Peter B49 5JA	Tomb chest, K	1586					A91
D3/395	London, Westminster	Abbey SW1P 3PA	Mural, J	1587	Cock pheasant crest. Rolled rush mat	Yes	Fauld	London	M445
D3/396	Pitchford, Shrops	Church, St Michael SY5 7DP	Slab, K,L	1587			Chellaston	John Tarbook (signed J.T 1587)	S40 GH2(12)
D3/397	Condover, Shrops	Church, St Mary and St Andrew SY5 7AA	Effigy, K,L	1587		No	Fauld		R199
D3/398	Coleshill, Warwick	Church, St Peter & Paul B46 3AD	Effigy, K,L	1587 (probably much later)				Possible Hollemans	R136
D3/399	Shelford, Notts	Church, St Peter & St Paul NG!2 1EN	Effigy, L	1587			Fauld	Royley	R70
D3/400	Woodbridge, Suffolk	Church, St Mary IP12 4LP	Mural, K	1587					A35
D3/401	Aubourn, Lincs	Church, Old Church LN5 9DZ	Effigy, K	1587			?		R219
D3/402	Stamford, Lincs	Church, St Martin PE9 2NT	Mural, C,L	1587				Cornelius Cure	M64

Number	Location	Building	Monument	Date	Armour and other features	Painted/collar	Source	Kerver	Notes
D3/403	Standon, Herts	Church, St Mary SG11 1LA	Mural, K	1587			Fauld		M150
D3/404	Quorndon, Leics (Quorn) – *see* Q2	Church, St Bartholomew LE12 8DP	Effigy, K,L	1587		No	Fauld	William Hargrave	R85
D3/405	Brocklesby, Lincs	Church, All Saints DN41 8PP	Mural, K,L	1587		Yes	Fauld	William Wright	M123
D3/406	Hainton, Lincs	Church, St Mary LN8 6LS	Mural, K,L	1587 (1559)		No	Fauld or Ledsham. Heavy veining		M85
D3/407	Packington, Leics	Church, Holy Rood LE65 1WL	Slab, C,L,L	1587				Garrett Hollemans	S9
D3/408	Clifton, Notts	Church, St Mary NG11 8NJ	Effigy, K,L,L	1587				Royley	R121
D3/409	Wentworth, Yorks	Church, Holy Trinity S62 7TW	Effigy, K,L	1587	Lion at feet		Chellaston		R275
D3/410	Wolstanton, Staffs	Church, St Margaret ST5 0HU	Tablet, -	1587 (1597)	No effigy				M634
D3/411	Aston Bottrell, Shrops	Church, St Michael WV16 6QX	Slab, C,L	1588					S71 L27 GH1(262)
D3/412	Wrotham, Kent	Church, St George TN15 7AD	Slab, C	1588				Epiphamus Evesham London	S201
D3/413	London, Westminster	Abbey, St Nicholas chapel SW1P 3PA	Mural with effigy, L	1588		Yes		Gerard Johnson	M122
D3/414	Gloucester	Cathedral GL1 2LX	Mural, C	1588					M58

Number	Location	Building	Monument	Date	Armour and other features	Painted/collar	Source	Kerver	Notes
D3/415	London	Church, St Martin in the Fields WC2N 4JJ	Effigy, K	1588	Rolled up mat	No			R49
D3/416	King's Norton, Warwicks	Church, St Nicholas B38 8RU	Slab, C,L	1588	French hood			Royley	S90 GH2(12)
D3/417	Warwick	Church, St Mary CV34 4RA	Mural with 2 effigies, R,L	1588 (1634)		Yes	Marble and alabaster	Credited to Nicholas Johnson or the Hollemans	A66
D3/418	Chesterfield, Derbys	Church, St Mary and All Saints S40 1XJ	Slab, K	1588		No	Chellaston	Garrett Hollemans (I)	S7 L7
D3/419	Hinton St George, Somerset	Church, St George TA17 8SP	Effigy, K	1588					R78
D3/420	Harrington, Northants	Church, St Peter & St Paul NN6 9NX	Mural, K,K,K,K,L,L	1588				Garrett Hollemans (I)	M220
D3/421	Warwick	Church, St Mary CV34 4RA	Effigy, R	1589	Rolled up mat	Yes	Alabaster and marble		R52
D3/422	London, Westminster	Abbey, SW1P 3PA	Effigy, L	1589		Yes		Richard Stevens (designed by Ralph Symons)	R139
D3/423	Leicester	Cathedral LE1 4LF	Slab (possibly ex tabletop), C	1589		No	Chellaston		S4
D3/424	Sibthorpe, Notts	Church, St Peter NG23 5PN	Effigy, C	1589			Fauld	Gabriel Royley (II)	A86
D3/425	Monk's Kirby, Warwicks	Church, St Edith CV23 0QX	Effigy, K,L	1589 (1547)				Royley	R113 (-)

Number	Location	Building	Monument	Date	Armour and other features	Painted/collar	Source	Kerver	Notes
D3/426	Boreham, Essex	Church, St Andrew CM3 3EQ	Effigy, K,K,K	1589			Contains alabaster touchstone and other minerals	Richard Stevens	R138
D3/427	London, Westminster	Abbey SW1P 3PA	Effigy, L,L	1589				Cornelius Cure	R155
D3/428	York	Minster YO1 7HH	Slab, C	1589					S261
D3/429	Canterbury, Kent	Cathedral CT1 2EH	Mural, K,L	1589					M486
D3/430	Worfield, Shrops	Church, St Peter WV15 5LF	Effigy, K,L	1589		No			R264
D3/431	Southwell, Notts	Minster NG25 0HD	Effigy, B	1590			Ledsham	York	A17
D3/432	Hornsey, Middx	Church, St Mary with St George N10 3AH	Slab, K,L,L	1590	French hood with front point			Jasper Hollemans	S10 GH2(19)
D3/433	Ashbourne, Derbys	Church, St Oswald DE6 1AN	Slab, K,L	1590				Royley	S91 L33 GH2(12)
D3/434	Sheffield, Yorks	Cathedral S1 1HA	Effigy, R	1590					R18
D3/435	Stoke Dry, Rutland	Church, St Andrew LE15 9JG	Effigy, C,L	1590	Dog in skirt. Chain collar	No. Children on tomb chest	Fauld	Royley	R122
D3/436	Cheam, Surrey	Church, St Dunstans SM3 8QH	Mural, L	1590		No			M147
D3/437	Chevening, Kent	Church, St Botolph TN14 6HG	Effigy, C,L	1590					R196
D3/438	Langar, Notts	Church, St Andrew NG13 9HG	Effigy, K	1590	Rolled up mat. Scrollwork on mat and frieze	Chain collar	Fauld	William Hargrave	R283

Number	Location	Building	Monument	Date	Armour and other features	Painted/collar	Source	Kerver	Notes
D3/439	Barking, Essex	Church, St Margaret. IG11 8AS	Tablet, L	1590					M624
D3/440	Stonton Wyville, Leics	Church, St Denys	Effigy, K	1590	Baby lies in own monument	Family on tomb chest	Fauld		A236
D3/441	Bottesford, Leics	Church, St Mary the Virgin NG13 0DA	Effigy, 4th earl, R	1591 (1594)	Rolled up mat			Gerard Johnson John Matthews Henry Kinder	R7
D3/442	Bottesford, Leics	Church, St Mary the Virgin NG13 0DA	Effigy, R 3rd Earl	1591 (1594)	Rolled up mat			Gerard Johnson John Matthews Henry Kinder	R29
D3/443	Swepstone, Leics	Church, St Peter LE67 2SA	Effigy (VI), K	1591			Fauld	Royley	GNP49 (-)
D3/444	Worcester	Cathedral WR1 2LA	Tomb chest, no effigy, B	1591			Uncertain	Anthony Tolly by signature	R183
D3/445	Ashbourne, Derbys	Church, St Oswald DE6 1AN	Slab, K,L	1591 (1537)				Royley	S256
D3/446	Acton Burnell, Shrops	Church, St Mary SY5 7PF	Effigy, K,L	1591			Fauld		R213
D3/447	Ashbourne, Derbys	Church, St Oswald DE6 1AN	Mural, K,L	1592		No	Fauld	Has London features	M392
D3/448	Throwley, Kent	Church, St Michael and All Angels ME13 0PJ	Effigy, K,L	1592		Part	Fauld	Gerard Johnson	R37
D3/449	Hackington, Kent	Church, St Stephen CT2 7AB	Effigy and demi-figure, K	1592	Rolled up mat under cadaver	Form of SS collar	Fauld	London probably Southwark	R193 L42
D3/450	Titchfield, Hants	Church, St Peter PO14 4AG	Effigy, K,L,K	1592		Yes	Fauld	Gerard Johnson (the elder)	R22

Number	Location	Building	Monument	Date	Armour and other features	Painted/collar	Source	Kerver	Notes
D3/451	Stenigot, Lincs	Church St Nicholas LN11	Mural, K	1592			Ledsham?		M65
D3/452	Glentworth, Lincs	Church, St Michael DN21 5DG	Mural, K,L	1592		No	Fauld and marble	Nicholas Johnson	M84
D3/453	Chesterfield, Derbys	Church, St Mary and All Saints S40 1XJ	Mural, -	1592		Shrouded figure and skeleton	Fauld	Possibly Garrett Hollemans	M116
D3/454	Mavesyn Ridware, Staffs	Church, St Nicholas WS15 3QE	Tabletop, K,L	1592	Inscription at foot of slab	No	Fauld	Jasper Hollemans	TT32 L8
D3/455	Easebourne, Sussex	Church, St Mary GU29 0AJ	Effigy, K,L,L	1592 (1598)		Yes. Garter	Alabaster and caen stone	Richard Stephens or Garret Johnson	R80
D3/456	Grendon, Warwicks	Church, All Saints CV9 3DP	Panels, K,L	1592				Royley	R123
D3/457	Ludlow, Shrops	Church, St Lawrence SY8 1AN	Mural, K,L	1592					M297
D3/458	Stratford on Avon, Warwicks	Church, Holy Trinity CV37 6BG	Effigy, K,L	1592 (1582)	Twisted pilasters	Part	Pale veining	Royley	R124
D3/459	Crich, Derbys	Church, St Mary DE4 5DJ	Slab, C,L	1592	Ruffs with feet on a unicorn and eagle. Walking attire	Curious hat Text at feet			S202 AO Fig 11
D3/460	Bradwell Juxta Coggeshall, Essex	Church, Holy Trinity CM77 8EP	Mural, K,K,L	1592 (1602)			Fauld	Southwark?	M165
D3/461	Eastling, Kent	Church, St Mary. ME13 0AX	Mural, K,L	1592					M603

Number	Location	Building	Monument	Date	Armour and other features	Painted/collar	Source	Kerver	Notes
D3/462	Ashley, Staffs	Church, St John the Baptist TF9 4LQ	Effigy, J,L	1593 (1612)		No	Fauld	Jasper Hollemans	R16
D3/463	Fulham, Middlesex	Church, All Saints SW6 3LA	Tablet, K	1593		No			M393
D3/464	Seighford, Staffs	Church, St Chad ST18 9PQ	Effigy, K,L	1593				Royley. Pevsner recorded	R125
D3/465	Blithfield, Staffs	Church, St Leonard WS15 3NL	Slab, C,L	1593			Chellaston	Royley	S63 GH2(12)
D3/466	Marchington, Staffs	Church, St Peter ST14 8LJ	Tabletop, K,L	1593	French hood with outer hood			Royley	TT19 Gh2(19) AO Fig 6
D3/467	Bushbury, Staffs	Church, St Mary WV10 8JP	Slab, C	1593				Royley	S98 GH2(19)
D3/468	Keele, Staffs	Church, St John the Baptist ST5 6QJ	Tablet, K,L	1593				Pevsner	M431
D3/469	Ingatestone, Essex	Church, St Edmund & St Mary CM4 9DU	Mural, K	1593	Shells	No	Fauld		M484
D3/470	Great Mitton, Lancs	Church, All Hallows BB7 9PH	Effigy, K,L	1594		No	Fauld	Gabriel Royley (II)	R222
D3/471	Bushbury, Staffs	Church, St Mary WV10 8JP	Slab, L	1594				Royley	S257
D3/472	Elstow, Beds	Church, St Mary and St Helen MK42 9XT	Mural, K,L	1594			Fauld or Ledsham		M90

Number	Location	Building	Monument	Date	Armour and other features	Painted/collar	Source	Kerver	Notes
D3/473	Titchfield, Hants	Church, St Peter PO16 7AB	Effigy, K,L	1594				Gerard Johnson (or Richard Stephens)	R81
D3/474	Mitton, Lancs	Church, All Hallows BB7 9PH	Effigy, K,L	1594 (1596)				Royley but *see* B86	R126
D3/475	Kirkby Mallory, Leics	Church, All Saints LE9 7QE	Slab, C,L,L	1594	French hood with outer hood			Royley	S99
D3/476	Hintlesham, Norfolk	Church, St Nicholas IP8 3NH	Mural, C,L	1594			Fauld heavy veining	Possibly Hollemans	M211
D3/477	West Malling, Kent	Church, St Mary the Virgin ME19 6NE	Tablet with brass insert, L	1594			Fauld	Gilles de Witt	M399
D3/478	London, Bishopsgate	Church, St Helen's EC3A 6AT	Tabletop, C	1594				William Kerwin (made for his own burial) or Epiphamus Evesham –*see* TT24	TT24
D3/479	Blackmore, Essex	Church, St Lawrence	Effigy, C,L	1594	Rolled up mat				A228
D3/480	Woodford, Essex	Church, St Mary	Mural, C	1595					M620
D3/481	Hainton, Lincs	Church, St Mary LN8 6LS	Effigy, K	1595	Rolled up mat	Yes	Fauld heavy veining	Possibly Hollemans	A57
D3/482	Egham, Surrey	Church, St John the Baptist TW20 9HL	Mural, C,L	1595					M160
D3/483	Radwell, Herts	Church, All Saints SG7 5ES	Mural, C,L	1595		Yes	Fauld	Maximilian Colt?	M102

Number	Location	Building	Monument	Date	Armour and other features	Painted/collar	Source	Kerver	Notes
D3/484	London, Westminster	Church, St Margaret SW1P 3JX	Mural, L	1595	Kneeling lady in front of prayer stall	Part	Fauld & marble		M400 *See also* M133
D3/485	Marston on Dove, Derbys	Church, St Mary DE65 5GB	Slab, C	1595				Royley	S259
D3/486	Kirkby Mallory, Leics	Church, All Saints LE9 7QE	Slab, K,L,L	1595				Royley	S260
D3/487	Chesterfield, Derbys	Church, St Mary and All Saints S40 1XJ	Effigy, K,L	1595		Stained	Probably Fauld	Garrett Hollemans (I)	R63 L7
D3/488	Chigwell, Essex	Church, St Mary IG6 7QB	Mural, K,L	1595			Fauld		M258
D3/489	Market Drayton, Shrops	Church, St Mary TF9 1AD	Slab, C,L	1595			Chellaston	Royley	S24 GH2(19)
D3/490	Hanbury, Staffs	Church, St Werburgh DE13 8TF	Tabletop, L,K,L	1595	Mary, Queen of Scotts hoods	Diagonal text strap	Fauld – brown veined	Royley	TT2 GH2(19) AO Fig 10
D3/491	Mersham, Kent	Church, St John the Baptist TN25 6NT	Tablet, L	1595				Epiphanius Evesham	M405
D3/492	Fenny Drayton, Leics	Church, St Michael & All Angels CV13 6BA	Mural, K,K	1596	No effigy	No		Jasper Hollemans	R43 X110
D3/493	North Leigh, Oxford	Church, St Mary OX29 6TX	Mural, K,L	1596			Fauld		M301
D3/494	Fletching, Sussex	Church, St Andrew and St Mary the Virgin TN22 3SR	Effigy, K,L	1596			Fauld		R251

Number	Location	Building	Monument	Date	Armour and other features	Painted/collar	Source	Kerver	Notes
D3/495	London, Westminster	Abbey SW1P 3PA	Effigy, C,L	1596		Yes		Bartholomew Atye or Isaac James	R40
D3/496	London, Westminster	Abbey SW1P 3PA	Mural, K	1596 (1603)		Some	Fauld and marble	London	M464
D3/497	Worcester	Cathedral WR1 2LA	Effigy, B	1596 (1604)		Yes			R184
D3/498	Shifnal, Shrops	Church, St Andrew TF11 9AB	Effigy, C	1596			Fauld		R214
D3/499	Ledbury, Hereford	Church, St Michael HR8 1PL	Slab, P	1596	Book and skull cap				S178
D3/500	Chichester, Sussex	Cathedral PO19 1PX	Mural, B	1596		Yes			M564
D3/501	Thorpe Mandeville, Northants	Church, St John the Baptist	Effigy, K,L	1597					A217
D3/502	London, Westminster	Abbey SW1P 3PA	Tomb chest, L	1597		Part			A142
D3/503	Melton Mowbray, Leics	Church, St Mary LE13 1AE	Slab C,L	1597		No			S31
D3/504	Peatling Magna, Leics	Church, All Saints LE8 5UH	Tabletop, K,L	1597	Large hood		Fauld	Royley	TT20 GH1 (276 & Fig 51) GH2 (19)
D3/505	London, Westminster	Abbey, St Nicholas Chapel SW1P 3PA	Mural, L	1597		Part	Possibly Ledsham with Ashford marble top	York carvers	M404
D3/506	Hythe, Kent	Church, St Leonard CT21 5DW	Mural, C	1597				Epiphanius Evesham	M180
D3/507	Marston on Dove, Derbys	Church, St Mary DE65 5GB	Slab, L	1597				Royley	S258

Number	Location	Building	Monument	Date	Armour and other features	Painted/collar	Source	Kerver	Notes
D3/508	Nettlestead, Kent	Church, St Mary ME18 5HA	Mural, L	1598 (1636)					M37
D3/509	Barton in Fabis, Notts	Church, St George NG11 0AA	Mural, K	1598 (1613)		Yes		Possibly Nicholas Stone	M403
D3/510	Stamford, Lincs	Church St Martin PE9 2NT	Mural K	1598 (1588)	Strapwork			Possibly by Cornelius Cure and completed by William Cure II	M66
D3/511	Breedon on the Hill, Leics	Church, St Mary & St Hardulph DE73 8AJ	Mural with effigies, K,L	1598 (1622)	Cadaver	No	Fauld	Garratt Hollemans or Gabriel Royley II	M95 L42
D3/512	Rochester, Kent	Cathedral ME1 1SX	Effigy, B	1598					R250
D3/513	Tittleshall, Norfolk	Church, St Mary PE32 2PN	Mural, L	1598					M178
D3/514	London, Westminster	Abbey SW1P 3PA	Effigy, L	1598		Yes	Fauld	Gerard Johnson	R151
D3/515	London, Westminster	Abbey SW1P 3PA	Effigy, J	1598		Yes		Gerard Johnson	R152
D3/516	West Hallam, Derbys	Church, St Wilfrid DE7 6GR	Effigy, K,L	1598					R249
D3/517	Condover, Shrops	Church, St Mary and St Andrew SY5 7AA	Mural, J,K,L,C	1598		Yes			M221
D3/518	Bottisham, Cambs	Church, Holy Trinity CB2 3NZ	Mural, K,L	1599					M228
D3/519	Claverley, Shrops	Church, All Saints WV5 7DS	Slab, C,L	1599				Jasper Hollemans	S20 GH2(19)

Number	Location	Building	Monument	Date	Armour and other features	Painted/collar	Source	Kerver	Notes
D3/520	Shipton Moyne, Gloucs	Church, St John the Baptist GL8 8PW	Effigy, J	1599		Yes			R177
D3/521	Great Brington, Northants	Church, St Mary NN7 4JB	Effigy, K	1599	Peaked mourning hood	Yes	Uncertain	Jasper Hollemans	R60
D3/522	London, Bishopsgate	Church, Great St Helens EC3A 6AT	Mural, K,L	1599					M402
D3/523	Uffington, Berks	Church, St Mary SN7 7RD	Effigy, K	1599	Canopy			London	R237
D3/524	London, Westminster	Abbey SW1P 3PA	Tablet, C	1599		Some colour	Black		M463
D3/525	Saundby, Notts	Church, St Martin DN22 9ER	Tomb chest without effigy, K,L	1599	Frieze	No	Fauld	William Hargrave	R284
D3/526	Boston Lincs	Church, St Botolph PE21 6NW	Effigy (VI), K	16th cent (1539–1566)	Scala Coeli			Cannot be identified	GNP57 X93 (-)
D3/527	Boston Lincs	Church, St Botolph PE21 6NW	Effigy (VI), L	16th Cent (1539–1566)	Scala Coeli			Cannot be identified	GNP58 X93 (-)
D3/528	Darley Dale, Derbys	Church, St Helen DE4 2GG	Slab, C,L	16th Cent (Poss 1540)					S175
D3/529	Quorndon, Leics (Quorn) – *see* Q2	Church, St Bartholomew LE12 8DP	Mural, K	16th Cent		No	Fauld		M593
D3/530	Norton, Derbys	Church	Slab, K,L	16th Cent		No			S273

Appendix D4 – 17th Century 1600 to 1699

GNP = Gothic Gardner 'no picture' list in file, G = Gothic Gardner with picture, R = Renaissance, T = Transition, M = Mural

Number	Location	Building	Monument	Date	Armour and other features	Painted	Source	Kerver	Notes
D4/1	Watford, Herts	Church, St Mary WD18 0EG	Mural with effigy, L	1600 (1619)				Isaac James – now in Chenies (D4/14)	*See* A161
D4/2	Fulham, Middlesex	Church, All Saints SW6 3LA	Tablet, C	1600		No			M394
D4/3	Faringdon, Berks	Church, All Saints SN7 7HW	Mural, K,L	1600 (1588)					M338
D4/4	Noseley, Leics	St Mary Chapel of Noseley Hall LE19 2JA	Slab, K	1600				Jasper Hollemans, worn	S69
D4/5	Waltham Abbey, Essex	Abbey church EN9 1XQ	Effigy, K,L	1600		Yes	Fauld	Bartholomew Atye and Isaac James	R42
D4/6	Shouldham Thorpe, Norfolk	Church, St Mary PE33 0ED	Slab, K	1600			Frame Inlayed image only. Fauld		S100
D4/7	Sudbury, Derbys	Church, All Saints DE6 5HT	Effigy, K,L	1600					R235
D4/8	Merton, Surrey	Church, St Mary SW19 3HJ	Mural, K,L,L	1600				Garratt Johnson	M144
D4/9	Montgomery, Powis	Church, St Nicholas SY15 6PT	Effigy, C,L	1600	Cadavers	Yes		Walter Hancock	M213 L42
D4/10	Tavistock, Devon	Church, St Eustacius PL19 0AG	Mural, K,L	1600		Yes			M406

Number	Location	Building	Monument	Date	Armour and other features	Painted	Source	Kerver	Notes
D4/11	Sandon, Staffs	Church, St Andrew ST18 0DB	Slabs, K,L,K	1600 (1474 and 1501)				Sampson Erdeswike *see* S80	S138
D4/12	Duffield, Derbys	Church, St Alkmund DE56 4BA	Mural with slabs, C,L,L,Ch	1600			Fauld		S203
D4/13	London, Westminster	Church, St Margaret SW1P 3JX	Mural, L	1600		Part		William Cure	M462
D4/14	Exton, Rutland	Church, St Peter & St Paul LE15 8AX	Mural, K,L	1600 (1591)	Double arch		Fauld		M32
D4/15	Chenies, Bucks	Chapel, St Michael WD3 6ER	Effigy, L	1601				Attributed to Isaac James	A161
D4/16	Charlecote, Warwicks	Church, St Leonards CV35 9EW	Effigy, K,L	1601			Fauld		R65 L10
D4/17	Weekley, Northants	Church, St Mary NN16 9UW	Effigy, J,L	1601 (1618)	Head on great helm	Part			A162
D4/18	Derby	Cathedral DE1 3GP	Mural, L	1601		Yes		John Smythson	M145
D4/19	Turvey, Beds	Church, All Saints MK43 8EP	Tomb chest, K	1601		Yes		Possibly Maximillian Colt	A159
D4/20	South Ockendon, Essex	Church, St Nicholas RM15 6NU	Mural	1601		Part painted	Fauld alabaster		M636
D4/21	Bunbury, Cheshire	Church, St Helen CW6 0AG	Effigy, K	1602		Yes			A163
D4/22	Bristol, Somerset	Cathedral BS1 5TJ	Effigy, K	1602				Sir Richard Berkeley (died 1602)	A164

Number	Location	Building	Monument	Date	Armour and other features	Painted	Source	Kerver	Notes
D4/23	Highclere, Hants	Church, St Michael & All Angels RG20 2RG	Effigy, K,L	1602		Yes	Some effigies are not alabaster	Isaac James and Bartholomew Ayte	R39
D4/24	Denton, Lincs	Church, St Andrew NG32 1LG	Mural, K,L	1602					M407
D4/25	Bristol, Somerset	Chapel, Lord Mayor's (St Mark) BS1 5TB	Effigy, K	1602			Chellaston		R34
D4/26	Norton, Northants	Church, All Saints NN11 5ND	Mural, L	1602	Strapwork	Yes		London	M408
D4/27	Withybrook, Warwicks	Church, All Saints CV7 9LS	Tabletop, K,L	1602					TT9
D4/28	Millbrook, Beds	Church, St Michael MK45 2JB	Effigies, K,L	1602 (1560, 1621)	French hood. Articulated pauldron	No	Chellaston	Trent Valley	R79 Appendix O
D4/29	Maldon, Essex	Church, All Saints CM9 5HN	Mural, L,K,L	1602		No			M132
D4/30	Wednesbury, Staffs	Church, St Bartholomew WS10 9DJ	Mural, K,L	1602			Fauld		M409
D4/31	Gresford, Denbigh	Church, All Saints LL12 8	Mural, L,L,L	1602		Part	Fauld		M263
D4/32	Ordsall, Notts	Church, All Hallows DN22 7TU	Mural with effigy, K	1603 (1613)		No		Nicholas Stone?	M40
D4/33	Old Dalby, Leics	Church, St John the Baptist LE14 3LB	Mural, K	1603	Rolled up mat	Chain collar	Fauld	William Hargrave	M324 L35

Number	Location	Building	Monument	Date	Armour and other features	Painted	Source	Kerver	Notes
D4/34	Bromham, Beds	Church, St Nicholas SN15 2JS	Effigy, K	1603	Rolled up mat. Canopy	No	Fauld	London	R252
D4/35	London, Westminster	Abbey, St Edmunds Chapel SW1P 3PA	Effigy and mural, K,L	1603 (1587)		Yes	Alabaster, touché and pink marble	Cornelius Cure	R48
D4/36	Cothelstone, Somerset	Church, St Thomas of Canterbury TA4 3DS	Effigy, K,L	1603	Knight has Bible and hand on heart	Yes	Watchet		R57
D4/37	Cheam, Surrey	Church, St Dunstans SM3 8QH	Mural, L	1603				An inventory drawing exists for this but the carver is unknown	M108
D4/38	Pembroke, Wales	Church, St Mary SA71 4DB	Mural tablet, Child	1603 (1610)					M196
D4/39	Bunny, Notts	Church, St Mary the Virgin NG11 6QW	Mural, C,L	1603		No	Fauld		M410
D4/40	Seckington, Warwicks	Church, All Saints B79 0LD	Mural, K,L	1603		Part	Fauld		M412
D4/41	Fulham, Middlesex	Church, All Saints SW6 3LA	Mural, L	1603	Seated facing forward	Chrisom	Fauld		M577
D4/42	Gazeley, Suffolk	Church, All Saints CB8 8RF	Mural with effigy, K,L	1604 (1613)				Nicholas Stone?	M14
D4/43	Trent, Dorset	Church, St Andrews DT9 4SL	Tablet, K	1604	And slate		Alabaster and slate	To William Gerard, pilasters and heraldic device	M369

Number	Location	Building	Monument	Date	Armour and other features	Painted	Source	Kerver	Notes
D4/44	Chenies, Bucks	Chapel, St Michael WD3 6ER	Effigy, L	1604 (1619)		Yes		William Cure	A165
D4/45	Kelstern, Lincs	Church, St Faith LN11 0RG	Mural, L	1604		No	Fauld	Possibly Cornelius Cure as there are similarities to R48	M87
D4/46	Gloucester	Cathedral GL1 2LX	Effigy, B	1604		Yes			R25
D4/47	Hardwick, Northants	Church, St Leonard NN9 5GZ	Mural, K	1604			Alabaster and slate		M413
D4/48	Sutton, Beds	Church, All Saints SG19 2ND	Effigy, K,L	1604			May not be alabaster		R30
D4/49	Chesterfield, Derbys	Church, St Mary and All Saints S40 1XJ	Effigy, child	1604		No	Probably Fauld	Jasper Hollemans	R64 L7
D4/50	Bramley, Hants	Church, St James RG26 5DF	Mural, K	1604					M414
D4/51	Lee, London	Church, St Mildred	Mural, K,L	1604					M565
D4/52	Crediton, Devon	Church, Holy Cross EX17 2AH	Mural, J	1605			Watchet		M177
D4/53	Romford, Essex	Church, Edward the Confessor RM1 3AB	Mural, K,L	1605			Fauld		M255
D4/54	Romford, Essex	Church, Edward the Confessor RM1 3AB	Mural, L	1605			Fauld		M257

Number	Location	Building	Monument	Date	Armour and other features	Painted	Source	Kerver	Notes
D4/55	Charlecote, Warwicks	Church, St Leonards CV35 9EW	Effigy, K,L	1605			Fauld	Isaac James and Bartholomew Atye	M120 L10
D4/56	London, Bishopsgate	Church, St Andrew Undershaft EC3A 8BN	Mural, C	1605		No	Effigy is Fauld alabaster	Believed to be by Nicholas Johnson	M208
D4/57	Englefield, Berks	Church. St Mark RG7 5EN	Mural, K,L & K,L	1605	Strapwork. Rolled up mat	No	Fauld	London	M44
D4/58	Malpas, Cheshire	Church, St Oswald SY14 8PP	Effigy, K,L	1605	Mary, Queen of Scots cap	No but may have been in the past	Fauld	Possibly Hollemans	R236
D4/59	Bisham Abbey, Berks	Church, All Saints SL7 1RW	Obelisk	1605	Figures of swans	Partial	Fauld		W3
D4/60	Coxwold, North Yorks	Church, St Michael YO61 4AD	Mural, with effigies, K,L	1605			May be in Magnesium limestone	Thomas Browne	M98
D4/61	Croxall, Staffs	Church, St John the Baptist WS13 8RA	Slab, K,L	1605	French hood. Farthingale		Fauld	Jasper Hollemans	S121
D4/62	Radwell, Herts	Church, All Saints SG7 5ES	Mural, L	1605	Lady facing forward with chrisom	Part. Six sons and four daughters	Fauld	Possibly Maximilian Colt	M100
D4/63	Fulham, Middlesex	Church, All Saints SW6 3LA	Mural, L	1605		Part			M395
D4/64	London, Westminster	Abbey SW1P 3PA	Effigy, J,(L)	1605				Garratt Johnson	R153
D4/65	Bath, Somerset	Abbey church BA1 1LF	Mural, K,L	1605		No	Fauld and touch	London	M27
D4/66	Hardingstone, Northants	Church, St Edmund NN$ 6BZ	Mural, K,L	1606					M415

Number	Location	Building	Monument	Date	Armour and other features	Painted	Source	Kerver	Notes
D4/67	Standon, Herts	Church, St Mary SG11 1LA	Mural, K,L	1606			Fauld		M151
D4/68	York	Minster YO1 7HH	Mural, B	1606		Yes			M50
D4/69	London, Westminster	Abbey SW1P 3PA	Effigy, K	1606				Isaac James	R41
D4/70	London, Westminster	Abbey, St Paul's Chapel SW1P 3PA	Mural, K,L	1606		Yes		Bartholomew Atye (mural) and Isaac James (effigies)	M106
D4/71	Wimborne, Dorset	Minster BH21 1EB	Effigy, K	1606		Part		London	M371
D4/72	Bristol, Somerset	Cathedral BS1 5TJ	Mural, L	1606 (1603)	-	Yes	Freestone (*see* note M146)	Samuel Baldwin	X10
D4/73	Lenton, Lincs	Church, St Peter NG33 4HF	Tablet, L	1606			Fauld		M88
D4/74	Greens Norton, Northants	Church, St Bartholomew NN12 8BN	Mural, K,L	1606			Fauld		M363
D4/75	Stanford on Avon, Northants	Church, St Nicholas NN6 6JP	Mural, K,L	1606 (1582)		Part	Fauld		M314
D4/76	Leaveland, Kent	Church, St Lawrence ME13 0NP	Mural, L, child	1606			Fauld	Southwark	M365
D4/77	Stanford on Avon, Northants	Church, St Nicholas NN6 6JP	Effigy, K	1606		Part			R218
D4/78	Green's Norton, Northants	Church, St Bartholomew NN12 8BN	Mural, K,L	1606		No	Fauld		M316

Number	Location	Building	Monument	Date	Armour and other features	Painted	Source	Kerver	Notes
D4/79	Norton in Hales, Shrops	Church, St Chad TF9 4AT	Mural, K,L	1606 and 1635		No	Fauld	Inigo Jones and Southwark school	M300
D4/80	Haugh, Lincs	Church, St Leonard	Mural, K,L	1606			Light veined		M548
D4/81	North Ockendon, Essex	Church, St Mary Magdelene RM14 3QH	Mural, K,L	1606					M638
D4/82	London, Westminster	Abbey, St John the Baptist Chapel SW1P 3PA	Mural, K,L	1607 (1603)		Yes			M152
D4/83	Stenigot, Lincs	Church St Nicholas LN11	Mural, K	1607					M67
D4/84	Uffington, Lincs	Church St Michael SN7 7RD	Mural, K,L	1607					M68
D4/85	Ashby Folville, Leics	Church, St Mary LE14 2TE	Effigy, K,L	1607		Yes	Very pale light brown veining		R221
D4/86	Dorney, Bucks	Church, St James the Less SL4 6QP	Mural, K,L	1607			Fauld		M377
D4/87	Shenley Church End, Bucks	Church, St Mary MK5 6LL	Mural, K	1607	On one elbow. Strapwork			Probably Southwark	M416
D4/88	Mackworth, Derbys	Church, All Saints DE22 4NF	Mural, K	1607		Was	Fauld or Chellaston	Edward Mundy	M103
D4/89	Narborough (Narburgh) Norfolk	Church, All Saints PE32 1TE	Mural with effigies, K,L	1607				John Key and William Wright	M119
D4/90	Cardington, Shrops	Church, St James SY6 7JZ	Mural, J	1607	The judge rests on one elbow	Yes. Children grouped on a panel	Fauld	Atye and James (or Key and Wright)	M141

Number	Location	Building	Monument	Date	Armour and other features	Painted	Source	Kerver	Notes
D4/91	Wellington, Somerset	Church, St John the Baptist TA21 8SF	Effigy, K,L	1607		Yes		Cornelius Cure	R163
D4/92	Cumnor, Berks (Oxford)	Church, St Michael OX2 9PE	Mural, K,L	1607	Rolled up mat				M417
D4/93	West Thurrock, Essex	Church, St Clements RM20 4AL	Effigies (was mural), K,L	1607 (1611)			Fauld	London	M387
D4/93	Holme next the Sea, Norfolk	Church	Mural, K	1607					M601
D4/94	Hougham, Kent	Church, St Laurence, CT15 7AH	Mural, K	1607					M606
D4/95	North Ockendon, Essex	Church, St Mary Magdelene RM14 3QH	Effigy	1607			Fauld alabaster		R287
D4/96	Oxnead, Norfolk	Church, St Michael NR10 4HF	Effigy, K	1608		No	Fauld on marble tomb chest	Possibly Key and Wright	R204
D4/97	Worcester	Cathedral WR1 2LA	Effigy, C,L	1608		Yes	Uncertain		R185
D4/98	London, Westminster	Abbey SW1P 3PA	Effigy, child (2)	1608 (1606)	Crib	Yes		Maximilian Colt	A166
D4/99	Hawnby, Yorks	Church, All Saints YO62 5QR	Tablet, Child	1608 (1617)		Yes-part	Fauld		M249
D4/100	Edgcote, Northants	Church, St James OX17 1AG	Effigy, K,L,L	1608?			Fauld	Royley?	R112
D4/101	Chilton, Bucks	Church, St Mary C010 2ZB	Effigy, K,L	1608		Yes	Fauld or Ledsham	Nicholas Stone or Nicholas Johnson	R31

Number	Location	Building	Monument	Date	Armour and other features	Painted	Source	Kerver	Notes
D4/102	Middle Claydon, Bucks	Church, All Saints MK18 2EY	Mural, C,L	1608			Fauld		M381
D4/103	Gawsworth, Cheshire	Church, St James SK11 9RJ	Effigy, K,L	1608		Yes. Cadaver			R46 L42
D4/104	North Walsham, Norfolk	Church, St Nicholas NR28 9BT	Mural with effigy, K	1608				William Wright and John Key	M107
D4/105	Rivenhall, Essex	Church, St Mary and All Saints CM8 3PQ	Effigy, K,L	1608	Rolled up mat			Southwark	R69
D4/106	Wells, Somerset	Cathedral BA5 2UE	Effigy, B	1608		Yes	Fauld		R194
D4/107	Yarnton, Oxford	Church, St Bartholomew OX5 1PY	Effigy, K,L	1609		Yes		Jasper Hollemans	R15
D4/108	Norwich, Norfolk	Church, St George Tombland NR3 1AF	Mural, C,L	1609		Yes			M140
D4/109	Great Waltham, Essex	Church, St Anthony and Lawrence CM3 1AR	Effigy, K,L	1609				Bartholomew Atye	R166
D4/110	Leicester	Cathedral LE1 4LF	Slab (possibly ex tabletop), C	1609		No			S5
D4/111	Ely, Cambs	Cathedral CB7 4DL	Effigy, B	1609	Carved cope	Yes	Fauld		M375
D4/112	Bishopsgate, London	Church, Great St Helen EC3A 6AT	Effigy, K,L	1609		Yes		It is suggest that the carver is Nicholas Johnson	R2

Number	Location	Building	Monument	Date	Armour and other features	Painted	Source	Kerver	Notes
D4/113	Broxbourne, Herts	Church, St Augustine EN10 7AU	Effigy, K,L	1609		Partial	Fauld	London features	A167
D4/114	South Harting, Sussex	Church, St Mary & St Gabriel GU31 5QB	Effigy, K	1609					R76
D4/115	Kedington, Suffolk	Church, St Peter & St Paul CB9 7NN	Mural with effigy, L	1609 (1613)	Square columns	No	Chellaston	London	M16
D4/116	Bisham Abbey, Berks	Church, All Saints SL7 1RW	Mural with effigies, L	1609	Iron grill. Coronets	Yes	Fauld	Southwark, London features believed to be the Cure workshop	M96 X53
D4/117	Fulham, Middlesex	Church, All Saints SW6 3LA	Tablet, K	1609					M396
D4/118	Bishops Hull, Somerset	Church, St Peter & St Paul TA1 5EB	Mural, K	1609			Fauld and Watchet	There are alabaster tablets to three children dated 1661–1673 and Sir George 1647–1660 both appear to be Watchet	M121
D4/119	Newstead Abbey, Notts	Abbey crypt NG15 8NA	Effigy, K	1609		Painted		William Hargrave	M391
D4/120	Ross on Wye, Hereford	Church, St Mary HR9 6QY	Mural, no effigies, C,L	1609			Chellaston	Samuel Baldwin	M182
D4/121	Eccleshall, Staffs	Church, Holy Trinity ST21 6BY	Mural, B	1609 (1603)					M293

Number	Location	Building	Monument	Date	Armour and other features	Painted	Source	Kerver	Notes
D4/122	London, Westminster	Abbey, St John the Evangelist Chapel SW1P 3PA	Effigy, K,K	1609 (1635)	Rush mat. Slab over supported by four knights	Yes	Marble and alabaster	Maximilian Colt	A180
D4/123	East Sutton, Kent	Church, St Peter & St Paul ME17 3DE	Mural, K,L	1609		No	Fauld	London features	M599
D4/124	Little Easton, Essex	Church, St Mary CM6 2JH	Effigy, K,L	1610					A60
D4/125	Streatham, London	Church, St Leonard SW16 1HS	Tablet, C	1610		Yes	Chellaston	A stonecutter near Charing Cross – Will entry. Most probably William Wright	A88
D4/126	Burton Pedwardine, Lincs	Church, St Andrew NG34 0BX	Mural	1610		No	Fauld		M319
D4/127	Elvaston, Derbys	Church, St Bartholomew DE72 3EP	Effigy, K,L	1610		Yes			R158
D4/128	Swineshead, Lincs	Church St Mary PE20 3JD	Mural, Children	1610					M69
D4/129	Penkridge, Staffs	Church, St Michael ST19 5AL	Effigy, K,L,K,L	1610 (1629)			Fauld		R88
D4/130	Hainton, Lincs	Church, St Mary LN8 6LS	Mural, C,L	1610		No	Fauld or Ledsham		M86
D4/131	Longford, Derbys	Church, St Chad DE6 3DS	Effigy, K,L	1610	Falling ruff		Chellaston		R36
D4/132	Harefield, Middlesex	Church, St Mary UX9 6DL	Mural, K	1610 (1614)	Skull. Strapwork in arch	Partial	Fauld	William White (or Wright)	M361

Number	Location	Building	Monument	Date	Armour and other features	Painted	Source	Kerver	Notes
D4/133	Betley, Staffs	Church, St Margaret CW3 9AP	Mural, C,L	1610		Partial	Fauld	Pevsner	M421
D4/134	London, Haringey	Church, St Olave N2 2TW	Mural, C	1610			Fauld		M433
D4/135	London, Tower of London	Church, St Peter ad Vincula EC3N 4AB	Mural, K	1610 (1564 or 74)				Cornelius Cure and William Cure II (An extension of the 1564 or 1574 tomb)	M329
D4/136	Kedington, Suffolk	Church, St Peter & St Paul CB9 7NN	Mural, K,L,L	1610 (1613)	Wives face each other in mural with knight recumbent	No. Strapwork	Chellaston	Possibly Nicholas Stone but certainly London	M15
D4/137	Fowey, Cornwall	Church, St Finnbarrus PL23 1AR	Mural with effigy, C	1610 (1624)			Fauld	Baldwin?	M143
D4/138	London, Chancery Lane	Chapel of the Rolls WC2A 1LR	Mural, K	1610 (1617)					M181
D4/139	Waterperry, Oxford	Church, St Mary OX33 1JZ	Mural, K,L	1610		Part	Fauld	Samuel Baldwin	M183
D4/140	Welford, Berks	Church, St Gregory RG20 8HA	Mural, L	1610	Chrisom and kneeling lady	Black columns	Fauld and Chellaston	Epiphanius Evesham	M204
D4/141	Hawstead, Suffolk	Church, All Saints IP29 5NT	Mural, L	1610			Chellaston		M571
D4/142	Fulham, Middlesex	Church, All Saints SW6 3LA	Mural, L	1610		Part			M578
D4/143	Beddington, Surrey	Church, St Mary SM6 7NH	Mural, K	1611		Garter	Fauld		M250

Number	Location	Building	Monument	Date	Armour and other features	Painted	Source	Kerver	Notes
D4/144	Norwich, Norfolk	Church, St Etheldreda NR1 2DF	Mural, C	1611					M139
D4/145	Boscastle, Cornwall	Church, St Merteriana PL34 0DL	Mural, C,L	1611		Partial	Fauld and slate		M418
D4/146	Bredon, Worcs	Church, St Giles GL20 7LE	Mural, K,L	1611		No	Fauld	Samuel Baldwin	M168
D4/147	Chenies, Bucks	Chapel, St Michael WD3 6ER	Effigy, L	1611					A184
D4/148	Wentworth, Yorks	Church, Holy Trinity S62 7TW	Mural, K,L,K	1611		Part coloured	Fauld		M575
D4/149	Little Gaddesden, Herts	Church, St Peter and St Paul	Mural, L	1611		Yes			M584
D4/150	Bakewell, Derbys	Church, All Saints DE45 1FD	Mural. K,L	1611					M594
D4/151	Averham, Notts	Church, St Michael and All Angels	Mural, K	1611	Frieze			William Hargrave	M595
D4/152	West Dereham, Norfolk	Church, St Andrew PE33 9RT	Tablet, K,K	1612	Shields in border. Skull		Fauld		M419
D4/153	Leyton, Essex	Church, St Mary the Virgin E10 5JP	Effigies, K,L	1612	On one elbow	Partially	Fauld		A168
D4/154	Didsbury, Lancs	Church, St James M20 2RQ	Mural, K,L,L	1612					M326 CMS-CG
D4/155	South Walsham, Norfolk	Church, St Mary NR13 6DQ	Mural, K	1612			Fauld		M420

Number	Location	Building	Monument	Date	Armour and other features	Painted	Source	Kerver	Notes
D4/156	Spilsby, Lincs	Church St James PE23 5DU	Effigy (II), K,L	1612	Standing man		Fauld and marble	John Taylor	M422 L20
D4/157	Ludlow, Shrops	Church, St Lawrence SY8 1AN	Mural, L	1612		No	Fauld	Bartholomew Atye	M298
D4/158	Windsor, Berks	Chapel, St George SL4 1NJ	Effigy, B	1612					A169
D4/159	Bottesford, Leics	Church, St Mary the Virgin NG13 0DA	Effigy, K,L	1612				Nicholas Johnson	R8
D4/160	Stallingborough, Lincs	Church St Peter & Paul DN41 8AA	Mural, C	1612					M70
D4/161	Easton Neston, Northants	Church, St Mary NN12 7HS	Mural and Effigies, K,L	1612 (1628)	Scalloped fan niche. Strapwork	Part painted. Children on tomb chest	Fauld	Jasper Hollemans	R17
D4/162	Easton Maudit, Northants	Church, St Peter & Paul NN29 7NR	Mural, K,L	1612					M202
D4/163	Grendon, Warwicks	Church, All Saints CV9 3DP	Mural, C	1612					M423
D4/164	Chiddingly, Sussex	Church, Unknown dedication BN8 6HT	Mural, J,L,K,L	1612	Resting on one elbow. Staning statues	Kneeling effigies with children grouped behind	Claimed as Battle but no evidence of mining in the 17th century, more likely Fauld	William Cure II and Garret Johnson	M131
D4/165	Egham, Surrey	Church, St John the Baptist TW20 9HL	Mural, L,L	1612		Yes	Fauld	Epiphamus Evesham	M161

Number	Location	Building	Monument	Date	Armour and other features	Painted	Source	Kerver	Notes
D4/166	Cranford, Middx	Church, St Dunstan TW5 9RZ	Mural, K,L,L	1612		Yes	Fauld, touch and marble	William Cure II	M157
D4/167	Wallington, Surrey	Church, Holy Trinity SM6 8BL	Mural, K,L	1612					M252
D4/168	Leyton, Essex	Church, St Mary E10 5JP	Mural, K,L	1612					M253
D4/169	Masham, Yorks	Church, St Mary HG4 4EQ	Mural, K,L	1612		No	Fauld		M264
D4/170	Blackburn, Lancs	Church, St John BB1 6DW	Mural, J	1612				Possibly Gerard Johnson	M446
D4/171	Worcester	Cathedral WR1 2LA	Mural, L	1613		Yes	Fauld	Samuel Baldwin	M184
D4/172	Youlgreave, Derbys	Church, All Saints DE45 1WS	Mural, K,L	1613	Strapwork	Partially	Fauld		M424
D4/173	Norwich, Norfolk	Church, St Andrew NR2 4AD	Effigy, K,L	1613			Fauld	Southwark workshops	R110
D4/174	Norwich, Norfolk	Church, St Andrew NR2 4AD	Effigy, K,L	1613			Fauld	Southwark workshops	R111
D4/175	Snarford, Lincs	Church, St Lawrence LN8 3SL	Mural, K,L	1613	Tiered with both effigies on one elbow	Strapwork. Part painted	Fauld	London	M71
D4/176	Keele, Staffs	Church, St John the Baptist ST5 6QJ	Effigy, K,L	1613				Pevsner	A170
D4/177	Abbess Roding, Essex	Church, St Edmund CM5 0PA	Mural, K,L	1613					M611

Number	Location	Building	Monument	Date	Armour and other features	Painted	Source	Kerver	Notes
D4/178	Horseheath, Cambs	Church, All Saints CB21 4QA	Mural and effigy, K,L	1613			Poss Fauld	Nicholas Johnson	M425
D4/179	Tunstall, Kent	Church, St John the Baptist ME9 8DX	Mural, K,L	1613		Yes			M124
D4/180	Stroud, Gloucs	Church, St Lawrence GL5 1AP	Mural, J	1613		Yes	Fauld	Samuel Baldwin when working in Stroud	M426
D4/181	North Stoneham, Hants	Church, St Nicholas SO50 9NW	Mural, J,L	1613		Yes			M173
D4/182	Burwell, Cambs	Church, St Mary CB25 0HB	Mural, K,L	1613					M334
D4/183	Stanford on Avon, Northants	Church, St Nicholas NN6 6JP	Mural, K,L	1613		No	Fauld		M313
D4/184	Wednesbury, Staffs	Church, St Bartholomew WS10 9DJ	Effigy, C,L	1613		No	Fauld		A172
D4/185	Chevening, Kent	Church, St Botolph TN14 6HG	Mural, L	1613					M217
D4/186	West Ham, Essex	Church, All Saints E15 3HU	Mural, K,K	1613 (1632)			?		M248
D4/187	Swinbrook, Oxford	Church, St Mary OX18 4DY	Mural, K,K,K	1613		No		Possibly William Byrd	M302
D4/188	Melbourne, Derbys	Church, St Michael with St Mary DE73 8JH	Slab, K,L	1613	French hood with hooped outer hood				S108

Number	Location	Building	Monument	Date	Armour and other features	Painted	Source	Kerver	Notes
D4/189	Fryerning, Essex	Church, St. Mary the Virgin and St. Edmund	Mural, C,L	1613					M617
D4/190	East Donyland, Essex	Church, St Lawrence	Mural, L	1613					M596
D4/191	Norton, Worcs	Church, St James WR5 2PX	Mural, K,L	1614				Samuel Baldwin – *see* page 351 of Llewellyn	M191
D4/192	Shipton under Wychwood, Oxford	Church, St Mary the Virgin OX7 6BP	Mural, C,L	1614	Tall hat	Traces	Fauld		M427
D4/193	London, Haringey	Church, St Olaves N2 2TW	Bust, C	1614		Yes			A63
D4/194	Stansted Mountfitchet Essex	Church, St Mary the Virgin CM24 8UB	Effigy, L	1614	Farthingale, lace collar, tall hat. Ornaments				A61
D4/195	Tortworth, Gloucs	Church, St Leonard GL12 8HF	Effigy, K	1614				Samuel Baldwin	R156
D4/196	Peatling Magna, Leics	Church, All Saints LE8 5UH	Incised tabletop, K,L,L	1614 (1605 or 1597)	Large hood		Fauld Brown veined	Royley	TT21 GH1(276)
D4/197	Nantwich, Cheshire	Church, St Mary CW5 5RQ	Effigy, K,L	1614		No	Fauld Brown veined		A65
D4/198	Framlingham, Suffolk	Church, St Michael IP13 9BJ	Effigy, K,L	1614 (1547)	Coronet at knee	Yes	Fauld	Maximilian Colt but *see* A32	A32 X100
D4/199	Flitton, Beds	Church, St John the Baptist MK45 5EJ	Effigy, K,L	1614	Coronet	Yes	Not Fauld. May well be Watchet	Possibly London	A70 A71

Number	Location	Building	Monument	Date	Armour and other features	Painted	Source	Kerver	Notes
D4/200	Spetchley, Worcs	Church, All Saints WR5 1RS	Effigy, K,L	1614		No	Fauld	Samuel Baldwin	R53
D4/201	Wells, Somerset	Church, St Cuthbert BA5 2AW	Mural, C	1614					M428
D4/202	Bradgate, Leics	Chapel LE12 8SS	Mural, K,L	1614					M205
D4/203	Quatt Malvern, Shrops	Church, St Andrew WV15 6QW	Effigy, K,L	1614		Part			R216
D4/204	Blakesley, Northants	Church, St Mary NN12 8RB	Mural, C,L	1614		Yes			M315 CMS-CG
D4/205	Stratford on Avon, Warwicks	Church, Holy Trinity CV37 6BG	Mural and effigy, C	1614				Gerard Johnson II	M343
D4/206	Tonbridge, Kent	Church, St Peter & St Paul TN9 1HD	Effigy, K,L	1615	Uncomfortable pose on one elbow	No	Fauld		R66
D4/207	Rolleston on Dove, Staffs	Church, St Mary DE13 9BE	Slab, P	1615					S44
D4/208	Leigh, Worcs	Church, St Eadburga WR6 5LB	Mural, K,L	1615					M429
D4/209	Keele, Staffs	Church, St John the Baptist ST5 6QJ	Tablet, C	1615				Pevsner	M430
D4/210	Gloucester	Cathedral GL1 2LX	Mural, C,L	1615	Corinthian columns	Yes. Origin paint on robe		Samuel Baldwin of Stroud	M60
D4/211	Truro, Cornwall	Cathedral TR1 2AF	Mural, C,L	1615	Tiered. Iron railings	Yes	Fauld		M432

Number	Location	Building	Monument	Date	Armour and other features	Painted	Source	Kerver	Notes
D4/212	Hulcote, Bedford	Church, St Nicholas MK17	Mural, K,L	1615					M34
D4/213	Berkeley, Gloucester	Church, St Mary GL13 9BN	Effigy, K,L,	1615	Portrait		Alabaster effigies and canopy on stone tomb chest	Samuel Baldwin	R1
D4/214	Great Malvern, Worcs	Church, priory WR14 2AY	Effigy, K,L	1615				Samuel Baldwin	R170
D4/215	Holme Pierrepont, Notts	Church, St Edmund NG12 2LD	Effigy), K	1615				John Smythson	R3
D4/216	Charterhouse, London	Chapel EC1M 6AN	Mural, C	1615 (1614)		Yes		Nicholas Stone	M7
D4/217	Charterhouse, London	Chapel EC1M 6AN	Mural, C	1615		No		Nicholas Stone	M8
D4/218	York	Minster YO1 7HH	Mural, K,L	1615		Yes		Nicholas Stone	M5
D4/219	York	Minster YO1 7HH	Mural, L	1615		Yes		Nicholas Stone	M51
D4/220	Avening, Gloucs	Church, Holy Cross GL8 8NL	Mural, C	1615 (1616)				Samuel Baldwin	M166
D4/221	Brewood, Staffs	Church, St Mary & St Chad ST19 9BT	Effigy, K,L	1615		Yes			R83
D4/222	Oxford	Chapel, Merton College OX1 4JD	Mural, K	1615		Pile of books	Some marble	Nicholas Stone	M164
D4/223	Bristol, Somerset	Lord Mayor's Chapel BS1 5TB	Mural, C	1615				Samuel Baldwin	M167
D4/224	Chevening, Kent	Church, St Botolph TN14 6HG	Mural, K,L	1615				Southwark	M216

Number	Location	Building	Monument	Date	Armour and other features	Painted	Source	Kerver	Notes
D4/225	London, Westminster	Abbey SW1P 3PA	Effigy, L	1615		No			A181
D4/226	Linton, Kent	Church, St Nicholas ME17 4AW	Mural, K,L	1615	Convex plinth. Vestige family tree	No			M450
D4/227	Lamport with Faxton, Northants	Church (demolished)	Mural tablet. Now in V&A Museum, K	1616	Part marble	Was	Fauld	Nicholas Stone	M3
D4/228	South Harting, Sussex	Church, St Mary & St Gabriel GU31 5QB	Effigy, K	1616	Ruff. Cross sash		Chellaston		R77
D4/229	Barton in Fabis, Notts	Church, St George NG11 0AA	Effigy, K.L	1616	Tudor plate armour. Great helm with feathers	No	Fauld	Hollemans	R19
D4/230	Caldecote, Warwick	Church, St Theobald and St Chad CV10 0UN	Mural, K,L,K,L	1616					M435
D4/231	Bletchley, Bucks	Church, St Mary MK3 6DZ	Slab, P	1616			Brass portrait	Dr Richard Haydocke	S181
D4/232	Wing, Bucks	Church, All Saints LU7 0NX	Mural, K,L	1616	Black columns	No	Fauld	Nicholas Johnson	M46
D4/233	London, Haringey	Church, St Olave N2 2TW	Mural, C	1616			Fauld	London workshops	M434
D4/234	Eyeworth, Beds	Church, All Saints SG19 2HH	Mural, L,K,L	1616		No	Fauld		M91
D4/235	Kentchurch, Hereford	Church, St Mary HR2 0DA	Effigy (check), K,L	1616				Samuel Baldwin	R171
D4/236	Worcester	Cathedral WR1 2LA	Effigy, B	1616					R186

Number	Location	Building	Monument	Date	Armour and other features	Painted	Source	Kerver	Notes
D4/237	Monken Hadley, Herefordshire	Church, St Mary EN5 5PZ	Mural	1616				Nicholas Stone I	M158
D4/238	Great Milton, Oxford	Church, St Mary OX44 7PN	Mural, K,L,K	1616 (1618)	Rolled up mat			Uncertain but Gerard Christmas, Epiphanius Evesham and Samuel Baldwin are all named	M174
D4/239	Droitwich, Worcs	Church, St Peter de Witton WR9 7AN	Mural, Serjeant	1616			May be marble	Samuel Baldwin	M189
D4/240	Fawsley, Northants	Church, St Mary NN11 3BS	Tablet, K,L,L	1616 (1619)		Part			M437
D4/241	Stratford on Avon, Warwicks	Church, Holy Trinity CV37 6BG	Mural, C	1616 (1623)		Yes		Gerard Johnson II	M344
D4/242	Appleby, Cumbria	Church, St Lawrence CA16 6QN	Mural, L	1616			Fauld effigy with black marble slab and alabaster surround	Maximilian Colt	M443
D4/243	Cowbridge, Wales	Church, Holy Cross	Mural, C	1616					M567
D4/244	Edensor, Derbys	Church, St Peter	Effigy, K,K	1616 (1626)	Cadavers		Chellaston		R277 L42
D4/245	Bolsover, Derbys	Church, St Mary S44 6HB	Mural, K,L	1617	Tiered	No		Maximilian Colt John Smythson	M142
D4/246	Harefield, Middlesex	Church, St Mary UX9 6DL	Mural, K,L	1617	Strapwork. Curtains			Southwark	M438
D4/247	Burton Joyce, Notts	Church, St Helen NG14 5DQ	Slab, K,L	1617					S235

Number	Location	Building	Monument	Date	Armour and other features	Painted	Source	Kerver	Notes
D4/248	Hawstead, Suffolk	Church, All Saints IP29 5NT	Mural, K,L	1617	No effigy		Chellaston	Nicholas Stone	M9
D4/249	Repton, Derbys	Church, St Wystan DE65 6FH	Mural, C,L	1617 (1614)					M42
D4/250	Riddlesworth, Norfolk	Church, St Peter IP22 2TA	Mural, K	1617	Veined	Partially	Fauld	Attributed to either Nicholas Stone of Maximilian Colt	M154
D4/251	Tombland, Norfolk	Church, St George NR3 1AF	Mural, C	1617		Yes		Nicholas Stone	M6
D4/252	Emneth, Norfolk	Church, St Peter & St Paul PE14 8AF	Effigy, K,L	1617				Nicholas Stone	R10
D4/253	Aldbourne, Wilts	Church, St Michael SN8 2EL	Mural, C	1617					M76
D4/254	Ash, Kent	Church, St Nicholas CT3 2EN	Mural, K,L	1617					M79
D4/255	Much Cowarne, Hereford	Church, St Mary HR7 4JQ	Effigy, K,L	1617	Possible likeness as beard has unusual features	No		Possible Baldwin	R253
D4/256	Bristol, Somerset	Church, Holy Trinity (or St Stephen) BS16 4RH	Effigy, C	1617		Yes		Samuel Baldwin	R35
D4/257	Falmouth, Cornwall	Church, King Charles the Martyr TR11 3DX	Mural, K	1617			Limestone and alabaster		M441
D4/258	Hereford	Cathedral HR1 2NG	Effigy, P (no tomb chest)	1617	Lion		Chellaston	Probably Southwark	R227

Number	Location	Building	Monument	Date	Armour and other features	Painted	Source	Kerver	Notes
D4/259	Hornchurch, Essex	Church, St Andrew RM12 6QP	Mural, K,L	1617	Strapwork	Part	Pale veined	Probably Southwark	M475
D4/260	Wield, Hampshire	Church, St James SO24 9RT	Effigy, K,L	1617	Tiered monument	No	Fauld		A191
D4/261	Cambridge	Chapel, Great St Mary	Tablet, C	1617	Demi-figure				M627
D4/262	Ash, Kent	Church, St Nicholas CT3 2EN	Mural, C	1618			Veined		M80
D4/263	Marsworth, Bucks	Church, All Saints HP23 4LX	Tomb chest panels, C	1618			Fauld	Epiphanius Evesham	X32
D4/264	Bath, Somerset	Abbey Church BA1 1LF	Effigy, B	1618		No		William Cure with some work by Nicholas Stone	R20
D4/265	Blore Ray, Staffs	Church, St Bartholomew DE6 2BS	Effigy, K,L	1618/1630	Mattress		Alabaster effigies and marble	Jasper Hollemans	M21
D4/266	Wroxeter, Shrops	Church, St Andrew SY5 6PH	Effigy, K,L	1618		Yes			R102
D4/267	Lincoln	Church, St Mary le Wigford LN5 7DN	Effigy, K,L	1618 (1630)				Maximilian Colt	R21
D4/268	Lynsted, Kent	Church, St Peter & St Paul ME9 0RH	Effigy, K,L	1618				Kemp suggests this is possibly Epiphanius Evesham	M35
D4/269	Peatling Magna, Leics	Church, All Saints LE8 5UH	Mural, C,L	1618		No	Fauld		M322

Number	Location	Building	Monument	Date	Armour and other features	Painted	Source	Kerver	Notes
D4/270	Southwark, London	Cathedral SE1 9DA	Mural, C	1618				Southwark	M149
D4/271	Bath, Somerset	Abbey church BA1 1LF	Effigy, B	1618 (1619)	Bishop's robes	No	Chellaston	William Cure II and Nicholas Johnson	R254
D4/272	London	Temple Church EC1A 2DE	Mural, C	1618		Yes	Fauld	William Cure II possibly repaired by the Stantons	M114
D4/273	London, Westminster	Abbey, St Edmunds Chapel SW1P 3PA	Effigies, K,L	1618		Yes	Marble and alabaster	William Wright	A179
D4/274	Litchborough, Northants	Church, St Martin NN12 8JG	Effigy, K	1618			Fauld		R217
D4/275	Brereton, Cheshire	Church, St Oswald	Tablet, –	1618					M476
D4/276	Faversham, Kent	Church, St Mary of Charity ME13 8GZ	Mural, K	1618		Part			M604
D4/277	Beckington, Somerset	Church, St George BA11 6TG	Tablet with bust, C	1619		No		London	M442
D4/278	Waltham Abbey, Essex	Church, Holy Cross & St Lawrence EN9 1XQ	Effigy, L	1619		No	Fauld		R255
D4/279	Woodham Ferrers, Essex	Church, St Mary CM3 8RF	Effigy, L	1619 (1611)		Yes		Nicholas Stone?	M4
D4/280	Snarford, Lincs	Church, St Lawrence LN8 3SL	Medallion portrait, K	1619	Demi-figure facing forward	Part	Fauld	Epiphanius Evesham	M72

Number	Location	Building	Monument	Date	Armour and other features	Painted	Source	Kerver	Notes
D4/281	Tichborne, Hants	Church, St Andrew SO24 0NA	Mural, child	1619		Yes – effigy	Fauld		M247
D4/282	Watford, Herts	Church, St Mary WD18 0EG	Mural, L	1619 (1599)				Nicholas Stone (but cannot be if date is 1599)	M12
D4/283	Portchester Castle, Portsmouth, Hants	Church, St Mary PO16 9QW	Mural, K	1619 (1604)		Part	Fauld. Purple veined and marble	Nicholas Stone	M13
D4/284	Gawsworth, Cheshire	Church, St James SK11 9RJ	Effigy, K,L	1619					A182
D4/285	Brooke, Rutland	Church, St Peter LE19 2JA	Effigy, K	1619	Rolled up mat	Yes	Uncertain	Attributed to William Hargrave of Bilborough	R282
D4/286	Truro, Cornwall	Cathedral, crypt TR1 2AF	Effigy, K,L	1620					R256
D4/287	Yougal, Co Cork Ireland	Church, St May Collegiate	Mural, K,L,L	1620		Yes	Uncertain	Alexander Hills	M214
D4/288	Otterden, Kent	Church, St Lawrence ME13 0BU	Mural, K,L	1620				Epiphanius Evesham	M355
D4/289	Felsted, Essex	Church, Holy Cross CM6 3DG	Effigy, K,L	1620			Stated as various stones	Epiphanius Evesham	R160
D4/290	Landwade, Suffolk	Church, St Nicholas CB8 7NF	Mural, K,L	1620	Knight on one elbow with lady recumbent	No	Pale, slightly veined	London	M339
D4/291	West Wickham, Kent	Church, St John the Baptist BR4 9HN	Effigy, K	1620			Fauld. Reported to be skilful use of veining		R257

Number	Location	Building	Monument	Date	Armour and other features	Painted	Source	Kerver	Notes
D4/292	St Osyth, Essex	Church, St Peter and St Paul CO16 8NX	Effigy, K,L	1620		Partially	Fauld and marble	William Wright	R68
D4/293	Kempsey, Worcs	Church, St Mary WR5 3JH	Effigy, K	1620			?	Samuel Baldwin	R157
D4/294	Oxford	Christ Church chapel OX1 1DP	Mural, C	1620		Yes	Fauld		M304
D4/295	Blunham, Beds	Church, St Edmund & St James MK44 3NQ	Effigy, L	1620	Fine detail on gown	No	Chellaston and Fauld and black marble		R258
D4/296	Tichborne, Hants	Church, St Andrew SO24 0NA	Mural, K,L	1621		Yes-effigy	Chellaston		M576
D4/297	Dalby, Lincs	Church, St Lawrence PE23 4PP	Mural, C,L	1621		Yes partially	Fauld. Lightly veined		M82
D4/298	Ufford, Cambs	Church, St Andrew PE9 3BH	Mural, L	1621					M332
D4/299	Salisbury, Wilts	Cathedral SP1 2EJ	Mural, K,L	1621 (1625)		Yes partially		William Wright	M105
D4/300	Norton, Worcs	Church, St Egwin WR11 4TL	Mural, K	1621				Samuel Baldwin	M192
D4/301	Exeter, Devon	Cathedral EX1 1HS	Effigy, B	1621					R144
D4/302	Attenborough, Notts	Church, St Mary the Virgin NG9 6AS	Tablet, C,L	1621		Part		Probably Burton	M373

Number	Location	Building	Monument	Date	Armour and other features	Painted	Source	Kerver	Notes
D4/303	Wantage, Berks	Church, St Peter and St Paul OX12 8BL	Tablet, C,L	1621				London	M447
D4/304	Ingatestone, Essex	Church, St Edmund & St Mary CM4 9DU	Tablet, K	1621	Demi-figure in oval frame	No	Fauld	Epiphamus Evesham or Maximilian Colt	M483
D4/305	Swarkestone, Derbys	Church, St James DE73 1JB	Effigies, K,L	1622	Great helm			Probably Burton	A38
D4/305	Tenterden, Kent	Church, St Mildred TN30 6AR	Mural, K,L	1622	Shields in arch. Strapwork	Yes	Fauld		M459
D4/306	Bray, Berks	Church, St Michael SL6 2AB	Mural, C,L	1622		Yes		Garret Johnson	M110
D4/307	Lynsted, Kent	Church, St Peter and Paul ME9 0RH	Mural and effigy, K	1622		Yes	Fauld	Epiphanius Evesham	M36
D4/308	Thornhill, Yorks	Church, St Michael WF12 0JZ	Effigy, K,L	1622				Maximilian Colt	A173
D4/309	Gloucester	Cathedral GL1 2LX	Mural, L	1622		Yes	Fauld	Samuel Baldwin	M55 Figure 121
D4/310	Eastchurch, Kent	Church, All Saints ME12 4BN	Effigy, C	1622					A223
D4/311	Great Wilne, Derbys (Separated from its church which is at Church Wilne)	Church, St Chad DE72 3QH	Mural, K,L	1622	Putti		Fauld		M448
D4/312	Carlton Curlieu, Leics	Church, St Mary the Virgin LE8 0PH	Effigy, K,L	1622 (1624 or 1629)	Great helm	No	Chellaston	Possibly Hollemans	R195

Number	Location	Building	Monument	Date	Armour and other features	Painted	Source	Kerver	Notes
D4/313	Tawstock, Devon	Church, St Peter EX31 3HY	Mural, K,L	1623	Kneeling figures at head	Yes	Fauld		M209
D4/314	Scarning, Norfolk	Church, St Peter & St Paul NR19 2PE	Mural, Child	1623	Child with head on skull	No	Fauld. Fractured	Epiphanius Evesham	M222
D4/315	Stanwell, Middlesex	Church, St Mary the Virgin TW19 9PF	Mural, K,L	1623	Drapes. Peer's robes		Fauld	Nicholas Stone	M380
D4/316	Newstead Abbey, Notts	Chapel NG15 8NA	Mural, K,L	1623 (1625)		Painted			M136
D4/317	London, Smithfield	Church, St Bartholomew EC1A 9DS	Tablet, C	1623					M279
D4/318	Chenies, Bucks	Chapel, St Michael WD3 6ER	Effigy, L	1623 (1641)		No	Fauld and touchstone	Cornelius Cure	R259
D4/319	Harefield, Middlesex	Church, St Mary UX9 6DL	Mural, K,L	1623	Strapwork	Part	Fauld	Southwark	M439
D4/320	Harlton, Cambs	Church, Assumption of the Blessed Virgin Mary CB23 1ET	Mural, C,K,L	1623		Yes		Maximilian Colt (William Wright)	M376
D4/321	Gloucester	Cathedral GL1 2LX	Mural, L	1623		Yes		Samuel Baldwin	M57 Figure 122
D4/322	Eyeworth, Beds	Church, All Saints SG19 2HH	Effigy, J,L	1623	Mourning hood		Fauld		A69
D4/323	South Cockerington, Lincs	Church St Leonard LE11 7EF	Effigy, K	1623				Epiphanius Evesham	R28

Number	Location	Building	Monument	Date	Armour and other features	Painted	Source	Kerver	Notes
D4/324	Tixover, Rutland	Church, St Luke PE9 3QL	Mural, K,L	1623					M455
D4/325	Eton College, Bucks	Chapel SL4 6DQ	Mural, C	1623		No	Alabaster and marble	Maximilian Colt	M126
D4/326	London, Westminster	Abbey, St Edmunds Chapel SW1P 3PA	Statue, K	1623 (1627)		Part	Limestone and alabaster	Nicholas Stone	R260
D4/327	Audley, Staffs	Church, St James the Great ST7 8HL	Effigy, C	1623				To check	R261
D4/328	Margam Abbey, Glamorgan	Abbey SA13 2TJ	Mural, K	1623				London	M477 X109
D4/329	Stowe Bardolf, Norfolk	Church, Holy Trinity PE34 3HT	Mural, K	1623		No	Fauld		M307
D4/330	King's Lynn, Norfolk	Chapel, St Nicholas PE30 1NH	Mural, C,L	1623		Yes	Fauld		M308
D4/331	King's Lynn, Norfolk	Chapel, St Nicholas PE30 1NH	Mural, C,C	1623		Yes	Fauld		M310
D4/332	Tong, Shrops	Church, St Bartholomew TF11 8PW	Mural, L	1624		Yes			M135
D4/333	West Hallam, Derbys	Church, St Wilfrid DE7 6GR	?, C	1624					M478
D4/334	Toft Monks, Norfolk	Church, St Margaret NR34 0EX	Tablet, C,L	1624 (1653)		No	Fauld		M259
D4/335	Cambridge	Chapel, Trinity College CB2 1TQ	Effigy, C	1624					R262

Number	Location	Building	Monument	Date	Armour and other features	Painted	Source	Kerver	Notes
D4/336	Wingham, Kent	Church, St Mary the Virgin CT3 1BB	Mural with statuary, C	1624	Two large winged angels	No	Fauld	Nicholas Stone	M480
D4/337	Hitcham, Bucks	Church, St Mary SL1 7DP	Mural, K	1624	Iron grill. Great helm	Partially. Soldiers holding back curtains			M386
D4/338	Hanbury, Staffs	Church, St Werburgh DE13 8TF	Mural, K	1624		No	Fauld	Pevsner	M481
D4/339	Ingatestone, Essex	Church, St Edmund & St Mary CM4 9DU	Mural, K,L	1624			Fauld	William Cure	M482
D4/340	Wiggenhall, Norfolk	Church, St Mary the Virgin	Mural with effigies, K,L	1624	Strapwork. Falling ruff	Part. Chrisom	Fauld	London	M628
D4/341	Gotham, Notts	Church, St Lawrence NG11 0JL	Mural with effigies, K,L	1624		Yes	Fauld	Hollemans	M24
D4/342	York	Minster YO1 7HH	Mural, K,L,K	1624 (1670)		Yes			M48
D4/343	York	Minster YO1 7HH	Mural, Lawyer	1624		Yes			M172
D4/344	Hintlesham, Norfolk	Church, St Nicholas IP8 3NH	Mural, K,L	1624		No	Fauld, heavily veined	Possibly Hollemans	M212
D4/345	Salisbury, Wilts	Church, St Thomas SP1 1BA	Mural, C,L	1624		Yes			M200
D4/346	Neen Solars, Shrops	Church, All Saints DY14 0AH	Mural, K	1624		No	Fauld		M299
D4/347	Everton, Beds	Church, St Mary SG19 2JZ	Tablet, J	1624		Part	Alabaster and black marble		M383

Number	Location	Building	Monument	Date	Armour and other features	Painted	Source	Kerver	Notes
D4/348	Ratcliffe on Soar, Notts	Church, Holy Trinity NG11 0EB	Effigy, K,L	1625 (1585)		Was	Fauld	Hollemans	R4
D4/349	Much Dewchurch, Hereford	Church, St David HR2 8DL	Mural, C,L	1625				Samuel Baldwin (Nicholas Johnson)	M185
D4/350	Ratcliffe on Soar, Notts	Church, Holy Trinity NG11 0EB	Effigy, K	1625		Was	Fauld	Hollemans	R5, X37
D4/351	Ratcliffe on Soar, Notts	Church, Holy Trinity NG11 0EB	Mural with effigies, L,L,L	1625		Was	Fauld Cockleshell	Hollemans	M2, X37
D4/352	Southwark, London	Cathedral SE1 9DA	Mural, C	1625		Yes		Southwark	M148
D4/353	Gotham, Notts	Church, St Lawrence NG11 0JL	Mural with effigies, K,L	1625		Partial	Chellaston. Cockleshell. Light veining	Hollemans	M23
D4/354	Nettlestead, Suffolk	Church, St Peter & St Paul IP8 4QS	Mural, K,L	1625 (1647)	Demi-figures with hands together and on one elbow	No	Fauld		M18
D4/355	Canterbury, Kent	Cathedral CT1 2EH	Mural, C	1625			Material uncertain	Nicholas Stone	M485
D4/356	Radwell, Herts	Church, All Saints SG7 5ES	Mural, K	1625		Part	Fauld and black marble		M101
D4/357	Radwell, Herts	Church, All Saints SG7 5ES	Tablet, L	1625		Part	Fauld and marble		M629
D4/358	Bletchingley, Surrey	Church, St Mary RH1 4PD	Tablet, C	1625			Fauld		M488
D4/359	Morley, Derbys	Church, St Matthew DE7 6DE	Slab, Child	1625	Small slab	Holding skull in his hands	Chellaston		S111 GH2(28) AO Fig 12

Number	Location	Building	Monument	Date	Armour and other features	Painted	Source	Kerver	Notes
D4/360	Barnwell, Northants	Church, All Saints PE8 5PX	Mural, Child	1625					M245
D4/361	Hornchurch, Essex	Church, St Andrew RM12 6QP	Mural, C,L	1625					M487
D4/362	Sutton at Hone, Kent	Church, St John the Baptist	Mural, K	1625		No	Castle Hay	London	M587
D4/363	Margaretting, Essex	Church, St Margaret. CM4 0EB	Mural, C	1625		Part			M619
D4/364	Wickhamford, Worcs	Church, St John the Baptist WR11 7SD	Effigy, K,L & K,L	1626 (1630)			Fauld but check Watchet	Samuel Baldwin	R67
D4/365	Chilton, Suffolk	Church, St Mary C010 2ZB	Mural, K,L,L	1626				Gerard Christmas	M138
D4/366	Bovey Tracey, Devon	Church, St Peter, St Paul and St Thomas TQ13 9EP	Mural, C,L,L	1626		No	Fauld	London?	M239
D4/367	Aston, Warwicks	Church, St Peter and St Paul WA7 3ED	Mural, K,L	1626				William Stanton	M276
D4/368	Worfield, Shrops	Church, St Peter WV15 5LF	Effigy, K,L	1626		No	Fauld		R265
D4/369	Gloucester	Church, St Nicholas GL1 2QT	Effigy, C,L	1626 (1620)		No	May not be alabaster	Samuel Baldwin	R263
D4/370	Tathwell, Lincs	Church St Vedas LN11 9SR	Mural, C,L	1626					M73

Number	Location	Building	Monument	Date	Armour and other features	Painted	Source	Kerver	Notes
D4/371	Gawsworth, Cheshire	Church, St James SK11 9RJ	Effigy, L	1626		Yes			R47
D4/372	Mersham, Kent	Church, St John the Baptist TN25 6NT	Mural, L	1626 (1625)	Drapes and angels Baldachino	No	Lightly veined	Nicholas Stone	M179
D4/373	London, Southwark	Cathedral SE1 9DA	Effigy, B	1626		Yes		Gerard Johnson	X4
D4/374	East Horsley, Surrey	Church, St Martin KT24 6RL	Effigy, K,L	1626		No	Chellaston		R207
D4/375	Exeter, Devon	Cathedral EX1 1HS	Effigy, B	1626					R143
D4/376	Wilton, Wilts	Church, St Mary and St Nicholas SP2 0DL	Mural, C,L	1626		Yes			M275
D4/377	Wrangle, Lincs	Church, St Nicholas PE22 9EP	Effigy, C,L	1626			Fauld	May be Burton	R161
D4/378	Marlborough, Wilts	Church, St Peter & St Paul SN9 4NQ	Mural, Children	1626		Yes	Fauld		M244
D4/379	Ilam, Staffs	Church, Holy Cross DE6 2AZ	Effigy, C,L	1626		Part			R208
D4/380	Paulerspury, Northants	Church, St James	Effigy, K,L	1626			Touch and alabaster		R280
D4/381	Theydon Mount, Essex	Church, St Michael, CM16 7QQ	Mural, K,L	1626	Tiered effigies	Children below	Fauld	London	M633 CMS-CG
D4/382	Cockayne Hatley, Beds	Church, St John SG19 2EA	Mural, K,L	1627					M490

Number	Location	Building	Monument	Date	Armour and other features	Painted	Source	Kerver	Notes
D4/383	Eastwell with Boughton Aluph, Kent	Church now V&A Museum	Tablet, L	1627				Nicholas Stone	M489
D4/384	Bristol, Somerset	Chapel, Lord Mayor's (St Mark) BS1 5TB	Mural, child	1627		No		Poss Samuel Baldwin	M243
D4/385	Bristol, Somerset	Church, St Stephen BS16 4RH	Tablet, C	1627	Cockleshell	Part		Samuel Baldwin	M171
D4/386	Woodbridge, Suffolk	Church, St Mary IP12 4LP	Mural, K,L,L	1627		Yes		Gerard Johnson (II)	M19
D4/387	Linton, Kent	Church, St Nicholas ME17 4AW	Mural, K,L,L	1627	Convex plinth	No			M449
D4/388	Thornhill, Yorks	Church, St Michael WF12 0JZ	Mural, K	1627	Straw mat, strapwork and straight canopy		Alabaster, touch and raunce	Maximilian Colt	M379
D4/389	East Bridgford, Notts	Church, St Peter NG13 8PG	Mural, K	1627 (1620)		Yes			M62
D4/390	Canterbury, Kent	Cathedral CT1 2EH	Mural, C	1627					M491
D4/391	Worcester	Cathedral WR1 2LA	Effigy, B	1627					R182
D4/392	Swarkestone, Derbys	Church, St James DE73 1JB	Effigy, K,L	1627			Fauld		R106
D4/393	Smisby, Derbys	Church, St James LE65 2TN	Mural, K,L	1627	Possible cockleshell inlays	Part. Sixteen children	Fauld	Possible Hollemans	M451
D4/394	Shinfield, Berks	Church, St Mary RG2 9BY	Mural, C,L,L	1627		Part	Fauld		M580

Number	Location	Building	Monument	Date	Armour and other features	Painted	Source	Kerver	Notes
D4/395	Dagenham, Essex	Church, St Peter and St Paul	Tablet, C	1627					M625
D4/396	Salisbury, Wilts	Church, St Thomas SP1 1BA	Mural, K,L	1628		Yes, stained to resemble oak			M273
D4/397	Melton Mowbray, Leics	Church, St Mary LE13 1AE	Slab, C,L	1628	Farthingale. No headgear	11 chirldren at feet. Ridged edge	Chellaston	London	S236 GH1(283)
D4/398	Salisbury, Wilts	Church, St Thomas SP1 1BA	Mural, K,L	1628		Yes, stained to resemble oak			M274
D4/399	Ampton, Suffolk	Church, St Peter IP31 1NX	Mural, C	1628	Demi-figure	No	Pale with black veins, possibly Watchet	Nicholas Stone	M452
D4/400	Burford, Oxfordshire	Church, St John the Baptist OX18 4RY	Effigy, J,L	1628		Yes. Cadaver		Gerard Christmas	R51 L42
D4/401	Fenny Drayton, Leics	Church, St Michael & All Angels CV13 6BA	Mural, K,L,L	1628 (1631)	Central columns	Children on tomb chest. Kneeling wives	Columns are marble		M99 X110
D4/402	Wimborne, Dorset	Church, St Giles BH21 1HT	Effigy, K	1628		Yes	Alabaster & clunch		M372
D4/403	York	Cathedral YO1 7HH	Effigy, B	1628		Yes			M104
D4/404	Saddington, Leics	Church, St Helen LE8 0QH	Slab, P	1628	Cassock and surplice	No			S179
D4/405	Salisbury, Wilts	Church, St Thomas SP1 1BA	Mural, C,L	1628		Yes			M199

Number	Location	Building	Monument	Date	Armour and other features	Painted	Source	Kerver	Notes
D4/406	Morley, Derbys	Church, St Matthew DE7 6DE	Slab, Child	1628	Small slab. Chrisom		Chellaston		S276
D4/407	Exeter, Devon	Cathedral	Effigy, J	1628	Judges robes and coif	Painted	Uncertain		A237
D4/408	Paston, Norfolk	Church, St Margaret NR28 9TA	Mural, L	1629	Reclining on one elbow	No. Railings		Nicholas Stone	M492
D4/409	Bramfield, Suffolk	Church, St Andrew IP8 4AT	Effigy, C,L	1629		No		Nicholas Stone	R164
D4/410	Noseley, Leics	St Mary Chapel of Noseley Hall LE19 2JA	Effigy, K,L	1629		Yes	Fauld		M20
D4/411	York	Minster YO1 7HH	Mural, L	1629					M52
D4/412	Ashby Folville, Leics	Church, St Mary LE14 2TE	Effigy, K,L	1629		Yes	Very pale light-brown veining		R220
D4/413	Chipping Campden, Gloucs	Church, St James GL55 6JG	Effigy, K,L	1629		The chest is black marble but the effigies are uncertain	Could this be Watchet alabaster?	Reputed to be Nicholas Stone.	M130
D4/414	Brocklesby, Lincs	Church, All Saints DN41 8PP	Effigy, K, L	1629	Tiered effigies	Part	Fauld	William Wright	M318
D4/415	Great Mitton, Lancs	Church, All Hallows BB7 9PH	Mural, C,L	1629					M327
D4/416	Great Wishford, Wilts	Church, St Giles SP2 0PH	Mural, K,L	1629			May not be alabaster	Possibly Baldwin	M272
D4/417	Checkendon, Oxford	Church, St Peter & St Paul RG8 0SR	Mural, K,L	1629		Part	Fauld	London	M494

Number	Location	Building	Monument	Date	Armour and other features	Painted	Source	Kerver	Notes
D4/418	Stratford on Avon, Warwick	Church, Holy Trinity CV37 6BG	Mural, K,L	1629	Coronets. Weapons on tomb chest	Yes	Pale veined and marble	Edward Marshall	M342
D4/419	Crediton, Devon	Church, Holy Cross EX17 2AH	Mural, C,L	1630					M176
D4/420	Sapperton, Gloucs	Church, St Kenelm GL7 6LQ	Mural, K,L	1630				Samuel Baldwin	M169
D4/421	Ledbury, Hereford	Church, St Michael HR8 1PL	Mural, C,L	1630		No		Samuel Baldwin	M186
D4/422	Kidderminster, Worcs	Church, St Mary DY10 2JN	Effigy, K,L,L	1630	Knight is on one elbow	No. Plain tomb chest			M109
D4/423	Bristol, Somerset	Cathedral BS1 5TJ	Mural, K	1630					M495
D4/424	Selston, Ashfield, Notts	Church, St Helen NG23 5JQ	Effigy, K,L	1630					M43
D4/425	Gloucester	Cathedral GL1 2LX	Mural, C	1630		Yes		Samuel Baldwin (but some say Southwark)	M59
D4/426	Watford, Herts	Church, St Mary WD18 0EG	Mural, K,L	1630				Nicholas Stone	M113
D4/427	Eastwell with Boughton Aluph, Kent	Church, now V&A Museum	Effigy, C,L	1630 (1634)	Lightly veined	No	Fauld	Nicholas Stone with William Cure	A56
D4/428	Brewood, Staffs	Church, St Mary & St Chad ST19 9BT	Effigy, C,L,C,L	1630		Yes. A son and six daughters			M134
D4/429	North Bradley, Wilts	Church, All Saints BA14 8TD	Mural, K,L	1630					M335

Number	Location	Building	Monument	Date	Armour and other features	Painted	Source	Kerver	Notes
D4/430	Eggesford, Devon	Church, All Saints EX18 7QU	Mural with one standing figure, L,L	1630		No			M230
D4/431	Bowdon, Cheshire	Church, St Mary WA14 3BN	Mural, C,L	1630		Part	Fauld	Gloucester or London	M496
D4/432	Rodney Stoke, Somerset	Church, St Leonard	Effigy, L	1630	Arched canopy		Pinkish. May be Watchet	Local historians suggest a Dutch carver	R278
D4/433	Wickhambrook, Suffolk	Church, All Saints	Effigy, K	1630		No		Nicholas Stone	R279
D4/434	Codsall, Staffs	Church	Effigy, K	1630				An Ashby de la Zouch workshop	R281
D4/435	Theydon Mount, Essex	Church, St Michael, CM16 7QQ	Mural, K,L,L	1631	Kneeling wives		Fauld	London	M616 CMS-CG
D4/436	Abergavenny, Gwent	Church, Priory of St Mary NP7 5ND	Effigy, J	1631		No		Samuel Baldwin (in part)	R180
D4/437	Frolesworth, Leics	Church, St Nicholas LE17 5EF	Effigy, K	1631		No	Fauld		R224
D4/438	West Ham, Essex	Church, All Saints E15 3HU	Mural, L	1631		No	Fauld		M254
D4/439	Dalby, Lincs	Church, St Lawrence PE23 4PP	Mural, C	1631	Lightly veined	Yes, partially	Fauld		M83
D4/440	Isfield, Sussex	Church, St Margaret TN22 5XR	Mural, L,K,L	1631		No		William Wright	R38
D4/441	Chilton, Bucks	Church, St Mary C010 2ZB	Mural, L	1631	Veined	Yes	Fauld or Ledsham	William Wright	M93

Number	Location	Building	Monument	Date	Armour and other features	Painted	Source	Kerver	Notes
D4/442	Easton Maudit, Northants	Church, St Peter & Paul NN29 7NR	Mural, K,L	1631		Pile of books		Possibly by Maximilian Colt	M201
D4/443	Prestwold, Leics	Church, St Andrew LE12 5SH	Mural, K,L	1631	Stuart armour on rolled up mat	Part	Fauld	London	M41
D4/444	Harlton, Cambs	Church, The Church of the Assumption CB23 1ET	Mural, L,K,S & L	1631		Yes	Very pink	Maximilian Colt	M453
D4/445	Coxwold, Yorks	Church, St Michael YO61 4AD	Mural, K,L	1631		No	Alabaster and marble	Nicholas Stone	M454
D4/446	Hurst, Berks	Church, St Nicholas RG10 0SN	Mural, L	1631					M33
D4/447	Chilham, Kent	Church, St Mary CT4 8DA	Monument, L	1631 (1632)		No		Nicholas Stone	R137
D4/448	Wroxton, Oxford	Church, All Saints OX15 6QE	Effigy, K,L	1631	White	Part	Chellaston	Samuel Baldwin	R154
D4/449	Inkberrow, Worcs	Church, St Peter WR7 4DZ	Effigy, C	1631				Samuel Baldwin	R266
D4/450	Chigwell, Essex	Church, St Mary IG7 6QB	Mural, K,L	1631			Fauld		M497
D4/451	London, St Paul's	Cathedral EC4M 8AD	Statue, C	1631	Depicting resurrection			Nicholas Stone	R197
D4/452	Newcastle upon Tyne	St Nicholas Cathedral NE1 1PF	Mural, K,L	1631		Yes			M498
D4/453	Margam Abbey, Glamorgan	Abbey SA13 2TJ	Effigy, L,K,L	1631				London	R231 X109

Number	Location	Building	Monument	Date	Armour and other features	Painted	Source	Kerver	Notes
D4/454	London, Westminster	Abbey SW1P 3PA	Tablet, C	1631	Bust	No	Fauld	Edward Marshall	M467
D4/455	London, Westminster	Abbey SW1P 3PA	Mural, L	1631	Skeleton	No	Black marble and pinkish alabaster		M473
D4/456	Fulmer, Bucks	Church, St James	Mural, K,L	1631		Yes	Marble and alabaster		M585
D4/457	Upton Hellions, Devon	Church, St Mary	Mural, C,L	1631					M589
D4/458	King's Norton, Warwick	Church, St Nicholas B38 8RU	Mural, K,L	1632		No	Fauld		M277
D4/459	Walthamstow, Essex	Church, St Mary E17 9RJ	Mural, L	1632				Nicholas Stone I	M159
D4/460	Elmley Castle, Worcs	Church, St Mary WR10 3HT	Effigy, L,C,C	1632	Veined	Baby in arms	Chellaston?	Samuel Baldwin	R54
D4/461	Hinxhill, Kent	Church, St Mary TN25 6NU	Mural, K,L	1632			Fauld	.	M500
D4/462	Acton Burnell, Shrops	Church, St Mary SY5 7PF	Mural, K,L	1632		No	Fauld	Nicholas Stone	M295
D4/463	Brewood, Staffs	Church, St Mary & St Chad ST19 9BT	Effigy, K,L	1632		Yes			R84
D4/464	Canterbury, Kent	Cathedral CT1 2EH	Mural, K	1632					M501
D4/465	Bottesford, Leics	Church, St Mary the Virgin NG13 0DA	Mural and effigies, K,L,L	1632	Crown	Yes			M89
D4/466	Tong, Shrops	Church, St Bartholomew TF11 8PW	Effigy, K	1632					R87

Number	Location	Building	Monument	Date	Armour and other features	Painted	Source	Kerver	Notes
D4/467	London, Westminster	Abbey SW1P 3PA	Effigy, K,L	1632				William Wright	R142
D4/468	Paston, Norfolk	Church, St Margaret NR28 9TA	Mural, C	1632			Fauld	Nicholas Stone	M493
D4/469	Greatham, Hants	Church, St John the Baptist GU33 6HB	Effigy, L	1632		No	Fauld	London	R285
D4/470	Sutton Cheney, Leics	Church, St James CV13 0AG	Effigy, K	1633	Corase scrolls	High tomb chest	Fauld	Possibly Hollemans	R191
D4/471	Radley, Berks	Church, St James OX14 2JW	Mural, K,L	1633				Nicholas Stone	M378
D4/472	Great Warley, Essex	Church, St Mary CM13 3JP	Mural, K,K	1633					M502
D4/473	Bradley, Staffs	Church, St Mary and All Saints ST18 9BD	Mural, C,L	1633			Chellaston		M223
D4/474	Forton, Staffs	Church, St Lawrence TF10 8BY	Mural, K,L	1633		No	Chellaston	Garrett Hollemans	M401
D4/475	Instow, Devon	Church, St John the Baptist EX39 4LU	Mural, C	1633		Part	Watchet	Barnstaple	M231
D4/476	Kinnersley, Hereford	Church, St James HR3 6QD	Mural, K,L	1633 (1635)	Semi-circular canopy	Part	Alabaster and black marble	Samuel Baldwin	M503
D4/477	London, Southwark	Cathedral SE1 9DA		1633				Nicholas Stone	X5
D4/478	East Lockinge, Berks	Church, All Saints OX12 8QY	Mural, L	1633		Yes			M45

Number	Location	Building	Monument	Date	Armour and other features	Painted	Source	Kerver	Notes
D4/479	Chipping Campden, Gloucs	Church, St James GL55 6JG	Mural, L	1633				John and Matthias Christmas	M54
D4/480	Hambleden, Bucks	Church, St Mary the Virgin RG9 6RX	Mural, K,L	1633	Civil War costumes	No. Children carry skulls		William Wright or John Hargrave	M504
D4/481	Bath, Somerset	Abbey church BA1 1LF	Mural, L,K	1633		No	Fauld and touch		M291
D4/482	Abbess Roding, Essex	Church, St Edmund CM5 0PA	Mural with demi-figure, L	1633					M612
D4/483	Barnstaple, Devon	Church, St Peter and St Mary EX31 1BH	Mural, C	1634		Yes	Watchet?	Barnstaple	M235
D4/484	South Acre, Norfolk	Church, St George PE23 2AD	Mural, K,L	1634	Charnel house			John and Matthias Christmas	A139
D4/485	Horndon on the Hill, Essex	Church, St Peter SS17 8NX	Mural, C,L	1634					M506
D4/486	Lydiard Tregoze, Wilts	Church, St Mary SN5 3PA	Effigy, K,L,L	1634		No	Poss Watchet	Samuel Baldwin	R165
D4/487	Lugwardine, Hereford	Church, St Peter HR1 4AT	Mural, C	1634			Fauld	Samuel Baldwin	M190
D4/488	Stoke by Nayland, Suffolk	Church, St Mary CO6 4QU	Mural, K	1634			Fauld	Attributed to Nicholas Stone but this is uncertain	M289
D4/489	Newcastle upon Tyne	St Nicholas Cathedral NE1 1PF	Mural, C,L	1634 (1653)		Part			M499

Number	Location	Building	Monument	Date	Armour and other features	Painted	Source	Kerver	Notes
D4/490	Ashby St Ledger, Northants	Church, St Leodegarius CV23 8UN	Mural, C,L	1634		No	Fauld		M311
D4/491	Sutton on the Hill, Derbys	Church, St Michael DE6 5JB	Mural, L	1634			Fauld	London	M460
D4/492	Holcombe Regis, Devon	Church, All Saints	Mural, K,L	1634					M579
D4/493	Barmston, Yorks	Church, All Saints YO25 8PR	Tabletop, K	1634	Four urns, supported slab		Black marble and alabaster		TT45
D4/494	Farthinghoe, Northants	Chapel of Steane Park to St Peter NN13 5PG	Effigy, L	1635				John and Matthias Christmas	A37
D4/495	Ludlow, Shrops	Church, St Lawrence SY8 1AN	Mural, C,L	1635				Edward Waites (1635) and Martha (1629)	M505
D4/496	Much Marcle, Hereford	Church, St Bartholomew HR8 2PL	Effigy, C,L	1635			Possibly marble	Samuel Baldwin	R178
D4/497	Spixworth, Norfolk	Church, St Peter NR10 3PR	Mural. C,L	1635		No	Fauld	Thomas Stanton or Edward Marshall Part by William Wright	M210
D4/498	Madingley, Cambs	Church, St Mary Magdalene CB23 8AF	Mural, child	1635	Chrisom Standing angels	No	Fauld		M226
D4/499	Wighill, Yorks	Church, All Saints LS24 8BG	Effigy, C,L	1635		No	Fauld		R205
D4/500	Compton Verney House, Warwicks	Chapel CV35 9HZ	Effigy, K,L	1636		No	Chellaston	Nicholas Stone	R267

Number	Location	Building	Monument	Date	Armour and other features	Painted	Source	Kerver	Notes
D4/501	Ross on Wye, Hereford	Church, St Mary HR9 6QY	Effigy, C,L	1636		Baby lying against skull		Samuel Baldwin	R167
D4/502	Hereford	Cathedral HR1 2NG	Mural, B	1636	Demi-figure	Was	Chellaston	London	M384
D4/503	Harefield, Middlesex	Church, St Mary UX9 6DL	Mural, L	1636 (1637)	Draped curtains	Partial	Fauld	Maximilian Colt	M440
D4/504	Framlingham, Suffolk	Church, St Michael IP13 9BJ	Tabletop with corner effigies, K	1636 (1638)		Part	Fauld and black marble	Francis Griggs	TT44 X100
D4/505	Nettlestead, Kent	Church, St Mary ME18 5HA	Mural, L	1636					M38
D4/506	Ely, Cambs	Cathedral CB7 4DL	Mural, P	1636		Yes			M374
D4/507	Gilston, Herts	Church, St Mary CM20 2 RJ	Mural, K,L	1636				Joshua Marshall	M517
D4/508	Amersham, Bucks	Church, St Mary HP7 0DB	Mural, Child	1636		Resurrection		Edward Marshall.	M356
D4/509	Bishops Cleeve, Gloucs	Church, St Michael and All Angels GL52 8BA	Effigy, K,L	1636		Yes		Samuel Baldwin	R162
D4/510	Holkham, Norfolk	Church, St Withburga NR23 1AB	Mural, L	1636		No	Watchet	Nicholas Stone	M305
D4/511	Hitcham, Suffolk	Church, All Saints CO10 0PQ	Tablet, K	1636			Fauld		M507
D4/512	Oxnead, Norfolk	Church, St Michael NR10 4HF	Mural, L	1636		No	Fauld (Pediment only)	Nicholas Stone	M586

Number	Location	Building	Monument	Date	Armour and other features	Painted	Source	Kerver	Notes
D4/513	Newton St Cyres, Devon	Church, St Cyr & St Julitta EX5 5BN	Mural, K	1637			Fauld		M509
D4/514	Yalding, Kent	Church, St Peter & St Paul ME18 6HU	Mural, C,L	1637			Fauld		M366
D4/515	Nottingham	Church, St Mary NG1 1HN	Mural, K	1637					M170
D4/516	Lugwardine, Hereford	Church, St Peter HR1 4AT	Mural, C	1637					M508
D4/517	Down Ampney, Gloucs	Church, All Saints GL7 5BD	Mural, K	1637				Samuel Baldwin	M187
D4/518	Ludlow, Shrops	Church, St Lawrence SY8 1AN	Effigy, J,L	1637 (1638)	Railings		Alabaster is stained a very dull yellow	Some say Francesco Fanelli but probably Baldwin	R268
D4/519	Wheathampstead, Herts	Church, St Helen AL4 8AA	Effigy, K,L	1637	Leopard at feet	No	Fauld	London	M630
D4/520	Ipswich, Suffolk	Church, St Stephen IP1 1DP	Mural, C,L	1637 (1639)		Part	Fauld	John and Matthias Christmas	M288
D4/521	Nottingham	Church, St Peter NG1 1HN	Tablets, L,L	1637		No			M600
D4/522	Great Brington, Northants	Church, St Mary NN7 4JB	Effigy, K,L	1638				Nicholas Stone	R269
D4/523	Gresford, Denbigh	Church, All Saints LL12 8RG	Mural, K,L	1638		Part	Fauld		M262

Number	Location	Building	Monument	Date	Armour and other features	Painted	Source	Kerver	Notes
D4/524	Hinton Ampnor, Hants	Church, All Saints SO24 0LA	Effigy, child	1638 (1601)		Yes	Chellaston	Possibly Southwark	R200
D4/525	Hornchurch, Essex	Church, St Andrew RM12 6QP	Mural, C	1638					M510
D4/526	Margam Abbey, Glamorgan	Abbey SA13 2TJ	Effigy, K,L	1638	Rolled mat		Fauld and black marble	London	R232 X109
D4/527	Cirencester, Gloucs	Church, St John the Baptist GL7 2NR	Mural, C,L	1638				Samuel Baldwin	M188
D4/528	Egham, Surrey	Church, St John the Baptist TW20 9HL	Mural, C	1638				William Wright	M162
D4/529	Ampton, Suffolk	Church, St Peter IP31 1NX	Mural, K	1638	Demi-figures	Yes		John and Matthias Christmas	M511
D4/530	Bottisham, Cambs	Church, Holy Trinity CB2 3NZ	Mural, Children	1638 (1635)		No	Fauld		M229
D4/531	Tilton on the Hill, Leics	Church, St Peter LE7 9LB	Mural, C	1638					M513
D4/532	Ellesborough, Bucks	Church, St Peter & St Paul HP17 0XG	Mural and effigy, L	1638					M175
D4/534	Eyeworth, Beds	Church, All Saints SG19 2HH	Mural, C,L	1638	Holding heart	No	Alabaster	Edward Marshall	M92
D4/535	Rolleston on Dove, Staffs	Church, St Mary DE13 9BE	Mural, K	1638			Fauld		M294
D4/536	Ledbury, Hereford	Church, St Michael HR8 1PL	Tablet, P	1638	Demi effigy Canopy	No		Samuel Baldwin	M514

Number	Location	Building	Monument	Date	Armour and other features	Painted	Source	Kerver	Notes
D4/537	Sotterley, Suffolk	Church, St Margaret NR34 8DB	Mural, K,L,L	1638		No	Fauld		M290
D4/538	Uxbridge, Middlesex	Church, St Margaret UB8 1PL	Mural, L	1638	Charnel house with hands clasping bars	Strapwork		Possibly made by the Christmas workshop	M512
D4/539	Morley, Derbys	Church, St Matthew DE7 6DE	Slab, K	1638	Cavalier in ringlets	Holding book	Chellaston		S204
D4/540	Stratton Strawless, Norfolk	Church, St Margaret	Mural, C	1638	Charnel house	No	Light veined	Possibly carved by the Christmas workshop	M559
D4/541	Leicester	Cathedral	Mural, C	1638		No	Alabaster and touch		M588
D4/542	Ightham, Kent	Church, St Peter, TN15 9NJ	Mural, K,K	1638 (1611)			Fauld		M607
D4/543	Wanstead, Essex	Church, St Mary the Virgin. E11 2SW	Mural, C	1638					M622
D4/544	Ruislip, Middlesex	Church, St Martin HA4 8DG	Mural	1638 (1647)	Busts in oval recess		Alabaster and marble	John and Matthias Christmas	M637
D4/545	Burton by Lincoln, Lincs	Church, St Vincent LN2 3PF	Mural, C,L	1639			Fauld		M320
D4/546	Gloucester	Cathedral GL1 2LX	Effigy, K,L	1639	Falling ruff. Eagle and mailed fist at feet	No	Fauld or Ledsham and black marble	Epiphanius Evesham or Edward Marshall or Samuel Baldwin	R26

Number	Location	Building	Monument	Date	Armour and other features	Painted	Source	Kerver	Notes
D4/547	Llanrwst, Denbigh, Wales	Church, St Grwst LL26 0LE	Mural, Child	1639		No	Chellaston		M225
D4/548	London, Westminster	Abbey SW1P 3PA	Tablet, L	1639	Death bed and curtains	No		Epiphanius Evesham	M516
D4/549	Holkham, Norfolk	Church, St Withburga NR23 1AB	Tablet, K	1639		No	Watchet or Fauld	Nicholas Stone. Signed RP (Robert Pook)	M306
D4/550	Ilston on the Hill, Leics	Church, St Michael and All Angels LE7 9ET	Tablet, L	1639		No	Fauld		M323
D4/551	Weddington, Warwicks	Church, St James CV11 6AU	Mural, K,K	1639					M515
D4/552	Newark, Notts	Church, St Mary NG24 1JS	Tablet, C	1639					M359
D4/553	Little Baddow, Essex	Church, St Mary the Virgin CM3 4BE	Mural, K	1639				John and Matthias Christmas	M614
D4/554	Stratfield Saye, Hants	Church	Mural, C,L	1640		Part	Fauld	John and Matthias Christmas	M581
D4/555	Morley, Derbys	Church, St Matthew DE7 6DE	Slab, L	1640	Coffin shaped		Chellaston		S237
D4/556	Scawby, Lincs	Church St Hybald DN20 9AE	Mural, C,L	1640	Fauld			Joshua Marshall	M74
D4/557	Leigh, Worcs	Church, St Eadburga WR6 5LB	Effigy, K,L	1640	Talbot emerging from coronet				A136

Number	Location	Building	Monument	Date	Armour and other features	Painted	Source	Kerver	Notes
D4/558	Shipton Moyne, Gloucs	Church, St John the Baptist GL8 8PW	Effigy, K,L	1640		Yes		Samuel Baldwin	R174
D4/558	Marlesford, Suffolk	Church, St Andrew IP13 0AT	Mural, K,L	1641		Part	Fauld		M286
D4/559	London, Smithfield	Church, St Bartholomew EC1A 9DS	Tablet, C	1641				Sometime attributed to Hubert le Seuer	M280
D4/560	Cranborne, Dorset	Church, St Mary and St Bartholomew BN21 5PP	Mural, Child	1641		No	Fauld	John Elliot depicted	M224
D4/561	Little Warley, Essex	Church, St Peter CM13 3EN	Mural, K,L	1641			Alabaster and marble		M127
D4/562	Churchover, Warwicks	Church, Holy Trinity CV23 0EW	Mural, C,L	1641					M111
D4/563	Belton, Lincs	Church, St Peter and Paul NG32 2LS	Mural, C	1641 (1650–1660)				Joshua Marshall	M81
D4/564	Colmworth, Bedford	Church, St Denys MK44 2JU	Mural, K,L	1641					M198
D4/565	Sheepstor, Devon	Church, St Leonard PL20 6PF	Tablet, L	1641	Death bed and curtains	No	Fauld	Epiphanius Evesham	M518
D4/566	Churchover, Warwicks	Church, Holy Trinity CV23 0EW	Mural, K,L	1641					M112
D4/567	Leigh, Essex	Church, St Clement SS9 2DA	Tablet, C	1641	Demi-figure holding globe		Fauld	Thomas Stanton	M519

Number	Location	Building	Monument	Date	Armour and other features	Painted	Source	Kerver	Notes
D4/568	Tatenhill, Staffs	Church, St Michael & All Angels DE13 9SG	Mural, L	1641				Said to be Burton	M520
D4/569	Ightham, Kent	Church, St Peter, TN15 9NJ	Mural, L	1641			Fauld	Edward Marshall	M608
D4/570	Willingale Doe, Essex	Church, St Christopher. CM5 0SJ	Mural, K,K,L	1641				William Wright	M618
D4/571	Chipping Campden, Gloucs	Church, St James GL55 6JG	Mural with standing effigies, K,L	1642 (1664)	Depicting resurrection		Chellaston	Joshua Marshall	M129
D4/572	Twickenham, Surrey	Church, St Mary TW1 3NJ	Mural, C,L	1642					M328
D4/573	Curry Mallet, Somerset	Church, St James TA3 6TD	Mural, K,L	1642					M535
D4/574	Burbage, Leics	Church, St Catherine LE10 2DE	Mural, K,L	1643			Alabaster and black marble		M521
D4/575	Brereton, Cheshire	Church, St Oswald CW11 1RY	Mural, K,L	1643					M522
D4/576	Gawsworth, Cheshire	Church, St James SK11 9RJ	Effigy, K,L	1643					R270
D4/577	London, Bishopsgate	Church, Great St Helens EC3A 6AT	Tablet, K	1643			Pink	Thomas Stanton	M523
D4/578	North Ockendon, Essex	Church, St Mary Magdelene RM14 3QH	Mural	1643					M639

Number	Location	Building	Monument	Date	Armour and other features	Painted	Source	Kerver	Notes
D4/579	Weekley, Northants	Church, St Mary NN16 9UW	Tablet, K	1644				May be attributable to the Stone workshop	M524
D4/580	Miserden, Gloucs	Church, St Andrew GL6 7JA	Effigy, K,L	1644			Chellaston	Samuel Baldwin	R56
D4/581	Gloucester	Church, St Nicholas GL1 2QT	Tablet, C	1645				Stephen Baldwin	M526
D4/582	Broad Hinton, Wilts	Church, St Peter ad Vincula SN4 9PA	Effigy, K	1645				Samuel or Stephen Baldwin	R175
D4/583	Oxford	Church, St Frideswide OX2 0BL	Tablet (check), C,L	1645				Epiphanius Evesham (but check date)	M525
D4/584	Barmston, Yorks	Church, All Saints YO25 8PR	Tabletop, C	1645	Six urns, supported slab		Black marble and alabaster		TT46
D4/585	Tunstall, Kent	Church, St John the Baptist ME9 8DX	Mural, Demi-figure, C	1647		Part	Fauld		M125
D4/586	York	Minster YO1 7HH	Mural, K,L	1648		Yes			M49
D4/587	Caldecote, Warwick	Church, St Theobald and St Chad CV10 0UN	Tablet, C	1648					M436
D4/588	Strubby, Lincs	Church St Oswald LN13 0LR	Mural, C,L,L	1648					M75
D4/589	Rothley, Leics	Church, St Mary & St John LE7 7PN	Mural, L	1648				Edward Marshall	M527

Number	Location	Building	Monument	Date	Armour and other features	Painted	Source	Kerver	Notes
D4/590	Eggesford, Devon	Church, All Saints EX18 7QU	Effigy, K,L	1648		No	Chellaston	Has Baldwin like features	R201
D4/591	Bishop Burton, Yorks	Church, All Saints HU17 8QB	Effigy, L	1649		Shrouded cadaver	On modern base	William Wright	R192 L42
D4/592	Brasted, Kent	Church, St Martin TN16 1HZ	Mural, J	1649 (1664)				Thomas Stanton	M260
D4/593	Lambourn, Berks	Church, St Michael and All Angels RG17 8PA	Plaque and medallion, R	1649				.	X54
D4/594	Stratford on Avon, Warwicks	Church, Holy Trinity CV37 6BG	Mural, L,C	1649					M590
D4/595	Wimborne, Dorset	Minster BH21 1EB	Mural, C,L	1650					M370
D4/596	Llandegai, Wales	Church, St Tegai LL57 4HY	Mural, B	1650					M528
D4/597	Crayford, Kent	Church, St Paulinus. DA1 4AE	Mural, C,L	1650 (1652)				Thomas Stanton	M602
D4/598	Skeffington, Leics	Church, St Thomas a Becket LE7 9YB	Tablet, K	1651	Figures holding back cutains	No effigy just inscription panels	Fauld		M325
D4/599	London, Tower of London	Church, St Peter ad Vincula EC3N 4AB	Mural, Children	1651			Check if alabaster	William White?	M330
D4/600	Ross on Wye, Hereford	Church, St Mary HR9 6QY	Effigy, K,L	1651				Stephen Baldwin	R169

Number	Location	Building	Monument	Date	Armour and other features	Painted	Source	Kerver	Notes
D4/601	Faversham, Kent	Church, St Mary of Charity ME13 8GZ	Mural, K,L	1651		Yes			M605
D4/602	Great Hale, Lincs	Church, John the Baptist NG34 9LF	Slab/Tablet, K,L,L	1652			Fauld	Anthony Cawdron	S183 GH1 (284)
D4/603	Shenfield, Essex	Church, St Mary CM15 9AL	Effigy, L	1652	Charnel house Chrisom	No	Fauld	Thomas Burman	A224
D4/604	Dagenham, Essex	Church, St Peter and St Paul	Tablet, C	1652					M626
D4/605	Kedington, Suffolk	Church, St Peter & St Paul CB9 7NN	Mural, K,L Demi-figures	1653 (1669)	The demi-figures have hand on skull and on one elbow	No	Chellaston	John Stone?	M17
D4/606	Coates by Stow, Lincs	Church, St Edith LN1 2DW	Mural, K	1653		No	Fauld		M321
D4/607	Barnstaple, Devon	Church, St Peter and St Mary EX31 1BH	Mural, C	1653		Yes	Watchet?	Barnstaple workshop	M234
D4/608	Chenies, Bucks	Chapel, St Michael WD3 6ER	Effigy, K,L	1653		Yes		Cornelius Cure	R271
D4/609	Middle Claydon, Bucks	Church, All Saints MK18 2EY	Mural, K,L,L,L	1653			Alabaster and white marble	Edward Marshall	M382 (R192)
D4/610	Tunstall, Kent	Church, St John the Baptist ME9 8DX	Effigy, K	1654		No except for tomb chest	White	Signed: William Sweet and M Miles	A59
D4/611	Swimbridge, Devon	Church, St James EX32 0PR	Mural, C	1654		Yes	Possibly Watchet	Barnstaple workshop	M232

Number	Location	Building	Monument	Date	Armour and other features	Painted	Source	Kerver	Notes
D4/612	Edmondthorpe, Leics	Church, St Michael LE14 2JZ	Mural, K,L,L	1655	Tiered monument	Demi-figures in round-headed niches	Fauld	William Byrd	M206
D4/613	Newark, Notts	Church, St Mary NG24 1JS	Tablet, C	1655					M357
D4/613	Leicester	Cathedral LE1 4LF	Mural, C,L,L	1656		Yes	Not possible to determine	Joshua Marshall	M77
D4/614	Audley, Staffs	Church, St James the Great ST7 8HL	Slab, C,L	1656					S267
D4/615	Pinner, Middlesex	Church, St John the Baptist HA5 3AA	Mural, C,L	1656					M336
D4/616	St Minver, Cornwall	Church, St Menefreda PL27 6QH	Mural, C	1657		No	Fauld	Poss Thomas Stanton	M236
D4/617	Gilston, Herts	Church, St Mary CM20 2 RJ	Mural, L	1657		No	May not be alabaster	Joshua Marshall	M456
D4/618	Ashby St Ledger, Northants	Church, St Leodegarius CV23 8UN	Mural, C	1657		No	Fauld		M312
D4/619	Frolesworth, Leics	Church, St Nicholas LE17 5EF	Effigy, L	1657 (1658)		No	Fauld		R225
D4/620	Standish, Lancs	Church, St Wilfred WN6 0XA	Effigy, K	1658			Chellaston?		R223
D4/621	Wistow, Leics	Church, St Wistan LE8 0QF	Mural, K	1658			Alabaster and black marble		M530
D4/622	Little Warley, Essex	Church, St Peter CM13 3EN	Mural, L	1658				Thomas Burman	M128

Number	Location	Building	Monument	Date	Armour and other features	Painted	Source	Kerver	Notes
D4/623	Darfield, Yorks	Church, All Saints S73 9JX	Mural, C	1658					M30
D4/624	North Witham, Lincs	Church, St Mary NG33 5LQ	Mural, L	1658				Joshua Marshall	M529
D4/625	St Brides super Ely, South Wales	Church, St Bridget CF32 0LF	Memorial, K,C,C	1658			Penarth (red)		M193
D4/626	Kirkleatham, Yorks	Church, St Cuthbert TS10 5NW	Mural, C,L	1659		May not be alabaster		Joshua Marshall	M531
D4/627	London, Smithfield	Church, St Bartholomew EC1A 9DS	Tablet, C	1659					M281
D4/628	Newark, Notts	Church, St Mary NG24 1JS	Tablet, C	1659					M358
D4/629	Walthamstow, Essex	Church, St Michael and All Angels. E17 6PQ	Tablet, C	1659					M623
D4/630	Noseley, Leics	St Mary Chapel of Noseley Hall LE19 2JA	Mural, K,L,L	1660 (1649)		Yes. Children carrying skulls	Fauld	William Wright	M39
D4/631	London, Smithfield	Church, St Bartholomew EC1A 9DS	Tablet, C	1660					M282
D4/632	Flaxton, Northants (demolished)	Church, St Denis (now in V&A)	Mural, K	1660				Nicholas Stone workshop	M317
D4/633	Morley, Derbys	Church, St Matthew DE7 6DE	Slab, C	1660					S112 GH2(28)

Number	Location	Building	Monument	Date	Armour and other features	Painted	Source	Kerver	Notes
D4/634	Great Parndon, Essex	Church	Tablet, L	1661					M615
D4/635	Draycott in the Moors, Staffs	Church, St Margaret ST11 9AG	Effigy, C	1662				Pevsner	R272
D4/636	West Hallam, Derbys	Church, St Wilfrid DE7 6GR	Mural, C	1662					M479
D4/637	Stutton, Suffolk	Church, St Peter IP9 2SD	Mural, C,L	1662	Black inscription panel	Two daughters and a son	Fauld	London	M632
D4/638	London, Westminster	Abbey SW1P 3PA	Tablet, P	1662			Fauld and black marble	London	M469
D4/639	London	Church, St Giles in the Fields WC2H 8LG	Effigy, L	1663				Joshua Marshall	R273
D4/640	Ratcliffe on Soar, Notts	Church, Holy Trinity NG11 0EB	Slab, C	1663			Chellaston		S128
D4/641	Temple Balsall, Warwicks	Church, St Mary the Virgin B93 0AN	Effigy, L	1663				Joshua Marshall	A185
D4/642	Egham, Surrey	Church, St John the Baptist TW20 9HL	Bust on pedestal, C	1663		Yes	Fauld	Thomas Stanton	M163
D4/643	Little Waltham, Essex	Church, St Martin CM3 3LS	Mural, C,C,L	1663					M613
D4/644	Owthorpe, Notts	Church, St Margaret NG12 3GA	Tablet, K	1663–1664 & *circa* 1681		No	Fauld		M219
D4/645	Uffculme, Devon	Church, All Saints EX15 3AX	Effigy, C	1663 & 1701		Yes			R202

Number	Location	Building	Monument	Date	Armour and other features	Painted	Source	Kerver	Notes
D4/646	Kedleston, Derbys	Church, All Saints DE22 5JH	Mural, K,L	1664	Demi-figures facing forward	Yes	Fauld	Possibly Hollemans	M26
D4/647	Fulham, Middlesex	Church, All Saints SW6 3LA	Tablet, C	1664		No			M397
D4/648	Beverley, Yorks	Church, St Mary HU17 8DL	Mural, C	1665–1670		Yes			M28
D4/649	Hampton Gay, Oxford	Church, St Giles OX5 1JT	Mural, L,C	1665			Alabaster and black marble		M474
D4/650	Framlingham, Suffolk	Church, St Michael IP13 9BJ	Tablet, -	1665		No	Fauld		M29
D4/651	Sprowston, Norfolk	Church, St Mary & St Margaret NR7 8AU	Effigy, K,L	1667	Tiered effigies. Reclining	Pseudo collar of SS with Tudor rose pendant	Fauld		R274
D4/652	Oxford	Chapel of St John's College OX1 3JP	Bust, C	1667					A186
D4/653	Throwley, Kent	Church, St Michael and All Angels ME13 0PJ	Mural tablet, C	1668		No	Fauld	William Stanton	M94
D4/654	Great Hale, Lincs	Church, John the Baptist NG34 9LF	Mural, C	1668			Lightly veined		M337
D4/655	Theydon Mount, Essex	Church, St Michael, CM16 7QQ	Effigy, K	1668	Restoration clothes and wig		Fauld	London	R286 CMS-CG
D4/656	Felbrigg, Norfolk	Church, St Margaret NR11 8PN	Mural tablet, C	1669				Martin Morley	M215

Number	Location	Building	Monument	Date	Armour and other features	Painted	Source	Kerver	Notes
D4/657	Barton in Fabis. Notts	Church, St George NG11 0AA	Mural tablet, C	1671			Watchet? White with black veins		M22
D4/658	Chalfont St Giles, Bucks	Church, St Giles HP8 4JH	Mural, K	1671				Attributed to Jasper Latham	M532
D4/659	Checkendon, Oxford	Church, St Peter & St Paul RG8 0SR	Tablet, C	1673		No	Fauld		M533
D4/660	Blithfield, Staffs	Church, St Leonard WS15 3NL	Slab, child	1673					S143
D4/661	Melbourne, Derbys	Church, St Michael with St Mary DE73 8JH	Slab, L	1673	Elliptical frame			London	S109
D4/662	Teversal, Notts	Church, St Katherine NG17 3JN	Tablet, K,L	1674	Latin inscription				M534
D4/663	King's Lynn, Norfolk	Chapel, St Nicholas PE30 1NH	Mural, C,L	1675			Fauld	Thomas Cartwright	M309
D4/664	Boxted Suffolk	Church, All Saints IP29 4LN	Statue, L	1675	–	–	Marble	*See* Boxted 1725 for details	A39
D4/665	London, Westminster	Abbey SW1P 3PA	Tablet with bust, C	1676 (1682)		No	Black marble in an alabaster frame. Pinkish		M472
D4/666	Narburgh, Norfolk	Chapel, Narburgh Hall PE32 1TE	Mural, K,L	1678					M261
D4/667	Stratton Strawless, Norfolk	Church, St Margaret	Mural, C,L	1678		No	Light veined		M560

Number	Location	Building	Monument	Date	Armour and other features	Painted	Source	Kerver	Notes
D4/668	Melbourne, Derbys	Church, St Michael with St Mary DE73 8JH	Slab, K	1679					S110
D4/669	Narborough (Narburgh), Norfolk	Church, All Saints PE32 1TE	Statue, –	1679		No	Fauld	Sir William Wilson (possibly)	L9
D4/670	London, Westminster	Abbey SW1P 3PA	Tablet, C,L	1681		No	Chellaston	London	M465
D4/671	Worcester	Cathedral WR1 2LA	Tablet, L	1682					M197
D4/672	Prestwold, Leics	Church, St Andrew LE12 5SH	Mural, C	1682			Watchet. White with black veins	London	M203
D4/673	Radbourne, Derbys	Church, St Andrew DE6 4LY	Mural, K	1684			Watchet	Grindling Gibbons and Arnold Quellin	M331
D4/674	Swinbrook, Oxford	Church, St Mary OX18 4DY	Mural, K,K,K	1686	Triple tiers	Reclining on one elbow	Castle Hay	William Byrd	M207
D4/675	Winchester, Hants	Cathedral SO23 9LS	Statue, C	1687		No	Fauld	Sir William Wilson	A58
D4/676	Sturton le Steeple, Notts	Church, St Peter & St Paul DN22 9HQ	Statue, L	1687	Fire damaged	No	?		A188
D4/677	Chatsworth, Derbys	Chapel DE45 1PP	Figures and reredos, –	1688			Castle Hay	Caius Gabriel Cibber design carved by Samuel Watson of Heanor	A130
D4/678	Stanton Harcourt, Oxford	Church, St Michael OX29 5RJ	Mural, C,L	1688		No	Fauld		M303
D4/679	Wirksworth, Derbys	Church, St Mary DE4 4ET	Tablet, C	1688				To Philip Gell (died 1688)	M348

Number	Location	Building	Monument	Date	Armour and other features	Painted	Source	Kerver	Notes
D4/680	Landwade, Suffolk	Church, St Nicholas CB8 7NF	Mural, K	1689			Pale veined	London	M340
D4/681	Bittadon, Devon	Church, St Peter EX31 4HJ	Mural, C	1691			Watchet	Barnstaple	M233
D4/682	Madingley, Cambs	Church, St Mary Magdalene CB23 8AF	Mural, L	1692	Rolled mat and cushion	No	Fauld and black marble	Edward Stanton	M227
D4/683	Ashprington, Devon	Church, St David TQ9 7UP	Mural, C,L	1692 (1711–1730)		No		John Weston.	A189
D4/684	Darfield, Yorks	Church, All Saints S73 9JX	Tomb chest, C,L	1695					A40
D4/685	Ogbourne St Andrew, Wilts	Church, St Andrew SN8 1SD	Mural, C,L	1695	Demi-figures facing three-quarters	No	Pinkish		M246
D4/686	Great Milton, Oxford	Church, St Mary OX44 7PN	Cartouche, L	1695					A190
D4/687	Stanford on Soar, Notts	Church, St John the Baptist LE12 5PY	Tablet, C,L	1695			Fauld		M345
D4/688	Thrumpton, Notts	Church, All Saints NG11 0AX	Mural/ tablets, C	1648, 1695, 1823,1838 *Circa* 1870	Italian. Fauld	No			A14
D4/689	Church Gresley, Derbys	Church, St George and St Mary DE11 9NR	Statue, K	1699				Sir Thomas Gresley by Sir William Wilson	A107

Number	Location	Building	Monument	Date	Armour and other features	Painted	Source	Kerver	Notes
D4/690	Wanstead, Essex	Church, Christchurch, E11 2LT	Mural with standing statue, K	1699					M621
D4/691	Little Warley, Essex	Church, St Peter CM13 3EN	Statue, –	17th cent				Father Time a fragment found in the churchyard	–
D4/692	Curry Mallet, Somerset	Church, St James TA3 6TD	Mural, L	17th cent	Reclining female figures	Part	Fauld		M536
D4/693	Noseley, Leics	St Mary Chapel of Noseley Hall LE19 2JA	Slab, L	17th cent					S102
D4/694	Great Hallibury, Essex	Church, St Giles	Statue, –	17th cent	Cadaver	No			X105
D4/695	Raglan, Monmouth	Castle chapel	Effigies, K,K	17th cent	Damaged	No			X106
D4/696	Hothfield, Kent	Church, St Margaret, TN26 1EP	Effigy, K	17th cent					A225

Appendix D5 – 18th Century 1700 to 1799

GNP = Gothic Gardner 'no picture' list in file, G = Gothic Gardner with picture, R = Renaissance, T = Transition, M = Mural

Number	Location	Building	Monument	Date	Armour and other features	Painted/Collar	Source	Kerver	Notes
D5/1	Tawstock, Devon	Church, St Peter EX31 3HY	Tablet, C	1700 (1702)	Oval inscription. Ionic columns	No	Slate and alabaster frame possibly Watchet	Barnstaple?	M237
D5/2	London, Smithfield	Church, St Bartholomew EC1A 9DS	Tablet, C,L	1704 (1727)					M283
D5/3	Lincoln	Cathedral LN2 1PX	Slab, B	1705					S264

Number	Location	Building	Monument	Date	Armour and other features	Painted/Collar	Source	Kerver	Notes
D5/4	London, Westminster	Abbey SW1P 3PA	Effigy, L	1708	Kneeling statue	No	Fauld		A192
D5/5	Owthorpe, Notts	Church, St Margaret NG12 3GA	Tablet, L,C,L	1713	Pinnacles with a device painted red		Watchet		M218
D5/6	Sutton Coldfield, Warwicks	Church, Holy Trinity B72 1TJ	Tablet, C	1715		No	Fauld		M457
D5/7	Exeter, Devon	Church, St Petrock EX1 1HJ	Tablet, C,L	1715 (1717)		Gilded	Watchet	John Weston	M238
D5/8	Sherborne, Dorset	Abbey DT9 3LQ	Tablet, C,L	1717					M368
D5/9	Wirksworth, Derbys	Church, St Mary DE4 4ET	Tablet, C	1719			Chellaston		M347
D5/10	Wombourne, Staffs	Church, St Benedict	Tablet, –	1720		No	Italian	Good Samaritans	X97
D5/11	Knowlton, Kent	Church, St Clement, CT3 1PT	Mural, L	1721		No			M609
D5/12	Whitchurch, Devon	Church, St Andrew PL19 9ED	Tablet, C	1722		No	Watchet white with black veins and pink	John Weston	M241
D5/13	Boxted, Suffolk	Church, All Saints IP29 4LN	Statue, L	1725			Chellaston. Green and red mottled		A39
D5/14	Long Buckby, Northants	Church, St Lawrence NN6 7QH	Bust, L	1726	In square niche		Marble bust in alabaster	John Hunt of Northampton	A134
D5/15	Dartmouth, Devon	Church, St Saviour TQ6 9DL	Tablet, C,C	1727 (1696)			Watchet white with black veins	John Weston	M240
D5/16	Langford, Norfolk	Church, St Andrew SG18 9QE	Effigy and statue, K	1727		No	White, possibly Chellaston	Christopher Horsnaile	A129

Number	Location	Building	Monument	Date	Armour and other features	Painted/Collar	Source	Kerver	Notes
D5/17	Newark, Notts	Church, St Mary NG24 1JS	Tablet, C	1727			Possibly Watchet		M360
D5/18	Hinton St George, Somerset	Church, St George TA17 8SP	Effigy, K	1728	Rolled up mat	No			R49
D5/19	Tawstock, Devon	Church, St Peter EX31 3HY	Tablet, K	1729		No	White with black veins so possibly Watchet	Thomas Jewell	M287
D5/20	Lincoln	Cathedral LN2 1PX	Slab, P	1732					S265
D5/21	Stratford on Avon, Warwick	Church, Holy Trinity CV37 6BG	Tablet, C,L	1732			Veined and blue lias		M591
D5/22	Denbury, Devon	Church, St Mary the Virgin TQ12 6DY	Tablet, C	1736				John Weston	M242
D5/23	London, Smithfield	Church, St Bartholomew EC1A 9DS	Tablet, L	1739					M284
D5/24	Tunstall, Kent	Church, St John the Baptist ME9 8DX	Mural, Demi-figure, C	1740		No	Uncertain		M537
D5/25	Bunny, Notts	Church, St Mary NG11 6QW	Mural, C	1741 (may be earlier)	Standing effigy. Black inscription	No	Fauld	Reputed to be designed and built by Thomas Parkyn	M411
D5/26	Gotham, Notts	Church, St Lawrence NG11 0JL	Tablet, C	1746		No	Redhill Ashford marble		M458
D5/27	Bradford, Yorks	Cathedral BD1 4EH	Tablet, L	1767		Possibly yes		John Francis Moore	M538

Number	Location	Building	Monument	Date	Armour and other features	Painted/Collar	Source	Kerver	Notes
D5/28	Christchurch, Hants	Priory BH23 1BU	Tablet, C	1784					M539
D5/29	Llansantffraid, Monmouth	Church, St Bridget	Panels, –	1786		No	Chellaston		X108
D5/30	Ashbourne, Derbys	Church, St Oswald DE6 1AN	Tablet, K,L	1789				Joseph Evans	A131
D5/31	Wirksworth, Derbys	Church, St Mary DE4 4ET	Tablet, C,L	1798			Fauld		M346

= details on henrymoore website

Appendix D6 – 19th Century Onward (1800 to date)

GNP = Gothic Gardner 'no picture' list in file, G = Gothic Gardner with picture, R = Renaissance, T = Transition, M = Mural

Number	Location	Building	Monument	Date	Armour and other features	Painted/Collar	Source	Kerver	Notes
D6/1	East Sutton, Kent	Church, St Peter & St Paul ME17 3DE	Tablet, L,C	*Circa* 1805				John Golden	A133
D6/2	Ashbourne, Derbys	Church, St Oswald DE6 1AN	Tablet, L	1805			Fauld		M540
D6/3	Crowcombe, Somerset	Church, Holy Ghost TA4 4AA	Tablet, C	1808		Yes	Fauld		M292
D6/4	East Sutton, Kent	Church, St Peter & St Paul ME17 3DE	Tablet, C	*Circa* 1810				Edward and Thomas Gaffin	A132
D6/5	Burley, Rutland	Church, Holy Cross LE15 7SU	Statue, L	1813 (1817–24)		No	Marble and alabaster	Francis Chantrey	A193
D6/6	Wirksworth, Derbys	Church, St Mary DE4 4ET	Tablet, L	1813					M351

Number	Location	Building	Monument	Date	Armour and other features	Painted/Collar	Source	Kerver	Notes
D6/7	Wirksworth, Derbys	Church, St Mary DE4 4ET	Tablet, L	1814					M350
D6/8	Wirksworth, Derbys	Church, St Mary DE4 4ET	Tablet, C,L	1819					M352
D6/9	Heanor, Derbys	Church, St Lawrence DE75 7AA	Tablet, C	1820			Fauld	White Watson	M631
D6/10	Wirksworth, Derbys	Church, St Mary DE4 4ET	Tablet, C,L	1836					M354
D6/11	Eccleshall, Staffs	Church, Holy Trinity ST21 6BY	Effigy, B	1843		No	Fauld		R210
D6/12	Gaddesby, Leics	Church, St Luke LE7 4WG	Mural, S	1848		No	Italian alabaster and marble	Joseph Gott	M541
D6/13	Welshpool, Montgomery	Church, St Mary SY21 7DP	Effigy, K	1853	Pink mottled	No	Chellaston	Edward Richardson and George Gilbert Scott	A62
D6/14	Ely, Cambs	Cathedral CB7 4DL	Tomb chest, P	1853	Figures at feet		Copper effigy. Tomb chest is alabaster, serpentine and marble	George Gilbert Scott (executed by Mr Philip)	A158
D6/15	York	Minster, south choir aisle YO1 7HH	Tablet, P,P	1854 and 1797				Francis Albert Skidmore	M270
D6/16	Dale Abbey, Derbys	Chapel, All Saints	Tablet, K	1855					M542
D6/17	Truro, Cornwall	Cathedral TR1 2AF	Tablet, C,C,C	1855			Uncertain		X44

Number	Location	Building	Monument	Date	Armour and other features	Painted/Collar	Source	Kerver	Notes
D6/18	Sudeley Castle, Gloucs	Chapel, St Mary	Effigy, L	1860	Replacement		Fauld and marble	John Birnie Philip and Gilbert Scott	A207
D6/19	Eversley, Hampshire	Church, St Mary RG27 0PX	Effigy, L	1862	Old lady	No	Chellaston		A195
D6/20	Woodchester Priory, Gloucs	Chapel	Effigy, K	1863	Knight of St Gregory			Messrs R L Boulton & Sons Cheltenham	A201
D6/21	Chester	Cathedral CH1 2DY	Effigy, B	1863			Chellaston alabaster and limestone	Designed by A W Blomfield and carved by Matthew Noble	R289
D6/22	Wirksworth, Derbys	Church, St Mary DE4 4ET	Tablet, C,L	1866					M353
D6/23	Hereford	Cathedral	Effigy, P	1867		Part	Fauld tomb chest with Carrara marble effigy	Matthew Noble carved the effigy	A218
D6/24	Deene, Northants	Church, St Peter NN17 3EJ	Effigy, K	1868		No		J E Boehm	A196
D6/25	Condover, Shrops	Church, St Mary and St Andrew SY5 7AA	Statue, C	1868	Kneeling effigy holding sword & a recumbent effigy	No	Chellaston	George Frederick Watts Reginald Cholmondeley	A123
D6/26	Wirksworth, Derbys	Church, St Mary DE4 4ET	Tablet, C	1869					M349
D6/27	Blickling, Norfolk	Church, St Andrew NR11 6NG	Effigy, C	1870	Large standing angels	No	Fauld or possibly Chellaston	G E Watts and J H Pollen	A122
D6/28	Tickhill, Yorks	Church, St Mary DN11 9LY	Effigy, L	1871	Effigies only	No	Fauld	William Calder Marshall	A101

Number	Location	Building	Monument	Date	Armour and other features	Painted/Collar	Source	Kerver	Notes
D6/29	Chipping Sodbury, Gloucs	Church, St John the Baptist BS37 6NB	Tablet, P	1872					M543
D6/30	Edinburgh, Midlothian	Cathedral, St Giles EH1 1RE	Wall tablet, P	1874				A Wallace & Co of the Shrub Place Marble Works. Designed by John Chesser	M544
D6/31	London, Westminster	Abbey SW1P 3PA	Tablet, K	1875	Bust	No	Fauld and white marble	Matthew Noble	M468
D6/32	Crawley, Sussex	Friary church, St Francis & St Anthony RH10 1HR	Effigy, C	1875	Friars robes	No	Chellaston or Fauld and Petworth	Wilfred Scawen Blunt and Neville Northey Burnhard	A121
D6/33	Tideswell, Derbys	Church, St John the Baptist SK17 8NU	Tomb chest, K	1876		No	Fauld	Possibly Gilbert Scott done at the same time as G57	A80
D6/34	London, Westminster	Abbey SW1P 3PA	Mural, C	1876	Demi-figure	No	Fauld	Richard Belt (Signed)	M466
D6/35	Ellough, Suffolk	Church, All Saints NR34 7TR	Tablet, C,L	1877		No	Fauld and Kingston		M285
D6/36	Middle Claydon, Bucks	Church, All Saints MK18 2EY	Mural, L	1877	Bust		Fauld		M545
D6/37	Worcester	Cathedral WR1 2LA	Tomb chest in High Altar, P	1877					A99
D6/38	Worcester	Cathedral WR1 2LA	Tomb chest, C	1878		No	Fauld and white marble	Attrib to James Forsyth	A97
D6/39	Lichfield, Staffs	Cathedral WS13 7LD	Effigy, B	1880			Chellaston and Fauld	Thomas Nichols of London	A197

Number	Location	Building	Monument	Date	Armour and other features	Painted/Collar	Source	Kerver	Notes
D6/40	Gotham, Notts	Church, St Lawrence NG11 0JL	Mural tablet, P	1881 (1900)		No	Local. Veined and poor quality		M25
D6/41	London, Westminster	Abbey SW1P 3PA	Effigy, C	1884		No	Marble effigy and Fauld alabaster chest	Sir Joseph Edgar Boehm	A178
D6/42	Wednesbury, Staffs	Church, St Bartholomew WS10 9DJ	Tablets, L	1885,1903 & 1910			Marble with alabaster borders		M546
D6/43	Rochester, Kent	Cathedral ME1 1SX	Tablet, C	1886			Fauld	James Currie and Temple Lushington Moore	M367
D6/44	Worcester	Cathedral WR1 2LA	Tomb chest, K	1888			White marble on Fauld alabaster.	Attrib to James Forsyth	A198
D6/45	Edinburgh, Midlothian	Cathedral, St Giles EH1 1RE	Effigy, K	1888		No		John and William Rhind. Robert Rowand Anderson	A95
D6/46	Worcester	Cathedral WR1 2LA	Tomb chest, K	1888		No	Fauld and white marble	Attrib to James Forsyth	A98
D6/47	Finchingfield, Essex	Church, St John	Tablet	1889			Fauld		M640
D6/48	Welshpool, Montgomery	Church, St Mary SY21 7DP	Effigy, K	1891		No	Chellaston Pink mottled	Possible involvement of George Gilbert Scott	A77
D6/49	York	Minster, north choir aisle YO1 7HH	Tablet, B	1891			Fauld	Farmer and Brindley	M271
D6/50	Chenies, Bucks	Chapel, St Michael WD3 6ER	Effigy, K	1891			Alabaster, and red and black marble		A183

Number	Location	Building	Monument	Date	Armour and other features	Painted/Collar	Source	Kerver	Notes
D6/51	Beddington, Surrey	Church, St Mary SM6 7NH	Tablet, P	1891			Brass with Chellaston frame		M574
D6/52	Westonbirt, Gloucs	Church, St Catherine GL8 8QG	Effigy, C	1892	Gothic style	No	Veined, possibly Italian	William Silver Frith	A49
D6/53	Louth, Lincs	Church St James LN11 9ET	Mural, C	1892	Bust		Veined alabaster possibly Fauld		M547
D6/54	Edinburgh, Midlothian	Cathedral, St Giles EH1 1RE	Mural tablet, K	1892		No		Robert Rowand Anderson	M195
D6/55	Colston Bassett, Notts	Church, St John the Devine NG12 3FE	Statue, L	1892		No	Chellaston?		X21
D6/56	Lincoln	Cathedral LN2 1PX	Effigy, P	1894			Fauld	Leon-Joseph Chavalliaud	A174
D6/57	St Albans, Herts	Abbey AL1 1BY	Effigy, B	1895			Fauld	John Oldrid Scott (effigy by James Forsyth)	A105
D6/58	Edinburgh, Midlothian	Cathedral, St Giles EH1 1RE	Effigy, K	1895			Fauld	Charles McBride and Thomas Beveridge	A92
D6/59	Norwich, Norfolk	Cathedral NR1 4DH	Effigy with alabaster tomb chest, B	1896				James Forsyth	M549
D6/60	Chichester, Sussex	Cathedral PO19 1PX	Effigy, B	1896		No	Fauld		A202
D6/61	Tewkesbury, Gloucs	Abbey GL20 5RZ	Tablet, C	1900				Messrs R L Boulton & Sons Cheltenham.	M561
D6/62	Chester	Cathedral CH1 2DY	Effigy, K	1902			Fauld alabaster and limestone	Designed by C J Blomfield and carved by F W Pomeroy	R288

Number	Location	Building	Monument	Date	Armour and other features	Painted/Collar	Source	Kerver	Notes
D6/63	Chichester, Sussex	Cathedral PO19 1PX	Tablet, C	1903		No	Fauld		M562
D6/64	London, Bishopsgate	Church, St Andrew Undershaft EC3A 8BN	Tablet, P	1903		No	Fauld		M610
D6/65	Hoar Cross, Staffs	Church of Holy Angels DE13 8QR	Effigies (2), C,L	1904		No	Chellaston	Farmer and Brindley and Leon-Joseph Chavalliaud	A126
D6/66	Southwell, Notts	Minster NG25 0HD	Effigy, B	1904 (1907)	Kneeling bishop	No	Fauld	Bronze by Pomeroy. Base by William Caröe	A81
D6/67	Edinburgh, Midlothian	Cathedral, St Giles EH1 1RE	Mural tablet, –	1904 (1900)		No	Fauld	Field and Allen	A93
D6/68	Gloucester	Cathedral GL1 2LX	Effigy, B	1905	Crocketted canopies on tomb chest	No	Fauld with effigy in uncertain stone	William Silver Frith (*See also* B167)	A194
D6/69	Chichester, Sussex	Cathedral PO19 1PX	Tablet, B	1907		No	Kingston	John Tweed	M278
D6/70	London, Westminster	Abbey SW1P 3PA	Tablet, C	1907		No	Possibly Kingston	Farmer and Brindley	M471
D6/71	Newcastle on Tyne	St Nicholas Cathedral NE1 1PF	Effigy, B	1908			Chellaston	Frederick William Pomeroy	A135
D6/72	Sherborne, Gloucs	Church, St Mary Magdelene GL54 3DJ	Mural tablet, C	1909		No	Probably Italian, Purple veined	However alabaster of colour consistent with Fauld	M61
D6/73	London	St Paul's Cathedral crypt EC4M 8AD	Mural, L	1910 (1916)	Cameo of a nurse attending a patient	No	Fauld frame with marble panel	Arthur George Walker	M156

Number	Location	Building	Monument	Date	Armour and other features	Painted/Collar	Source	Kerver	Notes
D6/74	Ufford, Cambs	Church, St Andrew PE9 3BH	Tablet, C	1911					M333
D6/75	Bradford, Yorks	Cathedral BD1 4EH	Tablet, L	1911			Red-brown		M550
D6/76	Cranham, Gloucs	Prinknash Abbey GL4 8EX	Tablet, C	1913			Brass with alabaster frame		M566
D6/77	Brocklesby, Lincs	Church, All Saints DN41 8PP	Mural, Soldier	1914	Kneeling soldier in a Stuart period frame	No	Fauld	Charles Jagger	M551
D6/78	Lanhydrock, Cornwall	Church, St Hydroc PL30 4DE	Tablet, C	1915		No	Fauld		M552
D6/76	Truro, Cornwall	Cathedral TR1 2AF	Tablet, C	1915			Fauld		M568
D6/77	York	Minster YO1 7HH	Tablet, Sailor	1916		No	Pink, may be Watchet	Frederick William Pomeroy	M265
D6/78	Stowting, Kent	Church, St Mary TN25 6BG	Mural tablet, Sailor	1916/17			Fauld	Conrad Jenkins who died at Scapa Flow in Dec 1916	M553
D6/79	Edinburgh, Midlothian	Cathedral, St Giles EH1 1RE	Mural tablet, Sailor	1918		No	Fauld		M194
D6/80	Hungerford, Berks	Church, St Lawrence	Tablet, Sailor	1918			Alabaster frame		M582
D6/81	Nuthall. Notts	Church, St Patrick NG16 1DA	Mural tablet, –	1919		No	Fauld		M554
D6/82	Eydon, Northants	Church, St Nicholas NN11 3PQ	Tablet, –	1919			Fauld		M555
D6/83	Bradford, Yorks	Cathedral BD1 4EH	Tablet, –	1919			Fauld		M556

Number	Location	Building	Monument	Date	Armour and other features	Painted/Collar	Source	Kerver	Notes
D6/84	Kendal, Cumbria	Church, St George LA9 7AS	Mural tablet, –	1920					M569
D6/85	Kendal, Cumbria	Church, St George LA9 7AS	Mural tablet, L	1920					M570
D6/86	Altrincham, Cheshire	Church, St John the Evangelist	Tablet	1921			Marble in alabaster frame		M641
D6/87	Welwyn, Herts	Church, St Mary AI6 9LX	Tablet, –	1923			Fauld		M557
D6/88	Heacham, Norfolk	Church, St Mary PE31 7HH	Tablet, –	1927					No add details
D6/89	Broome, Norfolk	Church, St Michael NR35 2HU	Tablet, –	1927					No add details
D6/90	Chichester, Sussex	Cathedral PO19 1PX	Tablet, C	1928		No			M563
D6/91	Rolleston on Dove, Staffs	Church, St Mary DE13 9BE	Tablet, C	1928		No	Fauld		M597
D6/92	St Davids, Pembroke	Cathedral SA62 6RD	Effigy, L	1932	Pet dog at feet	No	Fauld – veined	William Caröe, J O Scott and Frederick Brook Hitch	R71
D6/93	Eaton Bishop, Hereford	Church	Tablet, B	1942					A206
D6/94	London, Westminster	Abbey SW1P 3PA	Tablet, C	1947			Fauld and an unidentified white alabaster		M470
D6/95	Brightling, Sussex	Church, St Thomas a Beckett TN32 5HH	Tablet, C,L	1954					M558

Number	Location	Building	Monument	Date	Armour and other features	Painted/Collar	Source	Kerver	Notes
D6/96	London, Westminster	Abbey SW1P 3PA	Slab, C	1960					S263
D6/97	Corsham, Wilts	Church, St Bartholomew SN13 0BY	Effigy, L	1970	Girl at feet	No	Rose red and Fauld	Fred Kormis	A199
D6/98	London, Westminster	Abbey SW1P 3PA	Statue, L	1971		No	Calcite		A177
D6/99	Bradford, Yorks	Cathedral BD1 4EH	Tablet, –	1990		No	Fauld frame		A200

Appendix D7 – Undated

GNP = Gothic Gardner 'no picture' list in file, G = Gothic Gardner with picture, R = Renaissance, T = Transition, M = Mural

Number	Location	Building	Monument	Date	Alabaster	Painted/Collar	Source	Kerver	Notes
D7/1	St Albans, Herts	Abbey AL1 1BY	Effigy, –	?				Langhams – *see* page 85 of Saul	X6
D7/2	Nottingham	Church, St Mary NG1 1HN	Slab, P	?					S29

Appendix D8 – Others

Altars, screens, fonts, retables, reredos, pulpits, foreign effigies and other miscellaneous items

Number	Location	Building	Monument	Date	Armour and other features	Painted/Collar	Source	Kerver	Notes
D8/1	Long Melford, Suffolk	Church, Holy Trinity CO10 9DL	Tablet possibly reredos	1350				London	A21
D8/2	Flawford, Notts (now Nottingham Castle)	Church demolished NG11 6LG	Images	1380 (*circa*)				Nottingham	*See* Appendix H
D8/3	Durham	Cathedral DH1 3EH	Screen	1380					A19

Number	Location	Building	Monument	Date	Armour and other features	Painted/Collar	Source	Kerver	Notes
D8/4	Rome, Italy	Cathedral	Images	1382				Nottingham	A16, X18
D8/5	Seville, Spain	Cathedral	'carvings'	1390					X59
D8/6	Blunham, Beds	Church, St Edmund & St James MK44 3NQ	Statue	14th cent				Nottingham	X45
D8/7	Worcester	Cathedral WR1 2LA	Panel	1400				Nottingham	A23
D8/8	Washington, DC	National Gallery of Art	Statue	1400–1420					X97
D8/9	Fécamps, Normandy France	Cathedral	Blocks	1414		No	White Chellaston	Sutton/Prentys	Appendix V
D8/10	Montréal, Languedoc, France	Church	Retable	1420 to 1451		Yes	White Chellaston	Nottingham	Q1
D8/11	Boston, Massachusetts	Museum of Fine Arts	Image	1420 to 1450		Part	White Chellaston	Nottingham	Q3
D8/12	Santiago de Compostela, Spain	Church	Altarpiece	1456				Nottingham	X15 & X18
D8/13	Caerleon, Monmouth	Quarry	Image	15th cent	St Michael				X96
D8/14	Chicksands, Beds	Priory (MOD owned) SG17 5PF	Panels	15th cent				Flemish.	X76
D8/15	Whittlesford, Cambs	Church, St Mary and St Andrew CB22 4NX	Reredos panels	15th cent			Chellaston	Nottingham	A148
D8/16	Preston, E Yorks	Church, All Saints HU12 8SA	Panels	15th cent			Chellaston	Nottingham	A144
D8/17	Norwich, Norfolk	Church, St Peter Mancroft NR2 1QZ	Reredos panel	15th cent			Chellaston	Nottingham	A149
D8/18	Mabe (Falmouth), Cornwall	Church, St Laudus TR10 9JG	Reredos panel fragments	15th cent			Chellaston	Nottingham	A150

Number	Location	Building	Monument	Date	Armour and other features	Painted/Collar	Source	Kerver	Notes
D8/19	Grandborough, Bucks	Church, St John the Baptist	Reredos panel fragments	15th cent			Chellaston	Nottingham	X99
D8/20	Barling Magna, Essex	Church, All Saints SS3 0LS	Figures	15th cent			Chellaston		X77
D8/21	Amport, Hants	Church, St Mary SP11 8BG	Panel from reredos	1500		Yes		Nottingham	X60
D8/22	Plymtree, Devon	Church, St John the Baptist EX15 2JU	Panel	16th cent				Flemish	X78
D8/23	Risley, Derbys	Church, All Saints DE72 3SU	Font	16th cent					X82
D8/24	Barnard Castle, Durham	Bowes museum	Altarpiece	1643		No	White alabaster and wood	Isaac Tissenaken	X104
D8/25	Williton, Somerset	Church, St Peter TA4 4NS	Font	1666		No	Pink Watchet	Possibly Nicholas Stone and signed by his workmen	*See* Appendix M
D8/26	Hull, Yorks	Church, St Mary Lowgate HU1 1EJ	Bust in frame	1666	Demi-figure		Fauld		X33
D8/27	Breaston, Derbys	Church, St Michael DE72 3DX	Font	1720					X61
D8/28	Burton Agnes Hall, Yorks	Hall YO25 4NB	Chimney pieces	1727–1760					X55
D8/29	Newburgh Priory, Yorks	House YO61 4AS	Chimney piece	1766		Possibly yes	Green and red veined	John Francis Moore	X56
D8/30	Wreay, Cumberland	Church, St Mary CA4 0SA	Font	1840				Sara and William Losh	–

Number	Location	Building	Monument	Date	Armour and other features	Painted/Collar	Source	Kerver	Notes
D8/31	Dublin, Ireland	University church	Altar and reredos	1855		No	Chellaston	John Hungerford Pollen and John Newman	X30
D8/32	Flaxley, Gloucs	Church, St Mary the Virgin GL14 1JR	Reredos	1856				Philip John Birnie, designed by George Gilbert Scott	X62
D8/33	Bromsgrove, Worcs	Church, St John the Baptist B61 7JW	Reredos	1859		Part	Possibly Chellaston	Part alabaster dating from rebuilding.	–
D8/34	Derby	Church, St Peter DE1 1NN	Pulpit	1859				The alabaster work may date from 1923 by Temple Moore	–
D8/35	Alfreton, Derbys	Church, St Martin	Reredos	1860					X107
D8/36	Windsor, Berks	Chapel, St George SL4 1NJ	Reredos	1863				Philip John Birnie designed by George Gilbert Scott	–
D8/37	Bath, Somerset	Eyre Mortuary Chapel	Altar	1863		No	Alabaster, black and white marble	Messrs R L Boulton & Sons Cheltenham	–
D8/38	Chetnole, Dorset	St Peter	Reredos	1865				Dr A Salviati	A176
D8/39	Worcester	Cathedral WR1 2LA	Reredos	1867		No	Fauld and Chellaston	Gilbert Scott and James Forsyth	–
D8/40	Roath, Cardiff, South Wales	Church, St Margaret of Antioch CF23 5AD	Bricks and ornamentation Pulpit	1870			Penarth	William Clarke. Crossing of the church with other stones	–
D8/41	Lod, Israel	Church, St George	Tabletop	1870					X52
D8/42	London, St Paul's	Cathedral EC4M 8AD	Tablets in crypt	1872 to 1898			Fauld		X63

Number	Location	Building	Monument	Date	Armour and other features	Painted/Collar	Source	Kerver	Notes
D8/43	Worcester	Cathedral WR1 2LA	Pulpit	1873	-	No	Fauld and Chellaston	James Forsyth to a design by Gilbert Scott overseen by John Scott	A100
D8/44	Winchester, Hants	Cathedral SO23 9LS	Figures	1873	Angels				A209
D8/45	Birmingham, Warwicks	Church, St Martin B5 5BB	Reredos sculpture	1874		No	Chellaston	A gift from the congregation on when the refurbishment complete	X34
D8/46	London, Bayswater	Church, St Mary of the Angels W2 5DJ	Altars and reredos	1874					X31
D8/47	Baglan, South Wales	Church, St Catherine SA12 8PT	Church furniture and bricks and ornamentation	1875			Penarth	William Clarke (John Prichard)	X64
D8/48	Putley, Hereford	Church, no dedication HR8 2QP	Altar and reredos	1875			Fauld	Farmer and Brindley	A127
D8/49	Mackworth, Derbys	Church, All Saints DE22 4NF	Pulpit	1876		No	Chellaston (light brown veining)	On a limestone plinth and with green marble columns. R G Lomas	Appendix J
D8/50	Edinburgh, Midlothian	Cathedral, St Mary RC EH12 5EQ	Altar	1876			Chellaston and Barrowmouth	R Rowand Anderson	A94
D8/51	London, South Kensington	Church, Redcliffe Sq	Pulpit	1877			Marble and alabaster	Messrs R L Boulton & Sons, Cheltenham. Made in their new Wellington St workshop	–

Number	Location	Building	Monument	Date	Armour and other features	Painted/Collar	Source	Kerver	Notes
D8/52	Cheltenham, Gloucs	Church, All Saints	Reredos	1877				Messrs R L Boulton & Sons, Cheltenham. Designed by J Middleton	–
D8/53	Mackworth, Derbys	Church, All Saints DE22 4NF	Reredos	1878		No	Chellaston (light brown veining)	With blue john inlays. R G Lomas	Appendix J
D8/54	St John's Wood, London	Church, St Mark NW8 7NE	Reredos	1879		No	White Chellaston	Mr Underwood	A72
D8/55	Somercotes, Derbys	Chapel DE55 4LY	Font	1879			Chellaston	Mr Bird	–
D8/56	Stanton by Bridge, Derbys	Church, St Michael DE73 7GH	Reredos	1879					X65
D8/57	Chellaston, Derbys	Methodist chapel DE73 6TB	Font	1880			Chellaston		–
D8/58	Wednesbury, Staffs	Church, St Bartholomew WS10 9DJ	Altar	1880					A113
D8/59	Bakewell, Derbys	Church, All Saints DE45 1FD	Reredos	1880			White Chellaston	Mr Twigg of Ashford	–
D8/60	Lichfield, Staffs	Cathedral WS13 7LD	Font and reredos	*Circa* 1880			Derbyshire?	Robert Bridgeman	A117
D8/61	Chellaston, Derbys	Chapel, Methodist DE73 6TB	Reredos	1880			Chellaston	The Welpton memorial, Thomas Forman	A74
D8/62	London, Westminster	Abbey SW1P 3PA	Table	1880			Chellaston	Mr Terry	A75
D8/63	Edinburgh, Midlothian	Church, St Cuthbert EH1 2EP	Reredos	*Circa* 1880				Robert Bridgeman	A118

Number	Location	Building	Monument	Date	Armour and other features	Painted/Collar	Source	Kerver	Notes
D8/64	Luton, Beds	St Mary LU1 3JF	Pulpit and Reredos	1881				George Street and Dr A Salviati	A175
D8/65	Kemberton, Shrops	Church, St John the Baptist TF11 9LH	Pulpit	1882			Penarth		A143
D8/66	Ashbourne, Derbys	Church, St Oswald DE6 1AN	Pulpit	1882			Chellaston		X67
D8/67	Ashbourne, Derbys	Church, St Oswald DE6 1AN	Altar	1882			Chellaston		X67
D8/68	Saundby, Notts	Church, St Martin DN22 9ER	Altar and reredos	1885			Alabaster, enamel and red marble		X102
D8/69	Thurstaston, Wirral	Church, St Bartholomew LE3 3PF	Reredos Pulpit	1885			Chellaston	Nathaniel Hitch	–
D8/70	Pontardawe, South Wales	Church, All Saints SA2 0HN	Gables on reredos	1885			Penarth with white marble	William Clarke	X71
D8/71	St Peter Port, Guernsey	Church, St Stephens GY1 2DL	Reredos	1886			Veined	Harry Hems	X72
D8/72	Welford, Northants	Church, St Mary the Virgin NN6 6HB	Reredos	1888		No	Fauld or Kingston	William Forsyth. Designed by A Hill Parker	X73
D8/73	St Peter Port, Guernsey	Parish Church GY1 2DL	Pulpit	1889			Caen stone & alabaster		–
D8/74	Landogo, Monmouth	Church, St Oudoseus	Reredos	1889				William Clarke of Llandaff	–
D8/75	Manchester, Lancs	Church, Holy Name of Jesus	Altar	1890	Saints statues		Alabaster & green Russian malachite	Messrs R L Boulton & Sons, Cheltenham. Design by J S Hansom	X69

Number	Location	Building	Monument	Date	Armour and other features	Painted/Collar	Source	Kerver	Notes
D8/76	Aberavon, Wales	Church, St Mary	Reredos	1890			Alabaster with bright green columns	Kempston & Fowler designed by H H Armistead	–
D8/77	Hungerford, Berks	Church, St Lawrence	Pulpit	1891			Caen stone with alabaster cornice	Mr Stallwood of Reading and carved by Earls and Abbs of Lambeth	X90
D8/78	Albury, Herts	Church	Reredos	1891			Marble and alabaster		–
D8/79	Lockeley, Hampshire	Church, St John SO51 0JJ	Reredos	1892			White Chellaston and marble	Nathaniel Hitch	–
D8/80	Ilston, South Wales	Church, St Nicholas SA2 7LD	Pulpit and reredos	1892				George Eley Halliday	–
D8/81	Stanford on Soar, Notts	Church, St John the Baptist LE12 5PY	Font	1893–1894			Marble and alabaster		–
D8/82	Streatley, Berks	Church, St Mary RG8 9HU	Reredos	1893			Chellaston	Nathaniel Hitch	–
D8/83	Nicholaston, Wales	Church, St Nicholas SA3 2HL	Reredos	1894			Watchet? Pink. Irish red and green marble	Olive Talbot	–
D8/84	Peterborough, Cambs	Minster PE1 1XS	Reredos	1894			Chellaston or Fauld	Robert Davidson	A104
D8/85	Headingley, Yorks	Church, St Michael and All Angels LS6 3AW	Pulpit	1895			Chellaston	Nathaniel Hitch	–
D8/86	Daybrook, Notts	Church, St Paul NG5 6JD	Reredos	1895			Chellaston	Nathaniel Hitch	–

Number	Location	Building	Monument	Date	Armour and other features	Painted/Collar	Source	Kerver	Notes
D8/87	Treochy, Wales	Church, St George	Reredos	1895			Red Penarth	George Eley Halliday and William Clarke	–
D8/88	Maesteg, South Wales	Church, St Michael and All Angels	Pulpit	1895			Pink alabaster, green stone & Irish red marble columns	George Eley Halliday	–
D8/89	Maida Vale, London	Church, Catholic Apostolic W2 1TF	Altar and statue of Good Shepherd	1895–1896			Chellaston	Nathaniel Hitch	–
D8/90	Leeds, Yorks	Chapel of the Sacred Heart (Now Our Lady of Lourdes) LS6 3BJ	Reredos	*Circa* 1895			Chellaston	Panels in a worn condition	–
D8/91	Cowbridge South Wales	Church, St John the Baptist CF71 7JF	Pulpit	1896			Red Penarth	William Clarke	X16
D8/92	Ashbourne, Derbys	Church, St Oswald DE6 1AN	Retable	1896			Chellaston	T Hardy of Ashbourne	–
D8/93	Llanfleiddan, Wales	Church, St John the Baptist	Pulpit	1896			Penarth	Designed by fowler and made by W Clarke	–
D8/94	Cirencester, Gloucs	Church, St Peter	Altar	1896				Messrs R L Boulton & Sons Cheltenham	–
D8/95	Wells, Somerset	Cathedral BA5 2UE	Effigy, B, only tomb chest	1897		Yes	Fauld	Thomas Brock	A115
D8/96	Oakham, Rutland	Church, All Saints LE15 6AA	Reredos	1898		No	Fauld	James Forsyth	–

Number	Location	Building	Monument	Date	Armour and other features	Painted/Collar	Source	Kerver	Notes
D8/97	Dorchester, Dorset	Church, St Peter DT1 1UG	Reredos	1899					A156
D8/98	Woking, Sussex	Church, St Peter GU22 9JF	Figures	1899			Pink (Watchet) and North African marble	Nathaniel Hitch	–
D8/99	York	Church, All Saints Pavement YO1 8RZ	Reredos	19th cent			Kingston?		X40
D8/100	Ripley, Derbys	Church. All Saints DE5 3DA	Pulpit	19th cent			Alabaster and marble		–
D8/101	Caerleon, Monmouth	Church, St Cadoc	Reredos	19th cent					–
D8/102	Newport, Monmouth	Church, St Philip	Font	19th cent					–
D8/103	St John's Wood, London	Church, St Mark NW8 7NE	Altar	1900		No	White Chellaston		A73
D8/104	Pen y Fai, South Wales	Church, All Saints CF31 4LS	Reredos and pulpit	1900			Red Penarth	William Clarke (Goscombe John)	X79
D8/105	Kingston on Soar, Notts	Church, St Winfred NG11 0DA	Reredos	1900	-	No	Claimed as Chellaston but *see* note A96	Possibly Lomas of Derby	A96
D8/106	Rochester, Kent	Cathedral ME1 1SX	War memorial	*Circa* 1902			Veined		X81
D8/107	Mackworth, Derbys	Church, All Saints DE22 4NF	Candlesticks	1902		No	Chellaston (Pit Close)	R G Lomas & Co	Appendix J
D8/108	London, Westminster	Church, St Stephen SW1P 1LE	War memorial	1902			Penarth		–

Number	Location	Building	Monument	Date	Armour and other features	Painted/Collar	Source	Kerver	Notes
D8/109	Caerphilly, South Wales	Church, St Martin CF83 1EJ	Gables on reredos	1902			Penarth	George Eley Halliday	–
D8/110	Caerphilly, South Wales	Church, St Martin	Reredos gables	1902			Penarth	George Eley Halliday	–
D8/111	Mackworth, Derbys	Church, All Saints DE22 4NF	Pulpit	1903		No	Chellaston (Pit Close)	R G Lomas & Co	Appendix J
D8/112	Clydach, Wales	Church, St Mary	Reredos	1903 (1921)			Pink Penarth alabaster framing white marble relief		–
D8/113	Bridgend, Glam	Hope Baptist chapel	Baptistery	1906					X84
D8/114	Birmingham, Warwicks	Oratory	Statue	1908				Messrs R L Boulton & Sons, Cheltenham.	X70
D8/115	Alexandra Park, Manchester	Church of the English Martyrs M16 8GF	Reredos	1908–1918			Chellaston (green and white)		X66
D8/116	Glasgow	Church, St Francis	Pulpit	*Circa* 1910				Messrs R L Boulton & Sons, Cheltenham	–
D8/117	Keighley, Yorks	Church, St Anne	Pulpit	*Circa* 1910				Messrs R L Boulton & Sons, Cheltenham	–
D8/118	Durban, South Africa	Cathedral	Altar	*Circa* 1910				Messrs R L Boulton & Sons, Cheltenham	–
D8/118	Hopkinstown, South Wales	Church, St Davids CF37 2SG	Pulpit	1914			Penarth	George Eley Halliday	–
D8/119	Fulham, Middlesex	Church, All Saints SW6 3LA	War memorial	1918					M398

Number	Location	Building	Monument	Date	Armour and other features	Painted/Collar	Source	Kerver	Notes
D8/120	Uttoxeter, Derbys	Church, St Mary ST14 8AW	War memorial	*Circa* 1918			?	Nathaniel Hitch. Plaque of 5 panels	–
D8/121	English Bicknor, Gloucs	Church, St Mary GL16 7PG	War memorial	*Circa* 1918		Yes	Possibly Chellaston		X14
D8/122	Bradford, Yorks	Cathedral	War memorial	*Circa* 1918		Yes	Fauld		X58
D8/123	Hereford	Cathedral	War memorial	*Circa* 1918		Part	Fauld alabaster frame		M592
D8/124	Tutbury, Sraffs	Church, St Mary DE13 9JE	Reredos	1919		No	Chellaston	Cecil Greenwood Hare	X111
D8/125	Berkhamsted, Herts	Church, St Peter HP4 2AX	Reredos	1920			Red alabaster and green marble	Nathaniel Hitch	–
D8/126	Chelmsford, Essex	Shire Hall CM1 1RA	War memorial	1920			Dark colour	Marble with alabaster surround	–
D8/127	Temple Guiting, Gloucs	Church	War memorial	1920				Messrs R L Boulton & Sons, Cheltenham	–
D8/128	Chelmsford, Essex	Church, All Saints CM1 7HS	War memorial	1920			Fauld	Marble with ornate alabaster surround	–
D8/129	Pleshey, Essex	Church, Holy Trinity CM3 1HB	War memorial	1920			Fauld	Marble with alabaster surround	–
D8/130	Writtle, Essex	Church, All Saints CM1 3EN	War memorial	1920			Fauld	Brass on a plain alabaster plaque	–
D8/131	Derby	Church, St Peter DE1 1NN	War memorial	1920				Tracery	–

Number	Location	Building	Monument	Date	Armour and other features	Painted/Collar	Source	Kerver	Notes
D8/132	Brinsop, Hereford	Church, St George HR4 7AU	Reredos	1926 (1931)					X85
D8/133	Saltcoats, Ayrshire	Church, St Cuthbert	Reredos	1929		No	Fauld, white and red veined	Messrs R L Boulton & Sons, Cheltenham	X68
D8/134	Thornhill, Kirklees, Yorks	Church, St Michael WF12 0JZ	Font with figure	1931				Amy Lewis	X86
D8/135	Kingsbury, Middlesex	Church, St Andrew NW9 8RU	Reredos images	1932		No		James Redfern	A119
D8/136	Kingston on Soar, Notts	Church, St Winfred NG11 0DA	Font	1933	–		Brown veined Fauld with a Kingston kerb,	New Kingston Fine Arts workshop and William Lomas	A114
D8/137	London, Crouch Hill	Church, St Saviour	Tablet	1933					M572
D8/138	Hirwaun, Wales	Church, St Lleurwg	Font	1936					–
D8/139	Leicester	Cathedral LE1 4LF1	Altar	2015			Fauld	James Elliott. Installed for the re-interment of Richard III	X41
D8/140	Prestwold, Leics	Church, St Andrew LE12 5SH	Baptism font bowl	?			Watchet. White with black veining		X75
D8/141	South Normanton, Derbys	Church, St Thomas the Apostle DE23 8DE	Reredos	1890				Jack England	X87
D8/142	Hereford	Cathedral HR1 2NG	Heraldic shields	?	?				X88
D8/143	Clumber, Notts	Church, St Mary S80 3AZ	Altar				White		–

Number	Location	Building	Monument	Date	Armour and other features	Painted/Collar	Source	Kerver	Notes
D8/144	Illington, Norfolk	Church	Image fragments	?	?		White		X89
D8/145	Cardiff, South Wales	Church, St Catherine	Reredos	?	?			Kempson and Fowler	–
D8/146	Hanbury, Stafford	Church, St Werburgh DE13 8TF	Font	? (1770)			Fauld and Irish marble		X83

Appendix D9 – Vanished (index D9)

The following table is an incomplete list of alabaster work which has not survived. D9/0 to D9/2 pre-date the accepted date of the first alabaster effigies but contemporary texts including Weever, report them as alabaster and so are listed.

Number	Location	Building	Monument	Cent	Date	Details	Notes
D9/1	Canterbury, Kent	Cathedral CT1 2EH	Tomb chest	13th	1292	Isobel, Duchess of Athol. Tomb chest reported as having inlaid alabaster panels but these may well be later than the effigy which is not alabaster	Reported *circa* 1840 that the panels are 'wholly destroyed'
D9/2	Wells, Somerset	Cathedral BA5 2UE	Effigy	14th	1305	Henry Husee, Dean of Wells	A90
D9/3	Berkhamsted, Herts	Church	Effigy	14th	1306	Richard and Margaret Torrington once founder of church. This monument is described on page 586 of Weever's book	A number of ancient monuments were removed from the church in 1820. There was a report of this monument being one
D9/4	Ely, Cambs	Cathedral CB7 4DL	Effigy	14th	1337	Bishop John Hotham. The chest survives having been moved in current times.	St John Hope writes in 1901 as if the tomb effigy survived then. A stone canopy exists which once covered the tomb so some doubt remains
D9/5	Durham	Cathedral DH1 3EH	Image	14th	1341 (1347)	Durham records mention an alabaster image of the trinity and the virgin valued at 22s being the gift of Prior John Fosser	Almost certainly lost at the dissolution
D9/6	Tutbury Staffs	Priory	Effigy	14th	1343	Henry de Ferrers. The annals of Robert the Earl of Derby mention interring his bones beneath an effigy in alabaster	Monument lost when priory suppressed in 1538
D9/6A	Osberton, Notts	Church	Panel	14th	1350	A panel presented by Sir Godfrey Foljambe in 1350 as an altar-piece to Beauchief Abbey later transferred to Osberton church and then to the Foljambe residence	Current location unknown

Number	Location	Building	Monument	Cent	Date	Details	Notes
D9/7	Hereford	Cathedral HR1 2NG	?	14th	?	In 1841 the floor of the belfry was excavated when concern was expressed about the tower. Fragments of a 14th century tomb were found as fill but nothing was kept	Thrown away
D9/8	Old St Paul's, London	Cathedral	Effigy	14th	*Circa* 1358	John Lord Beauchamp KG (shown as No 10 on Holler's 1658 plan of the cathedral)	Destroyed in 1666 fire of London. Modelled on Sir Richard Pembridge's effigy. X103
D9/9	Grey Friars, London	Church	Effigy	14th	1359	William Ramsey	A44
D9/10	Windsor	Chapel, St George SL4 1NJ	Retable	14th	1367 (1371)	Peter the Mason, Chellaston alabaster	A10
D9/10A	Albury, Herts	Church	Effigy	14th	1370	Gough refers to a tomb to an unknown knight and lady *circa* 43 Edw III (1370). A great helm with a half angel, feet on lion and holding a heart in his hands. Gough suggests it is John de la Lee (Leye)	There is no trace of this in current lists of monuments for the church. John de la Leye is mentioned in respect of property deals in Northamptonshire *circa* 1361 but no connection with Albury can be made
D9/11	London, Charterhouse	Chapel EC1M 6AN	Effigy	14th	1371	To Sir Walter Mauny (or Manny) KG in the quire of the Carthusian Monastery of which he was the founder. In his will he specified that it was to resemble that of John Beauchamp who died in 1358. This too has not been found	Tomb not found. In 1947 a dig at the Charterhouse uncovered a lead coffin and skeleton which has tentatively been identified as Manny's. The Beauchamp tomb was in old St Paul's – *see* 1358 above. A64
D9/11A	Durham	Cathedral,	Tomb of St Cuthbert	14th	1372	London based order for a shrine of marble and alabaster costing in excess of £200	Destroyed in 1539 at dissolution according to Durham history
D9/12	Dover, Kent	St Radigund's Abbey	Effigy	14th	1374	To Lord Poynings. To be placed in the choir of the Abbey. Will directed that the effigy be of a knight in full armour in alabaster for which he left £100	Probably destroyed at dissolution
D9/13	Old St Paul's, London	Cathedral	Effigy	14th	1374–1376	John of Gaunt and wife Blanche (Duchess of Lancaster) designed by Henry Yeaveley and made by Thomas Wrek. Located north of the high altar (No 36 shown on Holler's 1658 plan). Illustration in *St Paul's, the Cathedral Church of London*, 2004, p604	It is believed that the tomb was destroyed in fire of London 1666 However the effigies may have been destroyed as early as the last quarter of the 15th century during the War of the Roses leaving only a tomb chest. A18, X103

Number	Location	Building	Monument	Cent	Date	Details	Notes
D9/14	Rouen	Cathedral	Effigy	14th	1376	Jean de Liege for Charles V of France. Destroyed in 1736	B129
D9/14A	Exeter, Devon	Cathedral, south transcept	Effigy, K,L	14th	1376	Hugh Courtney (or Courtenay) 2nd Earl of Devon and wife Margaret (Bohan). This exists but in 1785 Gough reported the effigies much damaged	It is believed the alabaster was replaced by freestone effigies but information is hard to locate. No alabaster was found by Gardner. A report to the Society of Antiquaries of 1869 says alabaster but also says recently restored and moved
D9/15	Durham	Cathedral DH1 3EH	Reredos	14th	1380	Caen stone carved by Henry Yeaveley and still extant but minus the figures which may well have been alabaster	L16 G7
D9/16	St Mary Graces, Liberty of the Tower, London	Church	Effigy	14th	1380	Now lost but mentioned in contract with Henry Lakenham. The monument was possibly that to Sir Nicholas Loveyne which is believed to be a freestone effigy on a 'marble' tomb chest	A43
D9/17	Guisborough Priory, North Yorkshire	Priory	Effigy	14th	1380	William Lord Latimer 'An alabaster tomb as he has devised'	Disappeared at dissolution *circa* 1536
D9/18	Old St Paul's, London	Cathedral	Effigy	14th	*Circa* 1381	Sir Alan Buxhill (not found on Holler's 1658 plan)	Possibly destroyed in 1666 fire of London but the absence in 1658 means it may have been lost earlier. X103
D9/19	St Michael, Crooked Lane, London	Church	Effigy	14th	*Circa* 1381	John Lovekyn several times mayor of London	Removed by mayor William Walworth *circa* 1560 and replaced by brass in order to provide more room in chapel
D9/19A	Rufford, Nottingham	Church	Effigy	14th	*Circa* 1383	Thomas Neville and wife Joan (Furnivall). Reported by Gough in 1785 but unclear if he was talking about an extant tomb. The male effigy had a bascinet and feet on lion and she has a cushion with angels	The only church at Rufford is a medieval one destroyed at the dissolution. Thomas expressed wish to be buried in Worksop Priory *circa* 1406. No trace can be found of any Rufford tombs
D9/20	Hereford	Cathedral HR1 2NG	Fragments	14th	?	Found in 1841 when the central tower was repaired	The 1841 report states that the fragments were from a tomb
D9/21	Preston in Holderness, Yorks	Church, All Saints	Panels	14th	?	Fragments of panels found buried near the pulpit in 1881–1882 during restoration of the church. The bits were assembled and found to be parts of nine panels formerly from a reredos or retable	Assembled by the rector E Evers but their current location is unknown.

Number	Location	Building	Monument	Cent	Date	Details	Notes
D9/22	Frolesworth, Leics	Church LE17 5EF	Slab	14th to 16th	1390 to 1582	These were seen by Burton and listed as Edmund Wolf (no date), John Wolf (1390), Katherine Wolf (1401), Robert and Elizabeth Walshall (1508), William Staresmore (1509), John Staresmore 1549 and Frances Staresmore (1582)	Slabs removed and converted for use as a pulpit according to Greenhill but this is not supported by local history
D9/23	Caldey Island, Pembroke	Settlement	Reliquary	15th	?	Dug up by accident in 19th century	Unknown but believed to be in private hands
D9/23A	Boston, Lincs	The Guild Hall	Statue and retable	15th	?	The inventory of the Guild of the Blessed Virgin Mary holds two references, one to a statue of our lady in alabaster and the other to a (re)table of alabaster with the story of doom	The guild was almost certainly suppressed in the mid-16th century and the items destroyed
D9/24	Dale Abbey, Derbys	Chapel, All Saints	Slab	15th	?	Dug up in 19th century. The slab has red colour in incised grooves	Unknown but believed to be broken up
D9/24A	Barrow on Trent, Derbys	Church	?	15th	?	A large number of alabaster monuments noted in the 18th century	It is recorded that most were removed in the 19th century and pounded to pieces to repair the local roads
D9/25	Uttoxeter, Staffs	Church, St Mary ST14 8AW	Slab	15th	1391–1405	John and Margaret Mynors *circa* 1400	After the chantry was made into a vestry the slab was found to be broken and it was agreed that the bits could be taken away to be crushed. *Circa* 1877
D9/26	Chellaston, Derbys	Church	Slabs	15th	*Circa* 1400	Slabs of Chellaston alabaster	Destroyed in 1819 when the church was reordered
D9/27	Nantes, France	Abbey	Effigy (II), K	15th	1399–1408	Duke de Bretagne (Brittany). The monument was made in England by Thomas Colyn, Thomas Holewell and Thomas Poppehowe who may be Trent Valley based. However, Edward Richardson offers the opinion that the three were London based	No longer in existence *see* A15. X18 and X23
D9/27A	Chesterfield, Derbys	Church	Slab	15th	1411	Slab to John Pupua, a priest. Formerly in the chancel it showed him in mass vestments and holding a book and chalice	Disappeared in the reordering of the chancel
D9/27B	Robertsbridge, Sussex	Church	Effigy	15th	1417	Sir John Dallingridge of Bodiam (died 1408) but contract not let till 1416 for installation in Robertsbridge Abbey in 1417. The carving and carriage to Small Hythe was to be borne by the carver, John Petit of London. By 1421 the work was incomplete and was subject to litigation, the executors being awarded £13 damages	Abbey suppressed on 16th April 1538. A mutilated torso was found with a SS collar which may well be that of Sir John. However, research into the tombs at Arundel suggests that a tomb was obtained for reuse in the church there *circa* 1430–1476 and this can be seen to the left in the FitzAlan chantry chapel. *See* A211

Number	Location	Building	Monument	Cent	Date	Details	Notes
D9/27C	Halesowen, Shrops	Priory	Effigy	15th	1417	Sir Hugh Burnell in his will desired to be buried in the choir under a fair tomb of alabaster near the body of his wife	Suppressed in 1538 and the tomb probably destroyed
D9/28	Tiverton, Devon	Church	Effigy	15th	1419	Edward 3rd Earl of Devon and Lady Maud. It is suggested that tombs of 1511 and 1527 were there also. All three were alabaster	Destroyed in the Civil War *circa* 1644 when the church was occupied by soldiers.
D9/28A	York	Minster	Effigy	15th	1423	Tomb of Archbishop Henry Bowet (died 1423)	The tomb niche exists but without effigy which was believed to have been damaged in the arson fire of 1829
D9/29	Chesterfield, Derbys	Church, St Mary and All Saints S40 1XJ	?	15th	1433	Thomas Foljambe MP who married the Loudham heiress	Disappeared in 1875 and may have been destroyed when Foljambe monuments regrouped. *See* X22
D9/29A	Epworth, Lincs	Axholme Charterhouse Priory	Effigy	15th	1434	John Mowbray of Millwood Park, Epworth (died 19th Oct, 1434). Reported of being in alabaster	Priory suppressed in 1538 and nothing known of the tombs
D9/30	Roche Abbey, South Yorkshire	Abbey	Effigy	15th	1440–1446	Maud, Countess of Cambridge 'a stone of alabaster and an effigy shall be raised like a tomb in a manner as described to my executors'	Disappeared at dissolution *circa* 1536
D9/31	Chesterfield, Derbys	Church, St Mary and All Saints S40 1XJ	?	15th	1451	Thomas Foljambe who married the Aston heiress	Disappeared in 1875 and may have been destroyed when Foljambe monuments regrouped. *See* X22
D9/31A	Wingham, Kent	Church	Slab	15th	1458	Robert Toste required that 'a marble stone be laid over me with an inscription to induce people to pray for my soul'	It is implied that the marble is likely to be alabaster but no slab to Toste can be found
D9/32	Chesterfield, Derbys	Church, St Mary and All Saints S40 1XJ	?	15th	1469	Thomas Foljambe who married the Longford heiress	Disappeared in 1875 and may have been destroyed when Foljambe monuments regrouped. *See* X22
D9/32A	Nottingham	Church, St Peter NG1 1HN	Slab	15th	1469	Found on removal of pews in 1819. To John Hunt, alderman in 1440 and mayor in 1467	Not found in 2016
D9/32B	Hawkeden, Suffolk	Church	Reredos	15th	1470s (1471)	Bequest of a panel of alabaster but may well be attributed to John Andrews, died 1471, who left 13s 4d according to Suffolk wills	No current trace and probably removed at Reformation

Number	Location	Building	Monument	Cent	Date	Details	Notes
D9/33	Elmore, Gloucs	Church	Tabletop	15th	1472	To John Guise. An inscribed slab in the shape of a knight	Reported *circa* 1880 in Gloucestershire notes but not found during the survey of monuments in 1985
D9/33A	Ickenham, Suffolk	Church, All Saints	Retable	15th	1472	Margaret Cratern and John Chyrcheman bequeathed 13s 4d for 'the buying of a panel called de alabaster'. Identified a reredos panel.	No current trace and probably removed at Reformation
D9/34	Worcester	Dominican Priory	Tablet	15th	1477	Wife of Sir John Beauchamp willed that a tablet of alabaster depicting the birth of the lord and the three kings of Cologne should be placed over her grave	Disappeared when the priory was suppressed in 1538
D9/35	St Albans, Herts Wallingford, Berks Newbury, Berks	Churches and priories	Tablets	15th	1481	Supply of panels or tablets for reredos or retables. Disputed payment with Burton alabasterers – *see* B21 and B22	Disappeared when the priories were suppressed in 1538
D9/36	Prestwold, Leics	Church, St Andrew LE12 5SH	Inscribed tabletop	15th	1487	William Ryddyns and wife Margaret of Prestwold, Leics died 1st Feb 1487	Disappeared sometime in the 18th or 19th century. The tomb chest may have survived – *see* TT23
D9/36A	Cranbrook, Kent	Church,	Retable	15th	1490	'I leave a table of Alabaster [another of the carved panels] to the altar of St Nicholas in the foresaid church of five marks value.'—Thomas Portreffe, 1490 (P.C.O., 33, Miles)	Probably remove at Reformation
D9/37	Leicester Greyfriars	Priory Chapel Site; LE1 4LF	Inscribed tabletop	15th	1495	King Richard III buried following Bosworth 1485 but tomb was not commissioned until 1494 and installed in 1495. Made in Nottingham by erver Walter Hylton	Disappeared with the suppression of the priory in 1538 but may have remained in the grounds until mid-16th century Also *see* A45 and TT3
D9/38	Warter, Yorks	Church	Slab	15th	1499	Thomas Bridlington, prior of Warter priory	The earthworks of Warter are in the current church grounds. The slab was discovered buried by St John Hope in 1899 and reburied
D9/39	Crich, Derbys	Church, St Mary DE4 5DJ	Slabs	15th	*Circa* 1490	Two alabaster slabs to the Wakebridge family.	Reported by Bassano in 1710 but now cannot be found
D9/40	Burton on Trent, Staffs	St Modwens Church then museum	Effigy	15th	14??	A fragment of an unidentified knight. Moved to the new church and then into the garden and then to the museum in 1924. Thomas Cox found this in 1738	GNP86. When the museum closed the fragment disappeared.
D9/41	Fountains Abbey, Yorks	Abbey	Reredos	15th	14??	During excavations in 1854 a panel was found which depicted the Coronation of the Virgin	This find was reported in 1860

Number	Location	Building	Monument	Cent	Date	Details	Notes
D9/42	Chichester, Sussex	Museum	Tablets	15th	?	Two tablets in Lagny or Chelles alabaster donated in the 19th century, one signed I T. Lagny and Chelles are 20 miles from Paris and produce yellow white stone	The collection was disbursed in the early 20th century and the whereabouts are unknown
D9/42A	Stutton Hall, Suffolk	Hall	Panel	15th	?	Noted on a tour in 1885 as a Nottingham alabaster panel of the Ascension	No trace in 2016
D9/43	Thetford, Norfolk	Priory	Effigy	16th	15??	2nd Duke of Norfolk, victor at Flodden	Disappeared at dissolution *circa* 1536
D9/44	Cowbridge, Wales	Llantrithyd Place	Chimney piece	16th	?		House derelict by mid-19th century and chimney piece lost except for two armorial shields now in the church
D9/45	Eastcheap, London	Church, St Michael	Effigy	16th	?	To John Loskin, fishmonger and four times mayor of London and wife	Stow reports in 1598 that the tomb was removed and replaced by a floor slab but no date is stated
D9/46	Faringdon, London	Church, Grey Friars	Effigies	16th	?	Stow reports in 1598 that there were nine tombs of alabaster in the choir and one in the nave	He also states they are all now pulled down
D9/47	Faringdon, London	Church, St Faith	Effigies	16th	?	Stow reports in 1598 that there are three tombs of alabaster to Robert Barton, Henry Barton and Thomas Mirfin	He observes that all three pulled down in 1549.
D9/47A	Beachamwell, Norfolk	Church, St Mary	Altar	16th	?	In 1765 the rector, Mr Ibbot found pieces of alabaster under the floor. One part of a cross and one St Peter	Not found in 2016
D9/48	Humberstone, Leics	Church, St Mary LE5 1AE	Effigy	16th	1500	Thomas Keble and his two wives located in the Kebles Chapel. Reported in 1638 as being 'all in Alabaster'	Disappeared in the rebuilding of 1857–1858. *See* note L6
D9/48A	Fornham, Suffolk	Church	Retable	16th	1500	Thomas Edwards bequeathed a table of alabaster in his will of 1500	No current trace and probably removed at Reformation
D9/48B	Burscough, Lancs	Priory	Effigy	16th	1504	Thomas, Earl of Derby, in his will of the 28th July 1504 specified a tomb for himself and his two wives	The priory was dissolved in 1536 and the tomb probably destroyed
D9/49	York	Church, St Saviours	Tablet	16th	1505	A bequest under the will of Sir John Gilliot of a table of alabaster for the high alters.	Any tables would have disappeared during the Reformation. St Saviours was made redundant in 1954 and is now the York Archaeological Trust Centre
D9/49A	Wollaton, Notts	Church	Tomb	16th	1505	Thoroton recorded 'An alabaster tomb under an arch in the middle of the church to Matilda wife of John Dabrishecourte'	Not found by Glynne in 1867 or Fellows in 1902

Number	Location	Building	Monument	Cent	Date	Details	Notes
D9/50	Hunworth, Norfolk	Church, St Lawrence	Tablet	16th	1506	A bequest under the will of John Colyn of a table of alabaster depicting the virgin and St Anne	Any tables would have disappeared during the Reformation
D9/51	Staveley, Derbys	Church, St John the Baptist S43 3TL	Slabs	16th	*Circa* 1509	Slabs to the Frecheville family	Reported in Kelly's guide to have been removed *circa* 1682 when the chapel was rebuilt
D9/52	Patshull, Staffs	Church, St Mary WV6 7HY	Slab	16th	1514	Anne Bagot wife of Lewis Bagot (S61). She is also mentioned at Blithfield	Lost during rebuilding
D9/53	Mottram, Cheshire	Church, St Michael	Tabletop	16th	1517	To the rector John Pyckton	Described in 1662 by Randle Holme who tabled a simple drawing of an inscribed figure. This has not currently been found
D9/54	Old St Paul's, London	Cathedral	Mural	16th	*Circa* 1519 but may be later	To John Colet (died 1519) and illustrated in William Dugdale's History of St Paul's in 1658. It was No15 on Holler's 1658 plan of the cathedral. The monument was a demi-figure facing forward with a recumbent skeleton (cadaver) below	The monument was destroyed in the fire of 1666. X103
D9/55	Cranbrook, Kent	Church,	Tabletop or retable	16th	1524–1525	To Thomas Colyer who wished to be buried in the chancel bequeathing £10 to its carving provided the church finds the rest. However, in light of the price, the item may refer to a retable.	Duncan in 1925 (Kent Archaeological Society Vol 37) failed to find this. The church has been much changed with monuments removed. *See also* 1550
D9/56	Coventry, Warwick	Church, St Michael CV1 5FB	Effigies	16th	1525 (1546)	*See* T12	On the night of the 14th November 1940 Coventry was blitzed completely destroying St Michael's church. Although some memorials remain T12 was not amongst them
D9/56A	Brampton, Derbys	Church	Slabs	16th	1525	Bassano in 1710 noted many slabs one of which was a Richard Br (?) and two to a Philip (?) with inscribed figures and children	These had disappeared by 1875
D9/57	Priories and Monasteries	Many	Many	16th	1530 to 1553	Destruction of tombs within religious houses	X29
D9/58	Lichfield, Staffs	Cathedral WS13 7LD	Effigy	16th	*Circa* 1530	To Bishop Geoffrey Blythe	Destroyed in Reformation

Number	Location	Building	Monument	Cent	Date	Details	Notes
D9/59	Prestwold, Leics	Church, St Andrew LE12 5SH	Effigy	16th	1531	An unknown effigy reported in antiquity	May well have disappeared during the many church reordering
D9/60	Bramley, Hants	Church, St Leonard RG26 5DF	Images	16th	1532	A travelling salesman sold several images. Entry says '... several images paid for out of church box – 9s'. The images were destined for the rood loft. It is clear the salesman had been come in search of orders as he had previously been paid 4d for 'a bargain' in 1531	Probably lost at Reformation
D9/61	London, Westminster	Abbey SW1P 3PA	Effigy	16th	1532	Abbot Islip represented by an alabaster skeleton in winding sheet under a canopy	The whole was destroyed during the Civil War
D9/62	Bury St Edmunds, Suffolk	Abbey Church, St Mary IP33 1RT	Effigy	16th	1533	Alabaster tomb to Mary sister of Henry VIII died 1533	Destroyed 1540 when Abbey dissolved. Body moved to parish church but tomb broken up
D9/63	Plumtree, Notts	Church, St Mary NG12 5ND	Slab	16th	1534	Thomas Wigfall, rector	Mentioned by Thoroton in late 17th century but not found
D9/64	Stone, Staffs	Priory	Effigy	16th	1537–1538	Ancestors of Lord Stone. Tombs in alabaster	In 1537 Lord Stone rescued the tombs of his ancestors from Stone but installed them in the Augustine House at Stafford only to lose them when that house was dissolved in 1538
D9/65	Kingston on Soar, Notts	Church	Effigy	16th	1537–1538	To Sir Thomas and Katherine Babington under the Babington canopy. Bequest made in Katherine's will and commissioned by her cousin Humphrey Welles (R95). As his tomb was made by Royley it is possible that the Kingston tomb was also by this carver	The current Babington tomb is stated as 'limestone' in all the village histories. The 'tomb' of alabaster mentioned by Katherine may then well relate to an effigy which has disappeared. Authors of the late 16th and 17th century failed to find a tomb. For discussion on this *see* A96
D9/66	London, Greyfriars	Priory	Effigies	16th	*Circa* 1537–1538	Nine tombs of alabaster and seven score tombstones sold for £50	Alderman Martin Bowers oversaw the sale. Antiquarian John Stow recorded sale in late 16th century from old records

Number	Location	Building	Monument	Cent	Date	Details	Notes
D9/67	Coventry, Warwick	Church, St Michael CV1 5FB	Tomb chest with tablet	16th	1539	*See* T25. A Richard Parker monument	On the night of the 14th November 1940 Coventry was blitzed completely destroying St Michael's Church. Although some memorials remain T25 was not amongst them. However, some authors claim that T25 was removed before 1939
D9/68	Livermore Magna, Suffolk	Church, Buckenham Chapel	Table	16th	1539	A bequest under the will of Anne Buckenham of a table of alabaster depicting the trinity, St Peter and St Nicholas	This would not have been there long as any table would have disappeared during the Reformation. *See* note X35
D9/69	Packington, Leics	Church, Holy Rood LE65 1WL	Slab	16th	1539	Thomas Leeson, vicar, as mentioned by Burton in 1622	Not found but may have disappeared *circa* 1894
D9/70	Cockersand, Lancs	Abbey	Table	?	1540	An alabaster table was noted by the commissioners of Henry VIII in the Lady Chapel	Disappeared when the Abbey was suppressed in the same year
D9/71	Canterbury	Priory	Effigies	16th	1540	Tombs to Thomas Arundel and John Buckingham	Cranmer authorised the closure of chantries and the destruction of the monuments there
D9/72	Mixbury, Oxford	Church	Slab	16th	1548	Sir John Wellesborne (died 1548) and wife Elizabeth and two daughters	Destroyed in restoration of church *circa* 1850 but some fragments remain. This slab is attributable to the Royley workshop
D9/73	Sudeley Castle, Gloucs	Chapel, St Mary	Tomb unknown	16th	1548	Catherine Parr wife of Henry VIII died 5th Sept 1548	Destroyed in 1649 during the Civil War. Nothing was left except an alabaster slab with no inscription later built into the wall. Later in 1728 the grave was discovered and marked by the current marble effigy. *See also* A207
D9/73A	Cranbrook, Kent	Church, St Dunstan	Tabletop	16th	1550	To Sir Walter Hendley (died 1550) who specified that a tomb of marble currently stored at Clerkenwell be used. This may well indicate reuse of a former tomb made for someone else	Duncan in 1925 (Kent Archaeological Society Vol 37) failed to positively identify this. The church has been much changed with monuments removed. A tomb believed to be in Purbeck in the corner of the chancel may be this tomb

Number	Location	Building	Monument	Cent	Date	Details	Notes
D9/74	Rochester, Kent	Cathedral	Table tomb unknown	16th	*Circa* 1550	Camden mentions that a tomb to a member of Somers family stood in the cathedral	Later recorded that the tomb was battered to pieces with only the alabaster shields recovered and reused and mounted on Richard Somers tomb of 1682
D9/75	London Possibly St Michael, Crooked Lane – *see* 1381 above	Church	Possibly a slab	16th	1562	William Walworth, fishmonger and mayor of London. On the 16th June 1562 the alabaster tomb was named during the Lord Mayor's Show referring to Walworth as 'The knight and fishmonger of London and mayor who was made knight by King Richard (II) for killing Jack Cade and Will Walle that came out of Kent'. The tomb was paid for by William Paris, also a fishmonger	It is believed the tomb was lost in 1666
D9/76	Old St Paul's, London	Cathedral	Effigy	16th	*Circa* 1569	To William Herbert Earl of Pembroke KG died 1569. Shown as No 37 on Holler's 1658 plan of the cathedral	The monument was destroyed in the fire of 1666 but was described in William Sinclair's book on St Paul's. Page 99 lists a number of monuments extant before the fire some of which will most certainly be alabaster. *See also* Note X103
D9/77	Caldecote, Warwicks	Church, St Theobald and St Chad CV10 0UN	Effigy	16th	1570	Michael Purefoy	The tomb was ejected in 1766 during repairs. It was not restored. Some fragments were placed in the cellar of the Chinese temple in Ansley Hall when this was built in 1778. In 1814 the parts were removed and made into a rockery. In 1960 the NCB gave permission for the fragments to be restored to Caldecote church
D9/78	Quorndon, Leics (Quorn) – *see* Q2	Church, St Bartholomew LE12 8DP	Slab	16th	1574	To Thomas Farnham (died 1574) and wife Anne Eyre in the south chapel	Reported by Nichols but now lost possibly broken up in 1887
D9/79	Warwick	Church, St Mary CV34 4RA	Effigy	16th	1577	A Royley tomb created for Thomas Fisher and his first wife Winifred is listed by Bayliss. The name of Wenceslas Holler has also been mentioned but the dates do not fit	Lost in fire of 1694

Number	Location	Building	Monument	Cent	Date	Details	Notes
D9/80	Prestbury, Cheshire	Church, St Peter SK10 4DG	?	16th	*Circa* 1577	Elizabeth Davenport wife of Thomas. The Davenports took over the chapel in the churchyard which became ruinous in the 17th century. Thomas was also buried there as was John Davenport in 1556	The alabaster tombs were reported present at the end of the 16th century. Earwaker writing in 1877 describes the tombs in the past tense leading to the assumption that they had disappeared
D9/81	Tettenhall, Staffs	Church, St Michael and All Angels WV6 9AH	Effigy	16th	1578 (1580)	A Royley tomb constructed for John Wrottesley and Elizabeth Astley	The monument was destroyed in the fire of the 3rd Feb 1950
D9/82	Rufford, Lancs	Church, St Mary L40 1TA	Effigy or mural	16th	1588	To Thomas Hesketh reported by Dodsworth in 1620 as an fair monument of a knight and his wife	The tomb was dismantled some time before 1908 (possibly 1869) as one effigy was then restored with a figure of a dog and a heraldic panel. There is some doubt as to whether the effigy was a brass
D9/83	Nether Alderley, Cheshire	Church, St Mary	Inscribed slab	16th	1591	A slab inscribed to Thomas Stanley. Ormorod states that his wife was Ursula the daughter of Richard Cholmondeley of Malpas	In 1597 one Edward Fitton defaced the slab by stabbing it with a dagger. Later in Feb 1598 he returned with retainers and did further damage such that the slab had to be buried and replaced by another on which the inscription was copied
D9/83A	Bilborough, Notts	Church, St Martin of Tours	Tomb	16th	1592	Alabaster tomb to Edmund Helwyn and his daughter	Tomb broken up in 1833 but the tablet from the top was affixed to the church wall – *see* X101
D9/84	Old St Paul's, London	Cathedral	Mural	16th	*Circa* 1592	To Sir Christopher Hatton. The monument was made by Richard Stevens but lay unfinished when he died in 1592. Fished by Maximillian Colt. A drawing was made in 1658 by William Dugdale and Holler shows this as No 28 on his 1658 plan. The tomb was mocked by ordinary people for its size 'Philip and Francis have no tomb for great Sir Christopher takes all the room' makes fun of the fact that Sidney and Walsingham buried nearby have no monument	The monument was destroyed in the fire of 1666. Hatton was one of only two paid members of Elizabeth's Privy Chamber and later lord chancellor. X103

Number	Location	Building	Monument	Cent	Date	Details	Notes
D9/85	Norwich	Cathedral	Effigy	16th	1594	A chest tomb to Bishop Edmund Scamler chaplain to the Archbishop of Canterbury with iron grate	There is a statement in that 'In the time of a rebellion by the Presbyterians the grate was taken away and the effigy and tomb chest demolished level with the floor'. The date of this is uncertain
D9/86	Old St Paul's, London	Cathedral	Mural	16th	*Circa* 1595	To Sir Thomas Heneage (died 1595). Vice Chamberlain to Elizabeth I. Shown as No 33on Holler's 1658 plan of the cathedral.	The monument was damaged in the fire of 1666 and the remains lie in the crypt of the current St Paul's. X103
D9/87	Beckbury, Shrops	Church, St Milburga TF11 9DG	Effigy	16th	1595	Tomb to Richard Haughton and wife in an alcove on north wall of chancel	Destroyed in 1856 when church rebuilt. *See* R188
D9/87A	Paulerspury, Northants	House	Chimney piece	16th	1595	Marble and alabaster piece made by the Johnson workshop in Southwark as recorded by Rowse in his book *Raleigh and the Throckmortons* (1962)	No trace of the house can be found
D9/87B	London	St Dunstans in the East	Monuments	15th & 16th	?	The church contains many monuments and alabaster tombs as listed in *Chronicles of a City Church, an Account of the Parish Church of St Dunstans in the East,* 1859 by Thomas Murray.	The book list 20 tombs from 1390 to 1580 many from their description are alabaster. The church was totally destroyed in the Blitz of 1941 leaving only the tower and spire
D9/88	Old St Paul's, London	Cathedral	Possiblya tablet	17th	1628–1634	Poet John Owen by Epiphamus Evesham. Not found on Holler's 1658 plan of the cathedral.	The monument was possibly destroyed in the fire of 1666 X103
D9/89	Skeffington, Leics	Church, St Thomas a Becket LE7 9YB	Mural	17th	1600	Tomb of Thomas Skeffington and Elizabeth (Byron) *circa* 1600. A 1790 drawing shows this to be a large mural with kneeling figures. http://www.leicestershirechurches.co.uk/skeffington-st-thomas-a-becket/	The monument was dismantled in the 19th century leaving only the alabaster figures
D9/90	London	St Giles, Cripplegate	Slab	17th	1602	Charles Langlie, ale brewer, shown kneeling at a desk with crutches	Destroyed in 1940 during an air raid
D9/91	London	St Giles, Cripplegate	Slab	17th	1606	Roger Mason and wife, vintner, shown kneeling	Destroyed in 1940 during an air raid

Number	Location	Building	Monument	Cent	Date	Details	Notes
D9/92	Kegworth, Leics	Church, St Andrews	Slab	17th	1606	One of the rare Reformation set of slabs one to John Ireton rector and the other to Edward Barwell	Found when the chancel floor was renewed (*circa* 1950s) but again buried. The records state that the graves were reused for later burial. *See* 'Report to Leicester Museum' 31st March 1960
D9/92A	Wanstead, Essex	Church	Mural	17th	1610	In 1830 a mural to William Waldegrave (died 1610) and wife Dorothy (died 1586) was reported as being in the church	No trace found
D9/93	Quarrendon, Bucks	Chapel, St Peter	Effigy	17th	1612	Tomb of Sir Henry Lee. The village of Quarrendon is an abandoned village. Lee was the champion of Elizabeth I from 1559 and held this role until his retirement tilt in 1590. Lee died in 1611. The tomb was probably erected before his death but the carver is unknown. The words of his inscription survive and can be found on page 318 of Llewellyn's book	The chapel was probably intact at the beginning of the 19th century but is now a ruin. However, there is some evidence that the tomb may well have been destroyed in the first quarter of the 17th century
D9/94	London, Sherehog	Church, St Bennet	Tablet	17th	1613	To Anne Ferrar. Believed to be a Southwark memorial	Destroyed in fire of 1666
D9/94A	Breadsall, Derbys	Church	Effigy	17th	1616	John Harpur and wife Dorothy attributed to William Hargrave of Bilborough	Removed from church in 1840 and later seen in the grounds of the priory in 1900. Now vanished
D9/94B	Husbands Bosworth, Leics	Church	Tablet	17th	1616	A black tablet in an alabaster frame attributed to Erasmus Smith and his two wives. Believed to be the work of Epiphanius Evesham	The tablet was removed from the chancel at the end of the 19th century and in the tower where it was damged by water.
D9/95	Mitcham, Surrey	Church, St Barnabus	Mural	17th	*Circa* 1623	To Theophilus Brereton (died 1638) and wife Mary	The monument was noted in the visitation of 1623. In 1820 the church was pulled down and the monument consigned to the cellar with only the inscription slab in the church. In 1896 the then vicar resurrected the bits but nothing is known since
D9/96	Letherington, Suffolk	Church	Effigy	17th	1628	Sir Robert Haunton. A monument by Nicholas Stone	Church derelict by 1730 and tomb robbed for parts but some has been recovered *see* http://www.suffolkchurches.co.uk/Letheringham.htm

Number	Location	Building	Monument	Cent	Date	Details	Notes
D9/97	Lilford, Northants	Church, St Peter	?	17th	1635	Thomas Elmes (died 1632) and Christian his wife (died 1635)	Church demolished in 1778 and the tomb has not been found. One monument was taken to Achurch but this is not Elmes
D9/98	Haddington, Lothian	Church, St Mary	Canopy	17th	1638	To John Earl of Lauderdale. The tomb is extant but the canopy of alabaster has been replaced in another stone	Appears to have been replaced *circa* 1785 when it fell into disrepair
D9/99	Berry Pomeroy Castle, Devon	Castle	Statuary	17th	1641	Reported in 1641 as having 'apartments adorned with splendid statues and figures in alabaster'	The castle was demolished by Sir Edward Seymour (1633 to 1708) and the alabaster destroyed or dispersed
D9/100	Peterborough, Cambs	Minster	Various	17th	1643	Various monuments to queens and bishops and the reredos	A regiment of horse under the command of Oliver Cromwell defeated a band of Royalists and destroyed all the monuments in the minster. Although no single alabaster monument can be identified the descriptions of 'marble' may well indicate that some was indeed alabaster
D9/101	London, Westminster	Abbey SW1P 3PA	Effigy	17th	1652	Henry Ireton and his wife Bridget. The sculptor was William Wright	Destroyed in 1661 when Ireton and Cromwell's remains removed from the abbey
D9/102	Withyham, Sussex	Church	Unknown	17th	1663	Sackville family tombs	Church struck by lightning and set on fire. Steward reports '... many monuments reduced to lime' indicating the presence of alabaster
D9/103	Wells, Somerset	Cathedral BA5 2UE	Tomb	17th	1679	To Robert Chrichton, canon of Wells, said to be buried in a side chapel	Not found
D9/104	Bletchley, Bucks	Church, St Mary MK3 6DZ	Slab	17th	1693	Rev Edward Taylor one of the last slabs to depict a clergyman. Believed to be alabaster but some doubt	Destroyed in a Victorian restoration in 1868
D9/105	Chatsworth, Derbys	House DE45 1PP	Carving	17th	1698	Samuel Watson carving alabaster for a tomb for the Duke of Newcastle	No trace of this can be found
D9/106	Chatsworth, Derbys	House DE45 1PP	Carving	18th	1711	Mask heads in alabaster carved by Samuel Watson I in the lower dining room	These are not to be found in the current Chatsworth house

Number	Location	Building	Monument	Cent	Date	Details	Notes
D9/107	Tong, Shrops	Church, St Bartholomew TF11 8PW	Slab	18th	1735	An alabaster slab to William Clay reported as being 'formally' in the church	Noted as missing in 1894
D9/108	Hartington, Derbys	Church, St Giles	Sculpture	19th	*Circa* 1856	A sculpture by James Redfern of a warrior and horse done as a commission for the vicar in alabaster	Not found
D9/109	Derby	Church, St Andrew	Reredos	19th	1867	A reredos in Chellaston alabaster designed by Sir George Gilbert Scott and possibly carved by J Bernie Philip. The reredos carvings have been likened to panels for the pulpit in Christchurch, New Zealand made by John Roddis and Aston and R I Clarke. The panels there were in tribute to Bishop Selwyn (A197). The Christchurch church was badly damaged in the recent earthquake	Whereabouts unknown. St Andrew's Church demolished in 1970. One fragment remains (location unknown). The survival of the pulpit in New Zealand is unknown
D9/110	Honiton, Devon	Church	Font	19th	1886	Alabaster and marble	Destroyed in fire of 1911
D9/111	Cardiff, South Wales	Theatre, Empire, Queens St	Tiles	20th	*Circa* 1900	Tiles made from red Penarth alabaster fitted inside an arch.	The theatre was pulled down in 1962
D9/112	Panton, Lincs	Church, St Andrew	Effigy	14th	?	Military effigy	Church redundant 1974 and converted to hay barn in 1980. Monuments believed lost
D9/113	Castle Donington, Leics	Church, St Edward King and Martyr DE74 2LA	Slab	15th	1500 onwards	A lady *circa* 1500 with one arm chiselled out and other unidentified	Slabs removed in 1877 and converted for use as a pulpit – *see* A145
D9/114	Blithfield, Staffs	Church, St Leonard WS15 3NL	Slab	15th		Reputed to be attributable to a John Colwich depicting a man and woman	Reported to have disappeared in 1737
D9/115	Breadsall, Derbys	Church	Pieta (Lady of Pity)	15th	?	Found in 1877 hidden and believed to be Nottingham but the panel had an embattled top which may be York	Current location unknown
D9/116	Rothley, Leics	Church, St Mary & St John LE7 7PN	Slabs	15th & 16th	1480 to 1516	A number of Kyngston slabs recorded by Nichols of which only one (TT7) remains in the church	Removed in 1860 at restoration of the church and broken for making ornaments to be sold to pay for restoration
D9/117	East Horndon, Essex	Church, All Saints	Monuments	15th and 16th	?	Chapel of the Tyrells	Damaged or dispersed in 19th and 20th century with exception of X38 and marble slab

Number	Location	Building	Monument	Cent	Date	Details	Notes
D9/118	Exeter, Devon	Exeter Cathedral then Sudbury	Statue	16th		An alabaster Madonna and child found buried in the garden of a house in Exeter in 1933. The statue is believed to have been hidden in the time of the Reformation. Restored by William Drinkwater Gough and given to St Georges, Sudbury	The church at Sudbury is deconsecrated and the location of the statue is unknown
D9/119	Tickhill, Yorks	Church, St Mary DN11 9LY	Slab	16th		Brothers Thomas, Richard and William Faunceys	Noted by Bassano in 1710 but destroyed when the old church was demolished for the new
D9/120	Sapcote, Leics	Church	Slabs	?	?	Three medieval slabs	Removed from the church in 1794 and placed in the courtyard of the rectory until 1808. They were broken and used to make ornaments for the house
D9/121	Derby	Church, St Werburgh	Slab	?	?	?	Slabs removed and converted for use as a pulpit according to Greenhill. The church is redundant and the current history states that the pulpit is wrought iron
D9/122	Tong, Shrops	Church, St Bartholomew TF11 8PW	Fragment	?	?	An alabaster shield supported by angels in the porch as found in 1892 under the floor, possibly from a destroyed tomb	Recorded in 1894 but currently not found
D9/123	Astley, Warwicks	Church, St Mary the Virgin CV10 7QS	Effigies	?	?	Reports of many alabaster monuments of which only three remain as G176, G177 and GNP92	The church was reported to be rich in monuments in 1608. The disappearance of the other tombs is not explained
D9/124	Canterbury, Kent	Cathedral CT1 2EH	?	?	?	In 1631 John Weever recorded a large number of monuments built in 'marble' many no longer listed as extant monuments. These are listed in his book, pages 197 to 307	
D9/125	Carmarthen, Dyfyd	Church, St Peter SA31 1LN	Effigy	?	?	The effigy of a Welsh knight	Destroyed by Nash to provide gypsum for repair of church ceiling
D9/126	Worksop, Notts	Church, St John the Evangelist S80 1QG	Reredos	?	?	Stone and alabaster erected in memory of G S Foljambe	Replaced by one in oak, *circa* 1932

Appendix D10 – Non-Religious House Alabaster Items

Number	Location	Building	Monument	Date	Material	Painted/ Collar	Source	Kerver	Notes
D10/1	Dijon, Cote d'Or	Palace, Duke of Burgundy	Effigy	1423 (1443–1456)			Uncertain – may well be Spanish	Jean de la Huerta and Antoine le Moiturier	A83
D10/2	Compeigne, France	Hotel de Ville	Altarpiece	15??					A22
D10/3	London	Victoria and Albert Museum	Effigies	1510			White	Spanish	A141
D10/4	Montresor, Indre et Loire, France	Mausoleum	Effigies	1523		No	White	Rebuilt by Francois Roguet and Michel Brueil *circa* 1875	A82
D10/5	Victoria and Albert	Museum	Model	1580		No	Italian honey calcite	Model for lid of tomb. Northern German Cat. No 1170–1864	–
D10/6	Arras, France	Museum of Fine Arts	Effigy	1585			English probably Fauld		A102
D10/7	Charlton, West Surrey	Charlton House	Chimney piece	1612					A203
D10/8	Los Angeles, California	Museum of Art	Statue	1750			Calcite	Lazar Widman, Saturn and two children	–
D10/9	Holkham Hall, Norfolk	Marble Hall	Columns	*Circa* 1756		No	Redhill	Joseph Pickford and Thomas Carter	W4
D10/10	Kedleston Hall, Derbys	Marble Hall	Columns Window architraves	*Circa* 1760		No	Redhill	Rough finished at Ratcliffe and finished at Kedleston	W1
D10/11	Brocklesby, Lincs	Mausoleum	Columns	*Circa* 1770		No	Redhill	Internal columns	W2
D10/12	Llandaff, South Wales	House, Insole Court	Archway	1880			Penarth	William Clarke	X80
D10/13	Cardiff, South Wales	University	Tiles	1903			Red Penarth	William Caröe	–
D10/14	London, Westminster	Windsor Hotel, Victoria St	Entrance	1908–1918			Chellaston (Alabaster Quarry)		X66
D10/15	Buxton, Derbys	New baths	Entrance	1908–1918			Chellaston (Alabaster Quarry)		X66

Number	Location	Building	Monument	Date	Material	Painted/ Collar	Source	Kerver	Notes
D10/16	London	St Thomas's Hospital	Mural	1917			Fauld	Arthur George Walker	M155
D10/17	Harewood House	Mansion LS17 9LQ	Statue	1938	-	No	Fauld – veined	Sir Jacob Epstein	A50
D10/18	Tate	Gallery	Statue	1940			Fauld	Sir Jacob Epstein	A51
D10/19	Kidwelly, Wales	Dyffryn House	Chimneypiece	15th cent				Moved from a house in England	–
D10/20	Nancy, France	Musee Historique Lorain	Retable	16th cent			English		A103
D10/21	Edinburgh, Midlothian	National Museum of Scotland	Panel	17th cent		No	Possibly Watchet	Alabaster fragment of Christ before Pilate from a small private retable – probably Flemish	–
D10/22	Bolsover, Derbys	Castle	Chimney pieces	Mid-17th cent (1620)		No	Fauld, Ashford marble and cockleshell	Robert Smythson	X47
D10/23	Bolsover, Derbys	Castle	Chimney piece	Mid-18th cent				Thomas Carter	B126
D10/24	Stamford, Lincs	Burghley House	Urns (pair)	18th cent		No	Italian		A116
D10/25	Waddesdon, Manor, Bucks	Billiard room	Panel	18th cent			Redhill	Panel above chimney piece	–
D10/26	Derby	House, St Helens, King St	Fireplace	19th cent				Graffiti from 1880s	–
D10/27	Cardiff, South Wales	Ely Rise House (now Conservative Club)	Chimney piece	19th cent				John Prichard	–
D10/28	Kenilworth, Warwick	Castle	Chimney piece					Joseph Pickford	–
D10/29	Thrumpton, Notts	Hall	Chimney piece	16th cent				Joseph Pickford	–
D10/30	Aston on Trent, Derbys	Hall	Chimney piece					Joseph Pickford	–
D10/31	Chatsworth, Derbys	House DE45 1PP	Door frames						–
D10/32	Kingston on Soar	Kingston Hall	Door frames	19th cent			Kingston		–

Appendix D11 – Significant Non-alabaster Effigies

Number	Location	Building	Monument	Date	Material	Painted/ Collar	Source	Kerver	Notes
D11/1	Bures, Suffolk	St Stephen's Chapel CO8 5LD	Effigy, K	1141 (1296) (1300)	Limestone	–	–	-	A25
D11/2	Worcester	Cathedral WR1 2LA	Effigies, R	1216	False marble	–	Purbeck quarries	London or Isle of Purbeck	X7
D11/3	Bures, Suffolk	Church, St Mary CO8 5AA	Effigy, K	1300	Wooden (oak)	–	–	-	X1
D11/4	Wells, Somerset	Cathedral BA5 2UE	Effigy, B	1329	False marble	Yes	Purbeck quarries	Isle of Purbeck	X26
D11/5	Wingfield, Suffolk	Church, St Andrew IP21 5RA	Effigy (?), K	1361	Limestone		Unknown		A36 (–)
D11/6	Chichester, Sussex	Cathedral PO19 1PX	Effigies, L	1293 to 1376	Undetermined	No	Unknown		X74
D11/7	Wingfield, Suffolk	Church, St Andrew IP21 5RA	Effigy (V), K,L	1415	Wood and Freestone		Unknown		X95
D11/8	Fyfield, Oxford	Church, St Nicholas	Effigy, K	1442	Stone	No	Local quarry		X92
D11/9	Warwick	Castle chapel CV34 3QU	Effigy, K	1456	Bronze	Gilded	–	William Austen	X17
D11/10	Gaddesby, Leics	Church, St Luke LE7 4WG	Effigy, –	1500	Grey sandstone	SS	Unknown	Unknown	–
D11/11	Worcester	Cathedral WR1 2LA	Tomb chest, R	1502	False marble	–	Purbeck quarries	London	X7
D11/12	Newark, Notts	Church, St Mary NG24 1JS	Tabletop, –	1532	Purbeck marble	–	Purbeck quarries	Possibly Burton	X43
D11/13	Staindrop, Durham	Church, St Mary DL2 3NJ	Effigy, K,L,L	1564	Oak			John Tarbotons	X51
D11/14	Bristol, Somerset	Cathedral BS1 5TJ	Effigy, L	1603	Freestone	–	–	Samuel Baldwin	X10
D11/15	Wootton Wawen, Warwicks	Church, St Peter B95 6BE	Mural, C	1605	Freestone		Uncertain material	London workshop	X46

Number	Location	Building	Monument	Date	Material	Painted/	Source	Kerver	Notes
D11/16	Leigh, Worcs	Church, St Eadburger WR6 5LB	Effigy, C	1606	Freestone	Yes			X48
D11/17	Barton in Fabis, Notts	Church, St George NG11 0AA	Chest tomb – no Effigy, K,L	1606	Freestone	Yes			X49
D11/18	Miserden, Gloucs	Church, St Andrew GL6 7JA	Effigy, K	1614	Freestone			Samuel Baldwin	X12
D11/19	Thornhill, Yorks	Church, St Michael WF12 0JZ	Mural, K,L	1614	Freestone				X50
D11/20	Gloucester	Church, St Nicholas GL1 2QT	Effigy, C,L	1626	Freestone			Samuel Baldwin	X11
D11/21	Wells, Somerset	Cathedral BA5 2UE	Effigy, C	1703	Marble	–		Robert Taylor I	X27
D11/22	Gloucester	Cathedral GL1 2LX	Statue, K	1713			Marble but uncertain	Thomas Green of Camberwell, London	X57
D11/23	Malmesbury, Wilts	Abbey SN16 0AA	Effigy, R	14th/15th cent	Limestone	–	–	–	X8
D11/24	West Leake, Notts	Church, St Helena	Effigy, –	14th/15th cent	Limestone	Possible guild robes	–	–	X94

Appendix D12 – Kings and Queens of England

Name	Reigned	Buried	Monument
Eathelstan	927 to 939	Malmesbury	A 14th or 15th century limestone tomb with gablette
William I	1066 to 1087	Rouen	Rouen – marble slab dating from 19th century
William II	1087 to 1100	Winchester	Rufus stone in New Forest
Robert Curthose	Usurped by both William II and Henry I	Gloucester Cathedral	Died in Cardiff. Bog oak monument made *circa* 1234
Henry I	1100 to 1135	Reading Abbey	None known probably lost at dissolution. His burial place, like Richard III is believed to lie beneath a car park
Stephen	1135 to 1154	Faversham Abbey	None known probably lost at dissolution suggestion that remains moved to St Mary of Charity

Name	Reigned	Buried	Monument
Henry II	1154 to 1189	Fontevraud Abbey, Anjou with Queen Eleanor	Fontevraud Abbey, Normandy – limestone, Plaster cast in V&A Museum London
Richard I	1189 to 1199	Fontevraud Abbey, Anjou	Heart is in a tomb at Rouen and the rest in a limestone tomb at Fontevraud Abbey
John	1199 to 1216	Worcester	Purbeck
Henry III	1216 to 1272	Westminster Abbey	Westminster Abbey – gilt bronze. Later the heart was removed and buried in Fontevraud Abbey
Edward I	1272 to 1307	Westminster Abbey	Westminster Abbey – Purbeck marble without effigy
Edward II	1307 to 1327	Gloucester	Gloucester – alabaster (G9)
Edward III	1327 to 1377	Westminster Abbey	Westminster Abbey – Formerly of wood showing effect of stroke later Purbeck with gilt-bronze effigy
Richard II	1377 to 1399	Kings Langley. Later removed to Westminster Abbey	Westminster Abbey – Purbeck or Sussex marble with gilt bronze effigy. Made in 1292–1294.
Henry IV	1399 to 1413	Canterbury	Canterbury. The effigies are alabaster (G97) Westminster Abbey – bronze
Henry V	1413 to 1422	Westminster Abbey	Westminster Abbey – gilt bronze. Later the heart was removed and buried in Fontevraud Abbey
Henry VI	1422 to 1461, 1470 to 1471	Chertsey Abbey then to Windsor St George's Chapel. Moved by Richard III	None
Edward IV	1461 to 1470, 1471 to 1483	St George's Chapel, Windsor	None
Edward V (Richard, Duke of York)	1483	The Tower of London possibly now Westminster Abbey when two skeletons were found in 1674	A white marble container designed by Christopher Wren contains the remains
Richard III	1483 to 1485	Greyfriars, Leicester, later Leicester Cathedral in 2015	Greyfriars – alabaster – destroyed *see* Appendix R – later Leicester Cathedral in Wharfedale stone
Henry VII	1485 to 1509	Westminster Abbey Also Elizabeth of York	Westminster Abbey – gilt bronze designed by Pietro Torrigiano and cast by Humfrey Walker and Nicholas Ewen
Arthur Tudor	Not crowned	Worcester	Worcester – chest tomb without effigy
Henry VIII	1509 to 1547	St George's Chapel, Windsor	Tomb not completed. A marble slab placed on vault in 1837
Edward VI	1547 to 1553	Westminster Abbey	None but a stone was placed in the floor in 1966
Lady Jane Grey	1553 – Not crowned	Executed in the Tower of London, buried St Peter ad Vincula	None
Mary I	1553 to 1559	Westminster Abbey	Westminster Abbey – marble erected by James I in 1606. Shared with Elizabeth I
Elizabeth I	1559 to 1602	Westminster Abbey	Westminster Abbey. Shared tomb with Mary I

Name	Reigned	Buried	Monument
Mary, Queen of Scots	Not crowned	Peterborough then Westminster Abbey in 1612	Westminster Abbey – marble. A copy is in the Edinburgh museum also in marble
James I	1602 to 1625	Westminster Abbey	None. A small plaque is in the floor
Charles I	1625 to 1649	St George's, Windsor	None known
Charles II	1660 to 1685	Westminster Abbey	None known. A wax effigy was placed on grave for some time. A plaque now marks the spot
James II	1685 to 1688	Not buried but remains held in coffin in Paris but disappeared in the French Revolution of 1789	None known but James expected to be buried in Westminster Abbey
Mary II and William III	1688 to 1702	Westminster Abbey	That to Mary was designed but not erected. A small plaque marks the spot. Both had wax effigies. William is buried in same vault
Anne	1702 to 1714	Westminster Abbey	None known
George I	1714 to 1727	Leine Castle, Hanover later Herrenhausen	None
George II	1727 to 1760	Westminster Abbey	None
George III	1760 to 1820	St George's, Windsor	None
George IV	1820 to 1830	St George's, Windsor	None
William IV	1830 to 1837	St George's, Windsor	None
Victoria	1837 to 1901	Frogmore, Windsor	None
Edward VII	1901 to 1910	St George's, Windsor	None
George V	1910 to 1936	St George's, Windsor	None
Edward VIII	1936	Frogmore, Windsor	None
George VI	1936 to 1952	St George's, Windsor	None
Elizabeth II	1952 to date	–	–

Notes to Appendices D1 to D12

Key to notes below:

A = General Notes not linked any other list. G = Notes in relation to photographs contained in Gardner. GNP = Notes in relation monuments which are contained in Gardner without photographs. L = Notes on linked monuments. M = Notes on mural monuments. R = Notes on Renaissance monuments. S = Slabs other than tabletops. T = Notes on transition monuments. TT = Notes on tabletop monuments. W = Notes on miscellaneous monuments not included in other groups. X = Notes on non-alabaster monuments which have affinity with alabaster working.

A1 Langar, Notts. Knight and lady. Sir John Chaworth (died 1558) and two wives Elizabeth and Mary. By the inscription the second wife Mary died in the same month and year but this is not true.

A2 Screveton, Notts. Knight. Richard Wallaye (Walley) died 1583. He had three wives all depicted in relief on the back panel. Erected by Barbara, his third wife. He has his feet on a whale as pun on his name. The monument was formerly in the chancel now in the tower. Walley obtained the procession of Welbeck Abbey in 1538. A supporter of Somerset he avoided his fate by paying a fine but was later imprisoned for experimenting with alchemy. He lost Welbeck in 1553 but regained it at the accession of Elizabeth. Barbara Walley married again and erected a monument to her second husband Edward Burnell at Sibthorpe in 1590 (A86).

It is reported that Screveton also has a stored tomb in the west tower which has been likened to that at Selby, Yorks. Nothing more is known about this tomb.

A3 Wollaton, Notts. Sir Henry Willoughby (died 1528), knight in alabaster on Purbeck marble base. The 17th century alabaster wall tablet dedicated to Percival and Bridget Willoughby reads:

One tomb in death as erst in life one bed
Holds man and wife in double wedlock bound
May he in whom our load of sin was laid
Pardon whate'er of sin in them was found

Bridget was the eldest daughter of Sir Francis Willoughby of Wollaton Hall and died 16th July 1629. Percival died 23rd August 1643. The tomb effigy is surrounded by small effigies of his four wives. There is a cadaver beneath. Conserved in 2009.

A4 Rothley, Leics. A number of monuments including Humphrey Babington (died 1544) and Eleanor Beaumont (of the family of Richard III). *See* TT6

A5 Nantwich, Cheshire. Sir David Craddock (died 1390). This was not found by Gardner as it was discovered buried in 1855 and is now restored on an ashlar tomb chest. The lower legs are missing.

A6 Wollaton, Notts. A tomb to Sir John Willoughby commissioned 1514 but not used until 1549 is reported to have been constructed by John Hippis of Lincoln, Thoroton recording the contract in Record Series Vol 21 P1-2 as dated 6th April 6H8 (1515)

A7 Spare

A8 Spare

A9 Spare

A10 Windsor, Berks. Reported in the 18th century as no longer in place. The retable like most others was probably destroyed in the mid-16th century. Cheetham records that William Burdon was paid £40 for painting a table in the chapel in 1369. There is a possibility that this is the same. The National Archives – Exchequer has an account of the expenses incurred in transport from Nottingham accession No E101/580/42. These documents span 25 Jan 1367 to 24th Jan 1368.

A11 Spare

A12 Ratcliffe on Soar, Notts. For details *see 'Incised Floor Slabs.doc'*. One slab has similarities with Stoke Dry, Rutland 1479, Breedon 1494, Rothley 1486, Holdenby, Northants 1490 and Gaddesby 1498. *See* L25

A13 Spare

A14 There are a number of mural monuments. They are mainly in white or black marble with veined alabaster surrounds probably from Fauld Mine. The reredos is white Italian alabaster in a Fauld surround dating from 1870s. The 1648 memorial to the Pigotts could be a Stone monument in white alabaster.

A15 Nantes (St Peter), France. T Rymer in *Foedera* Vol VIII comments of a passport granted for the export of a tomb to

Nantes, France in 1408 for John, Duke of Brittany the former husband of Joan of Navarre, queen to Henry IV who died in 1399. Made by Thomas Colyn, Thomas Holewell and Thomas Poppehowe. Destroyed in French Revolution *circa* 1789 but a picture was published in *Histoire de Bretagne* by Lobineau and on page 27 of Crossley. The merchant who was charged with its delivery to France was John Guychard who received a safe conduct from the king and it appears that the three carvers may well have travelled to Nantes with the consignment. Nigel Saul maintains that the three kervers were Trent Valley based but the support for this is thin, the evidence coming from the safe conduct which states '… three liege from one of the English counties who made the tomb namely …' followed by the names of the three carvers. Gardner likens the effigy to that of Staindrop (G105, 1425).

A16 Writ issued by King Richard II in 1382 allowed the pope's collector, Cosmato Gentilis to take three large images of the Virgin Mary, St Peter and St Paul and a smaller one of the Trinity to Rome. The export was though Southampton and believed to be a present for the Pope. St John Hope likens these to those at Flawford.

A17 Southwell Minster, Nottingham. Bishop Edwin Sandys of York (died 1588–1589) and tomb erected by son Samuel (R67). Was in the choir. It is believed to have been carved in York with Ledsham alabaster. Llewellyn casts doubt as to whether the effigy is a likeness but the visage is very close to the last portrait of Sandys which was available in York at the time of carving. The monument has been moved at least twice. The minster reports that the monument was damaged in the Civil War and the current head was carved by an Italian based on the portrait at Obersley, Worcs. The hands originally holding an open Bible were replaced at the same time. The monument is extremely well carved and wholly unlike those carved in the East Midlands or in London. The tomb chest depicts Cecily his wife (*see* tomb M4) and their eight children Samuel, Edwin, Myles, Thomas, Henry, George, Margaret and Ann. The bishop displays clerical robes which are considered in conflict with his Protestant beliefs but in the late 16th century. Such robes were not unusual for higher-status clerics and it has been suggested he later took to wearing vestments in protest for extreme puritanical views. *See also* X13.

A18 London, Old St Paul's. The tomb of John of Gaunt and his wife probably destroyed in the fire of London and therefore omitted by Gardner.

A19 Durham. Medieval screen made from Caen stone, Purbeck marble and alabaster made by Yeaveley in 1380.

A20 Bisham Abbey, Berks. This effigy is stated as being to Richard Hertcombe (died 1421) and his wife. However, Nigel

Saul and John Bayliss say that Hertcombe commissioned the effigies for the Earl of Salisbury his former employer. It was not found by Gardner and was assumed to have been lost. Documentary evidence exists that the effigy was made in Chellaston and the tomb chest in London by Robert Broun – *see* the list of kervers. *See also* Appendix W.

A21 Long Melford, Suffolk. An early horizontal panel depicting the Adoration of the Magi believed by Brian Harris to be 1350. It is likely that had been hidden from Edward VI commissioners as it was found hidden beneath the chancel in 1750. An ox and ass appear.

A22 Compeigne, France. One of the few complete two-tier altarpieces of Nottingham alabaster formed of nine panels grouped round a central panel. The Haddon Hall chapel has the remains of such a two-tier altarpiece.

A23 From Cheetham. He reports the panel depicts the Virgin and Child and that it has the original wooden frame. How this survived is not recorded.

A24 Daventry, Northants. Cheetham records that Henry IV knelt before a small image of St Anne on Palm Sunday 1471 in this church. It is unlikely to have survives the trauma of 1550.

A25 Bures, Suffolk. In the church at Bures there is an effigy in freestone which is outside the scope of this book but is worthy of comment. The Church Monument Society reports this third tomb in Bures reputedly of Robert de Vere the 3rd Earl of Oxford is *circa* 1300 but needs investigation. Lithographs are in Chancellor's *Essex*. It is reported that the tomb chest does not belong to the effigy. Paul Saul in his 2011 book (*see* bibliography) has a different viewpoint. He refers to a brief epitaph at the head which reads *Albericus de ver* … and observes that this indicates that it commemorates Aubrey de Vere, chamberlain of Henry I who did in 1141. He goes on to say that it cannot be his son, also Aubrey, who was created Earl of Oxford (died 1194) as the above citation would not be correct for that office. Significantly the shape of the figure and style of decoration point to a date no later than the third quarter of the 12th century. If correct then this effigy is one of the earliest English knightly effigies still in existence. However, the epitaph on the chest tomb and the mismatch of chest and effigy means that the identification remains suspect.

A26 Bury St Edmunds, Suffolk. Tomb of John Baret (died 1467). Baret was probably influenced by the writings of monk-poet John Lydgate who was himself influenced by the Danse Macabre painting in Paris. He therefore specified that his tomb show himself as a cadaver with inscription 'He that will sadly behold one with his eye / May see his own mirror and learn for to die' This tomb may not be alabaster but is included as it demonstrates the mid-15th century moralising.

The tomb includes a small figure dressed in his best attire and carrying an SS collar awarded by Henry VI. Figure 100 of Sally Badham's book *Seeking Salvation* shows this tomb and 'CMS Journal' Vol XXX, 2015, page 133, has a brief comment on the text.

A27 Bury St Edmunds, Suffolk. Tomb of Sir William Carew and wife. (Not known if alabaster.)

A28 Bury St Edmunds, Suffolk. Tomb of Sir Robert Drury (died 1535) and wife Anne (Calthorpe, died 1513). (Not known if alabaster.) This very similar to A27.

A29 Framlingham, Suffolk. Limestone. Thomas Howard, 3rd Duke of Norfolk (died 1554) and his first wife Anne (died 1511) daughter of Edward IV. The suggestion that this is his second wife Elizabeth daughter of Edward Stafford, Duke of Buckingham has been refuted. She is buried in Lambeth and in any case the estrangement between Thomas and Elizabeth in her later years makes this suggestion unlikely. The tomb chest with its shell-headed niches is continental but the carver is unknown but may well be Pietro Torregiano. Margaret Whinney offers the suggestion that the tomb chest was made by a carver from France the 3rd duke having seen the 1502 tomb of the Dukes of Orleans in Saint Denis or that of Francis II at Nantes. She goes further in saying that the effigy is of the Burton school but offers no other evidence. Also the date of the carving is unknown but Llewellyn says this may be mid-1530s or 1550s or even 1560. The tomb chest contains images of the saints or apostles and the monument displays transition attributes. Richard Marks (*Studies in the Art and Imagery of the Middle Ages*, 2012) also offers the opinion that the apostle figures are *circa* mid-1530 and show French influence but admits to infiltration of Renaissance forms which sets the ensemble as mid-1550s to 1560. The reader can make his choice but also *see* note X100. Marks also states that the survival of clear Catholic imagery at a time (1560s) when such adornment was official deemed iconoclastic makes this monument unique. The effigies are considered to be English and most likely Burton. There is a connection with Thetford in that a copy of parts of this tomb were made for the 2nd duke's tomb there of which nothing now is known and that two other bodies of Norfolk ancestors were recovered from the priory and reinterred here.

A30 Framlingham, Suffolk. Limestone. Henry Fitzroy, Duke of Richmond (died 1536) and his wife Mary Howard daughter of the Duke of Norfolk (died 1555 or 1557). The illegitimate son of Henry VIII. The chest has no effigy but has fluted pilasters, shields and angels. May be Renaissance. Margaret Whinney offers the suggestion that the tomb chest is by the same carver as A29 – certainly the date of Lady Mary's death fits the period. Richard Marks also comments on this tomb. The biblical figures also date from the mid-1530s whilst the tomb ensemble is a date close to that of A31 making it also a rare survivor. Lindley (*see* X100) notes contemporary graffito on the tomb chest which shows the date of 1555 and mason's marks. The tomb was moved from Thetford priory after it was suppressed.

A31 Framlingham, Suffolk. Limestone. Two effigies of the wives of Thomas Howard, 4th Duke of Norfolk (he is buried in St Peter ad Vincula). One is Margaret Audley the second wife (died 1564) – the other effigy is Mary FitzAlan his first wife (died 1557) although only Margaret is buried there. Their feet rest on a stag and dragon. There is a large space between the effigies. Tradition has it that this space was intended for the duke himself or Mary, Queen of Scots the proposed marriage of whom cost the duke his life in 1572.

A32 Framlingham, Suffolk. Henry Howard, Earl of Surrey executed 19th Jan 1547. Painted alabaster with kneeling children. He was first buried at All Hallows, Barking within sight of the Tower where many executed people found temporary graves but his son Henry Howard moved his body to Framlingham in 1614. It is likely that tomb chest and effigy dates from this time. Henry Howard was executed in the last days of Henry VIII and it may be that any tomb at All Hallows was simple, it being expedient not to commemorate a 'traitor' with a monument. The tomb was extensively restored in 1976 by John Green who determined that there were dowel holes intended for a coronet (never fitted). A new coronet was made from lead and gilded. The two large, kneeling figures represent Thomas 4th Duke of Norfolk and the Earl of Northampton. The base contains the following: 'Johanne Griffitho Nuper Comiti Northamtonae Ab Epistolis Curante'. John Griffiths was the secretary to the Earl of Northampton by whose direction the tomb was made. The centre inscription has some errors in the pedigree.

A33 Kedington, Suffolk. Knight and lady. Sir Thomas Barnardiston (I, died 1503) and wife Elizabeth (died 1526). The tomb chest indicates later construction date and may have been made when Elizabeth died.

A34 Kedington, Suffolk. Knight and lady. Sir Thomas Barnardiston (II, died 1520) and wife. Effigies on a plain tomb, children kneeling.

A35 Woodbridge, Suffolk. Thomas Sackford – tomb chest with open arcade and without effigy.

A36 Wingfield, Suffolk. Sir John Wingfield (died 1361). The effigies are in chalk made to look like alabaster. The founder of the collegiate church at Wingfield. Having no male heir the estates went via his daughter to the de la Pole family who continued to extend the church. One of the de la Pole descendants is also buried here in an alabaster tomb (G163).

Pointed ogee gable.

A37 Farthinghoe (Stean or Stene Park), Northants. Temperance Brown, died 1634, wife of John Brown. Monument carved by John and Mathias Christmas, signed and dated 1635.

A38 Swarkestone, Derbys. Sir John Harpur of Chellaston and Swarkestone Hall (died 1622) and wife Isabella (Pierrepont). Carver not yet identified. The tomb may date from 1627. Later Swarkestone was sacked by Parliamentary forces and the family settled at Calke Abbey. Seven sons and five daughters kneel in front of a prayer desk on the tomb chest.

A39 Boxted, Suffolk. Dame Abigail Poley (died 1652). Young offers the opinion that this monument carved in 1725 may have been the last alabaster memorial before the Victorian revival. Others agree with this conclusion. This was carved to accompany the marble monument to Sir John Poley of 1675 to 1680, but is less elaborate. The Boxted monuments were subject of a report in 1967: Suffolk Records Office FL530/3/15.

A40 Darfield, Yorks. William Wombwell 1695 and Elizabeth Copley 1742.

A41 Dorchester on Thames, Oxford. Judge Sir John Stonor, died 1354 – details unknown and may not be alabaster. The effigy is a good example of the attire of judges in the early part of the 14th century. He is shown in the knee-length collobium with wide elbow-length sleeves over a cassock extending to the ankles. A coif graces his head.

A42 East Neston, Northants. Richard Fermor, died 1552, and wife Alice.

A43 London, St Mary Graces, Liberty of The Tower. The tomb of Sir Nicholas Loveyne, died 1375. The extant contract for the carver offered for the tomb to be here or in Penshurst. The effigy was in freestone with a 'marble' tomb chest which could be Purbeck or alabaster.

A44 London, Grey Friars, Newgate. Queen Isabella, queen of Edward II commemorated in 1358–1359. She died 1358. The church was destroyed in the great fire and although rebuilt was again destroyed in the blitz. Isabella was the wife of Edward II (*see* G9) and the mistress of Roger Mortimer, Earl of March arrested and hung following his capture by Edward III at Nottingham in November 1330.

A45 Leicester, Greyfriars. In the Public Records Office copies of the Chancery Records there is a record dated 1 July 1496 stating that twelve months previously the Royal Commissioners Sir Reynold Bray (Chancellor of the Duchy of Lancaster) and Sir Thomas Lovell (Chancellor of the Exchequer) arranged for one Walter Hylton, a Nottingham alabasterman to build a memorial over the grave. Hylton was to receive £50 for the work payable in two instalments of £20 and the balance 'when the tomb is installed in the church (of Greyfriars) aforesaid'. There was also a payment of £10 1s to James Keyley but the purpose was not stated. He may have been a jobbing contractor or the carter from Nottingham. There was a dispute between Keyley and Hylton which went to be resolved in chancery in which the tomb is described as being in the 'Newarke' which is crossed out and replaced by 'friars'. There is no other description of this monument but in 1577 Raphael Holinshed recorded that it incorporated a picture (effigy?) in alabaster depicting his majesty. This may have been from recollections as the tomb is unlikely to have survived the suppression of the friary in 1538. William Burton writing in the 17th century recorded the same details probably taken from Holinshed. Sir George Buck, also in the 17th century, recorded the alabaster was 'of mingle coloured marble' meaning that the alabaster was veined but also added 'adorned by an effigy'. He may have seen a fragment but reference to an 'effigy' may have dual meaning. The carving depicting the king may have been an effigy or more likely an incised tabletop slab. The carver, Hylton, was a Nottingham alabasterman voted lord mayor in 1489–1490 and again in 1496–1497 – so someone of high status. Whilst Nottingham was famous for its small images, retable and reredos panels there is little or no evidence for effigy carving in the city this being the province of Burton and South Derbyshire. The transport issues of carrying large blocks of alabaster from the quarries or even up the steep hills of Nottingham meant that these were carved close to the quarries – a practice that continued until the end of the 16th century. However, there is a case for saying that Nottingham also acted as a retail and marketing centre for the Western workshops and may have contracted an effigy or large tabletop from these – hence the dispute with Keyley. The forinsec pleas of Nottingham have many records of disputes between alabastermen and carters and sub-contractors and indeed Hylton is named in one in 1482 over the staining of an image. Christopher Wren whilst visiting Leicester in 1612 claims to have seen in the garden which Greyfriars had become a 'stone pillar on which was a simple inscription' which Robert Hayrick mayor of Leicester had set up. No mention of an effigy or inscribed slab is made and by 1612 it is fair to say that whatever existed there in 1538 had gone. There the matter rests until further information can be obtained. The population of existing tabletop inscribed tombs is very small. There are many inscribed alabaster slabs in churches set into the floor but few on a tomb chest. A census shows that there are four from 1486 to 1510 (excluding that of Richard III), three 1510 to 1547 and three from 1550 to 1614 when the practice in tabletop tombs in alabaster seems to have died. For detail *see* the TT notes below. The tabletop tomb appears never to have been popular. On the 4th February 2013 the results of the archaeological investigation into a car park in Leicester which was on the site of Greyfriars was announced. This investigation unearthed a skeleton with severe war wounds. The conclusions were that the skeleton was without doubt that of the body of Richard III. The creation of the tomb post-burial for monarchs who death was un-natural is has strong precedents – for details *see* A55.

A46 Tickhill, Yorks. Effigy to a member of the FitzWilliam family and his wife. This may well be Sir Thomas (1513) who died at Flodden Field and wife Lucy (Neville) or to Richard FitzWilliam, died 1478, and wife Elizabeth (Clarell), died 1496. The tomb is said to date from 1525. The confusion over the depicted person is due to the inscription also mentioning Richard FitzWilliam but the consensus is that it is Thomas who is commemorated as he is mentioned in will for placement in the priory. Moved to the church on dissolution in 1538. Iron railings date *circa* 1780 to 1828 when it was noted by Hunter that the tomb was 'painted in a gorgeous colour'. Condition is poor. Routh observes that the 'tomb' is in a Renaissance style but this may relate only to the tomb chest. It is believed that moved monuments at the time of the dissolution were often placed on new tomb chests to remove the old Gothic features which were unacceptable at the time. Lucy made a tomb for her son by her marriage to Sir Anthony Browne in Battle, Sussex (T16) in full Renaissance detail with a copy of the rebuilt tomb chest in Tickhill. Thoroton offered the opinion that this tomb was Elizabethan and Gardner failed to list this in the Gothic pre-1560 list of monuments however the money for the tomb was bequeathed in Sir Thomas's will in 1513. The knight has a strange form of SS collar and the lady a gable hood which makes a pre-1510 date unlikely. The faces are badly damaged.

A47 Burghfield, Berks. A much mutilated pair of effigies. The man is thought to be Richard Neville, Earl of Salisbury who was killed or executed following the battle of Towton in 1460. The Neville arms can be discerned on the jupon. The lady is possibly the Countess of Salisbury but may not belong to the man. The lady effigy is believed to be taken from Bisham Abbey at dissolution. Saul believes that the monument cost 200 marks (£133). *See also* A20.

A48 Gloucester Cathedral. Thomas (or Sir John) Brydges of Coberley (*circa* 1400) and wife. Undated 15th century effigy on a 14th century tomb chest. Both effigies have SS collars. Hers is a short narrow collar and his broad leather strap with attached SS. Lion and collared dog at feet. This monument is not listed by Gardner as being found in Gloucester in 1940 and may not have been identified as alabaster as it shows signs of weather damage. The alabaster is dark in colour like the Hanbury effigy but needs investigation. The history of Gloucester quotes this monument as Sir John Brydges (died 1407).

A49 Westonbirt, Gloucs. Robert Stayner Holford (died 1892). A modern monument in possibly Italian alabaster in Gothic style but not a direct copy of a medieval monument. The church is now the chapel of a girls' school and only available for inspection on occasion. Holford was an MP and landowner/landscape enthusiast. Two angels kneel behind the cushion in a clear take on the medieval form.

A50 Harewood House. The huge statue of Adam by Sir Jacob Epstein *circa* 1938. The statue was purchased by Harewood in 1961 from Madam Tussaud's in Blackpool. The source of the alabaster is 'South Derbyshire' but the only mine open was Fauld in Staffordshire in the 20th century and is most likely source.

A51 London, Tate Gallery. Jacob and the Angels 1940.

A52 Dorchester on Thames, Oxford. Unknown bishop of uncertain material.

A53 Spare

A54 Leicester. This triptych (*see* page 408) was on display at the Richard III exhibition at the Guildhall in Leicester January/February 2013. This was intended for domestic use either in a bedroom or private chapel. The presence of suns and roses in the decoration dates it to 1461 to 1485 and is believed to have been owned by a Yorkist. The triptych is representative of the products of the Nottingham carvers and although the form varies the details are rarely identical. Here John the Baptist is show with a yellow beard. Below Christ is rising from the tomb with his left hand raised in blessing. The figure to the left of John is St Thomas Beckett with book and staff and the figure to the right St Peter holding a key. A canopy is over the top. This is a particularly fine example.

Triptych showing head of John the Baptist in Richard III exhibition Leicester 2013. Photo: the author.

A55 Richard III was not the only king to have been deprived of his kingdom and his life by violence. Prior to the 16th century, Edward II, Richard II and Henry VI all died un-naturally and were buried hurriedly and without pomp in a monastic setting, Edward II in Gloucester Abbey having died at Berkeley Castle, Richard II in the Dominican Priory of King's Langley and Henry VI in Chertsey Abbey. In all three cases the burial arrangements were upgraded later sometimes by the person who was instrumental in their downfall. Edward III subsequently built a lavish tomb now in Gloucester Cathedral in 1330 – *see* G9, Henry V transferred Richard II remains to a tomb in Westminster Abbey – a tomb which had been prepared in Richard's lifetime and Richard III himself transferred the body of Henry VI to a tomb in St George's Chapel, Windsor (despite him being a Lancastrian). It was therefore fitting that Henry VII should upgrade Richard III burial place and also fitting that the body will eventually be transferred to an established church.

A56 Formerly in Eastwell with Boughton Aluph, Kent but now in the V&A Museum as A.184–1969. This monument is to Sir Moyle Finch and Lady Elizabeth Finch (1630), Countess of Winchelsea, and comprises a large alabaster base and tomb chest. Black Carrara marble inlays, white marble effigies on black marble slab. There are eight circular column holders. Effigies are likenesses. A picture of the tomb in the ruined church appears on page 3 of Llewellyn's book and its first location in the V&A appears on page 4 although it has now been moved. The 1616 mural (M3) from Faxton and Lamport church can be seen on the wall behind although this is now in another gallery. The church at Eastwell suffered subsidence and was abandoned before being demolished. The monument formerly had a canopy whose columns fitted into the six circular platforms. Sir Moyle has Stuart armour which is finely carved and unlike the effigies of Baldwin or the Southwark group does not display any leather trim. *See* M489 for another ex-Eastwell monument.

A57 Hainton, Lincs. Sir George Heneage (died 1595). There is a report that in 1659 the executors of a later George Heneage (nephew) were instructed to repair the damage to this monument inflicted by Civil War soldiers. Sir George Heneage was in the service of Bishop of London Edmund Bonner famous for his attempt to indict Katherine Parr in 1545 and it was his probable Catholic leaning that led to his tomb being targeted. A fine carved effigy and tomb chest.

A58 Winchester Cathedral. Sir John Clobery MP (died 1687). A fine standing effigy in Fauld alabaster with black marble columns and panels.

A59 Tunstall, Kent. Effigy on one elbow to Sir Edward Hales (died 1654 aged 78). Unpainted alabaster on a painted tomb chest possibly as late as 1665. His first wife Deborah Harlakden is not depicted nor is his second wife the widow of James Cromer also depicted in the same church. The monument is signed. This is an unusual carving with the effigy lying on its side. The Henry Moore website offers the opinion that these were local carvers as the work was crudely done. The chapel was extended for this monument.

A60 Little Easton, Essex. Sir Henry Maynard (died 1610) and wife Susan (Pierson). Henry was MP for St Albans. The man is in plate armour and ruff with the woman in farthingale, ruff and hood. In front are kneeling figures of eight sons and two daughters, on wall at back, marble tablet with Ionic pilasters, entablature, achievement and two shields of arms.

A61 Stansted Mountfitchet, Essex. Hester (Middleton) Salusbury (died 1614) which is an uncertain coloured effigy on an alabaster tomb chest. The tomb has been moved from the chancel. The church contains the tomb of her father Thomas which is also in uncertain material. The church is in the care of the Church Conservancy Trust.

A62 Welshpool, Montgomeryshire. Edward Herbert, 2nd Earl of Powis, died 1848, but tomb not built till 1853. Edward was accidentally shot during a pheasant shoot by one of his sons. The effigy was designed by Sir George Gilbert Scott and carved by Edward Richardson (*see* B80). The alabaster is salmon coloured.

A63 St Olave's Church, London. A bust to Dr Peter Turner, physician, which formed part of a memorial (*see* below). This was removed from the church during the blitz in April 1941 and disappeared, to reappear in April 2010 in an auction in London having been sold by a dealer in Kent. The bust has been returned to St Olave's where restoration is being considered. Stone did work in St Olave's at this time and may well be the carver.

A64 London Charterhouse Suppression Inventory of 1538–1539 lists a number of alabaster items including a high altar of alabaster with images, a table of the resurrection and one of St Augustine in St John's Chapel and another in the chapter house. These would all be removed.

A65 Nantwich, Cheshire. Sir Thomas Smith of Hough (died 1614) and Dame Anne (Brereton). Tomb commissioned by Anne. The knight has long flowing hair and full beard. The lady has a hood and full ruff. The tomb is decorated by small figures in the same style as the recumbent effigies. The tomb is covered by a canopy with course scrolls.

A66 Warwick. Robert Dudley, Earl of Leicester (died 1588) and wife, Lettice Knollys, Countess of Essex (died 1634). Two effigies on decorated tomb chest protected by metal grill made by Nicholas Paris of Warwick in 1716. The tomb back is also highly decorated with four columns. The tomb is of 17th century design and most probably carved long on the death of Lettice. Some attribute this to Jasper Hollemans. The church also contains a monument to his son Robert who died aged three in 1584.

A67 Temple Church, London. Edmund Plowden (died 1585). Alabaster and marble. Semicircular coffered decorated arch with Italianate putti and a large heraldic device above. Small truncated pyramids. The tomb looks much later than 1585 and is likely to be *circa* 1600. The inscription records his classical education and dedication to the law. The tomb carries the inscription 'ETS repaired and beautified 1687'. The tomb may have been restored again by Edward Richardson in 1843 but this is uncertain. There is conjecture that the 1687 restoration was by the Stanton workshop the E being Edward and the T, Thomas.

A68 Blunham, Bedfordshire. Uncertain lady. May be Susanna (Longuevile), wife of the Earl of Kent or her daughter Susannah Grey date *circa* 1620. A fine white alabaster recumbent effigy in a semicircular niche with a veined alabaster back with raised images of praying figures and black marble inscription panel.

A69 Eyeworth, Bedfordshire. Sir Edmund Anderson (died 1605) and wife Magdalene (Smyth, died 1623). He was Judge at the trials of Mary, Queen of Scots and Sir Walter Rayleigh. The tomb chest is particularly heavily veined with raised figures of children in prayer. The columns are of black marble with a semi-circular canopy. There is a report that the effigy has an SS collar which needs investigation.

A70 Flitton, Bedfordshire. The de Grey mausoleum in Flitton church founded by Henry de Grey in 1605 is one of the largest sepulchral chapels in England and contains some 20 memorials only one of which contains alabaster. Access is by appointment.

A71 Flitton, Bedfordshire. Henry de Grey, 5th Earl of Kent and Lord Hastings (died 1614) and wife Mary (died 1580). She is buried in Great Goddesden, Herts. A fine alabaster monument with painted effigies and rich heraldic devices. Black marble panels and inscriptions. The alabaster is an unusual colour and merits further investigation but may well be Watchet meaning that the carving can be attributed to London.

A72 St John's Wood, London. The diary of Henry Forman of Chellaston on the 28th April 1879 records a purchase of blocks of alabaster by a Mr Underwood 'for Canon Duckworth's church, St Mark's at St John's Wood'.

A73 St John's Wood, London. The church records show an altar constructed of white alabaster with green (marble) inlays and the date given is 1900 and the person commemorated is Fernanda Wanamaker.

A74 Chellaston Methodist Chapel, Derbyshire. In 1880 Thomas Forman quarryman and carver supplied an alabaster reredos to the chapel. In Gothic style with three arches contains passages of scripture and a block below commemorates Mr W T Whelpton who was long a resident of the area. The chapel also has an alabaster font and pulpit both the work of Forman.

A75 London, Westminster Abbey. The monument to the Duchess of Westminster was carved by Sir Joseph Edgar Boehm in marble but the plinth is in Chellaston alabaster being supplied in June 1880 to a Mr Terry. The block was one of the largest excavated from the Chellaston quarry measuring 8ft 3 inches by 3ft 2 inches and weighing 5 tons 17cwt and was delivered some eight days after order. The plinth is not in good condition showing inclusions.

A76 Spare

A77 Welshpool, Montgomery. Edward James Herbert, 3rd Earl of Powis, died 1891. Similar to his father's tomb.

A78 London, Westminster Abbey. Philippa of Hainault (died 1369). The wife of Edward III. The tomb chest is touch marble from which the weepers have been lost but the effigy is alabaster. There is some damage mainly the right lower arm and hand which may well have held a sceptre. This is considered a portrait and is likely to have been carved by royal masons or in some quarters it has been suggested to be by Jean de Liege of Brabant. Crossley claims the carver was Hawkin of Liege. The tomb was formerly guarded by an iron grill. Curiously this monument is not listed by Gardner. It may well be that the order of alabaster from Chellaston in 1362 may be for this tomb which was known to have been carved in her lifetime. It is suggested that a model in marble and alabaster was made in 1850 by John Birnie Philip and Samuel Cundy (Abbey mason) for a proposed repair to this tomb. This was donated to the V&A as item A15-1973. The work was not carried out despite parliament voting £4500 for this to be done.

A79 Warwick. Robert Dudley, Lord Denbigh (aged 3, died 1584). A mural monument with effigy of child. Robert was the only son of Robert Earl of Leicester – *see* A66. His head is on a pillow and his feet on a bear. Sometimes called the *Noble Impe.*

A80 Tideswell, Derbys. A 1462 stone cadaver effigy to Sir Sampson Meverill rebuilt in 1876 into an alabaster frieze and a marble plinth surmounted by a Purbeck marble slab into which is inset a number of brasses. The tomb is located in the centre of the chancel. Some brass was disturbed in 1688 and restored *circa* 1702. The origin of the Purbeck slab is uncertain as it shows inscribed crosses in the corners and centre consistent with once being an altar mensa. It may well be that the tomb is a later construction with a recovered mensa slab from somewhere. One end of the 1876 frieze retains its original limestone panel.

A81 Southwell, Notts. Bishop Ridding (died 1904) a bronze statue and alabaster sarcophagus. Ridding was headmaster of Winchester and bishop 1884 to 1904. The monument may not have been erected until 1907. The monument may have been assembled by William Carȍe assistant to Ewan Christian, architect, who refurbished Southwell *circa* 1888. The alabaster carver is not known.

A82 Montresor, France. The mausoleum of Ybert de Bastarnay built in 1523. There are three effigies in pure white alabaster. The monument was ejected from the church in 1793 but restored in1875 and it is unclear how much is original. The three effigies lie on their back with clasped hands which are vertical. There are angels holding shields at the corners and the tomb chest has weepers in a Renaissance form. The style is wholly unlike English carvers but the original alabaster could well be Chellaston.

A83 Dijon, Cote d'Or. John the Fearless (died 1419) and his wife Marguerite de Baviere (died 1523). Black marble and alabaster. Polychrome. Originally in the Charterhouse of Champmol, Dijon, moved to the cathedral in 1792 and then to its current location in the duke's Palace in 1827. The tomb chest has Gothic features. John was assassinated.

A84 Holme, Notts. John Barton (died 1490–1491) and his wife Isabella. He was the patron of this church carrying much rebuilding. The effigies lie on a tomb chest beneath which is the carving of a cadaver. The tomb may well have been built during his lifetime *circa* 1485. His will is in the Nottingham Archives item DD/1609/6 accession number 4239. There is a rebus in the form of a tun + bar (Bar-ton).

A85 A commentator links the tomb at Berkeley (G87) with those at Thornton (G41 and G42). These may well be of the Burton on Trent workshops.

A86 Sibthorpe, Notts. Edward Burnell or Burnett (died 1589). A monument erected by his wife Barbara (*see also* A2) in 1590. Monument was moved in 19th century restorations. An unusual Renaissance tomb with a back panel of which the pediment has been broken (*circa* 1951) and now rests by the head. The effigy is in civilian robes and is not carved in the round being somewhat crude in carving. The robes cover the foot between which is a grinning skull. It is believed this is the work of Gabriel Royley (II) at a time when the quality of the Burton workshop was in decline. Margaret Whinney observes that the figures which sit beside the shields have their wings transposed into scarves.

A87 Tong, Shropshire. Henry Vernon (died 1515) and his wife Anne Talbot (died 1494). Gardner failed to record this monument and it may not be alabaster.

A88 Stratham, London. Edmund Tylney (died 1610), Master of Revels to James I. A wall tablet made in London 'close to Charing Cross' according to will and most probably William Wright. Tablet made to Tylney's own direction.

A89 Wells, Somerset. St Calixrus Chapel. Thomas Boleyn (died 1472), presenter of Wells. Behind this effigy is an inscription to Henry Husee (died 1305) – *see* Vanished Section and A90. Canopied. The tomb chest has alternating saints and shields in canopied niches. The left image is the annunciation with a vase and three-headed lily first seen in the 14th century (V&A A146–1946). At the effigy's head is what looks like the remains of a canopy which has been broken off. Although stated as 1472 the tomb chest and the head canopy may not belong to the effigy.

Photo: Stephanie Grimley 2015.

A90 Wells, Somerset. St Calixrus Chapel. In 1826 John Britton in his book recorded an effigy in alabaster to Henry Husee in a recess. This information was repeated by Henry Winkler in 1836 and in the reprint of his book in 1892. *See* bibliography. No carved alabaster effigy is known of this date and if it existed then it has vanished to be replaced by that of Thomas Boleyn (*see* A89). On the other hand the effigy of Boleyn could well have been confused with that for Husee. The style of Boleyn's tomb is most definitely 15th century. There are 15th century alabaster panels which are attributed to Nottingham. Images of these are shown in Crossley's book, page 149.

A91 Coughton Court, Warwick. Sir Robert Throckmorton (died 1586). A friend of Edmund Plowden (A67) the monument consists only of a tomb chest. A devout Catholic he was knighted under Mary I but disappeared from political life on the accession of Elizabeth in 1559. His home was searched a number of times. A nephew Francis Throckmorton was executed for his role in the conspiracy surrounding Mary, Queen of Scots in 1584.

A92 Edinburgh, St Giles. Archibald Campbell, 1st Marquis of Argyll (executed 1661). An elaborate memorial in marble and alabaster designed in 17th century style by Sydney Mitchell and Thomas Beveridge and unveiled 27th May 1895. The effigy is marble carved by Charles McBride. It cost £1000. The Marquis was formerly leader of the Covenanters in Scotland but changed sides after Charles I's execution in 1649. However, he was executed for his previous opposition to the monarchy.

A93 Edinburgh, St Giles. War memorial to the Royal Scots in South Africa 1900–1902. A tablet reported to be in marble but with a clear Fauld alabaster frame. Designed by W S Black and carved by Field and Allen who had a marble works in Edinburgh. The monument carries two obelisks of a form seen in the 17th century. The St Giles catalogue lists the monument as 1904 but Field and Allen ceased trading *circa* 1901.

A94 Edinburgh, St Mary. Altar designed and carved by Robert Rowand Anderson reputedly in Derbyshire and 'Whitehaven' (Barrowmouth) alabaster. This is the only recorded monument sourced from Cumbria (but *see* M195). Scotland's Churches Trust (SCT) suggests that the altar was moved to St Mary from the Catholic Apostolic Church following Vatican II (1962–1965) but the reports that the alabaster was rebuilt into the Baldachino (canopy) are false. *The Dictionary of Scottish Architects* confirms that the altar in the latter church was constructed in 1872 and Baldachino in 1894. SCT states that the alabaster is 'pale, varying from yellowy cream to mid brown'.

A95 Edinburgh, St Giles. James Graham, 1st Marquis of Montrose (hanged 1650). Montrose was a romantic figure and Royalist. He was hanged in 1650 and his body parts distributed over Scotland later to be recovered in 1660 and reburied in St Giles. This is another Robert Rowand Anderson design in 17th century style from 1888. The effigy is in Carrara marble with black marble columns but the rest is in alabaster. The cost was £1250.

A96 Kingston on Soar, Nottinghamshire. Reredos commissioned in 1900. It is in dark brown veined alabaster which was claimed to Chellaston by Brian Smith in 1990. The alabaster is not of good quality with inclusions and unlike that associated with Chellaston (*see* Mackworth church) and most likely to be from Fauld. This is the former church of the Babingtons later the Lords Belper and Howe who were long associated with local mining. The church was rebuilt *circa* 1900 and the chancel reordered. Although the family had no connection with the Staffordshire mines in the early 19th century, by 1900 the quarries and mines were coming under the sway of BPB and may well be the source. The will of Dame Katherine Babington (died 1537) specified the arch between the chancel and the chapel should contain an alabaster tomb for her husband and herself. The adjacent Babington monument is still in place and has been reported as 'alabaster' but the official history states limestone, a statement which is probably true. If this had an effigy then it would have blocked the access to the chancel as the church in the 16th century was, unusually, on a north-south alignment. There may well have been one installed but currently there is no trace. Involvement in the Babington Plot of 1586 caused the family to lose the estate and the manor fell to George, Earl of Shrewsbury who was at one time jailer to Mary, Queen of Scots. The History of Kingston on Soar reveals much friction between Shrewsbury and the villagers. In the immediate years following Shrewsbury's acquisition of the manor he was repeatedly reported to the Bishop of York for some unnamed abuses of the church. The disappearance of any tomb may well be dated to these years after 1586. Sally Badham on page 147 of her book observes that Katherine paid for a priest to sing for her soul and her husband for one year after her decease. It is interesting to speculate about the status of the church since that at Kingston on Soar and Thrumpton were chapelries of the mother church at Ratcliffe on Soar as stated in the 1536 Valor Ecclesiasticus Henry VIII page 167. In this, the priest there was named as Thomas Wynter, an appointee of Burscough priory who did not leave until 1543. Burscough was dissolved in 1536 whereupon the chapelries were split away becoming churches in their own right but the date for this is uncertain. In the absence of any other identifiable priest Thomas Wynter of Ratcliffe may well have carried out the requirements of Katherine's will.

A97 Worcester Cathedral. Lord George Lyttelton (died 1876). White marble effigy on alabaster tomb chest probably made 1878. A colonist famous for his support of settlements in New Zealand.

A98 Worcester Cathedral. Earl of Dudley (died 1888). White marble effigy on alabaster tomb chest.

A99 Worcester Cathedral. Dean Peel (died 1877). Incised cross with signs of Evangelists.

A100 Worcester Cathedral. Probably the finest pulpit in an English cathedral. The design was by Gilbert Scott about 1872 but supervised by his son John. The pulpit is alabaster and marble from various sources (as confirmed by correspondence F1395 of 1873). The plinth appears to be Purbeck marble with possibly Irish green marble columns and Fauld alabaster column tops. The carved panels are Chellaston alabaster. At that time the large alabaster could only be obtained from Fauld. The name of Farmer and Brindley is associated with the marble. Worcester Cathedral. Paid for by Lord Dudley.

A101 Tickhill, Yorks. Louise Blanche Foljambe (died 1871) and of second son, Frederick. Formerly in Hazelbech, Northants and moved to Tickhill in 1908. Carved by William Calder Marshall. Blanche cradles her son who lived only one day. There is a suggestion that some 68 monuments were placed in 38 churches to this lady.

A102 Museum of Fine Arts, Arras, France. The tomb of Oudart de Bournonville formerly in the church of St Martin de Henin-Beaumont, Pas de Calais. Discovered in 1840. Dr Kloppmann identifies this as English alabaster. The tomb is 1585 but Kloppmann has suggested the material is reused from an earlier monument. Paint traces.

A103 Musee Historique Lorain, France. A retable de la Deportation altarpiece identified as English alabaster but the carver is unknown but suggested as being Dutch.

A104 Peterborough Minster, Cambs. A fine baldachino and reredos installed in 1894 in place of the one destroyed in 1643. The cost is recorded as being £1307. In addition there is a mosaic floor of various English 'marbles' one of which is recorded as being Frosterley.

A105 St Albans Abbey, Herts. Bishop T Legh Claughton (died 1895). A tomb in Fauld alabaster with a white marble effigy. The tomb chest is Gothic in style.

A106 Ysbyty Ifan, Wales. Rhys ap Meredydd, his wife Lowri and son Robert. Three mutilated alabaster effigies in St John's Church is Chellaston alabaster. Rhys was the standard bearer at Bosworth who seized the standard when Henry VII's man William Brandon was cut down. This places the effigies post Aug 1485. Rhys was known locally as Rhys Fawr owing to his height. Gardner did not list these effigies.

A107 Church Gresley, Leics. Sir Thomas Gresley (died 1699) Baronet Drakelow. Kneeling effigy under an arch in wig and gown and with children as weepers. Heraldic devices of ancestors.

A108 Spare

A109 Worcester Cathedral. An unknown friar in an alcove

A110 Tydd St Mary, Lincs. William de Tidde (died 1390).

A111 Barlborough, Derbys. Joan Nevil (died 1399) wife of Sir Thomas Nevil. This is a slab and the inscription has been mostly lost. It was first installed in Worksop Priory and moved to Barlborough in a damaged state. However it was recorded in Bassano's church notes who stated that Nevil became Lord Furnival. In 1817 the monument was noted as a slab with shields.

A112 Ashby Folville Leics. An unidentified knight which may not be alabaster. Cusped chest side with shields. The church claims this to be Sir Eustace de Folville (died 1347) who erected a window as a thanks offering on being pardoned by the king following a duel. Head on cushion and feet on lion.

A113 Wednesbury, Staffs. A rather beautiful altar dating from *circa* 1880 in Fauld alabaster. Nottingham style niches with figures which may be Chellaston.

A114 Kingston on Soar, Nottingham. The marble font made in 1933 is almost certainly the product of the Kingston Fine Art Workshop and supervised by William Lomas (*see* Appendix L Section 8). Formerly located to the right of the entrance it was moved in 1980s to its current position. The base is in fine pale buff coloured, slightly translucent, alabaster which Vincent Brown (and Henry Woodfield) in the 1950s identified as coming from the Kingston mine. In 1971 a plaque was erected on the north wall of the nave to Richard Woodfield which was carved from the same alabaster which must have been some of the last to be obtained as the mine closed in May 1971. On the chancel north wall there is another tablet in Fauld alabaster fame to Edward and Elimy Strutt dated 1890.

A115 Wells Cathedral, Somerset. Bishop Lord Arthur Hervey (died 1894). Hervey's daughters were the ones who trained the mute swans at Wells to ring a bell on a chain for food. His effigy in white marble is in Gothic style complete with feet on lioness and head on cushion supported by angels. The tomb chest is in Fauld alabaster and is also in Gothic style with arcades and chamfered edges.

A116 Burghley house the seat of the Cecils has a pair of gadrooned urns about 38cm high dating from the 18th century. The alabaster is free of veining and may well be Italian by colour.

A117 Lichfield Cathedral. The reredos and font in 'Derbyshire' alabaster by Robert Bridgeman. B170 has details of two statues which may have been carved in the same period.

A118 Edinburgh, St Cuthbert, off Princes St. A version of the last supper by Da Vinci made by Robert Bridgeman *circa* 1880 in Chellaston alabaster. Placed in the semicircular apse of the chancel, it was assembled in three pieces. The church has a marble and Fauld alabaster pulpit from 1906.

A119 Kingsbury, Middlesex. The Church of St Andrew's was formerly in Oxford St, London and was moved complete with interior to Kingsbury in 1932. The reredos was dismantled and reassembled hence the date of catalogued date 1932 but the original carving was *circa* 1870. The church reconstruction was supervised by William Forsyth.

A120 London, St Paul's crypt. The crypt contains a number of tablets with Fauld alabaster surrounds. Amongst these is a plaque of 1872 commemorating the visit by Queen Victoria to St Paul's in thanksgiving for the recovery of the

Prince of Wales from illness, Rev Henry Venn 1873, Sir Henry Bartle Frere 1884, Bishop Piers Calverley Claughton 1884, Sir Harry Smith Parkes 1885, Sir Vivian Dering Majendie 1898, and Bishop Robert Claudius Billing 1898. *The Memorials of St Paul's Cathedral* by W M Sinclair 1909.

A121 Crawley Friary church, Sussex. Francis Scawen Blunt (died 1872). Blunt converted to Catholicism and is shown in friar's robes. The friary church was rebuilt in 1959 but encompassed the original church which contained the tomb which was installed in 1875. The tomb itself, designed by Wilfred Blunt. Francis's brother, consisted of an alabaster and Petworth marble tomb chest on a raised plinth on top of which is a recumbent effigy in veined alabaster recorded as Derbyshire but most probably Fauld. It is possible the alabaster was obtained from Derby hence the uncertainty of the source. The details of the tomb are contained in CMS Vol XXXVIII 2013 page 89 which states that the alabaster was obtained by George King a foreman of the South Kensington Museum (now the V&A) and that Neville Northey Burnard was also involved, then an itinerant sculptor. There is reference to the obtaining of Petworth marble via the intervention of Lord Leconfield and during later restorations the marble was found to have suffered from water damage and was replaced by Portland stone. In addition it is also unclear as who actual carved the alabaster, the papers of Lady Annabella (Anne) Blunt referring to Binden the Painter, Wilfred Blunt and a drunken fellow who can only be Burnard. The tomb was assembled by a stonemason called Holmes. Lady Anne observing the finished tomb for the first time expressed regret that alabaster and not white marble was used.

A122 Blickling, Norfolk. The tomb of the 8th Marquess of Lothian, erected by his widow in 1870. A fine effigy in winding sheet with two large angels at the head and feet. The tomb is in Gothic style with chamfered edge to the tomb top and script in English with Gothic letters.

A123 Condover, Shrops. Sir Francis Cholmondeley-Owen (died 1864) next to the recumbent effigy of his sister-in-law Lady Alice Cholmondeley (died 1868) created when that of Sir Francis was erected. It is suggested that Sir Francis was christened Thomas a fact which has caused some confusion. The effigy to Lady Alice was sculpted by her husband Reginald Cholmondeley (*see* B185) and includes a chrisom of girl. It is believed that Watts acted as adviser to Reginald (or vice versa) during the creation of the monuments. One author links this monument to the styles of Nicholas Stone but since the same author identifies the figure, incorrectly, as Thomas Cholmondeley (*see* above); this must be taken at face value.

A124 Tewkesbury, Gloucs. Edward, Lord Despenser (died 1375). The monument comprises a kneeling statue in alabaster and a canopy restored in 1827. The kneeling posture is unusual for the period.

A125 Seckington, Warwicks. In the tower is an effigy of a 14th century lady which is much damaged. The hands are missing and tradition established by Dugdale has it that it was always thus the hands being omitted because the lady had her hands cut off by her violent husband. There is also evidence that Hollar sketched this effigy but restored the hands on the assumption that they had been removed after carving.

A126 Hoar Cross, Staffs. Hugo Meynell-Ingram killed in a hunting accident in 1871and Emily Meynell-Ingram (died 1904). A monument to Hugo in marble made by Woolner was erected in the church by the widow, but in 1904 Emily contracted for her own tomb this time in alabaster but died before it was finished. Her executor Emily's brother asked architect Bodley to remove Hugo's effigy and replace it by a copy of that being created for Emily. The effigy is recorded as being made by Farmer and Brindley (B187) with the head by L J Chevalliard (B188). Information supplied by the church wardens of Hoar Cross. The altar is also of alabaster.

A127 Putley, Hereford. A magnificent altar and reredos dating from 1875.

A128 North Leigh, Oxford. Sir William Wilcote (died 1410) and wife Elizabeth (died 1445). Her two sons are also commemorated in the chantry chapel. The tomb chest is of stone but the effigies are in Chellaston alabaster. It has been suggested that the two effigies are of different dates although both are attributed to Prentys and Sutton. Lawrence Stone observes that the quality of the carving is superior to the other Chellaston effigies of the period and offers the opinion that the carving was done in Nottingham. He goes further to suggest the three carvers of the Duke of Brittany's tomb (A15) were Nottingham based and may well be responsible. This is currently unsupported by any documentary evidence and this author will argue that no effigy carving was carried out in that town (*see* elsewhere). If the effigies were carved at different times then there was 35 years between the demise of the two subjects. As Lawrence Stone's assertion is based on the carving of Elizabeth then this may explain the 'improved' quality and she may well have been carved after Sutton died.

A129 Langford, Norfolk. Sir Nicholas Garrard (died 1727). The tomb is of marble but the effigies are reported to be in alabaster the source of which is not determined. He reclines on one elbow in Roman dress with two standing statues of his father, Sir Jacob Garrard and grandfather, Sir Thomas Garrard, also clad as Romans. The carver is reported as Christopher Horsnaile a partner in the Stanton workshop who charged 400 guineas for its creation. In the 18th century, armour and banners and arms were displayed but these have long since disappeared.

A130 Chatsworth House chapel. The John Moore Dictionary quotes Faber (1926) as identifying the figures of Faith and Justice in the chapel as being carved by Caius Cibber *circa* 1688–1691 although this may only be the design. The same dictionary credits the actual carving to Samuel Watson. Firman claims the alabaster may well be from Castle Hay.

A131 Ashbourne, Derbys. Sir Brooke Boothby (died 1789) and wife Phebe (died 1788) by Joseph Evans of Derby. The monument probably made 1789. Signed *Jos H Evans fecit.* There is a monument to Maria Elizabeth Boothby made by E F Evans of Derby dated 1805 of which not details available. Any reader wishing to research the inscriptions is directed to Google Books, *Monumental Inscriptions in Ashbourn (sic) Church by Sir Brooke Boothby*. The Carrera marble effigy of Penelope Boothby, Sir Brooke Boothby's granddaughter is particularly fine.

A132 East Sutton, Kent. Edmund Filmer (died 1810) by Edward Griffin. The tomb is inscribed 'E Griffin, Regent St, London'.

A133 East Sutton, Kent. Dorothea (died 1793) and Beversham Filmer (died 1805) installed by Edmund Filmer. The tomb is inscribed 'J Golden FT'.

A134 Long Buckby, Northants. To Cilena l'Anson Bradley (died 1726, aged 12) by John Hunt of Northampton. The tomb is inscribed 'Jno Hunt North fecit'.

A135 Newcastle Cathedral. The fine tomb to Bishop Lloyd (died 1908). The effigy is in white alabaster and carved by Pomeroy whilst the canopy was erected by Oliver and Leeson of Newcastle. The bishop is buried in Benwell. The effigy and tomb chest is in Gothic style with angel weepers at the foot of the effigy.

A136 Leigh, Worcs. Walter Devereux (died ?) and wife Elizabeth (Knightly). Carved in 1642 before his death as dates not completed. A curious monument with the two effigies in a niche with two central columns supporting the niche top. Children carved in relief in side of tomb chest.

A137 Dorchester on Thames, Oxford. A knight with crossed legs thought to be William de Valence (died in battle 1282 in Wales). He was buried at Dorchester Abbey from whence the monument was moved at the Reformation. The current commentators are reticent about the stone for this monument which may well be limestone, but the images show an alabaster-like finish. If alabaster then it could pre-date that at Gloucester but the availability of good stone this early is questionable. On the other hand it may be contemporary with the effigy at Hanbury (1340), but in Chellaston alabaster indicating a rough date for the opening of workings there. Two earlier memorials one a bishop and the other a knight with canopy are in limestone.

A138 Oxford, Christ Church Chapel. Sir George Nowers (died 1425). The effigy and tomb chest do not belong having been married in the 17th century. The stone is limestone but merits inclusion as there seems to be alabaster repairs probably carried out when the monuments were reordered. There is much debate as to the identity of the effigy but the consensus is that it is Nowers although the armour is more in keeping with late 14th century styles. One tomb chest shield displays the coat of arms of Ralph Basset of Drayton, Leics killed at Evesham in 1262.

A139 South Acre, Norfolk. Sir Edward Barkham (died 1634) and wife. He was Lord Mayor of London and wears robes over armour. There is a charnel panel with skulls. Back wall has woman holding a wreath. Attributed to the Christmas workshop.

A140 Kilkenny Ireland. An image dating from the 15th century believed to be made in Nottingham. It is of the Holy Trinity, God the Father with his hands raised, Christ and the dove of the Holy Spirit. The latter is damaged. It was found in a bricked up niche in the abbey church in the 19th century. It is reported that this is one of only ten English alabaster sculptures found in Ireland. Of the other nine one is lost and two are Clongowes Wood College, Co Kildare. The others are not known to the author but all are triptych or reredos panels. *See 'Medieval Alabasters in Ireland'* by J Hunt and P Harbison 1976. One interesting aspect is the clear duplication of a Nottingham panel in a by a local freestone carver of Ennis, Co Clare. Located in the Franciscan priory the panel was commissioned by More Ni Brien in 1470 for her husband and shows the resurrection of Christ suitably modified to show Irish weapons and dress. Like England Ireland may well have suffered from English abuse of Catholic imagery but the feeling is that alabaster purchases by Ireland were few and far between.

A141 In 1906 the Church of San Pedro at Ocaňa near Toledo was declared unsafe. The memorials were acquired by the V&A and are on display (now in room 50a). The effigy of Don Garcia de Osorio (died *circa* 1502) holds a sword in front of him and his hat has the shell of St James or the order of Santiago de Compostela. The carver is most certainly Spanish, possibly Castilian and the alabaster from Catalonia. At his feet there is a woman in mourning resting on a helmet. This a paired with the effigy of a lady identified as Dona Maria de Perea, the wife of Don Garcia. She wears a simple dress and holds a rosary as symbols of piety. There is a bedesman in the folds of the dress.

A142 London, Westminster Abbey. A tomb chest for Elizabeth Cecil (died 1597) the wife of Robert Cecil who erected the monument. Alabaster with black marble top.

A143 Kemberton, Shrops. The church was built in 1882 and is reported to have a pulpit of Penarth alabaster and Irish red and green marble.

A144 Preston, Holderness, Yorks. In 1880 during restoration a number of pieces of a retable were found hidden under an arch in the nave together with a partial statue of a bishop. The pieces were sufficiently complete for it to be determined that they came from a retable of nine panels depicting the resurrection, the nativity, the Virgin Mary and a priest at an altar. These are preserved in the church. The consensus is that these are mid-15th century Nottingham.

A145 Castle Donington pulpit made in 1877 from incised slabs.

Photo: the author.

A146 Bingham, Notts. A fragment of a knight in Chellaston alabaster. Local history claims this is Sir Thomas de Bingham (died 1438). It is not listed by Gardner.

A147 Kingston upon Hull, Yorks. Believed to be Robert de Selby (died 1390) and wife. This identification is by no means certain and Gardner failed to list it. Sally Badham did a fine summary of the origins in CMS 'Monument of the Month' September 2012. The lady is likened to that at West Tanfield (G31). The date of the Hull tomb rules out it being a member of the de la Pole family proposed in some quarters.

A148 Whittlesford, Cambs. Fragments of a 15th century reredos panels now under glass in the nave. These were discovered *circa* 1872–1875 buried in the chancel walls where they were hidden during the Reformation.

A149 Norwich, Norfolk. St Peter Mancroft church. A fragment of a Nottingham alabaster panel depicting a group of female saints. These are believed to be Saints Magdelene, Hildegarde, Justine, Ursula, Margaret, Helen, Ethereda and Barbara.

A150 Mabe, Falmouth, Cornwall. Fragments of a medieval reredos which appears to be Nottingham. Said to have been found buried in the sedilia in 1869 and reported on by Rev W Iago in JRIC, Vol4, 1871. Subjects include St Erasmus and the flagellation of Christ but there are other interpretations. The suggestion that the alabaster is Watchet is questionable. Whole or fragments of panels also exist at Lostwithiel (St Bartholomew), Madron (rood screen), Cury, St Michael's Mount, St Neot and Treslothan (nativity) – all in Cornwall.

A151 Leicester, St Margaret. Bishop Penny (died *circa* 1496 but may be as late as 1519). It was noted by Leland in the 1520s but without any observation as to date. This was moved and restored in the late 19th century. It was not listed by Gardner. An alabaster effigy on a modern freestone tomb chest but was once covered by a canopy. Identified, wrongly, by Burton in 1622, as the marble tomb to Bishop John Middleton (died 1588).

A152 London, the Church of the White Friars. Robert Mascall, Bishop of Hereford (died 1416) at Hereford. Mascall was Carmelite friar from Ludlow and once confessor to Henry IV.

A153 Thornhill, Kirklees, Yorks. Sir Thomas Saville (died 1449) and wife Margaret. Weepers. There is a 1322 knight shown cross-legged which is not alabaster.

A154 Kidderminster, Worcs. Joyce Beauchamp (died 1473) uncertain material.

A155 Oakley, Hants. Hugh Wareham (died 1520) and wife Maryon (Colles). Alabaster effigies on a restored tomb chest. She wears a gable hood. The date is uncertain as this was not found by Gardner.

A156 Dorchester, Dorset. A reredos presented by Miss Ashley in memory of the Earl of Shaftsbury according to a brass plaque on the wall. The carving is based on the *Last Supper* of Leonardo da Vinci in Milan.

A157 Dijon, France. Philip the Bold (died 1404) but tomb may have been constructed as early as 1389. The tomb may also be to his wife Margaret. The tomb was dismantled in 1793 during the French revolution and remade in 1823–1825. The records of Claus Sluter show that two artisans took 272 days to polish the 40 figures in the arcades around the tomb chest. The current alabaster is white and most likely to be Chellaston. The original may well have been Chellaston too as the tomb is near contemporary with the Fécamp purchase. The current tomb is partial stained both the cloak and the cushion being in rich colour. Only 37 of the figures are present and 3 can be found in museums.

A158 Ely Cathedral, Cambs. Dr Hodge-Mill (died 1853), canon of Ely. A copper effigy on an alabaster, marble and serpentine tomb. The symbolism on the tomb reflects his time in India, as of the two figures, one is Asian and the other a student.

Dean Hodge-Mill (1853). Photo: the author.

A159 Turvey, Beds. Lewis Mordaunt, 3rd Baron Mordaunt (died 1601). A black slab with a painted alabaster pall.

A160 Bedale, Yorks. Sir Bryan FitzAlan and wife Muriel. She is in limestone and until recently his was considered to be in the same stone. In some quarters (Pevsner and many others) this is suggested as being alabaster but the CMS County Guide disagrees. Sir Bryan possibly died *circa* 1306 which makes it a bit early as it would pre-date both the Hanbury and Gloucester tombs. However it is included here just in case.

A161 Chenies, Bucks. The private Bedford Chapel attached to Chenies Manor House (M11 on 'The Heraldry of the Bedford Chapel'). Lady Bridget Hussey (died 1600) transferred from Watford Herts, St Mary's. Mural monument to Bridget Countess of Bedford who died 1600. The tomb is of alabaster and black marble but shows signs of being much later. The tomb contains an effigy of Lady Elizabeth Russell who died 1611. It has been suggested that this is a Stone monument dating from 1619 – *see* M10 but is unlikely as Margaret Whinney is clear that it has the features of the Isaac James workshop. Moved from Watford, St Mary in 1907. Associated with the Norris tomb in Westminster.

A162 Weekley, Northants. Edward Montagu chief justice (died 1601) and wife Elizabeth (died 1618). Recumbent effigies. The columns are freestanding outside the tomb chest. Decorated pilasters enclosing niches with shields.

A163 Bunbury, Cheshire. Sir George Beeston (died 1602) – a captain under Howard of Effingham.

A164 Bristol Cathedral, Somerset. Sir Richard Berkeley (died 1602).

A165 Chenies, Bucks. The private Bedford Chapel attached to Chenies Manor House (M12 on 'The Heraldry of the Bedford Chapel'). Anne Russell, Countess of Warwick (died 1603) wife of William Lord Russell, but may not have been constructed till 1619. This was moved from Watford, St Mary in 1907.

A166 London, Westminster Abbey. Princesses Sophia and Mary, daughters of James I (died *circa* 1606–1608). Sophia is in a crib and Mary behind resting on one elbow.

A167 Broxbourne, Herts. Sir Henry Cock (died 1609) and wife. Henry lies on one side while his wife lies recumbent on her back.

A168 Leyton, Essex. Sir Michael Hick(e)s (died 1612) and wife Elizabeth (died 1635) in mourning habit and holding a book. There is a suggestion that this was tiered monument but was moved *circa* 1859 and rebuilt along one wall as an effigial tomb. The attribution to Bartholomew Atye relates to a later monument of 1680 in the same church.

A169 Windsor, St George Chapel, Berks. Dr Giles Thomson, Bishop of Gloucester (died 1612).

A170 Keele, Staffs. William Sneyd (died 1613) and wife. Some damage.

A171 Spare

A172 Wednesbury, Staffs. Richard Parkes (died 1613) and wife. May be likeness as he has receding hair and a Greek nose. Square inscription panels and figures. Pevsner says the date is 1618. The carving is unusual as the robes show no sign of being draped giving the effigies a plump feature.

A173 Thornhill, Yorks. Sir George Saville (died 1622) and wife Ann.

A174 Lincoln Cathedral. Dean Butler (died 1894). Alabaster and red marble.

A175 Luton, Beds. St Mary's was restored from 1865. A marble and alabaster pulpit was installed by G Street in 1881 along with a mosaic reredos in an alabaster frame.

A176 Chetnole, Dorset. An alabaster reredos modified by Dr A Salviati *circa* 1865.

A177 London, Westminster. A statue to Sister Concordia Scott of Minster Abbey, Kent. The statue of a virgin and child was installed in 1971, the original, carved 1377, having disappeared several centuries ago. The alabaster appears to be calcite.

A178 London, Westminster. Arthur Penrhyn Stanley (died 1881), dean and wife Augusta (died 1876). The monument installed in 1884.

A179 London, Westminster. Edward Talbot, 8th Earl of Shrewsbury (died 1618), and wife Jane (Cuthbert) – died 1626. Talbot at his feet. Kneeling figure of child.

A180 London, Westminster. Sir Francis Vere (died 1609), and his brother Horace (died 1635). A very unusual tomb with the effigy lying on a rush mat with a slab above supported by four knights which contains his armour. The tomb is believed to be inspired by that of Count Engelbert II at Breda.

A181 London, Westminster. Lady St John of Bletso (died 1615. The monument originally had her two children but now only the effigy of the lady remains. This has been moved. Her head is on her right hand and she wears a ruff, stomacher and full skirt. Restored in 19th century.

A182 Gawsworth, Cheshire. Sir Edward Fitton (died 1619) and wife Anne with children.

A183 Chenies, Bucks. The private Bedford Chapel attached to Chenies Manor House (M8 on 'The Heraldry of the Bedford Chapel'). Frances Charles Hastings 9th Duke of Bedford (died 1891).

A184 Chenies, Bucks. The private Bedford Chapel attached to Chenies Manor House (M10 on 'The Heraldry of the Bedford Chapel'). Lady Elizabeth Long (died 1611). Believed to be moved from St Mary, Watford in 1906.

A185 Temple Balsall, Warwick. Lady Anne Holbourn (died 1663) restorer of Templar's church.

A186 Oxford, St John's Chapel. Richard Baylie (died 1667). Moved in the 1843 but restored in 1949. Believed to be likeness.

A187 Spare

A188 Sturton le Steeple, Notts. Dame Frances Earle (died 1687) known locally as The White Lady. A life-size statue in a framed doorway with side columns holding a mural entablature. The church was damaged by fire on the 24th Feb 1901 and the statue shows the effect of heat. The lady clutches a shroud and stands facing forward in Roman-like pose. The material is uncertain and some commentators state that the statue is in marble but Cornelius Brown identified the statue as alabaster in 1896. Moved in 1870.

A189 Ashprington, Devon. John Kelland (died 1679) and wife Susanna (died 1648). Poss only the upper cornice is alabaster. The monument is attributed to John Weston active 1711 to 1730 despite English Heritage listing the monument as 1692. The Royal Albert Memorial Museum has part removed in 1965 which shows The Last Judgement.

A190 Great Milton, Oxford. Joanna Meetkerke (died 1695).

A191 Wield, Hants. William Wallop (died ?) and wife Margery. A tiered monument.

A192 London, Westminster. Mary Kendall (died 1708) shown kneeling in alabaster. The effigy is in a niche supported by two columns more like a statue. The carver is not known but probably London based.

A193 Burley, Rutland. Lady Charlotte Finch (died 1813) who had been governess to the children of George III. A kneeling statue in marble with an alabaster pedestal.

A194 Gloucester Cathedral. Bishop Charles Ellicot (died 1905). A splendid effigial tomb with a Renaissance effigy and a retro tomb chest in Gothic style. The tomb chest is in Fauld alabaster but the effigy is uncertain. The tomb chest shows the cusped niches and bedesmen of the early 16th century work of the Trent Valley carvers.

A195 Eversley, Hants. Dame Marianne Cope of Bramshill House (died 1862).

A196 Deene, Northants. James Thomas Brudenell, 7th Earl of Cardigan of the 11th Hussars (died 1868). Reported as 'alabaster and coloured marbles, brass fillet, bronze end reliefs and corner seahorses'. Placed in line with the earlier alabaster monument (G128).

A197 Lichfield Cathedral. Bishop Selwyn (died 1880). He had strong connections with New Zealand. In the Forman records of Chellaston there is an entry dated 1st June 1880 which states 'Mr Nichols of London came about a block of alabaster for the late Bishop Selwyn's tomb in Lichfield Cathedral'.

A198 Worcester Cathedral. Earl of Dudley (died 1888). Alabaster tomb chest.

A199 Corsham, Wilts. Lady Eleanor Methuen (died 1958) but the tomb dated 1970. A gifted artist there is a depiction of her with a sketch pad.

A200 Bradford Cathedral, Yorks. A list of vicars from 1293 marble tablet in an alabaster frame. The tablet is surmounted by a statue in a Gothic pose.

A201 Woodchester Priory, Gloucs. William Leigh (died 1873) in the robes of St Gregory holding model of a church in his hands.

A202 Chichester, Sussex. Cathedral. Bishop Richard Durnford (died 1896). A fine tomb with an effigy in Fauld alabaster.

A203 Charlton House, Surrey. The 1612 chimney pieces are made from alabaster with some plaster work in lower status rooms. In particular the statues of Vulcan and Venus in the principal room have been admired. The carver is currently unknown.

A204 Saffron Walden, Essex. A panel recovered from a garden wall of the old vicarage in the 1900s. The panel is rare depicting Christ the Majesty. *See also* St Mary, Saffron Walden.

A205 Saffron Walden, Essex. A second panel fragment recovered also from a garden wall of the old vicarage in the 1900s. The panel is shows a centurion and is most likely a crucifixion. There is a label which would have held the line 'Vere filius Dei erat iste' (truly this was the Son of God).

A206 Eaton Bishop, Hereford. Lady Irva Keenan Pulley (1942).

A207 Sudeley Castle, Gloucs. Queen Dowager Katherine Parr (Seymour) died 1548. *See also* D9/73. A replacement tomb constructed in 1860 with a marble effigy and alabaster tomb chest in Gothic style.

A208 Ingham, Norfolk. Sir Roger de Bois (died 1300) and wife Margaret (died 1315), but the style indicates that the tomb was created some 30 to 40 years later. This 14th century tomb was not found by Gardner but is clearly identified as alabaster by the Stalham, Suttin and Ingham historians. They also claim that it was painted and produced an artist's impression of the tomb in the 14th century.

A209 Winchester, Hants. Bishop Samuel Wilberforce (died 1873). The tomb has six kneeling angels in alabaster.

A210 Oxford, St Aldate's. John Noble (died 1522) official to the archdeacon. The ancient description suggests that his head was tonsured but this is not immediately seen. The tomb was described by John Henry Parker in 1838. The tomb chest shows Trent Valley features with bedesmen and weepers. Sally Badham says that the tomb chest also shows kneeling figures of Noble's parents reciting from their Book of Hours an extract of which is inscribed on the ledge above.

A211 Bodiam, Robertsbridge and Arundel, Sussex. It is clear that a tomb was commissioned for Sir John Dallingridge (died 1408) in 1416 comprising a tomb chest and effigy and possibly intended for Robertsbridge Abbey, Sussex. This was made in London by carver John Petit whose poor delivery record was subject to litigation. It has been suggested that this would have been freestone and that the alabaster torso later found was a replacement from the Midlands. This is confused by *Sussex Archaeological Collections* 147 (2009, Nigel Saul) claim that a tomb was obtained by the FitzAlans for reuse *circa* 1430–1476 which they attribute to Richard Dallingridge (died 1471). However, they also suggest (page 7) that the tomb was a reject snapped up by the FitzAlans making the connection with that made for John in the 1420s, a strong one. The tomb in Arundel is currently without effigy but displays panelled sides with lozenges and shield. It is possible the effigy was the substandard item which was abandoned on transfer. On the other hand there is scant evidence for the tomb ever reaching Robertsbridge and may well have been intended for Arundel all along. There is much confusion about this. The torso currently resides in Bodiam Castle.

A212 Worksop, Notts. Lord Thomas Furnival (the Hasty, died 1366). A much mutilated torso once in Worksop Priory. Described by Gough but may have errors.

A213 Worksop, Notts. Lord Thomas Nevil (died 1406). A much mutilated torso once in Worksop Priory. Described in *Nottinghamshire History (1875) Worksop and the Dukeries*.

A214 Spare

A215 V&A Museum, London. Don Garcia de Osorio (died after 1502). His wife died in 1499. Formerly in the San Pedro de Ocana in Toledo, Spain and moved when that church became unsafe *circa* 1906.

A216 Rochester, Kent. Bishop John de Sheppey (died 1360). This was hidden and only discovered in the 19th century. Not found by Gardner and possibly in store at the time. Lawrence Stone has compared this with the freestone tomb of Bishop Ralph at Wells.

A217 Thorpe Mandeville, Northants. Thomas Kirton (died 1601) and wife Mary or Margaret (died 1597). Twelve children on tomb chest.

A218 Hereford Cathedral. Dean Richard Dawes (died 1867). A white marble effigy on a fauld alabaster tomb chest. A number of other marbles are used.

A219 Gnosall, Staffs. Two unknown tombs *circa* 15th century. One is small and may be a heart burial.

A220 Kinver, Staffs. Edward Grey (died 1528) and wives. A tomb chest without effigy. An etching in the William Library in Staffordshire Archives dated 1846 shows this tomb.

A221 Kinver, Staffs. John Hampton (died 1471). A much damaged tomb whose identity is suspect.

A222 Glenfield, Leics. Dame Joan Foulshurst (born 1370). A damaged effigy formerly in the old church at Glenfield and moved to the new church in 1952.

A223 Eastchurch, Kent. Gabriel Livesey (died 1622). Effigy.

A224 Shenfield, Essex. Elizabeth Robinson (died 1652) in her shroud with her baby in her arms. A recumbent effigy resting on one elbow with the baby cradled. An extraordinary carving in almost Baroque style. Carved by Thomas Burman. There is a charnel house built into the tomb chest sides.

A225 Hothfield, Kent. Effigy, unknown. In alabaster currently undated but has ruff possibly early 17th century.

A226 Theydon Mount, Essex. A tiered mural to Thomas Smyth (died 1577) and wife Philippa. Children below. His tabard and helm were in the church until the latter was stolen. The tomb has a shallow coffered arch, two ionic columns and two black obelisks.

A227 Fryerning, Essex. Effigy. Sir William Petre (died 1572) and second wife Anne (Browne). Rush mat. Cornelius Cure.

A228 Blackmore, Essex. Thomas Smythe (died 1594) and wife. Rolled mat.

A229 Patshull church, Wolverhampton, Staffs. Sir John Astley (died 1532) and wife Joan Orely. This was omitted from the Gardner's list. It is attributable to Richard Parker. The church is in the care of the Church Conservancy Trust. The tomb chest has round headed niches filled with figures and unusually figures at the corners. This has been grouped with the 1687 marble mural of Sir Richard Astley.

A230 Sheffield Cathedral. George Talbot, 4th Earl of Shrewsbury (died 1538) and wives Ann Hastings (died 1520) and Elizabeth Walker (died 1567). George specified that he should be buried without any pomp and his tomb erected by Elizabeth *circa* 1560–1565. Attributable to Richard Parker. Feet on Talbot. There are similarities to the Spencer tomb at Great Brington,

Northants.

A231 Etwall. Derbys. Sir John Port (died 1541) and two wives Jane FitzHerbert (died 1527) and Margaret Trafford. Bayliss attributes this to Richard Parker. Really a tabletop. English Heritage says that slab has a central band across the middle and a raised border. Llewellyn suggests this band was left due to structural weaknesses in the slab material. There are a small number of monuments with the centre section marked by a pillar or band.

A232 Morley Derbys. Katherine Sacheverell (died 23/8/1543) wife of Thomas Babington and daughter of Henry Babington. Bayliss attributes to Richard Parker.

A233 Boston (St Botolph), Lincs. Knight unknown. Believed moved from St John's Hospital, Boston. Gothic monument in recess. Four arcades with angels under an ogee arc with crocketted pinnacles. Much restored and re-cut in 1850. Feet on lion. Chain collar with Maltese cross pendant. Sword is an 1850 addition. The hands are vertical which is very unusual for the date.

A234 Saxilby, Lincs. Knight, possibly Sir Ralph d'Aubeney (died *circa* 1378) and wife Alice Montague. Or it may be Sir Giles d'Aubeney (died 1386) and his wife Alianore. Brought from the chapel at North Ingleby after it fell into disuse. Badly mutilated with much loss of limbs but the coat-armour shows the d'Aubeney heraldry. Conserved in 1993–1994. Bascinet with aventail and feet on lion.

A235 Clifton, Notts. Alice Clifton (Nevill) wife of Sir Gervaise Clifton. No inscription. A picture appears in Nottingham History by George fellows (1907).

A236 Stonton, Wyville. Edmund Brudenell (died 1590). A fine effigy with his child as a chrisom on its own chest on the right side (*see also* Exton Rutland).

A237 Exeter Cathedral. Judge John Doddridge (died 1628). Known as the 'sleeping judge' owing to his habit of closing his eyes whilst sitting.

G1 Wantage, Berks. Knight, and lady, Sir William Fitzwarren or Fitzwaryn (died 1361) and wife Amicia. Knight with legs crossed but not in crusader form as his arms are crossed on his chest. Feet on dog. Lady has frilled cap. It reported that the effigy carries a garter. Gardner suggests that this effigy is by a local carver, but that still leaves the problem of the transport of alabaster in the rough.

G2 Bunbury, Cheshire. Knight, Sir Hugh Calverley commander in the French wars (died 1394). The tomb has empty weeper niches and had iron railings (the tomb currently has railings which may be modern). Calf badges on jupon in relief, carved bascinet band. Calverley was a close companion of Ralph Basset and a mercenary of some repute. He also had a friendship with Sir Robert Knolles who was his executor and who almost certainly place the contract for the tomb in Bunbury, the Knolles armorial alternating with that of Calverley on the tomb chest. Stothard observed the monument in 1817 and recorded much coloured paint remaining but the armour was left unpainted. The sabatons have been repaired in plaster. Blair gives a good description of this tomb in http://www.bunbury.org.uk/papers/sir_hugh_frameset.html

G3 Barthomley, Cheshire. Knight, Sir Robert Foulshurst (died 1389). Tomb chest with angels which may not belong. The angels are standing holding shields and extended wings with serrated edges a feature not thought to be used for another 20 years. SS collar and orle.

G4 Greystoke, Cumbria. Knight, William the Good, 2nd Baron of Greystoke 1320–1358. Canopy (gablette) at head decorated with shields. The effigy is short about 38 inches long. The armour shows a camail and bascinet with feet on a dog. The gablette was a feature of the Trent Valley school but is too early for Chellaston.

G5 Durham. Bishop Thomas Hatfield (died 1381). Gardner likens this to that of William of Hatfield (G30) which has been attributed to John Orchard. Borders on chasuble. Durham accounts mention alabaster being 'imported' in 1372 and 1380 (but *see* G7). St John Hope suggests this is London carved. The tomb is unique in that the canopy contains the bishop's throne which was considered to once be the highest is Christendom. The British Library has a 1778 drawing to be found as shelf mark MS 15538.

G6 Durham. Knight. Ralph, Lord Nevill, the 1st Earl Westmorland (died 1367) and Margaret his first wife on the left of him and on the right Joan his second wife (but she is buried in Lincoln). Somewhat defaced. St John Hope suggests this is London carved.

G7 Durham. John Lord Nevill of Raby (died 1388) son of G6 and wife Matilda (or Maud). John Nevill was donor of the shrine and of the reredos. Examination of the 'alabaster imports' mentioned in G5 indicates that John Nevill was a major benefactor of the cathedral paying £200 for the 'new work in marble and alabaster' to go beneath the shrine of St Cuthbert which was boxed up in London and shipped via the Tyne. In respect of the reredos, this too was made in London for 200 marks (£133) and shipped via the Tyne in 1380. Reported as damaged in 1869.

G8 Layer Marney, Essex. The church of Layer Marney Towers. Sir William Marney (b.1370, d.1414). Son of Robert

Marney (died1400). The accepted date is 1360 but is likely to be much later. This tomb is believed to have been moved and shows repairs to the left leg and one foot which appears to be the classic casein filler. Arms on jupon. *See also* X3. John Bayliss maintains this monument dates from 1414 and is a product of the Trent Valley workshops.

G9 Gloucester Cathedral. King Edward II died 20th September 1327, but monument not erected until 1328–1330. What distinguishes the effigy is that it has a potential likeness to the king. The king's head is supported by angels believed to be the first depiction of this form and, due to this, it is considered that the tomb of John of Eltham (G18) is by the same carver. The tomb chest is in Purbeck marble and the canopy of Cotswold limestone (some say Caen). An observer comments that the canopy was influenced by the great reredos in Exeter Cathedral which is contemporary with the Gloucester monument. *See also* G10. The alabaster is clearly from the Staffordshire or Derbyshire beds and the tomb is unlikely to have been carved in London owing to the transport issues but on site in Gloucester, the monument being contemporary with the rebuilding of the abbey. The monument was erected at the behest of Edward III. Whilst not involved in Edward I's death he was concerned that a cult following had emerged around the tomb at Gloucester which he thought may be a focus for the disaffected followers of Mortimer. By erecting the effigy of Edward II in the 'new' material he 'took charge' of the cult and was able to curtail its actions. Edward's itinerary for 1328 shows that he stopped over at Tutbury Castle on the 3rd January when he may well have been shown alabaster carving. The weepers are placed against a dark substance which is mastic or dark plaster. The whole matter of Edward III's accession is complex. Edward II was deposed and imprisoned in Berkeley Castle and Roger Mortimer with Edward III's mother, Queen Isabella, as consort assumed regency with Edward III held in thrall. Edward II died and was buried with some pomp in Gloucester on the 20th December 1327. A tradition has it that he was tortured with a poker but this has largely been discounted and smothering is most likely to have been used. Edward III was not permitted to erect a memorial and later moved against Mortimer capturing him at Nottingham in Nov 1330 and arranging for his execution. The coincidences of Edward III's coronation and the erection of the tomb at Gloucester are noted.

G10 Tewkesbury, Gloucs. Knight and lady. Baron, Sir Hugh Despenser (died 1348) and Elizabeth Montague (died 1359). Knight in contemporary round-topped bascinet with camail and with feet on lion. Lady in framed headdress with tasselled cushion. This curious headdress is sometimes called a nebule or nebuly (*see* Appendix E). Kemp claims the tomb design was based on that of Edward II in Gloucester (G9). The monument has a magnificent decorated canopy with receding tiers of cusped arches and pinnacles. This, like that at Gloucester (G9), is believed to be influenced by the great reredos in Exeter. Although the alabaster appears to be Chellaston the carving does not appear to be Trent Valley. In view of the close support given to Edward III by Hugh Dispenser the tomb is likely to be the work of London or the royal masons especially as in some quarters there is an identification of this tomb with that for Edward II at Gloucester. The face may well be a likeness. Elizabeth remarried but chose to be buried with her first husband. The commissioning of the tomb therefore may be closer to the death of her than Hugh himself. The Despenser's have a bad press. Hugh's father, also Hugh, was executed in Hereford by Mortimer and Queen Isabella in 1326 due to his support for Edward II but his body was dismembered and some parts scattered. What may well be the main parts of his body were discovered in 2008 in the village of Abbey Hulton, Staffs in 2008 on the site of Hulton Abbey. The reason for this remote burial has not been determined. The Despensers were restored to the Baronetcy in 1338.

G11 Berkeley, Gloucs. Knight and lady. Thomas, 8th Lord Berkeley (died 1361) and wife. Thomas had the care of Edward II when he suffered his fate in 1327. The lady has a framed frilled headdress. The knight wears a hauberk reaching to the middle of the thighs with long sleeves, and gussets of mail at the armpits and under the elbows. Over it is a slightly shorter jupon, tight-fitting, and embroidered in front with the Berkeley Arms. A pointed bascinet has a small camail chain attached by a cord running through staples on the bascinet and the plate edging of the camail. The shoulders are further protected by epaulières of two plates; the arms by brassards and vambraces of cuir bouilli, with folded guards for the elbows. The hands are restored and are represented with gauntlets formed of a broad plate to the knuckles. The hands are also in the wrong position being vertical instead of horizontal. The legs are cased in cuisses and jambs of cuir bouilli, the latter being laced up tightly on the inner side. The genouillères are of plate, very convex and rounded, and feet have articulated sollerets of plate with rowel spurs strapped under the foot and buckled across the instep. A bawdric, handsomely jewelled in quatrefoils, encircles the hips, and is buckled and knotted on the right side; to it is fastened a misericorde with fluted pommel and plain cross-hilt. On the left side hangs a long sword with cross-hilt and pommel of very handsome decorative Gothic work. Railings removed 1864. This monument was commissioned by the widow (of Lord Cobham *see* G211) in 1364 and is linked to Lingfield.

G12 Winchester, Hants. Bishop William of Eddington (died 1366). Purbeck marble tomb chest and alabaster effigy. Fylfot (swastika) pattern on amice and maniple. Broken angels. The hands are missing, but were formerly in benediction and not in prayer. Chancellor under Edward III and offered the post of Archbishop of Canterbury, but declined and died shortly after.

G13 Hereford. Knight Sir Richard Pembridge (died 1375). Garter on left knee, crest of feathers. Reported similar to Lord Cobham's tomb (G211). In Hereford there is a spare wooden right leg displayed on an adjacent column. It is reputed to have been made when the right leg on the effigy was damaged but included the garter which is wrong and so could not be used. His will of the 31st May 1368 specified that his body be interred in Hereford and set out the details of the tomb but this has yet to be located by the author. Most likely to be a London workshop.

G14 Canterbury, Kent. Archbishop John Stratford (died 1348). One of the first ecclesiastical effigies in alabaster. Canopy over head, richly embroidered mitre, stole with double cushion. Page 222 of Weever refers. Has been damaged.

G15 Canterbury, Kent. Archbishop William Courtenay (or Courtney) died 1396 at Maidstone. Cushion with angels. It is reported that William Courtney is also buried at Maidstone, Kent. The face is sculptured and may well be a likeness. It is said that the carver was London based – *see also* G90.

G16 Canterbury, Kent. Joane, Lady Mohun (died 1390). This effigy is in the undercroft. The inscription is in French being 'pour dieu priez por l'ame Johane Burwaschs que fut Dame de Mohun'. Reported as being defaced by workmen who used the undercroft as a material store.

G17 Leicester, Leics. Believed to be Mary de Bohun first wife of Henry IV and mother of Henry V and as such it is suggested that the effigy was once in St Mary's College, but when this was suppressed in 1548 the tomb was moved to the chapel of Trinity Hospital. It is badly damaged and is dressed as a widow which makes the identification with Mary de Bohun doubtful. Local observers suggest that the effigy is one Dame Mary Hervey an early benefactor of the hospital.

G18 London, Westminster Abbey. Prince John of Eltham, Earl of Cornwall (died 1337) but effigy dates from 1340. Coronet on bascinet, cross-legged with feet on lion, short surcoat, cushion with angels. The tomb chest is penetrated by nine cusp-headed arches on each side with figures representing kings and queens with shields under. The canopy was demolished in 1760 (or possibly 1776). Mark Dowling page 116 has a drawing of monument dated 1723 and so does Crossley page 57. Considered to be the same carver as for Edward II (G9). The detail behind its creation supports this belief. John was the brother of Edward III and much like him. John died in Perth in 1337 during a campaign in Scotland in uncertain circumstances which gave rise to rumours from the Bruce camp that Edward had him murdered. The tomb is Westminster was commissioned probably to dampen these rumours and Edward certainly made large donations to the Abbey for its upkeep for some 30 years. This tomb was once identified as belonging to Henry Holland due to a misreading of the heraldic inscriptions.

G19 London, Westminster Abbey. Prince William of Windsor (or Hatfield) and Princess Blanche of the Tower (infant children of Edward III) died in 1348 and 1342 respectively. Contracted for by John Orchard in 1376. Small effigies 1ft 6i nches long.

G20 London, Westminster Abbey. Archbishop Simon Langham, cardinal (died 1376 but effigy may date from 1390). Angels at head, dogs at feet with little bells on collars (*see* X19). Langham died in Avignon but his bones were collected and reburied at Westminster. The monument had a canopy but was removed in 1714. A statue of Mary Magdelene former stood at his feet with his cardinal's hat suspended above. Both were probably lost at Reformation.

G21 East Harling, Norfolk. Knight and lady possibly John de Harling (died 1392). Framed headdress and unicorn on jupon. Feet on lion head on helm without crest. Purbeck marble tomb chest under cusp arch. Brass inscription mentioning a later Robert Harling *circa* 1435 which probably relates to the tomb chest. This can be likened to the tomb in Swine, Yorks (G189).

G22 Ashton, Northants. Knight. John de Herteshull

G23 Spratton, Northants. Knight, Sir John Swinford. SS collar (first effigy to display one), jupon laced at side. The pendant is a knot reminiscent of a hangman's knot and was recorded by Hartshorne. No other example of this exists. There is a fine decorated hip belt and the mail hauberk protrudes below the leather jupon.

G24 Willoughby on the Wolds, Notts. Judge Sir Richard Willoughby, chief justice (died 1362). Houppelande with high collar. He is clad in the robes of a judge considered so good that it was used as an illustration in Stothard's *Monumental Effigies* and in Fairholt's *Costume in England*. He has his head on a cushion supported by angels which are badly damaged. The head has side ringlets but he is shown bald on the top with a later plaster repair. This may well be a likeness but the date is more in keeping with 1410. The houppelande is secured around the waist with a decorated belt which folded over to hang in front. He does not have his hands in prayer and the right hand is raised as if taking an oath. There three effigies of stone here dating from the 13th century and from 1325. The chapel was reordered in 1984 and the tomb chest may not belong.

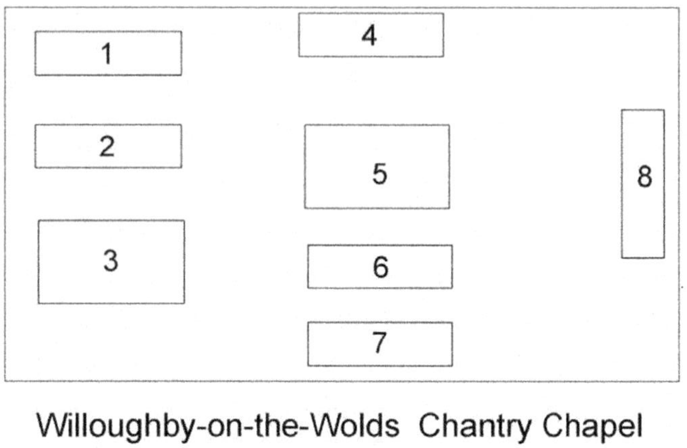

No's 1, 2 & 3 are 12th century and early 13th century freestone effigies. No 4 is Sir Richard Willoughby G24 (died 1362). No 5 is Sir Hugh de Willoughby G138 (died 1448) and his wife Margaret Freville (died 1493). No 6 is a slab to Isabel Foljambe first wife of GNP67. No 7 is Sir Richard de Willoughby GNP67 (died 1369 but tomb dates from 1395) son of G24. Drawing by the author

G25 Strelley, Notts. Knight Sir Sampson Strelley (died 1391) and Lady Elizabeth. Mail and plain collar, holds horn with Saracen head crest. Coronet with cauls, crespine with hands clasped. This was constructed 1405–1410 by his wife Elizabeth nee Hercy. The armour is of the early 15th century vintage with a 'pot' sheathed dagger and sword to left hand side. The head of Elizabeth shows the side trussed hair of the early 15th century heavily bejewelled and a coronet. This is considered unique. The dress is an open mantle held by a cord and with jewelled fastenings. They hold hands. Other tombs – an arch from the same carver as one in Wollaton church.

G26 Wells, Somerset. Bishop Ralph de Salopia or of Shrewsbury (died 1363), Bishop of Bath and Wells. This monument was moved *circa* 1546. This monument has similarities with that of Bishop Stratford (G14, 1348) and to Bishop Sheppey of Rochester (died 1360). The latter is reported as freestone but has been identified as alabaster and was rediscovered *circa* 1825 in an alcove. It can be assumed that these are likely to be London carved. The effigy in Chellaston alabaster sits on a modern plinth but the slab has an embattled edge. Much graffiti. Appears to be wearing gloves with a symbol on the back. Bishop's staff. Feet on playful puppies. The mitre is oddly hinged and has similarities to that of Bishop Harewell (G27). The tomb is covered by CMS 'Monument of the Month' September 2015.

Photo: Stephanie Grimley 2015.

G27 Wells Cathedral, Somerset. Bishop John Harewell (died 1386). Hares at feet in a pun on his name. In bishop's robes with staff. Harewell was treasurer and chancellor to the Black Prince during his rule over Aquitaine 1362 to 1372. Has a hinged mitre which is clearly a copy of that on G27. The tomb chest may well be a replacement as Frederick Crossley claimed that there exists a couchant alabaster lion, one of four, which once held Harewell's tomb. In 1921 this was owned by a Dr Philip Nelson and is shown on page 163 of Crossley's book. The use of such supports for English tomb slabs has no precedent. The Nelson lion has been in possession of the V&A since 1926.

The hares at the foot of Bishop Harewell's tomb 1386. Photo: Stephanie Grimley 2015.

G28 Hanbury, Staffs. Knight Sir Henry de Hanbury 1340. Gardner says this cross-legged effigy dates from 1300 and is John de Hanbury but this is disputed by Cheetham although in some places he is known to agree. Brian Harris in 2006 repeated the date as 1303 and stated the sword has an inscribed date of 1580. To add to the confusion Edward Richardson states that the effigy cannot be later than 1240. Brian Harris also says the alabaster came from Chellaston but without any documentary proof and he may well have been talking about the sword. All agree that this is the first (non-royal) effigy in alabaster but the date and alabaster source is still being debated. The knight has a mail, surcoat and shield and with legs crossed. He is in the act of drawing (or sheathing) a sword. Head on cushion with angels. The style is very like a crusader and Gardner believes it to be the work of a local stone mason. Saul gives some background to Henry. He was a justice of the Irish Bench in the 1320s and justice of the King's Bench from 1330. The normal attire of a judge is foregone in order to show Henry in armour more in keeping with his status as a lord than his calling as a judge. (A brass in Walsall to Sir William Hillary also shows a judge in armour and others in the early 14th century show that this was far from rare). This effigy remains an enigma as we do not know if it pre-dated or post dated the tomb of Edward II. If it pre-dated then there was some serious quarrying being done many years before the Duchy of Lancaster exploited the minerals. As yet we have no information to prove or disprove the date.

G29 Bures, Suffolk. St Stephen's Chapel, Bures and Colne Priory (for directions *see* G113). Knight. Thomas de Vere, 8th Earl of Oxford *circa* 1370 and formerly in Colne Priory. Colne Priory came to the de Vere family at the dissolution *circa* 1536. By the 17th century the priory building was derelict and therefore dismantled in 1736, all the De Vere tombs except for three being also broken up. The three tombs were transferred to the de Vere family house and later, in 1935–1938, to St Stephen's Chapel, Bures. *See also* G113. Time Team carried out a dig at Colne Priory which was shown on TV 3rd March 2012. This much repaired tomb is reputed to have been wider possibly holding two effigies. The de Vere arms of stars are displayed on jupon. *See also* note X28.

G30 York Minster. Prince William of Hatfield (Chase, near Doncaster) who died 1337–1344. He was the second son of Henry III and Philippa of Hainault. The date of the effigy is uncertain as it shows a boy of eight. Short embroidered jupon and long cloak. Cushion with damaged angels. Coronet. Feet on lion. Short, only 4ft 6 inches long. The date is uncertain. The monuments to his two siblings in Westminster Abbey date from 1376 and it is thought that this monument may be contemporary. It was first recorded in 1385. May also be by John Orchard. Gardner likens the tomb of Bishop Hatfield at Durham to this one in York.

G31 West Tanfield, Yorks. Knight Sir John Marmion (died 1386–1387) and his wife, Elizabeth (St Quentin, died 1400). Short but broad SS collar with loop pendant, jewelled band and feather crest, arms on jupon. The wife wears a close-fitting headdress and a mantle thrown open. Her head is supported by angels and her feet rest on a dog (but some say ape). The tomb has a wrought iron hearse surrounding it with prickets for candles at each corner and across the centre.

Figure 96 of Sally Badham's book *Seeking Salvation* shows this tomb. Sir John died in Spain. It is suggested that until 1859 the lady was on the right of the knight.

G32 Holy Trinity, Hull, Yorks. Knight Sir William de la Pole (died 1366) and Lady Katherine (Norwich, died 1381) according to Gardner and Routh. Bearded with long cloak in form of merchant's dress. Lady with veil which is shown starched which is unusual. Sally Badham offers the opinion that both William and his brother Richard can be ruled out. She offers the suggestion that the monument is to wool merchant Robert de Selby and his wife Emma and the date 1387 to 1390. This is supported by Leland who recorded Selby being there in mid-16th century. More contentious is the claim that the alabaster is Ledsham but no evidence for this is offered. There is no record of Ledsham being quarried before the late 16th century and although the monument is stained a dark honey it is most likely Chellaston. *See* CMS 'Monument of the Month' 2012. The style is not like any other and is likely to be London. Pointed ogee gable.

G33 East Shefford, Berks. Knight and lady. Sir Thomas Fettiplace (died 1442) and Beatrice (died 1447). Lady with horned headdress. Katherine Esdaile attributes this to the Trent Valley.

G34 Clifton, Beds. Knight and lady. Sir Michael Fysher. Hair curled over shoulder with heavy pauldrons. Lady with long hair and orle (may have been made 1519).

G35 Turvey, Beds. Knight and lady. Sir John Mordaunt (Bosworth and Barnet) died 1504 and wife Elizabeth (Latimer – died 1518). SS collar and mantle. Lady has long hair and an orle. Holes for brass inscription (lost). Uncertainty as to identification. It is possibly 1st Lord Mordaunt died 1562 and Elizabeth Vere (R240) who provided £60 for monument. The tomb chest is Purbeck. The tomb chest has spiral pilasters which lack the refinement of later Trent Valley tombs but the sides show lozenges with shields usually a feature of that centre of production.

G36 Windsor, Berks. Knight and lady. Sir George Manners (died 1513) and wife Anne (died 1526). She was niece of Edward IV. Weepers and angels and bedesmen. SS collar and large neck guard. Feet on unicorn. Short pediment and padded sleeves.

G37 Windsor, Berks. St George's Chapel. Knight and lady. Charles Somerset, Earl of Worcester (Elizabeth his wife died 1506). Has bronze screen of Flemish design. Garter robes and bedesmen. Loose hair and band.

G38 Aldermaston, Berks. Knight and lady. Sir George Forster (died 1533) and Lady Elizabeth Forster (died 1526). The tomb dates from 1526 as the date for Sir George is left blank. SS collar of unusual design. Cloth lining to helm. Pediment headdress and inscription. May date from 1536. Katherine Esdaile links this to the 1542 tomb in Bottesford (T7) and thereby indicates that this may be a Parker tomb. Crossley also links this to the Matthews tomb at Llandaff (GNP118) and Nash Ford (Berkshire History) links the Aldermaston tomb to that of Lord Roos in Windsor (G36) whose wife died in the same year as Lady Elizabeth.

G39 Haversham, Bucks. Lady. Lady Clinton (died 1390). Weepers in civilian dress with chaperons and angels, widow's barbe and veil.

G40 Bletchley, Bucks. Knight. Lord Grey of Wilton (died 1442). Restored *circa* 1890 (some say 1704 at the expense of Browne Willis) and not done well. SS collar and inscription.

G41 Thornton, Bucks. Knight. Believed to be John Barton (died 1437). Collar of twisted rope with a lion pendant possibly the Lion of March more in keeping with the Yorkist collar. The death of John preceded the advent of the Yorkist collar but since the carving is most probably 1468 the link to the House of York may be made then.

G42 Thornton, Bucks. Lady. Believed to be Isabella Barton (died 1457) the wife of John Barton. Flapped headdress. Isabella Barton's head rest on a cushion, held by two small figures, the one possibly remodelled in the Victorian period. Her cloak is held with a cord attached to two clasps. She wears a necklace of five cords and a cross. There are a number of rings on her hands. There are two little dogs at the feet of her skirt. The detail of her clothing is beautiful and there are traces of the original red colouring.

G43 Middle Claydon, Bucks. Lady. Margaret Gyffard or Giffard (died 1539). Pediment (gable hood) headdress, puffed sleeves. Gardner says this is Gothic but some commentators say there is Renaissance detail with Italianate baluster pilasters at the angels and with the inscription in mixed Gothic and Italianate characters. Large Gothic shields with foliated niches. Small shields on inscription panel.

G44 Over Peover, Cheshire. Knight and lady. Sir John Mainwaring (died 1410). SS collar, sacred name on bascinet, ass-headed crest, steel lined jupon. Lady with SS collar, high collar, crespine.

G45 Over Peover, Cheshire. Knight and lady. Sir Randal Mainwaring (died 1456) and wife. SS collar and orle, sacred name on bascinet, ass head crest on helm. Horned headdress. Nigel Saul claims this is the last effigy to emanate from Thomas Prentis's workshop. However, it is believed his son Robert carried on for about another decade at Chellaston before closure.

G46 Cheadle, Cheshire (Brereton chapel). Sir John Hondford. SS collar and orle. Bascinet and gorget. The local history group claim that the person depicted is Richard Bulkeley (died 1454). The latter date is in keeping with carving style.

G47 Cheadle, Cheshire (Brereton chapel). Knight. Sir John Hondford (II). SS collar. A duplicate of G46 except that there is slightly more modern armour and the effigy is bare headed. The local history group claim this to be Sir John Hondford (died 1460) attributed to G46. Again there is some justification to this claim.

G48 Macclesfield, Cheshire. Knight. Sir John Savage (I) (died 1463). SS collar.

G49 Macclesfield, Cheshire. Knight. Sir John Savage (II) *circa* 1480. Hair in roll, elaborate armour. Earwaker mentions this as a curious effigy quoting Randle Holmes's writing in 1592. The identification is not quite certain as Earwaker goes on to suggest that only the upper and lower part of the effigy is visible the middle of the trunk being obscured by part of the wall which is at variance with the effigy drawing on page 502. This observation may relate to G48.

G50 Macclesfield, Cheshire. Knight and lady. Sir John Savage (III) died 1495 and wife Catherine (Stanley). Kneeling weepers holding shields. Yorkist collar. Lady has collar with roses, butterfly headdress and hands clasped. Earwaker has a full description of this tomb on page 293 of his book. He offers the opinion that the shields had been changed at least three times.

G51 Macclesfield, Cheshire. Knight. Sir John Savage (IV) (died 1513). Chain collar and long hair.

G52 Macclesfield, Cheshire. Knight and lady. Sir John Savage (VI) (died 1527) and wife Elizabeth. SS collar. Angels and weepers. Lady has pediment headdress and padded sleeves. Inscription may be in English.

G53 Malpas, Cheshire. Knight and lady. Sir Rundle (Randle) Brereton (died 1530) and second wife Eleanor (Dutton). The local historian states that Sir Randle is buried here but that '… the tomb was ordered in his lifetime and is made from Burton alabaster'. In the original source document the word is Chellaston. The tomb inscription confirms that the tomb was constructed in 1522. Gardner claims it was badly restored by J Cookson the sculptor in 1841 (alabaster tile found in 1950 when monument moved). However, the author disagrees and this tomb remains one of the finest largely undamaged monuments of its time. Angels and weepers and bedesmen which are shown in Crossley's book page 142. Brereton was knighted for conspicuous valour in France for which he was permitted to wear the SS livery collar. Elizabeth has a long pediment headdress and dog toying with the skirt indicating fidelity. The Breretons were the parents of William Brereton executed by Henry VIII in 1536. This tomb may well have a duplicate in the Tower of

London chapel (T28).

G54 Callington, Devon. Knight. Lord Willoughby de Broke KG (died 1503). Garter robes and collar, bedesmen and feet on lion. The tomb chest has 'Honi soit qui mal y pense' inscribed.

G55 Millom, Cumb. Knight and lady. Angels with shields and kneeling weepers. Yorkist collar. Lady has flapped headdress.

G56 Barrow on Trent, Derbys. Priest unknown. Bare head and chasuble. The date for this is uncertain but the consensus is that it is 14th century

G57 Tideswell, Derbys. Knight and lady. Believed to be a Sir Thurstan (died 1423) and Margaret de Bower (although some doubt exists as to this identity). Damaged. SS collar with ring pendant and orle on bascinet. The bascinet carries the sign of Jesus of Nazareth. Sir Thurston served the Lancastrian cause at the Battle of Shrewsbury in 1403. The effigies sit on a modern tomb chest restored in 1873 by Messrs Innocent and Brown of Sheffield. The inscription is in English Gothic script and carved at the same time as the tomb chest. This is out of keeping for the period and is probably incorrect. The effigies have been moved twice. The effigy of the knight has been likened to that of Sir Thomas de Wensley (or Wendesley – GNP17) in Bakewell who was also killed at the Battle of Shrewsbury and there are similarities to that at Hoveringham (GNP68) too. The tomb chest may have been restored at the same time as A80. The lady is in a close-buttoned dress with cloak .She has a rosary round her neck and her hair is a in a first-quarter 15th century horned headdress. Both heads are on cushions supported by angels he with his feet on a lion and her on a dog.

G58 Ashbourne, Derbys. Knight and lady. Sir John Cockayne (died 1438) and wife Margaret (Longford). Angels holding shields. SS collar and orle. Horned headdress

G59 Longford, Derbys. Knight. Sir Nicholas de Longford (died 1416). SS collar and orle. IHS on bascinet. This effigy and GNP18 have been moved and lay side by side. There are three Nicholas de Longford effigies (GNP18, GNP121 and G59).

G60 Aston on Trent Derbys. Judge and lady. Possibly Thomas and Alice Hunt formerly of Aston Hall *circa* 1450. Saul and others observe that effigy is most likely of Thomas Tickhill, a lawyer whose will of 1419 requested burial in St Laurence Jewry, London. Thomas owned lands in Aston. He wears a chaperon and houppelande, hands clasped. Lady has crespine. Has Chellaston motif of angels holding shields, those at end are kneeling.

G61 Norbury, Derbys. Knight. Nicholas FitzHerbert 10th Lord Norbury (died 1473). Weepers with two wives at end one dressed as widows. Yorkist collar with boar pendant. Mailed fist on helm. Elaborate armour. His wife is shown on an incised slab in the same church. In 1662 Fuller reported that the alabaster had a blue tinge indicating the alabaster may well have come from the Fauld beds. One of these is reputed to be a death mask.

G62 Norbury, Derbys. Knight and lady. Ralph FitzHerbert, 11th Lord Norbury (died 1483) and Elizabeth (poss died 1491). Weepers and angels. Yorkist and armour with collar with Lion of March pendant. Hair curled, bedesmen perched on the lion at feet. Mailed fist on helm. Knight wears a standard of mail (neck protection). Lady wears Yorkist collar and has a butterfly headdress. The lady shows the looped cording associated with the Burton workshops. Sir Nicholas FitzHerbert's wife in a shroud is reputed to be depicted on an incised slab nearby *circa* 1491. The V&A index states that this monument has been removed into their care and can be found in sculpture room 46a.

G63 Kedleston, Derbys. Knight. Sir John Curzon *circa* 1406. SS collar. The effigy is in a recess with crocketted and ogee arch. Gardner has this as a Class IV which may be an error. Damaged with part of arms missing. Bowl crop hair and head on great helm. Hip belt may indicate a Trent Valley workshop.

G64 Youlgreave, Derbys. Knight. Thomas Cockayne (died 1488). Yorkist collar. Tomb about half normal size and may represent a youth although the effigy is in full armour. The local history group confirm that Thomas died in a duel with Thomas Burdett of Bramcote. It is said that Burdett killed his friend in error and in consequence paid for the memorial. Thomas Cockayne is shown small because he died before his father. Restored 1873.

G65 Dronfield, Derbys. Knight. Unknown. Angels holding shields. This may be Richard Barley (died 1593). Feet on dog. Has been moved and inscription lost.

G66 Radbourne, Derbys. Knight and lady. John de la Pole and wife (1491). SS collar. Lady with flapped headdress or maybe truncated cone. May now sit beneath the 1684 monument.

G67 Kedleston, Derbys. Knight and lady. Sir John Curzon (*circa* 1450) and wife Joan (Bagot). SS collar. Lady with flapped headdress or maybe truncated cone. Knight has feet on lion and head on great helm. Three seated saints and two standing angels. The face has a portrait like quality. Seventeen children. The style is Trent Valley and may be Chellaston.

G68 Sawley, Derbys. Priest. Prebendary of Lichfield, John Bothe (died 1496). Quire habit, but not mass vestments.

G69 Ashover, Derbys. Judge and lady. Thomas Babyngton of Dethick (died 1518) and Edith(a) daughter of Ralph and

Elizabeth FitzHerbert of Norbury. SS collar (although this being disputed) and long gown and script. Purse on belt and head on cushion supported by angels. The lady has a long pediment and dress held by a tasselled cord. Angels and saints some holding hands, St Catherine holding a wheel. Believed to have been commissioned during Thomas's lifetime from Burton probably in 1511 when Edith died. The monument has a palimpsest brass plate which has been inscribed on the reverse to a Robertus Prykke who was in the court of Margaret of Anjou. *See* 'Monument of the Month' of the Church Monument Society June 2010. There is also a slab to Thomas Babington and wife Isabella Dethick which may be explained by the fact that Thomas did not wish Edith's tomb opened for his body and specified he should be laid alongside under a slab. Cox gives a good description of this monument in 1875. He maintains the collar is plain made of square links and records the tomb as being painted but in recent times. Sally Badham observes that amongst Thomas's good deeds was one supporting young men destined for the priesthood.

G70 Duffield, Derbys. Knight and lady. Sir Roger Mynors (died 1536). SS collar and great helm. Lady has short pediment and padded sleeves. Bedesmen and angels holding shields. Repaired in 1732 by a friend of the Mynors family.

G71 Fenny Bentley, Derbys. Thomas Beresford (died 1573) and his wife Agnes (died 1467). A shrouded effigy with the shroud ties at head and feet. There are shrouded aspects of the children and it has been suggested that the sculptor lacked skills to carve the usual effigies. Llewellyn believes the monument to have been carved as late as 1580. Andrew Oliver in 1881 claims a slab of 1473 to the children of Thomas and Agnes Beresford which may be 1573 and cannot currently be found.

G72 Bakewell, Derbys. Tomb without effigy, possibly John Vernon (died 1477). Weepers and angels which classifies as (V).

G73 Great Cubley, Derbys. Sir Nicholas Montgomery died 1491 (grandson of GNP20) and wife Joan Delves. Tomb chest without effigy but with weepers and angels which classify this as (V). The effigies are reported as 'lost' but may have been brass. This has been identified as Harpur and Moorecock of Burton. The chest in under an arch. Daughter Isobel married Henry Sacheverell of Morley.

G74 Haccombe, Devon. Effigy of a boy about 2ft 2 inches long with angels holding a cushion, believed to be Hugh the son of Sir Hugh Courtenay died 1373–1374. The boy died whilst a student at Oxford. The torso displays a hip belt which may indicate a Trent Valley workshop.

G75 Exeter, Devon. Bishop Edmund Stafford (died 1419). He was the 19th bishop. Canopy over tomb and over head. The tomb canopy and tomb chest are believed to be a later addition to match those of Bishop Branscombe (basalt not alabaster) and dates from *circa* 1442. Branscombe does not have a head canopy. Stafford's effigy is believed to be the last ecclesiastic in Class III robes and Gardner states that he believes it to have been carved in Chellaston because of the likeness in the gablettes with Lowick.

G76 Horwood, Devon. Lady. Unknown but possibly Elizabeth Pollard (died 1430). Small figures of her children beside her skirt, horned headdress.

G77 Wimborne, Dorset. Knight and lady. John Beaufort, Duke of Somerset (died 1444) and Duchess Margaret. John was the grandson of John of Gaunt, grandfather of Henry VII. SS collar, garter below left knee and orle. Lady has SS collar and coronet over veil. Much graffiti including dates of 1644 and 1647 probably inscribed at the time of the Civil War.

G78 Marnhull, Dorset. Knight and two Ladies. John Carent (died 1478) and wives Alice and Margaret. Yorkist collar. Ladies have butterfly headdress with large flap. The tomb chest is a partial 19th century reproduction. Mentioned by Thomas Gerard in 1632. Moved 1898. The ladies have studded collars. One lady is damaged about the face reputedly to obtain a piece of alabaster. There is a fragment of the original tomb chest elsewhere in the church.

G79 Puddletown, Dorset. Knight. Gardner suggested that it is Sir William Martyn but the dates and presence of the Yorkist collar make this doubtful. In 2005 it was determined that it was Thomas Martyn who died 14th Sept 1485 probably from wounds received at Bosworth. Purbeck marble with alabaster canopy. Yorkist collar with Lion of March pendant and salet on his head. The shield is a later addition. Some restoration *circa* 1630, further restoration *circa* 2012.

G80 Melbury Sampford, Dorset. Knight. Reputed once to be Sir Giles Strangeways (died 1547) and wife Joan. However, Leland recorded the inscription before it was changed which indicates that it is to John Brouning the father of G81. Yorkist collar with salet of a unique design. There are Purbeck marble details. There is a suspicion that the tomb was purloined from the Brouning family *circa* 1467 which is consistent with the dated armour and Yorkist collar which would not be possible in 1547. *See* X24 and X25. The church is in private hands.

G81 Melbury Sampford, Dorset. Knight. William Brouning *circa* 1470. A duplicate of G80. Also to wives Katherine (Dru) and Alice (Burton). Reported to have been erected *circa* 1647 (for the second time?). The canopy and tomb chest is of Purbeck Marble with clear Gothic decoration but the effigy is in alabaster. *See* X24.

G82 Stourton Caundle, Dorset. Lady. Widow believed to be Agnes Fauntleroy with small figures of children in folds of skirt. She was the wife of Edward 6th Lord Stourton. Canopied. Barbe and veil. *See* X24 and X25.

G83 Dunmow Priory, Essex. Knight and lady. Church Monuments Society says this is Walter Fitzwalter (died 1432) and wife (died 1464). SS collar, ridged armour and large elbow and knee caps. Horned headdress, transition to butterfly with rose collar. T Dugdale writing in 1830 reported that these effigies had been moved and confirm representation of Walter Fitzwalter and one of his wives although he could not date them.

G84 Dunmow Priory, Essex. Lady. Unknown, possibly a Fitzwalter. Flapped truncated headdress. Necklace or SS collar with pendant. Legend has it that this is Matilda Fitzwalter but she existed about 1218 and as the tomb is a Class V the date variation is some 200 years and therefore unlikely. Another legend says the fingers are stained to represent poison but it is more likely to be vestiges of paint. Matilda Fitzwalter was the Maid Marion of legend. It is also stated that the early 15th century effigy sits on a late 15th century tomb chest. There are similarities to the tombs at Strelley, Notts.

G85 Wethersfield, Essex. Knight and lady. Unknown but may be Henry Wentworth, died 1482 and his wife Elizabeth (Howard – also died 1482). Tabard. Lady with Yorkist collar and flapped headdress. Somewhat battered. Elizabeth Howard was daughter of Henry Howard the uncle of John Howard, 1st Duke of Norfolk who was slain at the Battle of Bosworth 1485. The Howard connection may be the reason why Elizabeth is shown with Yorkist collar.

G86 Gloucester Cathedral. Priest. Abbott Seabroke (*circa* 1457). Mitre and mass vestments, feet on lion. His bishop's staff was found in his coffin in 1741. This has been moved at least twice but resides in its origin location.

G87 Berkeley, Gloucs. Two knights. James, 11th Lord Berkeley (died 1463) and his son also James killed in France (suggested 1452). Quatrefoils and shields. Both have Yorkist collars one with a Lion of March pendant. Gardner says the tomb style shows it was erected some 30 years after James senior's death (1493). Hair like Edward Stafford, Lowick 1499, rest or tomb like Sir Robert Harcourt at Stanton Harcourt. Like that of Holme Pierrepont the presence of a Yorkist collar post-1485 is questionable. The effigies are different sizes to signify the difference in ages.

G88 Gloucester Cathedral. Priest. Abbot William Parker (died 1539). Some sources say William Malvern as WM appears in the frieze above but this is believed to be an alias of Parker. Mitre, angels and cushion. Parker may be buried elsewhere but this is uncertain and wrongly based on the dissolution records which were written after his death. The effigy may have been carved in Parker's lifetime in 1535. The tomb when opened in 1919 held two coffins.

G89 Bristol, Somerset, St Mary Redcliffe. Mayor and priest. William Canynge died 1474 or 1467 and wife. There are two effigies – one in freestone. Canynge was mayor and after the death of his wife took holy orders. When he died there were two effigies one here and one in the collegiate church of Westbury on Trym (alabaster). This was transferred to St Mary Redcliffe after dissolution. This is shown in quire habit, feet on bearded man. Both look like portraits but not by the same hand.

G90 Winchester, Hants. Bishop, William de Wykeham (died 1404). A painted effigy restored 1894–1897. Hands vertical – unusual for period. Three clerks at feet and angels on cushion. The three Benedictine monks may refer to the provision for support of three monks in his will. Wykeham was an opponent of John Wycliffe. It is said that the same London carver carved the tomb of Bishop Courtenay in Canterbury. The Henry Moore database claims that William Byrd repaired the monument in 1664. Seeing that Winchester suffered during the Civil War it may be that the hands were replaced and put in vertical position. There is internet chatter that Nathaniel Fiennes, an officer of the Parliamentary army placed a guard on this monument. The dainty patterns on the dress were probably made from gesso – *see* Appendix S.

G91 Godshill, IOW. Knight and lady. Sir John Leigh died 1522 and wife Agnes (Hackett). SS collar and bedesmen at feet. Long pediment on lady angels with cushion. Agnes survived Leigh's death by some years and although buried separately, the tomb may have been constructed much later and may not be alabaster.

G92 Weobley, Hereford. Knight and lady. Sir John Marbury (died 1437) and his wife Agnes Croph. SS collar and orle with IHS on bascinet. Lady has SS collar and crespine headdress.

G93 Burghill, Hereford. Knight and lady. Sir John Milbourne (died 1450). Salet and orle. Lady has horned headdress.

G94 Eye, Hereford. Sir Roland Cornewall (died 1520) and wife Jane. An effigy on a later Fauld tomb chest. Long SS collar with Tudor rose pendant. Head on great helm and feet on lion with gauntlets at side. The annunciation is depicted similar to Ross on Wye, complete with three-headed lilies representing the Trinity. This may well have been moved. Smaller images of deceased as priant. The similarities in the features and in the ladies dress to the one at Ross (G96) make this a probable Parker monument and may date after 1530. The corners have spirals which are an early Renaissance feature. There is also in the church, a single alabaster angel holding a shield which may have come from the original tomb chest.

G95 Hereford. Priest, Dean John Harvey (died 1491) but tomb may be later. Much battered. On later limestone chest.

G96 Ross on Wye, Hereford. Judge and lady (although Llewellyn calls William a Serjeant at law). William Rudhall (died 1529–1530) and Ann his wife Ann (died 1556). There is an annunciation scene with angels with family kneeling behind under a canopy (Gardner identifies it as St Anne instructing the young virgin). Judge wears coif, lady a short pediment headdress. His head is on a great helm. Scrolls are believed to represent greeting by the angels and the response by the virgin. Further scrolls are held by Rudhall and his wife. The purpose seems to be to involve the viewer to take part in the prayers. The arcades have saints all of which were requested by Rudhall's will. This tomb is credited to Parker at Burton which presupposes a contract.

G97 Canterbury, Kent. King Henry IV (died 1413) and his second Queen Joan of Navarre (died 1437). Tomb may be as late as 1420. Formerly painted. Canopies over head and both have SS collars her with a short one like a necklace and he with the pendant broken off and partial obscured by the robe. Jewelled crown. King bearded and possible good likeness as was suggested when the tomb opened in 1832. He has feet on lion and her feet on dogs. Gardner did not list this tomb but the Canterbury Historical and Archaeological Society confirm that the effigies are alabaster. Interestingly, they suggest that the tomb was designed by Richard Beke and carved by Sutton and Prentys. Cheetham says the carver was Robert Brown (Broun) of London, a view supported by Lawrence Stone, but Nigel Saul says they have the angels and shields of the Chellaston school which supports the Canterbury suggestion. In some quarters the design is credited to Stephen Lote. A portrait of Thomas Beckett was painted on one panel and the coronation of the virgin on another. Henry wears a sleeved tunic known as a dalmatic, a mantle, crown of oak leaves. She has a crespine, coronet and wears a cotehardie and has creatures at her feet. The canopies are very late for a mid-15th century tomb. It is suggested that Joan's effigy was added on her death in 1437 so that the styles of the two effigies merit investigation. It is stated that Henry IV was the first king since Edward the Confessor to announce his coronation in English after which French was largely abandoned. Latin continued to be used for the inscription in tombs until the Reformation.

G98 Canterbury, Kent. St Michael's Chapel. Two knights and a lady. John Beaufort, Earl of Somerset, died 1410, Margaret Holland (or Holand), died 1437 (or 1440) and the Thomas, Duke of Clarence died 1421. Assumed erected 1437 by Margaret Holland as style is Class III. Grey Sussex marble with alabaster effigies. Knights have SS collar. Possibly linked to G166 and G168. Page 211 of Weever refers. The lady has coronet and is dressed in a kirtle, mantle and surcoat.

G99 Ash, Kent. Knight and lady. The Ash website claims these are John de Septvans (died 1458) and wife Katherine Martin (died 1498) – alabaster figures on a Purbeck marble tomb chest moved to Ash from Sittingbourne in antiquity but this does not gel with Gardner's Class V. SS collar with loop pendant and tabard, bald forehead, angels supporting helm. Widow's barbe.

G100 Minster in Sheppey, Kent. Knight. Unknown but may be George Duke of Clarence (1475). Has been seriously attacked probably by Tudor vandals – damage same as in St Anne's, Sutton Bonington, Notts. Yorkist collar but may be sun bursts rather than suns and roses. Later restored on Purbeck tomb chest. Feet on ram. George, Duke of Clarence was executed by Edward IV and is reported as being buried in Tewkesbury with his wife. Another claim to the tomb is Hugh de Badlesmere.

G101 Little Chart, Kent. Knight. Sir John Darell (died 1509). SS collar. Darell directed burial in will. Inscription explains why the lion at his feet should bear a trefoil on shoulder. The medieval church at Little Chart was destroyed by a V1 in 1944 and a new church was not built until 1955. Darell's effigy and great helm was rescued and installed in the new church. Darell had a part in Buckingham's revolt of 1483 and on being attainted by Richard III fled to join Henry Tudor and probably was at Bosworth. Knighted in 1497. The pre-war photographs show the knight with his feet on a lion with typical Harpur/Moorecock split tail on his sabatons except that on one there is a bedesman.

G102 Halsall, Lancs. Priest. Unknown but may be Richard Halsall. Amice with pendants.

G103 Bottesford, Leics. Knight. William, Lord Rous or Roos (died 1414). Downing comments that effigy taken from Belvoir Priory at dissolution. Partially restored. SS collar of the early short variety with a pendant and orle marked 'ihc Nazare'. Garter, peacock on great helm under head, fine detail, breastplate under jupon. Front-facing angels on tomb chest holding rectangular shields.

G104 Staindrop, Durham. Knight and two ladies. Ralph Nevill, Earl of Westmoreland (died *circa* 1425) and wives Margaret (Stafford, died 1370) and Joan (Beaufort, died 1440). Joan is buried at Lincoln and Margaret at Brancepeth (where she wears a Yorkist collar with boar pendant). Joan was daughter of John of Gaunt by Elizabeth Swynford. Panels with empty niches. SS collar and orle. Hair bunched over ears, coronets, clerks at desks at feet but with missing heads. The monument is ably described by Lipscombe's 1888 book *The History of Staindrop and its Monuments*. St John Hope attributes this to Sutton and Prentys despite the monument having no gablettes.

G105 Bottesford, Leics. Knight. John, Lord Rous or Roos (died 1421). Downing comments that effigy taken from Belvoir Priory at dissolution. This is similar to G103. SS collar, garter and orle marked ihc Nazare, fine detail. Angels holding shields. The tomb once had a peacock crest.

G106 Ashby de la Zouch. Pilgrim dated 1483 to 1530, possibly William brother of Edward 2nd Lord Hastings who died 1506. William and Edward were the sons of William, 1st Lord Hastings executed by Richard III in 1483. SS collar with hands holding a now broken palmer's staff. Pilgrim's hat, cloak with a script, shell or scallop under head and long hair. Dog at feet. The shell is believed to signify that the person has made a pilgrimage to St James the Greater at Santiago de Compostela, Spain (*see* X15). The pilgrimage had to be licensed, the Encyclopaedia Brittanica stating that in 1434, 2460 licenses were issued. The Church Monument Society says this is one of only two such monuments and the only one in England. The monument at Ashby has been moved during which its identity was lost. Hartshorne records that in 1506 Edward, Lord Hastings ordered 'placebo, dirge, commendations with mass requiem with orisons and prayers to be said for seven years for the benefit of his soul'. He bequeathed 10 marks a year to the priest for these observances.

G107 Leicester (St Margaret's), Leics. Bishop. Bishop Penney (or Penny) of Carlisle formerly Abbot of Leicester. He died in Carlisle but was buried in Leicester. Was badly painted.

G108 Thurlaston, Leics. Knight and lady. John Turville (died 1509) and wife Katherine (Staunton). SS collar. Lady also has SS collar and long hair under orle. Angels holding shields on tomb chest. The monument has been moved more than once probably in 1850 when the chantry was restored. The chantry which had been abandoned as a store for rubbish once held many more monuments some of which were lost in the restoration. For more details *see The History of Thurlaston, Leicestershire Including Normanton Turville* available on the internet. John's will of 1506 specified that 10 marks be set aside for a tomb of alabaster or marble but his executor appears to have exceeded his wishes with a more elaborate tomb.

G109 Lockington, Leics. Lady. Lady Elizabeth Ferrers died 1500. Six bedesmen and angels at end. Coronet over long hair. Dog on side of dress and cushion with angels. An inscription was recorded in 1795 but little remains.

G110 Prestwold, Leics. Two Ladies. Unknown and stated as *circa* 1520. Bedesmen and long pediment headdress consistent with period 1500 to 1520, but may well be earlier. It is reported that the monument once had a canopy. The two carvings are identical and the identity of the ladies has been elusive. Gardner quoting Chatwin says that this and North Aston (G143) are by the same Burton workshop but says that they are not the work of Harpur or Moorecock. The reason given is in the similarity of the friar-like 'weepers' or bedesmen but the two tombs have slightly different arcading although insufficient to challenge this assertion. The ladies have the slash and bow style down the front of the dress. Local tradition says that it is Gertrude and Grace Lacey of Hoton the discoverers of a miraculous well and some say they are the Nele sisters patrons of Swarkestone Bridge but the date of 1520 (given by Pevsner) rules this out. Philip White of the Wolds Historical Organisation gives a thorough and detailed analysis of these tombs in his *Two Unknown Ladies of Prestwold*. This monument poses more questions than answers as the style and design is in keeping with the second quarter of the 15th century.

G111 Castle Donington, Leics. Knight and lady. Robert Hazelrig and lady died 1536. Angels and bedesmen. SS collar and large neck guard. Lady has short pediment headdress and puffed sleeves. Pevsner believes that this is a duplicate of that at Clifton Campville (G161).

G112 Ashby de la Zouch, Leics. Knight and lady. Francis Hastings, 2nd Earl of Huntingdon (died 1561) and wife Katherine Pole (died 1576). Knight weepers under canopies alternating with shields. Bearded, coronet, garter robes and insignia. The tomb may date from 1561 as the 1576 date is added. Jon Bayliss attributes this to Richard Parker (Vol V 1990 CMS). It retains much Gothic detail unusual for the date however the heraldic signs are disproportionate to the effigies which is not a Gothic trait and so the monument is a mixture of styles. Gardner singled out this monument stating '… this exhibits much more Gothic than Italian feeling in its whole design and treatment apart from a few insignificant details'. This may seem odd today but at the time would not have raised any doubts in the mind of the observer. The Earl wears a collar of alternating roses and what seem to be gathered ribbons in pleats. A photograph on the wall of the church shows the tomb in its original position against the east wall butting up to a mural of alabaster depicting the Hastings coat of arms. The mural remains but detached from the monument.

G113 Bures, Suffolk. St Stephen's Chapel Bures ex Colne Priory. Knight and lady. *See also* G29. Reputed to be Richard de Vere, 9th Earl of Oxford (b.1385, died 1417) and his wife Alice Sergeaux (died 1452). St Stephen's Chapel is believed to be the place where King Edmund was crowned in 855AD and is not easy to find being hidden in a hollow about a mile north of Bures hamlet half a mile from the road to Assington. These effigies appear on one tomb chest which has been much repaired but a lithograph taken from Chancellor's *Essex* shows a male effigy different from that which is claimed by existing information. Edward de Vere sold the manor *circa* 1591. He is believed to be associated with Shakespeare being part owner of the Globe. Died 1604 and buried in Hackney, London. The chapel contains a third effigy of Robert de Vere, 3rd Earl of Oxford dating from 1296 which is not alabaster (*see* X2). *See also* X28.

G114 London, Great St Helen's Bishopsgate. John Oteswich (died *circa* 1400) and lady. A civilian in long gown buttoned to the neck, bearded with scrip and short sword. Veil with buttoned front. The tombs were originally in St Martin's, Outwich but were moved when the church was demolished in 1874. John's date of death is uncertain, but he was alive in 1387 when the advowson of St Martin's was purchased. The son of a surgeon. Saul observes that this is one of the rare effigies to civilians at a time when brass monuments became popular.

G115 London, Tower of London chapel. This monument was in St Katherine's but moved when the dock was constructed *circa* 1820 and erected in a chapel at Regent's Park. When that became the Danish Church in 1951 the monument was moved to the Tower. Civilian with two Ladies. John Holland, Duke of Exeter (died 1447) but monument may well be 1462 but some say 1432 on the death of his first wife Anne Stafford. It may well have been intended for only two effigies and third seen here has not been positively identified. However, Holland's third wife Anne Montague (died 1457) is reputed to have willed that she be buried with her husband and so may well be that lady. In that case the two lady effigies are some 24 years apart in date yet very similar. Canopy. All have coronets. Some restoration to ladies which may include new head and shoulders on the angels supporting the cushions. Unusually the order is C,L,L which indicates that this was always a wall tomb and this supported by a photograph (however in view of the fact that one lady was added later this may be the reason). Holland was constable of the Tower 1420 to 1447. The photograph shows the tomb chest side had a row of niches which may well have contained figures. This seems to have been repositioned above the canopy and is limestone. The ladies have horned headdresses. The whole is in Chellaston alabaster without any sign of waxing. It may be that this is a product of the Sutton and Prentys workshop. What is also odd is that despite the man being in civilian robes with a round neck collar, his head is on a great helm of unusual shape without crest.

G116 London, Great St Helen's, Bishopsgate. Sir John Crosby (died 1475 or 1476) and wife Agnes. Yorkist collar with Lion of March pendant. Orle over loose hair. Purbeck marble tomb chest. Has been restored by scrapping to remove graffiti which entailed loss of weapons. Feet on griffin. Inscription – *see* Mark Dowling page 87. He left £100 for the repair of Bishop's Gate and the nearby walls and his arms were marked on them.

G117 London, Westminster. Knight and lady. Sir Giles Daubeny KG (died 1506). Garter robes, bedesmen at feet. Orle over loose hair. Bloxham offers the opinion that the Coleshill tomb (G178) was carved in the same workshop.

G118 Abergavenny, Mon. Knight and lady. Sir William ap Thomas (died 1450) and wife Gwladys. A made up tomb from fragments. SS collar, lady with horned headdress with two small boys holding the mantle claimed to be Gwladys. His head was formerly on a great helm with a maiden's head crest but is now believed to be a Moorish woman in a turban. It was reported that the canopies over the heads of the effigies in poor condition, that over the lady is smaller than the knight. The inside face of the canopies were reported as painted red, blue and yellow. Symonds (1645) makes no reference to the canopies and the top edge is rough and unfinished giving rise to the possibility that like the effigies, the canopies are from another tomb now lost or even originally mounted horizontally over an image where the upper surface would not be visible. This is reinforced by the fact that the crest faces the canopy which is not how it would have been shown were the canopy related. It is suggested that the tomb chest sides are the former parts of an altar screen or reredos which was demolished during the Reformation and hidden. The damage to the tomb is reported as being done during the Civil War whereupon the tomb was reassembled post-1660 with the parts from the former altar. Restored 2012 with 'specially resourced Midlands's alabaster' and reopened Feb 2013.

G119 Abergavenny, Mon. Knight and lady. Sir Richard Herbert (died 1470) and wife Margaret. Yorkist collar. Some fragments added. Lady has orle over loose hair and is reputed to be Margaret. A Madonna is included in weepers. Like the observations made in G118 the panel depicting the virgin is considered from the lost reredos. He was the guardian of the young Henry Tudor later Henry VII.

G120 Abergavenny, Mon. Knight. Sir Richard Herbert (died 1510). SS collar with mutilated pendant. Seated angels and bedesmen, weepers in niches. It was reported that when cleaned a tomb revealed an alabaster bedesman – *see* picture in Abergavenny website. The chapel in which G118 to G120 are located was once a schoolroom which has resulted in serious damage to the monuments through initial-cutting. He was brought up with Henry Tudor and fought at Bosworth.

G121 Ashwellthorpe, Norfolk. Knight and lady. Sir Edmund de Thorpe (died 1417–1418) and wife Joan. Both have SS collars with loop pendant. Knight has orle and lady has crespine headdress and dogs at feet. Originally had wooden canopy which was removed *circa* 1865. Tomb chest has panels with angels holding shields which have been restored.

In 1817 Stothard reported that some details were brightly coloured with the SS collar having gold letters on a blue background but that much was left unpainted.

G122 Lowick, Northants. Knight and lady. Ralph Greene and wife Katherine (Malley) of 1419. Stag crest, fauld looks like square plates covered with leather. Lady has crespine headdress, hands clasped, canopy over heads. There is a surviving contract for this tomb – *see* Gardner. Cost reputed to be 50 marks (£40). Has angel and shield motif of the Chellaston school. Katherine in the contract called for the tomb to be 'gilded, painted and arrayed with colours'. Unless this tomb was transferred to Nottingham for staining it implies that Chellaston had resident stainers. Saul claims that the bascinet has 'Ihc' imprinted – *see* Appendix L. In 1840 Hartshorne attributed this monument to 1459 and to an Italian carver which acts as a warning to those who may take information at face value. The gablettes on this tomb are magnificent with the rear carved as detailed as the front. Crossley shows these in detail on page 102 of his book. Both Ewelme (G42, 1477) and Arundel (G167, 1416) have equally intricate gablettes.

G123 Lowick, Northants. Knight. Edward Stafford, Earl of Wiltshire (died 1498). SS collar and tabard, long hair, bedesmen at feet with inscription. Shields on tomb chest encircled with Staffordshire knot set in lozenges. Figure 90 of Sally Badham's book *Seeking Salvation* shows the bedesmen.

G124 Yelvertoft, Northants. Priest. Unknown mid-15th century priest in mass vestments. Possibly John Dycson rector 1439 to 1445 but in some quarters the date of 1470 or 1479 is given. Quatrefoils on canopy and pillow with angels. Clearly shows Trent valley features. Figure 51 of Sally Badham's book *Seeking Salvation* shows this tomb which has the unique feature of extending outside the church. The window above may, at one time, been fitted with stained glass.

G125 Dodford, Northants. Knight. Sir John Cressy (died 1444). Angels holding shields. SS collar and inscription indentifying all Cressy's offices in English-controlled France. This is one of the last tombs to display chivalric emblems. Cressy fought in France with the Duke of Bedford whose arms feature on the tomb. The inscription detailing the service of Cressy is rare for a tomb of this period.

G126 Greens Norton, Northants. Knight and lady. Sir Thomas Greene (died 1457) and wife Philippa. Both have SS collars and knight has head on great helm with dog crest and a bowl crop haircut. Lady has horned headdress. In 1840 Hartshorne reported these much defaced probably because they were removed from the church in 1826 and probably left outside. They were recovered in 1891 and restored to the church. Great grandparents of Catherine Parr.

G127 Fawsley, Northants. Knight and lady. Sir Ralph (or Richard) Knightley (died 1534) and wife Jane (Skenard). In good condition. Weepers, ladies dressed in Tudor costume with black background under crocketted arches. SS collar with tabard. Short pediment headdress much colour preserved. Jon Bayliss (Vol V 1990 CMS) has identified this as a Richard Parker carving. Ancestors of the Earls Spencer.

G128 Deene, Northants. Civilian and two Ladies. Sir Robert Brudenell (died 1531) and wives Margaret and Philippa. Chief justice of common pleas. Judges coif with colour preserved especially on red robe. Short pediment headdress. Widow's veil and barbe. The church is redundant and under the care of English Heritage.

G129 Upton, Northants. Knight and lady. Sir Richard Knightley (died 1537 or 1538) and first wife. Possible made earlier than 1537. SS collar with Tudor rose pendant and tabard. Loose hair under coif.

G130 Apethorpe, Northants. Knight. Sir Richard Dalton. He died 1442, but style of tomb looks like 1500. It is a small effigy 3ft 9½in long, tabard on slab 5ft 9½in long. Coronation of the Virgin placed over head. The Apethorpe monument is without parallel in respect of this adornment. (There is evidence of other monuments to Sir John Leigh *circa* 1606 and Rowland Woodward *circa* 1643.)

G131 Nuthall, Notts. Knight. Sir Robert Cokefield. Plate armour under jupon.

G132 Fledborough Notts. Knight. Unknown. Jupon laced at side. Possibly Sir John de Lisieux (died after 1359). The effigy is badly damaged with no legs. The chest of the effigy has inscribed mantled helm and crest. The bascinet is of third quarter 14th century form.

G133 Clifton, Notts. Knight. Possibly Sir Gervase Clifton but may be 15th century. Feet on lion. May be Robert Clifton *circa* 1491 but style does not fit but *see also* G134. [John Clifton died at the battle of Shrewsbury in 1403. He had married Katherine sister of Sir Hugh Cressy of Hodstock. All the Clifton are buried at Clifton – *see also* S127.]

G134 Clifton, Notts. Lady. Possibly Lady Alice Clifton (nee Nevill). Possibly wife of G133 and hair in crespine which dates it to late 14th century/early 15th century.

G135 Holme Pierrepont. Knight. Sir Henry Pierrepont (died 1499). Yorkist collar with cross pendant. An extract from the *Holme Pierrepont Trail* reads 'A tomb is of another Sir Henry (Henrie) Pierrepont who died in 1499. Sir Henry was a Yorkist who fought at the Battle of Bosworth.' Henry's will directs that 'A tomb of alabaster to be set up upon a sepulchre and graven by discretion of my executors'. The date of the tomb is very late for a Yorkist collar – *see* X25, but the explanation may lie in the often omitted final words of his will which reads '… if I make it not in my lif daies'. The tomb chest shows distinctive mid-Tudor features which together with the periodic reordering of the church may indicate that the tomb chest is a mid-16th century reproduction.

G136 Ratcliffe on Soar, Notts. Knight and lady. Sir Ralph Sacheverell. SS collar with Tudor rose pendant. The tomb of Ralph Sacheverell, died 1539 and one of his wives either Anna died 1528 or Cecilia Durance. The lady has a decorated gable hood dating from about 1520 to 1540 whilst the man has a 15th century Plantagenet haircut and plate armour but disports a Henry VIII esse Collar (SS collar) with a Tudor rose (*see* General Note 1). The man has his head on a great helm from which the crest has been removed. The tomb lies under a Tudor arch. The lady has a triple chain with a cross. Jon Bayliss suggests that the effigies are second hand and cites that fact that the inscription has been recut after the original was erased. The chamfered edge of the tabletop has been grooved and the letters cut in relief in crude form of Gothic script. Ratcliffe manor was bequeathed to Ralph on the death of his uncle Richard of Morley who died in 1534 and was buried in the Newarke at Leicester. This college was suppressed and closed at Easter 1548 and it is quite possible the tomb was recovered by Ralph's son Henry and set up in Ratcliffe as a monument to his father. This would explain the presence of the SS collar but does not explain the removal of the goat crest (unless this was later stolen). The lady's dress remains appropriate to the early 1530s (for discussion *see* CMS Vol XXVIII 2013 page 88 note 14. The lady sits on a reduced tomb chest and the main slab border is terminated short. It is possible she does not belong to the knight. All in this entire monument is an enigma. Atop the arch is a stone helm or armet held in place by a steel support. The presence of separate pieces of armour on monuments is discussed in a lengthy article in CMS Vol XXIX 2014.

G137 Nottingham, St Mary's. Civilian. John Salmon or Samon (mayor 1396–1397 and 1407–1408) died 1416. The effigies stands on the ground with a trefoil canopy above, the tomb chest having been destroyed in the 1840s (but *see* GNP70 and note 1 on 8.10). The effigy has a long buttoned high collar robe of a merchant. The effigy has a high hat with upturned flaps which usually indicates that he was once an apprentice at law but this cannot be confirmed. He did own a number of manors including a third interest in that at Gotham, Notts with the rights to appoint there every third time the living fell vacant. Samon's will was dated 10th August 1415 and left a fortune of £350 mainly gained through the wool trade. Samon is credited with the reconstruction of St Mary's in the late 14th century.

G138 Willoughby on the Wolds, Notts. Knight and lady. Sir Hugh Willoughby (died 1448) and wife Margaret Freville (died

1393). The first wife, Isabel Foljambe (died 1417) is believed to be commemorated by a slab (*see* sketch in note G24) but some references reverse the names on the tomb and slab. Early form of salet, feet on lion. Horned headdress, feet on dogs and cushion supported by angels which have been damaged. Cheetham says that the panel of the Trinity on the side of the tomb was formerly carved for an altarpiece. At the head and foot of the tomb is a pair of panels illustrating lessons on redemption of the world with the Trinity at the head and the Virgin at the foot. Saul has stated that these panels indicate Sir Hugh's interest in the Carthusian Order in which he was lay member probably of Beauvale. It is probable that this unusual form was specified either by Hugh or by his executor but it cannot be established for sure. All the tombs have received rough treatment due to the chapel being used as a punishment corner for the village school. Colonel Michael Stonhope is buried here, the victim of a skirmish between Royalists and Parliamentarians on the 5th July 1648.

G139 Strelley, Notts. Knight and lady. John de Strelley (died 1501–1502). Stone canopy. Knight has chain collar. An extract from *Tudor Trail* by Graham Beaumont. The tomb of John de Strelley and his wife dating from 1501. The man rests on a tilting helmet and his feet rest on a lion. Bedesmen. Figure 91 of Sally Badham's book *Seeking Salvation* shows the bedesmen. There is similarity in style of the bedesman on this tomb and that of the Redman tomb in Harewood (G206).

G140 Northleigh, Oxon. Knight and lady. Sir William Wilcotes (died 1411). Both have SS collars. Knight has orle and lady high collar and crespine with a houppelande. Saul claims that the bascinet has 'Ihc' imprinted – *see* Appendix L. William Wilcotes was a retainer, attorney and feoffee of the Earl of Warwick and his rights to wear armour is questionable and may be only by association with his lord.

G141 Stanton Harcourt, Oxford. Knight and lady. Sir Robert Harcourt KG (died 1471). Yorkist collar and garter robes. Lady has widows veil and barbe, Garter on left arm above the elbow. Bedesmen on tomb chest. Repainted in 19th century.

G142 Ewelme, Oxford. Lady. Alice de la Pole, Duchess of Suffolk (died 1475 or 1477). Four angels support the cushion and there is a cadaver under. Veil and barbe, garter on left wrist. Canopy is believed to have been added later in 15th century. The use of angels holding shields became popular in the 15th century. Sometimes they are shown seated in pairs holding a shield between them as at Methley. Alice was granddaughter of Geoffrey Chaucer. Figure 115 of Sally Badham's book *Seeking Salvation* shows this effigy and the text describes the good works of the duchess including almshouses and a school. Over her head is fine gablette.

G143 North Aston, Oxford. Knight and lady *circa* 1490. Unknown – possibly John and Alicia Anne. Angels and 14 bedesmen on the tomb chest. SS collar with a lion and loop pendant. Lady has flapped truncated headdress. Restored by Kelland Conservation. Figure 93 of Sally Badham's book *Seeking Salvation* shows the tomb chest. The niches do not have crocketted canopies and may indicate an earlier version of what later became a 'trade mark' form. In addition the bedesmen carry inverted candles. The tomb chest is clearly in Fauld alabaster.

G144 Chipping Norton, Oxford. Knight and lady. Richard Croft. Chain collar. Pediment headdress with long flaps at side.

G145 Oxford. Priest. John Noble of Broadgate Hall later Pembroke College. Angels. In university hood over shoulder.

G146 Kinlet. Lady. Unknown but possibly Isobel Lychefield (died 1410). Baby beside lady in swaddling clothes. Crespine headdress with plain band.

G147 Burford, Oxford. Lady. Princess Elizabeth (died 1426), daughter of John of Gaunt. Coronet over flowing hair.

G148 Tong, Salop. Knight and lady. Sir Richard Vernon (died 1451) and Benedicta de Ludlow. Fine SS collar orle and horse-head (boars head?) crest. Horned headdress. By this marriage the Vernons of Hadden Hall acquired Tong Manor. The tomb chest is sandstone but otherwise show the crocketted canopies of the Trent Valley. Saints and angels.

G149 Tong, Salop. Knight and lady. Richard Vernon (died 1517) and wife Margaret Dymmok. Weepers and bedesmen in niches. SS collar with Tudor rose pendant. Lady has long pediment. May show traces of colour. Margaret later married Sir Richard Manners forging a link with the Dukes of Rutland and with Bottesford. Figure 92 of Sally Badham's book *Seeking Salvation* shows the tomb chest. The niches alternate between those which are wide and contain shield and narrow which contain the bedesmen – a departure from the normal Burton form.

G150 Kinlet, Shrops. Knight and lady. Sir Humphrey Blount (died 1478) and wife Elizabeth. Weepers and annunciation. Yorkist collar. Butterfly with large flaps.

G151 Newport, Shrops. Civilian and lady. Unknown (died 1530) and wife. Angels, bedesmen on tomb chest and weepers. Twisted shaft at corners. Short pediment on lady.

G152 Wells, Somerset. Priest. Unknown. Annunciation and priests with shields. This and several other tombs moved to churchyard in the 18th century but returned to the church in 1860.

G153 Porlock, Somerset. Knight and lady. Lord Harrington (died 1418) and Elizabeth Courtney. Stone canopy. SS collar and orle. Angels supporting helm. Lady has horned headdress. He went to France with Henry V but died there. Monument dates from 1440.

G154 Glastonbury, Somerset. Civilian. Bursar of abbey, possibly a member of the Camel family, possibly John (died 1487). Bath stone tomb with alabaster effigy in St John's church. Mantle is open at sides and a full length tunic beneath with hat on shoulder. Scrip at side. The form of the attire indicates that the commemorated was a notary.

G155 Yatton, Somerset. Civilian and lady. Judge Sir Richard Newton (died 1449) and wife died 1475. Angels. Judges coif, robes and pouch and head on great helm which is unusual. Lady has butterfly headdress with flaps which may mean tomb erected *circa* 1475. The head of the judge has similarities to the priest at St Mary Redcliffe, Bristol.

G156 Wells, Somerset. Bishop Beckyngton or Beckington (died 1465). Stone cadaver beneath. Tomb possibly erected in 1451. John Britton in 1826 observed that the effigy was of wood. The tomb was restored in 1922. It has a railings round the tomb. The dainty patterns on the dress were probably made from gesso – *see* Appendix S.

G157 Ilton, Somerset. Lady. Unknown but possibly Elizabeth Popham. Collar of roses alone and butterfly headdress.

G158 Elford, Staffs. Knight and lady. Sir John Arderne (died 1408) and wife Matilda clasping hands. This has been attributable to Sir Thomas Arderne (1391) but it is now known that it was commissioned by his son John for himself by virtue of a will. Restored 1848 by Edward Richardson who published a commentary in 1852. Angels and weepers in three cusp niches. Both have short SS collar and he wears an orle. The collars have reversed 'S's and a tiret with a hanging jewel. Angels on helm, early crespine. Saul claims that the bascinet has Ihc imprinted – *see* Appendix L.

G159 Elford, Staffs. Knight and two ladies. Sir William Smythe (died 1525) and wives, Elizabeth (Isobel) Nevill (died 1516) and Anne Staunton. Elizabeth was niece of the Earl of Warwick (Kingmaker) and is also related to Richard III. Restored by Edward Richardson possibly in 1852. Bedesmen in niches. Long SS collar with cross pendant. Elizabeth has a coronet and Anne a long pediment. The crocketted niches are of a later design and may well be from the Harpur and Moorecock workshop near the end of their existence.

G160 Tamworth, Staffs. Knight and lady. Sir Thomas Ferrers (died 1512). Headless weepers. SS collar with Tudor rose pendant and lady with long pediment.

G161 Clifton Campville, Staffs. Civilian and lady. Sir John Vernon (died 1545) and wife Ellyn (Montgomery). Weepers and seated bedesmen. Twisted shafts. Frieze of animals and birds. Flat cap and chain collar. Short pediment and rosary at side. Pevsner believes that this is a duplicate of that at Castle Donington (G111). There is possible mason's mark on one pilaster comprising a buckle or garter. There is an unusual frieze of flowers and animals at base of chest. This allocated to Parker and the frieze may well indicate a growing Renaissance style. There may possibly have been paintings on the back of the tomb recess.

G162 Dennington, Suffolk. Knight and lady. Sir William Phelip, Lord Bardolf or Bardolph KG (died 1441) and wife. Fine SS collar. Feet on hawk, garter below knee and feather crest. Horned headdress and feet on wyvern. (Possibly linked to *circa* 1440 effigy at Weobley, Hereford.)

G163 Wingfield, Suffolk. Knight and lady. John de la Pole, Duke of Suffolk (died 1491) and Elizabeth Plantagenet (sister of Edward IV and Richard III). Coronet, garter and garter robes with cloak embroidered with the symbol of the order. Saracen's head on helm. Duchess has coronet and veil. A canopied wall monument in perpendicular style, it has a shallow arch and a horizontal crenulated top. A new book on the de la Poles is to be published in July 2015. It has been suggested that the effigies have moved position. It was noted by Jon Bayliss in Nov 2015 that the effigies have two very different quality of alabaster. The garter robes are tied with cords which are reminiscent of the Burton workshops.

G164 Chilton, Suffolk. Knight and lady. Robert Crane (died 1500) and wife Anne Ogard (died 1521), Lady Arundel. Tabard and unicorn at feet. Lady has a very short SS collar with a sun pendant and flapped headdress. The reason for the right to wear an SS has not been established but her father was for a long time linked with Richard of York hence the sun pendant. The unicorn had a horn originally dowelled. Great helm into which the crest (missing) was also dowelled. Lozenges with heraldry – modern painting.

G165 Chilton, Suffolk. Civilian. George Crane (died 1491). Long robe and script, long hair and liripipe over shoulders.

G166 Lingfield, Surrey. Knight and lady. Reginald, Lord Cobham (died 1446) and Anne Bardolf (2nd wife died 1453). Saracen's head on helm in veined alabaster as is the sea-wolf at the feet. Veil and widows barbe. The knight's will directed that his body to be buried before the altar. This is linked with G98 and G168. Possibly once polychrome.

G167 Arundel, Sussex. Civilian and Llady. Thomas Fitzalan, Earl of Arundel (died 1415) and Beatrix (daughter of John I of Portugal). Partly Purbeck. Gablettes and canopies over heads. SS collar, coronet and long robes. Bedesmen on tomb chest. Lady has coronet and elaborate crespine, dogs at feet playing with folds of skirt.

G168 Arundel, Sussex. Knight. John Fitzalan, Earl of Arundel (died 1435). SS and tabard. Close fitting bascinet with holes for visor, angels and cushions. Stone cadaver beneath slab. Linked to G98 and G168. Nigel Saul claims there are close links to two non-alabaster tombs to Archbishop Chichele in Canterbury and to the Hoo brothers in Herstmonceux, Sussex dating from 1446.

G169 Chichester, Sussex. Bishop Sherburne (died 1536). Angels at head supporting a cushion and lion at feet with bedesmen. Gilded mitre, crosier and full robes. Tomb made in lifetime of bishop according to his will which also confirms the alabaster came from Needwood Forest. There is another tomb to this bishop in the church at Rolleston on Dove (R128). Sherburne was responsible for many of the fine works in Chichester Cathedral.

G170 Easebourne, Sussex. Knight. Sir David Owen (died 1535). Will indicates that tomb ordered some 40 years before death (about 1502) which is consistent with Gardner's classification as Class V. SS collar and roses, Tudor rose pendant and tabard. Owen was Henry VII's half-uncle.

G171 Warwick. Knight and lady. Thomas Beauchamp, Earl of Warwick (of Crecy and Poitiers) died of the plague in France 1369 but monument may date from 1371. Wife Katherine (Mortimer) daughter of the Earl of March. Weepers but many plaster reproductions, breastplate under jupon, feet on bear. Clasped hands. Framed headdress and long hair. Strangely the knight was a Knight of the Garter invested 1373 but the effigy does not display this decoration. The effigies are stained and polished such that little of the alabaster can be seen. The tomb resides in the middle of the chancel.

G172 Meriden, Warwicks. Knight. Sir John Wyard died 1404. Richly decorated sword, arms on jupon, angels, and rosettes on hip belt. Hands at 45°.

G173 Merevale, Warwicks. Knight and lady. Edmund, Lord Ferrers of Chartley (died 1440). Early salet and orle, feather crest. Lady has horned headdress and dogs at feet.

G174 Wootton Wawen, Warwicks. Knight. John Harewell (died 1428). Band round bascinet or great helm with a hare crest, chain collar, feet on dogs. Four niches with shields two of which has been repainted.

G175 Polesworth, Warwicks. Lady. Isobel Cockayne. Shields and crespine headdress.

G176 Astley, Warwicks. Lady. Elizabeth, L'Isle (died 1486). Rose collar, loose hair and circlet. Was placed on Lord Ferrers's tomb but may have no connection.

G177 Astley, Warwicks. Cecily Bonneville, Marchioness of Dorset (died 1530). Long pediment.

G178 Coleshill, Warwicks. Knight and lady. Sir Simon Digby (died 1520) and wife Alice. Said to be made in his lifetime but see later. SS collar. Spiral pilasters with panels and shields. Lady has long pediment. The man has feet on a stylised lion and has his gauntlets to one side. Gardner links the monument to that at Youlgreave and offers the opinion that it has Flemish characteristics and may well be a Fleming working in Burton. GNP98 shows a lion of the same design. This is identified with Royley and although 1519 is too early for the Royley workshop may well be by the same carver. On the other hand the spiral pilasters place this after 1540 so uncertainty remains. To make things worse, Bloxham says that the Westminster tomb (G117, *circa* 1506) was carved by the same workshop.

G179 Alcester, Warwicks. Knight and lady. Sir Fulke Greville (died 1558) and wife Elizabeth Willoughby. The chest has weepers including a chrisom. His grandson (a third generation Fulke who died in 1628) was a friend of Sir Philip Sidney whose poetry he published after Sidney's death in 1586. Sidney is commemorated by a mural in St Paul's which is not alabaster and Sir Fulke Greville a marble monument in Warwick. The lady has folds of dress clearly defined and the lion has its head turned. Spiral pilasters and plain niches with inscribed shields. Sidney's funeral on 16th Feb 1587 is described in CMS Vol XXIX 2014. The original monument of unknown stone in St Paul's was lost in the fire of 1666 but the Greenwich helm which adorned it was saved and is now at Penshurst, Kent.

G180 Salisbury, Wilts. Bishop Mitford or Medford (died 1407). Purbeck marble tomb and alabaster effigy.

G181 Salisbury, Wilts. Knight. Lord Hungerford (died 1459 but tomb may date from 1464). SS collar, angels and cushions. The armour is Milanese and well carved.

G182 Salisbury, Wilts. Knight. Sir John Cheyne (standard bearer at Bosworth for Henry VII). SS collar with portcullis and Tudor rose pendant, garter robes, cloak with embroidered symbol of the order, long hair, angels and cushions. The cording on the robes has details which indicate a Trent Valley workshop possibly Harpur and Moorecock.

G183 Bromham, Wilts, Worcs. Knight. Richard Tocotes (died 1492), the second husband of Lady Elizabeth Beauchamp. Purbeck marble chest. SS collar, beavor and cap, large neck guard. The tomb to Lady Elizabeth Beauchamp (died 1491) is in Purbeck marble with a canopy but no effigy.

G184 Bromsgrove, Worcs. Knight and lady. Sir Humphrey Stafford (died 1450 or 1440) and wife Eleanor (may not have died until 1479). SS collar, boar's head crest. Lady has horned headdress. Bascinet with jewelled orle.

G185 Bromsgrove, Worcs. Lady. Attributed to Elizabeth Greystoke, later Lady Talbot of Grafton manor (died 1490). Some say 1517, but class makes this unlikely. Angels holding shields and tracery panels, loose hair and circlet which were originally jewelled. Surcoat hollowed out at sides with mantle over, open at the front and fastened by a cord. Hands and arms damaged. Angels and dogs at feet much damaged. She died in Whitchurch, Shrops.

G186 Kidderminster, Worcs. Knight and lady. Sir Hugh Cokesey (died 1445) and wife. SS collar, tabard and ridged salet with visor raised. Lady has horned headdress.

G187 Stanford on Terne, Worcs. Knight and lady. Sir Humphrey Selway, Salway or Salwey (died 1493) and wife Joyce. SS collar. Kneeling weepers once identified by shields with three grouped at end. Lady has truncated headdress and circlet. The monuments were formerly in the old church (now under the lake) but were removed in 1769 and have been turned round to face a different direction.

G188 Hornby, Yorks. Knight and lady. Sir John Conyers (died 1422) and wife Margaret. No tomb chest. Orle with 'ihc Nazare', pointed bascinet and fauld of lames. Lady has veil and wimple. John Bayliss has this as Trent Valley workshops. There are little dogs partially covered by folds of dress.

G189 Swine, Yorks. Knight and lady. Sir Robert Hilton (died 1372) and possibly wife Maud (of Campaigne, a Lascelles). Broken weepers and shield, chaplets of Lascelles on jupon, feather crest on helm. The west end cannot be seen as it is too close to the adjacent tomb. The head of the knight is in good order with a fine tapering moustache. This tomb is likened to that at East Harling, Norfolk (G21). The lady shows a barbe which can be compared with that on a tomb at Hornby, Yorks although this tomb is half a century later.

G190 Swine, Yorks. Knight and a lady. Believed to be Sir Robert Hilton (c.1410–1420) and possibly Joan (Constable). SS collar and orle. Chaplets of Lascelles on jupon, good armour. Lady has veil and wimple. Very similar to G191 in respect of tomb chest.

G191 Swine, Yorks. A knight possibly a member of the Hilton family (maybe also a Robert – c. 1420 or 1431). Tomb chest has pairs of angels holding shields which can be compared to those at Aston on Trent, John Cockayne, Ashbourne and Judge Gascoigne, Harewood (G193). Chaplets on jupon, very similar to G190. Lion.

G192 Harewood, Yorks. Harewood House church, Yorkshire. Knight and lady. Sir Richard Redman and his wife Elizabeth Aldburgh died 1434. Sir Richard was with Henry V at Agincourt. A native of Cumberland, Sir William acquired Harewood when his wife and her sister Sybil inherited the estate on the death of their brother William. The Redmans and Gacoignes intermarried so that Gawthorpe and Harewood became one. Harewood states that the church was built in 1410 but Arthur Gardner states the church rebuilt in 1430. It is believed that Sir Richard is buried elsewhere and the current tomb erected 1430–1434. The SS collar has interposed 'S's and flowers but pendant obscured by hands. The great helm has a horse's head and his bascinet has an orle. Angels and cushions, eagle buckle on hip-belt. Lady has crespine headdress, feet on dogs.

G193 Harewood, Yorks. Harewood House church. Civilian and lady. Judge Sir William Gascoigne (died 1419) and his first wife Elizabeth Mowbray. His second wife Joan Pickering was buried at Holme on Spalding Moor, Yorks. Close fitting coif and long robe. Lady has crespine headdress. Sir William was born at Gawthorpe the medieval home of the Gacoignes sited where the lake below Harewood House is today. He served Henry IV and has a fine reputation. There are antiquarian records which state that the tomb chest chamfer once held a brass inlay which gave the name and date of death. This was removed during the Civil War.

G194 Methley, Yorks, Waterton chapel. Knight and lady. Sir Robert Waterton died 1424 and wife Cecily (Fleming). Trinity, seated angels and shields. SS collar, bearded with a large orle like a turban – *see* L3. Saul claims that the orle has 'Ihc' imprinted – *see* Appendix L. The SS collar is unusual in that the S is alternated with crowns believed to be possibly indicating his fealty to the Lancastrian cause rather than an actual collar however it is probably that he was awarded a full collar during his lifetime.

G195 Barmston Yorks. Knight. Possibly Sir Martin de la Mare (died 1420) or William Monceux (died 1446). Angels holding shields and tracery panels. Orle with sacred name on bascinet. On the 18th October 1620 the church was visited by Roger Dodsworth, the antiquary who noted '… an ancient monument of alabaster. A man in armour thereon. No inscription. It came out of Brelington'. This is interpreted as stating it came from Bridlington Priory but the evidence for this is thin. The tomb chest indicates a Burton origin. Henry Lawrence in 1949 observed that '… the shop had this effigy on their hands carved for someone else and saw a chance of off-loading it to Barmston'. This is little more than a suggestion but Pauline Routh observes that the spurs have been sawn off and the great helm crest removed and a new one dowelled in which in turn has been lost. She also observes that an attempt has been made to remove the SS collar. Whilst none of this absolute proof the suspicion remains that the tomb is second hand.

G196 Harewood, Yorks. Knight and lady. Sir William Gascoigne (died 1465) and his wife Margaret Clarell of Rawmarsh, Yorks. The grandson of Judge Gascoigne (*see* G193). Appears to have supported the Lancastrian cause but was reconciled with Henry IV *circa* 1461 and therefore sports the Yorkist collar. The collar of suns and roses supports an animal pendant which is reputed to be a Lion of March. Lady Margaret married William as her third husband but there is some evidence of a clandestine affair as the marriage was very quickly after the death of her second husband. Their son William married into the Neville family and was knighted following the battle of Wakefield in 1466. The lady survived into her third widowhood and has veil and widow's barbe.

G197 Harewood, Yorks. Knight and lady. Sir William Gascoigne (died 1487) and his wife Margaret Percy (daughter of the Earl of Northumberland). The Earl had been killed at the battle of Towton in 1461. Involved in the marriage of Richard, Duke of York and made Knight of the Bath. Fought at Bosworth for Richard III, but reconciled with Henry VI and therefore allowed to wear the SS collar. Angels and weepers. The collar is mixed collar of SS and roses or suns indicating reconciliation between the houses of York and Lancaster fostered by Henry VI. The effigy has a tabard and bull's head crest on helm. Lady has veil and widow's barbe. Arthur Gardner identified this tomb as John Nevill of Womersley but this is now considered incorrect.

G198 Burton Agnes, Yorks. Knight and lady. Sir Walter Griffith (died 1481) and first wife Jane (or Joan). Saints and angels holding shields. SS collar, feet on griffin and great helm with a maiden crest. Lady has short SS collar, veil over loose hair, angels holding cushion and small figures of son and daughter on either side. These figures are exact miniature replicas of their parents. There are also saints under ogee gables. It is believed one figure was stolen in modern times. His second wife Agnes later married Sir Gervase Clifton of Nottingham and chose to be buried at Burton Agnes rather than at Clifton.

G199 Methley, Yorks. Knight and lady. Lord Welles KG. Knight killed at Towton 1461. Chain collar, tabard and garter robes. Lady has chain collar, horned headdress with wide forehead band.

G200 Ryther, Yorks. Knight. Sir William Ryther (died 1475). Weepers. Yorkist collar with Lion of March pendant and elaborate mail. May well have had a lady (Gough 1786). Three ogee canopies each with crockets and finials but have buttresses the full height at the corners, like Ashover.

G201 Thornhill, Yorks. Knight and lady. According to Pevsner it is Sir John Savill (died 1481) and his wife Alice (Gascoigne). However, Routh points out that the arms are those of a Thornhill and this is supported by Dodsworth (1620) and may well be Brian Thornhill and wife Joan FitzWilliam but doubt remains. The great helm shows the maiden crest of the Thornhills. Weepers – the ladies wear Yorkist dresses. Yorkist collar with Lion of March pendant places tomb post-1461. Lady has circlet over loose hair and head on cushion from which the angels have been removed. Dogs around the feet. Tomb chest has niches with shallow crocketted canopies. Crossley observes that the tomb was '… of the York school with weepers which are thin and wiry which makes them not good'. Gardner on the other hand disagrees. There is similar tomb at Llandegai, Wales (GNP112).

G202 Halsham, Yorks. Knight. Unknown but may be Sir John Constable. SS collar and rolled hair. It is suggested that the effigy came from Thornton Priory in Lincolnshire in the mid-16th century with the tomb chest of an earlier date.

G203 Sheriff Hutton, Yorks. Civilian. One time believed to be Edward, Prince of Wales, the son of Richard III (died 1484). Trinity and angels holding a shield to one side. The effigy is in civilian dress and a crown. Gardner says style is earlier than 1484 but could not come to conclusion. A review carried out by Dr Jane Crease in March 2013 and published in the 'Church Monument Society, Monument of the Month' proved that it could not be Edward but is likely to be a high status Neville child of the 1420s. The tomb is undersized and probably was once in the chantry chapel of the castle and may even have spent some time outside. Crease comments on the similarity of this monument with that at Methley (G194) and Harewood (G192). Firman believed the alabaster had texture similarities with that obtained from Rippon Park and this is agreed with by Crease except that she states the alabaster is 'local to York'. In fact Jane Crease states clearly the alabaster has small nodules of harder stone some of which has come to the surface. This is unlike the Trent Valley alabaster hence the attribution to Ripon. The style is unlike that of the Trent Valley particularly in respect of the niches and weepers and the consensus is that it was carved in York.

G204 South Cowton, Yorks. Knight. Possibly Sir Richard Conyers (died 1502). Tomb may date from 1509. SS collar with roses, Tudor rose pendant and band over hair.

G205 South Cowton, Yorks. Lady. Unknown. Flapped truncated headdress. May be Alice Wycliffe – *see also* GNP108, the wife of G204. The three effigies are without tomb chest and lie on metal frames.

G206 Harewood, Yorks. Knight and lady. Edward Redman of Levens (died 1510) and his wife Elizabeth Huddlestone (died 1529). Edward was great grandson of Sir Richard Redman with whom Gardner confused the effigy in 1940 noting that he said it did not look like 1476 but may 'later' in keeping with collar. The SS collar has intervening roses but sports a Tudor rose pendant probably introduced *circa* 1509. Widow's veil and barbe, bedesmen on lion at feet. Saints include St Lawrence, Edward the Confessor and St Stephen. The carver has used the bedesman to hide one plain sole of a sabaton popular at the end of the 15th century. The lion's tail is curved back to cover the other is a style reminiscent to the Harpur and Moorecock workshop.

G207 Batley, Yorks. Knight and lady. Sir William Mirfield (died 1497). Stone weepers. Lady has orle over loose hair. Noted by Dodsworth in 1620 as belonging to the Mirfield family. Pauline Routh has a fine description in her book (*see* bibliography).

G208 Penmynydd, St Gredifael, Anglesey. Knight and lady. Gronw Fychan (ap Tudor died 1382) and wife Myfanwy, ancestor of Henry Tudor. Forrester of Snowdonia, drowned in accident. Supporter of Owain Glyndwr in 1400. Empty niches. Fluted bascinet, small shield on camail over chin, breastplate under jupon. Lady has crespine and large string of buttons. This tomb was moved from Llanfaes Priory at the dissolution.

G209 Beaumaris, Wales. Knight and lady. Unknown. Salet with raised visor, SS collar.

G210 Howden, Yorks. Robert Partington (died 1491). Buried with father and mother before the altar.

G211 Cobham, Surrey. Reginald Lord Cobham (died 1361). Garter on left leg to which honour he was elected in 1352. Cobham was closely associated with other knights including Thomas Lord Berkeley whose tomb resembles that of Cobham's (*see* G11), Lord Burghersh, Sir Walter Pavely and the Earl of March. They are all represented on the tomb. The monument was commissioned by Joan, Cobham's widow who may also have commissioned Lord Berkeley's. The tomb at Cobham was repainted in modern times and it cannot be certain if the effigy is alabaster but it is included because of it forerunner status in the use of garter decoration. The tomb has the castellated top edge as seen on other monuments of the same era and currently has a metal railing.

G212 Ashbourne, Derbys. John Cockayne (died 1372). He was the senior administrator in the service of the Duchy of Lancaster supervising the estates north of the Trent which would have included the alabaster mining area of Tutbury and Fauld. He may well have been the steward instructed to obtain alabaster for John of Gaunt. The effigy is shown in the dress of a lawyer or attorney complete with coif. His tomb chest is 15th century freestone and is shared with the effigy of his son Edmund who was added in 1412. Edmund was killed at the Battle of Shrewsbury fighting for Henry IV. There are a number of shields showing links with other families some of which are disputed as the shields were repainted by Elias Ashmole in 1611. Jupon with three cocks.

GNP1 Acton, Cheshire. Knight Sir William Mainwaring (died 1399). SS collar with a sacred name on bascinet, ass head crest on helm. Inscription. Mainwaring was in military service in Aquitaine from 1369, dying there in 1399. He chose to be returned and buried in Acton, the proceeds from his time in France being used to pay for the monument. Low four-centred arch.

GNP2 Aylesbury, Bucks. Knight unknown. Breastplate under jupon. Not in good condition. This was believed to have found in the grounds of Aylesbury Greyfriars and was reported in 1885. It has been suggested that it is the founder of Greyfriars, James Boteler (Butler), the Earl of Ormonde but the heraldic remains do not support this.

GNP3 Newent, Gloucs. Knight and lady. Framed headdress.

GNP4 Kirby Bellars, Leics. Lady in widow's veil and barbe (*circa* 1360–1370).

GPN5 Kirby Bellars, Leics. Knight. Sir Roger Bellars (died 1380). Effigy in arched recess. Damaged and partially repaired. Great helm with coronet. Crest broken off. Hip belt.

GNP6 Huyton, Lancs. John de Winwick (died 1360) in quire habit. John who was rector of nearly Wigan and latterly treasurer of the Bishop of York founded the chantry in Huyton church in 1350. The effigy is tonsured. John de Winwick in his will specified that his brother Richard should oversee the founding of a college at Oxford known as St Mary's Hall (now part or Oriel) for which certain revenues from the sale of Ratcliffe on Soar church would be used. This earned censure from the pope for which Ratcliffe church was attacked on the evening of the 9th October 1381. For more details *see The Ratcliffe Chronicles* and *John de Winwick and his Chantry* by F Crooks, 1925.

GNP7 North Cockerington, Lincs. Knight *circa* 1380–1390 (may be John de Yerburgh of Cockington). The church is closed and under Churches Conservation Trust. The effigy is in bad condition with only torso and lion footrest remaining.

GNP8 Whatton, Notts. Knight Sir Adam (or Sir Hugh) de Newmarch (died 1377) with SS collar. There is heraldry on the jupon.

GNP9 Kingsbury, Warwicks. Knight unknown may have been lying on side with shield as per Hanbury but badly damaged. This may be a Bracebrigge.

GNP10 Aston, Warwicks. Knight unknown but believed to be Ralph Arden. Ornamental band on front of bascinet. Placed beside tomb of lady *circa* 1490 with whom he has no connection … Arcades without figures. The monument has been moved during a number of refurbishments. Gardner places monument at 1360, but current views place the carving later.

GNP11 Dorchester on Thames, Oxfordshire. Knight, Hugh Segrave died 1387. Band round bascinet. Tomb chest does not belong. Leland observed in 1543 'Here lieth a knight on the north side of the choir who the late Abbott believed to be a Seagrave. The image was in alabaster. However, I later heard that the knight was one Holcum'

GNP12 Orlingbury, Northants. Knight details unknown.

GNP13 Pickering, Yorks. Knight *circa* 1380 but only a fragment comprising head and torso. There is a repeated pattern of small castles like chess pieces round the margin of the bascinet which in some quarters is identified with the Roucliffe family. *Ryedale and North Yorkshire Antiquities* states that the depicted is a member of the Lascelles family of Keld Head. Gough described this tomb in 1785 and noted that the chapel was being used as a school with the tombs boxed up.

GNP14 Barthomley, Cheshire. Priest. Robert Foulshurst, rector (died 1529).

GNP15 Greystoke, Cumbria. Knight. John Greystoke, 4th Baron Greystoke 1389–1436. May be later than that recorded by Gardner as 1436 was date of will. SS collar and circle of flames round helm under head. Angels and saints displaced from origin position. Henry V hairstyle. This and G4 were stored outside and received vandalism from the local populace. Now moved inside in a specially constructed niche. CMS Vol XXIX 2014 has a brief description of John's funeral.

GNP16 Wetheral, Cumberland. Knight and lady. Sir Richard Salkeld died 1518 and Jane Vaux (died 1500). Tomb probably delivered in his lifetime. SS collar (check as some reports say Yorkist). Lady flapped headdress.

GNP17 Bakewell, Derbys. Knight. Sir Thomas Wendesley (or Wensley). SS collar and orle. Angels and cushions. He was killed at Shrewsbury in 1403. Linked to G57 and GNP68. Thomas Wensley was a close associate of John of Gaunt and one-time overseer of the duchy lands in the East Midlands.

GNP18 Longford, Derbys. Knight. Sir Nicholas de Longford (died *circa* 1350) and wife Alice. This effigy and G59 have been moved and lay side by side. There are three Nicholas de Longford effigies (GNP18, GNP121 and G59).

GNP19 Newton Solney, Derbys. Knight (*circa* 1375). Unknown, but thought to be Sir John de Solney. Angels supporting pillow and feet on lion.

GNP20 Great Cubley, Derbys. Knight. Sir Nicholas Montgomery died 1435 married Margaret Foljambe (Chesterfield and Bakewell). Severely damaged with missing legs. An SS collar was identified by Gardner but is believed to an early form of Yorkist collar which may indicate a carving date close to 1461. Orle. Feet on dog. The tomb chest has angels with shields.

GNP21 Ashbourne, Derbys. Knight and lady. Claimed by Ashbourne as Sir John Bradbourne (died 1483) and wife Anne (Vernon, died 1499). Moved in 1840.

GNP22 Repton, Derbys. Knight, believed to be Thomas Fraunceys (or may be Robert Francis, Lord of Foremark) died 1482. Yorkist collar.

GNP23 Norton, Derbys. Judge and Lady. William Blythe 1518. Erected by son Bishop Geoffrey Blythe of Lichfield *circa* 1530. Lady has long pediment. This is credited to Harpur and Moorecock and must have been carved in the final years. The slab has embattled edges and does not appear to have an edge inscription.

GNP24 Scropton, Derbys. Knight and two ladies. Nicholas Agard. Both ladies have long pediments. Knight has chain collar.

GNP25 Chesterfield, Derbys. Henry Foljambe (died 1510). Gardner said this was an unknown tomb chest with weepers and angels which classify this as (V). This has been identified as being made Harpur and Moorecock of Burton. It formerly had brasses (since Gardner wrote these have now been restored). The tomb is a tabletop with inlay and was to be modelled on that of Sir Nicholas Montgomery of Great Cubley, Derbys – for full transcript *see* X22. A 17th century effigy has been placed on the chest – *see* R64.

GNP26 Modbury, Devon. Knight. Unknown but possibly Sir John Champernowne (died 1503). Collar of roses. May have received damage during the Civil War.

GNP27 Puddletown, Dorset, Athelhampton chapel. Knight and lady. Unknown *circa* 1470, but probably a member of the Martyn family. Lady has butterfly. In Gardner's time one side panel with angels was placed above the effigy on the wall indicating that tomb is likely to have been moved. The knight has feet on ape. Mutilated and may indicate Tudor vandalism. Some blue colour remains. In 2005 the tomb was moved to the centre of the chapel and the side panel restored. The tomb chest has clear Trent Valley features.

GNP28 Netherbury, Dorset. Knight. Unknown. SS collar and long hair.

GNP29 Dalton le Dale, Durham. Knight. Possibly Sir William Bowes. There is an effigy to an unknown lady which is badly preserved which may not be alabaster.

GNP30 Redmarshall, Durham. Knight and lady. Thomas de Langton. SS collar and orle. Horned headdress.

GNP31 Christchurch, Hants. Knight and lady. Sir John Chidiock (died 1461) and wife Kathryn (Lumley). SS collar.

GNP32 King's Pyon, Hereford. Knight. Unknown (*circa* 1440). Placed beside a stone lady. Severely damaged with missing limbs.

GNP33 Weobley, Hereford. Knight. Believed to be Sir William Devereux (died *circa* 1430) SS collar and orle.

GNP34 Bredwardine, Hereford. Knight. Sir Roger Vaughan (died *circa* 1450). May be later as he was killed at Agincourt. SS collar and orle.

GNP35 Hereford. Bishop Stanbury or Stanberry (died 1474 at Ludlow). The tomb was badly damaged during the Reformation when all the faces including that of the bishop were removed. The tomb chest has angels holding shields. The tomb chest has Burton features.

GNP36 Kington, Hereford. Knight and lady. Thomas Vaughan (died 1469) and Ellen (Gethin). Yorkist collar. Lady has flapped headdress. Thomas was slain at Banbury (Edgcote Moor). He has feet on lion. Restored at some date. The tomb chest has niches with saints holding shields.

GNP37 Stoke Edith, Hereford. Lady *circa* 1482–1520 according to Gardner but 1470 by the *History of Hereford*. Unknown. Butterfly.

GNP38 Royston, Herts. Knight. Unknown. Gough suggests that the effigy was transferred from the local priory and was one of the founders, Eustace de la Mere or Ralph de Roucester.

GNP39 Minster in Sheppey, Kent. Knight. Sir Thomas Cheyne KG (died 1558), Lord Warden of the Cinque Ports. Small ruff and garter robes. Thomas was originally buried in St John's chapel but his son demolished the chapel in 1581 transfering Thomas's body to the church. It therefore uncertain if the tomb dates from 1558 and moved with the body or if it was installed in 1581. Marcus Herbert 2011 concludes that Cheyne died 1487 his tomb carries a Yorkist collar but the only Cheyne known to have died in that year was William Cheyne, Thomas's father. The tomb was said to be made in his lifetime circs 1473-1483 but Llewellyn claims a tomb was made in 1560 but without knowing the body was moved. He also claims the tomb shows '… a fashionable plainness'

GNP40 Warrington, Lancs. Knight and lady. Sir John Butler (or Botelier) who died *circa* 1462–1463 and wife Margaret. The tomb chest is a collection of bits made up when the church was restored in 1847. Plain collar and hands clasped. Lady has cauls and veil. The angels may have been assembled from an old retable. It is reputed that he was murdered at Bewsey in circumstances which remain unclear.

GNP41 Burscough, Lancs. Formerly in Burscough Priory (dissolved 1536). A Knight and lady believed to be a Stanley. Long hair, chain collar and tabard. Lady has coronet and veil.

GNP42 Ormskirk, Lancs. Knight and lady possibly another Stanley. This is a duplicate of GNP41.

GNP43 Halsall, Lancs. Knight and lady. Sir Henry Halsall. Sated by Gardner as 1490 but may be as late as 1523.

GNP44 Whitwick, Leics. Knight. Sir John Talbot (died 1365). In poor condition. The knight wears a pointed bascinet with attached aventail. The head rests on a great helm which may have had a dog (Talbot) crest. Sir John was reputed to be a giant and his effigy is 6ft 6½in long. At one time it was recorded that the forehead was marked 'Jesus of Nazarenus' but there is also a record of the full inscription being 'Misere Mei Deus Jesus Nazarenus Rex Judacorum'.

GNP45 Appleby Magna, Leics. Knight and lady. Sir Edward de Appleby (died 1396) and wife. Poor-quality workmanship. Knight has great helm with peacock's head. Feet on lion, a pointed bascinet with attached aventail, hip belt and spurs. Lady has framed (nebule) headdress. The existence of the nebule some years after it was largely abandoned as a style places the date in question.

GNP46 Melton Mowbray, Leics. Lady (*circa* 1420 to 1450). Unknown, but heavily restored. The lady has head on cushion supported by two angels. Crown headdress and wimple.

GNP47 Lutterworth, St Mary, Leics. Cleric and lady. Sir John Fielding (death unknown but post-1430) and wife Margaret Purefoy in arched recess. Partially restored. Long robe over armour which is unusual for a cleric. Plain collar. Lady has veil. The apex of arch has depiction of soul being carried to heaven in a napkin. A picture has now been obtained. (It is reported that inscription relates to John's death in 1403 but this is believed to be a misreading of his birth date).

GNP48 Prestwold, Leics. Incised slab on chest tomb. The chest is Class V and slab may look like the one in Hanbury, Staffs. *See also* TT10.

GNP49 Swepstone, Leics. Knight. William Humphrey (died 1591).

GNP50 Fenny Drayton, Leics. Nicholas Purefoy died 1554 and wife Jane (Vincent). Probably Burton school (this is a tabletop and therefore more details held in TT5). *See* similarities with S65.

GNP51 Spilsby, Lincs. Knight and lady. John, 3rd Lord Willoughby d'Eresby (died 1372) and Joan (or Cecily) his wife. Orle, lady with three dogs at feet. Much restored. Flanked by pillars with small monks or bedesmen. John Bayliss claims this for the Trent Valley workshops. Saul claims that the bascinet has 'Ihc' imprinted. *See* 'Manuscript Account of Monuments in Spilsby Church' Lincolnshire Archives ref 3-ANC/9/24 by Gervase Holles 1814. Gough describes this tomb in some detail.

GNP52 Spilsby, Lincs. Knight. Robert 4th Lord Willoughby d'Eresby (died 1396) and Elizabeth. Possible new tomb chest. Restored. Small figures in niches with restored heads. Saul claims that the bascinet has 'Ihc' imprinted. Gardner wrongly dates this tomb. *See* 'Manuscript Account of Monuments in Spilsby Church' Lincolnshire Archives ref 3-ANC/9/24 by Gervase Holles 1814. Gough page 188 describes this tomb in some detail.

GNP53 Broughton, Lincs. Knight and lady. Sir Henry Redford or Retford (died 1409) and wife Catherine (widow of Sir Ralph Paynell). Freestone tomb chest. SS collar with defaced pendant and orle. Right hand originally holding wife's right hand. Lion with scroll in mouth. Crespine headdress.

GNP54 Stamford, St Mary, Lincs. Knight. Unknown but may be John Browne (died 1442). Limestone tomb chest. The effigy is in poor condition with loss of arms and lower legs. Originally head on two cushions supported by angels.

GNP55 Wellingore, Lincs. Knight and lady. This is the 1435 effigy of Sir Richard de Buslingthorpe and Isabella. SS collar with loop and ring pendant and orle. Widow's barbe and veil. The knight's nose has had a large hole drilled in it. Legs broken and repaired by cement. Head on great helm.

GNP56 Harlaxton, Lincs. Judge, Thomas Ricard (died 1410) and lady. Chaperon hat, gorget and liripipe, houppelande. Crespine headdress.

GNP57 Boston, Lincs. Knight in poor condition (*circa* 1539–1566). Angels holding shields, lion and great helm. Restored but poorly done. Possibly Sir John Tilney. Moved in 1770 or taken from St John's Church, Boston when that was pulled down in 1626.

GNP58 Boston, Lincs. Unrelated lady in poor condition (*circa* 1539–1566). Headdress and two small dogs at feet. This is possibly the sister of GNP57 and also restored. Moved as per GNP57.

GNP59 Old Leake, Lincs. Knight in poor condition (16th century) lying in a 14th century niche. Possible a member of the Leake family.

GNP60 Newport, Mon. Knight in poor condition. 'The History of Monmouth' in 2000 reports that the niche contains the arms of Sir John Morgan 1493 but that '… it cannot be ascertained if the torso of the knight and head-less woman belong'.

GNP61 Norwich Cathedral, Norfolk. Bishop Goldwell. Just a fragment. The cathedral was desecrated during the Civil War and the tomb claims to have a musket ball in it.

GNP62 Irthingborough, Northants. Unknown civilian and lady, possibly John and Joan Pyel. Angels and shields otherwise not in good condition.

GNP63 Irthingborough, Northants. Unknown lady. Long pediment.

GNP64 Great Addington, Northants. Knight. Unknown but may be Henry de Vere (died 1493). SS collar.

GNP65 Chillingham, Northumberland. Knight and lady. Sir Ralph Grey (died 1443) and wife Elizabeth (FitzHugh) but tomb may date from 1450. He appears to have died in France. Figures and 14 saints but only the effigies are alabaster. Short SS collar with tiret enclosure, tabard, decorated hip belt, and ladder and cloak badges. Lady has horned headdress. The tomb has a Jacobin limestone mural entablature added of uncertain date but which contains a Royalist motto and is probably mid-17th century commissioned by Edward Grey. The existence of the figures of saints is unique in that it appears to have escaped the Reformation iconoclasts. St Ralph's face may be a likeness.

GNP66 Bothal, Northumberland. Knight and lady. Sir Ralph Ogle (died 1513) and wife Lady Margaret Gascoigne. Tabard and chain collar. Flapped truncated headdress. Lord Ogle had the task of accompanying Princess Margaret to Scotland to marry James IV. The cording on the dress of Margaret indicates a Burton origin.

GNP67 Willoughby on the Wolds, Notts. Knight. Sir Richard Willoughby. Son of G24 represented by a tomb *circa* 1395. He sports a moustache. The head is covered by an aventail but he appears not to wear a bascinet. A decorated belt is low over the salet.

GNP68 Hoveringham. Knight and lady. Sir Robert Goushill and his wife. SS collar and orle. Swelling breastplate. Sir Robert was murdered following the battle of Shrewsbury during Henry IV reign. The effigy of the man displays late 14th century plate armour, jupon, camail hood and hauberk and rests his head on a helm (or tilting helmet) with an orle or garland around the steel headpiece. One glove is removed and he once held the hand of his wife. He has an SS collar round his neck from which the pendant has been broken (*see* Appendix E). The wife is Elizabeth Fitzalan (died 1425) one time Duchess of Norfolk and her effigy displays a peeress mantle and ducal coronet. Tomb may not have been built till 1425. *See* picture on cover. Style is similar to that of Sir Hugh Calverley at Bunbury (G2).

GNP69 Holme Pierrepont, Notts. Knight *circa* 14th century. Unknown and fragmented, only the trunk and head remaining. The alabaster is white Chellaston. The effigy shows signs of being outside at some time. The remains of a great helm is evident as are a belt and crenulated jupon. (This effigy resides next to an even older sandstone effigy of a civilian).

GNP70 Nottingham, St Mary. In 1940 Gardner recorded the presence of a fragment of an unknown civilian in alabaster dated 1413 to 1456. In 2014 this fragment was not found nor could anyone remember it. However, there is a tomb at the end of the north transept which has a trefoil canopy identical to that of John Samon (G137). The history book of the church claims that this canopy and the tomb recess was created late in the 15th century but the tomb now in it is a composite of three other medieval monuments. The suggestion is that during one of the rebuilding projects (possibly that of the 1840s) opportunity was taken to use the parts from other destroyed monuments in this recess. The canopy is attributed to Thomas Thurland (died 1473), the slab made of Purbeck marble is attributed to William de Amyas (died 1350) and the alabaster tomb chest to John Tannesley (died 1413). On the tomb top there is a framed fragment from a tomb chest which has been identified by the church as formerly belonging to Robert English (died 1475) a former mayor. The tomb chest displays a rare lily crucifix and the Amyas slab shows the indentations which formerly held brass inlays. It is clear St Mary once had many more tombs most of which appear to be alabaster. The Gardner fragment is mentioned by both Thoroton and Deering who describe the tomb as having figures similar to that in the frame and the church offers the suggestion that the lost effigy was that of Robert English.

GNP71 Worksop, Notts. Lady. Unknown but may be Lady Maude Neville. In poor condition, hair in cauls.

GNP72 Southwell, Notts. Bishop. Unknown but may be Archbishop William Booth. Reported by Gardner in 1919 as being in poor condition and now located in the side aisle of the chancel.

GNP73 Sutton Bonington, Notts. Knight. Badly battered similar to Minster in Sheppey. Yorkist collar. Identity uncertain but probably a Staunton *circa* 1470.

GNP74 Broughton, Oxford. Lady. Possibly Lady Wykeham (*circa* 1456) but details uncertain. Restored in 1846. SS collar and crespine headdress. Possibly mid-15th century. She does not belong to GNP75 although currently set side by side. Fragmentary tomb chest with lost canopy.

GNP75 Broughton, Oxford. Knight. Sir Thomas Wykeham (died 1470 or 1471) and wife Margaret. His was killed at the battle of Barnet. Also restored. Yorkist collar which means this is likely to be the husband of the granddaughter of GNP74.

GNP76 Minster Lovell, Oxford. Knight. Lord Lovell. Possibly William 7th Baron of Tichmarsh died 1455. Weepers and saints (one St Margaret). Has been retouched in colour *circa* 19th century and so displayed coats of arms which may not be correct. It has been suggested that it may be his son John (died 1465).

GNP77 Stanton Harcourt, Oxford. Knight. Sir Robert Harcourt (*circa* 1490). Y collar with Lion of March pendant. Angels and bedesmen round tomb chest. Possibly painted in 19th century. It is reputed that Sir Robert died in a feud between the Harcourts and the Staffords.

GNP78 Burley, Rutland. Knight and lady. Unknown (maybe William de Plessington who died in 1457). Has been attacked at some time. SS collar and Orle. Lady has horned headdress and SS collar.

GNP79 Exton, Rutland. Knight and lady. Sir John Harrington (died 1524) and wife Alice (Southill). Collar with motto. Pediment headdress with long flaps. The tomb carries bedesmen at the feet which makes the date of 1592 quoted by some authorities unlikely. Spiral pilasters. There were a number of John Haringtons but the 1592 date appears to relate to James Harington. The lion at the feet of the knight has its tail split and attached to the sole of the sabatons which probably indicates a product of the Burton workshops.

GNP80 Ashwell, Rutland. Priest much defaced. Unknown. Eucharistic vestments.

GNP81 Tong, Salop. Knight and lady. Sir Fulke Pembrugge, lord of Tong 1371 to 1409 with wife Isabella de Lingen (died 1446). Orle. Lady has veil and barbe. Isabella founded Tong church, the chantry and college in 1410 in commemoration of Sir Fulke and her two later husbands Thomas Peyteveyne and John Ludlow. Isabella's daughter is commemorated by G148 by which marriage the Vernons of Hadden acquired Tong. It is suggested that the gap between the effigies may indicate that gablettes were originally placed over the heads.

GNP82 Shrewsbury, Shrops. Knight and lady. William Charlton (died 1532) and wife Alice or Ann Hoorde or Horde. This may well have been in Apley Castle before being transferred to Wellington church and when this was demolished in 1789 it was left outside and then brought into Shrewsbury Abbey. Possibly new head. Was painted. Angels and bedesmen. Lady has long pediment.

GNP83 Dunster, Somerset. Knight and lady. Sir Hugh Luttrell (died 1428) and wife. SS collar and orle. The effigies are damaged below the trunk.

GNP84 Elford, Staffs. Knight. Unknown but reputed to be Sir Thomas Latham (died 1382). When restored in 1852 by Edward Richardson the date given as 1470 which is clearly wrong taking into account the armour. Local history says this is Sir John Stanley (died 1474) but this too is probably incorrect. Near his head is an eagle and baby depicting a legend about an adoption of an illegitimate son. Nearby is a memorial to Sir John Stanley's grandson killed by a tennis ball in 1460 (this is not alabaster).

GNP85 Audley, Staffs. Knight. Unknown. This effigy is straight-legged and raised on freestone tomb. The monument was sketched in the 19th century and this can be seen in the William Salt Library of the Staffordshire Archives. The effigy has lost both arms but has feet on lion, a camail and chevron baldric. Possibly Sir John Tuchet (died 1360) who married Joan De Audley of Heleigh Castle. The effigy is reported as once holding a shield.

GNP86 Burton on Trent, Staffs. Knight. Unknown. Fragment with crossed legs and may have held a shield. This was in the museum and has been classified V by Gardner who was uncertain of the date states that it is *circa* 1470 or later. Gardner says he saw a shield which had a Tudor style. *See* effigy at Hanbury.

GNP87 Leigh, Staffs. Knight and lady. Unknown. Weepers in pairs and angels. Collar of roses. Lady has short pediment.

GNP88 Chichester, Sussex. Bishop John Rickingale (died 1428). This monument was formerly identified as being attributable to Bishop Storey (died 1503). A fine monument with a tomb chest with four lozenges containing shields which have been repainted.

GNP89 Birmingham, St Martin in the Bullring, Warwicks. Knight. Believed to be Sir John de Birmingham. Arcades without figures, band round bascinet. Gardner places monument at 1360, but current views place the carving later. The effigies in St Martin show wear on the top the work of centuries of window cleaners who stood on them.

GNP90 Aston, Warwicks. Knight and lady. Sir Thomas Erdington (died 1433) and wife (died 1460). Tomb is Class IV which indicates constructed at latter date. Both have SS collars although in the case of the knight there has been an attempt at removal. Lady had butterfly headdress.

GNP91 Aston, Warwicks. Knight. A member of Harcourt family possibly Sir William. Angels and Yorkist collar (may be responsible for damage to GNP90.

GNP92 Astley, Warwicks, Knight. Sir Edward Grey, Lord Ferrers of Groby (died 1457). SS collar.

GNP93 Grendon, Warwicks. Lady *circa* 1460. Unknown. Butterfly headdress.

GNP94 Birmingham, Warwicks St Martin. Priest (*circa* 1500) unknown in quire habit.

GNP95 Compton Winyates. Lady. Unknown, possibly Dame Werburge (Compton). Poor condition – lower part only.

GNP96 Compton Winyates. Knight. Sir William Compton (died 1528). SS and tabard otherwise in poor condition. Thomas Cox says that Compton ordered that his wife, mother and father should be buried in the same tomb. The tomb was specified in his will of the 8th March 1522.

GNP97 Monk's Kirby, Warwicks. Knight and lady. Sir William Fielding and wife Elizabeth (Poultney). Balding man. Lady has short pediment and ruff (which is early). Some question as to whether the knight has been reworked from an earlier effigy.

GNP98 Coleshill, Warwicks. Knight and lady. John Digby (died 1558) and wife Anne Thockmorton (died 1558). There are similarities with G178 in that the stylised lion seems to be from the same hand. GNP98 has been identified with the Royley workshop. There are twisted pilasters and shields in niches with arrow heads. Plain corner pilasters.

GNP99 Martley, Worcs. Knight. Sir Hugh Mortimer. Yorkist collar (a bit early making date of 1459 suspect).

GNP100 Bromsgrove, Worcs. Knight and two ladies. Sir John Talbot of Albrighton and his two wives. Sir John died 1501 and it is most likely that the tomb was built on death of second wife Elizabeth Wrottesley. First wife was Margaret Troutbeck. Knight has SS collar. One lady has a short pediment and the other a Queen of Scots cap.

GNP101 Pickering, Yorks. Knight and lady. Sir David Roucliffe (died 1407) and wife Margery. No tomb chest. Both have SS collars and the knight has an orle – much broken. Has a castle on his surcoat – *see also* GNP13. The knight's hands may well have held a heart.

GNP102 Selby, Yorks. Knight. John, Lord Darcy (will dated 1411). SS collar otherwise much worn. Moved in 1857 during which some parts were lost. It was dismantled again in 1890 and was in pieces when the fire of 1906 happened. The pieces were later assembled at an unspecified date. Routh likens the tomb chest to that on the Oxford tomb at Bures (G113), one at Ashbourne, Screveton (note on A2) and the Neville tomb at Staindrop (G104). The monument is in a poor state.

GNP103 Darfield, Yorks. Knight and lady. Sir John Bosville (died 1405). SS collar. Lady has net over hair, angels and cushions.

GNP104 Harewood, Yorks. Knight and lady. Sir William Ryther of Ryther Castle Yorks and his wife Sybil Aldeburgh of Harewood died 1440. Ryther is between Selby and Tadcaster. Sybil is co-heir of Harewood with Elizabeth (*see* G192). This union endured that the Ryther, Redman and Gascoigne families held Harewood jointly for some 200 years. The effigies are very similar to G192. The SS collar is formed of plain 'S's and like G192 the pendant is obscured by the hands.

GNP105 Wadworth, Yorks. Knight and lady. Sir Edmund FitzWilliam (died 1431) and wife Maud (died 1433) although the effigy shows no signs of widow's weeds. Headless angels holding shields. The knight has SS collar and orle. Lady has veil over caul. FitzWilliam may have held a serjeanty post as his tomb depicts a hunting horn. The tomb chest has angels holding shields but no niches, buttresses or canopies. Has been linked with the Gascoigne tomb at Harewood (G196) in respect of the tomb chest.

GNP106 Wentworth, Yorks. The tomb is in the old church now a chapel. Knight and lady. A member of the Gascoigne family.

Nothing is left of the old tomb chest except for one panel showing canopied niches which favour those at Harewood. Weepers. SS collar with trefoil pendant and tabard. The lady is badly battered, being only the torso and head and is not shown as widow. The crest on the great helm has disappeared. Pauline Routh has a long discourse on the identity of the occupant of this tomb but without firm conclusions. There are also unsubstantiated suggestions that the tomb was moved from Monk Bretton priory.

GNP107 Eastrington, Yorks. Civilian and lady. Sir John Portington (died 1462) and wife. Judges coif and robes over armour. Alabaster effigies on stone tomb chest. The lady is headless and of different length which is suspicious. Angels holding shields on tomb chest. The tomb is not well executed. There is a suspicion that this may well be a York carving.

GNP108 South Cowton, Yorks. Lady. Unknown but probably a Conyers (*circa* late 15th Cent) but Routh suggests that it may well be Eleanor Lascelles, the daughter of Richard Conyers and the second wife of Sir Richard Lascelles (died before 1498). Orle over loose hair. *See also* G205. This is an individual effigy but was once placed with G204. This is just the effigy and stacked with G205.

GNP109 Allerton Mauleverer, Yorks. Knight and lady. Sir John Mauleverer *circa* 1458 but may be some 40 years later. Beavor. On the 18th October 1620 the church was visited by Roger Dodsworth, the antiquary who noted in the north quire '… an ancient monument of alabaster with the portraiture of a young man in armour and a woman lying by him'. The effigies are still there but now mounted on a brick tomb chest. The effigies are crudely carved but may well prove to be an early Burton tomb. Pauline Routh (*see* bibliography) has affine description of this tomb.

GNP110 Whitkirk, Yorks. Knight and lady. Sir Robert Scargill (died 1530) and wife Jane (Conyers died 1547). Fought at Flodden. Weepers. Queen of Scots cap. Tomb erected as part of will of the lady *circa* 1546–1547. This may well be a transition tomb as it has spiral pilasters and columns. It is unclear if an effigy existed when Sir Robert died in 1530. Jane had requested that '… her executors within three years immediately ensuing my decease shall cause a tomb of alabaster to be made and set over the bones of my said husband and me … the same to be in fashion like the one erected within the college of Macclesfield'. Routh observes that of all the monuments in Macclesfield none resemble the Whitkirk tomb nor can any reason for the request be established.

GNP111 Montgomery, Wales. Knight. Unknown in poor condition and restored with stone. There may be a problem with the dating of this as the effigy shows a Yorkist collar which placing it late 15th century.

GNP112 Llandegai, Wales. William Griffith of Penrhyn *circa* 1480. Angels holding shields. Yorkist collar. Lady has butterfly with flap. This has been likened to that at Thornhill, Yorks (G201).

GNP113 Slebech, Wales. Knight and lady. Sir Henry Wogan (died 1475). Possibly restored. Yorkist collar. Lady has orle over loose hair. It is reported that this monument has been moved to the County Museum.

GNP114 Ruabon, Wales. Knight and lady. John ap Elis Eyton (died 1526) and his wife Elizabeth (died 1524). Fought at Bosworth having joined Henry VII. Angels and saints. SS collar with Tudor rose pendant. The Monuments of Wales identifies the tomb chest as being only 3ft 10 inches long. There are similarities to the Sacheverell tomb (R136).

GNP115 Llandaff, Wales. Knight. Sir.

David Mathew (died 1484). He was standard bearer to Edward IV at Towton. For full details *see*: http://www.walesonline.co.uk/lifestyle/nostalgia/welsh-history-month-tomb-david-3406443?pageNumber=13

GNP116 Llandaff, Wales. Lady. Unknown. Widow's veil and barbe. Known locally as 'Lady Audrey'.

GNP117 Llandaff, Wales. Knight and lady. Sir Christopher Mathews (died 1500) and wife Elizabeth (died 1526). Weepers. SS collar. Short pediment. Freestone ogee arch.

GNP118 Llandaff, Wales. Knight and lady. Sir William Mathew (died 1528) and wife Jenette (died 1530). Angels and bedesmen. An unusual SS collar formed of linked letters S on their side with a pendant which has not yet been identified. Short pediment. Crossley has a fine picture of this tomb on page 97.

GNP119 Montgomery, Wales. Knight. Unknown. Restored in stone and painted.

GNP120 Tenby, Wales. Alabaster tomb chest on which has been placed a stone effigy of Thomas Whyte. The chest has saints and family of original deceased.

GNP121 Longford, Derbys. Knight. Sir Nicholas de Longford (died *circa* 1404). This effigy lies on a tomb chest under a canopy arch. Pointed bascinet, SS collar and mail gorget, under head a great helm with the crest of the Longfords reputed to be three mushrooms. There are three de Longford effigies, all Sir Nicholas GNP18, GNP121 and G59.

GNP122 Alvingham, Lincs. Fragment – torso and lion with portion of tomb chest. No identification possible. Gardner listed this item and Pevsner mentions it in passing.

GNP123 Tong, Shrops. Fragment blocking old processional door. Angels holding shield possibly end panel from old tomb. A similar fragment can be found elsewhere in the church.

Links:

L1 Chellaston linked monuments, mainly Sutton and Prentys, include Elford (G158, 1408), Henry IV at Canterbury (G97, 1413), Bottesford (G103,1414), Thomas Earl of Arundel (G167, 1416), Ashwellthorpe (G121, 1417), Lowick (G122, 1419), Barmston (G195, 1420), Haversham (G39, 1422), Tewkesbury in freestone (1422), Merevale (G173, 1440), Dodford (G125, 1444), Ashbourne (G58, 1447), Willoughby (G138, 1448), Aston-on-Trent (G60, 1450), Tong (G148, 1451), Lingfield (G166, 1453) and Over Peover (G45, 1456). These have gablettes and/or angels in niches holding shields – *see* page 6 of Gardner and photograph of Lowick which shows both tabernacles over the heads of the angels (by contract) and canopy (gablette) over the heads of the effigies. The exception is the Greystoke gablette (G4, 1367) which is too early for these carvers and Barthomley (1389) but may well be from an earlier Trent Valley workshop. The Barthomley angels are crudely carved but have serrated edges to the wings. However, there is some evidence of the tomb chest being later than 1389 so some doubt remains. The dates of the recognised Chellaston tombs above span some 48 years which for the time is exceptional for a single group of carvers. The date of the death of either Sutton or Prentys is fugitive and it is possible the workshop continued under the management of sons of the original owners. Crossley is firm in the belief that the kneeling or standing angels holding shields before them clothed in albs with outspread wings with serrated edges is definitely a feature of the Chellaston workshops. In the case of Dodford and Tong the angels alternate with saints or apostles. The Dodford tomb has angels in pairs in the style of York which makes the identification of this tomb with Chellaston speculative although Crossley is firm in this score. For later angels and shields *see* L39.

L2 Harpur and Moorecock linked monuments include Foljambe tomb at Great Cubley (G73, 1491), Strelley (G139, 1501), Little Chart (G101, 1509), Harewood (G206, 1510), Chesterfield (GNP25, 1510), William Bythe at Norton (G94, 1510), Tamworth (G160, 1512), Tong (g149, 1517), Thomas Babington at Ashover (G69, 1518), Coleshill (G178, 1519), Tower of London (T28, 1521), Malpas (G53, 1522), Godshill IOW (G91, 1522), Madeley (TT28, 1522), Exton (GNP79, 1524), Elford (G159, 1525), Macclesfield (G52, 1528) and Llandaff (GNP118, 1528). Some have seated friars. Prestwold (G110, 1520) and North Aston (G143, 1490) may be of same school although Chatwin assigns them to Burton though not to Moorecock or Harpur.

L3 The York school 1400 to 1430 – *see* page 6 of Gardner but may well have started *circa* 1372. This group includes Swine

(G189, 1372 and G190, 1410 and G191, 1403). Harewood (G193, 1419 and GNP104, 1426) and Methley (G192, 1430 and G194, 1424). The seated angels with shields are believed to be a feature of this workshop. A later tomb at Burton Agnes (G198, 1481) has the same arrangement with two angels except the shield is mounted on the string course on the tomb end. Colin Rowntree writing at the eve of World War Two reports on the repair and reordering of the Swine monuments. They had been roughly repaired and suffered from damp. The work was paid for by the Pilgrim's Trust and Yorkshire Archaeological Society and was carried out by G W Milburn & Son at a cost of £53 8s 9d.

L4 Linked incised slabs include John Wydeville of Grafton Regis, Northants 1415 and Thomas Lovell of Clevedon, Somerset are the same. William Grevel 1440 of Drayton Oxon is the same as Richard Spicer of Claverley, Salop.

L5 G43 and G136 may have close links. Both are 1539.

L6 Notes on the monuments of Humberstone church. All but one of the medieval and the Tudor/Stuart memorials were swept away in the rebuilding of this church in 1857–1858. The one to remain is Hotoft's (*see* TT1). Why this should have survived is unclear. One other alabaster monument is mentioned *circa* 1638 and this is listed in the 'Disappeared List' below *circa* 1500. The remaining lost monuments included one for Joan Thistlewaite which may well have been a tabletop of freestone and Swithland slate. This monument was claimed by Lord Hastings in 1637 as having been illegally installed and therefore should be removed. The claim went before the Archdeaconry Court and dragged on for some 3 years. The details can be found in a paper Hastings V Thistlewaite – The Humberstone Monument Case 1637–1639 by Brian Burch dated 1982. The monument was without effigy or inscribed image and contained only English text being formulated by the parish clerk both local masons William Haswell (60) and his son Thomas (22) both of Leicester, being illiterate.

L7 Chesterfield, Derbys. The Foljambe tombs were removed from their original position and assembled in the former Lady Chapel (renamed Foljambe Chapel), at the Reformation, during the 19th century restoration by Gilbert Scott. *See* GNP25 and R62 to R64.

L8 Mavesyn Ridware, Staffs. The Church of St Nicholas has a number of alabaster slabs but it is recorded that Charles Chadwick in the late 18th century (reported as 1779) refurbished the north aisle by means of the addition of alabaster wall panels showing his ancestors and their deeds. However it is believed that a number of monuments were lost at this time. Other Hollemans slabs are at Queenhill (S8), Packington (S9), Claverley (S20), Croxall (1605) and Hornsey

(S10). The slabs at Noseley (S69) may also be from the same workshop.

L9 Narborough (Narburgh), Norfolk. On 27th August 1844 a traveller noted the monuments in Narburgh (*sic*) church. He describes one monument as '... a square pillar about 7ft high within which is vertically interred the body of Clement Spelman and upon which is a life-size statue of alabaster shown in robes of a recorder'. Spelman was the recorder for Nottingham and oyer and terminer for the Midland circuit. He died 30th January 1679 aged 72. The coffin was discovered in Victorian times (probably *circa* 1840) when the monument was moved from the centre of the chancel and the plinth shortened. Clement Spelman specified that he should be buried upright to avoid being walked on but is now buried elsewhere.

L10 Charlecote, Warwicks. The Lucy Chapel contains three notable monuments all to a Sir Thomas Lucy. Two are detailed in R65 and M120. The third is a fine marble monument made by the Nicholas Stone workshop in 1640.

L11 Merevale, Warwicks (G173, 1440), East Shefford (G33, 1440) and Willoughby on the Wolds, Notts (G138, 1448) appear to be linked although there are variations in the tomb chest.

L12 Harlaxton (GNP56, 1410), Harewood (G193, 1419), Aston on Trent (G60, 1450 – although may be earlier) appear to from same workshop – *see also* L1.

L13 Dunster (GNP83, 1428), Porlock (G153, 1440), Dennington (G162, 1446), Bromsgrove (G184, 1450), Tong (G148, 1451), Over Peover (G45, 1456) have similarities – *see also* L1. One feature is the horned headdress on the lady. Others with horned headdress include East Shefford (G33, 1440), Tideswell (G57, 1440), Ashbourne (G58, 1447), Horwood (G76, 1450), Dunmow (G83, 1460), Weobley (G92, 1457), Burghill (G93, 1450), Abergavenny (G118, 1450), Greens Norton (G126, 1457), Willoughby-on-the Wolds (G138, 1448), Merevale (G173, 1440), Kidderminster (G186, 1443), Methley (G199, 1461), Redmarshall (GNP30, 1440), Chillingham (GNP65, 1443) and Burley (GNP78, 1457). These span a period 1440 to 1460 and whilst horned headdresses were a common feature of a period in medieval history the close grouping of the effigies which depict this points to a single source. That source may well be Sutton and Prentys but more work has to be done to prove this. Greenhill states that there is a similarity in treatment of the knight's pauldrons which can also be found on the slabs at Newbold on Avon and at Dauntsey, Wilts. From the Fécamp purchase of 1414 it is known that Sutton and Prentys had premises in Nottingham as well as Chellaston and it possible that some carving was done there especially any slabs which would have been difficult to transport in a finished state from Chellaston.

L14 Cheetham says Holme Pierrepont (G135, 1499) and Strelley (G139, 1501) and Ratcliffe on Soar (G136, 1539) are from the same workshop. All three and Lowick (G123, 1498) show lozenge shaped sides to tomb chest and there are likenesses in the effigies.

L15 Bottesford (G103, 1414) and (G105, 1421) are from same workshop.

L16 It is believed that the great Durham reredos of 1380 was based on that for Exeter. The Durham reredos is made from Caen stone and carved in London and included 107 figures in an unknown material which may or may not have been alabaster. Gardner goes one further and suggests that the figures were Nottingham carved and sent to London before being reshipped to Tyneside. The niches which held these are now empty the legend being that they were removed at the Reformation and hidden never to be found. The reredos is the work of Henry Yeaveley and commissioned by Lord John Neville. Yeaveley's association with the alabaster of Needwood Forest makes the use of alabaster a distinct possibility.

L17 Gardner states that Batley (G207, 1496), Thurlaston (G108, 1509) and Abergavenny (G120, 1510) is in the same hand.

L18 Wethersfield, Essex (G85, 1490) and Chilton, Suffolk (G164, 1500) are stated to be in yet another hand. Gardner considered these differ from Northern schools. The ladies have respectively a Yorkist and SS collar but the husbands are without. Gardner has the opinion that the families copied one another and may be London origin.

L19 Spare

L20 Spilsby, Lincs. Current sources of information on St James Church are confused and the identity of the effigies is not completely established. Gardner in 1940 identifies two alabaster tombs, one undated to Robert but is classified as a Class II and therefore pre-1400. The second is William which he dates as 1420. Others identify three effigies to successive John d'Eresbys and claim the tomb to William is a brass. The description given by Holles in 1814 may clarify the situation but has yet to be viewed by the author. Margaret Whinney identifies the 1612 monument to Peregrine Bertie, 10th Lord Willoughby (died 1601) and his daughter Katherine (died 1610) in St James, Spilsby to John Taylor. Llewellyn observes that Willoughby shows no emotion and stands upright gazing into the distance with his baton in hand. Katherine died in childbirth and her baby lies in a crib at her feet. The monument M63 to Peregrine Bertie is also to Katherine Willoughby, Baroness Willoughby d'Eresby, formerly Duchess of Suffolk, who died in 1580. In 2015 Katherine was named as the potential 7th wife of Henry VIII by David Baldwin should Katherine Parr have died or been deposed.

L21 St John Hope (page 232) suggests that a group comprising Sir Thomas Greene (Greene Norton, G126, 1457), Aston, Warwicks (GNP90, 1460), Sir Robert Harcourt (Stanton Harcourt, G141, 1471) and Sir John Crosby (Bishopsgate, G116, 1475) are from the same workshop. This period was one of the few dominated by York workshops although the Chellaston workshop was still working, so a clear identification remains elusive.

L22 Spare

L23 Greenhill draws likeness in the inscribed tabletop slabs of the Chesterfield tomb of Henry Foljambe (GNP25) and that of Madeley Staffs to Randolph Egerton (TT28). Based on this assumption he links the slab at Turnastone (S51, 1522), Westhide, Hereford (S253, 1524), Noseley, Leics (S52, 1525) and Woodcote, Shrops (S220, 1527) all from the same workshop. He cites the handling of the sword hilt in all cases to be the same and not found on any other carving.

L24 Although Sutton and Prentys are renowned for their effigies, Greenhill makes a clear link between the slabs at Grafton Regis (TT22 of 1415) and that at Clevedon, Somerset also *circa* 1415.

L25 Greenhill states that Ratcliffe on Soar (S54, 1487) has similarities with Stoke Dry, Rutland (1479), Breedon on the Hill (1494), Rothley (TT7, 1486), Holdenby, Northants (S215, 1490) and Gaddesby, Leics (S216, 1498) although no workshop is named. The similarities are in the dress of the lady.

L26 A group comprises Lowdham (S1), King's Norton (S55, 1513) and Willesley, Leics (1505) – all priests from an unknown workshop.

L27 Another group includes Aston Botterell (1501), Penkridge (1502), Beckbury (S32, 1505), Blithfield (1508 or 1534), Staveley (1510), South Scarle (1510), Crich (1513), Cofton Hackett (1514), Tettenhall (1517) and Croxall (1521). These too are as yet unassigned to a workshop. However, Greenhill likens them to the group listed as L28.

L28 This group includes Brewood (1518), Draycott in the Moors (1522), Thakeham (1527) and Tong (1531).

L29 This group depicting strange armour includes Rothley (TT29), West Hallam (1530), Saxelby (S56), Langar (1537), Bulkington (TT30), Lockington (S58 and S59) and Kedleston (S60). S59 has been identified with the Royley workshop.

L30 Greenhill groups four slabs as possibly Leicester carved. These are St Mary de Castro (1543) thinly carved and poor, Peckleton (S65, 1544), Fenny Drayton (GNP50/TT5, 1545) and Breedon on the Hill (1545).

L31 A small group of two slabs unlike any others includes the 1558 slab at Stanton by Bridge (S66) and that at Kirk Langley (S68, 1559). The effigies are said to have elongated legs but otherwise of an exceptional standard.

L32 Greenhill links slabs S231 at Aston Flamville, Leics and TT33 at Coleshill and being replicas.

L33 Greenhill links the slab of Sir John Byron (TT16) in Newstead (formerly Colwick – moved 1937), that of Ipsley (S231) and Barbara, wife of Thomas Cockayne at Ashbourne (S91).

L34 Rothley (TT6) and Norton (S233) show ladies with a flat cap over a caul, the only slabs to show such a style although in the case of Rothley the cap is worn by one of the daughters.

L35 The church at Old Dalby, Leics was burnt down in 1834 and rebuilt in 1835. The chancel in which the monuments lie, survived the fire although the monuments were smoke blackened. When the church was rebuilt the old chancel now behind the altar, was converted into a lady chapel.

L36 The Brereton lady at Malpas (G53, 1522) has similarities with that of Elizabeth, Lady Cholmondeley (T28, 1521) except the tomb chest is wholly different. The local history at Malpas claims that the Cholmondeley Chapel at Malpas was constructed by Richard and Elizabeth Cholmondeley in 1514 and this is supported by the inscription surrounding the north chapel which reads in Latin 'Pray for the good estate of Richard Cholmondeley and Elizabeth, his wife, who built this chapel AD 1514'. There is no tomb to Richard Cholmondeley but the current chapel is occupied by the tomb of Hugh Cholmondeley (R236) although this is believed to have been moved from its original position. The Brereton tomb (G53) and the Cholmeley tomb in the Tower (T28) are the subject of a special investigation by the author in conjunction with George Roberts of the Tower of London, the results of which will not be available until after 2016 but are likely to suggest that T28 is a tomb formerly in Malpas and moved to the Tower of London in 1554 hence the duplicate entries in table D3 for 1521 and 1554.

L37 Jane Crease in her thesis states that the effigy at Sheriff Hutton is '… a small version of that at Methley and that of Sir Richard Redman at Harewood'. The Harewood (G192) and the one at Methley (G199) are clearly in Chellaston alabaster and display none of the inclusions seen on the Sheriff Hutton (G203) effigy. This does not preclude all three being the product of York workshops only that alabaster was sourced from a number of locations. The Welles tomb at Methley (G199) has reported similarities with Chideock tomb in Christchurch (GNP31) and Lord Hungerford's tomb at Salisbury (G181) – Pauline Routh. There is good reason to believe that this group is a product of Chellaston workshops.

L38 Lawrence Stone suggests that the tomb of Edward II (G19), John of Eltham (G18), John d'Ifield, Ifield, Sussex, Robert FitzEly, Waterperry, Oxford (1330), Lesnes Abbey, Kent (now in the V&A Museum) are made by the same carvers.

The last three are in Caen stone reinforcing the suggestion that the carvers were London based. To this list can be added the clunch tomb of a knight at Warkworth, Northants (1340) according to Count Paul Biver.

L39 Angels with shields are rare after 1460. The exceptions being Yatton (G155, 1475), Youlgreave (G64, 1488), Stanton Harcourt (GNP77, 1490) and Millom (G55, 1494). Amongst these there are some style similarities including serrations inside the wings. Crossley saw this group as indicative of another workshop 'near the quarries'. This is most likely to be Burton. In the case of Ewelme (G142, 1477) the angel has swallow-like wings and feathers. Two very late tombs are Abergavenny (G120, 1510) and Ashbourne (1538), a tabletop in brass to Francis Cockayne with freestone tomb chest. Whereas the latter two are almost certainly Burton the identity of the carver of the Ewelme tomb is not known. Crossley states 'Nottingham' with no conviction and in light of the status of the Duchess of Suffolk and the closeness of Oxfordshire to the capital, a London carver is more likely.

L40 The inclusion of bedesmen takes two forms. They may be part of the effigy carving or on the tomb chest. The appearance of bedesmen on the effigy on Bishop Wykeham tomb at Winchester (G90, 1404), in the form of three monks at his feet, is not repeated on an extant tomb until that at Norbury in 1493 (G62, 1493) in the form of a single bedesman sitting astride the back of the lion. This is repeated at Lowick (G123, 1498), Strelley (G139, 1501) and Tong (A87, 1515) where they appear on the soles of the sabatons. Bedesmen are more common on the tomb chest. The Earl of Arundel's tomb (G167, 1416) has a continuous row of bedesmen in the form of canons probably of his newly-founded college. Standing bedesmen can be found at North Aston (G143, 1490), Tong (G149, 1517) and Elford (G159, 1525) and seated at Stanton Harcourt (GNP77, 1490).

L41 Few medieval marriages were love matches. However a small number of monuments depict knights holding the hand of their wife. This appears very early as on the 1379 effigy in Warwick (G171) which shows this feature. Others include Strelley (G25), Hoveringham (GNP68) although the arms have been broken. Others are Elford (G158), Lowick (G122) and the non-alabaster tombs of Richard II, Wimborne and Ingham, all in the period 1400 to 1444.

L42 In the mid-15th century there started a vogue for momento-mori in the form of a cadaver either as the main effigy or in a chamber below the tomb slab. One on the first was the 1435 effigy at Arundel (G168). Other are at Wells (1456, G156), Bury St Edmunds (1467, A26), Ewelme (1477, G142), Holme (1491, A84). There is then a gap and the next appeared in 1528 at Wollaton (A3) followed by Kinlet (1548, M296), Hackington (1593, R193), Breedon (1598,

M95), Montgomery (1600, M213), Gawsworth (1608, R46), Edensor (1616, R277), Burford (1628, R51) and Bishops Burton (1649, R192). The now lost tomb of 1519 in Old St Paul's also included a cadaver (D9/54). Non-alabaster cadavers include the freestone effigies of precentor William Sylke at Exeter (1485), the undated Wakeham effigy at Tewkesbury, Feniton, Devon and Hemingborough, North Yorkshire. In a number the shroud is collected above the head and tied in knot.

M1 Bakewell, Derbys. Sir Godfrey Foljambe (died 1376) and wife. An early mural monument with demi-figures facing forward. The emergence of the mural was believed to be due to pressure on floor space especially when pews began to be installed. The Foljambe mural remains the sole example of this form until the late 16th century.

M2 Ratcliffe on Soar, Notts (*see also* R5). Henry Sacheverell (died 1625) and his three wives. This Class IX mural shows all the features of the Dutch school and may be the work of the Hollemans of Burton or Nicholas Stone school but this does not appear in his account books. It retains much of the original paint and the three ladies are in the dress of their period. Mary Gittings (died 1600) shows an identical Queen of Scots headdress which is contemporary with that on the effigy of Jane Ireton (R4). The second wife is Mary Copley and the third wife is Lucy Broughton who later married Sir Thomas Grantham (*see* R61). The squares above the columns are inlaid with cockleshell marble. The monument had railings when recorded by Stretton in 1819 but these had gone when visited by Godfrey in 1887. A wall bracket extant in 2012 is believed to have held the funeral armour of the deceased.

M3 Victoria and Albert Museum (Faxton with Lamport). Mural monument. Tablet to Sir Augustine Nicholls (1616). The church at Faxton, Northamptonshire fell into disrepair during the 20th century and was demolished, the V&A accepting the tablet as a gift needing significant repair. There are black marble sections and plain black marble inlaid squares.

M4 South Woodham Ferrers, Essex. Cecily Sandys (wife of A17). She died 1611, but tomb states not erected until 1619. The alabaster is close to that from Fauld and the monuments displays certain attributes of the Nicholas Stone workshop but is not listed in his workbook. Cecily was buried in the churchyard and a sandstone slab now resting against the church wall once marked her grave. Her son Samuel (R67) was christened in the church.

M5 York Minster. Sir Henry Belasis and wife Ursula. A mural monument complete with kneeling figures which was made for £150 in February 1615 which included a chimney piece in Newburgh Priory. The details of this are included in folio 3 or the Stone notebook. The memorial has two columns and inscription. Painted. Stone worked at York with 4 men over 15 days erecting monument. He was paid 1s a day for expenses for food whilst his men were paid 4d each with and 4s a day drinks between meals. A man called Benedick was paid £7 for painting the monument. In 1829 a fire damaged the monument and some shields fell to the floor. Those that could be recovered were replaced and new ones made but were installed without due regard to their correct position. This was later corrected in 1989. Repainted and re-gilding in 1946. For details of the inscription and shields *see Monuments in York Minster* by Ian Pattison and Hugh Murray 2001 monument No 43.

M6 Norwich, St George's Tombland, Norfolk. Alderman Thomas Anguish (*circa* 1617). A mural monument with a kneeling figure and with side columns. The Stone notebook folio 5 reports this was made for £20.

M7 London, Charterhouse. Mural tablet and effigy of Thomas Sutton (died 1611) invoiced in November 1615 at a cost of £400 but installed on 12th December 1614. This is recorded in Stone's notebook folio 2. The memorial construction was managed by Mr Nicholas Janson (Johnson) of Southwark but Sutton's executor John Law had a hand – *see* M8. A huge mural and chest tomb for which Francis Carter built a new aisle in the chapel in 1614. The tomb in 1919 was shown to be protected by railings. The effigy shows Sutton who made his fortune in coal mining, in the civilian damask robes (mentioned in his will) laying on a cushion with his hands in prayer.

M8 London, Charterhouse. Janson also completed a memorial to John Law in 1615 which is recorded in Stone's notebook folio 2. The tablet shows an effigy facing forward in civilian clothes and ruff in an oval surround supported by two female figures. The details of John Law and his management of the tomb of Thomas Sutton are contained in Biographica Brittanica (the lives of the most eminent persons Volume 6).

M9 Hawstead, Suffolk. The mural tomb of Sir Robert Drury killed in a duel in 1590 completed in 1617 for £140 and wife Ann Bacon. Recorded in Stone's notebook folio 5. The records of the Drury family say that Sir Robert Drury accompanied Lord Willoughby to France in 1589 to aid Henry IV and was killed in a duel with Sir John Borough. This unusual tomb displays un-Jacobean features and must have been commissioned by the Drury family some years after his death. The oval bust is of his father Sir William Drury.

M10 Watford, Herts, St Mary's. Mural monument to Sir Charles Morrison (died 1599), but memorial made 1619. Recorded in the Stone notebook folio 7 at a cost of £400. A very large mural monument with effigy. The effigy is leaning on one elbow dressed in plate armour and with ruff. The effigy is in marble but the surround and the two kneeling sons are in alabaster. The sons on one knee hold one hand on stomach. The daughter is dressed in peeress robes with coronet.

M11 Spare

M12 Watford, Herts, St Mary's. A third mural monument is not inscribed and attributable to 1580. A female figure kneeling at a prayer desk of alabaster and black marble but with two classical Stone columns with Corinthian tops shows signs of being much later. It is possible that this is a Stone monument also dating from 1619 – *see* M10. However, Llewellyn records that the Morrison Chapel was constructed in 1596–1597 and the first to be placed there was Dorothy (died 1599) wife of Sir Charles (M10).

M13 Portchester, Hants. Sir Thomas Cornwallis died 1604. Tomb made 1619 by Nicholas Stone recorded as folio10. Head and shoulders only looking forward. The monument is in veined alabaster formed into a circle within which the effigy in plate armour with a sash across left shoulder. The crest is above. The inscription is below in black marble.

M14 Gazeley, Suffolk. Mural tomb of Edmund Heigham (1604) and his wife Alice Pierson (1599). The mural has similarities to Ordsall.

M15 Kedington, Suffolk. Sir Thomas Barnardison (died 1610) and two wives. May be later than 1610. The knight is recumbent with two wives facing each other in mural setting.

M16 Kedington, Suffolk. Grissell daughter of M15 died 1609. Looks later. Kneeling lady, columns.

M17 Kedington, Suffolk. Sir Nathaniel Barnardison (1653) and wife (1669). Frontal demi-figures both resting heads on hands and elbows on pillow.

M18 Nettlestead, Suffolk. Samuel Sayer (died 1625) and wife Thomasine (died 1647). An unusual monument which may at one time may have been moved. The departed are depicted as demi-figures facing forward holding hands. The interesting point is that the heraldic device is separated and placed on the wall above the figures in Fauld alabaster but the shelf on which the figures stand is of a different alabaster and may well be Kingston. This may well have been repositioned *circa* 1870 to 1910 when the shelf was carved as the PO directory for 1865 states that the Sayer monument is 'a handsome monument' indicting that the monument was complete at that date. (*See* Dorothy Calthorpe 1693 at Ampton Suffolk for similar style). Also likened to that at Kedington (M17).

M19 Woodbridge, Suffolk. Mural in three tiers. Geoffrey Pitman, his two wives and two sons. The effigies face each other over prayer stalls. Pinnacles.

M20 Noseley, Leics. Sir Thomas Heselrigge died 1629–1630 and wife Frances Gorges. Tomb effigies with eight boys and six girls kneeling in prayer depicted on the back plate. The church is in private hands.

M21 Blore Ray, Staffs. William Basset tomb attributable to Jasper Hollemans *circa* 1618–1630.

M22 Barton in Fabis, Notts. Henry Sitwell (ancestor of the author family) died 7th March 1671 aged 30 and Katherine Sacheverell eldest daughter of Henry Sacheverell of Barton. This is plain mural tablet in black limestone with an alabaster surround and armorial device mounted above. The alabaster is white with black veins and may well be Watchet.

M23 Gotham, Notts. William St Andrew died 24th November 1624 aged 40. He had three wives but only one is depicted which is either Mary Skeffington who died 15th March 1605 aged 27 or Mary Pilkington of Stanton who died 7th July 1618 aged 27. His third wife Elizabeth Wedgewood (of the Staffordshire Wedgewood family) was still living in 1625. The memorial is claimed to be installed 5th April 1625. The memorial suffered in the same fire as M24 and was painted grey apart from the armorial which was tinted. Like M2 there is a cockleshell panel above both columns. The head of the lady bears great similarity to the right hand lady on M2 although one has a half ruff and the other a ruff-bib. There is an effigy of a baby in a crib which is original. The prayer stall is missing but the Bibles have survived and three children are represented by small figures in white alabaster although these are likely to be 18th century reproductions. The inscription is on black panels similar to M24 with poor spelling. The monument was cleaned in August 2015.

M24 Gotham, Notts. John St Andrew died 14th January 1624 aged 26. This mural memorial is contemporary with M2 and M23. The effigies kneel before prayer stalls and the inscriptions are inscribed in black panels. The alabaster is lightly veined or white consistent with that from Chellaston. The memorial suffered some fire damage in 1789 and the wall on which it is mounted was rebuilt. It is likely the columns were renewed at this time. The effigies have been painted grey. It is probably a product of Burton workshops.

M25 Gotham, Notts. A plain tablet in veined alabaster with inclusions. The memorial is to The Rev James Vaughan who was rector for 50 years and who died 30th November 1881. The alabaster is similar to that which was used to make the reredos of Kingston church and may indicate that the tablet was carved in the 20th century.

M26 Kedleston, Derbys. Sir John Curzon (died 1686) and wife Patience (died 1642). The tomb is believed to date from

1664 and has features such as the heavy scrollwork similar to that provided by the Hollemans workshop. The effigies face forward and their four sons and three daughters look out below facing forward.

M27 Bath, Abbey church, Somerset. Bartholomew Barnes (died 1605) and family.

M28 Beverley, Yorks. Michael Warton died 1655. Alabaster and black marble. There is a vague report of a tomb of white alabaster to Idonea Lady Percy about which nothing is known.

M29 Framlingham, Suffolk. A wall tablet to the Alexander family with various dates from 1633 to 1660 but with a carving date of 1665. Black touch panel with touch columns and alabaster frame.

M30 Darfield, Yorks. Reported as a Mr Godfrey and his lady but Darfield church claim that the tomb was transferred from Beauchief Abbey at the Reformation during which its identity was lost. The citation for the *Listed Building of England* states that the alabaster tomb in Darfield is Sir John Bosvile and wife dating from 1410. The tomb has shields in roundels with quartrefoils and the knight has his head on an uncrested great helm. The lady has her head on acushion flanked by angels . This monuments is therefore of uncertain provenance.

M31 Easton Neston, Northants. Mural to John Farmer (or Fermor) died 1577 and his wife Maude. Small figures kneeling at prayer desk, limestone and alabaster with arms above. *See*: http://360hugh.co.uk/panormas/the-english-church-2/

M32 Exton, Rutland. Sir James Harrington (died 1591) and wife, Lucy. Mural may date from 1600. A mural with effigies facing each over a prayer stall.

M33 Hurst, Berks. Mural monument to Lady Margaret Savile died 1631. Furled curtain held to one side by angels.

M34 Hulcote, Bedford. Richard Chernoke (died 1615) and two wives Mary (Pothenam) and Audrey (Tradsorn). A large mural in three tiers. Richard is shown kneeling with his two wives behind and (it is assumed) the children above and below.

M35 Lynsted, Kent. John Roper 1st Baron Teyneham died 1618 and Elizabeth Parke died 1567.

M36 Lynsted, Kent. Christopher Roper, 2nd Lord Teyneham (or Teynham) died 1622. The monument is labelled 'E Evesham fecit'. A good photograph of this monument is contained Figure 35, page 62 of Llewellyn's book. The depicted is shown on the point of death with his widow shown kneeling in mourning clothes with her children on the tomb chest. Evesham made a touching point as the children have their pets with them and the boys have hawks and hounds. This family group shows how far the monument styles have moved over the century from 1522.

M37 Nettlestead, Kent. Lady Elizabeth Stafford (died 1598) daughter of William Stafford whose first wife was Mary Boleyn. Lady Elizabeth was the first wife of Sir John Scott.

M38 Nettlestead, Kent. Lady Katherine Scott second wife of Sir John Scott died 1616 but monument may not have been built until 1636. Restored.

M39 Noseley, Leics. Sir Arthur Heselrigge (died in the Tower 7th January 1660) and wives. In marble and alabaster. Twelve children. The wives are Frances Elmes and Dorothy Greville. There is an inscription which mentions Arthur Heselrigge aged 12, son of Dorothy who died in 1649. There are three other Heselrigge in the church none of which have any alabaster. Arthur Heselrigge was one of the five members of parliament whose arrest was sought by Charles I, the event which started the Civil War. The tomb is very tall with a large oval description panel. One wife resides on her elbow.

M40 Ordsall, Notts. Unknown but thought to be Samuel son of Anthony Bevercotes 1603. This monument has been moved at least twice and has lost its backing stones. It was once in the chancel but was moved to the bell loft in 1831 and restored to the north aisle in 1931.

M41 Prestwold, Leics. Sir William Skipwith and Dame Jane (or Joanna) Skipwith *circa* 1631. Sir William died 3rd May 1610 in London although Prestwold parish register shows that he was buried on the 7th May 1610 but monument not commissioned until death of Jane in 1630 (the register has her name as Joanna). Jane occupied the manor at Cotes. William's first wife Margaret Cave is commemorated by an inscription. Her son was Sir Henry Skipwith (of Cotes) who attempted to make the Soar navigable in 1635. Symbols of time in back panel and angels within the arch. The family crest of a red turnpike is shown on the top of the monument.

M42 Repton, Derbys. George Wakelin of Bretby (died 1617) and his wife Ellen or Elizabeth (died 1614). A mural monument which has been moved a number of times – the last time in 1854. The monument shows them kneeling in front of a prayer stool with their son kneeling on a cushion below.

M43 Selston, Ashfield, Notts. William Willoughby (died 12th Dec 1630 aged 21) and Ann. Stretton observed this monument in 1813 and noted that the effigies were in poor condition. He also notes Willoughby's helmet and breastplate were hanging in the chancel as were his gauntlets and sword although by 1813 these had disappeared.

M44 Englefield, Berks. Sir John Englefield (died 1605) and wife, daughter and son. This is unusual in that John's father, also John (died 1567) and his mother, are depicted as a recumbent effigies above the panel showing his son and wife.

Strapwork in the pilasters indicate a London carver. Two over large black obelisks stand on the floor and two smaller, stand on the pediment. Erected by the wife.

M45 East Lockinge, Berks. Millicent Grace (died 1633). Wife of John Grace, vicar and daughter of Edward Needham of Ilston.

M46 Wing, Bucks. Baronet Robert Dormer (died 1616) and wife Lady Elizabeth Dormer (Brown, died 1630) and children kneeling in prayer. Unusually, Robert and Elizabeth are facing the same way.

M47 Youlgreave, Derbys. Mural plaque to Jane the wife of Robert Gylbert *circa* 1492. A knight and lady with seven sons and nine daughters are shown kneeling either side of a Madonna. Considered a rare 15th century mural. Gardner likens this to a tomb at Coventry (T25) and may well be from a Burton workshop. The local history group suggest this was once part of a larger monument, but cannot give further information. This is placed on the wall to act as reredos but this may well have not been its original position being, at one time, part of a chapel which included a screen. The depiction of the Madonna would have made it a target for damage in the mid-16th century making it a rare survivor. Robert Gylbert died *circa* 1499. Figure 14 of Sally Badham's book *Seeking Salvation* shows this mural.

M48 York Minster. Sir William Ingram (died 1623) and his wife Catherine and also his son Sir William Ingram (died 1670). Date of construction of monument uncertain. There is a full description of this monument in *Monuments in York Minster* by Ian Pattison and Hugh Murray 2001 monument No 41.

M49 York Minster. Sir William Gee (died 1611) and his wife Mary. The tomb was contracted for by Mary and may date from 1648 as there is an initial 'RL' and date on the east pedestal. Repainted and restored by Stoneyard *circa* 1979 at the cost of the Gee family. For details *see Monuments in York Minster* by Ian Pattison and Hugh Murray 2001 monument No 34.

M50 York Minster. Archbishop Matthew Hutton (died 1606). An altar tomb with the effigy resting on one arm and holding a book with the other. Damaged in fire of 1829 and restored in 1844 and again in 1977. For details *see Monuments in York Minster* by Ian Pattison and Hugh Murray 2001 monument No 33.

M51 York Minster. Anne Bennet (died 1602). A mural tablet made by Nicholas Stone in 1615 ordered by Anne's husband Sir John Bennet at a cost of £35. A demi-figure effigy in a round headed recess. For details *see Monuments in York Minster* by Ian Pattison and Hugh Murray 2001 monument No 31.

M52 York Minster. Mrs Frances Mathew (died 1629). A mural monument with composite columns and shaped cornice, two obelisks and a heraldic lozenge supported by two naked cherubs. Damaged in the 1829 fire but restored in 1844 when an alabaster cherubim from this monument was sold by the Minster for £3. The inscription was damaged by the fire but recorded in 1736. For details *see Monuments in York Minster* by Ian Pattison and Hugh Murray 2001 monument No 50.

M53 Spare

M54 Chipping Campden. Gloucs. Penelope Noel (died 1633).

M55 Gloucester Cathedral. Elizabeth Williams (died 1622 in childbirth) daughter of Bishop Miles Smith and widow of John Williams. This is a mural by Samuel Baldwin of Stroud. The effigy lies on one elbow with the child lying beside. There is a semi-circular canopy with black marble colonnades. Two panels beneath with a type of black mottled stone. This is linked to M57 as Margery Clent was her sister.

M56 Spare

M57 Gloucester. Margery Clent (died 1623) a daughter of Bishop Miles Smith and widow of James Clent. A mural (M55) also by Samuel Baldwin was her sister.

M58 Gloucester Cathedral. Richard Pate (died 1588). He was a founder of Pate's Grammar School in Cheltenham. This is an early mural tomb without effigies although the 'History of Gloucester' claims that it once did. The back panel has painted Elizabethan images in kneeling posture.

M59 Gloucester Cathedral. Alderman John Jones (died 1630). Registrar has ruff open at front. Alderman and mayor hanging sleeves same robes as machine doublet with slashings, good hands. Demi-figure. Time with scythe sitting on scull. Young boy painting inscription. Column globe-shaped cathedral surrounded by flames. Pile of docs dated 1600 to 1630. *See* Canterbury designed by Nicholas Stone and *also see* Orlando Gibbons. Decorated sword. Monument carved in lifetime but he died just as it was completed (it carries no date but one document is dated 1630 indicting he was continuing as registrar for the cathedral at the time).

M60 Gloucester Cathedral. Alderman Thomas Machen (died 1614) in the robes of Mayor of Gloucester and wife Christian (died 1615) and children. Mural dates from 1615 with kneeling children which shown in relief on tomb chest. The younger children are shown on the corner and end face of tomb chest. Repainted. Machen came from Stroud and so face may be a likeness. The carving of the lady has similarities to Sapperton (M169) and Great Malvern (R170).

M61 Sherborne, Gloucs. A small mural tablet in veined alabaster dating from 1909 to the Hon Charles Dutton. Inscription and image in the form of a medallion in light-coloured alabaster.

M62 East Bridgford, Notts. John Hacker (died 1620) and wife Margaret (died 1627). Mural memorial erected by their four sons and two daughters. Colonel Francis Hacker, a grandson, defended the Trent Bridge fortifications during Civil War and signed Charles I death warrant for which deed he was executed at Tyburn in 1660.

M63 Spilsby, Lincs. A large unusual mural which needs properly dating. It is credited to Thomas Goodlord a Lincolnshire carver believed to be only working in the 1580s. The mural depicts Richard Bertie (died 1582) his wife Katherine Willoughby d'Eresby (died 19th Sept 1580) and former Duchess of Suffolk. The Willoughby family fled during Mary I's reign and son Peregrine was born during this time. Three standing statues – two of a green man.

M64 Stamford, Lincs. Civilian. Richard Cecil (died 1587) and wife.

M65 Stenigot, Lincs. Francis Velles de Guevara (died 1592). The church is modern but contains two monuments both of Spanish origin, the family of Guevara coming to England with Catherine of Aragon. The other monument is to Sir John Guevara (1607).

M66 Stamford, Lincs. William Cecil, Lord Burghley (died 1598). A tomb comprised of several coloured marbles and an alabaster effigy on a rolled mat and with Greenwich armour and garter badge. Accredited to Cornelius Cure but may date from 1587–1588. Cure had a strong relationship with William Cecil.

M67 Stenigot, Lincs. Sir John de Guevara (died 1607).

M68 Uffington, Lincs. Roger and Olyver Manners (died 1607).

M69 Swineshead, Lincs. Only part remaining are the children of Sir John Lockton *circa* 1610.

M70 Stallingborough, Lincs. Civilian. Sir Edward Ayscough (died 1612) and wife.

M71 Snarford, Lincs. Sir George de Paule (died 1613) and wife Frances (Wray). A tiered monument with both effigies leaning on one elbow.

M72 Snarford, Lincs. Lord Robert Rich, Earl of Warwick (died 1619). Grandson of Sir Richard Rich (R160). A medallion portrait believed to be by Epiphanius Evesham.

M73 Tathwell, Lincs. Edward Hanby (died 1626) and wife.

M74 Scawby, Lincs. Richard Nelthorpe (died 1640) and wife Ursula (Gravener). A wall tablet with the depicted facing forward. Six smaller effigies of children, two of which are damaged.

M75 Strubby, Lincs. William Ballett and two wives Joan and Susanna he died in 1648 at 99.

M76 Aldbourne, Wilts. Mural monument to the Walrond brothers (died 1614 and 1617).

M77 Leicester Cathedral. Mural to John Watton and two wives dated *circa* 1656 and carved by Joshua Marshall (his name is shown above the central head). The mural is completely painted almost chocolate brown, so that no alabaster is visible. John Watton was a justice of the peace under Charles I. He and the two wives are shown as demi-figures. There are 15 other monuments with styles similar to this monument.

M78 Wingham, Kent. Mural with effigies to Sir Thomas Palmer Bart and Margaret Pole or Pooley dated 1624–1625. By Nicholas Stone. The monument may have cockleshell marble inlay. Painted columns. The alabaster may be pink.

M79 Ash, Kent. Mural to Sir Thomas Septvans (died 1617) and wife Bennett (died 1612). Effigies kneeling facing each other over prayer stall. Scroll base and children. Corinthian columns.

M80 Ash, Kent. Mural to Christopher Toldervey (died 1618). Similar to M79 but less ornate. Effigies kneeling facing each other over prayer stall. Scroll base and children. Corinthian columns.

M81 Belton, Lincs. Mural monument to Richard Brownlow (died 1638). An eminent lawyer who founded Belton House. Credited to Joshua Marshall the monument was probably made between 1650 and 1660. The monument shows a demi-figure in an arched niche.

M82 Dalby, Lincs. A mural to William Llandon (died 1621) and Alice his wife. A partial painted monument with square columns, text beneath and coat of arms over. Probably restored. The rectangular panels beneath the columns may be cockleshell marble.

M83 Dalby, Lincs. A mural to Julyan Llandon (died 1631). An unusual five-sided tablet mural in Fauld alabaster with the figure in relief, text and a coat of arms below. It appears to be that this has been repositioned in modern times.

M84 Glentworth, Lincs. Mural to Sir Christopher Wray (died 1592) and wife under a coffered arch. Kneeling effigy of son on top and four kneeling daughters beneath. The strapwork is particularly nice linking coats of armour in the columns. Attributed to Nicholas Johnson of Southwark.

M85 Hainton, Lincs. Large mural to John Heneage (died 1559) and wife Anne (died 1587). Date may be later. Two kneeling figures unpainted facing each other with an array of coats of arms on tomb chest. Two arcades with three columns.

M86 Hainton, Lincs. Large mural to William Heneage (died 1610) and two wives, Anne (died 1585) and Jane (died 1594). Children beneath. William was aged 91.

M87 Kelstern, Lincs. Elizabeth South (died 1604). A frontal effigy with putto and spade and putto with skull and extinguished torch.

M88 Lenton, Lincs. Jane Chaworth (died 1606) tablet memorial with strap work.

M89 Bottesford, Leics. Francis Manners, 6th Earl of Rutland died 1632 and two wives. Involved in witchcraft trial after unexpected deaths of sons. A mural with three prone effigies and two kneeling effigies of children.

M90 Elstow, Bedfordshire. Sir Humphrey Radcliffe (died 1566) and his wife Isabel (died 1594). Triple columned with two figures at prayer facing each other.

M91 Eyeworth, Bedfordshire. Sir Francis Anderson (died 1616) and two wives Judith (died 1608) and Audrey. He was the son of A69. The tomb chest is particularly heavily veined with raised figures of children in prayer. There are no columns supporting the semi-circular canopy. Unusually the figures of Sir Francis and his wives face forward.

M92 Eyeworth, Bedfordshire. Sir Edmund Anderson (died 1638) and wife Alice. A demi-figure mural with the effigies holding a heart in their hands between them. An image of their daughter Dorothy appears below in cameo. Alice remarried Sir Thomas Cotton and is buried at Connington, Cambs where she also has a memorial. The 'CMS Journal' Vol XXX 2015 has a description and commentary on the text. The text seems to indicate that Alice died broken hearted at the death of her husband but this may just be an emotional 'death' rather than physical.

M93 Chilton, Bucks. Elizabeth Tyreil (died 1631) and chrisom Dorothy. Attributed to William Wright. The lady is in cameo but the chrisom is an effigy.

M94 Throwley, Kent. Captain Thomas Sondes (died 1668). A fine tablet with a black marble inscription and a broken arch which includes a bust of Sondes. It is signed WS.

M95 Breedon on the Hill, Leics. George Shirley (died 1622) and family including his wife Frances nee (Berkeley) erected 1598. A large double tier mural with cadaver beneath. Some doubt as to details of this as it is stated George died 1588 and the tomb was erected by the Royleys) Wiki says that tomb built 1622 and rebuilt *circa* 19th century by Thomas Allt who signed the work. The confusion may arise because three generations are shown. George Shirley's grandfather may have died 1598 and this has been taken as the date of the tomb. Cadaver has rolled up mat.

M96 Bisham, Berks. Elizabeth (Cooke) widow of Sir Thomas Hoby (*see* R44) who later married Lord Russell and who died in 1609. This remarkably fine memorial has been restored and shows Elizabeth in widow's dress and with children kneeling behind and her husband in front. Both wear coronets. The canopy is straight and supported by two columns. Iron grill. There is evidence of the tomb being transported from Southwark by boat along the Thames. The tomb may well have been designed in Elizabeth's lifetime (*circa* 1607) as the images of her children reflect their size at the turn of the century. Linked to the 1612 tomb of Sir Roger Aston in St Dunstan's, Cranford. Brian Kemp shows a fine picture of the rear of the headdress (page 87, Figure 65 of his book).

M97 Coxwold, North Yorkshire. Thomas Viscount Fauconberg and Barbara his wife. The monument was made in 1631.

M98 Coxwold, North Yorkshire. Sir William (died 1604) and Lady Belayse. Some doubts about the material. Retains some colour.

M99 Fenny Drayton, Leics. George Purefoy (died 1628) and two of his three wives facing east and a recumbent effigy with kneeling children. Erected by his third wife Jane (Roberts) who is one of the wives depicted, the other being Mary (Knightly). The second wife Dorothy is omitted due to her having no children. The story goes that the Puritan congregation had refused to kneel to take communion but shortly after Jane created the tomb showing kneeling effigies as an imposition of strict Anglican authority.

M100 Radwell, Herts. Mary Plomer (died 1605). The lady is seated in late Elizabethan costumes facing forward with one foot on a skull and nursing a chrisom. There is an hour glass beside the lady. The tomb chest has the depiction of children in relief. The square columns surmounted by finials and strapwork. Such decoration makes it likely to be the work of Maximilian Colt. Mary died in childbirth whilst giving birth to her 11th child.

M101 Radwell, Herts. Sir William Plomer (died 1625). Sir William is depicted kneeling before a prayer stall. Unusually, the finials are placed at the side instead of the top of the columns and the usual heraldic device is on top of the cornice. It is reputed that this monument was stolen in 2000, but recovered and refitted.

M102 Radwell, Herts, John Parker (died 1595) and wife Mary (died 1574) and an un-named son possibly John. The current effigy of Mary is painted blue which if correct is an unusual departure from the normal black. The monument looks as if it has been restored. The columns are headed by finials and the usual heraldic device above. The decoration on the columns indicates that the monument may well be by Maximilian Colt which means that this is one of his early works.

M103 Mackworth, Derbys. Edward Mundy (died 1607). Effigy with six sons and two daughters on tomb chest.

M104 York Minster. Tobias (Toby) Matthew Archbishop of York (died 1628). The effigy was once part of a mural but was damaged during the fire of 1829. The effigy was recovered and placed on a new tomb chest designed by Sydney Smirke in 1844. The monument was placed on a plinth between 1880 and 1890 and painted in 1943. Nothing can be seen of the alabaster.

M105 Salisbury Cathedral, Wilts. Sir Edward Seymour (died 1621) Earl of Hertford and his first wife Catherine Grey (died 1567 or 1563). A very tall mural tomb with two effigies in stained alabaster. Catherine's effigy is raised above Edward's effigy as she is of royal lineage being the sister of Lady Jane Grey. The family has a long line of secret marriages which was against English law and which resulted in long period of imprisonment. Catherine was first buried at Yoxford but was moved to Salisbury on the death of Edward. Another secret marriage in the family involved Lady Arabella Stuart – *see* R50.

M106 Westminster Abbey. Monument to Sir John Puckering (died 1596) and his wife Jane Chowne but may not have been completed until 1606. Sir John Puckering was the Speaker of the House of Commons. This large monument of alabaster and marble was erected by his widow Jane. The tomb shows the effigies of John and Jane, he in black robes decorated with gold lace, with a ruff and curly hair, and she in widow's dress with an ermine lined blue mantle, a long stomacher, ruff and hood. At their feet are their crests of a hart (a type of deer) and a silver hand which once held an arrow or a sword. On the front of the tomb are depicted three sons and five daughters. One son and one daughter hold skulls denoting that they died before their parents. Various symbols appear on the tomb including a winged book, roses, fruit and spades.

M107 North Walsham, Norfolk. Sir William Paston (died 1610) but possibly built 1608. Alabaster, rance and black marble. Reported cost was £200. Paston rests on one elbow between twin Corinthian columns supporting a pediment with three large pinnacles and a heraldic device.

M108 Cheam, Surrey. Elizabeth D'Arcy (died 1618) wife of Baron Lumley. The tomb appears to be made long before her death possibly 1603 or as early as 1592. The robe is finely picked out in gold as is other parts of the monument.

M109 Kidderminster, Worcs. Knight and two ladies. Sir Edward Blount (died 1630) and his two wives. He is leaning on one elbow looking at wives.

M110 Bray, Berks. William (died 1609) and Joyce Goddard (died 1622). A well carved mural depicting two demi-figures facing forward which may well be likenesses. An antiquarian drawing in Bodleian Library MS Berks C49.114 shows this monument and Llewellyn suggests that this is or was modelled in plaster. However other sources state alabaster. It may well be that the figures are indeed painted plaster in an alabaster frame.

M111 Churchover, Warwicks. Charles Dixwell (died 1591) and his wife Abigail (died 1635) but not erected until 1641. This memorial in the north aisle has been moved from the chancel at some time. Five children William, Edgar, Humphrey, Barbara and Basil are depicted in demi form. Thought to be similar to Robert Price memorial in the same church (*see* M112).

M112 Churchover, Warwicks. Robert Price (died 1595) and his wife Mary Dixwell but date erected uncertain as it is very similar to M111. This memorial is in the south aisle. This unusual double mural also depicts Mary's parents Humphrey and Ann (e) Dixwell, her seven children and the three of her parents. Humphrey is believed to be the brother of Charles Dixwell.

M113 Watford, Herts. Sir Charles Morison, Bart (died 1628) and wife Mary (died 1643). Nicholas Stone recorded this monument in his notebook in the year 1630. It states the monument is to be made from 'good and pure white marble – in complete armour with sword and spurs according to the life – to consist of six foot in length of one entire whole stone'. It is likely the effigies are marble and the tomb alabaster with black Ashford panels.

M114 London, Temple Church. Mural to Richard Martin (1570–1618) the recorder of London and lecturer of the Middle Temple. He is shown kneeling at a prayer stall with one hand on an open book. Semi circular arch. The tomb bears the inscription 'ETS repaired and beautified 1687' in curved inlaid panel. The side columns display strap-work. The tomb may have been restored again by Edward Richardson in 1843 but this is uncertain.

M115 Chesterfield, Derbys. James Foljambe (died 1558) and also attributable to his first wife Alice Fitzwilliam and his second wife Constance Littleton but this is subject to a challenge. Bayliss attributes this to Garrett Hollemans (I) which dates the carving to post-1584.

M116 Chesterfield, Derbys. An allegorical mural which is dated 1592 is unattributable to any one person, but is likely for the Foljambe family. Probably the work of Garrett Hollemans and may well be associated with the 1595 memorial. The mural has a shrouded figure and a standing skeleton, as well as other symbols.

M117 Weston under Wetherley, Warwicks. Mary and Margaret Morgan (both died 1568) daughters of Thomas Morgan of Heyford, Northants. Probably one of the first memorials to be produced by the Hollemans workshops in Burton on Trent. There is an early monument to their grandfather Sir Edward Saunders which requires investigation.

M118 Spare

M119 Narburgh (Narborough) Norfolk. Sir Clement Spelman (died 1607) and family. Attributable to John Key and William Wright. *See* Llewellyn Fig 48 page 75. The mural has two effigies in echelon and leaning on right elbow. The mural panel is unusual in that it contains three arcades. The centre bears the inscription flanked by two effigies of children one in a crib and the other kneeling. The lady has a ruff and a Stuart hood which is shown stiffened. Hoods are common on monuments to about 1616.

M120 Charlecote. Warwicks. Sir Thomas Lucy (died 1605). A mural monument with a recumbent effigy and a kneeling figure of his wife. The contract for this tomb exists which includes '… himself to be made of good alabaster in armour and carved and the other of his ladies to be made of Tatternullstone'. The contract also appears to cover monument R39. Llewellyn identifies Tatternullstone as a chalky limestone of poor quality which compares unfavourably with alabaster.

M121 Bishops Hull, Somerset. George Farewell (died 1609). His wife, four daughters and five sons kneel beneath the tomb chest. He leans on one elbow. The tomb has an arch and a black inscription panel. Llewellyn identifies the alabaster for George as Chellaston for which there is some doubt as it may well be Fauld and says that the children are in 'local form' which may mean Watchet. A close examination indicates a white alabaster with black veining which makes this likely to be correct. This requires more detailed examination.

M122 London, Westminster Abbey. Anne Duchess of Somerset (died 1587). She was the second wife of Edward Seymour (executed 1553) brother of Jane Seymour. The tomb was erected by Anne's son the Earl of Hertford. Camden was to write about this monument '… a magnificent alabaster sepulchre 23ft high. The earl is buried at Salisbury in an equally magnificent tomb attributable to William Wright' (M105). This is linked to R151.

M123 Brockelsby, Lincs. Sir William Pelham (died 1587) and family. Kneeling effigies.

M124 Tunstall, Kent. Sir John Cromer (died 1613) and his wife Martha who erected the monument. The monument is in pieces with Sir John and Martha kneeling either side of a panel showing their children and with the heraldic device now fixed to the wall.

M125 Tunstall, Kent. Robert Cheke (died 1647). A wall tablet with demi-figure facing forward as if out of a window.

M126 Eton College Chapel, Bucks. Thomas Murray (died 1623), provost of Eton. A mural showing Murray as a demi-figure. Murray was the Provost of Eton. An elaborate architectural composition, executed in alabaster, with a niche containing a coloured portrait bust, and a carved wood skeleton in a recess in the base. The inscription is in Latin, and upon the monument are three cartouches of arms. In the north porch of the quire are monuments to Richard Allestree, 1680, Provost of Eton, with arms, and to Maria Bateman, 1657, also with arms. In the churchyard is the tomb of John Hales, 1659, and in the ante-chapel a large floor slab to Sir Henry Wotton, 1637, provost of Eton, with a shield of arms.

M127 Little Warley, Essex. Sir Denner Strutt (died 1641) and wife Dorothy. Built in two tiers with cherubs pulling back curtains attached to a canopy. The wife appears to be an effigy in alabaster and Sir Denner in white marble.

M128 Little Warley, Essex. Mary (2nd wife of Sir Denner Strutt) died 1658. Alabaster (mural) and marble (effigy) showing woman in shroud leaning on one elbow.

M129 Chipping Campden, Gloucs. Edward Noel, Viscount Campden (died 1642) and his wife Juliana (died 1664). Alabaster effigies with black marble surround and heraldic device on pediment. Statues in alabaster by Joshua Marshall. These are standing effigies in shrouds with the man holding the wife's hand. A tradition states that the monument has doors which were closed in the life of the wife and opened on her death in 1664.

M130 Chipping Campden, Gloucs. Sir Baptist Hicks, Lord Campden (died 1629) and wife. This is believed to be a Nicholas Stone monument.

M131 Chiddingly, Sussex. Sir John Jefferay (died 1578) and other members of his family. This monument was erected in 1612 and was carved by William Cure but Garratt Johnson may also have been involved. This monument occupies the width of the wall. There are two reclining figures with kneeling child. Sir John is clothed in his robes as a judge with an unidentified order. His elbow rests on a cushion and he holds a scroll. Dame Alice, his wife lies below. To the left is the standing figure of Sir Edward Montagu who commissioned the monument and to the right their daughter Elizabeth. This monument has some damage believed to have been caused by an attack by a mob in mistake for the monuments of the infamous Judge Jeffries. The Sculptors of Sussex database claims that the alabaster of the effigies was mined at Battle but this is fugitive as no record of mining here before 1872.

M132 Maldon, Essex. Thomas Cammocke and family erected 1602. A small mural showing Thomas facing forward and his two wives at either side. One wife is believed to be the sister of Lord Rich. A large number of children are shown under each wife. The inscription confirms that the memorial was erected jointly at the cost of his eldest son Robert and the surviving wife. A Lieutenant Hammond visited Maldon in 1635 was told the story of an elopement with Miss Rich whereby Cammocke escaped by crossing the Blackwater on his horse with the lady behind him pursued by Rich's retainers. The monument makes no reference to this romantic interlude but the Blackwater at low tide is shallow and so such a crossing is quite feasible.

M133 Bacton, Herefordshire. Blanche Parry (died 1590). Blanche was the chief gentlewoman to Elizabeth I and was buried twice once in St Margaret's Westminster and again in Bacton which consigned her bowels to the earth although the tomb is empty. This monument in Bacton was constructed during her lifetime. It shows Blanche kneeling beside a second figure which may be intended to be Elizabeth.

M134 Brewood, Staffs. Edward Moreton (died 1630) and wife (died 1633), three sons, three daughters and a chrisom. A two-tiered monument which also depicts Matthew Moreton (died 1669) and wife (died 1672), a son, six daughters and a chrisom. Restored *circa* 1851 by the Earl of Ducie.

M135 Tong, Shropshire. Ann Wylde (died 1624) daughter of Thomas Harries who died in childbirth. A mural monument with marble columns.

M136 Newstead Abbey, Notts crypt (now the gift shop). Sir John Byron (died 1623) and his wife Margaret (FitzWilliam – also died 1623). Also to son John (died 1625) and to daughter Alice. This was moved from Colwick Old Church in September 1937. Restored. The inscription says that the monument was created in 1625 by Alice who was married to Sir John Radcliffe and lived for 50 years after her marriage.

M137 Whitchurch, Denbigh (parish church of Denbigh). Sir Humphrey Lewyd (died 1568). Memorial installed much later. Known as the Father of Modern Geography, he piloted the translation of the Bible into Welsh. A kneeling effigy carved in relief with alabaster panels above. Touch columns.

M138 Chilton, Suffolk. Sir Robert Crane (died 1643) and two wives Dorothy (died 1624) and Susan (died 1681). Mural built in 1626 in Sir Robert's lifetime. Credited to Gerard Christmas and believed to have cost £50. Crane was the Chancellor of the Order of the Garter and his early commissioning of his monument was carried out when he was raised to the barony in 1626. Touchstone columns. Susan shows an open ruff like that of R5.

M139 Norwich, St Etheldreda, Norfolk. William Johnson (died 1611). This mural was moved from St Peter Southgate when that church was demolished *circa* 1887.

M140 Norwich, St George Tombland, Norfolk. John and Olive Symonds (*circa* 1609). This has been re-positioned and has lost its surround. Repainted at some time.

M141 Cardington, Shrops. Justice Sir William Leighton (died 1607). The effigy is lying on its side. Small panels depict wife and children beneath effigy – one is a chrisom resting on a skull. The monument was erected after his death by his four executors, all London men, who gave the work to London carvers in preference to the Hollemans.

M142 Bolsover, Derbys. Sir Charles Cavendish (died 1617) and his wife. The three sons are depicted below, all of the same size despite the third son, Charles, being a dwarf of which is said '… a little weak crooked man and nature not adaptable to court or camp, he took himself to the study of mathematics of which he became a grand master'. The inscriptions are particularly interesting and discussed in 'CMS Journal' Vol XXX 2015 pages 125 and 126.

M143 Fowey, Cornwall. John Rashleigh (died 1624). The effigy is in the robes of a merchant. The eldest son, Jonathon, is show alone on the monument owing to '… fit space there was none. The son whose only charge this was is therefore set alone'. There is also a suggestion a second son was mentally deranged, John Rashleigh charging his first son to maintain his brother for his remaining lifetime. John Rashleigh commenced to build Menabily House which was completed by his son and was the basis for Daphne du Maurier's Mandeley.

M144 Merton Surrey. Gregory Lovell (died 1597) and two wives, Joan Whitehead and Dorothy Greene. Lovell is shown on the dexter side (left as viewed) with the progeny for the first wife beneath him and that of the second wife beneath the ladies.

M145 Derby Cathedral. Elizabeth Talbot, Bess of Hardwick (died 1608). The monument was designed by John Smythson but the carver is unknown. Her famous husband George Talbot is buried in Sheffield (A230) but no mention is made of Bess on his monument. This is no surprise as George and Bess we estranged over their role as custodian of Mary, Queen of Scots and whereas husbands enthused over the dutiful role of their wives, Bess was neither obedient nor dutiful. The tomb at Derby was completed in 1601 some seven years before her death and it is recorded she paid frequent visits to appreciate her monument.

M146 Bristol Cathedral. Sir John Young (died 1585) and his wife Joan. This monument is freestone (*see* X10) but included because it is the first Baldwin monument and almost certainly intended for alabaster. In John Young's will he provided for a small monument based on that for William Bond of St Helen's Bishopsgate erected in 1576. He never got his way as the freestone tomb which was finally erected in 1606 by Samuel Baldwin was on a far grander style with Joan usurping the prime position with minor roles for Sir John and her first husband Sir Giles Strangeways. This challenge to the accepted rule is further compounded by the unusual order of the children which mixes male and female with one who died at birth not shown at all. This monument has been moved.

M147 Cheam, Surrey. Jane FitzAllen, Lady Lumley (died 1577) but memorial dated 1590 and stated to be 'incomplete'. The monument comprises three alabaster panels craved in relief with a black marble top. The top panel depicts Lady Lumley at prayer and the two lower panels her children. A very unusual mural.

M148 Southwark. London. John Bingham (died 1625) saddler to James I. A demi-figure facing forward. One of the 'bargainers' who oversaw the purchase of Southwark from James I.

M149 Southwark. London. John Trehearne (died 1618) gentleman porter to James I. A three-quarter figure facing forward. Gestures towards an inscription which describes his achievements. One two monuments to commoners which demonstrates the descent of monument building down the social scale.

M150 Standon, Herts. Sir Ralph Sadler (died 1587). No wife is depicted as his marriage may well have been bigamous. Jailer of Mary, Queen of Scots. The tomb is reputed to have once borne the trophies of the Battle of Pinkie Cleugh and these are listed in 1910 as two helmets, a sword, stirrups, halberd, spurs and banners. His children who were made legitimate *circa* 1546 are displayed in semi-relief on tomb chest.

M151 Standon, Herts. Sir Thomas Sadler (died 1606) and wife Gertrude (Markham). The tomb is similar to his father's (M150).

M152 London, Westminster Abbey. Henry Carey, 1st Baron Hunsden (died 1596) and his wife Lady Anne Carey (died 1607). This is the tallest monument at 36ft in the abbey and displays an amazing range of heraldry. Repainted in 1950.

M153 London, Westminster Abbey (Chapel of St Edmund). Katherine Knollys (died 1568) wife of Sir Francis Knollys and one of Elizabeth's ladies of the bedchamber. Katherine was daughter of Mary Boleyn and therefore cousin to Elizabeth I which earned her the right to be buried in Westminster. Moved in 1960. *See* http://www.westminster-abbey.org/

our-history/people/katherine-knollys.

M154 Riddlesworth. Norfolk. Sir Drue Drury (died 1617). An unusual mural with two figures holding back curtains to reveal Drury kneeling before a prayer stall. One of the jailors of Mary, Queen of Scots at Fotheringhay assisting Sir Amias Paulet from 1584. The inscription on the monument claims that Drury was 99 years old at his death but it is now accepted that his true age was 86. Both Stone and Colt have been mentioned as the carvers but this monument does not appear in Stone's notebooks and the design favours Colt.

M155 London, St Thomas's Hospital. Florence Nightingale (died 1910). A wall monument in plaster with a Fauld alabaster frame. This is believed to an exact copy of one in St Paul's Cathedral crypt except for the frame shape. M156 is by Arthur Walker and this may well be his work too.

M156 London, St Paul's Cathedral crypt. Florence Nightingale (died 1910). A wall monument in marble with a Fauld alabaster frame. *See also* M155.

M157 Cranford, Middlesex. Sir Roger Aston (died 1612), and wives Mary and Cardella and children. Aston was a Scotsman who came south with James I and was associated with Robert Cecil performing the role of Master Huntsman. The contract with Cure was signed before his will which indicates that Aston was illegitimate and of 'no breeding' which is in contrast to grandiose tomb he built for himself. This is one of several tombs of grand design by lowly people who were important to the Stuart court. Unlike Elizabeth's court that of James I was more relaxed and more open to such people who could rise through the ranks to become important in their own right. This led to the nobility pouring scorn on their monuments as will be seen in other monuments of the period. The accession of Charles I in 1625 saw a reversion to the old formal ways and few if any humble courtiers were to be commemorated by grand monuments at least for another 50 years. The Cranford tomb has linked with the marble tomb of Mary, Queen of Scots.

M158 Monken Hadley, Herefordshire. Sir Roger Wilbraham (died 1611) and his wife made by Nicholas Stone I in 1616. Two demi-figures facing forward with small statues of their children. A modest monument to another member of James I court Wilbraham being the master of requests.

M159 Walthamstow, Essex. Mary Merry (died 1632) wife of Sir Thomas Merry who commissioned Nicholas Stone to make the mural. This has similarities to M158 although carved some 16 years apart. Sir Thomas was yet another courtier of the Stuart court being the king's controller of the household. Again Stone has carved demi-figures facing forward this time in oval niches and with the children represented by busts.

M160 Egham, Surrey (*see also* X9). Richard Kellefet (died 1595) and his wife Cecily. A tablet in alabaster and marble. Kellefet was '… a most faithful servant to His Majestie, chief groome in the removing garderobe of beddes, and yeoman also of her standing garderobe, of Richemount'.

M161 Egham, Surrey (*see also* X9). Lady Cecily Denham (died 1612?) and Eleanor Moor, first and second wife of Sir John Denham. A tablet in alabaster and marble. The demi-figures are in an oval frame with pediment and columns and heraldic device above. One lady holds an infant and the figure of a boy in placed left of centre on the frame which holds the inscription. The carving is coarse and not well executed.

M162 Egham, Surrey (*see also* X9). Sir John Denham (died 1638) Royalist poet. This unusual and well executed mural has many notable features. The plinth which is inscribed 'Ex ossibus armati' has a frieze which depicts skeletons with figures of a man and woman who have regained their flesh, clearly indicating the resurrection. The main niche with side columns shows a nude man rising from the grave. The man sports a beard and is believed to be a likeness of Sir John. He is partly clothed in the shroud.

M163 Egham, Surrey (*see also* X9). Sir Robert Foster (died 1663). A small mural depicting a bust of Foster which may well be a likeness.

M164 Oxford, Merton College Chapel. Sir Thomas Bodley (died 1613) lecturer in Greek and founder of the Bodleian Library. The mural displays a mixture of religious and academic iconography the most interesting of which is the columns made from representation of two piles of stacked books. The others represent music, arithmetic, grammar and rhetoric. There is evidence that great helm now in the library was once mounted over the monument.

M165 Bradwell Juxta Coggeshall, Essex. Anthony Maxey (died 1592) and his wife Dorothy Bassett (died 1602). The monument was erected by their son Sir Henry Maxey. Two knights in plate armour and wives at prayer desks. Corinthian columns. There is a slab of a priest dated 1349 of which only lower half remains but this is unlikely to be alabaster.

M166 Avening, Gloucs. Henry Bridges or Brydges (died 1615). May not be alabaster. Shown as Figure 21 in Llewellyn's book. Bridges was a pirate, highwayman and smuggler but pardoned by James I. The head of the effigy is very fine.

M167 Bristol, Lord Mayor's Chapel. This was formerly the chapel to St Mark's Hospital. It is not under control of the diocese. John Aldworth (died 1615) and son Francis (died 1623). A Samuel Baldwin monument in alabaster and freestone. John was Sheriff of Bristol. An early Baldwin monument with Gothic features.

M168 Bredon, Worcs. Sir Gyles Reed or Read (died 1611) and wife Catherine Grenville (also died 1611). Alabaster and black marble. This has similarities to Plowden's monument in Temple Church, London (A67). In particular the strapwork and the grotesques within arches are common. Carved by Samuel Baldwin this monument is believed to predate that at Spetchley (R53). The children are shown as separate kneeling effigies. A nearby plaque records that the tomb was set up by Sir Gyle's son. The 'CMS Journal' Vol XXX 2015 page 151 has a good discussion on the inscription.

M169 Sapperton, Gloucs. Sir Henry Poole (died 1616) and Anne Wroughton. He was High Sheriff of Gloucestershire. The monument dates from 1630. Kneeling figures on one leg of predeceased sons Devereux and Giles. Also son Henry and daughter-in-law Beata and at base Anne, Eleanor, Francis and Dorothy. The material is uncertain. The carving of the lady has similarities to Gloucester (M60) and Great Malvern (R170). Devereux died in France in 1590 fighting for the Protestant forces (probably the Battle of Ivry of the 14th March).

M170 Nottingham. In 1637 a large mural monument was erected in the south transept of St Mary's Church to John Holles, Earl of Clare which was believed to be alabaster. This was removed in 1804 due to being in poor condition. It was replaced by a marble tablet flanked by two coats of arms in alabaster which may well have featured on the original tomb. The Holles tomb may well have attracted attention during the English Civil War.

M171 Bristol, St Stephen's. Martin Pringe (died 1626–1627). A wall tablet showing four muses: navigation – geometry – astronomy – grammar. Beneath is inscription of a beautification carried out by Hannah Oliver widow in 1793 probably to repair damage. Another repair carried out in 1773 by William Pugh has a plaster addition to the lower section depicting Hope as mermaid and Time as satyr. Also anchor and hourglass crossed by a spade and pick. Original monument is by Samuel Baldwin. The SB may have cockleshell marble panels and possibly columns. The figures of the mermaid and satyr copied from badge of Bristol Merchant Venturers. Two effigies at top Prudence and Fortitude somewhat damaged. It may well be a copy of Nicholas Stone's (M164) at Merton. This has music – arithmetic – teaching – rhetoric with grammar at bottom.

M172 York Minster. Sir Henry Swinburne (died 1624). Henry was lawyer and he is shown in lawyer's robes. The monument contains two small niches, one once held the kneeling effigy of his wife but which disappeared *circa* 1736 and the other intended for his son but appears never have to have been filled.

M173 North Stoneham, Hants. Sir Thomas Fleming (died suddenly 1613) and his wife Mary (died 1614) erected by his son. Thomas is shown in the robes of a judge having presided over the 1606 trial of Guy Fawkes. They had 15 children but only 8 are depicted on the tomb chest. The mural has much intricate scroll work which is seen on other monuments. Two large obelisks. The effigies are coloured and both rest on their elbows.

M174 Great Milton, Oxford. Sir Michael Dormer (died 1616), wife and father Sir Ambrose Dormer. The image of death as a skeleton appears holding a spear and an egg timer. Moved in 1860. Rolled up mat. Dormer is depicted as a soldier at a military camp in the Spanish wars. The use of such military reliefs was more prevalent on the continent and is rare in England. The likely carver is Samuel Baldwin.

M175 Ellesborough, Bucks. Bridget Coke (died 1638). A fine effigy which is shown reclining on one elbow.

M176 Crediton, Devon. John and Elizabeth Tuckfield (died 1630). An interesting monument with three arcades each with an image. The left is a portrait roundel of John. The centre has a seated figure of the widowed Elizabeth and the right a similar roundel of a surviving son. Inserted within an arch in the church, it has a broken pediment. One end of the tomb chest has a military engagement depicted.

M177 Crediton, Devon. Sir William Merriam or Perham (died 1604) but monument is attributed to 1605. He was one of the judges who sentenced Mary, Queen of Scots. An interesting monument is what is stated to be pink marble, but may be in Watchet alabaster.

M178 Tittleshall, Norfolk. Bridget Coke (died 1598) formerly Paston, the wife of Edward Coke. The effigy kneels at a prayer stall within an arch with rich Strapwork similar to that from the Southwark workshops. The children are shown in relief below the effigy. Nicholas Stone's workbook states Robert Pook '... also dismantled and moved the Elizabethan monument to Sir Edwards's first wife who died in 1598 and re-erected it elsewhere' indicating that this monument was moved in 1638.

M179 Mersham, Kent. Lady Bridget Knatchbull (died 1626). A Nicholas Stone wall mural made for £30. Draped baldachino with angels holding back curtains, cherub heads and obelisks.

M180 Hythe, Kent. John Collins (died 1597). The son of Gyles Collins he was many years the mayor. The monument is signed 'E Evesham fecit'.

M181 London, Chancery Lane, Rolls Chapel. Edward Bruce, Lord Kinloss, Master of the Rolls (died 1610). Head resting on one hand. His son the 2nd Lord Kinloss is kneeling before him. There is some question as to date as the chapel may not have been constructed until after 1617 and may well have been commissioned by son.

M182 Ross on Wye, Hereford. William Rudhall (died 1609) and wife Margaret (Croft). Alabaster and black marble. There is a central prayer desk but any effigies that knelt at it are missing.

M183 Waterperry, Oxford. Francis Curson (died 1610) and wife Anne Southcote daughter of R147. A small wall mural with the knight and his lady kneeling facing each other and their children in relief at the bottom.

M184 Worcester Cathedral, Abigail Goldsborough (died 1604), wife of Godfrey, the Bishop of Gloucester constructed 1613. She knees on a cushion without a prayer stall under a coffered arch with rose motifs.

M185 Much Dewchurch, Hereford. Walter Pye (died 1625) and wife Joan (Rudhall). Black and white marble and alabaster mural with kneeling figures across a prayer stall. Ionic columns. Walter was an attorney general from 1602. In some quarters the monument is credited to Nicholas Johnson and a copy of the Johnson carved tomb in Bottesford.

M186 Ledbury. Hereford. Edward Skynner (died 1630) and his wife Elizabeth (died 1628). Five sons and five daughters depicted on tomb chest. A baby is shown lying between the figures. Edward was a clothier. Monument erected by sons Edward and William. Legend has it that the baby was killed by the last wolf in England but this cannot be substantiated.

M187 Down Apney, Gloucs. Sir John Hungerford (died 1635). Erected by son Sir Anthony.

M188 Cirencester, Gloucs. George Monox (died 1638) and wife. Merchant of Cirencester.

M189 Droitwich, Worcs. George Wilde or Wylde (died 1616). He is shown in his red robes as serjeant-at-law.

M190 Lugwardine, Hereford. William Reed (died 1634). He is shown leading on one elbow.

M191 Norton, Worcs. Sir Thomas Bigg (died 1613–1614) and wife and nine children. High Sheriff of Worcester and justice of the peace. The inscription wrongly dates the construction as 1613 as Bigg died May 1614.

M192 Norton, Worcs. Sir Thomas Bigg (died 1621).

M193 St Brides super Ely, South Wales. An interesting wall mural to Captain William Jones (died 1658) and sons William (1640) and Robert (1650). This is reputed to be in Penarth alabaster but this is as yet to be confirmed.

M194 Edinburgh, St Giles. Captain Neil James Primrose (killed in the battle for the hill of Gezer, Palestine in 1917). There is a similar tablet in Christ Church, Epsom, but not quite so elaborate.

M195 Edinburgh, St Giles. John Inglis, Lord Glencorse (died 1891). An elaborate well crafted tablet in marble and alabaster. It follows a 17th century design with black columns with coat of arms over the cornice. The colour is strange being pink/buff. In light of Anderson's possible use of Barrowmouth alabaster on his other memorial (A94) this may well be from that source.

M196 Pembroke, St Mary. The 1603 (or 1610) monument to William Adams (aged eight) has a reused alabaster panel from a 15th century tomb which is a palimpsest in that it has been reversed. The rear shows angels and may well be the only known example in alabaster. The 24 inches by 36 inches panel dating from 1410 to 1450 was set in plaster but was discovered in 1879. The angels are holding shaped shields in front under a trefoil canopy reminiscent of the Burton workshops.

M197 Worcester, Cathedral. Frances Griffiths (died 1682). A wall tablet to the daughter of John Bromley. Her husband John Griffiths was a minor canon of the cathedral.

M198 Colmworth, Bedford. Sir William Dyer (died 1621) and his wife. A fine mural monument installed by his widow Catherine in 1641 who added a poem. Dyer rests on one elbow and there are three Corinthian columns. The family of four sons and three daughters face forward on the tomb chest. Faith, Hope and Charity are depicted. A baby, Henry her grandson, is depicted at Lady Dyer's feet who died in 1637.

M199 Salisbury, St Thomas. Thomas and Elizabeth Eyre. Thomas died 1628. This was formerly in the chancel and moved in the 18th century. Fourteen of their fifteen children are shown (the fifteenth is missing from a damaged panel) including three chrisoms. Thomas was mayor of Salisbury 1586–1587. The painting includes a resemblance to oak panelling.

M200 Salisbury, St Thomas. Christopher and Elster Eyre. Christopher (the son of M199) died 1624. This is also painted and includes a resemblance to oak panelling. A semi-circular arch depicts father time with scythe and hourglass.

M201 Easton Maudit, Northants. Sir Henry Yelverton (died 1630–1631) and wife Margaret Beale (died 1625). A large canopied tomb with the effigies one above the other on the north wall of the Yelverton chapel. The recumbent effigies rest on one elbow. Four sons and five daughters are depicted. Unusually there are bedesmen in black gowns.

M202 Easton Maudit, Northants. Sir Christopher Yelverton (died 1612) and wife Mary (died 1611). An elaborated canopied tomb in the centre of the Yelverton chapel. Four sons and eight daughters are depicted.

M203 Prestwold, Leics. Christopher Packe, Lord of Prestwold Hall died 1682. Packe was alderman of London in 1649 and lord mayor 1654–1655 being knighted in 1655. Packe is dressed as an alderman of the post-Reformation era and leans on one elbow. The face may well be a likeness. The alabaster is odd being black veined.

M204 Welford, Berks. Lady Parry (died 1585) but monument carved 1610. Kneeling lady with chrisom. Katherine Esdaile gives a long description of this monument.

M205 Bradgate Park, Leics. Henry Grey (died 1614) and wife Ann. Recumbent effigies on a tomb chest within a recess with columns and entablature. Strapwork. The chapel is in the grounds of Bradgate House a ruin mid way into the park and open at only certain times of the year. The House was the home of Lady Jane Grey.

M206 Edmondthorpe, Leics. Sir Roger Smith (died 1655) and two wives Jane (died 1599) and Ann (died 1652) and offspring. A three-tiered monument with the two wives on one elbow and demi-figures on either side depicting Edward (son died 1632) and Roger (grandson died 1646). There is red stain on the wrist of Ann which is probably a colouration of the stone. Ann had the reputation of being a witch who could turn herself into a cat. Tradition has it that one day the butler caught a cat in the pantry and hit it with a cleaver wounding it on the paw. Later Ann appeared with a bandage which on examination was a wound on the wrist. The red mark was said to be this event. The monument was restored in 2000 when an inscription 'WB 1658' for William Byrd was found on the rear of the cartouche.

M207 Swinbrook, Oxford. Edmund Fettiplace (die 1686) and his two predecessors. A strange tiered monument in marble and alabaster with the three effigies resting on one elbow and ranked one above the other. This is attributable to William Byrd who seems to have a liking to tiered tombs (*see* M206 above).

M208 London, St Andrew Undershaft. John Stow (died 1605). An effigy in ruff and gown facing forward seated at a writing desk. Probably a likeness. The monument commissioned by his wife is variously recorded as terracotta and alabaster. He holds a pen which is traditionally renewed every three years by the lord mayor.

M209 Tawstock, Devon. William Bouchier (died 1623) and wife Elizabeth. A fine mural with two recumbent effigies and three kneeling figures. Much strapwork and black panels with Latin inscriptions. Restored 1999 when mild steel rods which held the monument were replaced.

M210 Spixworth, Norfolk. William Peck (died 1634) and wife Alice. Two recumbent effigies both shrouded which is unusual. *See also* M559. The inscription is studies in an article in 'CMS Journal' Vol XXX 2015 page 138 to 139.

M211 Hintlesham, Norfolk. Thomas Timperley (died 1594) and wife Audrey Hare. An unusual mural monument with the effigies in relief. One son and several daughters also in relief. Large letters on pediment **** FILIA' and numbers

1 and 5. Heavily veined Fauld alabaster. Pilasters with inlaid black panels.

M212 Hintlesham, Norfolk. Nicholas Timperley (died 1624) and wife Ann Markham. An identical mural monument to M211 also with the effigies in relief. One son and two daughters also in relief. Large letters on pediment '**** FILIA' and numbers 6 and 8. Heavily veined Fauld alabaster. Pilasters with inlaid black panels.

M213 Montgomery, Powis. A finely decorated mural tomb to Richard Herbert (died 1596) and wife Magdalene (died 1627). She later remarried Sir John Danvers. Six sons are depicted amongst them are poets George Herbert and Lord Herbert of Chirbury. The tomb was completed in 1600 and attributed to Walter Hancock.

M214 Yougal, Co Cork, Ireland. A large mural tomb to Richard Boyle, 1st Earl Cork *circa* 1620. The earl rests on one elbow with his two wives one on each side. Large pediment with figures and obelisks. Painted and may not be alabaster.

M215 Felbrigg, Norfolk. Thomas Windham (died 1653) aged 82. Commissioned by his daughter Elizabeth in 1669 from carver Martin Morley of Norwich. Reported to have alabaster painted columns.

M216 Chevening, Kent. Sampson Lennard (died 1615) and wife Margaret (died 1611) later Baroness Dacre. Small effigies of children. Obelisks and coffered canopy.

M217 Chevening, Kent. Ann Herrys (died 1613). A wall mural with a kneeling figure and two small children. Angels hold back curtains. (There is a tablet to Robert Cranmer 1619 in uncertain material.)

M218 Owthorpe, Notts. A wall tablet to Elizabeth Norton (died 1713), Julius Hutchinson (died 1738) and Betty Hutchinson (died 1752) and various children. The tablet appears to have been erected in 1713 and added to in 1738 and 1752 with changes in script. The central panel is marble but the surround appears to be in alabaster with grey/black veining which may be Watchet. The pediment has two truncated obelisks with a red painted device on the top like a closed fist. Two putti appear on the bottom corners and a central skull on the bottom scroll.

M219 Owthorpe, Notts. A wall tablet to John Hutchinson (a regicide who died in Sandown Castle 1663), another (died 1659) which is not his wife Lucy (who died in 1681) and to various children. The church has a Hutchinson vault which extends the full width of the church containing 17 coffins all chained vertical. This has not been opened since 1859. The upper frame is Fauld alabaster much affected by water damage with an Ashford marble inscription panel. Two obelisks with skulls and laurel wreaths. The heraldic device is much damaged and unreadable. The lower inscription panel is marble or alabaster with a poor Ashford marble surround. There is a third tablet to Charles Hutchinson (died 1695) which is in marble.

M220 Harrington, Northants. (William) Saunders (died 1584). Two women and four men kneeling opposite each other. Images of Hope with an anchor and Faith with a shield. Probably erected by his son Edward just before he sold the estate in 1590. However, there us some belief that it is Edward Saunders who died in 1576. And his wife who died in 1588.

M221 Condover, Shrops. A two-tiered mural for Judge Thomas Owen (died 1598) and his son Sir Roger Owen – both on lower tier. The top tier has Jane Norton (daughter) who erected the monument with her husband Bonham Norton.

M222 Scarning, Norfolk. A mural monument to Edward Games (died 1623) an infant, son of John Games associated with the Middle Temple, London. The monument is signed 'Evesham fecit'. This monument has been moved *circa* 1869 and may have lost some parts. There is a recumbent effigy of a young child with his head on a skull above a slate or black marble plaque surmounted by a heraldic device. Two obelisks are present. There is full description in 'CMS Journal' Vol XXVIII 2013 page 133.

M223 Bradley, Staffs. Thomas Browne (died 1633) and his wife. Small figures facing each other in Chellaston alabaster partially painted. The monument formerly had a prayer desk as indicated by the chevron on the wall. May have been moved.

M224 Cranborne, Dorset. A wall mural to John Eliot (died 1641). A boy aged seven, son of John Eliot of Cornwall and erected by his grandmother. He is reported to have died suddenly at school. The mural has a frame of alabaster within which is an alabaster effigy of a seated boy with one elbow resting on a skull. A black panel with inscription and a heraldic device above.

M225 Llanrwst, Denbighshire. Sidney Wynn (e) (died 1639) aged one month the daughter of Owen Wynn (e). A modest-sized mural in Chellaston alabaster showing a chrisom and two shields in relief. A panel with a raised edge holds an inscription.

M226 Madingley, Cambs. Believed to be Elizabeth Stewkley (died 1635) aged one day, the daughter of John Stewkley who penned the inscription in Latin. A modest mural with a cornice held by two angels and a chrisom lying on its left side on a cushion. Black marble inscription. A crown inscribed Coronat Innocentia.

M227 Madingley, Cambs. Dame Jane Cotton (formerly Hynde, died 1692). A reclining effigy on a rolled mat and cushion on a shallow tomb chest. Swags and cherub heads and strapwork. Esdaile claims the work is by Edward Stanton.

M228 Bottisham, Cambs. Thomas Pledger (died 1599) and wife Margaret (died 1598).

M229 Bottisham, Cambs. Lionel and Dorothy Alington (died 1638). Two infants residing on their right side on black marble platforms. Two cherubs stand holding back the curtains.

M230 Eggesford, Devon. Dorcus Hill (died 1630) and Mary Digby, the wives of Arthur Chichester, 1st Earl of Donegal. He stands upright between the two ladies who lean on their elbows.

M231 Instow, Devon. John Downe (died 1640). The mural is rare being in Watchet alabaster in pink and white/black alabaster and an Ashford marble inscription panel. The effigy is in Bath stone and is painted being depicted waist upwards in an oval frame. He has his right elbow on as skull and a book in his left hand. The historian for Instow says that Watchet alabaster was only mined for 50 years. In light of the fact that we know mining was in hand in 1633 this means it ceased in 1683. There is similar monument in Barnstaple church and at Swimbridge (M232).

M232 Swimbridge, Devon. Tristram Chichester (died 1654 or 1672). This is claimed to be carved in Barnstaple and there are similarities with that at Instow (M231). The mural is painted and may be badly restored and may not be alabaster.

M233 Bittadon, Devon. Edward Pointz (died 1691). This like the monuments at Instow and Swimbridge is credited to Barnstaple workshops and to Watchet alabaster. The canopy and reclining angels are limestone and the oval Ashford marble.

M234 Barnstaple, Devon. Walter Tucker, merchant (died 1653). A mural monument in Barnstaple style with a demi-figure facing forward and one elbow on what maybe an hourglass and holding a skull. Beneath is an effigy of his daughter and her infant. Linked to M231 to M233.

M235 Barnstaple, Devon. Nicholas Blake (died 1634). A mural monument in Barnstaple style with a demi-figure facing forward and one elbow on a skull and holding a skull. Beneath is an effigy of his daughter and her infant. Linked to M231 to M234. The monument was erected by his father Martin Blake, vicar of Barnstaple.

M236 St Minver, Cornwall. John Roe (died 1657). A fine mural with a kneeling effigy in Fauld alabaster with what maybe clunch columns. Black inscription panel. This is quite a plain monument with no heraldic devices. Likened to a monument in St Leonard's Streatham to John Massingford and wife dated 1657 and may be accredited to Thomas Stanton.

M237 Tawstock, Devon. Edward Lovett (died 1700).

M238 Exeter, Devon, St Petrock. A wall tablet to Jonathon Ives (died 1717) and his wife Elizabeth (died 1698). The tablet appears to have an alabaster frame in black and white Watchet alabaster. This monument was moved from St Kerian Church, Exeter when that was demolished in 1873. It is reported that the *Last Judgement* plaque by the same sculptor is here. There is another in the Royal Albert Memorial Museum at Totnes was once part of this monument. The plaque in Totnes is reported as 'marble' but has a pinkish hue which is suspicious.

M239 Bovey Tracey, Devon. Elizaeus Hele (died 1626) and his two wives and son. He was a member of the Inner Temple but is buried in Exeter Cathedral. He lies on his side on his right elbow with his hand on a skull. The two wives knee in front of the tomb chest facing each other with the son behind. Fauld alabaster and probably the work of a London carver.

M240 Dartmouth, Devon, St Saviour. John Robert Vavasor or Vavasour (died 1694) and his son Henry. The wall tablet appears to be in Watchet white and black veined alabaster.

M241 Whitchurch, Devon. Francis Pengelly (died 1722). This tablet by John Weston appears to be in Watchet white with black veined alabaster with a trademark oval plaque in pink alabaster.

M242 Denbury, Devon. Joseph Taylor (died 1733) but monument not erected until 1736. This one of the last recorded works of John Weston and appears to be in Watchet alabaster. A naval man the monument has a battle scene depicted in the same style as the plaques on the earlier monuments. There is a large anchor. Said to be a copy of one in Westminster Abbey to Henry Priestman dated 1712 and carved by Francis Bird. This is in marble but depicts the anchor and with a head in relief within a medallion as does that at Denbury.

M243 Bristol, Somerset, Lord Mayor's Chapel. A mural monument showing a boy, John Cookin (died 1627) aged 11 on one knee and holding a book in his left hand. Nothing much is known about the subject but he may have been a pupil in the nearby Queen Elizabeth School.

M244 Marlborough, Wilts. Children, Robert, Francis and Elizabeth Hyde (died 1626). All three died within 32 days and may well have been the plague. Their parents are buried in Catherington (not alabaster).

M245 Barnwell, Northants. Henry Montagu (died 1625) aged three. He was drowned.

M246 Ogbourne St Andrew, Wilts. William and Elizabeth Goddard (died 1695). An interesting mural in pinkish alabaster worthy of closer examination.

M247 Tichborne, Hants. A mural monument to Richard Tichborne (died 1619) aged one. The lower part appears to be a recent repair in uncertain stone with a black inscription panel but the whole is surmounted by an arch of Fauld alabaster with a large heraldic device on top. The effigy is slightly unnatural lying on its right side and is painted but probably alabaster. He was the son of Sir Richard Tichborne.

M248 West Ham, Essex. John Faldo (died 1613) and his father Francis Faldo (died 1632). These two monuments are by the same hand and may not be alabaster.

M249 Hawnby, Yorks. Anne Tankard (died 1608). A child aged two, daughter of Sir Henry Tankard. A mural tablet in Fauld alabaster without any effigy. A dial is carved at the top and floral carvings which are coloured. There is a baby in a crib. There is later 1617 inscription detailing a later burial.

M250 Beddington, Surrey. Sir Francis Carew (died 1611). A mural monument with columns between which is the effigy in armour of a knight. The inscription refers to his adoption of Nicholas Throckmorton the son of Sir Nicholas Throckmorton, his brother-in-law to bear the name of Carew and inherit his estate. Below the effigy are other effigies of this Nicholas Carew (Throckmorton), the wife and four sons and two daughters. Nicholas commissioned the tomb.

M251 London, Aldgate, St Katherine Cree. Sir Nicholas Throckmorton (died 1571). He lies in armour and on a rolled mat. The inscription panel has a fretwork frame which is unusual.

M252 Wallington, Surrey. Sir Olliph Leigh (died 1612) and wife Jane (Browne). The monument originally erected to his father, John Leigh (died 1571) and grandfather Nicholas Leigh (died 1565). The effigies are the latter are in niches. Also shown in John's wife Joan and Nicholas's wife Ann, daughter of Sir Nicholas Carew. Also commemorated is Sarah, wife of Sir Francis Leigh (1691) and of her mother Elizabeth Lovel.

M253 Leyton, Essex. Sir Michael Hickes (died 1612 and wife Elizabeth (died 1635). The monument was moved in 1853 from the chancel. The monument has been rearranges along one wall of the chapel.

M254 West Ham, Essex. William Fawcet (died 1631) and wife and her second husband William Toppesfield (who erected the tomb). Fawcet is recumbent but the other two kneel in front of a prayer desk. Columns are black marble.

M255 Romford, Essex. A fine mural to Sir George Hervey (died 1605). Sir George kneels before a prayer desk with his wife in front and their four children. Two black Corinthian columns in marble. Sir George was lieutenant of the Tower.

M256 Romford, Essex. A fine mural to Sir Anthony Cooke (died 1576). Sir Anthony kneels before a prayer desk with his wife in front and their children. Restored 1873. This has similarities to the monument in St Peter ad Vincula in the Tower. Also similar to the Richard Allington monument in King's College London (possibly not alabaster).

M257 Romford, Essex. A fine mural to Ann Carew (died 1605). She lies on one elbow. Two black Corinthian columns in marble.

M258 Chigwell, Essex. Thomas Coleshill (died 1595) and wife Mary (Crayford, died 1599). They were married 50 years. Monument erected by daughters Susanna Stanhope and Anne Leeke.

M259 Toft Monks, Norfolk. John Bayspool (died 1624) and wife Elizabeth. A very unusual memorial comprising two carved heraldic devices in alabaster and an inscription with an alabaster frame surmounted by an alabaster obelisk. The bottom of the inscription carries the words 'Fecit Apri: An 1653' which indicates it was made in 1653.

M260 Brasted, Kent. Judge Robert Heath (died 1649) possibly not made until 1664 for which Stanton charged £60.

M261 Narburgh Manor Chapel, Norfolk. Sir Edward Barkham his wife Joan, two sons and three daughters. He lies on a mat in armour but also includes his robes and chain of office as mayor of London.

M262 Greshford, Denbigh. Sir Richard Trevor (died 1638) and wife Catherine. The tomb was created in his lifetime. The two depicted face forward in a kneeling pose. Catherine has a separate monument probably dated 1602.

M263 Greshford, Denbigh. Lady Catherine Trevor (died 1602) and her daughters. Catherine is shown kneeling with five daughters behind. *See also* M262.

M264 Masham. Yorks. Sir Marmaduke Wyvill (died 1612) and wife of Low Burton Hall. The effigies are recumbent on one elbow in two tiers. Rails are considered to be original.

M265 York Minster. Rear-Admiral Sir Christopher Cradock (died 1914). He engaged Admiral Von Spee and went down with his ship. There is another monument in Gilling West.

M266 Spare

M267 Spare

M268 Spare

M269 Spare

M270 York Minster. A tablet to two canons of the minster William Mason (died 1797) and William Dixon (died 1854) assumed to have been erected in the latter year. The monument is mainly metal, coloured marble but the figures of the

Good Shepherd and the angels are of alabaster.

M271 York Minster. A tablet to Archbishop William Conner McGee (died 1891). He had only a short tenure. A brass made by Bodley in an alabaster frame made by Farmer and Brindley. A Gothic tablet with pinnacles and a carved angel. McGee is buried in Peterborough.

M272 Great Wishford, Wilts. To Sir Richard Grobham (died 1629) and wife Margaret. Margaret went on to marry John St John of Lydiard Tregoze and she is also on the monument there. Although it cannot be confirmed that this is alabaster the association with Lydiard Tregoze makes it likely.

M273 Salisbury, St Thomas, Wilts. Christopher Eyre (died 1624 or 1628) and wife Ester. This is stained or painted to resemble oak. The two face each other over a prayer desk. Father time, a scythe and hourglass are included. Children including a chrisom are to be seen on the lower panels.

M274 Salisbury, St Thomas, Wilts. Thomas Eyre (died 1628) and wife Elizabeth (1617). This is stained or painted to resemble oak as is M273. The two face each other over a prayer desk. This was moved from the chancel at some point and has received some damage which has resulted one child to be lost.

M275 Wilton, Wilts. William Sharp (died 1626) and wife. They are small effigies facing each other over a prayer desk. The effigies are part of a larger monument which is not alabaster over the cloister door.

M276 Aston, Warwicks. Sir Edward Devereaux (died 1626) and Katherine (died 1627). Black and white marble and alabaster.

M277 King's Norton, Warwick. Sir Richard Gervis of Moseley (died 1632) and Lady Ann. The children are depicted in a panel above effigies.

M278 Chichester, Sussex. Cathedral. Bishop Earnest Wilberforce (died 1907). A fine tablet showing the bishop in prayer made by John Tweed. The frame and base is limestone but the relief of the bishop is in a semi-translucent alabaster which is very like that mined from the Kingston.

M279 London, St Bartholomew, Smithfield. Francis Anthony (died 1623).

M280 London, St Bartholomew, Smithfield. James Rivers (died 1641), a demi-figure holding a sword. Has been moved. It was covered in pitch at one time which was removed in 1912. It seems to have been a feature of this church as other monuments are so treated.

M281 London, St Bartholomew, Smithfield. Ellis Yonge (died 1659), a small tablet in alabaster. This may date from an earlier date as the inscription refers to him being a 'rembrancer who was in the 11th year of his majesties reign', 1659 being the last year of the Commonwealth.

M282 London, St Bartholomew, Smithfield. John Millett (died 1660). Millet appears to have been a mariner as the monument is decorated with mariner's instruments. Researchers may be confused by the number of John Millets associated with this church. This John probably died in Wandsworth and is likely to be buried there, the memorial being erected in keeping with the other Milletts who are buried in Smithfield.

M283 London, St Bartholomew, Smithfield. John whiting (died 1704) and his wife Mary (died 1727). An oval tablet with drapery, garlands and cherubs. The monument may date later than 1704.

M284 London, St Bartholomew, Smithfield. Margaret Fielding (died 1739). A small tablet.

M285 Ellough, Suffolk. Rev Richard Aldous Arnold (died 1877) and his wife Charlotte (died 1832 aged 37). A small tablet beneath a larger one which commemorates the restoration of the chancel. The frame of the larger tablet seems to be in Fauld alabaster and that of Arnold's in Kingston. Arnold was 80 when he died.

M286 Marlesford, Suffolk. William Alston (died 1641) and wife Avis (Pitman). The monument erected by their daughter, also Avis. The monument is unusual as it depicts the deceased as portraits in two carved wreaths with an ornate frame which encloses black marble inscription panel.

M287 Tawstock, Devon. Sir Henry Northcote (died 1729). A wall tablet is what looks like white alabaster with black veining. Credited to Thomas Jewell of Barnstaple.

M288 Ipswich, St Stephen, Suffolk. Robert Leman (died 1637) and wife Mary (also died 1637 on the same day). A part-painted and maybe restored mural with the two departed facing each other over a prayer desk. Children depicted.

M289 Stoke by Nayland, Suffolk. Sir Francis Mannock (died 1634). He was of a recusant family. His wife is commemorated by a brass in the floor. The knight lies on his back with kneeling figures at his head and feet. This is locally credited to Nicholas Stone but this does not feature in his workbooks.

M290 Sotterley, Suffolk. Thomas Playtor (died 1638) and his two wives both called Anne. By these he had 22 children who are all depicted on the panel beneath. The monument is very imposing with the knight, kneeling, facing forward and the wives facing to the side.

M291 Bath, Somerset, Abbey church. Lady Waller (died 1633). Lord Waller rests on one elbow and looks at his wife. Two kneeling children with other children in relief along the tomb chest.

M292 Crowcombe, Somerset. Robert Cranmer-Trollope (died 1808). A painted portrait in an alabaster frame.

M293 Eccleshall, Staffs. Bishop William Overton (died 1603). Two wives are shown kneeling in niches above the effigy, one Margaret Barlow and the other Mary Bradstock. The epitaph was written by Overton in 1603.

M294 Rolleston on Dove, Staffs. Sir Edward Moseley (died 1638).

M295 Acton Burnell, Shrops. Sir Humphrey Lee (died 1632) and wife Margaret (Corbet). Six children depicted in relief. Lee was the son of R213.

M296 Kinlet, Shrops. George Blount (died 1548) and wife Constantia. This six-poster monument with a cadaver beneath has a feel of being much later than 1548 and may well be 1580 or later.

M297 Ludlow, Shrops. Edmund Waller (died 1591) and wife Mary and children. This is a mural monument with high arch and strapwork which may be much later than 1591. The principal effigies are recumbent with small figures which are painted in a line at the foot of the monument. The whole in screened with an iron railing which is considered to be contemporary.

M298 Ludlow, Shrops. Dame Mary Eure (died 1612). The effigy rests on one elbow.

M299 Neen Solars, Shrops. Humfrey Conyngesby (died 1624). A slim Humfrey resides on one elbow gazing into the distance. The tomb chest has an odd design on the front panels.

M300 Norton in Hales, Shrops. Sir Rowland Cotton (died 1634) and wife Frances (died 1606). She died in childbirth and naked child is shown clutched to her breast. Column decoration and strapwork. The tomb was made *circa* 1609 and adapted for Sir Rowland in 1635. The cost was reputed to be £2000 but this is doubtful. The tomb was moved in 1864 to its current position. There is a suggestion that the tomb was designed by Inigo Jones based on a drawing in the Royal Institute of British Architects which has many similarities. Despite this the strapwork and other features point to the Southwark schools for its creation. The drawing L5/1 referred to above, is annotated *Design for Lady Cotton 1608* and has many of the normal mural features but has two tall columns standing on the floor and the effigy is semi-reclining with cherubs. The tomb chest is ornate with massive scroll work. It would appear that Jones may well have produced an idea of a tomb but its execution holds for the standard interpretation of the London carvers. There have also been similarities recognised in the Marshall non-alabaster monuments in All Saints Conington for which a number of papers have been written.

M301 North Leigh, Oxford. William Lenthall (died 1596) and wife Frances. They kneel in front of a prayer desk with four children in relief below.

M302 Swinbrook, Oxford. Sir Edmund Fettiplace (died 1613) and his father and grandfather. A three-tiered monument like M207. This is a bit early for William Byrd unless erected long after Edmund deceased. Unlike M207 it is not signed. The assumption is that this was not by Byrd and that M207 was commissioned as a copy.

M303 Stanton Harcourt, Oxford. Sir Philip Harcourt (died 1688) and wife. Moved from the chapel sometime prior to 1876. The monument has two oval laurel wreaths each containing a demi-figure facing forward. In some quarters the date is given as 1723, but the dress is clearly late restoration. The monument is highly decorated with swags and putti.

M304 Oxford, Christ Church chapel. William Goodwin (died 1620). A wall mural with the demi-effigy facing forward and holding a book. He was vice-chancellor of Oxford and preached to James I in 1614. The side columns have objects tied together by strapwork.

M305 Holkham, Norfolk. Meriall Coke (died 1636). Erected by her husband John. Unusually her parents Anthony Wheately and Anne Armiger and Grandparents William Wheately and Martha Skinner are depicted. At the foot are six sons and nine daughters in relief. The large memorial appears to be in Watchet alabaster. Coke himself appears in a demi-effigy facing forward in the top. In view of the material used it is assumed this is a London carving and some authors credit this to Nicholas Stone, he having possibly mined Watchet from 1633. *See also* M306.

M306 Holkham, Norfolk. Miles Armiger (died 1639). Uncle of M305. The monument is 'signed' Robert Pook who was the senior carver in the Stone workshop at Long Acre, London. Pook was illiterate but used a mason mark 'RP' (as noted in the Stone notebooks). This appears to be in Fauld alabaster but requires more research. Miles kneels and unusually has his head turned a quarter to the front. The arch has roses. *See also* note under Joseph Pickford.

M307 Stowe Bardolf, Norfolk. Sir Ralph Hare (died 1623). I fine mural with no effigy and with intricate strapwork. There is a simple non-alabaster tomb chest within which he is buried in the same church.

M308 King's Lynn, Norfolk. Thomas Snelling (died 1623) and wife Margaret. A wall mural with the depicted facing each other over a prayer desk. A well coloured memorial which may well have been repainted in recent times.

M309 King's Lynn, Norfolk. Thomas Greene and wife Susannah (Barker). A wall mural with the depicted facing forward in what is believed to be portrait images. The monument dates from the late 17th century and the clothes and hair are very well done. There are nine children all kneeling with heads turned forward which are also considered to be likenesses. This too is a well coloured memorial which may well have been repainted in recent times.

M310 King's Lynn, Norfolk. A family memorial with Richard Clarck (died 1602) on left and Matthew Clarck (died 1623) on right. There are five children beneath. This like the other wall murals is a well coloured memorial which may well have been repainted in recent times.

M311 Ashby St Ledger, Northants. Brian Ianson (died 1634) and wife Anne and 10 children. The inscription panel has a blank date.

M312 Ashby St Ledger, Northants. John Ianson (died 1657), son of M311 … An oval mural with the deceased shown in relief. The mural also names his first wife Sally and second wife Thomasine and four children.

M313 Stanford on Avon, Northants. Sir Thomas Cave (died 1613) and wife Eleanor (St John). Feet on greyhound. Margaret Whinney made observations about this tomb on page 37 of her book.

M314 Stanford on Avon, Northants. Henry Knollys (died 1582) and his wife Margaret (died 1606). The monument appears to have been created in the 17th century. Margaret rests on one elbow facing forward below her husband. Two daughters kneel on either side. These effigies are fully painted. Knollys was an adventurer and sometime pirate but died in Holland and died there aged 40.

M315 Blakesley, Northants. William Watts (died 1614) and wife Mary and two children. All effigies are headless in two tiers.

M316 Green's Norton, Northants. William Hicklinge (died 1606) and wife Frances (died 1603). A very unusual semi-circular wall mural like a bow window. The local guidebook suggests Nicholas Stone as the carver but there is no other support for this.

M317 Flaxton, Northants. Sir Nicholas Nicholls (died 1660). The church at Flaxton was demolished in 1958 and the monument which had suffered from exposure was transferred to the care of the V&A in 1965 and was restored for display in room 58a.

M318 Brockelsby, Lincs. Sir William Pelham (died 1629) and wife Anne. An interesting tiered monument with two recumbent effigies on a tomb chest which has a curve topped niche which contains images of the family. The inscription panel and heraldry is attached to the wall above the effigies.

M319 Burton Pedwardine, Lincs. Sir Thomas Horsman (died 1610).

M320 Burton by Lincoln, Lincs. Christopher Randes (died 1639) and wife Katherine (Moudeford). The figures are in relief and the columns have detailed strapwork.

M321 Coates by Stow, Lincs. A mural in alabaster to Brian Cooke (died 1653). A demi-figure facing forward under an arch holding a book in left hand.

M322 Peatling Magna, Leics. William Jervis (died 1618) and wife Elizabeth (Shepperd).

M323 Ilston, Leics. Elizabeth Nedham (died 1639) wife of John Nedham. Small figures on tablet.

M324 Old Dalby, Leics. Sir Andrew Noel (died 1603 or 1607), son of R132 and wife Mabel (Harrington). Effigy on rolled up mat. Raised by his son Edward Noel, Viscount Campden. Much damaged by the 1834 fire and the shield above the inscription panel is now lost. Nichols also has an etching of this tomb. The contract for the lost monument at Breadsall (*see* D9/94A) is believed to specify a copy of this tomb.

M325 Skeffington, Leics. Sir John Skeffington (died 1651). An ornate wall tablet with two inscribed panels. Large statues of angels holding back curtains to reveal the panels. *See*: http://www.leicestershirechurches.co.uk/skeffington-st-thomas-a-becket/

M326 Didsbury, Lancs. Sir Nicholas Mosley (died 1612) and wives Margaret (Whitbroke) and Elizabeth (Rookes) and sons Rowland and Edward.

M327 Great Mitton, Lancs. Richard Shireburn (died 1629) son of R222. He kneels in front of a prayer desk the other side being occupied by his mother Maude. There are other Shireburn monuments 1668 (Richard), 1689 (Richard), 1690(Richard) and 1693 (Isabel Ingleby) all stated to be by Thomas Stanton as is one of 1702 (Richard Francis). However, the sculptor was almost certainly William Stanton who carved them all the 17th century tombs in 1699 as a commission by Isabel at a cost of £253 and is stated to have crossed-legged knights. The monument to Richard Francis was carved in 1703 for a cost of £177. These have not yet been identified as alabaster.

M328 Twickenham, Surrey. Francis Poulton (died 1642) and wife Susan. Demi-portraits facing forward which may be likenesses. The effigies are grouped in an informal pose. The alabaster is referred to as ‘pinkish’ with a black central panel.

M329 Tower of London chapel, London. Tomb of Sir Richard Blount (died 1564) and his son Sir Michael Blount (died 1610). A mural tomb with kneeling effigies. Both were lord lieutenants of the Tower. The mural is early 17th century design incorporating a four or five-poster type showing French influence. Sir Richard was lieutenant from 1560 to 1564 and Sir Michael from 1590 to 1610. The 1564 is the work of William Cure II and it is believed that the later 1610 extension is the work of Cornelius Cure and William Cure II.

M330 Tower of London chapel, London. Mural to the children of George Payler. Samuel (died 1649), Maria (died 1646) and Robert (died 1651). George Payler was the surveyor of the ordnance for the tower.

M331 Radbourne, Derbys. Germaine Pole (died 1683) and possibly wife Anne and Germaine's mother and father. Appointed by his executors. A large sarcophagus with urns and drapery with effaced inscription. The stone appears to be in black veined alabaster but this is as yet to be confirmed. The figures below are part of G66.

M332 Ufford, Cambs. Dame Bridgett Carre (died 1621) with the lady semi-reclining under an arch with columns supporting a cornice with heraldic cartouche above. In Nov 2015 it was reported that the church is to be passed into the care of the Churches Conservation Trust who intend to conserve the monuments.

M333 Ufford, Cambs. Francis Lang (died 1911).

M334 Burwell, Cambs. Thomas Gerard (died 1617) and wife (died 1608) possibly made in 1613. Moved onto the north aisle wall in 1743.

M335 North Bradley, Wilts. Sir Edward Lewis (died 1630) and Lady Ann. Moved from within chancel rails.

M336 Pinner, Middlesex. Thomas Hutchinson (died 1656) and wife Margaret (Allanson). Alabaster and black marble.

M337 Great Hale, Lincs. Robert Cawdron (died 1665) and family. The monument created 1668 by his widow Elizabeth. A double-decked mural.

M338 Faringdon, Berks. Sir Edward Unton (possibly died 1582) and wife (died 1588). This wall mural was recorded at the time of the Civil War as having kneeling effigies or in some reports, demi-figures facing forward but these appears to have disappeared.

M339 Landwade, Suffolk (formerly in Cambs). Sir John Cotton (died 1620) and wife. He lies on his left elbow with his wife below him recumbent. The canopy is arched with roses.

M340 Landwade, Suffolk (formerly in Cambs). Sir John Cotton (died 1689). He rests in a semi-reclining fashion on his left elbow on a cushion and rolled up mat. The canopy is arched with cherubs. He wears armour which was becoming unfashionable at the time. It is believed this was done to keep in tune with other Cotton monuments – *see* CMS Vol XXIX 2014.

M341 Exeter Cathedral. Sir Peter Carew (died 1575). Originally located in the north choir, it was moved to the south transept in 1805. The mural shows Sir Peter kneeling with heraldry all around. The monument was described with the other Carew monuments in CMS Vol XXIX 2014 and in Vol XXX 2015 page 134. *See also* X42. He died in Ireland and is buried at Waterford.

M342 Stratford on Avon, Warwicks. George Carew, Earl of Totnes (died 1629) and wife Joyce (Clopton) who died in 1635. The pedigree of the Carews is discussed at length in CMS Vol XXIX 2014. The tomb was probably commissioned by Joyce and as for other Carew monuments is covered in heraldic shields. Coronets on head. *See* X42. The lower part of the tomb has ordnance in the form of gunpowder barrels and cannon.

M343 Stratford on Avon, Warwicks. John Combe (died 1614). Died a friend of Shakespeare and a bachelor. It is reputed that Shakespeare composed an epitaph but that on the monument is not original and therefore this cannot be proved.

M344 Stratford on Avon, Warwicks. William Shakespeare (died 1616) but the monument may be later. A wall mounted demi-figure facing forward in alabaster and black marble with the grave on the floor beneath. The attribution to Gerard Johnson (the younger) is based on the attribution of an engraving but which fails to show the pen and script – *see* below. The engraving was copied by Vertue *circa* 1620 which shows the monument as it was created with Shakespeare with his hand on a wool sack indicating his connection with the wool industry from which he is believed to have earned his wealth. Dr Adam White provided a fine description of this monument as CMS 'Monument of the Month' March 2010. The bust was painted white at some point which caused a stir and the paint was removed *circa* 1861.

M345 Stanford on Soar, Notts. Thomas Lewes (died 1695) and wife Anne (died 1694) and two infants. Moved to its current position in 1893. The tablet is oval shaped with putti in the margins and two skulls at the bottom. A very unusual memorial.

M346 Wirksworth, Derbys. A wall tablet in slate with an alabaster surround to Thomas Eley (died 1798) and his wife Mary (died 1801).

M347 Wirksworth, Derbys. A wall tablet in slate with an alabaster surround to John Low (died 1713) erected by his heir Charles Hurt in 1719. The tablet sides have carved symbols and the top and both have putti and a skull.

M348 Wirksworth, Derbys. A wall tablet to Philip Gell (died 1688).

M349 Wirksworth, Derbys. A wall tablet to Thomas Poyser (died 1869).

M350 Wirksworth, Derbys. A wall tablet to Lucy Gell (died 1814).

M351 Wirksworth, Derbys. A wall tablet to Harriet Eleanor Gell (died 1813).

M352 Wirksworth, Derbys. Stephen Hall (died *circa* 1819) and wife Ruth (died 1836). Slate with alabaster surround.

M353 Wirksworth, Derbys. Thomas Tomlinson (died *circa* 1866) and wife Mary (died 1866). She was daughter of M352. Also Jane (died 1847) and Mary (died 1901).

M354 Wirksworth, Derbys. William Webb (died *circa* 1890) and wife Ruth (died 1836). Alabaster with slate surround.

M355 Otterden, Kent. Sir Justinian Lewin (died 1620) and wife and child. The knight is recumbent but his wife kneels in front with his daughter. The effigies are plaster but the rest is marble and alabaster.

M356 Amersham, Bucks. Henry Curwen (died 1636 aged 14) by Edward Marshall. Shrouded figure emerging from tomb held open by angels. Restored 1980.

M357 Newark, Notts. Henry Trewman (died 1655). A wall tablet with a demi-figure facing forward. Trewman was the vicar of St Mary during the Civil War. Black marble in alabaster frame.

M358 Newark, Notts. John Johnson (died 1659). A wall tablet with a demi-figure facing forward. Alabaster frame.

M359 Newark, Notts. John Ramsey (died 1639). A wall tablet with a demi-figure facing forward. Alabaster frame. Ramsey was claimed to have died though being struck by lightning.

M360 Newark, Notts. Daniel Crayle (died 1727). A wall tablet which is in a black veined stone which may be Watchet alabaster.

M361 Harefield, Middlesex. Sir John Newdigate (died 1610). The monument was erected by the widow Ann Fitton (died 1618). It was recorded by a family member that the contract was with a William White and the carving was in 1614. Like the monument in the Tower of London the details of William White are elusive and it may well be that over the span of years the name 'White' has been taken for 'Wright'. *See also* M438 and M439 but there are style variations. The columns are rectangular and the strapwork is in the arch rather than the plinths and a skull is depicted on the prayer desk.

M362 Greens Norton, Northants. John Hicklinge (died 1558).

M363 Greens Norton, Northants. William Hicklinge (died 1606) and wife Frances (died 1603) – *see* English Heritage and CMS. Couple face each other over prayer stall with daughter behind. A plumes helmet is in niche.

M364 Hackney, London. Sir Thomas Rowe (died 1569) and wife Mary but may be dated to 1570. Page 6 of Llewellyn refers. Monument mentioned in will. There is a suggestion that this has been moved from a church known as St Augustine where it was recorded in 1752.

M365 Leaveland, Kent. Katherine Roper (died 1606) and her son Francis Herdson (by her first marriage). In Fauld alabaster and with strapwork of the Southwark school.

M366 Yalding Kent. Ambrose Warde (died 1637) and his wife Elizabeth (died 1679) and his eldest daughter Bennet (died 1656). Black marble and Fauld alabaster. The monument carved circ 1656 according to local history and the inscription for the wife would have been added later. Although the effigies kneel at a prayer stall their bodies are turned a quarter to front.

M367 Rochester, Kent. Joseph Maas (died 1886).

M368 Sherborne Abbey, Dorset. John Derbie (died 1713) and Mary (died 1717). Tassels, lamps and cartouche.

M369 Trent, Dorset. William Gerard (died 1604). Pilasters and heraldic device.

M370 Wimborne, Dorset. Thomas Hanham (died 1650) and wife.

M371 Wimborne, Dorset. Sir Edmund Uverdale (died 1606). On one elbow.

M372 Wimborne St Giles, Dorset. Sir Anthony Ashley (died 1628) and Jane his wife and Anne his daughter. Large tomb.

M373 Attenborough, Notts. Francis Jacques (died 1606) and his wife Jane (Roe of Ratcliffe on Soar) who died in 1621 when the tablet was placed in church by her son George. The tablet records that that Francis had an alias known as Gambard of Toton, but almost nothing is known of this. A small tablet with columns and a pediment and two curious pinnacles. The inscription panel is in limestone. Partially picked out in paint.

Dean Caesar (1636). Photo Janet State.

M374 Ely Cathedral, Cambs. Dean Caesar (died 1636). A kneeling effigy at an ornate prayer desk. The whole has been restored.

Bishop Dean Heaton (1609). Photo Janet State.

M375 Ely Cathedral, Cambs. Bishop Martin Heaton (died 1609). The bishop is recumbent with finely carved robes and lies on a cushion on top of a rolled up mat. The alabaster looks like Fauld, but merits closer examination.

M376 Harlton, Cambs. Henry Fryer (died 1631) flanked by his parents Thomas (died 1623) and Mary (died 1614) and a recumbent stepmother Bridget, Carotids flank either side.

M377 Dorney, Bucks. Sir William Garrard (died 1606) and wife Elizabeth (Roe). Elizabeth erected the monument but it was completed by her son-in-law Sir John Kederminster who added his name to the bottom.

M378 Radley, Berks. Sir William Stonehouse (died 1633) and wife. This Nicholas Stone monument cost £120 and appears in Stone's workbook. A son kneels at the head carrying a skull. He is believed to have died before his parents. Other children appear on the bases which according to Esdaile were carved by an assistant.

M379 Thornhill, Yorks. Sir George Savile (died 1627). Effigy on straw mat. Colt appears to have maintained the style popular some 30 years earlier and had not moved with the changes in fashion.

M380 Stanwell, Surrey. Lord Knyvett (died 1623) and wife Elizabeth (Haywood). White marble figures on alabaster sarcophagus. A particularly nice mural with the peer and his wife facing each other over a prayer desk. Black columns with drapes.

M381 Middle Claydon, Bucks. Uriah (died 1608) and Lettice Verney.

M382 Middle Claydon, Bucks. Sir Edmund Verney (died 1642) killed at Edgehill, his wife Margaret (died 1641) and Sir Ralph Verney (died 1696) and his wife Mary (possibly died 1640). The monument was set up by Sir Ralph and the commission given to Edward Marshall in 1650 but not completed until 1653. *See also* R192.

M383 Everton, Beds. Sir Humphrey Winch (died 1624). The judge is shown as a demi-figure in a semi-circular arch. The alabaster is a strange colour and merits closer examination. The Judge presided over the 1616 Leicester witchcraft trials which were subsequently proved to be a miscarriage of justice and which damaged his reputation.

M384 Hereford Cathedral. Bishop, Theophilus Field (died 1636). A demi-figure in a style popular in London.

M385 Hitcham, Bucks. Roger Alford (died 1580) and wife, Elizabeth (Ramsey, died 1598).

M386 Hitcham, Bucks. Sir William Clarke (died 1624). Recumbent effigy flanked by soldiers holding back curtains. Contemporary iron grill. Decorated obelisks.

M387 West Thurrock, Essex. Sir Christopher Holford (died 1607) and wife Mary (Vyner) died 1611. These are effigies lie separate the mural monument of which they were part having been dismantled. Both lie on their sides and the tomb may well have been two tiered indicating a London workshop. The lady wears a ruff and mourning hood which makes a 1607 date more likely for its carving.

M388 Greensted, Essex. Joan Wood (died 1585) wife of Alan Wood. A tablet with columns.

M389 Latton, Essex. James Altham (died 1583) and wife. Eleven children.

M390 Welford, Northants. Francis Saunders (died 1584) and his three wives, Elizabeth Carew, Helen Chaloner and Frances Pope (died 1594). This is a mural tablet in alabaster with polychrome heraldic devices and brass panel depicting the people. Inscription. Bayliss reports that there were formerly alabaster slabs in the floor in front of this monument.

M391 Newstead Abbey crypt (now the gift shop). Sir John Byron (died 1609) and his wife Alicia (Alice) Strelley (died *circa* 1599), the daughter of Sir Nicholas Strelley. This is painted. The man wears plate armour. Taken from Colwick Old Church in September 1937. Restored.

M392 Ashbourne, Derbys. Dorothy Cockayne wife of Sir Thomas Cockayne (died 1592). Distinctive headpiece and high necked ruff.

M393 Fulham, Middlesex. William Plumbe (died 1593). A mural tablet with inscription on a black Ashford marble slab. Corinthian columns with an entablature with coloured marbles.

M394 Fulham, Middlesex. Thomas Bonde (died 1600). A mural tablet with inscription on a black slate slab. Corinthian columns with an entablature with coloured marbles.

M395 Fulham, Middlesex. Katherine Hart (died 1605). A mural with a kneeling woman and children. She has her hand on the son of one son.

M396 Fulham, Middlesex. Thomas Smith (died 1609). A mural with a kneeling woman and children. She has her hand on the son of one son.

M397 Fulham, Middlesex. William Earlby of North End (died 1664).

M398 Fulham, Middlesex. 25th Cyclists Battalion, London Regiment. The alabaster is confined to the surround.

M399 West Malling, Kent. Jane, Lady FitzJames (died 1594).

M400 Westminster, St Margaret. Blanche Parry (died 1590) lady in waiting to Elizabeth I. There is a churchwarden receipt for 20s for license.

M401 Forton, Staffs. Sir Thomas Skrymsher (died 1633) and his wife Anne (Sneyd, died 1656). Five sons and four daughters are depicted. The tomb chest is freestone and the tomb has been renovated at some time.

M402 London, Great St Helen's, Bishopsgate. John Robinson (died 1599) and wife Christian. A two bay mural with Corinthian columns which enclose two kneeling figures in front of a prayer desk. Nine sons and seven daughters are depicted.

M403 Barton in Fabis, Notts. Henry Sacheverell (died 1598).

M404 London, Westminster Abbey, Elizabeth Cecil (died 1591) at the age of 16. She was the wife of Sir William Cecil. She resides on one elbow and wears a mourning hood.

M405 Mersham, Kent. Margaret Collyns (died 1595). Signed 'Evesham me fecit'.

M406 Tavistock, Devon. John Granville (died 1600) and wife Alicia.

M407 Denton, Lincs. John Blythe and wife *circa* 1602.

M408 Norton, Northants. Lady Elizabeth Seymour. Second wife of Sir Richard Knightly (died 1602). Black marble columns. A richly decorated tomb with much strapwork which gives a suggestion of the London workshops.

M409 Wednesbury, Staffs. Thomas Parkes (died 1602) and wife Elianor. Square pilasters. This unusual floor level mural shows the effigies carved in relief with an oval inscription which is a mixture of Latin and English.

M410 Bunny, Notts. Sir Richard Parkyn (died 1603) and wife Elizabeth (died 1608) – *see also* wrestler Sir Thomas Parkyn 1741 (M411). A nearby tablet to Humphrey Barley is reputed to be by William Hargrave and carved in alabaster on which the inscription has been lost. This was recorded by Thoroton in the 17th century and can be found in the transactions of the Thoroton Society.

M411 Bunny, Notts. Sir Thomas Parkyn (died 1741). According to Dr Tony Shaw Parkyn designed and (had) built his own memorial. The tomb is most unusual with the standing effigy in a wrestling pose. In the right bay there are figures of Time having felled Parkyn in a wrestling match. It would appear that Parkyn used local sources of alabaster and Ashford marble.

M412 Seckington, Warwick. Robert Burdett (died 1603) and wife Mary. A wall mural with the depicted facing each other over a prayer desk with children. The monument has two bays with a simple pediment and two obelisks. The heraldry and inscription is found below.

M413 Hardwick. Northants. Francis Nicholls (died 1604 but no two sources agree on the date). The monument also records the death of his son Sir Francis Nicholls in 1641.

M414 Bramley, Hants. Reginald Hannington (died 1604).

M415 Hardingstone, Northants. Stephen Harvey (died 1606) auditor of the Duchy of Lancaster and wife Anne (died 1590). Three sons. Alabaster and black marble.

M416 Shenley Church End, Bucks. Thomas Stafford (died 1607). He rests on one elbow with wife and children on tomb chest.

M417 Cumnor, Berks/Oxford. Sir William Sutton (died 1607) and wife.

M418 Boscastle, Cornwall. John Hender (died 1611) and wife Jane. Two small kneeling figures. May have been repaired with limestone.

M419 West Dereham, Norfolk. Robert Dereham (died 1612) and his father Thomas (died 1559). Black inscription panel and columns. It is unusual in that heraldic shields are carved into the border of the inscription. A skull is carved into the bottom scroll.

M420 South Walsham, Norfolk. Sir Wymond Carye (died 1612). Erected by his brother Edward Carye.

M421 Betley, Staffs. Ralph Egerton (died 1610) and wife Frances (died 1595). A wall mural with two kneeling effigies facing each other over a prayer desk. Only one child shown. Partially painted.

M422 Spilsby Lincs. A memorial to Katherine Lady Watson the daughter of Peregrine Bertie (died 1610). He is depicted on the monument (died 1601) with a daughter died in childbirth. Monument dates from 1612. The latter depicted semi-reclining with baby at feet in a crib. *See also* note B76 and L20.

M423 Grendon, Warwick. William Chetwynd (died 1612). Possibly set up in 1676 by Walter Chetwynd.

M424 Youlgreave, Derbys. Roger Rooe (died 1613) of Alport and wife. The wife wears a tall Stuart hat. They face each other over a prayer desk. A row of children are ranged below. Interesting strapwork on the side columns.

M425 Horseheath, Cambs. Sir Giles Alington (died 1613) and Lady Anne. Fig 46 page 73.

M426 Stroud, Gloucs. Thomas Stephens (died 1613). An early tablet mural made by Samuel Baldwin when he was still working in Stroud. This fine monument shows Thomas kneeling in front of a prayer stall.

M427 Shipton under Wychwood, Oxford. Timothy Stamp (died 1614) and wife. They face each other over a prayer desk with four children. She wears a strange tall hat with an orle which may be placed over a mourning hood.

M428 Wells, St Cuthbert, Somerset. Henry Llewellyn (Luellin, died 1614).

M429 Leigh, Worcs. William Coles (died 1615) and wife Mary (Palmer, died 1602). Twelve children.

M430 Keele, Staffs. Thomas Sneyd (died 1615).

M431 Keele, Staffs. Edward Brett (died 1593) and wife Sisley.

M432 Truro Cathedral, Cornwall. John Robarts (died 1615) and wife Philippa (Gavrigan). Moved from old parish church of St Mary. Effigies of a skeleton and a cherub. The depicted effigies lie on their side. Philippa clutches a rose.

M433 London, St Olave. Andrew Bayninge (died 1610). An unusual monument wrapped round a pillar in the church.

M434 London, St Olave. Paul Bayninge (died 1616), brother of M433. A wall mural with four effigies. Strangely, one effigy has her back turned to the deceased.

M435 Caldecote, Warwick. William Purefey (died 1613) and wife Catherine (Wigston, died 1616). Also their son Francis Purefey (died 1613) and his wife Eleanor (Baskerville).

M436 Caldecote, Warwick. George Abbott defender of Caldecote Hall in 1642 who died in 1648. He defended the hall against Prince Rupert with eight men, his mother and handful of maids.

M437 Fawsley, Northants. Richard Knightley (died 1615) and his two wives Mary (Fermor, died 1573) and Elizabeth (Seymour, died 1602). A tall tablet partially painted. Some doubt as to material.

M438 Harefield, Middlesex. Sir Robert Ashby (died 1617). A mural with the knight and his lady facing each other over a prayer stall with the children depicted beneath. The mural is unusual as it has red draped curtains secured to the black columns. The strapwork indicates a Southwark origin. There are similarities to M439. The earlier tomb attributable to William White (Wright) of 1610 (M361) is significantly different in style but still shows London features.

M439 Harefield, Middlesex. Sir Francis Ashby (died 1623) and wife Joan. A mural with the knight and his lady facing each other over a prayer stall with the children depicted beneath. The mural is unusual as it has red draped curtains secured to the black columns. The strapwork indicates a Southwark origin. There are similarities to M438. The earlier tomb attributable to William White (Wright) of 1610 (M361) is significantly different in style but still shows London features.

M440 Harefield, Middlesex. Alice Spencer, Countess of Derby (died 1637) made in her lifetime. Related to the Spensers of Althorpe. The draped curtains found on the other Harefield monuments are repeated here. This monument is attributed to Maximilian Colt who clearly was instructed to repeat the curtain design.

M441 Falmouth, Cornwall. John Killigrew (died 1617). A fragment noted by Pevsner but no further details known.

M442 Beckington, Somerset. Samuel Daniel, poet, died 1619. An unusual tablet with surmounted bust of the poet. It was commissioned by Lady Anne Clifford when she was Countess of Pembroke as recorded in her diaries published in 1992. The date of carving is unknown but is much later than 1619. According to the diary the monument was commissioned in London. Lady Ann commissioned a number of monuments as her diaries confirm.

M443 Appleby, Cumbria. Lady Margaret Clifford (died 1616). Her wish was to be buried in Alnwick but her will granted dispensation and she was buried in Appleby. The tomb shows evidence of being painted. Set up in 1617 and carved by Maximilian Colt in his Farringdon, London workshop. The transport issues from London to Appleby merit speculation. Although the River Eden runs through Appleby it has always been un-navigable therefore the most likely route is by sea to Carlisle and thence by road now the A66. A later tomb to daughter Lady Ann Clifford (died 1676) dated *circa* 1660 and carved in marble also resides in the church. Appleby church has a rather nice font of Frosterley marble.

M444 Westminster Abbey. Sir Richard Pecks all (died 1571) and two wives Alianor (Paulet) and Alianor (Cotgrave). Tomb erected by the latter. The tomb has suffered theft of the shields mainly in 1975 and 1978.

M445 London, Westminster Abbey. Chapel of St Paul. Sir Thomas Bromley (died 1587). He married Elizabeth (Fortescue) who is buried without monument in St Margaret's Westminster. Erected by his son Henry. The small effigies of his daughters have received some damage and had, at one time, plaster heads. Recently a more lasting repair with (Fauld) alabaster has been affected.

M446 Blackburn, Lancs. Judge Walmsley (died 1612) which is believed to be a copy of the tomb of the Duchess of Somerset in Westminster (M122). This may be carved much earlier. A confused report says that tomb vandalised during Civil War, but subsequently repaired.

M447 Wantage, Berks. John Wilson (died 1621) and wife Mary. A nice tablet with broken pediment and volutes, the work of a London workshop.

M448 Great Wilne (Church Wilne), Derbys. Sir John Willoughby (died 1605) and wife Frances (died 1606) but tomb not made until 1622. Tomb commissioned by Henry Willoughby.

M449 Linton, Kent. Sir Anthony Mayne (died 1627) and wives. The seated mourner is reputed to be a gardener.

M450 Linton, Kent. Sir Anthony Mayne (died 1615) and wives.

M451 Smisby, Derbys. Henry Kendall (died 1627) and wife Elizabeth (Armstrong). This has similarities to Gotham (M230) which may indicate a Burton origin.

M452 Ampton, Suffolk. William Whetall (died 1628). A mural with a demi-figure facing forward in an oval frame. The alabaster is pale with possible black veining.

M453 Harlton, Cambs. Sir Henry Fryer (died 1631), wife Mary (died 1613), son Henry and Henry's wife Bridget. The three main effigies are kneeling. Mary is dressed as an Elizabethan whilst Bridget shows Stuart clothes and rests on one elbow. Formerly had railings.

M454 Coxwold, Yorks. Thomas Viscount Fauconberg (died 1631) and wife Barbara (Cholmeley, died 1618). Some writers state 1652 but this conflicts with Nicholas Stone's workbook Plates XXXVIII (c) which states 'Mural monument for Coxwold, 11th Jan 1631, with two kneeling figures facing same way (east). Alabaster and marble. Robert Pooke carved for which he was paid £17. Mr Babbe (*sic*) is reputed to have carved the inscription and set up the monument for which he was paid £7'.

M455 Tixover, Rutland. Roger Dale (died 1623) his wife and two daughters. Finely carver kneeling effigy with ruff under a double arch.

M456 Gilston Herts. Bridget Gore (died 1657) the daughter of Sir John Gore. Although the standing figure is marble the surround has distinct alabaster flavour. This standing shrouded figure is made popular by John Donne's effigy in St Paul's London.

M457 Sutton Coldfield, Warwicks. George Sacheverell (died 1715). An ornate tablet with inscription in Latin.

M458 Gotham, Notts. Tablet to the Bridges family spanning 1710 to 1746 but probably made in the latter year. An Ashford marble inscription plaque with an alabaster surround lightly veined.

M459 Tenterden, Kent. Herbert Whitfield (died 1622) and wife Martha. The church also has an alabaster fragment of the resurrection from a reredos now mounted on the wall. The origin of this is stated to be Leigh Green in the late 19th century but the local historian suggests it may be a panel with an embattled top which indicates a possible York origin.

M460 Sutton on the Hill, Derbys. Judith Sleigh (died 1634). A mural monument with no effigies. In the usual place occupied by a recumbent effigy there is a black coffin. It was erected by her husband Samuel who left a space for his own epitaph which was never filled in. However there are also inscription to Gervase Sleigh and his wife Eliza who died in 1636 during childbirth. There is a number of alabaster slabs referred to but details are thin.

M461 Stoke Newington, London. John Dudley (died 1580) and wife Elizabeth and daughter Elizabeth.

M462 London, Westminster, St Margaret. Marie, Lady Dudley (died 1600) daughter of Lord Howard of Effingham. She first married Edward Sutton, Lord Dudley and then Richard Mompesson who erected the monument. He is shown kneeling. The tomb has been linked to the Founder's Tomb in Charter House Chapel.

M463 London, Westminster. A tablet to Robert Bingham (died 1599). Located in the south choir the Abbey Monument Archive describes the alabaster as 'black' without any explanation as to its origin which may well be Derbyshire Ashford marble.

M464 London, Westminster. A mural to Henry Carey, Lord Hunsdon (died 1596). Located in the chapel of St John the Baptist, the Abbey Monument Archive describes the tomb as the tallest in the abbey at 36ft. The monument was erected by his widow. He was the son of Mary Boleyn. There are others buried in vault beneath.

M465 London, Westminster. A tablet to Christopher Chapman chorister (died 1681) and his daughter Elizabeth (died 1680). Located in the cloisters.

M466 London, Westminster. A tablet with a demi-figure depicting the Rev William Conway (died 1876).

M467 London, Westminster. A tablet with bust depicting Michael Drayton (died 1631). Poet's corner.

M468 London, Westminster. A tablet to explorer Sir John Franklyn (died *circa* 1847). Franklyn died with his crew searching for the North-West Passage. The bust is white marble within an alabaster niche.

M469 London, Westminster. A tablet to Peter Heylyn (died 1662). The inscription in Latin was written by Dean John Earle.

M470 London, Westminster. A tablet to hymn writer Henry Francis Lyte (died in Nice). He wrote Abide with me.

M471 London, Westminster. A tablet to explorer Sir Leobold McClintock (died 1907). The tablet is close to that of Franklyn (M468) for whom he was commissioned to search for. He was the one who found the men where they had perished. The alabaster has the brown streaks of that extracted from the Kingston mine although a link between the Lichfield workshop that made it and the Nottinghamshire beds has not yet been established.

M472 London, Westminster. A tablet to historian Sir William Sanderson (died 1676). There is bust on top. The monument also to his wife Bridget (died 1682) which may indicate the date of carving.

M473 London, Westminster. James Hill (nee Stoteville) – died 1631. She kneels on a cushion with the effigy of a skeleton in a winding sheet behind.

M474 Hampton Gay, Oxford. Ann & Vincent Barry (*circa* 1665). A wall mural believed to be moved from an older church. Hampton Gay is an abandoned village and only the church remains. The mural shows the man and lady facing each other over a prayer stall with a smaller effigy to Lady Catherine Fenner to left and behind the lady. Alabaster effigies and black marble columns.

M475 Hornchurch, Essex. Francis Rame (died 1617) and wife Helen (died 1613).

M476 Brereton, Cheshire. A tall tablet to the Brereton family (installed 1618) when family remains were transferred from Astbury.

M477 Margam Abbey, Glamorgan. Sir Rawley Bussey (died 1623).

M478 West Hallam, Derbys. John Powtrell (died 1624).

M479 West Hallam, Derbys. Robert Powtrell (died 1662).

M480 Wingham, Kent. Charles Tripp (died 1624).

M481 Hanbury, Staffs. Sir Charles Egerton (died 1624). Sir Charles leans on one elbow cradling a great helm in his left arm and holding a shield with his right.

M482 Ingatestone, Essex. Erected by 2nd Lord Petre for his father John Petre (died 1613) and wife Mary (Waldegrave). The tall monument has two kneeing mourners.

M483 Ingatestone, Essex. Captain John Troughton (died 1621). He is believed to be a privateer.

M484 Ingatestone, Essex. Robert Petre (died 1593). He was the younger brother of William Petre.

M485 Canterbury, Kent. Orlando Gibbons (died 1625). He was an organist who came to Canterbury for the marriage of Henrietta Maria to Charles I but died of smallpox.

M486 Canterbury, Kent. Sir James Hales (died 1589) and wife Alice (Kempe, died 1592). Also Cheney Hales, their son. The monument was erected by Alice's second husband and may date from 1592. There are images of ships and of figures two of which appear to be placing a man in the sea probably associated with the role of constable of the Cinque Ports.

M487 Hornchurch, Essex. Humfrey Pye (died 1625) and wife. Humfrey was letter writer to King James.

M488 Bletchingley, Surrey. Nathaniel Harris (died 1625) in black marble with alabaster surround.

M489 Eastwell with Boughton Aluph, Kent, now in the V&A as A.185–1969. Frances Lady Finch (died 1627).

M490 Cockayne Hatley, Beds. Sir Patrick Hume (died 1627).

M491 Canterbury, Kent. Thomas Thornhurst (died 1627).

M492 Paston. Norfolk. Dame Katherine Paston (died 1628). Katherine rests on her right elbow. The carvings of the dress are superb. The effigy may well be marble but the rest is Fauld alabaster. A discussion of the inscription can be found in 'CMS Journal' Vol XXX 2015 page 140.

M493 Paston, Norfolk. Edmund Paston (died 1632). A large monument containing an urn.

M494 Checkendon, Oxford. Richard Braybrooke (died 1629) and wife. The depicted kneel at a prayer stall. Small effigies of children (one damaged).

M495 Bristol, Somerset. Sir Charles Vaughan (died 1630).

M496 Bowdon, Cheshire. William Brereton (died 1630) and wife Jane. Seven children.

M497 Chigwell, Essex. Thomas Coleshill (died 1595) and wife Mary (Crayford, died 1599). The monument put up by daughter Susannah Stanhope. The two deceased face each other over a prayer stall. He was inspector of customs to James I.

M498 Newcastle on Tyne, Northumberland. William Hall (died 1631) and Jane (died 1613) erected by only son Alexander.

M499 Newcastle on Tyne, Northumberland. Henry Maddison (died 1634) and Elizabeth (died 1653) and their parents.

M500 Hinxhill, Kent. Robert Edolphe (died 1632) and wife Cecily. Monument covered in plaster during Civil War and not found until 19th century.

M501 Canterbury, Kent. William Pride (died 1632) but nothing much known.

M502 Great Warley, Essex. Gyles Fleming (1623) and his son also Gyles Fleming (1633). Also to the latter's wife Susanna. A demi-effigy in frame.

M503 Kinnersley, Hereford. Francis Smalman (died 1633). *See* Broome item 41 and *British History Online* for description. The Baldwin memorial is mounted on the wall and has the depicted kneeling in front of a prayer stall. There is a semi-circular canopy with curtains. The children are shown in relief at the bottom.

M504 Hambleden, Bucks. Sir Cope d'Oyley (died 1633), his wife Martha (died 1618 in childbirth) and 10 children. Those who died before their father carry sculls. The dress of the children shows both Royalist and Puritan attire revealing differences in loyalty and may well indicate a much later date for the carving. Esdaile suggests John Hargrave is the carver but Geoffrey Fisher suggests William Wright. Hargrave was at the time attached to the Nicholas Stone workshop in Long Acre.

M505 Ludlow, Shrops. Edward Waites (died 1635) and wife Martha (died 1629).

M506 Horndon on the Hill, Essex. Daniel Caldwell (died 1634) and wife Alice (Mayn).

M507 Hitcham, Suffolk. Sir George Waldegrave (died 1636).

M508 Lugwardine, Hereford. John Best (died 1637) alabaster and slate.

M509 Newton St Cyr, Devon. Sir John Northcote (died 1637). A mural with a standing effigy and two more kneeling below at a prayer stall. There are two ovals with busts of ladies in relief.

M510 Hornchurch, Essex. Richard Blakstone or Blaston (died 1638).

M511 Ampton, Suffolk. A member of the Calthorpe family believed to evoke an emotional response. May be Sir Henry Calthorpe. Demi-figures holding hands.

M512 Uxbridge, Middlesex. Dame Leonora Bennett (died 1638). Reclining on one elbow and with a charnel house in tomb chest. Credited to the Christmas workshop it displays classic strapwork.

M513 Tilton on the Hill, Leics. Depicting Nichols family.

M514 Ledbury, Hereford. Dr John Hoskyns rector (died 1638) and wife Frances. A demi-figure facing forward with ruff and canopy over. Charles Hoskyns bequeathed 30s for repair in 1671. This is 49 in Broome list.

M515 Weddington, Warwicks. Humphrey Adderley (died 1598) and his son Humphrey (died 1637) erected by the latter's wife Jane and his son Humphrey in 1639.

M516 London, Westminster. Lady Jane Crewe (died 1639). The tablet is in relief showing Jane lying on her deathbed with her husband and children around a sarcophagus on which lies a child.

M517 Gilston, Herts. Sir John Gore (1659) or Bridget Gore (1657) needs sorting with M456.

M518 Sheepstor, Devon. Elizabeth Elford (died 1641). The tablet has a clear likeness to M516 which suggests Epiphanius Evesham as the carver.

M519 Leigh, Essex. Robert Salmon (died 1641). Salmon was master of Trinity House. Catalogued as M2946 in the Database of Maritime Memorials. A demi-figure in a circular frame with the depicted holding a globe.

M520 Tatenhill, Staffs. Margaret the wife of Henry Griffiths and his two daughters. She died in 1641. The church is under threat of redundancy.

M521 Burbage, Leics. Anthony Grey, 9th Earl of Kent (died 1643) and his wife Magdalena.

M522 Brereton, Cheshire. William Smethwick (died 1643) and wife Frances (died 1632).

M523 London, Bishopsgate. Martin Bond (died 1643). An interesting tablet with the deceased sitting and two sentries standing guard one with a horse.

M524 Weekley, Northants. Sir Edward Montague (died 1644).

M525 Oxford. William Brouncker (died 1645) and wife Winifred.

M526 Gloucester, St Nicholas. Samuel Baldwin (died 1645) but material uncertain. This modest memorial was carved by his son.

M527 Rothley, Leics. Anne Babington (died 1648).

M528 Llandegai, Wales. John Williams, Archbishop of York (died 1650).

M529 North Witham, Lincs. Elizabeth Sherard daughter of Brownlow of Belton (died 1658).

M530 Wistow, Leics. Sir Richard Halford (died 1658) with wooden rails from 1863. The deceased lies on his right side. The entablature is in black marble with alabaster columns and figures.

M531 Kirkleatham, Yorks. John Turner (died 1660) and wife Elizabeth.

M532 Chalfont St Giles, Bucks. Sir Thomas Tyrril (died 1671)

M533 Checkendon, Oxford. Henry Knappe (died 1673).

M534 Teversal, Notts. Sir Francis Molyneux (died 1674) and his wife.

M535 Curry Mallet, Somerset. John Pyme (died 1609) and wife Juliana (Towse, died 1628) erected in 1642 by their son.

M536 Curry Mallet, Somerset. A mural to an un-named lady with two reclining females.

M537 Tunstall, Kent. Edward Mores rector (died 1740). A tablet which is made from uncertain material.

M538 Bradford, Yorks. Hannah Gilpin Sharp (died 1767). The Moore Archive states the person depicted is Faith Sawrey but this has not been resolved.

M539 Christchurch, Hants. John Richman (died 1784). Black with alabaster frame.

M540 Ashbourne, Derbys. Maria Elizabeth Boothby (died 1805). A nice tablet with spiral columns.

M541 Gaddesby, Leics. Colonel Edward Hawkins Cheney (died 1848) and who fought at Waterloo in 1815. He is depicted astride a horse which has been injured. At Waterloo he had no less than four horses shot from under him. The statue is probably marble but the base and relief are in alabaster. The statue was formerly in Gaddesby Hall but moved in 1917 on log rollers to the church when the hall was sold. *The Melton Times* (4th June 2015) states that the statue was carved in Rome and dragged from the station to the hall by 15 horses but this may be speculation.

M542 Dale Abbey, Derbys. Philip Henry, 4th Earl Stanhope (died 1855).

M543 Chipping Sodbury, Gloucs. Rev Edward Walker (died 1872).

M544 Edinburgh, St Giles. Rev Robert Nisbet (died 1874).

M545 Middle Claydon, Bucks. Emily Fremantle (died 1877). An alabaster frame within which is a bust of the deceased.

M546 Wednesbury, Staffs. Tablets to Mary Ann Richards (died 1885), a marble tablet with a border of alabaster. Thomas Pritchard (died 1910) and Ellen Jones (died 1903).

M547 Louth, Lincs. James Fowler MP (died 1891). A bust in relief with a Fauld alabaster surround.

M548 Haugh, Lincs. Sir John Bolle (died 1606). A mural monument with lightly veined alabaster.

M549 Norwich Norfolk. Bishop Pelham (died 1896). Alabaster with marble effigy.

M550 Bradford, Yorks. Hannah Lambert (died 1911).

M551 Brocklesby, Lincs. Lord Worsley (died 1914). An interesting 17th century style mural.

M552 Lanhydrock, Cornwall. Thomas Agar-Robartes (died 1915).

M553 Stowting, Kent. Conrad Jenkins who died at Scapa Flow in Dec 1916.

M554 Nuthall, Notts. War memorial in alabaster and grey slate.

M555 Eydon, Northants. War memorial in alabaster frame and grey slate.

M556 Bradford, Yorks. War memorial in alabaster. Small statue of knight.

M557 Welwyn, Herts. A tablet to the Boothby family. Hugo Boothby died at sea 1881 on HMS *Wild Swan* which is shown on tablet.

M558 Brightling, Sussex. Thomas Percy Tew (died 1954) and wife Constance Mabel.

M559 Stratton Strawless, Norfolk. Thomas Marsham (died 1638). Thomas had separated from his wife at the time of his death so is depicted alone. He is shown in a shroud which he is throwing off as he pushes up on one elbow. A charnel house is shown below. These shrouded monuments were made popular following the style of Dr Donne's effigy made by Nicholas Stone *circa* 1631. Another shrouded monument is that to the Pecks in Spixworth dating from 1635 (M210). The tomb was renovated in 2005.

M560 Stratton Strawless, Norfolk. Henry Marsham (died 1678) and wife Anne. Henry is shown kneeling facing forward in restoration dress with his wife and son Henry kneeling between. A chrisom is to be seen on the right.

M561 Tewkesbury, Gloucs. Thomas Collins, a builder who died in 1900. A portrait in low relief.

M562 Chichester, Sussex. Charles Lennox (died 1903), a marble tablet in an alabaster frame.

M563 Chichester, Sussex. Gordon Lennox (died 1928), a marble tablet in an alabaster frame.

M564 Chichester, Sussex. Bishop Thomas Bickley (died 1596). A mural showing the bishop kneeling at a prayer stall.

M565 Lee, London. Bryan Annesley (died 1604) and wife Audrey (Tirrell, died 1591). Tomb erected by daughter Cirdelia Annesley.

M566 Cranham, Gloucs, Prinknash Abbey. Baroque style to John Rees (died 1913).

M567 Cowbridge, Wales. William Carne (died 1616). Rare for this part of Wales. Kneelers and prayer desk.

M568 Truro, Cornwall. Captain Thomas Agar-Robarts (died 1915) – *see also* Lanhydrock.

M569 Kendal, Cumbria. The Danvers family.

M570 Kendal, Cumbria. Clara Burra.

M571 Hawstead, Suffolk. Elizabeth Drury (died 1610, aged 14).

M572 Crouch Hill, London. Frederick George White (died 1933). A novel alabaster tablet. The church is under threat of redundancy.

M573 Chelsea, Middlesex. Robert Hungerford (died 1581) and wife Ursula (Sandes). A mural in alabaster and marble.

M574 Beddington, Surrey. Rector Alexander Henry Bridges (died 1891). The frame has quatrefoils in the corners containing symbols of the four evangelists.

M575 Wentworth, Yorks. Sir William Wentworth (died 1614) and wife Anna (died 1611). There is third effigy of Sir Thomas Wentworth, Earl of Strafford who was executed in 1641.

M576 Tichborne, Hants. Sir Benjamin Tichborne (died 1621) and wife.

M577 Fulham, Middlesex. Lady Margaret Legh (died 1603). A seated effigy facing forward holding a baby in her arms with a chrisom on her left. Her raised foot once rested on a skull.

M578 Fulham, Middlesex. Jane Payne (died 1610) and husband William. A mural seated effigy facing forward holding a baby in her arms with a chrisom on her left. Her raised foot once rested on a skull.

M579 Holcombe Regis, Devon. Richard Bluett (died 1634) and wife Elizabeth (Portman, died 1636). Squirrel crest.

M580 Shinfield, Berks. Henry Beke (died 1627). A truly magnificent mural with his two wives.

M581 Stratfield Saye, Hants. William Pitt (died 1636) and wife Edith (died 1633) but tomb not made until 1640. The effigies are in marble but the mural is in Fauld alabaster. The effigies lie on one elbow and the lady looks most uncomfortable.

M582 Hungerford, Berks. Captain Edward Dugdale D'Oyley Astley (died 1918).

M583 Albury, Herts. Thomas Hyde (died 1570) and son (died 1580). Three Corinthian columns with strapwork and skulls.

M584 Little Gaddesden, Herts. Elizabeth Dutton (died 1611), known as the Red Lady. Reported to be moved from St Martin in the Field, London in 1730.

M585 Fulmer, Bucks. Sir Marmaduke Darrell (died 1631) and Anne Lennard and daughter Mary. Kneeling children repainted.

M586 Oxnead, Norfolk. Katherine, Lady Paston (Bertie, died 1636). A monument in touch with a bust of the lady but with an alabaster pediment. By Nicholas Stone. There is a discussion on the inscription in 'CMS Journal' Vol XXX 2015 page 142.

M587 Sutton at Hone, Kent. Sir Thomas Smith (or Smythe, died 1625). A fine well carved monument with nice features such as the sleeves and costume. A discussion on the inscription can be found in 'CMS Journal' Vol XXX 2015 page 146. The monument was restored *circa* 2014 as a thanksgiving service was held on the 30th November 2014 for this work paid for by donations by the Worshipful Company of Skinners on behalf of Tonbridge School and the Japan 400 project. An ambassador to Russia he was well regarded.

M588 Leicester Cathedral. James Andrewe (died 1638). Now in St Dunstan's Chapel. There is brief observation on the inscription in 'CMS Journal' Vol XXX 2015 page 155. The article suggests that anagrams on monuments were commonplace but this is the only one which I have seen on an alabaster tomb. The mural shows Andrewe as a cameo reading in his study with the anagram of his name beneath stating *Reede I was man*.

M589 Upton Hellions, Devon. Richard Reynell (died 1631) and wife.

M590 Stratford on Avon, Warwicks. Judith Combe (died 1649) and husband Richard. The stone used for the monument is unclear but the history of the church states that the demi bust of Judith (and possibly Richard) is made from alabaster and carved by Thomas Stanton. Dugdale attributes the monument to Gerard Johnson but current observers suggest this is not to be trusted. Conserved in 2013 when layers of paint and grime and old wax were removed.

M591 Stratford on Avon, Warwicks. John Lacy (died 1732) and wife Hannah.

M592 War memorial to Lieutenant-Colonel Percy Archer-Clive died 8th April 1918. A Fauld alabaster frame with touch columns and marble panel.

M593 Quorndon, Leics. A wall mural now believed to be to John Farnham but the date is uncertain. Attribution to Robert de Farnham or to Thomas Farnham has been challenged.

M594 Bakewell, Derbys. Sir John Manners (died 1611) and wife, Dorothy (died 1584). The Manners are connected to both Haddon Hall and Belvoir Castle.

M595 Averham, Notts. Sir William Sutton (died 1611) and wife Susanna. An ornate mural tomb with two recumbent figures. A pair of ionic columns with a cornice which contains a frieze which has been identified with William Hargrave of Bilborough.

M596 East Donyland, Essex. Elizabeth Marshall (died 1613). A seated monument. East Donyland church was built in 1838 and the old church demolished. This monument was transferred from this. In some quarters the name is given as Mary Gray and the date 1627.

M597 Rolleston on Dove, Staffs. Oswald Moseley, 5th Baronet (died 1928). A tablet in Fauld alabaster.

M598 East Sutton, Kent. Robert Filmer (died 1585). A nice tablet clearly of London manufacture, with a skull in bottom left hand corner, columns and obelisks.

M599 East Sutton, Kent. Margaret Randolph (died 1609) commissioned by Edmund Randolph who also appears on the monument. A nice tablet clearly of London manufacture, with a skull in bottom left hand corner, columns and obelisks.

M600 Nottingham, St Peter. Two wall tablets with similar frames. One tablet is to Margaret Saunders (died 1633) and Jane Ellis (died 1637) both wives of John Locke of Hertfordshire.

M601 Holme next the Sea, Norfolk. Richard Stone (died 1607). Fourteen kneeling figures.

M602 Crayford, Kent. William Draper (died 1650) and Mary Draper (died 1652). Mural with effigies by Thomas Stanton.

M603 Eastling, Kent. Martin and Thomasyne James (died 1592), mural with kneeling figures – two sons and daughters. Mottled alabaster.

M604 Faversham, Kent. Edward Fagg (died 1618) and wife Anne Theobald. Mural with effigy. Daughters Marie and Anne. Painted. Ladies appear as half effigies. Unusual.

M605 Faversham, Kent. Thomas Stouthouse (died 1651) but monument may date from 1653. Painted.

M606 Hougham, Kent. Mural to William Hannington and family dated 1607.

M607 Ightham, Kent. Mural with reclining figures on one elbow. Sir William Selby (died 1611) and nephew also by same name (died 1638). Clearly Fauld alabaster.

M608 Ightham, Kent. Mural with demi-figure. Dorothy Selby (died 1641) by Edward Marshall. Alabaster surround. Clearly Fauld alabaster.

M609 Knowlton, Kent. Lady Elizabeth D'Aeth (died 1721) in childbirth. This looks like alabaster but needs investigation.

M610 London, St Andrew's Undershaft. Fauld tablet to William Frazer Nash (died 1903), curate and presenter of the church.

M611 Abbess Roding Essex. Sir Gamiel Capell (died 1613) and his wife kneeling at a prayer stall. Six sons and three daughters. Formerly in the chancel.

M612 Abbess Roding Essex. Mildred Capell (died 1633) wife of Sir William Lucklyn. A demi-figure resting on one elbow looking out of a curtained recess. The curtains are held back by cherubs and behind angels descend to place a crown on her head. Partially painted.

M613 Little Waltham, Essex. John Aleyne (died 1663) of Grays Inn and to his parents Giles and Elizabeth Aleyne. Alabaster and black marble with broken pediment. Mural.

M614 Little Baddow Essex. Henry Mildmay (died 1639) attributed to John and Mathias Christmas. Recumbent effigy with wives kneeling below. Entablature with broken pediment. Spiked railing which may be contemporary.

M615 Great Parndon, Essex. Mary Sparkes (nee Turner, died 1661) widow of Thomas. Tablet in an alabaster frame.

M616 Theydon Mount, Essex. Sir William (died 1631) and wives Helegenwagh (who carrys a skull) and Anne (Croft). A small effigy of his son was stolen along with a salamander but has since been recovered.

M617 Fryerning, Essex. John Lord Petre of Writtle (died 1613) and wife Mary (Waldegrave).

M618 Willingale Doe, Essex. Robert Wiseman (died 1641) and Richard Wiseman (died 1618) and his wife Mary (died 1635). William Wright.

M619 Margaretting, Essex. John Tanfield (died 1625). Part painted. Mural. A very well executed monument.

M620 Woodford, Essex. Rowland Elrington (died 1595). He was a haberdasher and merchant venture from London.

M621 Wanstead, Essex (Christchurch). Josiah Childs (died 1699). A large mural with standing statue.

M622 Wanstead, Essex (St Mary). Captain John Morice (died 1638).

M623 Walthamstow, Essex. William Conyers (died 1659). Tablet. Black marble with alabaster architrave.

M624 Barking, Essex. Elizabeth Hobart (died 1590). Tablet.

M625 Dagenham, Essex. Tablet. James Harvy (died 1627).

M626 Dagenham, Essex. Tablet. Jonathon Lloyd (died 1652).

M627 Cambridge, Great St Mary Chapel. William Butler (died 1617).

M628 Wiggenhall, Norfolk. Sir Henry Kerville (died 1624) and wife Mary. The church is now redundant. Sir Henry was the last of his line as he died without issue. He was also accused of being a papist.

M629 Radwell, Herts. Ann Plomer (died 1625). A tablet with curious figures on the top.

M630 Wheathampstead, Herts. Sir John Garrard (died 1637) and wife Elizabeth (Barkham). Also to Isabella Garrard (died 1677). In an unusual pose Elizabeth has her head turned to gaze at her husband.

M631 Heanor, Derbys. Samuel Watson (died 1715). A tablet made by his grandson White Watson in 1820.

M632 Stutton, Suffolk. John Jermy (died 1662) and wife Mary (Rowe, died 1664).

M633 Theydon Mount, Essex. Sir William Smyth (died 1626) and wife Bridget.

M634 Wolststanton, Staffs. William Younge (died 1587) and wife Susanna (Corbett). Alabaster and brass. No effigies.

M635 Cambridge, Gonville and Caius College. Dr John Caius founder of the college (died 1573).

M636 South Ockendon. Sir Richard Saltonstall (died 1601) and wife Susannah (Poyntz). Twelve children.

M637 Ruislip, Middlesex. Raphe Hawtrey (died 1638) and wife Mary (died 1647).

M638 North Okendon, Essex. Catherine Poyntz (died *circa* 1606) wife of John Maurice Poyntz.

M639 North Okendon, Essex. Sir James Poyntz (died *circa* 1623) and son Richard (died 1643). Kneeling fihures. It is believed the monument dates from 1643.

M640 Finchingfield, Essex. Rev Matthew Vaughan (died 1889). Erected by widow.

M641 Altrincham, Cheshire. Reverend Napier Malcolm (died 1921).

Q1 Montréal, Yonne, France. The centre panel represents the mass of St Gregory which has a distinct Nottingham flavour having a similar panel in the wall of St Mary's Nottingham (*See* paper by William Stevenson Transactions Vol XI 1907). The panels have also been likened to panels in Preston church, Holderness, East Yorkshire (A144).

Q2 The chapel at St Bartholomew Quorn belongs to the Farnham Trust and access is by permission. An assessment of all the monuments can be found on the CMS website as 'Monument of the Month' June 2015 and July 2015 by Moira Ackers and www.Quornmuseum.com/artifacts/pdf/1898.pdf. The name Quorndon has its roots in the Dark Ages and the point at which the modern accepted name, Quorn, came into use is uncertain. Nichols *The History and Antiquities of the County of Leicestershire* Vol III part 1 (1800) describes the monuments as they existed at the dawn of the 19th century. Significant reordering of the chapel has taken place since. Moira Ackers suggests that all the slabs now placed upright along the wall, were once tabletop tombs.

Q3 Boston, Massachusetts. An image of the Trinity dating from 1420 to 1450. English and probably exported to Spain and possibly from Jac Cathedral. Purchased in 1919 from an auction in Madrid and acquired by the museum in 1927. The museum also has a kneeling knight in alabaster which is Spanish. The knight is believed to be Dom Monzo Averesque. The alabaster seems to be black veined and probably Castilian. There are also Italian examples including a nice montage comprising carved alabaster and painted with oils. The scene is Joseph explaining his dream to his brothers and was painted by Antonio Tempesta. The alabaster is probably Tuscan. The museum at Boston has a fine website which shows details of all the items mentioned above.

R1 Berkeley, Gloucs. Knight and lady. Henry, 17th Lord Berkeley (died 1613) and Katherine (Howard). Constructed 1615 with canopy. Berkeley Castle has the bill of sale for this dated 5th July 1615 exists and states that Baldwin had to be responsible for repairs – *see From Gate to Gate* the in-house magazine for Berkeley Castle. This is the only surviving document for this workshop. For details *see*: www.stmarys-berkeley.co.uk/monuments. There may have had mural addition containing kneeling figures of sons and daughters (one small figure remains on a window sill). The tomb chest is stone but the canopy is alabaster. Believed to be a portrait of Henry. In light of the closeness of the Baldwin workshop to Berkeley this is a distinct possibility.

R2 London, Great St Helen with St Andrew Undershaft with St Martin Outwich, St Mary Axe and St Ethelburga, Bishopsgate. John Spencer (died 1609) and wife Alice Bromfield (died 1610) with effigy of daughter. Although John died in 1609 the tomb may be later. The ladies shown fine drum farthingales. (Access to St Andrew Undershaft is made by ringing 0207 2832231.)

R3 Holme Pierrepont, Notts. Sir Henry Pierrepont. Seven small figures holding shields. An extract from the Holme

Pierrepont Trail reads ‘A knight on Tudor armour depicting Sir Henry Pierrepont died 1615. He was the husband of Frances Cavendish the daughter of Bess of Hardwick. These are reputed to be from the Nottingham school of Kervers’. *See* Index of Kervers for John Smythson

R4 Ratcliffe on Soar, Notts. Knight and lady. The tomb of Henry Sacheverell (son of T9) died 1585 and his wife Jane Ireton. The gauntlets are at his feet and Jane’s effigy shows lace at the top of the gown. This tomb shows distinct similarities with that of his son (R5). The style and format is Class VIII and therefore much later than 1585. This is confirmed by the details of the will of Henry III (R5) who made provision for a tomb of his father. *See also* Coleshill (R136). The status of Jane is currently unclear being either the daughter or widow of Gervase Ireton of Attenborough. In addition the date of death of Henry II is not entered as no-one was alive at its creation who could remember him.

R5 Ratcliffe on Soar, Notts. Knight and Ladies. The chest tomb of Henry Sacheverell (son of R4), died 1625 and the wall plaque of his three wives Mary Gittings died 1600, Elizabeth Copley died 1616 and Lucy Boughton died 1667. The three wives show the dress of the period. There is some doubt as to whether the wall plaque is contemporary with the tomb as it covers the centre window of the chancel centred on the chest tomb. There is no reason why the chest tomb and plaque could not have been placed on a blank wall unless the plaque was an afterthought. However, the tomb is of the same style and therefore date as R4 and if it is believed that both this and R4 were assembled at the same time then the positioning of R5 is to keep the two tombs in line. In this case the mural had to be centred on the tomb and therefore over the window. The ladies show bum-rolls and Lucy has an open ruff like M138.

R6 Bottesford, Leics. Knight and lady. Henry Manners, 2nd Earl of Rutland and wife Margaret (1563). The tomb of the 2nd earl dating from 1563 is located under an Elizabethan ‘table’ of immense size. The carver of this is as yet un-identified. There is a legend that Earl Manners lent his table to be copied. It is also stated that design is similar to Braybrooke, Northants.

R7 Bottesford, Leics. John Manners 4th Earl of Rutland. The tomb of the 4th earl was created by Gerard Johanssen (Johnson) a London based Flemish sculptor. It is recorded that both tombs were carved in the same year 1591 (or 1594) and that Johansson spent time in Bottesford erecting the monument for which he was paid £100. It is likely the carving was done in London. This could still mean that Nottingham alabaster was used.[3] John Matthews of Nottingham was paid £20 in 1592 for staining both the 3rd and 4th Earl’s tombs. Henry Kinder, a Newark man, was paid 3s for giving advice. Llewellyn quoting a Rutland manuscript, states that in May 1590 a expert assessor earned 10s for travelling from Burton '… and back again to give his advice was for the placing of the tombs of the 3rd and 4th Earl'.

R8 Bottesford, Leics. Knight. Roger Manners, 5th Earl of Rutland (died 1612) and his wife Elizabeth. The tomb of the 5th earl was created by Nicholas Johnson the son of Gerard for £150 in 1612 which included the cost of transport from Boston.It would have come by coastal ship and then by cart taking the efforts of 17 men. It is reported that the Bottesford tombs were moved from Croxton Abbey and Belvoir Priory to Bottesford. *See also* Stone connection for Johnson. Roger Manners' wife, Elizabeth, was buried in St Paul's, London where the tomb there was destroyed in the Fire of London in 1666. The inscription makes reference to the death of his two sons by sorcery for which local women were blamed and which led to the Witches of Belvoir trials.

R9 Wysall, Notts. Formerly Thorpe in the Glebe. The tomb is that of Hugh Armstrong (died 22nd December 1572) and his wife. The wife is Mary Sacheverell the daughter of Henry Sacheverell II of Ratcliffe on Soar (*see* T9 below) who died 20th March (year damaged but is now known to be 1562). The Armstrong family lived at Thorpe in the Glebe now a lost village and only a few stones remain of the church there. However, it is uncertain when the village was depopulated the popular estimate being at the Black Death around 1349. Certainly the Valor Ecclesiasticus of 1535 stated the village as being deserted. The church may well have remained and it is possible that Hugh was buried there and the tomb placed in the church in 1572. Subsequently it fell into ruin but may still have been roofed in the 17th century. Throsby's drawing of 1790 shows only standing structure was the tower. So it is possible that the tomb was moved to Wysall but this had to be some time in the 17th century. The tomb table is particularly well done. Hugh has his feet on a lion and Mary her feet on a dog. He has a chain collar and head on a great helm. The children all hold shields except one who is believed to have remained unmarried and therefore having no coat of arms.

R10 Emneth, Norfolk. Sir Thomas Hewar and wife. A canopied alabaster monument which had railings and was carved in 1617. This was recorded in folio 5 of the Stone notebook and cost £95.

R11 Framlingham, Suffolk. Limestone. Elizabeth, daughter of the 4th Duke of Norfolk (died 1565). Small tomb with shields but no effigy.

R12 Wolstanton, Staffs. Sir William Sneyd (died 1571) and wife Anne (Barrow). Eleven children.

R13 Charwelton, Northants. Sir Thomas Andrews (or Andrewes died 1564) and two wives, Katherine Cave (1555) and

Mary Heneage. The tomb is attributed to Richard Parker and local history sources claim that the tomb was built on the death of Katherine in 1555. The effigy is reputed to show an SS collar with a Tudor rose pendant which is odd for a date post-1547, but may well be a trailing application. This requires further investigation.

R14 Great Brington, Northants. Sir John Spencer (died 1522). Possibly a Richard Parker.

R15 Yarnton, Oxford. Sir William Spencer (died 1609) and his wife. Attributed to Jasper Hollemans but erected post-1609. The tomb has an iron railing and a large heraldic device on the top.

R16 Ashley, Staffs. Sir Gilbert Gerard (judge) who died 4th Feb 1593 and his wife Lady Ann Ratcliffe. John Betjeman claimed the work was by Jasper Hollemans but not completed until 1612. Two adult children kneel at the head and two children in front of the tomb chest. Four women are shown in relief on the back panel.

R17 Easton Neston, Northants. Sir George Fermor (died 1612) and wife Mary (Curzon, died 1628). Attributable to Jasper Hollemans. Two recumbent effigies with a number of children shown on the tomb chest. The arch is supported by two Corinthian columns with obelisks. Fan decoration behind tomb.

R18 Sheffield, Yorks. George Talbot, 6th Earl of Shrewsbury (died 1590) husband of Bess of Hardwick.

R19 Barton in Fabis, Notts. William Sacheverell (died 8th March 1616) and Tabitha Spenser daughter of James Spenser. The lady has a Mary, Queen of Scots headdress and a late Tudor dress with a soft ruff. The man is dressed in dated Tudor armour and soft ruff. Neither effigy is carved in the round. The tomb chest depicts inscribed figures of two sons a daughter and a chrisom with the scribed marks filled with pitch. There is a black limestone inscription panel. The Sacheverells were related to those at Morley, Derbys and Ratcliffe on Soar.

R20 Bath, Abbey church, Somerset. Bishop James Montagu (died 1618). Effigy on raised table with freestanding columns at each corner surmounted by an armorial device. James Montagu was responsible for the rebuilding if the abbey from 1608.

R21 Lincoln, St Mary le Wigford. Sir Thomas Grantham (died 1630) and his wife Frances Puckenus (died 1618) was illustrated in Earl Marshall's *The Book of Monuments* MS1 (i) page 13, 'College of Arms', London and must have been sketched shortly after its construction. The sketch shows a mural monument with two effigies with black columns and a decorated frieze surmounted by armorial devices and figures. This monument formerly in St Martin's was damaged in 1644 during the siege of the city. The tomb had been moved to the basement, but was damaged by the collapse of the canopy. It remained in the ruins of the church until the 19th century when it was included in the rebuilt St Martin's. It was later removed to St Benedict Church where it was recovered by the family who firstly offered to the cathedral before being moved it to its current location. Sir Thomas Grantham's second wife Lucy is depicted on M2.

R22 Titchfield, Hants. Sir Thomas Wriothesley, 1st Earl of Southampton (died 1551), his wife Jane Cheyne (died 1574) and Henry Wriothesley, 2nd Earl (died 1581) but tomb may not have been constructed until 1592 or 1594. The tomb was constructed for £1000 left in the will of the 2nd Earl and the contract for this survives. The contract was for two monuments but only one was made or survives. Alabaster and marble. Long obelisks with corner peninsulas possible copied by Baldwin for Spetchley (R53). The vault beneath also holds the 3rd Earl and his son James (1624) and the 4th Earl Thomas (1667). The tomb is different in that it is on two tiers. The CMS County Guide has some excellent pictures.

R23 Thame, Oxford. Lord Williams and his wife *circa* 1559. A fine Renaissance tomb with visages which may well represent a likeness. The man is in armour with covering cloak. Their feet rest on a dog and a horse. The tomb chest was damaged during the Civil War and was repaired in the 19th century.

R24 Wing, Bucks. Sir Robert Dormer (died 1552) and wife Elizabeth. Tomb made by grandson *circa* 1567. Robert Dormer, 1st Baronet built this tomb and one to his father who died *circa* 1575. The latter tomb has true 'stone' figures. Margaret Whinney is of the opinion that this shows French features close to those attributed to Nicholas da Modena for the failed Henry VII tomb and to features at Fontainebleau as well as those believed to have been seen on the Palace of Nonesuch.

R25 Gloucester. Bishop Goldsborough (died 1604).

R26 Gloucester Cathedral. Alderman Abraham Blackleech (died 1639) and wife Gertrude. Black marble chest with possibly Ledsham alabaster effigies. British Library attributes this to the Baldwin workshop and the 'Biographical Dictionary 1560 to 1660' agrees. This is a finely carved pair of effigies with the man dressed in the Stuart clothes of the period. The CMS however attribute this to Edward Marshall (hands) or Epiphamus Evesham (faces) and I am inclined to agree that the style is clearly London. Was once located elsewhere in the cathedral. Unusually his feet rest on an eagle and his wife on a mailed fist holding a dagger.

R27 Snarford, Lincs. Knight. Sir Thomas St Paule (died 1582) and wife Faith (Grantham) . Two recumbent effigies with a canopy supported on six columns.

R28 South Cockerington, Lincs. Sir Adrian Scrope (died 1623). It is unclear how much is alabaster. Esdaile states that the side panels are alabaster and depict the children of the deceased.

R29 Bottesford, Leics. Manners 3rd Earl of Rutland died 1591. Tomb may date from 1594 – *see* R7.

R30 Sutton, Bedfordshire. John Burgoyne (died 1604) and wife Anne. Uncertain if alabaster. (There is a monument to Sir Roger Burgoyne (died 1679) by Grinling Gibbons with a white and black veined stone which needs investigation)

R31 Chilton, Bucks. Sir John Croke (died 1608) and wife Elizabeth (died 1611). A fine alabaster memorial with two recumbent effigies and six adult figures, a child and a chrisom. Black marble columns and pyramids with large heraldic devices. There is uncertainty over the carver both Nicholas Stone and Nicholas Johnson being named.

R32 Lillingstone Dayrell, Bucks. Paul Dayrell (died 1556) and Dorothy (died 1571). The lady has a farthingale. Both have hands which are not quite vertical. The tomb chest is unusual with columns at the corners and diminutive figures of children. Mary, Queen of Scots headdress and small ruffs. This is clearly Renaissance in style but has transition features. May well be a very late product of the Parker workshop.

R33 Wing, Bucks. Sir William Dormer (died 1575) and wife Dorothy (died 1613). First wife Mary Sidney not depicted. *See also* note in R24. Children depicted on tomb chest. A two-tiered tomb. He lies on a rolled-up mat. Restored 2011.

R34 Bristol, St Mark's Chapel. This chapel belongs to the city. Sir Richard Berkeley (died 1602). Recumbent effigy on tomb chest.

R35 Bristol, Holy Trinity or St Stephen, Trinity Road. Sir George Snygge (died 1617). Leaning on one elbow. Cartouche with allegorical figures. Strapwork like Plowden in Temple Church (A67). Repairs carried out by Thomas Hodges (grandson).

R36 Longford, Derbys. Sir Nicholas Longford (1610) and wife (1620).

R37 Throwley, Kent. Sir Thomas Sondes (died 1592) and wife Cecelia or Cyccyllte (died 1584). Two figures kneeling at a large prayer stall with built in inscription panel. A very similar monument to Sir Michael Sondes (brother) who died 1617 and his wife Mary (died 1603) is nearby. This latter tomb with two kneeling effigies with six sons and six daughters is by Nicholas Johnson and is in painted freestone and therefore not listed separately. There was a canopy over the tomb at one time but was removed in the 17th century. For details *see*: http://www.geograph.org.uk/snippet/5789. A fine painted and carved coat of arms.

R38 Isfield, Sussex. Sir John Shirley or Shurley (died 1631) and his two wives. This unpainted tomb has Shirley in between his wives on tiered tomb chests with a huge domed canopy. The front chest has eight figures of his children. Columns flank the tomb and angels and cherubs grace the pediment with a restrained heraldic device on the peak. There are a number of other Shirley tombs but none are alabaster. Saul shows this monument as Figure 37, page 64. Interestingly, Sally Badham suggests that the Shirley tomb of 1558 reuses a tomb slab from Lewes.

R39 Highclere, Hants. Richard Kingsmill (died 1601) and his wife. This was erected in 1602. The record shows this monument was part of the contract for Charlecote, Warwick – *see* R65. Llewellyn believes that the effigies are in a chalky limestone which was called Tatternullstone in an alabaster surround but the contract for its construction specified that one effigy (the male one) had to be in alabaster. It would appear that the person who commissioned the tomb, Thomas Lucy, had a fine tuned sense of status although Lady Lucy exacted her revenge when specifying the Charlecote effigies. The contract exists in Kew being referenced SP/46/23fo145-145d for £60. Dated 1st June 1601.

R40 London, Westminster Abbey, St Paul's Chapel. Sir John Puckering (died 30th April 1596). A tomb erected by his wife Jane who is also depicted. Restored in 1962. Latin inscription, 3 sons and 5 daughters are also shown on the tomb chest.

R41 London, Westminster Abbey. Henry 1st Baron Norris *circa* 1606. Possibly the work of Isaac James.

R42 Waltham Abbey, Essex. Edward Denny (died 1599) and his wife Margaret who died in 1647. The tomb was constructed under the commission of Margaret but she is buried in Bishops Stortford. A fine painted monument in Fauld alabaster showing the effigies leaning on one elbow with their children (one pair of twins) in line below. The tomb was inexpertly restored in the 19th century and after the paintwork began to be damaged by leeched salts was restored by Nimbus Conservation Ltd in the 20th century. They issued an undated online report (Denny Monument – Waltham Abbey) which is worth reading.

R43 Fenny Drayton, Leics. George Purefoy (died 1593) and Edward Purefoy (died 1594) erected 1596. An unusual mural memorial.

R44 Bisham, Berks. Brothers Sir Philip Hoby (died 1558) and Sir Thomas Hoby (died 1566). Contracted for by Thomas's widow. Probably carved late 1560s and has possibly Southwark features. Cornelius Cure, Samuel Baldwin and William Cure I have been credited with the carving from time to time but the consensus is the latter. However, the effigies have features close to those carved by Pierre Bontemps giving rise to speculation that they were carved in France or by a member of his workshop called to England by the widow. The brothers rest on their elbows under an arch. The tomb has unusual features in that the great helm is shown standing vertical and the armour is highly decorated along the seams with swirls which are repeated on the helm and painted gold. The tomb was commissioned by Elizabeth Hoby (Cooke, died 1609) whose tomb also lies in Bisham. M Whinney suggests that Pierre Bontemps may be the carver but research has dismissed this claim. The tomb is linked to that of the Duchess of Suffolk in Westminster and the Duchess of Shrewsbury in Erith, Kent neither of which is alabaster.

R45 Leyton. Essex. Sir Michael Hicks (died 1612) and his wife Elizabeth (Pervis) erected after his death. The effigies rest on one elbow and are unusual in that they reside feet to feet. The tomb chest is very long and the back has two semi-circular arches.

R46 Gawsworth, Cheshire. Francis Fitton (died 1608) and wife Katherine. A pair of painted alabaster effigies on a freestone tomb chest. The cadaver is wrapped in a winding sheet drawn over the head which has been damaged such that it appears to be headless. It is said the inscription cannot be read as it faces the wall but Earwaker copied the inscription from Holmes and can be found on page 554 of his book.

R47 Gawsworth, Cheshire. Dame Alice Fytton (or Fitton) who died in 1626. A strange monument with a single large seated effigy with two children fore and aft dated to 1627. This is a picture of melancholy with Alice holding her head in one hand. She is the widow of Sir Edward Fitton (died 1606).

R48 Westminster Abbey, St Edmund's Chapel. John Lord Russell (died 1584) and his daughter Elizabeth (died 1600). Monument erected in 1603 although some authors date it as early as 1587. The date confusion may arise from the fact that Elizabeth's memorial was added after her death and in all probability the earlier date is correct for the main tomb. In alabaster, touché and marble. Lord Russell has his effigy supported on one elbow and Elizabeth is shown seated. The monument was repainted in the 19th century and again in 1960. Small effigy of son Francis. It is suggested that Elizabeth pricked her finger on a needle from which she got blood poisoning but this has been discounted and she probably died of consumption. The alabaster block from which the male effigy is carved is exceptionally large allowing the full height of Lord Russell to be depicted. The block is just over 6ft long with the width at shoulder 22in. Similarities to the tomb of Ann Russell at Chenies.

R49 London, St Martin in the Fields and Hinton St George, Somerset. Sir Amyas Poulett *circa* 1588 but removed and taken to Hinton St George in 1728. Inscriptions on tomb chest in French. Rolled up mat. Poulett was the sometime guardian of Mary, Queen of Scots whom she detested. The mural addition dating from the 18th century is not alabaster.

R50 London, Westminster. Margaret Douglas, Countess of Lennox (died 1578). Erected after her death so may be later but was certainly in place by 1600. She is buried in same grave as son Charles. A fine painted effigy with French hood and ruff and red fur lined cloak over a dress of blue and gold. The tomb chest has figures of her three sons and four daughters most of which died young and is considered to be slightly old-fashioned for the period. A Latin inscription at the end can be translated as ‘this work was completed at the charge of Thomas Fowler executor of this lady 24th October 1578’ although this cannot be taken as the date of construction and is conflict with the statement that the monument was paid for by James I (then James VI of Scotland) although even this in questionable. Restored *circa* 1960. Charles Douglas married Elizabeth Cavendish and their daughter Lady Arabella Stuart who died in the Tower of London in 1615 is also buried in Mary, Queen of Scots’ vault close by. Her second son was Henry Lord Darnley the father of James VI and murdered husband of Mary, Queen of Scots.

R51 Burford, Oxfordshire. Laurence Tanfield. Lord chief justice (died 1625) and his wife Elizabeth. Tomb erected 1628 by Elizabeth. Alabaster and black marble. Lucius Cary, 2nd Lord Falkland is kneeling flanked by a demi-figure of Lady Tanfield. There is also a kneeling figure of their daughter Elizabeth. A skeleton (cadaver) is shown below the effigies. The effigies may be likeness.

R52 Warwick, Beauchamp Chapel. Ambrose Dudley, Earl of Warwick (died 1589). Alabaster and marble with an 18th century iron coronet. His head rests on a rolled up mat and his feet on a bear. This fine monument is richly painted to resemble bronze and is reputedly resting on a wooden platform. This deception was in order to resemble the nearby Beauchamp tomb at a fraction of the cost. The adjacent tomb the Countess of Leicester is made of wood to resemble brass.

R53 Spetchley, Worcs. Sir Rowland Berkeley (died 1611) and Katherine nee Hayward (died 1629) but monument erected 1614. Both have feet on dogs. The monument has an arch and corner plinths with very large pinnacles (obelisks). An unusual monument commissioned by the second-born son. The tomb was built between 1611 and 1614 and shows the development of the corner peninsulas from that produced for Joan Young at Bristol (X10). The alabaster is rich golden colour and may well be Victorian varnish but *see* Appendix S.

R54 Elmley Castle, Worcs. William Savage (died 1616), Giles Savage (died 1631) and his wife Mary (died 1647). Mary holds a baby in her arms. There are four male weepers (Thomas, William, Giles and John) at the foot of the effigies and a stag with its neck pierced by an arrow. The effigies rest on a black marble tabletop. There are two inscribed back plates on the wall. Monument restored by Sally Strachey at a date unknown and partially gilded. The monument is attributed to Samuel Baldwin but the date is uncertain and may well have been completed by Stephen Baldwin (Broome gives date as post-1632 and erected by daughter-in-law Catherine).

R55 Kidderminster, Worcs. Knight and lady. Thomas Blount (died 1568 – but may be 1569) and wife, Margery Poley (died 1591 – date added later). A part mural tomb with children on back wall in cameo.

R56 Miserden, Gloucs. Sir William Sandys (died 1640) and his wife Margaret Culpepper (died 1644). This monument was once mistaken for being imported. Children lying or kneeling round the tomb chest. The *Gentleman's Magazine* Vol 88 Part 1 quotes this tomb as costing £1000 in 1625 which was greater than the annual value of their estate at the time but this is in conflict with the carving date which Broome states is 1644. This man appears to be no relation of Edwin Sandys (A17).

R57 Cothelstone, Somerset. Sir John Stawell (died 1603) and his wife Frances Dyer. Reported by Ron Firman to be the first effigy carved in Watchet alabaster. The name sometime spelt Stowell. The carving is different in that the knight does not have his hands in prayer. One hand is across his chest and the other holds a book probably a Bible. He wears Stuart light armour and puff trousers pushed into naval thigh boots. His head is on a simple pillow as is his lady. The lady wears a Mary, Queen of Scots headdress and a neck ruff. The dress is full length. Her hands are in prayer. Sir John Stawell was strongly opposed to the Spanish Armada and raised militia in Somerset for the defence of the coast. This monument has been moved and formerly had a canopy. Frances and John were married in 1572. There is a freestone pair of effigies to an earlier Stawell of the 14th century.

R58 Nuneaton, Warwicks. Sir Marmaduke Constable (died 1560). This effigy is carved from a very thin block of alabaster.

R59 Great Brington, Northants. Sir John Spencer (died 1586) attributable to Jasper Hollemans but may be his father Garret. There is also a monument to Lord Spencer (died 1599-R60) and another Sir John Spencer also attributable to the Hollemans, both dated 1599. The Spencers later abandoned the Burton workshops for those of Nicholas Stone who also provided two monuments to Great Brington.

R60 Great Brington, Northants. Baron Spencer (died 1599) attributable to Jasper Hollemans but may be his father Garret.

The Spencers later abandoned the Burton workshops for those of Nicholas Stone who also provided two monuments to Great Brington.

R61 Spare

R62 Chesterfield, Derbys. Godfrey Foljambe (died 1585) and wife, Trothea Tyrwhitt. Bayliss attributes this to Garrett Hollemans (I). It is possible that this and M115 were commissioned at the same time.

R63 Chesterfield, Derbys. Godfrey Foljambe (died 1595) and wife, Isobel Wray. Bayliss attributes this to Garrett Hollemans.

R64 Chesterfield, Derbys. Thomas Foljambe (died 1604) aged 13. A strange kneeling effigy of a youth in decorated armour. Bayliss attributes this to Jasper Hollemans and states it was once on a pillar and was moved to the top of the grave of his great, great grandfather probably during the Scott refurbishment (but *see* below). At some time the head was damaged or stolen and the current head is a replacement. A note mounted in a frame in the current chapel states there were '... five stanzas on the alabaster pillar which stood in the Foljambe Chapel at the foot of Henry Foljambe's altar tomb until the end of the 18th century when it disappeared. The kneeling figure formerly on the square pillar or pedestal has since stood on Henry Foljambe's tomb – July 1899' and signed H. A further note says these stanzas '... appear to refer to Godfrey Foljambe Esq. Who died without issue June 14th 1595 and to when the large monument on the south wall and altar tomb were erected (during his lifetime in 1592) as he was 27 at his father's death on January 10th 1585–1586 having been born 21st November 1558 and Sir William Dugdale makes a note to this effect in his visitation in 1662 – July 1899' and signed H.

R65 Charlecote, Warwicks. Sir Thomas Lucy (died 1600) and his first wife Joyce Acton. The tomb with is recorded as being carved in 1595 when the wife, Joyce, died and later extended to include Lucy himself in 1600–1601. Lady Constance Lucy demonstrated her rights by placing the female effigy ahead of her husband – *see also* R39.

R66 Tonbridge, Kent. Sir Anthony Denton (died 1615) and his 'Deer and Doleful' wife Elizabeth. He was lay rector for the church. A helmet is mounted above. Sir Anthony in his commission to the carver specified alabaster for his effigy and freestone for his wife. He is depicted in most uncomfortable pose on one elbow and she below him.

R67 Wickhamford, Worcs. Sir Samuel Sandys (died 1623) MP for Ripon, his wife Mercy Culpepper (died 1629) and son Edwin (died 1626) and his second wife Penelope (died 1680). He was the son of Edwin Sandys (A17) and Cecily (M4). The monument is attributed to Samuel Baldwin. A pair of recumbent effigies the right one being Samuel and the left his son Edwin. There is a canopy supported by five black Corinthian columns. The canopy which has black inscription panels is surmounted by heraldic devices. The children are depicted in relief on the tomb chest is similar manner to A17. Samuel married Mercy at Southwell Notts in 1586. Son Edwin was the treasurer of the Virginian Company.

R68 St Osyth, Essex. John, 2nd Lord Darcy (died 1581) and his wife Frances. He is in Tudor armour with ruff and mantle although damaged below the knee. The name Griggs has also been mentioned but this may relate to a brass fixed on the wall.

R69 Rivenhall, Essex. Ralph Wyseman (died 1608) and Elizabeth (died 1594). Recumbent effigies with square pillars and pediment with heraldic device. He has feet on seahorse. She has farthingale. Children on tomb chest and listed by name. Some uncertainty as to date as the inscription makes no reference to Ralph's knighthood. They lay on a rolled up mat. Elizabeth was the granddaughter of Richard Rich of Felsted (R160). Llewellyn suggests that the monument was delivered in pieces eastwards down the Thames and then northwards to the Blackwater where it was landed at Maldon to reach its destination by ox-cart. He goes on to say that the 'simple' construction indicates this. The assembly was on site where it was finished by travelling carvers. For more observations on this monument *see Art of Death: Visual Culture in the English Death Ritual 1500 to 1800.*

R70 Shelford, Notts. Lady Ann Stanhope (died 1587) wife of Sir Michael Stanhope implicated in the fall of Somerset, lord protector and executed in 1552. She had eleven children and these are depicted on the tomb chest

R71 St David's Cathedral Pembroke. Countess of Maidstone (died 1932). A life effigy with feet on pet dog.

R72 Llanfarchell, Denbigh. Sir John Salusbury (died 1578) and his wife Jane. A strange monument in Renaissance style. The tomb chest has nine figures along one side, one in robes and the rest in armour. On the other are two chrisoms and two daughters. He has his foot on a lion and his head on a great helm with what appears to be a Saracen-head crest and an orle. Her head is on a cushion. The pleats in the skirt are finely carved. Margaret Whinney suggested that this was a product of the Midland workshops and links it to R119 at Chesterton, but the names Donbins offers no clue.

R73 Breedon on the Hill, Leics. Francis Shirley (died 1571) and wife Dorothy (Giffard). A Royley tomb in Fauld alabaster. The tomb chest has sons and daughters holding shields.

R74 Breedon on the Hill, Leics. John Shirley (died 1570). A Royley tomb erected in 1585 for which a contract is extant

– *see* Appendix W. The cost is recorded as being £22.

R75 Somerton, Oxford. Thomas Fermor (died 1580) and second wife Bridget Bradshaw for which a Royley contract is extant. Tomb constructed 1583 for a cost of £40. It is worth quoting parts of the contract:

'... a fair tomb of good and durable alabaster stone and of certain specified dimensions. A fair of well proportioned picture or portraiture of a gentleman representing the said Thomas Fermor. Also a fair picture or portraiture of a gentlewoman with a French hood, edge and habiliments with all other apparel, furniture, jewels and ornaments and things in all respect usual, decent and seemly for a gentlewoman'. The carver is '... to furnish devising, colouring, gilding, garnishing, workmanship, carriage, conveying, setting up, and full finishing of the said tomb, ... but the executor, George Shirley will provide wains, carts and cattle to draw the parts of the tomb to Somerton' for which the 'waynman' received £4 3s 4d from the executor. The executor also paid for setting up the tomb and painting. Dog toying with ribbon. Children with shields on tomb chest and carved shield in a roundel. *See also* Appendix W.

R76 South Harting, Sussex. Sir Edward Caryll (died 1609). A much damaged effigy in the ruined chancel. This roofless and in some cases wall-less building was attacked by Royalists in 1643 and partially destroyed leaving this and R77 in the open. It not known if the fragment survives.

R77 South Harting, Sussex. Sir Richard Caryll (died 1616). A much damaged effigy in the ruined chancel. This roofless and in some cases wall-less building was attacked by Royalists in 1643 and partially destroyed leaving this and R76 in the open. Richard's effigy was brought into the church in 1956.

R78 Hinton St George, Somerset. Sir Amyss Poulett (died 1588). This effigy was removed from St Martin's in the Fields, London during its refurbishment but the parishioners refused to allow it back so in 1728 it was moved here. Poulett is famous for being the guardian of Mary, Queen of Scots being described as '… one of the most zealous and pitiless man I have ever known' a factor which may well have played a part in the eviction decision.

R79 Millbrook, Beds. Reputed to be William and Mary Huett (both died 1602) but this is only by association with a tablet on the wall. This association was challenged by Pevsner – *see* Appendix O. The effigies are in Chellaston alabaster with the lady in mid Tudor dress with French hood headdress. He has well carved articulated pauldrons with leather edging but his left side is badly corroded from its time in the earth. The head is badly damaged and someone has gouged out one eye socket. The carving style is more mid-16th century than 17th and both the date of 1621and 1602 suggested by some is unlikely.

R80 Easebourne, Sussex. Anthony Browne, Viscount Montagu (died 1592 or 1598) and his two wives, Jane Ratcliffe (died 1552) and Lady Magdalene (or Margaret) Dacre (died 1608). This monument was formerly in Midhurst but moved in 1851–1852 to Easebourne. He is shown kneeling in armour with order of garter. A staunch Catholic serving Mary I but also a friend of Elizabeth I. In the move from Midhurst the monument was found not to fit. As a result the peninsulas and obelisks (like Spetchley) were omitted and the tomb rearranged with Anthony's effigy shown kneeling to one side and the wives' effigies ranged below.

R81 Titchfield, Hants. Henry and Mary Wriothesley. Henry died 1594. Mary may have been an infant aged four who died in 1615.

R82 Sutton Coldfield, Warwicks. John Harman or Vesey or Veysey (died 1554 reputedly aged 103), Bishop of Exeter but born in Sutton Coldfield. Moved in 1876 and possibly repainted. The monument was erected by Sir John Wyrley of Hampstead in Handsworth, Staffs, in memory of his great-uncle the bishop, and was repaired and beautified by the corporation in 1748. The inscription records that the bishop 'procured the town to be incorporate by name of Warden and Society of King's Town of Sutton Coldfield' and that he built 'two isles to the church and an organ, erected a Moot Hall with a prison below, a market place, 51 stone houses, 2 stone bridges, one at Curdworth and one at Water Orton, paved the whole town and endowed a free grammar school'. On the east wall above the tomb is a carved achievement of the Tudor royal arms with greyhound and dragon supporters, a crown and motto 'DOMINVS MIHI ADIVTOR' and below it the bishop's own arms.

R83 Brewood, Staffs. John Giffard (died 1615) and Joyce Leveson (died 1608). Tomb chest displays eight sons of which five are in armour and six daughters. John Giffard was imprisoned for his Catholic faith. One son was implicated in the Babington Plot of 1587.

R84 Brewood, Staffs. Walter Giffard (died 1632) and Philippa White (died 1636).

R85 Quorndon, Leics (Quorn). John Farnham (died 1587) and wife Dorothy (Walwyn). An unusual effigy tomb with the chest top inscribed with an inscription in a panel at the foot. According to Nichols the tomb had an inscription panel at the feet of the effigies when first constructed. At some point this panel was removed and placed at the head end. This panel was unusual for an effigial tomb and may well have been carved to mimic the Royley tombs. The attribution to Epiphanius Evesham has been contested and the name William Hargrave of Bilborough has also been suggested although little or nothing is known about him.

R86 Tong, Shropshire. Margaret Vernon and Thomas Stanley (died 1576). The son of Richard and Margaret (G149) died without heir leaving Haddon to daughter Dorothy and Tong to daughter Margaret who married Stanley. *See also* R87.

R87 Tong, Shropshire. Edward Stanley (died 1632) son of R86. This is the lower tier of a family tomb which included R86. Stanley was the last Vernon to own Tong the estate being sold in 1613 to Thomas Harries. The Renaissance tomb of 1576 was altered to accommodate Edward and includes huge obelisks which formerly stood on the floor. It has been suggested that the obelisks replace figures which were removed to niches although showing signs of damage.

R88 Penkridge, Staffs. Sir Edward Littleton (died 1610) and wife and his son Sir Edward Littleton (died 1629) and his wife. A unique double memorial with the son and his wife mounted above his father and mother.

R89 Penkridge, Staffs. Sir Edward Littleton (died 1574) and wife Alice Cockayne.

R90 Claverley, Shrops. Sir Robert Brooke, Chief justice of the common pleas (died 1559) and wives Dorothy Gatacre and Ann Waring. Sir Robert is in judge's robes. The judge wears a collar of alternating S and roses making it possible that the tomb was created long before his death. One wife wears a gable hood and the other a French hood reinforcing the view that the tomb is more 1530s than 1550s.

R91 Draycott in the Moors, Staffs. Sir Philip Draycott (died 1559) and wife Elizabeth FitzHerbert.

R92 Rushton, Northants. Sir Thomas Tresham (died 1559), Lord Prior of the Knights Hospitallers of Jerusalem. The tomb is dated 1562 and was first set up in St Peter's Church transferred to All Saints in 1799. He is shown in his priory robes. Tresham was appointed prior by Mary I when she revived the order. The prior died in the same year as Mary and never saw the order dissolved as it was soon after Elizabeth I accession.

R93 Shareshill, Staffs. Two effigies now separated. Humphrey Swynnerton (died 1562) and wife Cassandra Giffard (died 1570). His will in the Staffordshire Archives (D641/5/TS/4/6) requests he be buried in Swinnerton or Shareshill church 'before the places where images stood' and priests to pray for soul. Clearly Humphrey adhered to the old religion. The current effigies are reported not to be on their original tomb chest leading to the assumption they were moved at some time. Effigies much repaired.

R94 Stafford, St Mary. Sir Edward Aston (died 1568) and his wife Joan (Bollys). The monument is believed to have been erected in his lifetime. It is suggested it was moved from Tixall. The effigy of the man is headless although a drawing of the early 19th century shows this to be complete. Another drawing dated 1840 shows that the head had gone by that date. It is reputed that workmen accidentally beheaded the effigy when setting up a jury box. Tomb chest with weepers. *See also*: http://www.geograph.org.uk/photo/4461377

R95 Yoxall, Staffs. Humphrey Welles (died 1565) and wife Mary Chetwynd (died 1584). Possibly not erected until 1584. Reported to have been moved in 1827 and pushed into a corner. Welles oversaw the erection of a tomb at Kingston on Soar in 1537–1538 (*see* D9) and had long time associations with the Honour of Tutbury and the Duchy of Lancaster. She has French Hood and puffed sleeves. She holds a prayer book between the hands. He has a somewhat dated hair style and a beard.

R96 Spare

R97 Misterton, Leics. Sir Michael Poultney (died 1567). Great helm with Saracen's head. There is a tabletop also dedicated to a Poultney with an alabaster frame and a black marble top.

R98 Healaugh, Yorks. Thomas Lord Wharton (died 1568) and wives Ann Ratcliff and Anne Talbot. Edge Latin inscription mainly defaced. Two panels also with Latin inscriptions. Small cross carved into forehead of one wife. Tomb chest has large shields in circlet with standing effigies. Reported as similar to the 1556 limestone tomb at Kirkby Stephen also commissioned by Thomas.

R99 Spare

R100 Rothley, Leics. Thomas Babington (died 1567) and wife Eleanor Humphrey (died 1570).

R101 Wroxeter, Shrops. Sir Richard Newport (died 1570) and wife Margaret Bromley (died 1578). A richly painted monument. The tomb chest has spiral pilasters and figures holding shields to one side otherwise plain with chamfered plinth. He has feet on a lion with its head turned towards the effigy. The folds of Margaret's dress are cleanly carved and a bird is carved. English inscription.

R102 Wroxeter, Shrops. John Barber and wife.

R103 Leighton Bromswold, Hunts. Katherine Tyrwhitt (died 1567) wife of Sir Henry D'Arcy. Tomb chest is modern. *See also* R104.

R104 Leighton Bromswold, Hunts. Sir Robert Tyrwhitt (died 1572) and wife Elizabeth Oxenbridge (died 1578). Tomb may be as late as 1578. The effigies are damaged with the legs of Sir Robert missing. At some point *circa* 1626 the roof had fallen in and was rebuilt in 1632. The Tyrwhitts had interrogated Elizabeth I at Hatfield during Edward VI's reign over her contacts with Thomas Seymour and they never found favour again. The lady is very similar to R103.

R105 Swarkestone, Derbys. Richard Harpur, Justice of the Common Bench (died 1573 possibly 1577) and wife Jane Finderne. The tomb chest and with brass inlays was made in London. Harpur is reputed to have an SS collar. Harpur was a serjeant in 1558 and wears a coif.

R106 Swarkestone, Derbys. Sir John Harpur (died 1627) and wife Isabella Pierrepont. Seven sons and five daughters are inscribed on the chest with a double prayer desk. The tomb chest and with brass inlays was made in London. Harpur is reputed to have an SS collar.

R107 Wolverhampton, Staffs. John Leveson (died 1575) and wife Joyce (Ashfield died 1570).

R108 Wolverhampton, Staffs. Thomas Lane (died 1585) and wife Katherine Trentham (died 1589). Monument erected 1585. It has been moved. The tomb chest has a row of children two of whom are chrisoms.

R109 Whitchurch, Denbigh. This is also the parish church of Denbigh. Sir John Salusbury of Llewenni (died 1578) and his wife Joan Middleton (died 1588).

R110 Norwich, St Andrew's Church. Sir John Suckling (died 1627) and his wife Martha (died 1613). Monument erected in 1613. It is known that R111 was erected at the same time as R110 and therefore there is a strong possibility that this too was carved in the Southwark workshops.

R111 Norwich, St Andrew's Church. Robert Suckling (died 1589) and his wife Elizabeth Barwick (died 1569). Monument erected in 1613.

R112 Edgcote, Northants. Sir Toby Chauncey (died 1608) and wives Bridget Shelley (died 1579) and Elizabeth Risley (died 1619). Date is uncertain as Bayliss places this monument in the series constructed in the 1570s. There are children facing forward on the tomb chest. Two girls have Elizabethan ruffs.

R113 Monks Kirby, Warwicks. Sir William Fielding (died 1547) and his wife Elizabeth Poultney (died 1539). Gardner lists this but states it is Renaissance in styled. The knight has a bald spot and the lady wears a short pediment and ruff. Bayliss says that this effigy shows details of the Burton carving of the 1520s and also gives a date of 1547 which is hard to confirm. However, this may well be an older effigy which has been recut. This needs further work.

R114 Monks Kirby, Warwicks. Basil Fielding (died 1580) and his wife Godith Willington (died 1630?). The work is attributed to the Royley workshop which dates it prior to 1605. More work is needed to resolve date conflicts.

R115 Ashbourne, Derbys. Sir Humphrey Bradbourne (died 1581) and wife Elizabeth Turville. It is believed that the monuments were moved in 1882 into the Boothby Chapel and that some alabaster was reused elsewhere in the church. Sir Humphrey is believed to say that the Royleys were 'inexpensive and popular'. One of the figures round the tomb chest is Jane Sacheverell (*see* Ratcliffe on Soar and Morley, Derbyshire)

R116 Newbold on Avon, Warwicks. Edward Boughton (died 1548) and wife Elizabeth Willington (died 1583). Two-tier memorial.

R117 Rockingham. Northants. Sir Edward Watson and wife Ann Digby (died 1584).

R118 Edgcote, Northants. William Chauncey (died 1585) and wife Joan Bustard (died 1571).

R119 Chesterton, Warwicks. Humphrey Peyto (died 1585) and wife Ann Fielding. The children are arranged above the effigies. There are a number of animals, a dog curled up in the folds of the dress and another on which the knight is resting his feet shown howling. Margaret Whinney links this monument to that at Whitchurch (R72).

R120 Over Peover, Cheshire. Sir John Mainwaring (died 1515) and wife Katherine Hanford (died 1529). Monument erected by son Edward in 1586.

R121 Clifton, Notts. Sir Gervase Clifton (died 1587) and wives Maria Nevill (died 1564) and Winifred Thwaites. There is some question as to which Gervase this is. A Gervase married Mary *circa* 1530 and his son married Winifred at 14 dying at 20. [The son of the Clifton of the Wars of the Roses was born in 1516 and died *circa* 1587 having received the title of Gervase the Gentle].

R122 Stoke Dry, Rutland. Sir Kenelm Digby (died 1590) and wife Anne Cope. Eleven children. This Digby was the father of Everard Digby executed due to involvement in the Gunpowder Plot. One daughter is finely carved with over-large ruff and a smart hair style. Children on tomb chest including a chrisom.

R123 Grendon, Warwicks. John Cherwynd (died 1592) and wife Margery Middlemore. Panel removed from Ingestre, Staffs and set up in front of piscina.

R124 Stratford on Avon, Warwicks (Clopton Chapel). William Clopton (died 1592) and wife Anne (Griffith). The tomb chest has twisted pilasters. Repaired by daughter Joyce in 1630 and by Sir John Clopton in 1714. Above the tomb is a panel which depicts the children which include 3 chrisoms and Joyce whose tomb is also in the chapel (M342).

R125 Seighford, Staffs. William Bowyer or Bower (died 1592) and wife Mercy. Has been moved from original position.

R126 Mitton, Lancs. Sir Richard Sherburne (or Shirburne) – died 1594 and wife Maud Bowld (or Bold) – died 1558. Bayliss accredits this to the Royley workshop, but the records of the Stanton workshop also lay claim – *see* B86.

R127 Spare

R128 Rolleston on Dove, Staffs. Bishop Richard Shirburn (or Sherburne) of Chichester (died 1536). A curious effigy set in the wall like a coffin. The middle of the effigy is obscured by a stone block with a Renaissance decoration which justifies the classification as R. The effigy is turned almost on its side. Gardner declined to describe this monument. *See also* Standon church 1526 and Sherburne's other monument in Chichester (G169).

R129 Oxford, Trinity College. Sir Thomas Pope (died 1559) and second wife Elizabeth Blout. Pope was first buried in St Stephen's, Walbrook where his first wife Margaret (died 1538) was buried. His body with that of Margaret were moved to Oxford where the tomb was erected by Elizabeth as late as 1567 (records of Trinity College and *The Life of Thomas Pope* by Thomas Wharton *circa* 1772). The tombs at Walbrook were lost in the fire of 1666. Cleaned of wax and dirt by Cliveden Conservation.

R130 Hillesden, Bucks. Alexander Denton (died 1576) and wife (died 1574). Has a French feature.

R131 Stoughton, Leics. Thomas Farnham (died 1562) and wife Helen Chaloner (died 1569). Thomas was a teller of the exchequer under Mary I. The tomb was restored in 1739 by Arabella and Christina Beaumont and William Busby. Restoration accredited to Peter Scheemakers. Beard and close-cropped hair, head on great helm with crest, and feet on dog. Gauntlets at side. Helen with French hood. For other Farnham tombs – *see* Quorndon. It is interesting that the chapel there was secured by Thomas in 1553 but he is not buried there.

R132 Old Dalby, Leics. Andrew Nowell (or Noel died 1562) and two wives Dorothy Conyers (died 1548) and Dame Elizabeth Peryent (formerly Hopton) recorded as 'now living'. In fact it believed that Elizabeth commissioned the tomb from Richard Parker. The local history states that the pilaster on the north-east corner is placed upside down.

R133 Old Dalby, Leics. John Hopton (died 1580) and wife Clare and also to Sir Thomas Tyrell, second husband of Clare. The three effigies lie on a short tomb chest. The Hopton are the parents of the Elizabeth mentioned in R132. There is much uncertainty as to dates. The local history group state that the tomb was raised in 1562 at the same time as R132 which means that if 1580 is correct it was made prior to John's death. Nichols, in 1800, shows an etching of this tomb but shows only two effigies so that the provenance of the effigy of Tyrell needs some research.

R134 Spare

R135 Wirksworth, Derbys. Anthony Gell (died 1583). The son of Ralph Gell. A remarkable ornate 1584 tomb with the edges of the tomb slab richly carved. All the alabaster is Fauld except for the head which appears to be Chellaston and may well be a Victorian replacement.

R136 Coleshill, Warwicks. Sir George Digby (died 1587) and Lady Abigail Digby believed to have been erected some time after death. They are attended by standing figures of four sons, one in armour, two in boys' gowns and the fourth a swaddled baby. John's son, George (died 1587) and Abigail his wife are depicted in Elizabethan costume typical of the nobility of the time. There are the kneeling figures of four sons, the first an infant, the others with beards or moustaches and wearing armour and the figure of a daughter. The tomb chest style indicates a carving date much later than 1587 with polished plain corner pilasters and figures in profile in plain niches. The second son, Robert, is a good deal larger than George, Philip or John indicating that he had prominence since George died young and Robert having succeeded to the estate probably made the tomb. Robert died in 1614 which may well be the date of creation of Sir George's tomb in Coleshill when there was a growing tradition of sons honouring fathers at their own death.

R137 Chilham, Kent. Mary Kempe, Lady Digges (died 1631) erected by her Husband Sir Dudley Digges. The monument comprises a tomb chest with a large 11ft central column with an urn on top and four statues at each corner representing the four graces. The tomb is supposed to be based on Genesis chapter 35 vs16-20. Llewellyn reports this unusual monument as black and white marble but it is to be found in the workbook of Nicholas Stone who claims the monument has a pillar of alabaster. Such is the size that this could only have come from Fauld at that time. However, this is suspect and needs investigation. For Sir Dudley Digges the Palmer monument is in Bethersden marble. Column tombs are rare but two others are St Mary, Barton on Humber to Jane Shipsea (1626), wife of the Rev John Shipsea and to Rachel Sutton (1653) at Winterbourne Strictland, Dorset which is a half-column set as a wall monument.

R138 Boreham, Essex. Robert Radcliff (died 1542), Henry Radcliff (died 1557) and Thomas Radcliff (died 1583), the Earls of Sussex but not completed until 1589. The monument uses a number of different stones including touchstone, black and coloured marble and alabaster. Completed at Southwark at a cost of £266 13s 4d by Richard Stevens. Each side has three panels with moulded frames and panelled pilasters, the middle panel on the east, north and south sides has a shield with a garter, but the former brass shields are gone. One panel on the north, south and west sides have an inscription. The slab has a moulded edge and bears on rush mattresses three recumbent effigies of the three earls in enriched plate armour with peasecod breast plates, swords broken, feet against couchant apes each wearing a hat. There is a garter on left leg of each effigy, heads on cushions and behind them three couchant oxen, much mutilated, chained and collared with crowns. Remains of fixing of metal chains round neck of each effigy, and traces of red colour on collar of north effigy. The wife of Thomas Radcliff is commemorated by R139. The tomb components were carried to Boreham (40 miles) in twelve carts.

R139 Westminster abbey, St Paul's Chapel. Frances Sidney (died 1589) wife of Thomas Radcliff Earl of Sussex (*see* R138) probably erected at the same time.

R140 Ingatestone, Essex. Sir William Petre (died 1572), Order of the Garter and his second wife Ann Browne. Sir William has plate armour, head against helmet, feet against a crest and of lady with closed headdress, brocaded skirt, cloak and fur stole and feet on lozenge of arms. Both effigies lie on a rush mattress. The altar-tomb on two steps, sides divided into three panels by Doric columns of Purbeck marble and veined (marble?), each panel enriched with a shell-head and elaborate cartouche of arms; a similar panel at each end; in head of arch over tomb, ornamental ironwork supporting an alabaster oval plaque with achievement of arms surrounded by a chain with rose pendant encircled by a Garter. Sir William served four Tudor monarchs. The tomb may well have been erected by his son.

R141 Windsor, Berks, St George's Chapel. Edward Clinton, Earl of Lincoln (died 1584) and his wife Lady Elizabeth Clinton. Constructed possibly later in what was known, in 1811, as the Lincoln Chapel. Mixed stone. The effigies lie on a mat. He is in armour with feet on a greyhound and her with feet on a monkey. The sons and daughters are represented on their knees. The monument was defaced but restored *circa* 1789 at the cost of the Duke of Newcastle. Family arms in alabaster. Later fitted with grill.

R142 London, Westminster Abbey, St Paul's Chapel. Sir James Fullerton (died 1632) and his wife Magdalene. He lies on a rush mat with his feet on an otter (his crest). The wife is not buried in the abbey and so her inscription date is blank. Her effigy contains a miniature of her husband attached to her belt. Fullerton was a Scotsman and gentleman of the Stuart bedchamber. The recumbent effigies are somewhat old-fashioned and echoed the formal and traditional style which came forth with Charles I.

R143 Exeter, Devon. Bishop Valentine Carey (died 1626).

R144 Exeter, Devon. Bishop William Cotton (died 1621).

R145 Mamble, Worcs. Thomas Blout and family (*circa* 1561). An effigial monument in alabaster and freestone displaying some damage. *British History Online* claims that the effigy is full-size skeleton but this cannot be confirmed by the author.

R146 Spare

R147 Witham, Essex. John Southcote (died 1585) and his wife Elizabeth Robbins. A justice of the peace he remained a Catholic once resigning rather than condemn a priest.

R148 Long Melford, Suffolk. Sir William Cordell (died 1580). The alabaster effigy lies on a rolled straw mat under two coffered arches supported by marble Corinthian columns. There are four standing figures of Prudence, Justice, Fortitude and Temperance in shallow niches and the head of Bacchus can be found in the scrollwork at the top.

R149 Hackleton and Horton, Northants. Sir William Lane (died 1580) and family. A mural monument with strapwork, effigies facing each other with children behind, obelisks, pilasters and cartouche with winged skulls.

R150 Aylesbury, Bucks. Anne Lee, Lady Paget (died 1590) and daughter Mary.

R151 Westminster Abbey. Frances, Countess of Hertford (died 1598). Dressed in robes with lion at feet. She was the daughter of Howard of Effingham and wife of Edward Seymour who paid for the memorial. Restored 1960.

R152 Westminster Abbey. Judge Thomas Owen (died 1598). This has similarities to Temple (A67) and Bristol (R35).

R153 Westminster Abbey. Judge Sir Thomas Heskett (died 1605). This monument formerly had a kneeling wife, Juliana, which disappeared in the 19th century. This has similarities to Temple (A67) and Bristol (R35) as well as R152.

R154 Wroxton, Oxford. Sir William Pope, Earl Downe (died 1631) and wife Anne Hopton (died 1625). There are effigies of the sons William (died 1624) and Thomas (2nd earl) on one knee holding books. William is in Stuart armour. At the base is daughter Elizabeth with starched ruff raised at back and sloping at front. Hair in bun secured by a lace band. Both main effigies have falling ruffs. Possibly copied from Nicholas Stone to whom it is sometime credited but not in his workbook. Most likely the work of Samuel Baldwin. Very well carved effigies. Dog (greyhound) at feet of man and a spaniel with a very strange expression at foot of woman. The hem of the dress is particularly well done. The canopy and back panel is in alabaster with a black inscription panel.

R155 Westminster Abbey. Mildred Cecil, Lady Burghley (died 1589) and her daughter Anne, Countess of Oxford (died 1588). Kneeling figure of Robert Cecil. Although believed to be alabaster there is some evidence that wood is also used. The ladies have nice standing ruffs.

R156 Tortworth, Gloucs. Sir Thomas Thockmorton (died 1608 or 1609). Material uncertain. The effigy in armour shows a very high gorget and may have been copied from R159.

R157 Kempsey, Worcs. Sir Edmund Wylde (died 1620). High Sheriff of Herefordshire. At one time a horse chestnut tree grew out of monument. Material uncertain.

R158 Elvaston, Derbys. Sir John Stanhope (died 1610) and wife Catherine (Trentham).

R159 Westminster Abbey. William Thynne (died 1585). A fine alabaster and marble effigy made by a Southwark workshop. The effigy in armour displays a very high gorget also seen at Tortworth (R156). The tomb was restored in 1875 when the arch above was designed by Gilbert Scott.

R160 Felsted, Essex. Lord Richard Rich (died 1568), his wife and son Robert (died 1581). Reported as various marbles but the effigy is alabaster and said to have been constructed in 1620 after the death of his grandson in 1619. Rich was instrumental in the downfall of Sir Thomas More. Lord Rich in lord chancellor's robes turns his head to look at his son. Slate inscribed tablets showing events in his life. A grand memorial erected by Epiphanius Evesham in 1620. The monument is unusual as it depicts events from Rich's life.

R161 Wrangle, Lincs. John Reade (died 1626) and his wife Anne (died 1652). A large tomb with a Grecian pediment much damaged but protected by an iron railing when observed in 1843. Anne was his second wife and their children are depicted on the tomb chest with one chrisom over which looms the image of death. John was Sheriff of Lincolnshire and Anne was daughter of the Lord Mayor of London and 30 years younger than her husband.

R162 Bishops Cleeve, Gloucs. Sir Richard de Bere (died 1636) and wife Margaret. Two pairs of black columns supporting arch. Statues of Justice and Strength. She is thought to be a copy of a lady carved by Nicholas Stone at Watford (M113) with the gown trimmed to the knee and stomacher and mourning veil. The hood is without buckram stiffening and displays a soft turnback. May be portrait. He is in alderman's gown (but T Dugdale in 1830 says he displays the uniform of a serjeant at law) with two-tier ruff. Hands link heraldry. Snake biting tail as a symbol of eternity. Repaired in 1803.

R163 Wellington, Somerset. Sir John Popham (died 1607) and wife Amy Games. Unusually, at the west end his parents kneel at a prayer desk and at the east end his only son Sir Francis and his wife kneel in a similar way. On the south side kneel their six daughters and behind them three maidservants with different ruffs. On the north side the 13 sons and daughters of Sir Francis kneel again at a prayer desk. The tomb has been attributed to the workshop of Cornelius Cure but has been moved on two occasions but no trace of the grave was found. Attorney General and Lord Chief Justice Sir John Popham was involved in the trials of Mary, Queen of Scots, the Earl of Essex, Sir Walter Raleigh and the Gunpowder conspirators. Popham was also involved in investigating a Catholic plot to recruit Henry Sacheverell (R5) to the Catholic faith in 1603 – for details *see The Ratcliffe Chronicles* 2008. The monument has eight Corinthian columns and a canopy.

R164 Bramfield, Suffolk. Arthur Coke (died 1629) and wife Elizabeth (Waldegrave, died 1627). The effigies are well carved and polished. Can be compared with those at Lydiard Tregoze. She died in childbirth and holds her baby in her arms.

R165 Lydiard Tregoze, Wilts. Sir John St John (died 1648) erected 1634 in material including alabaster, chalk and limestone and so erected in his lifetime. Two wives Anne Leighton (died 1624) and her 13 children and Margaret (died 1637) who also has an effigy with her first husband Sir Richard Grobham at Great Wishford near Salisbury. Anne has the chrisom of her 13th child in her arms. Grand Samuel Baldwin tomb with good carved figures and massive canopy with figures and heraldic devices. The colour of the alabaster is interesting as it has a pink tinge and may well be Watchet. Has been wrongly attributed to Nicholas Stone in the past. The monument shows signs of repair especially to the figures of birds but the repair is crude and wrong colour. There is a report that the monument was damaged in transit from Gloucester. There are features including lace trim which makes it attributable to the Gloucester workshop. The monument includes a polyptych which shows the St John family.

R166 Great Waltham, Essex. Sir Anthony Everard (died 1614) erected on the death of his wife Anne (died 1609). Anne, who was reputed to be a cousin of Oliver Cromwell, is on a lower level. Two naked children hugging each other in a rare commemoration of children. Two coffins of unbaptised children are reported. Attributed to Bartholomew Atye. There is an 1893 alabaster font with wooden canopy.

R167 Ross on Wye, Hereford. John Rudhall (died 1636) and wife Mary (died 1668). High Sheriff of Hereford and MP. Erected by his wife. Effigy of baby and child.

R168 Spare

R169 Ross on Wye, Hereford. William Rudhall (died 1630) and wife Anne. Colonel in Royalist army. Erected by his wife in 1651.

R170 Great Malvern Priory, Worcs. John Knotsford (died 1586) and wife Jane (died 1582). Erected by Anne Knotsford (daughter) in 1615 who is shown kneeling at foot of monument. The carving of the lady has similarities to Sapperton (M169) and Gloucester (M60). In particular the deep vee of the bodice and pearls are copied from GJ. Jane's mother and father are there.

R171 Kentchurch, Hereford. John Scudamore (died 1616) and wife Amy (Starkie). She commissioned Samuel Baldwin to carve monument. His effigy in alabaster is shown reclining with a book but hers is in freestone. Effigies of eight sons, one daughter and an infant.

R172 Much Dewchurch. John (died 1547) and Walter Pye both of Mynde. Two males on one tomb.

R173 Spare

R174 Shipton Moyne, Gloucs. Sir Thomas Estcourt (died 1640) and wife Mary. Moved from Lasborough in 1825.

R175 Broad Hinton, Wilts. Francis Glanville (died 1645). The effigy is standing man in armour holding a standard. Glanville was a Royalist soldier killed at the siege of Bridgwater.

R176 Much Cowarne, Hereford. Edmund Fox (died 1617) and wife Ann. Three sons and seven daughters in relief excluding three chrisoms.

R177 Shipton Moyne Gloucs. Judge Thomas Estcourt (died 1599) and wife. Tomb chest shows nine children.

R178 Much Marcle, Hereford. John Kyrle (died 1650) and wife. High Sheriff of Hereford.

R179 Spare

R180 Abergavenny, Gwent. Judge Andrew Powell (died 1631). The badly weathered effigy is by Samuel Baldwin but the figure of a woman next to him is medieval and does not belong but some say Margaret. The church has several monuments made from fragments and the lady may well be from 1450 or 1470. Tomb chest is freestone and modern.

R181 London, Westminster Abbey. Winifred, Marchioness of Winchester (died 1586).Son of her first marriage Thomas Sackville kneeling. Daughter Ann and a chrisom.

R182 Worcester Cathedral. Bishop Thornborough (died 1641). Tomb started earlier possibly as early as 1627. Incomplete. The effigy has received much vandalism which may originate from the Civil War era. The face is blackened and the forearm is madly cut and marked with graffiti.

R183 Worcester Cathedral. Bishop Edmund Freake (died 1591). Tomb without effigy. It is claimed to one of the first signed tombs. It is by Anthony Tolly, a local carver. The chest is shorter than the alcove which is surmounted by a coffered arch more in keeping with several decades later. The material is uncertain.

R184 Worcester Cathedral. Bishop Richard Eedes (died 1604). Tomb with effigy with canopy held up by four columns. The material is uncertain. The tomb was erected by his wife Margaret with a punning epitaph. Reputed to be a playwright he was part author of the *King James Prayer Book* unfinished at his death.

R185 Worcester Cathedral. Robert Wilde (died 1607) and wife Margaret (died 1606). A 1608 tomb with two painted effigies in uncertain material. It does not have the fine lines of alabaster. Classical lion at feet unusual for period. The Wildes were clothiers and well respected and so allowed to be buried in the cathedral. Has been moved.

R186 Worcester Cathedral. Bishop Henry Parry or Parrie (died 1616). This is recorded as alabaster effigy in a 13th century niche into which it was removed losing much of the remaining parts of the tomb.

R187 Uppsala Cathedral, Sweden. The tomb of King Gustavus Vasa (died 1560) and his two of his three wives, Margaratas and Katharina. Commenced shortly after Vasa'a death, it is known that Flemish carver Willem Boy travelled to England to source alabaster in 1572 but it is not known from where he obtained his material. The monument was prepared in Mechelen in Belgium but was not installed until 1580. In 1702 one of the obelisks was damaged in a fire and a replacement was made which is reported to be plaster. Dr Wolfram Kloppmann has analysed a fragment of the original alabaster and the probable source is Fauld although some commentators declared the source to be Newark. The tomb has a recumbent man in coronet and robes and one wife at each side all in marble. The corners have alabaster obelisks some 6ft high (1.68m). The effigies were confiscated by the Dutch magistrates after Boy failed to attend a hearing to debate his bond for 1000 daler which he had taken out.

R188 Beckbury, Shropshire. Uncertain – Richard Haughton died 1595 and lady. *British History Online* claims this was destroyed in 1856 and the recess is now empty and heavily restored.

R189 Easton Maudit, Northants. Sir Henry Yelverton (died 1630–1631) and wife Margaret Beale (died 1625). A large canopied tomb with the effigies one above the other on the north wall of the Yelverton chapel. Four sons and Five daughters are depicted. Unusually there are bedesmen in black gowns.

R190 Thame, Oxford. Lord Williams of Thame (died 1559). Repaired by William Byrd *circa* 1670 who made a new unicorn and greyhound. He may have added strapwork

R191 Sutton Cheney, Leics. William Roberts the younger (died 1633). A strange chest monument in clear Renaissance style. Corner pilasters with strapwork and skull and the chest side have drapes and scrolls with a large black inscription. Knight in Stuart armour with falling ruff.

R192 Bishop Burton, Yorks. Rachel Gee (died 1649) wife of William Gee. Shrouded figure with one arm, hand and face exposed. Kneeling figure of girl. The figure was found under the floor in 1865 and is believed to once been part of a larger monument. The book *The Verneys: Love, War and Madness in Seventeenth Century England* by Adrian Tinniswood page 270–276 has an interesting account of Gee attempting to persuade Ralph Verney to have a tomb like that of Rachel's for his wife at Middle Claydon. In the end this was not adopted and after offering the work to Burman who estimated £200 the tomb (M382) was completed by Edward Marshall. In a comment made in 1650 by Burman to Verney's agent he stated that alabaster was 7s per foot and that a life-sized figure made from this would be a quarter of the cost of one made in marble.

R193 Hackington, Kent. Sir Roger Manwood (died 1592) chief baron of the exchequer, wife Dorothy and five children. Cadaver on mat. The tomb was made in his lifetime. The painted demi-figure of Sir Roger faces forward in his robes and shows a modified collar of SS with a Tudor rose pendant. Sir Roger was born in 1525 and his authority for wearing a livery collar long after it was apparently discontinued requires investigation. A detailed paper in 'Kent Archaeological Society Journal' by Edward Foss in 1858 which was spurred by the observation of the collar on Manwood's tomb, elicited the information that Justice Popham in 1594 observed that '... the nobility gathered resplendent in their collars of SS'. This may well reveal that at the end of Elizabeth I's reign the SS collar had a brief resurgence but this needs more research.

R194 Wells Cathedral, Somerset. Bishop John Still (died 1608).

R195 Carlton Curlieu, Leics. Sir John Bale (died 1622) and his wife Frances (died 1624). An unusual monument with the children depicted in relief above the effigies. The knight has his head on a great helm and she on a very plump cushion with a mourning hood. The wife is raised above the knight which may indicate a post-1624 date. Strapwork, shields and inscriptions on tomb chest. The hands are missing. The monument has similarities to M2. The Bale family is a distant relation to one of the authors.

R196 Chevening, Kent. The Stanhope Chantry which contains the effigy of John Lennard (died 1590) and his wife Elizabeth (died 1585). Lying on a mat.

R197 London, St Paul's Cathedral. The statue of the poet Dr John Donne (died 31st March 1631) in white marble in a grey marble niche in the south choir. The statue merits inclusion as it seems to in include an alabaster urn in pinkish stone. The statue was carved in 1631 from a portrait made earlier when Donne was close to death. The carver has been suggested a being Humphrey Moyer of the Nicholas Stone workshop. It is stated in the Walpole Society Volume 7 that Donne requested a life-sized portrait be painted for which he wrapped himself naked in a winding sheet and stood on a wooden urn. The statue was finished by Humphrey Mayer (B87) and the niche by Robert Flower. The statue (shown as No 14 on Holler's 1658 plan of the cathedral) is the only one to survive the 1666 fire crashing through the floor into the crypt which saved it from total destruction by fire. It was later reinstated in the south choir where it currently resides showing scorch marks on the urn. *See also* X103.

R198 Spare

R199 Condover, Shrops. Sir Thomas Scriven (died 1587) and wife Margaret. It is reputed that the tomb was moved here from St Chad's, Shrewsbury.

R200 Hinton Ampnor, Hants. Thomas Stewkley (died 1638 or some say 1601) aged nine days son of Thomas Stewkely of Martowne. A baby in a wrap with head on cushion and in niche with floral inserts.

R201 Eggesford, Devon. Edward Chichester (died 1648) and his wife Anne (Copleston) (died 1616) completed by his son Arthur Chichester, 1st Earl of Donegal (died 1675). *See also* M230.

R202 Uffculme, Devon. A curios monument with three demi-figures facing forward and a tomb chest with two portraits in ovals. The journal of the Rev Jeremiah Milles 1770, dean of Exeter, claims the figures on the monument are alabaster but this cannot be confirmed. The identity is uncertain as is the material as the whole is painted somewhat inexpertly. Above the monument is the recumbent effigy of a knight *circa* 1701 thought to be Sir William Waldron (died 1689). This monument is covered in detail in CMS Vol XVIII 2003 pages 65–90. One oval may be William Waldron (died 1627) and one the figures William Waldron (died 1650 or 1667) and wife Ursula (died 1698). Amongst the confusion of dates and identities is a claim that the monument was moved from Kentisbeare, Devon and none of the three components may have originally been together.

R203 Selling, Kent. Peter Heyman (died 1550) and wife Elizabeth and son William. The knight knees at the end of the tomb chest but is considered to once been on top.

R204 Oxnead, Norfolk. Sir Clement Paston (died 1608). He lies on a mat in Stuart armour with a small effigy of his wife kneeling in front of the tomb chest. There are some alabaster draperies which may be associated with the monument to Katherine Paston's tomb but this uncertain as the memorial is in marble.

R205 Wighill, Yorks. Robert Stapleton (died 1635) and wife. Unusually he has his feet on the family crest of a Saracen's head. Six children depicted on tomb chest.

R206 Tenbury Wells, Worcs. Thomas Acton (died 1546) and wife Mary (died 1564). Sons Gabriel and Lancelot are depicted as is daughter Joyce.

R207 East Horsley, Sussex. Thomas Cornwallis (died 1597) and wife Katheryn (died 1626). Their two sons Robert and Henry are shown with some damage.

R208 Ilam, Staffs. Robert Meverell (died 1626) and wife.

R209 Uttoxeter, Staffs. Elizabeth Hussey (died 1523) second wife of Thomas Kynnersley.

R210 Eccleshall, Staffs. Bishop James Bowstead (died 1843). A recumbent bishop in ecclesiastical robes and holding a mitre. He was Bishop of Sodor and Mona, Ely and Lichfield but died in Bristol. Although his obituary was printed in the *Gentleman's Magazine* for 1843 almost nothing can be learnt about the monument.

R211 Rolleston on Dove, Staffs. Thomas Caldwell (died 1555), wife and children. Monument believed to date from 1600.

R212 Standon, Staffs. Nicholas Hyde (died 1526) but may not be alabaster possibly by Richard Parker. *See* R128 for similarities.

R213 Acton Burnell, Shrops. Sir Richard Lee (died 1591) and wife. Unusually, the children are shown kneeling and facing forward behinds the effigies. He was the ancestor of Col Robert E Lee the Confederate leader. His son has a monument (M295).

R214 Shifnal, Shrops. Oliver Brigges (died 1596).

R215 Stoke upon Tern, Shrops. Sir Reginald Corbet, Justice of the King's Bench (died 1566) and wife Alice (Gatwood, died

1603). He was a justice of the King's Bench. The lion at the knight's feet has his tail curled back over its body but not divided. Stoke on Tern, Shrops.

R216 Quatt Malvern, Shrops. Francis Wolryche (died 1614) and wife Margaret who commissioned to tomb. Fine alabaster with gilded details with a black description panel. The tomb chest has reliefs of the children who are named in black lettering. Two the children are damaged.

R217 Litchborough, Northants. Sir John Needham (died 1618). Erected by his wife Elizabeth (Watson) at the time of her second marriage in 1633. It is possible this was once a mural as part of the entablature is mounted on the wall behind. The tomb chest is part alabaster and part a black marble.

R218 Stanford on Avon, Northants. Richard Cave (died 1606 in Padua). A kneeling effigy within an arched tomb.

R219 Aubourn, Lincs. Sir Anthony Meres (died1587). Only the upper torso remains of a destroyed monument which was found when the tower was demolished.

R220 Ashby Folville, Leics. Francis Smith (died 1629) and wife. A fine tomb with a canopy supported by four columns. The tomb chest has empty niches and it is claimed once had figures like R221. The alabaster has very pale veining unlike Fauld.

R221 Ashby Folville, Leics. George Smith (died 1607) and wife. A fine monument with a tomb chest which has figures in the niches. The alabaster has very pale veining unlike Fauld.

R222 Great Mitton, Lancs. Sir Richard Shireburn (died 1594) and wife Maude (Bold, died 1588). The local history records this as a Royley tomb. The end panel has shields supported by a griffon and a unicorn. He rests his head on a great helm with a horse crest and wears a chain collar and long pointed beard. His feet rest on a lion. She wears a strange type of skull cap and hair in ringlets and a curious ruff with over large folds. A chain hangs from her waist with a pendant which reaches down to her feet. All in all an unusual monuments.

R223 Standish, Lancs. Sir Edward Wrightington (died 1658). Pevsner states that this is the 'only noteworthy piece of 17th century work in Lancashire'. Only the effigy is alabaster as the tomb chest is various marbles. The man is in civilian clothes with head on a cushion and feet on a lion.

R224 Frolesworth, Leics. Francis Staresmore (died 1626) erected by his wife (*see* R225). Decorated pillow.

R225 Frolesworth, Leics. Frances Staresmore (died 1657) wife of R224. A curious effigy in a winding sheet reminiscent of the effigy of John Donne in St Paul's, London.

R226 Hackney, London. Lucy, Lady Latimer (died 1582). The tomb was formerly in the Church of St Augustine and was left damaged when that was demolished. The remaining part appears to be the tablet. It was restored by Farmer and Brindley which resulted in some alabaster being replaced by stone. There was minimal work on the effigy which still shows damage.

R227 Hereford Cathedral. Robert Bennett (died 1617). Effigy and parts of monument remain. The monument was mentioned in his will specifying that it should be '... of white alabaster with a picture of a man lying in a white sheet upon an altar of other stone. To be encompassed about with strong iron bars after the example of other tombs in the cathedral'. The tomb has been moved and the bars and tomb chest lost.

R228 Wirksworth, Derbys. Anthony Lowe (died 1558). An effigy in limestone with alabaster panels in tomb chest and in tablet on the wall behind the tomb. The panel states that Lowe served four monarchs. The tomb chest side depicts two angels holding a shield. The rest of the tomb chest is limestone. The panel is painted and the tomb chest side is partially painted – both may be restorations.

R229 Bristol Somerset, St John the Baptist, Tower Lane. The church is redundant. A merchant and his wife *circa* 1550 or later. A possible Renaissance tomb in the crypt except that the tomb chest has angels holding shields and may be much earlier than 1550. She has a late gable hood and he merchant's robes. The cushions may well have the remnants of angels which may also date the tomb to pre-Reformation.

R230 Chenies, Bucks. The private Bedford Chapel attached to Chenies Manor House (M2 on 'The Heraldry of the Bedford Chapel'). Lord Francis Russell (1585) 2nd Earl of Bedford and wife Margaret (St John 1562). There is a suggestion that this is carved by an Italian but the alabaster is deemed to be from the Trent Valley. The tomb has Venetian features. Great helm with goat crest and feet on lion. Considered a likeness including a droop in one eye damaged in 1523.

R231 Margam Abbey, Glamorgan. Sir Thomas Mansel (died 1631) and two wives. Daughters of stone and sons in alabaster.

R232 Margam Abbey, Glamorgan. Sir Lewis Mansel (died 1638) and wife. Dr Adam White observed that there is a similarity between this tomb chest and that supporting Maximillian Colt's 1607 effigy of Princess Mary in Westminster Abbey.

R233 Margam Abbey, Glamorgan. Sir Rice Mansel (died 1559) and wife Cecelia but monument may date from the 1650s. Cecelia was his third wife. He purchased Margam Abbey at the dissolution. The inscription claims they are buried in St Bartholomew (the Great), Smithfield, London.

R234 Checkley, Staffs. Listed in Pevsner. Godfrey Foljambe (died 1560) and wife Margaret (More). Uncertainty as to date and it may be that Margaret died in 1560.

R235 Sudbury, Derbys. John Vernon (died 1600) and wife Mary. Tiered tomb.

R236 Malpas, Cheshire. Sir Hugh Cholmondeley (died 1596) but the tomb may be made *circa* 1601 and second wife Mary. Mary was the widow of Sir Randall Brereton. A fine Renaissance tomb with realistic child carvings. Inscription reads (in Latin):

Hugh Cholmondeley of Cholmondeley the elder, Knight, Vice-Warden of the Welsh Marches, six times sheriff died in his 83rd year, 1596, and in this earth is buried. Also his son and heir, Hugh Cholmondeley, Knight attaining the age of 50 departed this life AD 1601 and lies here. Also his wife the Lady Mary who after the death of her husband, on account of her very dear affection for him, for love of him had this monument erected AD 1605.

R237 Uffington, Berks. Sir John Saunders (died 1599) but may be later. An altar tomb with canopy resting on pilasters with floral decorations, shields and long swags of flowers and fruit, spades and picks. Believed to be the work of a London workshop.

R238 Shottesbrooke, Berks. William Throckmorton (died 1535 but tomb later). The effigy is only 3ft 11 inches long and resides in a coffin. Doctor's flat cap and gown. Brass inscription plate affixed to a slab set across the middle of the effigy.

R239 Turvey, Beds. John Mordaunt, 2nd Baron Mordaunt of Turvey (died 1571) and two wives Eleanor (FitzLewis) and Joan (Fermor). A fine monument with a huge canopy supported by seven alabaster columns. The effigies retain much original paint. John's effigy is raised above those of his two wives. In the same church is a tomb to the 3rd Lord Maudaunt which is reported to have a 'black-painted alabaster pall' which has not been identified.

R240 Turvey, Beds. John Mordaunt, 1st Baron Mordaunt of Turvey (died 1562) and wife Elizabeth (Vere). A fine monument with two recumbent effigies under an arch. He is in civilian robes and she wears a gable hood considered late for the date of carving. The tomb chest has curved sides. The hands held in prayer are horizontal again late for the date. Brian Kemp claims this monument for a carver named as Thomas Kirby.

R241 Bosbury, Hereford. John Harford (died 1559). A very unusual tomb with the tomb chest suspended on animal effigies and a huge canopy supported by columns with a Greek pediment. This tomb is by John Gildon and made in 1573 and signed by him. Possibly the first tomb to carry a signature.

R242 Bosbury, Hereford. Richard Harford (died 1575) and wife Martha Harford. This tomb is by John Gildon and made in 1575.

R243 Wolverhampton, Staffs. John Leveson (died 1575) and wife Joyce. Children holding shields which are carved not painted.

R244 Madley, Hereford. To Richard Willison (died 1575) and wife Ann (Elton). Tomb made *circa* 1585.

R245 Margam Abbey, Glamorgan. Sir Edward Mansel (died 1585). Four kneeling figures. The Mansel Chapel contains a number of alabaster tombs.

R246 Dyrham and Hinton, Avon. Sir George Wynter (died 1581)

R247 Ludlow, Shrops. Sir Robert Townshend & wife Alice. A very ornate effigial tomb in a niche. Richly painted.

R248 Wolverhampton, Staffs. Thomas Lane (died 1582) and wife Katherine. Tomb dates from 1585. Children on tomb chest.

R249 West Hallam, Derbys. Walter Powtrell (died 1598) and wife Cassandra (Shirley).

R250 Rochester Cathedral. Walter de Merton, bishop 1274 to 1277. The bishop originally had a tomb which would not be alabaster. This was destroyed at the time of the Reformation and Sir Henry Savile had a replica in alabaster made in 1598. The bishop founded Merton College, Oxford. The college fathers did not like the effigy and resolved to replace it by a slab in 1849. This did not happen but the tomb was moved.

R251 Fletching, Sussex. Richard Leche (died 1596) and his wife Charity. May have been rebuilt following collapse in 1783.

R252 Bromham, Beds. Sir Lewis Dyves (died 1592). The tomb carved in 1603. The effigy resides on a tomb chest over which is a canopy supported by five columns themselves resting on square pilasters. Dyves grandson, also Lewis, prominent in the Civil War, escaped from the Tower of London in 1647. The tomb displays a rich honey colour but is probably Fauld alabaster.

R253 Much Cowarne, Hereford. Edmund Fox (died 1617) and wife Ann. Ten children grace the tomb chest with three chrisoms at the feet of the effigies. Unusually the chrisoms are in the tomb chest side. The top slab chamfer has a diagonal slashes.

R254 Bath, Abbey church, Somerset. Bishop James Montague (died 1618) but tomb made in 1619. He was the Bishop of Winchester and died there but is buried in Bath. The tomb chest is not alabaster.

R255 Waltham Abbey, Essex. Elizabeth Greville (*circa* 1619). A damaged effigy without tomb chest. Elizabeth was the aunt of Lady Jane Grey. Although generally thought to be 17th century the costume and style is more 16th century.

R256 Truro Cathedral crypt. Two kneeling figures of uncertain identity.

R257 West Wickham, Kent. Probably Samuel Lennard (died 1618). The inscription in Latin would appear to support this attribution but John Lennard has also been named.

R258 Blunham, Beds. Susanna Longueville (Grey), Countess of Kent (died 1620). John Donne (R197) was rector here 1621 to 1626 and almost certainly oversaw the installation.

R259 Chenies, Bucks. The private Bedford Chapel attached to Chenies Manor House (M4 on 'The Heraldry of the Bedford Chapel'). Frances Lady Chandos (died 1623) but tomb possibly dated 1641. The lady rests on one elbow with an embroidered or jewelled dress.

R260 London Westminster. Francis Holles (died 1622). A freestanding monument without canopy made by Nicholas Stone. Francis is depicted sitting on a drum pedestal in Roman armour. His uncle George Holles is also shown nearby also standing in Roman armour.

R261 Audley, Staffs. Edward Vernon, vicar of Welford Gloucs and founder of local school poss died 1623.

R262 Cambridge, Trinity College Chapel. Edward Woodrofe (died 1624). A picture is to be found on page 3 of Llewellyn.

R263 Gloucester. John Walton (alderman, died 1626) and wife Alice.

R264 Worfield, Shrops. Sir George Bromley (died 1589) and wife Jane Waverton.

R265 Worfield, Shrops. Sir Edward Bromley (died 1626) and wife Margaret Lowe.

R266 Inkberrow, Worcs. John Savage of Nobury and Egioke Broome (died 1631). Commissioner of the peace and High Sheriff of Worcs.

R267 Compton Verney House, Warwicks. Richard Verney (died 1636) and wife Margaret. A beautifully carved effigial tomb with likenesses of the deceased. The cushions are decorated and the dress and armour well detailed.

R268 Ludlow, Shrops. Sir John Bridgeman (died 1637). Effigial tomb with low back panels. The alabaster does not appear to have any veining.

R269 Great Brington, Northants. Lord William Spencer (died 1638) and wife. There is a claim that this monument is by Samuel Baldwin.

R270 Gawsworth, Cheshire. Sir Edward Fitton (died 1643) and wife Jane.

R271 Chenies, Bucks. The private Bedford Chapel attached to Chenies Manor House (M3 on 'The Heraldry of the Bedford Chapel'). Francis Russell, 4th Earl of Bedford (died 1641) and wife Catherine (bridges, died 1653).

R272 Draycott in the Moors, Staffs. An unknown member of the Draycot family dated 1662.

R273 London, St Giles in the Fields. Lady Frances Kniveton (died 1663) in shroud said to be effigy.

R274 Sprowston, Norfolk. Sir Thomas Adams (died 1667) and wife. A tiered monument.

R275 Wentworth, Yorks. Thomas Wentworth (died 1587) and second wife Margaret (Gascoigne). An unusual tomb chest which is plain apart from evenly spaced round columns. The effigies display high ruffs and the faces are in good order.

R276 Cobham, Kent. Sir George Brooke, Lord Cobham (died 1558) and his wife Ann (died 1561). A high Renaissance tomb with well carved tomb chest figures in shell-headed niches between ionic columns. This appears to be in Flemish style which has been compared with that of Count Antoine Lallaing in Hoogstratten, Holland which is also alabaster carved by Jan Mone. The tomb in Cobham was a shattered by a falling bean in the 18th century and repaired in 1840 by George Hammerton. Railing installed in 1843. Heraldic beasts at feet of effigies. Nevertheless there are strong similarities in the tomb chest and tomb slab.

R277 Edensor, Derbys. Henry Cavendish (died 1616) and William Cavendish, Earl of Devonshire (died 1626). An unusual effigial tomb with two cadavers under a table tomb. One lies on a rolled mat and the other on a cushion.

R278 Rodney Stoke, Somerset. Anne Rodney (died 1630) the daughter of Sir Thomas Lake(s). A fine effigial tomb with a high arched canopy decorated with stars and clouds. The tomb chest is a sarcophagus. Local Somerset historians suggest this is Watchet alabaster and carved by a 'Dutch' carver. In view of the fact that the Stone workshop may have been exploiting the cliffs at Watchet in this decade this may well be an uncatalogued Stone monument.

R279 Wickhambrook, Suffolk. Sir Thomas Higham (died 1630). He rests on one elbow. This is credited to Nicholas Stone.

R280 Paulerspury, Northants. Sir Arthur Throckmorton (died 1626) and wife. Reclining on one elbow facing each other.

R281 Codsall, Staffs. Walter Wrottesley (died 1630). It is suggested that this was made in a workshop at Ashby de la Zouch but the reasons are not clear. The tomb was erected by his son Hugh.

R282 Brooke, Rutland. Charles Noel (died 1619). A recumbent knight with much original paint intact. Attributable to William Hargrave of Bilborough. The Noel family was also associated with Exton also in Rutland.

R283 Langar, Notts. Sir George Chaworth (died 1589). The rolled mat is curled up under the feet as well as the head and the top surface is carved with scrollwork. This is indicative of the work of William Hargrave.

R284 Saundby, Notts. John Helwys (died 1599) and wife Mary. The strapwork frieze has been identifies with the work of William Hargrave.

R285 Greatham, Hants. Dame Marjory Caryll (died 1632). Formerly in the nave of Greatham Old Church there is a project to protect this in a rebuilt chancel. The current condition is not good having been exposed to damp. The tomb chest has slate inscriptions in niches with angel's heads and outstretched wings and a broken black marble slab. The tomb comprised of a recumbent effigy with a mural canopy with heraldic devices supported by columns in the usual manner. These have been disturbed. The tomb is subject to a conservation plan by SPAB.

R286 Theydon Mount, Essex. Sir Thomas Smyth Bart (died 1668 or 1688).

R287 North Ockendon, Essex. Gabriel Poyntz (died 1607) and Etheldreda (Cutts, died 1594). Large back panel with heraldry and straight canopy. There is a statement that the alabaster 'is imported from France' but it looks very like Fauld.

The magnificent Gothic tomb chest on the Hugh Lupus tomb.

R288 Chester cathedral. Hugh Lupus Grosvenor Duke of Westminster K.G (died 1899). The effigy is probably marble but the tomb chest is in Fauld alabaster with gothic crocketted arcades. The Duke was named after the Norman 1st Earl of Chester who died in 1101.

Two of the apostle heads on the Pearson tomb chest.

R289 Chester Cathedral. John Pearson, Bishop of Chester 1672 to 1686. A leading supporter of the 1662 Prayer Book and possible author of the Creed revised in 1659. The monument was erected in 1863 partly financed by funds raised by William Rollinson Wittingham, Bishop of Maryland, USA. Although principally limestone, the tomb chest include the heads of the twelve apostles in alabaster, four along each side and two at each end.

S1 Lowdham, Notts. Priest *circa* 1520 probably Nicholas Leverson. The inscription states that the priest was under the patronage (Rad Shae) of the Covent and Priory of Westminster. *See also* L26.

S2 Repton, Derbys. Incised slab formerly part of a table tomb now resting against the wall. Gilbert Thacker (died 1563) his wife Katherine, two children and a dog (Greenhill says it is a ridiculous lion but describes the slab on page 273 of GH1). Strange pointed shoes. Thomas Thacker (his father) was steward to Thomas Cromwell and was responsible for pulling down the old Repton Priory. Also a Katherine Blackwell and her children are named dated 1598. There is a second unidentified slab also in Fauld alabaster. The 1563 slab is likened to that at Egmanton, Notts.

S3 Tickhill, Yorks. Reported as three 15th century effigial slabs which need cataloguing. One 'Here lies John Sandford knight who died September of the year ...' *See* P. Farman, P. Hacker, S. Badham, and P. Ryder, 'Incised Slab Discoveries at Tickhill, Yorkshire', 'Transactions of the Monumental Brass Society', 17 (2008), 521–49.

S4 Leicester Cathedral. A 1589 inscribed slab now mounted on the wall of Lady Chapel to John Heyricke. This alabaster slab shows no signs of footfall and may once have been mounted as a tabletop. The source may be latter day Chellaston as the mottling is subdued.

S5 Leicester Cathedral. A 1609 inscribed slab now mounted on the wall of Lady Chapel to Robert Ormgood. This alabaster slab shows no signs of footfall and may once have been mounted as a tabletop. The source may be latter day Chellaston as the mottling is subdued.

S6 Burton on Trent, Staffs. A wall-mounted incised slab once forming part of a tabletop tomb depicting William Dethick and his wife Margaret dating from 1497. The Dethick home being Newhall. The alabaster is claimed to be Fauld by the town but is very pale and may well be Chellaston. The Burton History website claims Dethick was a priest and gives the history of the movement around the church. However, the Dethick family website claims that William was the patron and it was his son John who was the priest. It was placed upright in the bell tower in 1884. Horse head crest and feet on Talbot with children along the bottom edge.

S7 Chesterfield, Derbys. George Foljambe (died 1588). A slab attributable to Garrett Hollemans.

S8 Queenhill, Worcs. Henry Field (died 1584) and his two wives, Anna who died in 1572 and Sybil who survived him (as her date of death is left blank). An early slab from the Hollemans workshop. This was formerly in the floor but in 1913 was reported to be set against the south wall of the nave. This is reputed to be one of the earliest surviving Hollemans slabs. Greenhill describes this slab in Vol 1 but no picture is forthcoming.

S9 Packington, Leics. A slab to Ralph Leeson (died 1587) and his two wives, Elizabeth Dethick (died 1581) and Ursula Poole (died 1586). An early form of tall hat. John and Thomas Spencer recorded in 1894 that this slab was unknown until the brick floor was taken up to install an organ when this and two other slabs were found underneath. The slab was in good condition but broken. Bayliss has identified this as from the Hollemans workshop. Greenhill links this to Hornsey (S10). When this was buried is the subject of speculation. Burton, in 1622, makes no mention although he refers to the tomb of Thomas Leeson, 1539 but it appears that a new floor was laid and oddly seems to have buried this a two other slabs.

S10 Hornsey, Middlesex. George Rey born in Brewood Staffs died *circa* 1590 and two wives and kneeling son. A fine slab attributable to Jasper Hollemans. An image is shown as Greenhill Vol 2 fig 127a. The wives are slightly behind husband and display French hoods. Greenhill links this to Packington (S9).

S11 Everton, Notts. An unidentified worn slab with a Latin inscription which reads '… and Joan his wife daughter and one of the heiresses of the lady mother of Michael ... he died July 1440 and the said Joan died …'

S12 Whatton, Notts. Slab of Thomas Cranmer (died 1501). Thomas was the father of Archbishop Cranmer. Inscription in Latin. A squire in long robes with symbols of station. Long hair. Bell mouth cuffs of gown.

S13 Thakeham, Sussex. William Apsley (died 1527).

S14 Pitchford, Shropshire. Thomas Ottley (died 1534) and his wife Katherine. A fine well carved effigy of a knight in 15th century armour with the wife in a final version of the gable hood. Latin inscription. This slab is attributable to the Royley workshop and therefore likely to be post-1540 in light of the gable hood. Greenhill (Vol 1 page 21) suggests that this was the workshop's first slab. Unusually the effigy includes a pen holder attached by a sash to the waist band.

S15 Quorndon, Leics (Quorn). Francis Farnham (died 1557) recorder of Leicester and wife Margery (Cave). A finely carved slab showing a man in civilian robes and text in bottom third. MQS bonnet. Sally Badham in 2004 offered the opinion that the slab has been polychromed and gilded.

S16 Quorndon, Leics (Quorn). Robert Farnham (died 1560) and wife Mary Langham. A finely carved slab with man in civilian robes and bottom third covered in text. Sally Badham in 2004 offered the opinion that the slab has been polychromed and gilded.

S17 Belton, Rutland. Thomas Haselwood (died 1558) and wife Clemence Samwell possibly on old tomb chest. There are medieval stone effigies imbedded in the church perimeter wall. These are reported not to be alabaster but how they came to be used such is a mystery.

S18 Ipsley, Warwicks. Sir John Huband (died 1583) and wife Mary (Thockmorton). The slab may have been carved as early as 1558 as it attributed to the Royley workshop in that period. She has a long pediment headdress – odd for such a late date.

S19 Claverley, Shrops. William Gatacre (died 1577) and wife Helen (Mitton). A fine inscribed slab with a row of children at the feet of a knight and lady. Latin inscription but date in English. This slab is attributed to the Royley workshop. Compare with S20. Ruff.

S20 Claverley, Shrops. Possibly slab to Francis Gatacre (died 1599) and Elizabeth Swynnerton. This slab is attributed to the Hollemans workshop. A civilian and lady with inscription mainly in English at the foot of the carving. Words divided by dots. Compare with S19.

S21 Burbage, Leics. Richard Wightman (died 1578) and wives Mary Reynalds and Dame Margaret Booth widow of Marmaduke Constable. This slab has been removed from the floor and mounted on the wall possibly in 1857. French hood.

S22 Egmanton, Notts. Nicholas Powdrill, Justice of assizes (died 1573 or 1579) and two wives. Greenhill states that the carving is unskilled.

S23 Grendon, Warwicks. Margaret wife of William Chetwynd (died 1538). Slab dates from 1539. Pediment headdress, loose sleeves and long skirt. Hands in prayer with rosary. Chrisom which is named as William Chetwynd. Possibly brought from Ingestre along with R123. Margaret was the stepmother of William.

S24 Market Drayton, Shrops. Thomas Bulkeley (died 1595) and wife Elizabeth Grosvenor (died *circa* 1585). Possibly a tabletop at one time now hidden away in vestry and showing signs of a horizontal fracture. Thomas is in civilian robes and Elizabeth has high piled hair and tall hat. The Bulkeleys are reputed to be related to three presidents of the USA, Calvin Coolidge and both Georges Bush.

S25 Nailstone, Leics. Thomas Corbet (or Corbett) who died 1586 and who was chief sergeant of the pantry to the Tudors. Half effigy with curious verses. Inscription no longer legible but Nichols recorded details some 300 years ago.

S26 Teversal, Notts. Slab to Anne Greenehalghe (nee Babington). She died in 1538. This is believed to a cross slab in the old form of single large cross the entire length of the slab. This is unusually late for such a design. No carver is listed for this unlike Catherine's husband Roger who died in 1562 and which is described in S27. The date is in Latinised Roman and difficult to interpret.

S27 Teversal, Notts. Slab to Roger Greenehalghe (died 1562) husband of S26. This is believed to be a Parker slab in the conventional form. The slab is said to be place over the grave of Roger. He left a will and his executor was Gervase Clifton. Inscription begins 'Orate pro anima' or a prayer for the dead which is quite unusual for the date.

S28 Wells, Somerset. Bishop Beckington (*circa* 1465). The effigy is in wood but lies on a slab of alabaster. Beneath is freestone effigy depicting a copse in a winding sheet.

S29 Nottingham, St Mary's church. A slab showing St Thomas of Canterbury with Pope Alexander III found under the floor of the sanctuary and now set into the south wall of the chapel.

S30 Rolleston on Dove, Staffs. Sir John Rolleston (died 1485) and wife Margaret. Placed vertical in 1885 and possibly recut.

S31 Melton Mowbray, Leics. Slab to Edward Pate (died 1597) and his wife Katherine (died 1593) and their 11 children. He wears the robes of a master of the mint. A simple but fine cut slab.

S32 Beckbury, Shropshire. A slab to Richard Haughton (died 1505) and wife Margaret. *British History Online* claims this slab was moved to the north wall of chancel in 1856 'when the altar tomb on the north wall was destroyed'. *See* R188.

S33 Orton on the Hill, Leics. William Foster (died 1511) and wife. It is reported that another slab dating from 1515 to John Bradschawe and wife also remains in the church but this has yet to be found.

S34 Atcham, Shrops. Sir Edward Burton (died 1524) and wife Josai (or Joyce or Jocase). This slab was formerly in St Chad's Shrewsbury and moved *circa* 1788 after that church fell into disrepair. This is under suspicion for being recut. The lady's dress is probably original but the head seems to have been restored. The headdress shows a frontlet but no gable and the hair is long. Canopy, children, inscription are probably original.

S35 Rowington, Warwicks. John Oldnall (died 1558) bailiff and wife Isobel. The church has a number of inscribed slabs.

S36 Hope Under Dinmore, Hereford. Humphrey Conyngsbye (died 1559) and wife Anne Englefield. She has a French hood. Pevsner says slab is later than 1559.

S37 Wednesbury, Staffs. John Comberford or Comberforce (died 1559) and wife. The slab was exposed during the 1880s widening of the chancel.

S38 Wednesbury, Staffs. Richard Jennyngs (died 1521) and wife. The slab was exposed during the 1880s widening of the chancel.

S39 Pitchford, Shrops. A slab to William Ottley (died 1530) and wife Margery. Greenhill attributes this slab to the Royleys but either the slab is later than 1530 or this is in error.

S40 Pitchford, Shrops. A slab to Adam Ottley (died 1578) and wife Mary (died 1587). This is rare being signed by the carver. The style of carving is unlike the other two in the same church although one (to Richard Ottley who died 1686) is signed I.T. 1587– *see* S14 and S39. Also *see* B148. Greenhill praised the quality of these slabs and illustrated one as Vol 2 Fig 87a. The illustration shows a spiral border and heads slightly too small for the body. Fussy scrollwork at top and at bottom enclosing an inscription.

S41 Quorndon, Leics (Quorn). Thomas Farnham (died 1502) and wife Margaret Kingston. A slab with incised figures and text around the edge. It is described in the 'Antiquities of Leicestershire'. A knight in armour and a lady with a long pediment headdress with cinquefoil embroidered on lappet. It is likened to that in Rothley (TT7).

S42 Quorndon, Leics (Quorn). William Farndon (died 1548) and wife Dorothy Nevill. A fine carved slab with text on bottom third. Sally Badham in 2004 offered the opinion that the slab has been polychromed and gilded.

S43 Spare

S44 Rolleston on Dove, Staffs. Edward Rolston (died 1615), Rector, partially defaced. In civilian clothes.

S45 Shrewsbury, St Mary, Shrops. Nicholas Stafford (died 1471) and wife Catherine Merevell (died 1463).

S46 Bardney, Lincs. A slab attributed to Abbot Richard Horncastle (died 1508). The slab was originally in Barney Abbey (suppressed 1538) and was found during excavation 1914. This is a particularly nice slab with the abbot dressed in mass vestments and with his soul going up to heaven in a napkin beneath a canopy.

S47 Bardney, Lincs. A damaged slab of which only the words John and Joyce and the date 1446 can be read. The slab like S46 was originally in Barney Abbey and discovered in 1910. Figure is set on a tiled pavement.

S48 Ashby de la Zouch, Leics. Robert Mundy (died 1526) and wives both Elizabeth. This was removed from the floor when the church was reordered in 1829 and mounted vertical on the west wall. The slab is considered good for the period. This is the only slab of many which has survived the re-pewing of 1829. Greenhill observes that the cap shown under the frontlet of the gable headdress is much larger than normal. One lady has a striped bodice.

S49 Ashby Folville, Leics. Ralph Woodward or Wodford (died 1498). An unusual slab which may at one time been a tabletop. The image is one of a naked skeletal man in a winding sheet which is drawn across his lower body by his left hand. There are two foliated crosses and he has his feet on a greyhound. There is script in Latin on both the edges and in scrolls one of which is an extract from Job chapter 19. The slab dates from 1485 as the date of 1498 in the edge script is added in a smaller hand. Nichols observed in 1800 that this slab was headless and recent investigations indicate that this may well be true, the original carver failing to complete the head under the pitch applied for setting out the drawing. It may well be that as the slab was created in Ralph's lifetime the carver who delayed carving the head until the visage of Ralph in death was seen. In the intervening 13 years the carver himself may have died and on Ralph's death the missing head was not noticed. The Woodford family was in considerable disarray at the time. The slab is now complete with head which may well have been added later (after 1800). For more details *see The Woodforde Family – Sir Ralph Woodford 1430–1498* available on the internet. Figure 103 of Sally Badham's book *Seeking Salvation* shows this slab.

S50 Skeffington, Leics. Thomas Skeffington (died 1543) and Margaret (Stanhope died 1539). A drawing of this slab is shown in CMS-CG and shows a knight and his lady with children at their feet. It is badly worn and only the bottom part of the panel is discernible.

S51 Turnastone, Hereford. Thomas Aparri (died 1522) and wife. A slab believed to be by Harpur and Moorecock but by this date Moorecock had died. Apparri may translate to ap Harry.

S52 Noseley, Leics. Thomas Haselrige (died 1525). Attributed to Harpur and Moorecock but by 1525 the latter had died.

S53 Burton Joyce, Notts. Sir Brian Stapiltun (Stapleton) *circa* 1550. Greenhill considered this slab to be a unique if clumsy, depiction of Maximilian armour.

S54 Ratcliffe on Soar, Notts. Isobel Babington (died 1487). This slab is linked with other late 15th century slabs – *see* L25. The Babingtons lived in the manor of Kingston on Soar which in the 15th century had just a chapel which meant that they had to be buried in the mother church. Greenhill says that slab is under the organ which is now untrue as the organ has been moved. *See* Appendix X for details of inscription

S55 King's Norton, Warwicks. Humfrey Toye (died 1515). There was a sketch made in 1826 by the antiquary Dr Peter

Prattinton.

S56 Saxelby, Leics. Robert Brokesby (died 1531). Now set on the wall.

S57 Newbold on Avon, Warwick. Geoffrey Allesley (died 1401) and wife Alianor. Once was a tabletop and used for seating. Graffiti in the form of nine men's morris carved on top.

S58 Lockington, Leics. Thomas Malle (1509) and wife. Greenhill claims the surname is Whitby but no evidence for this can be found. He also gives the date as 1545.

S59 Lockington, Leics. William Mylnegate farmer (died 1555) and wife Agnes. Upper part damaged.

S60 Kedleston, Derbys. William Curzon (died 1547). This is linked to S58 as the effigy is very similar and only varies in small details.

S61 Blithfield, Staffs. Sir Lewis Bagot (died 1534) and three of his five wives. The first wife Emma is shown and second wife unknown of which only the head is visible. The lady has pediment lappets which are adorned with jewels. This has been reported as 1508 but is unlikely. The slab has only a narrow inscription on the perimeter. The knight has his head on a great helm with a goat crest. A large group of mourners which may well be the children at the bottom. These are well carved with different facial expressions. One wife Ann (Montgomery, died 1513) was intended to buried here but is in Patshull under a slab of her own. The central figure is shown as a head only and strangely has long hair usually only used to denote a maiden. The Lichfield list of 1532 (B200) gives Sir Lewis and names his wives as Emma and Margaret.

S62 Blithfield, Staffs. Jane daughter of Richard Astley of Patshull (died 1557). Wife of Thomas Bagot. The Lichfield list of 1532 (B200) gives Thomas and lists his wife Jane and children Margaret and Maud.

S63 Blithfield, Staffs. Francis Aston of Patshull (died 1593) and wife Mary. Outer hood over French hood.

S64 Blithfield, Staffs. Walter Broughton (died 1586) at the aged of three months the son of Richard Broughton. A strange slab with the inscription in the lower quarter in Old English script. The image shows death carrying away a small child. The arms of Broughton and Bagot are also shown. The Quorndon slabs (S15, S16 and S42) all show text in bottom quarter of the slab. The Blithfield slab is much cruder and may reflect the declining quality of the Royley workshop claimed in some quarters whilst retaining some of the original style.

S65 Peckleton, Leics. Thomas Harvey (died 1544) and two wives Philippa and Isabel. This is now mounted on the wall and may once have been a tabletop tomb. The styles of the two ladies show the changing fashion. The older woman has pediment long since discarded by the young, whilst the younger woman has a French hood without veil. The gowns of both are like that of Jane Purefey's at Fenny Drayton (GNP50).

S66 Stanton by Bridge, Derbys. William Sacheverell (died 1558) and wife Mary (Lowe). The local history claims that this was formerly a tabletop in the nave but is now set against the chancel wall probably in 1866. Greenhill says that this slab is particularly good and gives a long description in GH1 (266). For other Sacheverell tombs *see* Morley, Derbys and Ratcliffe on Soar and Barton, Notts.

S67 Stanton by Bridge, Derbys. Katherine Francis (died 1530) wife of Richard Francis. This is also set in the wall of the chancel probably in 1866.

S68 Kirk Langley, Derbys. Henry Poole (or Pole) MP (died 1559) and wife Alice (or Dorothy). An inscription names him as the church patron. Linked to S67.

S69 Noseley, Leics. Bertin Hazelrigg or Hasilrige (died 1565). A worn slab.

S70 Adwick le Street, Yorks. James Washington (died 1580) and wife. He wears a civilian hat. The treatment of the children on both this and the slab at Sprotbrough indicate the same workshop but whilst this slab has contemporary depiction of armour that at Sprotbrough has an armour style some 100 years out of date (TT31). The head is turned half sideways to show veil dropping down behind, ruff. Shield of arms placed over effigy.

S71 Aston Botterell, Shrops. John Botterell (died 1588) and wife Mary.

S72 Selby Abbey, Yorks. Bishop John de Shireburn (died 1407) in a mitre. He was the 27th abbot.

S73 Selby Abbey, Yorks. Bishop Laurence Selby (died 1504) in a mitre. This slab is badly worn.

S74 Lockington, Leics. Robert Scales, priest (died 1540) with chalice and wafer.

S75 Derby Cathedral. Canon John Lawe (died 1480). He is shown in the act of blessing the chalice. Derby was a former collegiate church. Greenhill praises this as one of the finest slabs. Side niches contain figures of coped priests each with a chalice and some seven mourners in a funeral procession. Virgin Mary and child are also depicted. Figure 89 of Sally Badham's book *Seeking Salvation* shows this slab.

S76 Noseley, Leics. Margaret Heron (died 1402 or 1406) but badly worn. Her daughter married a Hazelrigge and so Noseley passed into that family.

S77 Noseley, Leics. Thomas Hesylrige (died 1467) wearing a salet. The slab also shows his wife.

S78 Shrewsbury, Shrops. Nicholas Stafford (died 1471) and wife Catherine. Slab dates to 1473 and unusually shows a Yorkist collar of suns and roses. Moved in 1825 and possibly once a tabletop.

S79 Breedon on the Hill, Leics. Henry Wynter (died 1494) and wife. Partial slab with upper part missing. *See also* S81.

S80 Sandon, Staffs. Sampson Erdeswyke (died 1545) and wife Elizabeth. The Lichfield list of 1532 (B200) gives Samson and lists his wife as Elizabeth with children Richard, Frances, Amy, Hugh and John.

S81 Breedon on the Hill, Leics. A member of the Wynter family (died *circa* 1545), possibly Robert or George and wife of Worthington.

S82 Smisby, Derbys. William Kendall (died 1548) and wife Anne (Austrey). Damage to upper part of male effigy.

S83 Whitmore, Staffs. Edward Mainwaring (died 1580) and wife Alice. Made during lifetime. May now be hidden.

S84 Standon, Staffs. Francis Rose (died 1562) and wife. The name is also spelt Roos. A well-carved slab with fourteen children.

S85 Willesley, Derbys. George Abney (died 1571) and wife Ellen. Badly worn.

S86 Willesley, Derbys. John Abney (died 1505) and wife Maria. Badly worn.

S87 Prestbury, Cheshire. Jasper Worth (died 1572) and wife Alice Draycott (died 1596). Her date is added later. The slab is now in the wall having been removed when the church was cleared of all monuments. The inscription is contained in Earwaker's book page 195.

S88 Over Peover, Cheshire. Philip Meymmaringe or Mainwaring (died 1573) and wife Anne (Leycester). Children –all facing forward – are named with an apostrophe substituted for the letter 'n'.

S89 Over Peover, Cheshire. John Mainwaring (died 1515) and wife Katherine (died 1529). Thirteen sons and daughters are listed. This slab is listed by Greenhill as 1586 or 1589 and shows distinct Trent Valley features and so fits the Royley workshop (*see* S88). Why it was created some 60 years after the deceased is unclear. Amongst the small figures is clergyman John Mainwaring (son) in surplice and stole, clutching a book and with a chalice, flagon and wafer. John's head is on a great helm with an ass crest.

S90 King's Norton, Warwicks. Humphrey Littleton (died 1588) and wife Martha (Gower). Ruff and French hood.

S91 Ashbourne, Derbys. Sir Thomas Cockayne (died 1590 although in some quarters the date is given as 1537) and wife Barbara (FitzHerbert).

S92 Chellaston, Derbys. John Bancrofte (died 1557) and wife Alice. Worn. Bassano noted in 1710 that there were 'many monuments to the Bancroft family' nearly all illegible but none exist.

S93 Marston on Dove, Derbys. Francis Lathburye (died 1560) and wife. Part damaged.

S94 Matlock, Derbys. Anthony Woolley (died 1576) and wife, Agnes. Made during lifetime probably 1560.

S95 Packington, Leics. Robert Leeson (defaced) bailiff and wife Margaret (died 1560). MQS bonnet.

S96 Solihull, Warwick. Thomas Greswolde (died 1577) and three wives Alice (died 1537), Jane and Isobel. Slab found under seats in aisle in 1879.

S97 St Mary de Castro, Leicester. Richard Ruding (died 1582) and wife who may have died *circa* 1543. Stated as crude. Holding hands.

S98 Bushbury, Staffs. John Colley, son of Francis vicar of Bushbury (died 1593). Epitaph.

S99 Kirkby Mallory, Leics. Richard Dilke (died 1594) and wives Anne Robertes and Elizabeth Ashton. Widow's hood over French hood.

S100 Shouldham Thorpe, Norfolk. Thomas Buttes (died 1600) shown kneeling at a prayer desk. Mainly marble with inlays of alabaster. The old church was demolished *circa* 1857 and rebuilt. The slab is mounted on the wall like a tablet and it is possible the whole was reassembled when the church was rebuilt. The frame is alabaster as is the rectangular panel with the inscribed image.

S101 Noseley, Leics. Margaret Blaket (died 1406), wife of John Blaket. The image is shown in Greenhill Vol 2 Fig 141a. The lady is somewhat worn but shows a canopy. Possibly the first slab to show a woman in 15th century dress. Greenhill detected the remnants of an SS collar which is rare on a slab.

S102 Noseley, Leics. Mary Stafford (died *circa* 1610), wife of William Stafford. Only a fragment remaining.

S103 Croxall, Staffs. John Curzon (died 1350) and wife Inocentia. Reported to be one of 'several'. Pointed bascinet. This was at one point reported as lost.

S104 Doveridge, Staffs. Ralph Okeover (died 1495) and wife Agnes. Great helm.

S105 Radbourne, Derbys. Peter de la Pole (died 1432) and wife Joan. Possible has been moved.

S106 Little Wilne, Derbys. Hugo Willoughby of Risley (died 1491) and wife Isabella daughter of Gervase Clifton (died 1462). Hands are crossed. She may have a butterfly headdress. Church damaged by fire in 1917 and restored in the

1920s.

S107 Darley Dale, Derbys. John Rollesley (died 1513) and wife Elizabeth (Cheney). A very nice drawing of this can be found in 'The Andrew's Pages Picture Gallery: Derbyshire'. Canopy, sons and daughters. She has long pediment with the cap visible. Compare with S174.

S108 Melbourne, Derbys. Henry Hardie (died 1613) and wife Elizabeth. She displays a French hood with hooped outer hood. Said to be crude.

S109 Melbourne, Derbys. Anne Harding (died 1673) wife of Robert Harding. Half length in elliptical frame. Long hair falling in curls.

S110 Melbourne, Derbys. Sir Robert Harding (died 1679).

S111 Morley, Derbys. Ralph son of Jacinth Sacheverell (died 1625) holding a skull in his hands. A small slab.

S112 Morley, Derbys. Richard son of John Harpur, rector (died 1660) bust in oval.

S113 Long Whatton, Leics. Robert Whatton (died 1577) and wife Margaret. The slab is only a fragment with a shield and a few letters but has been researched by John Swift Whatton who states that both died in the same month of September and the same year.

S114 Croxall, Staffs. Edward Mynors (died 1530) in chrisom robes. A Mynor is believed to have married into the Curzon family but the background to this slab is obscure.

S115 Croxall, Staffs. John Howes (died 1554) in chrisom robes.

S116 Croxall, Staffs. John and Mary Curzon (*circa* 1480) children of Thomas Curzon.

S117 Croxall, Staffs. William Shepherd of Okeley (died 1500) and wife Elena. Worn.

S118 Croxall, Staffs. Thomas Curzon (*circa* 1485) and wife Margaret. Close on the floor to S116. The *Sketch of Croxall* printed in 1881 records another Thomas Curzon with wives Anne and Elizabeth but these are now believed to be lost.

S119 Croxall, Staffs. William Curzon (died 1487) son of John Curzon. Shown in chrisom robes.

S120 Croxall, Staffs. John Horton (died 1520) and Anna his wife.

S121 Croxall, Staffs. George Curzon (died 1605) in armour and wife Katherine. She displays a French hood and farthingale.

S122 Ratcliffe on Soar, Notts. James Eadmundson (died 1519) in chrisom robes. A small slab in the chancel. The details of the inscription were recorded by Thoroton but are now lost.

S123 Ratcliffe on Soar, Notts. A fragment of a 16th century lady close to the tomb of Ralph Sacheverell.

S124 Brooksby, Leics. Henry Villiers (died 1480) and wife.

S125 Hoby, Leics. Mary Sharpe (died 1567) wife of John Sharpe.

S126 Clifton, Notts. Eleanor Milford (*circa* 1520) reported to be a nun by Thoroton.

S127 Clifton, Notts. Isabel (Isabella) Clifton (died 1457) wife of Sir Gervase Clifton. Some damage to head. Latin inscription recorded by Thoroton. There is a slab fragment which is Rosslyn Bruce (*The Clifton Book*) could just read the name Isabelle and 1403 who is believed to be the wife of G133.

S128 Ratcliffe on Soar. Notts. Edward Trowell (died 1663), Yeoman. The slab was not found by Greenhill as it lay buried. During the positioning of two sandstone slabs the buried alabaster slab of Edward Trowell was found in the churchyard after the roots of an old elm which was blown down in a gale were excavated. It was recovered *circa* 1980 and placed in the church in a fragmented state. There is no image and the poor condition shows why alabaster was rarely used for external monuments. A stone sarcophagus was found at the same time and also lies in the church.

Photos: John Allen 1970.

S129 Thurlaston, Leics. Mary Turvyle (died 1440), daughter of William Turvyle partially lost.

S130 Staunton, Notts. Robert Staunton (died 1582) son of Anthony Staunton. A strange slab with a wide inscription border and no image. The incised motif is a shield with the letters R and S and a scroll with a motto and a panel with inscription.

S131 Winkburn, Notts. William Burnel (died 1570). Stiff pose with high-collared gown and coif. Large inscription lettering. An unusual slab which was once a tabletop as noted by Pevsner. He was auditor to Henry VIII.

S132 Mavesyn Ridware, Staffs. David Cordon (died 1557) and wife Maud.

S133 Mavesyn Ridware, Staffs. John Cordon (died 1477) and wife Elizabeth (died 1485). Daughters wearing turban head-dresses. Greenhill considered the work crude.

S134 Mavesyn Ridware, Staffs. John Cordon (died 1585).

S135 Mavesyn Ridware, Staffs. Hugo Davenport (died 1473 or 1478). Illustrated in Andrew Oliver's book Figure 4.

S136 Langar, Notts. Thomas Flowre (died 1537) a local bailiff. Upper part is effaced.

S137 Melbourne, Derbys. Unidentified slab to a Thomas (*circa* 1530) and wife partially effaced.

S138 Sandon, Staffs. The Erdeswike slabs *circa* 1600 made by Sampson Erdeswike (died 1603). The commemorated people are Hugh and Cecile Erdeswike (1473) and Hugh Erdeswike (1501). Sampson was an antiquary and probably just commissioned the slabs. He is also buried at Sandon (S80). The carver has depicted armour of an earlier time. In 1881 Andrew Oliver recorded three other slabs to Maybrow Walkerdyne (1433) and two other Erdeswike slabs none of which are currently known.

S139 Thurlaston, Leics. Richard Turville (died 1563) and Wife Babington (died 1584).

S140 Stapleford. Notts. Robert Teverey (died 1571) and wife Katherine. An alabaster floor stone near the monument in the south aisle. *See* Throsby Vol 2, 197; for the inscription. W.S. Sep. I, 1818. Farthingale which may mean the slab carved a little later.

S141 Blithfield, Staffs. John Bagot (died 1512) and wife Helen (Boteler). The inscription was incised but has been copied onto brass.

S142 Blithfield, Staffs. John Bagot (died 1480) and two wives Isabella (Curzon) and Agneta (Kniveton). The inscription is worn out and only the date of 14th Oct 1480 survives. Ashmole noted this.

S143 Blithfield, Staffs. Salusbury Bagot (died 1673) aged two. The son of Walter Bagot. Death carrying away a small child.

S144 Blithfield, Staffs. Sons of Thomas Colwich (died 1508). This broken slab depicts two knights in armour believed to be brothers one of which may be called Lodowici (Lewis) and who died in 1487. The inscription was incised but has been copied onto brass the details of which have been disputed and which refers to a lady called Jacose or Jocose.

S145 Blithfield, Staffs. Thomas Bagot (died 1541) and wife Jane (died 1557). It is unclear whether only Jane is depicted on the slab. She looks to the right instead of the conventional forward.

S146 South Scarle, Notts. Sir William Mering (died 1510).

S147 Noseley, Leics. William Hesilrige (died 1474) and wife. Upper part now lost.

S148 Dauntsey, Wilts. John Delvale (died 1455) and wife Joan (Dauntsey). John was her third husband. This is linked to that at Newbold on Avon (S149).

S149 Newbold on Avon, Warwicks. Eleanor and Geoffrey Allesley (*circa* 1441).

S150 Grove, Notts. Hugh Hercy (died 1455) and wife Elizabeth (Leake). A cartoon-like image showing Hugh in armour but with a merchant's hat with feathers. She has a steeple headdress shown at an angle. The facial features are unfinished and crude. A dog is carved at the foot of Hugh and at the bottom are tufts of grass. The slab has been poorly restored at some time in what seems to be in order to repair a crack. Oddly the repair appears to be in Chellaston alabaster.

S151 Strelley, Notts. John de Strelley (died 1421) and wife Joan.

S152 Strelley, Notts. Sir Robert de Strelley (died 1438).

S153 Norbury, Derbys. Henry Prynce or Prince (died 1500), rector. Wearing vestments and holding a challis. Head on cushion under a crocketted canopy.

S154 Barlow, Derbys. Robert Barley or Barlow (died 1467) and wife Margaret. This is now mounted vertically. A collar of suns and roses can be seen. Robert was the brother of the Anne who married Thomas Cockayne of Youlgreave (G64).

S155 Netherseal, Derbys. Roger Doulton (died 1500) rector.

S156 Doveridge, Derbys. Thomas de la Pole (died 1359), vicar in mass vestments. Andrew Oliver claimed this is Robert Kniveton in 1881.

S157 Ratcliffe on Soar, Notts. John Prescott (died 1497), priest in mass vestment and tonsure. Prescott was a nominee of Burscough priory, Lancs. His head is on a tasselled cushion to dexter of which is placed a chalice and to the sinister a clasped missal. The marginal inscription running from top sinister corner anti-clockwise is now much damaged and in places obliterated. There is a late 15th century fragment of a slab of which only 'Henric' can be made out.

S158 Ratcliffe on Soar, Notts. Hector Ryding (died 1505 aged 70), priest in mass vestment and tonsure. There was a canopy, challis and a scroll with a quotation from Job which now cannot be read. The chasuble has a psi orphrey. On the feet are round-toed shoes. The shaftless canopy was apparently of three gables of which only the dexter survives. The marginal inscription begins at top sinister corner running anti-clockwise.

S159 Sprotbrough, Yorks. Margaret Tatersall (died 1458). The inscription sates she was an anchoress of Doncaster which is believed to be St Edmund's Hospital.

S160 Hinton on the Green, Gloucs. William Halford (died 1490) abbot of Bordesley. In mass vestments but without mitre. Reputed to have been unearthed in 1740.

S161 Wawne, Yorks. Thomas Burton (died 1437) abbot of Meaux Abbey. A much damaged slab of an abbot credited with the writing of history of the abbey. The slab is believed to have been removed from the abbey and placed in a garden before finding a home in Wawne.

S162 Bardney, Lincs. Richard Horncastle (died 1508) abbot. Reported as being fine. Mass vestments.

S163 Clevedon, Somerset. Thomas Lovell (died 1415). Linked to that at Grafton Regis (TT22).

S164 Eastrington, Yorks. Thomas de Portington (died 1427) and Agnes his wife according to Greenhill.

S165 Rufford, Lancs. Thomas Hesketh of Rufford (died 1463) and wife Margaret.

S166 Malpas, Cheshire. Urian Davenport (died 1495) one time rector and vicar of Acton. He is in Eucharistic vestments with his head on a cushion. There is an edge inscription in Latin. The slab is much worn.

S167 Penkridge, Staffs. William Wynnesbury (died 1502) and wife Katherine. Long pediment.

S168 Etwall. Derbys. Richardus and Johana (surname illegible) *circa* 1503. Found during 1881 alternations and now filling the priests door. Greenhill (GH1 page 268) says the partial surname is ... hyll. Mourning dress without veil or barbe.

S169 Ashbourne. Derbys. John Cockayne (died 1504) and wife Ann (Vernon). Originally laid in the floor, it was later mounted on the wall but now shown as a tabletop. Only the shields can be seen.

S170 Whichford, Warwicks. Priest possibly John Merton (died 1510) but slab not made until 1537. Mass vestments. A fine slab. Greenhill claims that the fur lining of the cassock can been seen protruding from around the neck which he considers unique. Linked to TT4.

S171 Staveley, Derbys. John Frecheville (died 1509).

S172 Crich, Derbys. Reputed to be John Clay (died 1583) and wife Mary. A quaint note complains that one Joseph Mather, an ignorant fellow, who taught school in the church allowed the boys to climb on the tomb thus erasing the inscription. The slab may have been a tabletop and date from 1603. The lady displays a French hood. Greenhill suggests the slab was carved by a different hand to that of the former tomb sides. The church is fully carpeted and the slab is not visible.

S173 Crich, Derbys. Godfrey Beresford (died 1513). He was a servant to George, Earl of Shrewsbury. The church is fully carpeted and the slab is not visible.

S174 Darley Dale, Derbys. John Rollesley (died 1534) and wife Agnes (Hybalt) who died 1550. This lab is much smaller that the norm. It is like S107 but the canopy has been replaced by a curtain. Gable hood. This slab and S107 is a good study in changing styles bridging the Reformation changes. The daughters are shown in French hoods.

S175 Darley Dale, Derbys. A Columbell family slab of uncertain date which was reported to have been removed to the churchyard in 1877, but subsequently restored to the church as reported by Cox when it was placed in a vertical position in the south aisle. The local history speaks about this slab in the past and it may not exist. It may have been to Thomas and Agnes Columbell (1540) according to Andrew Oliver (1881).

S176 Norbury, Staffs. Benedicta FitzHerbert (died 1531) wife of John FitzHerbert. A badly worn slab which depicts the lady in a shroud.

S177 Edgmond, Shrops. Nicholas de Peshale (died 1425) rector. Greenhill reports that this slab had been cut in pieces to repair the fabric the details of which can be found in Vol 1 page 124.

S178 Ledbury, Hereford. Edward Cooper (died 1596) archdeacon of Hereford and master of St Katherine's Hospital, Ledbury. Partially coloured. This fine slab has been placed vertically for protection. The gown is not reminiscent of a cleric and he has a skull-cap and holds a book. Inscription.

S179 Saddington, Leics. Richard Holland (died 1628). One of the rare country Protestant clergy slabs. In cassock and surplice.

S180 Glossop, Derbyshire. William Deusnape (died 1572) but slab may date from 1560. A clergyman who served fewer than three monarchs but is shown in civilian dress. The slab is small being 2ft by 18 inches and is arranged as a family group depicting the parents, brother and sister. He holds a book and a hammer and trowel are to be seen. The slab was removed by Christopher Howe *circa* 1831–1833 and given to a surgeon on which to mix his ointments. It was then discarded and stood outside but rescued again in 1893 and is now in the church. There is an inscription. For more details see the 'Transactions of the Lancashire and Antiquarian Society 1886'.

S181 Bletchley, Bucks. Thomas Sparke (died 1616) rector. Brass inlay. Sons, daughters and other figures possibly congregation. The history of the church attributes the brass to engraver Dr Richard Haydocke, but the carver of the alabaster portion is unknown.

S182 Spare

S183 Great Hale, Lincs. Robert Cawdron (died 1652) and wives Anne and Mary. Greenhill classifies this as a slab but it is really a tablet. The family are inscribed as small figures at the base with the parents kneeling and their family ranged behind. He is shown in Stuart armour and jack-boots and spur leathers but no spurs. This is the penultimate slab monument to show a man in armour. The monument is attributed to Robert's son Anthony who may well have been an amateur carver as the work is coarse and without finesse.

S184 Great Grimsby, Lincs. William Weel (died 1410) and wife. Greenhill believes that this was carved by the same workshop as that for Pedde (S185). The inscribed effigy has a collar on which is just discernible two letter S leading some to believe that it shows a SS collar – one of the few slabs to do so.

S185 Great Grimsby, Lincs. Geoffrey Pedde (died 1408). Damaged in a WW2 air raid. Greenhill believes that this was carved by the same workshop as S184. Greenhill says that both effigies show a startled expression and in the case of Pedde he has his hands raised in supplication. Inscription almost effaced.

S186 Claverley, Shrops. Richard Spycer (died 1448), merchant and wife.

S187 Welford, Northants. A slab to a member of the Wyvile family (died 1454) and wife.

S188 Adbaston, Staffs. Reginald Bradoke (died 1441) and wife Matilda or Maud (died 1468).

S189 Stretton Sugwas, Hereford. Richard Grenewey and wife Maud (Harper) who died in 1473. Lady has butterfly headdress and both have feet on dogs. There is a canopy and a foot inscription which may suggest a Trent Valley carving.

S190 Ratcliffe on Soar, Notts. Civilian and wife *circa* 1480. The slab is cracked in several places and much patched with plaster, with a small horizontal strip near centre cut out and missing. The present reduced dimension is 82 inches by 40 inches. It bears the effigies of a civilian in long gown trimmed with fur at cuffs and along bottom edge and long pointed shoes. His head rests on a cushion and he wears baselard and purse. To dexter is his wife the upper part of her totally effaced. Beneath the feet of each is a bull-terrier the husband's with head turned backwards. The man's head and right arm are effaced as is also most of the marginal inscription (base Latin) which began at the top sinister corner running anti-clockwise. There is one other 1480 fragment which is unidentifiable except that it is a civilian called Henry and his wife.

S191 Peatling Parva, Leics. William Bradgate (died 1494), but slab carved *circa* 1480. Long hair and Baselard. Bradgate was instrumental in the provision of the church tower.

S192 Ashwell, Rutland. John Vernam (died 1481) and wife Rose (died 1479). Veil obscures the headdress. Much graffiti.

S193 Pusey, Berks. Henry Doggett (died 1491) and wife Amy (died 1485). The slab originally had the date left blank and so was created in his lifetime. The gown has embroidered hems, cuffs and top line. A girdle with a pendant.

S194 Croxall, Staffs. John Curzon (died 1490) son of Thomas and Margaret Curzon. Greenhill lists a slab of the same date to Mary daughter of the said Thomas and Margaret which has not yet been identified. This slab shows a lady with long flowing hair and gown with a train.

S195 Chipping Sodbury, Gloucs. Richard Colemor (died 1501) and wife Edith. The slab is sufficiently different to suggest this was carved away from the traditional workshops. The lady is in mourning and has a long cloak and the man a long gown obscuring all other dress. The effigies stand on a plinth with a large cross and stand under a pointed niche with crosses. Greenhill suggests that this is Bristol carved but without offering any other evidence.

S196 Penkridge, Staffs. Richard Littleton (died 1518) and Alice (Wynnesbury) who died 1529. Lady has a long pediment with the lower border decorated. A nice slab with fine carved effigies and coats of arms.

S197 Langham, Rutland. John Clarke (died 1533) and wives Jane and Anys. John was a reeve and attorney.

S198 Chellaston, Derbys. An ecclesiastical in a cope possibly Bawdon (or Bawredon) who died in 1523.

S199 Wirksworth, Derbys. Ralph Gell (died 1564) and two wives Godithe and Emma. The father of Anthony Gell (R135).

S200 Faringdon, Berks. Tobias Playdell (died 1583) and wife.

S201 Wrotham, Kent. Robert Rychers (died 1588) and family kneeling. A black marble slab in an alabaster frame attributable to the London workshops. Greenhill links this to the slab in St Helen's Bishopsgate (TT24).

S202 Crich, Derbys. Germaine Poole or Pole (died 1588) and second wife Margaret. Feet on griffin. Slab dates from 1592. Gloves and a walking stick. Greenhill offers the suggestion that the costume is a walking out attire. The slab used to stand on an altar tomb chest, but was dismounted *circa* 1800 and laid on the floor. In 1861 it was again moved to the chancel and fixed to the wall.

S203 Duffield, Derbys. An unusual mural monument in sandstone with alabaster panels. Anthony Bradshaw (Bradshawgh) who died in 1614. This 'little' monument made *circa* 1600, stands some 12 ft high and comprises panels commemorating himself, two wives (Griselda and Elizabeth) and 20 children. The panels appear to be in Fauld alabaster and are well carved carrying the initials of family member on each panel. Restored in 2002. Anthony is well dressed in high ruff and sleeved gown with shoulder length hair brushed up and beard. The male children dressed likewise but without beards. The ladies have hats perched on top of French hoods.

S204 Morley, Derbys. Henry Sacheverell (died 1638) and wife Dorothy. Shown as a civilian cavalier with long boots and falling collar and long hair. He holds an open book with both hands. Probably one of the last alabaster slabs to show a civilian and image slabs themselves become rare after 1650. Similar to that at Melbourne.

S205 Creich, Fife. Helen Douglas (died 1421). A freestone slab but the face and hands are cut very deep possibly indicating that part was inlaid with alabaster or brass. This church is roofless ruin and the existence of the slab us uncertain. 'Places of Worship in Scotland' states the slab may have been used to block an old doorway.

S206 Thorpe Salvin, Yorks. Katherine Sandford (died 1461) wife of John Sandford. Nine daughters shown on her skirt all wearing heart shaped headdresses.

S207 Spare

S208 Hereford Cathedral. Andrew Jones (died 1497) and wife Elizabeth, cider merchant and benefactor to the cathedral. The inscription is rarely quoted in full and is reproduced as follows: *Hic jacet Andreas Jonis quodam mcator hui ciuitatis et Elizabet vxor eius qui hanc domii carnarie diu desolata de nono reedificauit et repluit erga festu oim scor anno d'ni Mccccxcvii. Eciam ad tuc bn et laudabilii ordinauit capellanum futuris temporibz in eade defunct ti p aiabz benefactor et oim fidelium defunct quor aiabz propicietur deus. Amen.* A large slab with a heart headdress for the lady and the man with his feet on a barrel of cider. It now resides on a modern chest in the crypt.

S209 Banbury, Oxford. Lewis Grevell or Greville (died 1438) and wife Margaret. She has a horseshoe headdress. This was once in the chancel and now in the belfry but is much worn.

S210 Norbury, Derbys. Alice FitzHerbert (died 1460) wife of Sir Nicholas FitzHerbert. May be earlier.

S211 Spare

S212 Coates by Stow, Lincs. Henry Hansard (died 1470) and wife Joan. A worn slab but which shows a butterfly headdress.

S213 Lolworth, Cambs. Two ladies of the Langley family. A slab *circa* 1480 with a French inscription although the slab is clearly English.

S214 Dunster, Somerset. Lady Elizabeth Luttrell (died 1493), wife of Sir James Luttrell. There are suggestions that this is Watchet alabaster. *See* picture below. This is an interesting slab as Greenhill considered this to be the best English slab of the century. A drawing of the slab shows a lady in exquisite robes with what appears to be a little dog playing with the skirt. Her head is on a cushion supported by two angels. The whole is wholly unlike the normal offering of the Midland carvers and may well have been carved locally hence the suggestion that the alabaster may well be Watchet but in the absence of a colour picture this remains to be determined.

S215 Holdenby, Northants. William Holdenby (died 1490) and wife Margaret.

S216 Gaddesby, Leics. William Darby (died 1498) and wife.

S217 Denton Lincs. Agnes Denton (died 1440) but partially lost.

S218 Watton at Stone, Herts. John Butteler or Boteler (died 1480) and wives Elizabeth (1471) and Custans. His date is not filled in.

S219 Stanford on Soar. Notts. Ralph Illingworth (died 1498) and wife Agnes. Long pediment. Somewhat worn. Reported to have indents for brasses now lost.

S220 Woodcote, Shrops. Humphrey Cotes and wife Helen. Greenhill gives the date as 1527 but others 1500. Long pediment, canopies and nicely carved. Credited to the Harpur and Moorecock workshop but by 1527 the latter had died.

S221 Haughmond Abbey, Shrops. Ankareta Mynde (died 1528) wife of Richard Mynde. It is reputed she became a hermit. Broad band of fur down front of gown.

S222 Draycott in the Moors, Staffs. Sir John Draycott (died 1522) and wife Elizabeth. She appears to wear a heraldic mantle with arms of Eyre emblazoned, but this is not certain. Andrew Oliver claimed a slab to William Draycott of 1512 is in this church in 1881.

S223 Kirk Langley, Derbys. Widow Alice Beresford (died 1511) wife of Thomas. Not shown in widow's weeds. Handkerchief on right arm.

S224 Crofton Hackett, Worcs. William Leycester (died 1508) and wives Eleanor (Wyrley died 1514) and Anne (Hoord).

Long pediments.

S225 Tettenhall, Staffs. Richard Wrottesley (died 1517) and wife Dorothy. Sixteen children at feet. The church history has this as 1417. Feet on dog. Andrew Oliver claims this slab was supplied unfinished.

S226 Brewood, Staffs. Richard Lane (died 1518) and wife Anne (Harcourt). Uncovered during restoration 1879.

S227 Croxall, Staffs. John Horton (died 1520) and wife Anne.

S228 Tong, Shrops. Humfrey Vernon (died 1542) and wife Alice (Ludlow, who may have died 1531). A mixed effigy on the lady with an old style of dress, but modern gable hood. This may well be a tabletop tomb. The man has a dog at his feet and the lady a lion rampant at her head (for Ludlow). The interment of Humfrey is logged in the churchwarden accounts. Alice is associated with Haddon Hall, Derbys.

S229 Geddington, Northants. Richard Tresham (died 1533) and wife Isabel. Some sources give the date of 1433 but this is incorrect. The slab may have been recovered from St Faith's church Newton by Geddington, now a field centre.

S230 Norton, Derbys. John Selioke (died 1535) and wife. Gable hood.

S231 Aston Flamville, Leics. Sir William Turville (died 1549) and wife Jane (Warburton). Greenhill singles this slab out for special mention as set out in GH2 (266). CMS Vol XI 1991 has description.

S232 Ipsley, Warwicks. Nicholas Hubande (died 1553) and wife Dorothy (Danvers). This has been linked to Aston Flamville. . The Hubande website confirms that Nicholas died 16th May 1553. The slab has Nicholas with head on great helm and feet on greyhound. Dorothy is shown on Fig 44 in GH1 with a description on pages 266 and 267. A very late gable hood and a gown with exceptionally long sleeves reaching almost to knees.

S233 Norton, Derbys. William Selioke (died 1541) and wife Joyce. Greenhill has an image of Joyce as Fig 45 in GH1 page 268. This effigy shows the lady facing three-quarters front with a strange flat cap over a caul. The headdress can be seen on the Babington girls at Rothley (TT6, 1544–1547). The dress is also different with bell-mouthed sleeves, shoulder cape, decorated belt with large clasp. In all an interesting departure from the normal offering.

S234 Packington, Leics. William Leeson (died 1534) and wife Agnes. This was found by Greenhill and listed on page 268 but nothing of it can be found in 2015.

S235 Burton Joyce, Notts. George Lacock (died 1617) and wife Alice. Alice is kneeling with a hat over French hood on her head. Described by Thoroton but now very worn.

S236 Melton Mowbray, Leics. John Pate (died 1659) and wife Elizabeth (died 1628).

S237 Morley, Derbys. Dorothy Coke (died 1640) daughter of Jacinth Sacheverell. This is strange coffin shaped slab showing a young woman with long flowing hair.

S238 Knipton, Leics. John Eyre (died 1523) infant in chrisom robes. *See*: http://www.mbs-brasses.co.uk/Picture%20 Library%20Chrysoms.html#Eyre

S239 Ratcliffe on Soar. Notts. James Damport (died 1458). Son of Thomas Damport. This was not found by Greenhill but recorded by Thoroton.

S240 Ratcliffe on Soar. Notts. Joan Shirley date unknown. This slab listed the relationship with a number of lords stating: '... Joan daughter and heir to Thomas Basset son of Sir John Basset of Dr (ayton) the wife of Sir Ralph Shirley son and heir of Hugh Shirley'.

S241 Ratcliffe on Soar. Notts. Thomas Fynderne (died 1524) and wife. On floor of north aisle a large slab of alabaster 86 inches by 40¾in cracked into several pieces and central portion utterly effaced bearing effigies of an armed man (all but head and right leg and foot obliterated) his head on a cushion and wife to right wearing gable hood headdress with extremely long lappets apparently trimmed with lace partlet and gown with girdle and rosary slung from right arm her head on tasselled and embroidered cushion. Beneath their feet are small figures of five sons and one daughter and above their heads a quintuple canopy without shafts on which are three shields. Finderne took part in the Battle of East Stoke in 1487.

S242 Ratcliffe on Soar. Notts. An unknown civilian (died 1500) and wife Alice.

S243 Ratcliffe on Soar. Notts. An unknown civilian Robert D ... (died 1495) and wife Agnes. Children at feet.

S244 Willesley, Derbys. John Wylkins, Priest (unknown date but possibly 1540).

S245 Hartshorne, Derbys. Knight and lady unknown.

S246 Tettenhall, Staffs. Richard Wrottesley and wife Dorothy and 16 children (dated 1417 or 1408). Survived the fire of 1950.

S247 West Hallam, Derbys. Thomas Powtrell (died 1484). Formerly a tabletop this is now in the floor.

S248 Wormington, Gloucs. John Daston (died 1532) and two wives. Possibly once a tabletop and now set into the wall.

S249 Rock, Worcs. Richard Smith (or Smyth) priest (died 1554). Possibly tabletop now set in the wall. The slab is dated at 1554 but looks earlier. There is a canopy.

S250 Scropton, Derbys. William Schower (Shore) died 1494. Shore was a goldsmith whose wife was Jane Shore mistress to Edward IV. Although a London trader he was taken and buried in Scropton where a slab was placed in 1495.

S251 Prestbury, Cheshire. Robert Downes (died 1495) and wife Matilda (Bechton). Earwaker described this slab and reproduces the inscription from which we learn that Robert died during the vigil of St Laurence the Martyr on the 10th August. In 1877 the slab was reported to have been moved and stood against the wall in the chancel. It seems to have been reported as present in 2012 but this could not be currently confirmed. Crossley has a fine picture on page 104.

S252 Prestbury, Cheshire. Edward Warren (died 1573) and wife Matilda. Earwaker described this as a tabletop tomb which had disappeared by 1877 leaving the slab to be placed in the wall of the chancel. Like S251this seems to have been confirmed as present in 2012 but this could not be currently confirmed.

S253 Westhide, Hereford. Richard Monyngton (died 1524) and wife Alice. Eight sons and eight daughters. Alice has pediment headdress. The slab has a canopy. Credited to the Harpur and Moorecock workshop, but by 1524 the latter had died.

S254 Willesley, Leics. George Abney (died 1577) and wife Ellen Wolseley (died1571).

S255 Aymestrey, Hereford. Sir John Lingen (1506) and wife Elizabeth (Burgh 1522).

S256 Ashbourne, Derbys. Sir Thomas Cockayne (died 1537) and wife Barbara (FitzHerbert). Slab is believed to be late 16th century.

S257 Bushbury, Staffs. Believed to be Jane Alicock or Allicourt (died 1608). However, the dates do not fit.

S258 Marston on Dove, Staffs. Katherine Lathebery (died 1597).

S259 Marston on Dove, Staffs. Unknown (died *circa* 1595).

S260 Kirkby Mallory, Leics. Unknown knight with two wives *circa* 1595.

S261 York Cathedral. Matthew Pollard (died 1589).

S262 York Cathedral. Thomas de Castell (died 1403). Vicar choral of York Minster.

S263 Westminster Abbey. In 1960 the marble statue of James Watt (died 1825) was removed to the Institute of Mechanical Engineers and replaced by a bust at a high level and an alabaster slab on the floor. Unfortunately the close proximity of the 1507 tomb of Sir Giles Daubeny (G117) meant that visitors stood on the slab.

S264 Lincoln Cathedral. Slab to Bishop Gardiner (died 1705)

S265 Lincoln Cathedral. Slab to Sub Dean Gardiner (died 1732) and his daughter Susanna (died 1733).

S266 Radcliffe, Lancs. Possibly James Radcliffe (died 1410) and wife. A much worn slab not listed by Baines in 1833 but found and restored to the chancel in 1870–1873. The Radcliffes were the owners of what is now Radcliffe Tower.

S267 Audley, Staffs. Edward Eardley (died 28/2/1656).

S268 Bowdon, Lancs. Sir William Booth (*circa* 1519) and wife Eleanor.

S269 Haughton, Staffs. Nicholas Graviner (died 1520), rector. A priest in his mass robes and with a tonsure.

S270 Selby, Yorks. Abbot John Barwick (died 1526).

S271 Norbury, Derbys. Elizabeth FitzHerbert (nee Marshall, died 1491) wife of Ralph FitzHerbert. An unusual shrouded figure.

S272 Nuthall, Notts. Edward Boun (died 1558) and wife Isaballa Hunt (died 1562). A slab in Chellaston alabaster also showing five small children. Badly worn. In 1819 Stretton noted several alabaster slabs in the church entrance but only Boun's seems to have survived.

S273 Norton, Derbys. A much worn slab to Richard Blythe and wife Katherine of unknown date but *circa* 1500. The inscription is now illegible but could be read in 1780 as 'Orate pro anibus Ricardi Blith et Katherine exorus ejus quiquidem Ricardi obit xxiij die ... vicessimo quarto pp ... Amen'.

S274 Stoke Dry, Rutland. Jaquetta Digby (died 1496). Fragment. An excellent photograph can be seen on *Flickr*.

S275 Ratcliffe on Soar, Notts. Elizabeth (died 1505) wife of Anthony Babington of Kingston. A very strange slab probably the work of a local carver. The small effigy is basic and may be incomplete while most of the slab is taken up by coats of arms. The rest of the details of this slab is contained in Appendix X.

S276 Morley, Derbyshire. Richard Sacheverell (died 1628). A small slab showing a chrisom. Richard was the son of Jacinth and Elizabeth Sacheverell.

S277 Gedling, Notts. A very worn slab depicting a knight and partially under the altar which was identified by A E Lawson Lowe in 1903 as bearing the date of 1487. This has given rsie to speculation that the depicted knight died at the battle of East Stoke in that year. Further speculation has suggested that the slab depicts Francis Lovell, supported of Richard III who fled the field and whose burial place has never been found. In support of this it is pointed out that his mother was lord of the manor of Gedling although subject to attainder. The slab was not seen by Thoroton. Another alabaster slab is located next to this but bears no inscription.

T1 Lambourn, Berks. Knight and lady. Sir Thomas Essex (died 1558) and first wife Margaret (Sandys). Groups of children kneeling at end. Tabard, small ruff and chains. French cap and puffed sleeves. Jon Bayliss identifies this with carver Richard Parker (Vol V 1990 CMS). There is a dolphin at feet of knight and a damaged winged horse at the feet of the wife.

T2 Faringdon, Berks. Knight and lady. Sir Thomas Unton (died 1533) and wife Elizabeth (Yonge). The tomb is said to possibly date from 1540. Breastplate under jupon. The tomb chest has fine Renaissance features including niches with shields and wreaths. Great helm with dog crest and orle.

T3 Eye, Hereford. Knight and lady. Sir Richard Cornwall (died 1533 or 1535) and wife Jane Melbourn (died 1553). The tomb is considered to have been ordered earlier than Jane's death (possibly 1540 which is supported by the presence of the SS collar) but Gardner quotes the Christian name George so some uncertainty remains. Long SS collar with Tudor rose pendant and tabard. French cap and padded sleeves. There are similarities to Ratcliffe on Soar (G136) and St Peter ad Vincula (T28). The knight has his head on a great helm and feet on a lion as per G94 in the same church.

T4 Holme Lacy, Hereford. Knight and lady. John Scudamore (died 1571) and first wife Sybil Vaughan. Gothic on Renaissance chest. Chains round neck and short pediment. Jon Bayliss identifies this with carver Richard Parker (Vol V 1990 CMS). The inscription describes his place in the court of Henry VIII but the date is incomplete.

T5 Hereford Cathedral. Knight and lady. Sir Alexander Denton and first wife Anne Willison (died 1566). Attributable to Richard Parker. Ann died in childbirth aged 18 and a chrisom in to be found on the tomb. Sir Alexander, who died in 1576, is buried in Hillesden, Bucks. There is a suggestion that the monument was hauled over land from Burton to Hereford in pieces and erected on site but the evidence for this is not forthcoming. The alternative to this would be by boat down the Trent then by sea to one of the Severn ports and then up the Wye or hauled over land – a long and dangerous passage. It s suggested that this tomb was copied by John Gildon for the Willison freestone tomb at Hillesden in 1581.

T6 Wheathampstead, Herts. Knight and lady. Sir John Brockett (died 1543) and wife Margaret. The tomb may date from 1558. Gothic on Renaissance chest. The knight has long hair and a beard and his head on a helm. He has a chain around his neck which once had a cross 'patee' but is now obscured by plaster applied as a repair to support the hands. His feet rest on a lion and he has a sword and misericorde hanging from the sword belt by a cord. The head of the lady, which rests upon a pillow, has been much damaged; she wears a close-fitting cap and a necklace, a long dress fitting closely to the figure with sleeves puffed and slashed at the shoulders; the arms are broken off; the skirt is open in front and ornamented by rows of knots. A pomander hangs from the front of her waist by a long chain. Her feet rest on a dog or leopard, much broken. From her shoulders hangs a cloak, kept in position by cords tied in front and hanging down to her feet. The date and year of Margaret's death is omitted from the inscription. She died in 1560. The tomb chest has children holding shields.

T7 Bottesford, St Mary, Leics. Knight and lady. Thomas Manners, 1st Earl of Rutland (died 1543) and Countess Eleanor (Paston) – died 1550 and buried in Shoreditch. Weepers and Renaissance chest. Garter robes and collar. The 1543 effigy of the 1st earl was carved by Richard Parker of Burton on Trent who was paid £20 for its creation and erection. It is stated that John Lupton and his father who were 'rough masons' had to strengthen the floor to carry the weight and this took six months. It may be the total cost was £33 5s 8d. Renaissance decoration with long wreaths of bay and the corners marked by broad stumpy balusters in square bases. The effigies are straight Gothic with an attempt at portraiture. Hands in Catholic position. This may be Parker's only documented work the Rutland accounts showing the commission in 1539. The Manners were buried either in Croxton Abbey or Belvoir Priory but on suppression of these in 1538 and 1539, Thomas moved the earlier monuments of the Albany and Roos families to Bottesford.

T8 Stanford on Avon, Northants. Knight and lady. Sir Thomas Cave (died 1558) and wife Elizabeth Danvers. Kneeling family with Renaissance detail. Chain collar. Lady has Queen of Scots cap, puffed sleeves and shoulders. Tomb chest has spiral pilasters.

T9 Ratcliffe on Soar, Notts. Knight and lady. Sir Henry Sacheverell, son of G136. The tomb of Henry Sacheverell died 1558 and his wife Lucy Pool (or Pole – died 1554). Lucy appears also with a triple chain and puffed sleeve gown. The gauntlets are by his side and the head rests on a helmet with the Sacheverell crest of a goat. The chest is of Renaissance style with Gothic effigies. (Inscription reads: *Here lieth the tombe of Henry Sacheverell Esquire …*) Bayliss accredits this to Richard Parker but there is some doubt. The tomb chest chamfer is grooved like his father's tomb (G136) and has the same crude Gothic script giving rise to the possibility that this too is a reused tomb and by the same workshop.

T10 Kinlet, Shrops. Knight and lady. Sir John Blount (died 1531) and wife Katherine Peshall (died 1540). Weepers in groups. Renaissance detail in the form of dolphins in the arcades of the tomb chest. SS collar. Lady has short pediment (gable hood). May be much later than 1531. Jon Bayliss (Vol V 1990 CMS) has identified this as a Richard Parker carving. Parker started *circa* 1522 and therefore is most likely to be later than 1531, possibly 1540 as suggested by Gardner. Elizabeth Norton maintains Blount was buried in Greyfriars London and when his tomb there was destroyed the tomb in Kinlet was made as a replacement *circa* 1540 which would agree with Gardner.

T11 Wroxeter, Shrops. Civilian and Lady. Lord Chief Justice Thomas Bromley (died 1555) and wife Mabel (or Isabel). Bromley was a Serjeant at Law. Weepers with Renaissance detail such as spiral pilasters and child holding flower. Judges coif. Short pediment. Pheasants beside cushion. Jon Bayliss credits this monument to Richard Parker (Vol V CMS). The standing figure is daughter Margaret whose tomb is described in R101. Mabel wears a gable hood considered old-fashioned for the period. It may be the church is semi-derelict.

T12 Coventry, Warwicks. Knight, lady and civilian. Thomas Essex, Elizabeth Swillington (died 1546) and Ralph Swillington (died 1525). Ralph was attorney general and has head on a great helm. Renaissance tomb chest. Bearded with chain collar. Lady has short pediment. Civilian has long gown and chain collar. Monument erected during Elizabeth's lifetime. This is believed to have been destroyed during the Blitz – *see* Appendix D9. Ralph Swillington was also commemorated by a brass in Driffield, Yorks which was copy of one in the Temple Church, London neither of which survive.

T13 Bakewell, Derbys. Sir George Vernon (died 1566–1567) and two wives – Margaret Tailboys and Maud Longford. Attributable to Richard Parker.

T14 Hillesdon, Bucks. Thomas Denton MP (died 1558) and wife Margery (or Magdelen) nee Mordaunt. Thomas has lost his lower legs. The lady displays a farthingale. Both have small ruffs and Thomas has a chain collar from which the pendant has been broken. Margery was first married to Edmund Fettiplace of Besselsleigh, Berks and is depicted on a brass in Morcham church.

T15 Bristol, St John the Baptist. Merchant (unknown) and wife.

T16 Battle, Sussex. Sir Anthony Browne and his wife Alice (Gage). Anthony died in 1548. The alabaster is a pink colour. Part coloured. The tomb chest is tall and is believed to be in an Italian style possible observed by Browne when he was ambassador to the French court. The monument is also believed to have been made during his lifetime *circa* 1540 or earlier. Llewellyn believes this tomb shows similar traits to the Marney tombs (X3) which we made by Florentine Pietro Torregiano but this attribution has not been proved since he died in 1522. It has been suggested that this tomb was commissioned by Sir Anthony's mother Lucy Fitzwilliam (later Browne) of Tickhill, Yorks and it has similarities to the tomb there (A46). It should be noted that the Tickhill tomb is Gothic effigies on a new Renaissance tomb chest comprising flattened shell heads, candelabra balusters and shields and wreaths. There are putti which are considered to have been copied by later alabastermen but with less skill as seen on the tomb of Sir John Salusbury at Stanford on Avon (R72), Humphrey Peyto at Chesterton (R119) and Edward Burnett at Sibthorpe (A86). These tombs may have Torrigiano influences but are likely to be from a Burton workshop. One odd feature is the canopy over the head of the lady at Battle a practice which had ceased at least 100 years earlier.

T17 Albrighton, Shrops. Sir John Talbot (died 1555) and his wife Frances Gifford. Sir John is the father of George Talbot Earl of Shrewsbury and husband of Bess of Hardwick. There is a similarity to T9. The pictures show a SS collar which is unusual for such a late monument.

T18 Barcheston, Warwicks. William Willington (died 1555) and wife Anne Middlemore. A fine transition tomb is white Chellaston alabaster. The man is dressed in armour of the period and has ruffs at the neck and wrists and a chain about his shoulders: his hands are in prayer. His head rests on his helm, which has a maiden's-head crest, and his feet rest against a lion; his gauntlets lie by his side and he wears a sword. The woman wears a close Tudor cap, tight corsage and full skirt, ruffs at neck and wrists, close pleated sleeves, and has a chain about her neck with a pendant cross, and a girdle with a suspended sachet-case. Over all is a long mantle held together with points or tabs. The base has a moulded plinth, and top edge with the inscription: 'Here lies the bodyes of William Willington of Barson Esquyer and Anne his wyeffe which Will^{am} dyed the fyrste daye of Maye in the yere of our Lorde God M^{o} ccccc^{o} lv unto whose soules and Bodyes God graunte a joyfull resurrection. Amen.' The east and west ends are carved with shields of the Willington arms, a saltire vair, in a circular ribbon inscribed 'In God be all my truste'. The long sides are divided each into three bays by twisted pilasters: the middle bays have shields, in circular ribbons, charged with the arms of Willington impaling Middlemore of Edgbaston. The other four bays have standing figures of daughters in much the same costume as their mother; two in each bay except the north-western, which has one and also three in grave-clothes each bearing a child. Each living daughter has a shield on her left with a charge impaling Willington, and some hold pairs of gloves or bouquets.

T19 Brewood, Staffs. Sir John Giffard (died 1556) and two wives Jane Hoord and Elizabeth Greysley. Twisted baluster shafts and tomb chest depicting a son, 3 daughters and no less than 13 chrisoms.

T20 Brewood, Staffs. Sir Thomas Giffard (died 1560) and two wives Dorothy Montgomery and Ursula Thockmorton. A tomb chest depicting seven sons, six daughters and four chrisoms. The ladies each wear a gable hood and a French hood.

T21 Weekley, Northants. Sir Edward Montagu (died 1556). Reported to have had brass inlays. Plain tomb chest with just a shield.

T22 Spare

T23 Penkridge, Staffs. Sir Edward Littleton (died 1558) and wives Helen Swynnerton and Isabel Wood. Ladies have gable hoods. Part gilded. Sir Edward has long beard

T24 Enville, Staffs. Thomas Grey (died 1559) and wife Anne Verney. Great helm and feet on lion with head turned. Spiral pilasters and shield inside a circle.

T25 Coventry, St Michael, Warwicks. Julian Nethermyl (died 1539) and first wife Joan. This is a tabletop without effigy. There is a side which is similar to the monument at Youlgreave (M47) and shows Flemish traits. Gardner offered the opinion that it was made by a Fleming working for one of the Burton workshops. Nethermyl was a wealthy draper and mayor of Coventry. Thomas Sharp's Illustrated History of Coventry 1871 states that the tomb was removed 'in this year'. In any case T25 does not feature in the list of monuments surviving the 1940 blitz – *see* Appendix D9.

T26 Stowe by Chartley, Staffs. Sir Walter Devereux, Viscount Hereford (died 1558) and two wives – one Mary Grey (died 1537) and the other Margaret Garneys. A Fine effigial tomb accredited to Richard Parker. The figures, believed to be children on the tomb chest are particularly well carved. Strange spade-shaped footwear. He has head on great helm with feather crest and he wears the garter collar. One lady wears a gable hood and the other a French hood. Walter Devereux was the grandfather of the Earl of Essex, favourite of Elizabeth I. Has a similarity to Kinlet. The Lichfield list of 1532 (B200) gives Sir Walter and lists his wife as Lady Mary and children Richard, Walter, William, Catherine, Henry, Mary, Margaret and Dorothy.

T27 Hackleton and Horton, Northants. Lord William Parr (died 1546) and wife Lady Mary formerly a Salisbury (died 1555). The Parrs were the uncle and aunt of Catherine Parr. The church is currently redundant. Jon Bayliss has a full description in the 'CMS Journal' Vol XXVIII 2013 page 78. The tomb is a free-standing chest tomb in transition style but Jon Bayliss offers a suggestion that the effigies were second hand and originally carved by Richard Parker. He has his head on a great helm with a hand holding a wheatsheaf as a crest. He also shows a heavy beard and she wears a gable hood. The tomb chest is distinctive and Renaissance in style. The sides have foliated round-headed arches. Inside the arches on the ends are shields supported by cowled figures which are similar to bedesmen. The sides have figures facing forward. The use of bedesmen in 1548 is odd and this is one feature which gives support to the belief that the tomb was reused however, the inscription is believed to be post-1555 and it might well be that the effigies are *circa* 1530 but the tomb chest was new in 1555 when the effigies were moved to Horton and when bedesmen may have been acceptable to the Marian rights of the period. The wheatsheaf crest is *not* associated with the Parrs but can be found listed against the Gipp and Wheathill families but no appropriate tomb can be identified.

T28 London, Tower of London chapel. A very interesting tomb not listed by Gardner but showing clear Transition features. Sir Richard Cholmondeley (died 1521) and his wife Elizabeth (died 1546). He was knight lieutenant of the Tower. The tomb is suggested to have been in the Priory of the Crutched Friars located just north of the Tower (Thesis by Nick Holder 2011). It is reputed to have been reinstalled in the Tower chapel in 1554 but by his widow which appears to make its installation much earlier. However, the Tower records confirm the date but state that the installation was by his son. It is curious in that the tomb chest is basic Gothic but has spiral Renaissance pilasters. The effigy of the knight sports an SS collar with a Tudor rose pendant which was discontinued in 1547. The pendant style may not have been used before 1509. The hair style and armour is very similar to that at Ratcliffe on Soar (G136). The lady, on the other hand, displays a very long pediment headdress which would be considered unfashionably by 1510. There are traces of blue and red stain on the lady. The transfer of this monument when recovered from its original position may have resulted in some muddling of the components especially as the tomb may have been stored until the 1540s. The alabaster is Chellaston and with more work it may be possible to identify it as a Trent Valley product. Pictures show that the tomb has had (in the past) at least two styles of iron railings and has been moved within the chapel probably when it was dismantled for cleaning in 1876 and when a quartered font was found hidden inside. This is believed to be hidden *circa* 1650 and this is now restored to the chapel.

The Cholmondeley crest is believed to be a demi-griffon sergeant beaked, membered or holding between the claws a helmet as in the arms. The great helm carries a crest which appears to be just a war helmet. The north and east side of the tomb chest and the slab under the lady is modern limestone and it can be seen that although the knight's slab of alabaster continues along the west face the limestone has been let in. The suspicion is that the lady was, in antiquity, a fugitive from another tomb possibly third quarter 15th century. The presence of angels supporting the cushion and the dogs toying with the skirt support the early date. The ancient name for the family is Cholmeley. For further analysis *see* G53 and L36.

T29 Chenies, Bucks. The private Bedford Chapel attached to Chenies Manor House (M1 on 'The Heraldry of the Bedford Chapel'). John Russell, 1st Earl of Bedford (died 1555) and wife Ann (Sapcote, died 1559). Russell was created Earl of Bedford in 1550–1551 in recognition of his implementation of the order of the council against religious images.

T30 Whitchurch, Shrops. Sir John Talbot (died 1550). An interesting transition tomb. The tomb chest has cusped lozenges in a Gothic style but the canopy is in the form of a semi-circular arch with Renaissance elements. The effigy appears to be dressed in garter robes.

TT1 Humberstone, Leicester. Knight. Tabletop inscribed slab to Richard Hotoft (died 1451). For details of Humberstone monuments *see* L6. Many commentators quote this slab as being 1547, but the date on the border is clearly not 16th century being M⁰ CCCC⁰ Li. This was formerly a tabletop in the south aisle on what is reported as a plain tomb chest. In the last century it was repositioned on the east wall and the tomb chest demolished. The carving is crude but deep with the grooves filled with pitch and shows a knight in 15th century armour. The head is helmetless on a strange cushion. Feet on dog. The inscription, in Latin, is evenly spaced in the border with the date in a curious form of mixed Roman and Latin script. The quality of carving is not of Chellaston or Burton standard and may well be a product of Nottingham. The slab is cracked which happened when the slab was moved. Greenhill states that this is recut and comments of the armour in Vol 1 page 166. He says the spiked elbow and knee cops are unique in English slab carving.

TT2 Hanbury, Staffs. Ralph Adderley (died 1595) and wives Margaret (Bagot) and Philota (Milwarde). A tabletop in alabaster. A widow's hood over a French hood.

TT3 Greyfriars, Leicester. Tabletop to Richard III *circa* 1495 – *see* A45

TT4 Aldbourne, St Michael, Wilts. Inscribed tabletop *circa* 1510 to cleric and prebendary, John Stone, vicar of St Michael 1473 to 1510. Greenhill says this is Nottingham carved. Linked to S170.

TT5 Fenny Drayton, Leics. *Circa* 1545 – *see* GNP50 for some details. Gardner failed to identify this as a tabletop. Saul has picture Fig 50 (page 77) and shows a sandstone chest with figures in niches and a heraldic device. Greenhill also shows an image as Vol 2 Fig 89b and states that the Peckleton slab (S65) is from same workshop. The slab has Gothic script round chamfer and has been identified in some quarters as being carved by Parker. Unusually the couple hold hands.

TT6 Rothley, Leics. A tabletop monument to Humphrey Babington (died 1547–1549) and wife possibly Elizabeth (or Eleanor) Beaumont (Richard III family). *See also* A4. One daughter wears a flat cat over a caul.

TT7 Rothley, Leics. A tabletop monument to Bartholomew Kyngston (died 1486) and wife Agnes (some say Elyn). The slab contains parts of his will. This is the only remaining slab out of four which originally graced the church – *see* Appendix D9. Figure 7 of Sally Badham's book *Seeking Salvation* has a fine rubbing made by Greenhill. Likened to S41 at Quorn.

TT8 Swarkestone, Derbys. Richard Harpur of Chellaston (*circa* 1573) and later Calke Abbey. A tabletop tomb identified with Gabriel Royley of Burton on Trent. Young says that that the tabletop is clearly local but cannot be so sure about the chest. Llewellyn is clearer and attributes the tomb chest to the London workshops. He goes on to observe that the texts on both the chest and the slab carry the same inscription indicating that the Harpur family provided this and that the instructions were misunderstood and carved by both carvers.

TT9 Withybrook, Warwicks. Sir Christopher Wright (died 1602) and wife. A tabletop in alabaster which is unusual in that the inscription in the alabaster panel behind the slab begins in Greek and drifts into English in archaic Gothic. The inscription is by Wright's wife Jane who signed the inscription. Inscriptions in languages other than Latin and English are rare. Greenhill GH1 page 281 makes some observations about the shoes.

TT10 Prestwold, Leics. Sir Richard Nele (died 1486) and his wife Isobel (died 1476). Sir Richard was a justice of the common pleas and the carving shows a coil and robes of a justice. The lady has a gown with long straight sleeves with furred cuffs, divided veil and headdress. This incised slab is shown with canopies over their heads. A drawing of the slab is contained in *Prestwold and Its Church* by Philip White. On the two exposed south side of the tomb chest there are arcades containing monks with rosaries, two of which have also crutches. Also three angels with shields. The west side has a monk and two angels with shields. Isobel was a Ryddynges (Ruddynge or Ryddyns) by birth and it was through her that the Neles came to Prestwold. A drawing is also shown in Greenhill Vol 2 Fig 103a. The scroll over the judge's head reads 'Mother of mercy help us in this case' whilst that of the wife reads a more conventional 'Jesus mercy and thy grace'. Greenhill also observes that the judge wears such a sinister expression that the carver must have had a dislike of judges or Nele himself.

TT11 Shirland, Derbys. John Revell (died 1537) and wife Margaret (possibly Margery, said to have died 1500). The Revell family is linked to the Wilmots of Berkswell, Warwick whose descendents are the Cartlands of Carnfield Hall. The inscription is clearly marked with the year of the death of John as MCCCC trisecimo septimo (1537) but that of his lady is just MCCCCC indicating that the date of 1500 is in error and that the monument was made prior to the ladies death and not filled in.

TT12 Aston Flamville, Leics. Tabletop monument to Sir William Turville (died 1552) and second wife Jane Warburton. Greenhill links this with Quorndon (S42).

TT13 Cossington, Leics. Rev Dr Matthew Knightley (died 1561) – rector. The tomb was set up *circa* 1556 to 1558 in the deceased's lifetime. It contained a prayer for the dead which was subsequently cut away. The rector is shown in academic dress but which exposes the Royleys lack of understanding of the form attributable to a graduate of Cambridge. The slab was heavily criticised by Greenhill and a long critique can be found in Vol 1 page 116.

TT14 Eccleshall, Staffs. Richard Samson, Bishop of Lichfield (died 1553). He was also Bishop of Coventry. Part is reported as being lost.

TT15 Gayton, Northants. Francis Tanfield (died 1558) and wife Margery (or Bridget) Cave (died 1583). A tabletop by the Royley workshop dated from 1583. The tomb chest depicts their 18 children and is adorned with lozenges. Greenhill says that the slab was 'lost' and has been incorrectly restored.

TT16 Newstead Abbey, Notts crypt (now the gift shop). Sir John Byron (died 1567) and wives Isabel Shelton and Elizabeth Constantine (or Consterdine). The tomb was moved from Colwick Old Church in September 1937. The tomb may have been made in 1576 by his son also John causing confusion as to Sir John's date of death. However, Greenhill dates the carving to 1559 which could mean it was made in John's lifetime – *see* page 273 of GH1. Children inscribed on tomb sides. It is stated that Sir John held to the old religion and paid for a priest to sing mass for 10 years after his death for which he made a stipend of £10 per annum. The table slab may well have been used as an altar as two consecration crosses are visible in the corners.

TT17 Newbold on Avon, Warwicks. Thomas Boughton (died 1454) and wife Elizabeth. Greenhill says that this is Nottingham carved and is similar to the smaller slab at Dauntsey Wilts of 1455. Thomas has a salet. Greenhill studied the pauldrons and provided a link to six others – *see* L13.

TT18 North Mimms, Herts. Elizabeth or Mary Beresford (both died 1584). Some say the family name is Barford. Greenhill observes that by this date the Royley quality had declined. There are some fine points and some changes in that the ears are shown.

TT19 Marchington, Staffs. Walter Vernon (died 1592) and wife Mary Littleton. A drawing is shown in the Salt Library of Staffordshire Archives doc SV VII.64c. She wears French hood with outer hood.

TT20 Peatling Magna, Leics. William Jervis (died 1597) and wife Katherine Ward. Tabletop showing children facing forward. Inscription in English on chamfered edge of slab. The head of the lady is odd. She appears to be bald with ruff that looks like a beard. A over large hood.

TT21 Peatling Magna, Leics. William Jervis (died 1614) and wives Anne Purefoy and Frances Marston. Tabletop which was probably created some years earlier as the date has been added after carving. Inscription in English on chamfered edge of slab. Children facing forward. Widow's hood over French hood.

TT22 Grafton Regis, Northants. Sir John Wydeville (died 1397) great grandfather of Elizabeth Woodville, queen of Edward IV who married in Grafton in 1464. The alabaster slab is mounted on a freestone chest. The tomb is believed to have been erected *circa* 1415. John erected the church bell tower and this is referred to in the inscription. Hartshorne says that this incised effigy shows some 'curious points' which are detailed on pages 38 to 39 of his book. His main point is the absence of chain mail but he seems to have been unaware that the slab was carved some years after John's death. Greenhill, on the other hand, singles this out as a Prentys and Sutton slab and links it to that at Clevedon, Somerset (S163).

TT23 Prestwold, Leics. Nichols stated that between 1795 and 1815 in Vol 3 page 360 records 'The Rydding's monument ... was in the nave, a descent of two steps into the old chancel. It was an alabaster slab with figures of a man and a woman with her dog, cut-in and almost defaced'. The date of 1487 makes it contemporary with the Nele tabletop TT10. The spelling of Ryddings is fugitive and may well be Ruddyngs. His wife was Margaret and he appears to have died 1st Feb 1487.

TT24 St Helen's Bishopsgate. A tabletop to mason William Kerwin (died 1594) and son Benjamin made by himself. Tomb chest with lozenges and figures and carved pilasters. Restored 1868. Greenhill likens the effigy of the son to one at Wrotham (S201) and the father similar, making an attribution to Epiphamus Evesham a possibility.

TT25 Hornsea, Yorks. Rector Anthony St Quintin (died 1430). Tomb believed to be carved in his lifetime. This was not found by Gardner. The table has received much attention by graffiti artists including a number of 'footprints'. Blank shields in quatrefoils and partial inscription. The St Quintins were an important family in this part of Yorkshire.

TT26 Harpham, Yorks. William St Quintin (died 1349) and wife. An incised tabletop in black stone with an alabaster tomb chest. The style is much later than mid-14th century and is believed to have been set up by the rector of Hornsea which it resembles (*see* TT25). In fact Greenhill states the slab is dated 1384 and of York manufacture.

TT27 Uttoxeter, Staffs. Thomas Kynnersley (died 1538). The tomb has been variously dated at 1505 or 1550 but Jon Bayliss has investigated the likely construction and this can be found in CMS 'Brass of the Month' March 2013. Thomas's second wife is also in the church (R209).

TT28 Madeley, Staffs. Ralph (or Randolph) Egerton (died 1522) and wife Isabella. A tabletop believed to be from the Harpur and Moorecock workshop but by this time Moorecock had died. There are seventeen figures on tomb chest all badly worn. There are some old slabs with illegible inscriptions, one of which may be a lady of 1360.

TT29 Rothley, Leics. Knight and lady. Robert Vincent (died 1520) and wives Margery and Thomasina. Thomasina shows a modest necklace with a cross.

TT30 Bulkington, Warwick. Sir Christopher Sadeler (died 1530) and two wives, eight sons and two daughters.

TT31 Sprotbrough, Yorks. Philip Copley (died 1577) and wife. *See* S70 for similar slab. Greenhill says that this is a local carver depicting armour from an earlier period with wife in a 15th century dress with the children dressed in late Tudor. A confusing mix of styles.

TT32 Mavesyn Ridware, Staffs. Thomas Cawarden (died 1592–1593) and his wife Anne. A fine alabaster slab, the work of Jasper or Garrett Hollemans. The slab is reported by Greenhill to have been 'restored if not completely renewed' but this is currently disputed. The man is in armour and she is in late Tudor costume. .This was CMS 'Brass of the Month' August 2011.

TT33 Coleshill, Warwick. Sir Reginald Digby (died 1549) and wife Anne. Eight sons and Four daughters.

TT34 Swarkestone, Derbys. John Rolleston (died 1482) and wife Susan (some say Cicely) died 1460. Greyhound at feet of knight and two dogs at feet of lady. Also shown are seven sons and a number of daughters. A pomander hangs from the girdle.

TT35 London, Great St Helen's Bishopsgate. Sir Thomas Gresham (died 1579). There is some doubt as to whether this is alabaster. The top surface contains only the name and date. The sides of the chest are fluted and there is an effigy of a grasshopper. Unusual tomb.

TT36 Mavesyn Ridware, Staffs. Sir Robert Mavesyn (died 1403 at the Battle of Shrewsbury). A well cut slab in good condition in pale veined alabaster. Unusual inclusion of shields in the chamfer of the tabletop. A modern looking tomb chest – not alabaster.

TT37 Radbourne, Staffs. Ralph de la Pole (died 1454), Judge and wife Joan. Angels holding shields.

TT38 Eccleshall, Staffs. Bishop Thomas Bentham (died 1579) but may have been carved in 1578. A rare depiction of a post-Reformation bishop on a slab. The incised effigy is crude dressed in a long gown reminiscent of an overcoat with shoulder puffs. A close fitting coif and a book. The image is repeated on the tomb chest with his wife and four children. Drawings of this appear in the Staffordshire Archives William Salt Library SV-IV.125b

TT39 Forncett St Peter, Norfolk. Thomas Drake (died 1520) and wife Elizabeth (some say Ann). Spiral pilasters and lozenges with shields. Long pediment.

TT40 Leighton, Shrops. William Leighton (died 1540) and wife Margaret. Transferred from Buildwas Abbey.

TT41 Pentlow, Essex. Edmund Felton and wife Frances (Butler). Reported as a tabletop in 1916, the slab is rough cut with a date of 1542. The slab top may now be set against the north wall. The effigies are heavily overpainted such that he stone cannot be identified.

TT42 Fenny Drayton, Leics. Ralph Purefoy (died 1554) and wife Anne (Bingham). One of three slabs which may have been raised to tabletop tombs.

TT43 Bletchingley, Surrey. Thomas Cawarden (died 1559 in the Tower). A tabletop in uncertain material with brass fitted 19th century.

TT44 Framlingham, Suffolk. Sir Robert Hitcham (died 1636) made by Francis Griggs in 1638. An extremely unusual tomb with the slab made from black marble supported in the corners by what may be painted alabaster angels. Underneath the slab is an urn. The slab contains the signature of Francis Griggs on the western edge. Hitcham acquired the Framlingham estate in 1634 who, in turn, left it to Pembroke College, Cambridge who remain patron of St Michael.

TT45 Bramston, Yorks. Wife of Sir Matthew Boynton (died 1634). A tabletop in black marble supported by four alabaster urns. Reported as once used as a communion table until broken by a fallen beam and let into floor.

TT46 Bramston, Yorks. Peregrine Boynton (died 1645). A tabletop in black marble supported by six alabaster urns. The top is now lowered to the floor and the urns now support the rail under the chancel arch.

W1 Kedleston Hall. Mined in the Redhill mine (or quarry). Assheton Curzon owned the mine in 1750, his brother Lord Scarsdale purchased the alabaster and it was assembled by Adams. The Industrial Museum at Derby shows a model of the town in the late 17th century. The model shows Trent barges tied up at a wharf below the weir, the ground of which is now taken up by the Station Approach road. It is believed that barges negotiated the Derwent from Shardlow often being manually hauled. The alabaster probably travelled by barge to Derby from the wharf at Redhill (*see* A7) and thence to Kedleston by wagon. The Derby Canal built in 1792 removed almost all the river trade. Adams was assisted by Joseph Pickford of Derby the nephew of the Joseph Pickford of Holkham. *See also* Appendix M.

W2 Mined in the Redhill mine (or quarry). Mr Pelham, Lord Yarborough purchased alabaster which formed columns 20ft high in three pieces. Brocklesby is only a few miles from Barton on Humber to which the columns almost certainly came by boat down the Trent. There is some evidence of a causeway from the quarry to a wharf on the Trent now obliterated by the railway bridge. The assembly of the monument is contemporary with the opening of Trent and

Mersey Canal but the current Cranfleet and Beeston Cuts which bypasses Billy Stones shallows making river transport down the Trent easier, were not constructed until the 1790s. *See also* Appendix M.

W3 Bisham, Berks. Monument to Margaret wife of Sir Thomas Hoby (*see* R44). This unusual monument is an alabaster plinth crowned with a grey obelisk. At the corners are four swans the symbol of the Hobys. There were once four other obelisks at the foot of the plinth. The monument now stands on a modern marble platform.

W4 Holkham Hall, Norfolk. This Palladian mansion was designed by William Kent between 1734 and 1764. The work on the marble hall and other alabaster items was carried out by Joseph Pickford and Thomas Carter. The Hall records state that alabaster for the marble hall began to arrive from Castle Hay quarry in 1755 with the columns in 1756 (although it is not stated from which quarry the column alabaster was obtained). In Appendix M there is a discussion on possible sources.

X1 St Mary's Church, Bures, Suffolk. This effigy of an unknown knight reported to date from 1300 and carved in wood believed to be chestnut and displays many of the characteristics of the effigy in Hanbury, Staffs (*see* G28, 1340). The knight is carved in 'crusader' style with his feet on a dog and his head on a cushion supported by angels.

X2 St Stephen's Chapel, Bures, Suffolk. Robert de Vere (died 1296). For details of this chapel *see* G113 and G29. This may date from 1300 and is not carved in alabaster but may well be the source of St John Hope's misdating the first effigy carved in this medium in the early 20th century. It is also reported that the tomb chest does not belong.

X3 Layer Marney church, Essex. The tomb of Henry 1st Lord Marney (died 1523). Probably carved before his death. This effigy is not alabaster but is carved in black catacleuse stone from a quarry at St Endelion in Cornwall which was owned by the Marneys. The tomb canopy is in Gothic style in terracotta. The records are believed to indicate that the carver was Italian working in Renaissance style possibly Florentine Pietro Torregiano. A second effigy is of the 2nd Lord Marney who died 27th April 1525 at the age of 45. He played a significant part in the Field of the Cloth of Gold but does not display an SS collar. The effigy is also in black catacleuse from the same quarry as the 1st Lord and has many similarities. The allocation of the second monument to Torregiano is suspect since he died in 1522.

X4 London, Southwark. Bishop Lancelot Andrewes (died 1626). A tomb created by Gerard Johnson with canopy by Bloomfield and colouring by Sir Ninian Cowper. The tomb has been moved twice.

X5 London, Southwark. Joyce Austin monument by Nicholas Stone.

X6 There a number of accounts of St Albans – *see* Saul pages 85 and 86.

X7 Worcester Cathedral holds the earliest surviving monument to a king of England – that of King John (1216) and also Prince Arthur (1502), son of Henry VII and a number of others all in Purbeck marble. The *Gentleman's Magazine* Vol 88 Part 1 quotes John's tomb as 'alabaster' but this is incorrect. John is resting his head on a cushion supported by Bishops Wulfstan II and Oswald both Saxon bishops. The large use of Purbeck marble can be explained by the closeness of the cathedral to the Severn. The carvers were most likely London based and in the employ of the crown. When Arthur's tomb was carved Purbeck marble was in serious decline.

X8 Malmesbury, Wilts. The tomb of King Aethelstan (died 939). Although this is limestone and constructed in the 14th (some say 15th) century it shows much of the style of Gardner's Class II carving dating its probable construction to *circa* 1360.

X9 The Church of St John the Baptist, Egham Surrey was totally rebuilt *circa* 1817–1820 to which the Tudor and Stuart monuments were transferred from the old church. No information is forthcoming on their position and status there.

X10 Bristol Cathedral. At the west end of the nave is a freestone monument to Dame Joan Young (Wadham). This may well be the first monument carved by Samuel Baldwin *circa* 1603 when he set up his workshop at Stroud but also carries a date of 1606. This lacks the quality and fineness of his later monuments but displays certain features found on alabaster tombs. The monument has two peninsula extensions at 45° to the axis of the tomb chest on which reside two statues of bare-breasted women clutching timepieces. These peninsulas have appeared elsewhere but are surmounted by obelisks of various sizes but women in this pose are rare. The monument was installed in the old medieval sedilia in the chancel but it is clear that the Victorians found such images offensive as it was dismantled in 1861 and kept in pieces until re-erected *circa* 1900 at its current position. No-one has been able to explain the purpose of the images but they are likely to be classical depictions of the passage of time. Whatever the original purpose, Baldwin does not appear to have repeated the image style. Joan Young married two husbands one of whom was in permanent disputes with his fellow merchants. Both were originally depicted on the 1603 monument but are now lost.

X11 Gloucester, St Nicholas. Alderman John Walton (died 1626) and wife Anne (died 1620). Freestone. A later Samuel Baldwin which shows the development of Baldwin carving skills. Polychromed. Linen cap with steeple hat.

X12 Miserden, Gloucs. William Kingston (died 1614). Freestone. Possibly attributed to Samuel Baldwin. The monument has been moved but is notable for its fine carving and subject matter. The effigy rests his booted feet on a goat which is munching on greenery. His breeches have a garter – a feature of the SB workshop. The head may be a likeness and the beard is well carved. The effigy shows much colour remaining.

X13 The history of Edwin Sandys is very interesting. A staunch Protestant he had to flee abroad during the reign of Mary I to return after Elizabeth came to the throne. He was Bishop of London in 1571. In one of the twists of fate he was instrumental in the celebrations of the 7th October 1571 celebrating the Battle of Lepanto (Gulf of Corinth) when the naval forces of the pope defeated the Turkish fleet. This celebration took place on the 9th November 1571 when Sandys circulated prayers of praise and thanksgiving to be said in St Paul's and other parish churches. This unanimity with the Catholic Church appears out of character with his anti-Catholic stance but it seems he took his lead from Elizabeth who was 'no lover of the Turk'. Sandys owned a property in Woodham Ferrers Essex latterly known as Edwin's Hall and his family stayed there even after he was made Bishop of York. The monument at Southwell (A17) was probably contracted for by his son Samuel (R67) who also contracted for the monument to his mother (M4).

X14 English Bicknor, Gloucs. The war memorial in veined alabaster with central effigy of Christ on the cross.

X15 Other exporting evidence comes from records of the reredos depicting St James in the Cathedral of Santiago de Compostela presented by a priest named as John Gugguer (Goodyear) from Chale, IOW in 1456 and which, in 1940, was still extant. Cheetham says that the Santiago carving style is also to be seen in the Swansea altarpiece. *See also* X18.

X16 Llanblethian church, Cowbridge, South Wales. A rare use of Penarth alabaster. This pulpit made from Forest of Dean and Bridgend stone is faced with Penarth alabaster carved by William Clarke about 1900. The pulpit was later restored by C B Fowler.

X17 Warwick Castle chapel. Richard de Beauchamp (died 1439). Bronze made 1456 but not transferred to chapel until 1475. The armour is Italian being made in Milan. In the mid-15th century the armour of the armourers of northern Italy dominated the market. The style was latterly copied and permitted to rise of the South German armourers.

X18 The 'passport' issued for the effigy at Nantes (A15), the writ issued by the king for the images carried to Rome (A16), the reredos at Santiago de Compostela (X15) and the Dartmouth exports in 1390 all point to royal oversight on the export of alabaster in the latter part of the 14th century. In the 1414 purchase of alabaster for Fécamp there is no mention of any export controls and it can be construed that by the turn of the 15th century the need for controls had lapsed.

X19 There is no consistency as to which animal is depicted on tombs on which the effigy places its feet. The lion is popular for knights but so are dogs. Dogs were highly cherished. Most female effigies have their feet on a dog and sometimes a dog in the folds of the dress in playful mood and in the case of some brasses the dog is named with *Terri* as appearing at Deerhurst and *Jukke* at Ingham although this may well now be lost. For details of the passport *see* X23.

X20 The tomb of John Beauchamp (pronounced Beecham) of Holt and wife in Worcester Cathedral. This painted tomb does not appear to be alabaster but wholly made from limestone. Dated from 1400 as he was tried for treason and beheaded in 1388. The inclusion here is due to the unusual objects at the heads of the effigy. She has her head on a black swan and he on a great helm with a swan as the crest. There is a legend that he fought in Palestine and was caught and imprisoned and on being released was so emancipated that he was only recognised by his dog. His wife had dreamt that he would be returned riding on a black swan hence the head stones. Dogs are represented at feet.

X21 Colston Bassett, Notts. Statue to Alice Catherine Knowles (died 1892). The statue is in Carrera marble but is mounted in front of a panel which may well be Chellaston alabaster.

X22 Chesterfield Derbyshire. J Charles Cox reproduces the entire agreement on page 147 of his book. It states 'Henry Moorecock of Burton in Staffordshire to make a tomb for Henry Foljambe husband of Bennett in St Mary's Quire in the Church of All Hallows in Chesterfield and to make it as good as the tomb of Sir Nicholas Montgomery at Colley (*sic*) with 18 images under the table and the arms upon them and the said Henry in copper and gilt upon the table of marble with two arms at the head and two at the feet of the same and the table of marble to be a whole stone and all fair marble. The price to be paid is £5 and another £5 when all is performed signed this day 26th October 2nd Henry VIII'.

The date is 1510 and Cox believes the estimate was for only the stone part. Colley is Great Cubley, Derbyshire. Cox in 1875 reported that all the monuments had been re-grouped, but in the process three had been 'lost' – *see* Appendix D9.

X23 The passport for the 1408 export of a tomb to Nantes has survived. Written in Medieval Latin a translation is as follows:

The king, to all and individual admirals etc. To whom these letters shall be presented, greetings.

Know that we, at the request of our most dear consort (the Queen – Joan of Navarre) – who had made the Alabaster tomb for the deceased Duke of Brittany, her former husband in [*Piargea*] of Saint Nicholas of Nantes in Brittany, together with three of our English lieges, who were the carvers of that same tomb, namely Thomas Colyn, Thomas Holewell and Thomas Poppehowe, for the purpose of attending to and placing the aforementioned tomb in the church of Nantes in Brittany, – have given instruction for the sending [of a ship].

We have undertaken to provide safe and secure conduct for John Guychard, merchant and master of the aforementioned ship, and the 10 marine servants [sailors] in his company, for the crossing to Brittany, as has been said, and thence for returning the merchant to our kingdom of England, also the aforementioned ship, and her goods and any [equipment], and therefore we command you that you assist, protect, and defend the same John and his aforementioned servants and sailors in the crossing to Brittany and afterwards the merchant in returning to our kingdom of England, also the aforementioned ship and her goods and any [equipment] whatever, without interference, etc. So that [all things may be conducted as stated].

[The duration] of which etc. Lasting until the next Feast of the Nativity of Saint John the Baptist (24th June).

[Given] under the royal seal at [West?] monastery, the 24th day of February 1408 [in the ninth year of the reign of Henry IV].

By writ of private seal.

Comment: It is clear the three kervers accompanied the tomb to Brittany. Neither the ship nor the port of embarkation or the port to which the alabaster was delivered is named. Most probably St Nazaire was the French port and London the departure point. St John Hope was unable to trace any history of the three kervers.

X24 The two effigies at Melbury Sampford are enigmas. Gardner was puzzled. The Purbeck marble content of both tombs led him to suggest that they were carved by Isle of Purbeck carvers attempting to regain their lost trade in effigy carving. Certainly the style of both is unlike any others elsewhere. He suggests that if not Dorset then it may be Bristol. The problem is the source of alabaster. In the late 15th century the only working quarries were in the Trent Valley and as at the date of publishing distance has prevent any closer examination of the effigies. As regards the confusion on dates it may well be that both monuments were in Abbotsbury Abbey and transferred and reused by Sir Giles Strangeways in 1539. It is a problem still to be solved. The church is in private hands but can be accessed by prior arrangement with Melbury Hall.

X25 In 2014 Dan Jones in *History Magazine* looked at the Tudor propaganda post-1485. He made a compelling case that all the Tudor monarchs not least of which was Henry VIII, suppressed the Yorkist insignia. The merging of the red and white rose into the Tudor rose was a symbol of the new order as was the wearing of the SS collar. The appearance of the Yorkist collar on effigies after 1485 is therefore either incorrect in the dating of monuments or evidence of the old guard thumbing their nose at the Tudor upstarts – a risky practice. Amongst these monuments are those at Melbury Sampford in Dorset (1487), Youlgreave, Derbys (1488), Wethersfield, Essex (1490), Berkeley, Gloucs (1490), Millom, Cumbria (1494) and Holme Pierrepont, Nottingham (1499). It may be that the remoteness of these from London may have resulted in the owners taking the risk but the continued if spasmodic use of the Yorkist collar is strange.

Photo: Stephanie Grimley 2015.

X26 Wells Cathedral, Somerset. Bishop John Droxford (died 1329). A fine Purbeck marble effigy on a limestone base. The carving shows the peak of the Dorset carvers and is stained to represent the robes of office. This monument can be compared with that of his liege Edward II carved in alabaster at Gloucester about the same time.

X27 Wells Cathedral, Somerset. Richard Kidder (died 1703). A fine monument in a variety of stones some of which may be alabaster. Purbeck marble effigy on a limestone base. The effigy is Kidder's daughter in a somewhat risqué Baroque pose.

X28 In respect of the Bures, St Stephen monuments *An Inventory of the Historical Monuments in Essex* Vol 3, 1922 has photographs (plates 43 to 46) of the monuments whilst they were present in the De Vere house. It is clear that the monuments had been divided in order to provide a display with that of 'Thomas 1340' and 'Alice 1417' split from their respective partners and mounted against the wall. The tombs of 'Thomas 1371' and 'Richard 1417' were set into the wall side by side. The tomb chest of Richard and Alice both display the winged angels of the Chellaston carvers and were once most likely paired. The identity of the tombs is open to question hence the names in parenthesis above – *see* G29 and G113.

X29 Appendix H deals with the destruction of images and monuments during the Reformation but it is necessary to examine some claims in detail. Jon Bayliss in his 2013 paper on the Parr monument (T27) at Horton, Northamptonshire states clearly that he believes there to have been two phases of funeral monument destruction. The first phase starting in 1536 during the early suppression of the lesser houses and ending *circa* 1540 with the larger houses and a second phase of chantry closures mostly in parish churches, commencing in 1540 and peaking and 1547, but which may have continued until 1553. He also suggests that during the suppression of chantries parish church monuments also suffered from iconoclasts. In all some 625 religious houses were suppressed between 1536 and 1540 but the number of closed chantries and guild chapels is even higher at 2,374. That many monuments in dissolved houses disappeared with the fabric is without doubt and some are listed in Appendix D9 but Jon Bayliss has suggested that a number were removed for reuse and he cites Ratcliffe on Soar (G136), Middle Claydon (G43) and the Parr monument at Horton (T27) as examples. Evaluation of this claim is included in the note attached to each.

X30 University Church, Dublin. Built by john Newman with the help of John Hungerford Pollen *circa* 1855, the altar has an alabaster front in which are set two groups of six Derbyshire spar crystals. The alabaster may well be Chellaston as there is no sign of veining. Behind the altar is a wooden baldachino below which is band of alabaster and marble which also serves as a reredos.

X31 London Bayswater. This Catholic Church built in 1855 has had a number of additions amongst which is a marble and alabaster altar with reredos designed by J F Bentley in 1874. The north aisle has one too and as well as the chapel although the latter dates from 1912. There is a square alabaster and marble font and other minor alabaster additions.

X32 Marsworth, Bucks. Tomb to Edward West (died 1618). The tomb is signed 'Evesham fecit' unusually on a brass plate. The tomb has no effigy and has some five panels most of which are in Fauld alabaster. Two show foliated scrollwork on which are carved skulls. There is a wreath enclosing a heraldic shield and on the ends a shield with a carved heraldic device surmounted by a great helm with what appears to be a swan crest.

X33 Hull, Yorks. William Dobson (died 1666). An alabaster bust in an arch decorated with putti, skulls, fruit and flowers. Some wrought ironwork.

X34 Birmingham, St Martin in the Bullring, Warwicks. A Gothic set of panels, the gift of the congregation and freemen of Warwick to St Martin when the church was rebuilt in 1874.

X35 Freckenham, Suffolk. In the north aisle wall is panel from a reredos or retable which was recovered after being hidden in 18th century. It depicts St Eloy (Eligius) shoeing a horse and shows the chamfered frame used by London carvers in the 14th century. Some paint remains. The history of the church states that the church in Coddingham found an alabaster image in an attic in the village. Page 99 of Cheetham.

X36 The Norfolk Archives holds a letter from Dawson Turner dated 1847 describing how a crucifix and alabaster panel was found under the floor in the church. This is catalogue BEA 280 381 438x7.

X37 From the letters of John Raffle we learn that the Ratcliffe monuments (G136, M2,R5.T9) were stripped and cleaned and a new damp proof course laid in January 1974 by John Green who produced drawings of the monuments which are held in the Swindon Archives. For this work a grant of £2000 was obtained from the Pilgrim's Trust on the understanding that the organ was moved, a job completed on the 29th Sept 1973.

X38 East Horndon, Essex. Alice Tyrell (died 1422) wife of Sir John Tyrell. Limestone, possible not carved until 1440. The slab was removed from the church at East Horndon in 1969 for safe keeping but returned in 1976. Greenhill shows an image as Vol 2 Fig 142. Possibly of French manufacture and very fine.

X39 Hambleden, Bucks. Adoration of Christ which may be a relic of pre-Reformation.

X40 York, All Saints Pavement. This ancient church has a reredos which is stated by English Heritage to be 20th century although the east end was rebuilt in 1780 and remodelled in 1887. The monument is alabaster of a pale translucent type which may well be Kingston or adjacent quarry. The statuary is limestone and dates from same period.

X41 Leicester Cathedral. In 2012 the grave of King Richard III was found beneath a car park in Leicester. His re-interment took place in April 2015 in Leicester Cathedral for which a new altar was required. This was made by the same stonemason who carved the stone placed over Richard's grave in the chancel and who obtained the red/brown veined alabaster from the Fauld Mine in Staffordshire.

X42 Exeter Cathedral. The tombs in Exeter to the Carew family are made from an undisclosed stone which may or may not be alabaster. The CMS Vol XXIX 2014 has a long analysis of these monuments but fails to solve the origin. The reader is directed to this publication for more information.

X43 Newark, Notts. A tabletop in Purbeck marble to Robert Brown (*circa* 1532) which has Burton features such as the lozenges with painted central shields. Restored 1976.

X44 Truro Cathedral, Cornwall. A tablet containing three cartouches of Cornish statesmen. The date is uncertain as is the material which looks like Fauld alabaster. The depicted are John Elliot (1632), Sidney Goldolphin (1712) and Sir Eilliam Molesworth (1855). This beautifully carved monument has yet to be identified with a carver.

X45 Blunham, Beds. A 14th century statue of the Virgin minus head. The origins are uncertain but probably buried or hidden in the 16th century. Almost certainly Nottingham.

X46 Wootton Wawen, Warwick. Francis Smith (died 1605). This fine mural seems to be in freestone but is carved in the style of most alabaster tombs of the period. The form indicates a London workshop.

X47 Bolsover Castle chimney pieces. The castle interior was designed by Robert Smythson *circa* 1620 after the style of Italian Sebastiano Serlio. In all there are 15 decorated chimney pieces in the castle but *see* B126. The stone used varies but included Ashford marble, cockleshell marble and a 'pink' alabaster but at this stage it cannot be identified with Watchet. It is reported that the stone carries a high polish leading many commentators into thinking they are marble. The alabaster chimney pieces are in the Pillar Room, Star Chamber, Heaven Room, Cavendish Bedchamber, North West Room and South West Room, whilst the Marble Room and West Room is Ashford Marble and the Elysian Room has cockleshell marble in a sandstone surround.

X48 Leigh, Worcs. Edmund Coles (died 1606). Feet on lion. Some traces of paint.

X49 Barton in Fabis, Notts. Raffe Sacheverell (died 1605) and wife Emme (Dethick – died 1606). A tomb chest without effigy but with much heraldry. The material is uncertain but believed to be freestone or alabaster. There are similarities to a tomb in Appleby (*see* M443).

X50 Thornhill, Yorks. Sir George Saville (died 1614) and wife Ann. A report was made by Elliott Ryder Conservation in 2012.

X51 Staindrop, Durham. Henry Neville, 5th Earl of Westmoreland (died 1564) and his two wives, Ann daughter of Thomas Manners, Earl of Rutland and Anne daughter of Richard Cholmondeley of Malpas. The effigies in oak show a retrograde step into the Gothic for the date.

X52 Lod, Israel. The tomb of St George was constructed *circa* 1870 when the church was rebuilt. Photographs show distinct alabaster features but, at this time, it has not been possible to confirm the materials from which it was carved.

X53 For the tombs of the Hobys, Russells and Cliffords *see* Helen Crawford Gladstone's thesis 'Building an Identity – Two Noblewomen in England 1566 to 1666' available from Open Research Online

X54 Lambourne, Berks. A memorial medallion depicting Charles I with the figures of justice standing on chained roundheads or figures depicting tyranny. It is probably that this was hidden during the Commonwealth but was not placed in the church until 1920 when it was found in a house in the village.

X55 Burton Agnes Hall, Yorks. Several large chimney pieces variously reported as being transferred from Methley Hall and Barmston Hall *circa* 1762. A relief of the wise and foolish virgins is depicted on one.

X56 Newburgh Priory. A chimneypiece made by John Francis Moore in 1766. In green and red-veined alabaster. The piece is described in Wombwell Archives ZDVX15 (mic 1271).

X57 Gloucester Cathedral. Judge John Powell (died 1713). A fine standing statue by Thomas Green reported to be in marble but the material is uncertain.

X58 Bradford, Cathedral. War memorial with fluted side pilasters and broken pediment depicting a statue of a knight in armour.

X59 Seville, Spain. An application was made in 1390 by Henry and William Mayn, merchants, to export alabaster images to Seville in a ship called *George*.

X60 Amport, Hants. Head of John the Baptist with an angel holding his soul in a napkin, found in a cottage which was being demolished.

X61 Breaston, Derbys. Alabaster initialled IW or TW. Possible transferred from Risley Hall.

X62 Flaxley, Gloucs. Reputed to have been on display at the Paris Exposition.

X63 St Paul's Cathedral. The crypt contains a number of tablets mainly with frames of Fauld alabaster.

X64 Baglan, South Wales. The church contains a pulpit, font, reredos and porch ornamentation which appears to be formed from red Penarth alabaster. These mainly date from 1875. The pieces are small. This alabaster is also used in the church at Pen y Fai (X79).

X65 Stanton by Bridge, Derbys. Paid for by Edward Wright Whittaker in memory of his father the rector.

X66 Alexandra Park, Manchester. The use of Chellaston alabaster was recorded by Sherlock and Smith in 1918 who stated that the same material was used in the lounge of the Windsor Hotel in Westminster, the new baths at Buxton and possibly the reredos in Ely Cathedral.

X67 Ashbourne, Derbys. A pulpit and altar made from alabaster taken from the Bradbourne tombs.

X68 Saltcoats, Ayrshire. Recorded, incorrectly, as Italian alabaster in some publications. The local paper, The *Ardrossan and Saltcoats Herald* maintains the reredos is a replica of one provided to a church on the Isle of Wight by Edward VII in memory of Queen Victoria.

X69 Manchester, Lancs. Niches with statues of saints in Gothic style also made by Boulton.

X70 Birmingham, Oratory. A stature after a picture by Guido Reni.

X71 Pontardawe, South Wales. The gables on the reredos are Penarth red alabaster.

X72 St Peter Port, Guernsey. Memorial to Dr Lukis.

X73 Welford, Northants. In memory of the local vicar.

X74 Chichester, Sussex. Cathedral. The effigy of Joan de Vere (*circa* 1293) formerly in Lewes priory in Trent Valley style but whitewashed such that the material cannot be identified. A second effigy is to Richard FitzAlan, Earl of Arundel (died 1376) and wife Eleanor also once in Lewes. Eleanor is unusual in that she gas crossed legs and holds the hand of her knight. A third tomb is to Bishop Robert Stratford (died 1362). These have all been washed such that the material used cannot be identified and may well have been restored by Richardson in the 19th century.

X75 Prestwold, Leics. A font which once was in the nave now set aside.

X76 Chicksands, Beds. Five panels formerly in Chicksands Priory.

X77 Barling Magna, Essex. Found walled up in north aisle in 19th century. St John Hopes describes the first one as a figure of a bishop or abbot, headless, with painted gown and remains of staff. One hand formerly held something now lost. The second an image of St Dominic, also headless, in brown habit, black cloak and holding a large red book. A paternoster hangs from a girdle.

X78 Plymtree, Devon. Like Chicksands.

X79 Pen y Fai, South Wales. A fine Gothic reredos with figures carved by local sculptor known as Goscombe John.

X80 Llandaff, Insole Court, Wales. An archway in the dining room.

X81 Rochester Cathedral, Kent. To those that fell in the Boer War. This large tablet memorial appears to be carved from three blocks of brown alabaster which does not appear to be from the Needwood beds.

X82 Risley, Notts. This font is stated as being late Elizabethan. This font located in the west end of the nave has a moulded base and thick tapered stem with strapwork with an octagonal bowl which has the Willoughby arms. This is probably the oldest extant alabaster font.

X83 Hanbury, Staffs. This font is claimed to have a date of 1770 underneath but this is questionable.

X84 Bridgend, Hope Baptist Chapel, Glamorgan. The baptistery is made from white marble with an alabaster front which was the gift of Mrs Sam Llewellyn of Coed y Parc in memory of the Rev Thomas Cole.

X85 Brinsop, Hereford. A gilded alabaster reredos in commemoration of Hubert Delaval Astley and Richard Vincent Sutton.

X86 Thornhill, Yorks. An alabaster figure of a baby supporting a bowl brought from Rufford in 1948.

X87 South Normanton, Derbys. Made by Jack England in commemoration of Horold Lane. Formerly in All Angels.

X88 Hereford Cathedral. Seven shields placed against the east wall.

X89 Illington, Norfolk. Found in 1881 in the wall during refurbishments.

X90 Hungerford, Berks. Pulpit presented by the two Miss Lidderdale in memory of their parents and brother.

X91 Pauline Routh's Book 'Medieval Effigial Alabaster Tombs in Yorkshire' contains one of the best descriptions of this group of tombs and covers Allerton Mauleverer, Barmston, Batley, Burton Agnes, Darfield, Eastrington, Halsham, Harewood, Hornby, Hull, Methley, Pickering, Ryther, Selby, Sheriff Hutton, South Cowton, Swine, Thornhill, Tickhill, Wadworth, Wentworth, West Tanfield, Whitkirk and York.

Another good commentary is the website: http://diannesmedievalwriting.blogspot.com.au/2015/03/whats-with-medieval-tombs-part-8.html

X92 Fyfield, Oxford. The tomb to Sir John Golafre (died 1442). In local stone but shows an effigy lying on a slab with embattled edging under which is a tomb chest with column and which contains a cadaver.

X93 Two Boston wills mention that masses had to be said at the Scala Coeli (Ladder of Heaven altar) at Boston church on interment. It is not known if these tombs are the one but one person whose will exists was Hugh Schawe and the other Richard Shallock. The Scala Coeli pardon was attached to a church in Rome but was authorised for transfer to selected churches from 1476 by Pope Sixtus IV. Boston acquired theirs in 1516 but others include the St Thomas of Acre Hospital and the Crutched Friars in both London and Colchester (1516). That at Boston was attached to the chapel of the Guild of St Mary. The Scala Coeli pardon was believed to allow the deceased to be immediately released from purgatory. The Boston receipts grew fast after 1514 on the strength of this indulgence.

X94 West Leake, Notts. The church contains two effigial tombs in wall niches. Neither is identified or dated, but one with a canopy has a costume which is covered in St Andrew's crosses in what may be Guild Robes although none is known in the area.

X95 Wingfield, Suffolk. Michael de la Pole (died 1415), 2nd Earl of Suffolk and his wife. The effigies are of wood on a freestone tomb chest. The inclusion of this is due to Crossley's assertion (page 28) that the effigies were intended to be alabaster but that for some reason this was not carried through. Crossley bases this on the contract for the metal effigy for Lord Derby at Ormskirk, Lancs (now lost) which states '... and James Halys had for making the patron (pattern) of the image in timber one hundred shillings'. St John Hope, in 1920, also made the claim and added that the wooden effigies of Ralph Neville (died 1484) and wife at Brancepeth, Durham were likewise intended for alabaster. The Brancepeth effigies were destroyed in a fire in 1998. The making of wooden patterns for bronze casting is common practice the pattern being removed and replaced by wax which in turn is replaced by the molten bronze in what is known as the lost wax process. The Derby effigy was 5ft 6 inches long and weighed 5.5cwt (some 600lbs) and the foundry was paid £80, the gilding £35 and labouring £10. The existence of the Ormskirk contract does not make the making of a wooden pattern for alabaster certain but it is an interesting possibility.

X96 Caerleon, Monmouth. In 1660 a stone coffin was found in a quarry containing a skeleton in a lead sheet. Nearby was a broken image of alabaster partly gilding. It shows a figure in a coat of mail holding a sword in the right hand and in the left a set of scales the pans of which hold a maiden in one and a globe in the other. This was obtained by a ship's captain called Matthew Bird and donated to the Ashmolean in Oxford *circa* 1693 where it was seen and reported by Camden in 1695. Subsequently the scales were broken and lost. Discussion on the net offers the opinion that it dates from 1480 to 1530 and depicts St Michael weighing the soul of the departed. The carving is crude and unlike the work of Nottingham.

X97 Wombourne, Staffs. A relief tablet depicting the Good Samaritans brought to Wombourne by Sir Samuel Hellier.

X98 Washington, DC. A statue of a man on a horse *circa* 1400 to 1420 which may be St George. From the Samuel H Kress collection.

X99 Grandborough, Bucks. Crucifixion recovered from farmhouse wall now in church

X100 Notes on the Framlingham monuments. The Howard tombs have caused much debate as to their origins and many books. One of these is *The Howards and The Tudors – A Study in Science and Heritage* – a collection of essays by eight eminent authors edited by Phillip Lindley. This book looks at the history of the Howards and their association with Thetford Priory and subsequent location of the tombs in Framlingham. The book is commended but for the researcher into alabaster the omission of any observation as to materials used and their source means that certain lines of enquiry are missed. In 118 pages alabaster is mentioned only once and clunch twice. This note amplifies the essays in respect of the use of alabaster.

The Howards always intended to bury their ancestors in Thetford Priory. This plan was disturbed by the Reformation but Thetford was one of the last to be dissolved on the 16th February 1540 so it is possible that the church there stood for a number of years longer (it was visited in December 1546 when the heraldry was noted). The book suggests that the tomb chests of the wives of Thomas Howard (A31) and Henry Fitzroy and his wife May Howard (A30) were made in Thetford and later in the 1560s transferred to Framlingham. The design of both is similar and unlike any product from the Midlands and in any case is believed to be carved in clunch. Certainly Thetford held many burials. Page 25 of the book lists a number of names and also notes that an alabaster-man was paid 8d in 1501–1502 for some unspecified work. Alabaster fragments have been found in excavations over the years but no record of alabaster tombs has survived. John Howard the first Duke of Norfolk was killed at Bosworth in 1485 fighting for Richard III but his son Thomas changed allegiance and was restored to the dukedom as the 2nd duke in 1514 following his actions at Flodden. This 2nd duke died in 1524 and was buried at Thetford having commissioned a tomb from East Anglian master mason,

John Wastell of Bury St Edmunds, as its designer. Wastell died in 1514–1518 and therefore is unlikely to have been the actual carver of his tomb. The 2nd duke's will of 1520 mentions the tomb and states 'And a pictours (picture) of us and Agnes our wife to be sett togider (together) thereupon'. In the parlance of the time a 'picture' is often taken as meaning an incised slab and this may well have been alabaster or a brass although Phillip Lindley says that the tomb had Gothic trefoil arches in the tomb chest which bore a recumbent effigy of the duke without quoting the source for this suggestion. Lindley goes on to say that the wife Agnes did not appear and that she is buried at Lambeth in her own tomb but both the 2nd duke's and Agnes's tomb have been destroyed, one at the dissolution and the other during the Commonwealth. A drawing of the latter exists in the archives of Arundel Castle and shows a Purbeck marble chest and a brass under a triple canopy. Other members of the Howard family buried at Thetford include Anne (died 1511) but commemorated at Framlingham, Lord Thomas Howard, son of the 2nd duke, Thomas Howard, third duke, also commemorated at Framlingham and Henry Fitzroy likewise. That tombs existed is recorded in evidence given in 1539 by the third duke to Henry VIII in support of the retention of Thetford Priory church following dissolution. No tomb to the 3rd duke, who by that time was locked up in the Tower, was noted at Thetford in 1546 leading to the suggestion that his tomb (A29) was new to Framlingham. Although only Surrey's tomb is alabaster the group of monuments is worthy of inclusion due to their interesting history. Also on display at Framlingham is a helmet once thought to be used at the battle of Flodden in 1513 but now indentified as a Great Helm or jousting helmet.

X101 Bilborough, Notts. The panel in Fauld alabaster has the following inscription which states 'DMUNDE EXIGUO RESIDENS HELWISE SEPULCHRO EXTREMUM DOCEAS CORPORIS OMNIS ITER. NATA SIMUL DILECTA TIBI VI MORTIS INIQUAE RAPTA SUB HOC TUMULO CUM GENITORE JACET. SCILICET HIC MORTIS MOS EST MORTISQUE TRIUMPHUS GRANDAEVOS TENERIS TOLLERE SAEPE SIMUL. AETAS5 FLOS SERUS NON RUMPUNT VINCULA MORTIS NATA PATERQUE CADUNT TEMPORE NATA PRIOR'.

X102 Saundby, Notts. A reredos of alabaster and enamel mosaic was installed by the retired Rev C Hudson in 1885–1886 along with an altar of alabaster and red Verona marble.

X103 Old St Paul's, London. In 1658 the Bohemian engraver Wenceslas Holler produced a plan of the cathedral in which he identified some 31 tombs and monuments. The plan can be seen on *Wikipedia* under Wenceslas Holler. Amongst the tombs lost was that to John Hollis, Bishop Robert Braybrooke (mummified corpse of 1404 recovered for reburial),

Bishop Stephen de Gravesend (1338) and |John Acton, Goldsmith (1638).

X104 Barnard Castle, Bowes Museum. A Dutch altarpiece made by Isaac Tissenaken *circa* 1643 purchased by John and Josephine Bowes in the 19th century. This is an example of the small altarpieces in alabaster made by a number of Dutch and Flemish carvers from the 15th century.

X105 Great Hallingbury, Essex. A memento mori to the Morley family of uncertain date but not earlier than the 17th century. A standing cadaver between columns.

X106 Raglan, Monmouth. Castle chapel. Two much damaged effigies of knights believed to date from the first half of the 17th century and the remains of a canopy. Damaged by Parliamentary forces in 1646, they were further damaged by being left outside.

X107 Alfreton, Derbys. A reredos in marble but with a large Chellaston slab with date 1467. The slab was formerly in the floor but added to the reredos in 1860. The slab states 'Orate pro anima Roberti Barley nuper defunct qui obit in die assumpsionis beatae Maria Virginia item orate pro bono statu Margaretae uxoris suce' The slab was a tabletop in 1710. Three edges are chamfered which usually indicates a Mensa stone but no crosses are noted. There is also a brass inset in a slab of alabaster to John Oldfield dated 1682. There is a story that Robert Barley had a tomb in place in 1611 but gone by 1848.

X108 Llansantffraid, Monmouth. Two 15th cent panels set into the wall either side of the east window. These possibly came from Badney in 1786.

X109 Margam Abbey. The history of Margam states that the monuments in the Abbey church were studied by Thomas Dineley (Dingeley) who produced a book on these and other monuments. At the time of writing this has not been found.

X110 Fenny Drayton, Leics. *See*: https://www.le.ac.uk/lahs/downloads/FennyPagesfromVolume14-1-4.pdf

X111 Tutbury, Staffs. A Gothic reredos carved from a single block of what may be Chellaston alabaster. Three round headed arcades contain images with canopies.

Appendix E
The SS and Yorkist Collars, Decorations and Dress Styles

Introduction

This can only be an outline of the dress styles and the way effigies and images were decorated.

Symbols of rank were of much greater importance than personal features. Kings, princes, earls and dukes may wear a crown or coronet and bishops and abbots their mitre and mass vestments. Some priests may be represented by cope or quire habit (*see* slab of John Prescott, in Ratcliffe on Soar). Judges, lawyers and serjeants can be identified by their robes of office.

Ladies may assert their rank by wearing a coronet and in some cases a collar or even a garter.

Knights may wear robes over their armour but early Knights of the Garter may have this rank shown below the left knee (*see* later). On the rare cases where this honour was bestowed on a lady, this is shown on the left wrist or above the elbow – *see* Ewelme (G142) and Stanton Harcourt (G141).

The SS and Yorkist Livery Collar

(For more detail *see* The Heraldry Society – Livery Collars)

Alabaster was particularly suited to the carving of items of rank.[1] Most common is the 'Esse' or 'SS' livery collar on tombs constructed before 1547. Arthur Gardner reported in 1940 that some 115 alabaster effigies across the country displayed this decoration. The meaning of this decoration appears to be lost and Arthur Gardner discusses possible origins (page 27 to 31 of *Alabaster Tombs*) but without any firm conclusion. The collar had a pendant and this may give a better clue to the allegiance of the wearer. Unfortunately, Gardner did not think to record the form of the pendant and this aspect is still to be fully investigated.

John of Gaunt (1340 to 1399) was the 1st Duke of Lancaster and appears to have devised the collar formed of a row of letter S. The decoration seems to have been awarded to those specially attached to the household. The first confirmed use was before 1371 and Sir John Swinford's effigy in St Andrew's Church, Spratton, Northamptonshire (A29) of that year shows such a decoration (*see* G23 for details of pendant). John Swinford was a follower of John of Gaunt but his effigy may date from a little later that 1371 as the armour depicted is more in keeping with the last quarter of the 14th century. The SS collar appears as a buckling collar. Richard II and his followers had cause to fear John of Gaunt with his obvious military might and one chronicler observed that through '... their conspicuous livery collar of interlocking esses they thought they could gain riches before heaven and earth'. When John of Gaunt died in 1399 his son Henry Bolingbroke deposed Richard II and was crowned king on the 13th October 1399 as Henry IV.

The Heraldry Society observes that the inventory of Henry IV fails to mention that he owned a complete SS collar but does list figure 'S's made from 15 pearls for a 'collar' and a row of 'S's for a collar *'in the livery of Monsr de Lancaster'* reinforcing the link to John of Gaunt. However, the plain Gaunt collars were widely distributed after 1399 with 192 being awarded, 91 silver-gilt 81 in silver and the rest in an unstated base metal (possibly latten). It is suggested that some collars had the SS on their sides on some collars but none are to be seen on alabaster.

The *Complete Dictionary of Heraldry* mentions a roman Society of Simplicius whose emblem was a collar comprised of double SS and some European countries used the collar. Gough mentions that he saw such a collar on the tomb of Matilda Fitzwalter at Dunmow (G84) in Essex dating 'from the reign of King John' (early 13th century). The identity of this tomb is questionable as stated below.

Ashmole also mentions that an SS collar was around the neck of Margaret Pieto in Warwick in the early reign of Edward III (1327 to 1371). This was copied by an engraver into the *Antiquities of Warwick* but he misinterpreted the collar as a ruff. This has not been traced.

It is recorded by Favin that Henry V, following the battle of Agincourt made the declaration that '... for those present who are not gentleman, he would make them so ... that they be known from others ... by leave to wear a collar powdered with S'. It can be construed that Shakespeare's 'gentlemen of England still abed' speech owes much to this statement.

Selden refers to the ballad *The Tanner of Tamworth* with reference to making of esquires by the presentation of a collar by Edward IV. In Henry VIII reign in the year 1533 there was an act which specifically mentions the collar that they may '... publically wear the SS gold collar' but by then the award of the decoration was dying.

Figure 55. This shows the assumed tomb of Matilda Fitzwalter in Dunmow, Essex (G84). The collar is evident. The effigy is white Chellaston alabaster is believed to date from 1480 but this was at the time of the award of the Yorkist suns and roses collar so there is much doubt about both the date and person depicted. The looped cords are indicative of the Harpur and Moorecock workshop giving another reason for a later date. Photo: the author.

Meyrick in 1842 reports that the Lord Mayor of London had such a collar with interspersed red and white roses and knots with a portcullis pendant set with diamonds. He observes that this was a particular privilege as mayors were not knights. From the description it would appear that this was *circa* 1490 when Henry VII was anxious to promote union between the Houses of York and Lancaster. Later in the reign of Henry VII the lord mayor was again presented with a collar by Sir John Allen.

Another early depiction is that of Sir John Marmion at West Tanfield (G31) who died in 1386 again in late 14th century armour.

There is an SS collar on show round the neck of the effigy of Robert Goushill (*see* GNP68) who was knighted by Henry IV at the battle of Shrewsbury in 1403. He was murdered later that day for his possessions by his servant and his tomb may not have been carved until 1425 when his wife died. The collar appears to be of leather with embedded S letters but the pendant has been removed. The front cover of this book shows a picture of this effigy.

A Tudor rose SS collar is present on the tomb of Ralph Sacheverell in Ratcliffe on Soar (G136) similar to that shown on the portrait of Sir Thomas More. The tomb is believed to date from 1539 but may well be earlier – *see* discussion on G136 where Ralph's right to wear the decoration is challenged. An identical collar is to be found on the tomb of Richard Cholmondeley in the Tower chapel (T28).

As to structure, the collar appears to have been either made of leather stained green with imbedded letters of gilded latten (copper or zinc) or later linked letters to form a chain of gold or silver-like decoration with a pendant. Earlier examples have a short chain of 'S's but Tudor decorations appear to be longer. What determines a person's right to display the collar is not clear. It a clearly for some form of service rendered to a monarch descended from the House of Lancaster and were prized some being mentioned in the wills as a special bequest (Sir John Darrell). The wearing of the collar could also cause problems. The Herald Society records that Sir Thomas Swintone was deprived of his collar in 1377 by a London mob after Gaunt had angered the city and which led to other retainers to place theirs in hiding.

The Yorkists, in their turn, introduced a collar of suns and roses (and occasionally oak leaves) from 1461 during the reign of Edward IV until 1470 and from 1471 until the Battle of Bosworth in 1485. It is suggested that the roses and suns represent 'sun in splendour' following the sighting of a perihelion (ice crystals in the air giving impression of three suns) before the Battle of Mortimer's Cross 2nd Feb 1461. Examples of this can be seen at Norbury (G61), Wethersfield (G85), Harewood (G196), Sutton Bonington (GNP73), Minster in Sheppey (G100) and Holme Pierrepont (G135). The latter is interesting in that the tomb of a Henry Pierrepont erected in 1499 (or later) at least some 14 years after the fall of the House of York. Holme Pierrepont church is isolated and it may well be that the inclusion of a Yorkist collar was not noted by other than the Pierrepont retainers. On the other hand the tomb may be a 'changeling' in that the effigy may not be Henry but a 'liberated' effigy from another church or priory. Certainly the tomb chest gives the impression of being later but may be a feature of a post-Reformation reordering of the church.

Both the Minster in Sheppey and Sutton Bonington effigies have received more than the usual attention by vandals maybe indicating a campaign by Tudor sympathisers.[2]

In a few cases the collar is an amalgam of 'S's and roses (Harewood – *see* G206) and these all date from the reign of Henry VII and may be meant to represent the union of the Houses of York and Lancaster favoured by that monarch. In one case the 'S's have been removed from the collar (the 1433 tomb of Sir Thomas Erdington, Aston – *see* GNP90) for reasons which are unclear. In the case of an early Henry VII collar (Harewood, G197, 1487) the collar is a series of 'S's and 'O's but in this instance the collar is short and the pendant is obscured by the hands.

John of Gaunt's son, Henry Bolingbroke, deposed Richard II in 1399 following the death of his father and he reigned as Henry IV (1399 to 1413). A succession of Lancastrian kings followed with Henry V (1413 to 1422) and Henry VI (1422 to 1461 and 1470 to 1471). Each used the SS collar in a variety of forms. It lapsed in 1461 with the succession of the House of York. After the Wars of the Roses[3] in 1487, Henry VII, who had mixed Lancastrian and Tudor origins, resurrected the honour *circa* 1490 and although may have been allowed to lapse in the early 16th century was certainly reintroduced at the accession of Henry VIII and much used following the Field of the Cloth of Gold in 1520. Gardner considers that the collar was more elaborate after 1487 and cites Elford (G159) and Eye (G94) which display the broad leather band and are much longer. The comparison of the two effigies at Elford (G159 and G158) will demonstrate the evolution of the collar. It was not used after the death of Henry VIII in 1547.

Figure 56. The effigy of Edward Redman in Harewood church (G206, 1510) showing the composite collar of S and roses. It is unclear whether this was introduced by Henry VII or Henry VIII. The pendant is a fine Tudor rose which may well have been used from 1509. Certainly by 1530 the rose in the collar had again been discontinued and the use of the rose pendant dropped by 1547. Photo: Janet State.

It is the pendant by which the date of the collar can be identified. The collar shown on a painting of Henry VI in 1461 shows the pendant in the shape of a cross. Henry VII also used a portcullis, dragon or a leopard as pendants but in his 1505 portrait, when he was aged 48, Henry has a livery collar of unmarked links and a fox pelt pendant. Henry VII is also known to have used a swan as a pendant and although he established the Tudor rose which was an amalgamation of the red rose of Lancaster and the white rose of Yorkshire, its first use as a pendant was believed to be with Henry VIII from 1509 – *see* Harewood (G206). In the case of the Yorkist collar the principal pendant was the boar. During the investigations into the Bosworth battle site in 2009 and 2010 a silver-gilt boar badge or pendant was found close to Fen Lane which may well have been lost during the battle (*see Richard III – The Full Story of the King Under the Car Park* page 78 – History Magazine 2015).

Some pendants may be listed as follows:

Pendant	Dates	Introduced by	Applications	Notes
Swan	1390 to 1400	Henry Bolingbroke	Palazzo Ducal Mantua, Italy	Given to supporters of Henry in exile before he became Henry IV
Fetterlock	1401	Henry IV	None known	A D-shaped lock often used in heraldry 
Tiret[4] (no pendant)	1401 to 1413	Henry VI	Queen Joan at Canterbury. G104	Used alone. Later the tiret was used with pendants
Falcon and other beasts	1413 to 1422	Henry V	None known	Borrowed from chivalric orders. Reported by contemporary writers
Cross	*Circa* 1430 to 1460	Henry VI	G135. Sir John Lisle, Thruxton, Hants (not alabaster). Portrait of King Henry VI	Stated Sir John died 1407 but tomb later
Portcullis	*Circa* 1450	Henry VI	Mugginton Derbyshire (Purbeck marble)	Beaufort badge
Hog or boar	1461 to 1485	Edward IV and Richard III	G62, GNP73	
Black Bull of Clare	1461 to 1485	Edward IV and Richard III	No example are known to remain	Reported by contemporary writers
Oak leaves	*Circa* 1462	Henry VI	Joan Neville, wife of William Fitzalan at Arundel (not alabaster)	William died 1487 but research has dated the tomb to 1462 when Joan died
Lion of March	1463 to 1485	Edward IV and Richard III	G41, G61, G79, G87, G116, G143, G196, G200, GNP77. Joos de Bul at Bruges	
Rose (not Tudor)	1480	Edward IV	GNP112	
Lion	1490	Henry VII	G143	Portraits of Henry VII show him wearing the collar of the Golden fleece
Loop	1498	Henry VII	G99	
Tudor rose and portcullis	*Circa* 1509	Henry VIII	G182	
Tudor rose	1509 to 1547	Henry VIII	G53, G94, G129, G136, G170, G204, G206,R13, T3, T27, T28	One tomb dates to 1554 but is probably 1518

Figure 57. Sir Thomas More as the chancellor of the Duchy of Lancaster in 1527 showing the long Esse (SS) 'collar' and the Tudor rose. At this time the collar was of gold with linked S letters. More was a lawyer who was persuaded by Henry VIII to hold the post of lord chancellor. A devout Catholic he could not embrace Henry's reforms and in consequence was beheaded. This portrait shows him approaching the height of his power. He was chancellor of the Duchy of Lancaster from 1525 to 1529. From a picture by Hans Holbein.

SS collars are not restricted to alabaster effigies. CMS Vol XXIX 2014 has a description of the 1420 freestone tomb of John de Wittlebury at Marholm (Northamptonshire) which shows an SS collar on which the pendant is obscured. That at Isleham, Cambs to Robert Bernard *circa* 1434 shows a collar of flower heads with what appears to be a loop pendant.

Notes:

1. Freestone effigies also carry SS collars. That of an unknown knight at Gaddesby, Leics depicts a very long SS collar with a Tudor rose and may date from around 1500 but the date is uncertain. At Rippingale, Lincs the church has a much mutilated effigy to Sir Nicholas Bowet showing a short SS collar on a narrow band. The effigy is carved from limestone. Another limestone effigy is that of Richard de Shropshire dating from 1416 to 1421 at St Michael's, Uffington, Lincolnshire. He sports a short SS collar with a much worn pendant.
2. Despite the two monuments being some 130 miles apart the damage issurprisingly consistent.

3. From Rupert Matthews: The term 'Wars of the Roses' was coined by Sir Walter Scott in his novel *Anne of Geierstein.* Thereafter the term entered widespread use amongst historians. At the time of the conflict the combatants fought under their heraldic banner. The fable of the choice of a rose was created in Shakespeare's Henry VI part 1 where a scene was set in the temple garden in which the nobles chose a rose of colour to suit their allegiance. Henry VII when he married Elizabeth of York adopted a composite red and white rose to symbolise the union of the two houses. Therefore, until 1490 neither coloured rose had any significance. The composite rose became known as the Tudor rose much used by Henry VIII onwards.
4. The meaning of tiret is not clear. According to Fearnley and Crossley the tiret was the loop which held the bottom of the collar which could be round or with three cusps. The collar could be worn with a tiret but without a pendant.

The Order of the Garter

The successes of Edward III in France which culminated in the victory at the Battle of Crecy on the 26th August 1346 forged a comradeship between the knights who took part in the campaigns. A few months after Edward's return he commenced to found the Order of the Garter, the recipients being knights who had been with him in France. The first investiture was in 1348 with 26 knights receiving the honour.

The initial 1348 garter list comprised:

> Edward, Prince of Wales, Henry Plantagenet, Sir Miles Stapleton, Sir John de Grailly Sir John de Lisle, Thomas Beauchamp (G171), Ralph of Stafford, William Montague, Roger Mortimer, Earl of March, Sir Bartholomew Burghersh, Sir John Beauchamp, John 2nd Lord Mohun, Sir Hugh Courtenay, Sir Thomas Holland, Sir John Grey, Sir Richard FitzSimon, Sir Thomas Wale, Sir Hugh Wrottesley, Sir Male Loryng, Sir John Chandos, Sir James Audley, Sir Otho Holland, Sir Henry Earn, Sir Sanchet d'Abrishecourt, Sir Walter Paveley and Robert Ufford Earl of Suffolk. Later Reginald Lord Cobham (1352) and Sir William Fitzwaryne (1359) joined the list.

This was an elite order and to some it appears to be a means for expressing chivalric status. Richard Barber has clear views on this status of the garter knights. There is only one military clause in the statutes and that relates to a member being a 'respectable knight' which is rather vague. There is nothing which says there has to be an anniversary tournament but one was arranged at the beginning and periodically tournaments took place. The statutes are clear in that the members were to provide for the interment of deceased companion. So, the Order of the Garter was a religious fraternity of knights rather like a guild and a means for team building.

It is therefore not surprising that such decoration found its way on funerary art. One of the earliest effigies to show the garter was that of Reginald, Lord Cobham at Lingfield, Sussex in 1361 (*see* G211). Few monuments remain which depict the early knights but the order remains to this day and over the years some 14 alabaster monuments have the decoration. There is a curious feature in that two ladies wear the decoration on their wrist or arm with the monument at Stanton Harcourt (G141) and that at Ewelme (G142) from 1471 and 1477 showing the decoration. The reason for this is not yet clear.[1]

Some monuments which should have displayed the garter do not which may be attributed to the fact that the order may have been seen (incorrectly) as a chivalric club and not viewed with the same religious status that it later achieved. In addition, the garter emblem is sometimes shown on the tomb chest rather than on the effigy either round the edge or surrounding the coat of arms although none have been found on alabaster monuments.

Notes:

1. Saul offers a part explanation in that aristocratic women would require displays of status even in widowhood and this is demonstrated by the garter shown on the Duchess of Suffolk's tomb at Ewelme.

Great Helm Crests

The placing of the head of an effigy on a great helm emanates from the early 14th century. Before this the head resting on a cushion was the standard representation. Whilst the carver had to provide some support for the head, the opportunity was taken to use the support in a descriptive manner. The 1330s and 1340s saw a surge in tournaments under the guidance of the king. The knights involved dressed in exotic costumes which included great helms with crests. Not only did these helms hide the identity of the knight but also provided an opportunity to display crests which indicated the team of combatants to which each belonged. In death the comradeship that the tournament provided was represented in the depiction of the crest on the effigy great helm. It is therefore assumed that where effigies display the same crest that a relationship existed between the knights commemorated. Within the scope of this book crests have been identified as follows:

References in brackets relate to notes and indicate monuments in alabaster

Crest	Date	Person	Monument	Garter
Ass	1399 1410 1456 1515	Sir William Mainwaring Sir John Mainwaring Sir Randall Mainwaring Sir John Mainwaring	Acton, Cheshire (GNP1) Over Peover (G44) Over Peover (G45) Over Peover (S89)	
Bear	1522	Sir Randle Brereton	Malpas (G53)	
Boar	1450	Sir Nigel Stafford	Bromsgrove (G184)	
Broken crest	1380	Sir Roger Bellars	Kirkby Bellars (GNP5)	
Bull's head	1425 1487	Ralph Neville William Gascoigne	Staindrop (G104) Harewood (G197)	
Calf's head	1393	Sir Hugh Calverley	Bunbury (G2)	
Dog	1457 1499 1522 1615	Sir Thomas Greene Sir Henry Pierrepont Sir Randal Brereton Sir Henry Pierrepont	Greens Norton (G126) Holme Pierrepont (G135) Malpas (G53) Holme Pierrepont (R3)	
Eagle and child	1474	Sir John Stanley	Elford (freestone)	
Feathers	1372 1375 1386 1440 1441 1558	Sir Robert Hilton Sir Richard Pembridge Sir John Marmion Lord Ferrers Lord Bardolph Sir Walter Devereux	Swine (G189) Hereford (G13) (Note b) West Tanfield (G31) Merevale (G173) Dennington Suffolk (G162) Stowe by Chartley, Staffordshire (T26)	Yes, no date
Fist (boxing glove)	1572	Hugh Armstrong	Wysall, Notts (R9)	
Flower pot with flowers	1386	Sir Nele Loring	Chalgrave	
Fox	1378	Sir John Foxley	Bray, Berks	
Goat passant	1555	John Russell, 1st Earl Bedford	Chenies, Bucks (T29)	Yes 1539
Goat with long neck	1402	Sir Nicholas Dagworth	Blickling	
Hand holding a wheatsheaf	1548	William Lord Parr	Horton, Northamptonshire (T27) (e)	
Helmet	C1520	Sir Richard Cholmondeley	Tower of London (T28)	
Holly Bush	1506	Sir Giles Daubeny	Westminster (G117)	
Horse head (may be boar)	1451 1497 1484	Sir Richard Vernon William Dethick Richard Redman	Tong, Salop (G148) Stapenhill, Staffordshire (S6) Harewood (G192)	
Hunting horn	1395	Sir William de Brien	Seal, Kent	
Indent only	1417	Lord Berkeley	Wotton under Edge (Note a)	
Leg		The Foljambe family	Chesterfield	
Lion statant	1376	Black prince	Canterbury (d)	

Maiden-head	1481	Sir Walter Griffith	Burton Agnes (G198)	
	1555	William Willington	Barcheston, Warwicks (T18)	
Mailed fist	1473 1483	Nicholas Lord Norbury Ralph Fitzherbert	Norbury (G61) Norbury (G62)	
Man's head	C 1360	Sir John de Grailly (Captal de Buch of Windsor)	Died a prisoner	Inv 1348
Millstone	1408	Sir John de Lisle	Brass	Inv 1348
Peacock	1377 1391 1396 1414 1421	Edward III Sir Thomas Arderne Sir Edward de Appleby William Lord Roos John Lord Roos	Petworth marble Elford (G158) Appleby Magna (GNP45) Bottesford (G103) Bottesford (G105) missing	 Yes, no date Yes, no date
Saracen	1360 1361 1364 1391 1491 1567	John de Vere Reginald Lord Cobham Sir Miles Stapleton Sir Sampson Strelley John de la Pole Sir Michael Poultney	Brass Lingfield (G211) Brass Strelley, Notts (G25) Wingfield, Suffolk (G163) Misterton, Leics (R97)	 Inv 1352 Inv 1348 Inv 1472
Stag	1419	Ralph Green	Lowick (G122)	
Swan	1388	John Beauchamp	Worcester Cathedral (X20)	
Turk woman	1409	Fulke Pembrugge	Tong, Shrops (GNP81)	
Turnpike or turnstile	1631	Skipwith family	Prestwold (M41) (Note c)	
Broken crest	1380	Sir Roger Bellars	Kirkby Bellars (GNP5)	
No helm	1471	Lady Harcourt	Stanton Harcourt	Yes, no date
	1477	Duchess of Suffolk	Ewelme	Yes, no date

(a) This is a brass and only included for reference. There is an unusual collar sewn with mermaids, a reference to the arms of an earlier Berkeley.
(b) His great helm minus feathers is on display in the National Museum of Scotland, Edinburgh. Apart from those carved on effigial tombs this is reputed to be only one of three extant helms of the 14th Century. It was once displayed on the tomb (G13).
(c) The crest appears on the top of the monument. The medieval turnpike or barrier has been the crest of the Skipwith family for centuries but is only seen on M41.
(d) Bronze with replica helm above.
(e) The crest is not consistent with the Parr family and has yet to be identified but may relate to the Robertson, Gipps or Wheathill families.

Some of the above have clear tourney associations but those of the Pierrepont, Foxley, Norbury and Mainwaring family may be more associated with family crests than tournament teams. Later in the 16th and 17th century when tournaments had ceased this family association on helms is more evident as indicated by the list below which provides examples.

Crest	Date	Person	Monument	Other
Goat	1534 1539 1585 1625	Richard Sacheverell Ralph Sacheverell Henry Sacheverell (II) Henry Sacheverell (III)	Newarke, Leicester Ratcliffe on Soar (G136) Ratcliffe on Soar (R4) Ratcliffe on Soar (R5)	*See* G136 SS and Tudor rose

Tournaments had the same status as meeting to play golf has today. It was where you met and talked to people of your own social standing and in passing, work as a team. It was also a place where salesmen could promote their wares in the form of the latest armour and weapons.

Mottoes

A feature of 15th century effigies is the presence of mottoes. This may have a basis in tourneying and the most common is often an abbreviation of Jesus of Nazareth (Ihc Nazaren or Ihc Nazare) sometimes shortened to Ihc. It is mainly found on the upper edge of the bascinet or orle. A number of alabaster effigies have this as indicted in the lists contained in Appendix E. The practice is believed to date back to the 12th century and such an inscription is believed to be a protection against danger. The practice did not survive long in the 15th century.

Civilian Dress

Learned men especially those associated with the law are often depicted with a coif on the head. This was long before it was adopted by ladies. Judges can be found commemorated from the late 13th century, but the evolution of the courts introduced serjeants at law, men of legal expertise who could speak for clients at the bar. Later a new group of professional legal practitioners emerged known as apprentices (at law), serjeants and attorneys. The latter evolved into the now familiar role of solicitor.

The coif was the symbol of the serjeant and his selection was often referred to as being '*called to the coif*'. The dress consisted of a robe and furred cloak later adopted by judges. The coif is well represented by the tomb of Justice Gascoigne (G193) at Harewood, Yorkshire and Judge Storer at Dorchester on Thames, Oxon (A41). The Storer tomb of 1354 shows the attire of judges in the early 14th century.

The serjeants were never permitted to remove the coif even in the presence of the king but the coif had to be covered by a black cap if delivering a death sentence. However from 1350 significant changes were made to habit. The judges gave up the collobium in favour of a cloak or mantle sometimes known as 'chlamys' fastened over the right shoulder although the cassock and coif were retained. The website *Judiciary.gov* has a summary of robes worn. The robes of the 14th century evolved from court dress at the time of Edward III *circa* 1377 and comprised ermine, taffeta and silk. The colours were violet for winter, green for summer and scarlet for royal occasions. The last recorded use of green was 1534. The route to being judge was via practicing as a serjeant but by the end of the 15th century the serjeant's monopoly was being threatened by the rise of the apprentice-at-law. The first judge to be appointed from a route other than serjeantry was in 1519 and this became more frequent as the 16th century progressed.

Some judges preferred the trappings of lordship to that of the law. The effigy at Hanbury (G28) and others in brass and freestone show judges in armour and as late as 1472 the brass of Sir William Yelverton at Rougham, Norfolk depict a judge in armour with livery collar and coif. By mid-15th century commemorative etiquette had taken hold with the increasing status of the law so that armoured judges after this are rare. In 1635 the Judges' Rules were issued which made few changes but legalised that dress which was used at the time. This had evolved to a black robe faced with miniver (a light coloured fur) in winter and violet or scarlet robes faced with shot-pink taffeta in summer. A black girdle or cincture was worn with all robes. This had further changes in the 18th century which is outside the period of review.

The dress of serjeants evolved closely to that of judges consisting of a long robe or cassock, a hood, collobium and tabard, coif and fur collar. The main difference from judges was the omission of cloak or mantle. Serjeants began to decline at the end of the Tudor period with the rise of king's and queen's councillors but the role was not expunged until the 19th century with the Judicature Act of 1873.

Apprentices at law were neither young nor under instruction, but were a lower strata to the serjeant. These were not entitled to wear the coif or collobium, but learnt their trade by attending court. By Tudor times the apprentice was a graduate of the law and attached to an 'inn'. Their dress is elusive but seems to have included a turban-like hat such as those shown on Aston on Trent (G60), Methley (G194) and Harlaxton (GNP56) although two of these are stated as judges. That at Nottingham St Mary (G137) may also indicate apprentice status, but may just be the hat worn by a merchant. Saul offers the opinion that the first monument to show an apprentice hat was that of John Gour of 1380 at Pembridge (freestone?) who was the son of a serjeant whose tomb is also at Pembridge thus demonstrating the transition from one form to another over one generation.

The last group are the attorneys. These were usually dressed as civilians, but up to about 1380 may display a coif and in some cases of attorneys in the employ of high-status individuals, display additional items of status as shown on John Cockayne's monument at Ashbourne (G212).

Figure 58. Thomas Cromwell (1485–1540) was a Tudor lawyer and in this well-known portrait he is shown in the lawyer robes and coif cap. Lawyers were still being depicted in these robes into the 17th century. *See* Lord Kinloss Master of the Rolls (M181) and that of Humphrey Bridges of Cirencester, Gloucs although the latter is freestone. From a picture by Hans Holbein.

Notaries concerned with the drawing up and registration of documents whilst being dressed as civilians sometimes display the attributes of their trade including the pen and inkwell, or inkhorn, such as that at Glastonbury (G194).

Merchants and Civilians

Sumptuary laws passed in the reigns of Edward II, Edward III, Edward IV and Henry VIII restricted the use and cost of materials to certain classes. Thus whilst merchants may well be allowed to be depicted in rich clothes, those of lower ranks would be shown in a simple tunic. One popular item of dress in the middle ages was the chaperon headgear which became popular in the first half of the 15th century. A cloth roundlet with a broad piece of cloth called a gorget which could be draped round the neck or thrown over the shoulder and a narrow strap-like tail called a liripipe.

Effigies of lower ranks are rare.

Figure 59. A portrait by Jan van Eyck *circa* 1432 shows a merchant with a gorget and liripipe. These appear on effigies at Harlaxton (GNP56, 1410) and Aston on Trent (G60, 1450) and on the weepers on the tomb at Haversham (G39, 1422).

The liripipe appeared in common wear as the peasant hood covering the head and shoulders, but none appear on tombs.

Another item was the houppelande. This was a gown worn by both men and women the difference being in the length. It had a high stiff collar, long hanging sleeves and held in at the waist by a strap or girdle. The Oteswich effigy at St Helen's Bishopsgate (G114, 1400) is a good example as is the lady at Harewood (G193, 1419). *See* later.

An effigy at Nottingham, St Mary to John Salmon has a hat not found elsewhere (G137, 1416). It is a tall hat with an upturned brim.

Ecclesiastical

There are eight extant effigies of bishops in the period 1330 to 1420. They are shown in Eucharistic vestments and mitre. That of Archbishop Langham in Westminster (G20) is particularly good having also a crosier and pall.

The effigies of lesser clergy are few. The first may well be the 'friar' in Worcester Cathedral dating from 1385. This effigy is also in mass vestments of a simpler kind to the bishops. Another priest lies at Barrow upon Trent (G56, *circa* 14th century), bare headed and with a chasuble over the mass vestments. The effigy in friar's robes at Crawley (A121 of 1875) is modern.

It is probably on slabs that the dress of priests is best depicted. Mass or Eucharistic vestments were almost universally applied until the dissolution but in some cases quire or processional vestments appear. Such vestments can be seen on William Canynge tomb at St Mary Redcliffe (G89).

There are no extant alabaster effigies in monastic habit.

Hair

When bascinets and salets were worn (pre 1440) little or nothing of the knight's hair could be seen. It is assumed the hair was cut short but the portraits of Henry V (1413-1422) show the hair cut straight round the head above the ears with the back of the neck shaved in what is known as a bowl-crop (Figure 60).

The effigy at Dodford (G125, 1444) shows such a hair style indicating that such was the status of Henry V that some 20 years after his death his fashion was still being copied. This can also be seen at Macclesfield (G48, 1463). In another Macclesfield effigy the bowl-crop is retained but the hair is brushed back to form a fringe roll (G49, 1480).

It may well be that knights wishing to be identified with England's most famous warrior was the cause of effigies being bare headed.

Figure 60. The bowl crop.

In Edward IV's time the hair was shown longer at the back (Norbury G61, 1473) and curled at the front. Clean shaven images predominate. From Richard III's times the hair grew longer with a forehead fringe and draped over the ears being square cut at the back. The portraits of the king show this and this began to be emulated on effigies typified by that at Lowick (G123, 1498) and Little Chart (G101, 1509). This style continued into Tudor times the effigy of Ralph Sacheverell at Ratcliffe on Soar (G136, 1539) being particularly well carved. After the Reformation hair styles became more varied with long Tudor locks without fringes without any particular traits.

Ladies Fashion

Men's effigies followed fixed styles and the attire of their calling. Ladies effigies initially followed the same fixed styles but as soon as they began to influence the design of monuments then the fashion of the times became more evident.

Women are not depicted on tombs before the mid to end of the 13th century. They began to appear alone on tombs at the beginning of the 14th century when they were increasingly included on the tomb chests of their husbands. There is little evidence of the woman influencing the form of the effigy during the 14th century, but at the beginning of the 15th century there is clear evidence of tombs being planned jointly or by a widow on behalf of her deceased husband – *see* Lowick (G122).

The attire of women effigies played as an important role as that for men. The first 13th century effigies are simply attired – a long robe and a wimple covering the neck and chin. Even 75 years later the dress had only evolved to a kirtle and surcoat (surcote) with a veil and wimple showing that the form was still male dominated. Some effigies show long hair often on those commemorating unmarried women.

In the 14th century there is evidence of the commissioners of monuments, either men or women, wishing to have their status demonstrated. The appearance of the mantle (mantelet is a shortened version) secured by cords below the shoulders and the surcoat cut away to show the kirtle and with cloth strips hanging from the arms indicates increasing interest in the show of fashion as an indication of status.

The kirtle and surcoat were still in evidence in the early 15th century, but there was increasing use of the houppelande, a high, often fur-collared gown.

Figure 61. A 15th century houppelande in fashion 1420 to 1450. Dutch 15th century print.

The houppelande was sometimes shown with a mantle. A simpler form was in vogue from about 1380 and was often depicted with flaring sleeves sometimes dagged or cut into scallops or leaf patterns. The houppelande is the forerunner for academic costume.

In the later 15th century until the end of the Tudor period, the farthingale was popular. This was a framework firstly of cane and later of willow which allowed the skirt to take a certain shape. In late Tudor times, the farthingale was displayed in an excessive way and linked to the bum-roll which accentuated the buttocks.

Some Tudor monuments display a long girdle sometimes with a pomander hung from a neck-chain or belt, or attached to the girdle itself. The pomander was in use from the beginning of the 16th century to mid-17th century.

Very little documentary evidence has come down regarding fashion, but the Green monument at Lowick contract states clearly that the lady 'had to be counterfeit (copy) of a countess'. This was carried out to the letter by the Chellaston carvers.

Medieval Headdresses (14th and 15th century)
Summary over period of Alabaster carving:

Couvre-chef	Largely Norman comprising of a cloth and circlet
Wimple	Plantagenet from *circa* 1154 into 14th century
Barbette	Introduced by Eleanor of Aquitaine *circa* 1200 – like the couvre-chef, but off the brow
Fillet	Like the barbette but very narrow – late 14th century
Crespine	Net or caul worn with the barbette 1364 to 1419
Gorget	1272 to 1307 Linen placed under the chin and tied to the hair
Horned	1420 to 1450 Lancaster – metal mesh with cauls
Heart & turban	1430 to 1460 Lancaster – horned raised vertical later turban
Hennin	1460 to 1485 York – tall horns cater cones
Butterfly	The hennin evolved into cone with linen veil often starched
Barbe	1425 to 1480 Both York and Lancaster – pleated linen bib made fashionable in mourning
Nebule (nebuly)	Sometimes known as the framed headdress. In vogue 1360 to *circa* 1380

One clear indication of fashion and one which permits dating is the headdress.

The first alabaster tomb to include ladies shows the nebule or framed headdress. This was square or round and made of crimped frills. It gave the effigy an Egyptian look and looked curious. It is first seen on the Tewkesbury tomb (G10, 1349–1359), but the style was common long before that. Nebule headdresses can be seen at Berkeley (G11, 1364), Warwick (G171, 1371), Newent (GNP3, 1370) and East Harling (G21, 1370). The style vanished from tombs soon after which makes the date for the tomb at Appleby Magna of 1396 questionable.

In the 14th century the fashion was for the wimple and caul. The wimple is associated with the gorget or throat cloth attached to the hair and seen on the depiction of the Wife of Bath in Chaucer (sometimes known as a barbet). The caul (or crespine when made from metal) emerged about 1377 and held the hair in rolls with a net. The hair was often curled into buns at the side of the head. This style lasted until *circa* 1399.

The crespine and horned headdress featured in effigies of Class II. As the 15th century dawned the caul was stiffened and became larger evolving into the elaborate horns shown above. For good examples of the former, *see* Strelley (G25, 1391), Ashwellthorpe (G121, 1417) and Harewood (G193, 1419) and of the latter Dennington (G162, 1441), Tong (G148, 1451), Ashbourne (G58, 1447), Lowick (G122, 1419), Norbury (G62, 1483), Peover (G45, 1456), Swinbrook (not alabaster) and Horwood (G96, 1450). It is unclear as to when the horned headdress fell out of favour but it evolved into the butterfly by bringing the points of the horns together. The butterfly is described below.

Later the horns became a single steeple often with material connected to the point of the steeple. The steeple headdress did not suit alabaster carving for obvious reasons. The lady's effigy at South Cowton (G205) has a curious fez-type hat which may be a truncated steeple. Later 17th century effigies had a tall hat which could be considered to be a form of steeple.

Some headdresses had attached hanging cloth. Such headdresses were called 'flapped'. Later in the 15th century ladies fashion the caul and horned headdress evolved into a flapped headdress known as the 'butterfly'. A cap with flowing material with wires for stiffening and with long hanging folds often wrapped under chin. This was probably in vogue between 1420 and 1490.

Figure 62. Butterfly headdress.

Brass carvers struggled to depict the 'butterfly' but alabastermen found it suited the three dimensional effigy. Effigies with 'butterflies' include Methley (G199, 1461), Ilton (G57, 1470), London Bishopsgate (G116, 1474), Marnhull (G78, 1478) and Norbury (G62, 1483) Yatton (G155, 1449) and Macclesfield (G50, 1495) but most are in the period 1460 to 1480.

In all this fashion some ladies preferred a simple veil as seen at Lingfield (G166, 1453) and Harewood (G197, 1487).

A radical change takes place *circa* 1485 to 1490. The steeple and butterfly headdresses give way to a low cap with a ball ornament in a net which evolved into cauls often at the side. This in turn gave way to the Tudor hoods.

Tudor Headdresses

The gable hood was in vogue from about 1500 to about 1540 (although the evolution may have started about 1485 with the pediment sometimes known as the kennel, pyramidal or angular). A very English fashion, it had a wired or stiffened frame under which was worn a close cap the edge of which is sometimes visible. It sometimes had a veil at the back and in the early days and lappets which would fall over the shoulders. The picture (Figure 63) shows the form from about 1503. It had, at first, a plain braid edge known as a billiment, but this became complex and patterned from 1518. It became shorter in the 1530s and usually associated with the veil at the back. The picture below shows headdress with long lappets when it was also known as the English hood or pediment hood. In the following description the term 'pediment' has been used to identify hoods with lappets.

Figure 63. A long pediment headdress worn by a Beaufort Lady *circa* 1526. Orginal picture in National Portrait Gallery.

The long pediment was seen worn by Elizabeth of York in the 1490s and survived amongst older women into the 1520s. Long pediments are evident in the two ladies of Prestwold (G110, *circa* 1520, Figure 18). Until 1525 the cap permitted hair to be shown but from that date the under cap concealed all the hair as shown above. In younger women the gable hood was increasingly seen until it too was supplanted. The last effigy to display a long pediment was 1530. From *circa* 1518 the gable hood was raised to just below the chin and raised again to level with the cheek by 1530. The long pediment does not feature on continental effigies except for one lone example. The slab in the Museum of Boulogne to an English couple originally in the English town of Calais shows a pediment headdress although the carving is clearly French.

The coif was in fashion from about 1500 and sometimes had a veil at back. This died out *circa* 1550. The coif was a cap which fitted round the head without pediment with tab projections across the jawline. More often seen on lower ranks but an early drawing of Ann Boleyn exists which shows her wearing one. It has been known that a coif may have been worn under both gable and French hoods. A form of coif re-emerged in the 1580s to the early 17th century. The tab projections are also seen in the portrait of Thomas More and there is some evidence that some women may have worn this style of coif.

Figure 64. French (or Boleyn) hood. *Wikipedia.*

The French hood became popular amongst the young from about 1520. Ann Boleyn, who had been educated in France, popularised the headdress from 1530 and therefore is sometime known as a Boleyn hood. It outlasted both the coif and gable and the billiment became jewelled *circa* 1545 with a veil. A strap added from 1549 but it did not die out until 1580. The construction was with a stiff foundation and the hood was worn on the back of the head. The jewelled billiments were added early and were curved forward to cover the ears and trimmed with crimped cypress (a form of material like crepe).

Mary, Queen of Scots favoured a cap like a modified caul which came to a point over the forehead and curved round under the ears so that the hair projected from each side. Sometimes shown with veil.

Figure 65. Mary Stuart from a portrait by Robert Herdman. Depicting as she was *circa* 1560 en route to Edinburgh, with a modified coif later identified as a Mary, Queen of Scots cap. Mary had spend time in the French court and the cap probably emanated from there. From *The Story of the British People in Pictures* 1936 from a 19th century picture.

The vertigale, or bum-roll, remained in fashion until the 1620 but may have lingered in the upper classes and in rural areas much longer. In the case of the three ladies shown on the monument to Henry Sacheverell (M2) all three are shown with vertigales although the remaining dress is true to the period in which they died or when the monument was constructed.

Stuart Civilian Headdresses

The late Tudor headdresses continued for a while. One new feature introduced in the late Tudor years and carried forward to the 17th century was the stiff hood. This was made from buckram – cotton or linen soaked in starch and then stretched over a frame and left to dry. This produced a stiff, light hood seen on a number of tombs.

Tudor and Stuart female hat.

The late Tudor and Stuart female hat with stiff brim and flower-pot dome. The hat perched on the top of the head and held by a strap which passed at the back over the coif. The colour always seems to be black with a rope band. It is usually associated with a full ruff until the mid-17th century. This hat is associated with the Puritans except that, in that case, the hat has lost the rope band in exchange for a plain band and buckle. *See* monument at Cirencester to Humphrey Bridges *circa* 1620 and Pershore Worcs both in freestone and the two ladies at Hanbury (shown below).

Figure 66. Stuart civilian headdress.

The photo (Figure 66) from the author's collection shows Katherine Agard right (died 1620 or 1628) and her daughter Ann Woollocke left (died 1657) in the chancel of Hanbury church, Staffordshire. Although these are called 'Puritan' both display ruffs in keeping with the 1620s but not appropriate to the Civil War or commonwealth period. In fact Ann left 10s for the monuments to be cleaned and 10s for an annual sermon against popery and 10s to encourage the people to come and hear it. It is not possible to see if the hats carry a buckled or rope band. The carver is unknown but clearly both monuments are by the same hand. Katherine Agard died at the age of 66 leaving five daughters and six sons. The hat (sketched above) may have had its origins in the pilgrim hats where it was known as the cockle hat from the symbol used for pilgrimage associated with St James of Compostela, Spain. Also called a capotain.

An amusing story from Hanbury relates that Sir Charles Egerton (M481) stipulated that he should not be buried in the chancel where he would '... lie for eternity under the gaze of the Puritan ladies'. His wish was granted and he is buried at the east end of the nave where neither woman could see him. As Sir Charles died in 1624, four years after Katherine and some 20 years before Ann, it may indicate that Ann's monument was constructed in the 1620s alongside her mother which is why they are identical.

Ruffs

Ruffs make a frequent appearance on effigies. A feature of the Elizabethan age, this fashion of folded starched linen was to change shape until the open or wired-up ruffs died out *circa* 1635. The half ruff attached just to the shoulders is rare but can be seen on Lucy Sacheverell's effigy in Ratcliffe (M2, Figure 32). Later the starch was omitted allowing the ruff to fall loose over the upper chest, known as a falling ruff and this evolved into the lace collar. Older ladies adhered to a wide ruff known as the cart wheel ruff. Other fashions included the fan collar extending backwards from the shoulders which ended in the late 1630s. The fan collar was never seen on monuments. Hand ruffs can be seen but rarely after 1630 when they were replaced by turned-back cuffs. The dating of effigies by the ruff can be a problem as customer had their own preferences.

Barbe

Widows were often shown wearing the barbe. This was a veil drawn up over the chin and derived its name from the French word for beard. It was a development of the wimple. The sides were drawn up over the ears and pinned to the top or back of the head. The barbe developed into the barbette (little beard) where the cloth was worn under the chin. Tombs with fine barbes are Haversham (G32, 1422), Lingfield (G166, 1453), Stourton Caundle (G82, 1460), and Harewood (G197. 1487).

Figure 67. The fine effigy of 1487 in Harewood Hall church. The barbe made from crimped linen can be clearly seen along with the veil over the head. The kirtle cording can be seen, but differs markedly from the cording carved by Harpur and Moorecock. Photo: Janet State.

This brief journey through adornment is little more than a taster but I hope it gives the reader a feeling for the link between the carver and the requirements of the customer on one hand and the fashion seen on the streets which was copied for individual effigies on the other.

Appendix F

Index to Alabaster Monuments in the Nottingham and Leicester City Museums

See Unearthed, The Nottingham Medieval Alabasters by Francis Cheetham 2008

Nottingham

Number	Image	Subject	Cent	Date	Alabaster	Painted	Source	Kerver	Notes
1	Images	Three images: Virgin and child, St Peter as pope and a bishop	14th	1380–1390	Fine white	No	NCM 1908-146 NCM 1908-147 NCM 1908-148	English – Nottingham	
2	Panel	The annunciation	15th	*Circa* 1400	Honey	No	NCM 1960-24	English – Nottingham	
3	Panel	St Eloy shoeing a horse	15th	*Circa* 1450	Honey	No	NCM 1925-55	English – Nottingham	
4	Panel	The entry into Jerusalem	15th	*Circa* 1450	Honey	No	NCM 1961-180	English – Nottingham	
5	Panel (part)	St George	15th	*Circa* 1450 to 1500	Honey	No	NCM 1971-43	English – Nottingham	
6	Panel	The martyrdom of St Lawrence	15th	*Circa* 1450 to 1500	Honey	No	NCM 1952-16	English – Nottingham	
7	Panel (part)	St Peter	15th	*Circa* 1400 to 1450	Honey	No	NCM 1952-15	English – Nottingham	
8	Panel	The resurrection	15th	*Circa* 1400 to 1430	Honey	No	NCM 1925-43	English – Nottingham	
9	Image	The lamentation over the dead Christ	15th	*Circa* 1400 to 1450	Honey	No	NCM 1925-53	English – Nottingham	
10	Panel (part)	St Zita	15th	*Circa* 1450 to 1500	Honey	No	NCM 1932-27	English – Nottingham	
11	Panel	The holy church	15th	*Circa* 1450 to 1500	Honey	No	NCM 1967-144	English – Nottingham	
12	Panel	The head of St John the Baptist	15th	*Circa* 1450 to 1500	Honey	No	NCM 1932-29	English – Nottingham	

Number	Image	Subject	Cent	Date	Alabaster	Painted	Source	Kerver	Notes
13	Panel	St Peter receiving the souls of the blessed into heaven	15th	*Circa* 1450 to 1500	Honey	No	NCM 1925-223	English – Nottingham	
14	Panel	The assumption of the Virgin	15th	*Circa* 1450 to 1500	Honey	No	NCM 1989-902	English – Nottingham	
15	Panel	The coronation of the Virgin	15th	*Circa* 1450 to 1500	Honey	No	NCM 1959-75	English – Nottingham	
16	Panel	The adoration of the kings	15th	*Circa* 1460	Honey	No	NCM 1954-38	English – Nottingham	
17	Panel	The crucifixion	15th	*Circa* 1500	Honey	No	NCM 1932-28	English – Nottingham	
18	Panel	The entombment	15th	*Circa* 1450 to 1500	Honey	No	NCM 1925-54	English – Nottingham	

Leicester

This is just one example of panels and triptych carvings of Nottingham placed here for reference.

Number	Image	Subject	Cent	Date	Alabaster	Painted	Source	Kerver	Notes
1	Panel	The head of St John the Baptist	14th	1461–1485	Honey	No	A triptych in a wooden frame	English – Nottingham	A54

Appendix G
Index to Alabaster Workers

(For Timeline – *see* **The Alabastermen's Timelines 1 to 8**)

The alabaster worker emerged from the ranks of the mason's yard and turned their hands to any form of stone carving. By the mid-13th century there emerged a number of men who specialised in effigy and image carving but they never received a status beyond artisan before the latter part of the 16th century. As a result their humble existence means that the details of their lives and careers are hard to determine. Many authors mention carvers but these are often few in number. Those that are mentioned are listed below but the list has been expanded by names which appear in borough records, church warden's accounts, forinsec pleas, contracts, wills, church registers, official rolls and many others so that the list exceeds 300 names. From the late 16th century onward carvers began making their own records some of which survived.

The term 'alabasterer' and 'image maker' appears to be regularly interchanged. This does not reflect a progression, but more how the man is seen and the work he is doing at the time of the record. The term 'kerver' is used in the Middle Ages and seems to have been attributable only to those who carve in alabaster but researchers must also look for imager, marbler, image maker, tomb maker and ymager when accessing old records.

In addition the term 'painter' may also include the duties of polishing the monument which was accomplished by the use of sand.

The details of the requirements for monuments in the form of contracts in the pre-Reformation era are thin. Wills and bequests may specify the money to be allocated and may give general desires but early detailed contracts are restricted to the 1408 French and the 1414 Fécamps purchase and the 1419 Lowick tomb all in relation to the Chellaston workshop. Commissions were submitted by word of mouth indicating a form similar to an existing tomb. As a result much of the style is at the discretion of the carver and likenesses are restricted to royal tombs where a portrait was likely to exist. This freedom of style found its way into knightly effigy forms when carvers would be producing armour forms which were out-of-date for the period of construction. This was particularly true at times of protracted peace when carvers were unlikely to see knights in their latest German or Italian armour. Workshops probably purchased old suits of armour for erecting in their workrooms and which were copied by the carvers. In many cases the style of armour carving can lag the current styles by up to 50 years. Later customers asked for the more modern styles of armour to be used and it is quite possible that suits were loaned to the carver for use during the carving and later returned.

This was not true of ladies' or men's civilian dress. Ladies' fashion travelled quickly and would be seen every day by the carvers who may experience fashion first-hand in their own families. In 1590 a sculptor in brass submitted a design to a customer showing his ladies in the, then fashionable, farthingale. This form of dress was intensely disliked by the customer who insisted that straight skirts be shown. He had his way. Civilians such a lawyers or judges whose costume was seen and known of could be carved without recourse to models, but in some cases where special collars or other appurtenances were needed these may have required some research on the part of the carver or else specified by the customer.

In the following table, mention is made of Southwark, London especially in respect of immigrant Dutch carvers. In the 16th century Southwark was without the City of London and as there was prohibition of foreigners working within the city walls, Southwark was the closest they could get. The first to arrive was the Jannsen family remaining in Southwark until 1624 – *see* B106 for discussion on the name variations. Non foreign carvers were in East London usually Bishopsgate but from 1600 there was a general move westwards to Long Acre, St Martin's and St Giles where the large workshops of Stone, Marshall and Christmas families could be found.

In order to provide a trace on the periods in which carvers were active the table has been ordered by the first date of carving as near as can be established. The 302 names have been extracted from many sources some of which provide only fragmentary evidence of carving in alabaster. Where evidence is scant this has been stated and in a few cases there is no trace at all but the name has been retained because someone, somewhere, had cause to list it in relation to an alabaster carving. A few latoners (brass workers) appear as they are noted as fitting brass to alabaster slabs for which they may well have carved the recesses. The reader can choose to investigate or ignore as they see fit. The index below lists the carvers in alphabetical order against the sequence number in the date ordered list.

A

Name	Number	Name	Number	Name	Number	Name	Number
Ackers, Harry	180	Anderson, Robert Rowand	273	Austen, William	33	Ayte, Bartholomew	130
Alley, John	42	Ashby, Thomas	155	Aylde, John	47		

B

Name	Number	Name	Number	Name	Number	Name	Number
Backere, Giles de	28	Besnier, Isaac	184	Bounde, Robert	25	Broke, John	83
Baker, John	36	Besnier, Peter	184	Bourde, John	35	Brown, Richard	226
Baldwin, Samuel	144	Bolwell, Moses	164	Boy, Willem	106	Brown, Robert	20
Baldwin, Stephen	194	Blackwell, Thomas	214	Bridgeman, Chas William	296	Browne, Thomas	129
Basill, Simon	137	Blunt, Wilfred Scarwen	277	Bridgeman, Joseph	292	Burdon, William	7
Beke, Richard	30	Boehm, Joseph Edgar	261	Bridgeman, Robert	275	Burman, Thomas	197
Bellamy, William	80	Bonville, William	14	Brindley, William	286	Burnhard, Nevill Northey	278
Belt, Richard Claude	267	Bosher. Robert	55	British Alabaster Bowl	295	Bushnell, John	203
Benedick	163	Bott, William	61	Brock, Thomas	271	Burton, William	172
Bernini, Gian Lorenzo	165	Boughton, Harry	195	Brook, Robert	82	Byrd, William	193

C

Name	Number	Name	Number	Name	Number	Name	Number
Campion, John	201	Cheverton, Benjamin	241	Coffee, William John	230	Crosse, Robert	92
Caröe, William Douglas	287	Cholmondeley, Reginald	236	Colt, Maximilian	134	Cundy, Samuel	246
Carter, Thomas	224	Christmas, John	171	Colton, William Robert	263	Cure, Cornelius	107
Cartwright, Thomas	205	Christmas, Gerhard	151	Colyn, Thomas	17	Cure, William	98 & 145
Carver, Walter	79	Christmas, Mathias	171	Cookson, Joseph	243	Currie, James	251
Cawdron, Anthony	196	Cibber, Caius Gabriel	202	Cooper, Richard	46		
Chapman, John	99	Clark, William	272	Cottingham, John	74		
Chavalliaud, Leon-Joseph	285	Cleaver, Laurence	103	Cowebrigge, William	40		

D, E & F

Name	Number	Name	Number	Name	Number	Name	Number
De Keyser, Hendrick	189	Ellis, Anthony John	190	Fanelli, Francesco	152	Flynte, William	117
De Keyser, William	187	Else, Joseph	298	Farmer, William	288	Fox, William	213
Deymond, John	141	Epstein, Sir Jacob	300	Field and Allen	270	Frith, William Silver	265
Drawswerd, Thomas	68	Erdeswick, Sampson	139	Ford, Peter	269		
Egen, Gert van	131	Evans, Joseph	227	Forsyth, James	250		
Elliot, James	303	Evesham, Epiphanius	162	Forsyth, William	249		

G & H

Name	Number	Name	Number	Name	Number	Name	Number
Gaffin, Edward	233	Greenway, Thomas	149	Hems, Harry	260	Holewell, Thomas	18
Gaffin, Thomas	228	Griggs, Francis	191	Hepworth Barbara	298	Hollemans, Garrett	114 & 188
Gamman, Alan	101	Gough, William Drinkwater	281	Herteffeld, John	93	Hollemans, Joseph	136
Gildon, John	116	Hall, Joseph	222	Hill, Henry	257	Horsnaile, Christopher	209
Gillo, Philip	105	Halliday, George Eley	286	Hill, Nicholas	60	Howeton, William	31
Godeman, Nicholas	53	Hancock, Walter	138	Hill, Thomas	71	Hunt, John	219
Goldman, John	229	Hargrave, William	127	Hills, Alexander	154	Hurlbutt, Ricardus	51
Goodlord, Thomas	123	Harman, Cornelius	76	Hippis, John	81	Hylton, Edward	58
Gott, Joseph	245	Harpur, Henry	62	Hitch, Frederick Brook	294	Hylton, Walter	54
Green, Thomas	70	Havens, Theodore	102	Hitch, Nathaniel	274		

J, K & L

Name	Number	Name	Number	Name	Number	Name	Number
Jackson, John	192	Johnson, Jan	167	Lakenham, Henry	2	Lockwood, Richard	242
Jagger, Charles Sargeant	293	Johnson, Nicholas	133	Lakenham, Richard	2	Lomas, John Gilbert	259
Jakes, Elizabeth	52	Kerwin, William	119	Lambspring, Bartholomew	32	Lomas, William Edward	295
James, Isaac	140	Key, John	142	Larson, George	179	Lote, Stephen	12
Janssen, Geerart	113	Keyley, James	67	Latham, Jasper	211	Lovell, Margaret	302
Jewell, Thomas	208	Kinder, Henry	109	Lawrence, William	44	Lycett, Thomas	103

Johnson, Bernard	150	Kingsfield, Christopher	170	Legatt, Sir Francis	232	Lyngard, John	66
Johnson, Gerard	113 & 158	Kormis, Fred	291	Lende, John	43		
Johnson, Gerhart	173	Liege, Hawkin de	4	Lingherd, John	73		

M

Name	Number	Name	Number	Name	Number	Name	Number
Madden, Thomas	182	Marshall, Joshua	178	Michelson, Nicholas	16	Moore, Henry (London)	300
Mason, John	27	Marshal, William Calder	276	Mildenhall, John	24	Moore, John Francis	225
Mason, Peter the	5	Mathews, John	132	Miles, Michael	204	Moore, Temple, Lushington	279
Mason, William	29	Mauncey, James	128 & 157	Moderna, Niccolo da	96	Moorecock, William.	63
Mapilton, John	13	Maynard, Alan	112	Monday	169	Morley, Martin	206
Marshall, Edward	135	Mazzotti, Pellegrino	234	Moore, Henry (Derby)	235	Moyer, Humphrey	181

N, O & P

Name	Number	Name	Number	Name	Number	Name	Number
Nelson, Richard	146	Petit, John	22	Pomeroy, Fred William	290	Pritchard, John	239
Nicholson, John	90	Peyntour, John	26	Pooke, Robert	186	Pryce, Richard	156
Noble Matthew	252	Philip, John Bernie	253	Poppehowe, Thomas	19	Prylde, John	50
Orchard, John	9	Pickford, Joseph	223	Porter, William	88		
Owen, Nigel	301	Pierce, Edmund	216	Prentys, Robert	21		
Parker, Richard	85	Pollen, John Hungerford	266	Prentys, Robert (jnr)	39		

R

Name	Number	Name	Number	Name	Number	Name	Number
Raggi, Anthony	200	Redfern, James Frank	237 & 255	Rhind, John	240	Rosemond	120
Ramsey, Agnes	3	Reeve, Francis	212 & 217	Rhind, William Birnie	280	Rovezzano, Benedetto da	84
Ramsey, John	3	Reeve, Joseph	218	Richardson, Edward	238	Royley, Gabriel	95 & 126
Ramsey, Alma	299	Reeve, Stephen	215	Ropar, John	49	Royley, Richard	94 & 124
Ramsey, William	3	Remus, James	65	Ropar, Thomas	59	Russell, William	244

S

Name	Number	Name	Number	Name	Number	Name	Number
Salaboss, Melchior	125	Sluter, Claus	11	Starkey, Richard	89	Street, George Edmund	247
Salviati, Antonio	256	Smythson, John	160	Stephens, Richard	110	Sutton, Robert	23
Sani, Raffaello	268	Smythson, Robert	104	Steppyngleye, John	6	Sueur, Hubert le	176
Scott, John Oldrid	258	Spenser, John	69	Steppyngleye, Peter	5	Sweet, William	198
Scott, George, Gilbert	248	Stanton, Edward	210	Stonard, Robert	77		
Sherwood, Robert	57	Stanton, Thomas	183 & 210	Stone, Nicholas	159		
Skidmore, Francis Albert	254	Stanton, William	210	Stone, John	199		

T, U & V

Name	Number	Name	Number	Name	Number	Name	Number
Tallentire	100	Thomas, M	38	Tolly, Anthony	115	Tweed, John	289
Tarbotons, John	108	Thomson, John	177	Torrigiano, Pietro	75	Twyst, Gilbert	56
Tarbrook, John	122	Tissenaken, Isaac	143	Tomson, Edward	86	Ventris, Thomas	147
Taylor, John	153	Tissenaken, Tobias	143	Tull, Robert	64	Vickers, William	284

W, X, Y & Z

Name	Number	Name	Number	Name	Number	Name	Number
Wade, Robert	45	Warr, William	37	Weston, John	221	Witte, Gilles de	118
Walker, Arthur George	282	Waterton, Robert	75	Whatton, William	121	Woodrofe, Edward	174
Walker, Richard	87	Watson, Samuel	220	White, James	168	Woodroote, William	166
Walker, Richard	87	Watson, William	231	White, Richard	185	Wreck, Thomas	8
Wallace, Andrew	262	Watts, George Frederick	264	White, William	161	Wright, William	147
Walsh, William	91	Waycott, J F	283	Wildgoose, Nicholas	72	Yeaveley, Henry	1
Ward, William	41	West, William	10	Wilson, Sir William	207		

Number	Name	Active	Place	Title (Note 12)	Reference	Comments	Notes
1	Henry Yeaveley (Yevele) 1320–1400	1350 to 1400	London	Architect	*See* Saul page 63	Had family connections to Hanbury/Tutbury and may have used alabaster. Cheetham attributes John of Gaunt's tomb to this architect. Worked with Thomas Wreck (Wrek) and Stephen Lote	B61
2	Richard Lakenham and Henry Lakenham (died 1387)	*Circa* 1355 to 1387	London, St Paul's Churchyard	Marbler	*See* Saul page 63	Probably father and son. Recorded as a 'marblers' in respect of the tomb chest and effigy of Sir Nicholas Loveine in St Mary Grace's Church near the Tower	B128
3	William (1294–1349) and Agnes Ramsey (or Ramsay) Also John Ramsey (died 1371)	1359 (*see* B122) 1340 to 1371	London	Mason and marblers		Cited as making tomb of Queen Isabella, widow of Edward II. John Ramsey sometimes has the subscript III.	B122 B123
4	Jean de Liege (of Brabant) Possibly Hawkin of Liege (*see* Appendix W)	1360 to 1381	Paris and London	Sculptor	*See* the *Grove Encyclopaedia of Medieval Art*	Credited with the tomb of Philippa of Hainault in Westminster Abbey	B129
5	Peter the Mason (Peter Steppyngleye)	*Circa* 1367 to 1371 (1400?)	Nottingham and Chellaston	Kerver	Paper registered in the Nottingham Archives	Possibly Peter Steppyngleye of Bedford	B1
6	John Steppyngleye	1367 to 1375	Nottingham and Chellaston	Stonecutter	As above	Son of Peter	B1

Number	Name	Active	Place	Title (Note 12)	Reference	Comments	Notes
7	William Burdon	1369	Nottingham	Painter		Paid £40 for painting table at Windsor and may be the same one supplied by Peter the Mason	B43
8	Thomas Wreck (Wrek)	*Circa* 1374	London	Kerver	*See* Saul page 63	Cheetham attributes John of Gaunt's tomb to this carver. Worked with Henry Yeaveley	B135
9	John Orchard (died *circa* 1395)	*Circa* 1376 to 1395	London	Latoner		John Orchard may have been a brass worker but who inlaid the brass in alabaster	B29
10	William West (died 1453)	*Circa* 1380 to 1453	London	Latoner and marbler		Apprenticed to the Lakenhams and may well have taken over premises. Known mostly as a Latoner but later a marbler	B134
11	Claus Sluter 1340–1406	1385 to 1406	Brussels then Dijon, France	Sculptor		The tomb of Philip the Bold (A157)	B210
12	Stephen Lote	*Circa* 1398	London	Marbler		Worked with Henry Yeaveley	B61
13	John Mapilton	*Circa* 1390 to 1407	London	Marbler		Reported as working for the Lakenhams in 1376 but may well have used alabaster in his own workshop	B133
14	William Bonville	*Circa* 1400	Canterbury/Dorset	Mason		Reported as a marbler of Corfe and a member of an extensive Purbeck family	B62

Number	Name	Active	Place	Title (Note 12)	Reference	Comments	Notes
15	?	*Circa* 1400 to 1430	York	Kerver	*See* Saul page 68	An unknown reported as supplying the tombs at Methley and two (maybe three) at Harewood. Ceased production *circa* 1430	B118
16	Nicholas Michelson	*Circa* 1401	Burton on Trent	Image maker	Burton on Trent Archives		B36
17	Thomas Colyn	*Circa* 1408		Kerver		Noted in relation to Henry IV. Referred to in relation to Nantes Cathedral and the Duke de Bretagne	B50
18	Thomas Holewell	*Circa* 1408		Kerver		Noted in relation to Henry IV. Referred to in relation to Nantes Cathedral and the Duke de Bretagne	B50
19	Thomas Poppehowe (or Popplehouse)	*Circa* 1408		Kerver		Noted in relation to Henry IV. Referred to in relation to Nantes Cathedral and the Duke de Bretagne	B50
20	Robert Brown (or Broun)	*Circa* 1413 to 1421	London	Mason		Bisham Abbey and Canterbury tombs	B28
21	Thomas Prentys or Prentis	*Circa* 1414 to 1456	Chellaston/ Nottingham	Kerver		Lowick	B2, B3A
22	John Petit	*Circa* 1416 to 1423	London	Kerver		The Robertsbridge tomb – *see* A211	?
23	Robert Sutton	*Circa* 1419 to 1443	Chellaston/ Nottingham	Kerver		Lowick	B3, B3A
24	John Mildenhall	*Circa* 1420	Bury St Edmunds	Kerver		Will made in 1420. Work unknown.	?

Number	Name	Active	Place	Title (Note 12)	Reference	Comments	Notes
25	Robert Bounde (may be Broun)	*Circa* 1424	Burton on Trent	Image maker		Mentioned in Borough Records	B36
26	John Peyntour	*Circa* 1429 to 1430	Nottingham		Forinsec pleas		B33
27	John Mason	*Circa* 1429 to 1442	Nottingham	Kerver (Imager)	Forinsec pleas		B13
28	Gilles de Backere	*Circa* 1430	Bruges, Belgium	Carver		Sometime known as the Master of Rimini (from a stature carved for a church there)	B132
29	William Mason	*Circa* 1431 to 1432	Nottingham	Possible Imager		Son of John	B32
30	Richard Beke	*Circa* 1432 to 1458	London	Mason		Reported in connection with the Warrior Chapel in Canterbury	B136
31	William Howeton	*Circa* 1439	Burton on Trent	Painter and carver		Mentioned in Borough Records	B36
32	Bartholomew Lambspring, Dutch	*Circa* 1439	Possibly London or Warwick	Gilder		Mentioned in relation to Earl of Warwick effigy	B137
33	William Austen	*Circa* 1439	Possibly London or Warwick	Latoner		Mentioned in relation to Earl of Warwick effigy	B137
34	John Massingham	*Circa* 1439	Possibly London or Warwick	Kerver		Mentioned in relation to Earl of Warwick effigy	B137
35	John Bourde	*Circa* 1439 to 1457	Corfe or Isle of Purbeck	Carver		Purbeck for Earl of Warwick's tomb	B137
36	John Baker	*Circa* 1441	Late of Nottingham	Kerver		Mentioned in borough records	B12
37	William Warr	*Circa* 1441	Tutbury and Coventry	Mason		Joined the Coventry Guild Mentioned as a worker in alabaster	?

Number	Name	Active	Place	Title (Note 12)	Reference	Comments	Notes
38	M Thomas	*Circa* 1446	Nottingham	Kerver		Mentioned in the forinsec pleas for 1446	B11
39	Robert Prentys or Prentis	*Circa* 1456 to 1466	Chellaston	Kerver		Son of Thomas. Chellaston workshop may have closed 1466	B51
40	William Cowebrigge (Cowbridge)	*Circa* 1456 to1458	York	Alabasterer	York Guild register	Recorded as freeman	B109
41	William Ward (Warde)	*Circa* 1457 to 1458	York	Alabasterer	York Guild register	Freeman	B109
42	John Alley	*Circa* 1457	Bury St Edmunds	Kerver		Will of 1457. Work unknown	?
43	John Lende	1459	Burton on Trent	Image Maker		Burton records of the Marquess of Anglesey	?
44	William Laurence	*Circa* 1460	London	Kerver		Alabaster Kerver sued for debt by Thomas Taverner	?
45	Robert Wade	1460	Burton on Trent	Image Maker		Burton records of the Marquess of Anglesey	?
46	Richard Couper	*Circa* 1462	Burton on Trent later of Coventry	Kerver or painter		Supplied image for Coventry church	B20
47	John Aylde	*Circa* 1462 to 1465	York	Alabasterer	York Guild register	Recorded as freeman	B109
48	Henry Cuteis	*Circa* 1462 to 1468	York	Alabasterer	York Guild register	Recorded as freeman	B109
49	John Ropar (Roper) Died 1472	*Circa* 1462 to1472	York	Alabasterer	York Guild register	Recorded as freeman	B109
50	John Prylde	1464	York	Alabasterer	York Guild register	Greenhill found him listed as freeman in 1976	B109
51	Ricardus Hurlbutt	*Circa* 1472 to 1487	York	Alabasterer	York Guild register	Recorded as freeman	B109

Number	Name	Active	Place	Title (Note 12)	Reference	Comments	Notes
52	Elizabeth Jakes	1478	Bristol	Alabaster trader		Granted licence to export an alabaster reredos to Lisbon. The wife of Robert Jakes died 1475	B138
53	Nicholas Godeman or Goodeman or Goodman	*Circa* 1478 to 1479	Nottingham	Alabasterer		Mentioned in Borough Records	B7
54	Walter Hilton or Hylton	*Circa* 1480 to 1500	Nottingham	Kerver	Borough records of Nottingham	Mayor 1489–1490 and 1496–1497. Richard III	B16
55	Robert Bocher or Bosher or Boshur	*Circa* 1481	Burton on Trent	Alabasterer	Rolls of Edward IV	Burton records of the Marquess of Anglesey	B21
56	Gilbert Twyst or Twist or Twysse	*Circa* 1481	Burton on Trent	Alabasterer	Rolls of Edward IV	Burton records of the Marquess of Anglesey	B22
57	Robert Sherwood	*Circa* 1482	Nottingham	Image maker		Widow Emma sued by Walter Hylton for non-payment of fees for painting	B139
58	Edward Hilton or Hylton	*Circa* 1483–1488 and to 1512	Nottingham	Image maker	Borough records	Was sheriff 1484 possibly son of Walter	B17
59	Thomas Ropar (Roper)	*Circa* 1487 to 1490	York	Alabasterer	York Guild register	Recorded as freeman. Possible relation of John Roper	B109
60	Nicholas Hill	*Circa* 1490	Nottingham	Kerver (Image maker)		Mentioned in Borough Records	B5
61	William Bott	*Circa* 1490	Nottingham	Alabaster salesman		Possibly worked for Nicholas Hill	B5
62	Henry Harpur	*Circa* 1490 to 1529	Burton on Trent	Alabasterer	Foljambe tomb records	Chesterfield	B23 B200
63	William Moorecock	*Circa* 1490 to 1510	Burton on Trent	Alabasterer	Foljambe tomb records	Chesterfield	B24 B200

Number	Name	Active	Place	Title (Note 12)	Reference	Comments	Notes
64	Robert Tull	*Circa* 1493	Nottingham	Alabaster Carter?		Mentioned in Borough Records	B5
65	James Remus	*Circa* 1495	London, St Paul's Churchyard	Marbler		An unnamed testator ordered an epitaph. It may well be a continuation of the Lakenham workshop	?
66	John Lyngard	*Circa* 1495 to 1503	Nottingham	Alabasterer	Borough records		B19
67	James Keyley	1495	Nottingham/ Leicester	Bailiff for Henry Tudor	Rolls of Henry VII	Supervised the tomb of Richard III	B64 Appendix R
68	Thomas Drawswerd 1476–1529	*Circa* 1495 to 1528	York	Image maker	Newark wooden rood screen notes. Forinsec pleas	Mentioned with Nicholas George and William Drawswerd. Extent of alabaster work unknown but mentioned in alabaster dispute 1528	B140
69	John Spenser	*Circa* 1496	Nottingham	Image maker	Borough Records		B18
70	Thomas Green	*Circa* 1499	Beeston	Plasterer	Borough Records		B8
71	Thomas Hill (Hyll)	*Circa* 1499 to 1502	Nottingham	Alabasterman later Image maker	Borough Records	Paid 4d for license to trade	B35
72	Nicholas Wildgoose	*Circa* 1500	Nottingham	Alabasterman	Borough Records		B9
73	John Lingherd	*Circa* 1502	Nottingham	Image maker	Borough Records	Enrolled as a Burgess in the borough records	?
74	John Cottingham	*Circa* 1506 to 1530	Nottingham	Image maker	Borough Records	Brought action against John Nicholson	B10

Number	Name	Active	Place	Title (Note 12)	Reference	Comments	Notes
75	Robert Waterton	*Circa* 1507	York	Eteiler		Mentioned in respect of tombs in York but not yet known to be working in alabaster	B180
76	Cornelius Harman	1510 to 1540	Norfolk	Sculptor		Essex monuments	B73
77	Robert Stonard	*Circa* 1511	Bury St Edmunds	Kerver		Will dated 1511. Work unknown	?
78	Pietro Torrigiano Italian	*Circa* 1511 to 1525	London	Sculptor		Florentine	B60
79	Walter Carver (alias Bromflet)	*Circa* 1511	Ripon	Wakeman (nickname for the mayor of Ripon)		Listed by Collins in his Freemen of York as an alabasterman but more famous for the wooden carved choir in Ripon Cathedral	-
80	William Bellamy	*Circa* 1512	Bury St Edmunds	Kerver		Will dated 1512. Work unknown	?
81	John Hippis	*Circa* 1515	Lincoln	Marbler	Wollaton tomb	Brass worker but named in respect of Wollaton tomb	B30
82	Robert Brook	*Circa* 1520	Nottingham	Alabasterer	Borough Records	Mentioned in relation to images for Leverton for the rood loft. The purchaser was William Frankish	B141
83	John Broke	*Circa* 1521	?	Alabaster salesman otherwise called a factor		Mentioned by Lawrence Stone in 1955	?
84	Benedetto da Rovezzano Italian	In England *circa* 1524 to 1535	London			Italian	B55

Number	Name	Active	Place	Title (Note 12)	Reference	Comments	Notes
85	Richard Parker Died 1571	*Circa* 1522 to 1570	Burton on Trent (Horninglow St)	Kerver	Lichfield census of 1532	May have retired, Cheetham assigns Bottesford 1543 tomb to this carver	B25 B200
86	Edward Tomson (Thompson)	*Circa* 1524 to 25	York	Alabasterer		Recorded as freeman	B109
87	Richard Walker	*Circa* 1525	Burton on Trent	Carver		Mentioned by Greenhill in Vol 1	B26 B200
88	William Porter	*Circa* 1527	Burton on Trent (Horninglow St or Catte St or Bond End)	Alabasterman		Stepfather of Richard Parker	B199 B200
89	Richard Starkey	*Circa* 1529		Alabasterman			B15
90	John Nicholson	*Circa* 1530	Nottingham	Stainer			B6 & B10
91	William Walsh	*Circa* 1530	Nottingham and Chellaston	Alabaster Carter		Carriage of a cartload of alabaster stone from Chellaston to Nottingham	B6
92	Robert Crosse	*Circa* 1530 to 1540	Coventry	Marbler			B27
93	John Herteffeld	*Circa* 1533	Chester	Kerver		With Richard Herteffeld fined 12d by the sheriff for unspecified misdeed	?
94	Richard Royley (I) (Roiley)	*Circa* 1540 to 1614 *see* B131	Burton on Trent (Horninglow St)	Slab maker		Brother of Gabriel Royley (I)	B37, B40
95	Gabriel Royley (I) (Roiley)	*Circa* 1540 to 1614 *see* B131	Burton on Trent (Horninglow St)	Slab maker		Brother of Richard Royley (I)	B37, B40
96	Niccolo da Modona Italian	*Circa* 1540 to 1550	London			Italian	B55
97	Margery Walker (died1553)	*Circa* 1546 to 1553	Burton on Trent	Image Trader		Mother-in-law to Richard Parker	B26

Number	Name	Active	Place	Title (Note 12)	Reference	Comments	Notes
98	William Cure I 1514 to 1579 Dutch	1541 to 1559	Southwark, London	Sculptor		Dutch, invited to England possibly by Henry VIII in the 1540s (possibly 1541). Mason for Nonesuch Palace. Later patron was William Cecil. Son was Cornelius Cure	B46
99	John Chapman	*Circa* 1550	Bradford, Wiltshire	Stonemason		National Trust Inventory No. 996422 at Lacock	B142
100	Tallentire	*Circa* 1550	Durham	Sculptor		John Dakyn's tomb at Ravensworth	B143
101	Allen Gamman	1550 to 1560	London	?			?
102	Theodor Haveus Dutch or German	1550 to 1576	Norfolk and Cambridge or possibly King's Lynn	Sculptor		Dutch or German refugee	B74
103	Laurence Cleaver Thomas Lycett	1553	Burton on Trent	Possibly alabasterers		Mentioned in the will of Margery Walker (B26) as being owed money for wok completed	?
104	Robert Smythson 1535 to 1614	1556 to 1601	No fixed base, but mainly in Nottingham	Architect		Sons John, died 1634, Huntingdon, died 1648. Buried in Wollaton	B47
105	Philip Gillo	1558 to 1603	York	Mason		Freeman	B109
106	Willem Boy (Guillame Boyen) 1520 to 1592	*Circa* 1558 to 1592	Flanders	Sculptor		Flemish	B124
107	Cornelius Cure (died 1607)	*Circa* 1560 to possibly 1606	Southwark, London	Sculptor		Son of William Cure I. His son was William Cure II	B46

Number	Name	Active	Place	Title (Note 12)	Reference	Comments	Notes
108	John Tarbotons	*Circa* 1560 to 1563	Cumbria and Yorkshire	Sculptor		Carved wooden oak tomb in Staindrop church from 1563. Interesting in that it follows a Gothic style outdate for the year	B145
109	Henry Kinder	*Circa* 1560	Lincolnshire				B30
110	Richard Stephens (Stevens) 1541–1592 Brabanter	*Circa* 1567 to 1590	London, Southwark and St Martin in the Field	Sculptor		Dutchman who trained Epiphanius Evesham and Isaac James. Partnered Bartholomew Ayte	B52
111	Thomas Kirby	*Circa* 1562 to 1576	Possibly Bedford or Bucks	Sculptor		Lord Maudaunt's tomb at Turvey. Beds and Alexander Denton at Hillesden, Bucks	B206
112	Alan Maynard French	1563 to 1584	Hampshire and Wiltshire	Sculptor		French. Chimney piece carver. With Robert Smythson	B144
113	Gheerart Janssen (I) (Gerard Johnson) ? – 1611 Dutch	*Circa* 1567 to 1611	Southwark, London	Kerver		Later changed name to Johnson. *See* discussion B106	B4
114	Garrett Hollemans (I) Dutch	1568 to 1595	Burton on Trent	Tomb maker		Son Jasper (or Joseph)	B45
115	Anthony Tolly 1546 to 1594	*Circa* 1570 to 1591	Worcester and Gloucester	Tomb maker		Uncertain as to materials used. Carved tomb to Bishop Bullingham (died 1576) and Edmund Freake (died 1591) in Worcester. The former has a central column with an inscription across the effigy	B107

Number	Name	Active	Place	Title (Note 12)	Reference	Comments	Notes
116	John Gildon *Circa* 1530	*Circa* 1570 to 1585	Hereford	Tomb maker		Stated as only native tomb maker of the year	B75
117	William Flynte	*Circa* 1570 to 1590	Sussex	Freemason		Builder of Gatton church	?
118	Gilles (Giles) De Witte, Dutch Died 1614	*Circa* 1570 to 1610	Blackfriars, London	Sculptor		Dutchman	B146
119	William Kerwin (Kirwin) Died 1594	*Circa* 1570 to 1594	London, St Helen's, Bishopsgate. Workshop was at Holy Trinity, Aldgate	Sculptor and master mason to the queen		Possibly Dutch. Extent of work in alabaster uncertain but made statues to Elizabeth I in Ludgate. Later moved to a church. Tomb is in St Helen's, Bishopsgate	B147
120	Rosemond French	*Circa* 1580	Ledsham			Frenchman from Burgundy	?
121	William Whatton	1581	Burton on Trent	Alabasterer		Recorded as apprentice to the Royleys in the marriage register of Burton church	?
122	John Tarbook	*Circa* 1578 to 1587	Bewdley, Shrops	Carver		Pitchford St Michael slab	B148
123	Thomas Goodlord	*Circa* 1580 to 1581	North Lincolnshire	Tomb Maker			B76
124	Richard Royley (II) (Roiley)	*Circa* 1580 to 1589	Burton on Trent (Horninglow St)	Tomb maker		Son of Richard Royley (I)	B38, B40
125	Melchior Salaboss Milanese	*Circa* 1580 to 1590	Cheshire	Painter		Mentioned in respect of a triptych in Burford Shrops church	B216
126	Gabriel Royley (II) (Roiley)	*Circa* 1580 to 1605 (or 1614)	Burton on Trent (Horninglow St)	Tomb maker		Son of Richard Royley (II)	B39, B40

Number	Name	Active	Place	Title (Note 12)	Reference	Comments	Notes
127	William Hargrave	*Circa* 1587 to 1625	Bilborough, Notts	Tomb maker		Mentioned in relation to tomb of John Farnham (R85)	B209
128	James Mauncey	*Circa* 1590	London	Serjeant painter		Paid for painting the monument to Mary, Queen of Scots in Westminster	B94
129	Thomas Browne	1590 to 1630	York	Carver		*See* the Coxwold monuments	B149
130	Bartholomew Atye Died 1616	1590 to 1610	St Martin in the Fields, London	Sculptor		Associated with Isaac James on the Highclere monument and that at Charlecote and others	?
131	Gert van Egen	1591 to 1600	Amsterdam	Sculptor in alabaster		Panel in Wallace Collection London	B63
132	John Matthews	*Circa* 1592	Nottingham	Painter		Worked on the Bottesford tombs	B95
133	Nicholas Johnson ? – 1624	1592 to 1619	Southwark, London			Glentworth Lincs memorial of 1592. Son of Gerard Johnson (I). *See also* Bath Abbey church. *See* B106	B4
134	Maximilian Colt (Poultrain) (death uncertain but may be 1650 but more likely 1645) Arras and Utrecht	1595 to 1641	London, Smithfield and Bartholomew Close, Farringdon	Sculptor		King's master carver under James I. John Colt was his brother – *see* Toppesfield Essex 1633 but which may John Colt's son also John	B71
135	Edward Marshall 1598–1675	1619 to 1675	Fetter Lane, London from 1628 later White friars	Mason and sculptor		Master Mason to Crown from 1660. Unclear where he worked from until 1628	B48

Number	Name	Active	Place	Title (Note 12)	Reference	Comments	Notes
136	Joseph (or Jasper) Hollemans Died 1630	1599 to 1628	Burton on Trent	Kerver		Son of Garret Hollemans	B41
137	Simon Basill (Basil) Died 1615	*Circa* 1590 to 1615	London	Architect			B151
138	Walter Hancock	*Circa* 1600	Much Wenlock or Shrewsbury	Mason		Tomb to Richard Herbert in Montgomery, Powis	B150
139	Sampson Erdeswike 1553–1603	*Circa* 1600	Sandon, Staffordshire	Antiquary		Associated with the tombs to his ancestors (S138) but may well have only managed the commission	-
140	Isaac James (Harrar) (Dutch)	*Circa* 1600 to 1625	Southwark and St Martin's in the Fields, Westminster, London			Dutch born sculptor to whom Nicholas Stone was apprenticed	B72
141	John Deymond	*Circa* 1600 to 1620	Exeter, Devon and Dorset			Known as the Weller workshop? Credited with monument at Bickleigh, Devon to Elizabeth Eriseys 1618	B152
142	John Key (Keys)	1600 to 1610	London	Sculptor		Mentioned in relation to North Walsham monument and Narborough, Norfolk	B54
143	Tobias and Isaac Tissenaken (Dutch)	1600 to 1643	?	Sculptor		Makers of small altarpieces in wood with alabaster panel. An example is in the Bowes Museum, County Durham.	B223
144	Samuel Baldwin C1580–1645	*Circa* 1606 (1603) to 1645	Stroud, Gloucs Later Gloucester	Stonemason		Responsible for Berkeley tombs *See also* Stephen Baldwin, son. Died 27th August	B59

Number	Name	Active	Place	Title (Note 12)	Reference	Comments	Notes
145	William Cure II 15??–1632	*Circa* 1605 to1632	Southwark	Master mason		Son of Cornelius Cure. Often associated with Garrett Johnson	B46, B97
146	Ricardus (Richard) Nelson	1603 to 1625	York	Carver		Freeman	B109
147	Thomas Ventris	1603 to 1625	York	Carver		Freeman	B109
148	William Wright	*Circa* 1607 to 1640 possibly 1660	London, Charing Cross	Sculptor		Mentioned in relation to North Walsham monument and Narborough, Norfolk, and Kimbolton, Hunts. Also tomb of Henry Ireton in Westminster	B54
149	Thomas Greenway	*Circa* 1610	Lancashire or Bath	Carver			B153
150	Bernard Johnson Dutch	*Circa* 1610	Southwark, London	Architect		Son of Gerard Johnson (I). *See* B106	B4
151	Gerard Christmas 1576–1634	1610 to 1634	London, St Giles Cripplegate	Carver to the navy		Son of John Christmas (I) who may have immigrated from Northern Europe	B104
152	Francesco Fanelli 1590–1653 Italian	1610 to 1642	London	Sculptor		Florentine. Left in 1642 to return to Paris. Tomb monument in Ludlow church to Sir John Bridgeman	B154
153	John Taylor May have died 1651	1610 to 1620	London	Carver		*See* involvement in tomb in Spilsby Lincs otherwise little is known	?
154	Alexander Hills	1610 to 1630	London and Cork	Carver		*See* Yougal, County Cork	B155
155	Thomas Ashby	1610 to 1618	London	Tomb maker		Mentioned in relationship with Fulke Grenville marble tomb in St Mary Warwick	B156

Number	Name	Active	Place	Title (Note 12)	Reference	Comments	Notes
156	Richard Pryce	*Circa* 1611	London	Herald painter		Mentioned in respect of Lord Henry Norris monument in Westminster.	B96
157	James Mauncey	*Circa* 1612	London	Serjeant painter		Mentioned in relation to tomb of Mary, Queen of Scots	B96
158	Gerard Johnson (II) Dutch	*Circa* 1613 to 1625	Southwark, London			Pupil of de Keyser and arrived in England at same time as Nicholas Stone. Believed to be son of Gerard Johnson (I). *See* B106	B4
159	Nicholas Stone 1587–1647	*Circa* 1613 to 1647	Long Acre, London	Kerver	Notebook in John Soane Museum	Devon man, pupil of Hendrik de Keyser Snr in Amsterdam	B31 Appendix B
160	John Smythson Died 1634	*Circa* 1613 to 1634	Nottingham	Architect		Son of Robert Smythson. Designed Bess of Hardwick's tomb in Derby and the Pierrepont tombs as well as the castle chimney pieces at Bolsover	B14
161	William White	1614	London	Sculptor		In 1926 H S Cochran listed this man as a London sculptor. He credited with a tomb in the Tower of London (M330) and in Harefield (1610). Nothing can be found	B54
162	Epiphanius Evesham 1570–1634	*Circa* 1615 to 1634	Paris 1600 to 1615 then London, possibly Chancery Lane	Sculptor		*See* tomb at Lynsted, Kent. May have worked in London for a few years prior to 1600.	B53

Number	Name	Active	Place	Title (Note 12)	Reference	Comments	Notes
163	Benedick (Horsley)	*Circa* 1616	York	Painter		Painted Belasis tomb – *see* M5 for details. Listed as freeman 1612	–
164	Moses Bolwell	*Circa* 1618 to 1621	London (possibly Westminster where he was constable)	Sculptor		Mentioned in relationship with Fulke Grenville marble tomb in St Mary, Warwick 1621	–
165	Gian Lorenzo Bernini 1598–1680 Italian	1619 to 1680	Rome	Sculptor		Baroque style. No record of working in alabaster but listed because his work has been confused with that of Nicholas Stone. Had son Pietro	–
166	William Woodroote	*Circa* 1620	Cambridge			No trace	?
167	Jan Johnson	*Circa* 1620	London			Status unknown	?
168	James White	*Circa* 1620	Long Acre, London	Sculptor		Earl of Cork's monument in Deptford	B157
169	(?) Monday	*Circa* 1620	London	Herald painter		Earl of Cork's monument	B93, B96
170	Christopher Kingsfield	1620 to 1640	London	Master mason			B158
171	John (1599–1654) and Matthias Christmas (1605–1654)	*Circa* 1620 to 1640	London	Carvers to the navy		Sons of Gerard Christmas. Made mural memorials in Ampton church, Suffolk	B44
172	William Burton 1575–1645	*Circa* 1622 to 1641	Fauld, Staffordshire	Author		Whilst not in any way involved in carving Burton wrote extensively on the alabaster of Leicestershire and lived close to Fauld Mine	B98
173	Gerard Johnson (II) Dutch	1623	Southwark, London			Son of Gerard Janssen (I) *See* B106	B4

Number	Name	Active	Place	Title (Note 12)	Reference	Comments	Notes
174	Edward Woodrofe	1624	Cambridge	Kerver		Trinity College Chapel (R262)	B159
175	John Johnson Dutch	?	Southwark, London			Son of Gerard Janssen (I) *See* B106.	B4
176	Hubert Le Sueur 1580–1658 French	*Circa* 1610 to 1651	London	Sculptor in bronze. May have worked in alabaster		Huguenot from France but trained in Florence. Patron of Charles I but left for Paris with Fanelli in 1642 when war broke out. Marble bust of Charles I in V&A possibly only work in this material	-
177	John Thomson	1625 to 1649	York			Freeman	B109
178	Joshua Marshall 1629–1678	1654 to 1678	Fetter Lane, London	Mason and sculptor		Son of Edward Marshall and worked under Christopher Wren	B70
179	George Larson Dutch	*Circa* 1630 to 1650	London			Dutchman otherwise nothing known	?
180	Harry Ackers (Akers)	1630 to 1631	Long Acre, London			Worked for Nicholas Stone *circa* 1631	B88
181	Humphrey Moyer (Mayer) Died 1661	1627 to 1640	Long Acre, London			Assistant to Nicholas Stone *circa* 1627 onward	B87
182	Thomas Madden	1630	London			Nothing known	?
183	Thomas Stanton (I) 1610–1674	1630 to 1670	Holborn, London	Mason and sculptor		In Christopher Kingsfields workshop. Tomb of Jane Bacon in Culford, Suffolk for which he received £300 Had son Thomas who predeceased him and workshop went to William Stanton (*see* below)	B86 B158

Number	Name	Active	Place	Title (Note 12)	Reference	Comments	Notes
184	Peter (died 1693) and Isaac Besnier French	1631 to 1643 1661 to 1693	Covent Garden, London			French. Worked with Seuer on Westminster Abbey tombs but may only have sculptured in marble	B85
185	Richard White Died 1665	1638 to 1665	Long Acre, London	Mason	Notebook in John Soane Museum	Contract carver possibly foreman in Nicholas Stone's workshop	B57
186	Robert Pooke	1631 to 1643	Long Acre, London	Mason	Notebook in John Soane Museum	Contract carver, illiterate. In Nicholas Stone's workshop	B56
187	William de Keyser 1603–(1683) Dutch	1633	London and possibly Watchet Somerset	Alabaster miner and material purchaser	Notebook in John Soane Museum	Worked for Nicholas Stone and may be the 'Dutchman reported in Somerset in 1633'	*See* Appendix B B208
188	Garrett Hollemans (II) Dutch	1634 to 1656	Burton on Trent	Tomb maker		Maybe Gerrard – son of Joseph (or Jasper)	B42
189	Hendrik de Keyser 1613–1665 Dutch	1634 to 1647	Nottingham and London	Possible Kerver	Notebook in John Soane Museum	Brother in Law to Nicholas Stone	B31
190	Anthony John Ellis 1620–1671	1634 to 1668	London	Carver		Apprenticed to Nicholas Stone	B163
191	Francis Griggs	*Circa* 1638 to 1647	London	Mason		Made tomb monument in Framlingham, Suffolk at St Osyth 1640, and Braintree 1645	B160
192	John Jackson	*Circa* 1640 to 1661	Oxford			Provided estimate for repair of monument to Lord Williams in Thame church, Oxford in 1661	B84
193	William Byrd 1624–1690	1648 to 1690	Gloucester then Holywell in Oxford			Carved the Edmonthorpe monument in 1658	B130

Number	Name	Active	Place	Title (Note 12)	Reference	Comments	Notes
194	Stephen Baldwin *Circa* 1610–1662 (1667 or 1670)	*Circa* 1625 to 1667	Gloucester	Stonemason		Son of Samuel Baldwin. The date of his death is obscure. B113 shows evidence that Stephen died in 1670	B59 B110 B113
195	Harry Boughton	1640	London			Nothing known	?
196	Anthony Cawdron	1640	Lincolnshire			Recorded as Anne Cawdron's son and the carver of her slab in Great Hale, Lincs (S183). Otherwise little is known	?
197	Thomas Burman 1619–1674	1640 to 1670	Covent Garden, London	Sculptor		Apprenticed to Edward Marshall. In 1674 the workshop continued under his widow. Former apprentice John Bushnell who completed a monument to William Ashburnham may have done the carving	B83
198	William Sweet	1640 to 1665	London and Kent	Carver		Signed monument to Sir Edward Hales in Tunstall Kent. Believed to be a local carver	B161
199	John Stone	1642 to 1667	Long Acre, London	Kerver	Notebook in John Soane Museum	Son of Nicholas Stone	B31
200	Antonio Raggi 1624–1686 Italian	1647 to 1686	Rome	Sculptor		Pupil of Bernini. No record of any alabaster work but influenced the Renaissance style	B162

Number	Name	Active	Place	Title (Note 12)	Reference	Comments	Notes
201	John Campion	Before 1648 to 1675	Gloucester	Painter/Stainer		Associated with the Nicholls workshop and maybe that of the Baldwins – *see* Appendix S	B108
202	Caius Gabriel Cibber 1630 to 1700 Danish	1650 to 1700	London	Sculptor	Notebook in John Soane Museum	Worked for John Stone before branching out on his own. Known as Sieber or Cibo. Father of Colley Cibberooke	B105
203	John Bushnell 1630 to 1701	1668 to 1701	London	Sculptor		Apprentice to Thomas Burman. Worked on the Ashburnham monuments in marble	B217
204	(Michael) Miles	1650 to 1665	London and Kent	Carver		Signed monument to Sir Edward Hales in Tunstall Kent. Believed to be a local carver	B161
205	Thomas Cartwright I 1617–1702	1650 to 1701	London	Mason		Sons Thomas Cartwright II and Joseph. Masons to Sir Christopher Wren	B82
206	Martin Morley	1653 to 1669	Norwich	Sculptor		*See* Felbrigg, Norfolk	B164
207	Sir William Wilson 1614–1710	1659 to 1708	Nottingham and Leicester	Sculptor		John Clobery in Winchester. The Spelmans of Narborough, Norfolk	B99
208	Thomas Jewell the Elder Thomas Jewell the Younger	1690 to 1758	Barnstaple, Devon	Carver		Made five tablets in Tawstock church one of which (M287) is possibly Watchet alabaster	B222

Number	Name	Active	Place	Title (Note 12)	Reference	Comments	Notes
209	Christopher Horsnaile	1700 to 1742	London	Sculptor		Langford, Norfolk	B190
210	William Stanton 1639–1705 Thomas Stanton II Edward Stanton 1681–1737 Thomas Stanton III	1663 to 1705 1694 to 1734	Holborn, London	Stonemason		William was a nephew of Thomas Stanton (above) to whom he was apprenticed. Son of Thomas Stanton – predeceased him. Sons of William and great-nephews of Thomas Stanton (146). Over 140 monuments to their credit	B86
211	Jasper Latham 1610–1690	1663 to 1689	London	Sculptor/mason		Credited with an alabaster monument in Chalfont St Giles of 1671 (M532)	B207
212	Francis Reeve (I) 1639–1715	*Circa* 1664 to 1690 or beyond	Gloucester, St Nicholas	Stonemason	Gloucester apprentice register	Father may have been Joseph Reeve joiner of Tewkesbury but some uncertainty	B110 B111 B113
213	William Fox and son	*Circa* 1664	Twigworth and Gloucester	Mason	Gloucester apprentice register	The son was apprenticed to Stephen Baldwin but the father was also a mason	B110
214	Thomas Blackwell	*Circa* 1667	Gloucester	Stone carver	Gloucester apprentice register	Apprenticed to Stephen Baldwin 23rd March 1667. Later to Francis Reeve	B113
215	Stephen Reeve 1662–1724	*Circa*1680 to 1720	Gloucester	Stonemason	Gloucester apprentice register	Son of Francis Reeve	B111
216	Edmund (Edward) Pierce	*Circa* 1680	London	Painter/Stainer		A member of the Painter/ Stainer Company	B96
217	Francis Reeve (II) 1667–*circa* 1716	*Circa* 1682 to 1700	Gloucester but living in Ross on Wye in 1715	Stonemason		Apprenticed to his father Francis (I) 1675	B112

Number	Name	Active	Place	Title (Note 12)	Reference	Comments	Notes
218	Joseph Reeve 1669–1716	*Circa* 1690 to 1716	Gloucester	Stonemason		Listed by Llewellyn as being a monument carver	B111 B112
219	John Hunt	1696 to 1754	Northampton	Sculptor		Cilena l'Anson Bradley at Long Buckby	B69
220	Samuel Watson I 1662–1715 Samuel Watson II 1715 to 1778	1690 to 1715	Sudbury, Derbyshire	Carver	Chatsworth Archives Notebook	For cutting a monument in alabaster – two pieces for his grace the Duke of Newcastle. Chatsworth House	B77
221	John Weston	1712 to 1758	Exeter	Sculptor		The Ashprington monument to Kelland has alabaster components	B189
222	Joseph Hall	1725 to 1766	Derby	Sculptor	Kedleston Hall Archives	Attributed to the carving of the columns in Kedleston	B49
223	George Railton	*Circa* 1731	Carlisle	Alabaster merchant		Associated with Wragmire Bank quarry	-
224	Joseph Pickford I 1684 to 1762 Joseph Pickford II 1734-1782	*Circa* 1735 to 1762 *Circa* 1753 to 1782	London and Derby	Carver	Holkham Hall Archives	Worked with Thomas Carter. Noted in relation to the marble hall in Holkham Hall and Kedleston Hall	B125
225	Thomas Carter 1702 to 1756 Benjamin Carter 1719 to 1766	*Circa* 1735 to 1756	Portugal Row, London	Carver		Worked with Joseph Pickford. Associated with chimney pieces for Bolsover and Welbeck	B126
226	John Francis Moore ? to 1809 James Moore (son) ? to 1786	1760 to 1809	Berner St, London	Sculptor		English by born in Germany. Partner was one J Smith from 1786. Assistant was James Calvert.	B203

Number	Name	Active	Place	Title (Note 12)	Reference	Comments	Notes
227	Richard Brown 1736–1816 John Mawe 1764–1829	1760 to 1816	Derby	Spa carver		Traded as Brown and Mawe	B177
228	Joseph Evans	1770 to 1789	Derby	Sculptor		Sir Brooke Boothby memorial *circa* 1789 in Ashbourne	B66
229	Thomas Gaffin	1780 to 1855	London, Regent St	Sculptor			B67
230	John Golden	1780 to 1805	London, Holborn	Sculptor		Bevershal Filmer *circa* 1805	B68
231	William John Coffee 1773 to 1846	1792 to 1846	London then Derby and USA	Sculptor		Worked from 1810 but in 1816 immigrated to the USA. Mainly busts in alabaster	B165
232	White Watson 1760 to 1835	1800 to 1835	Bakewell, Derbyshire	Carver	Notebooks	Grandson of Samuel Watson. A carver making ornaments and tables in alabaster. White had preserved Samuel's notebooks and drawings from which much of the records are taken	B78
233	Sir Francis Legatt Chantrey 1781–1841	1808 to 1841	Curzon St, London	Sculptor		A prolific carver with some 538 works to his name. Mostly in marble the base of the statue to Charlotte Finch (A193) appears to be the only alabaster item.	?
234	Edward Gaffin	1819 to 1869	London, Regent St	Sculptor		Edmund Filmer *circa* 1810	B67

Number	Name	Active	Place	Title (Note 12)	Reference	Comments	Notes
235	Pellegrino Mazzotti 1794–1879	1822 to 1873	Wisbech, Ely and Cambridge	Modeller	*See* B0	Maker of small objects like vases in alabaster. Died in the workhouse in Wisbech	B218
236	Henry Moore	*Circa* 1825 to 1846	Greenhill, Derby	Painter and sculptor		Awarded a silver medal in 1825 from the Royal Society of Arts for his work in alabaster.	Appendix S
237	Reginald Cholmondeley 1827–1896	*Circa* 1830	Condover, Shrops and London	Sculptor		The Cholmondeley tombs in Condover church	B185
238	James Frank Redfern 1838–1876	*Circa* 1830	Hartington			Carved *A Warrior and Dead Horse* in alabaster	B172
239	Edward Richardson 1812–1869	1830 to 1866	London, Melbury Terrace, Marylebone	Sculptor		Edward, Earl of Powis at Welshpool. Presented papers	B80
240	John Prichard 1817–1886	1844 to 1886	Llandaff, Cardiff	Architect		Llandaff Cathedral and other churches	B205
241	John Rhind (Snr) 1828–1892	1837 to 1892	Edinburgh	Sculptor		Marquis of Montrose monument in St Giles	B117
242	John Howe & Co	*Circa* 1838	Carlisle	Alabaster dealers		Mentioned in relation to Cocklakes quarry	–
243	Benjamin Cheverton 1794–1876	1839 to 1876	London	Sculptor and inventor		Patented a machine for copying alabaster objects in 1844 and won gold medal at the Great Exhibition	B219
244	Richard Lockwood Boulton (and Sons) 1833–1906	1839 to 1977	Cheltenham, Birmingham and Worcester	Sculptors		The firm made the reredos in Saltcoats. Ayr (X68). Continued for a further 71 years after Richard's death.	B204
245	Joseph Cookson	1841	Tarporley	Restorer	Malpas church records	Repaired the Brereton monument at Malpas	B166

Number	Name	Active	Place	Title (Note 12)	Reference	Comments	Notes
246	William Russell	1842	Gloucester	Sculptor		Jane Velley alabaster monument in Gloucester Cathedral	B79
247	John and William Stuart Hamilton	1847 to 1858	Whitehaven	Alabaster Merchants		Mentioned as owing Barrowmouth mine	–
248	Joseph Gott Died 1860	1848	Yorkshire	Sculptor		The monument to Colonel Cheney in Gaddesby, Lincs (M541)	B220
249	Samuel Cundy 1816–1866	1849	London	Modeller and mason		Model for repair of Philippa of Hainault's tomb in Westminster Abbey	*See* A78
250	George Edmund Street 1824–1881	1849 to 1881	London, Bloomsbury	Architect		Installed much church furniture in alabaster	B202
251	George Gilbert Scott 1811–1878	1850 to 1878	London	Architect		Ely Cathedral and others. Supporter of the Gothic Revival and Chellaston Quarry	B90
252	William Forsyth 1834–1915	1851 to 1915	Worcester	Sculptor		Welford reredos in alabaster	B173
253	James Forsyth 1827–1910	1851 to 1907	Wells and London	Sculptor		The alabaster bases for two marble monuments in Worcester Cathedral, Witney and the font in Lichfield.	B171
254	James Currie 1836–1901	1851 to 1891	London, Oxford St Retired to Hampstead	Sculptor		The monument to Joseph Maas (M367) in Rochester Cathedral to the design of temple Moore	B197
255	Matthew Noble 1817–1876	1852 to 1876	Mayfair, London	Sculptor	Henry Moore database	London Westminster (M468)	B225

Number	Name	Active	Place	Title (Note 12)	Reference	Comments	Notes
256	John Bernie Philip 1824–1875	*Circa* 1856 to 1863	Derbyshire	Carver		Worked with Sir George Gilbert Scott on a number of commissions. Reredos in St George Chapel, Windsor and Flaxley, Gloucs.	B91
257	Francis Albert Skidmore 1817–1896	*Circa* 1854	Coventry	Sculptor		The monument to the canons of York Minster (M270)	B191
258	James Frank Redfern 1838–1876	1859 to 1876	London	Sculptor		St Andrew's, Kingsbury, Middlesex	B172
259	Antonio Salviati 1815–1890	1859 to 1890	Venice, Murano	Glass maker		Built and altered reredos in alabaster with glass mosaics	B201
260	Henry Hill	1860 to 1862	Hanbury	Trader in alabaster		Supplied Earley and Co Dublin	B181
261	John Oldrid Scott 1841–1913	1860 to 1913	Westminster, London	Architect		Son of George Gilbert Scott	B103
262	Robert Gilbert Lomas	1860 to *circa* 1905	37 King St, Derby	Sculptor		Mackworth church furniture (*see also* 214)	B92 Appendix K
263	Harry Hems 1842–1916	1861 to 1911	Exeter	Sculptor		Font at St Peter Port Guernsey	B120
264	Joseph Edgar Boehm 1834–1890	1862 to 1890	London	Sculptor		He is credited with the Earl of Cardigan's tomb in Deene which may be in alabaster	B127
265	Andrew Wallace	1866 to 1900	Leith Walk, Edinburgh	Sculptor		Various pieces in the Edinburgh area include St Giles	B115

Number	Name	Active	Place	Title (Note 12)	Reference	Comments	Notes
266	William Robert Colton 1867–1921	1867 to 1921	London	Sculptor		St Dunstan's, Cranbrook, Kent monument to Boyd and Claude Alexander	B168
267	George Frederick Watts 1817–1904	1867 to 1904	London	Sculptor		Tomb to the 8th Marquess of Lothian in Blickling (A122)	B184
268	William Silver Frith 1850–1924	1868 to 1924	London	Sculptor		Westonbirt Gloucs monument Ellicot monument in Gloucester	B167
269	John Hungerford Pollen 1820–1902	1868 to 1902	London	Designer and wood carver		Tomb to the 8th Marquess of Lothian in Blickling (A122)	B186
270	Richard Claude Belt 1851–1920	1869 to 1917	London	Sculptor	Mapping Sculpture	London, Westminster (M466)	B224
271	Raffaello Sani	1869 to 1881	London, Grays Inn Rd	Sculptor	Hampshire Telegraph *See* B0	Reported as exhibiting sculptures in alabaster in Portsea in 1869	B221
272	Peter Ford	1870 to	Uttoxeter, Staffordshire	Sculptor and alabaster trader		Owned part of Fauld alabaster mine	B119
273	Field and Allan	1870 to 1900	122 George St and 60 Bangor Rd, Edinburgh	Sculptors		War memorial in St Giles Edinburgh. Their premises were listed as artificial stone merchants	B169
274	Thomas Brock 1847–1922	1870 to 1922	London	Sculptor		The tomb chest to Thomas Hervey in Wells Cathedral	B175
275	William Clarke 1853–1923	1871 to 1915	Llandaff, South Wales	Sculptor		Worked for Llandaff Diocese	B114
276	Robert Rowand Anderson		Edinburgh	Architect		Altar in St Mary's, Edinburgh	B116

Number	Name	Active	Place	Title (Note 12)	Reference	Comments	Notes
277	Nathaniel Hitch 1845–1938	1871 to 1935	Battersea, London	Sculptor		Worked with John Loughborough Pearson	B101
278	Robert Bridgeman 1844–1918	1871 to 1911	Lichfield and Cambridge	Sculptor and Stonemason			B170
279	William Calder Marshall RA 1813–1894	1871	London	Sculptor		Louisa Foljambe tomb at Tickhill	B81
280	Wilfred Scarwen Blunt 1840–1922	1872 to1875	Crawley, Sussex	Sculptor		Led the work on the sculpting of the Blunt monument in the friary church in Crawley	B183
281	Neville Northey Burnhard 1818–1878	1872 to1875	Cornwall and later Crawley Sussex	Sculptor		Assisted in the sculpting of the Blunt monument in the friary church in Crawley	B182
282	Temple Lushington Moore 1856–1920	1875 to 1920	London	Architect		The monument to Joseph Maas (M367) in Rochester Cathedral with J Currie	B196
283	William Birnie Rhind 1853–1933	1878 to 1929	Edinburgh	Sculptor		Son of John Rhind Marquis of Montrose monument in St Giles	B117
284	William Drinkwater Gough 1861–1937	1881to 1937	London	Sculptor		Restored the Exeter Madonna and Child in 1933	B212
285	Arthur George Walker 1861–1939	1883 to 1936	London	Sculptor		Florence Nightingale *see* M155 and M156	B174
286	J F Waycott	*Circa* 1895	Paddington, London	Stone yard manager		Supplied Earbley and Co Dublin with alabaster	B213
287	William Vickers 1880–1922 William Vickers ltd	1883 to 1940	Birmingham and Glasgow, Cambridge St	Sculptor		Reredos in St Ninian's Church Pollockshields 1899. The workshop was opened by his father and continued in the family until 1940	–

Number	Name	Active	Place	Title (Note 12)	Reference	Comments	Notes
288	Leon-Joseph Chavalliaud 1858–1923	1890 to 1905 (in England)	Brixton	Sculptor		Sub-dean Butler in Lincoln Cathedral. Head of effigies in Hoar Cross, Staffordshire	B188
289	George Eley Halliday	1902 to1914 Poss 1888 to 1912	Llandaff and Penarth, South Wales	Sculptor		Pulpit in St David's Church Gyfelliwion, Hopkinstown, Pontypridd. Penarth alabaster	B176
290	William Douglas Caröe 1857–1938	1903 to 1932	Wales	Architect		Worked on tiles for Cardiff University in Penarth alabaster. Formed Caröe and Partners	B178
291	William Farmer 1825–1879 William Brindley 1832–1919	1904	London, Westminster Bridge Rd	Sculptors		Meynell-Ingram tombs in Hoar Cross (A126), tablet M271	B187
292	John Tweed 1869–1933	1907	Cheyne Walk, London	Sculptor		The Chichester tablet to Bishop Wilberforce (M278)	B193
293	Frederick William Pomeroy 1857–1924	1908 to 1916	London	Sculptor		Cradock monument in York Minster (M265)	B192
294	Fred (Fritz) Kormis (German) 1887–1986	1910 to 1977	Grenville Place London	Sculptor		Sarcophagus and effigy of Lady Methuen in rose alabaster dated 1970 in Corsham church	B121
295	Joseph Bridgeman 1881–1951	*Circa* 1912	Lichfield	Sculptor		Bridgeman and son	B170
296	Charles Sargeant Jagger 1885–1934	1914	Unsure but later Battersea, London	Military sculptor		Brocklesby church monument	B100

Number	Name	Active	Place	Title (Note 12)	Reference	Comments	Notes
297	Frederick Brook Hitch 1897–1957	1920 to 1957	Hertford	Sculptor		Son of Nathaniel Hitch	B102
298	British Alabaster Bowl Co	1921 to 1941	Weston on Trent, Staffordshire	Ornament maker	*See* note B0		
299	Charles William Bridgeman 1902–2004	*Circa* 1922	Lichfield	Sculptor		Bridgeman and Sons later Linford-Bridgeman	B170
300	William Edward Lomas 1863–	1926 to 1936	Lord Belper's New Kingston workshop, Nottingham	Sculptor		Possible related to Robert Gilbert Lomas as he came from King St Derby	*See* Appendix L Section 7
301	Barbara Hepworth 1903–1975	1926 to 1975	St Ives, Cornwall	Sculptor		Statues carved in alabaster	B227
302	Joseph Else 1890–1949	1927 to 1929	Nottingham	Sculptor	*See* note B0	Nottingham Council House frieze	B215
303	Henry Moore 1898–1986	1929 to 1986	London and Much Hadham Herts	Sculptor		Statues carved in alabaster	B226
304	Alma Ramsey 1907–1993	1930 to 1993	Warwick	Sculptor		Carver in alabaster	?
305	Sir Jacob Epstein 1880–1959	1939 to 1940	Loughton Essex	Sculptor		Harewood House *Adam* and *Jacob and the Angel* in the Tate	B179
306	Nigel Owen	1949 to Date	Yelvertoft, Northamptonshire	Alabaster Carver		Small item carver	B194
307	Margaret Lovell 1939	1960 to Date	Bristol	Sculptor		Carver in alabaster. Busts and other statues in what appears to be Watchet alabaster	B211
308	James Elliott	2015	Market Overton, Rutland	Carver and stonemason		The tomb to Richard III in Swaledale limestone and the alabaster altar in Leicester Cathedral	B195

B0 'Mapping the Practice and Profession of Sculpture in Britain and Ireland 1851 to 1951'. A website maintained by the University of Glasgow: http://sculpture.gla.ac.uk/view/organization.

B1 Reported as Peter Maceon or Peter the Mason. The payment made on the 6th June 1371 for the Windsor retable mentioned in the text was part payment. Peter's reputation would probably become known to King Edward III during one of his frequent visits to the town, and so secure him this large order, the execution of which, it may here be stated, cost £200 (equivalent to £4,800 in these days), and required 10 carts, 80 horses and 20 men to transport it to its destination (pipe rolls 41EdwardIII m41). The journey occupied seventeen days in the autumn of 1367 (20th October to 6th November) and the expenses of transport amounted to £30 or about £720 today. Peter is mentioned in the Nottingham borough rolls for 1360 to 1380. His residence in 1379 was stated as St Mary's Street (Via Beatrae Mariae). *See* main text for debate over Peter's identification with Peter Steppyngleye. Nottingham Borough Records states that a 'Peter' the mason was again licensed to trade in 1479 (Book ii page 306) and again in 1500 (Book xxix page 77).

B2 Thomas Prentis is recorded supplied block alabaster to Normandy, France in 1414. He is described as the kerver for the Lowick tomb indicating he was both quarryman and carver. The workshop may have closed *circa* 1450 as both Tong, Salop 1451 and Over Peover 1456 can be credited to Prentis workshops.

B3 Although Sutton and Prentis names are linked the relationship is claimed to a loose one with both kervers working in different workshops. Nigel Saul claims that the workshops were not large employing only a handful of carvers. Sutton is recorded as being sued by Sir Thomas Cumberworth for the supply of alabaster which was alleged to be 'impure'. This is taken as not being white. This was 1443 and may indicate that the pure white alabaster may have been difficult to obtain. The history of the Chellaston quarries indicate that new fields were opened from time to time and certainly white alabaster was still being produced in 1539. It is therefore most likely that Suttons current quarry was nearing exhaustion or that he was trying it on with Sir Thomas when he was sued. Later the 'impure' veined alabaster was seen to be decorative or irrelevant when the alabaster was stained.

B3A Nigel Saul says that the Sutton and Prentis trademark was a motif of a standing angel holding a shield placed in niches round the side of the tomb chest. This claim is made in 'Chellaston Standing Angels with Shields at Aston-on-Trent: Their wider Distribution 1400 to 1450' an article in *Derbyshire Archaeology Journal* 133, 1993 pages 69 to 90. The Lowick tomb has such a motif. The 'gablette' over the head of the effigy may also be another distinctive feature. Gablettes can be found on the tombs at Greystoke and at Arundel (G167). Mark Downing claims that another trademark is the highly decorated orle.

B4 The Janssens were Dutch/Flemish sculptors. They fled the Dutch/Spanish wars *circa* 1567 and settled in St Thomas the Apostle, Southwark London very close to where the Globe Theatre would be built. Gerard (I) had four sons, Bernard, John, Nicholas and Gerard (II) sometimes known as the younger. All were masons. Gerard (I) died 1611. Records say the Christian name is of the father is Garrett and the surname changed to Johnson which is the anglicised version of the Flemish name – *see* B106. Gerard Johnson the Younger carved the bust of Shakespeare at Stratford in 1623, Nicholas was the carver for the Bottesford, Leics tombs and Bernard was head mason for Northumberland House, Strand and Audley End, Essex. Records show that Johnson was boarded in the village of Bottesford from September to October 1591 when he was finally paid-off. Nicholas died in 1624. Gerard (II) is credited with the tomb of Jeffery Pitman in Woodbridge, Suffolk dating *circa* 1620. Sir William Dugdale wrote in his diary in 1593 'He lived in the parish of St Thomas and had his workshop close by the bishop's palace. In making the effigy of Andrews he must have seen his face and therefore the likeness (of the effigy) is good'. Dugdale went on 'Johnson sculpted the bust of Shakespeare and may have created more works in Southwark'.

B5 Borough Records. In 1490, Nicholas Hill, alabasterman, is recorded as delivering 58 heads of St John the Baptist, part of them being in tabernacles or niches. A great trade was done in these, which were, apparently, specialities in the town (Nottingham). There is a fine specimen of one in the Leicester Museum in its original oak case. On 31st October, 1491, the same man sued his salesman William Bott for failing to hand over all the proceeds of the sale of the heads. On the 6th June, 1493, he employed a Robert Tull (husbandman) to convey images of John the Baptist to London for 3s, but part defaulted in payment of 12d for which he was sued on the 7th January 1494. In 1498 Hill was called an image maker. In 1499 Hill appears as a defendant in a suit brought by Thomas Grene of Beeston – *see* B8.

B6 On the 27th May 1530, William Walsh, a carter, sued John Nicholson reported as a 'stainer' (one who painted and gilded the effigies) for failing to pay for the carriage of a cartload of alabaster hauled the 14 miles from Chellaston to Nottingham. He appears to have charged 1/6d. A note in the borough records states that the court found for Walsh. *See*: https://archive.org/stream/recordsboroughn14enggoog/recordsboroughn14enggoog_djvu.txt.

B7 In 1479 Godeman (or Goodeman) was charged VIII (8d) in fines (rates) for a license to allow him to continue with his trade in Nottingham. He was recorded as being neither a freeman nor a burgess. *See* forinsec pleas.

B8 In 1499 Nicholas Hill was again in trouble. Thomas Green of Beeston (a playsterer) sued Hill for a head of John the Baptist priced 16d.

B9 In January 1500 Nicholas Wildgoose died, his chattels comprising six heads of John the Baptist and a 'coffer' but were only valued at 8d. Wildgoose may have been a kerver.

B10 In May 1506 John Nicholson complained that John Cottingham, image maker, had 'detained' a head of John the Baptist unjustly. This dispute may again been due to the failure to pay a bill.

B11 Forinsec pleas 1446–1447, Nottingham Archives. Thomas (kerver of Nottingham) raised a complaint against his servant John Watson for trespass and contempt. It is unclear what the dispute was about but it was settled.

B12 Forinsec pleas 1441–1442, Nottingham Archives. John Baker, kerver, was sued by the Prior of Newstead in 1441. This appears again to be due to a dispute over payment. It seems that Baker produced some images for the prior but was also renting a cottage from the priory. The prior claims that Baker defaulted on the rent for the cottage and seized the images. Baker responded by breaking into the prior's house and recovered the images. Baker was summonsed for doing 40s worth of damage to the prior's house.

B13 Forinsec pleas 1431 – John Mason (image maker) and his son William with Richard Eyton sue Robert Dyke of Stapleford for debt. Forinsec pleas 1433 – John Mason was a juror in the suit between John Plumtre and John Wolaton of the 12 Nov 1433, being shown as an Ymager. He was again summoned for jury service 17th March 1434 (Court roll No 147) but appears not to have turned up. He was called again on the 12th May 1434 but again failed to appear earning the approbation of the bailiffs. He was called again 9th June

1434 but again failed to turn up. A John Mason appears again in 14th Dec 1441 in a dispute with the prior of a Carmelite priory over payment for some work (Court record 127). The matter came before the court on the 10th January 1442 but was postponed due to the jury not turning up.

B14 John Smythson was the son of Robert Smythson architect to Bess of Hardwick. The history of Holme Pierrepont records that he designed the tomb of Sir Henry Pierrepont (*see* Index) but the kerver is not mentioned. The chimney pieces at Bolsover Castle are magnificent and contain alabaster, Ashford black marble and cockleshell. A memorial to Robert Smythson is located in Wollaton Hall but he is buried in Wollaton church. Robert designed Wollaton Hall, Longleat and Burton Agnes as well as Hardwick but he died 1614.

B15 Borough records.

B16 Walter Hylton, image maker (1480–1497). Mentioned in a dispute over the staining of a tabernacle in 1482. Recorded as being commissioned by Henry VII to construct a tomb for Richard III at Greyfriars, Leicester which is likely to be 1495 but has been reported as late as 1500. This no longer exists but is recorded in the 18th century as being mingle coloured marble probably veined alabaster – *see* A45. The reporter probably only saw only a fragment. Like other Yorkist tombs that of Richard III probably received adverse attention either from Tudor supporters or by the commissioners of Edward VI. In 1496 Hilton was recorded as an alabasterman and mayor of Nottingham 1486–1487 and 1496–1497. There is also a Walter Hylton recorded as sheriff in 1463–1464. The skeleton of Richard III was discovered in 2012 when a car park which occupied the site of Greyfriars was excavated. *See* 'King Richard's Tomb at Leicester in The Richardian' Vol 3 1975 page 8–9, note A45 and TT3 and Appendix R.

B17 A sheriff's bond of 1488 mentions Edward Hilton as an image maker but in 1483 he was referred to as a paynter. This reflects the development of the trade. In 1503 he is again mentioned as an image maker and appears to have been a member of the council from 1500. In 1512 he contracted for some work at Ashton under Lyme church.

B18 John Spenser died *circa* 1496 but his widow Emma was sued by an Elizabeth Spenser for to the failure of John to deliver goods which had been ordered. The goods were described as 'divers altarpieces and other images of alabaster in her shop priced 20s'.

B19 Described as alabasterman in 1495 but an image maker in 1503.

B20 Variously described a paynter or corver of alabaster and sold a carving in Coventry. Cheetham reports that Couper moved to Coventry as early as 1444 but may have retained a workshop in both locations. The reference is unclear stating 'St Mary's altar 1462. It solute Coup(er) Burton super Trent peynter – image de Marie alabaster suitat apab Bablake xls'.

B21 Claimed payment for images from several religious houses – Blair and Ramsey – *Archaeological Journal* No 239, 1991. With Gilbert Twyst he claimed £11 from William, Abbot of St Albans, £10 from Anthony, prior of the house and Church of the Holy Trinity Wallingford and 8 marks (£5 6s 8d) from William Bray of Newbury, keeper of the Hospital of St Bartholomew. All the sums were owed and unjustly detained. The sums are small and probably relate to retables or reredos.

B22 Claimed payment for images from several religious houses – Blair and Ramsey – *Archaeological Journal* No 239 199. *See* B21 for details.

B23 Henry Harpur with William Moorecock also of Burton delivered a tomb to Chesterfield for Henry Foljambe in 1510. This has no effigy being surmounted by a brass. The weepers on the tomb table can be matched with Cubley, Derbyshire. Gardner believes the Babyngton tomb at Ashover and the Blythe tomb at Norton, Yorkshire are of the same hand and can be attributed to the same Burton carvers. The Llandaff effigies may also be of the Burton school. Almost no documentary evidence of the dates between which Harpur and Moorecock worked exists, except for the solitary contract for Chesterfield. It is clear that Foljambe would only have commissioned a tomb chest from established carvers and so it can be inferred that the two were well established by 1510. The Chellaston workshops may well have closed *circa* 1450 meaning that effigial carving moved west to Burton. On the basis of attributed monuments it seems the Burton workshop was active much before 1490 and was still working in 1529. The Harpur name does not appear in the list of Burton families in 1532.

B24 With Henry Harpur, William Moorecock was paid £10 for the Foljambe tomb *circa* 1508–1510. *See also* B23. Moorecock does not appear in the 1532 list of families and it is believed that he died in the 1510s but this cannot be confirmed. The Lichfield list does contain a Richard Morcoke (*sic*) living in Andenstaff Lane, Burton and a Richard Morekocke in church side, Burton but no family link can be established. *See* B200.

B25 Richard Parker is credited with the carving of the tomb of the 1st Earl of Rutland in 1543. He was believed to be the son-in-law of Margery Walker of Burton on Trent (B26) who was a trader in alabaster 'tables' according to her will made in 1546. The 'List of Families in the Archdeaconry of Stafford 1532' lists Richard Parker and his wife (uxor eius) Margaret with William Bradburne (Sp'us) living in Horninglow St (Hornying Low Strete). Parker is also credited with the Wroxeter and Clifton Campville monuments. Bayliss believes that Parker commenced carving in the 1520s probably under the direction of someone else (Church Monuments publication No 5 pages 39–56, 1990). In 2013 he suggested that person may be William Porter his stepfather or Richard Walker his father-in-law. There is a belief that an abrupt change in quality occurred between the Patshull monument (A229) and that a Fawsley (G127) *circa* 1532–1534 which may indicate that Parker had set out on his own (the list of families above shows the Parker family living separate from the Walkers). Bayliss also offers the opinion that the 'weepers' on the Fawsley monument show a lack of finish which, it is claimed, shows that he had few if any skilled assistants at that time and he was keen to complete the monument within budget. In any case the Parker workshops were well established by 1535 and closed on his death in 1571 but the 'good will' was probably acquired by the Royleys. The carving of monuments in which only the upper and lower parts of the effigy are shown the centre being obscured by a block which forms part of the surround is believed to be his design. Tombs in this group include Rolleston, Staffordshire (R128) and possibly Standon (1526) whilst the John Port slab at Etwall (A231) shows a variation on this theme. Nigel Llewellyn says that amongst the inventory of Richard Parker in 1571 was note which stated 'Item – unto one Mr Harford that I took in earnest for the making of a tomb'. This is taken as being a deposit of £4 for a tomb which may well have been for John Harford's first wife but was not completed due to Richard Parker's death. Parker tombs are noted for their decorative balusters at the corner of tomb chests.

B26 It is believed that Margery was a widow carrying on the trade of her husband – possibly Richard Walker. The 'List of Families In the Archdeaconry of Stafford 1532' lists Thomas Walker who may well be Richard Walker's son as there follows the name Margery with a cross and Margery (uxor eius) who is clearly Thomas's wife living in Horninglow St (Hornying Low Strete). There are children,

John, Joan, Isabel, Alice john, John, Emmot, Agnes, Thomas, John, Thomas, although the duplicate names indicate it is possible some were not living at the time of the record. There remains the possibility that Margery was trading in monastic spoils. Strangely her will of 1553 shows she rented a shop which is believed to be in Bristol for which she owed rent of 10/- to Edward Jonys (or Jenys). This may have been a warehouse storing work awaiting shipment. Bristol is mentioned elsewhere as a trading centre for the Iberian ports and Ireland. She is believed to be the mother-in-law to Richard Parker who married her daughter Margaret. Her will also showed that on her death she had debts of £13 6s 8d to Laurence Cleaver and £9 10s to Thomas Lycett both for tables of alabaster. As these are debts it is likely that both men were alabasterers although neither appears in the list of 1532.

B27 Crosse like Parker is reported to have workshops in both Burton and Coventry.

B28 Robert Brown (or Broun) is credited with a chest for the tomb of alabaster and stone to the Earl of Salisbury or Richard Hertcombe in Bisham Abbey *circa* 1421. After this date there is little documented record of London alabastermen until the middle of the 16th century. The commission for the Earl of Salisbury offer a rare glimpse of the executor in action, in this case Richard Hertcombe. He was charged with the organisation of the monument and gave it some thought as to where the work was to be carried out and the assignment of roles. The way this was carried out reveals the knowledge that had spread abroad in the first quarter of the 15th century. The chest went to Robert Broun for £22 13s 4d and the effigies to the Derbyshire carvers, Sutton and Prentys of Chellaston. It may well be that Hertcombe had seen the Lowick tombs of 1419 and like the customers from Fécamps in 1414, travelled to Nottingham to close the deal for 43 marks. Bisham is on the banks of the Thames near Maidenhead and the river may have provided the transport route of the effigies from the Midlands which may have eased the decision to place the commission in the North. The tomb of Henry IV in Canterbury (G97) is credited to Brown but the date is uncertain being stated as 1437 in some quarters which is later than the dates between which he carved.

B29 Nothing much is known about John Orchard's alabaster work and St John Hope points out that the rolls of Edward III state he is a Latoni (Latoner). B129 has details of John Orchard completing the tomb of Philippa of Hainault in Westminster receiving two payments of £5 on account of a total of £18 2s for 'various costs and expenses about the said tomb and in respect of two images of alabaster upon a little marble tomb for the son and daughter of the king'. These two images are those of William of Windsor and his sister Blanche of the Tower. The charge was also for a second-hand iron grate recovered from Bishop Michael of Norbury's tomb in St Paul's. The Whitewinds website claims that he commissioned the alabaster from another carver for the sum of 20s. As a result accreditation of the alabaster effigies can be challenged. The tomb of William of Hatfield in York may also be subject of clarification although he may well have added brass fittings to the alabaster tombs. Worked with Henry Yeaveley on several royal tombs. The Whitewinds website also has a modest description of Orchard as a Latoner. Other names associated with Orchard are Henry Lakenham and John Mapilton.

B30 Contracted with John Willoughby of Wollaton but the material is uncertain being referred to as 'Tombe of stone'. The 'City Register of Lincoln' for the years 1541 to 1564 records a charter of Painters, Gilders, Stainers and Alabastermen which states it was founded in 1525 in honour of Our Lord Jesus Christ, the Blessed Mary and All Saints and maybe St Luke the Evangelist. It appears to have survived the Reformation.

B31 Known as The Elder, born 1587 and died 1647. Trained in the Netherlands under Hendrik de Keyser (1565–1621) and was active in London from 1613 retiring in 1642, dying in 1647. Master mason for Windsor in 1626. Made many alabaster tombs. For details of the Stone 'school' *see* Appendix B.

B32 Forinsec pleas 1441–1442 – William Mason (Son of John – Imager) accused of withholding 4s 10d rent on a house in Nottingham belonging to Roger Hunt. On the 30th April 1432 judgement went against William Hunt being awarded the full rent plus 2d damages. William may have died in the intervening period as his case was put by John Corbette referred to as executor.

B33 Forinsec pleas 1429 – reported as an imager on a jury dated 8th Feb 1430.

B34 Ratcliffe on Soar, Henry Sacheverell.

B35 In 1501 he was fined 4d for a license to trade as an image maker. The term fine may well be allied to today's business rates.

B36 History of Staffordshire.

B37 The connection between Richard Royley (I) and (II) is unclear. *See* Church Monument Society VI 21–41.

B38 The name Cartwright is associated with Richard Royley (II) but the context is not clear. Opinions have been expressed that Richard (II) and his son Gabriel produced crude images but still were sought after. The tombs of the Shirleys at Breedon on the Hill (M95), that of Thomas Fermor at Somerton, Oxford (R75), Sir Humphrey Bradbourne at Ashbourne, Derbyshire and Sir John Salisbury at Whitchurch, Salop (R109) are attributed to Richard (II) and his son Gabriel. Richard died 1589.

B39 Son of Richard (II) – *see* B38. Gabriel died 1605.

B40 J Bayliss produced an appraisal of the Royleys in the Church Monuments publication dated 7th May 2006. Contracts exist for R74 and R75. Greenhill's study of the Royley slabs (Vol 1 page 177) suggests that the workshops had an almost monopoly of the Midlands alabaster trade in the period 1550 to 1585 although their time overlapped that of Richard Parker who seems to have ceased trading *circa* 1570. The workshop may have continued until 1614 although this is unclear and the last slab was produced *circa* 1597 (Peatling Magna, TT20). The quality of the product seems to have declined after 1585. Greenhill suggests that the virtual monopoly bred carelessness and that they failed to keep their patterns up to date so that a series of standard offerings were produced with declining skill. This may also be due to the decease of the older and more experienced Royley carvers. The slabs at Blithfield (S63) and Marchington (TT19) both 1593 especially witness this decline being classed a puerile by Greenhill who lists the final phase of Royley slabs as Blithfield (S63), Marchington (TT19), Kirkby Mallory (S99), Hanbury (TT2) and Peatling Magna (TT20).

B41 The son of Garrett Hollemans, he was trained in London but was working in Burton on Trent in 1599. The Great Brington, Northamptonshire tombs of Sir John Spencer (I) died 1586 and (II) died 1599 are attributed to him as are Sir William Spencer died 1605 at Yarnton, Oxford and Sir George Fermor died 1612 and his wife died 1628 at East Neston, Northamptonshire. Joseph also worked in stone and an example is believed to be that to Sampson Erdeswick at Sandon which dates from 1601. He was still working in 1612 but may have worked beyond this as he did not die until 1630. Source: Burton Archives.

B42 The son of Jasper Hollemans. Garrett (II) or Gerrard Hollemans inherited his father's business but the earliest record in 1634 and worked at least until 1656.

B43 Cheetham in *Unearthed* page 13. The tablet was in the upper chapel and the cost would tend to indicate that the work was extensive.

B44 John Christmas was born 1599 and died 1654. Matthias Christmas was born in 1605 and also died in 1654. Llewellyn has it that the Christmas workshop started in 1620 with Gerard. Details may be in *Walpole Anecdotes* Volume II page 38. There are 10 signed monuments including Archbishop George Abbott in Guildford (died 1633 but tomb erected 1640), Stean Northants (1633), Chipping Campden – M54 (1633), Farthinghoe, Northants – A37 (1635) and Ampton Suffolk.

B45 The Dutch family of Hollemans may have arrived in England as early as 1568 fleeing from the religious wars between the Dutch and the Spanish. To avoid clashes with the Janssens (Johnsons) they settled in Burton on Trent but the opening of the workshop here is uncertain. The earliest dated work is that of the Morgan family at Weston under Wetherley, Warwicks in 1584. The mural monument in Quorndon dated 1574 may well be from this workshop. Hollemans may well have started his work carving incised slabs (although this is disputed by Greenhill) and that for Thomas Cawarden in Mavesyn Ridware, Staffordshire dated 1592 is attributed to his workshop by then run by his sons – *see* B41 and B42. Garrett (I) died *circa* 1590. *See* Church Monument Society VIII 45–56.

B46 William Cure was of the Dutch school in Amsterdam. It is reported he was invited to England in the early 1540s by Henry VIII setting up a workshop in Southwark 'outside the control of the city companies'. A patron was William Cecil. The firm was continued by his son Cornelius. The birth year of Cornelius is not known. Adam White states that he was 'living' in 1574 suggesting that works earlier than this year are attributed to the father. Cornelius Cure being apprenticed to a marbler was a member of the Marblers Company but by 1584 this had dwindled to no more than a handful of carvers and so it merged with the larger Masons Company. William Cure II was Cornelius's son who worked with his father.

B47 The Smythsons were the architects for Hardwick Hall and Bolsover Castle. Although mainly building designers, RIBA has a drawing by Roberts Smythson *circa* 1601 for the alabaster tomb of Bess of Hardwick in Derby Cathedral. Bess died 1607 and is reputed to have viewed the tomb before her death. There is uncertainty as whether Smythson carved the tomb or if it was sub-contracted to the Hollemans of Burton or even the Johnsons of London. Smythson is buried in Wollaton church.

B48 Edward Marshall was apprenticed to John Clark (1585–1624) and having become free of the Mason Company in 1626 had his own workshop in 1628. Recorded effigies of Sir Edward and Lady Filmer in St Peter and Paul, East Sutton, Kent in 1629 and Henry Curwen in St Mary Amersham, Bucks in 1638 but has other memorials. His son Joshua is noted as producing cruder carvings.

B49 Kedleston. Joseph Hall, a Derby Sculptor is attributed with the carving of the columns in the Marble Hall in Kedleston. The detail of where and how these were carved is, as yet, unclear. Joseph Hall is mentioned in the *Gunnis Dictionary of British Sculptors 1660 to 1766*. Hall made a chimney piece for Melbourne Hall, Derbyshire in 1745 and has some association with the works at Ashford in the Water, near Bakewell. A picture of the works is recorded as DCHQ200196 in *Picturethepast* where it is recorded that Joseph Hall obtained an interest in Ashford machinery at Derby owned by Brown although the date of this is unclear. There is an association with James Gravenor who made wooden patterns for the Corinthian tops to the columns which were recorded as being in alabaster (Gunnis). The son of William Hall of Derby (supplied to Calke Abbey) he was in partnership with a Mr Chambers for a period during which they built the east wing of Kedleston (1761). He made a chimney piece for Tissington Hall in June 1757. His grandson also

Joseph married into the Brown family and inherited the marble works mentioned above in 1830. Joseph Hall exhibited alabaster from Chellaston and Ashford marble exhibits at the 1851 Great Exhibition.

B50 Nigel Saul maintains that all three kervers were Trent Valley based. *English Church Monuments AD 1150 to 1500* by F Crossley pages 26 to 27 reports the details of the passport which does not disclose the location of the three men. Octavius Morgan in his 1872 book says that the Duke de Bretagne died in 1399 and the monument was shipped in February 1408.

B51 It is reported that Thomas Prentis's son Robert carried on the Chellaston business for a decade after 1456.

B52 Reported as a sculptor working in alabaster 'in the Dutch style'. One of his pupils was Epiphamus Evesham. Stephens was born in 1541 and came to England from Brabant in the first wave of Dutch immigration in 1568. Still working in 1589 when the Boreham, Essex monument was completed. He died in 1592 part way through the construction of the tomb of Sir Christopher Hatton in Old St Paul's London which was likely finished by Maximilian Colt.

B53 Lived 1570 to 1634. Born in Wellington, Hereford to a large gentry family who moved to London in 1580. Studied under Richard Stephens, a Dutchman in Southwark *circa* 1590 and then in Paris 1600 to 1615. Created marble effigy to Archbishop Sens in Notre-Dame (now not traced). Credited with memorial to John Owen in St Paul and which was destroyed in the fire of 1666. Other monuments include Christopher Roper in Lynsted Kent 1620, Lady Parry in Welford church, Berks. Memorials to the Collyns family in Hythe, Kent and Mersham, Surrey, Lord Rich at Felsted, Essex (*see* Saul fig 45 page 72) and West Hanningfield, Essex.

B54 William Wright and John Keys are mentioned in the contract for the supply of a monument for Sir William Paston in North Walsham church, Norfolk. The monument was to a design by Sir Thomas Knyvett of Ashwellthorpe who oversaw the contract. The extant contract is interesting in its detail. The central effigy was specified to be a man in armour resting on one elbow above and around was to be three pyramids of fair black marble. The cost was to be £200 and the contract signed 23rd Feb 1608. A first instalment was paid on 26th May and the monument complete by the 2nd October. Paston paid the transport costs and those of the masons for meat, drink, bricks and mortar. Paston died 20th October 1610 aged 80. It is clear much of the preparation work was completed in just three months with the transport and assembly in eight months. It is not known if the monument contains any alabaster but the details indicate the adherence to the 'Dutch' style of tomb making. Wright is also mentioned in relation to the 1660 monument at Noseley, Leics (M39) but this may be tenuous. The monument at Narborough (or Narburgh) to the Spelman family is sometime credited to Key and Wright. This too has the effigies leaning on one elbow and has distinctive features in that the tomb chest is plain with a three-arcade mural above which contains a child and a chrisom. The classic heraldic devices are included. A sculptor named as 'William White' found in the same period may well be a misidentification of William Wright. William White (1825–1900) was a famous architect. Wright first trained as a haberdasher and is first mentioned in Charing Cross in 1607 where he partnered the obscure John Key. Wright continued with that to Edward Talbot, 8th Earl of Shrewsbury (*circa* 1619; London, Westminster Abbey), Sir Robert Gardener (*circa* 1620; Elmswell, Suffolk, St John the Baptist) and Edward Seymour, Earl of Hertford, and his Family (*circa* 1621; Salisbury Cathedral). He promoted the fashion for shrouded effigies, revealing a talent for figure sculpture in the tombs of Anne, Lady Deane (1634; Great Maplestead, Essex, St Giles) and Sir John Denham (*circa* 1639; Egham, Surrey, St John the Baptist). There are odd monuments of Sir

Richard Scott (1640; Ecclesfield, S. Yorkshire, St Mary), Sir Lionel Tollemache, Bart (*circa* 1640); Helmingham, Suffolk (St Mary) and Sir Robert Wiseman (*circa* 1641); Willingale Doe, Essex (St Christopher). Read more: http://www.answers.com/topic/william-wright#ixzz21w1RMOvA

B55 Torrigiano was followed by two other Tuscan sculptors Benedetto da Rovezzano and Giovanni da Maiano but they were gone by 1535 and later by Niccolo da Modona. Included because it is unclear as to whether they worked in alabaster.

B56 Travelling carver, polisher and installer of tombs. May have been in York for the Belasis tomb installation. May also have signed the font in Willington church Somerset.

B57 Countersigned the payment records of other carvers. His initials with that of Robert Pooke may be on the font in Willington church Somerset. Credited with the carving of 'a lady for Nicholas Stone' for £15.

B58 Mentioned in respect of Bishop Thomas Savage's tomb at York. Savage had his heart buried in Macclesfield amongst his relations who are commemorated by alabaster tombs. Whether Waterton worked in alabaster is yet to be established.

B59 Samuel Baldwin had workshop in Stroud Gloucestershire and is credited with some 60 monuments in a 40 mile radius (*see* John Broome, Church Monuments Society). He was a former joiner of Upper Lypiatt, Gloucs and was first active sometime between 1603 an 1606. He had moved to Gloucester by 1627. The works that are certainly his are the tombs of Dame Joan Young and her second husband (1606; Bristol Cathedral) and Henry, Lord Berkeley and his second wife (1615; Berkeley, Gloucs, St Mary). The former is crudely carved in local stone, whereas the latter, which has alabaster effigies, is fully up to the standard of much London-made sculpture of the time. Baldwin clearly made a close study of the tombs in Westminster Abbey, because the memorial to Sir Edmund Wylde (*circa* 1620; Kempsey, Hereford & Worcs, St Mary), which can confidently be attributed to him, is copied in almost every detail, except the effigy and cresting, from that of Sir Thomas Heskett (*circa* 1605) in the abbey. In the monument to Giles Reed and his wife (*circa* 1611; Bredon, Hereford & Worcs, St Giles) the subjects are shown beneath a huge canopy set against a wall such as had been erected in the abbey to Anne, Duchess of Somerset (*circa* 1587). Other monuments attributable to Baldwin's workshop are those of Sir Thomas Throckmorton (*circa* 1608; Tortworth, Gloucs, St Leonard) and William Kingston (*circa* 1614; Miserden, Gloucs, St Andrew). This body of work can in turn be related to other unattributed provincial sculpture, particularly in Bristol and Hereford, Worcester and Gloucestershire. Stephen Baldwin is stated to be his son but there are a limited number of works attributed to him and at present nothing in alabaster. The main works are four statues only one being in place. The Henry Moore Dictionary has:

In 1661 Stephen was paid £20 'for cuttinge and settinge up' a statue of King Charles II in Worcester Guildhall and he later received a further £8 12s for his 'men's wages in settinge up the Pediston and the Arch' (Worcester Audit of Account Books, 3, 1640–1669, cited by Gunnis 1968, 36) (2). The statue must either have been damaged or become worn, for Thomas White was paid for repairing it in 1712. Baldwin also replaced the damaged statue of King Charles I on Worcester High Cross, and his personification of Justice originally stood at the upper end of the High Street (1, 4). In 1662 the city of Gloucester ordered a similar figure of King Charles II (3). This was removed in the mid-18th century and was lost for many years before being discovered in pieces in a garden at Chaxhill in 1945. Memorial in St Nich Gloucester painted freestone).

B60 Pietro Torrigiano, a Florentine by birth, he was invited to London by Henry VIII to make his father, Henry VII's, tomb in Westminster *circa* 1511 to 1518 (but may have been as early as 1509). Whilst in London he was commissioned by Thomas Lord Marney to make his tomb in Layer Marney (*see* X3). Torrigiano is also credited with the Duke of Norfolk's tomb at Framlingham (A29) but this will need to be checked. Also credited with the monument in black marble and gilt bronze to Lady Margaret Beaufort in Westminster Abbey dated 1511 and the bronze medallion of Sir Thomas Lovell. He left England in 1520. For an assessment of Torrigiano *see* 'Foreign Influences on and Influences in the First half of the 16th Century' – a thesis by Nicola Jane Shilliam BA in Warwick 1986. Despite this there is no Renaissance work of the carver outside London and rather than found a style movement in England, the Renaissance elements that appeared in the 1530s was more Flemish than Italian.

B61 Henry Yeaveley (Yvele or Yeveley) was the King's master mason in 1398 and had an assistant, Stephen Lote (died 1418). The records of Canterbury mention both in relation with the building work at the cathedral and also with Lote as the architect for Edward the Black Prince (*circa* 1376), Edward III (*circa* 1386), Richard II (*circa* 1399) and Cardinal Langham tombs at Westminster and the tomb of Henry IV – *see* G97. Also the tomb of Archbishop Sudbury at Canterbury and the destroyed tomb of John of Gaunt (1376) in Old St Paul's. Lote is also referred to as a Latoner which may indicate he also worked in brass. Cheetham says that the family connection of Yeaveley with Yeaveley in Staffordshire means that the architect was familiar with the use of alabaster.

B62 Notes on the archaeology of Canterbury suggest that Purbeck marble was still in use in the third quarter of the 14th century despite competition from the alabastermen. However, the notes go on to suggest that the writing was on the wall for this stone and that the monuments in Christchurch were some of the last constructed.

B63 The Wallace Collection has a carved panel 14.9cm by 26cm in poor quality golden alabaster attributed to Van Egen. No source of the alabaster is given and the colour is unusual. The stone is badly fractured and may not be English but the carving is well executed.

B64 Referred to in relation to the tomb for Richard III in Greyfriars Church. Keyley was paid £10 1s for an unspecified task which may well have been for carting the alabaster from Nottingham to Leicester – *see* A45 and Appendix R. The chantry and a school commissioned by Keyley at Shenstone came under scrutiny in 1548 by Edward VI's commissioners. They determined that the payment for the chantry should cease but that the school supervised by Ralph Parker could continue at a cost of 5/-.

B65 Joshua Marshall succeeded John Stone as master mason of Windsor Castle and master mason to the crown on the retirement of his father in 1673. The construction of monuments tailed off following the great fire in 1666 after which he concentrated on buildings. He is credited with 10 pre-1666 memorials but Adam white attributes 56 others by virtue of style. His first memorial was late 1640s and he followed his father's design of demi-figures in a decorated niche – *see* M77.

B66 Joseph Evans is credited on the Henry Moore database with one memorial in alabaster which is believed to be designed by Boothby.

B67 The Gaffin workshop flourished in London's Regent St from about 1800 to 1900 and mainly worked in marble. They had other workshops around London. Their work is said to be competent but uninspiring and one monument to Edmund Filmer *circa* 1810 is registered as alabaster.

B68 John Golden was apprenticed to William Halfpenny but later set up on his own. A sculptor in coloured marble the Henry Moore database lists one alabaster memorial to Dorothea and Sir Beversham Filmer *circa* 1805.

B69 The Hunt family settled in Northampton from about 1670 and one alabaster memorial is credited to John Hunt jnr *circa* 1726 at Long Buckby.

B70 The son of Edward Marshall he is unkindly stated to be 'of little talent' – his designs relying heavily on his father. Ten monuments exist from the pre 1666 period but Adam White (Walpole Society Vol 61 (1999) pages 1 to 163) identifies 56 others which may be attributable to Joshua Marshall.

B71 Maximilian Colt (Coulte) was a Flemish born Huguenot from Arras and the sculptor of Elizabeth I's tomb in Westminster in 1605–1606 (*see* Llewellyn Fig 20 page 40) but his works in alabaster are as yet unclear but can be seen in that for Sir George Saville (M379) in 1627. He was born Poultrain but changed his name when he became a citizen of England in 1607. His arrival in England possibly with his brother Jean (John) is uncertain but the consensus is that it was in the last years of Elizabeth's reign *circa* 1595. A traditionalist adhering to the old styles of 20 to 30 years earlier and therefore lost custom. He was imprisoned for debt in 1641 and little information is available of his work thereafter. Tombs attributed include the marble monument to Robert Cecil at Bishops Hatfield, the Countess of Derby at Harefield Middlesex and Viscount Stormont at Scone Palace. John Poultrain (Colt) was also a carver but his work is unknown. Robert Cecil's monument includes a skeleton the whole costing £460.

B72 James family. Émigré Dutch established in London in the mid-16th century. Isaac James was active from 1600 being credited with Sir Edward and Lady Denny in Waltham Abbey, Sir Richard Kingsmill in Highclere, Hants (R39) and Henry Lord Norris and family in Westminster Abbey. In partnership with Bartholomew Atye in Westminster. One time he was associated with Nicholas Stone.

B73 Cornelius Harman, a Dutchman, possibly of Huguenot extraction is reputed to have come to England in 1510 and was active to late 1540s. He is credited with the monument in Touch marble to John de Vere the 15th Earl of Oxford of 1539 in Castle Hedingham, St Nicholas. Pevsner also suggests that the monuments at Saffron Walden (Audley, 1544) and Bodmin (Vyvyan, 1533) were by this carver (*see* Appendix H).

B74 Theodor Haveus (Theodorius de Have), Dutchman possible Huguenot. Arrived as refugee. Credited with memorial to Dr John Caius in Caius College, Cambridge. This was a sarcophagus under a canopy.

B75 John Gildon was a native of Hereford and worked extensively there. He worked mainly in freestone and has a number of signed monuments. For more information *see John Gildon of Hereford, a late 16th century Sculptor* by Lawrence Butler 1973. Two interesting monuments are those of Richard and John Harford in Bosbury, Hereford. John Harford died in 1559 although the signed tomb was not carved until 1573 with Richard's in 1575. These are in freestone but are interesting in that it shows the first venture into mural Renaissance style by a domestic carver having fluted columns which justifies his inclusion in this list. At Much Dewchurch he carved two male knights on one tomb (R172). Gildon was familiar with the alabaster works of Parker yet seems to have never wanted to import Midland's alabaster unlike Baldwin 50 years later. As a result the carvings are less well formed and have suffered from spalling.

B76 In respect of Goodlord, the records of Grimsthorpe Castle, Lincs has the following entry in the account book of Richard Bertie (and wife Katherine, Duchess of Suffolk) for September 1581. 'Prest cum lone, payments upon bills, including to Thomas Goodlord, the maker of the tombe in prest upon his bill £4 to my Lord Willoughby by way of a lone £10'. It is believed 'in prest upon his bill' means an advance to allow work to continue. It is also believed the tomb is for Katherine, Duchess of Suffolk who had died on 19th Sept 1580 and is located in Spilsby. There is an account of Spilsby monuments held in Lincoln's Archives 3-ANC/9/24 said to be credited the Gervase Holles dated 4th Feb 1814.

B77 The Chatsworth Archives has an entry that Samuel Watson was active at Chatsworth House between 1690 and 1711 mainly as a wood carver. The records speculate that some wooden carvings in the house were either carved by him or obtained as patterns from Grinling Gibbons. The reredos in the chapel and two mask heads for the dining room, both in alabaster, are credited to him. The work carried out for the Duke of Newcastle cannot be identified. The location of his workshop at Sudbury, Derbyshire was only a short distance from the alabaster quarries. The other carvings (probably wood) are in the Queen of Scots Lobby in Chatsworth. *The History of the County of Derby* Part 2 page 225 written in 1829 has extensive details on Watson's work which includes the statement that Watson studied under C Oakley in London. The book also observes that the dining room in Chatsworth has a doorway of alabaster and the walls lined with the same stone which may also be from this period. Samuel Watson II seems to have been only a wood carver but is credited with a stone cutting business in Bakewell at some time. Samuel Watson is buried in Heanor church with a tablet designed by his grandson White Watson (M631).

B78 The Watson notebooks are held at Cambridge University Library, Dept of Manuscripts and University Archives GBR/0012/ MSS Add 6304.

B79 Signed *Wm Russell Gloucs.*

B80 Medieval tomb restorer. Edward Richardson carved a statue to the late Earl Powis for Welshpool church, Montgomeryshire (*see* A62). A quote from the *Derby Mercury* for the 4th June 1851 is '… at last succeeded in obtaining a block of alabaster from the Chellaston quarry of George Wooton for the statue (effigy). The alabaster is pale salmon colour. Its length is 7ft 6 inches and it contains 41 cu ft and weights nearly 3 tons. It is the largest block for sculpture work that has been obtained since the mode of blasting the rocks with gunpowder has been used. Formerly all was obtained with picks and saws'. The effigy of the earl who died in 1848 was completed in 1853 and is still in the church. The medieval monumental effigies of the Temple Church were restored by him *circa* 1843 along with those at Elford, Staffordshire in 1852. He presented papers to the Archaeological Institute on English medieval alabaster sculpture in 1852 and the monuments in Chichester Cathedral in 1853. He wrote about the effigies of English kings at Fontrevault and Le Mans in 1854. Richardson lived at 17 Melbury Terrace, Marylebone from 1847 onwards. He died 17th May 1869.

B81 Calder appears to have been involved in only one alabaster monument and that may have been relocated.

B82 Thomas Cartwright. He was responsible for several monuments including Sir John Langham, Cottesbrooke, Northamptonshire, 1676 and Sir John Lewys, Ledsham, Yorkshire 1677 but the full extent of alabaster work is unknown. Also Purleigh Essex 1659 and Runwell, Essex 1692. The Biographical Dictionary lists 'eight figures of unidentified subjects seven of them alabaster' carved 1657 to 1659. These cannot now be traced.

B83 Apprenticed to Edward Marshall. Completed the effigy to Robert Devereaux 3rd Earl of Essex in 1646 which may well have been alabaster but this has vanished. He carried out some work for Nicholas Stone whose work he copied. Burman's monument in Sherborne, Gloucs to John Dutton has been compared with Stone's 1631 marble mural to John Donne in old St Paul's. Also may have worked at St John's College, Cambridge and at Walton on Thames. Credited with the monument to Lady Chandos (1623) in the Bedford Chapel at Chenies, Bucks. Bushnell had limited success and only two memorials are attributed before he became mentally unstable. He is credited with monuments in Shenfield, Essex 1652 (A224) and Little Warley, Essex 1658 (M128). He was also commissioned for the Verney tombs at Claydon, Bucks but was fired in 1653.

B84 Jackson appears to have been very active in and around Oxford. He is mentioned in relation to Brasenose College and may have worked there as early as 1634 in a minor role. The extent of any alabaster work is not yet known.

B85 The Besnier brothers assumed Sueur's mantle on his return to France until 1643 when the role was taken by Peter Benier alone. Peter was deprived of his commission by the Commonwealth but petitioned to be reinstated in 1660.

B86 The Stanton workshop appears to have been established by Thomas Stanton (I) *circa* 1631 but came to nephew William Stanton and his two sons Edward and Thomas (II) after the death of his son . Some 30 monuments are credited to Thomas (I) and 140 monuments are credited to the latter Stantons including that to Richard and Isabel Shireburn in Mitton, Yorkshire as well as chimney pieces in Aynho Park and Knowsley Hall. However, the Shireburn monuments are also accredited by Bayliss to the Royley workshop. William Stanton is associated with Belton House, Lincs. Marble was preferred medium but there are many tombs in alabaster. They may have repaired the tombs in Temple Church, London – *see* A67. K A Esdaile wrote a book *The Stantons of Holborn.*

B87 Apprenticed to Thomas Kingfield. Credited with assistance in the carving of the Stone monument to Dr Donne but his signed monuments are rare. That to Simon and Bridget Coston and possibly to Simon's parents in St Botolph's, Aldersgate, London *circa* 1637 is listed. The extent of alabaster work is not known but he was in the Stone workshop at the peak of alabaster carving there. The Simon and Bridget Coston monument is now in Greenford Middlesex.

B88 Listed in Stone's notebook as having carved the coats of arms on the monument to Sir George Villiers in Westminster Abbey but may well have carved others.

B89 Not a lot is known about Bartholomew Atye. He was in partnership with Isaac James for some years and is partly credited with the tombs at Highclere, Hants and to Henry Puckering in Westminster Abbey.

B90 Sir George Gilbert Scott is reported to have visited the Chellaston quarries by Farmer writing in 1916 (*Alabaster* by John Young 1990). Young reports that Scott was instrumental in the restoration of the reredos in Ely Cathedral for which Chellaston alabaster was used some of the figures being carved by J Bernie Philip who also worked with Scott on the St George's Chapel, Windsor reredos. There is correspondence between the Dean of Windsor and Philip about the delays in completion due to the failure of the quarry to find alabaster of the required quality (Windsor Archives). However, the quarry is not mentioned by name but the description fits Chellaston. The reredos in now demolished St Andrew's Church, Derby is believed to be carved from Chellaston alabaster.

B91 John Bernie Philip carved figures for Ely Cathedral and St George's Chapel, Windsor which are believed to be made from alabaster from Chellaston (*see* B90). He is also credited with the arch over the effigy of the 2nd Earl of Powis at Welshpool and repairing the monuments in All Saints, Chelsea in 1868. The alabaster reredos of 1864 in Lichfield is his in association with John Oldrid Scott.

B92 R G Lomas of Derbyshire. A respected monumental mason of Hall and Company of 37 King St, Derby. He worked with Emily Mundy to create a number of fine works in Mackworth church, Derbyshire. In 1860 he advertised that he had succeeded Joseph Hall as the proprietor of the Derby Marble Works and was using steam power for all kinds of work in marble, alabaster and stone. The 1851 catalogue of the Great Exhibition has the following entry:

Manufactures in Mineral Substances for Building or Decoration items 37 and 38. Hall J&T Marble Works Derby, Tennant J Strand. Specimen of articles manufactured by aid of steam machinery at the Derby Marble and Spa Works: of black marble, Derbyshire mottled alabaster, stalactite (oriental alabaster) and variegated alabaster (gypsum) and fluorspar.

The trade directory for Derby says that the workshop continued after Robert Lomas died and was still trading in 1925 – *see also* William Lomas (Appendix L Section 7).

B93 A painter called Monday was employed by James White to paint the monuments commissioned by the Earl of Cork in the 1620s. Those at Deptford are in alabaster. Monday is referred to as a herald painter and may have been mainly employed in painting the heraldic devices. The records of White reveal some interesting figures. Whilst White charged £100 for the monument to Cork's parents Monday added another £20 for painting.

B94 James Mauncey received £265 for painting the monument of Mary, Queen of Scots monument in Westminster Abbey for Cornelius Cure which was considered to about 30% of the cost. Mauncey is later referred to as a serjeant painter.

B95 John Matthews was paid £20 in 1592 for the painting of the tombs to the 3rd and 4th Earls of Rutland in Bottesford (17% of the total cost). The painting of the tombs made by Garret Johnson in 1591 may have been separately commissioned direct by the earl. Matthews was paid in instalments from February to November 1592.

B96 The medieval panels for which Nottingham was famous were painted or stained by workmen within the workshop and few names have survived. From the last quarter of the 16th century the emergence of interest in heraldry raised the status of monument decoration. In 1592 John Matthews of Nottingham was paid £20 for painting the Bottesford tombs. The painting was completed in stages from February to November. The reason for not allowing Garratt Johnson to paint the monuments is unclear but he may well have not wanted to remain in Leicestershire for this length of time. In 1612 James I commissioned Cornelius Cure to make a monument for his mother Mary, Queen of Scots. The painting of this tomb was allocated to James Mauncey who received £265 for the task, about 30% of the whole cost of the monument. In time the painters would be elevated to the status of gentlemen especially where heraldic painting was involved. So important did painting become that the heralds attempted to control the painting of tombs but with limited success. To combat the attempts by the heralds many sculptors held notebooks of heraldic styles (Llewellyn displays a page from the notebook of Epiphanius Evesham as Figure 103 page 144).

B97 William Cure II joined his father Cornelius in the workshop in Southwark in 1605. When Cornelius died in 1607 his prime contract which was the tomb of Mary, Queen of Scots was unfinished and this was completed by William. In 1621 William Cure's wages as Master Mason were withheld due to his failure to complete commissions. Inigo Jones was to complain that William had absented himself from contracted work for some five months. He claimed to be the carver of the memorial to Richard Martin in Temple Church (M114).

B98 William Burton born 1575 and died 1645. Born in Lindley he became interested in Leicestershire in 1597 and published his first history in 1622. He returned to Fauld in 1642 and died there in 1645 being buried in Hanbury church. Burton wrote in 1622 '... there is a quarry serving cutters and picture makers for statues, tombs and preparations discovered in Burton-on-the-Wolds the stone of which was scarcely so hard or so clear as that obtained from Tutbury or from the quarries at Fauld'.

B99 Sir William Wilson. A native of Leicester he appears to have worked mainly in the East Midlands carving a statue to the Duke of Newcastle in the grounds of Nottingham Castle subsequently destroyed in the riots of 1831. The Biographical Dictionary lists one alabaster statue by Wilson for John Cobery but the carving of the statue to Clement Spelman is uncertain.

B100 Charles Sargeant Jagger. A military sculptor of the First World War. He was commissioned to make a memorial to Lord Worsley when he was killed in 1914 now in All Saints Church Brocklesby, Lincs. Although not a user of alabaster he appears to have used this stone to create the monument in the style of the early 17th century in keeping with the memorials to the rest of the family in the same church.

B101 Nathaniel Hitch. A renowned carver of reredos during the Gothic Revival period. He appears to have used Chellaston alabaster.

B102 Frederick Brook Hitch. The St David's monument may be the only one in alabaster.

B103 John Oldrid Scott, the son of Gilbert Scott. He is recorded as designing the alabaster tomb chest for Bishop T Legh Claughton in St Albans although he may well not have been the carver. He is also credited with the mural memorials to Lord Sandford and professor Veitch in The University of Glasgow.

B104 Gerard Christmas. A sculptor credited with a few monuments but more associated for the sculptural decoration ships, a post which he took up in 1614. He designed the stage properties for the Lord Mayor's Show and was responsible for metal castings for statues. The two monuments credited include M138 (1626) and R51 (1628) although the former is stated to be 'his only surviving work'. His sons were John Christmas (II) and Matthias Christmas.

B105 Caius Gabriel Cibber was a Dane who worked for Peter de Keyser in Amsterdam in 1658. He came to England *circa* 1660 and worked for John Stone. When Stone visited Amsterdam to plead for a position with Charles II then making plans to return to England he suffered a stroke and it was Cibber who went to Holland and brought him home. He then started his own workshop. He is credited with the monuments to the 7th and 8th Earls of Rutland in Bottesford and the Sackville monument in Withyham, Sussex although any work in alabaster in uncertain.

B106 The names of this Dutch family is problematical. The surname is generally accepted as Janssen (sometimes Johansen) and at some point this was anglicised to Johnson. The elder carver who came to England in 1567 as a refugee is believed to have the Christian name of Geerart (in Dutch). As a result the Christian name has been anglicised to a range of English equivalents including Gerard,

Gerart, Garrett, Garet, Gerhard and Gerhart. Sometimes called Gerard the Elder. In 1613 his son also Geerart training in Holland, returned to England and assumed the Christian name of Gerard. He is known sometimes as the Younger. Another son was Nicholas who died in 1624. Other sons include Bernard and John. All were stone masons.

Oxford Dictionary of National Biography, Oxford University Press, 2004 (Nottingham Central Library 920.04103 2 Floor 3).

B107 Not a lot is known about Tolly but Worcester Archaeological Society Vol 19 1942 has a paper by Alec McDonald on Freake's monument.

B108 Campion was well respected in the Gloucester area and may well have contract painted for all the local workshops. The details are contained in Appendix S. On the 28th Sep 1672 he took his son, also John, as apprentice for seven years with a final payment of 20s. In 1674 John senior was listed as sheriff.

B109 York workshops. 'The Freeman Rolls of York' list a number of alabasterers from *circa* 1456 to 1650. Lawrence Stone, quoting Collins *Freemen of York* (1896), states that between 1423 and 1462 only five alabastermen were admitted as freemen of York. However, there were 15 between 1463 and 1502 and 27 in the years 1503 to 1542. The thesis written by Oliver Fearon called 'Pieces from Peaseholme – six medieval alabasters and their context in 15th century York' attributes the works at Harewood, Methley and Sheriff Hutton as well as the Peaseholme finds to this school. However, his observations on the source of York alabaster are suspect. Quoting R Firman he assumes that alabaster came from Hillam, a village on the edge of the Ledsham fields but reading the actual entry by Firman it states '... gypsum was formerly worked at Hillam … none of this is used for alabaster and there is no evidence that alabaster was worked in the Hillam/Sherburn area' (page 170). Firman does hypothesise that the Sheriff Hutton monument may have been sourced from Ripon Parks in the Permian beds but that the Methley tomb to Lord Welles is unlikely to be Ledsham due to the lack of evidence for quarrying before the 16th century is thin or non-existent. If either location can be proved then this reinforces the status of the York alabasterers but at this time it is mere speculation. The assumptions made by some academics as to sources of raw material often devalue the research made in that the transport and closeness of materials often dictates the location in which work is carried out. The case for the Peaseholme alabasters being York carved can be challenged.

B110 A memorial in St Nicholas Church Gloucester states that Francis Reeve died on the 7th Feb 1715 aged 76 which dates his birth to 1639. However, the apprentice register of Gloucester lists an apprentice whose indentures were taken out on the 14th Dec 1664. Francis Reeve, son of Joseph Reeve, joiner of Tewkesbury was indentured for eight years to Stephen and Mary Baldwin, stone carvers, with an end payment of 2s 6d. This calls into doubt the accepted date for the death of Stephen Baldwin as 1662.

In view of the note under B113 the assumption is that this Francis Reeve and founder of the Reeve workshop in Gloucester is the same. However, under the strict guild rules of Gloucester an apprenticeship at the age of 25 would not be possible so doubt remains. It may well be the birth date of Francis based solely on the memorial data is incorrect.

Later a second apprentice was indentured although neither his first name nor the day was recorded. This apprentice was surnamed Fox the son of William Fox, mason, of Twigworth (a village to the north of Gloucester with 13 houses assessed for Hearth

Tax in 1672). He too was indentured for eight years with an end payment of 2s 6d. It may well be that William Fox worked for the Baldwin workshop. *See also* B113.

B111 The *Biographical Dictionary of Sculptors* has an entry for the Reeves family of Gloucester. It lists seven Reeves from 1639 to 1768 but only Francis, Stephen and Joseph are of importance to this book. In addition to the Francis Reeve memorial in St Nicholas Church, Gloucester there is one to Joseph Reeve in which he is referred to as 'carver'. The date of this is 1716. Llewellyn lists Joseph Reeve as being monument carver of Gloucester from 1640 and gives date of death as 1690. This may be error as he appears to be referring to Francis and may well relate to his retirement as carver.

B112 On the 2nd April 1670 Thomas Saunders the son of Thomas Saunders farmer (deceased) of Gloucester was apprenticed to Francis and Hannah Reeve for seven years from the 28th Sept with an end payment of 10s. B113 sets out details of a transfer of apprenticeship in October 1670. The records continue with James Withenbury the son of James of Gloucester, carpenter, apprenticed to Francis and Hannah 3rd June 1672 and son Francis Reeve (II) likewise on the 2nd February 1675. In 1684 Francis Reeve apprenticed his second son Joseph to his profession. The indentures are dated 2nd February and were to last seven years. It is almost certain that the 1716 memorial is to this Joseph and his wife Sarah.

It is possible Francis Reeve may well have assumed the goodwill of the Baldwin workshop in 1670. Francis Reeve's will proved 16th Nov 1715 lists his workshop goods including an architectural book, models, his Westminster epitaphs and his stocks of stone including alabaster and marble. His son Stephen and his grandson Francis were to receive the goodwill of the Reeve workshop.

B113 The entry in the register of apprentices for 1667 lists Thomas Blackwell son of Thomas Blackwell of Rendcomb, yeoman, as being apprenticed to Stephen and Mary Baldwin for seven years on the 23rd March. This entry is annotated 19th October 1670 whereby Mary Baldwin releases Thomas Blackwell to Francis Reeve for the residue of his term. Reeve is to find him food, drink and clothing and give him at the end of the term 10s and two suits. Thomas's father is to give Francis 10s for clothing during and at the end of the term. In inference is that Stephen had died *circa* 1670 and that Mary had sold the business.

B114 William Clarke, sculptor of Llandaff, South Wales is credited with almost all the carving done in Penarth alabaster. The son of Edward Clarke a wood carver and sculptor, his older brother Robert was a sculptor of Hereford. His son Wyndham was apprenticed to him *circa* 1901.

B115 The Wallace firm of Edinburgh. Formed in Shrub Place, Leith in 1828 and trading under Wallace and White and Andrew Wallace and Co.

B116 Robert Rowand Anderson trained under Gilbert Scott before setting up his own business in Scotland. He is credited with a number of altars with canopies which contain alabaster as well a small number of monuments. What is significant is that much of the alabaster does not appear to be from the accepted sources. The memorial in St Giles (M195) and the altar in St Mary's (A94) may well be Barrowmouth whilst the altar at St John the Divine, Oban is stated to be 'pink' and the reredos and pulpit of 1872 at St Michael and All Angels, Helensburgh is also of unusual colour.

B117 John Rhind and his son William Birnie Rhind.

B118 A York workshop of the early 15th century is credited with the tombs at Methley, Sheriff Hutton and one at Harewood. Both Saul and Dr Jane Crease agree that this workshop has certain characteristics including the carving of miniature vaulting within the canopies finishing with a small boss and a slight convexity of the shields. The workshop appears to have ceased production *circa* 1430. It is significant that no alabasterers were admitted to the freedom of the city from 1272 to 1400 and only one between 1400 and 1449 with no less than six in the next 50 years.

B119 Peter Ford and Sons had a sculpting business in Uttoxeter, Staffordshire and leased land at Fauld in 1870 for extraction minerals including alabaster. It was an abandoned adit in Ford's mine that was used by the War Department for stock piling munitions. A 1904 a letter was addressed to an Earley and Co, a customer in Dublin, quoted a price of 18s 9d for 5cwt of alabaster (£3 16s a ton) with extra sawing 15ft at 7s 6d. Earley and Co were ecclesiastical decorators and one of their contracts was for the Church of Holy Name in Beechwood, Dublin which has a number of alabaster features including the coping of the pulpit.

B120 Harry Hems of Exeter had an extensive workshop and is noted for many Devon sculptures. He is credited with the alabaster font in St Peter Port church, Guernsey in 1886 and exhibited at the Paris Exposition of 1878 when he showed a statue entitled *Safe in the Arms of Jesus*.

B121 Fred Kormis was born (Fritz) in Germany in 1887. A Jew he fled Germany in 1933 and came to England via Holland. Pictures of his fine memorial are on the internet.

B122 Agnes Ramsey was the daughter of William Ramsey a mason who died during the Black Death plague of 1349. Although married to Robert Hubard (another mason) she continued to trade under her father's name and it is her who, in some quarters, is credited with the carving of the tomb of Queen Isabella the widow of Edward II for a cost of £100. A curious late 15th century painting (below) shows a female sculptor carving an effigy which may well be meant to represent Agnes. However, the painter clearly is unversed in the art of sculpting. The use of a large chisel on an obviously finished freestone effigy and the dress and attitude of the lady depicted on the tomb is out of keeping with the styles of the period. Nevertheless, the depiction of a female artisan in the brief period when women had some freedom to trade is interesting. Isabella died on the 22nd August 1358, but her tomb in the Franciscan church at Newgate, London did not survive the dissolution. *See also* B123.

Figure 68. Female carver. A 16th century print.

B123 John Harvey's book on Henry Yeaveley lists three William Ramseys (all masons) in the early 14th century one of which is associated with Gloucester Cathedral and one based in Norwich. It is not yet possible to refine this further. The association with Gloucester is interesting as it may give a lead to Edward II's tomb.

B124 Willem Boy was a Flemish carver recording as sourcing alabaster from England. He is recorded as making the tomb for King Gustavus Vasa in Uppsala Cathedral (R187) which was carved in Flanders despite Boy being located in Sweden. Few of the monuments have survived but another is that to Princess Isabella in Strangnas Cathedral, Sweden reputedly in alabaster.

B125 Joseph Pickford. Uncle and nephew. London based Joseph I is credited with work on the marble hall and chapel in Holkham Hall, Norfolk *circa* 1748 to 1756. Joseph I's brother is believed to have owned a quarry in 'Derbyshire' from which his son Joseph II selected and shipped alabaster. It is unclear where this quarry was and it may well be Redhill or Chellaston. Joseph II set up his workshop in Derby. It is clear that Joseph Pickford II sourced alabaster for his uncle as there are records of him 'going to Fauld for alabaster' which may well have been Castle Hay. In another reference we are told he went to another quarry which could be Chellaston or Redhill. Appendix M discusses the alabaster for the big houses and it may well be that Pickford used all three Midlands quarries. *See:* Derbycivicsociety.co.uk/doc/pickford_lecture_4_2014.pdf.

B126 Thomas Carter was a carver of elaborate chimney pieces and was London based. Of Thomas it is said he provided a design for a chimney piece at Welbeck Abbey which was a copy of one in Bolsover Castle '… composed of a great variety of English, Scottish and Irish marbles and alabaster and not one bit of foreign in it'. According to the Henry Moore sculptors dictionary the Welbeck design never proceeded beyond a drawing. He followed the practices of Inigo Jones. His brother Benjamin Carter had the premises next door in Portugal Row and it is to him that Thomas left his workshop and tools in his will. Both Carters are referred to in relation with Holkham and Uppark. Thomas Carter died before Holkham was completed.

B127 Joseph Edgar Boehm. A Viennese who came to England in 1862. Is credited with the Earl of Cardigan's tomb in Deene which may be in alabaster. Certainly the association with Cardigan is strong the V&A having a plaster cast of Lady Cardigan's hand and forearm made sometime after 1862. In the Recollections of Lady Cardigan she confirms Boehm's involvement but states clearly her effigy is in marble and placed beside that of her husband but without confirming the stone from which his is carved.

B128 Richard and Henry Lakenham. They are believed to be father and son and had a workshop in St Paul's churchyard until Henry died in1 1387. They are credited with the 1376 freestone tomb with a Purbeck marble tomb chest but who it was for is not known.

B129 Jean de Liege. Dutch sculptor working 1360 to 1381. Reported in Paris and then in London 1366 to 1367. Historians credit the tomb of Philippa of Hainault in Westminster to this man and claim the style was copied for his later works in France namely Charles V and Joanna of Bourbon in 1376 in St Denis Abbey and possibly Philip the Bold. In 1367 Liege carved an alabaster and marble tomb for Charles V in Rouen but this was destroyed in 1736. Another work is an alabaster statue to Philippe de l'Aulnoy in the church at Moussy le Vieux showing him dressed as burgess. It may be that many more works in alabaster may be uncovered in time. St John Hope claims that Liege was paid 200 marks (£133 6s 8d) for the tomb to Philippa which was not completed until 1376 when John Orchard added 'diverse figures of angels for it' at a cost of £5 – *see also* B29. St John Hope refers to Liege's Christian name as Hawkin (Norse hawk) from a Latin inscription and gives his origins as French.

B130 William Byrd. Apprenticed to mason William Nicholls of Gloucester and moved to Oxford in 1647. Experimented with staining and pigmentation (*see* Appendix S). Cole (Oxoniensia 1949) made an intriguing statement which has yet to be explored. It states 'He (Byrd) works whenever possible in alabaster, and, unlike his local contemporaries shuns the use of stone for monumental carving'. The Fettiplace effigies at Swinbrook of 1686 are in alabaster and the repairs to William of Wykeham's tomb in Winchester and Lord Williams of Thame are also of this material.

B131 The Royley workshop was in being from 1540 to 1614 and it is not always possible to determine which Royley worked when. Greenhill claims that one Richard died 1587 and one Gabriel died 1597.

B132 The Master of Rimini is an enigmatic alabaster carver of the 15th century which has been investigated a number of times. The name here is one of several and the best authority is Dr Kim Wood of the Open University.

B133 John Mapilton, London marbler. J Blair in 1980 named Mapilton as being associated with Henry Lakenham and contracts for tombs at the end of the 15th century.

B134 J Blair also names William West, marbler as assuming responsibility for the Lakenham workshop with another man called John Essex. It is possible that Essex was a Latoner but the covenant between the workers and the Earl of Warwick's executors *circa* 1439 mentions Essex as a marbler in respect of the Earl's tomb.

B135 Thomas Wrek or Wrewk is a shadowy kerver mentioned in relation to John of Gaunt and St Paul's Cathedral. He is reported to have charged £14 6s 8d for work in 1379 and £20 in 1381 the invoice being countersigned by Henry Yeaveley. Cheetham credits a monument in St Paul's to this carver but the details are unclear.

B136 Richard Beke. This mason designed and built the Warrior Chapel in Canterbury who was the appointed architect from 1432 to 1458 but it is uncertain if he had any hand in the alabaster tombs (G98) although this is suggested in some quarters.

B137 Bartholomew Lambspring and William Austen are both associated with the Beauchamp tomb in Warwick in respect of the gilding and casting of the bronze (latten) effigy of 1439 (although not completed until 1453–1457). John Massingham is also mentioned as a 'kerver' but the extent to which work was carried out in alabaster is uncertain. John Bourde of the Isle of Purbeck or Corfe provided the marble which he was bid to '… bring to Warwick and set it up there'. *See also* B134.

B138 Bristol seems to feature large in the export of alabaster with both Elizabeth Jakes (*circa* 1478) and Margery Walker (*Circa* 1535) managing trade to both Europe and Ireland. *Studies in English Trade in the 15th Century* by Eileen Power indicates the importance of Bristol as a trade centre singling out alabaster from as far afield as Nottingham as being important. Some merchants especially those in Coventry were free of tolls. It may also be significant that Elizabeth's husband Robert was mayor of Bristol and owned lands in Leicestershire. There are rumours that the richness of Bristol was exemplified in the 1490s when Henry VII paid a visit to find the wives of merchants so well dressed that he fined them for extravagance.

B139 On the 5th February 1482–1483 Walter Hylton sued Emma Sherwood widow of the late Robert Sherwood for an unpaid debt of 8s 8d. The debt was in respect of the gilding and painting of a tabernacle of St Philip for St Peter's Church, clearly of alabaster. Emma denied the suit. Robert Sherwood was also thought to be a kerver who had carved the tabernacle contracting with Hylton for the gilding but evidence is lacking. Hylton claimed that the gilding cost 6s and a 'mantletree' 2s with residual damages of 1s 2d with no claim for carving. A mantletree is a medieval term for the timber over a fireplace which is odd for a church.

B140 Thomas Drawswerd was the head of a family of image makers of York. The book *York Mercers and Merchant Adventurers 1356 to 1917* claims that the Drawswerd family had been carving alabaster for three generations. He may well have also carved wood as his most famous work is the rood screen in Newark completed in 1508. He provided a 'Doomsday' wagon for the York Mystery Plays and was rewarded by being admitted to the fraternity of the Holy Trinity. Drawswerd became a freeman *circa* 1495–1496, member of the Corpus Christi guild in 1500 (suppressed by Henry VIII), sheriff 1505 and mayor in 1514–1515 and 1522–1523. He was MP for York 1512. He worked on images for Henry VII's chapel in Westminster, but Crossley says that his designs were rejected in favour of those by Torrigiano. Although little is known of him after 1509, he justifies inclusion due to him being mentioned in a dispute over an alabaster item in 1528. The only recorded son is George but there is certainty that the other two, Nicholas and William are related. Endowed the last chantry in the diocese of York in 1529 having made his will on the 28th January of that year.

B141 The accounts for Leverton in Lincolnshire include the agreement with Robert Brook, believed to be of Nottingham, for the supply of alabaster items dated 1523 and 1526. In 1523 he was paid £8 for an alabaster 'table' plus 6d for expenses. In 1526 they called him to supply images for the rood-loft. *See* St John Hope's 1901 paper for full details.

B142 John Chapman was a Wiltshire stonemason working for the Thynne family at Longleat, at Lacock and at Dudley Castle. He carved chimney pieces and furniture and is believed to have used alabaster, but no extant items in this material have so far been traced. M Girouard made a suggestion that Chapman was working at Westminster in 1541 and Dartford in 1543 but this cannot be confirmed.

B143 Nothing is known about Tallentire apart from the signature on the Dakyn tomb.

B144 Alan Maynard is associated with Robert Smythson on a number of stately homes. He was a major carver of chimney pieces and is likely to have worked in alabaster, but no extant pieces of work can be identified.

B145 John Tarbotons signed the oak Nevill tomb in Staindrop and although work in alabaster is fugitive justifies inclusion as his carving represents a retrograde step back into Gothic form in the middle of the Renaissance period.

B146 Gilles de Witte came to England in 1585. Working in Blackfriars, a liberty within the city he appears to have provided alabaster memorial tablets with and without brass inserts. The alabaster and slate memorial in St Bartholomew the Great, London is also attributed to this carver.

B147 Vanessa Harding states that William Kirwin '… may well have made his own comely alabaster tomb' in St Helen's, Bishopsgate. The extent of any other monuments is uncertain.

B148 The church at Pitchford in Shropshire contains a number of alabaster slabs one of which is signed John Tarbook, carver of Bewdley and dated 1587. The inscription reads 'Draun and graven by Iohn Tarbook of Beudly carver anno 1587'. The style of carving is unlike any other in the same church. There is a second slab labelled 'I.T 1587' which is likely to be from the same workshop.

B149 Little is known of Thomas Browne except for the signature on the 1603 Coxwold tomb of Sir William Belayse which reads 'Thomas Browne did carve this tomb himself alone of Hesselwood stone'. Hesselwood stone is a magnesium limestone.

B150 Walter Hancock is well known for church and other building work in the Marches and Shropshire. He is credited with the tomb to Richard Herbert in Montgomery, Powis *circa* 1600, but no other work has come to light and it may be questioned if the carving was contracted out.

B151 Simon Basil or Basill was a Flanders architect and came to England *circa* 1600 under the patronage of Robert Cecil. His work in alabaster is currently unknown.

B152 John Deymond, a Devon carver with custom in Dorset and Devon churches including Bickleigh and Colyton St Andrew. *See*: 'Church Monuments of Devon and Cornwall 1660 to 1750' – A thesis by Clive James July 2006.

B153 The records of Bath show that a Thomas Greenway, carver, resided in Claverton St, Bath although the dates are uncertain.

B154 A sculptor in bronze but Christies claim to have sold reliefs in alabaster by Fanelli. The monument in Chipping Campden to Penelope Noel 1633 may well have an alabaster frame with the rest is in marble. The Ludlow monument to Sir John Bridgeman *circa* 1637 has also been credited to Fanelli, but may well be the work of Samuel Baldwin.

B155 Alexander Hills is credited with the mausoleum at St Mary's Collegiate Church, Yougal, County Cork to Richard Boyle *circa* 1620.

B156 Thomas Ashby is associated with John Smythson and Inigo Jones. He appears to have been the contract carver for these two architects and produced tombs and fireplaces one of which was in Arundel House, Strand *circa* 1618. The tomb of Fulke Grenville is by this carver, but this is not in alabaster.

B157 Epiphamus Evesham had commenced a work for the Earl of Cork but being in financial straits had ceased work. It is reported that James White of Long Acre completed the work which was erected in St Nicholas, Deptford.

B158 Thomas Stanton was apprenticed to Christopher Kingsfield described as a mason *circa* 1620 and so was Thomas Cartwright in 1637, but little else is known.

B159 Edward Woodrofe is credited with the tomb to Thomas Seckford in Trinity College Chapel dated 1624 which bears his signature. A full length effigy in academic robes. Not in good condition. An Edward Woodroffe (born 1622, died 1675) was an assistant to Sir Christopher Wren.

B160 Francis Griggs appears to have signed his monuments. At Biddenden, Kent a monument to Herbert Randolph is signed *Francis Grigs fecit anno 1645*, but both the Framlingham and St Osyth monuments are similarly signed.

B161 William Sweet may have lived in Rochester as he was charged for three 'chimneys' there under the hearth tax of 1664. He is associated with M(ichael) Miles. The Hales monument in Tunstall, Kent is considered to be crude according to Gunnis in 1968 which has led to the assumption they were local jobbing carvers.

B162 There are few monuments by this sculptor in England. One extant is the effigy to Lady Jane Cheyne in Chelsea old church which is not alabaster.

B163 Anthony Ellis was apprenticed to Nicholas Stone *circa* 1634 and is mentioned in his will of 1641 being described as his servant. John Stone commissioned him to carved heads for the Paston monument at Oxnead. Later emerged as a builder at Althorpe House.

B164 Martin Morley became a freeman of Norwich in 1653. He has only one known monument although several others have been attributed on the basis of style. The identified monument is to Thomas Windham (died 1654) *circa* 1669 in Felbrigg, Norfolk.

B165 A modeller for china workshops but set up in Derby where he modelled in all materials including alabaster. Emigrated in 1816 and became well known in the USA. None of the alabaster works have been traced but a 25 inches bust of Erasmus Darwin was sold at Christies in 1993.

B166 Cookson appears to have supervised a number of restorations to buildings but the Brereton tomb appears to be the only monument.

B167 The Bishop Ellicot tomb by William Silver Frith shows a clear reversal to Gothic styles with crocketted arcades and bedesmen. The chest table is chamfered but the effigy is Renaissance.

B168 Colton was born in Paris and came to England in 1870. He studied under William Silver Frith (B167) at Lambeth. The Cranbrook memorial may be the only one in alabaster.

B169 The Company seems to have moved a number of times. In 1870 they are listed as marble cutters but sculptors by 1880.

B170 Established his workshop in Lichfield in 1879. Son Joseph joined in 1910. Later Charles William Bridgeman, grandson, joined before selling out in 1968. The firm is recorded as carving in alabaster and a few works can be found. The font and reredos in Lichfield

Cathedral are two. The carving of the last supper at St Cuthbert in Edinburgh is another. Two interesting items are a 57 inches statue of Christ and a 59 inches statue of St Michael in what looks like Watchet alabaster offered for sale in 2014 and which was reported to have been 'standing in the Linford yard since 1964'. The backs of the statues is flat indicating that they formerly stood against a wall but the style is Gothic Revival and may well have been carved by Robert Bridgeman or by his son. *See also The Annals of a Century: Bridgemans of Lichfield 1878–1978* by Owen Keyte 1993.

B171 James Forsyth was born in Kelso with his brother William but moved to Wells in 1851. Worked with Theodore Phyffers until 1855. The reredos in Frome and pulpits in Worcester and Witney are attributed to him. He is also accredited with the 1860 alabaster relief of *Christ Appearing to his Disciples* in St Dionysius Church, Market Harborough latterly moved the Harborough museum.

B172 James Redfern was born in Hartington, Derbyshire in 1838 where he was commissioned by the local vicar to carve a warrior and horse in alabaster. As a result he was sent to Paris to study. He later carved the images for the reredos in the Oxford Street Church of St Andrew (*see* A119).

B173 William Forsyth was the brother of B171 and worked in Worcester.

B174 Arthur George Walker was born in Hackney, London. His only known works in alabaster are M155 and M156.

B175 Thomas Brock was born in Worcester. The only known works in alabaster is the Wells tomb chest.

B176 George Eley Halliday (often known only as G E) was the diocesan surveyor of Llandaff. The church at Ilston, near Swansea was rebuilt by Halliday in 1892 and in which we find a pulpit with carved alabaster figures and an alabaster reredos. Although not directly attributable these may be by this carver.

B177 Richard Brown was a Derby mason who worked with Derbyshire minerals. His apprentice was John Mawe (1764–1829) who became Brown's partner forming Brown and Mawe of Covent Garden and which sold objects made from 'Derbyshire marble'. Some objects reside in Derby museum. Mawe collected minerals for the King of Spain, most of the working English mines being represented. In 1800 the company owned the spa shop on Matlock Bath. They worked in Blue John making ornamental objects.

B178 Mainly an architect but oversaw some alabaster work.

B179 Epstein carved *Adam* in 1938 and *Jacob and the Angel* in 1940. There is no documented evidence as to the source of these large blocks of alabaster but from the colour and veining the source is the same for both statues. At this time Fauld was still in production and is the favourite and it was not until the explosion of 1944 that production was disrupted. According to Epstein's conceptual notes from 1940, the Jacob and the Angel sculpture began as a 6 ton block of alabaster and it is difficult to imagine such a block coming from anywhere but the Fauld Mine. Two earlier pieces in alabaster are *Elemental* carved in 1932 and *Consummat est* carved in 1936.

B180 Robert Waterton is mentioned in respect of York tombs but the work in alabaster is unknown. In 1512 he is mentioned in a covenant (Rolls of Henry VIII – York 1495) as Robert Waterton carver of York possibly in respect of an apprenticeship for Robert Norton son of Thomas Norton.

B181 The records of Henry Hill show an interesting list supplied to Earley in Dublin. They include 14th April 1860 three blocks totalling 52ft for £9 15s, 16th Nov 1861 four blocks totalling 40ft for £9, 11 Jan 1862 two blocks totalling 12ft for £2 14s 9d and 22nd Jul

1862 102ft for £26 5s.

B182 The son of a Cornish stonemason he became a sculptor in his own right making busts for the nobility. He became an itinerant *circa* 1870 but was commissioned to assist in the carving of the alabaster effigy of Francis Blunt (A121) between 1872 and 1875. No other work in alabaster is attributed to him.

B183 The brother of the person depicted. Wilfred Scawen Blunt was also a horse breeder famous for the Crabbet Stable, Sussex where he also carved the Blunt monument. He is not renowned for his sculpting activities but studied under George Frederick Watts (B184) alongside Reginald Cholmondeley (B185) for a time. Following the erection of the tomb to his brother he appears not to have done any more. Although many biographies state Blunt as being a sculptor the identification of other works has proved difficult. *See* 'CMS Journal' Vol XXVIII 2013 page 89.

B184 George Frederick Watts was famous for his painting but his sculpture works date from 1867 to his death in 1904 mostly in the last 13 years of his life. His sculpting in alabaster is hard to identify but the effigy of the 8th Marquess of Lothian in Blickling church, Norfolk (A122) and the kneeling figure of Sir Francis Cholmondeley in Condover (A123), Shropshire are certainly two. The Watts Museum also has a small alabaster model of larger work called Medusa.

B185 Reginald Cholmondeley onetime assistant to George Frederick Watts was a talented amateur sculptor.

B186 John Pollen was an assistant keeper at the South Kensington appointed in 1863. He was involved in the monuments at Blickling, Norfolk but in what capacity is uncertain. He is more known for carving in wood and it may be he prepared wooden patterns for George F Watts. He was active from 1844 but 1868 is his first known work involving alabaster.

B187 William Farmer and William Brindley founded the firm of Farmer and Brindley. In 1904 the firm carved the alabaster effigies of the Meynell-Ingrams in Hoar Cross, Staffordshire (A126). The firm merged with another in 1929 and their records were lost. Information supplied by the church wardens of Hoar Cross. The Westminster Cathedral website has a full history of the company. Brindley was an associate of Gilbert Scott and being born in Derbyshire would be fully aware of Derbyshire alabaster. *See also* Putley Hereford (A127). C J Allen (died 1956) was associated with the workshop.

B188 Leon-Joseph Chavalliaud was French but came to London between 1890 and 1905. He worked for Farmer and Brindley but was not renowned for his work in alabaster. Hoever his heads on the Hoar Cross effigies are considered superb. Also worked on the monument to Dean Butler in Lincoln.

B189 John Weston, carver of Exeter. Twelve monuments are credited in Devon and Cornwall, but only that at Ashprington has so far been identified as having alabaster components but others are believed to have some alabaster in their construction (*see* D5). The uncertain ones are Morebath, Devon to Nicholas Sayer 1712, Tiverton, Devon to John Newte 1715 and St Blazey, Cornwall to Henry Scobell 1729.

B190 Christopher Horsnaile. A sculptor working in the workshop of Thomas Stanton. The Langford memorial is particularly fine. Richard Hayward was apprentice to Horsnaile.

B191 York Minster records that the tablet to the canons (M270) was made by Skidmore more famous for his metalwork screens. It may well be that the alabaster figures were contracted out but independent confirmation of this is not currently forthcoming.

B192 York Minster also records that the tablet to Cradock (M265) was made by Pomeroy in 1916. Pomeroy made the fine effigy in Newcastle (A135) but is more famous for his statue of *Justice* on the top of the Central Criminal Court in London.

B193 Glasgow born John Tweed was a pupil of Auguste Rodin. It is not known as what other alabaster memorials were made by this sculptor.

B194 In 2001 Dennis Cox of Taylor Pearce Restoration Services stated that no alabaster was being mined in Britain but that Nigel Owen had a reserve of British alabaster. They now mined soapstone but 'found itself the owner of a spectacular *bin-end* of what is probably the last of Britain's stock above ground'. In 2001 this stock was expected to last until 2003 but from the website it is clear that alabaster items are still being made in 2014. The blocks are stated as being about a foot square. From the items seen the colour and translucence would seem to indicate Watchet and Kingston on Soar as the source.

Below is a pair of alabaster candlesticks signed 'Nigel Owen, Yelvertoft, Northampton' given as prizes *circa* 1983 by British Plasterboards to the church at Gotham, Nottinghamshire now in the possession of Chris and Jill Hind. The colour and translucence is very similar to objects in Kingston on Soar church which were stated as being mined in the Kingston by Harry Woodfield the last mine manager interviewed in the mid-1990s. It is noted that the Owen workshop advertises alabaster door stops with pink alabaster which may well be Watchet and red-brown veined alabaster which may well be Fauld.

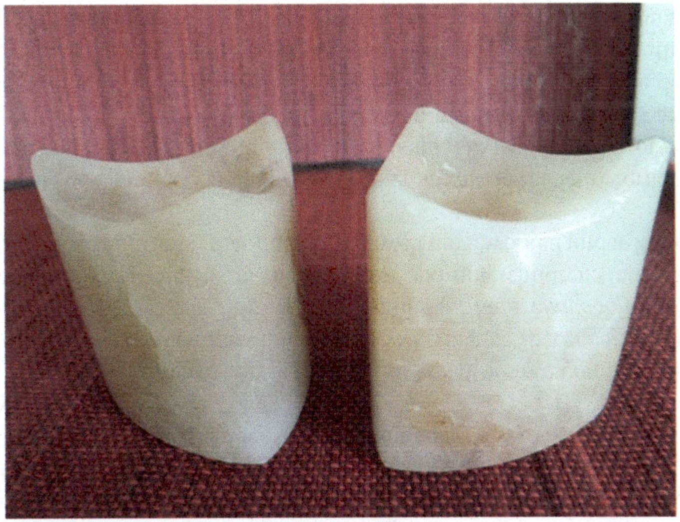

Figure 69. A Pair of alabaster candlesticks. Photo: the author.

B195 James Elliott's workshop is in Market Overton, Rutland and in conversation he confirms that the alabaster for the Leicester altar was obtained from the Fauld Mine in 2014. He states that the piece extracted was the largest block obtained for many years and he had to cut the block from the face himself (over mile underground).

B196 Temple Moore was born in Ireland and studied under Gilbert Scott being an advocate of the Gothic Revival.

B197 James Currie was born in Ayr, Scotland.

B198 Claus Sluter was a sculptor of Dutch origin probably working in Brussels before coming to Dijon in the employ of Philip the Bold, Duke of Burgundy. He was assistant to the court sculptor until 1389 when he succeeded the incumbent, until his death in 1406.

B199 Little is known about William Porter however *The List of Families In the Archdeaconry of Stafford 1532* lists him in Bond End, Burton on Trent where he resided with wife (uxor eius) Eleanor and nine children. Interestingly also 'residing' was one Richard Parker (sp-us) given credence to the suggestion that Parker may well have worked under Porter for a time. However please read note B200.

B200 The apparent census carried out by Lichfield Cathedral in 1532 is unique in that it recorded 51,000 family names in Staffordshire in what was one of the first master lists of county families in England. Divided by town or village and then by street, it provides an indication of the families living there. However, care must be taken in that many entities are annotated but without any indication as to why. It is believed by the author Ann Kettle in 1976 that some names were of people deceased and some of people who had at some time lived with the family such as apprentices, servants and in-laws. This is because the list appears to have been drawn up to record those families who contributed to some improvements in the archdeaconry in exchange for prayers both for the living and the dead. The annotation 'sp-us' attached to some males where the surname is not the same as the family name is obscure but the few that Kettle investigated showed that the sp-us indicated a former husband of a woman remarried into the new family. About 5% of the names have this attachment. In the case of the Porter family (B199) the name of Richard Parker is followed by nine children believed to indicate the offspring of the former marriage. This is compounded by the last entry which is 'parentes Ellen Herden' which has been identified as William Porter's mother-in-law. Unfortunately, no trade or occupation is listed. One final point is that the clerics who recorded the information placed the names in hierarchical order within a location. It is noted that within Horninglow St, Burton on Trent the Walker family (B25 and B26) head the list whilst Richard Parker (B23) comes 6th. There is, of course, no sign of the Royleys.

B201 Dr Antonio Salviati was a lawyer but was interested in glasswork. He opened his first workshop in 1859. Although not working in alabaster he installed a number of reredoses in alabaster frames and in some cases modified existing alabaster reredos with new mosaics.

B202 George E Street was an advocate of the Gothic Revival.

B203 John Francis Moore. Born in Germany to English parents he came to England in 1760 and had a prolific career with about 124 monuments and carvings to his credit but only two of which have been identified as alabaster (X203 and M538). He worked in polychrome at a time when unpainted monuments were the norm.

B204 R L Boulton and Sons worked much with Pugin where he was known as the architect's 'favourite sculptor'. Their work was widespread. The firm continued to trade ceasing sometime around 1977.

B205 John Prichard, architect for Llandaff Cathedral but influential over many churches throughout Wales. He was the supporter of the Gothic style and exploited local stones including Penarth alabaster and the Quarella and Radyr sandstones. He was in partnership with John Pollard Seddon between 1852 and 1863.

B206 Thomas Kirby, an obscure sculptor active between 1562 and 1576. Three monuments attributed to him display a sarcophagus but only two are alabaster. That of Lord Maudaunt at Turvey, Beds is the most competent. The others are to Anthony Cave at Chicheley, Bucks (not alabaster) and Alexander Denton at Hillesden, Bucks. These display French features. Nothing more is known about this carver.

B207 Jasper Latham appeared in the mason's lists about 1663. Mason-contractor for a number of churches but was carving a monument in Croydon to Archbishop Sheldon *circa* 1667–1669 with someone called 'Boune' possibly Jason Burne who was bound to Latham in 1668. Mentioned by Wren in 1689 as being a little deranged. He may well then have been over 80.

B208 William de Keyser. A person of this name was entered on the role of the Mason's Company on the 23rd Sept 1678. The list describes him as a foreigner who has paid his dues and is therefore elected.

B209 William Hargrave of Bilborough, Notts is mentioned by Jon Bayliss in regard to the tomb of John Farnham at Quorn, Leics (R85). Jon has done much work in identifying the works of this obscure carver which can be identified by the frieze. Hargrave appears to have worked at Wollaton Hall, Notts. Jon also identifies the tombs at Old Dalby (M324), Newstead Abbey (M391), Saundby (R284), Brooke, Rutland (R282), Bakewell (M594) and Langar (R283) as well as a lost tomb at Breadsall (D9/94A) and a tablet at Bunny (M410).

B210 Claus Sluter, a Dutchman who later moved from Brussels to Dijon where he worked for Jean de Marville and later court sculptor for Philip the Bold. Worked in limestone and may well have carved alabaster.

B211 Margaret Lovell is a carver in a variety of materials but some recent small works appear to use Fauld alabaster and some Watchet.

B212 In 1933 *The Tablet* reported that John Hugh Gough, the son of William had assisted in the restoration of an alabaster statue of a Madonna and Child found buried in the garden of a house in Exeter. The statue was given to St George, Sudbury, but the current whereabouts is now unknown – *see* D9/118.

B213 Named in the records of Earley and Son as a supplier of alabaster. Nothing more is known.

B214 Joseph Gott was born in Leeds but apprenticed to Flaxman in 1798. He later became an assistant to Canover in Rome arriving in 1822.

B215 Joseph Else made a frieze which depicted the alabaster industry in 1927 for the Nottingham Council House ballroom.

B216 Melchior Salaboss painted the Burford triptych which is in wood but there is a suggestion that alabaster items were painted by this Milanese painter.

B217 John Bushnell an eccentric carver with some good works remaining. After his death his family largely destroyed the sculptures in their possession. Worked a variety of materials and may well include alabaster.

B218 *Mapping the Practice and Profession of Sculpture in Britain and Ireland 1851 to 1951* maintains that his trade card read 'Alabaster ornaments neatly repaired and cleaned'.

B219 In the 1871 census he described himself as an 'artist in ivory and alabaster'. Pictures of his machines can be found on the internet.

B220 Joseph Gott born in Leeds went to Rome in 1822 and remained there until death in 1860 although he frequently visited England and received many commissions from clients in Yorkshire and the adjacent counties. The alabaster is probably Italian.

B221 The *Hampshire Telegraph* of the 20th Feb 1869 reported on an exhibition of alabaster in Portsea, Hants which it claims are Italian. Sani was in the habit of setting up in other towns. The details of the Portsea exhibition are not currently known.

B222 The Jewell family of Barnstaple, Devon appears to have been active from about 1690 to 1758 making tablets for the surrounding churches. There are no less than five attributions in Tawstock church which is one of the best West Country churches for monuments. The material used is not certain but the tablet to Henry Northcote (M287) appears to be in Watchet alabaster. Both Jewell the Elder and possibly his son Jewell the Younger (or Junior) are mentioned, but little of nothing is known about them.

B223 Tobias and Isaac Tissenaken. Dutch carvers of altarpieces. These were two of many Flemish and Dutch carvers who produced small devotional pieces. These two are listed as there is an example of their work in the Bowes Museum, Barnard Castle, County Durham.

B224 Richard Claude Belt. A London sculptor associated with Charles Lawes with who he had a number of disputes over the origins of certain works. Associated with Thomas Brock who also claim responsibility for some carvings but not M466.

B225 Matthew Noble. A pupil of John Francis he had a workshop in Mayfair in 1855. His custom mainly came from Lancashire and it not possible to determine how many pieces were in alabaster. M468 may be the only one.

B226 Henry Moore. Small pieces in a range of alabasters including Cumberland called *Four Piece* and *Girl with Clasped Hands*. *See* the Henry Moore Foundation.

B227 Barbara Hepworth. Small pieces in a range of alabasters including Cumberland which are *Mother and Child* (1934), *Two Heads* (1932) and *Three Forms* (1935) and *Head* (1931). Other objects are in Fauld and one in a pink alabaster which may be Watchet called *Pierced*. The latter is reported 'lost in the war'. *See* Tate Museum. Amongst the others, one called *Two Forms* (1933) is in a Redhill-like alabaster and *Two Forms* is in a white alabaster which may be Chellaston.

Photo: The author with permission of the New Walk Museum, Leicester.

Barbara Hepworth's sculpture *Head* which in all publications is stated as *Cumberland* alabaster, in the basement of the New Walk Museum in Leicester. The alabaster is a grey-brown colour and very hard which may indicate calcite. The colour is consistent with the sculptures made by Henry Moore (*see* B226) claimed to be in the same material. The mine from which this alabaster was obtained is fugitive as no publication states from where the alabaster was obtained. Appendix M Section 9 shows that alabaster was only mined for carving from Barrowmouth, Cocklakes (Wragmire Bank) and Stamphill and as Barrowmouth closed in 1908 the latter two are favoured as the source.

Appendix H
The Destruction of Images in the 16th Century and Beyond

In the second decade of the 16th century England's religion was firmly Catholic. Such was the standing of England that the pope had granted the title of Defender of the Faith on King Henry VIII for his attacks on the emerging Lutheran faith in Germany. Monasteries, priories and nunneries we all powerful and rich and held sway over many parish churches. Cathedrals were large and richly decorated.

These buildings together with many parish churches held symbols of the Catholic rites. The alter was often of stone, the windows glazed with stained glass, the walls painted depicting tracts from the Bible and images of the Virgin Mary, the crucifixion and the saints abounded. In some large monasteries and cathedrals monuments to saints existed which were subject to pilgrimage and in some cases they owned relics which had been purchased at some cost from the Holy Land. These relics were not always what they seemed and were used to absolve sinners and to cure illnesses often following a 'donation'. In one case a glass phial containing the blood of Christ which had a hidden valve which released the blood on demand but was really rabbit's blood which was topped up daily by the monks. Few relics had provenance but were useful in keeping the laity in thrall.

From the onset burials were allowed in monasteries. Llewellyn says that monasteries had a tumbarius whose job it was to be a keeper of the tombs. These were profitable and that the Worcester tomb keeper in 1532 earned £15 2s 3d. These men often gave guided tours. Ben Nilson in his book *Cathedral Shrines of Medieval England* observes that Worcester tumbarius records exist for the years 1375 to 1476 (Worcester Archive no's c453 to 472) when the role is stated as being the guardian of the tombs of Saint Oswald and Wulfstan. However, a tomb keeper is mentioned even earlier, in 1310, when he was allowed the use of a tenement.

The Catholic rite was in Latin and still conducted by the clergy in the sanctuary from which the laity were excluded. The sacrament was not distributed and the laity had little say or contribution to the church rites outside baptism, marriage and burial. In the Catholic rite the bread and the wine is taken as the body of Jesus. It was therefore important than no crumbs should remain from the distribution and no wine should be spilt. In fact to maintain this today the 'bread' is a wafer and the wine is not distributed to the laity. By the end of the 14th century an 'undercover' movement to publish the Bible in English was present. John Wycliffe's handwritten translation appeared in 1380 but which so infuriated the pope that 44 years after he died the pope had him dug up and the bones crushed. However, the first printed version was published by William Tyndale in 1525 most of which were burnt as soon as they were found. However, copies were squirreled away and one found its way to the library of Henry VIII. Tyndale was burnt at the stake in 1536.

The Reformation of the church which commenced about 1535 has been well documented and much blame has been placed on this event for the destruction of church property. This must be placed into its correct perspective. Whilst being adverse to the power of the monasteries and wishing to become the head of the English church Henry VIII was not anti-Catholic. Henry's will dated 30th December 1546 has two telling entries. It opens with the entreaty 'In the name of God and the glorious blessed Virgin Our lady Saint Mary' and later in the will he left £1266 to the dean and chapter of Windsor in exchange for daily Masses to be said for Henry's soul 'perpetually while the world shall endure'. This is hardly the words of a diehard reformer. His dispute with Thomas More was more about More's reluctance to recognise Henry as the head of the church than the emerging Reformation but with More's execution courtiers who were more extreme came to the fore. Amongst these were Thomas Cromwell and Thomas Cranmer, later Archbishop of Canterbury. They drove the fast pace of the Reformation often to the discomfort of Henry. In 1547 Cranmer introduced *The Book of Homilies* which was intended to be sermon material which was to be read at times of worship.

At this time there was no wholesale destruction of images and church decoration. Henry and Cromwell focused on the relics and other objects of pilgrimage. Relics were collected for ridicule or for destruction and some monuments destroyed. Amongst these were the tomb of St Thomas Becket at Canterbury and the stained-glass window to his memory in Grays Inn Chapel, London. Cromwell was the leader in opening the sacrament to the laity, publishing the Bible and prayer book in English and establishing church registers and some of these formed part of a Parliamentary Act passed on the 5th May, 1539. In the case of the sacrament the bread and the wine was distributed on the basis of remembrance of Jesus rather than the embodiment of his physical being. Despite Henry's support for the act he was still concerned over the pace of reform and when Cromwell mishandled the Ann of Cleves affair Henry let Cromwell's enemies have a free hand and in June, 1540 he was arrested and executed on the 28th July, 1540. Henry, forever fickle, was swayed by whatever party had his ear. This tended to be whichever family or retainers supported his current wife. Predominantly Catholic with Katherine of Aragon, Protestant with the Boleyns and Seymours and Ann of Cleves, he reverted to Catholic with the Howards and Protestant with Katherine Parr. Such was the faith of Katherine that both Gardiner and Bonner attempted to have her arrested and tried in 1546, but they were defeated by Henry VIII an event which subsequently earned Gardiner a spell in the tower although Gardiner had also earned

Henry's displeasure by refusing to 'donate' land to Henry's estate. He was removed from the Privy Council for this 'betrayal'. Neither Gardiner, Thomas Howard or the Earl of Surrey appears in Henry's will, all three having been set aside. Katherine Parr married Thomas Seymour after Henry VIII death and her cultivation of the Protestant rites is well documented.

In all this the progress of change had been uneven. In the southern counties change was largely unopposed but the largest opposition came from Lincolnshire, the North and from, surprisingly, the City of London where some images had to be removed in the dead of night.[5] In July 1541 Henry married Catherine Howard, but it was not to last, Catherine's infidelity leading to her imprisonment in November and subsequent execution. In 1544 Henry was absorbed by his spat with France over Boulogne which lasted until 1546 and the pace of reform slowed. The distraction of the French war allowed factions to emerge. Bishop Gardner and others attempted to persecute Protestants who openly criticised the function of the sacrament even to a spat of burnings and the banning of certain books. In this turmoil Anabaptists appeared. Hated by Protestants and Catholics alike they espoused the principal of adult baptism which meant that, unlike infant baptism, the person had a choice and in some cases a Christian path may not be followed. 1546 was a dangerous year. Henry was ailing and the factions used increasing desperate measures to gain ascendancy. In July 1546 Anne Askew and several others were burnt at the stake for their preaching of the gospel and questioning the sacrament. All this came to a temporary end early in 1547. The affect on tomb carving between 1530 and 1547 is hard to determine. In 1530 the presence of Catholic imagery on tombs was common but Renaissance elements were creeping in. By 1536 the Reformation was in full flow and between then and 1540 Catholic imagery was not only frowned on but that which already existed was occasionally removed. After the execution of Thomas Cromwell the traditionalist began to regain the ascendency and by 1546 some Catholic rites again began to emerge under the influence of Bishops Gardiner and Bonner and aristocracy such as Rich and Wriothesley. It is quite possible that style elements considered de rigour in 1540 were again acceptable in 1546. In that year William Lord Parr, an arch reformer, died and was buried in Hackleton and Horton church, Northamptonshire (T27) with a tomb chest containing distinct Gothic imagery leading one to conclude that not only was such features currently acceptable but that the tomb chest was probably second-hand recovered from some collegiate church or religious house. This period was one of confusion within the tomb-carving fraternity.[6]

King Henry VIII died on 28th January 1547. His will named his son Edward as successor followed by Mary and Elizabeth although true to fashion he hedged his bets by naming eight scenarios in which the succession would be managed – *See The King is Dead: The Last Will and Testament of Henry VIII* by Suzannah Lipscombe 2015. The new King Edward was then 10 when he succeeded to the throne. At Henry's deathbed

Edward's uncle, Edward Seymour, First Duke of Somerset, was named protector. He was an arch-reformist and drove the reform policy beyond anything which had gone before. However, Edward was himself full of reformist zeal. In 1549 at the age of 12, Edward wrote a treatise in which he criticised the papal supremacy although how much of this was influenced by Seymour is not disclosed. In 1547 about 20% of Londoners were Protestant but they were a vociferous minority and the stripping of images from City churches was complete long before such acts were proscribed by law. Elsewhere the extent of Protestants was patchy. In Kent, Sussex, Essex and Bristol the Protestant faith was well entrenched but elsewhere it had hardly progressed and apart from the pilgrimage shrines very little damage had been done.

The Duke of Somerset set about changing this. His first act was to reissue the details of Cromwell's 1539 Act. He went further banning the mass and closing chantries from side aisles in parish churches in 1547. Henry had paved the way for this in the Chantries Act of 1545, but he was more concerned at appropriating the chantry funds than the abolishment of the rites. Seymour's Act banned the rites themselves. More was to follow. In February 1549 an Act was passed[1&3] to remove all images from churches. This was to be enforced by commissioners called visitors and who were divided into six circuits. These visitors were to observe the destruction of images or in the case of reluctance, do the work themselves. The work was done quickly and all images were cleared by the end of 1549. In some case altars were jettisoned as well and records of the removal from 14 parish churches exists but a proviso in the Act was that destruction was not extend to '... such images that were in civil use or of a monumental kind' so that tombs were largely omitted from the vandalism. In December 1549 bishops who championed the old religion were stripped of their benefices and Gardiner and Bonner imprisoned the latter in the Marshalsea prison. Clergy were permitted to marry and in an Act of February 1549 all images in places of worship were banned.

That not all images were smashed is clear. At St Peter, Flawford in Nottinghamshire, the congregation and the priest on hearing about the approach of the visitors hid their images under the floor of the chancel to be forgotten about until the flagstones were lifted by Mr Cripwell in 1779. The church ceased to be used in 1718 and was approved for demolition in 1773. The images were donated in 1910 to Nottingham Castle by a Miss Percy of Beeston, Notts. St John Hope records that a similar image 'in the same hand' was found under the floor at Breadsall church, Derbyshire in 1877. This is illustrated in his 1901 paper but its current location is unknown. This was described latterly as a pieta or statue of the virgin cradling the body of Christ. St John Hope also suggests the 1382 images (A16) were also from the same school. It is quite possible that today many images lie under chancel floors in medieval churches. In 1848 work being carried out in St Mary's Church Nottingham uncovered a buried panel in the chancel. This panel depicted the Life of St Thomas Beckett and may have come from an altarpiece. A similar event occurred at Rustington, Sussex where a panel depicting the passion was turned on its back and placed in the chancel floor. Other examples include Brancaster, Suffolk where pieces of a destroyed reredos were found, assembled and installed in a panel on the wall sometime about 1904 and Kettlebaston, Suffolk where fragments of panels were extracted from the walls which when assembled depicted the Coronation of the Virgin, a photograph of one fragment being shown as Plate 146 in Lawrence Stone's book. This can be dated to the last half of the 14th century and clearly shows its London origins. An image of the Virgin Mary and Child holding a bird and a headless bishop holding a staff was found in the rood loft turret of Royston, Herts church in 1910.

Landed gentry who wished to preserve their ancestor's monuments moved them out of dissolved monasteries and priories. Examples of this are the FitzWilliams of Tickhill and the de Vere's of Earls Colne. Some sought to recover other artefacts. In 1547–1548 William Clopton of Long Melford, Suffolk bought a range of items including the images about the church and chapels of alabaster for 3s and the altar of alabaster in Our Lady's Chapel for 6s 8d. His family may well have donated the objects in the first place. In some cases recovered items were restored to the church during Mary I's reign only to be removed again after 1559.

There again others had an eye for a bargain. Many images were gathered together and shipped to France where there was a ready market. The calendar of state papers has reference to 'Three or four ships have latterly arrived from England laden with images which have been sold at Paris, Rouen and other places and being eagerly purchased gives to the ignorant people occasion to talk according to their notions which needed not had their lordship's command for defacing images on monuments been observed'. Clearly the writer did not approve of the recycling of images. Whether the church authorities conspired with this business opportunity is unclear but this trade continued through until 1553. In the records of Burton on Trent there are the details of a widow of an alabasterer named Margery Walker, who seems to be trading in 'liberated' images owning a shop there, one in Coventry and a warehouse in Bristol through which she was exporting alabaster work. Margery Walker is believed to be he mother-in-law of Richard Parker. The records of Bristol contain details of a licence to trade dated 1463 granted to merchants Powke and Bailly for exporting alabaster believed to be from Nottingham or Coventry. Alabaster images found in Ireland are believed to have been exported through Bristol by Elizabeth Jakes. There is other evidence. The church warden's 1548 accounts for St Andrew's and St Michael's in Lewes reads 'Item received, of Thomas Sentter who was put in trust by certain of the parish to make a sale of three altars of alabaster to the French men in party of payment of 30s whereupon they did …' St Michael's Chester made a similar entry in 1569 'Received of Sir John Savage for alabaster stone 26/8'.

Effigies in monastic buildings could be moved or destroyed or just left to decay. However, some were seen to be valuable. There is a strong case for the suggestion that the Cholmondeley tomb in St Peter ad Vincula in the Tower, the 1539 Sacheverell tomb in Ratcliffe on Soar, Notts and the Monceux tomb at Barmston, Yorkshire are all reuse of tombs originally located elsewhere and altered to conform to the new occupant. For details *see* G136, G195 and T28.

The attention of the reformers was clearly directed towards religious images. Floor slabs and effigies appear not to have been subject to serious vandalism. This may well have been true for rural churches but some high status pre-Reformation monuments were attacked. Loades in 1994 records that Edward VI's government in 1550 'abandoned to destruction' all the tombs of the earls and dukes of Lancaster at Leicester and the dukes of York at Fotheringhay. Those at Fotheringhay were not in the church but in the chapel attached to the castle. Those at Leicester were in the Newarke and although Henry VIII had resisted the dissolution of this house due to its long connection with the House of Lancaster, Edward VI had no such qualms. So too the tombs of Henry I at Reading Abbey and King Stephen's at Faversham. These were destroyed but these may also be due to the dissolution of those religious houses than a directed attack. He also observes that petitions from nobility to the government were occasionally submitted to save ancestors tombs and sometimes granted. The extent of this destruction is not known but the numbers of pre-Reformation monuments which survive indicate that the destruction was not universal.

In addition to images and effigies, wall paintings were obliterated from 1550 where a religious theme was considered inappropriate but stained glass was only broken out where it was the subject of pilgrimage. These would receive adverse attention from 1640 onwards.

At the same time the liturgy was under threat. In January 1549 the Act of Uniformity was passed by a divided parliament which enabled Cranmer's Book of Common Prayer to replace the Latin service. This did not receive overall public acclaim. In the same year Thomas Seymour, Edward's brother attempted an insurrection in which he sought to kidnap the king. This failed and earned him a date with the scaffold in March. Thomas had been the guardian of Lady Jane Grey.

During Mary's reign from 16th July 1553 to November 1558, attempts were made to resurrect the Catholic Church. Although Mary paid homage to the pope and obtained an Act of Parliament in 1554 which repealed the banning of images, the restoration of these in parish churches was patchy. This was not just because many had been destroyed or sold but the laity was, with a few exceptions, disinterested in the restoration of such ornaments despite the urging from the relevant diocese. In fact, Marian Catholicism was incomplete at the time of her death. Although the liturgical rites returned and religious art returned and received a partial Renaissance, the cult of saints, pilgrimages, chantries and belief in purgatory were casualties of Henry VIII and Edward VI propaganda. Mary was not helped by the ineffectiveness of the Archbishop of Canterbury. Reginald

Pole was made archbishop in 1555. Having fallen foul of Henry VIII and suffered attainder and a number of assignation attempts he was established in the See by Mary and attempted to re-establish Catholicism by force, some 287 burnings taking place between February 1555 and November 1558 when the laity were relieved of this brutality by Mary's and Pole's death. The disquiet of the laity to these events meant that the restoration of rites which included images was generally resisted.

In 1559 Elizabeth I came to the throne and the removal of images was resumed. Cheetham and St John Hope both record a case of prosecution for the concealment of images in Ripon on the 20th (or 29th) October 1567. The tables of alabaster were found by Archbishop Young during a visitation. It appears that five dissident clergy secreted the tables out of the minster in the dead of night for which one, Thomas Blackburn, was indicted. This spurred the diocese on an image hunt throughout the area. They were not entirely successful as in 1871 three remnants were found buried in the choir. Three more were found hidden in the tower in 1960 although these display Victorian restoration meaning that they were first discovered earlier. One other was added in 1896 from an unknown source but displays an embattled canopy as do two of the three tower panels which probably mean these were carved in York. These tables were almost certainly to have been hidden from Edward VI's commissioners in 1550 restored in 1553 and hidden again in 1559. The articles found in 1567 included 6 retable panels and 49 books, probably Marian manuals (one manual printed in York in 1553 resides in Dublin being the property of the church at Ratcliffe on Soar). It is not known if any of the 1567 panels are the ones current that lie in the minster. As late as 1574 images were still being unearthed as Nicholas Daniel, the vicar of Preston, reported to his bishop.

Not only images were attacked from 1559. Saul says that Protestant zealots again attacked effigial monuments but such practices were outlawed on the 19th September 1560 (not 1562 as some would have it). Hartshorne observes that the proclamation had to be repeated in 1573.

The proclamation in part reads:

> *The Queen's Majesty understanding that there hath been of late years spoiling and broken certain ancient monuments, some of metal, some of stone which were erected up only to show a memory to the posterity of the persons there buried or that had been benefactors to the buildings or donations of the same churches or public places, and not to nourish any kind of superstition by which means not only the churches and places remain at this present day spoiled, broken and ruinated (sic) to the offence of all noble and gentle hearts and the extinguishing of the honourable and good memory of sundry virtuous and noble person deceased.*

Weever's 1631 book page 52 has the full proclamation dated and sealed 'Windsor 6th September 1561'.

Nigel Llewellyn on page 269 of his book has an interesting interpretation on this proclamation which needed to be reaffirmed as early as 1570 (although Weever says 1573). It is unclear how much damage was done. Elizabeth's heralds described the tomb breakers as a certain rabble of men consigning them with a group of law breakers rather than reformers. The attacks where they occurred were at the heart on the assault of the doctrine of purgatory set out by Henry VIII in 1543 which questioned the value of intercession. Saul also claims that the assault was widespread both in cathedrals and parish churches but apart from some clear instances the damage may have been restricted to the defacement of religious images and the inscribed prayers. In an interesting twist the effigies which depicted Yorkist collars appear to have suffered specific damage as shown in the monuments at Minster in Sheppey, Kent (G100) and Sutton Bonington, Notts (GNP73). Bishop Sandys is recorded as saying in a letter dated 1st April 1560 'The Queen's majesty considered it not contrary to the Word of God, nay rather for the advantage of the Church, that the image of Christ crucified, together with those of the Virgin Mary and St. John should be placed as heretofore in some conspicuous part of the Church, where they might the more readily be seen by all the people' to which he adds, 'Some of us (Bishops) thought far otherwise'. Sandys is clearly commenting on the proclamation. His ultra-Protestant leanings are well known but as he was himself commemorated by a splendid tomb (A17) it is probably that he supported the banning of attacks on effigies. In the suit of the Stanley's versus Edward Fitton in 1598 over the defacing of a slab in Nether Alderley (*see* D9/83) the Stanley's evoked the 1560 proclamation with some success. The reason for Edward Fitton to attack the Stanley tomb was never stated.

In the 1530s monasteries and priories scheduled for closure were stripped of their monuments. Some were moved. The tombs to the de Vere family in Colne Priory were moved to the new house built close by and now reside in St Stephen's Church in Bures, Suffolk – *see* A25, G29 and G113.

In 1566, during a progress, Elizabeth stayed in Fotheringhay and it is alleged that as a result of her visit, the bodies of her York ancestors were exhumed from the castle and reburied in Fotheringhay church (*circa* 1573) where new tombs were constructed. Thanks to the intervention of a Tudor monarch many of the medieval monuments survive to this day but from 1560–1566 the purpose which they were intended changed. Gone were the prayers for the departed, the reference to saints, cadavers, mass vestments and the accoutrements of the sacrament. In came the cult of the individual, the achievements and character. Gardner called this period 'transition' as this change in emphasis coincided with the movement from Gothic to Renaissance style. The first transition monuments appeared in 1560 and by 1566 the Renaissance revolution was in full swing. Peter

Sherlock observes that the Renaissance style arrived in England by way of Holland with the introduction of *The Five Orders of Architecture* in 1562 along with pediments, cherubs, urns, scallop shells and garlands. The most prominent new shape was the semicircular arch.

See note 2 for a brief list of where images can be seen.

Renaissance monuments continued to be installed in churches throughout the second half of the 16th century. However, by the time the Renaissance style took hold, much of Nottingham's carved images were destroyed in the country of their creation which is why most work from the 14th and 15th century can be found only in France and Germany. Any depiction of Catholicism was heavily suppressed. In a statute of 1571 the receipt of any item blessed by the pope or his priests would lead to forfeiture of lands and goods and so such objects disappeared from monuments. Not that many items were specified, as the number of practicing Catholics was low (estimated at 40,000 in 1603 – less than 1% of the population). Penalties probably kept the numbers low as the fine for missing services in a Protestant church in 1581 could be as high as £20 (*God's Traitors* – Jessie Childs 2014). Those refusing were known as recusants (from the Latin recusare – to refuse). In 1593 the statute of confinement meant that recusants could not travel more than five miles from home without licence.

The defence of monuments extended to those abroad. In the 1580s the activities of the troops in damaging monuments in the Netherlands caused embarrassment. In 1596 English troops in France were commanded that '… none should use violence to any monuments'. This instruction appears to be more related to a concern that troops would acquire bad habits than any concern for the monuments themselves.

At the end of the reign of Elizabeth I, destruction of monuments abated. Nigel Llewellyn has a very thorough discourse on the attitudes of late Tudors and early Stuarts to the presence of imagery. Nevertheless isolated incidents of iconoclasm took place often against unpopular persons by mobs rather than any organised pogrom. Llewellyn cites the attack on the Jeffray tomb in Chiddingly, Sussex which appears to have been solely due to the mistaken belief that it was a relation of the unpopular Judge Jeffreys.

The reforms of Archbishop Laud after the accession of Charles I, spurred some minor iconoclasm amongst those who saw the reforms as a return to Roman Orthodoxy but the recorded damage is limited to the occasional defacing.

The growth of Puritanism concerned some. In 1640 Sir William Dugdale hired heraldic artists to tour the country and make drawings of glass, inscriptions and tombs. This was timely as in 1642 civil war broke out.

During the English Civil War and after (1642 to 1660) damage was done by Puritans and soldiers by removing images such a wyverns and angels from effigies and village youths saw much amusement by carving initials and stealing swords and hands and occasionally decapitating small figures. The extent of the damage done was dependent on the degree of local fanaticism and the presence of the Roundhead army. In August 1642 Colonel Sandys led his men into Canterbury where there were demolished '... many idols ... which were cast headlong and fell on their heads'. In December 1642 Sir William Waller carried out a similar action at Winchester and later Exeter where '... they defaced the Bishops' tombs'. Southwell Minster records damage to the monuments during the occupation of the Parliamentary forces involved in the siege of Newark. The details are included in A17. Most damage was simple vandalism and some was in order to change the layout of churches as exemplified by that at Holy Trinity, Hull where a de la Pole monument was destroyed in order to make a new doorway (this does not appear to be that of William which survives and is covered by G32). Nor was the damage restricted to the Parliamentary forces. The Royalists attacked South Harting church in 1643 destroying much of the building and leaving two monuments damaged – *see* R76 and R77. In August 1643 ordnance by the Commons decreed 'That all crucifixes, crosses and all images and all pictures of any one or more persons of The Trinity or of the Virgin Mary and all other images and pictures of saints ... shall be taken away and defaced'.

A specific case was the activities of William Dowsing (1596–1668) in East Anglia with his deputy Francis Jessop of Beccles. Dowsing was the Provost Marshall of the Eastern Association and was appointed by the Earl of Manchester to '... abolish all monuments of superstition idolatry' under the ordnance mentioned above. The remit included '... fixed altars, altar rails, chancel steps, crucifixes, crosses, images of the Virgin Mary and pictures of saints or superstitious inscriptions'. In May 1644 the scope of the ordinance was widened to include representations of angels (a particular obsession of Dowsing's), rood lofts, holy water stoups, and images in stone, wood and glass and on plate. Two hundred and fifty churches were visited in Cambridgeshire and Suffolk and damage was done often against the wishes of the parishioners who were charged one noble for the 'service'. His commission ceased late in 1644 when Manchester fell out of favour with Cromwell. He has left details of his actions in a diary which is available on line.

The first printed edition of this diary was in 1786 by a Woodbridge resident called Loder. His book has the following entry taken as effigy breaking:

> But the foulest and most inhuman action of those times was the violation of funeral monuments. Marbles which covered the dead were dug up, and put to other uses, tombs hackt and hewn a-pieces ; images or representations of the defunct, broken, erased, cut, or dismembered, inscriptions or epitaphs, especially if they began with an orate proanima, or concluded with cujus animce propitietur Deus. For greediness of the

> brass, or for that they were thought to be anti-Christian, pulled out from the sepulchres, and amboges; dead carcases, for gain of their stone or leaden coffins, cast out of their graves, notwithstanding this request, cut or engraven upon then, propter miserecordiam Jesu requiescant in pace.

The detail of Dowsing's diary fails to identify any effigy which was damaged as described by Loder. Monumental brasses were removed in large numbers mostly from slabs which may well have been of alabaster and it may be those to which Loder refers to as 'marbles' and his apparent rail against the defacing of effigies is therefore just a figment of his imagination.

In some cases the Civil War inflicted damage was political. In Hainton church, Lincolnshire the tomb of Sir George Heneage was targeted probably because of his service history with Catholic Edmund Bonner, Bishop of London. In 1659 instructions were given to restore the tomb 'which had been defaced in the time of trouble and war in this nation'.

In some cases where priory buildings had been incorporated into residential houses, monuments installed there were lost when the old buildings were demolished – *see* Colne Priory, Essex and Norton Priory, Cheshire. Even in country churches the peccadilloes of individual church wardens and incumbents could result in the removal of monuments. In Chellaston church, in the centre of alabaster mining, the churchwarden was permitted to remove the alabaster and pave his stable with them such that the Methodist chapel now has more alabaster than the parish church.

After the restoration in 1660 Royalists revenged themselves on those regicides that could be identified. The monuments at Westminster which included Ireton and Cromwell were opened and the bodies removed and the tombs destroyed. In the case of Henry Marten, his surrender to Charles II spared him the death penalty but revenge was taken out on his family tombs which were destroyed at Bray. Following this bout of destruction which was more political than religious, things died down with a few notable exceptions until the 19th century. However, indifference to our heritage resulted in some careless despoliation such as the removal of imagery at Westminster Abbey by Christopher Wren.

In 1766 the effigy of Michael Purefoy (died 1570) was ejected from Caldecote church, Warwickshire and not restored. The subsequent history is covered under Vanished Monuments (Appendix D9). There are other examples but insufficient to describe as iconoclasm. However, there appeared a new threat. The monument to the Greystoke family (G4 and GNP15) received attention from locals seeking stone for honing farm implements with some loss of parts.[4,7] Alabaster could also be rendered down into plaster and Nicholas Stone's monument to Sir Robert Haunton in Letherington Suffolk has received some disfigurement for this reason. The church was derelict by 1730 and the monuments systematically robbed. A support group has since restored the church and gathered as much of the monument parts as they could for display. Alabaster was also seen as having medicinal properties both in humans and in sheep and readily removed effigy parts disappeared for this reason.[8]

The Victorian Gothic Revival spurred later damage during well intentioned refurbishment of buildings. The alabaster monuments in Thrumpton church, Nottingham were moved from the nave and chancel to the tower in the 1872 rebuilding only to be restored in 1904 with some residual damage in the process. The damage to the Stanhope effigy (R70) in Shelford, Notts has been blamed on Parliamentary forces but is likely to have been done during the restoration in 1877. The condition of the Goushill effigy (GNP68) in Hoveringham, Notts is due to it being stored in the graveyard during the 1865 rebuilding and then 'doctored' to fit inside an alcove too small for the tomb chest.

Today all monuments are under protection.

Notes:

1. Cheetham says the Act was January 1550 and related to superstitious books and images. At this time the date of the Act is unclear. The Act states 'And be it further enacted by the authority aforesaid that if any person or persons of politic or corporate, that now have or hereafter shall have in his, her or their custody any books or writings of the sorts aforesaid or any images of stone, timber, alabaster, or earth, graven, carved or painted which heretofore have been taken out of any church or chapel or yet stand in any church or chapel and do not before the last day of June (1550) next ensuing deface and destroy or cause to be defaced and destroyed the same images and every one of them … and be thereof lawfully convicted, forfeit and lose to the King our Sovereign Lord for the first offence twenty shillings and for the second offence shall forfeit and lose being thereof lawfully convict four pounds and for the third offence shall suffer imprisonment at the King's will'.
2. St Mary's Church Nottingham. Panel of St Thomas Beckett.
   Victoria and Albert Museum. The Swansea Retable and panels – *see* Figure 9.
   Nottingham and Leicester Museum. Head of John the Baptist and Others – *see* Appendix E. The Flawford images comprising a figure of a bishop, a virgin and child and St Peter as pope presented in 1908.
3. Some prelates acted on their own. In Worcester, Bishop Blandford edict of the 10th January 1547 proscribed that all images at the high altar and throughout the church should be destroyed.
4. Although gypsum is found in the Eden valley the quarries do not produce alabaster and in any case the Eastern Uplands around Greystoke are a long way from Acorn Bank or Kirkby Thore.
5. John Leland recorded in his 'itinerary' of 1543 'There were diverse tombs of the lords of Stafford in Stone Priory made of alabaster. The images that lay on them were, after the suppression of the house, carried to the Friars Augustine in Forde Bridge'. This was of no avail as the tombs were lost when that house was suppressed. Leland states 'Burton on Trent has many marblers working in alabaster'.
6. The books by C S Sanson of which *Revelation, Lamentation* and *Dissolution* are just three, are recommended to the reader. Although fiction they accurately reflect the terrible years

of 1545 to 1547. This includes the arrest of shopkeepers trading on Sunday, the possession of the Bible in English, the pursuit of Anabaptists, burning at the stake for preaching reform and the destruction of tombs in dissolved religious houses.

7. **Bernard Miles in one of his Monologues in *Over the Gate* (*circa* 1950) described the use of effigy parts for sharpening – Ivinghoe, Buckinghamshire**

Author's observation: Ivinghoe church is not called St Mark's but St Mary's nor does it contain a crusader knight and his lady. It does contain an effigy in freestone of a priest one time thought to be the Bishop of Winchester but is most likely to be circa 1250. However, the practice of using the effigies as a means of sharpening farm implements was common as told by Bernard in this extract.

I'm church, myself, St Marks, what they calls perpendicular, that was built by the Vikings, in th' 'leventh century, afore the railway come. Tha's got some fine ole crusaders in un like these 'ere stone statutes where 'e lays underneath and they puts these 'ere stone statutes on the lid so's 'e'll reckernise 'isself.

Only I don't reckon nobody'll reckernise 'im cos us 'r' bin sharp'in' our sickles and faggin' hooks on 'im ever since I can remember, and 'e 'adn't got no face then. Us gets into church at night an' sharps our sickles an' faggin' hooks on this yer ole crusader, arr, all over 'im. They reckon that's the finest bit o' sharpening stone in 'Ertfordshire, only o' course nobody don't know, that's bin handed down like.

I had to laugh at our ole vicar, showin' some folks over the church. He said "This yer ole crusader" 'e says, "was," 'e says "defaced by Oliver Cromwell at the time of the Revelation." I had to laugh, haa. Arr, 'e lays there quite comfortable like with his ole woman alongside 'im. They reckon that's the finest bit of sharpening stone in 'Ertfordshire. Only 'is ole woman ain't no good. Can't get no edge out ov 'er.

He have a little dog lays at his feet, like a little crusading dog, wot used to follow after 'em down by the Crimea. Only I reckon tha's more like a whippet if you ask me. That stands over agin th' organ.

8. John Lloyd travelling in West Wales in 1905 was told about a man wandering the villages in 1802 carrying a stone which he called lysfaen and a knife. The person who recorded this meeting noted that the man claimed that the stone had magical properties and could cure 'canine disease' otherwise known as rabies. The stone could only be found on certain mountainsides in thunderstorms and his eye was trained to find it. The observer having some knowledge identified the stone as Glamorgan (Penarth) alabaster whereupon the man became angry to the amusement of the gathered villagers. The powdered alabaster was to be taken in milk for only nine days. The observer went on to say the stone was white with veined with a red-blue colour like a bruise. He also said that the name mentioned by the man was a corruption of 'cleisfaen' (Welsh for marble).

Appendix I
Cockleshell and Other False Marbles

Geologically, there is no true British native marble. Although true marble is a metamorphic rock of the limestone family, the English material called 'marble' is a crystalline form of limestone which has the appearance of natural marble. The term marble has been loosely used over the centuries beginning with Purbeck marble, a fossilised form of limestone composed of densely packed freshwater snails in limestone mud. Its likening to marble comes from its ability to hold a fine polish. Purbeck is not the only false marble for cockleshell, Frosterley, Ashford and Sussex marbles have also been employed in monument carving.

Monica Price's books such as *The Complete Source Book of Decorative Stone* show many forms of what she calls lumachelle and other fossiliferous limestones. The samples shown are from many parts of the world including Greece, North Africa, Asia, Turkey as well as Europe. For the purposes of this book we will consider only the British limestones. The following sections describe the different forms.

Cockleshell and Derbyshire Fossil Limestone

A number of 17th century alabaster effigies display inlaid panels of a dark mottled marble-like limestone. This is cockleshell 'marble' which is an iron rich non-marine lamellibranches or mussel band probably came immediately from above the cockleshell coal in the upper leaf of the Tupton coal seam and likely to have been from one of the Duke of Devonshire's colliery in the Rother Valley.[1]

This was only mined for a few years in the second quarter of the 17th century (possibly 1615 to 1630) before the seams ran out. Its presence allows the tomb or effigy to be accurately dated.

The cockles are fresh water molluscs.

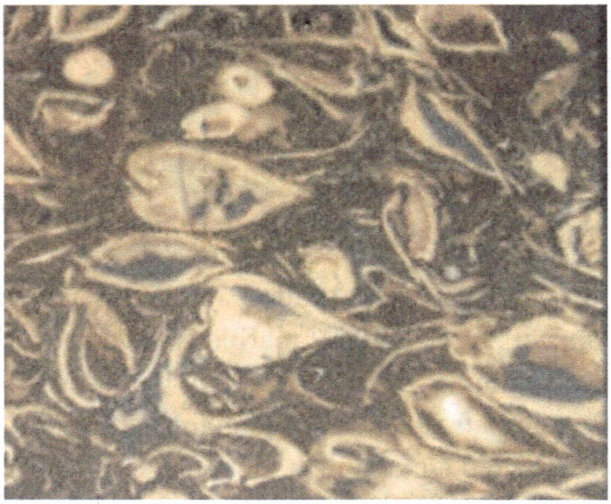

Figure 70. Cockleshell marble. Photo: the author.

Monica Price lists some Derbyshire limestones in this group. Page 170 of her book states that fossil limestone formed of sea creatures can be found at Hopton Wood from the 1750s and at Ricklow Dale where Monyash Marble was sourced but there are others. This can be identified separately from cockleshell as these are mainly buff or light grey and the crinoids have a distinct shape related to starfish and sea urchins. The stems of some are exposed when the stone is cut showing small white disks with a hole in the middle. Derbyshire limestones can be found at Chatsworth in the balustrade of some staircases and at Kedleston Hall but she lists the Houses of Parliament and the Bank of England as uses. To date no monuments have been found with Derbyshire limestone inlays. The proceedings of a conference in York in 2005 established that little exploitation of Derbyshire marble occurred before the late 18th century mainly because the movement of stone over the High Peak was difficult until the creation of the Cromford and High Peak Railway in 1831. Technically this marine limestone should be listed with Frosterley, but is discussed here due to its geographical closeness to the cockleshell seams.

Cockleshell marble can be found as follows:

- The tomb of Henry Sacheverell in Ratcliffe on Soar, Nottinghamshire dated 1625 (M2, R5). The marble appears within rectangular panels above the columns on the tomb.
- The tomb of St Andrews in Gotham church, Nottinghamshire (M23). The tomb is contemporary with that at Ratcliffe and has the marble in a similar position.
- Bolsover Castle rebuilt by Charles and William Cavendish from 1617 displays cockleshell marble within the design of one fireplace of the older part of the castle (X47).

- Chatsworth House as shown in an inlaid undated stone surfaced table in the South Sketch Gallery.
- Wellow Hall near Ollerton displays a fireplace with a fossil marble sometimes identified as cockleshell. The description includes the comments that the marble was obtained from quarries near Matlock or Uttoxeter but the date given for the quarrying of 1810 so it must be assumed this may well be Derbyshire fossil limestone.
- Holme Pierrepont church has a 1615 monument (R3) with an ovoid of what looks like cockleshell marble.

Frosterley

In Weardale, County Durham there are ancient quarries at Frosterley, near Stanhope. This produced similar grey-black marble-like limestone similar to the cockleshell but comprises marine molluscs and corals from the Carboniferous period. The Rogerley Quarry has worked for some 700 years and examples can be found in Durham Cathedral dating from 1242 (Chapel of the Nine Altars) and the old Frosterley Railway Station (*see* Figure 72). This is sometimes known as Stanhope Black marble. The local miners called it 'cockle' and the seam was often no more than 1m thick. Harehope Quarry is preserved as an educational centre and Broadwood Quarry is still occasionally worked. Frosterley church has a font carved in this marble. St Mary's Church at Eastington, Co Durham has an effigy made from Frosterley marble dating from 1300–1305. The effigy is a lady probably of the FitzMarmaduke family which, in some quarters, is stated as being Isabella Bruce the illegitimate daughter of William the Lion, King of Scotland and the wife of John FitzMarmaduke.

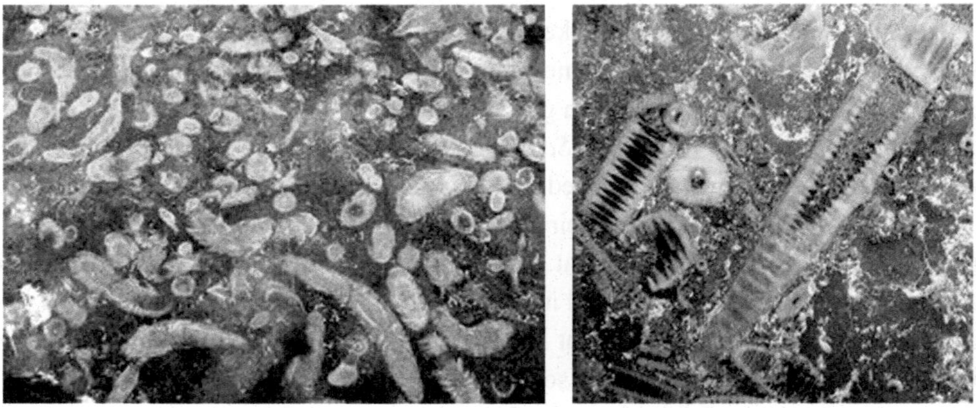

Figure 71. Frosterley Marble. These marine animals differ in shape to the fresh water ones found in cockleshell marble but note the white disks with a hole similar to Derbyshire limestone.
Photos: The author, taken at the Mining Museum, Keswick.

Figure 72. The block of Frosterley marble on the platform of Frosterley Station in July 2014. One portion is polished to show the marine molluscs. The nearby church of Frosterley has a font of the same material. Photo: Janet State.

Ashford

A black marble, really limestone with high bitumen content, was obtained at Ashford in the Water, Derbyshire, in the Rookery Plantation and also in the Arrock Mine in the 18th and 19th century. Although some samples contain fossils, the majority of objects made from Ashford marble are plain glossy black.

The Biographical Dictionary of Sculptors in Britain has an entry for John Lomas and Sons of Bakewell who flourished 1827 to 1881. They may well be related to the Lomas family of Derby (B92). Their Bakewell Marble Works were leased from the Duke of Rutland. Reported as being at Ashford until 1829 they later moved to Wye Mill, Bakewell where chimney pieces and monumental tablets were made. John Lomas also had an association with the quarry at Monyash (Ricklow – *see* Derbyshire limestone) with Richard Brown and Sons. The source for their white 'marble' monuments which were exhibited at Great Exhibition of 1851 is not known.

Sussex

In Kent, and East and West Sussex a type of stone has been quarried which is known as Sussex marble, Petworth marble or Bethersden marble so named after the local villages. It is sometimes known as winklestone. It is a fossiliferous freshwater limestone from the Cretaceous period and has a constituency like that of Frosterley marble but may be closer to Purbeck (it is formed of a pond snail called Paludina but of a different strain to Purbeck). It is wholly unlike alabaster or cockleshell marble. Its marble name came from its ability to be polished and therefore has been used for church monuments and furniture. The tombs of Edward III, Richard II and his queen are reported as being in grey Petworth marble indicating a use in the 14th century contemporary with Purbeck which is often used to repair damaged Sussex marble tombs. New quarries were opened as old ones were worked out and there is some evidence that the marble was mined as late as 1905. The monument to Lady Margaret Palmer who died in 1619 and resides in St Mary, Chilham is in Bethersden marble but the carver is unknown. The monument displays the style of the period with columns, pinnacles and heraldic devices. There is no effigy. A number of fonts are in the material including that at Trotton, Ardingley and West Chiltington. The church at Throwley, Kent is particularly interesting in that it has a 16th century Bethersden marble slab, a Purbeck marble tabletop tomb and two alabaster tombs of the London school the details of which are contained in the tables. The altar stone and Episcopal chair in Canterbury is reputed to be of Sussex marble. Other quarries are Kirdford, Northchapel and Laughton but Surrey can also lay claim at Charlwood, Outwood and Ewhust. All quarrying has ceased. Monica Price has a good picture of this marble on page 159 of her book.

Purbeck

Like all the examples in this appendix, Purbeck stone is not a marble but a fossiliferous limestone from the Upper Jurassic period only found in the Purbeck peninsular from which it gets its name. It was called a marble because it will take a fine polish but here the similarity with true marble ends. It was known to be mined in the Bronze Age but was much used in the Romano-British period (possibly as early as AD43) as witnessed in the villa at Fishbourne, IOW. It is in strata some 1 to 1.2m thick and like alabaster can be stained by oxides to give red, brown, green or blue varieties. Purbeck marble was first used for tombs from the 12th century and continued in use until largely overtaken by alabaster at the end of the 14th century. Even then tombs continued to be constructed with both materials with Purbeck used for the tomb chest and the more easily carved alabaster for the effigy. Mining continued spasmodically into the latter half of the 19th century and some quarrying has been carried for repair purposes as late as 1993.

Figure 73. The effigy of King John in Worcester Cathedral in blue/black Purbeck marble *circa* 1216 (X7). Purbeck stone was hard to carve and this fine effigy would have taken many months to carve. Purbeck effigies for commoners were less well carved and the availability of alabaster which was more easily carved and therefore less expensive but which could produce fine effigies saw the decline of Purbeck for all but simple structures. The two small effigies supporting the head are Bishops Wulfstan II and Oswald both of which had tombs in Worcester. Photo: the author.

Purbeck can be confused with Sussex marble (*see* below). It contains the shells of freshwater snails known as *Paludina carinifera* in a greenish- or bluish-grey limestone. Quarries include Worth Maltravers (Chapter House in Lincoln), Keates, St Aldhem's, Langton Maltravers, Herston and Swanage.

Catacleuse Marble

This is sometimes known as elvan formed in dykes around the Cornish granite. Most elvans are pink or grey but in the North there is a patch of 'blue elvan' which is of dolerite composition.

The monuments at Layer Marney church, Essex are described in X3. The effigies are carved in blue-black catacleuse stone from a quarry at St Endelion in Cornwall which was owned by the Marneys.

The monument to Prior Vyvyan at Bodmin, Cornwall (*circa* 1533) is also in this stone (*see* Saul, Fig 41 page 68 and Llewellyn page 199) and is attributable to Cornelius Harman who is also credited with the monument to Lord Audley in Saffron Walden dated 1544 and a monument in Castle Hedingham both of which are in black touchstone. Catacleuse is linked to Pentewan stone and is often known as greenstone. Pevsner suggests the name originates from a quarry near Padstow called Cataclew Point. This marble was still in use in 1660 when a grey elvan version was used for a tomb at St Tudy, Cornwall.

Some use is made of this stone for gravestones.

Other known English aliases[2]

Ashburton Marble,[3] Australian Marble, Bethersden Marble,[4] Bletchingdon Marble,[5] Breche Rose, Charlwood Stone,[6] Derby Marble,[7] Devon Marble,[8] Dundee Marble, Forest Marble,[9] Istrian Stone, Jaune Lamartine, Kilkenny Marble,[10] Large Paludina Marble, Laughton Marble,[11] Parian Marble, Pennon Marble, Pentelic Marble, Pink Verona Marble, Rance[12] or Belgian Marble, Sicilian Marble, Skyros Marble, Small Somerset Marble,[13] Paludina Marble, Teesdale Marble,[14] Tinos, Torquay Marble,[15] Tournai Marble,[16] Travertine, Verde Antico, Verde Fraye, Verona Marble, Westmorland Marble,[17] Yeovil Marble.

Other stones

Although not English false marbles, it is worth mentioning stone which is often found with alabaster. This is the Black Touch (sometimes Tournai) often imported from the Low Countries and Rance, a red mottled marble from Brittany and Belgium.

Notes:

1. Extracted from the records at Chatsworth House in respect of a table with inlaid cockleshell marble.
2. This may not be a complete list. Sir Ralph Verney around 1653 wrote 'It polishes like marble and there are several sorts and colours some are beautiful and lasting than others. (The source) is near me and so the carriage will cost little, and the stone being soft twill be wrought at an easy rate. It is not fit to pave a room nor stand wet nor in the air least it lose its polish and scale in time'. The Verney lands were near Claydon, Bucks and it is unclear as to which stone he was referring to. In 1653 Verney was negotiating for his tombs in the church and he was pressing sculptors Burman and Marshall on the merits of one stone over the other. The details of this remain unclear. (*See* Ralph Verney notes.)
3. The Devon limestone group including those of Newton Abbott and Buckfastleigh. Reputed to have been used for memorials but mainly used for cladding in high status buildings. Dark grey to black with white and red patches.
4. Not a limestone and mainly used in Kent and as far north as Buckinghamshire.
5. A Jurassic limestone in the same family as forest marble. The Tuscan columns at Neville's Court, Trinity College, Cambridge are in this stone, as is the columns in St John's College, Oxford and the pillars in the crypt of Anglesey Abbey.
6. A fossilised limestone much used for paving but does not carve well.
7. Hopton Wood (Matlock) gives cream colour, Haderne, Monyash (mottled grey). Ashford black marble is sometimes included but see the section on Derbyshire limestone above.
8. Quarries include Ketley (Yealinton) and Newton Abbott but both Ashburton and Torquay

are often included.

9. Effigies in Middle Jurassic forest marble are rare. Hartshorne in 1840 identified the 1265 cross-legged effigy of David de Esseby in Castle Ashby church, Northamptonshire as made from this material but later observers say Purbeck. Damage to the effigy means that clear identification is difficult. Hartshorne links the Ashby monument to one at Dodford to Sir Robert (or William) Keynes *circa* 1305 but again current observers say Purbeck. The name 'forest' was not coined until 1799 by William Smith. Sources of forest marble are restricted to Oxfordshire and Buckinghamshire where it is sometimes known as Wychwood, Kemble or Bradford and on the Dorset coast at Weymouth. Images of this marble show a varying coloured veined form wholly unlike Purbeck.
10. A black limestone from Ireland.
11. *See* Sussex marble.
12. Although mainly found in Belgium, Robert Plot recorded in 1686 that he had found a seam of rance in Needham (*sic*) Forest between the Trent and the Dore (Dove) in the same area as the principal alabaster beds. He also found Rance at Grindon on the estate of the Duke of Albemarle where the rance was '… of a white, hard, shiny grit striped red.' He went on to observe 'There are sources at Yelpersly Torr where the river Mangforld enters it'. He is referring to the Manifold Valley but Yelpersley Torr escapes identification.
13. Quantocks (grey and green), Cheddar (black) and Bristol (brown).
14. It is reported that the Church of St Mary in Barney has a Teesdale 'marble' font. Sometimes known as sugar limestone.
15. Also known as Pettitor and has grey, pink or 'spot' variety.
16. A black limestone from France.
17. Kendal (white with red veins), Ambleside (green and Kirby Lonsdale (black)).

Appendix J
Alabaster Images and the Mystery Play

The mystery play evolved from the 10th to the 16th century and peaked in the 15th century. The name 'mystery' has been variously identified with 'miracle' or with 'misterium' or 'craft' plays because of their close association with craft guilds. There is a link to the *Golden Legend (Aurea Legenda)* compiled by Bishop Jacobus de Voragine in the 13th century which contains a vivid account of the lives of saints and gospel stories which was one of the most published books in the 15th century. It is unlikely that the carvers would have been able to read this but the stories would have been presented by clergy and others to the laity.

With these stories circulating from about 1260 it would be natural to enact these in the form of a play or an adaptation of the scripture stories carried out in the church, later moving first to the churchyard and later to the market place.

The links with the alabastermen were explored by the antiquarian W L Hildeburgh. He concluded there is a close correlation between the events depicted in the plays and the alabaster tablets used on retables. He cites the V&A wood and alabaster triptych panel A193-1946 of 1400 as having parallels in illustrations of a mystery play. The presence of soldiers, especially on the panels dealing with the resurrection, has parallels with the soldier coming to check if Jesus was dead a popular event in the plays. In addition the extended top and bottom of some panels, sometimes embattled, is believed to have been used in plays to depict heaven and hell.

The mystery plays were latterly performed by craft guilds that would be responsible for the costumes and scenery. The blackening of the faces of villains on panel carvings and the depiction of feathered tights on the legs of St Michael are believed to have been drawn from the actors in the plays. In the same way headgear with projections which identified evil individuals has its basis in the characters.

Hildeburgh records that Nottingham carvers may have gone to Coventry for Corpus Christi where there was a fixed stage for performances.

Figure 74. Mystery play.
Pictures by A Foristiere from *The Story of the British People in Pictures*, 1936.

The mystery play migrated from the church or monastery into the market square and away from the control of the clergy to the laity, often the trade guilds. The actors were guild members. The depiction of hell shown left and below was often with 'effects'. The costumes used were of the style of the period rather than any attempt to depict the costumes of the Holy Land. The alabasterers may have taken part but in any case they would have seen the plays and obtained a visual format in support of the stories from the Golden Legend enabling them to form each scene depicted on the alabaster tablets.

In particular actors playing evil parts had their faces and limbs darkened whilst the 'good' guys were whitened. This practice was carried over into the Nottingham panel industry where all faces were unpainted (white) whilst those who were considered 'bad' were darkened – *see* Cheetham page 27.

Figure 75. The picture (right) shows a travelling theatre. Here the actors are playing a scene from the sacrifice of Abraham who is prevented from sacrificing his son by God in the form of an angel. The stages had little room and the actors would be close together and reliant on speech for effect. In the tablets the figures are also close together as a copy of the tight grouping seen in the plays. The local dignitaries are on a level with the stage and butterfly headdresses are very much in evidence. Pictures by A Foristiere from *The Story of the British People in Pictures*, 1936.

Occasionally costumes which may have been worn found their way onto tombs. Some of the angel weepers on the Ewelme (G142, 1477) tomb chest are shown wearing feathered tights which according to Professor Prior were a trait of the mystery plays.

The mystery plays have a modern equivalent in the 1995 *Lion Storyteller Bible* which is played out in infant and Sunday schools in a series of plays with simple props sometimes known as 'Open the Book' and performed by local villagers.

Figure 76. A medieval 15th century alabaster carved panel. The taking of Jesus in the garden. The soldiers have black faces whilst Jesus and a disciple are white. Photo: the author.

Appendix K
Modern Alabaster

In the mid-19th century alabaster decoration had resurgence. The Victorian's interest in Gothic architecture resulted in the provision of church furniture, altar screens, reredos and retables, many following the principles of the medieval carvers. The carvings of this period are sculptured and show a quality far superior to the arts and crafts techniques applied by their predecessors. The subjects include the crucifixion and the last supper but some depict the saints. The alabaster is often Italian but the Chellaston quarries were again working up until 1915.

A church of alabaster – All Saints, Mackworth with Markeaton

The church at Mackworth, Derbyshire contains much alabaster which can be attributable to the Mundy family. Sir John Mundy, a Lord Mayor of London *circa* 1522, purchased the Markeaton estate in 1516 and from that time until the early 20th century the Mundy family were great benefactors to Mackworth church.

An old incised alabaster slab was found buried in the floor in 1851 and is attributable to Thomas Touchet rector from 1381 to 1409 and is believed to be the work of the Chellaston workshops. In fact the Chellaston quarries feature largely as the source for most of the work. The slab had a Latin inscription and incised cross which is largely defaced and an 'opening' with a carving which may represent the head of the priest. The slab lies in an arched recess in the south wall of the south aisle where it was placed after discovery.

An effigy to Edward Mundy who died in 1607 lies in the south aisle having been moved from the chancel. It is in red/brown alabaster and in Renaissance form comprising of a recumbent civilian on a tomb chest. The effigy is carved from a single block of Fauld alabaster and the hands are parallel with the body. He wears a short ruff round the neck and at the wrists. His wife was Jane Burnell of Winkburn and the chest contains the images of their six sons and two daughters. It has been suggested that the effigy was once painted but no evidence of staining remains. Cox criticised the monument as being 'rather clumsily sculpted' but it is typical of the period and likely to be work of the Burton workshops in which case the alabaster was usually obtained from Fauld. The alabaster is not in good condition.

Much of the remaining alabaster is the work of carver R G Lomas a respected monumental mason of Hall and Company at 37 King St, Derby who worked to the ideas of Emily Mundy. Lomas started work in 1860 (*see* B92) and some of the earliest works for Mackworth are the pulpit of 1876 and the reredos of 1878.

The 1876 pulpit is reputed to be brown veined alabaster on a limestone (Purbeck) base but the provenance of this is uncertain. The panels and sills have a feel of red/brown veined marble. However, the carved frieze and lectern stand are white alabaster and the columns are green (Irish Connemara marble*). The alabaster is most likely to be from Chellaston. The pulpit shows an interesting use of mixed stones and this theme sets the church apart from the others.

* Irish green marble comes from Clifden, Connemara in the Recess and Streamstown Quarries.

Figure 77. The pulpit at Mackworth made in 1876. The base is Purbeck Marble as are the steps. The panels are veined marble with Connemara green marble columns, but the carved frieze and lectern stand are Chellaston alabaster. The whole assembly is the work of R G Lomas of the Derby Marble Works. Photo: the author.

The communion rails in cream alabaster are also a copy of a design found in Italy and contain Blue John from Derbyshire. These date from 1893.

Figure 78. The Mackworth communion rails in cream Chellaston alabaster. The vertical panel are Derbyshire Blue John. Photo: the author.

The vestry door has a surround of Chellaston alabaster which dates from 1877. The columns are engine turned with decorative inlays. The carver R G Lomas advertised his Derby Marble Works as being 'steam powered' from 1860.

The Mundy family are commemorated by four wall memorials in the chancel which are inlaid with Irish marble with white alabaster surrounds. These date from 1903 and 1929. Between the memorials on the south wall of the chancel there is a cross with an alabaster surround and inlaid stone. This was erected to commemorate Emily Mundy which resulted in a former cross of Connemara marble being moved to the south wall of the south aisle. There is no alabaster on this memorial.

Figure 79. The 1877 ornate surround over the vestry door. This extraordinary confection is in Chellaston alabaster. Photo: the author.

Figure 80. Detail of the inlayed and carved columns on the 1877 ornate surround over the vestry door. Photo: the author.

Two 8ft standard 'candlesticks' stand either side of the chancel. These were granted by Emily Mundy to Mackworth and are also believed to be the work of R G Lomas. Dating from 1902 they are in cream alabaster. By this date the non-veined alabaster must have been hard to find and Young speculates that a new quarry may have opened at Chellaston which had some limited quantities of good pure alabaster which was exploited by Lomas (this may well be Pit Close – *see* notes on the Chellaston quarries). The capitals of the candlesticks were carved separately from the columns which show signs of engine turning. The capital of the left candlestick is a non-translucent alabaster and may be from a different quarry to the rest of the artefact.

Figure 81. One of the extraordinary 'candlesticks' in the chancel of Mackworth church. This would have been made in three sections and the spiral column is probably engine turned. Once again this is Chellaston alabaster. Photo: the author.

The lectern of 1903 is again attributable to R G Lomas and is of the same quality as the candlesticks. It was granted by Emily Mundy for 39 years of married life and is reputedly carved from a single block of Chellaston alabaster. This may also be from Pit Close quarry but may well have been cut as early as 1884 when there are records of blocks of white/cream alabaster being produced some of which was recorded in the Thomas Forman's diary as being 'sent to Chellaston Methodist Chapel for Mr Lomas'. It is clear that Lomas was a good customer of Forman's Pit Close Quarry. The intricate carving is good.

Figure 82. The magnificent lectern in the nave of Mackworth church. Believed to have been carved from a single block of Chellaston alabaster by R G Lomas. The 1607 alabaster effigy of Edward Mundy lies beyond. Photo: the author.

The reredos which extending across the full width of the east end is also described as Derbyshire alabaster and the lower panels display some of the inclusions found in Chellaston stone as the quarries became worked out. The design of the reredos is claimed to be copied from one in a church in Pavia, Italy the idea being brought back from one of Emily Mundy's foreign tours. The inlays are in a variety of stones. For a full description *see* 'Record of Church Furnishing' – The Association of Decorative and Fine Arts Societies – All Saints Mackworth.

Figure 83. The ornate inlayed reredos which extends across the full width of the chancel. The stone inlays include many coloured limestones and marbles as well as panels of alabaster. The alabaster panel below the level of the altar is in panels is fractured alabaster. Photo: the author.

Worthy of study are:

- Thrumpton church, Nottinghamshire displays an alabaster reredos dating from 1871 when the church was rebuilt by the Byrons. It depicts the crucifixion. The carver is unknown but the alabaster is Italian.
- Thurcaston church, Cheshire displays an alabaster reredos dating from 1885. The reredos was carved by Nathaniel Hitch to the instruction of J L Pearson.

- Sydney Cathedral. The reredos was carved in 1885 by Nathaniel Hitch to the instruction of J L Pearson.
- Lockerley church, Hampshire reredos in alabaster and marble. The reredos was carved in 1892 by Nathaniel Hitch to the instruction of W Colson and depicts the last supper.
- Streatley church reredos in alabaster. The reredos was carved in 1893 by Nathaniel Hitch to the instruction of J L Pearson.
- St Paul's Church Daybrook, Nottinghamshire. Alabaster reredos depicting the last supper. Carved by Nathaniel Hitch in 1895 in conjunction with J L Pearson.
- Kingston on Soar church has a font and reredos in Kingston alabaster. That in the reredos shows the same faulting as that in Mackworth. These date from 1905.

Figure 84. The reredos in Kingston on Soar church in Fauld alabaster. This reredos was installed when the church was refurbished by the Lord Belper in 1905, at which time he was a director of the Fauld Company. To the right is the Babington tomb in limestone. This canopied tomb may have once held an effigy of Thomas Babington but this not supported by documentary evidence. After the execution of Thomas the manor was acquired by George, the Earl of Shrewsbury whose affinity for Mary, Queen of Scots was well known. The 1585–1586 presentments of the church wardens to the Bishop of York record that George did something nasty in the church the details of which were not made clear. Local legend has it that this entailed removal of Thomas's effigy which would have been in alabaster but this cannot be proved. Photo: the author.

Also worthy is the altar screen in the parish church of Barrow on Soar, Leicestershire, which, whilst in sandstone and not alabaster, displays a close resemblance to the medieval style although much more carefully crafted. This too was carved by Nathaniel Hitch under instruction from W D Caröe.

Nathaniel Hitch was born in 1845 and died in 1938.

Figure 85. Part of the reredos depicting the resurrection in Streatley church. Photo: the author.

Appendix L
Armour and the Carver

The section is not a discourse on armour. For that I would recommend *A Short History of Costume and Armour* by Francis M Kelly and Randolph Schwabe published by Dover Publications of New York.

However, it is necessary to explore how carvers understood armour design, the mistakes they made and the way they depicted the deceased knight on the effigy.

The majority of male effigies in the period preceding the Reformation depict the man in armour and many after. This not only reflects the fact the monuments were commissioned by gentry and minor nobility all of whom were expected to provide military duties but also those who wished to demonstrate their heroic and chivalric roles in life.

It is almost certain that the people depicted on effigies would have worn armour at some time in their lives. The exception is for effigies of judges, lawyers, clerics and clergy although even here there are exceptions. After the Reformation the right to wear armour was less justified as we will discuss. One issue which is self evident is that the armour carved in great detail is not always correct for the period in which the depicted died or in some cases lived and there tends to be a lag in the styles which is associated with the ability of the carver to observe the evolution of the armour industry.

In today's world of images of anything being immediately available online it is easy to dismiss the problems that a carver had in depicting armour. The wearing of armour in times of peace simply did not happen. It was extremely uncomfortable, hot and debilitating. War when encountered would be far from the populace and even more remote from the centres of carving. In the beginning the carver would draw on effigies carved in the centuries before alabaster became popular mainly in the 13th century. Crossley summarises the armour periods as follows:

- 1250 to 1250 The crusaders
- 1250 to 1320 Edward I
- 1320 to 1350 The experimental years
- 1350 to 1413 The French wars
- 1413 to 1435 Agincourt
- 1435 to 1500 Wars of the Roses
- 1500 to 1550 Early Tudor

Crossley, like Gardner did not stray beyond the Reformation. The period to the point at which armour had lost its popularity may be grouped as:

- 1550 to 1600 Late Tudor
- 1600 to 1640 Stuart
- 1640 to 1660 Civil War

The crusader and Edward I periods (1250 to 1320 above) are pre-alabaster and very little of the armour from this period carried over onto the alabaster effigy. The hood of mail, shield and cross-legged pose from this period appeared for a short time.

The period 1320 to 1350 is a time of diversity in armour development. The long surcoat was abandoned as it obstructed the knight when on foot for a shorter version slit at the sides and sometimes known as a cyclas, later becoming increasing figure hugging as it started to become the jupon. Mail shirts continued but the steel helmet known as a round bascinet appeared with the head mail now attached and known as a camail covering the neck and shoulders. A padded garment under the mail gave a slightly bulbous aspect to the chest and abdomen and elbow cops appeared normally round.

From 1350 the bascinet became pointed and decoration in the form of an orle appeared. The tunic now became tight and was shortened to become a jupon placed over a plate breastplate which often retained its bulbous appearance indicating a padded undershirt. The belt known as a baudric appeared.

From 1415 the camail disappeared but the mail shirt and jupon were retained but were now adorned by taces. A skirt of short plates appeared as did a bavier over a chin piece on the breastplate. The round elbow cops became fin-like.

The bulbous breastplate vanished about 1450 to be replaced by an armet and gorget with pauldrons laminated to permit the arm to be raised. At the end of the 15th century foreign armour appeared especially Milanese. Elbow cops lost their fins but became large. The head was still covered by a bascinet which became less conical.

From 1500 the armour became standard and the pauldron was turned up at the neck to provide defence against pike trusts. Effigies from this period are shown bare headed with a tilting helmet under the head.

Gauntlets varied over the period but by the start of the 16th century were no longer worn. Shoes also varied from mail through to plated and then to laminated steel with long points. Later a plain square-ended shoe known as a sabaton was employed.

Kelly offers the opinion that the armour shown on brasses which were cheaper to produce than effigies applied to lesser gentry and are therefore unlikely to show the latest modes of armour. Therefore they cannot be taken to represent the armour of the period. Effigies in stone or bronze are more likely to be noble individuals and therefore depicted in current styles. Kelly is true up to a point. The writer takes no account of the fact that it is the carver that needs to see the armour irrespective of that owned by the deceased and this was sometimes difficult.

It is quite possible that armour was loaned to the carver especially where the deceased requested such action in his will. Although there are no known wills for knights specifying this, there are such wills for civilians such as judges so this practice may have been common. Suits of armour were sometimes displayed alongside tombs in churches.

On the other hand, where no samples were provided the carver was left to his own devices. He may have drawings of armour or other effigies in production or if a city carver such as those in the mid-16th century in London there may have been opportunities for copying. Otherwise, the carver could purchase old armour and set this up in his workshop which may account for a tendency for armour carving to lag in time the evolving styles.

Following the end of the Wars of the Roses in 1487 there was a period of peace within Britain. From that time ordinary people would not normally see knights so attired, as wearing armour was uncomfortable. What battles there were occurred in the far north with the defeat of the Scottish army in 1519 and the suppression of the Pilgrimage of Grace in 1536 in Yorkshire and Northumberland. Later, following the accession of Elizabeth, musters were instituted in which the local gentry would parade with their followers usually in armour.

Even so provincial carvers had few opportunities to observe changes in armour style in the period 1487 to about 1550. Armour in this period tends to look old-fashioned and more like late Plantagenet than Tudor. Henry held tilts but these were localised to London and its surroundings. After the accession of Elizabeth her accession day was celebrated from 1581 by processions and tilts from each year until her death on or around 17th November 1602. Descriptions of these have survived in the records of Leopold von Wedel and others. The London tilts were probably the high point with some 12,000 people squeezed into the tilt-yard at Whitehall now Horse Guards Parade each paying 12d for entry. These tilts allowed gentry to see and order new armour. Musters increased in numbers from 1588 following the defeat of the Spanish Armada.

Carvers would therefore have an opportunity to see and copy the latest modes as they had done with ladies fashions. The armour depicted on tombs from 1580 have a more up-to-date feel.

The dominant armourers in the 15th century were Italian and German. English armourers were relegated to repairs except for helms and bascinets until Henry VII imported Italian and German workers to make armour in England, hence the appearance of Milanese armour on some effigies. Later Henry VIII created an armoury at Greenwich using continental armourers. For more detail on this *see* publications on the Greenwich armoury.

The wearing of full armour went into decline in the late 16th century yet the individuals continued to be shown so attired on their effigies. In the case of Henry Sacheverell (R4), he was a businessman with land and mine interests who never went to battle. He did attend musters when he may well have worn armour. His monument shows him dressed as a knight in Stuart armour more in keeping with the 1620s than the 1580s when he died, mainly due to his tomb being commissioned by his son in 1625. The carver clearly had lost the knowledge of Elizabethan armour at this time.

The period 1590 to 1650 are the peak years for alabaster effigy carving and it is to the credit of carvers that they had by this time got the styles more or less right. By the first quarter of the 17th century the emergence of firearms meant that armour had to be bullet proof. The Civil War from 1642 saw light armour used, much of which had been tested by point-blank shot but at the end of the war armour all but disappeared from effigies and it is interesting to note that this coincided with the decline in alabaster use.

The main centre of carving from 1390 to 1560 was the East Midlands. This location was remote from the place of power and government centred on London and the South East where the style changes of armour would have been most evident.

Reviewing the period from the first alabaster carving in 1329–1330 to 1360 the effigies were made by London carvers or those in royal service all of whom would have access to armour of high quality and of recent design. They may also have been loaned the actual armour of the depicted for copying. There is an important exception. The effigy at Hanbury (G28) is clearly by a local carver and Longford, Derbyshire (GNP18) and Stamford, Lincs (GNP54) may also be local.

The Hanbury effigy shows a knight in a cross-legged pose and in armour which is popularly identified with 'crusader' attire. By 1340 when the effigy is believed to have been carved, the crusades had been consigned to history and the cross-legged pose, so common in 12th and 13th century limestone and Purbeck marble effigies such as those in Temple Church, London, had long since declined in popularity. In fact this and the 1337 effigy of John of Eltham (G18) and the 1361 effigy of Sir William Fitzwarren at Wantage (G1) are the only surviving alabaster effigies in this style although the one at Dorchester is cross-legged but of uncertain material. The armour shows the close-fitting hauberk with coif, integral sleeves, mail hose and gloves with a surcoat open at the sides and drawn to one side. The shield is triangular and reaches below the waist – a form which had been discarded for battle in the previous century. The effigies of Prince William of Hatfield in York dating from 1346 (G30) and Sir Hugh Despenser in Tewkesbury of 1349 (G10) dispense with both the cross-legged pose and the shield although the hauberk style is retained in modified form.

The abandonment of the cross-legged style about the commencement of alabaster carving not only reflects changes in style but also that the crossed leg became vulnerable to damage when carved in the round and the shield demanded a larger block with high wastage. All 'Gothic' effigies from 1361 are straight-legged. It is suggested that the venerable carvers of the Hanbury and Westminster cross-legged effigies were experimenting with the new alabaster material having been schooled in the harder but less demanding stones but soon found that straight legs were more suitable. Alabaster became attractive to carvers as it permits finer carving of the detail of armour and so, to embrace this new material, styles of carving had to change to allow this to be used.

It is necessary to explain the term 'Gothic'. It was unknown as a term before the 18th century when it was coined as a term of reproach in the sense of Goths equals barbarous and uncouth and was applied to the styles and architecture of the medieval period. A few decades later the term 'Gothic' became honourable as appreciated by the 19th century designers and architects. At some point the term was used to describe armour and today is widely used for the period from mid-14th to early 16th century (*see* Gardner) although technically it should relate to the period 1455 to 1485 when armour design acquired graceful curves and fluting commensurate with medieval building styles. I have no problem with applying Gothic to the entire period prior to 1560.

Coincident with start of alabaster carving was the evolution of the bascinet steel helmet. Hugh Despenser's effigy (G10) displays a round-topped bascinet helmet over the mailed coif or camail which now is reduced to covering the head, neck and shoulders. The use of a steel helmet is earlier than the date of this effigy (1349) but the first types with a flat top or flared rim (like a WWI helmet) do not appear on any known British alabaster effigy. The bascinet in the form of a close-fitted skull-cap worn over a hauberk or camail was to change shape over the duration of the 14th century. The second half of that century saw the bascinet rise to point like a sugar-loaf depicted at Spratton (1371, G23), Greystoke (1367, G4).

Many effigies sport an orle or chaplet (garland or wreath). In the first half of the 15th century the knights display the orle often jewelled around the bascinet. Examples can be seen at Dennington (G162, 1441), Bromsgrove (G184, 1450), and Tong (G148, 1451). Strangely, the orle does not seem to be a feature of brasses of the period.

In some cases a larger helmet was worn over the bascinet. This is depicted in most popular images of medieval knights and was known as the 'great helm' which carried the crest of the wearer. The great helm as a fighting appurtenance died out *circa* 1380 and no effigy exists which shows someone wearing one. However, the great helm was used in tournaments and tilts into the 16th century and may not have finally died out until 1600 (*see* the lost effigy of Sir Henry Lee at Quarrendon, D9/93). If not shown on the head of an effigy, the helm, as a device, appears on many effigial carvings used as a substitute for a pillow under the head of the knight and usually bearing the crest. This persisted into the 17th century.

The bascinet also evolved. About 1380, it acquired a visor with a pointed front called a houndskull or pig-faced bascinet and the mail coif was modified to no longer go over the head but be attached to the underside of the bascinet by metal lace which falls over the shoulders. The lowered houndskull would obscure the face so there are no known effigies which have this feature.

There are other features. The embossed hip belt (sometimes called a bawdric or baldric) is common on alabaster effigies as it provided an opportunity for the carver to demonstrate his skills. Gardner suggests this was a feature of the Trent Valley workshops. The hip belt supported only the misericorde (dagger) and the belt seems to have been retained long after the real knights moved over to the shoulder or sword belt. In brasses the dagger is just laid beside the knight but the alabastermen could carve a dagger in its proper position. Many were vulnerable to damage and in some cases restorers have replaced the missing item. Misericordes can be seen on the effigy at Berkeley (G11) and Wheathampstead (T22) showing that the feature had a long lifespan in this case from 1362 to 1558. Decorated hip belts can be seen on the effigies at Hoveringham (GNP68), Swine (G191) and at Meriden (G172).

The period covered by Class II (1360 to 1420) saw the abandonment of the chain mail and linen surcoat and the arrival of the camail (aventail) and jupon (gipon). The change was not sharp. The Despenser effigy at Tewkesbury (G10) is an early example and overlaps other effigies which maintain the chain mail. This may reflect the fact that the carver may well be London based and the carving closer to 1360 than 1348. The jupon was a padded surcoat without sleeves and which was shorter than that used with chain mail. It would be called today a three-quarter length. The jupon was leather, padded and often was decorated, fringed or scalloped at the bottom. There are cases where the jupon swells out over the breast indicating that a metal breastplate was worn under the jupon. This can be seen in the picture of Sir Robert Goushill at Hoveringham (GNP68, 1403) included as a frontispiece. The jupon has a scalloped bottom and is shaped at the waist with a low decorated hip belt and a bawdric. Others are the Warwick tomb (G171) and Elford (G158). Even if the jupon does not swell it is likely the jupon is steel lined. The jupon was a godsend to the carver as it gave him scope for decoration and design.

The Despenser effigy also is one of the first to display the bascinet and like the jupon the changes from the mailed head cover overlapped in date. The carver maintained the fiction of the mailed head covering by carving a round top to the bascinet which was sometimes worn under the great helm until that was discarded in warfare. By 1360 the bascinet was well established and became pointed or fluted as seen on the effigy at Penmynydd (G208).

Gardner cites the effigies at Bunbury (G2) and Meriden (G172) as the final development of the Class II style with richly decorated jupon, jewelled hip belt and trimmed bascinet before the introduction of plate armour. Others of the same class type are Barmston (G195) and Layer Marney (G8).

From 1400 the bascinet became a means of decoration. In the de Vere effigy (above) the bascinet is plain and has only a narrow band where the aventail is attached. This band gradually became wider and fatter and the plain surface provided scope for decoration. This change can be seen by observing the band on the bascinet of Sir Hugh Calverley at Bunbury (G2, 1393) which has a decorated crown but a plain band and comparing it to the rich broad band round the rim of the bascinet on William, Lord Roos at Bottesford (G103, 1414).

Figure 86. The 1370 tomb of Thomas de Vere in Bures, St Stephen (G29). The jupon has a star carved on the breast. The jewelled hip belt and the aventail hung on the pointed bascinet are classical features of the early transition phase of Gardner's Class II. The alabaster is Chellaston and most likely carved in the Trent Valley delivery being by ship via the Colne estuary probably to Wivenhoe. This tomb was in Colne Priory until the dissolution. Photo: Janet State.

The approach of the effigies of Class III is heralded by one of the last in Class II – that of Sir Samson (Sampson) Strelley in Strelley Notts (G25, *circa* 1410–1415). His wife Elizabeth displays the new fashion in headdresses which has two tightly bound cauls at the side of the head as shown in the photograph attached to G25. 1415 sees the transition from jupon and mail to plate armour. Sir Samson has a bascinet but the camail attached to it is not carved and ends across the shoulder in what appears to be a plate. There is a scalloped jupon but it too appears to be placed under a steel breastplate. On the whole the effigy is unsatisfactory as if the carver being used to soft jupons is coming to terms with the new plate armour but has not mastered the subject. By 1419 the camail was being discarded and this is missing from the Green tomb at Lowick (G122) although it is suggested that it is beneath the gorget by the lower end showing.

The Class III armour of 1420 onward is one in which plate dominates. One of the first changes was the gorget which was designed to rest on the shoulder and cover the neck. At Lowick (G122) the gorget is narrow across the shoulders and comes up high on the chin in a shaped curve to deflect a blow to the head. It can be seen again at Ashwellthorpe (G121) from about the same date. Later the gorget is merged with the breastplate and the jupon and surcoat disappear as seen on the effigy at Tong (G148, 1451). With the jupon gone the thighs are protected by plates usually held by leather straps (lames) – the whole is called a fauld. The effigy at Dennington (G162, 1441) has particularly well carved lames and a narrow fauld and may be linked to Weobley (G92, 1437 or later). In fact the Dennington effigy has a number of changes including shaped elbow-cops, pauldrons and poleyns and is a very good example of early plate armour.

Figure 87. The elbow-cops (shown) are decoratively shaped, the pauldron (overlapping plates which protect the upper arm but allow the arm to be raised) is indicated but the means of articulation was omitted (this would emerge later) and the poleyns (knee-cops) are hinged so that the knee can be bent. Photo: the author.

The knights of the mid-15th century wore a salet rather than a bascinet. One of the first was the effigy at Merevale (G173, 1440), but by 1445 the salet was appearing more often. The undated effigy at Beaumaris (G209), Kidderminster (G186, 1445) and Willoughby on the Wolds (G138, 1448) all show forms of this helmet and this continues to 1470 with Puddletown (GNP27).

Figure 88. The Willoughby on the Wolds effigy of 1448 (G138) showing the salet with orle. The salet was a light fighting helmet which was brought down low over the neck. Photo: John Allen.

Figure 89. The decorated salet at Melbury Sampford, Dorset. A very nicely carved effigy with a gorget and the Yorkist collar prominent. The 16th and 17th dates for the two monuments at this place, has to be incorrect as no carver would carve a Yorkist collar after 1485. © Mike Searle.

The effigies of Melbury Sampford (G80 and G81) show salets (above) of a unique style. These two monuments in alabaster and Purbeck marble are duplicates and clearly date from *circa* 1470 despite the suggested dates of 1547 and 1647 which is nonsense. The effigies at Kidderminster and Beaumaris are recorded as having salets with visors which are shown in the raised position.

Before 1440 it was rare for effigies to be depicted without a helmet of some kind. As the next decade progressed helmeted effigies became increasingly rare so that by 1455 mainly bare-headed knights are shown. The Melbury Sampford knights (above) are one exception. The Cheadle knights (G46 and G47) are duplicates except that G46 has a bascinet and orle and G47 is bare headed (there are other detail differences). The local historians place the date of G46 at 1454 and G47 at 1460 which is in keeping with the change in style. The few remaining effigies which display helmets on the head show a salet but by 1485 this was over. However, the martial aura of the departed was maintained by the head resting on a great helm sometimes with crest then only used in the tilt. Few if any of those depicted by then actually took part in jousts but it was good for the image.

The period to the end of the Wars of the Roses (1485–1487) saw the final evolution of the Gothic armour. With much decoration on parts such as the elbow-cops, pauldrons and the faulds. This can be seen on the armour of Sir John Savage at Macclesfield (G49, *circa* 1480)

Observers looking at effigies carved in first quarter of the 16th century may note that the carver has taken liberties with the pauldron. The knight on the Tower of London tomb (G115), Malpas (G53) and Ratcliffe on Soar (G136) have pauldrons which show no signs of laminations such that if worn as shown the knight would be unable to raise his arm. This can be compared with those of a century later where the carver has taken care to show laminations hinged to permit the plates to telescope. In many cases the underlying leather is shown by scallops protruding from under the laminations.

Figure 90. The pauldron on the effigy of Ralph Sacheverell at Ratcliffe on Soar *circa* 1534 (G136). What appears as plate armour has only faint lines representing the lamination and the cut-out under the armpit gives the impression of a solid piece which in reality would have been near impossible to manufacture. In this state the knight would be unable to raise his arm. This is a Parker of Burton tomb and it is clear that the understanding of some functions of the armour was deficient although the effigy is well carved. (Photo: John Allen)

Later effigies from this carver were better formed. This may well have been copied from an earlier workshop as the Malpas tomb (G53) and that one in the Tower of London chapel (G115) carved by the Harpur and Moorecock workshop some 10 years earlier show the same error. Photo: John Allen.

Figure 91. The pauldron on effigy of Henry Sacheverell *circa* 1625 (R4). The plate armour is cut away showing the laminations which would be hinged along the edge of the pauldron so that as the arm was raised they folded in. The elbow has the same arrangement with a decorated elbow cop. Although almost certainly a Burton carved effigy it shows that the workshop had achieved a good standard of armour carving towards the end of the industry in that town. Henry's son who commissioned the tomb is attired in a similar fashion. Photo: John Allen.

However, the laxness in carving of the pauldron was also evident in the effigies of Sir John Savage at Macclesfield (1470, G49) and Sir Ralph Fitz Herbert at Norbury (1483, G62).

Summary of some styles:

Feature	**Dates**	**Monument**
Camail	1349	G10, G21, G22, G29, G104, G189, G208, M1
Cross-legged	1337–1361	A137, A160, G1, G18, G28
Orle	1370–1481	A234, G103, G121, G140, G158, G190, G191, GNP51, GNP52, GNP53, GNP81, GNP101
Pointed bascinet	1350–1425	G21, G23, G103, G104, G121, G189, G188, G208, GNP44, GNP45, S103
Round-top bascinet	1320–1350	G10
Salet	1445–1470	G80, G93, G138, G186, GNP27, G209
Ihc(s) Nazare (*see* below)	1360–1440	G8, G57, G103, G105, G122, G140, G158, G188, G191, G195, GNP44, GNP51, GNP52, GNP55,

IHC(S) Nazare. A feature of 15th century effigies is the presence of mottos. This may have a basis in tourneying and the most common is often an abbreviation of Jesus of Nazareth (Ihc Nazaren or Ihc Nazare) sometimes shortened to Ihc. This is a transliteration of the Greek J, E and S misunderstood in the conversion to Latin as the Greek letter eta and Latin H being similar. It is mainly found on the upper edge of the bascinet or orle. A number of alabaster effigies have this as indicated in the lists contained in Appendix E. The practice is believed to date back to the 12th century and such an inscription is believed to be a protection against danger. The practice did not survive long in the 15th century in England.

Armour on alabaster tombs is worthy of more detailed research than can be covered by this Appendix.

Appendix M

Alabaster Formations and the English Quarries and Mines (with a brief word on Continental sources)

Contents;

Introduction

The geological sequence of the formation of the gypsum and alabaster beds is complex and for more details refers to the BGS report of 1996. The section following gives a simplified description.

Keuper marl or Keuper waterstone is the obsolete name for the multiple layers of mudstones and siltstones of the Triassic period. The common name is included in the Mercian Mudstones Group but variations of this will be apparent. The deposits are generally featureless and contain few fossils and the colour can be red, green or grey. The extent of the deposit is shown below and generally follows the river valleys.

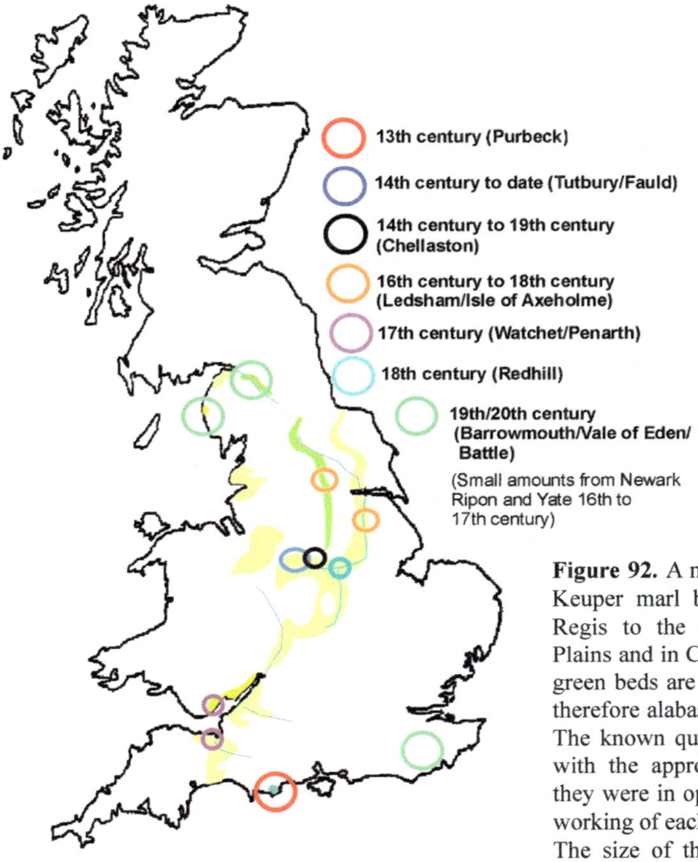

Figure 92. A map of England showing the Keuper marl beds in yellow from Lyme Regis to the Tees and in the Cheshire Plains and in Cumbria and Lancashire. The green beds are Permian marl. Gypsum and therefore alabaster is not found universally. The known quarries and mines are shown with the approximate centuries in which they were in operation. More details of the working of each centre are discussed below. The size of the circles has no relevance. Drawn by the author.

The Mercian Mudstone Group (named after the Saxon East Midlands kingdom) in which the largest deposits can be found, has been subject to a number of sub-classifications over the years for which reference to the 1996 BGS report is recommended. The report settles on the following:

- Blue Anchor formation
- Cropwell Bishop formation (CBp). This includes the Newark and Tutbury gypsum beds within which alabaster is found covering Derbyshire, Leicestershire and Nottingham
- Edwalton formation
- Gunthorpe formation
- Radcliffe formation
- Sneinton formation

All the mudstone formations produce siltstone or sandstone but only CBp has gypsum.

The detailed analysis of the Cropwell Bishop plate (CBp) would indicate that the deposits east of the River Soar have sporadic layers of Newark and Tutbury gypsum but in many places these have only gypsum in nodular form rather than seams. This may account for why workable alabaster was only found at Redhill at the far westernmost edge of the beds those further east being only worked for plaster.[1,2] From Chellaston westward to the Needwood Forest which includes Tutbury and Fauld the deposits is Tutbury gypsum ranging in thickness from a few metres to a maximum of some eight metres.

The Permian marl beds are some 50 million years older than the Mercian mudstones and gypsum was formed when the lands was covered by a shallow sea. Gypsum is found in Ripon, Yorkshire where the stone has dissolved leaving voids. Further south near Pontefract, gypsum is found which contains deposits of alabaster. The Eden Valley contains deposits of gypsum which are still being worked but any alabaster is of poor quality and not used for carving.

In 1984 Firman noted that the selenite output in Great Britain was in the order of 3 to 4 million tons per year but only a few hundred tons could be described as alabaster and most of this rendered to plaster. He observes that its present rarity must be reconciled with its apparent abundance in the past.

Notes:

1. Gypsum (hydrated calcium sulphate or $CaSO_4.2H_2O$) and anhydrite ($CaSO_4$) was one of the salts formed as the Permian Sea underwent periods of desiccation (140 to 280m years ago). These were buried by younger sediments especially in river valleys. Pressure at depth drove off the water molecules within the gypsum crystals and the anhydrous form of calcium sulphate, anhydrite was formed. This can be reversed by uplift in the presence of water. If the reaction takes place slowly, larger defined crystals can form gypsum. However, if the reaction is relatively rapid, a microcrystalline, massive form develops and this appears as alabaster.

   Alabaster formed only where water was present within the bedrock such as river valleys.

   Observation: In the BGS maps the extent of the Mercian Mudstone Group is evident and an overlay of the known alabaster quarries and mines shows all the deposits are river or sea facing. In the case of Redhill the deposits are associated with the uplift caused along the Normanton Hills Fault the section on the BGS map 141 clearly showing the Newark and Tutbury gypsum having been raised from much deeper layers.
2. A Saga of British Industry 1959 is the history of British Plasterboards who owned most of the mines in the East Midlands. R P Cafferata, one of the founding members, mined gypsum at Beacon Hill near Newark from 1858 and later at Hawton. Both these sites were open quarries. No trace can be found of Fellow's Wheatley workings which, if they existed, would be further to the east near Collingham.

The following section summarise the history of alabaster working by location in rough chronological order:

The Needwood Forest and Staffordshire beds

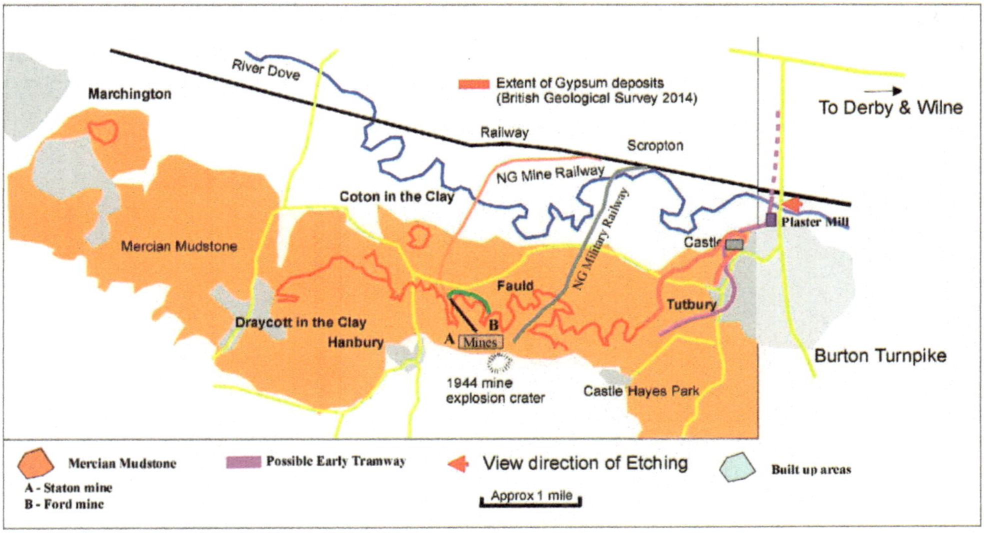

Figure 93. Needwood Forest alabaster beds. Drawn by the author.

First reports:	1160 at Tutbury
First use:	Tutbury church west door arch and footings
Exploitation:	Duchy of Lancaster for royal tombs (*see* Camden 1911)
Date of first effigy:	1330 Gloucester Cathedral tomb of Edward II[1]
Quarries/mines:	Tutbury Hill, Draycott in the Clay, Marchington, Coton in the Clay, Coton under Hanbury (later Fauld) and Castle Hayes[2] (Burton on Trent is mentioned but a search has not revealed any location in that area except for a place called Tatenhill which does not appear to have any workable alabaster, despite Llewellyn's claims on page 200 of his book)[3]
Last quarry/mine:	Fauld (still working in 2013 but not producing alabaster)[4]
Peak years:	Early 16th century to later 19th century
Last use:	The Breakers Mansion, Rhode Island, USA (1895) and statue of *Adam* (1938) and *Jacob and the Angel* (1940) both by Jacob Epstein. The altarpiece (reredos) in the chapel at Chatsworth House is recorded as being sourced from Castle Hayes and carved in Heanor in 1694.[5,6] However blocks were still be

	obtained in 1951 – *see* text below. In 2014 a block was obtained by James Elliott for the new altar in Leicester Cathedral – *see* B195 and X41.
Major event:	Munitions explosion in Fauld Mine 1944
Carvers:	Mainly Burton on Trent – *see* carver list
Colour:	Red/brown and white with brown veining
Maps:	Plan of estate at Fauld 1840, Stoke and Staffordshire County Records Office accession No D5226/7. Also 1843: D3453/7/18. Lease of the railway 1899: 4996/C/4

Figure 94. Fauld alabaster extracted 2015. Photo: the author.

Notes:

1. An effigy in Hanbury church (G28) has been identified with John de Hanbury (died 1300) and is in Staffordshire alabaster but there is uncertainty as to the date of carving and may well be *circa* 1340. The Gloucester monuments (G9) are the earliest confirmed use for monumental carving.
2. The reference to Castle Hayes (or Hay) needs some explaining. A hamlet by that name exists south-west of Tutbury but no quarry is evident here. The land above Fauld Mine was known as Upper Castle Hayes and the reference may relate to a side quarry off the main Fauld workings. However, William Burton mentions Castle Hay 'Park' so some doubt remains.
3. This is not to be confused with Totternhoe stone which is a clunch too soft for exterior use and quarried close to the River Lea and is of the chalk family. Tombs at Sparsholt and Sonning, Bury St Edmunds, Lullingstone and Wooton Wawen are all in clunch. *See* diagram below.
4. Allan Baker in 'The Narrow Gauge' No 164 Spring 1999 has a full description of the

mines in the 19th century. John C Staton exploited the mine (A) at Fauld in 1838 and had acquired the rights from Thomas Orm. There was another mine (B) nearby owned by Peter Ford a sculptor and stone mason from Uttoxeter. A disused section of the latter mine was used for munitions storage from 1937. A map in 'The Narrow Gauge' page 4, shows six adits, one at Fauld, three at Ford's and two new ones for the munitions storage. *See also* the *Scropton Tramway and Fauld Gypsum Mines* in two parts by Allan C Baker.

5. For similar blocks in Holkham Hall Norfolk *see* under Redhill.
6. The Henry Moore database attributes the chapel to Caius Gabriel Cibber *circa* 1688–1691.

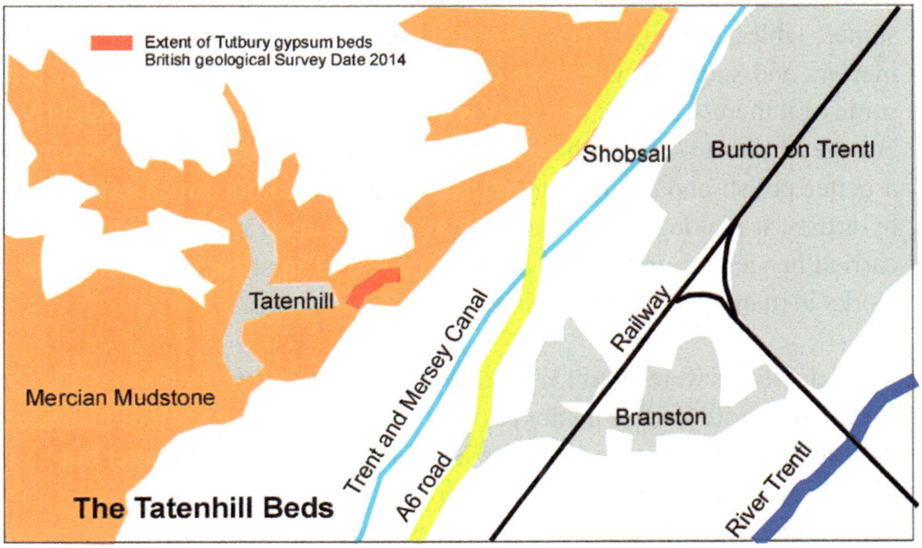

Figure 95. The Tatenhill beds. Drawn by the author.

History

Despite the lack of modern records (*see* first diagram above), alabaster was probably found during excavations for Tutbury Castle in the 12th century and the suitability for carving was instrumental in its use in the Norman doorway of the adjacent church where it was protected from the weather. Tutbury Museum reports that the footings of the church are on alabaster which is an unsuitable material for this use. In addition the museum reports an ancient mine adit into the hill mound.

Little is known about further use until the lands became part of the estates of the Duchy of Lancaster when alabaster was acquired for the royal masons for the tomb of Edward II in Gloucester Cathedral *circa* 1330. The success of this caused further investigation along the Forest of Needwood ridge and the effigy in Hanbury church dating from *circa* 1340 is probably in alabaster from Coton under Hanbury quarry (later known as Fauld). Firman states that the Hanbury effigy being Sir John Hanbury, dates from 1303 but other sources, mainly Cheetham dispute this. The Staffordshire quarries became the main source of stone for the Burton workshops leading to the following entry Robert Plot's *The Natural History of Staffordshire,* 1686. After a discourse on wattle and daub plaster and flooring on page 174, he states:

> This sort of alabaster, yet of a courser sort, is found also at Coton under Hanbury (Fauld) and there has it been dug at Draycott in the Clay: indeed the whole bank of red marl between the Forest or Chase of Needwood and the river Dove from Marchington to Tutbury has alabaster in it. But that at Castle Hayes (*sic*) is incomparably the best of which they make gravestones, tables, paving stones, chimney pieces etc and in smaller things: mortars and salts and they turn candlesticks, plates and fruit dishes. In some of it there are veins of a dirty red colour which are yet not unsightly but they have a sort which is harder and stronger than the rest bearing a better polish and finely watered with a bluish colour much esteemed by artists, it making as good a work as marble upon which account it is carried hence at a great charge and made use of in some of the choicest works in many parts of the nation.

It is claimed the seams were 10 to 15ft thick (*Nottingham and its Region*, 1966). Thomas Cox (1738) later wrote 'In this manor (Coton) is found a coarse form of alabaster'. He also observed that alabaster was also quarried in Fradswell near Uttoxeter but '... it was only used for plaster and ceilings in needlework (*sic*) houses'.

In 1984 Firman stated that in 1440 seventy carts of alabaster were sold from the east tower of Tutbury Castle at 9d a load but fails to disclose from where this information was obtained. He goes on to observe that according to Sommerville in 1960 the tower was being rebuilt at the time and the alabaster was most likely dug from the foundations. He also notes that Stebbing Shaw in 1801, quoting from a survey of Tutbury dating from 1563, said that Tutbury Castle was situated on a round rock of alabaster. Firman did not expand on the extent of alabaster at Tutbury but since then (1984) the British Geological Survey (BGS) has updated its maps and gypsum bearing mudstone is now shown encompassing the castle mound.

In his 1622 *Description of Leicestershire*, William Burton (1575 to 1645) writes 'Within his Lordship (of Burton on the Wolds) have been found quarries of alabaster and white stone serving for cutters and picture makers for statues, tombs and proportions (figures) but not altogether so hard or clear as that stone which is gotten in Castle-Hey Park (*sic*) near Tutbury or the quarries at Falde (Fauld) near adjoining'. He goes on enigmatically to say '... where in a mount called *Nantmorehull* (I) myself have a rock of the same stone'. This location has yet to be identified. What most authors omit is the preamble. This reads 'Burton, in the Hundred of Goscote upon the side of Nottinghamshire'.

The precise location of Castle Hay is difficult to determine. Edward Richardson writing about 1850 in the *Archaeological Journal*, 'At Fauld, near Tutbury, not only are there pits in full work yielding every variety, but pits long since abandoned are in many places observable, extending to the summit of the ridge on which Hanbury stands. This slope is called The Castle Haye and extends north-east from Hanbury towards Tutbury. It forms part of the Duchy of Lancaster.' He goes on to observe, 'In the times of Philip and Mary (mid-16th century) the park of Castle Haye has been disparked and the herbage kept for the King's use. The compass thereof exceeded four miles and in it were plaster pits, the rent of which with the herbage by the year was £5 5s, a considerable sum in those days'.

Llewellyn attributes the 'lordship's' quarries to Burton on Trent, but no trace of alabaster quarries here can be found. In fact the Hundred of Goscote, Leicestershire contains only one Burton and that is Burton on the Wolds. Thomas Spencer in 1894 confirms that the quarries were indeed at Burton on the Wolds near Barrow on Soar and British Gypsum currently mine gypsum close by making this quite possible. Discussion on these Charnwood beds is continued in the next section. Firman, too identifies the Burton on the Wolds area but the extent of the deposits he illustrates have been extended east by the BGS maps and Google Earth (not available to Firman) discloses what may be workings close to the village. These are under investigation.

In his 1622 publication William Burton dedicates the book to George Villiers, 1st Earl of Buckingham and it is significant that he adds his address which is 'Falde (Fauld) near Tutbury Staffordshire, 30th October 1622'. Burton's book may well have been written some 18 years before publication as a previous preamble was dated 1604. *See* note B98 for further details of William Burton.

William Camden in his 1592 *Britannia* refers to the alabaster of the region. He says '... the Trent which continues on its course eastwards till it meets the River Tame from the south in conjunction with which it runs through places abounding in alabaster to the north, that it may soon receive the River Dove and almost encompass Burton (on Trent), formerly a town, remarkable for its alabaster works'. Llewellyn has chosen to assume that Camden was speaking about Burton's decline in the alabaster industry but the words can be taken to refer to Burton's status as a town. In 1592 Burton was still active and the London alabaster industry had yet to take off.

Firman states that the alabaster slabs for the chapel in Chatsworth House were quarried from Castle Hayes in 1694 and carved in Heanor, Derbyshire (by Samuel Watson although the design may be by Cibber) quoting R Christian 'The Alabaster Industry in the Trent valley 1959', *Derbyshire Countryside* Vol 24 pages 14 to 16 as the source.

There is a report of marl beds at Eastcliff, Tatenhill, south-west of Burton (*see* diagram above). *A History of the Parish of Tatenhill* by Sir Reginald Hardy 1907 records that outcrops of gypsum can be seen where the marl has been eroded by water over the centuries but fails to confirm that alabaster is present. He refers to the alabaster trade in Burton but indicates that the source is Tutbury and Fauld. He also refers to the trade still flourishing in 1722 but no evidence for this claim is given. A statement made by Sir Oswald Moseley made *circa* 1850 to Edward Richardson is odd. He said: 'The last person to have a works there (Burton), for toys rather than effigies and tombs was named Burnett who had a manager by the name of Ineley from Suffolk. After 20 years the business failed and was taken over by a man named Cunningham. He moved to Derby in 1820. I think the carving of effigies ceased during the Civil War'.

Farey, in his 1811 book on Derbyshire, noted that Fauld was active and sold alabaster at 10/- or 12/- per ton. He goes on to say that Castle Hay was working, as was Row-Bank at Coton and Hound Hill at Marchington. He also mentions Horninglow but this is almost certainly Horninglow St the centre of Burton carving although the *History of Staffordshire* states that alabaster was mined in 1546 from a pit north of Horninglow which produced sufficient for a chimney piece for Sir William Paget's house and that it was still being dug into the 18th century. No independent confirmation of this can be found.

Firman quoting Trafford-Wynne's writing in 1907 observes that 18 blocks of 15 ton each have been obtained from Fauld (234 cu ft^2) and that in 1951 Bray reported that the average size of block obtained was 4 tons going on to say that 900 tons were produced in that year. Firman when commenting on the alabaster at Ledsham, Yorkshire observed that he estimated the minimum size of block for *two* medieval effigies would be 6ft x 3ft x 4ft (72cu ft or 4.5tons).[7] It is probable that only Fauld and Chellaston could produce such blocks until the end of the 17th century. In 1984 Firman observed that Fauld was by then (1951) the only quarry/mine able to produce alabaster even in small quantities.

These authors all underpin the importance of the Staffordshire alabaster deposits.

The British Geological Survey states that at Fauld the gypsum bed averages 2.5m thick and is some 65 to 70m below the green marl layer. The Bagots borehole south-west of Fauld notes the gypsum at 37m and with a seam thickness of 6m. The survey data does not distinguish between alabaster and gypsum.

Some of the Fauld deposits were developed in the 19th century by Peter Ford, a sculptor from Uttoxeter. He worked on the restoration of Hanbury church. His main customer for alabaster was the British Alabaster Bowl Co whose main products were trinkets, ornaments and memorial tablets but invoices exist for alabaster sent to Earley & Co of Dublin. Ford's mine was taken over by BPB in 1936. In 1948 the tenants of the Duchy of Lancaster presented Princess Elizabeth with a lampshade made from Fauld alabaster as a gift for her wedding. The British Alabaster Bowl Company traded at Weston on Trent and closed in 1941. It is believed they may have used Fauld alabaster.

Also present was the firm of J C Staton and Co. From small beginnings in 1838 the firm moved to Shrobnall. In 1870 they too took out a lease on a quarry at Fauld and drove an adit into the hill. Staton was acquired by BPB in 1935.

Notable alabaster extractions include blocks mined for the Vanderbilt's mansion called The Breakers on Rhode Island, USA and for Jacob Epstein – *see* below.

In 1889 the Fauld Quarry/Mine was connected to the North Staffordshire Railway at Scropton by a 3ft narrow-gauge railway described in detail in *The Narrow Gauge No 164* (1999) and *The Scropton Tramway and Fauld Gypsum Mines* of 2010 both written by Allan C Baker.

The Staton mine entrance was depicted *circa* 1950 with a diesel locomotive and three blocks of what must be alabaster since gypsum would not be removed in block form. Diesels were introduced in 1933. The size is not easy to estimate but the nearest block appears to be some 5ft x 5ft x 4ft. The destination of blocks is unknown. The photo can be viewed on the Fauld Mine and Tutbury Museum website.

Figure 96. Blocks of alabaster stand in Scropton Sidings, North Staffordshire Railway on the 18th June 1894 awaiting transfer to Liverpool for shipment to New York. The wagons were loaned by the MR. The sizes of the blocks can be gauged by the size of the nearest block stencilled on the side which is approximately 14ft x 4ft x 3ft.[8] Only Fauld was able to produce such large blocks at this time. The North Staffordshire Railway opened its line through Scropton in 1848. The blocks are labelled E.K. & Co, New York[9] but the identity of this firm has not been established. They are believed to be stone importers. There were 18 blocks in all each weighing 15 tons. Photo: Richard Keene, Burton on Trent, 1894 now in the Tutbury Museum.

Figure 97. A train emerges from the Fauld Mine in 1950. The wagons carry large blocks of alabaster but it has not been possible to identify to whom they were destined. Photo: Tutbury Museum with permission of the Fauld Mine.

Figure 98. The Staton workings *circa* 1890 with the mine entrance beyond the shed in the distance. The loco is a Bagnall 0-4-0 of 1890 which at the time ran without cab. Photo: Tutbury Museum.

One as yet unexplained issue is a picture in the possession of the small museum in Tutbury. The picture is reproduced below:

Figure 99. The picture is clearly Tutbury as the river and castle on the hill are unmistakable. The drawing shows a loaded wagon being hauled by a horse over a bridge whose decking is flat in keeping with that required by a tramway. Indeed an observer standing today at the vantage point from which the artist made the drawing will see the piers of such a bridge which did carry a standard gauge railway from Tutbury station sidings to the plaster mill at Tutbury but was rebuilt to take locomotives. The picture is by H Warren (1794–1879).[10] Picture: Tutbury Museum.

Alan Baker in his 1999 article on the railways in the Tutbury area says that a water-powered cotton-mill existed on the left of the bridge built between 1781 and 1790 but may well have been on the site of an earlier mill from the times of Henry VII. This mill was latterly owned by the Lyon family trading as the company Fine Spinners but had ceased production in 1888 but not before that it had built a half mile branch from the North Stafford Railway probably in 1848. The branch was horse worked and the picture (Figure 99) might be from that era. In 1890 the mill was purchased by Staton and converted to mill plaster. In 1899 the branch was strengthened to take locomotives and it is likely the bridge was rebuilt then. The plaster mill is shown on the diagram at the start of this section.

The gypsum mill closed in 1968 and was demolished. The big wheel which drove the drum is shown below.

As stated elsewhere the records of Holkham Hall say clearly that some of their alabaster came from Castle Hay but the cartage contracts only call for collection from the Burton Turnpike suggesting that the quarry delivered the stone to that location. At a time when transportation was a charge on the customer the inference is that the quarry had a means of carrying stone loads to what is now Hatton but how this was accomplished is not known.

Referring to the picture the current A511 road bridge was built in 1817 replacing an earlier bridge a short distance to the west whereupon the old bridge was demolished. The aspect of Warren's picture (Figure 99) would suggest he was standing on the old bridge which together with the shape of the wagon might suggest the presence of a wagonway earlier than 1848. This remains a puzzle to be solved.

In 2012 with the discovery of Richard III's body in a Leicester car park it was decided to bury him in the cathedral for which the existing altar had to be removed. A new altar (X41) was designed and made by stonemason James Elliott (B195) and alabaster was obtained in 2014 from the Staton mine at Fauld. This was probably the largest block obtained from the mine in the last 50 years and indicates that veined alabaster can still be obtained. It also provides irrefutable evidence of the colour and form of the Staffordshire selenite.

Notes:

7. Assumes a density of 143lb/cu ft.
8. These are huge. The Vanderbilt blocks of 1894–1895 were 168cu ft or 10 tons. It begs the question as to whether Trafford-Wynn had got his sums right. A weight of 15 tons would not present the main railways with any difficulty but the narrow gauge railway from the mine would struggle with such a weight. *The History of the British Plasterboard Co* states that 18 blocks were produced and were 'moved by pony and wagon' indicating that the blocks were moved to Scropton by road. The photograph below shows Jack Key cutting the alabaster rock face in Fauld Mine in 1945 showing how the blocks were produced.

9. One side is labelled 'Roussel, New York' and the other 'E K Co, New York'. The columns in The Breakers mansion can be viewed in Figure 119. On the 17th October 2016 The Breakers identified E K as Ellen and Kitson masonry contractors for the mansion.
10. Henry Warren became president of the Royal Institute of Artists in Water Colour in 1839.

Figure 100. A miner at Fauld cuts an alabaster block from the face *circa* 1945.
Photo: the author's collection.

1. The Charnwood beds (Burton on the Wolds, Leicestershire)

First reports:	1592 at Burton on the Wolds
First use:	Not yet known
Exploitation:	Mining or quarrying in the 16th century
Date of first effigy:	Not known
Quarries/mines:	Plasterpit south of the village and at Burton Bandalls
Last quarry/mine:	Not yet known
Peak years:	1592 to 1623, but dates uncertain
Last use:	Possibly 1834
Major event:	Two killed in roof falls
Carvers/miners:	William Pratt, Edward Stewart and Gulielmus Werall (otherwise known as Black Will)
Colour:	White

The BGS geological maps of the area show a small patch of CBp at Burton Bandalls (near Cotes, Leicestershire) which extends north and south of Burton on the Wolds. There are records of gypsum mining here. Google Earth discloses a pit and spoil heaps south of the village close to Burton Hall and two other possible locations, one behind a barn known as Plasterpit. The Burton Bandalls site was later a brickyard and is now a natural burial ground. These are shown on the diagram below.

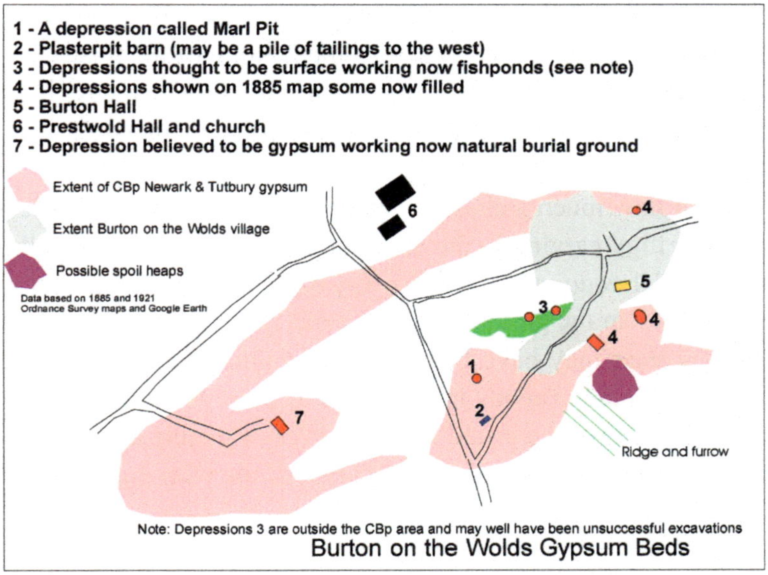

Figure 101. Burton on the Wolds, Leicestershire. Drawn by the author.

Leland in 1543 mentions 'fair quarries of alabaster stone four or five miles from Leicester'. He fails to be more precise. However, Holinshed's Chronicles written in 1579 states '... if marble will not serve then we have the finest alabaster that may elsewhere be had as about St David's of Wales also near to Beau Manor which is about four or five miles from Leicester and taken to be the best although there are diverse quarries hereof beyond the Trent, as in Yorkshire and fully as good but whose names at this time are out of my remembrance'. It clear that Leland had Beau Manor in mind. Beau Manor is close to Woodhouse Eaves and the Leicester Archaeological Society report finding alabaster in a dig at nearby Shelthorpe.

Reports elsewhere are considered to be confused with quartz. The works of William Burton (*see* B98 and the Needwood Section above) refer to alabaster being mined in Burton on the Wolds in 1604 and Burton's observations would seem to confirm the stone was used by 'Cutters and Picture makers for statues, tombs and proportions' although there are no indications as where these were located. The common pleas of

1512 record a dispute between the Neles of Prestwold and a farmer called Swillington for damage to his land which included Prestwold men loading eight cartloads of marl[1] and six cartloads of stone without permission. This indicates that extraction of minerals was established in early Tudor times. The Prestwold church records also indicate that on the 22nd July 1592 one Edward Stewart (or Steward), labourer, was digging deep into the earth when a movement of the earth dashed him to pieces and he was killed. The same fate befell William Pratt on 22nd June 1603. In 1614 Mattheus Gisbourne of Tutbury died in Burton and on the 1st May 1623 Gulielmus (William) Werall otherwise known as 'Black Will of the plasterpits' also died. None of the quarries appear large and the two accidents above may well relate to mining in which case it would almost certainly be a drift mine. The association with Tutbury with alabaster working and the plasterpits is strong.

It is not known how much alabaster was produced or to whom it was sold. There is no evidence of effigy carving in the area but picture makers may well relate to the carving of slabs which required less in the way of workshop facilities. It is significant that Prestwold church in the grounds of Prestwold Hall contained two tabletop tombs and that local alabaster may have been used. Certainly the sale brochure of Burton Hall in 1834 refers to the grounds having thick beds of alabaster and limestone '... to a great extent in parts of the estate which are very valuable and may be gotten at a moderate expense'. It is assumed that the location of the workings was known but not being worked.

For the above information I am indebted to Joan Shaw of Burton on the Wolds

Note:

1. Marl is a loose term defining a mixture of mudstone and calcium carbonate in the form of limestone. The mudstones of the CBp where formerly Keuper marl (e) and so the marl extracted might well be calcium sulphate in the form of gypsum in its crystallised form – alabaster.

2. The Derbyshire beds (Chellaston and Aston)

First reports:	1370 at Chellaston but may be much earlier
First use:	Tomb of the wife of John of Gaunt in old St Paul's, London *circa* 1370–1376
Exploitation:	Duchy of Lancaster which acquired the manor at Chellaston
Date of first effigy:	1376 St Paul's (lost in Great Fire of 1666)
Quarries/mines:	Alabaster Quarry, Woodlands, Pit Close, Leys, Aston Glebe (California), Chellaston Glebe, Parsons Pit and Chellaston Covert (*see also* note below)
Last quarry/mine:	Pit Close 1915

Peak years:	1370 to 1450 and 1850 to 1915
Last use:	Mackworth church furniture – *see* Appendix K
Major event:	The Fécamps purchase of 1414
Carvers:	Thomas Prentys and Robert Sutton, but much stone transferred to Nottingham for the kerver trade – *see* Appendix C
Colour:	Cream white, translucent pale yellow, pale pink, green later light brown veined like that of Staffordshire but paler

Note:

The BGS report of 1996 gives more details of the names of both quarries and mines and the dates of operation and a summary is given below:

Alabaster Quarry	Opened 1908, closed 1938, filled in 1938, owners H Forman and Son. The records of the Forman quarries are held in the archives at Kew cat No D4417.
Woodlands Clay Pit or Brickpits	The likely site of the 14th and 15th century workshops. The later quarry was in existence in 1918 and worked until 1938. Owners J Stapleford and, Chellaston Minerals Ltd.
Aston Brickyard	Opened 1931, closed *circa* 1940. Minerals mined as adits still visible in 1964.
Chellaston Mine	Unsure when opened, abandonment plans issued 1878
Weston on Trent Mine	No details of opening but abandoned in 1877. Owned by the Chellaston Mining Company.
Chellaston Glebe Mine	Unsure when opened, abandonment plans issued 1874. Includes Parsons Pit.
Aston Glebe (sometimes known as Aston No 1 or California).	Opened 1835, abandonment plans dated 1937. Part of this mine was known as The Duddles. Reported as owned by Pegg & Co.
Duddle Plantation	Believed to be an eastern extension of Aston Glebe reached by an inclined plane. Abandoned at same time.
Aston	This appears to be an unknown mine separate from the others as separate abandonment plans issued in 1879. Worked by John Stephens and Son and had its own tramway.
Aston Holme	No details but appears on the abandonment plans for 1904. Appears to have been a large mine close to Aston Brickyard which latterly broke into the adit.
Bellington Hill (north of Aston)	A small quarry working 1915.

History:
See Alabaster by John Young ISBN 0 90675. 3 18x 1990.

Alabaster was found close to the surface in the late 14th century. There are vague mentions of alabaster at Woodlands being extracted by monks but from which priory and when is unclear. The records of the Duchy of Lancaster indicate they were looking for other sources of alabaster following the discovery of the Staffordshire beds *circa* 1370. The BGS report records discovery, in 1850, of some wedge-shaped picks 8 to 12 ins long and the remains of an oaken ladder and an unmoved slab of sawn alabaster some 16ft below the surface. The report concludes that that this shows extensive earlier workings.

By the early 15th century mining was well established with the Sutton and Prentys workshops established nearby. The importance of Chellaston was highlighted by the Fécamp purchase of 1414 (reported in full in Appendix V) and the existing contract for the Lowick monuments of 1419. It is clear that Chellaston was one of the main suppliers to both Nottingham and Burton into the mid-16th century.

The records of mining of alabaster in Chellaston in the 17th and 18th century is fragmentary or totally absent (*see* Firman). It may well be that with Ledsham, Watchet and Fauld producing alabaster close to the centres of carving and with easier transport issues, the quarries at Chellaston was set aside. In the 19th century with both canals and railways close by, the commercial attractiveness of Chellaston again emerged. Glover states that alabaster was being extracted in 1829, the four proprietors being Sir George Crewe, Henry Orton, George Wotton and a perpetual curate in lieu of tythes. It is not stated for which purpose the stone was extracted but Glover states it was carried away to the potteries by canal so the assumption is for industry. However, during the Gothic Revival which preferred the fine white alabaster which Chellaston could provide mining for monuments again commenced. Smith's map of 1918 shows the workings at Chellaston mainly in an area known as Chellaston Covert. The BGS report also records that blocks 3ft thick and 10 to 11ft long were extracted by machine-driven wire saw with an average weight of 2 to 3 tons. The principal alabaster quarry in the later 19th and early 20th century was Foreman's quarry. This produced very fine white and translucent alabaster – *see* Mackworth church. Firman offers the opinion that this was not discovered earlier due to the thick overburden of glacial deposits which needed modern machinery to remove.

Chellaston is mentioned in Farey's 1811 book on the agriculture and minerals of Derbyshire. He reported that south east of the village were four working pits owned by Robert Wright, Gilbert Hutchinson and George Wooton (two). It was sold at 9/- per long ton (2400lbs) to the potters of Stoke being carted the mile and a half to Cuttlebridge Wharf on the Trent and Mersey Canal. Fine blocks of white alabaster were sold at 20/- per ton to the makers of alabaster ornaments. Further down the pile was the gypsum mixed with red and green earth which was sold at 7/- a ton for gypsum flooring. At the bottom was the fibrous gypsum sold at 2/- per ton for walls and paths. Farey makes reference to a pit at Aston and one at Adbaston and observes that these two and Chellaston are the only places in Derbyshire where gypsum is obtained.

The book Derbyshire (England) of 1817 written by Lyson has a paragraph on the quarries at Chellaston stating that much was raised for all manner of carving at 20s per ton. In 1800 some 800 tons of gypsum was raised of which 500 went to Staffordshire potters but this had risen to 1000 tons by 1817. He mentions Aston which produced only gypsum and Elvaston and Adbaston '... which for several years have been closed'.

The programme listing the exhibitors of stone products at the Great Exhibition of 1851 lists Joseph Hall of Chellaston showing alabaster products. Edward Richardson reports on investigations with a Mr Upton, the agent for Messrs Smith, into the Chellaston workings *circa* 1850–1851. He reports finding wedge-shaped iron picks 8 to 12 inches long, an oak ladder, S-hooks and a fine abandoned slab of alabaster of length 7ft 3 inches by 2ft 6 inches by 7 inches skilfully sawn and in sound condition.

As for Aston on Trent, there is evidence of some quarrying of alabaster in the 17th century by John Hunt (*circa* 1630). Richard Brown and Son announced the opening of an alabaster quarry in 1796 and these may be shown on the estate map of 1795. Humfrey Moore was paying rent for the quarries in 1809 and he built a tramway from Aston Hill to the Trent and Mersey Canal at near Hicken's Bridge. The tramway appears to have been constructed by Charles Holden for £500 but may not have been completed until 1812. A Samuel Storey was shown as 'working the quarries' in 1811. John Brookhouse (plasterer) and Joseph Johnson (coal merchant) appears to have leased the tramway in 1818 but it appears to have been derelict by 1825. The tramway was revived, extended and seems to have continued until just before the First World War, the gypsum (and alabaster) being carried down the canal to King's Mill where there was a plaster mill.

The Aston on Trent quarries which were working in 1909 are mainly, Glebe and Duddle Plantation. These were set aside by 1919 and only worked fitfully thereafter. The quarries were filled in by 1938. Smith records that much of the alabaster output of the Aston quarries what shipped by rail to Derby where it was used for ornaments, statuary and the production of electric light bowls. This would indicate that the alabaster was in small pieces and not the large blocks which could be obtained from Chellaston alabaster quarry.

Other examples of fine Derbyshire alabaster are the green and white alabaster used in reredos church of the English Martyrs, Alexandra Park, Manchester, the lounge of Windsor Hotel, Victoria St, Westminster, Buxton new baths and the lectern of All Saints Church, Mackworth, Derbyshire.

An extract from *The History of the County of Derby Part 2* is interesting. At Chellaston there are 890 acres of good corn land with a marl substratum in which fine alabaster is found. Many thousands of tons are conveyed by canal. The alabaster quarries are in the lands owned by Sir George Crewe, Henry Orton, George Wotton and the curacy of the church in the form of tithes.

The book goes on to say that the church was once paved in alabaster and that when it was re-pewed *circa* 1813 the church warden took the slabs and paved his stable with them.

The *Lost Leicestershire Industry* by J A Daniell and *A Brief History of Whitwick* by Sheila Smith, pages 30 and 31 have details of the alabaster ornament industry.

These publications reveal an interesting side use of Chellaston alabaster. In about 1836 a new industry became established in North Leicestershire. Old directories refer to the existence of a number of Spa Ornamental Manufactories. Locally the products from these were known as 'baubles' or 'bawbles'. Loosely translated a bauble is something decorative but which has no practical use. Although the raw material was alabaster from Chellaston, this term was never recognised and the locals used the word 'spa'. Why the small towns of Whitwick, Thringstone and Coleorton should adopt this industry is unclear as there was no natural market nor was the industry close to the source of materials. Daniell suggests the trade was imported by Derbyshire men relocating to Whitwick in the early 19th century but firm evidence is missing.

The baubles were sold to Mount St Bernard's Abbey but many were sent for sale at the seaside amongst which was Weston super Mare, Bridlington and Great Yarmouth. Extraordinarily, crates were sent to America each year which included at least one to Niagara Falls. The crates left Whitwick by rail but it was not unknown for one or more of the proprietors to take a barrow to a seaside resort.

Bauble makers are also recorded in Loughborough. In 1841 Thomas Spink was so named and later John Cunningham whose business did not close until 1863. A Henry More was recorded in Wards End, Loughborough. In the community of Whitwick a William Rooms and James Peters described their occupation as ornamental spa manufacturers and it is known that at least one of these came from Derbyshire. Some carving is recorded in Shardlow and Barrow on Trent both in Derbyshire and this may well have been the original centre of bauble production.

The alabaster was carried in block by horse and cart from Chellaston, cut into rectangular pieces in the workshop and then turned on a lathe. The object was finished with candle wax (reputedly from candle 'tailings' from the local church) and polished with fuller's earth.

Figure 102: Leicestershire 'baubles'. Photo: Permission from Martin Bird.

Amongst the items made were candlesticks, jugs, vases, ink stands, spill holders, egg cups and 'views'. These were spa peep-shows (Stanhopes) in which a picture or engraving was mounted in a recess in the spa which was carved and polished to provide a magnifying lens.

When the demand for plaster increased, pits were reopened near Chellaston and the Woodlands Quarry was shown on the 1835 one-inch ordnance survey map. In 1857, Pegg Harper and Co of Derby and Robert Meakin of Chellaston and its offices, engine houses, shafts etc., together with land and mines, were leased by Winterbottom to the Derby Plaster Co. In 1919 they were sold as the Glebe or California Mine to the Gotham Co Ltd (later BPB), together with the plaster mill, its engine, dynamo rooms, stone dressing sheds, head to mine shaft, winding house, kiln house with four large plaster and cement kilns and several other rooms. An attempt was made to revive the alabaster trade but it was found that large blocks could no longer be extracted and the activity died out in 1936, the plaster trade being transferred to Gotham.

All the quarries were filled in later in the 20th century.

3. The Yorkshire beds

First reports:	*Circa* 1570 at Ledsham near Pontefract
First use:	Earliest known tomb is that of Archbishop Sandys in Southwell Minster carved *circa* 1588
Exploitation:	York carvers exploited the beds
Date of first effigy:	1588 Southwell Minster
Quarries/mines:	Fairburn, Fairburne or Fierborn, Hillam, Buttercrambe, Scrayingham, Ledston
Last quarry/mine:	Still working in 1860 but alabaster output small and last extracted 1829

Peak years:	*circa* 1580 to mid-17th century
Last use:	Not known
Major event:	Opening of tunnel to link to canal *circa* 1822
Carvers:	Not known but might well be the York school (*see* B109)
Colour:	White with purple-red veining. The strata are Permian.

History:

Quarries at Buttercrambe are mentioned to have produced alabaster but there is no record of any carving from this source and all output appears to have put towards the making of plaster. Greenhill observes that the location may well be Scrayingham which is found on the Buttercrambe map, and where there are plaster pits on the east side of the Derwent.

As regards the Ledsham area, Vertue in 1742 (Walpole Society 1930) wrote (quoting Fuller):

> At Fairborne near Ledsham by Leeds are several quarries of alabaster – the finest is used for images (to be cut) and funeral monuments – for which are dug up pieces of a ton weight – sometimes two or three tons weight.

Firman observes that this establishes Ledsham as an alabaster source but comments that the blocks were small as compared with those obtained from Fauld (*see* estimates under Fauld above for block estimates). Nevertheless, based on these estimates, a 2 ton block would be sufficient for a single effigy as seen at Southwell (A17). Greenhill observes that plaster pits were shown on the map of Ledston about half a mile west of Ledsham.

Despite these respected authors observations there is no supporting evidence of carvable alabaster from any source other than Ledsham and Fairburn.

A Topographical Dictionary of England by Samuel Lewis *circa* 1845 states:

> FAIRBURN, a township, in the parish of Ledsham, union of Preston (under Gilbert's act), Upper division of the wapentake of Barkstone-Ash, W. Riding of York, 2¼ miles (N. N. W.) from Ferry-Bridge; containing 523 inhabitants. This township, which is situated on the river Aire, comprises about 1380 acres, chiefly the property of Lord Palmerston, who is lord of the manor. The substratum abounds with limestone and alabaster, both of which are quarried to a great extent; kilns have been erected for burning the limestone, and large quantities of lime are sent to various places in the surrounding district. A tunnel 305 yards long has been formed, which

> extends under the village to the canal communicating with the river Aire. The York and North-Midland railway passes through the place, in an excavation 48 feet in depth, and nearly three-quarters of a mile in length.

In an 1822 article on Yorkshire the 300 yd tunnel is stated as 'about to be driven' to communicate with the canal and to facilitate the operation of the lime works of Lord Palmerston. In 1838 the tunnel was reported as being in full operation with the village noted for its extensive quarries of excellent limestone and alabaster suitable for both plaster and funeral monuments. The population was stated as 465.

Rail succeeded the canal *circa* 1858 for the carriage of limestone. The tunnel ceased to be used but its entrance can still be traced. In 1926 the stone plinth which was used to mount the winch by which trucks were hauled through the tunnel was removed and used for the base of a village cross. This would indicate that the tunnel was at some point converted to a tramway.

The evidence for a tramway has been explored by the Fairburn Historical Society and has been published in their paper *web.onetel.net.uk/~gedburnell/fairburnrail.htm (gedburnell@yahoo.com)* although in some quarters a canal cut is still referred to.

It is plain that alabaster was mined for funerary monuments from the late 16th century as the above correspondents make plain clear. From the early 17th century the painting of monuments became widespread and it may be that much Ledsham alabaster lurks under paint. As a result, evidence of monuments made from Ledsham alabaster is fragmentary. The unpainted Southwell tomb to Edwin Sandys (A17) displays a vein colour which is not found in the East Midlands or Somerset quarries and as the carving is also different to that of either London or Burton, there is strong possibility that the carving was from the York workshops and from local (Ledsham) alabaster.

The 1822 article indicates that alabaster was extracted in the early 19th century for funerary monuments but this may not be tombs and the alabaster may well have been largely worked out the seams now only thick enough to be used for small objects. By 1845 the reference to funerary items has been dropped and although alabaster was mined it was, in all probability, directed towards the lime kilns.

Hillam is a small village to the east of Ledsham. R Firman is quoted as mentioning alabaster here but without a date. The thesis written by Oliver Fearon called 'Pieces from Peaseholme – six medieval alabasters and their context in 15th century York' attributes the works at Harewood, Methley and Sheriff Hutton as well as the Peaseholme finds to the York school. However, his observations on the source of York alabaster as being Hillam are suspect. The pieces and the tombs mentioned above are in white alabaster and of a size more in keeping with the Derbyshire quarries. Roger Firman agrees. He states that it seems improbable that the Methley tombs were made from Ledsham alabaster.

At the time of publishing the search for items made from Ledsham alabaster has proved difficult. The Sandys tomb at Southwell, Nottinghamshire (A17) is the best candidate and should the work with Dr Kloppmann prove successful this may yet prove to be the case.

A mention must be made of Ripon. This too is within the Permian strata and Firman observes that although the extraction of alabaster is difficult to prove the dark selenite structure of the tombs at Sheriff Hutton (G203) are close match for the seams at Rippon (*sic*) Park.

Finally reports of alabaster at Sherburn and Hillam are unsubstantiated and although Smith in 1974 reported gypsum production at 250,000 tons, none was used for alabaster.

4. The North Somerset and Penarth beds

First reports:	1633 at Blue Anchor
First use:	Font at Williton and Eworthy church, Sir John Stawell tomb in Cothelstone church Somerset
Exploitation:	Dutch workshops, exported through Blue Anchor and Barnstaple
Date of first effigy:	Possibly Sir John Stawell early 17th century
Quarries/mines:	Blue Anchor, Alabaster Cliffs Watchet, Penarth, Leckwith, Lavernock, Llandough
Last quarry/mine:	Alabaster Cliffs Watchet still provides some alabaster as does Penarth
Peak years:	1633 to 1670
Last use:	May be mid-18th century in the churches around Barnstaple
Major event:	None
Carvers:	Nicholas Stone workshops, De Keyser family, local carvers – *see* Appendix C. Also the Barnstaple workshops.
Colour:	Pink, white with black veining, rose red at Penarth

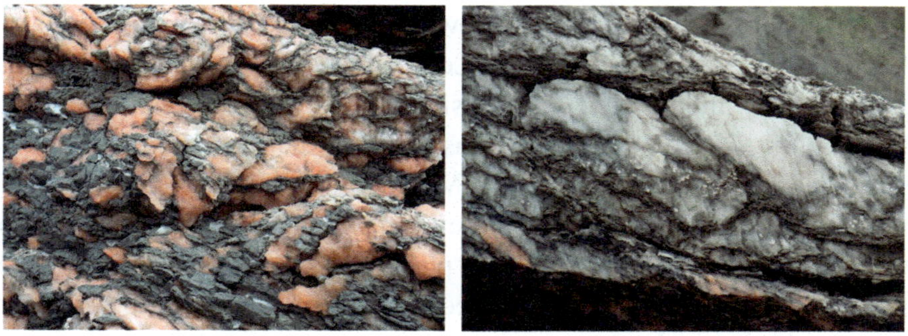

Figure 103. Watchet and Blue Anchor alabaster showing the pink and white with black veining. Photo: the author.

Figure 104 (left). The Williton font in pink dating from 1666 signed RP and RW possibly Nicholas Stone's carvers Robert Pooke and Richard White and **Figure 105 (above)** the 18th century Prestwold baptism font in black veined alabaster. Photos: the author.

History:

Firman records that a traveller called Thomas Gerard of Trent, Somerset who, in his travels through Somerset in 1632 or 1633, commented on Minehead which he confused with Watchet. He gives the impression that the discovery of alabaster was recent. He stated:

> At this place <u>in our time</u> a **Dutchman** hath found out mines of excellent alabaster which they use much for tombs and chimney pieces. It is somewhat harder than ye Derbyshire alabaster but for variety of mixtures and colours it passes any I dare say of this Kingdom if not others, for here shall you have pure white, others spotted with red, white spotted with black, red spotted with white and a perfect black spotted with white.

The observation on colour above is interesting. The red may be more like pink (but *see* Penarth) and black and white can still be seen. Black alabaster is unusual. At present Watchet alabaster is hard to locate.

The name Blue Anchor is believed to have derived from the alabaster in the water indicating that mining here is ancient but no records exist of mining before Gerard's observation in the 17th century. Firman observes that the alabaster deposits were probably known in medieval times but that alabaster of pure white quality was favoured until the onset of painted memorials made the veining and colour irrelevant.

P Cockerham in 2007 offered the opinion that Watchet alabaster was shipped along the coast to Cornwall with Barnstaple as the carving centre. He observes that the local English gentry preferred the Plymouth workshops but that Cornish had a taste for Barnstable using alabaster mined in Somerset.

A thesis completed in 2006 identifies the Jewell family as having a workshop in Barnstaple from about 1690 to 1758 and a number of monuments close to the town can be attributed to them. The records of Tawstock mention a Thomas Jewell the Younger of Barnstaple who made the monument to Henry Northcote in 1729 (M287) but there are other attributions to a Thomas Jewell the Elder. The identification of alabaster monuments is more difficult. That at Swimbridge (M232), Bittadon (M233) and Tawstock (M237) are believed to be in Somerset alabaster and some are attributed to the Jewell workshop. However, all three locations are within easy reach of Barnstaple and the church there has many monuments some of which are clearly both locally made and in alabaster. The five Tawstock monuments are Sir Bouchier Wrey (1696), Lady Rolle (1705), Robert Lovett (1710), Florence Lady Rolle (1724) and the Northcote tablet mentioned above.

The Stawell tomb at Cothelstone dates from 1603 and appears to be in black veined alabaster but may well have been carved much later. Its style is unlike others of the period and points to a hand which may well be Barnstaple but the date rules out the Jewells. The male effigy has a distinct nautical flavour with his costume and that of his wife, Frances, being late Elizabethan or early Stuart.

The fonts at Williton and at Elworthy are recorded locally as being made from 'Watchet' alabaster. A photograph of the Williton font is shown above. This font carries initials RP and RW which are attributed to the local church wardens. However, no church wardens with those initials are suggested. Both these are pink.

The old font at Prestwold, Leics has a bowl made from black veined alabaster and Barton in Fabis, Nottingham has a wall tablet made from the same material. Also in Prestwold church there is a large mural monument to Christopher Packe dating from 1682. This displays black veining in the effigy and columns and may indicate that this was from a London workshop with Watchet alabaster.

Figure 106. The head of Christopher Packe in Prestwold church, Leicestershire showing the black veining which is also visible in the panel behind. This monument from 1682 is almost certainly carved in London and the obtaining of Watchet alabaster would not be difficult by sea from Blue Anchor. The mining was well in hand by 1633 and large blocks are stated to have been liberated from the cliffs over the next century. Photo: Janet State.

Figure 107. The columns from Christopher Packe's 1682 memorial in Prestwold church showing the black veining associated with Watchet. Photo: Janet State.

The reference to a Dutchman in 1632–1633 is interesting in that this is the time of the height of Dutch carving fame in London. The identity of this 'Dutchman' is fugitive. One interesting piece of evidence is the records of Nicholas Stone who records in his note book two exports of alabaster. On the 21st August 1632 he records:

> 'Sent to Peter de Keyser (in Amsterdam) 4 blocks of alabaster the length of which came to 76ft'

There is an identical entry for 24th August 1634.

If the entry on the dispatch of alabaster in 1632 and 1634 is to be believed then the source of this alabaster is a matter of conjecture. Four blocks totally 76ft (23m) mean that on average the blocks were no less than 19ft (5.8m) long. Assuming the cross section was 3ft x 3ft this would indicate a weight of at least 10 tons per block.

This is no mean length and weight and one must consider the transport issues involved. In the first quarter of the 17th century there were no alabaster sources suitable for carving in Southern England. The prime quarries were in the East Midlands (Tutbury/Fauld and Chellaston) and Ledsham (near Pontefract, Yorkshire). The former is selenite from the Keuper marl beds of the Trent Valley and the latter selenite from the Permian marl beds of the Wharfe. These have distinct properties.

Significantly, Nicholas Stone had two travelling carvers in Robert Pooke and Richard White. Stone's notebook shows that Pooke, despite being illiterate, signed his work RP and the RP and RW on the Williton font may well be the work of these two carvers.

A 19th century writer commenting on a storm said 'it liberated house size blocks of alabaster from the cliffs at Watchet'. This comment and the presence of alabaster in the cliffs of Penarth across the Bristol Channel indicate that this stone exists in volume in this part of England. The report of 'carvers of alabaster in Barnstaple' above may just mean the carving of trinkets (baubles) and from the recent evidence of carved alabaster ornaments the colour of the Watchet alabaster is light pink or white with black veining and is good enough to be carved and polished to a high standard. The two photographs above show veins of pink and white with black in the cliffs near Blue Anchor. The alabaster at Penarth is a violent pink to red and has been used for decorative items (*see* later) but now is so soft as to be only used for rockeries.

Therefore there is circumstantial evidence that the 'Dutchman' may well be a member of the Nicholas Stone workshop possibly Peter de Keyser who we know from Stone's workbook was seeking alabaster. The alabaster cliffs at Watchet are very close to Blue Anchor from which, it is alleged, alabaster was shipped. Therefore, there is some evidence that the Stone workshop may well have obtained its alabaster by sea from Somerset for export to Amsterdam. The movement of blocks of 10 tons off the beach at Watchet merits comment. The lifting of the block by means of tripod and block and tackle is well within the technology of the time as is the placing it on a raft which is then floated at high tide and towed a mile or so to Blue Anchor where the process is reversed onto a coastal barque. More information of the sources of alabaster for the Stone workshop may be forthcoming once the known monuments by Stone are studied in greater depth.

One possible candidate for the Amsterdam blocks is the Reinout Van Brederode monument at Veenhuizen in the Netherlands. This effigy in alabaster and black marble dates from 1633–1634 and is the work of Peter de Keyser (the same who was seeking raw materials). The coloured pictures available show a largely white effigy with very thin to no veining and that veining which is present shows a very pale brown and may even be a dark pink colour. This alabaster is wholly unlike that obtained from the East Midlands but at present the identity of the alabaster is uncertain but there remains the likelihood that this was alabaster shipped by Stone in 1632 or 1633. The tomb of William of Orange in the Nieuwe Kerk in Delft has columns believed to be alabaster although some commentators quote these as being marble. This was made by Hendrik de Keyser but the date is 1614 and a bit early for Watchet.

The Somerset Heritage Centre has details of a license granted to John Halliday of Chapel Cleeve, Old Cleeve to take alabaster from the beach at Blue Anchor to supply Alfred G Barham of Bridgewater between 1857 and 1860. This has accession number DD/DP/53/4. Barham was one half of Barham Brothers later a tile and brick manufacturer of Bridgwater which was formed in 1857 but seems to have traded in alabaster at one time (*see* below). Halliday was a local land owner.

The claims for Watchet alabaster have to be tempered with a modicum of care. In 1889 a writer called Ussher categorised the cliffs as being formed of selenite, alabaster and satin spa obscuring the fact his texture group covered such a wide range which could be attributed to the whole of the Somerset deposits. In 1906 the geologist Woodward described the cliffs at Watchet as being of alabaster and gypsum used for plaster. The identification of objects made from Watchet alabaster remains fugitive and care has to be taken to take some of these historical references to as being ambiguous.

A letter from Walter Trevelyan, at Taunton to Henry Thomas De la Beche, geologist, dated 5th September 1848 asks 'Do you wish any blocks of alabaster from Watchet?' No answer is known.

As to Penarth the rose red alabaster is coarse and considered unsuitable for monumental carving. Its use is mainly in the form of a veneer and in this form is often referred to as 'pink'. However, the Welsh Stone Forum issued a Newsletter on the 2nd October 2004 which contains an excellent analysis of the South Wales alabaster trade.

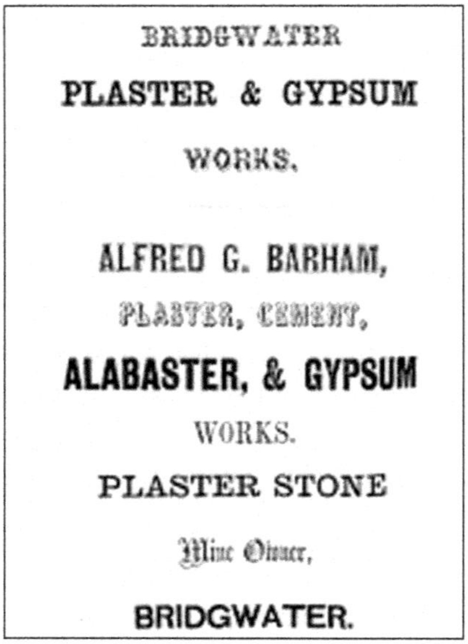

A mid-19th century advertisement for Barham's Works.

They identified 13 places where they believe Penarth alabaster had been used mainly at the direction of Llandaff Diocesan architect John Prichard and carver William Clarke, *circa* 1870 to 1910. However, George Eley Halliday and William Caröe are also mentioned. The most intriguing is that at St Brides super Ely which is recorded as being Penarth alabaster and dated 1658. The wall mural is simple but the carver is unknown and it merits further investigation. A letter is recorded from Thomas Johnes to Iolo Morganwg (antiquarian Edward Williams) dated January 18th 1808 says: 'I thank you very much for your account of the Marbles etc. It is the alabaster I would wish to have, if of a fine colour, and in single blocks, provided the expenses per column do not amount to more than I have allowed. I was to have some prodigious fine ones from Italy but these (Napoleon) problems have now totally prevented me.'[1] The stone was intended for library columns and a staircase at Hafod.

F J North in *The Minerals of Glamorgan* dated 1916 noted that the Cardiff University tiles were mined at Lavernock but this quarry cannot now be found as it was filled and grassed over. The Stone Forum confirms that the alabaster in the cliffs at Lavernock is poor and unlikely to have been the source for the 13 location using Penarth alabaster.

Notes:

1. Edward Williams of Glamorgan is recorded as being an accomplished carver including chimney pieces and memorials amongst them being the memorial to Anthony Jones at Llantwit Major and the tombstone to his father in Gileston cemetery. A letter written in 1880 from Owen Pughe is addressed to Edward Williams, Marble Mason, Flimston, near Cowbridge. It is quite possible that the correspondence with Williams was about Penarth alabaster.

The Aust Cliff beds of Gloucestershire

Stated to be of the Blue Anchor formation it is therefore no surprise that this is a pinkish hue in the same form as Watchet. Samuel Lewis in 1833 wrote that '… the Aust Cliff in the parish of Henbury, there is a fine of gypsum and alabaster which furnishes a plentiful supply for stuccoing to the masons of Bristol, Bath and other places but is inferior to that of Derbyshire'. Eric Garrett in 2008 offered the opinion that the collection of alabaster was by means of picking up fallen blocks rather than any quarrying indicating a use for plaster rather than carving. No evidence can be found of carving using Aust alabaster.

5. The Redhill, Nottinghamshire beds

First reports:	1750 at Redhill, Ratcliffe on Soar, Nottingham
First use:	Marble Hall, Kedleston Hall, Derbyshire
Exploitation:	Lord Scarsdale, Curzon family
Date of first effigy:	Not yet known
Quarries/mines:	Redhill[1]
Last quarry/mine:	*Circa* 1811 when use of alabaster for plaster, some local mining for plaster mills to the end of the 19th century[2]
Peak years:	1760 to 1780
Last use:	The mausoleum at Brocklesby[3]
Major event:	The Marble Hall at Kedleston,[4] possibly Holkham Hall, Norfolk
Carvers:	Not known but may have been Derby
Colour:	White with light brown veining

Notes:

1. Despite Lowe's comments there is some uncertainty as whether Redhill was a mine or quarry. Fellows offers the opinion that the Sacheverell tombs were made from alabaster obtained from Redhill. However, there is no evidence that mining at Redhill was in hand before the mid-18th century long after the Sacheverell tombs were constructed. In addition the colour and form of the Redhill alabaster is unlike that from which the tombs are formed.
2. The earliest attempts to provide a view of building stone was commissioned by the Board of Agriculture. One was the survey by John Farey published in 1811 as *A General View of Agricultural and Building Materials of Derbyshire.*

3. Firman notes that there are similar columns in Holkham Hall in Norfolk dating from 1753. These were identified by Christian in 1959 as coming from Tutbury but the source is more likely to be Redhill. This is discussed below. Holkham website notes that the alabaster was Derbyshire and carried down the Trent by barge and transhipped to coastal barque at Gainsborough but seeing that alabaster was sourced from more than one location there is a possibility that some came from Redhill.
4. The archives at Kedleston have failed to find any records of the mining activities of the Curzons. It would appear the records were burnt by one member of the family in the 19th century for reasons which are not immediately apparent.

History: In 1964 Roger Firman suggested that the monuments in Ratcliffe on Soar church dating from 1539 to 1625 were made from Redhill alabaster. In 1984 he changed his mind correctly identifying the alabaster as Chellaston and Fauld. The lords of the manor were the Sacheverells who had extensive mining interests in Derbyshire but no apparent interest in gypsum. A hundred years later the manor came into the possession of the Curzons of Kedleston and in particular Assheton Curzon who had interests in stone mining. There is strong evidence that quarrying in the outcrop which faces the Soar at Redhill was being carried out by 1750 and Throsby in 1795 observed that Redhill was the source of alabaster for '… Kedleston, Staunton Harold and Stanford Hall as well as chimney pieces for many country residences'. Greenhill observes that the incident with William Walsh (B6) in 1510 indicates that '… much of the material for Nottingham doubtless came from Redhill quarries'. This interesting aside is unfortunately, without any supporting documentation.

The outcrop at Redhill is the most westerly side of the Mercian Mudstone Group in which the mines at Gotham, Barton and Thrumpton were later to be found. Pushed up by the movement of the Normanton Hills Fault the cliffs have been eroded by the waters of the Trent and Soar for centuries and the outcropping is very clear. Possibly exploited for plaster making it was clear there was a significant deposit of alabaster which the Curzons developed for their own use and to provide stone for other houses.

Farey in 1811 in his description of the agricultural scene of Nottinghamshire observed 'At Redhill there are extensive quarries which yield gypsum and alabaster. The latter is extracted by the use of gunpowder the explosions of which not only disturbs the locals but renders the alabaster in such small pieces that it can only be used for plaster making'. Edward Richardson observes the '… disuse of this fine material after three centuries ... may be attributable partly to the introduction of gunpowder into the pits in lieu of the medieval saw and picks whereby the increased quantity of the material was obtained but of unsound quality and unfit for the purposes of sculpture'.

In his book on Derbyshire also dated 1811, he observes that Mr William Acton (the occupier) had plaster kilns here which he sold at 1/- a bushel. The farm and land at Redhill was later acquired by the Sheppard family who were instrumental in developing the Gotham mines which evolved into British Gypsum (now British Plasterboards). Some minor extraction continued but nothing of any consequence.

Reports of alabaster being extracted from the mines at Gotham appear from time to time. No supporting evidence is forthcoming and the small items claimed for Gotham may well have come from the bauble industry of Leicestershire (but *see* Kingston below). Nichols in 1795 reported that some alabaster is being obtained from a quarry at Thrumpton. There is indeed a quarry (later a mine) and the alabaster seam here narrows and emerges at ground level about a mile east of Redhill. This was uncovered during the excavations for the A453 widening but amounts would be small although one large nodule weighing some 11 tons was extracted. The road builders promised a nodule for display in the village of Ratcliffe on Soar and several for Gotham and samples of between 3 and 4 tons were earmarked. The Ratcliffe nodule was in place in 2016 but the Highway Authority refused permission for the two at Gotham. Small nodules of between 15 to 20lbs have been obtained and display white with light-brown veining.

The photograph (Figure 69, Appendix G) shows two small candlesticks presented by British Gypsum to Gotham church in 1980 and now in the possession of Chris and Jill Hind of Gotham. The suggestion is that this was made from alabaster from the Gotham mines and as the base carries a label of a carver in Yelvertoft in Northamptonshire so this cannot be proved. *See* the bauble industry under Derbyshire (Chellaston) above.

6. Kingston on Soar, Gotham, East Leake and Bunny, Nottinghamshire

First reports:	1905
First use:	Kingston on Soar church reredos, tablets and font
Exploitation:	Lord Belper of Kingston
Date of first effigy:	No effigy known
Quarries/mines:	Kingston, Weldon, Winser, Cuckoo Bush, Glebe, Silver Seal (Bunny) and Marblaegis (East Leake)
Last quarry/mine:	*Circa* 1963
Peak years:	1930s
Last use:	1936 but some retained until 1960s
Major event:	Dispute with highways agency over damage to local roads. Irregular shot blasting causing rocks to fall on Bunny village
Carvers:	Kingston Fine Arts
Colour:	White with dark brown veining, buff translucent with red brown mottling

History: The high ground to the east of the Soar is rich in gypsum but the presence of alabaster is generally thought to be uncertain. There is much anecdotal talk about alabaster being extracted from the Gotham mines and at East Leake (Marblaegis) and Bunny (Silver Seal) but there is no documentary evidence.

Figure 108. The adit 11 entrance to Silver Seal Mine at Bunny, Nottinghamshire *circa* 2000. This is now linked underground with the Marblaegis Mine at East Leake but this entrance is still used to transport equipment into the mine complex. The shallowness of the working can be seen in the low overburden. Photo: *Wikipedia.*

In 1990, Brian Smith in his history of the village of Kingston on Soar interviewed a number of people involved in the mines amongst them being Harry Woodfield, the Kingston mine manager. Around 1929 Lord Belper who owned Kingston Hall formed Fine Art Company which was installed in the farm buildings off the West Leake road. This company fashioned small objects (baubles) from local stone amongst which was onyx, Blue John and alabaster. The workshop produced ashtrays, vases, book-ends and light shades and these went on display in the showroom. Woodfield managed the business and also supplied the alabaster from the Kingston mine, blocks being removed and taken by rail to West Leake level crossing where they were carried the mile or so to the farm. In front of the farm cottage was a saw pit where the blocks were cut into manageable sizes.

Woodfield recorded the names of people involved including Jack Bent, Nora Limb of West Leake and Muriel Moore of Ratcliffe on Soar. The latter started in 1930 then aged 17 and made beads of onyx for a wage of 17/6d a week. Another carver was Stan Newbold and the overseer was William Edward Lomas of 41 King St Derby who had, at one time made alabaster wood-pigeon decoys. The London Gazette records that

William was descendant of R G Lomas of Mackworth fame and may have fallen on hard times as he had been declared bankrupt in 1927 but discharged in 1928.

Woodfield recalled a commission from Lord Belper in 1933 for a new font for the church in Kingston. Despite this, demand declined and the workshop closed *circa* 1936.

In Kingston church and also in Thrumpton church there are wall tablets to local gentry (one to Harry Woodfield himself) in a buff coloured semi-translucent alabaster which cannot be attributed elsewhere and may well have come from the Kingston mine. The alabaster reredos in the same church dating from 1905 is not Kingston but opaque Fauld, the lord of the manor having interests in the Staffordshire mines as well as those local to Kingston. A small vase in the same semi-translucent material was purchased from a charity stall in Essex in 2014 and may well have been a product of the Fine Art Company. An image of this is shown below:

Figure 109. The vase about 8 cm high is made from semi-translucent alabaster with pale brown veining. The alabaster is possibly mined from the Kingston mine. This is typical of the baubles made for sale at seaside resorts. The block of alabaster would be rough cut and then turned on a lathe and polished. The base would be squared and smoothed on a sandstone. Photo: the author.

7. The Cumbrian beds

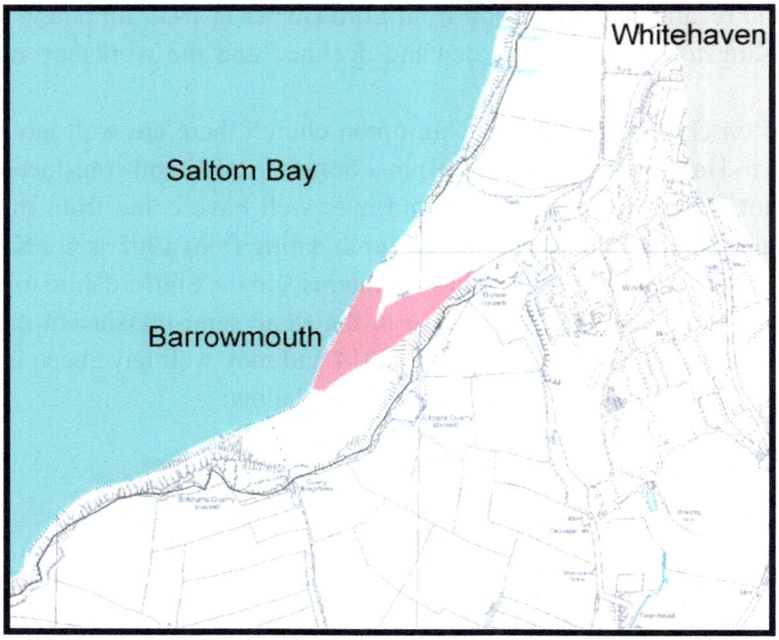

Figure 110. The location of the Barrowmouth quarry and mine south of Whitehaven. Drawing by BGS. Keyworth modified by the author.

In Cumbria the Eden Valley, Carlisle and Barrowmouth all in Cumbria, appear as alabaster sources although an obscure record of 1682 makes reference to an alabaster quarry at Sandwith Baugh (about half a mile from Barrowmouth). The Cumbria Archives has a lease (YDS 60/77/1) dated 26th Oct 1739 to Daniel Benn and William Williamson, masons, to mine freestone and alabaster on the seashore at Sandwith for seven years at an annual rent of 30s for three years and 35s each year thereafter. The lease was granted by the governors of St Bees School. The lease was renewed in 1753 (YDS 60/77/2), this time for 14 years at an annual rent of £6 10s. Clearly the working had proved profitable for in 1767 the lease (YDS 60/77/3) was renewed for a third time at £12 pa except that only Daniel Benn[1] was named. In 1777 the lease was issued to John France, John Grayson and William Thompson in which time the rent had been reduced to £7 and in 1784 it was again renewed, this time to Alexander Coltert, mason, for three years at £7 7s, and to John Barns and John Wilson in 1786 for the same sum. The leases continue with a 1796 lease to Thomas Smith, mason of Whitehaven at £21 pa, to Henry Thompson, Edward Johnstone and Andrew Spittal, all grocers and Joseph Benn, mariner in 1803 at a now inflated rent of £97 pa and in 1811 to Henry Birley, merchant and Joseph Barker, soap boiler at £60 pa. In 1818 the lease was transferred to Abraham Bell, stone mason of Whitehaven for £50. Joseph Benn died 1814. These leases are to be found in Cumbria Archives (YDS 60/77/4 to 11). The connection with these lessees over a century provides a tenuous link to alabaster carvers and in some cases it is clear that freestone was the driver. The Benns had contracts for repairing Cumbria's bridges and alabaster is wholly unsuitable for this purpose. Nevertheless, the names are worth noting as in time links may be forthcoming.

This is particularly relevant when it is noted that another writer called Gilpin, in a letter dated 1698, refers to carvable alabaster from Cumberland but fails to say where. This may be Sandwith.

Tyler records that the date of the first volume alabaster extraction is uncertain but names Knothill (Carlisle), Barrowmouth, Wragmire Bank and Stamphill as being quarried. He observes that the term 'alabaster' could have been loosely applied to fine-grained gypsum or anhydrite used for plaster and that the latter two were very small operations.

The most reliable records relate to Barrowmouth a short distance south of Whitehaven. It is clear that a small quarry was open here in 1794 but some authors say that alabaster was being worked as early as 1739 (*see* the lease mentioned above). There may be some confusion between Sandwith and Barrowmouth. In 1812 the lease on the quarry limited the extraction to an annual output of 400 tons. In 1832 the quarry was visited by Professor Sedgewick who produced a geological paper on his findings (yet to be found). By 1847 the quarry was owned by the Hamilton family of Whitehaven who are recorded as alabaster merchants. John, William and 'Billy' Hamilton extracted gypsum and alabaster until *circa* 1888 when they sold out to John Thomlinson of Knothill who continued mining until 1907. Around 1847 the Hamiltons renamed the area around the quarry as Port Hamilton and built a summer retreat landscaping the cliffs with pathways, ponds and alabaster statuary.

In 1850 Port Hamilton and the quarry was subject of guide, this time by Joseph Hodgson called *A High Victorian Guide to Port Hamilton and Fleswick Beach*[2] (*see* a slightly different name in bibliography section Cat 204/5 in Cumbria Archives).

Tyler says that very little of Cumbrian alabaster was used for carving owing to its open matrix, the only record being a few small pieces from Barrowmouth from 1847 to 1880. Other authors (Cranstone survey of 2007) confirm this, saying the alabaster was used for 'monumental' purposes. The pieces must have been small as the alabaster had to be carried up the cliff paths by packhorse until an inclined plane railway was constructed in 1896. The Hamiltons traded from an office in Whitehaven where they could ship out their products by ship or the Furness Railway. The only confirmed church use of Barrowmouth alabaster is the altar at St Mary's, Edinburgh (A94). This is recorded as Whitehaven alabaster since this was the trading town and the place from which the alabaster would be shipped. From the date of 1872 this could only have been supplied by the Hamiltons and come from Barrowmouth. Cranstone says that the colour of the processed gypsum was pink which caused some problem with plaster making and the Scottish Churches Trust say that the alabaster on A94, as noted in 2014, was 'pale yellow to a cream buff'. At the time of writing the altar (A94) is the only known extant use of Barrowmouth alabaster. A plan of the mine at Barrowmouth is to be found in the Cumbria Archives YBSC/21/5/7/1 to 3 and YDB 40/49 dated 1898 attributed to the Backermet Mining Co.

Enquiries of Cumberland Archives produced the fact that they knew of no extant objects made from locally mined alabaster.

One item for investigation is a number of sculptures in the Norwich Castle Museum dated 1931 and 1934 in 'Cumberland alabaster' which are not assigned to a carver but may be attributable one of the carvers named below.[3] However more reliable are the Henry Moore Centre, who record a number of carvings in Cumberland alabaster, and the statues carved by Barbara Hepworth. Both these carvers seem to have used alabaster from a number of sources. Moore's *Four Piece* and *Girl with Clasped Hands* and Hepworth's *Mother and Child* (1934) are labelled Cumberland and show an all-over grey-brown colour with brown veining as shown in this slab sample.

Photo: the author.

Of the principal gypsum mines and quarries the details are:

Sandwith	Working in 17th century – closed 1984. Close to Barrowmouth and mainly credited with gypsum and anhydrite.
Barrowmouth	Working 1794 – closed 1908. The only mine from which alabaster was definitely extracted but adits blocked when mine closed.
Knothill	Working 1685 – closed 1921. No alabaster recorded.

Wragmire Bank	Working 1685 – incorporated into Cocklakes. Early reports of alabaster.
Cocklakes	Working 1774 – closed 1966. Owned by John Howe and Company of Carlisle in 1838 named as alabaster dealers. The Pigg family was associated in 1850 and on the partnership being dissolved the family moved 'to continue to work alabaster further south'.
Acorn Bank	Working 1880 – closed 1937. No alabaster recorded.
Long Meg	Working 1870 – closed 1976. No alabaster recorded.
Kirkby Thore	Working 1829 – still open. Alabaster mentioned in 1829 in the Potts Well pit but nothing since.
Stamphill	Closed 1975. Reported as producing alabaster.

Notes:

1. The *Whitehaven Daily Advertiser* for 1st November 1777 has the following entry: 'Mr Daniel Benn aged 66 died last Monday at his house in Chapel St, Whitehaven. He was a much respected architect and master mason under whose direction the works in the harbour have been carried out. The St James Chapel, Castle and Westmorland Gaol are also monuments to his ability'. In respect of St James Chapel Daniel Benn oversaw the purchase of materials for the chapel construction noting about April 1752 that 'alabaster was obtained from Barrowmouth'. To what purpose is not mentioned but some £63 was expended on 'ornaments'.
2. Hodgson gives a detailed description of the mine. He reports that it was adrift mine working three seams of gypsum and alabaster varying from 12 to 20 ft thick and the output was put to making plaster or 'plastic art'. The mine was worked on the pillar and stall method, the former being 8 yards square and the latter being 5 to 6 yards wide. The roof was 8 to 12 ft high and freestanding. He names two miners who were William Watson (born 1810 and killed 8th July 1875 in an accident) and Joseph Craig. Apart from the reference to 'plastic art' Hodgson makes no mention of the alabaster being provided for carving.
3. During the visit to the New Walk Museum on the 17th Oct 2016 one sculpture was identified by Simon Lake as being *Composition* by Henry Moore stated as being Cumberland alabaster.

8. Battle Sussex Notes

Gypsum was found at Mountfield, Robertsbridge, Sussex in 1872 (closed 1990). The seam is several feet thick. Mining ceased in 1906 but restarted at a second mine at Brightling which opened in 1950. This mine still worked. The presence of alabaster is uncertain. The Sussex database says that the monument at Chiddingly was made from Mountfield alabaster but no supporting evidence is provided and the dates do not match.

9. The other Welsh beds

St David's, Pembroke is mentioned in 1579.

10. The other English beds

Yeovil, Hurcot and Somerton, all in Somerset, appear but all known authors state that no carvable alabaster was produced. In 1829 Thomas Moore wrote 'The alabaster which is found in the cliffs at Beer, Salcombe, Branscombe and Sidmouth makes good plaster of Paris but is in too small a quantity to become an object of attention. It is collected by a poor labouring man who hardly makes a living out of it'.

In 1791 Young wrote that alabaster was being sold at 2s 6d per cwt from the Hurcot quarry. This does not sound like carving alabaster and the fact it was being sold by the cwt indicates the use for plaster. Later a geological map of Hurcot was engraved with the name alabaster but no further evidence is forthcoming

The writing of Leland *circa* 1543 to 1550 records a 'fair quarry of alabaster at Beau Manor about 4 miles from Leicester'. No further information is available. Strangely John Leland also mentions the Isle of Axholme but fails to mention either the Derbyshire or Staffordshire quarries. Again the confusion as to the use of the word alabaster in the early writings reappears.

Firman reports gypsiferous strata in the Clarborough area of Lincolnshire. These Triassic beds contain fibrous gypsum none of which can be called alabaster. Further north, in the Isle of Axholme, the beds thicken to possible yield alabaster. The Leland report of 1543 discloses alabaster at Epworth and Burnham but he observes that the seam thickness would not support sculpture. He says '... plentiful quarries of alabaster commonly called plaster' leading one to assume he is referring to fine-grained gypsum rendered to plaster making. To further confuse the issue, Cameron in 1890 stated that large blocks were being extracted from the two quarries which does not sound like gypsum extraction but fails to use the word alabaster or describe the use to which the blocks were put. The history of 'Axholme Alabaster' remains obscure until further evidence is forthcoming.

11. Foreign beds

In 1339 Beatrice de Louvain ordered weepers for her tomb to be 'de boin fin alebastre' but nothing further is known. The book *Materials of Sculpture* by Nicholas Penny gives details of alabaster from Vizille near Grenoble and black polished limestone from Dinant. In 1392 Claus Sluter travelled to Paris to obtain the same for a tomb of the Philip le Hardi (the Bold), Duke of Burgundy once in Champmol now in the museum at Dijon (damaged in French Revolution but now restored) and obtained its alabaster from a Genoese merchant there and probably Italian. Tournai sculptor Claus de Haine is also associated with the Dijon tomb being described as 'ouvrier d'ymages de pierre d'alabastre'. Tonnerre near Auxerre is also named as a source. Other sources are Catalonia (Spain), Netherlands, France and Germany but almost certainly these are calcite. This is reputed to be harder to carve and therefore not exported and hence no continental alabaster trade developed.

The many churches in Barcelona have alabaster items. The province of Catalonia was mining alabaster in the 13th century and the Monastery de Santa Maria de Pedralbes was founded in 1326 in a worked-out alabaster quarry. The English translation of Pedralbes is white stones and the items display a cream to off-white alabaster with minimal visible veining. The founder of the monastery, Queen Elisenda, was buried there in 1364. She is commemorated by an alabaster tomb located in a side cell in the wall between the chapel and the cloisters. In the cloister passage is a nice alabaster slab with an effigy carved in cameo dated 1566.

Figure 111. The monastery cell commemorates five Catalonian ladies. The one shown right is that of Elisenda in which she is depicted half in nun's habit and half in royal robes. Her soul is being transported to heaven in a napkin. Photo: the author.

The Catalonian effigies show certain features. The tomb chest is usually wall mounted and has a pitched lid on which the effigy is carved so that it can be seen. In addition the hands are never carved in prayer but shown crossed as can be seen in the left picture above.

In the Basilica de Santa Maria del Mar in Barcelona, there is a tomb to Bishop Ramon d'Escales (died 1398) which was carved in 1406 (or 1411) by Antonio Canet. It is located in the Capelle de Les Animes Del Purgatori and like the others is wall mounted on a pitched-top tomb chest. This has English overtones in that the chest has eight bedesmen in niches with crocketted canopies.

Figure 112. The 1406 (or 1411) tomb to Bishop Ramon d'Escales in the Basilica Santa Maria del Mar, Barcelona. This was carved by Antonio Canet (died 1431) and shows some English features in the niches of the tomb chest. Photo: the author.

The crypt of same Basilica contains the alabaster sarcophagus of the remains of Santa Eulalia, the patron saint of Barcelona, carved in 1327 by a resident of Pisa, Italy. In addition, the Basilica holy water free-standing bowls are in Catalonian alabaster as are those in the church of the Sagred Cor in Tibidabo.

Figure 113. The alabaster stoup in Sagred Cor church Tibidabo, Barcelona.

It would seem that alabaster was widespread in Spain with extant examples in Miriflores, Pamplona, Valencia and Zaragoza amongst others associated with the name of Damian Forment.

Dr Wolfram Kloppmann who has undertaken isotope fingerprinting of alabaster identifies ancient quarries in the Jura and Alp ranges, Provence, Burgundy and Lorraine and Aragon and Catalonia in Spain. He claims that some sculptures have been identified with continental quarries but has only described one item as a 'tombstone of English origin'. Kloppmann was writing in 2011. Since then a more detailed paper published in January 2013 has been obtained. This produced clear evidence that the footprint of East Midland's alabaster is wholly different from continental alabasters when comparing sulphur (or sulfur) and strontium isotope ratios which has allowed him to link the monument of Uppsala in Sweden (R187) with the quarries west of Nottingham. Further samples have now been provided and research work is continuing.

In all this the evidence for foreign alabasters in England is thin prior to the 19th century and despite suggestion by authors such as Lawrence Stone that some non-standard effigy and panel carving in England is the work of continental workshops no support for this has been found.

Monica Price mentions Capo Circeo, Lazio, Italy which coarse and granular, Lano Montaione, Tuscany, Italy, Busca, Piedmont, Italy, Brown calcite from Gibraltar and Oran, Algeria used to great effect in the Garnier Opera House in Paris. The latter is cream with thin orange/yellow veining. Many of the previous mentioned quarries are no longer worked.

The Grove Encyclopaedia of Medieval Art lists some 50 continental monuments that contain(ed) alabaster but only in one case was the source identified.

Claims of there being Dutch quarries are suspect. The writings of Antoni Van Leeuwenhoek in the 17th century state that alabaster for Dutch carving was imported from England and Germany (Thuringia) and occasionally Italy.

Details of the Mexican and other North American beds drift in. Kevin Butler who had examined the area around St George's, Utah reports a range of alabasters from the calcite beds varying from white to pink, red and brown stained and green. Monica Price again notes that both Mexico (Baja California) and Yavapai County, Arizona have working quarries producing white, green and brown stained alabaster from which candlesticks and paperweights are made locally. At this time no details of monumental carving from the American beds has been uncovered.

For a further detailed list *see* mindat.org.

12. Status of alabaster

16th and 17th century authors on minerals used hierarchical interpretation in the ranking of materials. This inferred that all materials had an inferior or superior ranking in the ladder of God's creation. High quality minerals such as true marble were described as superior with some regarded as 'noble' whilst alabaster was at the other end being designated 'bastard-alabaster' due to its veining. In the grand order the precious stones came first followed by the metals with gold in prime position followed by marble, granite, sandstone and finally the limestones.

This was all very well but it took no account of the suitability for or the ease of carving. It also took no account of the mineral's ability to stand weathering or paint. Then there was the matter of cost. England has no natural marble and discerning customers who wanted this had to have it imported. This may be seen to have started with the Southwark carvers from the late 16th century. Later in the mid-17th century marble costs reduced to the point that it would displace alabaster as the choice of the customers.

Alabaster would stand much undercutting such that effigies could be carved in the round, it could be polished to a high finish and not being porous would take paint which would be long lasting. Despite its low hieratical status alabaster was preferred but where possible components which required less carving such as the tomb chest may well be in freestone for low cost or Purbeck marble for higher status although it must be stated that this is also from the limestone family despite its name. Observers in the 17th century comment on rare effigies cut from a single stone and the difficulty in this offers more for the appreciation of value than for aesthetics. The Nicholas Stone memorial to Sir Charles Morison in St Mary's Church, Watford is carved from a single block with the effigy resting on one elbow. This entailed a block some six feet long and about twice the normal height. The cost was £400 or approximately twice the normal charge for such a memorial.

Appendix N

Notes on Terminology

In the Gothic period (1330 to about 1560) there were few artistic commentators and contracts were placed on the basis of observation and recommendation from existing carvers. Terminology was incomplete and vague. The customer may specify an 'image' or 'picture' meaning an effigy and a tomb chest or table and possibly a canopy. Position within the church was important but the rest was left to the carver. The carver would list the details of the work and one extant contact is from Pietro Torrigiano for Henry VIII and the tomb of his father Henry VII dated 1511. He mentions '… pillars, bases, chaptrels, gablettes, crokkettes, anelles, finials, orbs, housings, Scocheons, graven with portecoleyses and Roses, all of copper …'

Cardinal Wolsey patronised the arts but from the 1540s the interests of Henry VIII in Renaissance architecture meant that there emerged a group of observers who began to describe the styles and forms they saw. However throughout the 16th century the terminology used was incomplete and lacked consistency. The term pillar could be used for any vertical structure and as late as the second quarter of the 17th century the notebooks of Nicholas Stone show only limited consistency in terminology. The table below, although incomplete, tries to set out the range of terminology used and explain its use.

Term	Alternative	Meaning/Use
Arcade		A series of arches supported by columns. Has tendency to be modern
Arch		Curved surround over a tomb usually freestanding
Architrave	Lintel	Not used before 1600. The main beam across the top of the columns
Arms *See* note below	Armorial, Heraldic supporters, Cartouche, Escutcheon	Comprising coats of arms, helm, mantling and motto. Sometimes mythical beasts or animals. The purpose has changed, The great displays start with the Dutch influence from the late 16th century. Cartouche is much used to describe the names in Egyptian hieroglyphics
Borders		The decorative edge
Canopy		A roof like assembly over the whole tomb. Occasionally in Gothic tombs there may be a canopy over the head and shoulders of an effigy.
Capitals	Chaptels, Pillar heads	The decorative ends of columns
Cherubim	Putti	Figures of children used as decoration
Column	Pillar	The support for the entablature. Columns were not common in the Gothic period and were a late 16th century import from Holland
Cornice	Corona	The upper horizontal moulded edging of a entablature
Demi-figure	Half statue	The 17th depiction of an effigy showing only the head and shoulders or from the waist upwards. Such effigies usually face forward
Effigy	Image, Picture, Representation, Proportions, Portrait, Lying Statue	The old reredos kervers were known as image makers, imagers (1466 to 1563) or ymagers (from *circa* 1500). As later as 1624 the term 'picture' was being used. Sometimes effigy was not related to a three-dimensional carving but related to an inlaid carving or stamping. From the late 17th century the term effigy became universal except when a vertical representation was used in which case statue became established
Entablature		The horizontal assembly complete with frieze, cornice and architrave supported on columns
Epitaph	*See* inscriptions	
Festons	Festoons	Leaves or flowers incorporated in one or more of the entablature or supports
Finials	Pyramids, Pinnacles	Part of the decoration of an entablature
Freize	Freeze	Decorated part between the architrave and the cornice
Gablette	Canopy	The small canopies over the heads of medieval effigies
Image		Medieval for effigy

Inscriptions	Epitaph, Epitates, Writings, Superscription	Epitaph seems to have taken hold from the first quarter of the 17th century. Tomb chests in the Gothic period had their upper corners chamfered to take text and this continued into the transition period but with the text now in English. Renaissance tomb chests had a tendency to have their inscription in panels. Later mural monuments were all epitaphs in frames
Lintel		Another name for the architrave. Lintel is more common in the modern world
Lozenge		The shaped decoration on a Gothic tomb chest containing a figure or shield
Moulding		A shape formed by manipulating a flexible material. Less applicable to stone monuments
Mural		A high tomb built like a picture against the wall. Introduced early 17th century
Niche		An alcove into which a monument is placed. In Gothic period the tomb chest may have niches into which figures are placed
Obelisk		A tapered column sometimes decorated by orbs, spikes or pikes
Pedestal		The base of a column or statue on which it is mounted
Pediment	Frontispiece	A triangular mounting supported by columns in the classical style
Picture	*See* effigy	The medieval term for an inscribed effigy on a slab
Pilaster		Generally taken as referring to a rectangular column at the corner of a tomb chest. Can also be round or spiral
Pillar	*See* Column	
Pinnacles	Finials, Pyramids	*See* Finials
Plinth	Basis, base, plynt or steppe	A low platform on which the tomb chest sits first used *circa* 1620
Prie-dieu	Prayer stall	A 17th century representation of a prayer bench
Pyramids	Finials, Pinnacles	*See* Finials. The studies in the mid-17th century began to alert the populace to the pyramid's Egyptian origins
Relief	Stories, Histories, Basso relieve	The cutting away of the surface to give the impression of the carving being raised above the surface of the panel
Spandrills	Spandrels	Triangular space formed by a horizontal lintel and the outer edges of arches often decorated
Strapwork		Stylistic representation of leather straps carved into the vertical faces of tombs
Tabernacle	Ledge, Ledger	A niche or the horizontal slab on which the effigy lies. The term ledge or ledger from which the term ledger stone derives. At some point ledger became associated with the mineral touchstone
Table		A tomb chest with open sides reminiscent of table with four legs. Table sometimes relates to the inscription panel
Tabletop		Refers to a tomb chest without an effigy but with a plain or carved slab
Tomb chest	Coffin, Urn or Vase	The box-shaped chest on which the effigy is set.

The advent of heraldry

The heralds were one of the first observers of monuments. The College of Arms was founded by Richard III in 1484 they were a small but influential group whose power was mainly exercised in the 16th and 17th century. Whilst ruling and preserving the social ranks they were able to approve the use of heraldic badges even where the origins were somewhat fictitious, it being considered that order and pedigree was better than disorder.

Heralds were instrumental in preserving some monuments. They campaigned against the iconoclasts claiming they were just ignorant masses who could not understand the purpose. In 1568 Elizabeth I ordered that no crest or badge should be displayed except by authority of the heralds. This in turn led to an accusation of corruption being thought to claim descent of clients from august families being invented instead of from registers and written records. Gervase Piggott of Thrumpton Nottingham sought the assistance of Dugdale, then Norroy King of Arms in the 1660s, to establish his ancestry. Dugdale concluded that the Pigotts were descended from the Picots of Hedon in Essex and of Ratcliffe on Soar, Nottingham so permitting him to display on his monuments the three picks of that family. Current research fails to support this belief but in the 17th century this was a coup – *see also* Appendix Q.

As the 17th century drew to a close the influence of the heralds was such that most wealthy families would ensure that their monuments were the means of preserving the pedigree of the family through heraldic display.

The heralds claimed there were degrees of society from the lowly to the most senior and that their displays indicated virtue reinforced by costume. Henry VIII involved the heralds in funerals and there was a dictatorial ruling which established the rules including the numbers of mourners by class. The value of monuments for establishing order was set out by Elizabeth in 1560 (*see* Appendix H) and further proclamations mainly in 1618 in which all heraldic devices had to be approved by the college. Heralds were encouraged to tour the country and make notes of monuments during visitations. It is for this reason than many drawings of monuments exist today. For further discussion – *see* Appendix Q.

The church at Millbrook, Bedfordshire is dedicated to St Michael and all Angels. It stands on the scarp of the Greensands Ridge some 200ft above the village.

APPENDIX O
THE STRANGE CASE OF THE MILLBROOK EFFIGIES

Figure 114. The 15th century church from the south. The church stands some 350ft above sea level and above the village. The later pitched roofed chancel can be seen to the right of the original tower and nave. The church is reached by a farm track off the A507 road or by a steep path from the village. Photo: the author.

The effigies reputed to be those of William and Mary Huett who died in 1602 stood against the north wall of the chancel on a tomb chest which also contained effigies of two of their children. By 1857 the chancel and the Huett tomb were in bad repair and William Butterfield was brought in to supervise restoration. This resulted in the alabaster effigies being removed from the chancel. They were never restored to their position in the church due to financial constraints.

So the effigies remained at one side in the church but soon after the repairs were completed, strange noises were heard. There sprung up a belief that the effigies were angry at their treatment and to overcome this, the rector had the effigies moved to the rectory cellar. The noises continued and to make matters worse the rectory maids would not go into the cellar and would barricade the door to their bedrooms.

In desperation the rector had the effigies buried in the churchyard. However, the noises continued. Then in 1888 the chancel roof was condemned due to death watch beetle infestation which was probably the cause of the noise.

In 1919 Reverend Pollard decided to dig them up. However, no-one quite knew where they had been buried. Seventeen members of the Bedford Archaeological Society, Mr Henman and Reverend Langdon carried out exploratory excavations but nothing was found until Mrs Bunker, an elderly widow whose husband was the Sexton, pointed to the spot where her husband's spade had hit some stone work. The effigies were then recovered from their grave, the male figure minus his legs and head. It transpires that Mrs Bunker was using the head as a door stop and that lady could only be persuaded to part with after a visit from a Huett ancestor. They now reside in the chancel floor although there are plans to restore them.

For additional comments *see* R79 and website:
http://virtual-library.culturalservices.net/webingres/bedfordshire/vlib/0.digitised_resources/millbrook_church_effigies.htm

Figure 115. The effigies reputed to be William and Mary Huett (died 1602) but showing evidence of a much earlier date. The alabaster is Chellaston and the lady wears a French hood largely out of fashion by the mid-16th century. There are strange protrusions from behind the neck which cannot be explained. The remains of tomb slab lies underneath. Photo: the author.

Figure 116. The effigy of the knight showing the damage inflicted during its burial. The armour has a mid to late Tudor feel and the remnant of a ruff is apparent. The head has received much damage from its time as a door stop. Photo: the author.

Appendix P
Patronage

In the period to the Reformation the people were concerned about the afterlife. In many cases patrons commissioned their tombs within their lifetime to ensure that prayers for their souls would be carried out. Wills would also commission chantries.

Alternatively tombs would be commissioned by executors of the deceased in accordance with wishes contained in wills. Less common were tombs commissioned by the deceased's relations unless these were also executors.

The attitude of patrons in this Gothic period was to ensure the focus of intersession was on assisting the commemorated through the dangers of purgatory. The presence of spouses, angels, bedesmen and saints focused attention on this role. The use of chantries is a matter of discussion. Often confused with chapels there is some doubt as to whether this is a spiritual ritual or a physical entity. The use of perpetual in front of chantry would indicate the former as this was intended to refer to the daily saying of the mass on behalf of the deceased.

This changed at the Reformation. Patrons were now focused on remembrance. Wills were written to ensure executors would enable monuments in case their heirs were negligent in their duty. Alongside remembrance there was need to record continuity of the blood line and legitimacy of ownership of territory. The rise of heraldry demonstrated that tombs could be used to establish inheritance and ancestry especially when such status items as coats of arms were being debated.

It therefore became the fashion to show children and also first and second (and sometimes third) wives usually in attitudes of prayer. This was a symbol of stability and the number of children a point of high standing within the social arena as well as an indication of continuity of the blood line.

In another change the patronage of tombs drifted down the social scale. Lesser gentry, clergy, lawyers and merchants now saw monuments as part of their right although this was, in some quarters, decried. Some conservatives saw that monuments should relate to blood lines rather than people such as merchants who had bought their right by the judicious application of something as low as trade.

Sometimes, it all went wrong. In the 1620s, a London carver by the name of Nicholas Hare died and appointed a fellow traveller Captain John Harvey as his executor. Hare's will provided for £200 to be granted to St Dunstans in the West for the relief of the poor as well as a substantial sum for a monument. A monument was made, possibly by the Johnson workshop but Harvey absconded with the rest of the money including the parish bequest, disappearing to Virginia where he was later elected governor. Legal claims were made by the church wardens involving Dr John Donne, John Chamberlain and Sir Dudley Carleton but by the time this was resolved Harvey had spent all the money. The monument to Hare has not survived.

Tomb commissioning was seen as a masculine role. Nigel Llewellyn describes the patriarchal approach and even when the commissioning was carried out by the matriarch it is clear she was taking advice as shown by the directions given by Jane Scargill for her tomb at Whitkirk (GNP110) in which she wishes the tomb to be copied from another. The aspects of this are worth summarising in that the tomb to be copied was in Macclesfield, Cheshire, the alabaster source Derbyshire, the carver Royley of Burton on Trent, Staffordshire and the destination Whitkirk in Yorkshire demonstrating how widespread the industry had become by mid-16th century. Jane must have received recommendation regarding the Royley workshop from some male relative or friend.

Some tombs were commissioned long after the demise of the occupant. In Ratcliffe on Soar, Henry Sacheverell made provision in his will for his tomb and his father's, also named Henry (R4 and R5). When he died in 1625 these tombs were commissioned by his executor but had an odd result in that no one was alive who could remember Henry's father let alone the date of his death. Therefore the year and date of death, which was some time in 1585, remained blank on the tomb inscription. Such errors on the part of the patron have resulted in much confusion over the years.

Appendix Q
Continuity and Order

Introduction

From Norman times and especially from 1330 to the Commonwealth in 1650 the maintenance of continuity and order outweighed all other considerations. This spilt over into the erection of monuments and their preservation with some notable periods of iconoclast attack (*see* Appendix H). After 1650 during the period of Puritan domination which saw heresy in imagery and after, when patrons saw the need to 'improve' churches, the monuments suffered destruction, eviction and neglect.

Before the Reformation the existence of purgatory (discussed elsewhere) determined the content of monuments and their form. Order was maintained by directing the observer towards the need for intercession. However, long before the Reformation disturbed this order memento mori began to appear on tombs as symbols of the preparation for the afterlife. The appearance of a cadaver or skeleton represented the ultimate destiny of the body whilst the soul was sped out of purgatory by prayer. After the Reformation the memento mori became more common and diverse. Skulls, hour glasses, Father Time wielding a scythe, Death poised with an arrow demonstrated the inevitability of death. These objects were not condemned as papist symbols even when carried by a statue because they were not seen as the representation of religious figures and because they conveyed to the observer examples of virtue. Even then the use of memento mori was muted until the fourth quarter of the 16th century when the European styles of monument became established. The monuments of Plowden (A67) and other show figures and symbols which a few years earlier might well have been considered idolatrous.

Monarchy

The monarchs saw that order was more important than bitterness and revenge and it is an interesting fact that a number of kings constructed tombs to their fallen predecessors or to those who had no progeny or descendants to see that it was carried out. Henry IV erected a fine tomb to Richard II, Edward III to Edward II, Henry VII to Richard III (*see* Appendix R) and James I to Elizabeth I in 1607 – a tomb to a monarch who had overseen the death of his mother. A 1260 wooden monument to Robert Curthose (Curthose), the eldest of William I's three sons, can be found in Gloucester despite the failure of his obvious right to accede to the English throne having been overturned by firstly William II and then Henry I. Robert died as Duke of Normandy in 1134 after being held captive in Cardiff Castle from 1106. His commemoration occurred during the reign of Henry III.

The need to ensure the commemoration of princely predecessors predominated in the minds of successor monarchs. These monuments to royalty were seen by some commentators 'as pieces state politic' a fact not lost on Oliver Cromwell who declined to allow a monument for the executed Charles I and probably earned for him and for Henry Ireton, the horror of disinterment and ritual 'execution' at the restoration. In addition to blocking new monuments, Cromwell oversaw the destruction of King Stephen's tomb at Faversham and that of Henry I at Reading.

It is a matter of interest that no Stuart monarch is commemorated by a tomb monument. It is too easy to put this down to parsimony or accident but there is most likely to be a more deep-seated reason. The Stuart period was very troubled. Commencing with the Gunpowder Plot in 1607 followed by Charles I's dispute with parliament, Civil War, the Commonwealth, the fall of James II and the shaky reign of Mary when linked to the growing magnificence of nobles memorials meant that no opportunity existed for the creation of a grand monument to outshine that of the grandest duke or in some cases the humblest artisan. In Southwark Cathedral there are fine wall tablets to James I's saddler John Bingham dated 1625 (M148) and John Trehearne dated 1618 (M149). These were saddlers and porters. Such commemoration to such lowly persons would be unheard of 25 years earlier but shook the established order in Stuart times with which the nobility found hard to compete. The changing art styles also meant that commemoration was established by means of statuary rather than tombs. This discussion takes us out of the period in which alabaster was used as a material since true marble became competitive in price and more in keeping with continental practices.

Appendix H discusses the destruction of church imagery during the Reformation in the 16th century but little damage to effigies seems to have been carried out until the accession of Elizabeth I in 1559 and even here the maintenance of continuity ensured that she soon put an end to that. The Plantagenet monuments which display the Yorkist collar seem to have come in for more than their fair share of abuse as indicated by damage to that at Sutton Bonington (GNP73) and Minster in Sheppey (G100).

Patriarchy

As to formal arrangement of effigies, patriarchal dominance is demonstrated by the raising of male effigies above that of female where both are shown. In murals where both are shown kneeling the male figure is shown to the viewers left which is the heraldic senior side. Even when the male is a recumbent effigy the kneeling wives are still shown facing to the left (*see* R5). There are exceptions. Where more than wife is shown the order of the effigies is in the order of marriage – again *see* R5 in which the carver has taken care to dress the wives in the style to which they would have been accustomed within their lifetime. In the case of Lucy,the third wife at Ratcliffe on Soar (M2), she is shown in the dress of the 1620s with half ruff, a fashion which would soon be replaced by more practical styles and probably caused her some discomfort over the years. Lucy remained at Ratcliffe until her death in 1667.

In a similar vein the children are often shown with the progeny of the first wife taking precedence over the later ones. The rule of patriarchy was fiercely defended into post-Reformation England. The placing of the powerful below the weak, the right below the left was seen as disruptive and monuments were designed to maintain the status quo. This did not mean that there were exceptions. Powerful women could establish dominance over lowly born spouses but could also justify the position as a result of extemporary virtues.

Heraldry

Commencing in the 16th century there was a growing number of historians and antiquaries who used inscriptions on monuments as a source for family and county histories. Amongst these were Hearne, Camden, Leland and Aubrey. In the 17th century interest in heraldry resulted in heralds using such inscriptions for the determination of family links in the process of authorising coats of arms which were a prominent feature of mural monuments. These were often manufactured and sometimes had dubious historical connections. Even at the onset of the English Civil War Sir William Dugdale was touring the country and making notes and drawings of monuments as well as arbitrating on heraldic matters.

I have to thank these dedicated men for some of the material which has allowed the shape and design of the monuments to be recorded for posterity. Their purpose was to establish the ancestral lineage of families in keeping with the maintenance of order and continuity. Where this could not be easily done the fabrication of an ancestral line was resorted to rather than leave a lord of the manor with dubious connections. In the case of Dugdale himself, it is recorded that he visited Gervase Piggott at Thrumpton Hall, Nottingham in 1660 with a view to establishing his line. After some time he ruled that Piggott was descended from the Norman Picot family despite that family having no connection with the area after 1313. He agreed that the Pigotts could display the emblem of the Picots which was three picks and this was subsequently emblazoned on the Piggott memorials in the local church. It is clear that a questionable link was far more important than to leave his friend dangling, a situation which was unlikely to be challenged for centuries if at all.

Symbolism

During the 15th century there emerged a desire to demonstrate the ultimate fate of the body. In this the normal clothed recumbent effigy is repeated as a cadaver or corpse beneath the tomb chest which was cut away or left open to reveal the second effigy. The purpose is obscure but may allude to the words in the Book of Common Prayer which states 'while our bodies lie in the dust our soul may rest with thee'. Examples include, Bishop Richard Fleming's 1431 tomb in Lincoln, the Golafre 1442 tomb in Fyfield (X92) and that to Archbishop Henry Chichele in Canterbury of 1443 which are early examples but not alabaster. The tomb to John Earl of Arundel of 1442 (G168), the Duchess of Suffolk in Ewelme (G142), John Barton at Holme (A84) and that of Bishop Beckington in Wells (G156) are however of this type but rendered in alabaster. In the case of Holme there are two clothed effigies and one cadaver as there are in Wollaton, Nottinghamshire in stone except that the two clothed effigies are in brass. There appears no simple explanation as to how this practice evolved but it seems that it was simply imported as a style from France. Such memento mori would appear in different forms later but the cadaver, as a feature, was rare after the mid-1500s. Two exceptions with a recumbent alabaster cadaver associated with kneeling effigies, are that at Kinlet, Shrops to St George Blount (1584, M296) and Breedon on the Hill to George Shirley (1588, M95). After this death was depicted by a shrouded figure such as that to the Foljambe family at Chesterfield *circa* 1592 (M116) and the Beresford family at Fenny Bentley (G71) or a recumbent skeleton such that at Hackington, Kent (R193). One of the oddest in this group is that to John Donne in St Paul's Cathedral (1631, R197) after which this depiction was rare with the exception of that to William Peck at Spixworth, Norfolk (1635, M210). Such depiction ceased at the restoration.

The allegory of the soul rising to heaven is repeated in the depiction of the soul being carried aloft in a napkin and this can be seen at Lutterworth (GNP47) and at Bardney (S46) and also in the panel of John the Baptist at Amport (X60). After the Reformation such depiction of souls and even angels was considered imprudent.

This medieval symbolism was replaced by one of resurrection in the 17th century. Amongst these are St Paul's Cathedral (1631, R197), Amersham (1636, M356) and Chipping Campden (1642, M129). This group includes that at Stratton Strawless (M559) in which the depicted is rising from a charnel house of bones and the tomb at Egham (M162) in which the depicted as a skeleton awaits the call to resurrection. Resurrection is often accompanied by angels blowing trumpets.

Language

Latin is the predominant language on alabaster tombs up to the Reformation. The use of this language limited the ability of the ordinary populace to understand the words. This was countered by the use of heraldry which most could recognise. Sally Badham points out that one of the first inscriptions in English was that on a brass in Wanlip, Leicestershire to Sir Thomas and Lady Walsh of 1397-1421. It is significant that the first monarch to use the English language in official documents was Henry V 1413–1422 (*History Magazine* September 2016 page 60). This not only widened the scope of intersession but listed the couple's good works so that more prayers would be forthcoming. Sir Thomas Walsh was also of the lesser gentry rank but English was to remain rare until the middle of the 16th century. Latin continued to make periodic appearances right through to the current time.

Heraldry

In the absence of literacy, knights and gentry could be identified by their heraldry. Long before alabaster was used heraldry was beginning to be organised and in the mid-15th century the principals which saw the creation of heralds was formulated in Italy. These were applied in heraldic disputes in that century and formalised in the time of Henry V and Richard III. The *Heraldic Miscellany* by Sir William Dugdale was published in 1486. In early tombs namely those at Hanbury (G28) and Westminster (G18) the knight carries a shield on which would be emblazoned the coat of arms. Time has erased these and in the case of Hanbury it has prevented the knight to be positively identified and dated. The kite-shaped shield beloved on the Purbeck carvers can be seen in the Temple Church in London but the alabaster shields are square and sometimes have a notch for the lance. Shields later migrated to the tomb chest and still later to back and top of mural tombs.

The alabastermen produced shields held by angels and one of the first was Elford in 1390 (G158). The details of angels are contained in notes L1, L3, and L39. Occasionally the heraldry would be carved instead of painted and later restorers often repainted those devices which could be identified.

Early alabaster tombs depicted the knight with his head on a cushion but by the mid-14th century this had been replaced by the great helm often with a crest. As stated elsewhere the great helm had largely been replaced in battle but was still used for tournaments. The crest was a heraldic feature and the main text above details those crests and their owners which can be identified. The earliest alabaster knight to employ a great helm was that of the Despenser at Tewkesbury (G10, 1349) but cushions continued to appear for some years. It is noted that some have mantles with dagged ends representing the scarf which received cuts at the joust. Amongst these are Fitzherbert (G62), Stafford (G184), Cholmondeley (T28) and Brereton (G53).

In addition to shields the arms of knights was sometimes emblazoned on jupons and tabards. If painted they may well have disappeared but in some cases the arms were formed of gesso so that they stood proud of the surface. Few if any have survived.

The ultimate sign of heraldry was a crown. Not just restricted to kings and queens these can be found on the effigies of nobility. A crown can be found on the first alabaster tomb at Gloucester (G9), Henry IV (G97), Duke of Norfolk (A29), Duke of Suffolk (G163), Earl of Arundel (G167), Earl of Rutland (M89), and at Swine (G189 to G191). Ladies include the Duchess of Suffolk (G142) and Lady Smythe (G159).

Appendix R
Hilton (Hylton) Family of Nottingham-Alabastermen

Historical Note

Richard III was buried in Greyfriars, Leicester without ceremony in August 1485. His discovery in 2012 show that he was buried in a rough-cut grave little more than a foot deep in the choir of the chapel but without any indication of any coffin, shroud or slab. In 1491 there was a belief the grave was covered by a bare slab but in 1495 Walter Hilton (Hylton) was paid £50 for a tomb and a James Keyley, probably the bailiff was paid £10 1s for some unspecified work which was later disputed in chancery.[1] One author Holinshed in an article, made after the tomb was destroyed wrote 'Henry VII caused a tomb to be made and set up over the place where he was buried in the church of the Greyfriars at Leicester with a picture of alabaster representing his person'. The alabaster was later described as 'mingled'.

From the details above it can be assumed that 'mingled' refers to the veined alabaster then found in the quarries of Needwood Forest. In addition the term 'picture' was attributable to an image inscribed on a slab rather than an effigy. There is broad agreement to this. The tomb was probably a type called a tabletop.

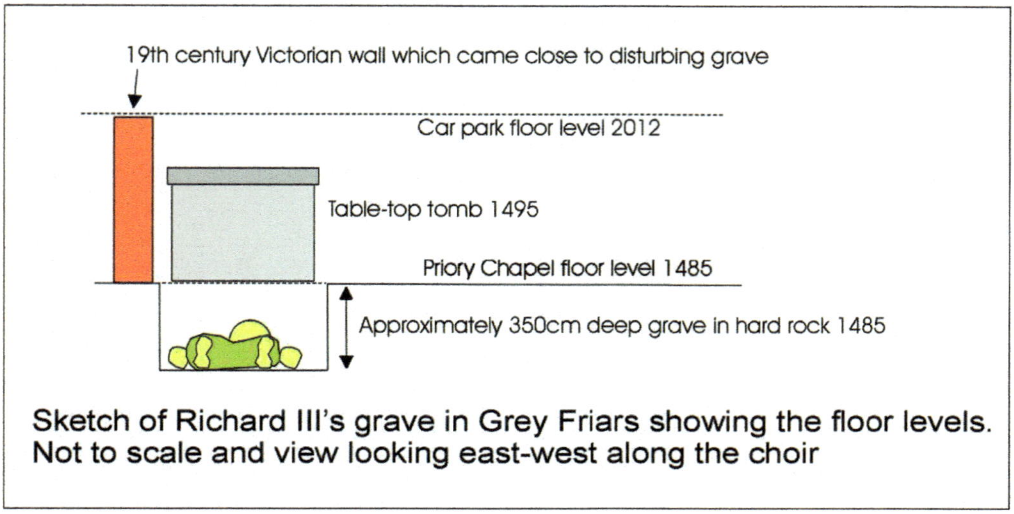

Figure 117. The tomb of Richard III in Grey Friars, Leicester. Drawn by the author.

Analysis

In the following section Borough Records ii or iii represent volumes in the Nottinghamshire Archives. The name Hilton is also spelt Hylton.

The borough records for Nottingham in the 14th and 15th century list few people working in the alabaster trade. One group which appears more frequently than others is the Hilton or Hylton family. Walter Hilton is recorded as sheriff in 1463–1464 (*Borough Records ii*) but this may well have been the father of Walter Hilton the alabasterman. John Hilton was sheriff in 1475–1476 (borough records iii, page 301) but there are no records of him as an alabasterman.

Walter Hilton was assessed in 1472–1473 for tax at 2s 8½d in respect of his freehold at Nottingham (*Borough Records ii*, page 293). Which property is not clear but may have been the family home on the banks of the River Leene.

The first record of Walter Hilton the alabasterman was as a 'carpenter' working on the construction of New Hall[2] in 1478–1479 but may well be poor reporting as he was probably associated with the stone work. However, in 1480 Walter applied for a lease of land on the south side of the Waters of Leene and north side of Walters's garden (*Borough Records ii*, 419). This may well be a planned extension of the family property but it was not the last to be mentioned.

In 1480 Walter's son or his brother Edward was recorded as an image painter and may well have been working alongside Walter as in 1482 there was a dispute with Emma Sherwood. Emma was the widow of Robert Sherwood another alabasterman (called an image maker). It appears that Walter carried out some work for Robert that was completed before he died but Walter claimed he was not paid. He subsequently sued Emma Sherwood (widow and executrix of Robert's estate) on the 5th February 1482 claiming a sum of 8s 8d for gilding and painting an altarpiece (tabernacle) in St Peter's Church, Nottingham. He said the money was for work on an image of St Philip for which it had been agreed to pay 6s. The rest was for a mantelpiece to the value of 2s. These were almost certainly to be alabaster. The remainder of the claim (8d) was for 'residual damage'. Emma denied the charge. The outcome is not recorded but it is likely that Walter's claim was upheld. Any tabernacle in St Peter's Church would not have survived the Reformation. The mantelpiece is probably a triptych similar to that in the Leicester museum.

By 1484–1485 Edward is recorded in borough records as an image maker. It was not unusual for alabastermen to start at the bottom as painters, work their way up to carvers and then to foremen/owners. A commentator in the following century noted that Edward was an image maker between 1488 and 1502 – but *see* later. In 1500 Edward's name appears on the list of town council members (*Borough Records ii*, page 431).

Walter Hilton was, in Aug 1486, enfeoffed of properties in Nottingham of the gift and grant of Thomas Bradmer (*Borough Records iii*, page 427). Later in the records these were described as two cottages in High Pavement, two in Pylchergate, a messuage in Narrow Marsh, a garden opposite Friars Minor (Listergate), a garden near Milneholes (east of Brewhouse Yard) and rood and a half of meadow land near le Roche Yard (also in Brewhouse Yard) and a meadow near Sheepbridge (a bridge in the Meadows) and other lands mostly meadows.

In 1488 Walter Hilton acquired a right to three messuages near the Woman's Market in Nottingham from William in the Wroo (a Glover) but he may well have been the leasee earlier. The Women's Market was for poultry, butter and other consumables sold by farmer's wives. It was held at Hen Cross or Hennecrosse which is now the intersection of The Poultry, Bridlesmithgate, High St and Victoria St. Most of the 14th and 15th century alabastermen were concentrated in St Mary's Gate, and the streets to the north. From 1550 when the Nottingham trade was destroyed there appears to have been a migration away to Burton but later, in the 17th century there are records in Stony St. Alabaster work in Nottingham terminates in 1647.

By 1488 Walter Hilton was an important person in Nottingham which probably led to his appointment as mayor 1489–1490.

In the meantime Edward Hilton was elected sheriff in 1484–1485 and seems to have occupied a property on the south side of the Market Place (now South Parade) as a few years later the Borough records state 'Edward Hilton enfeoffed of a messuage on the southern side of the Saturday market' and in 1504 he was taxed £5 4s 'to the subsidy' for this (*Borough records iii*, page 436). In 1488 he stood bond of £100 for Thomas Warber recorded as a 'litster'[3] (*Borough records iii*,page 17).

In 1492–1493 Walter's name is entered in the list of aldermen and he was again elected mayor in 1496–1497.

In the chancery records[4] there is an entry dated 1st July 1496 that 12 months earlier (summer 1495) Walter Hilton had been contracted to construct a tomb for Richard III in Greyfriars, Leicester – *see* note 5 and sketch of grave above. It is worth speculating as to how this may have come about. We now know that Richard III was buried without ceremony and that Henry VII appears to have been concerned with this and appointed Sir Reynold Bray and Sir Thomas Lovell to oversee the provision of a tomb over the burial place. These two high status individuals appear to be highly regarded as they were also Cecily Neville, dowager Duchess of York's executors.

The choice of Hilton needs some explanation. In the first half of the 15th century the centre of effigy making was a Chellaston but after the start of the Wars of the Roses, York seems to have dominated for the focus to revert to Nottingham in the last quarter. Whether this was chance or due to the influence of a Yorkist king cannot be ascertained but by the last quarter Nottingham was again in full production with effigy carving moving westward from Chellaston to Burton on Trent – *see* Index of Carvers.

Nottingham remained the source for panels, triptychs and church images yet it was a Nottingham carver who was chosen for the task of building the tomb of Richard III.

Henry VII was known to be in Leicester in September 1495. It is possible that he passed through Nottingham some time previously (to which he appears to have been favourably disposed since its help in the Battle of East Stoke[6]) and would have met Walter Hilton then a leading light having been mayor and the senior alabasterman in the city. Henry, forever parsimonious, would have noted that the carvers of Nottingham could produce a more cost-effective tomb than their counterparts in Burton and specified the city to his councillors. This decision was made despite Walter probably never having constructed a tomb before. Walter could not carve an effigy but would be able to incise (or obtain) a slab and so this was probably what was done. The subsequent payment to James Keyley has yet to be fully explained.[7]

The contract for the tomb is generally accepted as being £50 paid in two instalments of £20 and the balance on assembly in Greyfriars. The extant chancery document cost figures can no longer be read and for the amount we are reliant on old historians whose accuracy cannot be determined. This requires some examination. John Ashdown-Hill in his book (*The Last Days of Richard III*, ISBN 978 0 7524 9305 6) states that a plea in chancery states that one Rauf (Ralph) Hill, a grocer,[8] brought a suit against Walter Hilton for using his (Hill's) name in the indentures with Bray and Lovell in which the £50 is alleged to appear. Whatever the figure Ashdown-Hill draws parallels with the prices quoted on the few surviving contracts (page 100).

These are poor comparisons. The one effigial tomb quoted (Lowick) was carved within the quarry from which the alabaster was won and some 70 years before that of Richard III whilst the Chesterfield tomb was a tabletop and again carved close to the Fauld quarry from which the alabaster was won and in any case the price quoted may not have included the chest or brass and is a plain and simple slab. The two clearly Nottingham carved items (the retable and image) were small. The retable was probably a domestic triptych little more than 9 inches high and the image a statue about 18 inches high similar to the Flawford virgin.

Ashdown-Hill goes on the make the suggestion that Richard III's tomb had an alabaster effigy (his book, page 101 and Figure 25). He also states that '... alabaster tomb effigies were ten-a-penny ... whilst incised slabs from this period were much rarer'. These statements are questionable. Appendix D2 lists 18 extant alabaster slabs between 1485 and 1499 and 32 effigial tombs which, whilst making slabs the minority, hardly makes them rare.

Clearly Leicester University also does not agree with Ashdown-Hill as their CGI demonstrator of the Greyfriars Chapel in the Richard III Exhibition, Leicester shows an incised slab on a tomb chest. Unfortunately, care was not taken to research existing late 15th century slab designs and so CGI image shows a form of tomb chest most unlike that which would have been produced. A typical inscribed slab is s shown in the Humberstone slab below. There again the 1495 slab may well still exist. It is a case in point that there are instances when a slab has been reused by turning it over and carving the back in a form of palimpsest. It may be that the slab of Richard III may yet turn up on the back of an incised slab to someone else – one can dream. If a king can be found in a car park his slab can be found in some English country church.

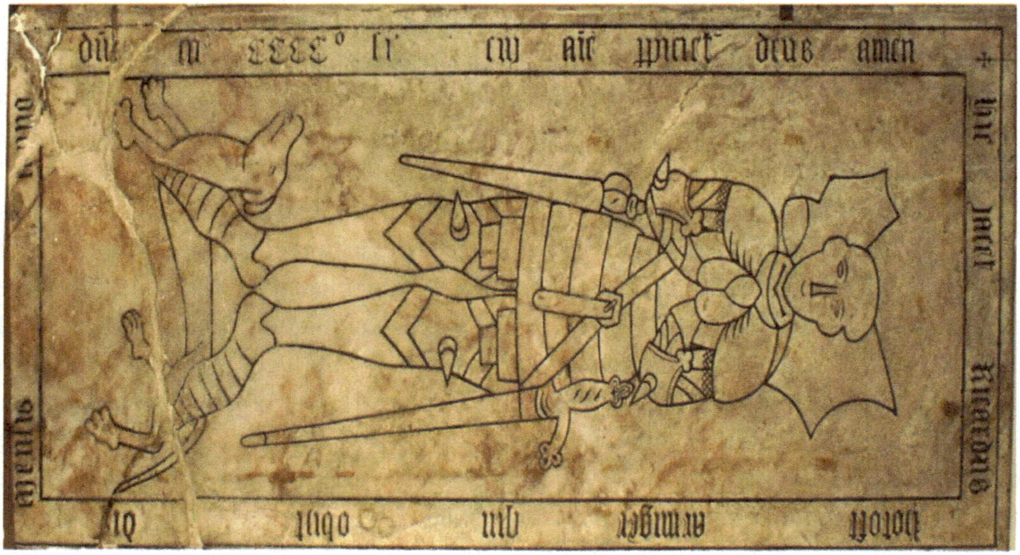

Figure 118. The slab in Humberstone church to Richard Hotoft died 1451 (TT1) which is typical of the inscribing of an image of a knight on alabaster. The slab was probably a tabletop but has now been mounted vertical on the wall. Such slabs from the period after 1595 could hide on their back, the inscribed 'picture' of Richard III. Photo: John Allen.

The one important issue is that there are no records of any effigial monuments being carved in Nottingham. There is a good reason for this. The workshops were small and not suited for the large blocks that would be needed and the cost of transport from the quarries would make the carving of effigies uneconomic. To get from the quarries by road to Nottingham meant the crossing of two maybe three rivers. This would be no problem with pack horses carrying small slabs of alabaster for retables, reredos and images in panniers, but for 4 ton blocks of alabaster, this would either be outrageously expensive or impossible. Nor could the river be used. Whereas Nottingham was reachable from Trent Falls (where it meets the Humber) for about 300 days each year, navigation upstream was obstructed first by the Billy Stones (Thrumpton) shallows and by a second succession of shallows until fully blocked by a weir at King's Mill. Navigation may well be just possible when the river was running but no reliance could be placed on this and the weir could be only be bypassed if the miller would allow a 'flash' which was rare. Therefore, navigation from Burton to Nottingham was a hit or miss affair and rarely used except when the river was 'running'.

Walter Hilton may well have contracted for a slab tomb in the form of a tabletop from the western Chellaston or Burton workshops, the enhanced price being due to the fact that obtaining such a slab from the western quarries would have cost him £10 to £20 in mining and cartage costs, the price of an uncut slab. He may then have carved the tomb sides and ends himself which was his normal level of business. The slab may well have been delivered direct from the western workshops involving only the crossing of the Trent which was easy in the 15th century.

We have seen that cartage to site was the responsibility of the purchaser and so the costs for uncut transport incurred by the western kervers was negligible. We have no reliable figures for charges for effigies from them at the end of the 15th century. However, it's most likely with good alabaster being harder to find in large blocks the price of a single effigial tomb may well have been in the order of £70 to £90 or twice that paid to Hilton.

Walter Hilton died 12th October 1502. In 1503 Walter's widow Joan released her right to three cottages near Hennecrosse held of the town (*Borough Records iii*, 434). Nottingham bridge wardens record an account for 3s 4d from a bequest of Joan wife of Walter Hilton (*Borough Records iii*, 95). The records describe the premises as being on the northern side of the King's Highway of the Woman's Market between the lands of Gervase Bampton on the east and the land of the late John Babington on the west. The cottages Walter Hylton occupied had been received from William Wroo son and heir of John in le Wroo (glover) '... which John had them by demise of the mayor and community'.

In the meantime Edward Hilton continues to appear despite the suggestion he ceased trading in 1502. He is mentioned in respect of litigation over an altarpiece in 1512 for Ashton under Lyne church but appears to have died *circa* 1520 as 'Edward Hylton left his house and bakehouse to found an image of St Luke in St Mary's Church and wax for candles and is willed to be buried in the church' (*Borough Records iii*, page 93). One final odd entry states Ralph Palmer has willed to be buried in a church 'near my father Edward Hilton' – will dating from 1529 (*Borough Records iii*, page 94). Like that at St Peter's the image will have disappeared in the destruction of 1550.

Notes:

1. A James Keyley was sued in 1480 for failure to give up two silver 'cooporteria' to William Smith which he had 'detained'. Keyley and his wife Margaret are reported to be formerly of Lichfield now of Shenstone, Staffordshire. They did not appear and the sheriff issued a warrant for their arrest. Jon Bayliss has more details of this in CMS Spring 2013.
2. Cannot be sure where this was but a John Clerk of Nottingham was recorded in 1479 as 'supervising the building of New Hall'. It may well be Newhall in south Derbyshire rebuilt about that time. In St Peter's Church, Stapenhill, Burton upon Trent there is an incised slab recorded as that of William Dethick of Newhall and his wife Margaret. William Dethick died in 1497. His slab is claimed to be in Fauld alabaster and was once a tabletop tomb but was let into the floor in 1822. It is now imbedded in the wall. The juxtaposition of the date of this slab with that of Richard III is interesting and might well be from the Hylton workshop. Despite this, the identification of New Hall remains fugitive.
3. An Old English name for a dyer. The Nottingham cave system in the Narrow Marsh was frequented by tanners and dyers.
4. BM ADD 7099 Folio 129 – *see also* note 6.
5. Leicester, Greyfriars. In the Public Records Office copies of the chancery records there is a record dated 1 July 1496 stating that twelve months previously the Royal Commissioners Sir Reynold Bray (Chancellor of the Duchy of Lancaster) and Sir Thomas Lovell (Chancellor of the Exchequer) arranged for one Walter Hylton, a Nottingham alabasterman to build a memorial over the grave. Hylton was to receive £50 for the work payable in two instalments of £20 and the balance 'when the tomb is installed in the church (of Greyfriars) aforesaid'. There was also a payment of £10 1s to James Keyley but the purpose was not stated. He is most likely to be the bailiff in charge and the charge for the carter from Nottingham. There was a dispute between Keyley and Hylton which went on to be resolved in chancery in which the tomb is described as being in the 'Newarke' which is crossed out and replaced by 'friars'. There is no other description of this monument but in 1577 Raphael Holinshed recorded that it incorporated a 'picture' in alabaster depicting his majesty. This may have been from recollections as the tomb is unlikely to have survived the suppression of the friary in 1538. William Burton writing in the 17th century recorded the same details probably taken from Holinshed. Sir George Buck, also in the 17th century, recorded the alabaster was 'of mingle coloured marble' meaning that the alabaster was veined but also added 'adorned by an effigy'. He may have seen a fragment but reference to an 'effigy' may have dual meaning. The carving depicting the king may have been an effigy or more likely an incised tabletop slab. The carver, Hylton, was a Nottingham alabasterman voted lord mayor in 1489–1490 and again in 1496–1497 – so someone of high status. Whilst Nottingham was famous for its small images, retable and reredos panels there is little or no evidence for effigy carving in the city this being the province of Burton and South Derbyshire. The transport issues of carrying large blocks of alabaster from the quarries or even up the steep hills of Nottingham meant that these were carved close to the quarries – a practice that continued until the end of the 16th century. However, there is a case for saying that Nottingham also acted as a retail and marketing centre for the western workshops and may have contracted for an effigy or large tabletop from these – hence the dispute with Keyley. The forinsec pleas of Nottingham have many records of disputes between alabastermen and carters and sub-contractors and indeed Hylton is named in one in 1482 over the staining of an image. Christopher Wren whilst visiting Leicester in 1612 claims to have seen in the garden which Greyfriars had become a 'stone pillar on which was a

simple inscription' which Robert Hayrick Mayor of Leicester had set up. No mention of an effigy or inscribed slab is made and by 1612 it is fair to say that whatever existed there in 1538 had gone. There the matter rests until further information can be obtained. The population of existing tabletop inscribed tombs is very small. There are many inscribed alabaster slabs in churches set into the floor but few on a tomb chest. A census shows that there are four from 1486 to 1510 (excluding that of Richard III), three 1510 to 1547 and three from 1550 to 1614 when the practice in tabletop tombs in alabaster seems to have died. For details *see* the TT notes above. The tabletop tomb appears never to have been popular. On the 4th February 2013 the results of the archaeological investigation into a car park in Leicester which was on the site of Greyfriars was announced. This investigation unearthed a skeleton with severe war wounds. The conclusions were that the skeleton was without doubt that of the body of Richard III. The creation of the tomb post burial for monarchs who death was un-natural has strong precedents – for details *see* A55.

6. Almost all the Nottingham gentry rallied to Henry VII's cause to meet the forces of the pretender Lambert Simnal at East Stoke, Nottinghamshire in 1487. Several were knighted and Henry's chronicler stated 'We were led to the battle by six good men and true of the village of Ratcliffe who showed the way and the places of ambush'.
7. The extract from the *Privy Purse* reads 11th September 1495 'To James Keyley for King Richard's tomb £10 1s'. Jon Bayliss provided details of Keyley in CMS Newsletter Spring 2013. He concluded that he was the bailiff placed in charge of supervising the tomb's installation. He is associated with Shenstone church where he founded a chantry. The cartage of the parts of the tomb from Nottingham (or Burton) would be a charge to the crown. It may well be this payment to an unnamed carter – the delivery having to be by road as river carriage was impossible in the late 15th century.
8. Ralph Hill was sheriff of Nottingham 1481–1482.

Appendix S
Painters and Stainers

The painting or staining of alabaster appears to have been carried out from early in the 14th century. However details of this process and the materials used are difficult to uncover. There is no doubt that patrons would see staining and gilding as an essential part of the delivered tomb. However, there was also a desire for the translucent features of alabaster which was close to normal skin colour and so staining would be restricted to cloths and hair and other features. In addition the fact that many tombs cannot be identified is largely down to the fact that inscriptions were painted and over time these have yielded to time.

Painting and staining took off with the retable and reredos panels produced in Nottingham from the late 14th century. The panels were coloured to enhance the story and many extant panels retain their colour after some 700 years. The borough records of Nottingham record painters (peynters) and stainers (steyners) as well as imagers, imaginer, ymager and imaginatours although this group is more associated with the carving. There is a belief that in some workshops painting was part of the duties of the imager.

Nottingham does not appear to have had a guild but Francis Hill's book on Tudor and Stuart Lincoln refers to the creation of a guild for painters in that city as follows 'When the council came to the painters, gilders, stainers and alabastermen they adopted the pre-Reformation charter written for better understanding in English'. This would be post-1560.

In the medieval period the term staining and painting was freely exchanged but today we consider that painting is the application of colour and staining, the application of dyes or transparent varnishes or wax.

In discussing the finishing of sculptures it is necessary to mention gesso. This was much used in wooden and some stone carving as a mixture of animal glue and white paint and filler in the form of chalk, gypsum or other powder. This formed a stiffish paste which was brushed on and allowed to set. It formed an absorbent base for painting and gilding. Sometimes linseed oil was used and the finished base may be coated in shellac. There is scant evidence that this was ever used on alabaster carvings as the surface of the stone was already suitable for direct painting with the exception for details such as daisy patterns especially on the background for tomb chest panels.[1]

The details of paint or stain are hard to find. However in 1747 there was published a specification for the staining of marble which had its roots in the early 17th century if not earlier. The specification was written in Latin but loosely translated in 1775 and appears in the account book of one Thomas Watts of High Wycombe.

The original specification is the work of William Byrd (1624–*circa* 1690). Byrd was a 'stone cutter' of Gloucestershire who had served his apprenticeship under Walter Nicholls another 'stone cutter' who worked extensively in Gloucester and the neighbourhood. Byrd came to Nicholls at the age of 15 in 1640 and served 8 years. Nicholls died in 1648 and in that year Byrd moved to Oxford (Holywell). In 1669 he presented to Charles II marble which he had impregnated with stain, breaking it to demonstrate how far the stain had penetrated into the material. This process appears to be a crude form of vacuum-pressure impregnation of porous objects much used in electrical industry today. He made a statement in 1682 in respect of the lawsuit over the mansion at Cuddeston stating he was 57 years old and had been born in St Nicholas parish Gloucester. The entry goes on to state he was well known as a carver of monuments and stained chimney pieces.

Where Byrd acquired this knowledge is unclear. Walter Nichols was a close friend of John Campion of Gloucester whom he left a bequest in his will. Campion is best known as a 17th century painter/stainer who did a good deal of contemporary work in the Gloucester area and from which Byrd may well have learnt the details of the staining. Campion is recorded as gilding and staining the decorative case for the organ at Gloucester Cathedral in November 1664. Masse's publication about the cathedral written in 1899 confirms Campion's status as a 'celebrated Gloucestershire stainer and painter of heraldic subjects'.[2]

The Latin version of the specification mentioned above opens with a warning that alabaster is a less suitable medium for staining than other 'softer' marbles and for some reason this was not included in the English translation. The specification in English reads:

Colouring of Marble

In order to succeed in it the pieces of marble on which the experiment is tried must be well polished and clear from the least spots or vein the harder the marble is the better it will bear heat necessary in the operation upon. Heat is always necessary to opening of pores in marble so as to render it fit to receive the colours but the marble must never be made red hot for then the texture of the marble itself is injured and the colours burnt and lose their beauty. Too small a degree of heat is as bad as too great for in this case though the marble receives the colour it will not be fixed in it not strike deep enough. Some colour will strike even cold but is never so well as when a good degree of heat is used. The proper degree is that without making the marble red will make the colour boil upon its surface. The menstruums[3] used to strike in the colour must (be) varied according to the nature of the colour to be used. A lixivium made with horses or dog's urine with four parts quick lime and one part potash is excellent for some colours. Common ley of wood ashes does very well for some others. For some, spirits of wine is best and finally for others oily liquors or common white wine. The colours that have been found to succeed best with the peculiar menstruums are these – stone blue dissolved in 6 parts of spirit of wine or of the urinous lixivium[4] and that colour that the painters call litmose dissolved in common ley of wood ashes and extract of saffron and that colour made of buckthorn berries and called by the painters sap green both succeed well dissolved in urine and quick lime tolerably well in spirits of wine. Vermilion and a fine colour power cochineal[5] succeed also very well in the same liquor. Dragon's blood[6] succeeds very well in spirits of wine[7] as does also a tincture of log wood (dogwood) in the same spirits. Alkanet[8] root gives a fine colour, but the only menstruums to be used for this are oil of turpentine for neither spirits of wine, nor any lixvium will do with it. There is another kind of Sanquis Dragonis called Dragon's Blood in Tears which mixed with urine alone gives a very elegant colour phi. Trans No 268.[9] Besides these mixtures of colours and menstruums there some colours to be laid on dry and un-mixed. These are Dragon's Blood of the purest kind for a red gamboge for a yellow green, wax for a green, common brimstone pitch and turpentine for a brown colour. The marble for these experiments must be made considerable hot[10] and the colours are to be rubbed on dry in the lumps.[11]

Notes:

1. For hands and feet a mortar composed of quicklime or gypsum mixed with casein (skimmed milk cheese) was devised. This provided for a strong adhesive for alabaster and marble products throughout the 17th century and may still have been employed into the 19th century. Casein, a phosphoprotein, is well known in the manufacturer of some paints and was used in binding safety matches. It was also used for gluing some wooden-framed aircraft including the Mosquito.
2. The register of apprentices for the city of Gloucester lists John Campion, son of John Campion painter stainer as being apprenticed to his father on the 28th Sept 1672 for seven years with a final payment of 20s. John Campion is shown as city sheriff 1674–1675.
3. Menstruum is the generic name for a solvent used for the extraction of compounds from plants or animal tissue.
4. Lixivium is the liquid produced by leaching wood ash with water sometimes known as lye.
5. Cochineal is a crimson colour from an insect found in Mexico and South America. It was used by the Maya and Aztec peoples. The conquest of the Americas in the 15th century introduced this dye to Europe.
6. Dragon's Blood is a resin obtained in the 14th century from the Canary Islands used in dyes and varnishes.
7. Spirit of wine otherwise known as aqua vitae is distilled from ordinary wine. Sometimes called brandy.
8. Alkanet is plant of the borage family and can give a yellow, red or green pigment.
9. The meaning of this sentence is not known but may be a translation error.
10. The action of heating the stone drives off any water vapour and can create a partial vacuum

in the pores, cracks or veins. The application of the stain to the surface causes the vacuum to draw the liquid into these. Careful heating should not damage the stone as both marble and alabaster were formed under heat. Alabaster may well have fewer surface defects and the staining may penetrate less than in fissured marble hence the warning. However this should not prevent this process being carried out on that stone.

11. We can conclude that the primary colours were red, green and blue.

There is no proof that this process was extensively used on alabaster. The warning produced in the mid-17th century, mentioned above, indicates that it was at least tried as an experiment and therefore included here as an example of the stainer's techniques.

It is clear that Campion was well known by the Nicholls workshop and it is worth speculating that he may well have worked for other Gloucester workshops including that of the Baldwins which was operational until 1662.

Looking further back into medieval times the painting and staining of panels for reredos and retables as well as figures produced in the Nottingham workshops was universal. William Burdon was recorded as being employed in painting the Windsor retable in 1369 (B43) and painter/stainers appear spasmodically over the next 200 years – *see* Appendix G. Francis Cheetham in his brilliant analysis of medieval alabasterers covers the art of painting (pages 26 to 27). Many of the alabastermen were responsible for their own painting as indicated by the disputes of the 15th century involving the Hilton workshop (Appendix R) and that of Nicholas Hill and William Bott (B5). However, this does not mean the carvers did the painting and the workshop may well have employed journeyman painters.

One of the best descriptions of staining is given as part of the contract for the Green monument at Lowick (G122). The contract states that the tomb, images and arch shall be '… gilded, painted and arrayed with colours well and sufficiently in the pure and honest and profitable manner that pertains to such work'. Only the hands and faces were to be left unpainted. It is impugned by the extract that monuments in the early 15th century were totally painted.

Cheetham lists the colours used including red, green, black, brown, gold, white, pink and blue. Appendix IV of Cheetham's book gives details of paint analysis carried out in Nottingham and within the Victoria and Albert Museum in the 1960s and 1970s. Discussions with Cathy Littlejohn of Hare and Humphreys in February 2014 have indicated that minerals dried and powdered with a pestle and mortar and then mixed with animal glue and other bases/mediums existed in times past.

The following list from several sources summarises the colours and materials:

Colour	**Source**	**Medium**
Red	Red mercuric sulphide	Animal glue
	Red oxide	None
	Red iron oxide[12]	None
	Red lead[12]	Oil,[15] glue tempera[16]
Pink	White lead with red above	*See* above
Gold	Gold leaf on red ground	Oil[15]
	Gold and silver	Oil[15]
	Gold leaf on yellow ground[11]	Oil[15]
Silver	Rare and source unknown	
Blue	Azurite and white lead[14]	Animal glue
Green[13]	Copper oxide	Turpentine[17]
Black	Carbon black	Animal glue, water glue
White	White lead	Oil[15]
Brown	Not defined	

Notes:

13. Blue and blue-green smalt, yellow ochre, white lead and carbon black may be later paint.
14. Azurite can degrade to a green. Ferric oxide with silicon and aluminium (does not seem to have been used as a colour in its own right).
15. Believed to be linseed oil or walnut oil rather than mineral oil.
16. Water glue and egg.
17. This is resin turpentine sometime called Venice – a naturally occurring substance of high acidity.

In the early period of tomb making it is possible the tombs were uncoloured apart from the painting of coats of arms. Evidence of polychroming seems to indicate that this may have started at the end of the 15th century and it is most likely that the same pigments as used on panels was also used for effigies.

Some effigies have no evidence of paint but have a deep hue, deeper than that of the original alabaster. In the case of Holme Pierrepont effigy of 1499 (G135) the alabaster is an even golden colour, too regular to be attributed to atmospheric pollution. There is a suggestion that beeswax may have been used to give a polished sheen on the effigy which over the years would darken. Whatever is the cause of the darkening the result is not unpleasant and merits further research.

A periodical called *Mechanics* of 1829 had an odd entry covering the treatment of alabaster. In an article by Mr Henry Moore of Greenhill, Derby he describes marking the block of alabaster for carving and then painting the uncarved portions with wax dissolved in turpentine and with white lead. After being allowed to dry the object is immersed in rain water for 48 hrs which etches the un-waxed parts. The wax is then removed by a pad soaked in turpentine and then dusted with plaster of Paris. He says that this was the treatment given to '... a vase made from alabaster from a quarry in Chellaston about 4 miles from Derby'. He recommends cleaning using turpentine and then dusting with plaster of Paris being much preferred to '... cleaning in the usual way using fish skins and Dutch rushes'.

The *Transactions of the Royal Society of Arts* Vol 42-43 refer to the presentation of a silver medal to Moore for this article dated 26th March 1825. It says the vase referred to above was placed in the society's repository.

The 1938 statue of Adam in Harewood House (A50), showed a few years ago, a uniform mid-brown stain which was attributable to the atmosphere and was cleaned and stripped of this staining in 2011. It is believed by the author that the staining is unlikely to have been atmospheric and was probably applied by the carver in 1940. If this was a finish applied by the carver (Epstein) the constituents are not known but could well be wax or even shellac.

Shellac is the secretion of an insect and introduced mid-19th century as a replacement for oils and waxes. It has very good water-resisting characteristics which, with its good electrical resistance, made it desirable for early electric equipment. It was sometimes mixed with beeswax.

Painters and stainers were organised into guilds in some cities and towns. In London it was the Worshipful Company of Painter-Stainer incorporated in 1581 and which exists in name today.

Later in the 19th and 20th century it became necessary to look at cleaning the monuments. In the archives of the City of Westminster there is a letter from artist and sculptor Frederick Cruikshank (1800–1868) dated 1st January 1846 to Mr Henry Moore of Greenhill, Derby regarding the cleaning of alabaster. This can be accessed through Accession No 988/20. Moore's process can be seen in *Mechanics Magazine* Volume 5 1826 and whilst applicable to small objects and statues, needs some interpretation for large monuments. The process involves covering the object with a mixture of wax dissolved in spirits of turpentine and white lead. Allowed to dry the object is then immersed in rain water for two days and then cleaned off with turpentine, dried and brushed with a soft brush dipped in plaster of Paris. He remarks that the objects he applied this to were made from alabaster which '... came from a quarry in Chellaston about 4 miles from Derby'. He finally observes that this process is '... quicker that that previously applied which comprised of using fish skins and Dutch rushes'.

Some of the current population of alabasters have received attention from inexpert restorers. In addition iron staples and pins can rust causing severe damage to the monuments. It was for this reason that the medieval alabastermen used non-ferrous latten wires. The beauty with alabaster is that it rarely permanently stains and will take cleaning well. Modern recommendations are for a mixture of white spirit, de-ionised or distilled water and a small quantity of non-ionic detergent[18] and cotton wool swabs. After cleaning the alabaster should be protected by an application of cosmolloid wax (Cosmolloid 80H).[19]

Note:

18. Such as Ovus Soap
19. Larson, 1979 – *The Conservator* Vol 3 pages 28–33 sometimes known as Renaissance wax

Specific references:

'A Calendar of the Register of Apprentices in the City of Gloucester 1595–1700'. The Bristol and Gloucester Archaeological Society 1991

'A Calendar of the Registers of the Freemen of the City of Gloucester 1641–1838'. The Bristol and Gloucester Archaeological Society 1991

Appendix T
Linked Monuments

This table lists monuments with similar styles where one or more are otherwise unidentified to a workshop or carver.

Location	Note	Date	Link	Common feature	Carver/workshop Association
Canterbury	G14	1348	L1	Gablette (head canopy)	London
Greystoke	G4	1367			Trent valley – with shields
Canterbury	G97	1413			Chellaston/Sutton & Prentys
Arundel	G167	1416			
Lowick	G122	1419			
Exeter	G75	1419			
Abergavenny	G118	1450			Possibly from earlier tomb
Apethorpe	G130	1500		Gablette in the form of a group	
Ashwellthorpe	G121	1417	L1	Standing angels holding shields	Chellaston/Sutton & Prentys and successors
Ashbourne	G58	1447			
Tong	G148	1451			
Canterbury	G98	1435		Freestone cadaver under tomb at Arundel, Canterbury 1423 and Wells Herstmonceux 1447 and Canterbury 1443 are all freestone but included for comparison. Others to sort	Gardner states these are a group but not all have cadavers
Arundel	G168	1435			
Herstmonceux	–	1447			
Canterbury (Bishop Chichele) in place 1423	–	1443			
Wells	G156	1451			
Lingfield	G166	1453			

Location	Note	Date	Link	Common feature	Carver/workshop Association
Dennington	G162	1441		Feet on wyvern	
Weobley	G92?	1440			
Coleshill	G178	1519		Lion carving	
Coleshill	GNP98	1558			
Youlgreave	G64	1488		Linked with G178 and GNP98	
Bakewell	GNP17	1403		?	
Hoveringham	GNP68	1403			
Tideswell	G57	1440			
Swine	G191	1403		Kneeling angels	York workshops
Sheriff Hutton	G203	1420			
Methley	G194	1424			
Harewood	G192	1430			
Merevale	G173	1440		Rudimentary tassels on fauld and bascinet with long back	Tomb chest by different hand but effigy by same carver
East Shefford	G33	1440			
Willoughby on the Wolds	G138	1448			
Harewood	G193	1419	L12	Flying angels supporting shields	York? May well be Chellaston
Harlaxton	GNP56	1410	L1		Credited to Chellaston
Aston on Trent	G60	1450			May be earlier than 1450
Porlock	G153y	1440	L13	Horned headdress? Others G33/G57/G58 G76/G83/G92/G93/G118 G126/G138/G173/G186 G199/GNP30/GNP65 GNP78	Chellaston – Sutton workshop
Dennington	G162y	1441			
Bromsgrove	G184y	1450			
Tong	G148y	1451			
Over Peover	G45y	1456			
Windsor	G36	1513		Figures and weepers	Fawsley, Northamptonshire attributed to Richard Parker
Fawsley	G127	1534			
Aldermaston	G38	1539			

Location	Note	Date	Link	Common feature	Carver/workshop Association
Cubley	G73	1491	L2	Weepers	Harpur and Moorecock of Burton. Contract for Chesterfield specifies 'like Cubley'
Chesterfield	GNP25	1510			
Ashover	G69	1518	L2	Weepers	Burton 'school' possibly Harpur and Moorecock
Norton, Derbyshire	GNP23	1530			
Lowick	G123	1498	L14	Tomb chest lozenges	Burton 'school' possibly Harpur and Moorecock. Later copied by Parker
Holme Pierrepont	G135	1499			
Strelley	G139	1501			
Ratcliffe on Soar	G136	1539			
Chilton	G164	1500	L18	Knights with tabards and heavily wrought. Ladies alike but wear different livery collars. Flapped headdress	Gardner claims that these are sufficiently different to possibly be London
Wethersfield	G85	1490			
Wingfield	G163	1491			CMS links this with the other two
Castle Donington	G111	1529		Bedesmen on tomb chest	The Clifton monuments have been identified with Parker but Castle Donington is identical
Clifton Campville	G161	1545			
Norbury	G62	1483		Bedesmen on animal under feet of effigy	Probably Burton school. Norbury and Harewood are very similar but some 27 years apart
Strelley	G139	1501			
Callington	G54	1503			
Harewood	G206	1510			
Godshill	G91	1522			

Appendix U

The Latter Day Stately Houses

This 18th century saw an acceleration of the building of stately houses. Baroque had given way to Palladian with its huge columns and architects cast around for suitable minerals. Mention of Kedleston, Brocklesby, Holkham and The Breakers has been made in the previous sections but it is necessary to expand on this work to place it in context.

It is unclear when an architect first considered alabaster. Large blocks of 3 to 4 tons had been cut since the late 14th century but the sizes required for the mansions were some three to four times this weight. As the 18th century dawned the only quarries listed in Appendix M that could produce blocks of that size were Chellaston, Fauld/Castle Hay and possibly Watchet. However, it has previously been stated that in the 17th century Watchet provided Nicholas Stone with alabaster column blocks which could not be less than 19ft (6m) in length in 1633 and 1634. It was also reported that 'house-size' blocks were liberated in storms early in the 1700s. The Stone blocks were destined for Amsterdam so Watchet could also provide blocks of some size. But before that Flemish carver Willem Boy had visited the East Midlands to obtain alabaster for columns on the tomb of Gustav Vasa in Uppsala Cathedral *circa* 1562–1583 although the alabaster was delivered to Mechelen in Belgium. Scientific analysis of a portion of this stone has identified it coming from 'quarries south-west of Nottingham' although some sources say Newark but this is in error. The report of the analysis can be found at the archaeometry website at Kloppmann_etal_alabaster_multi-isotope_2014.pdf

The uncertainty is Redhill. From early times repeated floods had eroded the cliffs facing the River Trent and Soar exposing the red Mercian mudstone (formerly Keuper marl) in which was buried nodules of alabaster-grade gypsum. At some point in time a large seam of alabaster was discovered at a point in the cliff where the Soar meets the Trent. Here a quarry was established. This was convenient as unlike the quarries at Chellaston and Fauld/Castle Hay the Soar/Trent junction was below the restrictions on navigation and so products could be easily transported by water except in the very driest of seasons.

Transport in the 18th century would be vastly improved by the building of canals from the 1750s but in the first half of that century the carrying of bulky objects weighing several tons was a problem. Appendix C deals with this in detail.

Returning to Redhill, we know that the parish of Ratcliffe on Soar in which Redhill is located became the property of the Curzons of Kedleston Hall *circa* 1714. This was the date of the construction of the new manor house in Ratcliffe by Nathaniel Curzon who is recorded as pulling the old one down in 1719. We also know that the quarry was working about 1750 but may well have been mined much earlier. The problem we have is that a later Curzon, in strange fit, made a bonfire of the Curzon mining records in the early 19th century so the only one remaining is the building of the marble hall. From this we know that Robert Adams used Redhill alabaster.

In the previous centuries the alabastermen had sought white or cream alabaster for their memorials but by the 15th century this was increasingly difficult to obtain and so alabaster with veining was used which was stained (painted) so that the veining was of little matter. The architects of the 18th century saw this veining as decorative and utilised the colours in the stone to great advantage. As a result the columns in the stately houses were unstained and polished to show the richness of the colour.

Of the stated houses the first one seems to be Holkham Hall. The chronology of the building of the hall has an entry for 1755 saying 'alabaster from Castle Hay arrives – Benjamin Carter and Joseph Pickford carving chimney pieces'. The name Benjamin is not yet explained as the carver is widely known by the name Thomas. It can be inferred that the first delivery of alabaster was reasonably small blocks for the chimney pieces. This is supported by records in Derby of Joseph Pickford's nephew also Joseph Pickford (*see* Appendix G) who was 'travelling to Fauld to select alabaster for Holkham' and later 'selecting alabaster from Chellaston from a quarry owned by his father' In the former case Castle Hay and Fauld are not much more than a mile apart in the group of quarries in the Forest of Needwood. In the latter case we do not know if the Chellaston alabaster was used for Holkham.

Another entry in the Holkham records dated 1756 says 'More alabaster delivered – alabaster columns being delivered' and in 1758 'William Atkinson is carving the alabaster door surrounds'.

Turning to Kedleston the design for the marble hall (Figure 41) was the idea of Robert Adams but the construction lags that of Holkham by some four years. The records state that Adams was assisted by Joseph Pickford, which is assumed to be the nephew of Holkham's Pickford who as noted above was the purchaser of alabaster for Holkham. There is therefore a design link between Holkham and Kedleston which is borne out by the fluting and similarities in colour. Whereas it is known that Kedleston's stone came from Redhill that of Holkham is stated to be 'Derbyshire' but as the Derbyshire county boundary is not more than 200m from the quarry face at Redhill it may well be that the Holkham alabaster came from Redhill the observers being unclear as to the precise location.

In a strange twist the existence of an old etching in the museum at Tutbury shown in Appendix M, Section 1, shows a bridge over the River Dove, a wagon and horses and Tutbury castle. The local records state this is an 18th century etching but without any provenance to this effect. What makes it odd is that it is on the line of a later tramway serving a plaster mill but the bridge shown is not the one used by the trams neither were horses used in this 19th century railway. Appendix M has a more detailed evaluation of this. The Castle Hay quarry was about a mile beyond Tutbury Castle. Wagonways were first introduced into the East Midlands in 1604 when the Wollaton Wagonway brought coals the two miles from Strelley to the turnpike at Wollaton. The track was wooden, horse drawn and had a gauge of 4ft 6in. With Castle Hay in an isolated position on the ridge it is quite possible that a wooden wagonway was built to bring gypsum and alabaster down to the Derby by road since the road down from the quarry into Tutbury being very steep and dangerous for loaded road wagons.

Returning to Holkham we are told that on the 20th October 1756 carters John Mather and William Repton carried alabaster from Castle Hay to Wilne Ferry being 4 tons 16cwt for a cost of £3 and on the 4th March 1757 George Cooper and Thomas Sumers were paid 8/- a ton for carting six blocks weighing 4 tons 13cwt from 'the pits' to the Burton Turnpike. Both these dates are too late to be identified with the columns and are likely to be panels. These weights are what would be expected of such items but as to the columns, if these were, say, 20ft x 4ft x 4ft the weight would be 21 tons, way outside the manageable wagons of the carters of Staffordshire.

The Breakers, Rhode Island, USA

Appendix M also has a discussion on the movement of 18ft blocks of alabaster from Fauld Mine for The Breakers the mansion on Rhode Island, USA. Although carried to Liverpool by rail and the sidings at Scropton being rail connected to the mine, the mine railway is considered to be incapable of carrying blocks of this size across the river. It is assumed that the mine railway moved the blocks to the mine entrance from where they were carried by road to Scropton and loaded by means of A-frames in the station yard.

More pictures of The Breakers can be seen on: http://www.newportmansions.org/explore/the-breakers

Figure 119. The ornate dining room in The Breakers mansion showing the alabaster columns. Photo: © John Corbett, for the Preservation Society of Newport County.

The Corinthian columns seen above are formed from two blocks. The photograph of the blocks awaiting shipping (Figure 96) show that there were two sizes and the two together made one column.

Other Houses

There are records of Derby-made chimney pieces made from alabaster in Kenilworth Castle, Warwick, Thrumpton, Nottinghamshire and Aston Hall. Alabaster door frames are to be found in Chatsworth and Kingston Hall, Nottinghamshire. In the former case it is suggested that the alabaster came from Castle Hay and in the latter from Kingston Mine. There are certainly others not yet found.

Appendix V
The 1414 Alabaster Purchase by the Abbey of Fécamp

Notes on sources:

The original text was found in the archives of the Abbey of Fécamp *circa* 1902 and preserved in Department de Seine-Infereure where the archivist M Charles de Beaurepaire published the text in *Notes sur les Architectes de Rouen* in the *Bulletin des Amis des Monuments Rouenais* for 1902 pages 85 to 87. Mr John Bilson of Hull reprinted the works in the *Archaeological Journal* for 1907 but failed to translate the French text to English. The text was translated by William Stevenson of St John's College, Oxford and published in the Thoroton Transactions Vol XI pages 89 to 98 also in 1907 from which the following is drawn.

The archives of Fécamp contained two documents. The first is a remit or charter for the group who travelled to England which Stevenson called the 'Charter Party'. The second is the report made by Alexander de Berneval to the Lord Abbot of Fécamp, Estard d'Estouteville, after the return of the travellers. The records are unique and therefore worthy of reproduction here with clarification notes.

The Charter Party

> In the name of God, Amen. Know all persons who shall see or hear this charter of freightment divided by A,B,C[1] that Dan Nicholas Ducroq a monk in the abbey of Fécamp has freighted for and in the name of the reverend father of God the Lord Abbot and the convent of Fécamp the ship called *Friday* whereof is master after God Walter Nyessem (Neasham) dwelling in England in the town of Newcastle on Tyne, and belonging to it, to depart and sail from the port of Harfleur at the first suitable weather that God shall send to him forthwith to the said country of England to the Port of Hull properly laden. And the said master shall be bound to take with him and bring back in his company safely and securely four persons servants of the said lord abbot this is to say Alexander de Berneval, Martin Lausse, Ralph le Pappe and John de Paris at the expense of the said abbot that is to say that the said master shall load or cause to be loaded in his said ship alabaster-stone and other merchandise of all and such cargo as the ship can carry or as the said servants or one of them shall cause to be loaded in he said ship when all shall have been delivered to the said

master on board the said ship by the said servants and at their expense.

And after the said ship shall have been charged as is above said, she shall sail and come forthwith to the port of Fécamp, Harfleur or to places in their neighbourhood and the said master shall deliver the said merchandise to the said lord abbot and convent or to his order, unless prevented by shipwreck and he shall load and reload as quickly as possible. And the said master acknowledged and confessed that he has received the sum of 200 ecus of gold from the said abbot by the hands of the said Dan Nicholas Ducroq to be employed in mechanise for the profit of the said abbot and by the said servants. And in the case the said servants shall not buy anything and they do not see in it the profit of the lord abbot the said master shall not be able to compel them to buy anything, but he shall be bound to take them across the sea and to be paid his freight as shall pertain to him. And in this case the said master shall be bound to render and store the said sum of 200 ecus after deducting his said freight and salary. And in order to fulfil and complete the said voyage the said master ought to have for every ton burthen the sum of 5 or 6 ecus of gold by the ordinance of Dan Richard de Beaunay, monk of the said place of Fécamp. And if the said master shall pay any money for the said abbot at the request of the said servants of the abbot, the said abbot shall be bound to render and restore it to the said master. And after the discharge and delivery of the said merchandise if there be any merchandise the master shall be paid all his freight and what he shall have paid for and in the name of the said abbot well and properly without contradiction. And if the said servants shall have any hindrance on the other side, Jaquelin de Bouchier, Burgess of Harfleur binds himself to release them and to discharge them at his own cost and expense. And firstly and before all by the expenditure of the said master all towage and pilotage, great and small shall fall upon the said abbot for the use and customs of the sea and of the river Seine.

For the observing, fulfilment and completing of all the above-said things and each of them in all their points in the manner aforesaid, the said master charges his body, his ship, her tackle and rigging, and all his movable goods and inheritances, present and future and the said Dan Nicholas Ducroq for and in the name as above, charges all the said merchandise and the goods of the said abbot and convent wherever they may be, present and to come. And for this he said Dan Nicholas Ducroq found as sureties William Dubois and the said Jaquelin le Bouchier, Burgess of Harfleur.

This was done and performed in the town of Harfleur by the accord and consent of the said parties in the year 1414 on 9th July in the presence of

William Dugardin and of me John Descamps clerk commissary of Oliver Gabart, clerk, notary sworn by our Lord the King in the district of Harfleur who have here set my sign manual (by hand) in witness of the truth.

O Gabart. J Descamps

The Report on the Party's Return

Memorandum of the appointment and bargain for the freight of a ship to journey to England to the town of Newcastle on Tyne etc as appears by a charter party. Be it known that in the year 1414 on the 13th July,[2] Master Alexander de Berneval, mason, Martin Lause, Ralph le Pape and John de Paris in his company departed to go to England by the commandment and ordinance of the reverend father in God the lord of Fécamp for the time being.[3] And they departed on the said day in the company of Walter Nyessem (Neasham), an Englishman, their conductor to the country of England in his ship called the *Friday.*[4] And they departed from Harfleur and he conducted them to the harbour of the said place of Newcastle on Tyne and arrived there on Wednesday following and they stayed there for the space of 7 or 8 days[5] at the expense of the said Englishman.[6] And they left there on the day of St Christopher[3] and arrived on the third day at Nottingham.[7] And from there the said Englishman took them to the village of Chaleston (Chellaston) where the alabaster is found and he there found the merchant who sells it named Master Thomas Prentys with who the said Englishman trafficked to have delivered to him certain pieces of alabaster at a certain price by agreement between the two in the presence of those above in such wise that the said Prentys received 40 ecus of gold beforehand, promising to deliver the said stone at the port of Hull in England. And the agreement was made between the two English merchants in the town of Nottingham in England.[8] And immediately after this the said English merchant[9] conducted the said Master Alexander and those of his company to the port of Vicenesey (Winchelsea) in England and caused them to cross the sea to Dieppe. And everything was done at the cost and expense of the said Walter, the Englishman, from the time that they left Harfleur until their return to this side at Dieppe with four horses bought by the said Englishman and they lived in the time aforesaid during the said journey for the space of five or six weeks at the expense of the said merchant as is aforesaid with the money for the said horses, etc.

This memorandum is made and written by the saying and relation of the said master Alexander who affirmed that he had a good and fresh memory thereof.

Notes:

1. The medieval form of contract was to have a document through which a wavy line was drawn and then cut in such a way that when the two (or more portions) were matched then it was seen that the document was authentic. This was often known as a 'charter parti' or divided charter and is the origin of our word indenture.
2. The 13th July was a Friday. The journey therefore took five days the arrival being the Wednesday 18th July.
3. It is believed that only one could speak English.
4. We do not know what sort of ship was the *Friday*. The history of the hanseatic trade states that the predominant type was the 'cog' used for Baltic and European trade from the 13th century and not superseded until the late 15th century. This deep-hulled, single-masted ship was built with an aft castle and later afore castle and was square rigged and may well have been flat bottomed for beaching where no harbour was present. It would have had a stern rudder. The cog reached its size limit late in the 14th century and was replaced by the hulk or holk and later the caravel, but many continued to trade into the 16th century.

Figure 120. A model of a cog without fore castle showing the flat bottom and stern rudder. *Wikipedia.*

5. They remained in Newcastle until the 25th July which was also a Wednesday. So the Nottingham arrival was the 28th July, 1414.
6. The detail of the funding is uncertain. It is believed in some quarters that the Abbot had advanced to Neasham 200 gold crowns. Neasham may have acted as purse-bearer, but again there is reference to an 'English Merchant at that port (Newcastle) who was their purse-bearer'. What is suspicious is that Neasham took them to Newcastle instead of Hull. Newcastle was the home port of the *Friday* but why Neasham should want to have to transport the party through Durham and Yorkshire seems odd unless he wanted to cut a deal with a partner in the town. The suspicion is that the Newcastle merchant was the person who advanced the money against a 'Charta-parti' which would have had to be drawn up by a notary hence the seven days in the town.
7. Lodging in Darlington, York and Doncaster and entering Nottingham by means of the Mansfield Road.

8. The mention of two merchants gives a clear indication that Sutton was also present. The deal was closed in Nottingham where there was probably a notary on hand to oversee the closing of the contract. At the time Sutton and Prentys were carving effigies in Chellaston but may well have had premises in Nottingham which would be the shipping place for Hull. There is a William Prentys resident in Nottingham in 1404 whose role was an 'appraiser' of goods who may well have been a family member. Stevenson says that in Nottingham the party would have seen panels and images being carved by a 'large number of alabastermen'. This is pure guesswork as this is not borne out by borough records despite Stevenson being the editor of all the volumes of the said records.
9. The word merchant implying that either Sutton or Prentys did the conducting. It is unlikely that either would want to be away from his workshop for this task and it was more like Neasham who had the responsibility of seeing the visitors on a ship to France.

Appendix W
Tomb Costs and Contracts

Some authors maintain that the design of a tomb was agreed between the customer and carver in the form of a detailed contract. So few contracts have come down to us that this cannot be firmly established. Lawrence Stone writing in 1955 makes firm statement that few specific features were specified beyond the general requirements of social position and genealogical connections. This would include such detail as armour, dress and awards but little else. Like all statements this has exceptions but the evidence for the detail requirements for design is thin.

Some writers also hypothesize that tombs were speculatively carved, the detail of social position being added as required. Again Lawrence Stone offers the suggestion that this is unlikely for it is rare that tombs are exactly alike and the workshops were unlikely that workshops would care to tie up capital on such a venture. There were times when contracts failed and under these circumstances the reuse of tombs may well have taken place. This excludes the period from 1536 when dissolution meant that tombs were moved and in some cases reused as their original locations were destroyed.

In the period 1328 to 1540 there are about 15 surviving contracts covering just 10 tombs out of the 462 extant alabaster tombs and slabs. Not all are for alabaster tombs. Only two of these relate to tomb carving outside London, one for a local church and the other remote. Of the London-carved tombs only one is remote the others are all for London churches. Therefore seven were carved for churches within a few miles of the workshop involved and of the ten tombs, seven give delivery months as August and September being the drier months and one gives April. It is therefore such a small sample that firm conclusions on the extent of intervention in design by the customer or the extent to which the carver was responsible for the carriage is possible.

Some of the contracts are:

Bronze of Queen Philippa of Hainault, wife of Edward III, 40 Edward III (1369)
Abbreviated – Contained in the Pell Records, Michaelmas 40 Edw III (1369). Made in London for Westminster Abbey:

> January 20 to Hawkin Liege from France … in discharge of 200 marks for making the tomb by writ £133 6s 8d. Issue roll 50 Edw III May 21 (1379) to John Orchard Latoner (brass worker) for making angels for the tomb of Queen Philippa by writ £5. The status of this is uncertain. The current effigy is alabaster but that of Edward III is bronze.

Bronze tomb for Sir Richard Beauchamp, Earl of Warwick, St Mary Warwick 1453

Abbreviated. Made in London and Isle of Purbeck for Warwick

> Some six contracts exist for this tomb between 1448 and 1456. An abbreviated set of contracts is contained in Crossley's book pages 30 and 31. That of 16th March 1456 and appears to be for the Purbeck marble tomb chest from John Bourde of Corfe. The tomb to contain in length 4ft and in breadth 4ft and in thickness 7 inches the tomb to bear in height 4ft and a half and in and about the tomb to make 14 principal housings and under each housing a goodly quarter for a escutcheon of copper and gilt to be set in according to a portraiture[1] delivered him and the carriages and bringing to Warwick[2] and there to set the same up where it shall stand. After the entailing he shall pullish (polish) and clense (cleanse) the tomb and shall have for it in sterling money £14.[3]

Notes:

1. A clear indication that a drawing was supplied.
2. This indicates that carriage to site was included in the price. The carriage of Purbeck marble was largely by sea and in this case the somewhat perilous navigation of Lands End and transhipment to boats capable of navigating the Severn and Warwick Avon would be indicated.
3. In 1829 the cost of moving 6 tons of cargo from Newcastle to London was £6 17s. The sea distance from Purbeck to Bristol and onward is about the same and taking inflation into account the cost in 1456 would be about £1. It is quite possible that cost of delivery was included in the price quoted in the indenture. Road transport would be from 2½ to 5 times as expensive seriously eroding the profit.

Bronze tomb for the Margaret Beaufort, Countess of Richmond and Derby, Westminster, 3 Henry VIII (1511)
Abbreviated – original in *Archaeologica* Vol 66, 1915. Made in London for Westminster

> The indenture is for a bronze tomb to be made by Pitir Thoryson of Florence but the contract was let through Pietro Torrigiano who was paid the sum of £400 sterling. In addition the merchants Leonard Fristo and John Cawalcant both of Florence were bound to the said executors for £500.

Bronze to Henry VII 1518
Text of the contract with Pietro Torrigiano is in *Archeaologia* Vol 16 pages 84 to 88. The contract included a tomb for Henry VIII and Queen Katherine of Aragon.

Alabaster tomb for Ralph Greene, Lowick, Northamptonshire: February 14, 6 Henry V (1418–1419). Translated from French by St John Hope
Abbreviated – *see* G122

> An indenture between Katherine who was the wife of Ralph Greene, Esq., William Aldwyncle and William Marshall, clerks on the one part and Thomas Prentys and Robert Sutton of Chellaston in the county of Derby, kervers, on the other part, witnessing that the said carvers have covenanted and agreed to make and carve well, honestly[1] and profitably a tomb of stone called alabaster, good, fine and pure, containing in length nine feet and in breadth four feet, two inches[2] upon which tomb shall be made two images of alabaster the one a counterfeit[3] of an esquire armed at all points containing in length seven feet with a helm under his head and a bear at his feet and the other image shall be the counterfeit of a lady lying in her open surcoat with two angels holding a pillow under her head with two little dogs at her feet: the one of the said images holding the other by the hand with two tabernacles called gablettes at their heads which tomb shall contain at the sides with the ledgerment three feet on which sides shall be images of angels with tabernacles bearing shields according to the device of the said Katherine, William and William. And also the said carvers shall make an arch of alabaster above all said tomb in length and breadth with pendants and knots and crest of faytes and other work pertaining to such a tomb, the

which images, tomb and arch shall be proportioned, gilded, painted and arrayed with colours well and sufficiently in the pure, honest and profitable manner that pertains to such work.[4] And all the said works shall be raised by the said Thomas and Robert in the parish church of Lowick in the county of Northampton at the costs and peril of the said Thomas and Robert in all manners between now and the feast of Easter in the year of our grace 1420.[5] For doing and performing which works in manner aforesaid the said Katherine, William and William shall pay or caused to be paid to the said Thomas and Robert or either of them, forty pound sterling of which there shall be paid at the making of these indentures, 10 marks, and at the feast of Easter next coming, 10 marks, and at the feat of John the Baptist[6] then following, 10 marks, and at the feat of St Michael[7] then following, 10 marks, and the remaining 10 marks shall be paid when all the works shall be done and set up in manner aforesaid.[8]

Notes:

1. Honestly = competently.
2. This clearly means the tomb chest.
3. Counterfeit = copy.
4. A clear indication that the tomb was coloured.
5. This would imply some 14 months from signing the indenture to completion. Care has to be taken as the year did not end until the 31st March but Easter Sunday in 1420 was the 9th April so the duration of the contract is probably correct.
6. June 24, 1419.
7. September 29, 1419.
8. A mark was valued at 13s 4d which means that the total came to approximately £33. St John Hope abbreviated the extract and it may well be that the missing £7 (another 10 marks) was for transport. Transport is not mentioned elsewhere in the translation. The value today of the suggested £7 would be some £3300 (for a longer discussion *see* Appendix C).

Alabaster tomb for Thomas Fermor and wife, Somerton, Oxford: February 14, 13 Elizabeth I (1582). Translated from French by St John Hope

Abbreviated – original in *Archaeologica* Vol 8, page 177. Made in Burton for Somerton – *see* R75.

Richard and Gabriel Roiley for and in condition of ye sum of money – £40 sterling do undertake to articially[1], cunningly, decently and substantially to devise, work, set up and perfectly and fully finish a very fair tomb of very fair well-chosen and durable alabaster stone containing in length six feet and a half and of ye breadth of four feet and of ye height of five feet by ye standard with two ends and one uttermost side all throughout adwrought adorned, gilded, engraved, portrayed and set forth with usual pictures of one son and two daughters with their several names of baptism over or under ye said pictures with escutcheons in their hands whereof ye said son to be pictured in armour and as living and ye one of ye said daughters to be pictured in decent order and as living and ye other daughter to be pictured a dying in ye cradle or swathes. And they shall work, make, lay and place artificially, durably and decently in or on ye uppermost part of ye said tomb a very fair and decent and well-proportioned picture of a gentleman with furnatuure and ornaments in armour and about his neck a double chain of gold with crest and helmet under his head with sword and dagger at his side and a lion at his feet and in or on the uttermost part of the uppermost part of the said tomb a decent and perfect picture of a fair gentlewoman with a French hood, edge and abilliment with all other apparel, furniture, jewels ornaments and things in all respects usual, decent and seemly for a gentlewoman. And about ye said tomb four shields or escutcheons one ye very true arms of Thomas Fermor and Francis ye first wife, the third the arms of Thomas and Bridget his second wife and the fourth the arms of ye said Bridget only. And further they shall work, make, ingrave and set out with good and convenable oils, gold and colours round about the edge and crest of ye said tomb with or in one row of great and fair gilt engraben letters ye epitaph. As also all ye and all manner of ye devising, colouring, gilding, garnishing, workmanship, carriage, conveying, setting up and full finish shall be all thoroughly at or by the only peril, pain, travel, costs and charges of ye said Richard and Gabriel. That ye said George Shirley within one month next after request be made shall find and send to Burton convenable and sufficient waines, carts and cattle to draw, lead, carry and bring all ye pieces and parts of ye said tomb and also to cause ye foundations of ye said tomb to be made by a mason at his own charges. And that five pounds be paid within eight days next after the ensealing thereof, another five pounds within within 20 days then next after, ten pounds at or before ye feast day of the nativity next coming after another twelve pounds at or before ye feast of Easter and another twelve pounds at such time and when ye said tomb shall be finished. 27th day of October 1582.

Notes:
1. Articaly = artfully .

Alabaster tomb for John Shirley, Breedon on the Hill, Leics, 16 Elizabeth I (1585)

Made in Burton for Breedon by Richard and Gabriel Royley.

Alabaster tomb for Henry Foljambe, Chesterfield, Derbyshire, 1 HenryVIII (1510). *See* GNP25

Identified as being made Harpur and Moorecock of Burton. The tomb is a tabletop with inlay and was to be modelled on that of Sir Nicholas Montgomery of Great Cubley, Derbyshire as specified by the customer – for full transcript *see* X22.

Alabaster tomb for Sir Walter Manny, Charterhouse, London (1371). Now lost – *see* D9/11

Manny's will specified '... une tombe d'alabastre ... fait ove un chivaler de mes armes tiel come est faite sur monsire Johan de Beauchamp a seint Poul en Londre'. It is believed this was translated into a contract.

Alabaster tomb for Richard Hertcombe, Bisham, Berks, 9 Henry V (1421). *See* A20 and B28

The Society of Antiquaries of London 1949 has a copy of the contract with Robert Broune who made the tomb chest for the effigies. The customer specified that the effigy be a counterfeit of that made for his 'patron' and this has given rise to the suggestion that this was the Earl of Salisbury. The effigies came from the Chellaston workshops but were displaced in time from the delivery of the tomb chest. The contract is quite specific in terms of how the customer expected it to look but again this is more towards the dimensions, material, quality and delivery. However, Hertcombe did provide sketches showing how the figures in the niches of the tomb chest should look and may well have had an idea of the sort of tomb chest from existing tombs. It is questionable as to whether Broun(e) the lead contractor was responsible for caving the niche figures as this is also a feature of the Chellaston workshop and whether Broun(e) just built the vault for the bodies the foundations and carried out the assembly.

Values 1325 to date:

£1 in Year	**Present day value**	**Event**	**Comment**
1325	£304	Edward II	First alabaster effigy
1350	£430	Black Death	Carvers may have fled London
1375	£304		SS livery collar
1400	£401	Henry Bolingbroke	
1420	£472	Henry V	
1450	£520		
1460	£530	Wars of the Roses	Collar of suns and roses
1485	£560	Bosworth	
1500	£501	Tudor	
1530	£466	Reformation	Damage to some monuments
1550	£243	Marian	Partial restoration of Catholicism
1560	£213	Elizabethan	Elizabethan decree to protect monuments
1600	£141	Stuart	Mural monument style well established
1650	£88	Commonwealth	Further attacks on monuments
1660	£98	Restoration	Alabaster falls out of favour
1700	£130	Georgian	Baroque period
1800	£52	Industrial Revolution	Gothic regains popularity
1900	£77	Empire	The rise of the alabaster tablet

Appendix X
Latin Inscriptions

The Latin inscriptions on medieval effigial and incised slabs were fairly regularised up to the Reformation. This was because the main purpose was to incite intersession as well as identifying the individuals for who intersession was required. A typical Latin inscription which is worth repeating here (the version in *Archeaologia Cantiana* Vol 48, 1936 is incomplete). The example is taken from the margin of John Sprott's marble slab in Crundale church, Kent.

> ***Orate Pro a(n)i(m)a d(omi)ni Joh(ann)is Sprot bacularii Iuris Canonictam Conjugato(rum) quo(n)d(a)m Rectoris Hui(us) eccl(es)ie qui legavit cuil(ibe)t/ parochiano(rum) suor(um) tam conjugate(rum) q(ua)m viduato(rum) xl denarios cuil(ibe)t immaritato(rum) xii d(e) nario(s) et obiit nono die mensis Decembris Anno D(om)ini M CCCC lxvi Cui(us) a(n)i(m)e propicietur D(eu)s Amen***
>
> ***Pray for the soul of Sir John Sprott, Bachelor of Canon Law, once rector of this church who left to each of his parishioners, both married and widowed, 40 pence, to each of the unmarried 12 pence and died 9th December in the year of our Lord 1466, on whose soul God have mercy. Amen***

There were two Latin verses which could not be deciphered but one may well be:

> ***Pastor quidem sobrius gregis hic fuit ille … sibi finis***
>
> ***He was indeed a faithful shepherd of his flock here (and came to a suitable) end***

The three essential requirements of the tomb are ably demonstrated. Firstly the person is identified with the date of his death, secondly the observer is requested to pray for the soul and thirdly, to be sure, the good deeds as rector and benefactor to the village were listed.

On another slab (S54) at Ratcliffe on Soar we have:

> ***[Hic jacet] Isabella Babington quanda (m) uxor Ioh(ann)is Babington de [Dethick] ar(migeri) ac Domini de Kingston quae Obiit[1] (piece at corner cut away but Thoroton says [18 mar anno Dom 1486] ... p(ro) piciet(ur) deus amen***

By modern standards this dates to 1487.

Straight translation:

> ***Here lies Isabella Babington wife of John Babington of Dethick arms bearer (knight) and Lord of Kingston who died March 18 1486 gracious to God Amen***

In another slab we have:

> ***Hic Jacet Elizabeth uxor Abthonii Babington Ar filis et una haeredum Johanne Ormond, filise et haeradum Willeli Chaworth militas ac unius consanguinaeum st haeradum Roberti Lathome, ... Caltoft, Johannis Bret, Thomas Aylesbury, Thomas Keynes Militum, ac Rad(olphus) Basset et Johannis Engaines, Baronum, quae Elizabeth ob 28 Nov anno 1505'***

> ***Here lies Elizabeth wife of Anthony Babington, the daughter and sole heir of John Ormond, son and heir of William Cha(r)worth, soldier and also sole kinsman and heir of Robert Lathome (John de) Caltoft, John Bret, Thomas Aylesbury, Thomas Keynes men-at-arms, and also Ralph Basset and John Engaines, Baron, and that of Elizabeth, died 28th November 1505***

Here the person who commissioned the slab wished a whole range of linked ancestors to be named so that their descendants would see the connection and add their prayers.

Latin inscriptions can mislead. In the case of the 1521 tomb, T28, Figure 23 in St Peter ad Vincula in the Tower of London, the inscription has misled observers for several centuries. The inscription along the south side reads:

> ***Jacent Corpora Richardi Cholmondeley Militis (et) Dominae Elizabethae conjugis suae. Qui***

> ***Lies the body of Richard Cholmondeley knight and his wife Dame Elizabeth. That or Who ...***

The damage has removed the word Hic (Here) but the name Cholmondeley in incorrect, the tomb being intended for Richard Cholmeley. The two Richards are cousins both with wives called Elizabeth. This has caused Richard Cholmeley, the true Constable of the Tower, to have his name misspelt for several centuries (*see* T28).

The inscription continues on the east side:

Ricus obiit die mensis

Richard died the day of (the) month

This is odd as it appears the day, month and year have been removed. The north side is blank as the tomb on this side has a Victorian repair. The west side continues:

Qui Quorum aiabus Deus propieter Amen

God be merciful to those who are earnest. Amen! or (on) Those who are earnest may God have mercy. Amen!

The inscription which starts so well and in conformity with the standard of the time descends into nonsense lending fuel to the suggestion in T28 that the tomb is that of Richard Cholmondeley of Malpas, Cheshire recovered and reused and placed in St Peter *circa* 1554.

Notes:

1. 'Obiit' is based on the Latin for 'to go away', but in medieval parlance became a noun meaning 'to die' and with is derivatives can be taken as 'died' or 'dying'.

Appendix Y

The Baldwin Workshop of Stroud and Gloucester

Profile

Stroud, Gloucestershire 1603 to *circa* 1627
Gloucester city 1627 to *circa* 1662
Workers – Samuel and Stephen Baldwin (*see* B59) and may have used a painter/stainer called John Campion (*see* Appendix S).
Extant works – 59 to 65 mainly in Oxfordshire, Worcestershire, Herefordshire, Gloucestershire and Wiltshire.

John Broome in a paper to the Church Monuments Society in 1995 (*see* bibliography) described the work and timeline of this workshop. Since then further analysis has amplified this account of the work of the workshop.

The most important issue is that apart from the monument to Joan Wadham (X10) and the Berkeley tombs (R1 and R53) and an unassigned drawing, there are no extant documents. Therefore attribution is by means of identification of styles and forms.

It is believed that Samuel Baldwin who was born *circa* 1480 worked in the Johnson workshop at Southwark before returning to Stroud sometime before 1603. Samuel's son Stephen who was born *circa* 1610 is also believed to have been apprenticed in London, this time under Nicholas Stone in Long Acre. This would be *circa* 1625 to 1630 but his name does not appear in the Stone workbooks held by the John Soane Museum in London.

It is not intended to repeat Broome's arguments for the assignment of the Baldwin workshop to the five score monuments listed but he omits the material used from his evaluation and so I have tabled an adaption of Broome's list showing the material as far as can be determined.

Index

The full details are contained In Appendix D.

Notes on form:

C = Canopy

KE = Kneeling effigy

M = No effigy

ME = Mural with effigy. (RE) recumbent (SE) lying on side (KE) kneeling effigies

RE = Recumbent effigy or effigies without entablature (n) represents the number of effigies

SE = Effigy lying on one elbow (n) represents to number of effigies

S = Statue

T = Wall tablet without effigy (–) or with small kneeling effigy (KE)

Location	Date	Material	Person	Reference	Form
Bristol	1603	***Freestone***	Joan Wadham	X10	RE (1)
Ross on Wye, Hereford	1609	Chellaston Alabaster	William Rudhall	M182	M
Waterperry, Oxford	1610	Fauld Alabaster	Francis Curson	M183	T (KE 2)
Bredon, Worcs	1611	Fauld Alabaster	Giles Reed	M168	ME (RE 1)
Spetchley, Worcs	1614	Fauld Alabaster	Roland Berkeley	R53	ME (RE 2)
Berkeley, Gloucs	1615	Alabaster	Henry Berkeley	R1	RE (2)
Worcester Cathedral	1613	Alabaster	Abigail Pope (Goldsborough)	M184	ME (KE 1)
Miserden, Gloucs	1614	***Freestone***	William Kingston	–	RE (1)
Tortworth, Gloucs	1614	Alabaster	Thomas Throckmorton	R126	ME (RE 1)
Stroud Gloucs	1613	Fauld Alabaster	Thomas Stephens	M426	T (KE)
Gloucester Cathedral	1615	Alabaster	Thomas Machen	M60	ME (KE 2)
Great Malvern, Worcs	1615	Alabaster	John Knotsford	R170	RE (2)
Bristol Lord Mayor's Chapel	1615	Alabaster	John Aldworth	M167	ME (RE 1)
Norton, Worcs	1613	Alabaster	Thomas Bigg	M191	ME (KE 2)
Eckington, Worcs	1616	***Freestone***	John Hanford	–	ME (KE 2)
Avening, Gloucs	1616	Alabaster	Henry Brydges	M166	ME (RE 1)
Droitwich, Worcs	1616	***Freestone***	George Wylde	–	ME (RE 1)
Kentchurch, Hereford	1616	Alabaster	John Scudamore	R171	RE (SE 2)
Great Milton, Oxford	1616	Alabaster	Sir Michael Dormer (uncertain)	M174	RE (3) C
Kempsey, Worcs	1620	Alabaster	Edmund Wylde	R157	ME (1)
Badsey, Worcs	1617	***Freestone***	Richard Hoby	–	ME (KE 2)
Bristol, St Stephen	1617	Alabaster	Sir George Snygge	R35	ME (SE 1)
Droitwich, Worcs	1620	***Marble***	Sir Walter Blout (lost)	–	–

Location	Date	Material	Person	Reference	Form
Cirencester, Gloucs	1620	***Freestone***	Humphrey Bridges	–	ME (RE 2)
Norton, Worcs	1621	Alabaster	Thomas Bigg	M192	ME (RE 2)
Gloucester Cathedral	1622	Alabaster	Elizabeth Williams (nee Smith)	M55	ME (SE 1)
Gloucester Cathedral	1623	Alabaster	Margery Clent (nee Smith)	M57	ME (KE 1)
Painswick, Gloucs	1623	***Freestone*** Note 1	John Seaman	–	KE (2) C
Much Cowarne, Hereford	1624	***Freestone***	Sybil Reed	–	ME (RE 1)
Cropthorne, Worcs	1624	***Freestone***	Francis Dingley	–	KE (2) C
Miserden, Gloucs	1624	***Freestone***	Anthony Partridge	–	T (KE 2)
Whitminster, Gloucs	1625	***Freestone***	Rebecca Hinson	–	T (KE 2)
Much Dewchurch, Hereford	1625	Alabaster	Walter Pye	R5, X37	ME (KE 2)
Gloucester, St Nicholas	1626	Alabaster	John Wallton	R263	RE (2)
Bristol Lord Mayor's Chapel	1626	Alabaster	Martin Pringe	M243	ME (KE 1)
Ledbury, Hereford	1630	Alabaster	Edward Skynner	M186	KE (2) C
Ledbury, Hereford	1629	***Freestone***	Dr Thomas Thornton	–	KE (1)
Great Wishford, Wilts	1629	Alabaster	Sir Richard Grobham	M272	ME (RE 2)
Sapperton, Gloucs	1630	Alabaster	Henry Poole	M169	ME (KE 4)
Wickhamford, Worcs	1630	Fauld or Watchet Alabaster	Samuel Sandys	R67	RE (2)
Spelsbury, Oxford	1631	***Freestone***	Henry Lee	–	RE (2) C
Wroxton, Oxford	1631	Alabaster	William Pope	R154	RE (2)
Abergavenny, Gwent	1631	Alabaster	Judge Andrew Powell	R180	RE (2)
Inkberrow, Worcs	1631	Alabaster	John Savage	R266	RE (1) C
Elmley Castle, Worcs	1632	Alabaster	William Savage	R54	RE (1)
Strensham, Worcs	1632	***Freestone***	William Russell	–	RE (2)
Lugwarden, Hereford	1634	Alabaster	William Reed	M190	ME (SE 1)

Location	Date	Material	Person	Reference	Form
Lydiard Tregoze, Wilts	1633	Uncertain possibly freestone	Giles Mompesson	–	ME (seated 2)
Lydiard Tregoze, Wilts	1634	Alabaster	John St John	R165	RE (3) C
Kinnersley, Hereford	1635	Alabaster	Francis Smalman	M503	T (KE 2)
Much Marcle, Hereford	1635	Alabaster	John Kyrle	R178	RE (2)
Ross on Wye, Hereford	1636	Alabaster	John Rudhall	R167	S
Bishop's Cleeve, Gloucs	1636	Alabaster	Richard de la Bere	R162	ME (RE 2)
Down Ampney, Gloucs	1637	Alabaster	John Hungerford	M187	ME (KE 2)
Ledbury, Hereford	1638	Alabaster	John Hoskyns	M514	KE (2) C
Cirencester, Gloucs	1638	Alabaster	George Moxon	M188	M (busts)
Gloucester Cathedral	1639	***Freestone***	Abraham Blackleech	(R26)	RE (2)
Castle Frome, Hereford	1640	***Freestone***	William Unett	–	RE (2)
Shipton Moyne, Gloucs	1640	Alabaster	Thomas Estcourt	R174	RE (2) C
Miserden, Gloucs	1644	Alabaster	William Sandys	R56	RE (2)
Gloucester, St Nicholas	1645	Alabaster	Samuel Baldwin	M526	T
Broad Hinton, Wilts	1645	Alabaster	Francis Glanville	R175	T
Lydiard Tregoze, Wilts	1645	Uncertain	Edward St John	–	S
Cropthorne, Worcs	1646	***Freestone***	Edward Dingley	–	T
Ross on Wye, Hereford	1651	Alabaster	William Rudhall	R169	RE (2)

Other notes:

1. It is believed that the 1623 monument was broken up in the 18th century and the effigies placed on a tomb chest.

One feature immediately apparent is the majority of the monuments are in alabaster. Whilst the land around Stroud and Gloucester are rich in limestone all alabaster had to be 'imported'. It is therefore worth speculating from where the Baldwins obtained their supplies, an aspect which no other writer appears to have covered. If Samuel Baldwin worked at Southwark he will have noted the arrival of good quality alabaster delivered by sea to London from Hull. This had to be alabaster from Chellaston, Fauld or later Ledsham all of which was exported through the port of Hull.

It can be assumed that the Baldwin workshop also obtained their supplies by sea but the voyage would be dangerous and probably require more than one transhipment. The road distance from the quarries to Gloucester is 90 miles. The alabaster required would be beyond the capability of the packhorse and so a covered wagon would be used. Travel in the autumn and spring would be avoided due to the mud but even then a wagon carrying 4 to 5 tons would make the trip in about nine days. A single cart could deliver 15 tons in two months and an analysis of the material required for the monuments listed above indicates between 200 and 300 tons would be required (based on Roger Firman's estimates – *see* Section 4). Over the 42 years of the workshop this indicates only an average delivery rate of between 5 and 7 tons per year with the peak years in the 1630s at a rate of 9 tons required. This is only approximate as the Broome list may not be a complete list but in any stretch of the imagination 9 tons does not seem to be a difficult proposition.

Reviewing the Baldwin monuments a mixture of Chellaston and Fauld alabaster is noted based on colour but that at Lydiard Tregoze (R165) may be Watchet. As stated elsewhere the mining at Watchet is known from about 1633 but as it is believed to be managed by the Nicholas Stone workshop at which Stephen Baldwin is associated, the use of Watchet alabaster is quite feasible post Stephen's return to Gloucester *circa* 1630. Delivery of alabaster by Severn trow from the harbour at Blue Anchor to the Gloucester wharfs is not difficult.

Gallery

Figure 121. Gloucester Cathedral – Lady Chapel, left side. Elizabeth Williams (M55, died 1622 in childbirth) daughter of Bishop Miles Smith and widow of John Williams. This is a mural by Samuel Baldwin of Stroud before he moved to Gloucester. The effigy lies on one elbow with the child lying beside. There is a semi-circular canopy with black marble colonnades. Two panels beneath with a type of black mottled stone. This is linked to M57 as Margery Clent was her sister.
The monument effigy is painted but the face, gloves and child are left bare. Photo: Janet State.

Figure 122. Gloucester Cathedral – Lady Chapel. Margery Clent (M57, died 1623 in childbirth) a daughter of Bishop Miles Smith and widow of James Clent. A mural (M55) also by Samuel Baldwin, was to her sister. Although smaller than that of Elizabeth Williams the style is similar in that the same decoration appears on the arch face and the black marble domes. Photo: Janet State.